The Oxford Introduction to Proto-Indo-European and the Proto-Indo-European World

The Oxford Introduction to Proto-Indo-European and the Proto-Indo-European World

J. P. Mallory and
D. Q. Adams

OXFORD
UNIVERSITY PRESS

OXFORD
UNIVERSITY PRESS

Great Clarendon Street, Oxford OX2 6DP

Oxford University Press is a department of the University of Oxford.
It furthers the University's objective of excellence in research, scholarship,
and education by publishing worldwide in

Oxford New York

Auckland Cape Town Dar es Salaam Hong Kong Karachi
Kuala Lumpur Madrid Melbourne Mexico City Nairobi
New Delhi Shanghai Taipei Toronto
With offices in
Argentina Austria Brazil Chile Czech Republic France Greece
Guatemala Hungary Italy Japan South Korea Poland Portugal
Singapore Switzerland Thailand Turkey Ukraine Vietnam

Published in the United States
by Oxford University Press Inc., New York

Reprinted 2009

ISBN 978-0-19-929668-2

Printed in the United Kingdom by
Lightning Source UK Ltd., Milton Keynes

Contents

List of Maps

List of Figures

List of Tables

List of Abbreviations and Acronyms

(All dates are approximate)

Alb = Albanian (16th century onwards).
Arm = Armenian (5th century onwards).
Av = Avestan, Iranian (1st millennium BC).
Bakhtiari = a Southwest Iranian language (modern).
Bret = Breton, Celtic (6th century AD onwards).
Bulg = Bulgarian, a south Slavic language (11th century onwards).
Corn = Cornish, Celtic language of Cornwall.
Cretan Grk = the variety of ancient Greek spoken on Crete.
Czech = Czech, a western Slavic language (11th century onwards).
Doric Grk = Doric Greek, one of the principal groups of the West Greek dialects.
Gallo-Roman = the Latin spoken in Gaul after the Roman conquest.
Gaul = Gaulish, a Continental Celtic language (3rd–1st centuries BC).
Goth = Gothic, an eastern Germanic language (4th century AD).
Grk = Greek (8th century BC onwards).
HierLuv = Hieroglyphic Luvian, an Anatolian language (1300–700 BC).
Hit = Hittite, an Anatolian language (1650–1190 BC).
Homeric Grk = the Greek dialect of the Homeric poems (800 BC).
Ibero-Celtic = the variety of Celtic spoken in Iberia (3rd–1st centuries BC).
Illyr = Illyrian.
Ishkashmi = a Southeast Iranian language (modern).
Kashmiri = Indic language of Kashmir (14th century onwards).
Khot = Khotanese, an Eastern Iranian language (5th–10th centuries AD).
Khowar = Dardic/Northwestern Indic language (modern).
Khufi = a Southeast Iranian language (modern).
Kurd = Kurdish, a North-west Iranian language (modern).
Lat = Latin (7th century BC onwards).
Latv = Latvian, Baltic (16th century onwards).
Ligurian = presumably Celtic language of north Italy.
Lith = Lithuanian, Baltic (18th century onwards).
Luv = Luvian, Anatolian language (17th–8th centuries BC).

Lyc = Lycian, Anatolian language of southwest Anatolia (6th–4th centuries BC).

Lyd = Lydian, Anatolian language of west central Anatolia (6th–4th centuries BC).

Maced = Macedonian, a language closely related to Greek.

MDutch = West (Low) Germanic (*c* 1300 to 1500).

ME = Middle English, Germanic (12th–15th centuries).

Messapic – non-Italic language of southeast Italy (6th–1st centuries BC).

MHG = Middle High German (AD 1050–1500).

MIr = Middle Irish, Celtic (AD 900–1200).

Mitanni = Hurrian (non-IE) language of the upper Euphrates with elements of Indo-Aryan (15th–14th centuries BC).

MLG = Middle Low German (AD 1050–1350).

MPers = Middle Persian, Southwestern Iranian (200 BC–AD 700).

MWels = Middle Welsh, Celtic (AD 1200–1500).

Myc = Mycenaean, earliest attested Greek (16th? –13th centuries BC).

NDutch = modern Dutch, West Germanic (1500 onwards).

NE = New (Modern) English, Germanic (1500 onwards).

NHG = New High German, Germanic (1500 onwards).

NIce = New Icelandic, North Germanic language (1400 onwards).

NIr = New Irish, Celtic (1200 onwards).

Norw = Norwegian, North Germanic (1800 onwards).

NPers = New Persian, Southwestern Iranian (8th century AD onwards).

OBrit = Old British, Celtic (until 8th century AD).

OCS = Old Church Slavonic, Slavic (9th–13th centuries).

OCzech = Old Czech, West Slavic (13th–16th centuries).

OE = Old English, Germanic (800–1150).

OHG = Old High German, West Germanic (750 to 1050).

OIr = Old Irish, Celtic (600 to 900).

OLat = Old Latin (6th–2nd centuries BC).

OLith = Old Lithuanian, Baltic (16th–18th centuries).

ON = Old Norse, Germanic (1150–1550).

OPers = Old Persian, Southwestern Iranian (6th–5th centuries BC).

OPol = Old Polish, West Slavic (13th–15th centuries).

OPrus = Old Prussian, West Baltic (16th–18th centuries).

ORus = Old Russian, East Slavic (1050–1600).

Osc = Oscan, Italic (5th–1st centuries BC).

Oss = Ossetic, Northeast Iranian (modern).

OSwed = Old Swedish, North Germanic language (13th–14th centuries).
OWels = Old Welsh, Celtic (9th–12th centuries).
Pal = Palaic, Anatolian (*c.* 16th century BC).
Parth = Parthian, Northwest Iranian (3rd–1st centuries BC).
Pashto = Southeast Iranian (modern).
Phryg = Phrygian (8th–3rd centuries BC and 1st century AD).
PIE = Proto-Indo-European.
Pol = Polish, Western Slavic (13th century onwards).
Roshani = Southeast Iranian (modern).
Runic = language of the earliest Germanic inscriptions (3rd–6th centuries AD).
Rus = Russian, East Slavic (*c.* 1050 AD onwards).
RusCS = Russian variety of Old Church Slavonic.
Sanglechi = Southeast Iranian (modern).
Sarikoli = Southeast Iranian (modern).
SC = Serbo-Croatian, South Slavic (19th century onwards).
SGael = Scots Gaelic, Celtic (13th century onwards).
Scyth = Scythian, Iranian.
SerbCS = Serbian variety of Old Church Slavonic.
Shughni = Southeast Iranian (modern).
Skt = Sanskrit, Indo-Aryan (1000 BC onwards)
Slov = Slovene, South Slavic (16th century onwards).
Sogdian = Northeast Iranian (4th–8th centuries).
Swed = Swedish, North Germanic (15th century onwards).
Thessalian Grk = classical Greek dialect of Thessaly.
Thrac = Thracian (5th century BC).
TochA = Tocharian A (7th–10th centuries AD).
TochB = Tocharian B (5th–13th centuries AD).
Umb = Umbrian, Italic (3rd–1st centuries BC).
Waigali = Nūristāni, Indo-Iranian (modern).
NWels = New Welsh, Celtic (1500 onwards).

Introduction

The *Oxford Introduction to Proto-Indo-European and The Proto-Indo-European World* fills the need for a relatively concise introduction to the full range of reconstructed vocabulary of the language that gave rise to the world's largest language family. It addresses two levels of readers. The first comprises general readers and students who want to know more about the Indo-Europeans and how they spoke, as well as professionals in disciplines such as archaeology who need to deal with the early Indo-Europeans. The second consists of linguists interested in refining, challenging, or adding to our understanding of Proto-Indo-European.

The book is broadly divided into two parts. The first, aimed principally at the first group of readers, gives concise introductions to: the discovery and composition of the Indo-European language family (chapters 1 and 2); the way the proto-language has been reconstructed (chapter 3); its most basic grammar (chapter 4); the interrelationships between the different language groups (chapter 5); and the temporal position of the Indo-European languages (chapter 6). Some of the difficulties involved in reconstructing a proto-language are described in chapter 7.

The second part, aimed at all readers, provides accounts by semantic field of the Proto-Indo-European lexicon. Where the evidence suggests that an item may be reconstructed to full Proto-Indo-European antiquity, we provide a summary table giving the reconstructed form, its meaning, and its cognates in English and in the three 'classical' languages of Latin, Greek, and Sanskrit. Our survey of semantic fields travels first into the natural world of the earth and heavens, fauna, and flora, before moving into the human realms of anatomy, kinship, architecture, clothing, material culture, food and drink, and social organization. It then looks at the more abstract notions of space, time and quantity, before turning to considerations of mind, perception, speech, activity, and finally religion. This organization reflects Carl Darling Buck's in his *A Dictionary of Selected Synonyms in the Principal Indo-European Languages*, and we have indeed aimed to do for Proto-Indo-European something of what Buck did for the individual Indo-European languages.

The final three chapters describe some of the commonest grammatical elements of Proto-Indo-European, survey the methods used to reconstruct the mythology of the Proto-Indo-Europeans, and examine the various attempts at locating the Proto-Indo-European homeland. In addition to standard indexes, the book also contains two word lists: a Proto-Indo-European English list and a list of the Proto-Indo-European vocabulary arranged by its English meaning (which should at least facilitate those who delight in such tasks as translating Hamlet into Klingon).

Students and general readers will be able to gain a broad knowledge from this book of the ancient language that underlies all the modern Indo-European languages. We hope that the arrangement of evidence by semantic group here will also stimulate research by linguists. One cannot be confronted with a list of, say, verbal roots all with the same 'reconstructed' meaning without wondering how their semantic valence may have differed in the proto-language and to what extent it might be possible to recover something of their earlier nuances. Although we frequently allude to attempts to discuss the data according to some system of folk taxonomy, this is obviously another area that has been insufficiently examined in the study of Proto-Indo-European. The various regional ascriptions of cognates will doubtless be subject to further scrutiny: the discovery of an Iranian cognate, say, to a word otherwise only found in European languages would change our conception of Proto-Indo-European itself. Other areas for further investigation include quantitative approaches to the Indo-European vocabulary (for example, phoneme preferences and investigation of sound symbolism by semantic class), and the comparison of Proto- Indo-European with other reconstructed proto-languages.

The Proto-Indo-European field of study opens a window on a distant past and presents the scholar and student with many opportunities for investigation and discovery. We hope the present guide will reveal something of its vibrancy, challenge, and endless fascination.

1

Discovery

1.1 Language Relations

One of the first hurdles anyone encounters in studying a foreign language is learning a new vocabulary. Faced with a list of words in a foreign language, we instinctively scan it to see how many of the words may be like those of our own language. We can provide a practical example (Table 1.1) by surveying a list of very common words in English and their equivalents in Dutch, Czech, and Spanish.

A glance at the table suggests that some words are more similar to their English counterparts than others and that for an English speaker the easiest or at least most similar vocabulary will certainly be that of Dutch. The similarities here are so great that with the exception of the words for 'dog' (Dutch *hond* which compares easily with English 'hound') and 'pig' (where Dutch *zwijn* is the equivalent of English 'swine'), there would be a nearly irresistible temptation for an English speaker to see Dutch as a bizarrely misspelled variety of English (a Dutch reader will no doubt choose to reverse the insult). When our myopic English speaker turns to the list of Czech words, he discovers to his pleasant surprise that he knows more Czech than he thought. The Czech words *bratr*, *sestra*, and *syn* are near hits of their English equivalents. Finally, he might be struck at how different the vocabulary of Spanish is (except for *madre*) although a few useful correspondences could be devised from the list, e.g. English *pork* and Spanish *puerco*.

The exercise that we have just performed must have occurred millions of times in European history as people encountered their neighbours' languages.

Table 1.1. *Some common words in English, Dutch, Czech, and Spanish*

English	Dutch	Czech	Spanish
mother	*moeder*	*matka*	*madre*
father	*vader*	*otec*	*padre*
brother	*broer*	*bratr*	*hermano*
sister	*zuster*	*sestra*	*hermana*
son	*zoon*	*syn*	*hijo*
daughter	*dochter*	*dcera*	*hija*
dog	*hond*	*pes*	*perro*
cow	*koe*	*kráva*	*vaca*
sheep	*schaap*	*ovce*	*oveja*
pig	*zwijn*	*prase*	*puerco*
house	*huis*	*dům*	*casa*

The balance of comparisons was not to be equal, however, because Latin was the prestige language employed both in religious services and as an international means of communication. A medieval monk in England, employing his native Old English, or a scholar in medieval Iceland who spoke Old Norse, might exercise their ingenuity on the type of wordlist displayed in Table 1.2 where we have included the Latin equivalents.

The similarities between Latin and Old English in the words for 'mother', 'father', and 'pig', for example, might be explained by the learned classes in terms of the influence of Latin on the other languages of Europe. Latin, the language of the Roman Empire, had pervaded the rest of Europe's languages, and someone writing in the Middle Ages, when Latin words were regularly being imported into native vernaculars, could hear the process happening with their own ears. The prestige of Latin, however, was overshadowed by that of Greek as even the Romans acknowledged the antiquity and superior position of ancient Greek. This veneration for Greek prompted a vaguely conceived model in which Latin had evolved as some form of degraded Greek. Literary or chronological prestige then created a sort of linguistic pecking order with Greek at the apex and most ancient, then the somewhat degenerate Latin, and then a series of debased European languages that had been influenced by Latin.

What about the similarities between Old English and Old Norse? Our English monk might note that all ten words on the list appeared to correspond with one another and in two instances the words were precisely the same ('pig' and 'house'). We have no idea whether any Englishman understood why the two languages were so similar. But in the twelfth century a clever Icelandic

Table 1.2. *Comparable words in Old English, Old Norse, and Latin*

English	Old English	Old Norse	Latin
mother	*mōdor*	*mōðir*[a]	*māter*
father	*fæder*	*faðir*	*pater*
brother	*brōðor*	*brōðir*	*frāter*
sister	*sweostor*	*systir*	*soror*
son	*sunu*	*sunr*	*fīlius*
daughter	*dohtor*	*dōttir*	*fīlia*
dog	*hund*	*hundr*	*canis*
cow	*cū*	*kȳr*	*bōs*
sheep	*ēowu*	*ær*	*ovis*
pig	*swīn*	*svīn*	*suīnus*
house	*hūs*	*hūs*	*domus*

[a] The Old English and Norse *ð* is equivalent to a 'th' in English, e.g. *this*.

scholar, considering these types of similarities, concluded that Englishmen and Icelanders 'are of one tongue, even though one of the two (tongues) has changed greatly, or both somewhat'. In a wider sense, the Icelander believed that the two languages, although they differed from one another, had 'previously parted or branched off from one and the same tongue'. The image of a tree with a primeval language as a trunk branching out into its various daughter languages was quite deliberate—the Icelander employed the Old Norse verb *greina* 'to branch'. This model of a tree of related languages would later come to dominate how we look at the evolution of the Indo-European languages (see Section 5.1).

The similarities between the languages of Europe could then be accounted for in two ways: some of the words might be explained by diffusion or borrowing, here from Latin to the other languages of Europe. Other similarities might be explained by their common genetic inheritance, i.e. there had once been a primeval language from whence the current languages had all descended and branched away. In this latter situation, we are dealing with more than similarities since the words in question correspond with one another in that they have the same origin and then, as the anonymous Icelander suggests, one or both altered through time.

Speculation as to the identity of the primeval language was largely governed by the Bible that provided a common origin for humankind. The biblical account offered three decisive linguistic events. The first, the creation of Adam and Eve, provided a single ancestral language which, given the authority and origin of the Bible, ensured that Hebrew might be widely regarded as the 'original' language from which all others had descended. Hebrew as a common language, however, did not make it past the sixth chapter of Genesis when the three sons of Noah—Shem, Ham, and Japheth—were required to repeople the world after the Flood. These provided the linguistic ancestors of three major groups—the Semites, the Hamites (Egyptians, Cushites), and the offspring of Japheth to whom Europeans looked for their own linguistic ancestry. By the eleventh chapter of Genesis the world's linguistic diversity was re-explained as the result of divine industrial sabotage against the construction crews building the Tower of Babel.

During the sixteenth century pieces of the linguistic puzzle were beginning to fall into place. Joseph Scaliger (1540–1609), French (later Dutch) Renaissance scholar and one of the founders of literary historical criticism, who incidentally also gave astronomers their Julian Day Count, could employ the way the various languages of Europe expressed the concept of 'god' to divide them into separate groups (Table 1.3); in these we can see the seeds of the Romance, Germanic, and Slavic language groups. The problem was explaining the relationships between these different but transparently similar groups. The initial catalyst for this came at the end of the sixteenth century and not from a European language.

By the late sixteenth century Jesuit missionaries had begun working in India—St Francis Xavier (1506–52) is credited with supplying Europe with its first example of Sanskrit, the classical language of ancient India, in a letter written in 1544 (he cited the invocation *Om Srii naraina nama*). Classically trained, the Jesuits wrote home that there was an uncanny resemblance between Sanskrit and the classical languages of Europe. By 1768 Gaston Cœurdoux (1691–1777) was presenting evidence to the French Academy that Sanskrit, Latin, and Greek were extraordinarily similar to one another and probably shared a common origin. A glance at our wordlist (Table 1.4), now extended to include Greek and Sanskrit, indicates just how striking those resemblances could be.

The correspondences between the language of ancient India and those of ancient Greece and Rome were too close to be dismissed as chance and,

Table 1.3. *Scaliger's language groups based on their word for 'god'*

DEUS GROUP	GOTT GROUP	BOG GROUP	THEOS GROUP
Latin *deus*	German *Gott*	Russian *bog*	Greek *theós*
Italian *dio*	Dutch *god*	Ukrainian *bog*	
Spanish *dio*	Swedish *gud*	Polish *bog*	
French *dieu*	English *god*	Czech *buh*	

Table 1.4. *Comparable words in the classical languages and Sanskrit*

ENGLISH	LATIN	GREEK	SANSKRIT
mother	*māter*	*mḗtēr*	*mātár-*
father	*pater*	*patḗr*	*pitár-*
brother	*frāter*	*phrḗtēr*	*bhrā́tar-*
sister	*soror*	*éor*	*svásar-*
son	*fīlius*	*huiús*	*sūnú-*
daughter	*fīlia*	*thugátēr*	*duhitár-*
dog	*canis*	*kúōn*	*śván-*
cow	*bōs*	*boûs*	*gáu-*
sheep	*ovis*	*ó(w)ïs*	*ávi-*
pig	*suīnus*	*hûs*	*sūkará-*
house	*domus*	*dō̂*	*dā́m*

although similar equations had been noted previously, history generally dates the inception of the Indo-European model to 1786 when Sir William Jones (1746–94), Sanskrit scholar and jurist, delivered his address to the Asiatic Society in Calcutta and observed:

> The Sanskrit language, whatever be its antiquity, is of a wonderful structure; more perfect than the Greek, more copious than the Latin, and more exquisitely refined than either, yet bearing to both of them a stronger affinity, both in the roots of the verbs and in the forms of grammar, than could possibly have been produced by accident; so strong indeed, that no philologer could examine them all three, without believing them to have sprung from some common source, which, perhaps, no longer exists: there is a similar reason, though not quite so forcible, for supposing that both the Gothic and the Celtic, though blended with a very different idiom, had the same origin with Sanskrit; and the old Persian might be added to the same family, if this were the place for discussing any question concerning the antiquities of Persia.

Jones's remarks contain a number of important elements. First, they suggest that there is a language 'family' that comprises Sanskrit, Greek, Latin, Persian, Gothic (Germanic), and Celtic. All these languages or language groups are derived from a common ancestor—Jones is uncertain whether this common ancestor is still spoken somewhere. And reprising an earlier tradition, he also imagines that Germanic and Celtic are in some ways adulterated languages that sprang from the blending of the original language with other elements that made them appear less closely related to the three classical tongues.

Critical to this entire model is the actual evidence that the various languages belong to the same family. Jones did not base his conclusions on the transparent similarities found in wordlists but rather on the correspondences also found in grammar (Gaston Cœurdoux also employed grammatical evidence). This was a critical insight because items of vocabulary may well be borrowed from one language to another (e.g. we have English *penicillin*, Irish *pinisilin*, Russian *penitsillín*, Turkish *penisilin*) and there is no question that Latin loanwords have indeed enriched many of the languages of Europe. But while a word may be borrowed, it is far less likely that an entire grammatical system will also be borrowed. A comparison of the present conjugation of the verb 'carry' in Sanskrit, Greek, and Latin indicates that systematic correspondences go beyond the similarity of the roots themselves (Table 1.5).

Table 1.5. *The verb 'to carry' in Sanskrit, Greek, and Latin*

	SANSKRIT	GREEK	LATIN
I carry	*bhárāmi*	*phérō*	*ferō*
You carry	*bhárasi*	*phéreis*	*fers*
He/she carries	*bhárati*	*phérei*	*fert*
We carry	*bhárāmas*	*phéromen*	*ferimus*
You carry	*bháratha*	*phérete*	*fertis*
They carry	*bháranti*	*phérousi*	*ferunt*

1.2 Indo-European

By 1800 a preliminary model for the relationship between many of the languages of Europe and some of those of Asia had been constructed. The language family came to be known as Indo-Germanic (so named by Conrad Malte-Brun in 1810 as it extended from India in the east to Europe whose westernmost language, Icelandic, belonged to the Germanic group of languages) or Indo-European (Thomas Young in 1813).

Where the relationships among language groups were relatively transparent, progress was rapid in the expansion of the numbers of languages assigned to the Indo-European family. Between the dates of the two early great comparative linguists, Rasmus Rask (1787–1832) and Franz Bopp (1791–1867), comparative grammars appeared that solidified the positions of Sanskrit, Iranian, Greek, Latin, Germanic, Baltic, Slavic, Albanian, and Celtic within the Indo-European family. Some entered easily while others initially proved more difficult. The Iranian languages, for example, were added when comparison between Iran's ancient liturgical texts, the *Avesta*, was made with those in Sanskrit. The similarities between the two languages were so great that some thought that the

Avestan language was merely a dialect of Sanskrit, but by 1826 Rask demonstrated conclusively that Avestan was co-ordinate with Sanskrit and not derived from it. He also showed that it was an earlier relative of the modern Persian language. The Celtic languages, which displayed many peculiarities not found in the classical languages, required a greater scholarly effort to see their full incorporation into the Indo-European scheme. Albanian had absorbed so many loanwords from Latin, Greek, Slavic, and Turkish that it required far more effort to discern its Indo-European core vocabulary that set it off as an independent language.

After this initial phase, which saw nine major language groups entered into the Indo-European fold, progress was more difficult. Armenian was the next major language to see full incorporation. It was correctly identified as an independent Indo-European language by Rask but he then changed his mind and joined the many who regarded it as a variety of Iranian. This reticence in seeing Armenian as an independent branch of Indo-European was due to the massive borrowing from Iranian languages, and here the identification of Armenian's original Indo-European core vocabulary did not really emerge until about 1875.

The last two major Indo-European groups to be discovered were products of archaeological research of the late nineteenth and early twentieth centuries. Western expeditions to oasis sites of the Silk Road in Xinjiang, the westernmost province of China, uncovered an enormous quantity of manuscripts in the first decades of the twentieth century. Many of these were written in Indic or Iranian but there were also remains of two other languages which are now known as Tocharian and by 1908 they had been definitely shown to represent an independent group of the Indo-European family. It was archaeological excavations in Anatolia that uncovered cuneiform tablets which were tentatively attributed to Indo-European as early as 1902 but were not solidly demonstrated to be so until 1915, when Hittite was accepted into the Indo-European fold. Other Indo-European languages, poorly attested in inscriptions, glosses in Greek or other sources, or personal and place names in classical sources, have also entered the Indo-European family. The more important are Lusatian in Iberia, Venetic and Messapic in Italy, Illyrian in the west Balkans, Dacian and Thracian in the east Balkans, and Phrygian in central Anatolia.

If we prepare a map of Eurasia and depict on it the various major groups of Indo-European languages (Map 1.1), we find that they extend from the Atlantic to western China and eastern India; from northernmost Scandinavia south to the Mediterranean and the Indian Ocean. The family consists of languages or language groups from varying periods. As we are currently painting our Indo-European world with a broad brush, we can divide the Indo-European groups into those in which there are languages still spoken today and those that

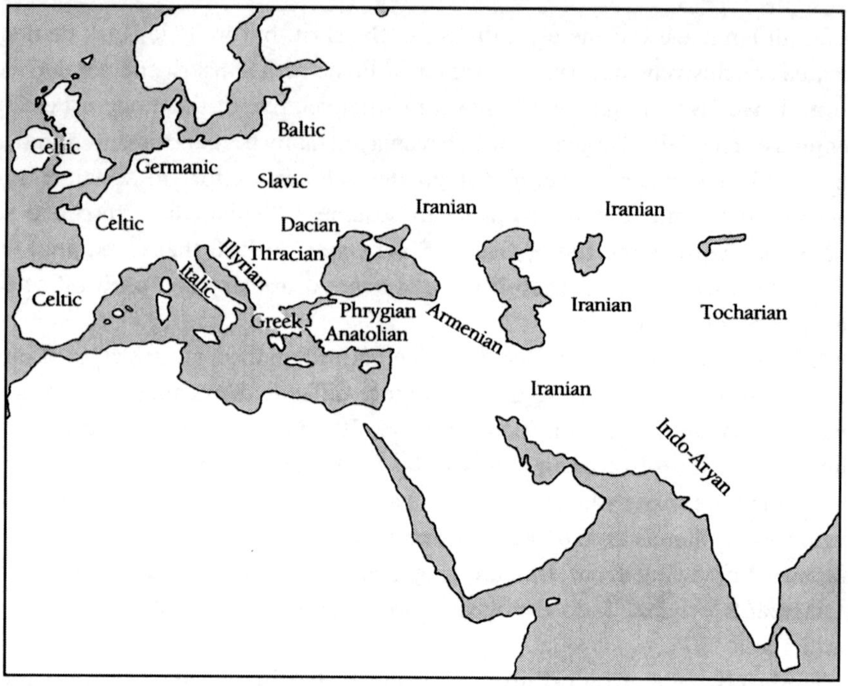

Map 1.1. Map of the Indo-European world

are extinct (Table 1.6). In some cases the relationship between an ancient language such as Illyrian and its possible modern representative, Albanian, is uncertain.

The map of the surviving Indo-European groups (Map 1.2) masks the many changes that have affected the distribution of the various language groups. Celtic and Baltic, for example, once occupied territories vastly greater than their attenuated status today and Iranian has seen much of its earlier territory eroded by the influx of other languages.

The map of the Indo-European languages is not entirely continuous as there are traces of non-Indo-European languages in Europe as well (Map 1.3). Even before a model of the Indo-European family was being constructed, scholars had begun observing that another major linguistic family occupied Europe. Before 1800 the Hungarian linguist S. Gyármathi (1751–1830) had demonstrated that Hungarian, a linguistic island surrounded by a sea of Indo-European languages, was related to Finnish (Hungarian did not take up its historical seat until the Middle Ages). He accomplished this primarily on the basis of grammatical elements, rightly realizing that vocabulary offers the least trustworthy evidence because it may be so easily borrowed. Linguists, including the irrepressible Rask, established the constituent elements of the Uralic

Table 1.6. *Status of Indo-European groups*

Surviving Groups	Extinct Groups
Celtic	Anatolian
Italic	Tocharian
Germanic	Phrygian
Baltic	Thracian
Slavic	Dacian
Albanian	Messapic
Greek	Venetic
Armenian	Illyrian(?)
Iranian	
Indic	

language family. In Europe this comprises Finnish, Karelian, Lapp (Saami), Estonian, Hungarian, and a number of languages spoken immediately to the west of the Urals such as Mordvin and Mari. Its speakers also occupy a broad region east of the Urals and include the second major Uralic branch, the Samoyedic languages.

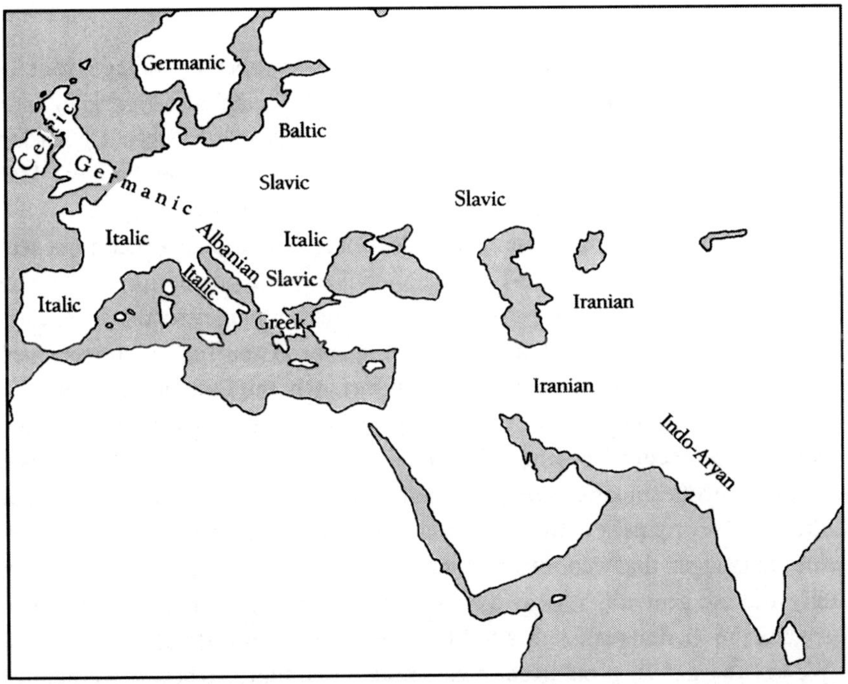

Map 1.2. Surviving Indo-European groups

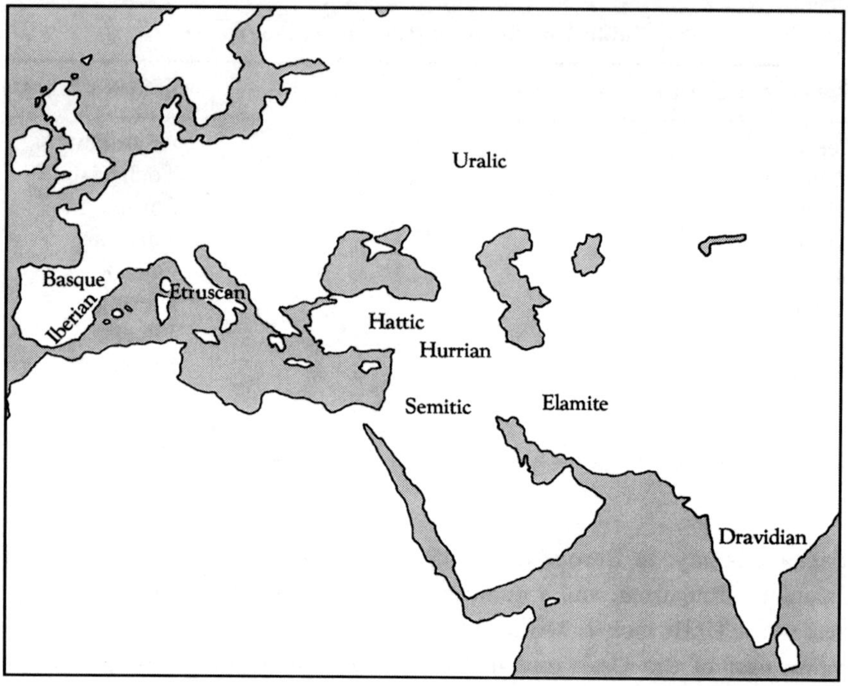

Map 1.3. Major known non-Indo-European groups in Europe and western Asia

The Caucasus has yielded a series of non-Indo-European languages that are grouped into several major families. Kartvelian, which includes Georgian in the south and two northern varieties, Northern and North-Eastern Caucasian, both of which may derive from a common ancestor. What has not been demonstrated is a common ancestor for all the Caucasian languages.

In Anatolia and South-West Asia Indo-Europeans came into contact with many of the early non-Indo-European civilizations, including Hattic and Hurrian in Anatolia, the large group of Semitic languages to the south, and Elamite in southern Iran. The Indo-Aryans shared the Indian subcontinent with two other language families, most importantly the Dravidian family.

The major surviving non-Indo-European language of western Europe is Basque, which occupies northern Spain and southern France. The other spoken non-Indo-European languages of Europe are more recent imports such as Maltese whose origins lie in the expansion of Arabic. There are also poorly attested extinct languages that cannot be (confidently) assigned to the Indo-European family and are generally regarded as non-Indo-European. These would include Iberian in the Iberian peninsula and Etruscan in north-central Italy.

We have seen that speculations concerning the similarities between languages led to the concept of an Indo-European family of languages comprised of twelve main groups and a number of poorly attested extinct groups. This language family was established on the basis of systematic correspondence in grammar and vocabulary among its constituent members. The similarities were explained as the result of the dispersal or dissolution of a single ancestral language that devolved into its various daughter groups, languages, and dialects. We call this ancestral language Proto-Indo-European.

Further Reading

For the history of language studies see Robins (1997). The history of the development of Indo-European is covered in Delbruck (1882) and Pedersen (1931). The spread of knowledge of Sanskrit to the West and the precursors to Jones's observations can be found in Amaladass (1992).

2

The Elements

2.1 The Indo-European Languages

We have seen how the Indo-European language family is comprised of twelve major groups and a number of languages, attested in antiquity, whose relationship to the major groups is uncertain or whose own evidence is quite meagre. All the groups are listed in Table 2.1 in very approximate geographical order, reading west to east (Map 1.1; Table 2.1).

The present geographical distribution of the languages, although it highlights some of the potential developmental history and interrelationships between the different groups, is not the way historical linguists might choose to order their material. As we have already seen, in some cases we are dealing with the limited survival of language groups that once enjoyed vastly larger distributions, e.g. Celtic, which was once known over most of western and much of central Europe but is now limited to the fringes of Great Britain, Ireland, and Brittany, or we find the more recent historical expansion of languages, e.g. Germanic and Slavic, once far more confined in space. While there are linguists who are interested in the interactions between current IE languages, e.g. French loanwords in English, the primary interest of the Indo-Europeanist concerns the origins of the Indo-European proto-language and its

Table 2.1. *Major and minor groups of Indo-European languages*

MAJOR GROUPS	MINOR GROUPS
Celtic	Lusitanian
Italic	Rhaetic
Germanic	Venetic
Baltic	South Picene
Slavic	Messapic
Albanian	Illyrian
Greek	Dacian
Armenian	Thracian
Anatolian	Macedonian
Iranian	Phrygian
Indo-Aryan	
Tocharian	

evolution into the different Indo-European languages. This means that an Indo-Europeanist will focus on the earliest attested Indo-European languages as a source closer in time and more valuable in content to the main research agenda. One might then rearrange the list in terms of the antiquity of each group's earliest (usually inscriptional) attestations (Table 2.2).

The antiquity of attestation is at best only a very rough guide to the value of each language group to the Indo-Europeanist. A handful of inscriptions may be useful but often the main body of textual evidence must be drawn from periods long after the earliest attestation, e.g. the earliest evidence of Celtic dates to *c.* 600 BC but most of our Celtic textual evidence dates to the Middle Ages, some 1,300 years later. In Indo-European studies, the comparative linguist will generally focus on the earliest well-attested stage of a language, e.g. Old English (*c.* AD 700–100), and only move into increasingly more recent forms of the language (Middle English at *c.*1100–1450 or New English *c.*1450–) when and if the latter stages of a language contribute something that cannot be recovered from the earlier. Where a language is extraordinarily well attested in its ancient form—Latin, Greek, and Sanskrit—there is seldom cause to present the later evidence of these language groups—Italian, Modern Greek, or Hindi/Urdu. On the other hand, where the evidence for the ancient language tends to be more limited, e.g. early Iranian languages such as Avestan and Old Persian, then recourse to more recent Iranian languages can help fill in the gaps.

The antiquity of attestation or even main textual evidence, however, is not a complete guide to the utility of a language group to contribute to our understanding of the development of Indo-European. One of the most recently

Table 2.2. *Antiquity of earliest attestation (in units of 500 years) of each Indo-European group*

2000–1500 BC	Anatolian
1500–1000 BC	Indo-Aryan
	Greek
1000–500 BC	Iranian
	Celtic
	Italic
	Phrygian
	Illyrian
	Messapic
	South Picene
	Venetic
500–1 BC	Thracian
	Macedonian
AD 1–500	Germanic
	Armenian
	Lusitanian
	Tocharian
AD 500–1000	Slavic
AD 1500–2000	Albanian
	Baltic

attested Indo-European groups, Baltic, contributes far more to discussions of Indo-European then a number of the earlier attested groups. One way of measuring the contribution of each group to Indo-European studies is to measure the frequency of its citation in the modern handbooks of Indo-European culture. There are two of these: Thomas Gamkrelidze and Vyacheslav Ivanov's *Indo-European and Indo-Europeans* (1995=G-I) and J. P. Mallory and D. Q. Adams's *Encyclopedia of Indo-European Culture* (1997=M-A). If we take the indices of words cited by language group across both encyclopedias (Table 2.3), the results are reasonably comparable. The Germanic languages have been well studied and a variety of them are routinely employed in Indo-European studies. Nevertheless, no single Germanic language is anywhere near as important as Greek. The Baltic languages, although attested the most recently, play a major part in Indo-European linguistics as does Indo-Aryan, here overwhelmingly Sanskrit. We will examine later how each language group contributes to the reconstruction of the proto-language.

The purpose of this chapter is to provide a brief survey of what constitutes the main linguistic groups employed by Indo-European linguists in their

Table 2.3. *Language group citation frequency in two Indo-European encyclopedias*

	G-I	M-A
Germanic	2,168	5,691
Greek	1,847	2,441
Baltic	1,019	2,376
Sanskrit	1,822	2,139
Italic	1,339	1,902
Celtic	687	1,823
Slavic	1,101	1,429
Iranian	1,122	1,408
Tocharian	377	1,111
Anatolian	1,341	765
Armenian	327	595
Albanian	163	445
Other	56	167
Total	13,369	22,292

Note: Gamkrelidze and Ivanov 1995 = G-I; Mallory and Adams 1997 = M-A.

reconstruction of the earliest relations and culture of the Indo-European family. The evidence will be arranged here according to its approximate geographical position, west to east.

2.2 Celtic

The Celtic languages represent one of the more attenuated groups of Indo-European. In the first centuries BC Celtic languages could be found from Ireland in the west across Britain and France, south into Spain, and east into central Europe. Celtic tribes raided the Balkans, sacked Delphi in 279 BC, and some settled in Anatolia in the same century to become the Galatians. The expansion of the Roman Empire north and westwards and the later movement of the Germanic tribes southwards saw the widespread retraction of Celtic languages on the Continent.

The Celtic languages are traditionally divided into two main groups—Continental and Insular Celtic (Table 2.4; Map 2.1). The Continental Celtic languages are the earliest attested. Names are found in Greek and Roman records while inscriptions in Celtic languages are found in France, northern Italy, and

Spain. The Continental evidence is usually divided into Gaulish, attested in inscriptions in both southern and central France, Lepontic, which is known from northern Italy in the vicinity of Lake Maggiore, and Ibero-Celtic or Hispano-Celtic in the north-western two-thirds of the Iberian peninsula. The inscriptions are very heavily biased toward personal names and do not present a particularly wide-ranging reservoir of the Celtic language. The earliest inscriptions are in the Lepontic language. Celtic inscriptions may be written in the Greek script, modified versions of the Etruscan script, the Roman script, or, in Iberia, in a syllabic script employed by the non-Indo-European Iberians. Where the inscriptions do have value is illustrating the earliest evidence for Celtic speech in its most primitive form. This latter point is quite significant as most of the Insular Celtic languages have suffered such a brusque restructuring that many of the original grammatical elements have either been lost or heavily altered.

Table 2.4. *The evidence of Celtic*

CONTINENTAL CELTIC
Gaulish (*c.* 220–1 BC)
Lepontic (*c.* 600–100 BC)
Ibero-Celtic (*c.* 200–1 BC)
INSULAR CELTIC
Ancient British (*c.* AD 1–600)
Welsh
Archaic (*c.* AD 600–900),
Old Welsh (900–1200),
Middle Welsh (1200–1500)
Modern Welsh (1500–)
Cornish
Old Cornish (*c.* AD 800–1200)
Middle Cornish (1200–1575)
Late Cornish (1575–1800)
Breton
Primitive Breton (*c.* AD 500–600)
Old Breton (600–1000)
Middle Breton (1000–1600)
Modern Breton (1600–)
Irish
Ogam Irish (*c.* AD 400–700)
Old Irish (*c.* AD 700–900)
Middle Irish (*c.* AD 900–1200)
Modern Irish (1200–)

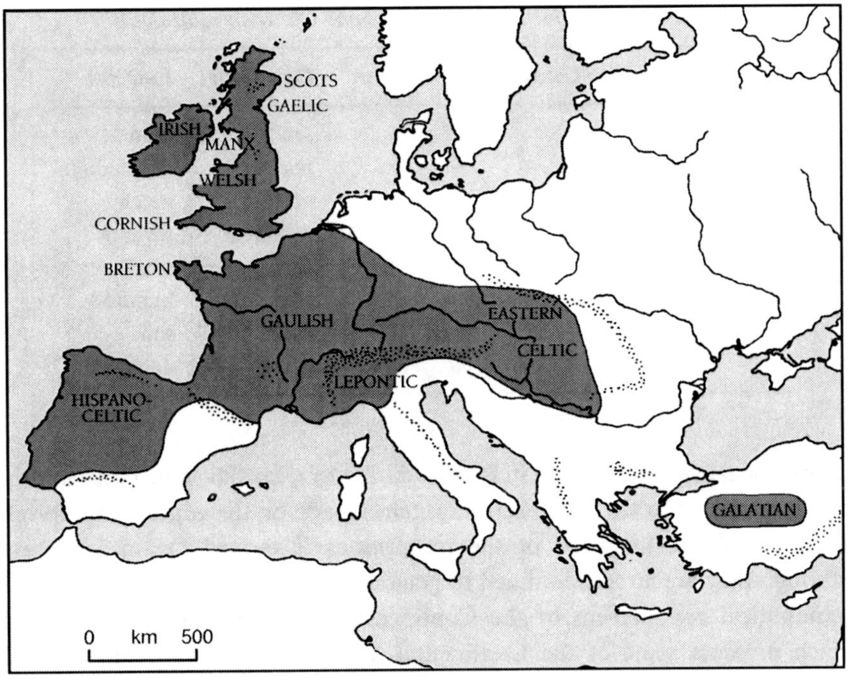

Map 2.1. Distribution of the Celtic languages

The Insular Celtic languages, so named because they were spoken in Britain and Ireland, are divided into two main groups—Brittonic and Goidelic. The first comprises the languages spoken or originating in Britain. The early British language of the first centuries BC, known primarily from inscriptions and Roman sources, evolved into a series of distinct languages—Welsh, Cornish, and Breton. Welsh developed a rich literary tradition during the Middle Ages and the main body of Welsh textual material derives from the Middle Welsh period. Cornish, which became extinct by the end of the 18th century, yields a much smaller volume of literature, and most of our Cornish data derives from the Middle Cornish period (which also serves as the basis of the Modern Cornish revival). Breton originated in Britain and was carried from southern Britain to Brittany during the fifth to seventh centuries where, some argue, it may have encountered remnant survivors of Gaulish.

The Goidelic languages comprise Irish and two languages derived from Irish—Scots Gaelic and Manx—that were imported into their historical positions in the early Middle Ages.

From a linguistic standpoint, the most important of the Celtic languages is Old and Middle Irish, as the quantity of output for these periods was quite large (the dictionary of early Irish runs to more than 2,500 pages). There is also

Table 2.5. *Continental Celtic and some Old Irish equivalents*

GAULISH	IBERO-CELTIC	OGAM IRISH	OLD IRISH	ENGLISH
uiros	*uiros*	—	*fer*	man
uenia	—	—	*fine*	descendants
ollon	—	—	*oll*	much
sextametos	—	—	*sechtmad*	seventh
decametos	—	—	*dechmad*	tenth
canto(n)	*kantom*	—	*cēt*	hundred
mapo-	—	*maqi*	*maic*	son
—	—	*inigena*	*ingen*	daughter

inscriptional evidence of Irish in Ireland dating to *c.* AD 400–700. These inscriptions are written in the ogam script, notches made on the edges of an upright stone, hence the language of the inscriptions is termed Ogam Irish, and although they are largely confined to personal names, they do retain the fuller grammatical complement of the Continental Celtic inscriptions. Table 2.5, which presents some of the Continental and Insular inscriptional evidence compared with the equivalent words in Old Irish, indicates something of the scale of change in Old Irish compared with the earlier evidence for Continental Celtic languages.

2.3 Italic

Latin is the principal Italic language but it only achieved its particular prominence with the expansion of the Roman state in the first centuries BC. It is earliest attested in inscriptions that date from *c.* 620 BC onwards (Table 2.6; Map 2.2) and are described as Old Latin. The main source of our Latin evidence for an Indo-Europeanist derives from the more familiar Classical Latin that emerges about the first century BC. The closest linguistic relation to Latin is Faliscan, a language (or dialect) spoken about 40 km north of Rome and also attested in inscriptions from *c.* 600 BC until the first centuries BC when the region was assimilated entirely into the Latin language.

South of Rome lay the Samnites who employed the Oscan language, attested in inscriptions, including graffiti on the walls of the destroyed city of Pompeii, beginning about the fifth century BC. There are also about two hundred other documents, usually quite short, in the Oscan language. Oscan finds a close relation in Umbrian, which was spoken north of Rome, and, after Latin, provides the next largest corpus of Italic textual material (Table 2.7). Although

Table 2.6. *The evidence of the Italic languages*

LATIN-FALISCAN
Latin
Old Latin (*c.*620–80 BC)
Classical Latin (*c.*80 BC–AD 120)
Late Latin (AD 120–*c.*1000)
Faliscan (600–100 BC)
OSCO-UMBRIAN
Oscan (500–1 BC)
Umbrian (300–1 BC)

there are a number of short inscriptions, the major evidence of Umbrian derives from the Iguvine Tablets, a series of seven (of what were originally a total of nine) bronze tablets detailing Umbrian rituals and recorded between the third and first centuries BC. In addition to these major Italic languages, there are a series of inscriptions in poorly attested languages such as Sabine, Volscian, and Marsian. While these play a role in discussions of Italic languages, it is largely Latin and occasionally Oscan and Umbrian that play the greatest role in Indo-European studies.

The so-called Vulgar Latin of the late Roman Empire gradually divided into what we term the Romance languages. The earliest textual evidence for the various Romance languages begins with the ninth century for French, the tenth century for Spanish and Italian, the twelfth century for Portuguese, and the sixteenth century for Romanian. As our knowledge of Latin is so extensive, comparative linguists rarely require the evidence of the Romance languages in Indo-European research.

2.4 Germanic

The collapse of the Roman Empire was exacerbated by the southern and eastern expansion of Germanic tribes. The Germans first emerge in history occupying the north European plain from Flanders in the west to the Vistula river in the east; they also occupied at least southern Scandinavia.

The Germanic languages are divided into three major groups: eastern, northern, and western (Table 2.8). Eastern Germanic is attested by a single language, Gothic, the language of the Visigoths who settled in the Balkans where the Bible in the Gothic language (only portions of which survive) was prepared by the Christian missionary Wulfilas. This fourth-century translation

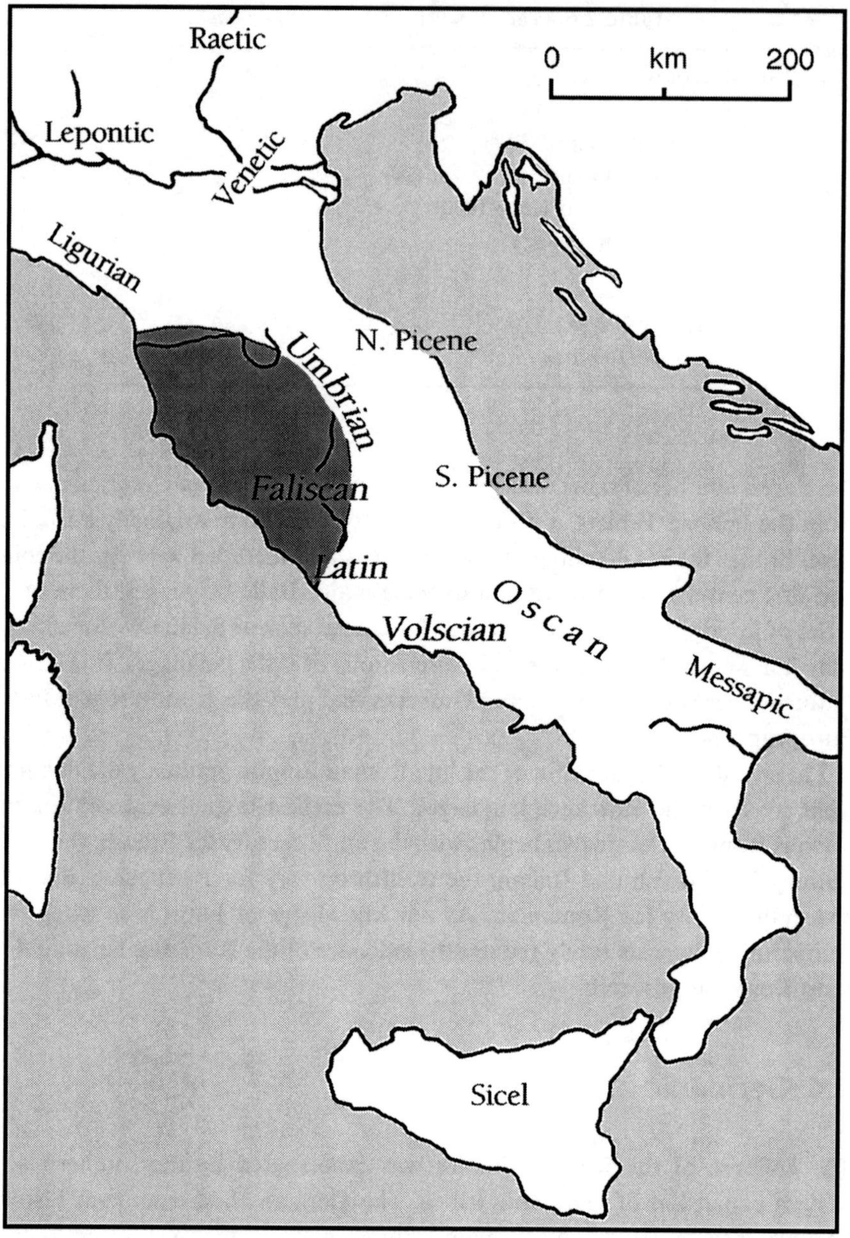

Map 2.2. Distribution of the Italic languages and Etruscan (shaded area)

Table 2.7. *Some IE cognates from the main Italic languages*

LATIN	OSCAN	UMBRIAN
pater 'father'	*patir*	pater
cānus 'grey'	*casnar* 'old'	—
lingua 'tongue'	*fangva-*	—
testis 'witness'	*trstus* 'third'	—
vir 'man'	—	*ueiro-*
avis 'bird'	—	*avi-*
probus 'good'	—	*prufe* 'properly'
—	*puklum* 'son'	—

survives primarily in a manuscript dated to *c.* AD 500. Eighty-six words of the language of the Ostrogoths were recorded in the Crimea by Oguier de Busbecq, a western diplomat to the Ottoman Empire, in the sixteenth century. Because of its early attestation and the moderately large size of the text that it offers,

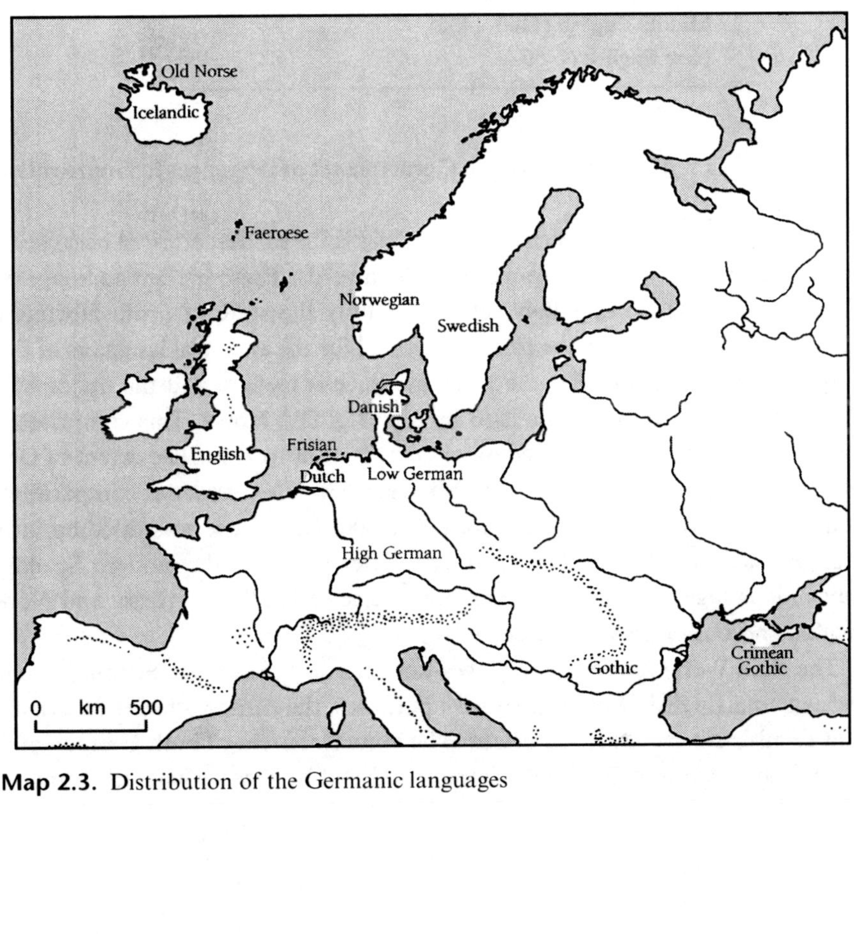

Map 2.3. Distribution of the Germanic languages

Table 2.8. *The evidence of the Germanic languages*

EAST GERMANIC
Gothic (350–1600)

NORTHERN GERMANIC
Runic (*c.* AD 300–1700)
Norse
  Primitive Norse (300–700)
  Old Norse (700–1350)

WEST GERMANIC
German
  Old High German (750–1050)
  Middle High German (1050–1350)
  New High German (1350–)
Dutch
  Old Dutch (–1150)
  Middle Dutch (1150–1500)
  Modern Dutch (1500–)
English
  Old English (700–1100)
  Middle English (1100–1450)
  New English (1450–)

Gothic plays a significant part of the Germanic set of languages in comparative linguistics.

The northern group of Germanic languages is the earliest attested because of runic inscriptions that date from *c.* AD 300 onwards. These present an image of Germanic so archaic that they reflect not only the state of proto-Northern Germanic but are close to the forms suggested for the ancestral language of the entire Germanic group. But the runic evidence is meagre and the major evidence for Northern Germanic is to be found in Old Norse. This comprises a vast literature, primarily centred on or composed in Iceland. The extent of Old Norse literature ensures that it is also regarded as an essential comparative component of the Germanic group. By *c.*1000, Old Norse was dividing into regional east and west dialects and these later provided the modern Scandinavian languages. Out of the west dialect came Icelandic, Faeroese, and Norwegian and out of East Norse came Swedish and Danish.

The main West Germanic languages were German, Frankish, Saxon, Dutch, Frisian, and English. For comparative purposes, the earliest stages of German and English are the most important. The textual sources of both German and English are such that Old High German and Old English provide the primary

Table 2.9. *Some basic comparisons between the major early Germanic languages*

GOTH	ON	OHG	OE	NE
fadar	*faðir*	*fater*	*fæder*	*father*
sunus	*sunr*	*sunu*	*sunu*	*son*
daúhtar	*dōttir*	*tohter*	*dohtor*	*daughter*
dags	*dagr*	*tak*	*dæg*	*day*
wulfs	*ulfr*	*wolf*	*wulf*	*wolf*
sitls	*setr*	*sezzal*	*setl*	*settle*

Note: Goth=Gothic, ON = Old Norse, OHG = Old High German, OE = Old English, NE = New English.

comparative evidence for their respective languages (cf. Mallory–Adams where only 23 Middle English words contribute what could not be found among the 1,630 Old English words cited). Incidentally, the closest linguistic relative to English is Frisian followed by Dutch.

2.5 Baltic

The Baltic languages, now confined to the north-east Baltic region, once extended over an area several times larger than their present distribution indicates. The primary evidence of the Baltic languages rests with two subgroups: West Baltic attested by the extinct Old Prussian, and East Baltic which survives today as Lithuanian and Latvian (Table 2.10; Map 2.4).

The evidence for Old Prussian is limited primarily to two short religious tracts (thirty pages altogether) and two Prussian wordlists with less than a thousand words. These texts date to the sixteenth–seventeenth centuries and were written by non-native speakers of Old Prussian.

Table 2.10. *The evidence of the Baltic languages*

WEST BALTIC
Old Prussian (*c.*1545–1700)
EAST BALTIC
Lithuanian (1515–)
Latvian (*c.*1550–)

Map 2.4. Distribution of the Baltic (shaded area) and Slavic languages

The evidence for the East Baltic languages is also tied to religious proselytization and it might be noted that the Lithuanians, beginning to convert to Christianity only in the fourteenth century, were among the last pagans in Europe. Unlike Old Prussian, however, both Lithuanian and Latvian survived and have full national literatures. There is considerable evidence that Latvian spread over an area earlier occupied by Uralic speakers, and within historic times an enclave of Uralic-speaking Livonians has virtually disappeared into their Latvian environment. Although attested no more recently than Albanian, the Baltic languages, especially Lithuanian, have been far more conservative and preserve many features that have disappeared from many much earlier attested Indo-European languages. For this reason, Lithuanian has always been treated as a core language in comparative Indo-European reconstruction (Table 2.11).

Table 2.11. *Some cognate words in the Baltic languages*

OPrus	Lith	Latv
alu 'mead'	*alùs* 'beer'	*alus* 'beer'
anglis 'charcoal'	*anglìs*	*ùogle*
lynno 'flax'	*lìnas*	*lini*
muso 'fly'	*musìs*	*muša*
sagnis 'root'	*šaknìs*	*sakne*
wissa 'all'	*vìsas*	*viss*
woble 'apple'	*obuolỹs*	*âbuol(i)s*

Note: OPrus = Old Prussian, Lith = Lithuanian, Latv = Latvian.

2.6 Slavic

In the prehistoric period the Baltic and Slavic languages were so closely related that many linguists speak of a Balto-Slavic proto-language. After the two groups had seen major division, the Slavic languages began expanding over territory previously occupied by speakers of Baltic languages. From *c.* AD 500 Slavic tribes also pushed south and west into the world of the Byzantine Empire to settle in the Balkans and central Europe while other tribes moved down the Dnieper river or pressed east towards the Urals and beyond (Map 2.4).

The initial evidence for the Slavic language is Old Church Slavonic which tradition relates to the Christianizing mission of Saints Cyril and Methodius in the ninth century. Their work comprises biblical translations and was directed at Slavic speakers in both Moravia and Macedonia. The language is regarded as the precursor of the earliest South Slavic languages but it also quite close to the forms reconstructed for Proto-Slavic itself. The prestige of Old Church Slavonic, so closely associated with the rituals of the Orthodox Church, ensured that it played a major role in the development of the later Slavic languages (Table 2.12).

The Slavic languages are divided into three main groups—South, East, and West Slavic. The South Slavic languages comprise Bulgarian, Macedonian, Serbo-Croatian, and Slovenian. The earliest attestations of these languages, as distinct from Old Church Slavonic, begin about AD 1000–1100.

The East Slavic languages comprise Russian, Byelorussian, and Ukrainian, and their mutual similarity to one another is closer than any other group. Here too the prestige of Old Church Slavonic was such that the three regional developments were very slow to emerge, generally not until about 1600.

The West Slavic languages were cut off from their southern neighbours by the penetration of the Hungarians into central Europe. The language that

Table 2.12. *The evidence of the Slavic languages*

SOUTH SLAVIC
Old Church Slavonic (*c.* 860–)
Macedonian (1790–)
Bulgarian
Old Bulgarian (900–1100)
Middle Bulgarian (1100–1600)
Modern Bulgarian (1600–)
Serbo-Croatian (1100–)
Slovenian (1000–)
EAST SLAVIC
Russian
Old Russian (*c.*1000–1600)
Russian (*c.*1600–)
Byelorussian (*c.*1600–)
Ukrainian (*c.*1600–)
WEST SLAVIC
Polish (*c.*1270–)
Czech (*c.*1100–)
Slovak (*c.*1100–)

Polish, Czech, and Slovak replaced was Latin, not Old Church Slavonic, which had been used in Bohemia-Moravia but was replaced very early by Latin. Unlike the case with East and South Slavic, Church Slavonicisms are almost entirely absent from West Slavic.

The abundance of Old Church Slavonic material, its conservative nature, and the fact that subsequent Slavic languages appear to evolve as later regional developments means that linguists generally find that Old Church Slavonic will suffice for Indo-European comparative studies although its evidence can be augmented by other Slavic languages (Table 2.13).

2.7 Albanian

The earliest reference to an Albanian language dates to the fourteenth century but it was not until 1480 that we begin to recover sentence-length texts and the first Albanian book was only published in 1555. The absorption of so many foreign words from Greek, Latin, Turkish, and Slavic has rendered Albanian only a minor player in the reconstruction of the Indo-European vocabulary,

Table 2.13. *A comparison of some cognate terms in Old Church Slavonic (OCS) and Russian (Rus) with Lithuanian (Lith), a Baltic language*

LITH	OCS	RUS
alùs 'beer'	*olŭ* 'beer'	*ol*
anglìs 'charcoal'	*ǫglĭ* 'charcoal'	*úgolĭ*
lìnas 'flax'	*lĭnĕnŭ* 'linen'	*len*
musìs 'fly'	*mŭšĭca* 'gnat'	*móška*
obuolỹs 'apple'	*(j)ablŭko* 'apple'	*jábloko*
šaknìs 'root'	*socha* 'pole'	*sokhá* 'plough'
vìsas 'all'	*vĭsĭ* 'all'	*vesĭ*

and of the 'major' languages it contributes the least number of Indo-European cognates. However, Albanian does retain certain significant phonological and grammatical characteristics (Table 2.14).

Table 2.14. *The basic Albanian numerals are cognate with other IE numbers*

One	*nji*
Two	*dy*
Three	*tre*
Four	*katër*
Five	*pesë*
Six	*gjashtë*
Seven	*shtatë*
Eight	*tetë*
Nine	*nëndë*
Ten	*dhjetë*

2.8 Greek

The earliest evidence for the Greek language comes from the Mycenaean palaces of mainland Greece (Mycenae, Tiryns, Pylos) and from Crete (Knossos). The texts are written in the Linear B script, a syllabary, i.e. a script whose signs indicate full syllables (*ra*, *wa*, etc.) rather than single phonemes, and are generally administrative documents relating to the palace economies of Late Bronze Age Greece (Table 2.15). With the collapse of the Mycenaean

Table 2.15. *Linear B and Classical Greek*

MYCENAEAN	GREEK
a-ka-so-ne 'axle'	*áksōn*
do-e-ro 'slave'	*doûlos*
e-re-pa 'ivory'	*eléphās*
i-qo 'horse'	*híppos*
pte-re-wa 'elm'	*pteléā*
ra-wa-ke-ta 'leader'	*lāgétās*

civilization in the twelfth century BC, evidence for Greek disappears until the emergence of a new alphabetic writing system, based on that of the Phoenicians, which developed in the period *c.*825–750 BC. The early written evidence indicates the existence of a series of different dialects that may be assigned to Archaic Greek (Table 2.16). One of these, the Homeric dialect, employed in the *Iliad* and *Odyssey*, was an eastern dialect that grew up along the coast of Asia Minor and was widely employed in the recitation of heroic verse. The Attic dialect, spoken in Athens, became the basis of the classical standard and was also spread through the conquests of Alexander the Great. This established the line of development that saw the later emergence of Hellenistic, Byzantine, and Modern Greek.

The literary output of ancient Greece is enormous and the grammatical system of Greek is sufficiently conservative that it plays a pivotal role in Indo-European comparative studies.

Table 2.16. *The evidence of the Greek language*

Mycenaean (*c.* 1300–1150 BC)
Greek
Archaic Greek (*c.* 800–400 BC)
Hellenistic Greek (*c.* 400 BC–AD 400)
Byzantine Greek (*c.* AD 400–1500)
Modern Greek (1500–)

2.9 Anatolian

The earliest attested Indo-European languages belong to the extinct Anatolian group (Map 2.5). They first appear only as personal names mentioned in

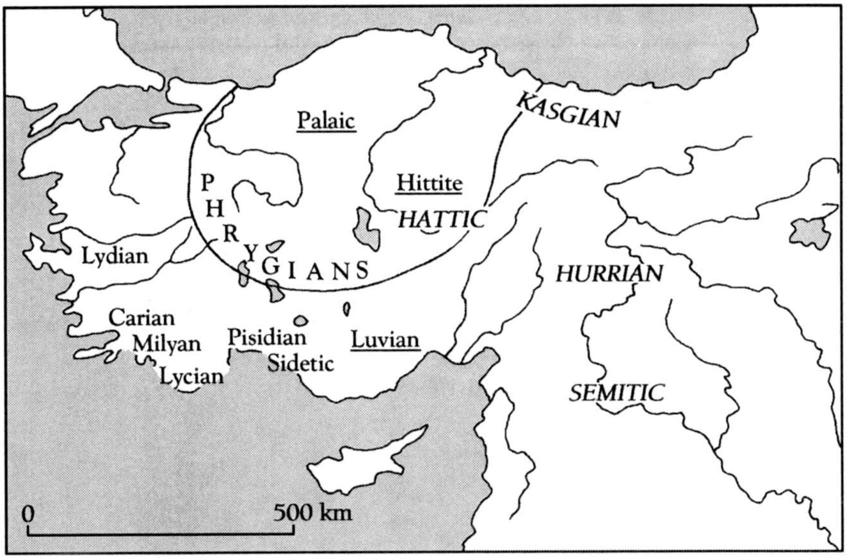

Map 2.5. Distribution of the Anatolian and Phrygian (lined area) languages

Assyrian trading documents in the centuries around 2000 BC. By the mid second millennium texts in Anatolian languages are found in abundance, particularly in the archives of the Hittite capital at Hattuša in central Anatolia.

The Anatolian languages are divided into two main branches: Hittite-Palaic and South/West Anatolian (Table 2.17). The first branch consists of Hittite and Palaic. Hittite is by far the best attested of the Anatolian languages. There are some 25,000 clay tablets in Hittite which deal primarily with administrative or ritual matters, also mythology. The royal archives of the Hittite capital also yielded some documents in Palaic, the language of the people of Pala to the north of the Hittite capital. These are of a ritual nature and to what extent Palaic was even spoken during the period of the Hittites is a matter of speculation. It is often assumed to have become extinct by 1300 BC if not earlier but we have no certain knowledge of when it ceased to be spoken.

In south and west Anatolia we find evidence of the other main Anatolian language, Luvian. Excepting the claim that the earliest references to Anatolians in Assyrian texts refer explicitly to Luvians, native Luvian documents begin about 1600 BC. Luvian was written in two scripts: the cuneiform which was also employed for Hittite and a hieroglyphic script created in Anatolia itself. Primarily along the south-west coast of Anatolia there was a string of lesser-known languages, many if not all believed to derive from the earlier Luvian language or, if not derived directly from attested Luvian, derived from unattested varieties of Anatolian closely related to attested Luvian. These include Lycian which is known from about 200 inscriptions on tombs, Lydian, also

Table 2.17. *The evidence of the Anatolian languages*

HITTITE-PALAIC
Hittite
Old Hittite (1570–1450 BC)
Middle Hittite (1450–1380 BC)
New Hittite (1380–1220 BC)
Palaic (?–?1300 BC)

SOUTH/WEST ANATOLIAN
Luvian
Cuneiform Luvian (1600–1200 BC)
Hieroglyphic Luvian (1300–700 BC)
Lycian (500–300 BC)
Milyan (500–300 BC)
Carian (500–300 BC)
Lydian (500–300 BC)
Sidetic (200–100 BC)
Pisidian (AD 100–200)

known from tombs and some coins as well, Pisidian, which supplied about thirty tomb inscriptions, Sidetic about half a dozen, and Carian, which is not only found in Anatolia but also in Egypt where it occurs as graffiti left by Carian mercenaries.

Anatolian occupies a pivotal position in Indo-European studies because of its antiquity and what are perceived to be extremely archaic features of its grammar (Table 2.18); however, the tendency for Anatolian documents to include many

Table 2.18. *Selected cognate words in Hittite (Hit), Old English (OE), and New English (NE)*

HIT	OE	NE
gēnu	*cnēo(w)*	*knee*
hāras	*earn*	*erne (eagle)*
kēr	*heorte*	*heart*
nēwas	*nīwe*	*new*
tāru	*treōw*	*tree*
wātar	*wæter*	*water*
yukan	*geoc*	*yoke*

items of vocabulary from earlier written languages, in particular Sumerian and Akkadian, has militated against a comparable importance in contributing to the reconstruction of the Proto-Indo-European vocabulary. All too often we do not know the actual Hittite word for a concept because that concept is always expressed as a Sumerian or Akkadian phonogram (which the Hittite speaker would have pronounced as the proper Hittite word much in the way an English speaker says 'pound' when confronted with the Latin abbreviation *lb*).

2.10 Armenian

As with many other Indo-European languages, it was the adoption of Christianity that led to the first written records of the Armenian language. The translation of the Greek Bible into Armenian is dated by tradition to the fourth century, and by the fifth century there was a virtual explosion of Armenian literature. The earliest Armenian records are in Old or Classical Armenian which dates from the fourth to the tenth century. From the tenth to nineteenth century Middle Armenian is attested mainly among those Armenians who had migrated to Cilicia. The modern literary language dates from the early nineteenth century.

As we have seen, the Armenian vocabulary was so enriched by neighbouring Iranian languages—the Armenian-speaking area was regularly in and out of Iranian-speaking empires—that its identification as an independent Indo-European language rather than an Iranian language was not secured until the 1870s. It has been estimated that only some 450 to 500 core words of the Armenian vocabulary are not loanwords but inherited directly from the Indo-European proto-language (Table 2.19).

Table 2.19. *Selected cognates in Armenian (Arm), Old English (OE), and New English (NE)*

Arm	OE	NE
akn	*ēage*	*eye*
cunr	*cnēo(w)*	*knee*
hayr	*fæder*	*father*
kin	*cwene*	*quean (woman)*
mukn	*mūs*	*mouse*
otn	*fōt*	*foot*
sirt	*heorte*	*heart*

2.11 Indo-Aryan

The ancient Indo-European language of India is variously termed Indic, Sanskrit, or Indo-Aryan (Map 2.6). While the first name is geographically transparent (the people of the Indus river region), Sanskrit refers to the artificial codification of the Indic language about 400 BC, i.e. the language was literally 'put together' or 'perfected', i.e. *saṃskr̥ta*, a term contrasting with the popular or natural language of the people, Prākrit. Indo-Aryan acknowledges that the Indo-Europeans of India designated themselves as Aryans; as the Iranians also termed themselves Aryans, the distinction here is then one of Indo-Aryans in contrast to Iranians (whose name already incorporates the word for 'Aryan').

The earliest certainly dated evidence for Indo-Aryan does not derive from India but rather north Syria where a list of Indo-Aryan deities is appended to a

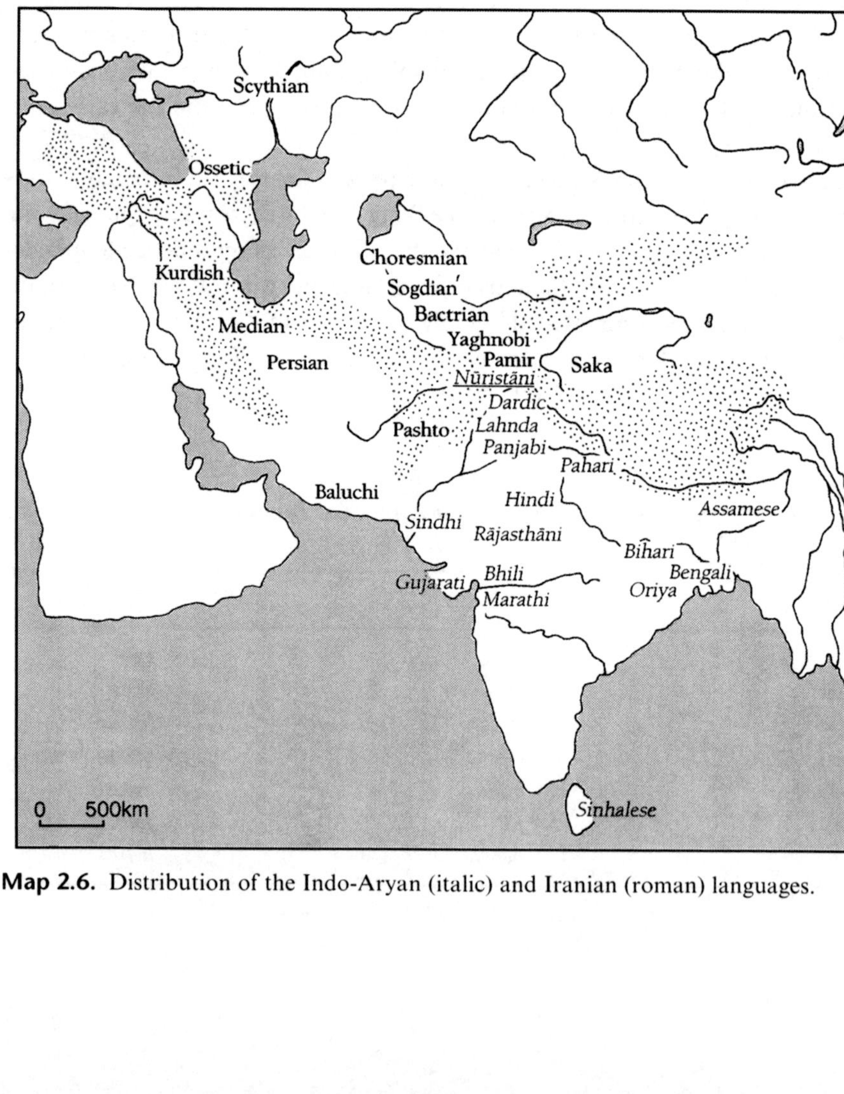

Map 2.6. Distribution of the Indo-Aryan (italic) and Iranian (roman) languages.

treaty between the Mitanni and the Hittites. This treaty dates to *c*.1400–1330 BC and there is also other evidence of Indo-Aryan loanwords in Hittite documents. These remains are meagre compared with the vast religious and originally oral traditions of the Indo-Aryans. The oldest such texts are the Vedas (Skt *veda* 'knowledge'), the sacred writings of the Hindu religion. The *Ṛgveda* alone is about the size of the *Iliad* and *Odyssey* combined and this single work only begins a tradition of religious literature that runs into many volumes. These religious texts, however, were not edited and written down until the early centuries BC, and dating the composition of the Vedas has been a perennial problem. Most dates for the *Ṛgveda* fall within a few centuries on either side of *c*.1200 BC. Because of the importance of the Vedas in Indic ritual and the attention given to the spoken word, the texts have probably not suffered much alteration over the millennia. A distinction may be made between Vedic Sanskrit, the earliest attested language, and later Classical Sanskrit of the first millennium BC and more recently. Sanskrit literature was by no means confined to religious matters but also included an enormous literary output, including drama, scientific treatises, and other works, such that the volume of Sanskrit documents probably exceeds that of ancient Greece and Rome combined.

By the middle of the first millennium BC we find evidence for the vernacular languages of India which, as we have seen above, are designated Prākrit. The earliest attested Indo-Aryan documents are in Prākrit and these provide the bases of the modern Indo-Aryan languages, e.g. Hindi-Urdu, Gujarati, Marathi, Sinhalese.

2.12 Iranian

In the first millennium BC the distribution of the Iranian languages was truly enormous and not only comprised Iran and Afghanistan but also all of central Asia and the entire Eurasian steppe from at least the Dnieper east to the Yenisei river. The Iranian languages are divided into two major groups, Eastern and Western (Map 2.6).

The Eastern branch is earliest attested in the form of Avestan, the liturgical language of the religion founded by Zarathustra, or Zoroaster as he was known to the Greeks. The *Avesta* is a series of hymns and related material that was recited orally and not written down prior to the fourth century AD. Unlike the *Ṛgveda*, the integrity of its oral transmission was not nearly so secure and there are many difficulties in interpreting the earlier passages of the document. These belong to the *Gathas*, the hymns reputedly composed by Zarathustra himself; there is also much later material in the *Avesta*. The dates of its earliest elements are hotly disputed but generally fall *c.*1000 BC and are presumed to be roughly contemporary with the *R̥gveda.*

Eastern Iranian offers many other more recently attested languages that belong to the Middle Iranian period. In central Asia, Bactrian, Sogdian, and Choresmian were all spoken and occasionally recorded from about the fourth century AD onwards until the Turkish conquest of the region. The European steppelands were occupied by the nomadic Scythians in the west and the Saka in the east, and what little evidence survives indicates that these all spoke an East Iranian language as well. The Saka penetrated what is now western China and settled along the southern route of the Silk Road in the oasis town of Khotan where they have left more abundant documents known as Khotanese Saka. Most of these East Iranian languages have disappeared except for those spoken by peoples who occupied mountainous regions and have survived into the New Iranian period. On the European steppe, East Iranian tribes settled in the Caucasus where they survive today as the Ossetes, and Ossetic provides a valuable source for East Iranian. Sogdian has a distant descendant in the Yaghnobi language of Tadjikistan while the remnants of the Saka languages survive in the Pamirs. The most important modern East Iranian language is Pashto, the state language of modern Afghanistan.

The West Iranian languages were carried into north-west Iran by the Persians and Medes. Old Persian is attested primarily in a series of cliff-carved inscriptions in cuneiform. This material is not particularly abundant and is often repetitively formulaic but it does offer significant additional evidence to Avestan for the early stages of Iranian. By the Middle Iranian period we find Middle Persian, markedly changed from the earlier language. After the Arab conquests of the region (and a major Arabic impact on the Persian language), New Persian arose by the tenth century.

Iranian is closely related to Indo-Aryan and because the latter is far better represented in the earliest periods, there is a greater emphasis on Indo-Aryan

Table 2.20. *Selected cognates in Sanskrit (Skt) and Avestan (Av)*

SKT	AV
ákṣi 'eye'	*aši-*
dā́ru 'wood'	*dāuru*
hŕ̥d- 'heart'	*zərəd-*
jā́nu 'knee'	*zānu-*
mū́ṣ- 'mouse'	NPers *mūs*
ójas- 'strength'	*aoǰah-*
yugám 'yoke'	*yugam*

among comparativists than on Iranian (Table 2.20). Within the wider context of Iranian itself, there are far more languages than have been summarized here. Because the *Avesta* and the Old Persian documents are meagre compared to the volume of Sanskrit material, scholars often exploit the vocabularies of the Middle and even the Modern Iranian languages in order to fill out the range of Iranian vocabulary.

2.13 Tocharian

At the end of the nineteenth century, western expeditions to Xinjiang, the westernmost province of China, began to uncover remains of what are known as the Tocharian languages (Table 2.21). The documents date from the fifth century AD until Tocharian was replaced by Uyghur, a Turkic language, by the thirteenth century AD. There are approximately 3,600 documents in Tocharian but many of these are excruciatingly small fragments. The documents are primarily translations of Buddhist or other Indic texts, monastery financial accounts, or caravan passes. There are two Tocharian languages. Tocharian A, also known as East Tocharian or Agnean, is recovered exclusively from around Qarashahr (the ancient Agni) and Turfan and gives some the impression that it may have been a 'dead' liturgical language by the time it was recorded. Tocharian B, otherwise West Tocharian or Kuchean, was spoken from the oasis town of Kucha east across Tocharian A territory. It is better attested and more conservative than Tocharian A. The application of the name 'Tocharian' to the remains of the documents is controversial: the Tocharians of classical sources were one of the peoples who occupied Bactria, and the presumption that these were the same people (or a closely related group) as those who lived in the Tarim and Turfan basins derives from several manuscript readings which have been rejected as often as they

Table 2.21. *Selected cognates in Tocharian (Toch), Old English (OE), and New English (NE)*

Toch B	OE	NE
ek	*ēage*	*eye*
käryā	*heorte*	*heart*
keni	*cnēo(w)*	*knee*
keu	*cū*	*cow*
ñuwe	*nīwe*	*new*
or	*trēow*	*tree*
pācer	*fæder*	*father*

have been accepted. For convenience sake, Tocharian has remained the common designation for this group by most but not all linguists.

2.14 Minor Languages

The expansion of literacy (or at least inscriptions) coupled with the occasional recording of foreign words by Greek authors provides us with our evidence for a number of poorly attested languages, largely found in the periphery of the earliest literate civilizations in the Mediterranean. Dacian, for example, was spoken in the territory roughly approximating modern Romania, and the residue of its language comes to us primarily through personal and place names and a few glosses recorded in Greek; to this one might include the hunt for 'substrate' words in modern Romanian. About twenty to twenty-five Dacian words have had reasonable though not certain Indo-European etymologies proposed. To its south, roughly in modern Bulgaria, was the Thracian language, again attested primarily in the form of personal and place names, about thirty-odd glosses in Greek sources, and a few impenetrable inscriptions in the Greek script. Along the west Adriatic (Dalmatia, Croatia, Bosnia, Albania) lay Illyrian which is almost entirely known from personal and place names, most of which have not been easy to etymologize. That Illyrian occupied the territory in which we later find Albanian suggests that it may be a predecessor of Albanian, but the evidence for Illyrian is so meagre that this cannot be demonstrated. These three Balkan languages then are extremely minor in terms of the reconstruction of Proto-Indo-European but they were hardly minor languages during the periods when the groups speaking them were flourishing. All of them were associated with major tribal confederations and kingdoms of the Iron Age and it is only their early absorption into the Roman Empire and concomitant Latinization that accounts for why we regard them today as minor Indo-European languages.

The expansion of Latin also meant the loss of a series of languages of somewhat uncertain affiliation (although Indo-European) in Italy. In Sicily there is the barely attested Siculan. Closely related to Illyrian (it is believed) is Messapic, spoken in south-eastern Italy (Map 2.2). There are about 260 short inscriptions that date from the sixth to the first centuries BC. Northwards along the Adriatic we find Southern and Northern Picene, again languages known from some inscriptional evidence beginning in the sixth or fifth centuries BC. South Picene is definitely Italic while Northern Picene is anybody's guess. Still further north we encounter Venetic with its two hundred inscriptions dating from the sixth to first centuries BC; some see it as a possible Italic language while others have suggested that it occupies a more independent position. To its north lies Rhaetic, again known from a small number of inscriptions, and its linguistic position is even more insecure. In north-west Iberia we find traces of the Lusatian language, apparently an Indo-European language lying somewhere between Italic and Celtic.

Of all the minor languages, Phrygian has probably the greatest claim to consideration (Map 2.5). The Phrygians carved out a substantial kingdom in north central Anatolia by the ninth century BC, superimposing themselves on earlier Anatolian-speaking populations. The language appears in two forms: Old Phrygian, some 250 inscriptions dating from the eighth to third centuries BC, and New Phrygian, written in the Greek script, and numbering about a hundred inscriptions, dating from the first century AD.

Further Reading

Basic surveys of the Indo-European languages can be found in Lockwood (1972), Baldi (1983), Ramat and Ramat (1998), and Bader (1997), which is particularly good at covering some of the minor attested languages. There are also several general synthetic studies of Indo-European culture, e.g. Mallory (1989), Sergent (1995).

Useful, often essential, works on the various Indo-European groups are listed below by language group.

ALBANIAN: Demiraj (1993, 1997), Hamp (1966), Huld (1984), Mann (1948, 1977), Newmark (1982), Orel (1998, 2000).

ANATOLIAN: Carruba (1970), Drews (2001), Friedrich, Kammenhuber, and Hoffmann (1975–), Kronasser (1962), Laroche (1959), Melchert (1994, 2004), Puhvel (1984–), Sturtevant (1951), Tischler (1977–).

ARMENIAN: Clackson (1994), Godel (1975), Hübschmann (1897), Mann (1963), Schmitt (1981), Solta (1963).

BALTIC: Endzelins (1971), Fraenkel (1950, 1962), Stang (1970).

CELTIC: Delamarre (2003), Lewis and Pedersen (1937), McKone (1996), Schrijver (1995), Vendryès and Lambert (1959–).

GERMANIC: Bammesberger (1979), DeVries (1962), Holthausen (1934), Kluge (1975), Lehmann (1986), Lloyd, Lühr, and Springer (1988–), Nielsen (2000), Prokosch (1938), Robinson (1992).

GREEK: Chantraine (1968–80), Frisk (1960–72), Horrocks (1997), Rix (1976), Schmitt (1977), Sihler (1995).

ILLYRIAN: Katičić (1976), Krahe (1964*a*), Mayer (1957–9), Polomé (1982).

INDO-ARYAN: Burrow (1973), Macdonell (1910), Masica (1991), Mayrhofer (1956–80, 1986–2001), Turner (1966–9).

IRANIAN: Bailey (1979), Bartholomae (1904), Beekes (1988), Jackson (1968[1892]), Kent (1953), Reichelt (1909), Schmitt (1989).

ITALIC: Baldi (1999), Bammesberger (1984), Buck (1928), Ernout and Meillet (1967), Meiser (1998), Palmer (1954), Schrijver (1991), Solta (1974).

MESSAPIC: Haas (1962), De Simone (1964).

PHRYGIAN: Brixhe (1994), Diakonoff (1985), Haas (1966), Orel (1997).

SLAVIC: Charlton (1991), Comrie (1993), Lunt (2001), Trubachev (1974–), Vaillant (1950–77), Vasmer (1953–8).

THRACIAN: Detschew (1957), Georgiev (1977), Polomé (1982), Katičić (1976).

TOCHARIAN: Adams (1988*a*, 1999), Krause and Thomas (1960), Pinault (1989), van Windekens (1976).

VENETIC: Beeler (1949), Lejeune (1974).

3

Reconstructing Proto-Indo-European

3.1 The Comparative Method

Anyone with even the sketchiest notion of phonetics who considers the alphabet of the western languages cannot but be struck by its utter randomness. Vowels are scattered here and there in no sensible order, there is little similarity of sound in respect to placement, nor is there any sense that the more useful letters are gathered together in one place. The arrangement of a Qwerty keyboard (the standard typewriter or computer keyboard, named after the order of the first half of the upper row of letters) makes more sense than the order of the alphabet. This haphazard arrangement, however, is not characteristic of the Sanskrit (or Devanāgarī) alphabet which unlike the Phoenician and Greek alphabets (and their descendants, Latin and Cyrillic) would appear to have been systematically created and arranged on the basis of a thoroughgoing analysis of the phonetics of the language for which it was intended. The Sanskrit alphabet begins with the simple vowels in series between short and long, e.g. *a*, *ā*, *i*, *ī*, then the diphthongs (e.g. *āi*, *āu*), and then the consonants which are as arranged in Table 3.1.

The consonants are arranged by place and method of articulation. First come the velars, those where the sound is made with the back of the throat, i.e. gutturals; then the palatals where the upper surface of the tongue is applied

Table 3.1. *The Sanskrit alphabet*

	unvoiced	unvoiced aspirate	voiced	voiced aspirate	nasal
velars	*k*	*kh*	*g*	*gh*	*ṅ*
palatals	*c*	*ch*	*j*	*jh*	*ñ*
retroflex	*ṭ*	*ṭh*	*ḍ*	*ḍh*	*ṇ*
dental	*t*	*th*	*d*	*dh*	*n*
labial	*p*	*ph*	*b*	*bh*	*m*

to the hard palate; then the retroflexes, a sound made with the tip of the tongue pressed against the palate, rather than the upper surface of the tongue as in the case of the palatal series; then the dentals, the sounds made by pressing the tongue against the teeth; and finally, the labials where the lips are employed in making the sound. The consonants may be voiced, i.e. involve a vibration of the vocal cords, or unvoiced. They may also be aspirated, accompanied by a breath, or unaspirated. Finally, they have nasal equivalents.

This same exemplary rigour was applied to the analysis of words and their constituent elements. Sanskrit grammarians described in detail the root, stems, and endings of verbs or nouns and both the internal and external changes that might alter their meaning or grammatical function. When western scholars began their study of Sanskrit, they not only acquired a new language but also learned a good deal about how to undertake grammatical analysis.

The early comparative philologists, armed with their better understanding of how languages might be studied, set out to demonstrate the systematic correspondence between phonological (sound) and morphological (grammar) elements in the Indo-European languages. In so doing, they invented the techniques of the comparative method. As an introduction to the method and the problems involved, we will take three words from a series of the Indo-European groups and explore how they are related (Table 3.2).

If we take the word for 'carry' in the first column and examine the root of the word, we arrive at the list of correspondences given in Table 3.3.

If we wished to describe this in as general terms as possible, we would say that the common shape of this root was LABIAL + VOWEL + R.

We could now investigate how stable some of these correspondences are and note in the second column, where we can now add a Lithuanian example as well, that the correspondences for the labial sound (*b* = *f* = *ph* = *bh* = *p*) remain precisely the same in the word for 'brother' as they do in the word 'I carry'. When we look to the third column we encounter two easily overcome obstacles. The word for 'brow' in Old Irish is obviously part of a compound word here so

Table 3.2. *Comparison of three Indo-European words*

	'I CARRY'	'BROTHER'	'BROW'
OIr	*beru*	*brāthair*	*forbrū*
Lat	*ferō*	*frāter*	—
OE	*bere*	*brōðor*	*brū*
Lith	—	*broterė̃lis*	*bruvìs*
OCS	*berǫ*	*bratrŭ*	*brŭvĭ*
Grk	*phérō*	*phrḗtēr*	*ophrûs*
Skt	*bhárāmi*	*bhrā́tar-*	*bhrū́-*
TochB	*parau*	*procer*	*pärwāne*

we ignore the *for*. In Greek we see that there is an *o* before the labial and we may presume that this reflects a particular development in Greek. Otherwise, all other correspondences hold. Obviously, we could do the same for the *r*.

If the pattern is correctly identified, we expect a predictive relationship so that where we find, for example, a *bh* in Sanskrit, we should expect a *ph* in Greek. So when we look further and compare the Sanskrit and Greek words for 'cloud', i.e. Sanskrit *nábhas-* and Greek *néphos*, or 'divide, share food', i.e. Sanskrit *bhájati* and Greek *phageîn*, we are not surprised to find the same correspondences of Skt *bh* = Grk *ph*. This process provides us with our initial stage of reconstruction: we have determined a system of correspondences for one of the labial sounds across the Indo-European languages. We have also shown that irrespective of the word, the same sound correspondences are in operation between each of the languages.

We now come to the first real crunch of the comparative method: how should we represent the correspondences that we have found? It is obviously far too cumbersome to drag out a list of the sound equivalences in each language of the twelve main Indo-European groups. We could, of course, suggest a simple algebraic symbol to express the correspondence. For example, we might propose the symbol L^1, i.e. labial correspondence type 1, so that we have (and here is the full series):

L^1 = OIr, OE, Lith, OCS, Alb, Arm, Av *b* = Lat *f* =Grk *ph* = Skt *bh* = Hit, Toch *p*

Table 3.3. *Selected sound correspondences across the Indo-European languages*

OIr, OE, and OSC *b* = Lat *f* = Grk *ph* = Skt *bh* = TochB *p*
OIr, Lat, OE, OCS, Grk *e* = Skt, TochB *a*
OIr, Lat, OE, OCS, Grk, Skt, TochB all share *r*

Returning to our first column and the verb 'I carry', we could then suggest a symbol for the corresponding vocalic set such that V^1, i.e. vowel correspondence type 1, would give us:

V^1 = OIr, Lat, OE, Lith, OCS, Grk, Arm, Hit *e* = Alb *ja/je* = Av, Skt *a* = TochB *(y)a/yä*.

We could then express the root of the verb to carry as $^*L^1 V^1 r$- but, mercifully, we do not.

The issue here is that although the relationship is abstract and can be expressed in a formula, we know that there was once a language or closely related language group that had a word 'I carry' which altered somewhat to give us the transparently similar words we find in all of the different Indo-European groups. It is both an uncontrollable and reasonable temptation to 'reconstruct' as closely as possible the original sound.

The reconstruction itself is based on a combination of common sense and observations on how sounds tend to develop in other languages. Common sense indicates that as all twelve groups demonstrate a labial, it is probable that the sound (our L^1) was also a labial in the proto-language. Now was it a voiced (*b/bh*) or an unvoiced (*p/ph*) labial? Eight of the twelve groups suggest that it was a voiced labial. If we look to the two languages (Hittite and Tocharian) that show an unvoiced labial (*p*), we would also discover that neither of these have a voiced labial in their respective languages to begin with, i.e. there could be no other outcome in Hittite or Tocharian for a Proto-Indo-European labial but an unvoiced one. As we also know that most of those languages that show a voiced labial also have an unvoiced labial, we can conclude that they do provide the evidence to distinguish which labial was in the proto-language, and so it appears that both Hittite and Tocharian have simplified the original sound. Can we determine this for certain?

One test would be to look for other words that show the unvoiced labial such as a *p* in Sanskrit and the other languages. When we do so, we note that Tocharian also gives a *p*, e.g. Tocharian B *pācer* 'father' = Sanskrit *pitár-*, Latin *pater*, etc. So the other languages show a contrast between the voiced (*b*) and unvoiced labial (*p*) whereas Tocharian does not. Furthermore, the devoicing of consonants is a frequently observed phenomenon throughout the linguistic world.

The odds are in favour then of a voiced labial and the main question is now whether it was aspirated (*bh*) or unaspirated (*b*). Most of the evidence suggests an unaspirated labial, and if we performed a simple head count, it would be seven groups who opt for *b* and only one, Sanskrit, with an aspirated *bh*. Numbers alone, however, do not provide a sufficient argument to conclude that the proto-form was a *b* because all those languages with only a *b* do not themselves possess an aspirated labial (*bh*) in the first place; this distinction is limited to Sanskrit, and there are sound reasons to imagine that it is Sanskrit that retained the original situation while the other Indo-European stocks lost the distinction between aspiration and non-aspirates. How do we know it was not the other way round, i.e. that it was Sanskrit that split the Proto-Indo-European voiced labial into an aspirated (*bh*) and unaspirated (*b*) form?

In deciding in favour of Sanskrit linguists use the tenet of the regularity of sound change, the fundamental discovery of late nineteenth century linguists. In short it states that, if a sound in an earlier stage of a language (here say a *b*) changes into a different sound (*bh*), that change will happen to all instances of that sound, not to just a random subset of its occurrences. It is possible that a single older sound might come to be pronounced in two different ways (i.e. that a *b* might become a *bh* in some situations but a *b* in others), but only in predictable conditions. Such conditions, for example, can be seen in the development of Latin into Spanish, where Latin /k/ (written 'c') remained /k/ in Spanish before back vowels (i.e. *a*, *o*, *u*), e.g. in Latin *cantō* 'I sing' which became Spanish *canto* 'I sing', but became Spanish /s/ or /θ/ (depending on dialect) before front vowels (i.e. *i* and *e*), e.g. Latin *centum* (/kentum/) 'hundred' became Spanish *ciento* (/syento/ or /θyento/). But in the question of *bh* versus *b*, we find no evidence of any special situations obtaining where some cognates give a *b* in Sanskrit and others a *bh*; we uniformly find a Skt *bh* regardless of the following sound among cognate words between Sanskrit and other IE languages. When two sounds are not predictably related to one another on the basis of their (original) environments, we must assume that they are independent of one another. If these two sounds are not distinct in some related language, then that non-distinction must reflect a merger of the two originally distinct sounds. This consideration alone should alert us to the probability that it is Sanskrit that retains a distinction between *b* and *bh* which has been lost in the other IE languages. Moreover, the evidence of Greek also supports the primacy of *bh* in that it returns an aspirated *p*, i.e. *ph*.

Comparativists in the nineteenth century, therefore, settled on the voiced aspirate as the form to be reconstructed for the proto-language in the situation where Sanskrit had *bh*, Greek had *ph*, and Slavic had *b*, etc. Because this form is reconstructed and not actually attested—there is no such thing as a Proto-Indo-European document—it is preceded with an asterisk to indicate its hypothetical status, hence Proto-Indo-European **bh*. We already know that the root will end in **r* so we must now turn to the question of the vowel, our V^1.

As we have seen, the verb 'carry' has as its vowel *-a-* in Sanskrit (and Avestan) but *-e-* in Celtic, Latin, Germanic, Slavic, and Greek. Despite the fact that the majority of Indo-European traditions showed *e* here, early Indo-Europeanists tended to follow the evidence of Sanskrit and reconstruct a Proto-Indo-European **a* on the presumption that Sanskrit had changed least of all from the proto-language. The principle of the regularity of sound change, however, finally convinced linguists that this time it was Sanskrit that had changed. The problem of blindly accepting Sanskrit as the most archaic language came to a head when linguists had to sort out the PIE velars.

In the example drawn from Spanish above, the nature of the following vowel dictated how Spanish would reflect an earlier Latin *c* /k/. In Sanskrit cognates involving the velars that we now reconstruct as *k̂* and k^w might be represented by a *k* or a *c* (/č/, as the first and last consonant in New English *church*) in Sanskrit but unlike Spanish, the following vowel was always *a* when followed by a Proto-Indo-European front vowel, e.g. Lat *quod* 'what' and Skt *kád* 'what' but Lat *-que* 'and' and Sanskrit *ca* 'and'. The unchanging Sanskrit outcomes made no sense unless one compared the following vowels in Latin, Greek, and other IE languages where we would find /e/, /a/, and /o/ where Sanskrit itself made no such distinction and only gave /a/. The other languages indicated that when the word had a front vowel (e.g. /e/) then the outcome of the velar in Sanskrit was *c*, but when it was a back vowel in Greek or Latin (i.e. /a/ or /o/), then Sanskrit gave a *k*. In this case it was evident that it was Sanskrit that had merged *e*, *a*, and *o* in a single /a/.

Thus linguists came to understand that, in this instance at least, Sanskrit was less conservative than its sisters Greek and Latin, and by the last quarter of the nineteenth century Proto-Indo-European **e* was reconstructed where Sanskrit showed *a* but Greek and Latin showed *e*, and likewise **o* was reconstructed where Sanskrit again showed only *a* and Greek and Latin showed *o* (e.g. Sanskrit *aṣṭā́*, but Old Irish *ocht*, Latin *octō*, Greek *oktṓ* all 'eight'). Proto-Indo-European **a* was reserved for those cases when all three groups showed *a* (e.g. Sanskrit *ájra-* 'field, plain', Old Norse *akr* 'field', Latin *ager* 'field', Greek *agrós* 'field'). An example of all three Proto-Indo-European vowels is to be seen in Greek *dédorka* 'I saw' which may be compared with its Sanskrit cognate *dadárśa*, with its uniform *a*.

As a result of these and other interlocking arguments we can confidently reconstruct the root of the Proto-Indo-European verb 'carry' as **bher-*. We can push reconstruction a bit further to see how one reconstructs the morphological system. Returning to **bher-* we can show the verbal endings for the singular of the present active indicative from some of the Indo-European languages (Table 3.4). The ending of the first person is *-*ō* (which in turn reflects an earlier *-oh*$_2$, the last symbol to be explained below in Section 3.3); the exception is Sanskrit, which has attached the first personal ending (*-mi*) of a different class of verbs to the original ending. The second person shows a sibilant ending (*-s*) while the third person shows evidence of a dental (*-t*). The sequence is reconstructed as: **bherō*, **bher-e-si*, and **bher-e-ti* where **bher-* is the root, *-e-* is the stem vowel, and *-si*/*-ti* are the endings of the second and third

Table 3.4. *The singular endings of the verb 'carry' in Indo-European*

	LATIN	GOTHIC	OCS	GRK	SKT
I carry	*ferō*	*baira*	*berǫ*	*phérō*	*bhárāmi*
you carry	*fers*	*bairis*	*bereši*	*phéreis*	*bhárasi*
she/he carries	*fert*	*bairiþ*	*beretŭ*	*phérei*	*bhárati*

persons. In very simplified terms, the earliest reconstructions tended to look very much like slightly modified Sanskrit. As we have noted, by the beginning of the twentieth century reconstructions tended to look more like Greek vowels inserted between Sanskrit consonants. This is when Karl Brugmann published his *Grundriss der vergleichenden Grammatik der indogermanischen Sprachen* (1897–1916), which reflected the current status of Indo-European studies, and the term 'Brugmannian' is popularly employed by Indo-Europeanists to describe 'traditional' reconstructions.

3.2 Schleicher's Tale

A good measure of the changing appearance of Indo-European reconstructions can be seen in what is known as 'Schleicher's Tale'. August Schleicher (1821–68) was one of the great comparativists of the mid nineteenth century. As an exercise he sifted through the reconstructed Indo-European of his day for enough usable words to compose a short narrative tale in Proto-Indo-European. The tale was published in 1868.

Schleicher's Tale

Avis, jasmin varnā na ā ast, dadarka akvams, tam, vāgham garum vaghantam, tam, bhāram magham, tam, manum āku bharantam. Avis akvabhjams ā vavakat: kard aghnutai mai vidanti manum akvams agantam.

Akvāsas ā vavakant: krudhi avai, kard aghnutai vividvant-svas: manus patis varnām avisāms karnauti svabhjam gharmam vastram avibhjams ka varnā na asti.

Tat kukruvants avis agram ā bhugat.

A sheep that had no wool saw horses—one pulling a heavy wagon, another one a great load, and another swiftly carrying a man. The sheep said to the horses: 'it pains my heart seeing a man driving horses.'

The horses said to the sheep: 'listen sheep! it pains our hearts seeing man, the master, making a warm garment for himself from the wool of a sheep when the sheep has no wool for itself.'

On hearing this the sheep fled into the plain.

It is useful to watch how this tale has been updated through time so let us take a closer look at the first line:

avis,	*jasmin*	*varnā*	*nā*	*ast,*	*dadarka*	*akvams,*
sheep	to whom	wool	not	was	saw	horses

The first thing that strikes us about Schleicher's reconstructions is the unremitting use of the vowel *a*, a clear sign of the predominance of Sanskrit in reconstruction. The first word, **avis* 'sheep', is attested in Old Irish *oī*, Latin *ovis*, Old English *ēowu*, Lithuanian *avìs*, Old Church Slavonic *ovĭnŭ*, Greek *ó(w)ïs*, and Sanskrit *ávis*. By 1939, the linguist Hermann Hirt provided an updated ('Brugmannian') version whose first line ran as follows:

owis, jesmin wblənā ne ēst, dedork'e ek'wons,

Some of the changes were purely notational, e.g. *w* (or *u̯*) is preferred today rather than the *v* of Schleicher's reconstructions (and the Sanskrit language). We now also see that with more attention to the other Indo-European languages the vocalic system is primarily *e* and *o*. There are several other reconstructions, however, that are also new. The words for 'saw horses' (*dedork'e ek'wons*) both indicate a *k* with an apostrophe, Hirt's notation for what is more commonly written as **k̂* today. We have already seen the problem of distinctive sounds in Proto-Indo-European being simplified to single sounds, e.g. PIE **e*, **o*, and **a* > Sanskrit *a*. The velars in Indo-European presented the opposite problem: there were fewer forms in the daughter languages than were being reconstructed to Proto-Indo-European. We can see an example of this when we take three sets of cognate terms in Latin and Sanskrit. Latin *centum* 'hundred', *coxa* 'hip', and *quod* 'that' are cognate with Sanskrit *śatám* 'hundred', *kákṣa-* 'side, flank', and *kád* 'that'. If we place these in series, we reconstruct three different initial velars.

Lat	***c**entum*	***c**oxa*	***qu**od*
Skt	***ś**atám*	***k**ákṣa-*	***k**ád*
	velar 1	velar 2	velar 3

We appear to have a situation where we can match the Latin–Sanskrit correspondences as follows:

vel^1 = Lat **c** = Skt **ś**
vel^2 = Lat **c** = Skt **k**
vel^3 = Lat **qu** = Skt **k**

We seem to need three velars to explain things but, unfortunately, not one of the Indo-European languages has more than two velars. The first velar (our vel^1) would seem to have become palatalized in Sanskrit, a process that happens quite frequently, e.g. whether one pronounces Celtic as /keltik/ or /seltik/.

By Hirt's time this was written as a palatal velar, i.e. *k̂ or **k'* as Hirt's notation. Our second velar (vel^2) gives the same results in Latin as Sanskrit and is left alone as a pure velar (*k*). The final velar (vel^3) is a labiovelar in Latin but a pure velar in Sanskrit. Latin appears to have merged the outcomes of vel^1 and vel^2 while Sanskrit merged the outcomes of vel^2 and vel^3. These two patterns are commonly distinguished as the centum : satem split, taking their names for the words for 'hundred' in Latin (where Latin *c* is always the hard /k/ sound) and Avestan where we have the *s*-sound, *satəm* as also in Indic. The centum groups, those that retain the /k/ sound, are Celtic, Italic, Germanic, Greek, Anatolian, and Tocharian; the satem group, the ones that yield a palatalized sound, comprises Baltic, Slavic, Armenian, Iranian, and Indic. Before the discovery of Hittite and Tocharian, the split was seen as a straightforward east–west split. The question of whether there were actually three velars in the proto-language or whether there were only two that behaved differently in different environments is still a topic of major argument. The evidence of the Anatolian language Luvian strongly suggests a three-way distinction. As suggested above, the three velar series are commonly reconstructed as palatal *k̂*, velar *k*, and labiovelar k^w. However, the centum group's change of a palatal to a velar would be phonologically unusual, and one might also suppose that Proto-Indo-European's three velars were *k*, *q* (dorso-uvular as the Arabic sound usually transcribed <q>), and q^w.

We move on to a third translation of Schleicher's tale which was published in 1979 by Winfred Lehmann and L. Zgusta.

owis, kʷesyo wl̥hnā ne ēst, ek̂wons espek̂et,

There are two major aspects of this translation that give us an indication of further changes in reconstruction. The first is word order. In the previous translations, the final phrase of the first line (Hirt: *dedork'e ek'wons* or here *ek̂wons espek̂et*) translates as 'saw horses'. The subject of the sentence, the sheep, is at the head and so the order of elements is the subject (S), then the verb (V) and then the object (O), i.e. SVO, i.e. 'sheep saw horses'. Since then, however, analysis of Anatolian and other Indo-European languages has suggested that the order of elements in Proto-Indo-European was more normally SOV with the verb at the end, and this is how Lehmann and Zgusta have put it although they have replaced Schleicher's verb with **espek̂et* which means the same as **dedork'e*. The other matter of interest is the word for 'wool' which has altered considerably since Schleicher's time. The shift from Schleicher's *r* to *l* in the reconstruction was simply another correction of the over-reliance on Sanskrit which largely merged the two sounds. More importantly, however, is that the 1979 version (**wl̥hnā*) has an *h*. The recognition of this sound in Proto-Indo-European has been called 'the most important single discovery in the whole history of Indo-European linguistics' and it was made by Ferdinand de Saussure (1857–1913) when he was 21 years old.

3.3 Laryngeal Theory

To understand de Saussure's discovery we need a little background. In English (and the other Germanic languages) we can alter the meaning of a word both by adding endings, e.g. sing/sing**ing**/sing**er**, or by changing the root vowel, e.g. sing/s**a**ng/s**u**ng/s**o**ng. The second pattern is termed ablaut and it involves a variation in the root vowel. It is a fundamental operation in Sanskrit and Greek as well as Germanic. In our first sentence we have the verb **dedork'e* in Hirt's translation. The Greek equivalent here is *dédorka* and we will take our example from Greek since it is the vowels that we need to follow. In Table 3.5 is found the ablaut pattern for the verb 'to see' in Greek and below each form the root has been isolated, and below that the actual vowel involved. The ablaut pattern here then is **e** ~ **o** ~ **ø** and these are known as *e*-grade, *o*-grade, and zero-grade. Ablaut is a fundamental part of Indo-European grammar.

The interesting problem arose when one considered other ablaut patterns that appeared to involve long vowels. Another example from Greek is given in Table 3.6. The ablaut pattern here would then be **ē** ~ **ō** ~ **e**. Similar patterns were observed with other vowels and there appeared to be two different systems: the first with short vowels that went down to the zero-grade and a second system where long vowels graded down to a short vowel. De Saussure devised a way of explaining them both as part of the same system. He proposed that the long vowels were originally a combination of a short vowel plus a sonant (written **E** in the example below) that was appropriate to each vowel (one for *e*, one for *o*, etc.). This meant that for the two examples given above, the systems ran as follows:

e ~ o ~ ø
eE ~ oE ~ E

Eventually, the logic of this proposition was accepted and the missing particles were identified as laryngeals, a sound made by closing the glottis such as the initial

Table 3.5. *Short vowel ablaut patterns in Greek*

dérkomai 'I see'	*dédorka* 'I have seen'	*édrakon* 'I saw'
derk-	*dork-*	**dr̥k-*
e	**o**	**ø**

Table 3.6. *Long vowel ablaut patterns in Greek*

títhēmi 'I put'	*thōmós* 'heap'	*thetós* 'put'
thē-	*thō-*	*the-*
ē	**ō**	**e**

'catch' (in phonetic notation/ʔ/) at the beginning of both syllables of the negative 'uh-uh', or the ordinary English h (a laryngeal fricative), or pharyngeals, sounds made in the pharynx. Collectively the laryngeals and pharyngeals are usually called just laryngeals. Another possibility is to see these consonants as the fricatives corresponding to the velars *k̂*, *k*, and k^w (just as *s* corresponds to *t*). Thus some would reconstruct x̂ (the initial sound in *huge*), x (as in German *Bach*) and x^w or as χ, and χ^w, where χ is the fricative corresponding to q. The laryngeal theory as it was called played a significant part in resolving many problems of Indo-European linguistics, although it also threw up some problems of its own. The problem with it was that the various Indo-European languages did not have laryngeals and so their existence was hypothetical. This situation remained until analysis of the Hittite language, which offered the earliest evidence of written Indo-European, revealed that it preserved some laryngeals, normally written in the form of an *h*. We can now reconsider the word for 'wool', i.e. **wl̥hnā*. The word is attested in Hittite as *hulana-*, perhaps an unfortunate example as this requires metathesis, that is the Hittites have altered the sequence of the initial syllable and so the pre-Hittite form was actually **ulhna*.

We can now look to our final translation, prepared by Douglas Adams in 1997:

$h_2$ówis, k^wésyo wl̥$h_2$néh$_4$ne (h_1é) est, $h_1$ék̂wons spék̂et

By now the notation of reconstruction looks positively algebraic. The simple *h* of Lehmann and Zgusta has become h_2, which merely identifies it as the second laryngeal type, i.e. the one that colours vowels *a*, e.g. the Latin word for 'wool' is *lāna*. We also note that laryngeals have been placed before the words for 'sheep' and 'horse' where previously they began with simple vowels. This addition was in order to ensure that the root began with a consonant. Analysis of the root structures of reconstructed Proto-Indo-European revealed that the root was limited in the form it could take and always began and ended with a consonant (C). If we let 'e' stand for any vowel (it was the most common vowel in Indo-European), then an Indo-European root could only be *CeC* or *CCeC* or *CeCC*. There were two other limitations on the structure of the root: two voiced stops could not occur together in the root, e.g. **deg-* and **bed-* would be impossible roots in Proto-Indo-European, and an unvoiced consonant and an aspirated consonant could not occur together, i.e. **tebh-* would also be against 'root-law'. A laryngeal could be treated as a consonant so even when there was no evidence for them in any surviving Indo-European language except Hittite and its close relatives (and not always there), they would be added in front of the initial vowel. In the case of the word for 'horse' (*h_1éḱwos) it is theoretical but in the case of 'sheep' (*$h_2$ówis) it is entirely justified as Luvian, another of the Anatolian languages to retain laryngeals, preserves the Proto-Indo-European word for 'sheep' as *hāwa/i-*, i.e. with an *h*. There are different schools of laryngeal use and argument over how many laryngeals should be reconstructed: opinions range from none to as many as six; three or four tend to be the general consensus.

3.4 Reconstruction and Reality

This chapter began with the reconstruction of Proto-Indo-European **bh* and this is where we must return to understand one of the other major current issues of reconstruction. How real are our reconstructions? This question has divided linguists on philosophical grounds. There are those who argue that we are not really engaged in 'reconstructing' a past language but rather creating abstract formulas that describe the systematic relationship between sounds in the daughter languages. Others argue that our reconstructions are vague approximations of the proto-language; they can never be exact because the proto-language itself should have had different dialects (yet we reconstruct only single proto-forms) and our reconstructions are not set to any specific time. Finally, there are those who have expressed some statistical confidence in the method of reconstruction. Robert Hall, for example, claimed that when examining a test control case, reconstructing proto-Romance from the Romance languages (and obviously knowing beforehand what its ancestor, Latin, looked like), he could reconstruct the phonology at 95 per cent confidence, and the grammar at 80 per cent. Obviously, with the much greater time depth of Proto-Indo-European, we might well wonder how much our confidence is likely to decrease. Most historical linguists today would probably argue that reconstruction results in approximations. A time traveller, armed with this book and seeking to make him- or herself understood would probably engender frequent moments of puzzlement, not a little laughter, but occasional instances of lucidity.

The reality of the reconstructions has emerged in particular because of problems with the structure of the traditional Indo-European phonological system. The consonantal system (and semivowels) of the traditional system may be reconstructed as in Table 3.7.

There are several problems with this system. The first is that **b* is (almost?) non-existent, i.e. it is extremely difficult, though not altogether impossible, to

Table 3.7. *The Proto-Indo-European consonant system*

	unvoiced	voiced	voiced-aspirate
Labial	*p*	*b*	*bh*
Dental	*t*	*d*	*dh*
Palatal velar	*k̂*	*ĝ*	*ĝh*
Palatal	*k*	*g*	*gh*
Labio-velar	k^w	g^w	g^wh

find a solid case for reconstructing a Proto-Indo-European **b*. Second, if one reviews the languages of the world, there is not a single well-attested one known that does not have voiceless aspirates if it has voiced aspirates as well. There are no voiceless aspirates, e.g. **ph*, **kh*, **th*, reconstructed to Proto-Indo-European so it is typologically unique and thus, from the standpoint of its critics, an implausible reconstruction. Another way of looking at the apparent anomaly is to think of each of the distinctive sounds of Proto-Indo-European (or any other language for that matter) not as indivisible units but rather as aggregates of phonological features. For instance, when comparing *p* and *b* we can say that *b* is distinguished from *p* by the presence of voicing while in the case of *p* and *ph* the latter is distinguished from the former because it is characterized by aspiration. We illustrate the phonological relationships in Table 3.8 where + indicates presence and—shows absence of a feature.

A language with these three kinds of stops is a typologically expected one (and a well-attested type) containing one sound without special characterization (*p*), and two others minimally characterized (*b* with voice and *ph* with aspiration). The traditional reconstruction of Proto-Indo-European, however, is problematic precisely because it has a doubly characterized *bh* but not singly characterized *ph* (Table 3.9).

In order to render the reconstructed system of Proto-Indo-European more realistic, that is, more like the range of systems encountered in the living languages of the world, Thomas Gamkrelidze and Vyacheslav Ivanov proposed the Glottalic theory. This theory suggests that the plain voiceless series that is reconstructed above was actually comprised of voiceless aspirated stops,

Table 3.8. *Normal marking of labials*

p	*b*	*ph*
– voice	+ voice	– voice
– aspiration	– aspiration	+ aspiration

Table 3.9. *Proto-Indo-European labials*

p	***b***	***bh***
– voice	+ voice	+ voice
– aspiration	– aspiration	+ aspiration

and that the other two series were voiceless glottalized stops, and voiced aspirated stops respectively, i.e. instead of **p* - **b* - **bh* one should reconstruct **ph* - **p*' - **bh*. In this reconstruction the presence of aspiration is held to be non-distinctive, that is phonetically present but not a basic part of the phonological description of the sound (which is, admittedly, cheating a bit), and we might prefer (as some do) to transcribe the sounds as *p*(*h*), *p*', and *b*(*h*) and array them as in Table 3.10. Others have suggested different revisions of the traditional system to make it typologically more realistic. All of the proposed revisions, however, have their critics. All of them also force one to assume that the attested sounds in the various branches have undergone changes which have few or no parallels or are otherwise complicated (how does one get from Proto-Indo-European **p*(*h*) and **b*(*h*) to the attested Greek *p* and *ph* for instance, or why do the majority of Indo-European branches have **p*' and **b*(*h*) falling together as *b*?). Thus the revisions would seem to fail the test of providing typologically appropriate transitional phases between Proto-Indo-European and the attested Indo-European languages. Finally there are rare but attested systems which show the same sort of imbalance of features necessitated by the traditional reconstruction of Proto-Indo-European. Thus in the Chinese of a large region of China around Shanghai, called Wu, we have *p*, *ph*, and *bh* which are displayed in Table 3.11. This system provides a kind of mirror image to that traditionally reconstructed by Indo-Europeanists (i.e. Proto-Indo-European had **bh* but no **ph* while Wu has *bh* but no *b*). Given the existence of a rare system such as that of Wu, it is hard to deny the possibility of an equally rare system in Proto-Indo-European.

Table 3.10. *The labials in the glottalic system*

***p*(*h*)**	***p'***	***b*(*h*)**
– voice	– voice	+ voice
– glottal	+ glottal	– glottal

Table 3.11. *The labials in Wu*

p	*ph*	*bh*
– voice	– voice	+ voice
– aspiration	+ aspiration	+ aspiration

Table 3.12. *The traditional Proto-Indo-European system and its glottalic equivalents*

Traditional	Glottalic	Traditional	Glottalic	Traditional	Glottalic
p	$p^{[h]}$	b	(p′)	bh	$b^{[h]}$
t	$t^{[h]}$	d	t′	dh	$d^{[h]}$
k̂	$\hat{k}^{[h]}$	ĝ	k̂′	ĝh	$\hat{g}^{[h]}$
k	$k^{[h]}$	g	k′	gh	$g^{[h]}$
k^w	$k^{[h]o}$	g^w	k'^{o}	g^wh	$g^{[h]o}$

Fortunately, one can interchange the reconstructed forms between the traditional system and the variety of newly proposed systems in a relatively mechanical fashion (Table 3.12). The traditional system is understood by all, and until the weight of scholarly opinion dismisses it for a single new system (if, indeed, that should happen), it remains the one most often cited (as it is in the remainder of this book for which, in any case, the exact phonological shape of words is of secondary importance). The reconstructed phonemes and their outcomes in the main Indo-European groups are summarized in Appendix 1.

Further Reading

There are a number of good introductions to the comparative method in linguistics such as Anttila (1972), Bloomfield (1933), Hock (1991), Hoenigswald (1960), Lehmann (1992), and Campbell (1998) and, at a more exhaustive level, Joseph and Janda (2003). The Glottalic theory is found most extensively in Gamkrelidze and Ivanov (1995) and more recent discussion of it in Salmons (1992), Barrach (2002, 2003). For reality in reconstruction see Hall (1960).

4

The System

4.0 The System

Over two centuries of research into the structure of the Indo-European proto-language have produced an enormous body of scholarship about the structure of Proto-Indo-European, and the purpose of this chapter is merely to introduce an extremely basic outline of the phonology and grammar of Proto-Indo-European.

4.1 Phonology

We have already discussed the reconstruction of Proto-Indo-European and we can provide a roster of the Proto-Indo-European phonological system (Table 4.1). This amounts to about thirty-two phonemes, i.e. distinctive sounds, although this could be increased depending on whether one wanted to admit other sounds, e.g. diphthongs such as **ay*, **ey*, etc. We might remind ourselves that the English language possesses forty-six phonemes (among the world's living languages the number of phonemes may range from about a low of eleven to a high of 141).

In the last chapter we have already seen that there are a number of issues still very much under debate. The Glottalic theory would alter the reconstructed forms of the first five series. Argument still persists on whether there were three

Table 4.1. *The Proto-Indo-European phonological system*

	unvoiced	voiced	voiced aspirate
labials	*p*	*b*	*bh*
dentals	*t*	*d*	*dh*
palatals	*k*	*g*	*gh*
velars	*k*	*g*	*gh*
labiovelars	k^w	g^w	g^wh
sibilants	*s*		
laryngeals	h_1	h_2	h_3 h_4
liquids	*r/3*	*l/C*	
nasals	*m/i*	*n/*	
semivowels	*i/y*	*u/w*	
vowels	*e*	*o*	*a*
	ē	*ō*	*ā*

series of velars (palatal-, pure, and labio-) and, if there were not, what precisely were the original velars. Many would only reconstruct the first three laryngeals; a few would require six laryngeals. Of the laryngeals presented, *h_1 leaves an adjacent vowel unchanged while an *h_3 will change an adjacent *-*e*- to an *-*o*-, e.g. **dideh$_3$*- > Greek *dídōmi* 'I give'. Both *h_2 and *h_4 change an adjacent *-*e*- to *-*a*- (e.g. **peh$_2$s*- 'protect' > Latin *pāscō* 'I protect' and **h$_4$elbhós* 'white' > Latin *albus* 'white' and Hittite *alpā*- 'cloud'). Only word initially can we distinguish *h_2 and *h_4, and then only when we have an Anatolian cognate. For **h$_2$e*- we have *ha*- in Hittite *harkis* 'white' (cf. Greek *argós* 'bright'), for **h$_4$e*- we have *a*- (as in *alpā*-). (Some have suggested that initial *h_4 is preserved in Albanian as *h*-, e.g. *herdhe* 'testicle' from **h$_4$orĝhiyeh$_a$*- beside Hittite *ark*- 'mount sexually'). Where we cannot distinguish between *h_2 and *h_4 we will use the symbol *h_a-. In some instances where a laryngeal is posited but we are uncertain which laryngeal should be indicated we will employ *h_x to indicate the unknown laryngeal.

The liquids, nasals, and semivowels are listed in both their consonantal and vocalic forms, i.e. if they are found between two consonants, they behave like vowels (*i*, *u*), but when they are found next to a pure vowel they behave like consonants (*y*, *w*; also written *i̯ and *u̯). When the other forms behave like vowels, this is indicated with a small circle below the form (*m̥*, *n̥*, *l̥*, *r̥*). Of the pure vowels, there are some who argue there was no PIE **a*; others suggest that there are no original long vowels: these are short vowels + a laryngeal.

4.2 The Noun

The English noun is a poor place to start for discussing the structure of the Indo-European noun. It distinguishes two numbers—singular and plural, e.g. *man/men*—and only two cases, i.e. the nominative (subject) and the genitive (possessive), e.g. *man/man's* and *men/men's*; it does not distinguish grammatical gender as do many other modern languages such as French or German. Proto-Indo-European distinguished three numbers (singular, dual, and plural), there is (disputed, but generally accepted) evidence for grammatical gender, and it distinguished eight cases. The dual, attested in a number of the historical Indo-European languages, was employed for pairs, often natural pairs, e.g. 'eyes', 'ears'.

If we look at the Indo-European noun from purely a mechanistic standpoint, we would begin with the root which would have to obey the rules laid down in the preceding chapter regarding its structure, i.e. (C)CeC(C)-. To the root might be added a variety of suffixes to create a *stem* and then finally the case endings depending on number and perhaps gender. In some cases, the so-called root-nouns, there are no suffixes before the case ending. Using R for 'root', S for 'stem-creating suffix', and E for 'case-number-ending', we might establish the formula for an inflected word in Proto-Indo-European as R-(S)-E. The suffixes sometimes still convey an earlier underlying meaning, e.g. the suffix **-trom* tends to indicate an instrument, e.g. **h$_2$erh$_3$-trom* 'plough' from a verb **h$_2$erh$_3$ye/o-* 'to plough', while kinship names tend to have the suffix **-er-* or **-ter-*, e.g. **sués-ōr* 'sister', **bhréh$_2$-tēr* 'brother'. The commonest suffixes and their functions are indicated in Table 4.2.

The basic case endings are outlined on Table 4.3. Most securely reconstructed are the nominative, vocative, accusative, and genitive of the singular and plural.

The nominative indicates the subject of the sentence and is formed either with an *-s* or no ending, e.g. *The father sees* (**ph̥$_a$tḗr*). The vocative is used in address, e.g. *O father!* (**ph̥$_a$ter*). The accusative denotes the direct object, e.g. *I saw the father* (**ph̥$_a$térm̥*); the genitive indicates possession, e.g. *the father's cow* (**ph̥$_a$trós*). The final four cases are the least well preserved and many languages have abandoned them. The ablative indicates motion from some place, e.g. *I ran from father* (**ph̥$_a$trós*); the dative shows motion to somewhere, e.g. *I ran to father* (**ph̥$_a$tréi*); the locative indicates position, e.g. *the flea was on the father* (**ph̥$_a$tér(i)*); and the instrumental indicates the means by which something is done or accompaniment, e.g. *he went with his father* (**ph̥$_a$tréh$_1$*).

The case endings are added directly to the root or to one of the suffixes. The final sound of the stem is used to define which particular type of declension the

Table 4.2. *Common Indo-European suffixes*

ACTION NOUNS:
-o-, *- eh_a-*, *-men-*, *-es-* [all root stressed], *- ti-*, *-tu-*, *- tr/tn-*, *-r/n-*, *-wr/wn-*, *-yeh_a-*

AGENT NOUNS:
-ó-, *- tér-*, *-mén-*, *-és-* [all stem stressed]

NOUNS OF INSTRUMENT:
-tro- (also *-tlo-* , *-dhro-*, *-dhlo-*)

DEADJECTIVAL VERBS:
-eh_a- ('become X'), *-eh_1-*('be X')

DEVERBAL VERBS:
-se/o-, *- eye/o-* (iteratives, intensives)
-new-, *- eye/o-* (causatives)
-$h_1$se/o- (desideratives)

ADJECTIVES:
-o-, *-yo-*, *-no-*, *o-*, *- k̂o-*, *-ro-*, *- lo-* [all adjectives of appurtenance]
-to-, *-wo-*, *-went-*[adjectives of possession, 'having X']
-en-, *- $h_1$en-* ['characterized by X']

noun belongs to, e.g. **nép-ōt* 'grandson' is a *t*-stem. If we look more closely at the nominative, accusative, and genitive of **nép-ōt* (Table 4.4) we note another feature of Indo-European nouns—a shift in the accent and ablaut of the pattern ō ~ o ~ ø.

The complicated patterns of stress and ablaut are not found in the *o*-stems (Table 4.5), the only stem forms to end in a vowel (if one presumes that the *ā*-stems are really *eh_2*-stems) and which have their own set of endings (Table 4.6).

Table 4.3. *Basic case endings of the Indo-European noun*

	singular	plural	dual
nominative	*-s*, *-ø*	*-es*	*-h_1(e)*
vocative	*-ø*	*-es*	*-h_1(e)*
accusative	*-m*	*-ns*	*-h_1(e)*
genitive	*-(o)s*	*-om*	*-h_1e/oh_xs*
ablative	*-(o)s*; *-(e)d*	*-bh(y)os*	*-h_1e/oh_xs*
dative	*-ei*	*-mus*	*-me/oh_x*
locative	*-i*, *-ø*	*-su*	*-$h_1$ou*
instrumental	*-(e)h_1*	*-bhi*	*-$bhih_1$*

Table 4.4. *Accent shift in case forms*

nominative	**nép-ōt*
accusative	**nép-ot-i*
genitive	**nep-t-ós*

The dative of the *o*-stems reveals one of the more obvious instances of dialectal differences in Indo-European. The dative plural ending **-oibh(y) os* is supported by Sanskrit, e.g. dative-plural *vr̥k-ebhyas* 'to the wolves', but Germanic (e.g. Gothic *wulf-am*), Baltic (e.g. Lithuanian *vilk-ams*), and Slavic (e.g. Old Church Slavonic *vlĭk-omŭ*) support the alternative ending **-omus*.

The *o*-stems were the most productive form of declension. By this is meant that through time, especially at the end of the Proto-Indo-European period and into the early histories of the individual Indo-European languages, the *o*-stems appeared to proliferate and replace other stem types. In Vedic Sanskrit, for example, they constitute more than half of all nouns. High productivity is often interpreted as evidence that the *o*-stems are a later declensional form than many of the other stems. Highly productive forms are ultimately capable of replacing many other forms as they provide the most active model by which speakers might decline a form. For example, in Old English, plurals were formed in a variety of ways, e.g. *cyning* ~ *cyningas* ('king/kings') but *cwēn* ~ *cwēne* ('queen/queens'), *feld* ~ *felda* ('field/fields'), *spere* ~ *speru* ('spear/spears') and *assa* ~ *assan* ('ass/asses'). All of these were levelled out to the first form with the *s*-ending (that of the Proto-Indo-European *o*-stems) which became the most productive. Regarding the last form, although many common enough words were given an *-an* ending for the plural, e.g. *guman* 'men', *froggan* 'frogs', *naman* 'names', *tungan* 'tongues', only one of these has survived, i.e. Old

Table 4.5. *Endings of o-stem nouns*

	Singular	Plural
nominative	*-os*	*-ōs* (< **-o-es*)
vocative	*-e*	*-ōs* (< **-o-es*)
accusative	*-om*	*-ons*
genitive	*-os*	*-om*
ablative	*-ōd* (< **-o-ed*)	*-om*
dative	*-ōi* (< **-o-ei*)	*-oibh(y)os/-omus*
locative	*-oi*	*-oisu*
instrumental	*-o*h_1	*-ōis* (< **-o-eis*)

Table 4.6. *h_2- (or ā)-stem endings*

	Singular	Plural
nominative	*-eh₂*	*-eh₂es*
vocative	*-eh₂*	*-eh₂es*
accusative	*-eh₂m*	*-eh₂ns*
genitive	*-eh₂os*	*-eh₂om*
ablative	*-eh₂os*	*-eh₂om*
dative	*-eh₂ei*	*-eh₂mus*
locative	*-eh₂i*	*-eh₂su*
instrumental	*-eh₂eh₁*	*-eh₂bhi*

English *oxa* ~ *oxan*, though Middle English created a few new *n*-plurals by adding the *-n* to nouns like *childre*, the plural of *child* 'child' to give modern *children*.

The h_2-stems are associated with feminine nouns, e.g. Lat *dea* 'goddess' and, because of their absence in this use in Anatolian, these stems have been regarded by many as late formations. The fact that Proto-Indo-European also forms collectives in *-h_2- (e.g. the Hittite collective *alpaš* 'group of clouds' from a singular *alpaš* 'cloud') has suggested that this was its original use and that it later developed the specifically feminine meaning.

4.3 Adjectives

The adjectives are constructed and declined very much like the nouns, i.e. a root, a stem, and an ending, with masculine and neuter endings corresponding generally to the *o*-stems and the feminine endings utilizing the h_2- endings. They are declined according to gender with masculine, feminine, and neuter forms, e.g. from the root **new-* 'new', we have the nominative singular endings **néw-os* (masculine), **néw-om* (neuter), and **néw-eh₂* (feminine), e.g. Latin *novus, novum, nova*, Greek *néos, néon, néā*, Sanskrit *návas, návam, návā*, and Old Church Slavonic *novŭ, novo, nova*. The comparative suffix was either *-*yes*- or (later) *-*tero*- while the superlative suffix was *-*isto*- or (again later *-(*t*) *mo*-).

4.4 Pronouns

Pronouns are one of the core elements of vocabulary. The evidence for pronouns in Indo-European is abundant and includes personal pronouns (*I, you,* etc.), reflexive pronouns (*one's self*), interrogative (*who, which, how many*), relative (*which*), and demonstrative (*this one, that one*).

Proto-Indo-European had special personal pronouns for the first and second numbers (*I, you*) but not for the third (*he, she, they*) and instead employed a demonstrative pronoun (*that one*) where we would use a personal pronoun. As was the case with nouns, the personal pronouns (Table 4.7) were declined in the singular, dual, and plural.

The first person singular and the first and second persons plural had two roots, one for the nominative and one for the other cases. That situation is still preserved in New English 'I' but 'me' and 'we' but 'us' ('you' historically represents the non-nominative only). However, there has been a strong tendency in the various Indo-European groups for one, usually the non-nominative, to replace the other. Thus Sanskrit retains the Proto-Indo-European situation (i.e. *ahám* 'I' but *mā́m* 'me', *vayám* 'we' but *nas* 'us', and *yūyám* 'you [nom.]' but *vas* 'you [acc.]') but in later Indic all three show replacement of the nominative by the non-nominative. The same threefold replacement pattern is shown by Old Irish at its earliest attestation. In both Italic and Greek we find the first and second persons plural with the same replacement at their earliest attestations. In Slavic it is only the second person plural that is affected while in Tocharian the non-nominative of the first person singular is extended to the nominative while the nominative and non-nominative of the first and second persons plural merge so completely that it is hard to say which was the dominant ancestor (e.g. Tocharian B *wes* 'we/us' from Proto-Indo-European **wei* + **nos*, *yes* 'you' from **yuh$_x$s* + **wos* (one should note that Tocharian *-e-* is the regular outcome of Proto-Indo-European **-o-*). Given that nominative pronouns were normally only used for emphasis (the person and number of the subject was normally adequately expressed by the ending of the verb), it is not surprising that the much more frequent non-nominative shape would win out. What is a bit surprising is that in Baltic it is the nominative shape that replaces the non-nominative one in the first and second persons plural.

The reflexive pronoun, used to refer back to oneself, was **séwe*.

The Indo-European languages do not agree on a single relative pronoun, e.g. *the man <u>who</u> killed the bear*, and there are two forms that were widely used, i.e. **yo-* in Celtic, Balto-Slavic, Greek, and Indo-Iranian but **k^{w}o-* or something

Table 4.7. *Personal pronouns*

	SINGULAR	DUAL	PLURAL
First	**h$_1$eg/*h$_1$éme*	**nóh$_1$*	**wéi/*nos*
Second	**túh$_x$*	**wóh$_1$*	**yuh$_x$s/*wos*

similar in Italic, Germanic, Albanian, Armenian, Anatolian, and Tocharian. This latter form is also found among the interrogatives, e.g. *who?*, *which?*, all of which begin with *k^w- (which we find in Old English as *hw-* which then metathesizes in the spelling [shifts the order of elements around] in New English as *wh-*). For example, we have PIE *k^wós, OE *hwā*, and NE *who*; PIE *k^wód > OE *hwæt* > NE *what*; and PIE *k^wóteros > OE *hwæþer* > NE *whether*).

As there was no third personal pronoun this function had to be served by a series of demonstrative pronouns such as **so* (masculine), *seh_a (feminine), and **tód* (neuter) 'that (one)', the latter of which survived as Old English *þæt* > *that*. An emphatic pronoun was also employed, i.e. *$h_1$éi 'he, this (one)', *h_1ih_a- 'she, this (one)', and *$h_1$id. The latter survives in New English as *it*. New English *he* derives from another demonstrative pronoun, **kís* 'this (one)'. For every question of 'where', 'when', 'how much', there was a corresponding pronoun to indicate 'there', 'then', 'that much', e.g. PIE **tór*~**tḗr* > OE *þǣr* > NE *there* or PIE **tóti* 'so much, many' > Lat *tot* 'so much' (see Chapter 24).

4.5 Numerals

Numbers tend to be one of the more stable elements of any language (although even these can be replaced) and some of the basic numerals are presented in Table 4.8 (see Section 19.1).

Volumes have been written about the Indo-European numerals as they provide evidence for the construction of a counting system. The number 'one'

Table 4.8. *Some basic numerals*

1	*$h_1$oi-no-s	NE *one*, Lat *ūnus*, Grk *oínē* 'ace on dice'
2	*dwéh₃(u)* → *$dwéh_3(u)$	NE *two*, Lat *duo*, Grk *dúō*, Skt *dvà* ~*dvé*
3	**tréyes*	NE *three*, Lat *trēs*, Grk *treîs*, Skt *tráyas*
4	*k^wétwor-	NE *four*, Lat *quattuor*, Grk *téssares*, Skt *catvā́ras*
5	*pénk^{w}e	NE *five*, Lat *quínque*, Grk *pénte*, Skt *páñca*
6	*(s)wéks	NE *six*, Lat *sex*, Grk *héks*, Skt *ṣáṣ*
7	**septḿ̥*	NE *seven*, Lat *septem*, Grk *heptá*, Skt *saptá*
8	*h_xoḱtṓ(u)	NE *eight*, Lat *octō*, Grk *oktṓ*, Skt *aṣṭā́* ~ *aṣṭáu*
9	*$h_1$newh_1m̥	NE *nine*, Lat *novem*, Grk *ennéa*, Skt *náva*
10	**déḱm̥(t)*	NE *ten*, Lat *decem*, Grk *déka*, Skt *dáśa*
20	*wīḱm̥tih$_1$	Lat *vīgintī*, Grk *eíkosi*, Skt *viṃśatí*
30	*trī-ḱomt(h_a)	Lat *trīgintā*, Grk *triā́konta*, Skt *triṃśát*
100	**ḱm̥tóm*	NE *hundred*, Lat *centum*, Grk *hekatón*, Skt *śatám*
1000	*tuh$_a$s- ḱm̥tyós-/*ghesl(iy)os	NE *thousand*; Grk *khī́lioi*, Skt *sahásram*

is singular, 'two' is dual, and 'three' and the higher numerals are plurals except for the number 'eight' which appears to have originally been a dual. This apparent anomaly presupposes one to imagine 'eight' as 'two fours' and that *h_3*eḱteh*$_3$(*u*) 'eight' contains the basal element **k*^{w}*et*- in 'four', but the phonological distance is very great. When we examine the numerals 'ten', 'twenty', etc., we see the element *-*ḱm̥t*- which was no doubt an abstract counting concept, a unit of some kind, on which were based 'ten' (two-units), 'hundred' (big unit), and, in some areas of the Indo-European world (including Germanic), 'thousand' (fat hundred).

4.6 Particles and Conjunctions

The Indo-European languages preserve a number of earlier particles of speech. For example, negation was made with the particle **ne* 'not' or **ĝhi* 'certainly not' or **meh*$_1$ if it were a prohibition, i.e. 'do not!'. There were also particles of time and place that have changed little, e.g. **new*- 'now'. The main connective particle was *-*k*^{w}*e* 'and', e.g. Latin -*que*, which would be suffixed to the final word in a series (e.g. *Senatus Populusque Romanus* 'the Senate People-and Roman'; see Section 24.5).

4.7 Prepositions

In English we require prepositions to indicate position or motion; in Proto-Indo-European these would not have been so much required because the different case endings already indicated location (locative), motion to (dative) or from (ablative), and accompaniment (instrumental). Nevertheless, prepositions were required to specify more closely location or movement and there is a fairly large number reconstructed to Proto-Indo-European, e.g. **ni* 'downward', **peri* 'over', **pro* 'before', **som* 'together' (see Section 18.2).

4.8 Verbs

The reconstruction of the verbal system is the most complex feature of the Proto-Indo-European language. Difficulties arise both because of its internal complexity and because it would appear that there were more dialectal differences involving the verb within Proto-Indo-European than was the case with the other major grammatical classes. In consequence there is less agreement among Indo-Europeanists about the verb than there is about the noun or adjective. These are some of the basic features almost all would agree with:

1. As was the case with the noun, the verb was also conjugated in three numbers: the singular (*I eat*), the plural (*we eat*), and the dual (*we two eat*).
2. There were two voices, i.e. indications of whether the subject acted on something else or (on behalf of) himself. There was, therefore, an active voice (*I wash the child*) and a medio-passive (also called the 'middle') voice (*I wash myself*). There is no pure passive in Proto-Indo-European (*The child was washed by the mother*) but the medio-passive could, in the proper context, be used passively as well as medio-passively.
3. The tenses included the present (*I eat*), the aorist (*I ate*), and the perfect (*I have eaten*)—though the perfect has left no trace in Anatolian and many Indo-Europeanists, therefore, would take the perfect to be a late addition to the Proto-Indo-European verbal repertoire of tenses, added only after the separation of pre-Anatolian from the rest of the Indo-European community. In another restricted set of languages there was yet another past, the imperfect (*I was eating*). The best evidence for an inherited imperfect comes from Indo-Iranian, Greek, and Armenian, and thus this imperfect may reflect a south-eastern innovation; other IE groups having the imperfect, Slavic, Italic, and Tocharian, may all have innovated independently. There is only scattered evidence of a future (*I will eat*) and, again, that evidence is not from Anatolian but it does occur on both the extreme east of the Indo-European world (Balto-Slavic and Indo-Iranian) and the extreme west (Celtic) so it may have been another late addition in Indo-European—otherwise the future must have been rendered with the present or the optative.
4. There may have been four moods: indicative (plain statement of objective fact), injunctive (perhaps mild commands or prohibitions), optative (intentions or hoped for action), and imperative (commands). In the Anatolian languages there is only a distinction between the indicative and imperative. In non-Anatolian Indo-European there are greater or lesser traces of a fifth mood, the subjunctive (potentiality, possibility).
5. A series of derivational suffixes could be employed to alter the meaning, e.g. the suffixes **-eye/o-* and **-neu-* could be added to form a causative, e.g. **ters-* 'dry' but **torséye/o-* 'to make dry'; *-eh$_2$-* changed a noun or adjective into a verb with those qualities, e.g. *new-* 'new' but **neweh$_2$-* 'make new' (e.g. Latin *novāre* 'make new', Greek *neáō* 're-plough', Hittite *newahh-* 'make new').

The personal endings of the verb were divided into two major conjugations, each with a primary and a secondary set of endings (Table 4.9). The conjugations are distinguished by the shape of the singular person endings in the present tense. The first conjugation is traditionally called the 'athematic' conjugation

Table 4.9. *Proto-Indo-European personal endings*

	Active			Middle	
	First Conj	Second Conj Thematic		First Conj	Second Conj
	sec/prim	prim	sec	sec/prim	prim/sec
1st	*-m(i)*	*-oh₂*	*-om*	*-h₂é(r)*	*-oh₂e(r)*
2nd	*-s(i)*	*-eth₂e*	*-es*	*-th₂é(r)*	*-eth₂e(r)*
3rd	*-t(i)*	*-ei*	*-et*	*-ó(r)*	*-eto(r)*
1st	*-me(s)*	*-omes*	*-ome*	*-medhh₂*	*-omedhh₂*
2nd	*-te*	*-ete*	*-ete*	*-dhwe*	*-edhwe*
3rd	*-ent(i)*	*-onti*	*-ont*	*-ntó(r)*	*-onto(r)*

(there being no theme-vowel between the root or stem and the person-number ending) while the most important subtype of the second conjugation is the 'thematic' verbs (which have an **-e-* or **-o-* after the root or stem and before the person-number endings). The primary endings were used in the present (and future) of the indicative. The secondary endings were used for the non-present tenses of the indicative, and for the injunctive, optative (and subjunctive). The difference between the primary and the secondary endings of the First Conjugation active is basically the addition of the particle **-i*, which is argued to be the same particle seen in the locative case and hence it carried (once) the meaning of 'here and now'. First conjugation verbs generally have a singular where the root vowel is *e* and a plural which shows a zero-grade. This interchange can be seen in the verb **h₁es-* 'to be' (Table 4.10). The reflexes of this verb are also shown for Latin, Greek, Sanskrit, and Hittite; we can see that Sanskrit has been the most conservative in preserving the interchange of a full-grade and a zero-grade in this verb.

Table 4.10. *The verb *h₁és- 'to be' in the present active indicative*

PIE	Latin	Grk	Sanskrit	Hittite
Singular				
1. **h₁és-mi*	*sum*	*eimí*	*ásmi*	*ēsmi*
2. **h₁és-si*	*es*	*eî ~ essí*	*ási*	*ēssi*
3. **h₁és-ti*	*est*	*estí*	*ásti*	*ēszi*
Plural				
1. **h₁s-més*	*sumus*	*esmén*	*smás*	*eswani ~ esweni*
2. **h₁s-té*	*estis*	*esté*	*sthá*	*esteni*
3. **h₁s-énti*	*sunt*	*eisí*	*sánti*	*asanzi*

Table 4.11. *Second conjugation of *bher- 'to carry' in the present active indicative*

PIE	Latin	Greek	Sanskrit
Singular			
1. **bhér-oh$_2$*	*ferō*	*phérō*	*bhárāmi*
2. **bhér-eth$_2$e*	*fers*	*phéreis*	*bhárasi*
3. **bhér-ei*	*fert*	*phérei*	*bhárati*
Plural			
1. **bhér-omes*	*ferimus*	*phéromen*	*bhárāmasi*
2. **bhér-ete*	*fertis*	*phérete*	*bhárata*
3. **bhér-onti*	*ferunt*	*phérousi*	*bháranti*

We have already encountered a second conjugation thematic verb in **bher-* 'carry' and its forms are indicated in Table 4.11, along with the reflexes in Latin, Greek, and Sanskrit (Hittite has no simple thematic verbs).

In addition to suffixes and endings, there were changes that could be made to the beginning of the verb as well. These comprise the augment and reduplication. The augment was merely the addition of a particle **h$_1$e-* to the beginning of the root. This was used to indicate the past tense and was therefore associated with the imperfect and the aorist, e.g. Sanskrit *á-bharam*, Greek *é-pheron*, Armenian *e-ber* indicate a Proto-Indo-European **h$_1$e-bher-om* 'I carried'.

The second technique of changing the beginning of the word is reduplication which involves, more or less, repeating the initial consonant followed by the vowel *e* or *i*, e.g. the verbal root **derk̂-* 'see' yields Sanskrit *dadarśa:* Greek *dédorka* < Proto-Indo-European **dé-dork̂e* 'he/she has seen'. In some cases nearly the entire root would be reduplicated, e.g. Sanskrit *várvarti* 'turns' <**wer-w(e)rt-*.

The participles formed from verbs were of great importance and were formed by the suffixes **-e/ont-*, e.g. **bher-* 'carry' but **bher-ont-* 'carrying', **-wes-* for the perfect and **-mh$_1$no-* for the middle. The participles were then declined like adjectives.

4.9 Derivation

Proto-Indo-European clearly had a rich system of both verbal and nominal derivation, the description and illustration of which would require a large book in itself. However a couple of examples of the derivational processes will give the reader a partial insight into the system and allow him or her better to understand and evaluate the lexical evidence offered up in later chapters in support of the reconstruction of various semantic fields.

Table 4.12. *Nominal and verbal derivatives of* *steh$_2$- 'stand'

Present Tense	*stí-steh$_2$-ti 'he/she stands (up)' [cf. Skt *tíṣṭhati*, Av *hištati*, Grk *hístēsi*, Lati *sistit*]
Aorist Tense	*h$_1$é-steh$_2$-t 'he/she stood (up)' [cf. Skt *ásthāt*, Grk *éstē*]
Verbal Derivatives	
(1) Stative	*steh$_2$-eh$_1$-ti 'he/she is standing' [cf. Lat *stat*, OHG *stāt* ~ *stēt*, OIr *tā* 'is', OCS *stoitŭ*]
(2) *w*-derivative (no apparent change in meaning)	
	*steh$_2$-w- 'stand' [cf. Lith *stóvia* 'stands', Goth *stōjan* 'to stand', Grk *stoā́* 'marketplace' (< 'where one stands')]
Nominal Derivatives	
(1) -*ó*-	*-sth$_2$-ó- 'standing' [cf. Skt *pra-stha-* 'stable, firm, solid', OIr *ross* 'promontory']
(2) -*tó*-	*sth$_2$-tó- 'standing, placed' [cf. Skt *sthitá-* standing', Lat *status* 'placed', Grk *statós* 'standing, placed', OIr *fo-ssad* 'strong', ON *staþr* 'obstinate'
(3) -*tí*-	*sth$_2$-tí- 'standing, erection' [cf. Skt *sthíti-*'stay, sojourn', Grk *stásis* 'place, setting, erection [of a statue]', Lat *statim* 'firmly, steadfastly', NE *stead*]
(4) -*tlo*-	*sth$_2$-tlo- 'something standing' [cf. Lat *obstāculum* 'obstacle', OE *staðol* 'support', Wels *distadl* 'worthless', Lith *stãklės* [pl.] 'loom']
(5) -*no*-	*stéh$_2$-no- 'standing, place' [cf. Skt *sthāna-* 'place', Grk *ástēnos* 'unfortunate', Lith *stónas* 'place', OCS *stanŭ* 'stand']
(6) -*men*-	*stéh$_2$-men- 'place for standing' [cf. Skt *sthā́man-* 'seat, place', Grk *stḗmōn* 'warp', Lat *stāmen* 'warp', Lith *stomuõ* 'statue']

The first example (Table 4.12) shows a number of productive nominal and verbal derivatives from Proto-Indo-European *steh$_2$- 'stand'. Each of the derivatives illustrated is reflected in at least three Indo-European groups which makes it relatively likely that the derivation dates to Proto-Indo-European times, rather than being the result of independent creations in the stocks where it is attested.

Table 4.13. *Derivational tree of* *h_2eh_x- *'be hot, burn' (cf. Palaic hā- 'be hot')*

First 'Generation' Derivatives	Second 'Generation' Derivatives	Third 'Generation' Derivatives
(1) *h_2éh_x-ti- 'heat' [cf. OIr *āith* 'kiln']		
(2) *h_2éh_x-mr̥ 'heat' [cf. Grk *êmar* 'day', Arm *awr* 'day' (< *'heat of day')]		
(3) *h_2eh_x-ter- 'burner' > 'fire' [cf. Av *ātarš* 'fire']	(3*a*) *h_2eh_x-tr-o- 'burnt' [cf. Lat *āter* 'black']	
	(3*b*) *h_2éh_x-tr-o- 'fiery, hot' [cf. Latv *ātrs* 'quick, sharp, hot']	(3*b*i) *h_2ē$h_x$tró- 'quick' [cf. OHG *ātar*-]
	(3*c*) *h_2eh_x-tr-eh_a- 'fire-place, hearth'	(3*c*i) *h_2eh_x-tr-iyo- 'of the hearth' [cf. Lat *ātrium* 'atrium' < *'fire-hall',
	(3*d*) *h_2eh_x-ter-ye/o- 'make fire, kindle' [cf. Arm *ayrem* 'kindle']	
(4) *h_2eh_x-s- 'burn'	(4*a*) *h_2eh_x-s 'ash' [cf. Hit *hās* 'ash, potash']	(4*a*i) *h_2eh_x-s-o- 'ash' [cf. Skt *āsa*- 'ash']
	(4*b*) *h_2(h_x)-s-tér- 'burner' > 'ember' > 'star' [cf. Grk *astḗr* 'star', Lat *stēlla* 'star', NE *star*]	
	(4*c*) *h_2eh_x-s-eh_a- 'burning place, hearth' [cf. Lat *āra* 'altar; hearth', Hit *hāssa* 'hearth, fire-altar']	
	(4*d*) *h_2eh_x-s-no- 'fiery' [cf. OIr *ān* 'fiery']	

(Cont'd.)

Table 4.13. (*Cont'd.*)

FIRST 'GENERATION' DERIVATIVES	SECOND 'GENERATION' DERIVATIVES	THIRD 'GENERATION' DERIVATIVES
	(4e) *h_2eh_x*-s-dh-* 'burn' (no detectable difference)	(4ei) *h_2eh_x*-s-dh-*eh_1- 'be burning' [cf. Lat *ardeō* 'burn'] (4eii) *h_2eh_x*-s-dh-ro-* 'burning' [cf. Toch B *astare* 'pure']

The second illustration is presented in the form of a (sideways) tree diagram (Table 4.13) and attempts to demonstrate the progressive nature of Indo-European derivation where one derivative presupposes another. In this example some of the derivatives are supported by only one Indo-European branch but the nature of the derivational process is such that derivatives at one point in the 'tree' presuppose derivatives 'higher up' (i.e. to the left) in the tree.

A final illustration (Table 4.14) gives examples from Old English and Greek of the role that ablaut, the interchange of vowels, plays in Proto-Indo-

Table 4.14. *Illustration of Indo-European ablaut in derivation (PIE *sed- 'sit' and *pet- 'fly')*

	Old English	Greek
Vowel		
ø	*nest* 'nest' < **ni-sd-ós* 'sit down [place]'	*pterón* 'feather'
e	*sittan* 'sit' < **sed-ye/o-* *setl* 'settle' < **sed-lo-*	*pétomai* 'fly'
o	*gesæt* 'act of sitting' < *-*sódos*	*potáomai* 'fly hither and thither'
ē	*sǣt* 'lurking-place' < **sēdeh*$_a$-	
ō	*sōt* 'soot' < **sōdos* 'what settles'	*pōtáomai* 'fly about'

European derivation. If we take the vowel *-*e*- as basic, the system of ablaut might be diagramed as follows:

ø ~ e > o, ē > ō.

Table 4.15. *Schleicher's Tale*

G^{w}r̥h$_x$ḗi h$_2$ówis, k^{w}ésyo wl̥h$_2$néh$_a$ ne h$_1$ést, h$_1$ék̂wons spék̂et, h$_1$oinom ghe g^{w}r̥h$_x$úm wóĝhom wéĝhontm̥ h$_1$oinom-k^{w}e méĝh$_a$m̥ bhórom, h$_1$oinom-k^{w}e ĝhménm̥ h$_x$ṓk̂u bhérontm̥. H$_2$ówis tu h$_1$ek̂woibh(y)os weuk^{w}ét: 'k̂ḗr h$_a$eghnutór moi h$_1$ék̂wons h$_a$éĝontm̥ h$_a$nérm̥ widn̥tbh(y)ós: h$_1$ék̂wōs tu wewk^{w}ónt: 'k̂ludhí, h$_2$ówei, k̂ḗr ghe h$_a$eghnutór, n̥sméi widn̥tbh(y)ós: h$_a$nḗr, pótis, h$_2$éwyom r̥ wl̥h$_2$néh$_a$m sebhi k^{w}r̥néuti nu g^{w}hermóm wéstrom néĝhi h$_2$éwyom wĺ̥h$_2$neh$_a$ h$_1$ésti.'

Tód k̂ek̂luwṓs h$_2$ówis h$_a$égrom bhugét.

Vocabulary

bhér-	'carry'
bhóros	'what is borne, a load' (from **bher-*)
bheug-	'flee'
ĝhmén-	'man'
ghe	intensifying particle
g^{w}hermós	'warm'
g^{w}r̥h$_x$-	'hill'
g^{w}r̥h$_x$u-	'heavy'
h$_1$ék̂wos	'horse'
h$_1$ést	'is'
h$_1$oinos	'one'
h$_2$ówis	'sheep'
h$_a$éĝ-	'drive, pull'
h$_a$éĝros	'field'
h$_a$eghnutór	'pains, is painful'
h$_a$nḗr	'man'
h$_x$ōk̂u	'fast'
k̂ḗr	'heart'
k̂leu-	'hear'
k^{w}e	'and'
k^{w}ós	'who' (genitive *k^{w}ésyo*)
k^{w}er-	'make'
méĝh$_a$-	'large'
moi	'me'
ne	'not'
néĝhi	'not at all'

(*Cont'd.*)

Table 4.15. (*Cont'd.*)

nu	'now'
n̥sméi	'us'
pótis	'master'
r̥	intensifying contrastive particle
sebhi	'for oneself'
spéḱ-	'see'
tód	'that one'
tu	'then'
wéĝh-	'move'
wéstrom	'clothes' (< **wes-* 'to dress')
wek^w-	'speak'
weid-	'see'
wóĝhos	'wagon' (< **weĝh-*'to move')
wĺ̥$h_2$neh$_a$-	'wool'

Any further discussion takes us into realms of detail unintended for this book. But as an exercise in some of the principles, the reader is invited to tackle, with attendant glossary, the complete text of Schleicher's tale (Table 4.15).

Further Reading

Good recent surveys of Proto-Indo-European can be found in Fortson (2004), Meier-Brugge (2003), Szemerenyi (1996), Tichy (2000), and Beekes (1995); see also Lockwood (1969); the most noteworthy earlier classical accounts can be found in Meillet (1937) and Brugmann (1897–1916). Specialist studies include Benveniste (1935, 1948), Jassanoff (2003), Kuryłowicz (1964, 1968), Lehmann (1952, 2002) Lindeman (1987), Mayrhofer (1986), Schmalstieg (1980), Specht (1944); syntax is discussed in Friedrich (1975) and Lehmann (1974). For Schleicher's tale (Schleicher 1868), see also Lehmann and Zgusta (1979); other examples of extended Proto-Indo-European text can be found in Sen (1994), Danka (1998), and Macjon (1998).

Etymological dictionaries of Indo-European include Buck (1949) and Delamarre (1991) which are both arranged semantically, and Pokorny (1959) which remains the starting point for most discussion; there are also Mann (1984–7) and Watkins (1985); encyclopedic presentations are to be found in Gamkrelidze and Ivanov (1995) and Mallory and Adams (1997). An index of the roots ascribed to Proto-Indo-European can be found in Bird (1993).

5

Relationships

5.0 Linguistic Relationships

The Indo-European languages share both internal and external relationships. The internal relationships are expressed as dialectal relationships among the different Indo-European languages while the external relationships are primarily concerned with the Indo-European language family and how it relates to others of the world's language families.

5.1 Internal Relationships

We have already seen that within any of the Indo-European groups, there are also subgroups. For example, the East Slavic languages of Russian, Belorussian, and Ukrainian are all much more closely related to one another than any of them is related to Polish or Serbo-Croatian, two other Slavic languages. This situation represents subgrouping (Eastern Slavic) within an Indo-European language group (Slavic). What interests us here is, to what extent can we speak of subgroupings within Indo-European itself? August Schleicher (1861–2) proposed one of the earliest models of the relationship between the different Indo-European groups (Fig. 5.1) that portrayed the groups as branches stemming from a common trunk (*Stammbaum*), and the concept of a family tree, although often maligned as oversimplistic, is still the primary method

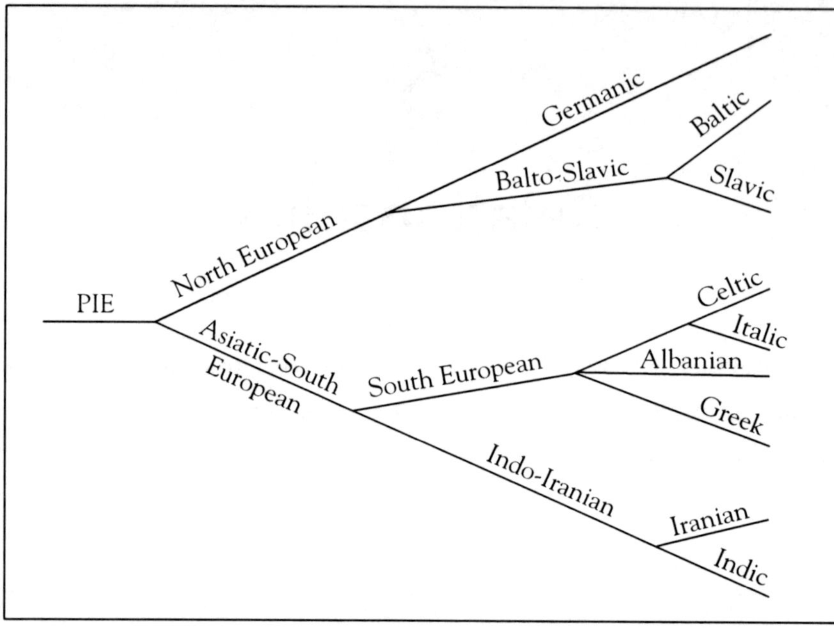

Figure 5.1. Schleicher's family tree of the Indo- European languages

employed in indicating the interrelationships of the Indo-European languages. The problem with the tree's simplicity is that the branching of the different groups is portrayed as a series of clean breaks with no connection between branches after they have split, as if each dialectal group marched away from the rest. Such sharp splits are possible, but assuming that all splits within Proto-Indo-European were like this is not very plausible, and any linguist surveying the current Indo-European languages would note dialectal variations running through some but not all areas, often linking adjacent groups who may belong to different languages. This type of complexity, which saw each innovation welling from its point of origin to some but not all other speakers (dialects, languages), is termed the 'Wave theory' (*Wellentheorie*). A detailed example is provided in Figure 5.2.

The 'Wave theory' provides a useful graphic reminder of the ways different isoglosses, the lines that show the limits of any particular feature, enclose some but not all languages. However, their criteria of inclusion, why we are looking at any particular one, and not another one, are no more solid than those that define family trees. The key element here is what linguistic features actually help determine for us whether two languages are more related or less related to one another. A decision in this area can be extraordinary difficult because we must be able to distinguish between features that may have been present throughout the entire Indo-European world (Indoeuropeia has been employed

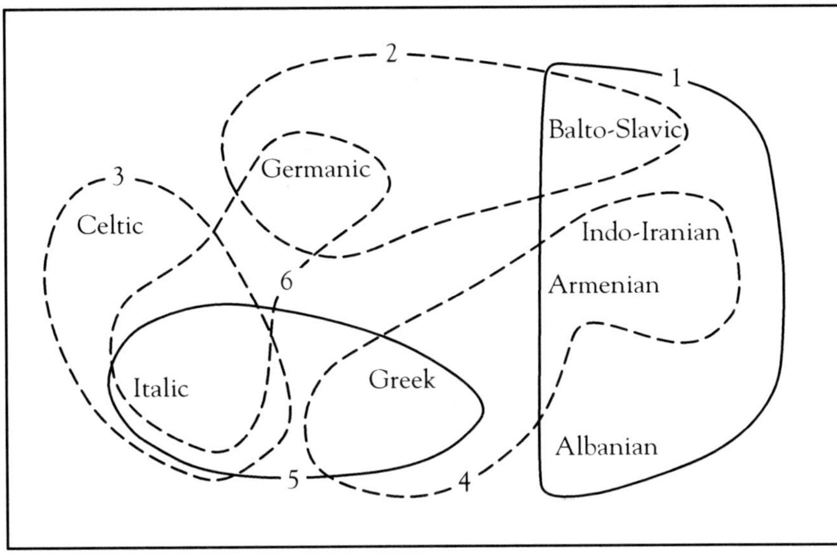

Figure 5.2. A 'wave model' of some of the interrelationships of the Indo-European languages

to describe this concept) and have dropped out in some but not others against those features that are innovations in only some of the different groups. The historical linguist is principally looking for shared innovations, i.e. are there traces of corresponding developments between two or more language groups that would indicate that they shared a common line of development different from other language groups? Only by finding shared innovations can one feel confident that the grouping of individual Indo-European linguistic groups into larger units or branches of the tree is real.

Before looking at the picture as a whole, we will review the evidence for those relationships that finds fairly general consensus.

5.1.1 Anatolian and Residual Indo-European

Most linguists will argue that Proto-Anatolian was the first Indo-European language to diverge from the continuum of Proto-Indo-European speakers; there are also a considerable number who would argue that the split was made so early that we are not dealing with a daughter language of a Proto-Indo-European mother but rather a sister language (Fig. 5.3). Acceptance of this latter model is the foundation of the Indo-Hittite hypothesis, though many linguists who believe in the early separation of Proto-Anatolian would not use the term 'Indo-Hittite' but rather continue to use the term Indo-European.

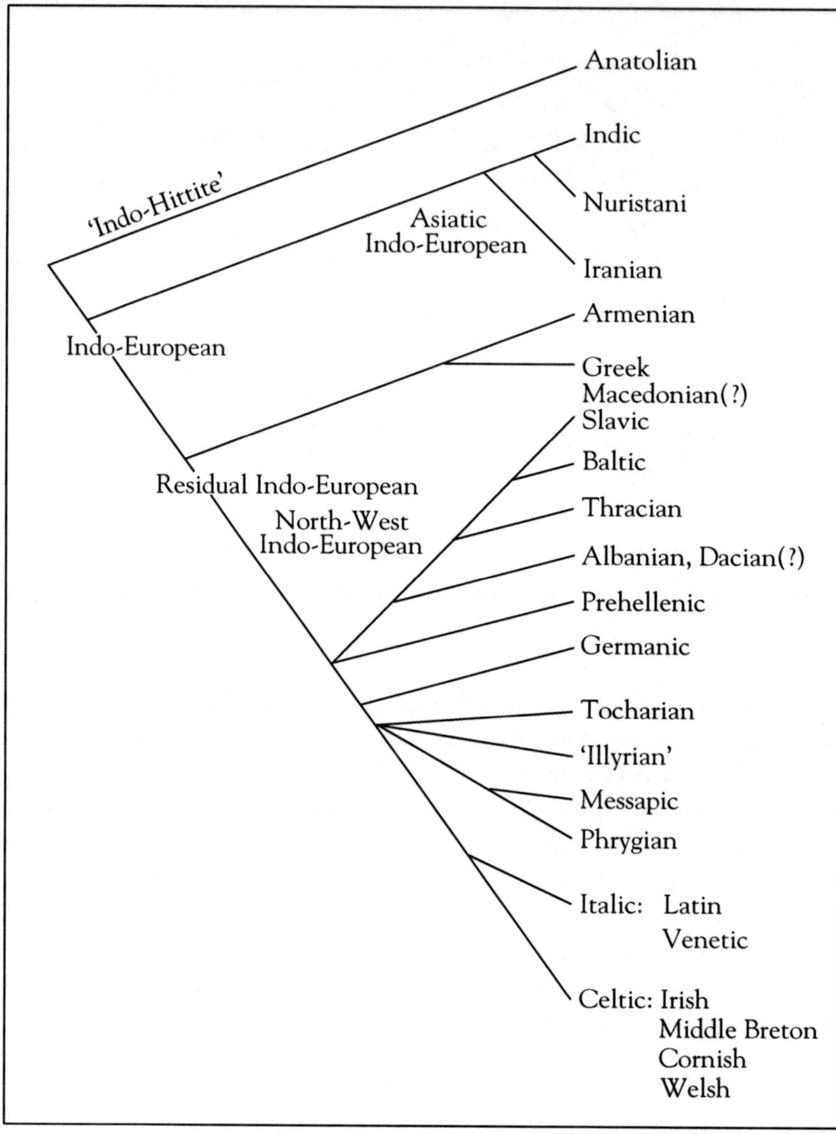

Figure 5.3. A modern tree diagram of the Indo-European languages suggested by Eric Hamp (1990).

The antiquity of the separation of Anatolian from the rest of Indo-European is argued on several grounds. The first is obviously Anatolian's own antiquity: it is the earliest Indo-European group attested in the written record which begins *c.*2000 BC. More important is the fact that when Hittite (the earliest and most substantially attested Anatolian language) is compared with the other

Indo-European languages, especially with its closest contemporaries, Indo-Iranian and Greek, it reveals on the one hand strikingly conservative features and on the other hand an absence of forms that one would have expected in an Indo-European language attested so early—how these absences are explained is one of the fundamental issues of determining the relationship between Anatolian and the other Indo-European languages.

Among the conservative features of Anatolian is the preservation of one laryngeal (*h_2) and traces of another (*h_3). Another is its productive use of what are known as heteroclitic nouns. One of the more curious types of declension reconstructed for Proto-Indo-European is nouns that have a stem in **r* in the nominative but in **n* in all other cases. While few traces are found in other Indo-European languages (where the stem is generally levelled one way or the other, for example, OE has *r* in *wæter* but ON has levelled the same word to *n* in *vatn* 'water'), Hittite maintained this type as an active declension pattern (e.g. Hit *wātar* 'water' in the nominative but genitive *witenas*). Another conservative trait of Anatolian is the preservation of two separate conjugational types characterized by different person-number endings. One type, easily recognized as cognate with the type found in other Indo-European languages, has *-mi*, *-si*, *-ti* as the endings of the first, second, and third persons singular. The other type, which has left only traces in the other IE groups, has the endings *-hi*, *-ti*, and *-i* instead.

On the other hand, Anatolian has no dual (as found in both Greek and Indo-Iranian), its verb has no subjunctive or optative (again unlike its Bronze Age neighbours), and it is questionable (arguments go both ways) whether there are any traces of a feminine in Anatolian. The augment **e-*, which is found in the other Bronze Age languages (Indo-Iranian, Greek) and all the surrounding languages, i.e. Phrygian, Armenian, with possible traces elsewhere, is not found in Anatolian. The combination of conservatism on the one hand with absence of features found in the other two groups to emerge in the Bronze Age has led some to suggest that Anatolian did not share in a number of the developments that we find in any of the other Indo-European languages because it was not part of the Proto-Indo-European world when these developments occurred. This supposition then leads to the hypothesis that Proto-Anatolian and Proto-Indo-European were siblings of an earlier Proto-Indo-Hittite language.

Opponents to this theory are highly sceptical of employing *absence of features* in Anatolian as evidence for greater antiquity. They have long argued that as there were non-Indo-European languages in central Anatolia, it is just as likely that the original features were lost as Anatolian was taken up by the substrate population or employed initially as a trade language whose grammar was simplified to facilitate intercommunication.

5.1.2 Indo-Iranian

The sole uncontroversial subgrouping of Indo-European is Indo-Iranian, the super-group, if you will, that unites the Indo-Aryan and the Iranian languages. We have already seen that the similarities between Avestan and Sanskrit were such that there was a period in Indo-European research when Avestan was regarded as a dialect of Sanskrit. Table 5.1 illustrates this similarity in a much cited comparison between a verse from the *Avesta* and its literal transposition into Sanskrit. A comparison between the two texts reveals similarities that are so strong that often one need do no more than make an expected sound change in one language to effect a translation into the other. The two languages are so closely related that we can derive them from a common Indo-Iranian proto-language. This means that between Proto-Indo-European and the Indo-Aryan and Iranian groups, there was also a Proto-Indo-Iranian stage. To this group, it might be noted, belongs one further subgroup. Only recorded since the nineteenth century, the five Nūristāni (also termed Kafiri, a term that means 'infidel' and is hardly politically correct today nor since their conversion to Islam is it any longer true) languages of the Hindu-Kush have provided evidence that their ancestor does not appear to have been either Indo-Aryan or Iranian but is more likely to derive directly from Proto-Indo-Iranian and possibly represents a third 'branch' of the super-group although there are arguments that set them closer to either Indo-Aryan or Iranian.

Precisely when this stage existed we cannot say, but we already have evidence by *c.*1400 BC for the existence of a separate Indo-Aryan language. The evidence

Table 5.1. *Yašt 10.6 from the Avesta and a Sanskrit translation*

Avestan	*təm amavantəm yazatəm*
Old Indic	*tám ámavantam yajatám*
Proto-Indo-Iranian	**tám ámavantam yaǰatám*
	This powerful deity
Avestan	*sūrəm dāmōhu səvištəm*
Old Indic	*śū́ram dhā́masu śáviṣṭham*
Proto-Indo-Iranian	**ću̇̄ram dhā́masu ćávištham*
	strong, among the living the strongest
Avestan	*miθrəm yazāi zaoθrābyō*
Old Indic	*mitrám yajāi hótrābhyaḥ*
Proto-Indo-Iranian	**mitrám yaǰāi ǰháutrābhyas*
	Mithra, I honour with libations

is intriguing in that it does not come from India but rather from northern Syria which was controlled by an ancient people known as the Mitanni. The Mitanni were contemporaries of the Hittites and their language was Hurrian, a non-Indo-European language attested to the south of the Caucasus in eastern Anatolia. But some of their leaders bore Indo-Aryan names, and in a peace treaty between themselves and the Hittites, they appended to a long list of deities guaranteeing the treaty the names of Indara, Mitraśil, Naśatianna, and Uruvanaššil which would have been rendered in India as Indra, Mitra, Nāsatya, and Varuṇa, principal gods of the Vedic religion. How much further back the Indo-Aryan languages separated from the Iranian we cannot say but there seems to be a general impression that sets the split to sometime around 2000 BC. Before this period we might imagine the period of Proto-Indo-Iranian.

The grouping of Indo-Iranian together is not based solely on the obvious similarities between the languages but also certain common innovations. There are a number of words that occur in both Indic and Iranian but not in any other Indo-European language. Some of these concern religious concepts, e.g. Proto-Indo-Iranian **atharwan-* 'priest', **r̥ši-* 'seer', **ućig-* 'sacrificing priest', **anću-* 'soma plant'. Both the ancient Indo-Aryans and Iranians drank the juices of the pressed soma plant (Indo-Iranian **sauma* > Sanskrit *soma* and Avestan *haoma*). Moreover, there are also some names of shared deities as well as a series of animal names (hedgehog, tortoise, pigeon, donkey, he-goat, wild boar, and camel), architectural names (pit, canal, house, peg), and a variety of other terms. These common elements suggest that the Proto-Indo-Iranians borrowed certain words from a presumably non-Indo-European culture before they began their divergence into separate subgroups.

5.1.3 Balto-Slavic

Although there are still some (more often Balticists than Slavicists) to contest the close association of Baltic and Slavic, majority opinion probably favours a common proto-language between Proto-Indo-European and the Baltic and Slavic languages, i.e. during or after the dissolution of Proto-Indo-European there was a stage of Proto-Balto-Slavic before the separation of the two language groups. This proto-language may not have undergone a simple split into Proto-Baltic and Proto-Slavic. Another possibility often put forward is that Balto-Slavic became divided into three subgroups: East Baltic (Lithuanian and Latvian), West Baltic (Old Prussian), and Slavic. In any case the two groups (Baltic and Slavic) or the three groups (East Baltic, West Baltic, and Slavic) remained in close geographical and cultural contact with one another and have continued to influence one another long after the initial division into separate groups. They share a number of items of vocabulary not found in other Indo-European groups as well as new grammatical features such as the definite adjective built on the adjective plus the relative pronoun **yos*, new accent and comparative adjective patterns, etc. (Oszwald Szemerényi lists fourteen although more than half are disputed). What is particularly interesting is that the Balto-Slavic languages are satem languages like Indo-Iranian and some suggest some form of historical connection between the two super-groups. In addition to satemization, all these groups obey what is known as the *ruki*-rule, i.e. **s* is palatalized to **š* after **r*, **u*, **k*, or **i*, e.g. Grk *térsomai* 'I become dry' but Skt *tr̥ṣyáti* 'he thirsts', Av *taršna-* 'thirst', Lith *tir̃štas* 'thirst'.

5.1.4 Contact Groups?

There are a number of other proposed relationships. Some argue that similarities between Greek and Armenian are such that there was a common Graeco-Armenian, while Italo-Celtic has been another long suggested and just as frequently rejected proposition. In both of these cases, we do not require a proto-language between Proto-Indo-European and the individual languages as we do with Indo-Iranian, and so the case for these other sets is simply not as strong as it is for Indo-Iranian and Balto-Slavic. Generally, when similarities between Greek and Armenian, say, or Italic and Celtic are found, it is presumed that they may have been a result of contact relations between the ancestors of the different languages, and these relationships may have been intense, but insufficient to view these similarities as evidence for discrete Proto-Graeco-Armenian or Proto-Italo-Celtic. Here, the concept of the 'Wave theory' probably has a significant role to play.

A major group presumably created or maintained by contact is labelled the North-West group and comprises Germanic, Baltic, and Slavic (as one chain whose elements may have been in closer contact with one another), and additionally Italic and Celtic. The link between these languages is largely that of shared vocabulary items: thirty-eight were originally proposed but more recent studies list up to sixty-four lexical innovations, although they do not cross all languages uniformly. Items include words such as 'rye' (ON *rugr* 'rye', OE *ryge* 'rye' (> NE *rye*), Lith (pl.) *rugiaĩ* 'rye', OCS *rŭžĭ* 'rye' from an earlier **rughis*), the type of 'culture word' that could be introduced into one area and then spread through a larger region along with the item itself. The evidence suggests that this spread occurred at some time before there were marked divisions between these languages so that these words appear to have been 'inherited' from an early period.

In some cases the loans are obviously late and involved an alien phonetic shape that challenged each language, e.g. the word 'silver' (Ibero-Celt *śilaPur* (/*śilabur*/) 'silver', ON *silfr* 'silver', OE *seolfor* 'silver' (> NE *silver*), Goth *silubr* 'silver', Lith *sidãbras* 'silver', Rus *serebró* 'silver') where the best we can reconstruct is **silVbVr-* where V stands for unknown vowels.

5.1.5 Family Trees

We can now return to the concept of a family tree and the relationships between the different Indo-European languages.

1. Anatolian is generally recognized as the first Indo-European language to have separated from the remaining languages (or, alternatively, the rest of Indo-European moved away from Anatolian). Whether one wishes to see this separation as an event so early that Anatolian did not share innovations developed by all other Indo-European languages (the Indo-Hittite hypothesis) or whether Anatolian simply departed somewhat earlier but may still be analysed like any other Indo-European language is, as we have seen, still debated.
2. The Indo-Iranian languages form a distinct super-group.
3. The Balto-Slavic languages, although somewhat more questionable than Indo-Iranian, are generally held to form a single super-group.
4. The Indo-Iranian and Balto-Slavic languages share both satemization and the *ruki*-rule and may have developed as some form of west–east (or north-west–south-east) continuum with certain features running through them.
5. There were close contact relations between Greek and Armenian at some period of their existence prior to their emergence as discrete language groups. This contact is plausible as many would see both their origins to lie in the Balkans, so that their ancestors were once more closely situated to one another than their present distribution suggests. There are also connections between this Graeco-Armenian group and Indo-Iranian, particularly with regard to what are probably late Proto-Indo-European morphological innovations, but there are also a series of lexical isoglosses confined to Greek and Indo-Iranian.
6. There were contact relations between the ancestors of Italic and Celtic. Again such contact is entirely plausible as the two groups were historically adjacent to one another in west central Europe.
7. The North-West European languages (Germanic, Baltic, Slavic, Celtic, Italic) shared a series of common loanwords (probably created among themselves as well as derived from some non-Indo-European source) at some period in their antiquity before they emerged as distinct Indo-European groups.

8. The position of Tocharian with respect to the other Indo-European groups is a major issue of contention. However, there is no grammatical evidence that it was strongly associated with its nearest neighbour, Indo-Iranian. Many suggest that its connections appear to lie further west, with Germanic in particular, or that Tocharian represents a peripheral language that separated from the other Indo-European groups at a very early date (Fig. 5.4).
9. In time sequencing Indo-European developments, there has been a tendency to see the more peripheral languages such as Celtic in the west and Tocharian in the east as the language groups that separated earliest (after Anatolian).

How the various relations were played out in three-dimensional (geographical) space is nearly impossible to determine. The assumption that Italo-Celtic relations occurred on the Italian–French border, for example, is purely presumptive and the actual relationship could have been developed distant from both Italy and France/Switzerland before either language group had achieved its historical position. Similarly, the common innovations of other contact groups may have occurred long before the component language groups emerged in their earliest historically attested locations.

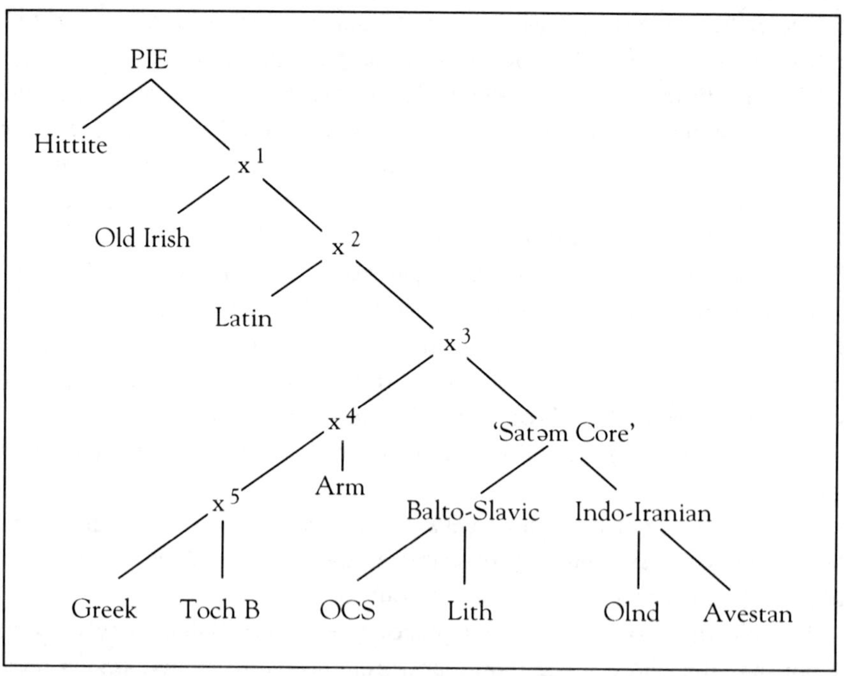

Figure 5.4. A recent family tree of the Indo-European languages prepared by D. Ringe, T. Warnow and A. Taylor (1995).

5.2 External Relations

Indo-European is but one of the world's language families and it obviously had non-Indo-European neighbours both before and over the course of its expansions. There are two ways in which Indo-European may have related to these neighbours: through contact or through genetic inheritance.

A contact relationship would occur when two languages were adjacent to one another and there were loanwords, possibly even grammatical or phonological borrowing, between the two. It should be emphasized that the movement of loanwords need not be the result of direct contact, i.e. Indo-European with language X, but may have been the result of indirect contact, i.e. language Y passes a word to language X which then passes it on to Indo-European (a good example of the circuitous route a loanword might take through space and time is the Avestan word *pairi-daēza-* 'enclosure' that was borrowed into Greek as *parádeisos* 'garden' then into Late Latin as *paradīsus* whence into Old French *paradis*, and, finally, into English *paradise*). Secondly, the contact relationships may have occurred during differing stages of each language family's evolution, e.g. the loan may be between the proto-language of one family and a late descendant of another family.

A genetic relationship is one in which Proto-Indo-European would be seen as a constituent element of a still larger family of languages, i.e. the Proto-Indo-European tree is reduced to a bundle of branches on a still larger linguistic tree.

5.2.1 Indo-European-Uralic

Indo-European shares Europe with one other major language family—Uralic, the family to which Hungarian, Finnish, Estonian, and a number of other languages found to both the west and east of the Urals belong. Relationships between the two have been proposed for many years and primary debate concerns: (1) whether they are evidence of an earlier genetic relationship or contact-induced loanwords, and (2) to which stage precisely of both Indo-European and Uralic these loanwords belong. Károly Rédei offers a total of seven words that are attributed to the earliest period (PIE **mei-* 'exchange': PU **miγe-* 'give, sell'; PIE **mesg-* 'dip under water, dive': PU *muśke-* 'wash'; PIE **$h_1$nómn̥* 'name': PU *nime* 'name'; PIE **snéh$_1$wr̥* 'tendon': PU *sene* 'vein, sinew'; PIE **deh$_3$-* 'give': PU *toγe-* 'bring' (note the representation of the PIE laryngeal by PU *-ɣ-); PIE **$h_a$weseh$_a$-* 'gold': PU *waśke* 'some metal'; PIE **wódr̥* 'water': PU *wete* 'water'). Some of these words have been also employed to argue a genetic rather than contact relationship between Indo-European and

Uralic. Subsequent loanwords are reputed to be between various stages of Indo-European, generally Indo-Iranian, and the Finno-Ugric languages, i.e. a subgrouping of Uralic, or even more recent stages of the Uralic languages. For example, Finnish *parsas* 'pig' could only have come from a satem language such as Iranian (Proto-Iranian **porśos* 'pig') rather than an earlier form such as PIE **pórk̂os* 'pig'. A number of these later words concern exchange relationships, e.g. 'value', 'portion', 'hundred', 'thousand', 'commodity', words associated with agriculture, e.g. 'grain', or stockbreeding, e.g. 'pig', 'ox', and suggest that at various stages of Indo-European, Uralic speakers were absorbing some elements of a farming economy and probably more complex social concepts from Indo-Europeans to their south.

5.2.2 Indo-European and Semitic

Unlike the relationship between Indo-European farmers and Uralic hunter-fishers, the Indo-Europeans were likely to have been economically less advanced and socially less complex than contemporary Semitic societies. Relationships with Semitic, one of the subgroups of the Afro-Asiatic language family that spanned the Near East and northern Africa, including ancient Egyptian, have been long discussed in Indo-European studies. The better-known Semitic languages are Hebrew, Arabic, and Aramaic.

In their study of Indo-European origins, Thomas Gamkrelidze and Vyacheslav Ivanov suggest that the Semitic vocabulary borrowed into Indo-European is primarily concerned with farming, technology, and numerals. They list seventeen potential loanwords such as 'bull', 'goat', 'lamb', 'monkey', 'grain', 'grinding stone', 'honey', 'axe', 'boat', 'sacrifice', 'star', and 'seven'. Some of these comparisons are far more speculative than others, e.g. the Proto-Indo-European word for 'goat' (**ghaidos*) that is compared with Proto-Semitic **gadyi-* is only attested in Latin and Germanic and it is far more easily assumed to be a regional word of North-West Indo-European rather than Proto-Indo-European. If such is the case, the resemblance of **ghaidos* and Semitic **gady-* would be entirely accidental. Similarly, the words for 'monkey' occur in only two Indo-European languages, Greek *kêpos* and Sanskrit *kapí-*, but these are far more easily explained as late loans from some Semitic language than as an inheritance from Proto-Indo-European: the export of monkeys as a prestigious gift was known in the eastern Mediterranean from the Bronze Age onwards. The more significant Semitic-Indo-European comparisons are Proto-Indo-European **médhu* 'honey': Proto-Semitic **mVtk-* 'sweet'; Proto-Indo-European **tauros* 'wild bull, aurochs': Proto-Semitic **ṯawr-* 'bull, ox'; Proto-Indo-European **septḿ̥* 'seven': Proto-Semitic **sab'atum*; and Proto-

Indo-European **wóinom* 'wine': Proto-Semitic **wayn* 'wine' (although this last word could also claim to have a decent IE pedigree).

The correspondences between Indo-European and Semitic are generally explained as flowing from Semitic into Indo-European at the level of the Indo-European proto-language itself. As for the mechanics of such loanwords, some maintain that they could only have been made if the Proto-Indo-European- and Proto-Semitic-speaking populations were living adjacent to one another (presumably somewhere in South-West Asia) or that these loanwords had passed through other intermediaries over a greater distance. Lesser claims for borrowing into or out of Proto-Indo-European have been made with reference to Sumerian, Kartvelian, and other Caucasian languages.

5.3 Genetic Models

It is logically imperative that Proto-Indo-European had its own prehistory and was descended from earlier languages and was likely to have had its own linguistic siblings. Attempts to substantiate such hypothetical relationships have been made on the small scale, e.g. with Proto-Indo-Uralic or Proto-Indo-Semitic, and on much larger scales where a series of language families have been combined into a single unit. The evidence for genetic constructs relies heavily on the same type of evidence that others adduce for contact relationships, e.g. that Proto-Indo-European and Proto-Uralic both share a common term for something as basic as 'water'. But further evidence derives from morphological comparisons which, in the attempt to distinguish between borrowing and inheritance, we already know count for far more. For example, in Table 5.2, we see again the reconstructed Proto-Indo-European pronouns compared with those in Proto-Afro-Asiatic and Proto-Uralic.

Rather than relations between Indo-European and one other family, most effort along these lines is now devoted to the reconstruction (and the confirmation

Table 5.2. *Pronouns in Proto-Indo-European, Proto-Uralic, and Proto-Afro-Asiatic*

	PIE	PUralic	PAfro-Asiatic
I	**h₁eĝ/*h₁éme*	**me*	**ma-/*mə-*
we two	**nóh₁*		**na-/*nə-*
we (plural)	**wéi*	—	**wa-/*wə-*
you	**túhₓ*	**te*	**t[h]a-/*t[h]ə-*
who	**kʷós*	**ku/*ko*	**kʷ[h]a-/*kʷ[h]ə-*

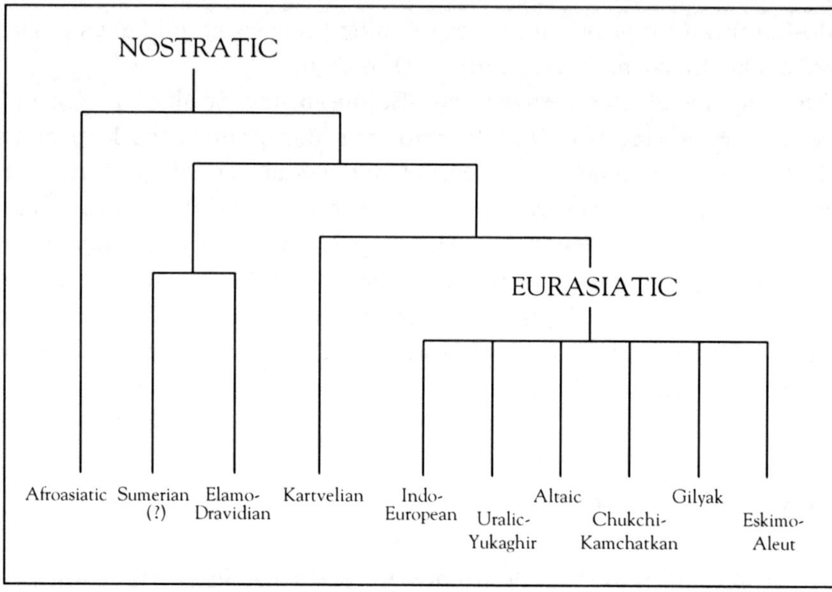

Figure 5.5. The Nostratic languages according to A. Bomhard (1996).

of the existence) of Eurasiatic and Nostratic. Eurasiatic as a hypothesis comprises Indo-European, Uralic-Yukaghir, Altaic, Korean, Japanese, Ainu, Gilyak (Nivkh), Chukotian (Chukchi-Kamchatkan), and Eskimo-Aleut in a single large genetic unit. In its most recent formulation it is based on 72 grammatical features and 437 items of vocabulary. Nostratic is the proposed mega-family that would unite Indo-European, Afro-Asiatic, Uralic, Altaic (Turkish, Mongolian, etc.), Kartvelian (Georgian), and Dravidian (languages of the southern third of India), and possibly several other families (some would exclude Afro-Asiatic and Dravidian from this list). In the dictionary of Nostratic published by Allan Bomhard, there are about 650 Nostratic roots which have been proposed to underlie Indo-European roots. One notes that evidence cited to establish contact relations can find itself being reinterpreted in terms of genetic relations, e.g. Nostratic **madw-/mədw-* 'honey, mead' is cited as the proto-form for the words for 'honey' not only in Indo-European but also Afro-Asiatic and Dravidian.

The Nostraticists propose that Nostratic existed about 15,000–12,000 BC, among hunter-gatherers, generally somewhere in South-West Asia (Fig. 5.5). They have opponents in abundance who challenge the entire concept of Nostratic, and most certainly one's ability to reconstruct proto-languages at such a time depth and the entire issue of time are so critical that we devote the next chapter to it.

Further Reading

The internal relationships of the Indo-European languages can be found in Porzig (1954), Meillet (1967), and Stang (1972). There is a large literature devoted to external relations: they are discussed at length in Gamkrelidze and Ivanov (1995); for IE-Uralic connections see Collinder (1974), Rédei (1988), and the papers to be found in Carpelan, Parpola, and Koskikallio (2001); for IE-Semitic relations see Brunner (1969), Levin (1973), Bomhard (1977), and D'iakonov (1985); for IE-Kartvelian see Klimov (1991); for Eurasiatic see Greenberg (2000–2); and for Nostratic see Bomhard and Kerns (1994), Bomhard (1996), Dolgopolsky (1998), and the many papers in Renfrew and Nettle (1999).

6

A Place in Time

6.0 The Fourth Dimension

We have considered the conceptual space of the Indo-European groups, their interrelationships with one another, and now it is time to enter the fourth dimension and consider their place in time or, as it is usually expressed in linguistics, time depth. Establishing time depth involves a combination of serenely difficult theoretical issues and some extraordinarily tricky practical problems. The theoretical problems stem from the fact that we are ultimately attempting to discuss the absolute dates, i.e. BC/AD dates, of a hypothetical construct. There are a lot easier things to do.

6.1 Time Depth

Many linguists adhere to the concept that Proto-Indo-European in the sense of the linguistic forms that we reconstruct is a hypothetical abstraction. This abstraction goes beyond the argument between those who maintain that our reconstructions are merely formula and those who assert that these formulas are still fair approximations of a real language. Rather, it can be argued that the abstract formulas, even if they are approximations, are not approximations set in real time, i.e. they do not go back to a common point or a single language but rather simply reflect reconstructable words, morphological forms, and syntactic processes that need not have been contemporary. We can discuss their relative order but this is not the same as the reconstruction of the entire state of a language at a particular moment in time. This concept of the proto-language as a timeless conglomeration of linguistic fragments is contrasted with the idea that there must have been a speech community that spoke a real language that was ancestral to the historically known Indo-European languages. Real people speak real languages in real time. It is interesting that linguists sceptical of joining reconstructed Proto-Indo-European with "real" Proto-Indo-European have tended to rediscover these distinctions every generation since at least the late nineteenth century. Their arguments may be correct but they have not become any better.

Generally, when one attempts to straddle the demands of the pure linguist and the logical needs of the cultural historian who is looking for a prehistoric Proto-Indo-European, the definition is then cautiously reshaped to describe the final state of the Proto-Indo-European language before its break-up and the dispersal or formation of the various daughter groups. The looseness of this definition also has its problems since "dispersal" is not necessarily equivalent to language change although, in time, it will stimulate differentiation.

The bottom line then becomes: what is the latest date that Proto-Indo-European could have existed? This question is partly answered by examining the earliest date that any of the Indo-European groups did exist. The three earliest are Anatolian at *c.* 2000 BC, Indo-Iranian at *c.*1400 BC (Mitanni treaty), and Greek at *c.*1300 BC or somewhat earlier (Linear B tablets). If we presume a Proto-Indo-European that includes Anatolian (rather than the Indo-Hittite hypothesis, which makes Anatolian a sister of Indo-European rather than a daughter), then Proto-Indo-European must be set before 2000 BC when Anatolian is historically attested. How long before? Once we ask this question, we enter the slippery world of intuitive extrapolation. The more cautious will not venture far. For example, Stefan Zimmer urges linguists and archaeologists not to use the word Proto-Indo-European for anything 'linguistic or archaeological' older than *c.* 2500 BC, but such caution, which in any case may well be misplaced, is not shared by most linguists who venture into the area of time depth.

In this chapter we will review the attempts to push beyond 2500 BC and clarify the chronology, both relative and absolute, of Proto-Indo-European. Relative is all some linguists will grant us anyway so we will begin there.

6.2 Relative Chronologies

A relative chronology simply expresses a relationship between two or more 'events', i.e. it seeks to determine whether A is older or younger than B. For at least the past century there have been linguists who have been attempting to discern the different layers of Indo-European and here we can employ the archaeological term 'seriation' to describe this process of ordering layers. There have been three basic techniques of linguistic seriation: morphological, semantic, and geographical; these are very crudely equivalent to an archaeologist attempting to order a sequence of artefacts by typology (style), context, and by distribution.

6.2.1 Morphological Seriation

If we consider the morphology of plural formations in English, we would note that the names of many of our most basic livestock tend to have irregular plurals, i.e. not the simple *-s* plural, or, if they do have it, they may still retain older formations, e.g. *cow/kine*, *sheep/sheep*, *ox/oxen*. The conclusion drawn from this situation is that the domestic animals obviously belong to a relatively archaic layer of the English vocabulary.

From time to time linguists such as Alfons Nehring and Franz Specht have attempted to apply similar techniques to the reconstructed morphology of Proto-Indo-European. For example, the heteroclitic nouns, those that have an *-r* ending in the nominative singular but then an *-n* in all the other cases, e.g. **wód-r̥* 'water' but genitive singular **wéd-n̥-s*, are seen to be among the earliest layers of Indo-European nouns. This proposal was supported, it was argued, by the fact that the semantic fields of these heteroclitics are among our most basic vocabulary, e.g. 'light', 'day', 'year', 'water'. The next level would be the root-nouns and the consonantal stems, with a third and final period marked by our *o*-stems and *-ā-* (or *-eh_2-) stems. This scheme always worked better in theory than in practice because there were too many *o*-stems that seemed to belong to pretty basic layers of the Indo-European vocabulary. For example, beside the domestic animals of the reconstructed lexicon, there also lurk the **h_2ŕ̥tḱos* 'bear' and **wĺ̥k^wos* 'wolf', and the forest revealed the **bherh$_x$ĝos* 'birch'. These basic items of the lexicon required explaining away and of course explanations were offered. For instance, the names of fierce animals were *o*-stems because they were not the real names of the animals but rather late circumlocutions, e.g. the word for bear could be derived from a root meaning 'destroy', and wolf is the adjective 'dangerous' changed into a noun with a shift in accent (Chapter 9). The birch word could be explained as the 'bright one'. In all these cases, so it is argued, we are reconstructing words of no great antiquity that may have been created either to avoid tabu, i.e. names of fierce animals are often governed by tabu (you don't say the name of you-know-what or you might find yourself its next meal), or they are derived from poetic language. The conundrum here is fairly obvious—if these words, tabu replacements or poetic epithets, were created to replace another word, they presuppose the existence of the earlier word, i.e. Indo-Europeans surely knew of bears and wolves and had a name for the animals before they replaced it with another word; alternatively, at an equally early date, the Proto-Indo-Europeans burst into a rapture of poetic metaphor in first encountering a wolf or bear. Thus this technique can decide the antiquity of the formation but not of the actual object. An older word might not only be replaced by a newer epithet but also might be rebuilt to look like a newer word itself. Certainly the histories of all attested branches of Indo-European show a pattern of replacement whereby other stem-types are replaced by (the descendants of) *o*-stems, e.g. the history in New English whereby *cow/kine* (where *kine* has itself replaced Old English *cȳ*) has been replaced by *cow/cows*. And, there is no reason to suppose that Proto-Indo-European itself was immune to this same tendency, and therefore a reconstructed *o*-stem may not be a new word at all but merely the morphological renewal of an old word. A good example comes from the word for horse, *h_1*éḱwos*, since one might presume that the wild horse was known to the Proto-Indo-Europeans. F. Specht got around this by regarding the horse word as a remodelled *u*-stem, i.e. it was an old word in the proto-language with a relatively archaic shape in earlier stages of the language that was then changed to an *o*-stem in a later period.

Other attempts to seriate the Indo-European lexicon argued that we could divide the words between those that indicated ablaut of the root and those that did not and thus were more recent. In this case the reconstructed word for 'birch' provides a good example. While some branches of Indo-European would appear to have words for 'birch' that reflect a Proto-Indo-European **bherh*$_x$*ĝos*, others would appear to reflect a Proto-Indo-European **bhr̥h*$_x$*ĝos*. The alternation of a full-grade (*-*er*-) and a zero-grade (*-*r̥*-) makes it reasonable to suppose that the *o*-stem formation of both is a later addition, albeit one of Proto-Indo-European age, to an older ablauting paradigm without it (i.e. something like **bhérh*$_x$*ĝs* [nominative], **bhr̥h*$_x$*ĝós* [genitive]). Hans Kuhn added that the reconstructed PIE **a* was another marker of a more recent layer of Indo-European and this could be confirmed by its frequent presence in words associated with agriculture. Robert Beekes and some other linguists would argue that the **a* is not Proto-Indo-European at all but indicates a later formation or loanword from a non-Indo-European substrate. This association of **a* with newness is today not nearly so strong, as many of the *a*-vocalisms are now treated as the result of an *a*-colouring laryngeals on an adjacent **-e-*.

What then can the morphological system really say about the antiquity of the concept? Probably less than frequently claimed. An archaic formation such as the heteroclitics can support a case for antiquity but the problem still remains, older than what? Older than an *o*-stem noun? If it means that the formation may be older, this may well be true, but unless the concept itself is inherently related to its morphological class, then very little intelligent can be concluded or, worse, something very unintelligent may be deduced. We can survey the English language and note that *cow* has a regular plural in *cows* but *ox* has a more archaic plural as *oxen*. Does this mean that oxen are older in English culture than cows? From the standpoint of linguistic history, such a conclusion is absurd, as both 'cow' and 'ox' derive from Proto-Indo-European words, *g^{w}ṓus* and **uk$^{(w)}$sen-* respectively.

6.2.2 Semantic Seriation

Another approach to discerning the layers of Indo-European vocabulary has been the analysis of the different semantic stages of the reconstructed vocabulary. For example, Sanskrit *ayas* clearly indicates 'copper' or 'bronze' in earlier Indic texts but comes to mean the technologically later 'iron' in later texts. This shift in meaning is an example of semantic change within a particular stock where our records of the language can confirm the change over time. The same kind of problem can arise when comparing two or more stocks: while comparative analysis may recover but a single proto-form, the different stocks may reflect different underlying meanings. Thus it has long been observed that PIE **h_aeĝros* 'field' revealed a semantic split between Indo-Iranian where it meant 'plain' and the European languages where the same root invariably referred to a 'cultivated field'. Wilhelm Brandenstein regarded this semantic divergence as evidence that the Indo-Europeans had dispersed at various stages of the evolution of the Indo-European vocabulary and that the Indo-Iranians had separated before the word for 'field' had come to mean 'cultivated or arable field'. He collected a large body of lexical evidence to distinguish between what he regarded as an early phase of Indo-European which was primarily pastoral and where its population lived where there were hills, swift running water, and warm weather and then, after expansion into Europe, revealed semantic shifts to colder, wetter weather and the adoption of farming. His conclusions were far more than the slender weight of evidence could carry and were very much anchored in a highly doubtful model of the origins of agriculture, i.e. that nomadic pastoralism preceded settled agriculture, that is generally not found creditable today.

6.2.3 Geolinguistic Seriation

A once popular school of comparative linguistics, perhaps more so in Italy than elsewhere, was *geolinguistics*, an approach to languages which emphasized that one could determine the antiquity of a word from its spatial distribution. According to the geolinguists, the centre of language areas tended to be where innovations developed and then spread, perhaps not entirely, to the periphery; conversely, peripheries tended to be more conservative of earlier layers of speech. A classic for adherents of this school was to be seen in the words for 'fire' in Proto-Indo-European. We reconstruct two words as seen in Table 6.1.

Giulio Bonfante argued that the two words were in contrasting distributions (he did not have all the lexical data at hand at the time) and that the more 'central' term was *$p\acute{e}h_2ur$ while the more peripheral word was *$h_x\underset{\circ}{n}g^wnis$. Originally, all the languages should have possessed the second term, which appears in Indic as the name of a deity and indicates fire in its 'animate' form, while *$p\acute{e}h_2ur$ was seen to have spread from the centre toward the periphery and begun to replace the more animate word with 'fire as instrument'. This explanation fails to convince on a number of grounds. To begin with, if the Indo-Hittite hypothesis has any force, then the presence of the innovative form in Anatolian is hardly indicative of its more recent date. One might also note for instance that Tocharian, as far out on the periphery as any Indo-European language, attests only *$p\acute{e}h_2ur$, supposedly the innovative, central form. It is also surprising that, in this pair, the supposedly innovative word *$p\acute{e}h_2ur$ is of the archaic heteroclitic form while the presumably more archaic *$h_x\underset{\circ}{n}g^wnis$ belongs to what is usually thought to be a younger morphological type. Today, the distinction between animate (*$h_x\underset{\circ}{n}g^wnis$) and instrument (*$p\acute{e}h_2ur$)

Table 6.1. *Indo-European words for 'fire'*

PIE	*PÉH$_2$UR 'FIRE'	*H$_x$ N̥G^{W}NIS 'FIRE'
Italic	Umb *pir* 'fire'	Lat *ignis* 'fire'
Germanic	OE *fȳr* 'fire'	—
Baltic	OPrus *panno* 'fire'	Lith *ugnìs* 'fire'
Slavic	Czech *pýř* 'ashes'	OCS *ognĭ* 'fire'
Greek	Grk *pûr* 'fire'	—
Armenian	Arm *hur* 'fire'	—
Anatolian	Hit *pahhur* 'fire'	—
Tocharian	TochB *puwar* 'fire'	—
Sanskrit	—	*agní-* 'fire'

would still be made, but these would be regarded as two contrasting concepts both attributed to the proto-language where one or the other stabilized in a particular group. In the case of Italic, the loss of contrast between **péh$_2$ur* and **h$_x$n̥g^{w}nis* must have occurred after the break-up of that group, since Umbrian shows generalization of the former word and Latin generalizes the latter. A second example leads to the same conclusion. The fact that the word often reconstructed as 'king', **h$_3$rḗĝs*, is attested only in Celtic (Gaul *rix*, OIr *rī*), Italic (Lat *rēx*), and Indo-Iranian (Skt *rāj-*) suggested to the geolinguists that Proto-Indo-European society had once been ruled by strong kings but a democratic revolution of the centre had replaced them, and hence the absence of the word in the centre of the Indo-European world. However, while the absence of an inherited word for 'king' may indeed betoken a major social change, it may also simply reflect a change in the designation of the ruler, whose social function continued largely as it had been. In any case, if the lack of the inherited word for 'king' in certain Indo-European branches is due to a social revolution, the revolution would appear to have been independently produced in all of those branches where it took place because the 'central area' shows no common replacement terminology.

There are certain core–periphery phenomenon in Indo-European but there would be few if any convinced today by the socio-chronological arguments of the geolinguists.

6.3 Absolute Chronologies

The relative dating of the evolution of Indo-European is all that many linguists might not only aspire to but admit as a possibility. On the other hand, unless Proto-Indo-European can be provided with an approximate absolute date, i.e. a date in years BC, then it will prove impossible to relate the Indo-European languages as a linguistic phenomenon with the prehistoric record. Linguists have proposed four different techniques for assigning an absolute date to a proto-language.

6.3.1 External Contact Dating

A modern English dictionary will reveal that the English language contains the word *sputnik* which refers to any number of artificial satellites. The term need not refer specifically to a Russian satellite but might be loosely employed for any satellite. The date of its introduction into English was 1957 with the launch of the first Russian satellite bearing that particular Russian name. This is a loanword then that carries with it a specific date. It has been suggested (and rejected) that we might discover similarly datable words in Proto-Indo-European that might suggest an approximate date for the proto-language itself.

The credibility of using loanwords to date Proto-Indo-European rests largely on our ability to date the loanwords in the first place. We already know that Indo-European languages had already differentiated by *c.* 2000 BC because that is the time when we encounter our first evidence of the Anatolian languages. If we seek a language earlier than *c.* 2000 BC, there are not many recorded that we can confidently read other than Egyptian, Sumerian, Elamite, Hurrian, and Akkadian. In 1923 Günther Ipsen thought that he could find such a datable relic when he proposed that Proto-Indo-European *$*h_2st\acute{\bar{e}}r$* 'star' (putting his reconstruction in modern symbols) be derived from Akkadian *istar*, attested *c.* 2000 BC, and not from any other earlier Semitic form, e.g. Proto-Semitic **a̱ttar* ~ **aθtar*. In so doing, he thought that he had proved that Proto-Indo-European had survived at least until 2000 BC when the form *istar* first appeared in Akkadian texts. Of course, this conclusion is contradicted by the existence of a separate Anatolian stock already by 2000 BC, and there is hardly a step in the reasoning regarding the 'star' word that has not been challenged, e.g. some derive it from Proto-Semitic, others claim that the word in Semitic only came to mean 'star' (in general) at a later date and hence the meanings are not comparable, and some maintain that the Indo-European word for 'star' is home-grown and not a loanword and can be derived from Proto-Indo-European *$*h_2eh_x$-s-* 'burn' (see Section 8.4). By and large there are no credible loanwords ascribed to Proto-Indo-European that can provide an absolute date for it unless one wishes to trust the absolute dating of others' proto-languages (blind leading the . . .).

Günther Ipsen's foray into dating Proto-Indo-European demonstrates how the technique is employed, and the use of external contacts is very much with us in the dating of prehistoric language phenomena. For example, there are Indo-Iranian (or later) loanwords in the Uralic languages and it has been presumed that as Indo-Iranian as a subgroup of Indo-European first formed *c.* 2500–2000 BC, this is the period to which the loanwords should be ascribed. Unfortunately, this argument rests entirely on the presumption that we have the date for Indo-Iranian correct.

6.3.3 Glottochronology

At about the time that physicists discovered that the constant disintegration of the isotope $_{14}C$ (radiocarbon) could be employed to date organic remains in archaeology, the American linguist Morris Swadesh was working on a similar technique to date languages. Swadesh reviewed the speed at which various languages changed through time by comparing their vocabulary either across their own time trajectory, e.g. Old English to Middle English to New English, or between closely cognate languages, e.g. English, German, and Swedish. He used a comparative wordlist of 200 lexical items which he thought were basic to any human language (e.g. *animal, blood, father, I, mother, sew, tree, two*) and thus resistant to cultural borrowing. Later, feeling that he had been optimistic about how many words were truly resistant to borrowing, he used a 100-word list (wherein, among others, *animal, father, mother*, and *sew* were excluded). This study was empirical and the surprising result that he announced was that no matter what the language family considered, there appeared to be a constant rate of attrition of the basic core vocabulary—after a period of 1,000 years, 86 per cent of the core vocabulary appeared to remain. He employed this technique (which is called *glottochronology*) against the major Indo-European languages to determine when Proto-Indo-European dissolved and what the chronological differences were between the various Indo-European stocks. He presented his results with the minimum of methodological discussion and even less empirical evidence and we are far better off illustrating the results of the method with a more recent example of the technique published by Johann Tischler in 1973 (Table 6.2).

A glance at Tischler's results should sober any optimist, and by and large the technique of glottochronology has had almost no currency among Indo-Europeanists although it may be found in use among linguists studying other language families (generally where there is no written evidence that might contradict the results), and there seems to be a particular fascination for publishing the results of glottochronology in science periodicals (where there are no apparent linguistic referees). The problem with glottochronology is that it rests on three assumptions, all of which have been challenged, sometimes not only challenged but apparently demolished. The first assumption is that there is a core vocabulary that one can examine to measure linguistic disintegration. However, experience has repeatedly shown that there is not a core vocabulary that is constant across all languages, culture areas, and times. There is no large part of the vocabulary of any language that can be trusted to behave in a consistent manner from which linguists can isolate out a set of words which will yield Swadesh's expected results. Swadesh employed wordlists of decreasing size, starting with 500 and then to 200 and finally the famous 100-word list. Tischler shows us the results of employing both the 200- and 100-word lists where Hittite gains over two thousand years of antiquity by using the 100-word list as opposed to the 200-word list, Albanian moves nearly 3,000 years, and other languages change their relative ordering of antiquity. The shift to the smaller wordlist was stimulated by the fact that so many of the words on the

Table 6.2. *Dates of separation from Proto-Indo-European based on the 100- and 200-word lists (after Tischler 1973)*

200-WORD LIST	DATE	100-WORD LIST
	9000 BC	
		Hittite (8800)
	8000	
	7000	
		Albanian (6600)
		Old Irish (6500)
Hittite (6400)		
	6000	
		Armenian (5700)
	5000	
Armenian (4700)		Greek (4700)
		Latin (4400)
	4000	
Greek, Albanian (3800)		
		Sanskrit, Gothic (3700)
Latin (3500)		
		Lithuanian (3400)
	3000	
Sanskrit, OCS (2900)		OCS (2900)
Lithuanian (2200)		
	2000	

longer list were seen not to be 'culture-free'. Even this shorter list has been recently modified by Sergey Starostin who has replaced ten words from the list which were regarded as less cultural-free. Starostin also recognizes a super core list of thirty-five and a somewhat less diagnostic list of sixty-five words. Glottochronology must be about the only scientific technique where the accuracy of one's results is enhanced by the removal rather than the augmentation of data! Moreover, the smaller the list, the more an error concerning any individual item on it will affect the accuracy of the result.

A second assumption is that, assuming there is a culture-free list of however many words one wants to propose, it changes at a constant rate. Where the technique can be tested closely, it reveals markedly differing results. Closer examination of changes in English for instance indicates a retention rate not of 86 per cent but 68 per cent, while Icelandic has remained far more conservative with a 97 per cent retention rate over the same period. Finally, the very means of calculating the separation is methodologically difficult. One seeks to match cognates between the different languages but how cognate must the words be? In some cases residues of the word may remain but in a different semantic form. For example, the Old Irish cognate of the Indo-European word for 'sun' only survives in the meaning 'eye', i.e. the sun seen as a large eye in the sky. And, finally, how does one convincingly address the problem of comparing languages whose own attestation is separated by great periods of time: how do we compare the 'basic vocabulary' of Lithuanian (attested only from the sixteenth century AD onwards) with Hittite which had been dead for over two thousand years?

So what do we get with glottochronology? A series of dates, generally cited to a precision of a century. The level of precision far exceeds anyone's confidence in the method, so one might imagine that these dates have about the comparable value of a radiocarbon date with a large statistical error, e.g. a date of 5000 ± 100 BP (years before present) indicates that a sample should have lived (with 95 per cent probability) somewhere between 4035 and 3541 BC. Glottochronology cannot even provide this level of precision since the rate of decay is simply not that well fixed. But we cannot avoid the allure of producing a list of the hundred words with their Proto-Indo-European forms and an indication of whether a particular stock shares this form (Table 6.3).

This list, indeed any list, would be far from definitive because there are numerous problems in establishing true cognate terms. Although we may derive the cognate set from the same root morphemes, a number of the sets require us to group together very different endings, dialectal forms, or more distant derivation, e.g. *$h_1$oi- is the root morpheme for 'one' but the forms underlying the different IE languages include *$h_1$oi-no-, *$h_1$oi-wo-, and *$h_1$oi-ko-. In other cases we find that we cannot be sure of the precise meaning of our reconstructed form, e.g. *pleu- 'swim' but it only means 'swim' in Greek and Indo-Iranian; in the other groups it may mean 'move', 'float', 'rain', 'wash', or 'flow'. In a number of instances there are multiple candidates for the PIE root, e.g. *twéks 'skin' rather than *péln-, or *sméru- 'oil, grease' and/or *$h_1$opús '(animal) fat' rather than *sélpes- 'fat, grease'; to select a different candidate would result in an entirely different series of correspondences and putative dates of separation.

6.3.4 *Informed Estimation*

George Trager, unimpressed by the claims of glottochronology, argued that a linguist's hunch, that is, "informed judgement" based on one's experience with known language separations and the structure of the language one was dealing

Table 6.3. *The 'basic' vocabulary of Proto-Indo-European and its attestation in the major Indo-European groups*

Word	PIE	Ct	It	Gm	Bt	Sl	Al	Grk	Arm	An	Ir	Ind	Toch	Total
I	**h_1eĝ*	+	+	+	+	+	+	+	+	+	+	+	+	12
You	**túh_x*	+	+	+	+	+	+	+	+	+	+	+	+	12
We	**wéi*	+	+	+	+	+	+	+	+	+	+	+	+	12
This	**so*	+	+	+	+	+	+	+	+	+	+	+	+	12
That	**k̂ís*	+	+	+	+	+	+	+	+	0	0	0	0	8
Who	**k^wós*	+	+	+	+	+	+	+	+	+	+	+	0	11
What	**k^wíd*	0	+	0	0	+	0	0	+	+	+	+	0	6
Not	**ne*	+	+	+	+	+	0	0	0	+	+	+	+	9
All	**wik̂-*	0	0	0	+	+	0	0	0	0	+	+	0	4
Many	**pél$h_1$us*	+	+	+	0	0	0	+	0	0	+	+	0	6
One	**$h_1$oin-*	+	+	+	+	+	+	0	0	+	+	+	0	9
Two	**dwéh_3(u)*	+	+	+	+	+	+	+	+	?	+	+	+	12?
Big	**meĝh_a-*	+	+	+	0	0	+	+	+	+	+	+	+	10
long	**dl̥$h_1$ghós*	0	+	+	+	+	+	+	0	+	+	+	0	9
Small	**pau-*	0	+	+	0	0	0	+	0	0	0	0	0	3
Woman	**g^wénh_a*	+	0	+	+	+	0	+	+	+	+	+	+	10
Man	**h_1nḗr*	+	+	0	0	0	+	+	+	+	+	+	0	8
Person	**dhĝhm-ón-*	+	+	+	+	0	0	0	0	0	0	0	0	4
Fish	**dhĝhuh_x-*	0	0	0	+	0	0	+	+	0	0	0	0	3
Bird	**$h_a$ewei-*	+	+	0	0	0	+	+	+	0	+	+	0	7
Dog	**k̂(u)wōn*	+	+	+	+	+	0	+	+	+	+	+	+	11
Louse	**lu-*	+	0	+	+	+	0	0	0	0	0	+	0	5
Tree	**dóru*	+	+	+	+	+	+	+	0	+	+	+	+	11
Seed	**se$h_1$men-*	+	+	+	+	+	0	0	0	0	0	0	0	5
Leaf	**bhel-*	0	+	+	0	0	0	+	0	0	0	0	+	4
Root	**wr(h_a)d-*	+	+	+	0	0	+	+	0	0	0	0	0	5
Bark	**lóubho/eh_a-*	+	+	+	+	+	+	0	0	0	0	0	0	6
Skin	**péln-*	0	+	+	+	+	0	+	+	0	0	+	0	7
Flesh	**(s)kwé$h_x$tis*	+	+	+	+	0	0	+	0	0	0	0	+	6
Blood	**$h_1$ésh_2r̥*	0	+	0	+	0	0	+	+	+	0	+	+	7
Bone	**$h_2$óst*	+	+	0	0	0	+	+	+	+	+	+	+	9
Grease	**sélpes-*	0	0	+	0	0	+	+	0	0	0	+	+	5
Egg	**h_aō(w)iom*	+	+	+	0	+	0	+	0	0	+	0	0	6
Horn	**k̂er-*	+	+	+	+	+	0	+	+	+	+	+	+	11
Tail	**puk(eh_a)-*	0	0	+	0	0	0	0	0	0	0	+	+	3
Feather	**pet(e)r-*	+	+	+	0	0	0	+	+	+	0	0	0	6
Hair	**k̂ripo-*	0	+	0	0	0	+	0	0	0	+	+	0	4
Head	**k̂r̥rḗh_2*	0	+	+	0	0	+	+	0	+	+	+	+	8

(*Cont'd.*)

Table 6.3. (*Cont'd*)

Word	PIE	Ct	It	Gm	Bt	Sl	Al	Grk	Arm	An	Ir	Ind	Toch	Total
Ear	**h$_a$óus-*	+	+	+	+	+	+	+	+	0	+	0	0	9
Eye	**h$_3$ok^w*	+	+	+	+	+	0	+	+	0	+	+	+	10
Nose	**h$_x$náss*	0	+	+	+	+	0	0	0	0	+	+	0	6
Mouth	**h$_{1/4}$ óh$_1$(e)s-*	0	+	+	0	0	0	0	0	+	+	+	0	5
Tooth	**h$_1$dónt-*	+	+	+	+	+	0	+	+	0	+	+	0	9
Tongue	**dn̥ghuh$_a$-*	+	+	+	+	+	0	0	+	0	+	+	+	9
Claw	**h$_3$nogh(w)-*	+	+	+	+	+	0	+	0	0	+	+	+	9
Foot	**pḗds*	+	+	+	+	+	+	+	+	+	+	+	+	12
Knee	**gónu*	+	+	+	0	0	+	+	+	+	+	+	+	10
Hand	**ĝhes-r-*	0	+	0	?	0	+	+	+	+	0	0	+	7?
Belly	**udero-*	0	+	0	+	0	0	+	0	0	+	+	0	5
Neck	**moni-*	+	0	+	0	0	0	0	0	0	+	+	0	4
Breasts	**psténos/speno-*	+	0	+	+	0	0	+	+	0	+	+	+	8
Heart	**k̂ḗrd*	+	+	+	+	+	0	+	+	+	+	+	+	11
Liver	**yék^{w}r̥(t)*	0	+	0	+	0	0	+	0	0	+	+	0	5
Drink	**peh$_3$(i)-*	+	+	0	+	+	+	+	+	+	+	+	0	10
Eat	**h$_1$édmi*	+	+	+	+	+	0	+	+	+	+	+	+	11
Bite	**denk̂-*	0	0	+	0	0	+	+	0	0	+	+	+	6
See	**derk̂-*	+	0	+	0	0	+	+	0	0	+	+	0	6
Hear	**k̂leu-*	+	+	+	+	+	+	+	+	0	+	+	+	11
Know	**weid-*	+	+	+	+	+	0	+	+	0	+	+	0	9
Sleep	**swep-*	+	+	+	+	+	+	+	+	+	+	+	+	12
Die	**mer-*	0	+	+	+	+	0	+	+	+	+	+	0	9
Kill	**nek̂-*	+	+	+	0	0	0	+	0	+	+	+	+	8
Swim	**pleu-*	+	+	+	0	+	0	+	+	0	+	+	+	9
Fly	**pet-*	+	+	0	+	0	0	+	+	0	+	+	0	7
Walk	**h$_1$ei-*	+	+	+	+	+	0	+	0	+	+	+	+	10
Come	**g^{w}em-*	0	+	+	+	0	0	+	0	0	+	+	+	7
Lie	**k̂ei-*	0	0	0	0	0	0	+	0	+	+	+	0	4
Sit	**sed-*	+	+	+	+	+	0	+	+	0	+	+	0	9
Stand	**(s)teh$_2$-*	+	+	+	+	+	+	+	+	0	+	+	+	11
Give	**deh$_3$-*	0	+	0	+	+	0	+	+	+	+	+	0	8
Say	**wek^w-*	+	+	+	+	0	0	+	+	0	+	+	+	9
Sun	**séh$_a$ul*	+	+	+	+	+	+	+	0	+	+	+	0	10
Moon	**méh$_1$nōt*	+	+	+	+	+	+	+	+	0	+	+	+	11
Star	**h$_2$stḗr*	+	+	+	0	0	0	+	+	+	+	+	+	9
Water	**wódr̥*	+	+	+	+	+	+	+	+	+	+	+	+	12
Rain	**h$_1$wers-*	+	0	0	0	0	0	+	0	+	+	+	0	5
Stone	**h$_4$ék̂mōn*	0	0	0	+	+	0	+	0	+	+	+	0	6

(*Cont'd.*)

Table 6.3. (*Cont'd*)

Word	PIE	Ct	It	Gm	Bt	Sl	Al	Grk	Arm	An	Ir	Ind	Toch	Total
Sand	?*samh̥$_x$dhos	0	+	+	0	0	0	+	0	0	0	0	0	3
Earth	*dhéĝhōm	+	+	0	+	+	+	+	0	+	+	+	+	10
Cloud	*nébhes-	+	+	+	+	+	0	+	0	+	+	+	0	9
Smoke	*dhuh$_2$mós	0	+	0	+	+	0	+	0	0	0	+	0	5
Fire	*péh$_2$ur	0	+	+	+	+	+	+	0	+	0	0	+	8
Ash	*h$_2$éh$_x$ōs	0	0	+	0	0	0	0	+	+	+	+	0	5
Burn	*dheg^{w}h-	+	+	0	+	+	+	+	0	0	+	+	+	9
Path	*póntōh$_2$s	+	+	0	+	+	0	+	+	0	+	+	0	8
Mountain	*g^{w}orh$_x$-	0	0	0	+	+	+	?	0	0	+	+	0	6
Red	*h$_1$reudh-	+	+	+	+	+	0	+	0	0	+	+	+	9
Green	*k̂yeh$_1$-	0	0	+	+	+	+	0	0	0	+	+	+	7
Yellow	*ghel-	+	+	+	+	+	0	+	0	0	+	+	0	8
White	*h$_4$elbhós	0	+	+	+	+	0	+	0	+	0	0	0	6
Black	*k ^{w}r̥snós	0	0	0	+	+	+	0	0	0	0	+	0	4
Night	*nek^{w}t-	+	+	+	+	+	+	+	0	+	0	+	+	10
Hot	*g^{w}hermós	0	+	+	+	0	+	+	+	0	+	+	0	8
Cold	*gel-	0	+	+	0	0	0	0	0	0	0	0	0	2
Full	*pl̥h$_1$nós	+	+	+	+	+	0	0	+	0	+	+	+	9
New	*néwos	+	+	+	+	+	0	+	0	+	+	+	+	10
Good	*h$_1$(e)su-	+	0	0	+	+	0	+	0	?	+	+	0	7?
Round	*serk-	0	+	0	0	0	+	+	0	+	0	0	+	5
Dry	*saus-	0	+	+	+	+	+	+	0	0	+	+	0	8
Name	*h$_1$nómn̥	+	+	+	+	+	+	+	+	+	+	+	+	12
Total		64	82	75	71	62	42	80	48	46	76	82	49	

with, was a far more reliable guide. But how can this task be accomplished? Generally, we find some form of triangulation based on the earliest attested Indo-European languages, i.e. Hittite, Mycenaean Greek, and Indo-Aryan, each of these positioned somewhere between *c.* 2000 and 1500 BC. Given the kind of changes linguists know to have occurred in the attested histories of Greek or Indo-Aryan, etc., the linguist compares the difference wrought by such changes with the degree of difference between the earliest attested Hittite, Mycenaean Greek, and Sanskrit and reconstructed Proto-Indo-European. The order of magnitude for these estimates (or guesstimates) tends to be something on the order of 1,500–2,000 years. In other words, employing some form of gut intuition (based on experience which is often grounded on the known separation of the Romance or Germanic languages), linguists tend to put Proto-Indo-European sometime around 3000 BC plus or minus a millennium.

The explicit reasons for these estimations, however, are hardly clear, never really quantifiable, and there seems no way of testing the validity of such guesses. For this reason, some suggest that these are not informed estimates but groundless guesses and that Proto-Indo-European might go back to 10,000 BC or earlier. Most linguists would probably argue, however, that such a long chronology is even more speculative than the estimates of change between Proto-Indo-European and Hittite, say, as it requires a rate of linguistic change in all descendant groups to be slower than any known historically from *any* attested Indo-European or non-Indo-European family. Unless we are prepared to believe that prehistoric language change is different by an order of magnitude from historic change, it is better to work with a more realistic and shorter chronology than one going back to 10,000 BC.

Of course any assumptions about rate of change (including those upon which glottochronology is built) are only as good as the data upon which they are based. In actuality we have long observable histories of language change only for a very few languages (e.g. Greek, Indo-Aryan, Egyptian, Chinese) and none longer than about 4,000 years. And all of these observed languages are naturally enough languages of high civilizations which have had long histories of interaction with other cultures and languages. It is possible that these interactions have caused a higher rate of change than would have been the case with languages of groups less in the limelight. On the other hand, one might also expect that the weight of the written tradition of these literate societies might have had the effect of slowing change.

6.3.5 Archaeological Estimation

If linguists have hunches, archaeologists sometimes propose theories with far greater hubris and far less credibility. The characteristic approach here is to presume that if the archaeologists can identify the archaeological equivalent of the proto-language, then the dates for the archaeological culture must provide us with the dates of the proto-language. When it comes to dating, between an archaeologist and a linguist, there is no contest. The archaeologist has an arsenal of techniques to date prehistoric remains with various degrees of precision. The usual technique employed with respect to the prehistoric record is radiocarbon dating which, for the general time depth that we have been discussing, should be able to come up with a date within about 400 years of the target. And unlike glottochronology, the date is replicable and capable of being tested against even more precise dating techniques such as tree-ring dating. But the archaeologist is normally dating some form of organic remains—wood, charcoal, bone—which can then be employed to date the archaeological culture (an entity of ambiguous if not dubious social reality) that provides a context for the remains. He or she is not dating a proto-language and the only way the archaeological date then comes into play is if one accepts that the culture in question coincides with the remains of the people who spoke the proto-language. So if one accepts, for example, that Proto-Indo-European was spoken by the first farmers to enter Europe (and only by them), then the archaeologist can put a date of *c.*7000 BC on the event and, hence, the proto-language. Alternatively, if one suggests that Proto-Indo-European was carried into south-eastern Europe with the spread of horse-riding pastoralists from the steppelands and the earliest evidence for this incursion dates to *c.* 4500 BC, then we have another date for Proto-Indo-European.

It takes little thought to realize that this entire means of dating requires one to accept some archaeological identification of the Proto-Indo-Europeans, and when one considers that there is no consensus on this issue after two centuries, there is precious little reason for optimism. Moreover, archaeological cultures, the entities that the archaeologist plays with, for the time in question, say *c.*7000–2000 BC, generally exist for periods of about 600 years, although some cultures can extend for up to 1,500 years. Every culture will have a predecessor (*Homo sapiens sapiens* has been around for *c.*100,000 years in the Near East and about 40,000 years in western Europe). If an archaeologist selects Culture X which dates to *c.*3500–3000 BC as the one to be associated with the spread of (Proto-)Indo-European, you can bet that there was a Culture W that may have occupied the same general area *c.* 4000–3500 BC. Now why has X been selected to date Proto-Indo-European and not the earlier W? Generally, because it is only Culture X that has transcended its earlier borders, which is then read by the archaeologist as an expansion (= linguistic expansion). If so, then the archaeologist is not even pretending to date the proto-language but what he or she takes to be the linguistic dispersal, i.e. an event which defines the break-up of the proto-language rather than the proto-language itself.

6.3.6 Lexico-cultural Dating

Although there is plenty of room to make mistakes or devise erroneous conclusions, lexico-cultural dating does offer at least some hope for generating approximate dates for a proto-language, provided that one's conclusions are properly framed. Much of material culture is time factored, that is, items of material culture have been added to the inventory of human knowledge over time (while some items have been discarded). Elements of the environment might also be time factored in that plants, particularly trees, have followed a regular and datable procession since the last Ice Age; the spread of domestic plants and animals to different regions of Eurasia also occurred over a specific time. The dating of a proto-language might then be attempted by comparing certain items of the reconstructed vocabulary with the archaeological record, here the general archaeological record rather than one specific to a certain region. For example, we reconstruct terminology associated with wheeled vehicles in Proto-Indo-European and from an archaeological standpoint we know that our earliest evidence for wheeled vehicles anywhere in Eurasia (actually anywhere on this planet) dates to the fourth millennium BC. We also know that dates might be pushed back somewhat in time—discoveries in archaeology are a growth business—and hence the actual date for a particular item may obviously antedate somewhat any of our existing evidence. But if the Proto-Indo-European vocabulary had words pertaining to wheeled vehicles, these should not have come into existence much earlier than *c.* 4000 BC on the basis of our present archaeological knowledge. The presence of words for wheeled vehicle does not date the proto-language to *c.* 4000 BC but it does tell us that any date long anterior to this becomes increasingly implausible. That the proto-language may have existed long after 4000 BC goes without saying; the archaeologist can provide a terminal date (in this case a *terminus a quo*) but there is no reason whatsoever why a proto-language should be correlated with the earliest occurrence of an item of material culture.

So, is there a consistent dating horizon for the reconstructed Proto-Indo-European vocabulary? In broad terms, there is certainly conclusive evidence that the Indo-European languages shared what an archaeologist might term a Neolithic vocabulary. There is a full range of domestic animals (cattle, sheep, goat, pig, dog; the horse was certainly known but its status as a domestic animal is arguable) and cereals (grain, barley) and the tools and techniques to process them (plough, harrow, sow, thresh, chaff, grind) and store the result (pot). The Neolithic economy appears in the Near East by about 8000 BC and in Europe it appears by the seventh millennium BC where it spreads both north and west to reach the western and northern European periphery by about 4000 BC. Although claims are occasionally made—sometimes with an amazing sense of audacity—that Proto-Indo-European should date back to the Palaeolithic or Mesolithic, periods before the advent of a mixed farming economy, such a dating can only be made if you ignore all the linguistic evidence to the contrary. Only archaeologists are likely to make such a gross mistake (there is a reason for making this mistake which we will see later).

What is the most recent date the lexicon offers for Proto-Indo-European? We have already seen that wheeled vehicle terminology tends to be part of the vocabulary and this tends to be no earlier than *c.* 4000 BC. Wool, the product of selectively bred sheep, would also appear to be largely a development of the fourth millennium BC although it was known somewhat earlier in the Near East. The plough may also join this list of relatively late developments. If silver be admitted as inherited from Proto-Indo-European, its presence would similarly point to a date in the fourth millennium BC. As we mentioned before, any discovery can be advanced in age and so we might imagine that the earliest we are going to be able to set Proto-Indo-European is about the fifth millennium BC if we want it to reflect the archaeological reality of Eurasia. We have already seen that individual Indo-European groups are attested by *c.* 2000 BC. One might then place a notional date of *c.* 4500–2500 BC on Proto-Indo-European. The linguist will note that the presumed dates for the existence of Proto-Indo-European arrived at by this method are congruent with those established by linguists' 'informed estimation'. The two dating techniques, linguistic and archeological, are at least independent and congruent with one another.

6.4 The Dark Ages?

If one reviews discussion of the dates by which the various Indo-European groups first emerged, we find an interesting and somewhat disturbing phenomenon. By *c.* 2000 BC we have traces of Anatolian, and hence linguists are willing to place the emergence of Proto-Anatolian to *c.* 2500 BC or considerably earlier. We have already differentiated Indo-Aryan in the Mitanni treaty by *c.*1500 BC so undifferentiated Proto-Indo-Iranian must be earlier, and dates on the order of 2500–2000 BC are often suggested. Mycenaean Greek, the language of the Linear B tablets, is known by *c.*1300 BC if not somewhat earlier and is different enough from its Bronze Age contemporaries (Indo-Iranian or Anatolian) and from reconstructed PIE to predispose a linguist to place a date of *c.* 2000 BC or earlier for Proto-Greek itself. So where we have written documentation from the Bronze Age, we tend to assign the proto-languages to an earlier period of the Bronze Age, i.e. earlier than at least 2000 BC if not 2500 BC.

When we turn to western and northern Europe, however, both our attestation of the different groups and the estimates of their proto-languages tend to be shallower. The Germanic languages, for example, are all derived from Proto-Germanic. Now the earliest runic inscriptions are so close to reconstructed Proto-Germanic that there is a tendency to date the Germanic proto-language to about 500 BC. Similarly, if we examine the earliest Celtic inscriptional evidence, be it Continental or even the much more recent Irish ogam stones, these inscriptions are not that far removed from the reconstructed Proto-Celtic and again we tend to have dates suggested on the order of 1000 BC. The Slavic languages only began differentiating from one another during the historical period, and Proto-Slavic is generally set to about the beginning of the

Christian era while Proto-Baltic and Proto-Balto-Slavic (assuming its existence) are probably envisaged as a second millennium BC phenomenon. In short, where the Indo-European groups are more recently attested, we tend to find that they are also regarded as having differentiated at a more recent time, i.e. between *c.*1500 and 500 BC.

One explanation for the relatively short time depths of the attested northern and western Indo-European groups is that these groups are the only survivors of a long process of linguistic assimilation that has occurred as small demographic and linguistic groups moved, interacted, and merged. We can see precisely such a process in action in the historic period as Latin assimilated and replaced all the other Italic languages, Umbrian, Oscan, etc., and then went on to assimilate and replace much of the Celtic languages. Also within the historic period Slavic assimilated and replaced such other Indo-European languages as Thracian, and Koine Greek replaced nearly all other varieties of Greek. If we had only contemporary data to work with, we would have to conclude that both Proto-Italic (now equivalent to Proto-Romance) and Proto-Greek flourished around the beginning of the Christian era. These 'extinction events' in the history of Italic and Greek had the effect of 'resetting' the time depth of the proto-language. This process must have been repeated time and again in the prehistoric period.

A second alternative is that the differences in chronology between the European languages and those of the Aegean-Anatolia and Asia may be an illusion fostered by the lateness of our written sources for most of Europe, i.e. linguists have a tendency to place proto-languages cautiously about 500 to 1,000 years before first attestation, and hence the later the earliest written evidence, the more recent the estimated time depth.

Finally, it might be argued that we should take the time depths of the various Indo-European groups at face value and envisage a process which led to a relatively recent spread of most of the Indo-European languages of Europe, some time after Indo-European languages had been established in Greece, Anatolia, and South-West Asia.

Further Reading

The most recent large-scale discussion of time depth can be found in Renfrew, McMahon, and Trask (2000). Specific discussions on Indo-European can be found in Zimmer (1988) and Mallory (1997*a*, 2002). Morphological seriation is discussed by Nehring (1936), Specht (1944), Arumaa (1949), Kuhn (1954), and most recently in Lehmann (2002). A major attempt at semantic seriation is seen in Brandenstein (1936). Geolinguistics in Indo-European is discussed in Bonfante and Sebeok (1944) and Devoto (1962). A rare instance of external contact dating and Proto-Indo-European is seen in Ipsen (1923). The literature on glottochronology is vast: the original application to Indo-European can be found in Swadesh (1960) but a better treatment is Tischler (1973); Bergsland and Vogt (1962) was among the first major criticisms. Trager's 'hunch' is quoted from Trager (1967) while an example of estimate triangulation can be found in Milewski (1968). There have also been attempts to classify different morphological and temporal stages within Proto-Indo-European in Meid (1975) and Adrados (1982).

7

Reconstructing the Proto-Indo-Europeans

7.1 Approaches to the Past

There is only one route to the reconstruction of Indo-European culture that offers any hope of reliability and that is language. Although we might compare cultural traditions, behaviour, or material culture among the different Indo-European groups, this exercise would be a very uncertain plunge into comparative ethnography or archaeology and we would be forced to compare peoples at vastly different time depths. For example, a number of Indo-European groups, from whatever period they are attested, indicate the existence of warrior bands or sodalities, *Männerbunde* for those who prefer the German expression. One could (and has) accumulate(d) accounts of these bands from Irish, Germanic, Greek, or Indic sources which themselves extend over a period of some 1,500 years at least. We could then generalize about the characteristics of such groups, e.g. a tendency to represent warriors as wolves with berserker-like behaviour, and then back-project this generalization to the Proto-Indo-Europeans. But why should Proto-Indo-Europeans in, say, 4000 BC have behaved like Irish or Germanic war-bands over 4,000 years later? Had nothing really changed in the structure, tactics, and behaviour of warriors and warrior units in so many thousand years? Could the similarities be merely independent developments? After all we find comparable institutions among unrelated Amerindians or African tribes. Or are we dealing with something in between—actual remnants of inherited social institutions but, by the time of our earliest written sources, these have been elaborated in similar ways that were independently generated in the different traditions? It is nearly impossible to know at what point to draw the line between acknowledging the existence of the institution and fleshing it out with our ethnographic parallels. Even when the evidence comes from roughly similar temporal horizons we find ourselves confronting dubious ethnographic comparisons. During the Iron Age both the early Celts and the steppe Iranians attest the practice of head-hunting. But so do many other peoples, and there are few if any who would regard this as sufficient evidence to project head-hunting to the time of the proto-language. Clearly we need something more directly associated with the people we are trying to deal with (those who existed at the time of the proto-language) and for that, there is only one, admittedly problematic, source: the reconstructed lexicon offers us our best hope of glimpsing the world of the speakers of Proto-Indo-European. Of course there is a catch, in fact, several catches. The first concerns the very reconstruction of the Indo-European vocabulary.

7.2 How Many Cognates?

How many cognates do we need to declare a word Proto-Indo-European? There are very few instances in which we find a cognate in every major IE group, and Table 7.1 indicates the items that are so fully attested.

The list poses no real surprises as most of the words belong to those regions of the lexicon that are quite basic and more resistant to loss. Of this list five are pronouns, four are numerals, and the rest are some of the more basic nominal concepts. But we should not imagine that this list necessarily indicates word frequency. We might compare it, for example, with the most frequent words in English which, other than pronouns, are primarily confined to prepositions (whose function would usually be met by case endings in PIE), conjunctions, and articles (absent from PIE), i.e. *you, that, it, he, of, to, in, for, on, as, with, the, and, a*, and *is*.

As we have just seen those reconstructions based on evidence from the full range of IE groups are very much in the minority and if we consider the 1474 reconstructions found in Mallory and Adams (1997) we can gain a rough idea of the size of the cognate sets that form the basis of our reconstructed lexicon (Table 7.2).

Only 1 per cent of the reconstructed lexicon is based on a cognate from all twelve major language groups. Most cognate sets are comprised of far fewer

Table 7.1. *Cognates that are found in all major Indo-European groups*

*wódr̥	'water'
*g^{w}ṓus	'cow'[a]
*pṓds	'foot'
*dhwṓr	'door, gate'
*tréyes	'three'
*pénk^{w}e	'five'
*septḿ̥	'seven'
_*$h_1$néwh_1m̥_	'nine'
*swep-	'sleep, dream'
_*$h_1$nómn̥_	'name'
_*h_1eĝ-_	'I'
*wéi	'we'
_*túh_x_	'thou'
_*yuh_xs_	'ye'
_*so_	'that (one)'

[a] A putative Albanian cognate for cow (*ka*) is uncertain.

language groups, with 75 per cent of the reconstructed lexicon based on six or fewer groups and half of our reconstructions based on between four and five groups.

With most of our cognate sets founded on half or less of the various language groups, how do we know that the word existed in Proto-Indo-European and not some later stage of development? There is no hard and fast rule accepted by

Table 7.2. *Number of cognate sets attested per number of groups sharing a cognate*

Language Groups	Cognates	Percentage
12	16	1
11	23	2
10	52	4
9	59	4
8	78	5
7	137	9
6	181	12
5	252	17
4	274	19
3	238	16
2	164	11

all linguists as to what constitutes a solid reconstruction and we feel that one needs to be fairly explicit about what criteria are employed. Because a cognate might exist in two language groups, e.g. Celtic (Old Irish *rucht* 'tunic') and Germanic (Old English *rocc* 'overgarment'), this does not mean that the ancestor of this word (**ruk-*) was also known in Proto-Indo-European. A word confined to Celtic and Germanic might more probably be assigned to a late development in western Europe long after the Indo-European languages had differentiated. There are many such regionally confined cognates (or early borrowings), and to the Celtic-Germanic correspondences we can also add cognate words from Italic (primarily Latin), Baltic, and Slavic. There are so many of these words that are confined within these five language groups (Celtic, Italic, Germanic, Baltic, and Slavic) that most linguists would regard cognates found *exclusively* between any two or among all of these groups as specifically North-West Indo-European and not demonstrably Proto-Indo-European. To accept a series of cognates as reflections of a PIE word requires that the evidence come from further afield than a series of contiguous language groups in Europe.

How about an isogloss between Celtic and Greek? That would be better than a North-West isogloss but this would still leave the word confined to two European groups. It is not that the word *might* not derive from Proto-Indo-European, but there are some fairly popular models of Indo-European dispersals that would see the prehistoric European languages moving west while the Asian languages dispersed south and east, and hence one might well expect innovations to emerge purely among the European (or Asian) groups that were never part of the shared Proto-Indo-European vocabulary. For convenience we will label these non-North-Western groups, that is, the Balkan languages (only Albanian attested in any significant sense), Greek, and Armenian (as we have seen, the suspiciously large number of isoglosses between Greek and Armenian leads many to group these two together), as the 'Central' languages. To this we might add Phrygian (it will not add much anyway) because it is generally recognized as a western intruder into Anatolia. Cognates may occur within the four Central languages (where they will be labelled 'Central') or between languages of the North-Western group and the Central group where they will be labelled here as 'West Central', but not positively Proto-Indo-European.

As we have seen, Anatolian is the earliest attested Indo-European group and is widely but not universally regarded as one of the first if not the first group to have separated from the rest of the Indo-European continuum. For those who accept the concept of Indo-Hittite, this separation, in terms of the evolution of Indo-European, may be even earlier. For this reason, one might propose that if there are cognates between Anatolian and any other Indo-European language, it may be accepted as Proto-Indo-European. Just such an example would be

Hittite *tanau* 'fir', OHG *tanna* 'fir', or, similarly, Hittite *hates-* 'adze, axe, hatchet', NE *adze*. This rule will not please everyone but it will be applied here.

The Asian languages are critical in defining Proto-Indo-European, especially when there is no Anatolian cognate (and given the paucity and nature of our Anatolian sources, such a lack is a very frequent occurrence). From our discussion of internal relationships, we see that the Asian languages must be divided into two groups, i.e. Indo-Iranian and Tocharian. We are not overly concerned if the word occurs in only one Indo-Iranian language since if it has a cognate in another Indo-European language, it is likely then that the word existed in Proto-Indo-Iranian and it is pure luck or loss that we do not find it in the other Indo-Iranian branch. A general rule of thumb would admit as Proto-Indo-European any word that shared cognates in a European language and an Asian language on the argument that they are dispersed so widely that it is unlikely that they are later innovations. Actually, the rule cannot be quite so hard and fast and we need some fine-tuning. An Irish-Indic cognate looks a damn sight stronger than a Greek-Iranian and linguists have long noted that there are a whole series of words that seem to be confined largely to Greek and Indo-Iranian. Here this pattern will be designated GA, i.e. Graeco-Aryan, which does not indicate a special branch of Indo-European but a pattern of isoglosses that we may feel cautious about assigning to full Proto-Indo-European antiquity without additional evidence. A cognate set involving Tocharian places us in the nightmare of determining the internal relationship between Tocharian and the other IE languages. Some would argue that it is merely a North-Western language while others, emphasizing its position so far to the east of the Indo-European world, would suggest that it constitutes independent evidence of an Asian language; this latter interpretation will be followed in the course of this book, i.e. a cognate set found in a European (or Anatolian) language and Tocharian will be regarded as Proto-Indo-European (PIE). On the other hand, in those very few cases where we have a word only in Indo-Iranian and Tocharian, these will be termed Eastern (E). We can summarize these relationships in Figure 7.1.

7.3 Reconstructed Meaning

A second major catch to our recovery of the Proto-Indo-European lexicon concerns the reconstructed meaning of a word. Sometimes there is uniformity across all or almost all the groups offering cognates. Take for example the cognate set of animal names indicated in Table 7.3 in which the odds are pretty well stacked in favour of reconstructing the proto-meaning as 'sheep'.

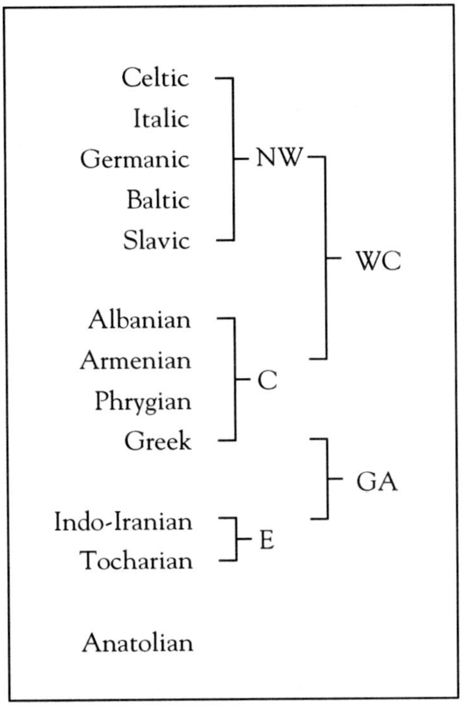

Figure 7.1. The levels of Indo–European reconstruction

On the other hand, Table 7.4 illustrates one of the classic problems of reconstruction in Proto-Indo-European.

In some instances the level of ambiguity appears truly perverse, especially when the cognates suggest what might seem to be diametrically opposed meanings as we find in Table 7.5.

Here we find the more central groups of Baltic, Slavic, and Greek indicating the process of washing or bathing while the more peripheral groups (Celtic, Indo-Iranian) suggest dirt/urine. The proto-meaning is usually taken to indicate 'wash' and the more contradictory meanings are explained as either the target or residue of washing (i.e. the filth one washes away) or, possibly, the use of urine to wash with, a cultural practice that includes several groups of IE speakers.

A third type of problem is when the range of meanings is obviously related but so disparate that we can only hazard a vague proto-meaning which might underlie the original word. Table 7.6 provides an example of a word that we can only reconstruct as 'some form of tool' (it is a nominal derivative of *k^w*er*- 'do, make').

Table 7.3. *Cognates of *$h_2$ówis*

OIr	*oī*	'sheep'
Lat	*ovis*	'sheep'
ON	*ær*	'sheep'
OE	*ēowu* (> NE *ewe*)	'sheep'
OHG	*ou* ~ *ouwi*	'sheep'
Lith	*avìs*	'sheep'
Latv	*avs*	'sheep'
OCS	*ovĭnŭ*	'sheep'
Grk	*ó(w)ïs*	'sheep'
Luv	*hāwa/i-*	'sheep'
Skt	*ávi-*	'sheep'
TochB	*āu*	'ewe'

7.4 Semantic Fields

We also find ourselves reconstructing multiple words to fill out a single semantic field. It has been observed that in English, for example, nouns are often organized according to some principle of meronomy, i.e. they may be arranged as subparts of a larger entity such as body > leg > foot > toe. While there may be some contrast at each level, e.g. 'foot' versus 'claw', there is unlikely to be a great proliferation of terms for a single referent. On the other hand, verbs tend to be generated according to a system of troponymy where each is nuanced in a particular way. The reconstructed PIE vocabulary illustrates both of these principles. For example, the reconstructed lexicon provides us simply with **pṓds* 'foot' (similarly *Collins Roget's International Thesaurus* simply lists *foot*) but when we come to a verb like *speak* the *Thesaurus* provides us with an enormous number of terms. Here is a fraction: *speak*, *talk*, *patter*, *gab*, *say*,

Table 7.4. *Cognates of *bheh$_a$ĝós*

Gaul	*bāgos*	'?beech'
Lat	*fāgus*	'beech'
ON	*bōk*	'beech'
OE	*bōc*	'beech'
OHG	*buohha* ~ *buocha*	'beech'
Rus	?*buz*	'elder'
Alb	*bung*	'oak'
Grk	*phēgós*	'oak'

Table 7.5. *Cognates of *m(e)uh$_x$-*

MIr	*mūn*	'urine'
OPrus	*aumūsnan*	'wash'
Lith	*máudyti*	'bathe'
Latv	*maudât*	'bathe'
OCS	*myjǫ*	'wash'
Grk	*mulásasthai*	'wash oneself'
Av	*mūθra-*	'dirt'
Skt	*mū́tra-*	'urine'

utter, vocalize, state, declare, remark, allege, give tongue, relate, recite, announce, proclaim, blurt out. One can readily appreciate how difficult it might be to retrieve the precise meanings of each of these terms after several thousand years, yet this difficulty is what confronts the linguist who sorts through the twenty-four odd roots that express for Proto-Indo-European or some subsequent phase the concept of 'speak' (Table 7.7). In some cases we can distinguish the differences in the underlying nuance of the word but often we cannot and hence our reconstructed meanings can only be vague approximations (indicated by ±) of what the word might have meant to its prehistoric speakers.

7.5 Folk Taxonomies

Many semantic fields of a language are structured by its speakers into a hierarchical system of categories. In English, for example, we tend to divide the natural world into three categories, animal, vegetable, and mineral, and these may be further subdivided, sometimes in reasonably Linnaean fashion but also according to different, folk taxonomic, criteria, e.g. Herman Melville's Ishmael who was adamant that a whale was a fish or the common tendency for English speakers to classify the tomato as a vegetable (a 'veg') rather than a fruit (even the US Supreme Court has ruled that tomatoes are 'vegetables') or refer to a spider as an insect or bug. Typical areas of folk taxonomies include colour terms, the (five) senses, the (four) seasons, the (four) directions, plants,

Table 7.6. *Cognates of *k^{w}r̥wis*

Lith	*kir̃vis*	'axe'
Rus	*cervĭ*	'sickel'
Skt	*kr̥vi-*	'weaving instrument'

Table 7.7. *Verbs concerned with speaking in Proto-Indo-European*

*wek^{w}-	'speak'
*(s)wer-	'say, speak'
*h_1eĝ-	'say'
*ter-	'± speak out'
*wed-	'raise one's voice'
*mleuh_x-	'speak'
*rek-	'speak'
?*g^{w}et-	'say'
*gal-	'call out, speak'
*ĝar-	'shout, call'
*neu-	'± cry out'
*ĝheu(h_x)-	'call to, invite, invoke'
*kelh_1-	'call out to'
*k̂euk-	'cry out (to)'
*k̂eh_1-	'declare solemnly'
*k̂e(n)s-	'declare solemnly'
*h_1/$_4$ōr-	'speak a ritual formula'
*(s)pel-	'say aloud, recite'
*yek-	'± express, avow'
*$h_1$erk^{w}-	'praise'
*$h_1$eug^{w}h-	'speak solemnly'
*weg^{w}h-	'speak solemnly'
*g^{w}erh_x-	'praise'
*kar-	'praise loudly'

animals, geometric shapes, or aspects of material culture, e.g. crockery, silverware. Modern English speakers tend to accept the canonical number of seasons, directions, and senses but these are a product of culture and it is perfectly possible to find examples of two seasons (summer versus winter) or to find taste as merely an aspect of touch (with the tongue). The level of taxonomy may operate with a single conceptual division where there are at least two terms in complementary distribution (e.g. the early Germanic system is reputed to have divided the year into only two seasons—'winter' and 'summer') but may form a multilevel system, e.g. from the main taxonym 'colour' (Level 0) we may then descend to a Level I basic colour term such as *red*, then a Level II variety of *red* such as *crimson* or *scarlet*, and then to a Level III specialized term such as *ruddy* which is generally confined to the human complexion. In the following chapters we will be mindful of some of the folk taxonomies that have been proposed for the various semantic fields.

7.6 Level of Reconstruction

The level of reconstruction varies depending on how much evidence we can extract from our cognate forms. In some cases we have sufficient evidence to reconstruct the entire 'word', i.e. the root, any extensions, and its nominative case ending (e.g. _*g^{w}ṓus_ 'cow') or the present indicative of the verbal form (e.g. _*$h_1$éiti_ 'he/she goes'). In many instances, however, the evidence for the nouns may be ambiguous with regard to the original declension (especially if we lack evidence from Latin, Greek, and Indo-Iranian which maintained so much of the original declension system) and we can only reconstruct the root morpheme, e.g. _*sem-_ 'summer'. In some cases, there will even be ambiguities about elements of the root morpheme, e.g. as both Hittite and Tocharian merged the PIE labials, a word reconstructed solely from cognates from these two languages must be unclear as to the nature of any labial, e.g. Hit _warpa_ 'enclosures', TochA _warp_ 'enclosure' permits us to reconstruct a PIE _*worPo-_ where the 'P' may indicate a _*b_, _*bh_, or _*p_.

In some instances the reconstruction will be based on cognates drawn from both nouns and verbal forms and sometimes from nouns alone (e.g. _*$h_1$nómn̥_ 'name' or _*$h_2$ówis_ 'sheep'). Occasionally there are sets of nouns that look very much as though they should be derived from a verb but no verb is found. Such is the case with _*yéw(e)s-_, the common PIE word for 'barley'. On the basis of similar words for 'grain' (including _corn_ and _grain_ itself) we might expect it to have meant *'ripe (grain)' or the like and it certainly looks like a banal derivative of _**yeu-_. Not until Tocharian AB _yu-_ 'ripen, mature' was discovered was either the semantic or the morphological hypothesis confirmed.

In some instances we will find cognate sets that would appear to agree perfectly, almost too perfectly, to be regarded as evidence for the reconstruction of a Proto-Indo-European word. This situation is likely to arise when, for example, we find a widely attested noun that has been clearly formed from a well-attested verb by processes active in most of the Indo-European groups. For example, Grk _edanón_, Hit _adanna-_, and Skt _ádanam_ could all be derived from a PIE _*$h_1$edonom_ 'food', but as all these words are fairly banal extensions of the widespread PIE root _*$h_1$ed-_ 'eat' (hence the word literally indicates a noun 'eats') we may be dealing with independent creations of a noun from an inherited verbal form.

7.7 Root Homonyms

In the basic vocabulary of English, say among the first 1,000 words or so, we might expect about 10 per cent of the words to be homonyms, i.e. two (or more)

Table 7.8. *Some PIE 'homonyms'*

*der-	'sleep'
*der-	'tear off, flay'
*h_1erh_1-	'quiet, at rest'
*h_1erh_1-	'row'
*mel-	'harm'
*mel-	'good'
*sed-	'sit (down)'
*sed-	'go'
*wel-	'grass'
*wel-	'die'
*wel-	'see'
*wel-	'wish, want'
*wel-	'turn, wind, roll'

different words sharing the same pronunciation such as *write/right* or *bough* (of a tree)/*bow* (to bend oneself). We find that our reconstructed lexicon indicates about the same percentage, although we have to be mindful that our reconstructions can never be regarded as even approximating phonetic transcriptions. Table 7.8 indicates some of the more peculiar homonyms.

In general, linguists attempt to reduce homonyms if possible under the presumption that what we reconstruct as several roots might, in fact, be a single root. In some cases we find attempts to nudge the proto-sememes (meanings) closer together, e.g. **wel-* has been discussed within the context of IE death beliefs where one might imagine that to die (**wel-*) meant that one went to live in fertile meadows or grass (**wel-*). Needless to say, many of these problems are products of root reconstructions; had we been able to reconstruct more of the word (i.e. its declensional or conjugational membership), we would generally have found that they were not actually homonyms.

7.8 How Long a Text?

We have seen how Schleicher's tale represents an attempt to reproduce in Proto-Indo-European an extended narrative, and a number of similar exercises have been attempted since Schleicher's time. But what is the longest text that we can actually reconstruct to Proto-Indo-European from its daughter languages? The answer: not very long, generally two words in combination. The problem here is that the IE languages have been separated for so long before we encounter them that any common text, e.g. a poem, prayer, or aphorism, that existed in the proto-language has either disappeared or been so much altered that we cannot reconstruct the original text. To give a familiar example, we can recover from Celtic, Germanic, Anatolian, and Sanskrit a specific medical incantation for rejoining a dismembered body. Its basic structure runs something like: 'joint to joint, limb to limb, blood to blood, skin to skin, etc.' In Germanic the expression in OHG goes *Ben zi bena, bluot zi bluoda, lid zi geliden* ... ('bone to bone, blood to blood, limb to limb ...). In Irish we have *ault fri halt di & féith fri féth* ('joint to joint, and sinew to sinew'). In Sanskrit the charm runs: *sáṃ te majjā́ bhavatu sá u te páruṣa páruḥ* 'marrow with marrow should be together, and joint with joint ... ' and we find similar spells in Hittite, i.e. *hastai-kan hastai handan* 'bone (is) attached to bone'. The structure is generally the same but nowhere do we find lexical cognates to permit us to reconstruct the text to Proto-Indo-European.

In order to reconstruct beyond the single word we must make recourse to poetic diction, the frozen phrases of poetry which have survived. Generally our evidence comes from those few groups that provide us with extensive poetic traditions when we first encounter their texts, i.e. Indo-Iranian and Greek, although some expressions have also survived in other language groups, occasionally as proper names. Many of these frozen expressions concern the main theme of poetry, the fame of the hero (Table 7.9).

Another expression reconstructed to PIE is *$(h_1e)g^wh$ént $h_1$óg^whim* 'he killed the serpent', a statement concerning one of the most central mythic deeds of the IE warrior god/hero. It is lexically only attested in Indo-Iranian, i.e. Av *ǰanaṯ ažīm* '[who] killed the serpent' and Skt *áhann áhim* 'he killed the serpent', and then with a substituted verb in Grk *kteine hóphin* 'he slew the serpent' and a new noun in Hit *illuyanka kwenta* 'he killed the snake'; cf. OIr *gono mil* 'I slay the beast' which has replaced both noun and verb.

7.9 Vocabulary—What's Missing?

To what extent does the reconstructed vocabulary mirror the scope of the original PIE language? The first thing we should dismiss is the notion that the language (any language) spoken in later prehistory was somehow primitive and restricted with respect to vocabulary. Counting how many words a language has is not an easy task because linguists (and dictionaries) are inconsistent in their definition or arrangement of data. If one were simply to count the headwords of those dictionaries that have been produced to deal with nonliterate languages in Oceania, for example, the order of magnitude is somewhere on the order of 15,000–20,000 'words'. The actual lexical units are

Table 7.9 *Some examples of poetic diction built on* *k̂léwos 'fame'

PIE **k̂léwos n̥dhg^{w}hitom* 'fame everlasting'
Grk *kléos áphthiton*
Skt *śrávas ... ákṣitam*

PIE **k̂léwos wéru* 'wide fame'
Gaul *Verucloetius*
Grk *kléos eurú*
Skt *urugāyám ... śrávo*

PIE **k̂léwos meĝh$_{a}$-* 'great fame'
Grk *mégas kléos*
Skt *máhi śráva-*
Cf. OIr *clū mōr* 'great fame'
Cf. ON *mikil frægð* 'great fame'

PIE **k̂léwos wésu* ~ **k̂léwos h$_{1}$esu* 'possessing good fame'
Illyrian *Vescleves-*
Grk *Eukleḗs*
Skt *Suśráva-*
Cf. OIr *sochla* (< *so+clū*) 'of good fame'
Cf. Av *vaŋhāu sravahī*

PIE **k̂léwos deh$_{1}$-* 'acquire fame'
Grk *kléos katathésthai*
Skt *śráva- dhā-*

PIE **dus-k̂lewes-* 'having bad repute'
Grk *duskleḗs*
Av *duš-sravahyā-*

PIE **k̂léwos h$_{a}$n̥róm* 'fame of (real) men'
Grk *kléa andrôn*
Skt *śrávo ... nr̥ṇā́m*

greater because a single form might have a variety of different meanings, each of which a speaker must come to learn, e.g. the English verb *take* can mean 'to seize', 'to capture', 'to kill', 'to win in a game', 'to draw a breath', 'imbibe a drink', 'to accept', 'to accommodate' to name just a few of the standard dictionary meanings. Hence, we might expect that a language spoken *c.* 4000 BC would behave very much like one spoken today and have a vocabulary on the order of 30,000–50,000 lexical units. If we apply fairly strict procedures to distinguishing PIE lexical items to the roots and words listed in Mallory and Adams's *Encyclopedia* or Calvert Watkins's *The American Heritage Dictionary of Indo-European Roots* (1985) we have less than 1,500 items. The range of meanings associated with a single lexeme is simply unknown although we occasionally get a hint, e.g. **bher-* indicates both 'carry (a load)' and 'bear (a child)'. So the PIE vocabulary that we reconstruct may well provide the basis for a much larger lexicon given the variety of derivational features in PIE.

Yet we know that our reconstructed lexicon falls far short of the full language, e.g. we can reconstruct 'eye' and 'eyebrow' but not 'eyelash'. We can most easily gain an impression of what may be missing when we consider modern ethno-botanical studies. In Proto-Indo-European we can offer about thirty-two plant names and an additional twenty-six tree names. In contrast, Brent Berlin examined the languages of ten traditional farming societies and found that the average number of botanical taxa reported in each language was 520. If we were to treat such comparisons at face value this would suggest that we are recovering only about 11 per cent of the probable botanical lexicon known to the Proto-Indo-Europeans. Or compare, for example, the fact that we can reconstruct only a few terms relating to the horse in Proto-Indo-European; in English this semantic field includes *horse*, *pony*, *nag*, *steed*, *prancer*, *dobbin*, *charger*, *courser*, *colt*, *foal*, *filly*, *gelding*, *hack*, *jade*, *crock*, *plug*, and many more terms, including the many specific terms describing the colour of the horse, e.g. *bay*, *chestnut*, *sorrel*, *pinto*. There is no reason to suspect that PIE did not behave similarly. The following chapters thus present a very incomplete record of Proto-Indo-European; nevertheless, this record brings us about as close to the speakers of the language as we can hope for.

Further Reading

Good discussions of folk taxonomies can be found in Anderson (2003) and Berlin (1992). For classic treatments of Indo-European poetic diction see Schmitt (1967, 1973), Meid (1978), and Watkins (1995).

8

The Physical World

8.1 Earth

We begin our review of the reconstructed Indo-European world with a survey of the four elements—earth, fire, water, and air (though there is no evidence that this fourfold division of nature can be dated to Proto-Indo-European times itself). Table 8.1 provides a summary view of the Indo-European lexicon that pertains to the solid world of the earth. It lists the PIE form, the reconstructed meaning, and representative examples drawn from Latin, New English (occasionally well-known forms from other Germanic languages), Greek, and Sanskrit to illustrate the phonological development of the proto-form.

The word for 'earth' (**dhéĝhōm*) also underlies the many formations for designating humans, either in the sense that they are 'earthly' (and not immortals) or that they were fashioned from the earth itself. Thus for 'earth' itself we find OIr *dū* 'place, spot', Lat *humus* 'earth', Lith *žẽmė* 'earth', OCS *zemlja* 'earth', Alb *dhe* 'earth', Grk *khthṓn* 'earth', Hit *tēkan* 'earth', Skt *kṣam-* 'earth', Toch A *tkaṃ* 'earth'. In the meaning 'human being' we have OIr *duine* 'human being', Latin *homō* 'human being' (and the adjective *humānus* 'human'), Lith *žmuõ* 'human being', Phrygian *zemelō* 'human being' and 'earthly'; it survives also in NE *bridegroom* where *groom* < OE *guma* 'man' which was remodelled after folk etymology.

Table 8.1. _Earth_

*dhéĝhōm	'earth'	Lat _humus_, Grk _khthṓn_, Skt _kṣam-_
*ml̥dho/eh$_a$-	'clay'	NE _mould_, Grk _málthē_, Skt _mr̥d-_
*tk^{w}reh$_1$yot-	'clay'	Lat _crēta_
*reh$_1$mós	'dirty; dirt, soot'	Skt _rāmá-_
*solh$_x$-	'dirt; dirty'	NE _sallow_, Lat _salebra_
*tih$_x$n-	'(be) dirty'	
_*pē(n)s-_	'dust'	Skt _pāṃsú-_
*bherĝh-	'high; hill'	NHG _Berg_, NE _barrow_
*g^{w}orh$_x$-	'mountain; forest'	Skt _girí-_
_*h$_4$éḱmōn_	'stone'	Grk _ákmōn_, Skt _áśman-_
*péru	'rock'	Skt _párvata-_
*pel(i)s-	'cliff'	Grk _pélla_, Skt _pāṣī-_
*dhólh$_a$os	'valley; vault'	NE _dale_, Grk _thólos_ 'vault'
*lónko/eh$_a$-	'valley'	

The first word for 'clay'(_*ml̥dho/eh$_a$-_) is tolerably well established (e.g. OE _molde_ 'sand, dust, soil' [NE _mould_], Grk _málthē_ 'modelling mixture of wax and pith', Skt _mr̥d-_ 'clay, loam'). The second word for 'clay' (_*tk^{w}reh$_1$yot-_) is found on the western and eastern fringes of the Indo-European world, but nowhere in the centre (e.g. OIr _crē_ 'clay', Lat _crēta_ 'chalk', Toch A _tukri_ and Toch B _kwriye_, both 'clay'). It is difficult to reconstruct an ordinary word for 'dirt'. All the possibilities suggest 'dirtiness' in contrast to cleanliness. So we have PIE _*reh$_1$mós_ (e.g. OE _rōmig_ 'sooty', Skt _rāmá-_ 'dark, black' and _Rāmá-_ 'Rama') and _*solh$_x$-_ (e.g. OE _salu_ 'dark, dusky' [NE _sallow_], _sol_ 'dark, dirty', Lat _salebra_ 'dirt', Toch B _sal_ 'dirty', and perhaps Hit _salpa-_ 'dog-dung'). A verb for 'be dirty' (_*tih$_x$n-_) occurs in Tocharian (Toch B _tin-_ 'be dirty') and in Slavic in a derived noun (OCS _tina_ 'mire, filth'). There is also _*pē(n)s-_ 'dust' (e.g. OCS _pěsŭkŭ_ 'dust', Av _pąsnu-_ 'dust', Skt _pāṃsú-_ 'crumbling soil, sand, dust').

The word for 'hill' or 'mountain' (_*bherĝh-_, seen, for example, in MIr _brī_ 'hill', NE _barrow_, NHG _Berg_ 'mountain', Rus _béreg_ 'river-bank', Av _bərəz-_ 'hill') derives from the adjective 'high' while _*g^{w}orh$_x$-_ (seen for instance in OCS _gora_ 'mountain', Alb _gur_ 'rock', Av _gairi-_ 'mountain', Skt _girí-_ 'mountain', and possibly Grk _boréas_ 'northwind' [if < *'mountain wind']) uniformly means 'forest' in the Baltic languages (e.g. Lith _girià_), a common enough semantic shift as forests are often found or survived after the introduction of agriculture in upland locations.

Certainly, one of the most troublesome words is _*h$_4$éḱmōn_ 'stone' as reflexes of this same word in a number of Indo-European groups render 'sky' or 'heaven' (e.g. Grk _ákmōn_ 'anvil', Skt _áśman-_ 'stone' [also 'heaven'?], OPrus *asman-* 'heaven', Lith *akmuõ* 'stone', OCS *kamy* 'stone', and, in the view of some, the Germanic words for 'heaven', e.g. NE *heaven*). This semantic convergence has been variously explained by assuming that the Proto-Indo-Europeans believed that they lived under a stone vault, that the stone hills and mountains rose to the sky, or that stone axes fell out of the sky, i.e. as thunder-stones (e.g., Lith *Perkūno akmuõ* 'thunder-stone' [lit. 'Perkūnas' stone', where Perkūnas is the god of thunder]). Restricted solely to the meaning 'stone' is PIE **péru* (e.g. Hit *perunant-* 'rocky', Av *paurvatā* 'mountain', Skt *párvata-* 'rock, mountain'). Meaning something like 'cliff, rock outcrop' was PIE **pel(i)s-* (e.g. OIr *ail* 'cliff' [< **pelis*], MIr *all* 'cliff' [< **pl̥so-*], ON *fjall* 'cliff' [< **pelsó-*], Grk *pélla* 'stone', Pashto *parša* 'steep slope', Skt *pāṣī-* 'stone' [< **pelsih*$_a$*-*]).

Words for 'valley' are **dhólh*$_a$*os* and **lónko/eh*$_a$*-*. The first has reflexes across the geographical spectrum of Indo-European (e.g. NWels *dôl* 'valley, meadow', NE *dale*, Rus *dol* 'valley, under side', Grk *thólos* 'vault' [a sort of 'upside-down valley'], Sarikoli [an Iranian language of the Pamirs] *δer* 'ravine') while the second is more restricted, occurring in Baltic (e.g. Lith *lankà* 'valley, river-meadow'), Slavic (e.g. OCS *lǫka* 'gulf, valley, meadow, marsh'), Tocharian (e.g. Toch B *leṅke* 'valley'), and Late Latin (< Gaulish?) **lanca* 'depression, bed of a river'.

Geographically more restricted words include: North-Western **mai-* 'soil, defile' (e.g. NE *mole*, Lith *miẽles* 'yeast'); West Central **h*$_1$*er-* 'earth' (e.g. NE *earth*, Grk *érā* 'earth'); **gloiwos* 'clay' (e.g. NE *clay*, Grk *gloiós* 'clay'; cf. Lat *glūten* 'glue'); **leu-* 'dirt' (e.g. Lat *polluō* 'soil, defile', Grk *lûma* 'dirt'); **grúĝs* 'dirt' (e.g. NE *crock* [as in 'that's a bunch of *crock*'], Grk *grúks* 'dirt under the nails'); **lep-* 'stone' (Lat *lapis* 'stone' [with unclear *-a-*], Grk *lépas* 'stone'); **leh*$_1$*w-* 'stone' (OIr *līe* (gen. *līāc*) 'stone', Homeric Grk *lâas* (gen. *lâos*) [rebuilt from (**lēwas, lawasos*?)], *léusō* 'stone' (vb.), Alb *lerë* 'rubble'); **kolh*$_1$*-ōn* 'hill' (e.g. NE *hill*, Lat *collis* 'hill', Lith *kálnas* 'mountain', Grk *kolōnós* 'hill'—these are all derivatives of **kelh*$_1$*-* 'rise, stand'); a similar development is seen in the connection between OE *swelle* 'slope, rise in land' and Toch B *ṣale* 'mountain', both from PIE **swelno-* 'slope'; **samh̥*$_x$*dhos* 'sand' (e.g. NE *sand*, Lat *sabulum* 'sand', Grk *ámathos* 'sand').

8.2 Fire

There are two words that explicitly refer to 'fire' but have long been seen to stand in semantic contrast. The first, **h*$_x$*n̥g*^{w}*nis*, is masculine and is generally understood to indicate fire as an active force; it is deified in India as the god Agni. The second term, **péh*$_2$*ur*, is neuter and hence regarded as 'inactive', i.e. fire purely as a natural substance without the personification implicit in the first

Table 8.2. *Fire*

h_xn̥g^wnis	'fire'	Lat *ignis*, Skt *agní-*
péh$_2$ur	'fire'	NE *fire*, Grk *pûr*
$h_2$eh$_x$tr̥	'fire'	Lat *āter*
$h_2$éh$_x$ōs	'ash'	NE *ash*
?*kenh$_x$is*	'ash'	Lat *cinis*, Grk *kónis*
$h_x$óngl̥	'charcoal'	Skt *áṅgāra-*
deh$_a$u-	'kindle, burn'	Grk *daíō*, Skt *dunóti*
$h_a$eidh	'burn; fire'	Lat *aedēs*, Grk *aíthō*, Skt *indhé*
$h_a$el-	'burn'	Lat *altar*, Skt *alātam*
$h_2$eh$_x$-	'burn, be hot'	Lat *āra*
dheg^{w}h-	'burn'	Lat *foveō*, Grk *téphrā*, Skt *dáhati*
?*k̂eh$_a$u-*	'burn'	Grk *kaíō*
$h_1$eus-	'burn, singe'	Lat *ūrō*, Grk *heúō*, Skt *óṣati*
swelp-	'burn, smoulder'	Lat *sulphur*
?*preus-*	'burn'	Lat *prūna*, Skt *ploṣati*
teh$_a$-	'to melt'	Lat *tābeō*, NE *thaw*, Grk *tḗkō*
(s)mel-	'give off light smoke, smoulder'	
dhuh$_2$mós	'smoke'	Lat *fūmus*, Grk *thūmós*, Skt *dhūmá-*
g^{w}es-	'extinguish'	Grk *sbénnūmi*, Skt *jásate*

term. The different Indo-European groups or even languages within a single group generally settled on the exclusive use of one or the other term, i.e. *h_xn̥g^wnis* is found in Lat *ignis*, Lith *ugnìs*, Latv *uguns*, OCS *ognĭ*, Rus *ogónĭ* and Skt *agní-*; *péh$_2$ur* survives in Umb *pir*, Germanic (e.g. NE *fire*), OPrus *panno*, Czech *pýř* 'ashes', Grk *pûr*, Arm *hur*, Hit *pahhur* (genitive *pahhenas*) and Tocharian (e.g. Toch B *puwar*). Another word for 'fire' (*$h_2$éh$_x$tr̥*) is only marginally attested but with cognates in Europe and Asia (e.g. Lat *āter* 'black' [< *'blackened by fire'], *ātrium* 'atrium' [< *'chimney space over hearth'], Av *ātarš* [genitive *āθrō*] 'fire') it is securely reconstructed. It derives from the verbal root *$h_2$eh$_x$-* 'burn, be hot' (see below) which also gives us a word for 'ash', *$h_2$éh$_x$ōs* 'ash' (e.g. NE *ash*, Hit *hās* 'potash, soda ash, ashes'). Another word for 'ash, combustion product' is PIE ?*kenh$_x$is* (Lat *cinis* 'ash', Grk *kónis* 'dust, ash', Toch B *kentse* 'rust, verdigris'). There is also *$h_x$óngl̥* 'charcoal' with cognates in NIr *aingeal* 'light, fire', Baltic (e.g. Lith *anglìs* 'charcoal'), Slavic (e.g. OCS *ǫglĭ* 'charcoal'), and Indo-Iranian (e.g. Skt *áṅgāra* 'charcoal').

The abundance of terms for 'burn' suggests semantic distinctions, only few of which we can hazard a guess for the proto-language. Getting a fire started may have been indicated by *deh$_a$u-* 'kindle, burn' with cognates in Celtic (e.g. OIr *doud* 'burning'), Grk *daíō* 'kindle, burn', Skt *dunóti* 'kindles, burns', and Tocharian (e.g. TochA *twās-* 'kindle, ignite, light'). A verbal root *$h_a$eidh- 'burn; fire' supplies both verbs and nouns, e.g. OIr *āed* 'fire', Lat *aedēs* 'temple', OE *ād* 'heat, fire', Grk *aíthō* 'burn', Skt *indhé* 'kindle'. PIE *$h_a$el- 'burn' is based on cognates in Italic (Lat *altar* 'altar' and *adoleō* 'burn a sacrifice'), Germanic (Swed *ala* 'blaze, flare up'), and Skt *alātam* 'firebrand, coal'. Our root *h_2eh_x- 'burn, be hot' is attested as such only in Palaic *hā-* 'be hot' but, as we have seen, has left a wealth of derivations, including *h_2éh_xōs 'ash', *h_2e$h_x$tr̥ 'fire', and *h_2e$h_x$mer- 'heat (of the day)' (Grk *hēmérā* 'day', Arm *awr* 'day'). The verb with the meaning 'burn' that is most widely spread in Indo-European is *dheg^{w}h- (e.g. OIr *daig* 'flame', Lat *foveō* 'heat, cherish', Lith *degù* 'burn', OCS *žegǫ* 'burn', Alb *djeg* 'burn', *ndez* 'kindle', Grk *téphrā* 'ash', Av *dazaiti* 'burns', Skt *dáhati* 'burns', Toch *tsäk-* 'burn'). Perhaps also belonging here is Proto-Germanic **dagaz* 'day' (e.g. NE *day*), if from 'heat of the day' as in *h_2e$h_x$mer- (above) and Toch B *kauṃ* 'day' from another word for 'burn', PIE *keh_au-, as in Grk *kaíō* 'burn'. There is also *$h_1$eus- 'burn, singe' indicated by cognates in Lat *ūrō* 'burn', Germanic (e.g. ON *ysja* 'fire'), Alb *ethe* 'fever', Grk *heúō* 'singe', and Skt *óṣati* 'burns, singes'. A PIE **swelp-* 'burn, smoulder', which occurs as an attested verb in Tocharian (i.e. *sälp-* 'be set alight, burn'), has an old nominal derivative **swélpl̥* (genitive **sulplós*) that shows up in both Germanic (e.g. OE *swefl*) and Lat *sulphur* as the word for 'sulphur', i.e. 'that which burns'. There is a possible PIE *?*preus-* 'burn' if one accepts that Lat *prūna* 'glowing coals' and Alb *prush* 'glowing' have a reliable cognate in Skt *ploṣati* 'burns'. We will encounter related words for 'burn' when we examine the vocabulary of cooking in Chapter 16. But to these words for 'burn' we should add *teh_a- 'to melt' which is attested in Celtic (NWels *toddi* 'melt'), Lat *tābeō* 'melt', Germanic (e.g. NE *thaw*), OCS *tajǫ* 'melt', Grk *tḗkō* 'melt', Arm *t'anam* 'moisten', and a single Indo-Iranian cognate in Oss *tajyn* ~ *tajun* 'melt'.

An isogloss of the NW and Tocharian can be found in **(s)mel-* 'give off light smoke, smoulder' which is seen in Celtic (Middle Irish *smāl* ~ *smōl* ~ *smūal* 'fire, glow, ashes'), Germanic (NE *smoulder, smell*), Baltic (Lith *smilė̃kti* 'give off light dust or smoke'), Slavic (Sorbian *smališ́* 'singe') and Toch B *meli* [pl.] 'nose'. The best word for 'smoke' is *dhu$h_2$mós 'smoke' with Lat *fūmus*, Lith *dū́mai*, OCS *dymu*, Skt *dhūmá-* all 'smoke', and Grk *thūmós* 'spirit'.

Finally, there is wide agreement in meaning, if not in phonetics, for a verb *g^{w}es- 'extinguish' seen in Baltic (e.g. Lith *gèsti*), Slavic (OCS *ugasiti*), Grk *sbénnūmi*, Anatolian (Hit *kist-*), Skt *jásate*, and Tocharian (Toch B *kes-*), which all indicate 'go out, extinguish'.

To these words may be added North-Western **swel-* 'burn' (e.g. OE *swelan* 'burn', Lith *svilù* 'singe', Grk *hélā* 'heat of the sun' [and it is presumably this **swel-* which underlies the extended **swel-p-* above]); **ker-* 'burn' (*ker-h_x- in

Goth *haúri* 'coal', ON *hyrr* 'fire' OE *heorþ*, whence NE *hearth*, Lith *kùrti* 'heat', OCS *kuriti sę* 'smoke'; **kr-em-* in Lat *cremō* 'burn' (borrowed in NE *cremate*); and perhaps **ker-s-* if Skt *kaṣāku-* ~ *kuṣāku-* 'fire, sun' belongs here; **perk-* 'glowing ash, coal' (OIr *riches* [< **pr̥ki-stā-*] 'glowing coal', Lith *pir̃kšnys* [pl.] 'ashes with glowing sparks'); **g(e)ulo-* 'fire, glowing coal', found only in Celtic (e.g. OIr *gūal* 'coal') and Germanic (e.g. NE *coal*). From the West Central region we have **(s)meld-* 'to melt' (e.g. NE *melt*, Grk *méldomai* 'melt'); ***k^w*ap-* 'smoke, seethe' (e.g. Lith *kvãpas* 'breath', Grk *kapnós* 'smoke'); and **(s)m(e)ug(h)-* 'smoke' (e.g. NE *smoke*, Grk *smū́khō* 'burn in a smouldering fire', Arm *mux* 'smoke'); **kseros* 'dry' (Lat *serescunt* 'they dry', *serēnus* 'clear, bright, fair [of weather]' < *'dry [of weather]', OHG *serawēn* 'become dry', Greek *kserón* 'dry land', *ksērós* 'dry, solid').

8.3 Water

The main word for 'water' was **wódr̥* which is attested in most language groups (e.g. OIr *uisce* 'water' [> NE *whiskey*], Lat *unda* 'wave', NE *water*, Lith *vanduõ* 'water', OCS *voda* 'water' [and the Russian derivative *vodka*], Alb *ujë* 'water', Grk *húdōr* 'water', Arm *get* 'river', Hit *wātar* [genitive *witenas*] 'water', Skt

Table 8.3. *Water*

**wódr̥*	'water'	NE *water*, Grk *húdōr*
***h_2*eP-*	'living water'	Lat *amnis*, Skt *āp-*
**wel/oh*$_x$*r*	'water'	Lat *ūrīnārī*, Skt *vār(i)*
**suh*$_x$*-*	'rain'	Grk *húei*
***h_1*wers-*	'rain'	Grk *eérsē*, Skt *várṣati*
**n̥bh(ro/ri)-*	'rain'	Lat *imber*, Skt *abhrá-*
**dhreg-*	'rain/snow lightly'	NE *dark*
**sneig*^{w}*h-*	'to snow'	Lat *nīvere*
**yeg-*	'ice, icicle'	NE *icicle*
*?**h_1*eih*$_x$*(s)-*	'ice'	NE *ice*
**ghel(h̥*$_2$*)d-*	'hail'	Grk *khálaza*
**rṓs*	'dew, moisture'	Lat *rōs*
**spoh*$_x$*ino/eh*$_a$	'foam'	NE *foam*, Lat *spūma*
**deh*$_a$*nu-*	'river'	
**drewentih*$_2$*-*	(river name)	
**móri*	'sea'	NE *mere*, Lat *mare*
**weh*$_x$*p-*	'body of water'	Skt *vāpī-*
**penk-*	'damp, mud'	Skt *pánku-*

udan- 'water') while **h_2eP-* (the labial appears sometimes voiced, sometimes voiceless) is preserved as 'river' in a number of languages, more generally as 'water' in others (e.g. OIr *ab* 'river', MWel *afon* 'river' [and thus from British the various English river names *Avon*], Lat *amnis* 'river', OHG river names in *-affa-*, OPrus *ape* 'river', Hit *hāpa-* 'river', Av *āfš* 'water', Skt *āp-* 'water', Toch AB *āp* 'water, river'). The combination of attested meanings suggests an original 'living water', i.e. 'water on the move'. Thus these two words for 'water' act in much the same way as do the two for 'fire'. **we/oh$_x$r* offers divergent meanings, e.g. 'water' (Luv *wār(sa)*), 'rain' (Av *vār*, Skt *vār(i)*, ON *ūr* 'fine rain'), 'pool' (OPrus *wurs*), 'moist' (OE *ūrig*), 'marsh' (Arm *gayṙ*), so that its underlying meaning is extremely obscured.

Judging by the number of words for it, 'rain' was something with which the Proto-Indo-European community had considerable experience. We are able to reconstruct the verbs **suh$_x$-* 'rain' (e.g. Grk *húei*, OPrus *suge* 'rain', Toch AB *su-* 'rain', and perhaps Alb *shi* 'rains'); **h$_1$wers-* 'rain' (e.g. Grk *eérsē* 'dew', *ouréō* 'urinate' [< *'make rain'], Hit *warsa-* 'rainfall'), Skt *várṣati* 'rains'; **n̥bh(ro/ri)-* 'rain' (e.g. Lat *imber* 'shower', Skt *abhrá-* 'rain-cloud', and probably Grk *ómbros* 'rain', Toch B *epprer* 'sky'); and **dhreg-* 'rain/snow lightly' (e.g. NE *dark*, Lith *dérgti* 'be slushy, sleety', ORus *padorog* 'stormy weather', Toch B *tarkär* 'cloud'). The root **sneig^{w}h-* (e.g. OIr *snigid* 'snows, rains', Lat *nivit* ~ *ninguit* 'snows', OE *snīwan* 'to snow', Grk *neíphei* 'snows', Av *snaēžaiti* 'snows') gives both the verb 'to snow' and two different noun formations of which the zero-grade (**snig^{w}hs* in Lat *nix* 'snow' and Grk *nípha* [accusative] 'snowflake') is presumed to be the older while Germanic, Baltic, Slavic, and Old Indic yield a full-grade root (**snoig^{w}hos*). 'Ice' would appear to be represented by two roots, **yeg-* 'ice, icicle' (e.g. OIr *aig* 'ice', NE *icicle*, Hit *eka-* 'ice', Sarikoli [an Iranian language of the Pamirs] *yoz* 'glacier') and *?*h$_1$eih$_x$(-s)-* 'ice' (e.g. NE *ice*, Lith *ýnis* 'glazed frost', Rus *ínej* 'hoarfrost', Av *aēxa-* 'frost, ice'). The meanings of the various reflexes of these words might suggest that the first meant 'solid expanse of ice' whereas the second was '(hoar)frost'. We also have a possible word for 'hail' in PIE **ghel(h̥$_2$)d-* which is found in Slavic (e.g. OCS *žlědica* 'freezing rain'), Grk *khálaza* 'hail', and NPers *žāla* 'hail'.

The root for 'dew', **rṓs* (e.g. Lat *rṓs* 'dew', Lith *rasà* 'dew', Rus *rosá* 'dew', Alb *resh* 'it is precipitating', Skt *rása-* 'sap, juice'), underlies a number of river names in Indo-Iranian, including the mythical world river of the ancient Indians (*Rasā-*). The word for 'foam', **spoh$_x$imo/eh$_a$* (e.g. Lat *spūma* 'foam', NE *foam*, Lith *spáine* (with dissimilation of *p... m* > *p... n*) 'foam (of beer)', may originally derive from the verb 'to spit'.

The names for 'river' are difficult; often elements in river names are offered as potential roots but it is seldom clear that they really derive from a Proto-Indo-European form. Aside from **h_2eP-* which apparently includes 'river' among its possible meanings, we have *$*deh_a nu$*, which is most famously attested in the river names 'Danube' and 'Don' (from Iranian, e.g. Av *dānu-* 'river'), while *$*drewentih_2$-* can be seen in river names as widely separated as Gaul (*Druentia*) and India (*Dravantī*).

The word for 'sea', **móri*, is firmly attested in Celtic (e.g. OIr *muir* 'sea'), Italic (e.g. Lat *mare* 'sea'), Germanic (e.g. NE *mere*), Baltic (e.g. Lith *mãrė* 'sea'), and Slavic (e.g. OCS *morje* 'sea') which would leave it a North-Western word were it not for a possible cognate in Ossetic (*mal* 'deep standing water'), an East Iranian language of the Caucasus, which would provide an Asian cognate. Hit *marmar(r)a-* 'swamp' may be a reduplicated version of the word and, if so, would secure this word to Proto-Indo-European. The semantics of the word pose difficulties as well since it only means 'sea', i.e. salt-water sea, in Celtic, Italic, and Slavic while Germanic often suggests a 'lake'. Generally we find that most Indo-European languages have innovated or borrowed terms to indicate the sea, e.g. Germanic, Greek, Indic, and so the balance of opinion suggests that the word referred originally to an 'inland sea' or 'lake' and was later extended to mean 'salt water sea'. However, excepting for a moment Germanic, it is noteworthy that those Indo-European groups with maritime locations (Italic, Celtic, Baltic, and Slavic) have the meaning 'sea', while those with an inland location (Ossetic and Hittite) have the meaning 'lake'. Either meaning could have been developed from the other to reflect the local environment. It is languages like English whose speakers live in a maritime environment but use the inherited **móri* for inland waters that tip the balance in favour of an original non-maritime meaning. Another word which could mean anything from a 'river' to a 'lake' is *$*weh_x p$-* 'body of water' found in Baltic (Lith *ùpė* 'river'), Slavic (OCS *vapa* 'lake'), Hit *wappu-* 'wadi, river bank', and Skt *vāpī-* 'large pond'. The existence of **penk-* rests on the evidence of Germanic (e.g. OE *fūht* 'wet') and Skt *pánku-* 'mud, mire'.

There are a considerable number of sub-PIE words, e.g. North-Western *$*h_a ek^w eh_a$-* 'water' (e.g. Lat *aqua*, NE *island*); **preus-* 'frost' (e.g. NE *frost*, Lat *pruīna* 'hoarfrost', with uncertain cognates in Celtic (e.g. OIr *reōd* 'strong cold') and possibly Indic (Skt *pruṣvā́-* 'hoarfrost' or 'dew, drop'?); *$*h_3 eust(y)o$-* 'estuary, river mouth' (Lat *ōstium*, Lith *úostas* 'river mouth, harbour', Rus *ustĭje* 'river mouth'); **pen-* 'water' (e.g. OIr *en* 'water', NE *fen*, OPrus *pannean* 'peat-bog'); West Central *$*yuh_x$-r-* 'water' (e.g. Lith *jūrės* 'sea', Thracian *iuras* [a river name]); *$*h_a eghlu$ (ĝh?)* 'rain' (OPrus *aglo* 'rain, Grk *akhlū́s* 'fog, cloud'); **mregh-* 'rain softly, drizzle' (e.g. Latvian *merguôt* 'rain softly', Grk *brékhei* 'rains'); **k̂er(s)no-* 'hoarfrost, frozen snow' (e.g. Lith *šarmà* 'frost', Rus *séren* 'frozen snow', Arm *sar̃n* 'ice'; **grōdo-* 'hail' (Lith *grúodas* 'frost', OCS *gradŭ* 'hail', and with unusual derivations, Lat *grandō* 'hail', Arm *karkut* [< **gagrōdo-*] 'hail'); *$*bhreh_1 wr̥$* (genitive *$*bhruh_1 nós$*) 'spring' (e.g. OE *brunna* 'spring' [> NE _burn_], Grk _phréār_ 'fountain', Arm _albiwr_ 'spring'); _?*kr̥sneh$_a$_ 'spring, wave' (e.g. OE _hræn_ 'spring', Grk _krḗnē_ 'spring'); _*sreumen_ 'flowing, streaming (in river names)' (NE _stream_, Rus _strúmenĭ_ 'brook', Grk _rheûma_ 'flow, river'); _*h$_a$eh$_x$-peros_ (?) 'river bank, shore of sea' (e.g. OE _ōfer_ 'bank', Grk _ḗpeiros_ 'shore', Arm _ap'n_ 'shore'); _*lokús_ 'lake, water, pond' (e.g. OIr _loch_ 'lake', Lat _lacus_ 'lake, cistern', OE _lagu_ 'water, lake, river', OCS _loky_ 'pool', Grk _lákkos_ 'pond, cistern'); _*tenh̥$_a$g-_ 'shallow water?' (e.g. Latv _tîgas_ 'deep spot in water', Grk _ténagos_ 'shoal, shallow water', possibly Lat _stāgnum_ 'standing water, pool, swamp'); _*h$_x$ih$_x$lu-_ 'mud; swamp' (Rus _il_ 'mud', Grk _īlū́s_ 'mud, swamp'); Graeco-Aryan _*séles-_ 'marsh' (e.g. Grk _hélos_ 'marsh, meadow', Skt _sáras-_ 'lake, pond', and possibly Celtic cognates e.g. NWels _hêl_ 'river meadow'); and Eastern _*h$_a$élmos_ 'spring' (Skt _árma-_ 'spring', Toch B _ālme_ 'spring').

8.4 Air

The word for the 'sun', _*séh$_a$ul_ (genitive _*sh$_a$wéns_), is old (e.g. Lat _sōl_ 'sun', NE _sun_, Lith _sáulė_ 'sun', OCS _slŭnĭce_ 'sun', Grk _hēélios_ 'sun', Av _hvar_ 'sun', Skt _svàr_ ~ _sū́r(y)a-_ 'sun'); the Old Irish cognate _sūil_ means 'eye', a concept also reprised in both Greek and Indic mythology.

The main word for 'moon', _*méh$_1$-nōt_ (or _*meh$_1$-n(é)s-_), derives from the verb _*meh$_1$-_ 'to measure', and indicates a functional conception of the moon, i.e. marker of the month. The meaning of the reflexes may be 'moon' or 'month' or both (e.g. OIr _mī_ 'month', Lat _mēnsis_ 'month', NE _moon_, _month_, Lith _mė̃nuo_

Table 8.4. _Air_

*séh$_a$ul	'sun'	NE _sun_, Lat _sōl_, Grk _hēélios_, Skt _svàr_
*méh$_1$-nōt	'moon'	NE _moon_, Lat _mēnsis_, Grk _mḗn_, Skt _mās-_
*(s)kand-	'moon'	Skt _candrá-_
_*h$_2$stḗr_	'star'	NE _star_, Lat _stēlla_, Grk _astḗr_, Skt _tāras_
*nébhos	'mist, cloud; sky'	Lat _nebula_, Grk _néphos_, Skt _nábhas-_
*sneudh-	'mist, cloud'	Lat _nūbēs_
*wápōs	'vapour, steam'	Lat _vapor_, Skt _vāṣpá-_
_*h$_3$meigh-_	'drizzle, mist'	NE _mist_, Grk _omíkhlē_, Skt _meghá-_
_*h$_2$weh$_1$-yús_	'wind'	Skt _vāyú-_
_*h$_2$weh$_1$-nt-_	'wind'	NE _wind_, Lat _ventus_, Skt _vā́ta-_
*(s)tenh$_x$-	'groan; thunder'	NE _thunder_, Lat _tonere_, Grk _sténō_, Skt _stanáyati_

'moon, month', OCS *měsęcĭ* 'moon, month', Alb *muaj* 'month', Grk *mḗn* 'month', Arm *amis* 'month', Av *må* 'moon, month', Skt *mā́s-* 'moon, month', Toch B *meñe* 'moon, month'). The other widely found noun, **(s)kand-* (Alb *hënë* 'moon', Skt *cándra-* 'moon'), derives from the verb **(s)kand-* 'shine'. The word for 'star', **$h_2$stḗr* (e.g. MIr *ser* 'star', Lat *stēlla* 'star', NE *star*, Grk *astḗr* 'star', Arm *astl* 'star', Hit *hasterza* 'star', Skt *tā́ras* 'stars'), has long been the subject of debate as to whether it was borrowed from a Semitic source (see Section 6.3.1). Such an origin seems doubtful as one might offer a purely Indo-European etymology for the word and derive it from **h_2eh_x-s-* 'burn' (i.e. PIE **$h_2(h_x)$-s-tér-* 'ember', with a semantic development like that of Alb *yll* 'star' when compared to OE *ysle* 'glowing ash'; both words are from PIE **$h_1$usli-*, a derivative of **$h_1$eus-* 'burn').

Words such as **nébhos* refer primarily to clouds but have often developed secondary meanings of 'sky' (e.g. OIr *nem* 'heaven', Lat *nebula* 'mist, fog', OE *nifol* 'dark', Lith *debesìs* 'cloud', OCS *nebo* 'sky', Grk *néphos* 'sky', Skt *nábhas-* 'mist, cloud; sky', Hit *nēpis-* 'sky') while **$h_3$meigh-*, originally 'drizzle', comes to mean 'cloud' in some languages (e.g. NE *mist*, Lith *miglà* 'mist', Rus *mgla* 'mist, darkness', Grk *omíkhlē* 'cloud', Skt *meghá-* 'cloud') as does the more weakly attested **sneudh-* with NWels *nudd* 'mist', Lat *nūbēs* 'cloud, mist', and Av *snaoδa-* cloud'. Slightly different semantically is the word for 'steam, vapour' (**wápōs*) seen at opposite ends of the Indo-European world in Lat *vapor* 'vapour, steam' and Skt *vāṣpá-* ~ *bāṣpá-* (< **vāpṣá-*) 'vapour, steam; tears'.

The atmosphere was not all doom and gloom as derivatives of the verbal root **dei-* 'to shine' were also employed to indicate both 'day' (Chapter 18) and 'sky' as well as a sky deity (Chapter 23); in the specific meaning of 'sky' (but with different extensions) we have Lat *dīum* 'sky', and Skt *dyáuṣ* 'sky'. The words for 'wind', **h_2weh_1-yús* (Lith *vė̃jas* 'wind' and Skt *vāyú-* wind') and **h_2weh_1-nt-* (e.g. NWels *gwynt*, Lat *ventus*, NE *wind*, Av *vā̊ta-*, Skt *vāta-*, Toch B *yente*, Hit *huwant-*, all 'wind'), both derive from the verb 'to blow'. A verbal root 'to groan, to thunder' is **(s)tenh$_x$-* (e.g. Lat *tonāre* 'to thunder', OE *þunor* 'thunder' (> NE *thunder*), OCS *stenǫ* 'groan', Grk *sténō* 'thunder', Skt *stanáyati* 'thunders').

The regional words include the following: North-Western **louksneh$_a$-* 'moon' (Lat *lūna*, OCS *luna* 'moon', OPrus *lauxnos* 'stars'); **meldh-* 'lightning'; West Central **(s)ḱeh$_1$w(e)r-* 'north wind' (NE *shower*, Lat *caurus* 'north wind', Lith *šiáure* 'north wind', *šiū́ras* 'cold, northern', OCS *sěverŭ* 'north', Arm *c'urt* 'cold; shower'); **ghromos* 'thunder' (possibly an independent formation in those languages where it occurs, OCS *gromŭ* 'noise', *vŭz-grĭměti* 'to thunder', Grk *khrómos* 'noise', from the verb **ghrem-* 'groan').

8.5 The Physical Landscape of the Proto-Indo-Europeans

The picture provided by the reconstructed lexicon is not very informative concerning the physical environment of the speakers of the ancestral language, although there have been scholars enough who have tried to press the slender evidence into revealing the precise location (or type of location) inhabited by the Proto-Indo-Europeans. That they had words for hills, mountains, or swift rivers may suggest a broken topography but hardly indicates, as has been suggested, that the Proto-Indo-Europeans themselves must have lived atop high mountains. The difficulties inherent in recovering a certain meaning for **móri-* 'sea' or 'lake' have been often rehearsed and consensus is probably still in support of projecting an original meaning of 'inland body of water' that was changed to 'salt water sea' in some language groups, e.g. Celtic, Italic, and Slavic. In our earliest attested languages we either find a potential cognate in Hit *marmar(r)a-* which refers to a body of shallow standing water or, in the case of the Greeks and Indo-Aryans, they borrowed words for 'sea' from non-Indo-European sources which has suggested that the Proto-Indo-Europeans did not originally know or have a word for 'sea'.

As for the rivers, there is a vast literature on the river names of Europe and Asia that has attempted to discern both a system of river names and, often, their origin. Much of modern discussion takes Hans Krahe's 'Alteuropäisch' as its point of departure. Krahe envisaged a hydronymic system that embraced the linguistic ancestor of what we might term the North-West Indo-European languages coupled with Messapic and Venetic. This system was extended back to Proto-Indo-European by W. P. Schmid, while more recently much of the same hydronymic system has been ascribed to Basque by Theo Venneman. All these systems are comprised of a wide variety of river names that are generally derived from exceedingly small bases (conjectural roots such as **el-*, **al-*, **er-*, **or-*, etc.) that may belong to any number of different languages or language families and whose underlying meaning simply cannot be verified to any confident degree. The actual number of river names that can be reasonably reconstructed to Proto-Indo-European, as we have seen above, is extremely few.

The terms associated with weather attest a basic range of atmospheric phenomena but nothing decisive as to where precisely the Proto-Indo-Europeans lived. One might compare the fairly basic lexicon associated with cold weather in Indo-European with that of the Indo-Europeans' northern neighbours who spoke Proto-Uralic and from whose reconstructed lexicon we can recover words for 'thin ice' (**ćaka*), 'hard snow' (**ćäke*), 'thin snow' (**kum3*), 'fine snow' (**kura*), and other terms that are clearly associated with a colder environment than one commonly reconstructs for the Proto-Indo-Europeans. But generally, those concerned with locating the Indo-European homeland through its lexicon tend to employ the evidence of its reconstructed fauna (Chapter 9) and flora (Chapter 10).

Finally, the astral vocabulary of the Indo-Europeans disappoints in its meagreness. While the night sky may alter gradually through time one might have hoped that the Indo-Europeans would have retained their names for stars and constellations reasonably well compared with, for example, terms for flora and fauna that might alter over the course of their migrations into different environments. This does not seem to be so, and whatever the original Proto-Indo-European view of the heavens was, it seems largely beyond recovery. Such potentially major sources of astral knowledge as Greek seem to have been remodelled on the basis of Babylonian astronomy. The most solidly 'reconstructed' Indo-European constellation is Ursa Major, which is designated as 'The Bear' (Chapter 9) in Greek and Sanskrit (Latin may be a borrowing here), although even the latter identification has been challenged. Eric Hamp has suggested that we can also reconstruct a second constellation, a 'Triangle' (and not the constellation Triangulum). This is suggested by Av *tištriya-* 'three-star' that may be cognate with Grk *Seírios* 'Sirius, the dog-star' thus suggesting a 'three-star' constellation involving Sirius. Hamp proposes a constellation that would embrace bright stars in Orion (Betelgeuse), Canis Major (Sirius), and Canis Minor (Procyon)(hence we may have a celestial 'Dog' contrasted with a 'Bear'; neither of these is in the Babylonian zodiac where we find instead animals such as the lion, bull, and scorpion).

Further Reading

All natural phenomena are handled in the basic IE handbooks, e.g. Schrader–Nehring (1917–28), Gamkrelidze–Ivanov (1995), Mallory–Adams (1997). For individual topics see the following: earth (Schindler 1967, Hamp 1990*a*), stone (Maher 1973), mountain (Hamp 1967), water (Watkins 1972*b*), rain (Bonfante 1989), snow (Benveniste 1956*b*, Gonda 1955*a*, Hoffman 1965), sun (Beekes 1984, Huld 1986, Hamp 1990*b*), moon (Beekes 1982, Hamp 1983), and star (Scherer 1953, Watkins 1974, Parvulescu 1977, Bomhard 1986, D'iakonov 1985 [against Semitic borrowing]); the fullest description of the Indo-European night sky is to be found in Scherer (1953); see also Hamp (1972*a*) for an additional constellation and Parvulescu (1988*a*: against Ursa Major in Vedic). For the vast topic of river names see Krahe (1964*b*), Kuhn (1967), Schmid (1968, 1972), Georgiev (1966), Blok (1971), and Vennemann (1994).

9

Indo-European Fauna

9.1 Reconstructing Environments

Many attempts to fix the location of the Proto-Indo-European world have depended heavily on the reconstructed vocabulary that pertains to the environment, both floral and faunal. It is often reasoned that if the reconstructed environment is specific enough, it can either indicate where the Proto-Indo-Europeans once dwelled or at least exclude territories that are incompatible with the reconstructed vocabulary. The problem with utilizing such data is logically self-evident. If an item is severely restricted in space, for example, the camel, then any Indo-European group who moved beyond the natural territory of the camel might do one of three things with their original word 'camel':

1. They might simply abandon the word altogether as they and their linguistic descendants were not likely to encounter a camel for the next several thousand years.

2. They might use the name 'camel' when they came across another animal that they were unfamiliar with but which bore some similarity in appearance or function. From the perspective of the historical linguist, we might then have to confront a situation where the original meaning 'camel' was (or was not) retained in those groups who lived where camels have always dwelled while other languages developed a totally different meaning for this word. The other

languages might well outnumber those who retained the original meaning or, worse, no language might retain the original meaning.

3. The population might retain the name and the meaning of 'camel' for thousands of years as a gesture of benevolence to future historical linguists.

Now, put so baldly, a scenario such as number three is impossible. However, it is certainly not the case that an animal or plant has to be native to the area where a particular language is spoken for the speakers of that language to have or retain a name for it. The lion has been extinct in Europe since classical times (and before then was, in any case, restricted to the Balkans) and the elephant and leopard have never shared Europe with modern humans. Nevertheless all medieval European languages had words for all three and at least the lion and the leopard played important roles in medieval and modern heraldry. Similarly, although snakes have always been absent from Ireland (even before St Patrick!), the Irish retained two inherited Indo-European names for the snake.

Illustrative of both points two and three is the history of English *elk*. When the Angles and Saxons invaded Britain from their continental homes, they were familiar with both *Alces alces* (the 'elk' of European English and the 'moose' of North American English) and *Cervus elaphus* (the 'red deer' of European English and the 'elk' of North American English) and applied those designations to members of the same two species which were also present in Great Britain. By about AD 900 *Alces alces* was extinct in Great Britain but the loss of local referents did not mean that the word 'elk' disappeared since the species was still familiar to some speakers because of its continued existence on the Continent (e.g. Scandinavia, Germany). However, for most speakers the referent was pretty vague, something like 'large deer' or the like. By 1600 or so the inherited designation for *Cervus elaphus* had been replaced by the innovative and descriptive *red deer* and by about the same time or so the species itself had disappeared from most of southern Britain except for a small number kept for the chase. At that point for most speakers of southern British English there were two terms for large deer, 'elk', and 'red deer', without well-known referents.

When some of these southern British English speakers emigrated to New England at the beginning of the seventeenth century they came to live in an environment again with both *Alces alces* and *Cervus elaphus* and they needed names for both. 'Red deer' was not suitable for either since neither *Alces alces* nor the North American variety of *Cervus elaphus* was noticeably red. However, 'elk' was available and was assigned to the commonest large deer in the new environment, *Cervus elaphus*, while a borrowing from the local Algonquian language, 'moose', was pressed into service for *Alces alces*.

In terms of Indo-European as a whole this case is probably not the only one whereby a word, relegated to the periphery of the lexicon and to a vague referent by environmental change, was reassigned to a new referent by yet another environmental change. In any case all three of our options pose real problems in recovering really specific evidence for the one and only Proto-Indo-European world.

9.2 Mammals

As a semantic class, the names for animals, at least mammals, are fairly abundant in the reconstructed lexicon. In reviewing the names associated with mammals, it is not always certain whether one is dealing with a domestic or a wild animal and hence all the words associated with mammals are treated together in Table 9.1.

Table 9.1. *Mammals*

*k^w*etwor-pod-*	'animal'	Lat *quadrupēs*, Grk *tetrápous*, Skt *cátuṣpad-*
**ĝhwēr*	'wild animal'	Lat *fera*, Grk *thḗr*
**pék̂u*	'livestock'	Lat *pecu*, NE *fee*, Skt *páśu-*
*(*s*)*teuros*	'large (domestic) animal'	NE *steer*
**wrētos*	'flock, herd'	Skt *vrā́ta-*
**demh$_a$-*	'tame, subdue'	Lat *domō*, NE *tame*, Grk *dámnēmi*, Skt *dāmáyati*
*g^w*yéh$_3$wyom*	'animal'	Grk *zō̂on*
**h$_{2/3}$wédr̥*	'creatures, (wild) animals'	
**léuh$_x$ōn*	'animal'	Grk *léōn*
**wételos*	'yearling'	Lat *vitulus*, Grk *ételon*, Skt *sa-vātára-*
*?*per-*	'offspring (of an animal)'	Grk *pór*(*t*)*is*, Skt *pr̥thuka-*
**k̂oph$_2$ós*	'hoof'	NE *hoof*, Skt *śápha-*
**k̂r̥nom*	'horn'	Lat *cornum*, NE *horn*
**k̂érh̥$_2$s*	'horn'	Grk *kéras*
**k̂érh̥$_2$sr̥*	'horn'	Lat *crābrō*
**k̂óru*	'horn'	Lat *cervus*, NE *hart*, Grk *kórudos*
**k̂em-*	'hornless'	NE *hind*, Grk *kemás*, Skt. *śáma-*
**h$_1$eĝhis*	'hedgehog'	Grk *ekhînos*
**k̂asos*	'hare'	NE *hare*, Lat *cānus*
**werwer-*	'squirrel'	Lat *vīverra*
**bhébhrus*	'beaver'	Lat *fiber*, NE *beaver*
**mūs*	'mouse'	Lat *mūs*, NE *mouse*, Grk *mûs*, Skt *mū́ṣ-*

(*Cont'd.*)

Table 9.1. (*Cont'd*)

*pélh$_x$us	'mouse'	
*g̥l̥h$_1$ís	'dormouse?'	Lat glīs, Grk galéē, Skt girí-
*wl(o)p-	'(red)fox'	Lat volpēs, Grk alōpós
*wl̥k^{w}os	'wolf'	Lat lupus, NE wolf, Grk lúkos, Skt vŕ̥ka-
*wl̥k^{w}íh$_a$-	'she-wolf'	Skt vr̥kī́-
*h$_2$ŕ̥tḱos	'bear'	Lat ursus, Grk árktos, Skt ŕ̥kṣa-
*ḱ(u)wōn	'dog'	Lat canis, NE hound, Grk kúōn, Skt śvā
*udrós	'otter'	Lat lutra, NE otter, Grk énudris, Skt udrá-
*keḱ-	'polecat'	Skt káśa-
?*lōḱ-	'weasel'	
?*bhel-	'± marten; wildcat'	Lat fēlis, Skt bharuja-
*h$_1$éḱwos	'horse'	Lat equus, Grk híppos, Skt áśva-
*h$_1$éḱweh$_a$-	'mare'	Lat equa, Skt áśvā-
??*os(o)nos	'ass'	Lat asinus, Grk ónas
*sūs	'pig (wild or domesticated)'	Lat sūs, NE sow, Grk hûs ∼ sū́s, Skr sūkará-
*pórḱos	'young pig, piglet'	Lat porcus, NE farrow
?*tworḱós	'boar'	
*h$_1$elh$_1$ēn	'red deer'	Grk élaphos
*h$_x$ólḱis	'elk/American moose'	Lat alcēs, NE elk, Skt ŕ̥śya-
*g^{w}ṓus	'cow'	Lat bōs, NE cow, Grk boûs, Skt gáu-
*h$_1$eĝh-	'cow'	Skt ahī-
*woḱéh$_a$-	'cow'	Lat vacca, Skt vaśā́-
*uk$^{(w)}$sēn-	'ox'	NE ox, Skt ukán-
?*domh$_a$yos	'one to be tamed, young bull'	Skt damya-
*tauros	'aurochs; bull'	Lat taurus, Grk taûros
?*usr-	'aurochs'	Skt usrá-
*h$_2$ówis	'sheep'	Lat ovis, NE ewe, Grk óis, Skt ávi-
*h$_2$owikéh$_a$-	'ewe'	Skt avikā́-
*wr̥h$_1$ēn	'lamb'	Grk arḗn, Skt urán-
*moisós	'ram, sheep; fleece, skin'	Skt meṣá-
?*(s)ḱegos	'sheep/goat'	NE sheep, Skt chā́ga-
*h$_1$eri-	'sheep/goat'	Lat ariēs, Grk ériphos, Skt āreya-
*díks	'goat'	
*h$_a$eiĝs	'goat'	Grk aíks
*bhuĝos	'buck, he-goat'	NE buck, Skt bukka-
*h$_a$eĝós	'he-goat'	Skt ajá-
*kápros	'he-goat'	Lat caper
*h$_4$eli-	'he-goat'	
??*(y)ebh-	'elephant'	
??*lebh-	'ivory'	

Terms for mammals, both wild and domesticated, are relatively abundant compared with many other semantic categories. There are a number of basic terms for animals that focus on different aspects. For example, *k^w*etwor-pod-* 'animal' is transparently a 'four-footer' and the word is attested in six different groups (Lat *quadrupēs*, Lith *keturkõjis*, Alb *shtazë*, Grk *tetrápous*, Skt *cátuṣpad-*, Toch B *śtwerpew*). The word **ĝhwēr* 'wild animal' (e.g. Lat *fera* 'wild animal', Lith *žvėrìs* 'wild animal', OCS *zvěrĭ* 'wild animal', Grk *thḗr* 'wild animal'; cf. the derived verb in Toch B *śeritsi* 'to hunt' [wild animals]') contrasts in meaning with **péḱu* 'livestock' which exclusively denotes domestic animals or possessions (e.g. Lat *pecu* ~ *pecus* 'cattle, livestock', OE *feoh* 'livestock, property, money' [> NE *fee*], Lith *pẽkus* 'cattle', Av *pasu* 'cattle', Skt *páśu-* 'cattle'). The *(*s*)*teuros* 'large (domestic) animal' is attested in Germanic (e.g. NE *steer*), Iranian (e.g. Av *staora-* 'large [domestic] animal [i.e. horse, cow, camel]'), and Alb *ter* 'bullock' (in meaning this word has been drawn to the phonetically similar **tauros* 'aurochs, bull'). The term for an animal collective may have been **wrētos* 'flock, herd' although cognates are limited to Germanic (e.g. OE *wrǣþ* 'herd of swine') and Skt *vrā́ta-* 'flock, swarm' which may have been formed on the verbal root **wer-* 'bind'. The nuanced meaning of *$demh_a$- 'tame, subdue' is of considerable interest and difficulty. The word is supported by cognates in seven groups: Celtic (OIr *damnaid* 'binds, breaks [a horse']), Lat *domō* 'break, tame', Germanic (e.g. NE *tame*), Grk *dámnēmi* 'break', Hit *damaszi* 'presses, pushes', NPers *dām* 'tamed animal', Skt *dāmáyati* 'subdues'. There are specific associations with horse-breaking in Celtic, Latin, Greek, and Indic, e.g. the Sanskrit agent noun *damitár-* '(horse) breaker'. But the meanings also extend to other animals, e.g. OIr *dam* 'ox', and frequently refer to the subduing of human opponents in Greek and other groups; also the Hittite cognate does not have a specific association with the maintenance of animals. This word has variously been seen to be an independent root or an o-stem derivative of *dem(h_a)- 'build (a house)' on the argument that the act of taming is literally 'domestication'.

PIE *g^w*yéh₃wyom* 'animal' (Grk *zṓon* 'animal', Toch B *śaiyye* 'sheep/goat') is built on the root *$g^w yeh_3$- > *$g^w eih_3$- 'to live' and hence relates to living beings while the poorly attested (in ON *vitnir* 'animal, wolf' and Hit *huetar* 'creatures, [wild] animals, wolfpack' only) *$h_{2/3}$*wéd-* 'creatures, (wild) animals, wolves' also seems to derive from an unattested verb 'to live', *$h_{2/3}$*wed-*; it is a heteroclitic *r/n*-stem which argues for antiquity and it has some possible Slavic cognates associated with 'werewolves' (e.g. Slov *vedevec* 'werewolf'). Proto-Indo-European *$léuh_x ōn$ 'animal' rests only on Greek (*léōn* 'lion') and Tocharian (e.g. Toch B *luwo* 'animal') evidence and gives us ultimately through a series of loans (Greek > Latin > English) our NE word *lion*. A yearling, **wételos*, is attested in three stocks (e.g. Lat *vitulus* 'calf, yearling', Grk *ételon* 'yearling', Skt *sa-vātára-* 'having the same calf') and gives us, among other words, the name of Italy, i.e. 'land of young cattle'; a related formation gives NE *wether*. The status of **per-* 'offspring (of an animal)' is doubted because a number of groups may have created nouns from the verbal root **per-* 'appear, bring forth' independently (e.g. OE *fearr* 'bullock, steer', Grk *póris* ~ *pórtis* 'calf, heifer', Skt *pr̥thuka-* 'child, young of an animal').

A number of anatomical terms apply specifically to animals. The word for 'hoof', **k̂oph$_2$ós*, is attested in Germanic (e.g. NE *hoof*), Slavic (e.g. Rus *kopýto* 'hoof'), and Indo-Iranian (e.g. Av *safa-* 'hoof', Skt *śápha-* 'hoof, claw'). There are a number of words for 'horn' but all built out of the same basic root, **k̂er-* 'horn', i.e. **k̂r̥nom* (e.g. Lat *cornum*, NE *horn*), **k̂érh̥$_2$(s)* (e.g. Grk *kéras*, Toch B *karse* 'stag' [< *'horned one']), **k̂érh̥$_2$sr̥* (e.g. Lat *crābrō* 'hornet', Lith *širšuõ* 'hornet', Toch B *krorīya* 'horn'), and **k̂óru* 'horn' (e.g. Lat *cervus* 'stag', Lith *kárvė* 'cow', Rus *koróva* 'cow', Grk *kórudos* 'crested lark', *koruphḗ* 'crest [of mountain or horse]', Av *srva-* 'horn; claw, talon'). There is a wide range of animals designated **k̂em-* 'hornless' (Skt *śáma-* hornless'), e.g. 'hind' in English and Greek (*kemás* 'young deer'), 'sheep' in Old Prussian (*camstian*), and 'horse' in Russian (*konĭ*) and Old Prussian (*camnet*). The hornless sheep in Old Prussian and the 'hornless' horses of Russian and Old Prussian are both presumably in contrast to the other major domesticated animal, horned cattle.

The number of wild mammals' names attributable to Proto-Indo-European is reasonably extensive. If we work our way systematically beginning with the insectivores, we have only the 'hedgehog', **h$_1$eĝhis*, whose name survives in Germanic (e.g., OE *igil*), Baltic (e.g. Lith *ežỹs*), Slavic (e.g. Rus *ež*), Grk *ekhînos*, Arm *ozni*, Phrygian *ezis*, and Iranian (Oss *wyzyn*).

The sole lagomorph is the **k̂asos* 'hare' (e.g. NE *hare*, OPrus *sasins*, Skt *śaśá-*), whose name derives from the adjective 'grey' (or, just possibly, the adjective 'grey' was originally 'hare-coloured' or the like)—compare Lat *cānus* (< **k̂asnos*) 'grey'.

Several rodents are known and these comprise the 'squirrel', **werwer-*, attested in six groups, e.g. ScotsGael *feòrag*, Lat *vīverra*, OE *āc-weorna* (<*'oak-squirrel'), Lith *vėverìs*, Rus *véverica*, and OPers *varvarah*; the 'beaver', **bhébhrus* (e.g. Gaul *bebru-*, Lat *fiber*, NE *beaver*, Lith *bebrùs*, Rus *bobr*, Av *bawra-*), which also exhibits a derivative **bhebhrinos* 'pertaining to beavers'. (India lacked the beaver and there we find a *babhrú-* 'mongoose'.) There are three words for the mouse, i.e. the ubiquitous (nine groups) **mūs* 'mouse' (e.g. Lat *mūs*, NE *mouse*, OCS *myšĭ*, Alb *mi*, Grk *mûs*, Arm *mukn*, NPers *mūs*, Skt *mū́ṣ-*, all 'mouse', and Toch B *maścītsi* 'mice, rats') that derives from the verb **meus-* 'steal'; **pélh$_x$us*, another name presumably derived from the adjective 'grey' (e.g. OIr *luch*, Rus *polokhók*, Shughni [an Iranian language of the Pamirs] *pūrg*); and **gl̥h$_1$ís* (Lat *glīs* 'dormouse', Grk *galéē* 'weasel' [< *'mouser'],

Bakhtiari [an Iranian language] *girza* 'rat', Skt *girí-* 'mouse') which possibly specified the 'dormouse'.

The major carnivores, at least those that preyed on livestock or were a potential threat to humans, are well represented although often showing substantial independent re-formation. This is the case with **wl(o)p-* 'fox' (e.g. Lat *vulpēs*, Lith *lãpė*, Grk *alṓpēks* ~ *alōpós*, Arm *aluēs*, Hit *ulip(pa)na-* 'wolf', Av *urupis* 'dog', *raopi-* 'fox, jackal', Skt *lopāśá-* 'jackal, fox'), for example, which boasts at least six different potential proto-forms. The word for 'wolf', **wĺ̥k^{w}os* and its feminine *i*-stem derivative, are widely attested (**wĺ̥k^{w}os* is found in ten groups: Lat *lupus*, NE *wolf*, Lith *vil̃kas*, Rus *volk*, Alb *ujk*, Grk *lúkos*, Av *vəhrka-*, Skt *vŕ̥ka-*, Toch B *walkwe*). The word uniformly means 'wolf' in all groups but Anatolian (e.g. Luv *walwa/i-*) which preserves a meaning 'lion', and the word has been variously explained as a nominalization of the unattested adjective 'dangerous' (**wl̥k^{w}ó-*) or derived from a verbal root **wel-* 'tear'. In either case, the different semantic specifications of 'the dangerous one' or 'the tearer' in Anatolian and the rest of Indo-European may suggest semantic shift as one (the Anatolians) or the other (residual Indo-Europeans) moved into a new territory (as Greece and the Balkans also possessed lions, it is perhaps more likely that it is the Anatolians who innovated). The word for 'bear', *h_2ŕ̥tḱos (e.g. OIr *art*, Lat *ursus*, Alb *ari*, Grk *árktos*, Arm *ar*, Av *arəša-*, Skt *ŕ̥kṣa-*, all 'bear', and Hit *hart(ag)ga-* 'a cultic official, bear-man'), has been similarly explained as a nominalized 'destroyer'. The root, *$h_2$retḱ-, is otherwise seen only in Skt *rákṣas-* 'destruction, damage; night demon'. The Bear also is used to designate *Ursa Major* (the Plough or Big Dipper) not only in Latin but also in Greek and Sanskrit. The word for 'dog', **ḱ(u)wōn*, is one of the most widely attested words in Indo-European (OIr *cū*, Lat *canis*, OE *hund* [> NE *hound*], Lith *šuõ*, Rus *súka* 'bitch', Grk *kúōn*, Arm *šun*, Av *spā*, Skt *śvā*, Toch AB *ku*, all 'dog', Hit *kuwan-* 'dog-man'). While it may seem somewhat surprising that in contrast to words for cattle, sheep, goats, and pig, we have only one solidly attested word for the dog, the oldest domesticated animal, in Indo-European, English is similarly served and once we have worked our way through the usual 'pooch', 'bow-wow', 'puppy', 'bitch', 'cur', and 'mongrel' in *Roget's International Thesaurus* most of the remaining words are attributive, e.g. 'police dog', 'sniffer dog'. The selective breeding of dogs does not appear to have begun till the later prehistoric period.

The smaller carnivores include the **udrós* 'otter' (attested in seven groups: e.g. Lat *lutra*, NE *otter*, Lith *ū́dra*, Rus *výdra*, Grk *énudris*, Av *udra-*, Skt *udrá-*) which is formed from the word for 'water', **wódr̥*; the **keḱ-*, attested in only Baltic (e.g. Lith *šẽškas*) and Indic (Skt *káśa-*), refers to a 'polecat' or 'weasel' respectively. The original referent may have been specifically the 'polecat' if one accepts the Balto-Slavic-Iranian correspondence (e.g. Latv *luoss*, Rus *láska*,

NPers *rāsū*) that presupposes Proto-Indo-European **lōk̂-* which uniformly designates the 'weasel'. Far more ambiguous is the root **bhel-* which is found in NWels *bele* to mean 'marten', Lat *fēlis* to mean any small carnivore (from marten to wild cat), and just possibly Skt *bharuja-* 'jackal'. It could mean either a 'marten' or a 'wild cat' or possibly some other small carnivore.

The ungulates are the best attested of the mammals. The word for 'horse', *h_1*ék̂wos,* is nearly universal (e.g. OIr *ech*, Lat *equus*, OE *eoh*, Grk *híppos*, Av *aspa-*, Skt *áśva-*, Toch B *yakwe*, HierLuv *azu*(*wa*)-, all 'horse', Lith *ašvíenis* 'stallion', perhaps Arm *ēš* [this may be an unrelated loanword for 'ass'], and perhaps surviving in Alb *sasë* 'horsetail rush, *Equisetum spp*' [presuming a compound where *h_1*ék̂wo-* is the first element]). absent only in Slavic for sure, while the feminine form,*h_1*ék̂weh*$_a$- 'mare', is known from four groups (Lat *equa*, Lith *ešvà* ~ *ašvà*, Av *aspā*, Skt *áśvā-*). The status of the animal, whether wild or domesticated, is a major issue of Indo-European studies and will be dealt with later. The word for the 'ass' (*?*os*(*o*)*nos*) is a long shot that requires a genetic relationship between Lat *asinus*, Grk *ónos*, and Luv *tarkasna-* (if from a compound **tarka-asna-* 'draft-ass'), when there are grounds to suspect that the word was borrowed among these different languages. Far more solid attestation comes for the words for the 'pig', **sūs* (eight groups: e.g. Lat *sūs* 'pig', NE *sow*, Latv *suvēns* 'young pig', Alb *thi* 'pig', Grk *sū́s* ~ *hûs* 'pig', Av *hū-* 'pig', Skt *sūkará-* 'pig, boar', Toch B *suwo* 'pig'), and its young, **pórk̂os* 'young pig, piglet' (e.g. MIr *orc* 'young pig', Lat *porcus* 'young pig', OE *fearh* 'pig' [cf. NE *farrow*], Lith *par̃šas* 'young pig; castrated male hog', Rus *porosënok* 'young pig', Av *pərəsa-* 'young pig'), which appears to derive from a root **perk̂-*'dig, root up the earth' (which is not attested as a verb but which also appears in NE *furrow*); this word was also borrowed into the Uralic languages (e.g. Finnish *parsas* 'pig'). Less certain (only an OIr *torc* and Av *θβərəsa-*, cognate) is **twork̂ós* 'boar'.

The 'red deer' or 'elk' (to North Americans), *h_1*elh*$_1$*ēn,* is well attested in eastern and central Europe and has an Asian cognate in Tocharian which designates 'gazelle' (e.g. Lith *élnis*, Rus *olenĭ*, Grk *élaphos*, all 'red deer', Arm *eln* 'hind', Toch B *yal* 'gazelle'); the larger 'elk' or for North Americans, 'moose', *h_x*ólk̂is,* shows a similar pattern of semantic shift where it means 'elk' in the European languages but refers to 'wild sheep' or 'antelope' among the Asian groups (e.g. NE *elk* [Lat *alcēs* is borrowed from West Germanic], Rus *losĭ* 'elk', Khot *rūś-* '*Ovis poli*', Skt *ŕ̥śya-* 'male of antelope'). This whole group of words is presumably related to *h_1*elu-* 'dull red' (Section 20.4) and the animals denoted by the colour of their hair (cf. the British English designation 'red deer').

Terminology relating to cattle is abundant and includes three different words for 'cow', i.e. *g^w*ṓus* (e.g. OIr *bō*, Lat *bōs*, NE *cow*, Latv *guovs*, ?Alb *ka*, Grk *boûs*, Arm *kov*, HierLuv *wawa-*, Av *gāuš*, Skt *gáu-*, Toch B *keu*, all 'cow', OCS *govęždĭ* 'of cattle'); *$*h_1eĝh$-* (e.g. OIr *ag* 'cow', Arm *ezn* 'cow', Skt *ahī-* 'cow'); and *$*wok̂éh_a$-* (Lat *vacca* 'cow', Skt *vaśā́-* 'cow') with no clear semantic difference between the three although the first is found in virtually all major groups of Indo-European. The male is more specifically designated by *$*uk^{(w)}$sēn-* 'ox' as in OIr *oss* 'stag, cow', NWels *ych* 'ox', NE *ox*, Av *uxšan-* 'bull', Skt *ukṣán-* 'bull', Toch B *okso* 'ox' (another term for 'bull', *$*domh_a$yos* 'one to be tamed; young bull', is known only from Alb *dem* 'bull, steer' and Skt *damya-* '[young bull] to be tamed', and they may be independent creations). The name of the wild cattle of Eurasia, **tauros* (e.g. OIr *tarb* 'bull', Lat *taurus* 'bull', OPrus *tauris* 'bison', Lith *taũras* 'bull; aurochs', Rus *tur* 'aurochs; mountain goat', Grk *taûros* 'bull', Alb *tarok* 'bullock', Khot *ttura-* 'mountain goat'), preserves such a meaning, i.e. 'aurochs' where the aurochs survived as a species until the historic period but otherwise shifted to 'bull', most probably because the aurochs was much larger and more aggressive than early domestic cattle (alternatively, sexual dimorphism among aurochsen was such that the bulls were very much larger than the cows). A more controversial set of possible cognates supports a PIE **usr-* 'aurochs' (which retains such a meaning in Germanic, e.g. OE *ūr* 'aurochs', OHG *ūro* ~ *ūrochso* 'aurochs', but in the putative Indo-Iranian cognates may mean anything from 'bull' to 'camel', e.g. Skt *usrá-* 'bull', *usrā-* 'cow', Pashto *ūṣ̌* 'camel'). It may be significant for emphasizing the long-standing association of Indo-European peoples and their cattle that we can possibly reconstruct a word, *$*g^w$ou-sth$_2$-ó-*, for 'sheltered place where cattle can lie down for the night' on the basis of Skt *goṣṭhá-* 'sheltered place for cattle' and Celtiberian *boustom* '± cattle stall' (presuming these are not independent creations).

The word for 'sheep', *$*h_2$ówis*, comes a close second to the word for 'cow' as it is attested in eleven of the main groups (e.g. OIr *oī* 'sheep', Lat *ovis* 'sheep', NE *ewe*, Lith *avìs* 'sheep', OCS *ovĭnŭ* 'sheep', Grk *óis* 'sheep', Arm *hoviw* 'shepherd', Luv *hāwa/i-* 'sheep', Skt *ávi-* 'sheep', TochB *āu* 'ewe'). The feminine derivative, *$*h_2$o-wikéh$_a$-* 'ewe', is found in three groups (e.g. NWels *ewig* 'hind', OCS *ovĭci* 'ewe', Skt *avikā-* 'ewe') while the young, *$*wr̥h_1$ḗn* 'lamb', is found in Grk *arḗn*, Arm *gaṙn*, Indo-Iranian (Av *varən-*, Skt *urán-*), and perhaps Tocharian (Toch B *yrīye*) and may be a later regional term. A product of the sheep is suggested by **moisós* which can mean both 'ram, sheep' but also 'fleece, skin' (e.g. Lith *maĩšas* 'bag', Rus *mekh* 'skin', Av *maēša-* 'ram', Skt *meṣá-* 'ram, sheep; fleece, skin', Hit *maista-* 'strand of wool'). Reconstruction of a PIE **(s)k̂egos* 'sheep/goat' depends on relating a series of Germanic words (e.g. NE *sheep*, OE *hēcen* 'kid') to a strong set of Indo-Iranian ones (e.g. Oss *sæγ* 'she-goat', Skt *chā́ga-* 'he-goat'). Another word for 'sheep/goat' (*$*h_1$eri-*) gives words for 'lamb/kid' in Grk *ériphos* 'young of a goat', Baltic (OPrus *eristian* 'lamb', Lith *ė̃ras* 'lamb'), Arm *oroǰ* 'lamb', and perhaps Tocharian (Toch B _yrīye_ 'lamb') and words for 'ram' in Italic (e.g. Lat _ariēs_), Indic (Skt _āreya-_), and Tocharian (Toch B _ariwe_); in Celtic the same word is extended to fallow deer (OIr _heirp_ 'she-goat; fallow deer').

Words for 'goat' are never quite so abundantly attested as those for the economically more important 'sheep' but four words can be assigned to Proto-Indo-European antiquity. PIE _*díks_ 'goat' can designate the 'she-goat' in several languages (e.g. OE _ticcen_ 'kid', Alb _dhi_ 'she-goat', ?Grk _díza_ 'she-goat', Ishkashmi [an Iranian language of the Pamirs] _dec_ 'goatskin bag') and a similar range of meaning is associated with _*h_$_a$_eiĝs_ 'goat' with a range of cognates such as Alb _edh_ 'kid', Grk _aíks_ '[she-]goat', Arm _ayc_ '[she-]goat', and Av _izaēnā-_ 'goathide'. All the other terms relate to the male, i.e. _*bhuĝos_ 'buck, he-goat' (OIr _boc_ 'buck', NE _buck_, Arm _buc_ 'lamb', Av _būza-_ '[he-]goat', Skt _bukka-_ '[he-]goat'); _*h_$_a$_eĝós_, which would appear to derive from the verbal root _*h_$_a$_eĝ-_ 'drive' (e.g. Lith _ožỹs_ 'he-goat', Av _aza-_ 'he-goat', Skt _ajá-_ 'he goat'); _*kápros_ (e.g. OIr _gabor_ 'he-goat', Lat _caper_ 'he-goat', OE _hæfer_ 'he-goat', NPers _kahra_ 'kid') which derives from _*kápr̥_ 'penis'; and _*h_$_4$_eli-_ (Toch B _āl_ 'ram, he-goat', Hit _aliyan_(_a_)- 'roebuck'—one should note that roebuck have very undeerlike horns, horns that are closer to those of goats than to those of other deer).

Words associated with the elephant receive some attestation, i.e. _*_(_y_)_ebh-_ 'elephant' (Lat _ebur_, Skt _íbha-_) and _*lebh-_ 'ivory' (Myc _e-re-pa_, Grk _eléphās_ and Hit _lahpa-_). There are those who would claim that they are both Proto-Indo-European (and indicate an Asian homeland), but the word for elephant is close enough to the Egyptian word (_3bw_) to suggest a _Wanderwort_ and objects of ivory were widely traded in the eastern Aegean during the Bronze Age, and borrowing is usually, and surely correctly, suspected here as well.

Regional sets of cognates for mammals include the following: [North-Western] _*k̂ormon-_ 'weasel, ermine/stoat' (e.g. OHG _harmo_ 'stoat', Lith _šarmuõ_ 'wild cat; ermine, weasel'); _*meli-_ 'badger' (Lat _mēlēs_, Slovenian _melc_ 'badger'); _*kat-_ 'cat' (Lat _cattus_, but a late loanword perhaps associated with the spread of the domestic cat from Egypt, cf. Nubian _kadīs_ 'cat', which was in turn widely borrowed by many other European languages); _*márkos_ 'horse' (e.g. OIr _marc_ 'horse', NE _mare_) and attested only in Celtic and Germanic—some would attempt to relate it to words of east Asia, e.g. Mongol _morin_; _*keul-_ 'pig' (Celtic [MWels _Culhwych_, a mythological figure associated with swineherds and boar-hunting] and Baltic [Lith _kiaũle_ 'pig']); _*h_$_1$_elh_$_1$_níh_$_a$- 'hind/cow-elk' (e.g. NWels _elain_, Lith _élnė_, OCS _lani_ ~ _alni_, all 'hind'), the feminine derivative from the more widely attested PIE _*h_$_1$_elh_$_1$_ēn_ 'red deer'; _*wis-_ and/or _*ĝ_(_h_)_ombhros_ 'bison' (the first is found in Germanic, e.g. OHG _wisant_ [whence by borrowing Lat _bisōn_], the second in some of the Baltic languages, e.g. Lith _stum̃bras_, Latv _subrs_, and Slavic, e.g. Rus _zubr_, while OPrus _wis-sambris_ 'bison', combines the two); and _*ghaidos_ 'goat' (e.g. Lat *haedus*, NE *goat*). Those words with a West Central distribution include **meh₁l-* 'small animal' (e.g. OIr *mīl* '(small) animal), NDutch *maal* 'young cow', with an initial *s*-mobile, this root gives us NE *small*, Grk *mêlon* 'sheep, goat'); **dibhro-* ~ **dībhro-* '(sacrificial) animal' (Gothic *tibr* 'sacrifice', OE *tīber* 'offering', MHG *ungezibere* 'vermin' [< 'animals unsuited for the sacrifice']), OHG *zebar* 'offering' [the only form requiring **dibhro-*], Arm *tvar* 'male sheep, herd of cattle'), perhaps a compound whose second member is **bher-* in the latter's meaning of 'offer sacrifice' but the initial part is obscure; **ghḗr* 'hedgehog' (Lat *ēr*, Grk *khḗr*), the regional word in Latin and Greek; **sw(o)r-* or **sworaks* 'shrew' (e.g. Lat *sōrex*, Latv *sussuris*, Bulg *səsar*, Grk *húraks*, all 'shrew'); possibly **(s)koli-* 'young dog' (e.g. Lith *kãle* 'bitch', Alb *këlysh* 'young dog', Grk *skúlaks* 'young dog; young animal'); **wailos* 'wolf' (an Irish-Armenian isogloss, OIr *fāel* 'wolf', Arm *gayl* 'wolf', possible from the 'wail' of the wolf); **dhóh$_a$us* '± wolf' (Phryg *dáos* 'wolf', Grk *thṓs* 'jackal; wild dog; panther', a derivative of which gives Lat *faunus* 'deity of forests and herdsmen' with its neo-Lat *fauna*); **(h$_a$) wiselo-* 'weasel' (e.g. Nir *fial* 'ferret', NE *weasel*) may be a North-Western word if one does not accept a potential Greek cognate (*aiélouros* 'cat; weasel'); **luk̂-* 'lynx' (e.g. OIr *lug*, OE *lox*, Lith *lū́šis*, Rus *rysĭ*, Grk *lúgks*, Arm (pl.) *lusanunk'*, all 'lynx'; NE borrows its *lynx* from Greek rather than continues the inherited form in OE *lox*); **li(w)-* 'lion' (in Slavic, e.g. Rus *lev*, and Greek, i.e. *lís*, the latter suspected by some to be a borrowing from Hebrew *layiw* 'lion'); **mú(k)skos* 'ass/donkey' (e.g. Lat *mūlus* 'mule', ORus *mŭskŭ* 'mule', Grk *mukhlós* 'he-ass'); **h₁eperos* 'boar' (e.g. Lat *aper*, OE *eofor*, Rus *veprĭ*), a North-Western word whose distribution may be extended by a possible Thracian cognate (*ébros* 'buck'); **bhrentós* 'stag' (Germanic-Messapic isogloss, e.g. Swed *brinde* 'stag', Messapic *bréndon* 'stag'), a Celtic-Greek **yórks* 'roedeer' (e.g. NWels *iwrch*, Grk *zórks*); **loh$_a$po-* 'cow' (Baltic-Albanian, i.e. Latv *luõps* 'cow', Alb *lopë* 'cow'); **h$_a$eg^{w}hnos* 'lamb' (Lat *agnus*, NE *yean*, OCS *(j)agnę*, Grk *amnós*); and possibly **koĝhéh$_a$-* 'goat' (Slavic-Albanian, e.g. OCS *koza* 'she-goat', Alb *kedh* 'kid'). There are a handful of words confined to the Indo-European centre such as **mendyos* 'horse' (where the Romanian *mînz* preserves a Dacian word and is compared to Alb *mëz* 'foal') and **ĝhor-* 'young pig' (Alb *derr* 'pig, hog, swine', Grk *khoîros* 'young pig; swine'). There are also several isoglosses that span the centre and east, e.g. **ĝhéyos* 'horse' (Arm *ji* 'horse' and Skt *háya-* 'horse', both derived from **ĝhei-* 'impels, drives'). Several big cat words have exclusively Central and Eastern distributions, e.g. **sinĝhós* 'leopard' (where it means 'leopard' in Arm *inj* ~ *inc* but 'lion' in Skt *siṃhá-*); and **perd-* 'panther, lion' (where there are several Iranian cognates, e.g. NPers *palang*, and Grk *párdalis* which may be a loanword). Finally, there is **gordebhós* 'wild ass', an Eastern word which is attested in Skt *gardabhá-* and Toch B *kercapo*.

Table 9.2. *Birds*

$h_a$ewei-	'bird'	Lat *avis*, Grk *aietós*, Skt *vi-*
**pipp-*	'young bird, nestling'	Lat *pipō*, Grk *pîpos*, Skt *píppakā-*
h_aō(w)i-om	'egg'	Lat *ōvum*, NE *egg*, Grk *ōión*
**ger-*	'crane'	Lat *grūs*, NE *crane*
**kVr-C-*	'crow; raven'	Lat *corvus*, NE *rook*
**wer-*	'crow'	
**kukū*	'cuckoo'	Lat *cucūlus*, NE *cuckoo*
h_an̥$h_a$ti-	'duck'	Lat *anas*, Grk *nêssa*, Skt *ātí-*
**pad-*	'duck, teal?'	
$h_3$or-	'eagle'	NE *erne*, Grk *órnis*
**teter-*	'gamebird'	Grk *tetráōn*, Skt *tittirá-*
**ĝhan-s*	'goose'	Lat *ānser*, NE *goose*, Grk *khḗn*, Skt *haṃsa-*
**kerk-*	'hen'	Grk *kérkos*, Skt *kr̥ka-vā́ku-*
$h_1$epop	'hoopoe'	Lat *upupa*, Grk *épops*
**kik̂-(y)eh$_a$-*	'jay'	Grk *kíssa*, Skt *kiki-*
$h_{2/3}$uh$_1$e/olo-	'owl'	NE *owl*
?**b(e)u-*	'owl'	Lat *būbō*, Grk *búas*
?**ulu-*	'owl'	Lat *ulu(c)us*, Skt *úlūka-*
**sper-*	'?sparrow'	NE *sparrow*, Grk *sparásion*
(s)ter-	'stork'	NE *stork*
(s)p(e)iko/eh$_a$-	'bird, woodpecker'	Lat *pīcus*, Skt *piká-*

9.3 Birds

The primary word for 'bird' (*$h_a$ewei-*) is well attested and found in Celtic (e.g. NWels *hwyad* 'duck'), Italic (e.g. Lat *avis* 'bird'), Alb *vida* 'dove', Grk *aietós* 'eagle', Arm *haw* 'bird; chicken', Indo-Iranian (e.g. Av *vīš*, Skt *vi-*). As we can see, it reveals semantic shifts to a variety of very different species, e.g. 'duck', 'dove', 'chicken', and 'eagle'. The word for the young bird, **pipp-*, is transparently onomatopoeic (e.g. the Latin derivative means 'peep') and is attested in Slavic (e.g. Slov *pípa* 'hen), Alb *bibë*, Grk *pîpos* 'young bird', and Indic (Skt *píppakā-*) as well. The word for 'egg', *h_aō(w)i-om* (attested in Celtic (e.g. NWels *wy*), Italic (e.g. Lat *ōvum*), Germanic (e.g. German *Ei*), Slavic (e.g. OCS *ajĭce*), Grk *ōión*, and Iranian (e.g. Av *-āvaya* 'having eggs'), is suspiciously close to the primary word for 'bird' (*$h_a$ewei-*) and, indeed, a fairly transparent derivative of it; if so, it provides a proxy answer to the age-old question since here the bird came first and the egg second. NE *egg* does not derive directly from the proto-form (as did *ǣg* in OE) but is a loanword from Old Norse (see Section 13.2 for 'nest').

The name of the 'crane' (**ger-*) is one of the better-attested bird names and is found in Celtic (e.g. NWels *garan*), Italic (Lat *grūs*), Germanic (e.g. NE *crane*), Baltic (e.g. Lith *gérvė*), Slavic (e.g. Rus *žeravlĭ* 'crane, goose'), Arm *kṙunk*, and, securing an Asian cognate, Oss *zyrnæg*. The word for 'crow', **kVr-C-*, is more problematic in that it is clearly onomatopoeic and the root vowel is unclear. It is attested in Italic (e.g. Lat *corvus*), Germanic (e.g. NE *rook*), Slavic (Bulg *krókon*), Grk *kóraks*, and Skt *karaṭa-* ~ *karāva-*. The same root, probably independently, gave rise to other bird names such as MIr *cerc* 'brood hen' (see below). The second word for 'crow', **wer-*, is found in Baltic (e.g. Lith *várna*), Slavic (e.g. Rus *voróna*), and Tocharian (Toch B *wrauña*). Almost the ultimate in onomatopoeia is the name for the 'cuckoo', **kukū*, attested in Celtic (e.g. OIr *cūach*), Italic (e.g. Lat *cucūlus*), Germanic (e.g. NE *cuckoo*), Baltic (e.g. Lith *kukúoti* 'to cuckoo'), Slavic (e.g. Rus *kukúša*), Grk *kókkuks*, Arm *k(u)ku*, and Indo-Iranian (e.g. NPers *kuku*, Skt *kokilá-*). Similar words are found in other language families, e.g. Akkadian *kugu* and Turkish *guguk*.

There are two words for 'duck'. The first, **h_an̥$h_a$ti-*, is found in Italic (Lat *anas*), Germanic (e.g. OE *ened*), Baltic (e.g. Lith *ántis*), Slavic (e.g. Rus *útka*), Grk *nêssa*, Iranian (e.g. Oss *acc* 'wild duck'), and Indic (Skt *ātí-*); the second, **pad-*, is less certain as it is attested primarily in modern languages, e.g. Spanish *pato* and SC *patka* are the sole representatives of Italic and Slavic respectively; it is also known from Arm *bad* 'drake' and NPers *ba*. Similar sounding names occur in Arabic and Georgian (e.g. *batti*) and this similarity suggests onomatopoeia. In other words, Indo-European ducks probably did not say 'quack, quack' but rather 'pad, pad'.

The name of the 'eagle', **$h_3$or-*, is preserved with the meaning 'eagle' in five groups, i.e. Celtic (e.g. OIr *irar*), Germanic (e.g. NE *erne*), Baltic (e.g. Lith *erẽlis*), Slavic (e.g. Rus *orël*), and Anatolian (Hit *hāras*); derivatives are also found in Grk *órnis* 'bird', and Arm *urur* 'kite', *oror* 'gull', and *ori* 'raven'. The word does survive in Modern English but citation of *erne* would send most readers to an English dictionary.

The precise meaning of **teter-* is uncertain but the range of meanings suggests a large gamebird such as the capercaillie, pheasant, or partridge; it is attested in Celtic (MIr *tethra* 'hooded crow'), Germanic (e.g. ON *þiðurr* 'capercaillie'), Baltic (e.g. Lith *tetervà* 'capercaillie'), Slavic (e.g. OCS *tetrěvĭ* 'pheasant', Rus *teterev* 'capercaillie'), Grk *tetráōn* 'capercaillie', Iranian (NPers *tadharv* 'pheasant'), and Indic (Skt *tittirá-* 'partridge'). The 'goose', **ĝhan-s*, is well attested and is found in Celtic (e.g. OIr *gēis*), Italic (e.g. Lat *ānser*), Germanic (e.g. NE *goose*), Baltic (e.g. Lith *žąsìs*), Slavic (e.g. Rus *gusĭ*), Grk *khḗn*, and Indic (Skt *haṃsa-* 'waterfowl'); some have derived it from the verbal root **ĝhan-* 'gape, yawn'. The 'hen', **kerk-*, which appears in Europe *c.* 3000 BC, is found in Celtic (MIr *cerc* 'brood hen'), dialectal Grk *kérkos* 'rooster',

Iranian (Av *kahrka-* 'hen'), Indic (Skt *kr̥kara-* 'a kind of partridge', *kr̥kavā́ku-* 'rooster'), and Tocharian (Toch B *krañko* 'chicken'); obvious is the suggestion that the name of the bird may be onomatopoeic (compare NE *cluck*) and so its reconstruction is not entirely certain. Unquestionably onomatopoeic is the name of the 'hoopoe', $*h_1$*epop*, which is found in Italic (Lat *upupa*), Germanic (e.g. NE *hoopoe*), Baltic (e.g. Lith *pupú̃tis*), Slavic (e.g. Pol *hupek*), Grk *épops*, Arm *popup*, and Iranian (NPers *pūpū*). In Aristophanes' *Birds*, the hoopoe cries '*epopoi popopopopopopopoi*'. The name of the 'jay', **kiḱ-(y)eh*$_a$*-*, is found in Italic (only in Italian *cissa*), Germanic (e.g. OE *hig(e)ra*), Grk *kíssa*, and Skt *cisa-* 'roller'. The names of the 'owl' are expectedly onomatopoeic, i.e. $*h_{2/3}$*uh*$_1$*e/olo-* in NE *owl*, NHG *Eule* 'owl', and Hit *huwalas* 'owl'; *?*b(e)u-* in Italic (Lat *būbō*), Slavic (Bulg *buk*), Grk *búas*, Arm *bu* ~ *bueč*, and Iranian (NPers *būm*) and *?*ulu-* (Italic, i.e. Lat *uluc(c)us*, and Indic, i.e. Skt *úlūka-*). 'Sparrow' is probably too specific for **sper-* which means 'sparrow' only in Germanic but 'crow' in Celtic (Corn *frau*), 'starling' in dialectal Grk *sparásion*, and some form of unidentified bird in Tocharian (e.g. Toch A *ṣpār*). The name of the 'stork', **(s)ter-*, would be confined to Germanic (e.g. NE *stork*) if it were not for the cognate form *tarlā* which occurs in Hittite; under one proposal there may also be cognates in Greek and Indic. Finally, **(s)p(e)iko/eh*$_a$*-* means 'woodpecker' in Italic (Lat *pīcus* 'woodpecker' but *pīca* 'jay; magpie') and Germanic (e.g. OHG *speh* 'woodpecker') but 'Indian cuckoo' in Indic (Skt *piká-*).

There are about a dozen regional names of birds. From the North-West we have $*h_a$*emes-l-* 'blackbird' (e.g. NWels *mwylach*, Lat *merula*, OE *ōsle* [> NE *ousel*]); **kap-* 'hawk, falcon' (e.g. NE *hawk*, Rus *kóbec* '[type of] falcon') derived from **kap-* 'seize'; **ḱarh*$_x$*keh*$_a$*-* 'magpie' which is found only in Baltic (e.g. Lith *šárka*) and Slavic (e.g. Rus *soróka*); the onomatopoeic **kắu-* 'howl; owl' (NWels *cuan*, OHG *hūwo*); **storos* 'starling' (Lat *sturnus*, NE *starling*, OPrus *starnite* 'gull'); and **trosdos* 'thrush' (e.g. Lat *turdus*, NE *thrush*, Lith *strãzdas*, Rus *drozd*, and perhaps Grk *stroûthos*). From the West Central area we have **bhel-* 'coot' (e.g. Lat *fulica*, OHG *belihha*) which has a Greek cognate as well (*phalarís*); **(s)pingo-* 'finch' (NE *finch*, Grk *spíggos* 'finch') but perhaps Proto-Indo-European if one accepts Skt *phingaka* 'shrike' as cognate; $*h_1$*orh*$_x$*deh*$_a$*-* which is some form of waterbird such as the 'heron' (e.g. Lat *ardea* 'heron', ON *arta* 'teal', SC *róda* 'stork', Grk *(e)rōdiós* 'heron; stork'); and $*h_1$*el-* 'waterbird, swan' (e.g. OIr *ela*, Lat *olor*) which has a questionable Greek cognate indicating the 'reed warbler' (*eléā*); **kopso-* 'blackbird' is confined to Slavic (e.g. OCS *kosŭ*) and Grk *kópsikhos*. **g*^{w}*l̥tur-* 'vulture' is found in Lat *voltur* ~ *volturis* ~ *volturus*, and Greek *blosur-ōpis* 'vulture-eyed'. A Greek-Armenian-Indo-Iranian isogloss is found in **ḱyeino-* 'bird of prey, kite?' (Grk *iktînos*, Arm *c'in*, Av *saēna-* 'eagle', Skt *śyená-* 'eagle') while the name of the 'quail', **wortok*^{w}*-*, is a Greek-Indic isogloss (Grk *órtuks*, Skt *vartaka-*).

9.4 Fish, Reptiles, and Amphibians

The reconstructed vocabulary pertaining to fish in Proto-Indo-European is quite small, and even when words are reconstructable, the precise meaning may be quite ambiguous. It is an area of the Indo-European vocabulary where Asian cognates are so few that one cannot even reconstruct a generic word for 'fish' that meets our full requirements of Proto-Indo-European. The general word for 'fish' with the widest potential distribution is **pik̂sk̂os* 'fish' with cognates in Celtic (e.g. OIr *īasc*), Lat *piscis*, Germanic (e.g. NE *fish*), and Skt *picchā-* 'calf of the leg'. The Indic cognate is semantically far removed but is commonly justifed on the widespread folk association of the calf of the leg with the belly of a fish filled with roe. The word is generally derived from **pik̂-sk̂o-* 'spotted' or the like, a derivative of **peik̂-* 'paint, mark', and the original referent is taken to be the 'trout' which, given its ubiquity across Eurasia, developed into the more general meaning of 'fish'. Other cognate sets include a word for 'carp', **k̂óph$_a$elos*, which is attested in Baltic and Old Indic only (e.g. Lith *šãpalas* 'chub', Latv *sapalis* 'chub, Dvina-carp', Skt *śaphara-* 'carp'). A PIE **ghérsos* is attested in Germanic (e.g. Norw *gjørs* 'pikeperch'), Slavic (e.g. Rus *zérekh* 'asp'), and possibly Indic with a wide range of meanings (e.g. Skt *jhaṣá-* 'a kind of large fish'). Equally problematic is *?*k̂ónkus* which depends on comparing the ON *hār* 'shark' with an Indic word referring to some kind of aquatic animal or fish (Skt *śankú-*). Far more secure is **lók̂s* which is attested in Germanic (e.g. OE *leax* 'salmon', OHG *lahs* 'salmon' [> NE *lox*]), Baltic (e.g. Lith *lãšis* 'salmon'), Slavic (e.g. Rus *losósĭ* 'salmon'), Arm *losdi* 'salmon trout', Iranian (Oss *læsæg* 'salmon trout'), and Tocharian (e.g. Toch B *laks*, where it has become the general word for 'fish'), although its specific referent, be it the Atlantic salmon (*Salmo salar*) or the salmon trout (*Salmo trutta*), has been the subject of major debate, similar in many ways to the beech-argument summarized in Chapter 10. Proponents of the first meaning employed the reconstructed word for 'salmon' to set the Indo-European homeland adjacent

Table 9.3. *Fish, reptiles, amphibians*

**pik̂sk̂os*	'trout, fish'	Lat *piscis*, NE *fish*, Skt *picchā-*
**k̂óph$_a$elos*	'carp'	Skt *śaphara-*
**ghérsos*	'asp' or 'pikeperch'?	
*?*k̂ónkus*	'a kind of fish'	Skt *śankú-*
**lók̂s*	'salmonid, salmon(trout)'	cf. NE *lox*
**(s)k^{w}álos*	'sheatfish, wels'	Lat *squalus*, NE *whale*
**h$_1$óg^{w}his*	'snake'	Grk *ékhis*, *óphis*, Skt *áhi-*

to the Baltic Sea while those preferring the anadromous types of salmon trout took it to indicate the Black or Caspian seas. Attempts to also include a range of Indic cognates (e.g. *lākṣā-* 'lac', if < *'reddish' < *'salmon-coloured') have also been widely discussed. The precise meaning of **(s)k^wálos*, reconstructed on the basis of Italic (Lat *squalus* '± shark'), Germanic (e.g. NE *whale*), Baltic (OPrus *skalis* 'sheatfish'), Greek (dialectal Grk *áspalos* 'fish'), and Iranian (e.g. Av *kara-* 'a kind of fish'), is not entirely secure, but the large 'sheatfish' whose meaning is attested in Middle High German and Baltic is far more probable than 'whale'; the Greek and Iranian cognates simply refer to some kind of fish.

The only reptile securely reconstructed is the 'snake', **h_1ó$g^wh$is*, which is retained in Celtic (e.g. NWels *euod* 'sheepworm'), Germanic (e.g. OHG *egala* 'leech'), Greek (e.g. *ékhis* 'viper', *óphis* 'snake'), Arm *iž* 'snake, viper', Iranian (e.g. Av *aži-* 'snake'), Indic (Skt *áhi-* 'snake'), and probably Tocharian (Toch B *auk*).

There are some regional cognate sets for some of the fish, reptile, and amphibian names. From the North-West we have: **krek-* 'fish eggs, frogspawn' in Germanic (e.g. ON *hrogn* 'roe'), Baltic (e.g. Lith *kurkulaĩ* 'frogspawn'), and Slavic (e.g. Rus *krjak* 'frogspawn'); the NE *roe* is a loanword from Old Norse which does exhibit the cognate form); *?* h_aeḱú-* 'perch' is found in Germanic (e.g. ON *ǫgr* 'sea-bass') and Baltic (e.g. Lith *ešerỹs* ~ *ašerỹs* 'perch') but, as the word derives from **h_aeḱ-* 'sharp' (the perch has spiny fins), it may have been independently created in the two groups. The same root underlies **h_aeḱe(tro)-* 'sturgeon' (e.g. Lat *acipēnser*, Lith *eškėtras*, Rus *osëtr*); **str̥(h_x)yon-* means 'sturgeon' in Germanic (e.g. OE *styri(g)a*) but refers to the 'salmon' in Celtic (Lat *sariō*, borrowed from Gaulish). An alternative name for the 'snake', **né$h_1$tr-* ~ **n$h_1$tr-* 'snake', is found in OIr *nathir* [gen. *nathrach*] 'snake' (which indicates retention of a name that transcended Irish geography although not necessarily experience as snakes are native to neighbouring Britain), Lat *natrix* 'watersnake; penis', Goth *nadrs* 'snake, viper', OE *nædre* 'adder' [ME *a nadder* > NE *an adder*]); a Western innovation meaning 'the twister' from **sneh_1-* 'twist, turn'.

In the West Central region we have a generic word for 'fish', **dhĝhuh_x-*, in Baltic (e.g. Lith *žuvìs*), Grk *ikhthûs*, and Arm *jukn* which exhibits an archaic shape that suggests it may have been the word for 'fish' in Proto-Indo-European but was replaced by other words on the extremities of the Indo-European world. The root **mn̥h_x-* (e.g. NE *minnow*, Rus *menĭ* 'burbot', Grk *maínē* '*Maena vulgaris*') appears to have meant something like 'minnow; small fish'. The word for 'eel', **h_xVnghel-*, is reasonably widely attested with cognates in Italic (Lat *anguilla*), Baltic (e.g. Lith *ungurỹs*), Slavic (e.g. OCS *ǫgulja*), and Grk *égkhelus*. A second word for the 'sheatfish', **ḱámos*, is found in Baltic (e.g. Lith *šãmas*), Slavic (Rus *som*), and Grk *kamasếnes* [pl.] 'a kind of fish'. The distribution of a word for the 'tench', *(*s*)*lei-*, is built on the root of the same shape meaning 'slimy' and is well attested in Baltic (e.g. Lith *lýnis*) and Slavic (e.g. Rus *linĭ*), possibly in Grk *lineús* 'blemy'; Germanic uses the same root to form the word for 'tench, mullet' (e.g. OE *slīw*) but this may be an independent creation. The name of the 'frog', **worh*$_x$*d-i/o-*, is found in Baltic (Latv *var̃de*) and Arm *gort*; a similar word (**worh*$_x$*do-*) gives us the words for 'wart' in Germanic (e.g. NE *wart*), Baltic (e.g. Latv *ap-vir̃de* 'abscess'), Slavic (e.g. Rus *véred* 'abscess'), and Iranian (e.g. NPers *balū* 'wart') which suggests that the association between warts and frogs is quite old. Another regional name for 'snake', i.e. **h*$_a$*éng*^{w}*his*, is found in Celtic (OIr *esc-ung* 'watersnake'), Italic (Lat *anguis*), Germanic (OHG *unc* 'snake'), Baltic (e.g. Lith *angìs* 'snake'), Slavic (Rus *už* 'snake'), Illyr *ábeis* 'snakes', and Arm *awj* 'snake' while **ghéluh*$_x$*s* 'tortoise' is found in Slavic (e.g. OCS *žely*) and Grk *khélus*. If we were able securely to reconstruct the tortoise to Proto-Indo-European, we would have another marker for the Proto-Indo-European homeland, in that the tortoise is not found further north than southern Scandinavia and central Russia. However, there are abundant reasons otherwise for not assuming a far northern homeland for the Proto-Indo-Europeans and thus the reconstructibility of the tortoise does not tell us much. Finally, playing loose with our strictly zoological classification, we can note that **dr̥k̂-* 'dragon' is attested in Celtic (MIr *muirdris* 'sea-monster') and Grk *drákōn* 'dragon' (whence, via Latin, NE *dragon*); it derives from the verbal root **derk̂-* 'see' as the dragon fixes its opponent with its baleful gaze.

9.5 Insects, Worms, and Shellfish

The reconstructable names of IE insects are largely a list of nuisances rather than an indication of economic importance. The nuisance factor suggests a certain emotional valence associated with a number of the insects which may well account for many of the phonologically irregular outcomes and metaphorical shifts to other referents. For example, there is no single stable word for 'ant' but rather three different (and clearly related) forms: **morwi-* supplies Celtic (e.g. OIr *moirb*), Slavic (e.g. OCS *mravi*), and Iranian (Av *maoirī*); **morm-* underlies the forms in Lat *formīca* and Grk *múrmos*; **mouro-* gives us the Germanic (ON *maurr*); while even more distorted is **worm-* which gives us an alternate Greek form *hórmikas*, Skt *valmī́ka-*, and Toch B *warme*. Despite the variety of forms, all are agreed in indicating the 'ant'. There has also been considerable change in the articulation of **plus-* 'flea'. The Latin word, for example, requires metathesis from **plusek-* to **puslek-* to achieve the historical

Table 9.4. *Insects, shellfish, etc.*

**morwi- ~ *morm- ~ *mouro-*	'ant'	Lat *formīca*, Grk *múrmos*, Skt *valmī́ka-*
**plus-*	'flea'	Lat *pūlex*, ?Grk *psúlla*, NE *flea*, Skt *plúṣi-*
**mok̂o-*	'gnat, stinging insect'	Skt *maśaka-*
**ĝelu-*	'leech'	Skt *jalūkā-*
lu-* (lus-*)	'louse'	NE *louse*, Skt *yū́kā*
**rik-*	'nit, tick'	Lat *ricinus*, Skt *likṣā́*
*$h_{2/3}$*wobhséh*$_a$-	'wasp'	Lat *vespa*, NE *wasp*
*k^w*r̥mis*	'worm, insect'	Skt *kŕ̥mi-*
**mat-*	' ± worm, maggot, insect'	NE *moth*, Skt *matkuṇa-*
**km̥h*$_a$*ros*	'crayfish'	Grk *kámaros*
**kark-*	'crab'	Lat *cancer*, Grk *karkínos*, Skt *karkaṭa-*
**k̂onkh*$_a$*os*	'mussel (-shell) etc'	Grk *kógkhos*, Skt *śaṅká-*

form of **pūlek*; and the possible Greek cognate would seem to require a development **plusy(e)h*$_a$- > **psuly(e)h*$_a$ - > *psúlla*. Baltic and Slavic go one further (e.g. Lith *blusà*, OCS *blŭcha*) and require **blusyeh*$_a$-. The precise designation of the **mok̂o-* eludes us although all cognates are agreed in using this word to designate some stinging insect. Lith *mãšalas* and Skt *maśaka-* can both mean 'gnat' (the Sanskrit word can also refer to the mosquito) but MPers *makas* refers to the 'fly' and Latv *masalas* to the 'horsefly'. Again we find dialectal variation in a by-form without a palatal, i.e. **moko-* which gives Lith *mãkatas* 'gnat' and Skt *mákṣ-* 'fly'. An Indo-Iranian form was borrowed into Finno-Ugric to provide the name for the 'bee', e.g. Hungarian *méh* 'bee'. A word for the 'leech', **ĝelu-*, depends on a Celtic-Indo-Iranian cognate set, e.g. OIr *gil* and Skt *jalūkā-*, both 'leech', which apparently derives from a verbal root **ĝel-* 'swallow'. The word for 'louse', *lu-*, has seen massive reshaping with more expected outcomes from Celtic (NWels *llau*) and Germanic forms such as NE *louse* but dialectal forms such as Lith *víevesa*, Rus *voši*, and Skt *yū́kā*. The young of the louse, the 'nit' (**rik-*), is reconstructed on the basis of an Italic-Indo-Iranian set, e.g. Lat *ricinus*, Skt *likṣā́*. Well attested is the *$h_{2/3}$*wobhseh*$_a$- 'wasp' with cognates in Celtic (e.g. MWels *gw(y)chi* 'drones'), Italic (Lat *vespa*), Baltic (e.g. OPrus *wobse*), Slav (e.g. OCS *osa*), and Iranian (e.g. MPers *vaβz-*); the noun derives from the verbal root *$h_{2/3}$*webh-* 'weave', i.e. one who weaves a wasp nest. The PIE *k^w*r̥mis* is perhaps best translated as a 'wug', i.e. a category that comprises both worms and bugs. It has a 'worm' meaning in many of the cognates, e.g. Celtic (OIr *cruim*), Baltic (Lith *kirmìs*), Slavic (OCS *črĭvĭ*), Alb *krimb*, and Indo-Iranian (e.g. Skt *kṛ́mi-*) but it can also designate anything from a 'mite' (OPrus *girmis*) to a 'dragon' (Lith *kirmìs*). The PIE **mat-* also has a wide range of meanings and yields both OE *maða* 'worm, maggot' and OE *moþþe* (> NE *moth*) as well as Arm *mat'il* 'louse' and Av *maδaxa-* 'grasshopper'.

The **kṃ$h_a$ros* is reflected with absolute phonological regularity in both Grk *kámaros* and ON *humarr*. In both languages it means 'lobster' but such a meaning cannot be correct for Proto-Indo-European, almost no matter where it was originally spoken. The only reasonable hypothesis is that the word meant 'crayfish' in Proto-Indo-European, and in both Germanic and Greek, as these groups adopted a maritime orientation, the word was transferred to the larger, and more important, lobster. A reconstructed **kark-* 'crab' is based on Lat *cancer* (< **karkro-*?), Grk *karkínos*, and Skt *karkaṭa-* (< **karkṛto-*) and *karkī-* 'cancer (as a sign of the zodiac)'. Another possible crustacean is the **k̂onkh$_a$os* 'mussel' and any related shellfish. The main cognate set is Grk *kógkhos* 'mussel(shell)' and Skt *śaṅká-* '(conch)shell' (with Latv *sence* 'mussel' as a derived form).

The North-West offers **bhi-k^{w}ó-* 'bee, stinging insect' on the basis of cognates in Celtic (e.g. OIr *bech*), Germanic (e.g. NE *bee*), and Slavic (e.g. OCS *bĭčela*) and, with a different suffix in **-tih$_a$-* we have Baltic cognates such as Lith *bìtė*; the underlying etymology is **bhei(h$_x$)-* 'strike, attack'. We also have a word associated with the product of the 'bee', **wos(h$_x$)-ko-* 'wax' (NE *wax*, Lith *vãškas* 'wax', OCS *voskŭ* 'wax'). For the 'butterfly' we have **pelpel-* with related forms in Lat *pāpiliō* and Germanic (e.g. OE *fīfalde*) that have been clearly altered. Etymologically transparent is **k̂ṛh$_a$sro-(h$_x$)on-* 'hornet' from **k̂ṛh$_2$s-* 'horn' with cognates in Lat *crābrō*, Germanic (NDutch *horzel*), Baltic (e.g. Lith *šìršė*), and Slavic (e.g. OCS *sĭrsenĭ*), all 'hornet'. Finally, there is **webhel-* ~ **wobhel-* 'weevil, beetle' seen in Germanic (e.g. NE *weevil*), Baltic (e.g. Lith *vãbalas*), and Slavic (Rus *veblica* '(intestinal) worm'). The West Central area offers a range of insect names: there are several words for the 'drone' such as the clearly onomatopoeic **dhren-* 'drone' (< 'buzz') found in Germanic (e.g. NE *drone*, Grk *thrṓnaks*) and **kṃh$_x$p-h$_a$-* 'drone' which is meagrely attested in OHG *humbal* and Grk *kēphḗn*; **mus/h$_x$-* 'fly; gnat, midge, mosquito' with cognates in Italic (Lat *musca*), Baltic (e.g. Lith *muša*), Slavic (e.g. OCS *mŭšĭca*), Grk *muîa*, and Arm *mun*; *?*kóris* ' ± biting insect' where the root **(s)ker-* 'cut' is believed to underlie OCS *korĭ* 'moth' and Grk *kóris* 'bed-bug'; **h$_1$empis* 'gnat, stinging insect' which is debatedly attested in OE *ymbe* 'swarm of bees' and a possible cognate Grk *empís* 'gnat'; **g^{w}elōn* 'insect's stinger' found in Baltic (e.g. Lith *geluõ* 'stinger') and Grk *déllithes* 'wasps'; **k̂(o)nid-* 'nit, louse egg' which is well attested with cognates in Celtic (e.g. OIr *sned* 'nit'), Germanic

(NE *nit*), Baltic (e.g. Lith *glìnda*), Slavic (Rus *gnída*), Alb *thërije*, Grk *konís*, and Arm *anic*; *h_x*orki*- 'tick' with cognates in Baltic (e.g. Lith *érkė*), and Arm *ork'iwn*; **diĝ(h)*- 'tick' found in Celtic (MIr *dega* 'stag beetle'), Germanic (e.g. OE *ticia*), and Arm *tiz*; **sleimak*- 'snail, slug' from a root *(*s*)*lei*- 'be slimy' which gives Rus *slimák* 'snail' and Grk *leímaks* 'slug'; and **wr̥mis* 'worm, insect' which overlaps phonologically with one of the 'ant' words above but also yields Lat *vermis*, NE *worm*, Lith *var̃mas* 'mosquito', OCS *vermije* 'grasshoppers', and Grk *rhómoks* 'woodworm'. Finally, there are several words restricted to the Central region: **melítih*$_a$- 'honey-bee' where one of the words for honey, **mélit*, provides the basis for Alb *bletë* and Grk *mélissa*, both 'honey-bee'; *h_x*orghi*- 'nit', a regional variant of *h_x*orki*- which is seen in Alb *ergjëz* and Arm *orǰil*; and **demelís* 'worm' or whatever will cover the proto-meaning of Alb *dhemjë* 'larva, caterpillar, maggot' and Grk *demeléas* 'leeches'.

9.6 Indo-European Fauna

The roster of animal names reconstructed to Proto-Indo-European is more extensive than that for plants and we can ascribe about seventy-five names to various animal species. This roster does not come anywhere close, however, to the numbers encountered in the lexicons of traditional societies. Brent Berlin examined a sample of seventeen languages which yielded an average of 435 names of animals per language. Be that as it may, Proto-Uralic also has a sizeable number with about sixty names altogether. It is instructive then to compare the structure of the two reconstructed lexicons in terms of the major orders of animals identified (excluding general names) (Table 9.5).

The differences between the two reconstructed lexicons derive primarily from the difference in the respective economies. The Proto-Indo-Europeans possessed a Neolithic economy with extensive references to domestic livestock

Table 9.5. *Animal names in Proto-Indo-European and Uralic*

	PIE	%	URALIC	%
Mammals	42	56	15	25
Birds	17	23	20	33
Fish	6	8	9	15
Reptiles/amphibians	1	1	2	3
Insects etc.	9	12	14	22
Total	75		60	

(cattle, sheep, goat, pig; possibly horse) while the Proto-Uralics were primarily hunter-gatherer-fishers. It is natural then that the Proto-Uralic vocabulary would reflect these differences with a limited number of mammals (four words for reindeer, marten, hare, fox, squirrel, etc.), and a more extensive vocabulary pertaining to birds (about a third of the words refer to some form of duck) and fish.

The designation of animals has been the focus of taxonomic studies and Cecil Brown has proposed a stadial sequence of expected animal names. Stage 1 lacks any 'life form' term (or word naming a large general category of living beings such as 'mammal', 'fish', etc.) while stages 2 to 4 see the addition of 'fish', 'bird', and 'snake' (in any order) and stages 5 and 6 see the introduction of a specialized term for 'mammal' and 'wug'. We have already used this term to define PIE **kʷr̥mis* as an animal that comprises both worms and bugs (it might be noted that *insect* did not appear in English until after 1600 and from 1650 it defined a 'wug'). Earl Anderson suggests that Proto-Indo-European was a stage 4 language where it lexicalized terms for 'bird' (**h$_a$ewei-*), fish (**dhĝhuh$_x$-*, **pik̂sk̂ŏs*), and 'snake' (**h$_1$ógʷhis*) and had a covert category, i.e. one without a linguistic label, for 'mammal' whose existence is predicated by the fact that Proto-Indo-European made a further (Level Ia) distinction between 'wild animal' (**ĝhwēr*) and 'domestic animal' (**pék̂u*). In some instances we may be in doubt as to whether the word had a generic or more specific meaning. For example, NE *deer*, which today specifies a cervid, derives from OE *dēor* which also covered the meaning 'wild animal' (cf. the cognate NHG *Tier* 'animal'). Multiple meanings or polysemy have been widely observed in animal taxonomies where the name of a focus animal may serve at both the species and a much higher level. That **pik̂sk̂os* may have originally designated the 'trout' and was then abstracted to 'fish' in general is a possible example. Similarly PIE **lók̂s* 'salmon trout' becomes Toch B *laks* 'fish'.

In their major study of Indo-European culture, Gamkrelidze and Ivanov proposed a hierarchical classification of plant and animal life forms in Proto-Indo-European that makes the distinction seen above between 'wild' (**ĝhwēr*) and 'domestic animal' (**pék̂u*). The wild animals are then divided into three classes depending on mythic location, i.e. an Upper World (birds), Middle World (beasts), and Lower World (vermin, snakes, fish). The domestic animals (which includes humans) are distinguished into rational and speaking humans (with their own subclasses) and quadrupeds. The latter are distinguished as those which are ritually close to humans and which may then be divided into those that are horned (cattle, ovicaprids) and not-horned (horse, donkey); the ritually distant animals are the dog, pig, and cat. Anderson regards such a system as too complex in comparison with those evident throughout the world and finds it unusual for any system to classify humans (and gods) along with animals. On the other hand, it does encompass a series of oppositions or polarities that may have formed either covert or lexicalized slots in Proto-Indo-European, e.g. **k̂érh̥$_2$s* and related words for 'horn' vs. **k̂em-* 'hornless'

As for the wild mammalian fauna, our ability to reconstruct words hardly recovers all the animals likely to have been distinguished in the proto-language. Certain species are found so widely over Eurasia that they should have been familiar to the Proto-Indo-Europeans irrespective of where their homeland lay. These would include the mole, bat, a variety of rodents (voles, mole rats, etc.), the badger, and the wild cat. The twenty or so bird names (compare this with the fact that the ancient Greeks knew over 500 bird names!) comprise those that were probably economically salient, e.g. ducks and geese, those that were culturally salient, e.g. eagle, and those where onomatopoeia has supported their survival, e.g. hoopoe.

The ten or so fish and shellfish names are extremely meagre (the ancient Greeks knew at least 570 names and even such a damaged resource as Old Prussian can return twenty-five) nor are they particularly revealing of the location of the IE homeland, although names such as 'salmon' and 'eel' have been employed to do just that. The salmon or 'Lachsargument' as it is known in German was, along with the beech-argument (see Chapter 10), one of the pivots of a north European homeland for the Indo-Europeans under the presumption that PIE **lók̂s* indicated specifically the Atlantic salmon (*Salmo salar*) that frequented the waters of the Baltic and North Atlantic. More recent opinion has suggested that **lók̂s* simply indicated a salmonid for which the salmon trout (*Salmo trutta*) was the more likely original referent and that it was later extended to include the Atlantic salmon by the ancestors of the Germans, Balts, and Slavs. Salmon trout are much more widely found across Eurasia than the Atlantic salmon.

The extensive vocabulary concerning domestic animals is pivotal in establishing, along with the words for cereal agriculture, that the Proto-Indo-Europeans possessed a mixed economy based on livestock and arable agriculture, i.e. had achieved at least a Neolithic mode of subsistence. The presence of two words for what was probably the domestic pig, i.e. **sūs* and **pórk̂os*, suggests that the economy was not, at least originally, that of pastoral nomads, as swine are notoriously difficult to herd over long distances. On the other hand, within any culture, and especially an area as large as that probably inhabited by the earliest Indo-Europeans, there might have been a wide range of economic regimes that also included various degrees of mobility.

In addition to the pig, ovicaprids, the sheep and goats, are also of special interest because these were not native (in their wild state) to much of the later Indo-European world prior to the expansion of the Neolithic economy from

South-West Asia. The route by which sheep spread into Europe certainly included the Balkans and probably also the Caucasus (to the steppelands); much less likely, although sometimes suggested, was the eastern Caspian steppe (to account for early Neolithic sheep in the southern Urals). Terms for sheep such as *$h_2$ówis* (and also 'wool' as we will see in Chapter 14) are virtually ubiquitous across the IE world and that ubiquity can only be explained with reference to the spread of a language whose speakers possessed stock-raising (and wool-procuring) skills.

Of all the (potentially) domestic animals, the main focus of debate has often been the status of *h_1éḱwos* 'horse'. That some form of horse can be ascribed to the earliest Proto-Indo-Europeans (and with Anatolian cognates in Hieroglyphic Luvian *azu(wa)-* and Lycian *esbe-* we may include the concept of Indo-Hittite) seems secure. Also secure is the importance of the horse in the cultures of the earliest IE groups and their mythologies and rituals. What is not secure, however, is whether we can reconstruct *h_1éḱwos* as 'domestic horse' or simply 'horse' and, in the event that we can reconstruct the proto-meaning as 'domestic horse', whether we can locate in space and time the location of the earliest domestic horses. The linguistic evidence for 'domestic horse' is not strong (nor could it be since there is no absolutely clear linguistic marker of a domestic animal) and relies primarily on the contrast between the feminine form, also of PIE date, which employs an *-*eh_a*- suffix (i.e. *h_1éḱweh$_a$*- 'mare') which stands in opposition, some argue, to the feminine of a more certain wild animal, the 'she-wolf' (**wl̥kʷih$_a$*-) with an *–*ih_a*- suffix. All other arguments rest on non-linguistic matters such as the presumed location of the homeland, the nature of its economy, and the apparent 'depth' at which the concept of a domestic horse appears to be embedded in Indo-European culture, e.g. in rituals, personal names. In terms of the prehistoric exploitation of the horse, the major centre would appear to be across the steppe and forest-steppe from the Dnieper east to the Ural and somewhat beyond, and this is generally the region where most would place the earliest domestication of the horse in the fifth or fourth millennium BC (there are heated arguments as to precisely when and what constitutes clear evidence). Remains of presumably wild horses are known outside the steppelands in Iberia, Atlantic, and northern Europe to the Danube; some horse remains have also been recovered from Early Neolithic Anatolia. There is a general absence of horse remains until the Bronze Age in Greece, most of the Balkans, and Italy. The lack of the horse in these regions has been pressed by some to suggest that the Indo-Europeans were hardly likely to have been resident in these areas until the Bronze Age.

Further Reading

Basic coverages of Indo-European fauna can be found in Schrader–Nehring (1917-28), Gamkrelidze and Ivanov (1995), Mallory–Adams (1997). General surveys of livestock can be seen in Benveniste (1949), Diebold (1992), and Blažek (1992). Useful articles on individual species include: bear (Delamarre 1992), beaver (Hamp 1972*b*), cow (Zimmer 1981), deer (Adams 1985*a*, Witczak 1994*a*), dog (Schlerath 1954, Hamp 1980*a*, Melchert 1989), fox (Adrados 1985, Schrijver 1998), horse (Hänsel and Zimmer 1993, Hamp 1990*c*, Bonfante 1996, Huld 2004, Parvulescu 1993*b*; for horse domestication, see Levine 2005), lion (Adams 1984), pig (Benveniste 1973*b*, Hamp 1987*a*), sheep (Hamp 1984*a*, 1987*b*, Lindeman 1990*a*), squirrel (Hamp 1972*c*), wolf (Klimas 1974, McKone 1985, Lehrmann 1987). The IE fauna is discussed archaeologically in Mallory 1982.

The word for 'bird' and 'egg' is treated in Schindler (1969); other species include the blackbird (Hamp 1982*a*), duck (Hamp 1978), hen (Schlerath 1953), thrush (Hamp 1981*a*), and birds from both an Indo-European and archaeological viewpoint in Mallory (1991).

Literature on the fish includes Adams (1985*b*), Bammesberger (1996), Diebold (1976, 1985), Hamp (1973*a*), Krause (1961), Krogmann (1960), Sadowsky (1973), Seebold (1985), Sevilla Rodriguez (1989), Thieme (1954), and Winter (1982); from an archaeological viewpoint see Mallory (1983).

The 'bee' is the subject of Hamp (1971*a*).

For folk taxonomies see Anderson (2003), Berlin (1992), Brown (1984); the count of Greek bird and fish names is based on Thompson (1895, 1947); the Uralic evidence is derived from Häkkinen (2001).

10

Indo-European Flora

10.1 Trees

As with animals, there is also an extensive reconstructed vocabulary relating to the various forms of plant life in Proto-Indo-European.

The general name for 'tree', **dóru*, is attested in eleven different groups, either under its root form (e.g. OIr *daur* 'oak', Grk *dóru* 'tree trunk; wood; spear'. Hit *tāru* 'tree, wood'. Av *dāuru* 'tree, tree trunk; wooden weapon'. Skt *dā́ru* 'wood'. Toch AB *or* 'wood') or in derivation (NE *tree* is a derived form as are, e.g. Grk *drûs* 'tree, oak', OCS *drŭva* 'wood', Alb *dru* 'wood, tree', *drushk* 'oak', OCS *drěvo* 'tree'). In Celtic and Greek, it tends to mean specifically the 'oak' and has religious connotations, e.g. a *druid* is a 'tree-knower'. The word for 'forked branch', *$\hat{k}\acute{o}h_1k\bar{o}h_2$ (e.g. Goth *hōha* 'plough', Lith *šakà* 'branch', Rus *sokhá* '(primitive) plough', Arm *c'ax* 'branch', NPers *šāx* 'branch', Skt *śā́khā* 'branch'), has secondary meanings as 'plough' in a number of languages as primitive ploughs were originally made from forked branches. The concept of plough also extended to another of the 'branch' words, **k̂ank-* (e.g. OIr *cēcht* 'plough', NWels *cainc* 'branch', ON *hār* 'thole-pin', Lith *atšankė̃* 'barb; crooked projection from a tree', Rus *suk* 'branch, knot', Skt *śankú-* 'peg'). The third word for 'branch' reconstructable to Proto-Indo-European is *h_2*ósdos* (e.g. OHG *ast* 'branch', Grk *ózos* 'shoot', Arm *ost* 'branch', Hit *hasduēr* 'twigs, branches') which has been analysed by some as a compound of the verb *sed-* 'sit', i.e. *h_2*o-sd-os* 'what one sits upon', the branch from the

Table 10.1. *Trees*

*dóru	'wood, tree'	NE *tree*, Grk *dóru*, Skt *dā́ru*
*k̂óh_1kōh_2	'(forked) branch'	Skt *śā́khā*
*k̂ank-	'branch'	Skt *śankú-*
*$h_2$ósdos	'branch'	Grk *ózos*
*$h_4$loĝ-	'branch'	Grk *ológinos*
*$h_x$ósghos	'knot (in wood)'	Grk *óskhos*, Skt *ádga-*
*bhlh_ad-	'leaf'	NE *blade*
*$h_a$ógeh_a-	'± berry, fruit'	NE *acorn*
*g^welh_a-	'acorn'	Lat *glāns*, Grk *bálanos*, Skt *gula-*
?*sap- /*sab-	'sap'	NE *sap*, Lat *sapa*, Skt *sabur-dhúk-*
*g^wétu	'pitch'	NE *cud*, Lat *bitūmen*, Skt *játu*
*sok^wós	'sap, resin'	Grk *opós*
*werno/eh_a-	'alder'	Skt *varaṇa-*
*$h_a$éliso-	'alder'	NE *alder*, Lat *alnus*
*$h_a$ebVl-	'apple'	NE *apple*
*me$h_2$lom	'apple'	Lat *mālum*
*$h_3$es(k)-	'ash'	NE *ash*, Lat *ornus*, Grk *oksúē*
*$h_{2/3}$osp-	'aspen, poplar'	NE *aspen*, ?Skt *sphyá-*
*bherh_xĝos	'birch'	NE *birch*, Lat *farnus/fraxinus*, Skt *bhūrjá-*
*wi(n)ĝ-	'elm'	NE *wych-*[*elm*]
*pteleyeh_a-	'elm?'	Lat *tilia*, Grk *pteléā*
*dhonu-	'fir'	NHG *Tannenbaum*
*péuk̂s	'(Scotch) pine, conifer'	Grk *peúkē*
*k̂óss	'(Scotch) pine'	Grk *kônos*
*pit(u)-	'(some form of) conifer'	Lat *pīnus*, Grk *pítus*, Skt *pītu-*
*$h_2$ed(h)-	'hawthorn'	
*h_2ēkr̥	'maple'	Lat *acer*, Grk *ákastos*
*mórom	'blackberry'	Lat *mōrum*, Grk *móron*
*weit-	'willow'	Lat *vītis*, Grk *ītéā*, Skt *veta-*
*$h_1$eiwos	'yew'	NE *yew*
*taksos	'yew'	Lat *taxus*, Grk *tókson*

bird's point of view so to speak. The fourth word for 'branch', *$h_1$loĝ-, also seems at times to cover the notion of 'vine, tendril' as well (e.g. Rus *lozá* 'vine, tendril, shoot', dialectal Grk *ológinos* 'branchy', Av *razura-* 'forest, thicket', Hit *alkista*(*n*)-'branch'). The place where the branch joins the tree, the 'knot' or 'joint', was *$h_x$ósghos (e.g. OIr *odb* 'knot', Grk *óskhos* 'sucker, sprout, vine branch', NPers *azy* 'branch'. Skt *ádga-* 'knot, joint'). The word for 'leaf', *bhlh_ad-, is restricted to Germanic (e.g. NE *blade*) and Tocharian (e.g. Toch B *pilta* 'leaf'). The word for some type of 'fruit', *$h_a$ógeh_a-, probably underlies

NE *acorn* (and e.g. Lith *úoga* 'berry', Rus *jágoda* 'berry', Toch A and B *oko* 'fruit'). The 'acorn' itself, *g^w*elh*$_a$*- (e.g. Lat *glāns*, Lith *gìlė*, Rus *želudĭ*, Grk *bálanos*, Arm *kalin*, Skt *gula-*), has the secondary connotation of the 'head of the penis' (*glāns penis*) in Latin (and medical English) and Indic (where it is the only meaning; and, no, we have no evidence for circumcision in Proto-Indo-European) and the presence of this word assures us that the Proto-Indo-European community was acquainted with the 'oak', even though a general Proto-Indo-European word specifically meaning 'oak' is not recoverable. One word for 'sap', **sap-* (e.g. Lat *sapa* 'must, new wine boiled thick', OHG *saf* 'sap'), has a variant **sab-*, which gives NE *sap* and a possible Indic cognate (*sabur-dhúk-* 'yielding nectar or milk') which would give this word Proto-Indo-European status. A second 'sap' or 'pitch' word is *g^w*étu* (e.g. Lat *bitūmen* 'mineral pitch, bitumen', OE *cwidu* ~ *cudu* 'mastic' [> NE *cud*], Skt *játu* 'lac, gum') and shows relationships with the birch tree in NWels *bedw* 'birch' and Lat *betulla* 'birch' (< Gaulish) wherein the latter is the 'sap-tree' because of the use of birch sap as a food or as a glue. Finally we have **sok^{w}ós* 'sap, resin' seen in Lith *sakaĩ* [pl.] 'resin', Rus *sok* 'juice, sap, sapwood', Alb *gjak* 'blood', Grk *opós* 'sap, resin', and Toch B *sekwe* 'pus'.

The number of trees strongly attested to the level of genus or species is not great because, as we have seen above, the environments of Europe and Asia often differ significantly so that recovery of a common tree name is made more difficult. An additional difficulty with the Asian side of the equation is that the attested records of Tocharian provide almost no tree names so our Asian evidence is restricted to Indo-Iranian.

The word for 'alder', **werno/eh$_a$*- (e.g. MIr *fern* 'alder', Alb *verr* 'alder', Arm *geran* 'alder'), does have an Indic cognate (i.e. Skt *varaṇa-* '*Crataeva roxburghii*') whereas the secure Proto-Indo-European status of **h$_a$ éliso-* (e.g. Lat *alnus*, Lith *alìksnis*, Rus *ólĭkhna*) depends on acceptance of Hit *alanza(n)* 'type of tree' as cognate (and that would depend on the exact meaning of the Hittite word which is not yet recoverable); a Proto-Germanic **aluzo-* gives us NE *alder*. Some argue that **h$_a$ éliso-*, if not reflected in Hittite, is actually a substrate term picked up by the Indo-Europeans in central and western Europe.

Both words for 'apple' may be regional terms of the West and Centre of the Indo-European world and are only extended to Proto-Indo-European if one accepts in the case of **h$_a$ebVl-* (e.g. OIr *uball*, NE *apple*, Lith *obuolỹs*, Rus *jábloko*, all 'apple') some possible Indo-Iranian cognates (e.g. Pashto *maṇá* 'apple', if from **amarna-* <**abarna-*) and in the case of **meh$_2$lom*, the Hittite word *mahla-* which may only mean 'grapevine' (cf. also Lat *mālum*, Grk *mêlon*, Alb *mollë* [borrowed from Latin or Greek?], all 'apple').

Similarly, the status of **h$_3$es(k)-* 'ash' outside of the West Central region (e.g. OIr *uinnis* 'ash', Lat *ornus* 'mountain ash' (*Sorbus aucuparia*), NE *ash*, Lith *úosis* 'ash', Rus *jásenĭ* 'ash', Alb *ah* 'beech', Grk *oksúē* 'beech; spearshaft') depends on acceptance of Hit *hassikk-* 'some form of tree with edible fruit'. As the ash was a preferred wood for shafts, it often also carries the meaning 'spear(shaft)'.

The word for 'aspen', *$h_{2/3}$osp-* (e.g. NE *aspen* (*Populus tremula, P. alba*), Lith *apušė̃* 'ash (*P. nigra*)', Rus *osína* 'ash (*P. tremula*)', Arm *op'i* 'poplar (*P. alba*)', is Proto-Indo-European if one accepts Indo-Iranian cognates that denote an 'oar' or 'shovel' (e.g. NPers *fih* 'oar', Skt *sphyá-* 'oar, pole, shovel').

The 'birch' word, *bherh$_x$ĝos* (e.g. Lat *farnus/fraxinus* 'ash', NE *birch*, Lith *béržas* 'birch', Rus *berëza* 'birch', Oss *bærz* 'birch', Skt *būrjá-* 'birch'), is generally derived from an adjective meaning 'bright, shine' and has a long association in several Indo-European groups with virginal purity. Gamkrelidze and Ivanov have used this connection to suggest that Hit *parku-* 'ritually pure; innocent' actually derives from the word for 'birch' although the Hittites had lost the arboreal term itself.

A Kurdish (Iranian) cognate, *viz* 'a kind of elm', helps secure *wi(n)ĝ-* 'common elm (*Ulmus glabra*)' to Proto-Indo-European rather than a West Central word (cf. NE *wych-elm*, Lith *vìnkšna* 'elm', Rus *vjaz* 'elm', Alb *vidh* 'elm'). There may be a second word for 'elm' in *pteleyeh$_a$- /pteleweh$_a$-* (e.g. MIr *teile* 'linden', Lat *tilia* 'linden', Grk *pteléā* 'elm', *ptélas* 'wild rowan', Arm *t'eli* 'elm', Oss *færwe* 'alder') but the wide range of meanings makes one cautious.

The word for 'fir' (**dhonu-*) is secured by a German-Hittite correspondence (OHG *tanna* 'fir' [> NHG *Tannenbaum*], Hit *tanau* 'fir') but the other conifers depend largely on the evidence of more recently attested Indo-Iranian languages to secure their ascription to Proto-Indo-European. Thus we have **péuk̂s* 'pine' (or some combination of 'pine', 'fir', and/or 'spruce'—and likewise with the next two words) attested in OIr *ochtach* 'pine, fir', OHG *fiuhte* 'fir', Lith *pušìs* 'pine, fir', Grk *peúkē* 'pine, spruce', and, on the Asian side, Waigali *puc* 'species of pine'. **k̂óss* 'pine' by itself is seen only in OE *haraþ* 'wood' and Khot *sara-cara* '*Barleria cristata*', but in the derivative **k̂e/osno-* in OE *cēn* 'torch (of resinous pinewood)', Rus *sosná* 'pine', Grk *kōnos* 'pinecone', *kōna* 'pitch', *kṓneion* 'hemlock', Khot *sānā-* '*Celosia cristata*'. Finally, **pítu-* 'pine' is to be seen in Lat *pīnus*, Alb *pishë* 'spruce, pine, fir', Grk *pítus* 'pine, spruce', and Skt *pītu-* 'deodar-tree'.

The word for 'hawthorn', *$h_2$ed(h)-*, is secured by an Old Irish (**ad-*, genitive *aide*)-Hittite (*hat(t)-alkisnas*) set, both of which also have ritual or magic connotations.

There is one word at least for 'maple', *h_2ēkr̥*, attested by Lat *acer* 'maple', OHG *ahorn* 'maple', Grk *ákastos* 'maple', Hit *hiqqar* '± maple'. The word for 'blackberry', **mórom*, in many languages also serves for the 'mulberry' (NWels *merwydd* 'mulberry', Lat *mōrum* 'mulberry, blackberry', Grk *móron* 'mulberry, blackberry', Arm *mor* 'blackberry', Hit *muri-* '[bunch of] grapes').

'Willow', **weit-*, is well attested in nine groups and frequently displays a meaning 'withies' or anything that might be produced from bending osiers, e.g. felloes of a tyre (e.g. OIr *fēith* 'some kind of twining plant', Lat *vītis* 'vine', NE *withy*, Lith *vytìs* 'willow', Rus *vítina* 'branch', Grk *ītéā* 'willow', Av *vaēiti-* 'willow', Skt *veta-* 'reed').

The primary word for 'yew' (**$h_1$eiwos*) is restricted to naming the tree (e.g. OIr *ēo* 'yew', OPrus *iuwis* 'yew', Lith *ievà* 'bird cherry', Rus *íva* 'willow', Hit *eya(n)-* '±yew'). The second of the 'yew' words, **taksos*, has shifted in meaning to 'bow' in Greek and Iranian (e.g. Lat *taxus* 'yew', Rus *tis* 'yew', Grk *tókson* 'bow', NPers *taxš* 'bow'). This shift is not surprising, given the well-known excellence of yew-wood for the manufacture of bows.

If one does not accept some of the more dubious Eastern cognates, some of the Proto-Indo-European tree names are only North-Western or West Central in distribution. There are also many regional words in their own right. From the North-West we have **widhu* 'tree, forest' (e.g. OIr *fid* 'tree', NE *wood*); **k^wrésnos* 'tree; brush(wood)' (e.g. OIr *crann* 'tree', Grk *prînos* 'holm-oak [*Quercus ilex*]'); **skwēis* '±needle and/or thorn' (e.g. OIr *scē* 'hawthorn', Lith *skujà* 'fir-needle and cone', Rus *khvojá* 'needles and branches of a conifer'); **ghabhlo/eh$_a$-* 'fork, branch of tree' (e.g. OIr *gabul* 'fork', OE *gafol* 'fork' [> NE *gavel*]); **kneu-* 'nut' (e.g. OIr *cnū* 'nut', Lat *nux* 'nut', NE *nut*); **$h_1$élem* 'mountain elm (*Ulmus mantana*)' (e.g. MIr *lem* 'elm', Lat *ulmus* 'elm', NE *elm*, Rus *ílem* 'mountain elm'); **kós(V)los* 'hazel' (e.g. OIr *coll* 'hazel', Lat *corulus* 'hazel', NE *hazel*, Lith *kasùlas* 'hunter's stick, spear; bush'); **kléinus* 'maple' (e.g. OE *hlīn*, Lith *klēvas*, Rus *klën*, Maced *klinó(s)trokhos*—possibly West Central if a potential Greek cognate, *glīno-* 'a type of maple', is accepted); **pérk^{w}us* 'oak' (Gaulish *érkos* 'oak-forest', Lat *quercus* 'oak [particularly *Quercus robur*]', ON *fjor* 'tree'); *?*pr̥k$^{(w)}$eh$_a$-* 'pine' (Italian *forca*, NE *fir*); a questionable **dhergh-* 'sloetree, blackthorn' (e.g. OIr *draigen* 'sloetree', OHG *dirn-baum* 'cornel cherry', Rus *derën* 'cornel cherry'); **sal(i)k-* '(tree) willow' (e.g. OIr *sail* 'willow', Lat *salix* 'willow', OE *sealh* 'willow').

From the West Central region comes **némos-* '(sacred) grove' (e.g. OIr *neimid* 'sacred grove', Lat *nemus* 'sacred grove', Old Saxon *nimidas* 'sacred grove', Grk *némos* 'wooded pasture, glade'); **$h_x$óiwo/eh$_a$-* '± berry, fruit' (Lat *ūva* 'bunch of grapes, fruit', Grk *óā* 'service-berry', Arm *aygi* 'grapevine'); *?*sre/oh$_a$gs* '± berry, fruit' (Lat *frāga* 'strawberries', Grk *hrṓks* ~ *hrā́ks* 'berry, grape'); **lóubho/eh$_a$-* 'bast, bark' (e.g. Lith *luõbas* 'rind, bark', Rus *lub* 'bast, bark', Alb *labë* 'rind, bark, crust', and related Lat *liber* 'bast; book' [because bast, especially beech-bast, provided an early writing medium], OHG *louft* 'bark, bast'); **wr(h$_a$)d-* 'root; branch' (e.g. Lat *rādīx* 'root', *rāmus* 'branch', Grk *hrā́dix* 'branch; palm-frond', ON *rōt* 'root' [NE *root* is borrowed from Old Norse], OIr *frēn* 'root', OE *wyrt* 'herb, plant' [> NE *-wort*], Grk *hríza* 'root', and perhaps Toch B *witsako* 'root'); **gwésdos* 'branch' (e.g. OHG *questa* 'tuft of branches', OPol *gwozd* 'mountain forest', Alb *gjeth* 'leaf'); **gol-* 'branch' (Rus *golíjá* 'branch', Arm *kolr* 'branch'); **wr̥b-* 'branch, sprig, twig' (e.g. Lat *verbēna* 'leaves and saplings for sacral use', Lith *vir̃bas* 'twig, switch', Grk *hrábdos* 'twig, rod'); **bhóliom* 'leaf' (e.g. Lat *folium*, Grk *phúllon* 'leaf; plant'); **dhal-* 'sprout' (e.g. NWels *dail* 'leaf', Alb *dal* 'arise, appear, emerge', Grk *thállō* 'bloom', Arm *dalar* 'green'); **$h_2$er-* 'nut' (e.g. Lith *ruošutỹs* 'nut', Rus *orékh* 'nut', Alb *arrë* 'walnut, nut tree', dialectal Grk *árua* 'nut') perhaps Proto-Indo-European if Hit *harau-* 'poplar' is cognate but the Hittite meaning is certainly distant; **g^wi$h_3$wo-* 'resin, pitch' (i.e. the plant's 'living material' from **g^wyeh_3-* 'live'; *cf.* OIr *bī* 'pitch', Rus *živicá* 'soft resin', Arm *kiv* 'tree pitch, mastic'); **pik-* 'pitch' (Lat *pix* ~ *picea* 'tar, pitch', OCS *picĭlŭ* 'tar, pitch', Grk *píssa* 'tar, resin'—this word may be related to one of the designations for conifers (**peuḱ-*) in Proto-Indo-European); **kle-$h_a$dhreh_a-* 'alder' (dialectal NHG *Lutter* 'mountain alder', Grk *klḗthrā* 'sticky alder'); **bheh_aĝós* 'beech' (e.g. Gaul *bāgos* '?beech', Lat *fāgus* 'beech', OE *bōc* 'beech; book' [> NE *book*], *bēce* [> NE *beech*], Alb *bung* 'durmast oak [*Quercus petraea*]', Grk *phēgós* 'Valonia oak [*Q. aigilops*]'), and perhaps Rus *buz* 'elder' but phonologically and semantically irregular; **kr̥nom* 'cherry' (Lat *cornus* 'cornel cherry', Lith *Kìrnis* 'divine protector of the cherry', Grk *krános* 'cherry'); **(s)greh_ab(h)-* 'hornbeam' (e.g. Umb *Grabovius* 'oak god', OPrus *wosi-grabis* 'spindle-tree', Lith *skrõblas* 'hornbeam', Rus *grab* 'hornbeam', Modern Grk *grabúna* 'hornbeam', and possibly Lat *carpīnus* 'hornbeam'); **$h_1$elew-* 'juniper, cedar' (Rus *jálovec* 'juniper', Grk *elátē* 'pine, fir', Arm *elevin* 'cedar'); **lenteh_a-* 'linden' (e.g. NE *linden*, Lith *lentà* '(linden) board', Rus *lut* '(linden) bast', Alb *lëndë* 'wood, material'); **$h_a$ebi-* 'fir' (e.g. Lat *abiēs* 'silver fir', dialectal Grk *ábis* 'fir'); **wikso-* 'mistletoe, birdlime' (e.g. Lat *viscum* 'birdlime', OHG *wīchsila* 'black cherry [*Prunus cerasus*]', Rus *víšnja* 'cherry', Grk *iksós* 'mistletoe'); **$h_a$eig-* 'oak' (NE *oak*, Grk *aigílōps* 'Turkey oak (*Quercus cerris*)', and perhaps Lat *aesculus* 'mountain oak [*Quercus farnetto*]'); **weliko/eh_a-* 'willow' (NE *willow*, Grk *elíkē* 'willow').

10.2 Wild Plants

The vocabulary of the wide variety of non-arboreal taxa of the Proto-Indo-European world has barely survived except for those plants specifically associated with agriculture which we will examine separately. A series of vague meanings, e.g. 'marsh-grass', 'flower', 'field', contribute to the vagueness of the proposed semantics of **$h_2$éndhes-* '±flower' (e.g. Fris *åndul* 'marsh-grass',

Table 10.2. *Plants (non-domesticated)*

*$h_2$éndhes-	'±flower'	Grk *ánthos*, Skt *ándhas-*
*$h_a$er-	'reed'	Lat *harundō*, Grk *áron*
**nedós*	'reed, rush'	Skt *nadá-*
**tr̥nu-*	'thorn'	NE *thorn*, Skt *tŕ̥ṇam*
*k̂ólh$_x$ōm	'stalk, stem, straw'	Lat *culmus*, Grk *kálamos*
*$h_a$enkulos	'shoot'	Skt *aṅkurá-*

Alb *ëndë* 'flower', Grk *ánthos* 'flower', Arm *and* 'field', Skt *ándhas-* 'a herb; the soma plant; grassy ground'). There are at least two words for 'reed': *$h_a$er- generally preserves the general meaning of 'reed' or 'rush' (Lat *harundō* 'reed', Grk *áron* 'arum', Khot *arā-* 'reed, rush') while **nedós* sees the Arm cognate *net* make the unsurprising shift to 'arrow' (cf. also Lith *néndrė* 'reed', Luv *nātatta-* 'reed', NPers *nai* 'reed', Skt *nadá-* '±reed'). The ascription of 'thorn' as the proto-meaning of **tŕ̥nu-* relies heavily on the evidence from Germanic (e.g. NE *thorn*) and Slavic (e.g. OCS *trŭnŭ* 'thorn') as Indo-Iranian exhibits a meaning 'grass' (e.g. Khot *tarra-* 'grass', Skt *tŕ̥ṇam* 'grass'; Finnish *tarna* 'sedge, grass' is borrowed from some early form of Indo-Iranian). The word for 'stalk' or 'stem', *k̂ólh$_x$ōm, is found in six groups, including Tocharian (e.g. Lat *culmus* 'stalk, stem, straw', OE *healm* 'stalk, stem, straw', Latv *salms* 'stalk, stem, straw', Rus *solóma* 'stalk, stem, straw', Grk *kálamos* 'reed', Toch A *kulmänts-* 'reed, rush'). A possible word for 'shoot', PIE *$h_a$enkulos, rests on a pair of cognates comprising ON *ōll* 'bud, shoot' and Skt *aṅkurá-* 'young shoot' that may derive from the verbal root *$h_a$enk- 'bend'.

Other plant names are more regionally confined as follows. [North-Western] **k̂wéndhr/no-* 'angelica' (e.g. SGael *contran* 'wild angelica', Lat *combretum* [an unidentified aromatic plant]. ON *hvonn* '*Angelica silvestris*'). Lith *švéndras* 'reed; reed-mace'; ?*bhloh$_x$dho- 'flower' (e.g. MIr *blāth* 'flower', OHG *bluot* 'flower', a derivative gives us NE *blossom*); **bhel-* 'henbane' (Gaul *belénion*, OE *beolone*, Rus *belená*); **mēus* 'moss, mould' (e.g. Lat *muscus* 'moss', NE *moss*, Lith *mùsos* [pl.] 'mould', Rus *mokh* 'moss'); **yoinis* 'reed, rush' (e.g. MIr *aīn* 'reed', Lat *iuncus* 'reed', *iūniperus* 'juniper', ON *einir* 'juniper'); [West Central] **kemeros* '± hellebore' (e.g. OHG *hemera* 'hellebore', Lith *kemẽras* 'marigold', ORus *čemerŭ* 'hellebore', Grk *kámaros* 'larkspur'); **ned-* 'nettle' (e.g. MIr *nenaid* 'nettle', NE *nettle*, Grk *adíkē* 'nettle', Lith *nõterė* 'nettle', Slovenian *nât* 'nettle'): *meh$_a$k- 'poppy' (OHG *maho* ~ *mago*, OPrus *moke*, Rus *mak*, Grk *mḗkōn*, all 'poppy'); **trus-* 'reed, rush' (e.g. Lith *tr(i)ušis* 'reed, horsetail', Rus *trostĭ* 'reed, cane', Grk *thrúon* 'reed, rush'); ?**don-* 'reed' (Latv *duonis* 'reed', Grk *dónaks* 'reed'); **kaulós* 'stalk' (e.g. Lat *caulis* 'stalk', OPrus *caules* 'thorn', Lith *káulas* 'bone', Grk *kaulós* 'stalk'); **wreh$_a$gh-* 'thorn' (e.g. MIr *fraig* 'needle', Lith *rãžas* 'dry stalk, stubble; prong of fork', Grk *hrākhós* 'thorn-hedge', *hrákhis* 'spine, backbone'); **alogh-* 'thorn' (e.g. SC *glog* 'thorn', Grk *glôkhes* [pl.] 'beard of grain', *glōkhīs* 'point, end', *glôssa* 'tongue'); and [Eastern] *?*g(h)rewom* 'reed, rush', which is attested only in Av *grava-* and Tocharian (e.g. Toch A *kru*).

10.3 Domesticated Plants

There are two words for 'field'. The first, **h$_2$érh$_3$wr̥* (e.g. OIr *arbor* 'seed', Lat *arvum* 'ploughed field', Grk *ároura* 'field', Arm *haravunk'* 'field'), can be assigned to Proto-Indo-European if one accepts the somewhat irregular Indo-Iranian cognates, e.g. Skt *urvárā-* 'fertile soil', and its underlying meaning is a ploughed field as it derives from **h$_2$érh$_3$w-* 'plough'. The second term (**h$_a$eĝros*) has caused much discussion as the European cognates indicate a cultivated field (e.g. Lat *ager*, OE *æcer* [> NE *acre*], Grk *agrós*, Arm *art*, all 'field') while the Skt *ájra-* means simply 'plain' with no indication of agriculture. This divergence of meaning led to the proposal that the Indo-Iranians separated from the Europeans before they had gained agriculture so that we might posit a pastoral Indo-Iranian world and an agricultural European. Such a distinction is not borne out by the abundant evidence that Indo-Iranians also shared in an agricultural vocabulary, e.g. the Iranian descendants of **k̂āpos* indicate a cultivated field, e.g. Roshani (an Iranian language of the Pamirs) *sēpc* 'cultivated field' (compare OHG *huoba* 'piece of land', Grk *kêpos* 'garden'). The word for 'meadow', **wélsu-* (e.g. Hit *wēllu-*), includes the Grk *Elysian* (*ēlúsios*) fields and would appear to be derived from one of the Proto-Indo-European words for 'grass', namely **wel-* (e.g. NWels *gwellt* 'grass', OPrus *woltis* 'head of grain', Hit *wellu(want)-* 'grass'), as 'grassy place' or the like.

There are a number of words for 'grain' that are difficult to specify further. For example, **h$_2$ed-* gives Lat *ador* 'emmer wheat', Goth *atisk* 'grain field', Arm *hat* 'grain', Sog *āδuk* 'crop, cereals', but Lyc *χθθahe* 'hay, fodder', Toch B *atiyo* 'grass'; **ses(y)ó-* gives 'barley' in NWels *haidd* but 'rye' in Ligurian (*asia*) and 'grain' in other languages (e.g. Hit *sesa(na)-* 'fruit', Av *hahya-* 'providing grain', Skt *sasyám* 'grain, fruit'). The meanings of **yéw(e)s-* are similarly disparate and although it does indicate 'barley' in Hit *ewan*, NPers *ǰav*, and Skt *yáva-* 'grain, especially barley', it means 'wheat' in Grk *zeiaí* 'einkorn or emmer wheat' and 'millet' in Oss *jæw* and Toch B *yap* (if from **yébom* by manner of dissimilation from **yéwom*) as well as the less specific 'grain' in other languages (e.g. Lith *javaĩ*, Av *yava-*). The word derives from the verbal root **yeu-* 'ripen, mature' while another root **ĝerh$_a$-* 'ripen' underlies **ĝr̥h$_a$nóm* 'grain' (e.g. OIr

Table 10.3. *Domesticated plants*

*$h_a$érh$_3$wr̥	'field'	Lat *arvum*, Grk *ároura*, Skt *urvárā-*
*h_aeĝros	'field, pasture'	NE *acre*, Lat *ager*, Grk *agrós*, Skt *ájra-*
*k̂āpos	'piece of land, garden'	Grk *kêpos*
?*wélsu-	'meadow, pasture'	Grk *ēlúsios*
*wel-	'grass'	
*$h_2$ed-	'cereal crop, grass'	Lat *ador*
*ses(y)ó-	'grain, fruit'	Skt *sasyá-*
*yéw(e)s-	'grain'	Grk *zeiaí*, Skt *yáva-*
*ĝr̥$h_a$nóm	'grain'	NE *corn*, Lat *grānum*
*dhoh$_x$néh$_a$-	'(harvested) grain'	Skt *dhānā́s*
*dr̥h$_x$weh$_a$-	'±grain'	NE *tare*, Skt *dū́rva-*
?*$h_{2/3}$(e)lĝ(h)-	'grain' (or 'millet'?)	Grk *áliks*
*prók̂som	'grain'	
*$h_a$ek̂es-	'ear of grain'	NE *ear*, Lat *acus*, Grk *ákhnē*
*$h_a$ek̂stí-	'±awn, bristle'	
*pelo/eh$_a$-	'chaff'	Lat *palea*, Skt *palā́va-*
*ĝhrésdh(i)	'barley'	Lat *hordeum*, Grk *krīthḗ*
*$h_2$élbhit	'barley'	Grk *álphi*
*meiĝ(h)-	'barley' ('grain'?)	
?*pano-	'millet'	
*kéres-	'millet, grain'	Lat *cerēs*
*rughis ~*rughyo-	'rye'	NE *rye*
*$h_a$ewis	'oats'	Lat *avēna*
*$h_a$éreh$_a$-	'±ryegrass'	Grk *aírai*, Skt *erakā-*
*ālu-	'±esculent root'	Lat *ālium*, Skt *ālú-*
*k̂eh$_1$kom	'edible greens' (< *'foliage'?)	Skt *śā́ka-*
?*kaulós	'±cabbage'	Lat *caulis*, Grk *kaulós*
*sepit	'wheat'	
*ga/ondh-	'wheat'	
*wóinom	?'wine'	Lat *vīnum*, Grk *oînos*

grān, Lat *grānum*, NE *corn*, Lith *žìrnis* 'pea', OCS *zrĭno*, Alb *grurë* 'wheat', Pashto *zaṇnai* ~ *zaṛai* 'kernel, seed'). PIE *dhoh$_x$néh$_a$- is found in Baltic (e.g. Lith *dúona* 'bread'), Iranian (e.g. NPers *dāna* 'grain'), Skt *dhānā́s* [pl.] 'kernels of grain, fried grain reduced to powder', and Toch B *tāno* 'grain, kernel'). It has been argued that in distinction from terms indicating a species of grain such as *yéwos, *dhoh$_x$néh$_a$- refers specifically to grain processed for consumption, i.e. 'cereal' in the sense of 'breakfast cereal'. A fifth word for 'grain', *dr̥h$_x$weh$_a$-, may not be a word for 'grain' at all but rather for 'tare' (e.g. Gaul *dravoca* 'darnel, ryegrass', NDutch *tarwe* 'wheat', Skt *dū́rva-* 'panic-grass' [related to millet]). A sixth possible word for 'grain' (or perhaps 'barley' or even 'millet') is *$h_{2/3}$*(e)lĝ(h)-* (Hit *halki-* 'barley; grain', NPers *arzan* 'millet', Grk *áliks* 'spelt' [borrowed from some Anatolian language?]); Toch B *lyekśye* 'barley' has also been suggested as a possible cognate. Another 'grain/millet' word is seen in Slavic. e.g. Rus *próso* 'millet', and Toch B *proksa* [pl.] 'grain', reflecting PIE **prok̂som* [sg.] ~ **prok̂seh*$_a$ [pl.]. The word for 'ear of grain', **h*$_a$*ek̂es-*, is attested in three European languages (e.g. Lat *acus*, NE *ear*, Grk *ákhnē*) and Tocharian (e.g. Toch B *āka* [pl.] 'barley') and comes from the root **h*$_a$*ek̂-* 'point, sharp'. A derivative, **h*$_a$*ek̂stí-*, gives the word for 'awn, bristle' (e.g. NWels *eithin* 'furze', Lith *akstìs* 'spit (for roasting)', Rus *ostĭ* 'awn, bristle', and perhaps Toch B *āśce* 'head'). A second word for 'millet' may be **kéres-* found in both Germanic (e.g. NHG *Hirse* 'millet') and Indic (e.g. Kalasha *karasha* 'millet'); in Italic, however, we have Lat *cerēs* 'bread, grain' (also *Cerēs* 'goddess of agriculture') with a much more generic meaning. 'Rye' is found mostly in the North-West (e.g. NE *rye*, Lith *rugỹs*, Rus *rožĭ*) but also in the Iranian Pamir languages (e.g. Shughni *roγ̌z* 'ear of rye'). The word for chaff **pelo/eh*$_a$*-* (e.g. Lat *palea*, Lith *pela* [pl.], dialectal Rus *pelá*, Skt *palāvās* [pl.]), is attested in Old Indic and appears to be related to words for 'dust'.

Of the actual plants that were brought into cultivation at various times over Eurasia, there is generally some uncertainty about the specific meaning of the proto-form. **ĝhrésdh(i)*, for example, means 'barley' in Lat *hordeum*, Germanic (e.g. German *Gerste*), and Grk *krî* ~ *krīthḗ*; 'wheat' in its possible Hittite cognate (*karas*); and cereal grain in Alb *drithë*. PIE **h*$_2$*élbhit* 'barley' (Grk *álphi* 'barley-meal', Alb *elb* 'barley') exhibits the same suffix found in Hit *seppit* 'wheat'. **meiĝ(h)-* 'barley' ('grain'?) can be counted Proto-Indo-European rather than North-Western (OIr *mīach* 'measure of grain, bushel', Lith *miẽžiai*) only if one accepts a Khotanese word for 'field' (*mäṣṣa-*) as cognate. A word for 'millet', **pano-*, rests on a Latin-Iranian isogloss (Lat *pānicum*, Shughni [an Iranian language of the Pamirs] *pīnj*). The weed, **h*$_a$*éireh*$_a$*-* '± ryegrass', survives in Proto-Indo-European (Latv *aîres* 'ryegrass', Grk *aírai* 'ryegrass', Skt *erakā-* 'sedge'). As **ālu-* '± esculent root' is only found in Lat *ālium* ~ *allium* 'garlic' and Skt *ālú-* '*Arum campanulatum* (an esculent root)' and, as its meanings are disparate, it is uncertainly reconstructed. The cognates of **k̂eh*$_1$*kom* 'edible greens' (e.g. ON *hā* 'aftermath, second cutting of hay', Lith *šẽkas* 'green fodder', Skt *śā́ka-* 'potherbs, vegetables') reveal that it was consumed by animals in the West and people in Asia. The distribution of **kaulós* '± cabbage' is confined to the Mediterranean world (Lat *caulis* 'stalk of the [cabbage] plant', Grk *kaulós* 'cole, kail, cauliflower', Hit *kaluis(sa)na* 'some sort of vegetable').

Wheat was the premier cereal of both the ancient and modern world but is not all that well attested. The word **sepit* 'wheat' is only found in Hittite and has no other cognates, but the archaic and unproductive morphology would argue that the word could not have been created in Anatolian but must be earlier, while **ga/ondh-* 'wheat' is confined to Anatolian (Hit *kant-* '[einkorn?-] wheat'), Indo-Iranian (e.g. Av *gantuma-* 'wheat'), and Tocharian (Toch B *kanti* 'bread') and may have some Asian source. Although included here among the domesticated plants, it is likely that the original referent for **h$_a$ewis* indicated the wild rather than domesticated oats as domesticated oats do not appear in the archaeological record until the second millennium BC. The word is attested in Lat *avēna* '(wild) oats', Baltic (e.g. Lith *ãvižos* 'oats'), Slavic (e.g. OCS *ovĭsŭ* 'oats'), and Iranian (Khot *hau* 'some form of cereal'). The word for 'wine', **wóinom*, is found in Lat *vīnum*, Alb *verë*, Grk *oînos*, Arm *gini*, and Anatolian (e.g. Hit *wiyana-*) and would appear to be old in Indo-European; it may derive from the verbal root **wei(h$_x$)-* 'twist', hence originally 'that of the vine' (see below).

There is a considerable number of regional terms associated with fields and the plants that might grow in them. [North-Western] **lendh-* 'open land, waste' (e.g. NE *land*, OIr *lann* 'open land', OPrus *lindan* 'valley', Rus *ljadá* 'overgrown field'); **polk̂éh$_a$-* '± fallow land' (e.g. Gaul *olca* 'fallow land', NE *fallow*, Rus *polosá* 'strip of arable land'); **seh$_1$men-* 'seed' (e.g. Lat *sēmen*, OHG *sāmo*, OPrus *semen*, OCS *sěme* from the root **seh$_1$-*, i.e. *'what is sown'; [West Central]: **rēpéh$_a$-* 'turnip' (e.g. Lat *rāpum*, OHG *ruoba* ~ *rāba*, Lith *rópė*, Grk *hráp(h)us*); **póh$_x$iweh$_a$-* 'open meadow' (Lith *píeva* 'meadow', Grk *póā* 'grass, grassy place') which is possibly from the verb **peh$_2$-* 'nourish'; **h$_1$ét(e)no-* 'kernel' (MIr *eitne* 'kernel' [< **h$_1$eteniyom*; NIr *eitne* and dialectally *eithne*], Grk *étnos* 'thin soup made from peas or beans'). The semantic equation is excellent, but the usual Irish *-t-* is phonologically irregular (expected is *-th-*); **k̂oino-* 'grass' (Lith *šiẽnas* 'hay', OCS *sěno* 'hay, fodder, grass', dialectal Grk *koiná* 'hay');*?*k^{w}et-* 'chaff, bran' (e.g. MIr *cāith* 'bran, needle', dialectal Grk *pḗtea* 'chaff'): **bhárs* 'grain' (e.g. NE *barley*, Lat *fār* 'grain; coarse meal', Rus *bórošno* 'ryemeal'), a North-Western word with possible Greek (*phêros* 'food of the gods') and Albanian (*bar* 'grass') cognates—it has been derived from both the Near East and a European substrate; **bhabheh* - 'bean' (e.g. both Lat *faba* 'bean', NE *bean* [reflecting a Proto-Indo-European **bhabhneh$_a$-*], OPrus *babo* 'bean', Rus *bob* 'bean'—cf. also Alb *bathë* 'bean' and Grk *phakós* 'bean' from PIE **bhak̂ó/eh$_a$-*); **k̂ik̂er-* 'chickpea' (Lat *cicer* 'chickpea', Maced *kíkerroi* 'birds' pease', Arm *sisen* 'chickpea'); these would be phonologically regular from the proposed PIE form but are also usually taken as borrowings from some non-Indo-European language); **linom* 'flax' (e.g. NWels *llin* 'linen, flax', Lat *līnum* 'linen, flax', Lith *linaĩ* [pl.] 'linen, flax', Rus *len* 'linen', Grk *línon* 'flax, thread, linen'); *?*kannabis* 'hemp' (both Lat *cannibis* and NE *hemp*); ?**melh$_2$-* '± grain, millet' (Lat *milium*), problematic since the cognates may simply be independently formed from the verb 'to grind' (*$melh_2$-) (see below); ?*$h_1$$ereg^w$o- 'pea' (e.g. Lat *ervum* 'pea', OHG *araweiz* 'pea', Grk *órobos* 'pea'), seen by many as a Near Eastern loanword. There is *$kremh_x$us '(wild) garlic' (e.g. MIr *crem* 'wild garlic', Grk *krém(m)uon* ~ *króm(m)uon* 'onion', a derivative gives us, e.g., dialectal NE *ramsom* '(bulb of the) broad-leaved garlic', Lith *kremùšė* 'wild garlic', Rus *čeremšá* 'wild garlic'); **mr̥k-* '± carrot' (e.g. dialectal NE *more* 'carrot', Rus *morkóvĭ*, Grk *brákana* 'wild vegetables'); *puh_xrós 'wheat' (e.g. Lith *pūraĩ* 'winter wheat', Slov *pîr* 'spelt', Grk *pūrós* 'wheat'); **tris-* '±vine' (e.g. SC *trs* 'grapevine; reed', Alb *trishë* 'offshoot, sapling, seedling', Cretan Grk *thriniā́* 'vineyard'). Dialectal Greek preserves another word for 'grapevine', namely, *uiḗn* (< Proto-Indo-European *wih_iḗn), which may well be old as it would seem to be the underlying noun from which the word for 'wine', **wóinom*, is derived (see above).

10.4 Agricultural Terms

There are a number of terms associated with the processing of presumably domesticated cereals. Taken in order of processing, we can begin with *$h_{1/4}$ek- 'rake, harrow'. It appears as a verb in Lith *akė́ti* 'harrow' and in derivatives meaning either 'rake, harrow' (e.g. NWels *oged*, Late Lat *occa*, OE *eg(e)ðe*, *ecgan*, dial Grk *oksína*) or 'furrow' (e.g. Grk *ógmos*, Oss *adæg* [< **agæd*]). Hit *akkala-* is semantically indeterminate; it may mean 'furrow' or 'type of plough'. PIE *seh_1- 'sow' is, an extension of the meaning 'throw' which is seen in Hit *sā(i)*-'sow, throw'. The other verbal cognates are restricted to Lat *serō*, Germanic (e.g. NE *sow*), Baltic (e.g. Lith *sė́ju*), and Slavic (OCS *sějǫ*); a derived noun *$sóh_1$r̥ has produced words for 'millet' in Baltic (e.g. Lith *sóra*) and the word for 'to plant' in Toch AB *sāry-*. An extended form of this root, *seh_1i-,

Table 10.4. *Agricultural terminology*

*$h_{1/4}$ek-	'rake, harrow'	Lat *occa*, Grk *ógmos*
*seh_1-	'sow'	NE *sow*, Lat *serō*
**kerp-*	'pluck, harvest'	NE *harvest*, Lat *carpō*, Grk *karpós*, Skt *kr̥pāṇī*
*h_2meh_1-	'mow'	NE *mow*, Grk *amáō*
**peis-*	'thresh, grind'	Lat *pīnsō*, Grk *ptíssō*, Skt *pináṣṭi*
**wers-*	'±thresh'	Lat *verrō*
*$h_2eh_2$er-	'thresh, rake'	Lat *ārea*
*$melh_2$-	'grind'	NE *meal*, Lat *molō*, Grk *múlē*, Skt *mr̥ṇā́ti*

however, appears in a number of derivatives in both the east and west of the IE world, e.g. Skt *sī́ra-* '(seed-) plough', *sī́tā-* 'furrow', Toch B *ṣito* '±grainfield', Grk *sîtos* 'grain (both wheat and barley)' (with *s-* preserved as in *sū́s* 'pig'). Another basic verbal root *(*s*)*ker-* 'cut', underlies **kerp-* 'pluck, harvest'. The semantics of the cognates vary from instruments that might be employed in cutting, e.g. MIr *corrān* 'sickle', Latv *cir̃pe* 'sickle', Skt *kr̥pāṇī* 'sword', to the act of plucking, e.g. Lat *carpō* 'pluck', to the object being gathered, e.g. Grk *karpós* 'fruit', to the actual act (NE *harvest*) or the period of the harvest (OE *hærfest* 'autumn'). A word for 'mow' (**h_2meh_1-*) is secured with cognates in Germanic (e.g. NE *mow*), Grk *amáō*, and Hit *hamesha-* 'spring, ±early summer' (i.e. 'mowing [time]', **h_2meh_1-sh_2o-*) and provides the basis for several regionally attested terms. The process of 'threshing' is indicated by several words. A PIE **peis-* is supported by cognates in Italic (Lat *pīnsō* 'thresh'), Baltic (e.g. Lith *paisýti* 'thresh'), Slavic (e.g. OCS *pĭchati* 'hit'), Grk *ptíssō* 'winnow', and Indo-Iranian (e.g. Skt *pinásti* 'grinds, threshes'). We also have the semantically more ambiguous **wers-* '±thresh' seen in Lat *verrō* 'sweep (grain after threshing)', Baltic (Latv *vãrsmis* 'unwinnowed heap of grain'), Slavic (OCS *vrěšti* 'thresh'), and Hit *warsi* 'plucks, harvests'. A root **h_2eh_2er-* 'thresh, rake' is attested only in Lat *ārea* 'threshing floor; open field' (and source of the more generalized in meaning NE *area*) and Hit *hahhar*(*a*)- 'rake'. Finally, the actual grinding of the cereal is indicated by the widely attested **$melh_2$-* 'grind' which is found in most IE groups, i.e. Celtic (e.g. OIr *meilid*), Italic (Lat *molō*), Germanic (e.g. NE *meal*), Baltic (e.g. Lith *malù*), Slavic (e.g. OCS *meljǫ*), Grk *múlē* 'mill', Arm *malem*, Hit *mall*(*a*)-, Indo-Iranian (e.g. Skt *mr̥ṇāti*), and Tocharian (e.g. Toch B *mely-*).

There are also a number of regional terms associated with agriculture. From the North-West we have two words for 'furrow': **pr̥ḱeh-* and **l*(*o*)*iseh-*. The first is attested in Celtic (e.g. NWels *rhych*), Lat *porca* 'a ridge between two furrows', and Germanic (e.g. NE *furrow*); it has related forms in other languages, e.g. Skt *párśāna-* 'chasm', but only the North-West region evidences a specifically agricultural meaning. The term is related to the word for 'pig' (**porḱos*) and there is the widespread notion of the pig as an animal that leaves a furrow-like track as it roots up the ground. With regard to **l* (*e/o*)*$iseh_a$* Lat *līra* preserves the meaning 'furrow' (or 'track' and 'to go off the track/out of the furrow' is *de-līrus*, i.e. 'insane', the source of NE *delirious*). OE *līste* 'fringe, border' (> NE *list*) is also cognate along with OPrus *lysa* and OCS *lěcha*, both 'field bed'. All of these would appear to be derivatives of an unattested verbal root **leis-* '±leave a trace on the ground'. In the North-West we have **h_2met-* 'mow', an enlargement of an unattested **h_2em-*, like **h_2meh_1-*, which is seen in Celtic (e.g. OIr *meithel* 'reaping party'), Lat *metō* 'mow, harvest', and Germanic (NE *meadow*). From the West Central region we have **worwos* 'furrow', which is seen in Lat *urvāre* 'to mark out a boundary with a furrow' and Grk *oûron* 'range (of area that could be ploughed up in a day)'; *$h_2$merg-* 'gather, harvest', another enlargement on putative *$h_2$em-* which is attested in Lat *mergae* 'reaping boards' and Grk *amérgō* 'gather, harvest'; **neik-* 'winnow' with cognates in Celtic (NWels *nithiaf*), Baltic (e.g. Lith *niekóti*), and Grk *likmáō*, all 'winnow'. The aberrant initial of the Grk form (*l* instead of *n*) is due to dissimilation. From this region we also have **ghrendh-* 'grind' seen in Lat *frendō* 'gnash the teeth', Germanic (e.g. NE *grind*), Baltic (Lith *gréndu* 'scrape, scratch (off)'), and Grk *khóndros* 'grain' with another example of dissimilation (from **khrondrós*). From the Graeco-Aryan region we have *$h_4$el-* 'grind down' with cognates in Grk *aléō* 'grind', Arm *alam* 'grind', and Skt *aṇu-* 'fine (< ground down); *Panicum miliaceum*'.

10.5 Proto-Indo-European Flora

As with the ethno-zoological system (see Chapter 9), the reconstructed vocabulary associated with plants is not extensive if we compare this semantic class with that of living 'natural' languages in the world which tend to average about 500 generic taxa, roughly the same number that the Greek philosopher Theophrastus (372–287 BC) managed to describe. On the other hand, it may be the right order of magnitude for a reconstructed language. The Uralic-speaking peoples who occupied the forest zone of Eurasia provide evidence of fewer than thirty species of plants (largely trees) from their proto-lexicon and about another twenty-five words identifying the parts of plants.

Linguistic-anthropologists have examined the ethno-botanical systems of many peoples in an attempt to determine whether there existed any universals in their folk taxonomies. What has been observed is a series of stages where we might expect the creation of specific words (lexicalization) for various degrees of botanical distinction. For example, at stage 1 there would be no generic name for life forms. At stage 2 the one generic word would be 'tree' (and in two-thirds of the languages that lexicalize 'tree', the same word also means 'wood'). At stage 3 a new word will appear to designate either 'grass' or non-grassy herbaceous plants (i.e. a grerb < grass +herb). At stage 4 a third generic plant name would be introduced—'grass', 'grerb', 'vine', or 'bush'. Modern English possesses a stage 6 taxonomy with its basic plant forms of tree, plant, grass, vine, and bush. Earl Anderson has suggested that Proto-Indo-European was a stage 2 language with one life form lexicalized, i.e. **dóru* which, according to expectations, does mean both 'tree' and 'wood'. As the word means specifically 'oak' in Celtic and Greek, he suspects that this was originally its meaning (in a pre-PIE Stage 1 system, where there was no generic name for 'tree' but only specific names for the different species of trees) and that it shifted to fill out the stage 2 taxon (note that many North American Indian languages possess a word meaning both 'tree' and 'fir'). More controversially, he suggests the existence of a covert taxon, grerb. A covert taxon is a classification that is not lexicalized (no word exists for it) yet is recognized by its speakers. There is a variety of ways in which such a covert category might be discerned, e.g. when types are routinely grouped together or in a consistent pattern that suggests a kinship between the objects being referred to even if there is no specific word to describe the group. For example, although we may commonly lump frogs and toads or alligators and crocodiles together into related groups, we do not actually employ any specific term for these groupings, e.g. crocogators. In Anderson's scheme, grerb would comprise both the terms for wild plants (note, however, the paucity of these words in Proto-Indo-European) and also, under another taxon, *h_2*ed-* 'grain'. Actually, assessment of the generic term for 'grain' is difficult in that there is not a single term that does not also refer to a species, e.g. Lat *ador* refers more commonly to 'emmer wheat' and there would certainly be other candidates for the generic term, e.g. **ĝr̥$h_2$nóm* 'grain' which serves as the basic form in Germanic. Indeed, there very well may be a more complex system of folk taxonomy evident in the distinctions between the uses of the different cereals grains, e.g. **dhoh*$_x$*néh*$_2$- '(harvested) grain'. The two principal grains were wheat and barley and although barley may have frequently overtaken wheat in terms of production (it is a much hardier plant and tolerant of poorer soils and temperature), wheat was also the preferred grain, and where we find the two paired in early Indo-European literature, we generally find that wheat is mentioned first, e.g. Hit *seppit euwann-a*, Grk *puroì kaì krīthḗ* both 'wheat and barley'.

What can we tell about the environment of the Proto-Indo-Europeans from their arboreal vocabulary? The more extensive treatments of this semantic class reveal very different takes on the nature of the Indo-European forest. Paul Friedrich's *Proto-Indo-European Trees* (1970) sees the arboreal evidence very much at home in the forests of eastern Europe while Thomas Gamkrelidze and Vyacheslay Ivanov set their arboreal landscape in the highlands of South-West Asia. In fact, most of the Indo-European arboreal vocabulary is not geographically very diagnostic—trees such as the alder, ash, and birch are known broadly over much of Eurasia from at least the Rhine to the Urals and through the Caucasus and highlands of west Asia. On occasion, some plants are not attested in the southern Mediterranean, e.g. the birch is absent in general from southern Italy, and here we find that the ancestors of the Latins shifted the meaning of the 'birch' word, *fraxinus*, to 'ash'.

The possibility of reconstructing a word for the 'beech', **bheh*$_a$*ĝós*, has historically been used as an argument for restricting the possible Proto-Indo-European homeland to an area west of a line drawn from Kaliningrad (= Königsberg) to Odessa since that line demarcates the easternmost range of the common beech (*Fagus silvatica*). However, this traditional 'beech-line argument' ignores (1) the presence of closely related species of beech in the Crimea (*Fagus taurica*) and the Caucasus and northern coast of Anatolia (*Fagus orientalis*) and the presence of *Fagus silvatica* itself in the forests that line the major rivers of the Ukraine and southern Russia; (2) the possibility that * *bheh*$_a$*ĝós* referred to a variety of oak in Proto-Indo-European (as it does in Albanian and Greek which were spoken in territories where the beech itself is abundantly attested): and (3) the absence of cognates of **bheh*$_a$*ĝós* in Anatolian or any of the other Asiatic groups which robs it of a secure Proto-Indo-European ancestry. Any of these reasons prevents the 'beech-argument' from restricting the potential Proto-Indo-European homeland to central and western Europe.

If there really does not seem to be a single diagnostic tree name that nails down the location of the Proto-Indo-European speakers, can the arboreal evidence be utilized in any other way to help locate the proto-language? While we cannot employ negative evidence, i.e. the absence of arboreal terms, to shed light on the prehistoric situation, it has been suggested that we can perhaps draw some conclusions from semantic shifts. We have already seen that Latin shifts what is unequivocally the word for 'birch' in all the other Indo-European languages to 'ash' and we have also seen that there are good ecological grounds to explain this shift, i.e. the ancestors of the Latin speakers migrated into a land that lacked birch trees. Paul Friedrich has argued that an even stronger case for semantic shift can be found in Greek. In some cases we find semantic shifts that pertain to species, e.g. PIE **h*$_2$*es*(*k*)-(Grk *oksúē*) 'ash' shifted to 'beech' and PIE **bheh*$_a$*ĝós*, the so-called 'beech word' (Grk *phēgós*), became 'oak'. Other shifts see replacement of the arboreal meaning with a technological one, e.g. PIE **taksos* 'yew' becomes *tókson* 'bow' in Greek (they borrowed an apparently non-IE word *smī́laks* to designate the yewtree); and PIE **h*$_3$*es*(*k*)- 'ash' not only designates the 'beech' but also becomes 'spear'. In terms of species shifts, Albanian also agrees with Greek with respect to changes in both the 'beech' word and 'ash'. These would be admittedly limited arguments that the earliest Indo-Europeans did not live in Greece and the southern Balkans—assuming, of course, that these were real shifts of meaning and that they were motivated by a regional ecology different from that of the Proto-Indo-Europeans.

The reconstructed vocabulary for domesticated plants forms a restricted part of the botanical vocabulary as a whole although it is clear from the approximately twenty lexical items that the Proto-Indo-European community was familiar with cereal agriculture, particularly with wheat and barley, and there are at least half a dozen strongly reconstructed terms associated with planting, harvesting, and processing cereal grains. While this has little geographical importance it does indicate that Proto-Indo-Europeans must have had at least a Neolithic subsistence base, i.e. date no earlier than *c.* 8000 BC, and that there is no question of their adhering to some form of (largely mythic) pure pastoral economy. Assigning exact referents to the several words meaning 'grain' or 'wheat' or 'barley' is not easy, in large part because of the ease by which the designation of a specific grain may become the word for grain in general or vice versa (PIE**ĝr̥h*$_a$*nóm* > American English *corn*, i.e. maize), and also because the natural development of these words is likely to have been disturbed by interdialect borrowing as new varieties, or even new species, were passed from group to group. In this context it is significant too that at least two of the ubiquitous weeds that infest wheat and barley, that is, ryegrass and (wild) oats, are also reconstructable. The rest of the Neolithic 'agricultural package', namely flax, pea, and chickpea, were probably also present in the Proto-Indo-European community, but the reflexes of their designations are found only regionally in the surviving Indo-European branches, principally those of the Mediterranean (Latin, Greek), which raises at least the possibility that they may derive from a non-IE substratum. 'Millet' as either an original meaning or a specific designation of a more generic word for 'grain' is interesting since it is not normally assigned to the early Neolithic package that entered Europe from the Near East but may have rather originated in central or east Asia (it is also found in the Harppan culture of India) and entered Europe across the steppelands.

Further Reading

The main summary source for arboreal terms is Friedrich (1970). For words for 'branch' see Knobloch (1987*a*). For individual trees see: apple (Joki 1963, Hamp 1979*a*, Adams 1985*c*, Gamkrelidze 1986, Markey 1988); ash (Normier 1981); beech (Krogmann 1955, 1957, Eilers and Mayrhofer 1962, Lane 1967); hawthorn (Watkins 1993); oak (Hamp 1989*a*); pine (Itkonen 1987); arboreal names as non-Indo-European substrates are in Huld (1990). Discussion of agricultural terminology and the names of cereals can be found in Diebold (1992), Mallory (1997*b*), Markey (1989), Puhvel (1964, 1976*a*), Watkins (1973, 1977), Witczak (2003), Woitilla (1986); for specific topics see; barley (Hamp 1985); oats (Stalmaszczyk and Witczak 1991–2); wine (Bonfante 1974, Beekes 1987*a*). For folk taxonomy see Anderson (2003), Berlin (1992), and Brown (1984).

11

Anatomy

11.0 The Body

We are able to reconstruct a substantial number of words for human and animal anatomy. This ability reflects both the natural human interest in the human body and the practical knowledge gained by butchery. Nevertheless, it is not altogether surprising that the vocabulary for the various parts of the external anatomy is better represented than that referring to internal organs. The terms for the external features were, of course, known to everyone while those concerned with at least some of the internal organs were a rather more restricted portion of the population. The number of words we can reconstruct in this area also reflects the relative stability of this particular set of words. Most of them are among the first words an infant learns and are thus particularly resistant to replacement.

11.1 The Head

There are four words attested for 'head'. The most widely distributed is *$\hat{k}$ *r̥rēh*$_2$ and its derivatives that are found in seven different groups, including Anatolian (e.g. ON *hjarsi* 'crown of the head', Lat *cerebrum* 'brain' [< *'(marrow) of the head' as opposed to 'bone-marrow'], Alb *krye* 'head', Grk *kárē* 'head', *karárā*

Table 11.1. *The head*

**k̂r̥ēh*$_2$	'head	Lat *cerebrum*, Grk *krānion*, Skt *śíras-*
**ghebhōl*	'head'	NE *gable*, Grk *kephálē*
**kapōlo-*	' ± head, skull'	Skt *kapā́la-*
**m̥lh*$_2$*xdh-o-*	'crown of the head'	Skt *mūrdhán-*
**h*$_1$*éni-h*$_3$*k*^{w}*-o/eh*$_a$*-*	'face'	Grk *enōpḗ*, Skt *ánīka-*
**próti-h*$_3$*(ō)k*^{w}*-o/eh*$_a$*-*	'face, front'	Grk *prósōpon*, Skt *prátīka-*
**h*$_2$*ent-*	'forehead'	Lat *ante*, Grk *antí*, Skt *ánti*
**bhólom*	'forehead'	Skt *bhālam*
**h*$_3$*ok*^{w}	'eye'	Lat *oculus*, NE *eye*, Grk *ómma*, Skt *ákṣi-*
**bhrúh*$_x$*s*	'eyebrow'	NE *brow*, Grk *ophrûs*, Skt *bhrū́-*
**h*$_x$*náss*	'nose'	Lat *nāris*, NE *nose*, Skt *nā́sā*
**h*$_a$*óus-*	'ear'	Lat *auris*, NE *ear*, Grk *oûs*
**h*$_{1/4}$*óh*$_1$*(e)s-*	'mouth'	Lat *ōs*, Skt *ā́s-*
**h*$_x$*oust-eh*$_a$*-*	'mouth, lip'	Lat *ōstium*, Skt *óṣṭha-*
**stómn̥*	'mouth'	Grk *stóma*
**dn̥ĝhuh*$_a$*-*	'tongue'	Lat *lingua*, NE *tongue*, Skt *jihvā́-*
**h*$_1$*dónt-*	'tooth'	Lat *dēns*, NE *tooth*, Grk *odṓn*, Skt *dánt-*
**ĝómbhos*	'tooth, set/row of teeth'	NE *comb*
**ĝénu-*	'jaw'	Lat *gena*, NE *chin*, Grk *génus*, Skt *hánu-*
**smek̂-*	'chin, jaw'	Lat *māla*
**men-*	'chin'	Lat *mentum*
**monis*	'neck'	NE *mane*, Lat *monīle*, Skt *mányā-*
**g*^{w}*rih*$_3$*w-eh*$_a$*-*	'neck'	Skt *grīvā́-*

'head', *krānion* 'crown of the head' [> via Latin into NE *cranium*], Av *sāra-* 'head', *sarah-* 'head', Skt *śíras-*'head', Toch B *krañiye* 'neck' [< *'occiput'], Hit *kitkar* 'headlong'). The second word, **ghebhōl*, is found in at least three groups (e.g. ON *gafl* 'gable, gable-side' [whence, via Old French, comes NE *gable*], Grk *kephálē* 'head', Toch A *śpāl* 'head') and yields the meaning 'gable' as well as 'head' or 'skull' in the Germanic languages. PIE **kapōlo-* is attested only in OE *hafola* 'head' and Skt *kapā́la-*and in the latter it means both 'head' and 'cup', an association found elsewhere among the Indo-European languages, e.g. French *tête* 'head' derives from Lat *testa* 'pot'. The 'crown of the head', **m̥lh*$_x$*dh-o-*, is found in at least three groups (e.g. OE *molda* 'crown of the head', Av *kamərəδa-*'head of a demonic being', Skt *mūrdhán-* 'head').

There are two words, both compounds indicating 'what is in front of the eye', that describe the 'face', i.e. **h*$_1$*éni-h*$_3$*k*^{w}*- o/eh*$_a$*-* (e.g. OIr *enech* 'face', Grk *enōpḗ* 'face', Av *ainika*-'face', Skt *ánīka*-'face, front') and _*próti-h_3(ō)k^wo/eh$_a$-_ (e.g. Grk *prósōpon* 'face', Skt *prátīka*-'face', Toch B *pratsāko* 'chest'). There are also two words for 'forehead', the first, _*$h_2$ent-_, being the 'front, the part before' (e.g. OIr *ētan* 'forehead', Lat *ante* 'in front of, before', Grk *antí* 'in front of, opposite', Hit, *hant*- 'face, forehead, front part', Skt *ánti* 'in front of, opposite', *ánta*- 'end, limit', Toch B *ānte* 'surface, forehead') while _*bhólom_ 'forehead' (OPrus *ballo*, Alb *ballë*, Skt *bhālam*, all 'forehead') may derive from the verbal root _*bhel-_ 'shine'. Such a basic concept as 'eye', _*$h_3$ok^w_ (e.g. OIr *enech* 'face', Lat *oculus*, NE *eye*, Lith *akìs*, OCS *oko*, Grk *ómma*, Arm *akn*, Av *aši*-(dual) 'eyes', Skt *ákṣi*-, Toch B *ek*, all 'eye'), is attested in ten Indo-European groups while _*bhrúh$_x$s_, 'eyebrow', can be found in at least nine groups (e.g. OIr *forbrū*, NE *brow*, Lith *bruvìs*, Rus *brovĭ*, Maced *abroûtes*, Grk *ophrûs*, Av *brvat*-, Skt *bhrū́*-, Toch B *pärwāne*, all 'brow(s)'). Two other major sense organs, _*$h_x$náss_ 'nose' (e.g. Lat *nāris* 'nostril', *nārēs* [pl.] 'nose', NE *nose*, Lith *nósis* 'nose', OCS *nosŭ* 'nose', Av *nāh*- 'nose', Skt *nā́sā* [dual] 'nostrils') and _*$h_a$óus-_'ear' (e.g. OIr *ō*, Lat *auris*, NE *ear*, Lith *ausìs*, Rus *úkho*, Alb *vesh*, Grk *oûs*, Arm *unkn*, Av *uši* [dual], all 'ear(s)'), are attested in at least nine Indo-European groups. For 'mouth' we find three words of antiquity: _*$h_{1/4}$óh$_1$(e)s-_ (MIr *ā* 'mouth', Lat *ōs* 'mouth', ON *ōss* 'mouth of a river', Hit *a(y)is*-'mouth', Av *āh*- 'mouth', Skt *ā́s*- 'mouth'), _*$h_x$oust-eh$_a$-_ (Lat *ōstium* 'mouth of a river', OPrus *austo* 'mouth', Lith *uostà* 'mouth of a river', OCS *usta* [pl.] 'mouth', Av *aušt(r)a*- 'lip', Skt *óṣṭha*- 'lip'), and _*stómn̥_ (NWels *safn* 'jawbone', Grk *stóma* 'mouth', Hit *istaman*- 'ear', Av *staman*- 'maw'), which tempt one to find some semantic distinction between the different words. The first two mean both 'mouth' and 'mouth of a river' with the second word also including 'lip' in Indo-Iranian. The third word, _*stómn̥_, means 'mouth' in Celtic, Greek, and Iranian but 'ear' in Anatolian (where the presumed proto- Anatolian meaning may be 'orifice'). The word for 'tongue', _*dn̥ĝhuh$_a$-_, is widely attested (e.g. OIr *tengae*, OLat *dingua*, NE *tongue*) but also widely remodelled, probably by the initial sound in the verb 'to lick' (we have three words and they all begin with an 'l'), e.g. Lat *lingua* but in Old Latin it was *dingua* while Lith *liežùvis* and Arm *lezu* also begin with an initial 'l'. There is also metathesis, e.g. Proto-Tocharian _*käntwo_ (Toch A *käntu*, Toch B *kantwo*) reverses the syllable-initial consonants of the expected _*tänkwo_. Both OPrus *insuwis* and OCS *językŭ* show the loss of the Proto-Indo-European _*d-_before _*n̥_, while Av *hizū*-and Skt *jihvā́*- show even more reformation. There are two words for 'tooth'. The presumably older (attested in nine groups) is _*$h_1$dónt-_ (e.g. OIr *dēt*, Lat *dēns*, NE *tooth*, Lith *dantìs*, Grk *odṓn*, Arm *atamn*, Av *dantan*-, Skt *dánt*-, all 'tooth', and Rus *desná* 'gums') which was originally a participle from the verb _*$h_1$ed-_ 'eat' (cf. Hit *adant*-'eaten'); _*ĝómbhos_ is found in seven groups (e.g. NE *comb*, Latv *zùobs* 'tooth', OCS *zǫbŭ* 'tooth', Alb *dhëmb* 'tooth, tusk', Grk *gómphos* 'large wedge-shaped bolt or nail', Skt _jámbha-_ 'tooth', Toch B _keme_ 'tooth'). There are several words for 'jaw' and 'chin'. Clearly old is _*ĝénu-_ (nine groups: OIr _gin_ 'mouth', Lat _gena_ 'cheek', NE _chin_, Grk _génus_ 'chin, jaw', Phryg _azēn_ 'beard', Av _zānu-_ 'jaw', Skt _hánu-_ 'jaw', Toch A _śanweṃ_ [dual] 'jaws'). We have already seen how _*smek̂-_ may mean 'chin' as well as 'beard'; the reconstruction of _*men-_ requires acceptance that the apparently cognate forms in Celtic (MWels _mant_ 'mouth, jaw'), Italic (Lat _mentum_ 'chin'), and Anatolian (Hit _mēni-_ 'chin') were not independent derivatives from _*men-_ 'project'. The two words for 'neck' seem to offer some semantic distinction in that _*monis_ (e.g. OIr _muin_ 'neck', Lat _monīle_ 'necklace', NE _mane_, OCS _monisto_ 'necklace', Av _manaoθrī_ 'neck', _minu-_ 'necklace', Skt _mányā-_ 'nape'), possibly also a derivative of _*men-_ 'project', yields derivatives meaning 'necklace' (the neck viewed from the outside) while _*$g^{w}rih_{x}w$- eh_{a}-_ (e.g. Latv _griva_ 'river mouth', Rus _gríva_ 'mane', Av _grīvā-_ 'neck [of a demonic being]', Skt _grīvā́-_ 'neck'), possibly derived from the verb _*$g^{w}er(h_{3})$-_ 'swallow', suggests the neck viewed from the inside, i.e. the throat.

The regional Indo-European vocabulary is not nearly so extensive. From the North-West we have _*káput_ 'head' (e.g. Lat _caput_ and less clearly derived NE _head_); _*leb-_ 'lip' (e.g. Lat _labium_ 'lip', NE _lip_, cf. Hit _lipp-_ 'lick'); _*$ghéh_{a}(u)$-mr̥_ 'interior of mouth (gums, palate)' (e.g. NE _gums_, Lith _gomurỹs_ 'palate'); and _*kólsos_ 'neck' (e.g. MIr _coll_ 'head, chief', Lat _collus_, OHG _hals_ 'neck'). From the West Central area are _*$\hat{g}onh_{a}dh$-o-s_ 'jaw' with cognates in Baltic (e.g. Lith _žándas_ 'jaw, cheek'), Grk _gnáthos_ 'jaw, mouth', and Arm _cnawt_ 'jaw'; _*ghelu-neh_{a}-_ 'lip' (e.g. ON _gjǫlnar_ 'jaws', Grk _khelū́nē_ 'lip', Arm _jelun_ 'palate') and _*h_{a}enĝh(w)ēn-_ 'neck' (e.g. Rus _vjazĭ_ 'nape', Grk _ámphēn_ ~ _aukhḗn_ 'nape', Arm _awjikʻ_ [pl.] 'neck'; from _*h_{a}enĝh-_ 'narrow'). A Greek-Indic isogloss (Grk _oûlon_, Skt _bársva-_) is seen in _*wólswom_ 'gums' (from _*wels-_ 'bulge').

11.2 Hair

The abundance of words pertaining to 'hair' is quite striking and in this section we will include both head hair and body hair as the two concepts occasionally overlap (or are too difficult to distinguish). The hair of the head was _*k̂ripo-_ (e.g. Lat _crīnis_ 'head hair', Alb _krip_ '[short] head hair, facial hair', _krife_ 'mane', Av _srifā-_ 'plume', Skt _śíprā_ [dual] 'moustache and beard') while the oldest word for 'beard' was _*smók̂wr̥_ (e.g. Alb _mjekër_ 'beard, chin', Arm _mawrukʻ_ 'beard', Hit _z(a)munkur_ 'beard', Skt _śmáśru_ 'beard, [especially] moustache') which also might mean 'chin' (e.g. Lith _smakrà_ 'chin', Alb _mjekër_ 'beard, chin', and in OE _smǣras_ [pl.] it came to mean 'lips'). Body hair in general, including especially pubic hair, was _*pou-m-s-_, and in several traditions marks the coming of

Table 11.2. *Hair*

**k̂ripo-*	'±head and facial hair'	Lat *crīnis*, Skt *śiprā*
**smók̂wr̥*	'chin, beard'	Skt *śmáśru*
**pou-m-s-*	'(human) body hair'	Lat *pūbēs*, Grk *pṓgōn*, Skt *púman-*
**pulos*	'(a single) hair'	Grk *púligges*, Skt *pulakās*
**pilos*	'(a single) hair'	Lat *pilus*, Grk *pîlos*
**k(e)*h_a*isVr-*	'mane'	Lat *caesariēs*, Skt *késara-*
**ghait(so)-*	'hair, mane'	Grk *khaítē*
**yók̂u*	'(animal) body hair'	Skt *yā́śu*
**gówr̥*	'(animal) body hair'	Skt *guṇá-*
**réumn̥-*	'horsehair' or 'fleece'	Skt *róman-*
**wendh-*	'(a single) hair'	Grk *íonthos*
**we/ondhso-*	'facial hair'	
**dhrigh-*	'±a (coarse) hair'	Grk *thríks*
**dek̂-*	'thread, hair'	NE *tail*, Skt *daśā́-*
**koik̂-*	'cut hair'	Skt *kéśa-*
**werĝ-*	'shave, shear'	
**wólos*	'tail hair (of a horse)'	Skt *vā́la-*
**puk(eh*$_a$*)-*	'tail'	NE *fox*, Skt *púccha-*
**wl̥*h_2*neh*$_a$*-*	'wool'	Lat *lāna*, NE *wool*, Grk *lênos*, Skt *ū́rṇā-*

adult age, e.g. Lat *pūbēs* also designates 'adult, one able to bear arms' while the Sanskrit cognate *púmān* means 'man, male' (cf. also dialectal Lith *paustìs* 'animal hair', Rus *pukh* 'down', Alb *pushem* 'begin to grow a beard, body hair', Grk *pṓgōn* 'beard', Shughni *pūm* 'down, fluff'). Related in some way are various words for 'a single hair', **pulos* and **pilos* (e.g. MIr *ulu* 'beard', Grk *púligges* [pl.] 'hairs of the body', Kurd *pūr* 'head hair', Skt *pulakās* [pl.] 'bristling hairs of the body', and Lat *pilus* '[a single] hair [of the human body]' *pilleus* 'felt', OCS *plŭstĭ* 'felt', Grk *pîlos* 'felt'). The word for 'mane' (the meaning in most cognate sets except Latin where *caesariēs* means 'long flowing hair') was **k(e)*h_a*isVr-* (e.g. Skt *késara-*, Toch A *śiśri*). Less secure in original meaning is **ghait(so)-* which means 'stiff hair' in MIr *gaīsid*, 'mane' in Grk *khaítē*, and 'curly hair' in Av *gaēsa-*. The body hair, probably of animals, seems to underlie words like **yók̂u* (e.g. Arm *asr* 'wool', Skt *yā́śu* ' ± pubic hair', Toch AB *yok* 'body hair, wool'), **gówr̥* (e.g. MIr *gūaire* '[animal] hair, bristles', Lith *gaũras* 'down, tuft of hair', Av *gaona-* 'body hair, colour', Skt *guṇá-* 'thread, string'), and **réumn̥-* 'horsehair' or 'fleece' (e.g. OIr *rōn* 'horse's mane', Rus *runó* 'fleece', NPers *rōm* 'pubic hair', Skt *róman-* ~ *lóman-* 'body hair of men or animals'). The root **wendh-* designated '(a single) hair' (e.g. MIr *find* 'a single hair', OHG *wint-brāwa* 'eyelash', Grk *íonthos* 'hair root, young beard; acne') while the inclusion of a suffix seen in **we/ondhso-* indicated 'facial hair' (e.g.

MIr *fēs* 'lip; beard; pubic hair', OPrus *wanso* 'first beard', OCS *vǫsŭ* 'mustache', Khot *vatca* 'facial hair'). The quality of hair can be seen in **dhrigh-* '± a (coarse) hair' (e.g. MIr *gairb-driuch* 'bristle, rough hair', Grk *thríks* 'a single hair', Khot *dro* 'hair') while **dek̂-*, which originally meant 'thread', was extended to mean 'hair' (e.g. OIr *dūal* 'lock of hair', NE *tail*, Goth *tagl* 'a single hair', ON *tāg* 'thread, fibre', Khot *dasa-* 'thread', Skt *daśā-* 'fringe', Toch A *śāku* 'head hair'). Finally, we have two words associated with the cutting of hair, i.e. **koik̂-* 'cut hair' (in Baltic, e.g. Lith *káišiu* 'scrape, shave', Alb *qeth* 'cut hair, shear', and Indic, i.e. Skt *kéśa-* 'head hair') and the poorly attested (an Armenian-Tocharian isogloss) **werĝ-* 'shave, shear' (e.g. Toch B *wärk-* 'shear', Arm *gercum* 'shave, cut hair'). The hair of animals is also attested in the sense that we have two words for 'tail', **wólos* (e.g. Lith *valaĩ* [pl.] 'tail of a horse', Skt *vā́la-* ~ *vā́ra-* 'tail of a horse; horsehair') and **puk(eh$_a$)-* (e.g. NE *fox*, Torwali *pūš* 'fox', Skt *púccha-* 'tail', Toch B *päkā-* 'tail, chowrie'). The first is attested only in Lithuanian and Old Indic and in both languages specifies the 'tail hair of a horse'. The second is found in Germanic, Indic, and Tocharian and gives us our word 'fox'. Nine different groups (including Anatolian) attest the Proto-Indo-European word for 'wool', **wĺ̥h$_2$neh$_a$-* (e.g. NWels *gwlan*, Lat *lāna*, NE *wool*, Lith *vìlna*, Rus *vólna*, Grk *lênos*, Hit *hulana-*, Av *varənā-*, Skt *ū́rṇā-*, all 'wool').

From the North-West we have **bhardh-eh$_a$-* 'beard' (e.g. Lat *barba*, NE *beard*, Lith *barzdà*, all 'beard', Rus *borodá* 'beard, chin'); **k̂er(es)-* '± (rough) hair, bristle' (e.g. NE *hair*, Lith *šr̃ys* 'bristle, animal hair', Rus *šerstĭ* 'wool, animal hair').

11.3 The Upper Body and Arms

There is a single word for the 'body' in general, **kréps*, which is attested in Celtic (OIr *crī* 'body, flesh'), Italic (Lat *corpus* 'body'), Germanic (e.g. OE *hrif* 'belly, womb' [> NE *midriff*]), and Indo-Iranian (Av *kərəfš* 'body', Skt *kr̥p-* 'form, beauty'). Of very indeterminate meaning (and not only with respect to body parts) is **poksós* 'side, flank' but with meanings as variable as Latv *paksis* 'corner of a house', Rus *pákh* 'flank, loins', *pakhá* 'armpit', Oss *faxs* 'side', Skt *pakṣá-* 'wing, flank, side', and possibly OIr *ucht* and Lat *pectus*, both 'breast'. The semantic range of words relating to 'skin', be it human or animal, is not always clear. The word **twéks* means 'skin' in Indic (Skt *tvák-*), 'self' in Hit *tuekka-* (also 'body, person'), and 'shield' (< skin shield) in Grk *sák(k)os*. Both **(s)kwéh$_x$tis* (e.g. NWels *es-gid* 'shoe' [< 'foot-hide'], NE *hide*, Lith *kiáutis* 'skin', Grk *skûtos* 'skin, leather, hide', Toch A *kāc* 'skin') and **h$_1$owes-* (e.g. Lat *ōmentum* 'fatty membrane or caul covering the intestines', Toch B *ewe* 'inner skin, hide') derive from verbs meaning 'to cover', i.e. **(s)keuh$_x$-* and

Table 11.3. *The upper body and arms*

*_kréps_	'body'	Lat _corpus_, NE _midriff_, Skt _kr̥p-_
*_poksós_	'side, flank'	?Lat _pectus_, Skt _pakṣá-_
*_twéks_	'skin'	Grk _sákkos_, Skt _tvák-_
*(_s_)_kwéh_$_x$_tis_	'skin, hide'	NE _hide_, Grk _skûtos_
*h_1_owes-_	'(inner) skin'	Lat _ōmentum_
*_kérmen-_	'skin'	Skt _cárman-_
*h_a_eĝínom_	'hide'	Skt _ajínam_
*$h_{1/4}$_ómsos_	'shoulder'	Lat _humerus_, Grk _ômos_, Skt _áṃsa-_
*(_s_)_k̂up-_	'shoulder'	Skt _śúpti-_
*h_a_ek̂s-_	'shoulder (joint); axle'.	Lat _axis_, Grk _áksōn_, Skt _ákṣa-_
*h_a_ek̂sleh_$_a$-	'shoulder'	Lat _āla_, NE _axle_
*_pl_(_e_)_t-_	'shoulder (blade)'	Grk _ōmoplátē_
*h_2_épes-_	'limb, part of the body'	Skt _ápsas-_
*_kók̂s-o/eh_$_a$-	'hollow of (major) joint'	Lat _coxa_, Skt _kákṣa-_
*h_a_érh_$_x$_mos_	'arm, forequartcr'	Lat _armus_, NE _arm_, Skt _īrmá-_
*_bhāĝhus_	'(fore)arm, foreleg'	NE _bough_; Grk _pêkhus_; Skt _bāhú-_
*_dous-_	'(upper) arm, shoulder'	Skt _dóṣ-_
*h_3_elVn-_	'elbow, forearm'	Lat _ulna_, NE _ell_, _elbow_
*_ĝhés-r-_	'hand'	Lat _hīr_, Grk _kheír_
*_ĝhós-to-s_	'hand'	Lat _praestō_, Skt _hásta-_
*_méh_$_a$_r̥_	'hand'	Lat _manus_, Grk _márē_
*h_3_nogh_(_w_)-	'(finger- or toe-)nail'	Lat _unguis_, NE _nail_, Grk _ónuks_, Skt _nakhá-_
*_pet_(_e_)_r-_	'wing, feather'	Lat _penna_, NE _feather_
*(_s_)_pornóm_	'wing, feather'	NE _fern_
*_pérk̂us_	'±breast, rib'	Skt _párśva-_
*_psténos_	'woman's breast, nipple'	Grl _stēnion_, Skt _stána-_
*h_1_óuh_$_x$_dhr̥_	'breast, udder'	Lat _ūber_, NE _udder_, Grk _oũthar_, Skt _ū́dhar-_
*_pap-_	'±mother's breast, teat'	Lat _papilla_, Skt _pippala-_
*_kúh_$_x$_los_	'back'	Lat _cūlus_, Skt _kū́la-_
*h_3_nobh-_	'navel, nave'	Lat _umbilīcus_, NE _navel_, Grk _omphalós_, Skt _nā́bhi-_

*h_1_eu-_ respectively, while *_kérmen-_ (e.g. OPrus _kērmens_ 'body', Av _čarəman-_ '[animal] skin, leather', Skt _cárman-_ 'skin') derives from the verb *(_s_)_ker-_ 'cut (off)'. Clearly associated with animal hide is *h_a_eĝínom_ (OCS (_j_)_azno_ 'hide, leather', Skt _ajínam_ 'hide') which derives from *h_a_eĝós_ 'goat' thus originally 'goat-hide'.

There are several words to indicate the 'shoulder'. The primary one, attested in seven groups from Italic to Tocharian, is *$h_{1/4}$_ómsos_ (e.g. Lat (_h_)_umerus_ 'shoulder', Goth *ams* 'shoulder', Grk *ômos* 'shoulder', Arm *us* 'shoulder', Hit *an(as)sa-* 'hip, buttocks; upper back', Skt *áṃsa-* 'shoulder', Toch B *āntse* 'shoulder'); **(s)k̂up-* is also reasonably widely attested (MLG *schuft* 'shoulder blade of cow or horse', Alb *sup* 'shoulder', Av *supti-* 'shoulder', Skt *śúpti-* 'shoulder'). The 'shoulder joint' is found in **$h_a$ek̂s-* and its derivative **$h_a$ek̂-sleh$_a$-*. The first indicates both the 'axis' and the 'axle' of a vehicle while the derivative is more closely associated with the 'shoulder' itself (e.g. Lat *axis* 'axis, axle', *āla* 'shoulder, wing', *axilla* 'armpit', OE *eax* 'axle, axis', *eaxl* 'shoulder', Lith *ašìs* 'axle, axis', OCS *osĭ* 'axle, axis', Grk *áksōn* 'axle, axis', Av *aši-* 'shoulder', Skt *ákṣa-* 'axle, axis'). The adjectival root **plet-* 'broad' gives a noun **pl(e)t-* in Celtic, Slavic, Greek, and Anatolian that means 'shoulder' or 'shoulder blade' (MIr *leithe* 'shoulder', Rus *plečó* 'shoulder', Grk *ōmo-plátē* 'shoulder blade', Hit *paltāna-* 'shoulder'). There are a few general terms for 'limb' or 'joint', i.e. **$h_2$épes-* (e.g. Hit *hapessar* 'limb, joint, part of the body', Oss *æfcæg* 'projecting part of the body, neck', Skt *ápsas-* 'protruding part of the body, breast, forehead, tusk', Toch A *āpsā* [pl.] 'limbs'), an admittedly banal derivative of **$h_2$ep-* 'to fit, fasten', and the hollow part of a joint, the **kók̂s-o/eh$_a$-*, with a challenging semantic spread, e.g. OIr *cos* 'foot', Lat *coxa* 'hip', OHG *hāhsa* 'back of knee', Av *kaša-* 'armpit', Skt *kákṣa-* 'armpit, loins', and Toch B *kakse* 'loins'. Perhaps it originally meant something like 'hollow of (major) joint'.

The upper limb has a number of words associated with it. Attested in six language groups is **$h_a$érh$_x$mos* 'arm' which may derive from **$h_a$érh$_x$-* 'attach' and several languages attest a meaning 'shoulder' which suggests that the semantic field for this word may have originally been the 'upper arm' (e.g. Lat *armus* 'forequarter, shoulder [of an animal]', NE *arm*, OPrus *irmo* 'arm', OCS *ramo* 'shoulder', Av *arəma-* 'arm, forearm', Skt *īrmá-* 'arm'). But **bhā-ĝhus* which can also indicate the shoulder is also reasonably well attested (e.g. OE *bōg* 'shoulder, arm, bough' [> NE *bough*], Grk *pêkhus* 'elbow, forearm', Av *bāzu-* 'arm; foreleg', Skt *bāhú-* 'forearm, arm, forefoot of an animal', Toch B *pokai-* 'arm; limb') and **dous-*, attested in five groups, may mean 'upper arm' or 'forearm' (e.g. OIr *doē* 'arm', Latv *pa-duse* 'armpit' [< 'that under the arm'], Slovenian *paz-duha* 'armpit', Av *daoš-* 'upper arm, shoulder', Skt *dóṣ-* 'forearm, arm'). Six groups attest **$h_3$elVn-* 'elbow, forearm' (e.g. OIr *uilen* 'corner', Lat *ulna* 'forearm, ell', NE *ell, elbow*, Grk *ōlénē* 'forearm', dialectal Grk *ōllón* 'elbow', Arm *oln* 'spine', Toch B *aliye* 'palm'; note that in both Latin and Germanic it also indicates the 'ell', a unit of measurement) and there are some semantic shifts, e.g. Tocharian 'palm'. Six groups, including Hittite, give us **ĝhés-r-* 'hand' (e.g. Lat *hīr* 'hollow of the hand', Alb *dorë* 'hand', Grk *kheír* 'hand', Arm *jeṙn* 'hand', Hit *kissar* 'hand', Toch B *ṣar* 'hand') while a derivative, **ghós-to-s*, is found in four groups (Lat *praestō* [< **prai-hestōd*] 'a hand',

Lith *pa-žastìs* 'armpit', Av *zasta-* 'hand', Skt *hásta-* 'hand'). Another word for 'hand', **méh*$_a$*r̥* (oblique stem **meh*$_a$*n-*), has been seen to have an underlying semantic connotation of 'power' as in 'hand over' (e.g. Lat *manus* 'hand', OE *mund* '[palm of the] hand, protection', Goth *manwus* 'at hand, ready', Grk *márē* 'hand', *iómōros* 'having arrows at hand', and the related Alb *marr* 'take, grasp', Hit *māniyahh-* 'hand over', *māri* 'manual tool, weapon'). The word for 'nail', **h*$_3$*nogh(w)-*, is nearly ubiquitous across the Indo-European world (e.g. OIr *ingen*, Lat *unguis*, NE *nail*, Lith *nãgas*, OCS *nogŭtĭ*, Grk *ónuks*, Skt *nakhá-*, Toch B *mekwa* [pl.], all 'nail'). In some groups the meaning has been generalized to 'foot' (e.g. Lith *nagà* 'hoof', Rus *nogá* 'foot, leg', Skt *ánghri-* 'foot'). For birds we have two words associated with 'wing' or 'feather', **pet(e)r/n-* (e.g. OIr *ēn* 'bird', Lat *penna* 'feather', NE *feather*, Grk *pterón* 'wing', Arm *t'rč'im* 'fly', Hit *pittar* ~ *pattar* 'wing') and **(s)pornóm* (e.g. NE *fern*, Lith *spar̃nas* 'wing', Av *parəna-* 'feather', Skt *parṇá-* 'feather'; also OCS *pero* 'feather', Toch B *parwa* [pl.] 'feathers'). The first derives from the verbal root **pet-* 'fly'.

The mid section has **pérk̂us* which may mean either 'breast' or 'rib' (e.g. dialectal Lith *piršys* 'forepart of a horse's chest', Rus *pérsi* [pl.] 'breast, chest [especially of a horse]', Alb *parz* ~ *parzëm* 'breast', Av *parəsu-* 'rib', Skt *párśu-* 'rib', *pārśvá-* 'region of the ribs, side') while a 'woman's breast' is indicated by cognates extending from Greek eastwards in **psténos* (e.g. dialectal Grk *stḗnion*, Arm *stin*, Av *fštāna-*, Skt *stána-*, Toch B *päścane* [dual], all 'woman's breast'; we will find a derivative in the North-Western languages). For animals largely we have **h*$_1$*óuh*$_x$*dhr̥* 'breast, udder' (e.g. Lat *ūber* 'udder, teat, [lactating] breast', NE *udder*, Lith *pa-ū̃dre* 'abdomen', Grk *oũthar* 'udder', Skt *ū́dhar-* 'udder'); the root **pap-* (e.g. Lat *papilla* 'teat, nipple, breast', MHG *buoben* 'breast', Lith *pãpas* 'breast', Skt *pippala-* 'nipple') looks like a continually reinvented children's word (cf. NE *pap* and *boob*). The word for 'back', **kúh*$_x$*-los* (OIr *cūl* 'back', Lat *cūlus* 'rear-end', Skt *kū́la-* 'slope, back; rear of army'), is derived from the root **keuh*$_x$*-* 'be bent (convexly)' (apparently distinct from **keuh*$_x$*-* 'hollow'; see also 'hernia' [Section 11.7]). Finally, **h*$_3$*nobh-* 'navel' also yields the meaning 'nave', and although 'navel' is the original meaning, a number of languages form their word for 'navel' by applying an extension, e.g. OE *nafu* 'nave' but OE *nafela* 'navel' (cf. also OIr *imbliu* 'navel', Lat *umbilīcus* 'navel', *umbō* 'boss on a shield', OPrus *nabis* 'nave, navel', Grk *omphalós* 'navel', Skt *nā́bhi-* 'navel', *nábhya-* 'nave').

The regional vocabulary includes North-Western words such as the Celtic-Germanic isogloss **letrom* 'leather' (e.g. OIr *lethar* 'leather', NE *leather*); **pólik(o)s* 'finger, thumb' (e.g. Lat *pollex* 'thumb', Rus *pálec* 'finger, toe'); **pn̥(k*^{w}*)stí-* 'fist' (e.g. NE *fist*, Lith *kùmstė* [< **punkstė*] 'fist', OCS *pęstĭ* 'fist') which may derive from the word for 'five' (**penk*^{w}*e*); and **speno-* '(woman's) breast, nipple' (e.g. OIr *sine* 'teat', OE *spanu* 'breast', Lith *spenỹs* 'teat') which appears to be a metathesized and simplified Western version of Proto-Indo-European **psténos* listed above. The West Central region also exhibits several words for 'skin', i.e. **péln-* 'animal skin, hide' (e.g. Lat *pellis* '[animal] skin, hide', NE *fell* and also *film*, Lith *plėnė̃* 'film [on milk], scab', Rus *plená* 'pelt', Grk *erusí-pelas* 'red inflammation of the skin'); and possibly **nák(es)-* '± pelt, hide' (e.g. OE *næsc* 'dressed fawn's skin', OPrus *nognan* 'leather', Grk *nákos* ~ *nákē* 'pelt, fleece, hide of deer or goat'). Other isoglosses include **méles-* 'limb' (e.g. Breton *mell* 'knuckle', Grk *mélos* 'limb'); *h_3*elek-* 'elbow, forearm' (a regional variant of the more widespread *h_3*elVn-*, e.g. Lith *úolektis* 'ell', *alkū́ne* 'elbow', Rus *lokótĭ* 'elbow, ell', dialectal Grk *álaks* 'forearm', Arm *olok'* 'shin, leg'); **pólh*$_a$*m̥* 'palm of the hand' (e.g. OIr *lām* 'hand', Lat *palma* 'palm', OE *folma* 'palm, hand', Grk *palámē* 'palm'); **dhénr̥* 'palm (of the hand)' (OHG *tenar* 'palm', Grk *thénar* 'palm, sole [of the foot]'), **dheh*$_1$*lus* 'nourishing, suckling' and **dhh*$_1$*ileh*$_a$*-* 'teat, breast' (e.g. Lat *fēlix* 'fruitful, prosperous, happy', Grk *thêlus* 'nourishing', Skt *dhārú-* 'suckling', MIr *deil* 'teat', OE *delu* 'nipple, teat'), both banal derivatives of the verb **dheh*$_1$*(i)-* 'suckle'; and possibly *teig*^{w}*-* '± side' with OIr *tōib* 'side' and Arm *t'ekn* 'shoulder'. Finally, there is the Indo-Iranian-Tocharian isogloss **mustí-* 'fist' (Av *mušti-*, Skt *muṣṭí-*, Toch B *maśce*, all 'fist').

11.4 The Lower Body and Legs

There is no unambiguous word for 'hip' although **k̂lóunis* may mean 'hip' in some languages where it also may indicate the 'haunch' or 'thigh' (e.g. NWels *clun* 'haunch', Lat *clūnis* 'buttocks, haunch [of animals]', ON *hlaun* 'buttocks, loin', OPrus *slaunis* 'hip', ?Alb *qênjë* 'belt', Grk *klónis* 'os sacrum', Av *sraoni-* 'buttock', Skt *śróṇi-* 'buttock, hip, loin'); the other possible word for 'hip' is **srēno/eh*$_a$*-* but this is limited to Baltic (e.g. Lith *strėnà* 'loin') and Iranian (e.g. Av *rāna-* 'thigh'). The part of the body covered by **sók*^{w}*t* certainly seems to include '(upper) leg' (as it is in Hit *sakutt(a)-* 'upper leg') but it may also mean 'hip' in Slavic and Avestan (e.g. Rus *stegnó* [< **segdno* < **sektno*] 'hip, groin, thigh', Av *haxti-* 'hip', Skt *sákthi* 'thigh'). There are two words for 'loins', **isĝhis-* (e.g. Grk *iskhíon* 'hip', *iksús* 'loins, groin', Hit *iskis(a)-* 'loins', Lat *īlia* [pl.] 'abdomen below the ribs, groin, flanks') and **lóndhu* (e.g. Lat *lumbus* 'loin', OE *lendenu* [pl.] 'loins', Rus *ljádveja* 'loin, hip', Skt *rándhram* 'loins'). The first is found both in the form given and metathesized as **iĝs-*, e.g. Grk *iksús*. There are two words for 'rear-end' or 'rump': *h_1*órs(o)-* (e.g. NE *arse/ass*, Grk *órros* 'rump', Arm *oṙ* 'rump', Hit *ārra-* ~ *ārri-* ~ *arru-* 'rump') and **bulis* (e.g. Lith *bulìs* 'rump', Skt *buli-* 'vulva; anus').

Table 11.4. *The lower body and legs*

**k̂lóunis*	'±haunch, hip'	Lat *clūnis*, Grk *klónis*, Skt *śróṇi-*
**srēno/eh$_a$-*	'±hip, thigh'	
**sók^{w}t*	'(upper) leg'	Skt *sákthi*
**isĝhis-*	'loins'	Lat *īlia*, Grk *iskhíon*
**lóndhu*	'loins'	Lat *lumbus*, Skt *rándhram*
**h$_1$órs(o)-*	'rear-end'	NE *arse*, *ass*, Grk *órros*
**bulis*	'±rump'	Skt *buli-*
**ĝónu*	'knee'	Lat *genū*, NE *knee*, Grk *gónu*, Skt *jā́nu*
**kenk-*	'±hock, back of knee'	NE *hough*, *hock*
**pṓds*	'foot'	Lat *pēs*, NE *foot*, Grk *poús*, Skt *pád-*
**leh$_a$p-eh$_a$-*	'foot, paw'	
**pérsn-eh$_a$-*	'heel'	Grk *ptérna*, Skt *pā́rṣṇī-*
**pēnt-*	'heel'	
**spr̥h$_x$-ó-*	'heel'	NE *spur*, Grk *sphurón*
**péses-*	'penis'	Lat *pēnis*, Grk *péos*, Skt *pásas-*
**kápr̥*	'penis'	Lat *caper*, Grk *kápros*, Skt *kápr̥th*
**putós*	'±vulva, anus'	Grk *púnnos*, Skt *putau*
**kutsós*	'anus, vulva'	Lat *cunnus*, Grk *kūsós*
**pisdo/eh$_a$-*	'vulva'	
**kuk̂is*	'±(female) pubic hair, vulva'	
**g$^{(w)}$elbhus*	'womb'	NE *calf*, Grk *delphús*, Skt *gárbha-*
**h$_4$órĝhis*	'testicle'	Grk *órkhis*
**h$_1$endrós*	'egg, scrotum'	Skt *āṇḍá-*

The word for 'knee', **ĝónu*, is a textbook word, attested in ten groups (e.g. OIr *glūn*, Lat *genū*, NE *knee*, Alb *gju*, Grk *gónu*, Arm *cunr*, Hit *gēnu*, Av *žnu-*, Skt *jā́nu*, Toch B *kenī(ne)* [dual], all 'knee'). The back of the knee or 'hock' is represented by a less widely attested word **kenk-* (e.g. NE *hock*, Lith *kenklė̃* 'hock, back of the knee', Skt *kankāla-* 'bone, skeleton'). For '(human) foot' in general we have the extremely well-attested **pṓds* (e.g. Lat *pēs* 'foot', NE *foot*, Lith *pãdas* 'sole of foot', Rus *pód* 'ground', Grk *poús* 'foot', Arm *otn* 'foot', Hit *pata-* 'foot', Av *pad-* 'foot', Skt *pád-* 'foot', Toch B *paiyye* 'foot') while for '(animal) foot, paw' there is the less widely attested **leh$_a$p-eh$_a$-* (e.g. ON *lōfi* 'palm', Lith *lópa* 'paw', Rus *lápa* 'paw', Kurdish *lapka* 'paw') and three words for 'heel': **pérsn-eh$_a$-* (e.g. Lat *perna* 'haunch', OE *fiersn* 'heel', Grk *ptérna* 'heel', Hit *parsna-* 'upper thigh', Av *pāšna-* 'heel', Skt *pā́rṣṇi-* 'heel', Toch B *porsnai-* 'ankle'), **pēnt-* (e.g. OPrus *pentis* 'heel', Rus *pjatá* 'heel', Pashto *pūnda* 'heel'), and **spr̥h$_x$-ó-* (e.g. OE *spor* 'footprint' [> NE *spoor*], *spure* 'heel', *spur*

'spur', Grk *sphurón* 'ankle[bone]', Toch B *sprāne* [dual] 'flanks', with the same kind of semantic development seen in Hit *parsna-*).

Terminology associated with genitalia survives rather well. There are two words for 'penis': **péses-* and **kápr̥*. The first is attested in five groups, including Anatolian (e.g. Lat *pēnis* 'penis', OHG *fasel* 'penis', Grk *péos* 'penis', Hit *pisna-* 'man' [i.e. 'one provided with a penis'], *pisnatar* 'penis', Skt *pásas-* 'penis'); it has been variously analysed as deriving from a verb 'rub', a verb 'penetrate', and, most recently, from **pes-* 'blow, swell', i.e. a swelling forth of liquid. The second word is basically attested by derivatives, in that Old Indic alone retains a meaning 'penis' (Skt *kápr̥th*) while in the other groups an *o*-stem derivative (i.e. 'one provided with a **kapr̥*') indicates either a 'he-goat' (Celtic, e.g. OIr *gabor*, Italic, e.g. Lat *caper*, Germanic, e.g. OE *hæfer*) or 'boar' (Grk *kápros*), i.e. these are archetypically 'male' animals. The best-attested word for 'vulva' is **putós*, found in Germanic (e.g. MHG *vut* 'vulva'), Grk *púnnos* 'anus', and Skt *putau* [dual] 'buttocks'. The crossing of 'anus' and 'vulva' also occurs in **kutsós* (e.g. Lat *cunnus* 'vulva', dialectal Grk *kūsós* 'vulva; anus', NPers *kūn* ass, backside; compare the similar semantic crossing in NE 'ass' and the Sanskrit descendant of **bulis* above). Another word for 'vulva', **pisdo/eh$_a$-* (e.g. Lith *pyzdà*, Rus *pizdá*, Alb *pidh*, Nūristāni *pəṛí*, all 'vulva'), is analysed as an old compound *(*h$_1$e*)*pi-* + *s*(*e*)*d-* + *-o-* 'what one sits on'. A Baltic-Iranian isogloss (e.g. Lith *kūšỹs* 'female pubic hair, vulva', NPers *kus* 'female genitals') supports the existence of **kuk̂is* 'female pubic hair, vulva'. The 'womb' is seen in **g$^{(w)}$elbhus* ~ **g$^{(w)}$ólbhos* (e.g. Grk *delphús*, Av *garəwa-*, Skt *gárbha-*, all 'womb') with frequent semantic shifts to 'newly born animal' (Av *gərəbuš*), either a lamb (OE *cilfor-lamb* 'ewe-lamb') or, in its *o*-stem form, **g$^{(w)}$olbho-*, the young of a cow, e.g. NE *calf*. The word for 'testicles', **h$_4$órĝhis* (e.g. MIr *uirge*, Alb *herdhe*, Grk *órkhis*, Arm *orjik'*, Hit *arki-*, and Av *ərəzī*, all 'testicle(s)'), is a deverbative from **h$_4$órĝhei* 'mounts (sexually)' (e.g. Hit *ārki* 'mounts', Rus *jërzajet* 'fidgets, wiggles, moves in coitus', Grk *orkhéomai* 'make lascivious motions, dance'; for the semantic relationship cf. American English 'balls', i.e. both 'testicles' (noun) and 'copulates' (verb)). The word for 'egg' or 'scrotum', **h$_1$endrós*, is built on a preposition and indicates 'that which is inside' (Rus *jadró* 'kernel, scrotum', Skt *āṇḍá-* 'egg, scrotum', [dual] 'testicles'.

Regional terms from the West Central region include **kónh$_a$m̥* 'lower leg, shin' (e.g. OIr *cnāim* 'leg', NE *ham*, Grk *knḗmē* 'tibia, spoke of a wheel'); **n*(*o*)*h$_x$t-* '±rear-end' (Lat *natis* 'human buttocks', Grk *nôton* 'back'); a Greek-Armenian isogloss **pr̥h$_3$k̂tós* 'anus' (Grk *prōktós*, Arm *erastank'* [pl.]). We also have two Greek-Indic isoglosses: **ĝhn̥ghéno/eh$_a$-* '±buttock' (Grk *kokhṓnē* 'crotch', Skt *jaghána-* 'hind end, buttock, pudenda') and **muskós* 'male or female sex organ' (dialectal Grk *múskhon* 'male or female sex organs',

Skt *muṣká-* 'testicle, scrotum; [dual] vulva'), a word like 'muscle' that ultimately derives from 'mouse', i.e. a moving bulge under the skin.

11.5 Internal Organs

As mentioned above, we know rather less about the designations for internal organs in Proto-Indo-European than we do about the external parts of the anatomy. Among the internal organs the word for the heart is particularly well reflected in the descendent languages. The liver is also well represented while the lungs and kidneys are less so. It is significant that we can reconstruct at least

Table 11.5. *Internal organs*

**mosghos*	'marrow, brain'	NE *marrow*, Skt *majján-*
**gutr̥*	'gullet, throat'	Lat *guttur*
**udero-*	'abdomen, stomach'	Lat *uterus*, Skt *udára-*, Grk *úderos*
**ud*^{s}*tero-*	'abdomen, stomach'	Grk *hustérā*
**wenVst(r)-*	'(ab)omasum'	Lat *venter*, Grk *ḗnustron*, Skt *vaniṣṭhú-*
**reumn-*	'rumen'	Lat *rūmen*, Skt *romantha-*
**pant-*	'stomach, paunch'	Lat *pantex*
**g*^{w}*étus*	'stomach, womb'	Lat *botulus*
**h*$_1$*en-t(e)rom*	'innards'	Grk *éntera*, Skt *antrā́-*
**gudóm*	'intestines'	Skt *gudá-*
**ĝhorh*$_x$*neh*$_a$*-*	'entrails'	Lat *haruspex*, NE *yarn*, Grk *khordḗ*, Skt *híra-*
**wn̥d*^{s}*tí-*	'bladder'	Lat *vēs(s)īca*, Skt *vastí-*
**ĝhóln-~ *ĝhólos*	'gall'	Lat *fel*, NE *gall*, Grk *khólos*
**h*$_2$*eh*$_2$*(e)r-*	'±kidney'	
**yék*^{w}*r̥(t)*	'liver'	Lat *iecur*, Grk *hêpar*, Skt *yákr̥t*
**lesi-*	'liver'	
**sploiĝh*$_2$*- ḗn*	'spleen'	Lat *liēn*, Grk *splḗn*, Skt *plīhán-*
**pléumōn*	'lung'	Lat *pulmō*, Grk *pleúmōn*, Skt *klóman-*
**h*$_1$*eh*$_1$*tr-*	'±lung, internal organ'	Grk *êtor*
**k̂ērd*	'heart'	Lat *cor*, NE *heart*, Gkt *kardíā*, Skt *hŕ̥daya-*
**h*$_1$*ésh*$_2$*r̥*	'(flowing) blood'	Lat *aser*, Grk *éar*, Skt *ásr̥k*
**kréuh*$_a$	'blood, gore'	Lat *cruor*, Grk *kréas*, Skt *kráviṣ-*
**h*$_2$*óst*	'bone'	Lat *os*, Grk *ostéon*, Skt *ásthi*
**mūs(tlo)-*	'(little) mouse; muscle'	Lat *mūsculus*, Grk *mûs*
**snéh*$_1$*wr̥*	'sinew, tendon'	Lat *nervus*, Grk *neûron*, Skt *snāvan-*

some words for parts of the complex digestive system of ruminants. The relationship between Proto-Indo-European speakers (and their descendants) and their domesticated animals has been a long and close one. We know almost nothing of what Proto-Indo-European speakers might have called nerves and blood vessels. It is quite possible that there was no very elaborate Proto-Indo-European vocabulary for this part of the anatomy.

The word(s) for 'brain' and 'marrow' are often combined in Indo-European. The only one with a sure claim to PIE status is **mosghos* which means 'marrow' in Germanic (e.g. NE *marrow*), both 'marrow' and 'brain' in Baltic, Slavic, and Indo-Iranian (e.g. Lith *smãgenės* 'marrow', *smẽgenys* brain', OCS *mozgŭ* 'marrow, brain', Av *mazga-* 'marrow, brain', Skt *majján-* 'marrow').

The 'gullet' or 'throat', **gutr̥*, is attested as a Latin-Hittite isogloss (Lat *guttur* 'gullet, throat, neck', Hit *kuttar* 'nape of neck'). The stomach, of humans or animals, is well attested in Indo-European. **udero-* (e.g. Lat *uterus* 'abdomen, womb', Grk *húderos* 'dropsy' [<*'swollen stomach'], Av *udara-* 'stomach', Skt *udára-* 'stomach') and **ud^{s}tero-* (e.g. Grk *hustérā* 'womb', *hústros* 'stomach', Toch B *wästarye* 'liver') both derive from **ud* 'out', i.e. it is the outer or superficial abdomen in distinction to the 'entrails'. The 'omasum' or 'abomasum', the third and fourth chambers of a ruminant's stomach, is attested in **wenVst(r)-* (e.g. Lat *venter* 'belly', OHG *wenist* 'belly, omasum', Grk *ḗnustron* 'abomasum', Skt *vaniṣṭhú-* 'part of the entrails of a sacrificial animal') while the first stomach, the rumen, **reumn-*, may also be ascribed to Proto-Indo-European (e.g. Lat *rūmen* 'gullet, rumen', Baluchi *rōmast* 'rumination', Skt *romantha-* 'rumination'). A Latin-Hittite isogloss (Lat *pantex* 'belly, paunch, guts', Hit *panduha-* 'stomach') gives us **pant-* 'stomach'. PIE **g^{w}étus* yields cognates with meanings such as 'stomach', 'womb', and 'intestines' (e.g. OE *cwiþ* 'belly, womb', Lat *botulus* 'intestines, sausage', Toch B *kātso* 'belly, womb'). The 'entrails' themselves are seen in three roots: **$h_1$en-t(e)rom* (e.g. ON *innr* 'entrails', OCS *jętro* 'liver', Grk *éntera* [pl.] 'entrails', Arm *ənderk'* 'entrails', Skt *antrá-* 'entrails'), literally the 'inner part' (cf. NE *innards* and **$h_1$entrós* above); **gudóm* (Low German *küt*, Macedonian *góda*, Skt *gudá-*, all 'intestines') which may derive from the verbal root **geu-* 'bend, twist'; and **ĝhorh$_x$neh$_a$-* where Germanic, Greek, and Indic suggest the connotation 'string of gut', e.g. NE *yarn*, Grk *khordḗ* 'string of gut; sausage', Skt *híra-* 'band, strip' (cf. also Lat *haruspex* 'entrail-seer', ON *gǫrn* 'guts', Lith *žarnà* 'guts').

The 'bladder', **wn̥d^{s}tí-*, rests on an Italic-Indic correspondence (Lat *vēs(s)īca*, Skt *vastí-*). The word for 'gall', **ĝhóln-* ~ **ĝhólos* (Lat *fel*, NE *gall*, Grk *khólos* ~ *kholḗ*, Av *zāra-*, all 'gall'), is a transparent derivative from **ĝhel-* 'yellow'. The 'kidney' is seen in **h_2eh_2(e)r-* if that is the correct proto-meaning (in Hittite the *hah(a)ri-* is some paired organ and Toch B *arañce* means 'heart'—cf. OIr *āru* 'kidney, gland', and maybe Lat *rēnēs* [pl.] 'kidneys'). Two words indicate the 'liver': **yék^{w}r̥t* is ancient and a heteroclitic (e.g. Lat *iecur*, Lith *(j)ẽknos* [pl.], Grk *hêpar*, Av *yākarə*, Skt *yákr̥t*, all 'liver'); **lesi-* is problematic in that it occurs only in Hit *lissi-* and Arm *leard* and while a cognate with Anatolian normally presumes Proto-Indo-European status, this word could be an early loan between two neighbouring languages. The 'spleen' is designated by **sploiĝh_2-ḗn* (e.g. OIr *selg*, Lat *liēn*, OCS *slězena*, Grk *splḗn* [> via Latin in NE *spleen*], Arm *p'aycaln*, Av *spərəzan-*, Skt *plīhán-*, all 'spleen'), though, for whatever reason, it has undergone an unusual amount of irregular phonological development.

The 'lung' was designated by **pléumōn* (e.g. Lat *pulmō* 'lung', Grk *pleúmōn* 'lung', Skt *klóman-* 'right lung'), which derives from **pleu-* 'float', i.e. the lung was the 'floater'. (One might compare the old-fashioned butchers' term for 'lungs' in English, namely *lights*.) A second word, **h_1e$h_1$tr-*, poses horrendous problems of semantic reconstruction as it means, among other things, 'entrails' (Celtic *inathar*), 'vein' (Germanic, e.g. OHG *ād(a)ra*), 'heart' (Grk *ē̂tor*, and also *ē̂tron* 'belly, abdomen'), and 'comfort' (Av *hv-āθra-*); its association with the lungs is presumed purely because the root appears to be related to **h_1e$h_1$tmén-* 'breath' (e.g. OE *ǣðre*, Skt *ātmán-*) and so we might suppose that it had something to do with the lungs. The word for 'heart', **k̂ērd* or **k̂r̥dyeh$_a$-*, is found in eleven groups (e.g. OIr *cride*, Lat *cor*, NE *heart*, Lith *širdìs*, Rus *sérdce*, Grk *kē̂r* and *kardíāñ*, Arm *sirt*, Hit *kir*, Av *zərəd-*, Skt *hŕ̥d-* and *hŕ̥daya-*, Toch B *käryāñ* [pl.], all 'heart[s]'). There are two semantically distinct words for 'blood'. **$h_1$ésh_2r̥* indicates 'flowing blood' (e.g. archaic Lat *asser*, Grk *éar*, Arm *ariwn*, Hit *ēshar*, Skt *ásr̥k*, Toch B *yasar*, all 'blood') while **kréuh$_a$* indicates 'blood outside the body' and yields meanings such as 'gore', 'raw flesh', 'piece of meat' (e.g. MIr *crū* 'blood', Lat *cruor* 'thick blood, gore', Lith *kraũjas* 'blood', Rus *króvĭ* 'blood', Grk *kréa* 'raw flesh', *kréas* 'piece of meat', Skt *krávis̩-* 'raw flesh'). The word for 'bone', **$h_2$óst*, is seen to be archaic in form and is found in eight groups (e.g. Lat *os*, Alb *asht*, Grk *ostéon*, Arm *oskr*, Hit *hastāi-*, Av *asti-*, Skt *ásthi*, Toch B *āsta* [pl.], all 'bone[s]', and OIr *esna* ~ *asna* 'ribs'). The word for 'muscle', **mūs(tlo)-*, is closely associated with the word for 'mouse' (it means 'little mouse'), and words for 'mouse' may also mean 'muscle' in various Indo-European groups (e.g. Lat *mūsculus* 'little mouse; muscle' [> NE *muscle*], OHG *mūs* 'mouse; muscle [especially the biceps]', Grk *mûs* 'mouse; muscle', Arm *mukn* 'mouse; muscle', Khotanese *mūla-* 'mouse; muscle'). The verbal root **snéh$_1$(u)-* 'turn, twist' is the basis for **snéh$_1$wr̥* 'tendon, sinew' (e.g. Lat *nervus* 'sinew, tendon, nerve, muscle' [> NE *nerve*], Grk *neũron* 'sinew, tendon, gut', Arm *neard* 'tendon', Av *nāvarə* 'tendon', Skt *snāvan-* 'tendon', Toch B *s̩ñor* 'tendon, sinew').

From the West Central region we have **mréghmen-* 'brain' (e.g. OE *bregen*> NE *brain*, Grk *brekhmós* 'forehead'); **bh*$_e$*rug-* 'gullet' (Lat *frūmen*, Grk *phár-u(g)ks* 'gullet', Arm *erbuc* 'breast'); **n̥g*^{w}*én-* ' ± (swollen) gland' (e.g. Lat *inguen* 'groin, swelling of the groin', OHG *ankweiz* 'pustules', Grk *adḗn* 'gland'); **ghelĝheh*$_a$*-* 'gland' (Rus *železá* 'gland', Arm *geljk'* [pl.] 'gland'); **neg*^{w}*hrós* 'kidney' (e.g. ME *nēre* 'kidney', Grk *nephrós* 'kidney'); and there is an Eastern **móstr̥* 'brain, marrow' (e.g. Av *mastrəγan-* 'skullwall' [< *'brain-case'], Skt *mastíṣka-* 'brain', Toch A *mäśśunt* [pl.] 'marrow').

11.6 Vital Functions

The verb 'to live' is **g*^{w}*eih*$_3$*-* (e.g. Lat *vīvō* 'live', Lith *gyjù* 'become healthy', OCS *živǫ* 'live', Av *ǰvaiti* 'lives', Skt *jī́vati* 'lives', Grk *zṓō* 'live', Toch B *śāw-* 'live'; NE *quick* is related to this root) and the concept of 'vital force' or 'life' is seen in **h*$_a$*óyus* (see below).

There are several words relating to the sexual act. A PIE **h*$_4$*órĝhei* 'mounts' is found in Germanic (e.g. ON *ergi* 'lascivious behaviour'), Baltic (e.g. Lith *ar-žùs* 'lascivious'), Slavic (e.g. Rus *jërzajet* 'fidgets, moves in coitus'), Grk *orkhéo-mai* 'makes lascivious motion', Ht *ārki* ~ *arga* 'mounts (used with respect to a male animal)', Skt *r̥ghāyáte* 'is impetuous'. The verbal form also underlies **h*$_4$*órĝhis* 'testicle', suggesting that the Proto-Indo-Europeans shared the same semantic mindset that yields American slang 'balls' to indicate both 'testicles' and the sexual act. We also have **yébhe/o-* 'enter, penetrate' in the specific meaning 'copulate' which is seen in Rus *jebú*, Grki *oíphō*, and Skt *yábhati*, all 'copulate(s)'; this meaning appears to be a later semantic development which did not take place in Anatolian or Tocharian (e.g. Toch B *yäp-* 'enter, set [of sun]'), nor is it found in the West. There is also a series of words for the concept 'bear young'. The most widespread is **bhére/o-*, the verb that can mean 'carry' as well as 'bear a child' (e.g. OIr *beirid* 'bears', Lat *ferō* 'bear', NE *bear*, OCS *berǫ* 'gather', Alb *bie* 'bring, take', Grk *phérō* 'bear', Arm *berem* 'bear', Av *baraiti* 'bears', Skt *bhárati* 'bears', Toch AB *pär-* 'bear'; a derivative gives the NE *bairn* 'child'). Another verb is **seu(h*$_x$*)-* (e.g. Av *hu-* 'bear a child', Skt *sū́te* 'bears, begets') which also has nominal derivatives, e.g. NE *son*, Grk *huyús* 'son', Skt *sūnús* 'son', Toch B *soy* 'son'. **ĝenh*$_1$*-* gives rebuilt transitive forms (e.g. OLat *genō* 'beget', Lat *gignō* 'produce', OE *cennan* 'beget', Grk *gennáō* 'beget', Skt *jánati* 'begets') but there is an underlying intransitive form, 'be born', that is found in Lat *gnāscor* 'am born', Grk *gígnomai* 'am born', Skt *jajána* 'am born'. The verb **tek-* 'bear a child' (Grk *tíktomai* 'bear, beget') provides the base of a noun **tek-men-* that gives NE *thane* and Skt *tákman-* 'child, offspring'.

Table 11.6. *Vital functions*

*$g^w eih_3$-	'live'	Lat *vīvō*
*$h_a$óyus	'vital force, life, age of vigour'	Lat *aevus*
*$h_4$órĝhei	'mounts'	Grk *orkhéomai*, Skt *r̥ghāyáte*
*yébhe/o-	'enter, penetrate, copulate'	Grki *oíphō*, Skt *yábhati*
*bhére/o-	'bear (a child)'	Lat *ferō*, NE *bear*, Grk *phérō*, Skt *bhárati*
*seu(h_x)-	'bear a child'	Skt *sū́te*
*ĝenh$_1$-	'beget a child; be born'	Lat *genō*, Grk *gennáō*, Skt *jánati*
*tek-	'bear or beget a child'	Grk *títkomai*, NE *thane*, Skt *tákman-*
*$h_a$eug-	'grow'	Lat *augeō*, NE *eke*, Grk *aéksō*, Skt *úkṣati*
*$h_a$wokséye/o-	'grow'	NE *wax*, Skt *vakṣayati*
*ĝerh$_a$-	'grow, age, mature'	Grk *gēráskō*, Skt *jī́ryati*
*$h_1$leudh-	'grow'	Lat *līber*, Grk *eleútheros*, Skt *ródhati*
*k̂er-	'grow'	Lat *crescō*, *creō*, Grk *korénnūmi*
*meh$_1$(i)-	'grow'	Skt *mímīte*
*bhenĝh-	'grow, increase'	Skt *baṃhayate*
*wredh-	'grow, stand, take shape'	Grk *orthós*, Skt *várdhate*
*$h_a$énh$_1$mi	'breathe'	Skt *ániti*
*$h_1$eh$_1$tmén-	'breath'	Skt *ātmán-*
*$h_a$énh$_1$mos	'breath'	Lat *animus*, Grk *ánemos*
*k̂wésh$_x$mi	'breathe deeply, sigh'	Lat *queror*, Skt *śvásiti*
*dhwésmi	'breathe, be full of (wild) spirits'	Lat *furō*, NE *dizzy*
*bhes-	'± blow'	Grk *psūkhḗ*, ?Skt *-psu-*
*k^weh$_a$s-	'cough'	NE *wheeze*
*denk̂-	'bite'	NE *tong*, Grk *dáknō*, Skt *dáśati*
*$h_1$reug-	'belch'	Lat *ērūgō*, Grk *ereúgomai*
*wémh$_x$mi	'spew, vomit'	Lat *vomō*, Grk *eméō*, Skt *vámiti*
*(s)py(e)uh$_x$-	'spew, spit'	Lat *spuō*, NE *spew*, Grk *ptúō*, Skt *ṣṭhīvati*
*(d)h$_2$ék̂ru	'tear'	OLat *dacruma*, Lat *lacrima*, NE *tear*, Grk *dákru*, Skt *áśru-*
*sweid-	'sweat'	Lat *sūdō*, NE *sweat*, Grk *idíō*, Skt *svédate*
*$h_4$elh$_1$-n-	'sweat' (noun)	
*$h_3$méiĝhe/o-	'urinate'	Lat *meiō*, Grk *omeíkhō*, Skt *méhati*
*sók̂r̥	'(human) excrement'	Grk *skōr*
*kerd-	'± defile, defecate'	Lat *-cerda*
*g^wuh$_x$-	'defecate'	Skt *gūtha-*
*ĝhed-ye/o-	'defecate'	Grk *khézō*
*k̂ók^{w}r̥	'excrement, dung, manure'	Grk *kópros*, Skt *śákr̥t*
*pérde/o-	'fart'	NE *fart*, Grk *pérdomai*, Skt *párdate*

The semantic sphere of 'grow' or 'increase' is abundantly covered in Proto-Indo-European. *$h_a$eug-* is known in seven groups (e.g. Lat *augeō* 'augment, increase', NE *eke*, Lith *áugu* 'grow', Grk *aéksō* 'increase', Av *uxšyeiti* 'grows', Skt *úkṣati* 'strengthens', Toch B *auk-* 'grow, increase') while its derivative, *$h_a$wokséye/o-*, is attested in three (e.g. NE *wax*, Av *vaxšaiti* 'grows', Skt *vakṣayati* 'grows'); both of these have the connotation 'increase'. The root *ĝerh$_a$-* suggests a meaning 'grow old' (e.g. OCS *zŭrěti* 'ripen', Grk *gēráskō* 'age, grow old', Skt *jī́ryati* ~ *jū́ryati* 'grows old, becomes decrepit', Toch AB *kwär-* 'age, grow old') and provides the base for words meaning 'old man' (e.g. Grk *gérōn*, Arm *cer*, Skt *járant-*). *$h_1$leudh-* also suggests growth in terms of maturation (e.g. OIr *lus* 'plant', Lat *Līber* 'god of growth', OE *lēodan* 'spring up, grow', Av *raodaiti* 'grows', Skt *ródhati* 'grows') and in nominal forms it may mean 'children' (Lat *līberī* [pl.] 'children'), 'free' (Lat *līber*, Grk *eleútheros*) or 'people' (e.g. NHG *Leute* 'people', Lith *liáudis* 'common people', Rus *ljúdi* 'people, servants'). The semantic field of **k̂er-* more precisely concerns the growth of plants; the name of the Latin goddess *Cerēs* derives from this root (cf. also Lat *creō* 'create', Grk *korénnūmi* 'satisfy', *koûros* 'adolescent', Arm *sirem* 'bring forth', Tocharian *kärk-* 'sprout'). The root **meh$_1$(i)-* (e.g. Hit *māi-* 'grow', Skt *mímīte* 'is conceived, grows [of the fetus in the womb]', Toch B *maiwe* 'youth') has a derivative **meh$_1$ro-* 'large' (see Section 19.2). PIE **bhenĝh-* 'grow, increase' appears as a verb only in Skt *baṃhayate* 'causes to grow' but its derivative, **bhénĝhus* 'thick, abundant', has left a widespread progeny (see Section 19.2). Finally, **wredh-* is also associated with the concepts of 'standing up(right)' and 'taking shape' (e.g. Latv *rãdît* 'bear', Rus *rodítĭ* 'produce', Grk *orthós* 'upright, straight, true', Av *vərədaiti* 'grows', Skt *vr̥dháti* 'grows, increases, becomes strong', *vrādhant-* 'upright', Toch AB *wrāt-* 'form, shape').

Respiratory activities are well attested with the verb **$h_a$énh$_1$-*, first person singular **$h_a$énh$_1$mi*, 'breathe' (Goth *uzanan* 'breathe one's last', Skt *ániti* 'breathes', Toch B *anāsk-* 'breathe [in]') providing the basis of the noun **$h_a$énh$_1$mos* 'breath' (e.g. Lat *animus* 'spirit, wind', Grk *ánemos* 'wind', Arm *holm* wind'). A second word for 'breath', **$h_1$eh$_1$tmén-* (e.g. OHG *ātum* 'breath', Skt *ātmán-* 'breath, soul', Toch A *āñcäm* 'self, soul' [phonologically conflated with the previous word]), lacks an underlying verb although it does appear to be related to **$h_1$eh$_1$tr-* which may have meant 'lung' (see Section 11.4); the distinction between the two words is unclear (both can also mean 'spirit' in some languages). The verb **k̂wésh$_x$mi* can also mean 'lament' or 'sigh' and so suggests a very audible breathing (e.g. Lat *queror* 'complain, lament', Av *suši* [dual] 'lungs', Skt *śvásiti* 'breathes, sighs', Toch B *kwäs-* 'lament, bewail'). A wide range of meanings is to be found associated with **dhwésmi*, e.g. 'rage' (e.g. OIr *dāsacht*, 'rage fury', Lat *furō* 'rage'), 'ghost' (e.g. MHG *tuster* 'ghost, spectre', Lith *dvasià* 'ghost, spirit), 'gasp', 'expire' (e.g. Lith *dvesiù*), and there is the suggestion of some form of animated breathing, a suffusion of wild spirits; derivatives give us general names for 'wild animals', including NE *deer*, Lat *bēlua* 'wild animal'. Possibly onomatopoeic is **bhes-* which may have meant something like 'blow' (Grk *psūkhḗ* 'breath, spirit', Skt *-psu-* 'breath'). The word for 'cough' would appear to be **$k^w eh_a s$-* (e.g. MIr *casachtach* 'act of coughing', OE *hwōsan* 'cough' [related in some way is NE *wheeze*], Lith *kósiu* 'cough', OCS *kašĭlĭ*'cough' [noun], Alb *kollë* 'cough' [noun], Skt *kā́sate* 'coughs', Toch B *kosi* 'cough' [noun]).

The verb 'bite', **denḱ-*, yields 'tongs' and 'pinchers' in Germanic (e.g. NE *tongs*) and Alb *darë* 'tongs' but its underlying meaning is retained in Greek, Indo-Iranian, and Tocharian (e.g. Grk *dáknō*, Skt *dáśati*, Toch B *tsāk-*, all 'bite'). The root **$h_1$reug-* 'belch' is found in seven groups (e.g. Lat *ērūgō*, OE *rocettan*, Lith *riáugmi*, Rus *rygátĭ*, Grk *ereúgomai*, Arm *orcam*, NPers *ā-rōγ* [noun], all 'belch') and 'spew' or 'vomit' is indicated by two roots: **wémh$_x$mi* (e.g. Lat *vomō*, Lith *vémti*, Grk *eméō*, Av *vam-*, Skt *vámiti*, all 'vomit') and **(s)py(e)uh$_x$-* (e.g. Lat *spuō* 'spit', NE *spew*, Lith *spiáuju* 'spew', OCS *pljują* 'spew', Grk *ptúō* 'spit out, disgorge', Skt *ṣṭhī́vati* 'spews'; a derivative of the latter is NE *spit*. The noun 'tear', **(d)h$_2$éḱru*, is problematic and some groups indicate an initial **d-* and others give no indication of such a form. Those stocks without a **d-* include Baltic (e.g. Lith *ašarà*), Anatolian (Hit *ishahru*), Indo-Iranian (Av *asrū-*, Skt *áśru-*), and Tocharian (e.g. Toch B *akrūna* [pl.]); those with an initial **d-* comprise Celtic (e.g. OIr *dēr*), Italic (e.g. OLat *dacruma*, Lat *lacrima*), Germanic (e.g. NE *tear*), and Grk *dákru*, i.e. there is roughly an East–West dialectal split. The **d-* may either be a prefix or a misdivision, e.g. **tod h$_2$éḱru* 'this tear' (cf. NE *newt* from a misdivision of the earlier *an ewte*). For the concept 'sweat' we have both a widely attested verbal root **sweid-* (e.g. Lat *sūdō*, NE *sweat*, Latv *svîstu*, Alb *dirsem*, Grk *idíō*, Skt *svédate*, Toch B *sy-*, all 'sweat') and the much more confined (Celtic-Anatolian) **h$_4$elh$_1$-n-* (OIr *allas* 'sweat' [noun], Hit *allaniye-* 'sweat' [verb]).

The verb 'to urinate', **h$_3$méiĝhe/o-*, is widely attested (eight groups) while the nominal formation appears to be later and secondary (e.g. Lat *meiō* ~ *mingō*, OE *mīgan*, Lith *minžù*, Serbo-Croatian *mȉžati*, Grk *omeíkhō*, Arm *mizem*, Av *maēzaiti*, Skt *méhati*, all 'urinate'). There are two words associated with excrement that are strongly attested to Proto-Indo-European (and others more regionally attested). The strongest is **sóḱr̥* with cognates in six groups (e.g. OE *scearn* 'dung, manure', Latv *sãrni* 'slag', Rus *serú* 'defecate', Grk *skôr* '[human] waste, excrement', Av *sairya-* 'dung'), including Anatolian, e.g. Hit *sakkar* 'excrement'; the base meaning of **kerd-* may have been more general, e.g. 'defile, dirty' as well as 'defecate' (e.g. Lat *mūs-cerda* 'mouse droppings', *bu-cerda* 'cattle dung', MPers *xard* 'clay', Shughni *šarθk-* 'defecate', Skt *kardama-* 'mud, slime, mire, dirt, filth', Toch B *kärkkālle* 'swamp, mire'). We may also add *$*g^wuh_x$-* 'defecate' (Arm *ku* 'dung, manure', Av *gūθa-* 'dirt, excrement', Skt *gūtha-* 'dung'), whose Proto-Indo-European status would be enhanced if proposed Lat *imbūbināre* 'defile with menstrual blood' and Germanic (OHG *quāt* 'dirt, excrement') be admitted; there is also **ĝhed-ye/o-* 'defecate' which is based on cognates from Alb *dhjes*, Grk *khézō*, and Skt *hadati*. The noun *$*\hat{k}\acute{o}k^w\underset{\circ}{r}$* 'excrement, dung, manure' is found only in Baltic (Lith *šikù* 'defecate'), Grk *kópros* 'dung, manure', and Indo-Iranian (Skt *śákr̥t* 'excrement, dung'), and it may be semantically related to PIE **sókr̥̂* 'human excrement' as 'animal dung'.

Finally, widely distributed (eight groups) also is **pérde/o-* 'fart' (e.g. NWels *rech*, NE *fart*, Lith *pérdžiu*, Rus *perdétĭ*, Alb *pjerdh*, Grk *pérdomai*, Av *pərəδ-*, Skt *párdate*, all 'fart').

Regional terms for natural functions are well attested. In the North-West zone we have **dher-* 'shit' with cognates in Lat *foria* [pl.] 'swine dung', *foriō* 'defecate', Lith *derė̃kti* 'besmirch with filth', and from the extended **dhreid-* in Germanic we have OE *drītan* 'defecate', NE *dirt* [<**drit-* <**dhrid-*], dialectal Russian *dristátĭ* 'suffer from diarrhea').

The West Central area includes *$*pelh_x$-* 'bear young', a term applied to animals (e.g. NE *foal*, Alb *pjell* 'give birth to, produce', *pelë* 'mare', Grk *pôlos* 'foal', Arm *ul* 'kid, young of deer or gazelle'); *$*h_ael$-* 'grow' (e.g. OIr *ailid* 'nourishes', Lat *alō* 'grow' and the NE derivative *old* and Lat *altus* 'high'). Of obvious onomatopoeic origin is **pneu-* 'snort, sneeze' which underlies a Germanic (OE *fnēosan* 'sneeze') -Greek *pnéō* 'breathe' isogloss. There are words associated with 'excrement', i.e. *$*\hat{k}uh_xd\acute{o}s$* 'dung' (Lith *šū́das* 'dung, muck', dialectal Grk *hus-kuthá* 'pig-dung') and *$*kak(k)eh_aye/o$-* 'defecate' (e.g. MIr *caccaid* 'defecates', Lat *cacō* 'defecate', Rus *kákatĭ* 'defecate', Grk *kakkáō* 'defecate', Arm *k'akor* 'excrement') which was originally a children's word, e.g. NE *caca*, which became the primary word for 'bad' in Greek, i.e. *kakós* (compare the semantic development of 'shitty' in contemporary NE). Finally, there is a phonetic variant of **pérde/o-* 'fart' seen in **pesd-* 'fart' (some have claimed the distinction is material, a **perd-* being louder than a **pesd-*) seen in Lat *pedō*, perhaps NHG *fisten*, Lith *bezdù*, Rus *bzdetĭ*, and Grk *bdéō*, all 'fart'.

11.7 Health and Disease

As one might expect there are a number of words we can reconstruct for various skin diseases and physical deformities. On the other hand, there are no words we can reconstruct for invisible diseases, such as a heart attack, stroke, cancer, etc.

Words for 'strength' in Proto-Indo-European are testosterone driven. For example, *$h_a$énr̥ (as a derivative *h_anḗr) yields 'man' in seven groups (e.g. Alb *njerí* 'person', Grk *anḗr* 'man', Phryg *anar* 'man', Arm *ayr* 'man, person', Luv *annar-* 'man', Av *nār* 'man', Skt *nár-* 'man, person') and other derived meanings

Table 11.7. *Health and sickness*

*$h_a$énr̥	'(manly) strength, vitality'	Grk *anḗr*, Skt *nár-*
*wéih_x(e)s-	'strength, vitality'	Lat *vīs*, Grk *ī́s*, Skt *váyas-*
*$h_a$óyus	'vital force, life, age of vigour'	Lat *aevus*, Grk *aiṓn*, Skt *ā́yu(ṣ)-*
*bélos	'strong'	Lat *dēbilis*, Grk *bélteros*, Skt *bálam*
*weĝ-	'strong'	Lat *vegeō*, Skt *vā́ja-*
*ken-	'fresh'	Lat *recēns*, Grk *kainós*, Skt *kanī́na-*
*sólwos	'whole'	Lat *salvus*, Grk *hólos*, Skt *sárva-*
*$h_{1/4}$eis-	'refresh'	Grk *ierós*, Skt *iṣirá-*
*med-	'heal, cure'	Lat *medeor*
*losiwos	'weak'	NE *lazy*
*$h_a$epus	'weak'	
*k̂emh_a-	'grow tired, tire oneself with work'	
*leh_1d-	'grow slack, become tired'	Lat *lassus*, Grk *lēdeîn*
*streug-	'be fatigued, exhausted'	Grk *streúgomai*
*seh_4i-	' ± be angry at, afflict'	Lat *saevus*, NE *sore*, Grk *haimōdíā*
*$h_a$éghleh_a-	'affliction'	NE *ail*, Skt *ághrā*
*$h_a$énĝhes-	' ± suffering, grief, fear'	Lat *angor*, Skt *áhas-*, NE *anger*
*$h_1$édwōl	'pain; evil'	
*swergh-	'be ill'	
*sokto-	'sickness'	
*$h_1$ermen-	'sickness'	
*$h_3$ligos		
*$k^{(w)}$leik̂-	'suffer'	Skt *kliśyate*
?*(p)k̂órmos	' ± grief, shame'	NE *harm*
*$h_a$em(h_x)-ī-weh_a-	'suffering'	
*k^weh_as-	'cough'	
?*pster-	'sneeze'	Lat *sternuō*, Grk *ptárnumai*
?*skeu-/kseu-	'sneeze'	Skt *kṣáuti*
*kl̥$h_x$wos	'bald'	Lat *calvus*
*ne/og^{w}nós	'bare, naked'	Lat *nūdus*, NE *naked*, Grk *gumnós*, Skt *nagná-*
*$h_a$endhós	'blind'	Skt *andhá-*

(*Cont'd*)

Table 11.7. *Health and sickness (Cont'd)*

*kolnós	'one- eyed'	Skt *kāṇá-*
*káikos	'one- eyed'	Lat *caecus*, Skt *kekara-*
*bhodh$_x$rós	'deaf'	Skt *bodhirá-*
*mū-	'dumb'	Lat *mūtus*, Grk *mukós*, Skt *mū́ka-*
*melo-	'bad'	
*méles-	'fault, mistake'	Lat *malus*, Grk *méleos*
*mendo/eh$_a$-	' ± (bodily) defect'	Lat *menda*, Skt *mindā*
*(s)keng-	'limp'	Skt *kañj-*
*sromós	'lame'	Skt *srāmá-*
*skauros	' ± lame'	Lat *scaurus*, Skt *khora-*
*dedrús	'tetter, skin eruption, leprosy'	NE *tetter*
*kl̥nos	'callosity'	Lat *callus*
*worh$_x$do-	'wart'	NE *wart*
*wr̥h$_x$os	'pimple'	Lat *varus*
*kreup-	' ± rough, scabby'	NE *rough*
*h$_1$élk̂es-	' ± ulcer'	Lat *ulcus*
*kéuh$_x$l̥	'hernia'	Grk *kḗlē*
*ster-	'barren, infertile'	Lat *sterilis*, Grk *stériphos*, Skt *starī́-*
*wédhris	'castrated'	Grk *ethrís*, Skt *vádhri-*
*wolno/eh$_a$-	'(bloody) wound'	Lat *volnus*, Grk *oulḗ*, Skt *vraṇá-*
*h$_a$éru(s)-	'wound'	Skt *áruṣ-*
*peles-	'wound'	Grk *ápelos*
*swero-	'(suppurating) wound'	
*mer-	'die'	Lat *morior*, Grk *émorten*, Skt *mriyáte*
*mr̥tós	'dead; mortal'	Lat *mortuus*
*mr̥tís	'death'	Lat *mors*, Skt *mr̥ti-*
*mr̥tóm	'death'	NE *murder*
*móros	'death'	Grk *móros*, Skt *māra-*
*nek̂-	'perish, die'	Lat *necō*, Skt *náśyati*
*nek̂s-	'death'	Lat *nex*, Grk *néktar*
*nék̂us	'death; dead'	Grk *nékus*
*wel-	'die'	
*dhg^{w}hei-	'perish, destroy'	Grk *phthínō*, Skt *kṣīyáte*
*néh$_a$wis	'corpse'	
*g^{w}es-	'extinguish'	Grk *sbénnūmi*, Skt *jásate*

include 'will' (Lith *nóras*), 'violently' (Hit *innarā*), and 'sexually potent' (Hit *innarawant-*); similarly, *wéih$_x$(e)s- 'strength, vitality' (e.g. Lat *vīs* 'power', Grk *ī́s* 'power', Skt *váyas-* 'vitality, growth') has the related *wih$_x$rós 'man' (e.g. OIr *fer* 'man', Lat *vir* 'man', NE *werewolf*, Lith *výras* 'man, husband', Av *vīra-* 'man', Skt *vīrá-* 'man, husband'). The noun *$*h_a$óyus* is more closely associated with the concept of 'lifespan' (e.g. OIr *āes* 'life, age', Lat *aevus* 'lifespan, age', Goth *aiws* 'time, eternity', *aiṓn* 'vitality, lifespan', Av *āyū* 'lifespan', Skt *ā́yu(ṣ)-* 'life, lifespan'). The adjectives for 'strong' are both problematic in that **bélos* (e.g. Lat *dēbilis* 'weak, infirm', OCS *bolĭjĭ* 'larger', Grk *bélteros* 'better', Skt *bálam* 'power, strength') requires a Proto-Indo-European **b-* which is exceedingly rare (some would argue non-existent) while **weĝ-* is limited to Lat *vegeō* 'enliven, stir up' and Indic (Skt *vā́ja-* 'strength'), although there are several other controversial cognates. The word for 'fresh' (with also meanings of 'young (animal)'), **ken-*, may be a regional term (West Central: e.g. MIr *cana* ~ *cano* 'young animal [of wolf, dog, etc.]', Lat *recēns* 'fresh, just arrived' [> by borrowing NE *recent*], OCS *začęti* 'begin', Grk *kainós* 'young') if one does not accept the proposed Indic cognate (Skt *kanī́na-* 'young'). Words for 'healthy' or 'whole' can be seen in PIE **sólwos* which is found in Lat *salvus* 'whole, well', Alb *gjallë* 'living, agile, deft', Grk *hólos* 'whole', Indo-Iranian (Av *haurva-* 'entire', Skt *sárva-* 'all, whole'), and Tocharian (Toch A *salu* 'complete'); a West Central regional word, *$*kóh_a$ilus* (NE *whole* and, borrowed originally from a Scots dialect, *hale*, OPrus *kailū-sitkan* 'health', OCS *cělŭ* 'healthy', dialectal Grk *koîlu* 'good'), is found in Greek and the Western languages (Celtic, Germanic, Baltic, and Slavic) which suggests to some two competing dialectal terms. There are two words of Proto-Indo-European status that refer to 'healing'. *$*h_{1/4}$eis-* (e.g. Grk *ierós* 'manifesting divine power, holy, hallowed', *iáomai* 'heal', Av *īš-* 'strength', Skt *íṣ-* 'refreshment, comfort, strength', *iṣirá-* 'strong, lively') finds cognates in Anatolian indicating 'salving' or 'anointing' (Hit *iski(ya)-*) while **med-* (which also gives Lat *medicus* 'doctor', Av *vī-mad-* 'healer') is probably a specialized development of PIE **med-* 'measure'.

There are a number of words indicating 'weakness, tiredness' and related concepts. A different formation of **losiwos* (Goth *lasiws* 'weak', Toch B *leswi* 'attacks of weakness') provides NE *lazy*. Some associate *$*h_a$epus* (e.g. Grk *ēpedanós* 'fragile, weak; maimed, halting', Skt *apuvāyáte* 'becomes ill, spoils') with *$*h_a$épo* 'backwards'. The state of 'being tired' is indicated by *$*\hat{k}emh_a$-* (e.g. MIr *cuma* 'grief', Grk *kámnō* 'be tired, work hard at', Skt *śā́myati* 'becomes quiet, fatigues, ceases') and *$*leh_1$d-* (e.g. Lat *lassus* 'tired', OE *læt* 'sluggish', Lith *lěnas* 'lazy, gentle', OCS *lěnŭ* 'lazy', Alb *lodhet* 'becomes tired', Grk *lēdeîn* 'be tired', Toch B *lāl-* 'exert oneself, tire oneself'), the latter also meaning 'grow slack' and possibly an extended meaning of the verb of the same form meaning 'let go'. The verb **streug-* is a Greek-Tocharian isogloss (Grk *streúgomai* 'am exhausted, worn out; suffer distress', Toch B *sruk-* 'die').

Words associated with 'pain' are abundant enough. *$*seh_4$i-* is to be seen in OIr *saeth* 'pain, sickness', Lat *saevus* 'fierce', NE *sore*, Latv *sīvs* 'sharp, biting',

Grk *haimōdíā* 'kind of tooth-ache', Hit *sā(i)*- 'be angry at, resent', Toch B *saiwe* 'itch'. *$h_a$éghleh$_a$*- is found in Germanic (e.g. NE *ail*) and Indo-Iranian (Av *aγrā* 'type of disease', Skt *ághrā* 'affliction'). *$h_a$énĝhes*- gives ON *angr* 'grief' which was borrowed into English as *anger*, as well as Lat *angor* 'fear', Av *ązah*- 'oppression', Skt *áṃhas*- 'fear'; the word derives from *$h_a$enĝh*- 'narrow' and brings together the underlying meaning of 'constriction'. Some form of searing 'pain' is indicated by *$h_1$édwōl* (e.g. Hit *idālu*- 'evil', Toch B *yolo* 'evil'; cf. also OIr *idu* 'pains, birthpangs', Grk *odúnē* 'pain, suffering') from a root *$h_1$ed*- 'eat' or 'bite'; the word means 'evil' in both Anatolian and Tocharian. The wide distribution and close semantic cluster of *swergh*- 'be ill' guarantees its PIE status: it is attested in Celtic (OIr *serg* 'illness'), Baltic (e.g. Lith *sergù* 'am ill'), Alb *dergjem* 'lie ill', and Tocharian (Toch B *särk*- 'illness'). A rare Celtic-Hittite isogloss suggests *sokto*- 'sickness' where we have OIr *socht* 'silence, stupor' compared with Hit *saktāizzi* 'takes care of, performs sick maintenance'; the word perhaps derives from the root *sek*- 'dry', i.e. sickness as a form of dryness. Some form of physical illness is suggested by *$h_1$ermen*- 'sickness' which is seen in Germanic (e.g. OE *earm* 'weak, wretched'), Alb *jerm* 'stupor', Arm *olorm* 'pity', and Hit *arman*- ~ *ērman*- 'sickness'. Another word that may indicate 'ill' is *$h_3$ligos* where a medical meaning is retained in Baltic (e.g. Lith *ligà* 'illness') and Alb *lig* 'bad', while the sense of 'smallness' is suggested by Grk *olígos* 'few' and Toch B *lykaśke* 'small, fine'; a Greek *o*-grade form with the expected loss of the initial laryngeal, *loigós*, does indicate 'ruin, harm'. The word *$k^{(w)}$leik̂*- is largely Eastern (Balto-Slavic, e.g. Lith *klìšės* 'crab-claw', Rus *klestítĭ* 'press', and the Asian languages, e.g. Skt *klíśyate* 'suffers, is tormented', Toch B *klaiks*- 'shrivel, wither'). The questionable ascription of *(p)k̂órmos* to Proto-Indo-European rests on a Germanic-Slavic-Iranian isogloss (e.g. NE *harm*, Rus *sórom* 'shame', Av *fšarəma*- 'shame') while *$h_a$em(h_x)-ī-weh$_a$*- is attested as a noun only in Greek (Grk *aníā* 'grief, sorrow, trouble') and Indic (Skt *ámīvā* 'suffering, sickness') but there are underlying verbal forms in other Indo-European languages (e.g. ON *ama* 'bother, pester, molest').

There are a number of words for specific ailments or conditions. The best-attested word for 'cough' is *k^weh$_a$s*- (from Irish to Tocharian—see above) while there are two others, *pster*- (e.g. OIr *srēod* 'sneeze', Lat *sternuō* 'sneeze', Grk *ptárnumai* 'sneeze', Arm *p'rngam* 'sneeze') and *kseu-/skeu*- (e.g. Lith *skiaudžiu*, Skt *kṣáuti*), that have reasonable distributions but have been regarded as onomatopoeic and hence possibly independent creations. We have seen that there are many words for 'hair' in Proto-Indo-European but only one for 'bald', *kl̥$h_x$wos* (Lat *calvus*, Av *kaurva*-, Skt *áti-kūrva*-, all 'bald') which is possibly related to the regional (West Central) *glo(h_x)wos* 'bare, bald' (e.g. NE *callow*, Rus *gólyj* 'bare'). The word for 'naked', *ne/og^{w}nós* (e.g. Grk *gumnós*, Hit *nekumant-*, Av *maγna-*, Skt *nagná-*, all 'naked'), yields a derivative **nog*^{w}*edho-* from which we obtain both Lat *nūdus* and NE *naked*). The word for 'blind', **h*$_a$*endhós*, is poorly attested and rests on comparing a Gaulish term for a gladiator who fights blind with a helmet without eye-openings (*anda-bata*) with Indo-Iranian (Av *anda-* 'blind', Skt *andhá-* 'blind'). There are two possible words meaning 'one-eyed', **kolnós* and **káikos*, the status of the first resting on a putative Celtic cognate (OIr *coll* 'having lost the right eye', otherwise a Greek-Indic isogloss, dialectal Grk *kellás* 'one-eyed', Skt *kāṇá-* 'one-eyed') and the second on a late Indic form (Skt *kekara-* 'cross-eyed') extending an otherwise North-Western distribution (e.g. OIr *cāech* 'one-eyed', Lat *caecus* 'blind', Goth *haihs* 'one-eyed'). A strong Celtic-Indic isogloss, **bhodh*$_x$*rós* 'deaf' (e.g. OIr *bodar*, Skt *bhadirá-*), does secure the word for this infirmity while the word for 'dumb', **mū-* (e.g. Lat *mūtus* 'dumb' [> by borrowing NE *mute*], Norwegian *mua* 'be silent', dialectal Grk *mukós* 'dumb', Arm *mun* 'dumb', Skt *mū́ka-* 'dumb'), is more problematic and may be sound-symbolic (cf. NE 'keeping *mum*').

Defects may be moral, e.g. **melo-* and **méles-* (e.g. MIr *mell* 'mistake', Lat *malus* 'bad', Lith *mẽlas* 'lie', Grk *méleos* 'miserable, fruitless, vain', Arm *melk'* 'sin', Av *mairya-* [an epithet of demonic beings]) or physical **mendo/eh*$_a$*-* with meanings ranging from 'stain' to 'defect of the body' (e.g. OIr *mennar* 'spot, stain', Lat *menda* 'bodily defect', Lyc *mẽte-* 'damage, harm', Skt *mindā* 'defect of the body'). A word for 'lame' or a 'limp' is seen in *(*s*)*keng-* (e.g. OHG *hinkan* 'limp', Grk *skázō* 'limp', Skt *kañj-* 'limp') and possibly **sromós* (a Slavic-Indo-Iranian isogloss, e.g. Rus *khromój* 'lame', Skt *srāmá-*, but possibly a loanword in Slavic from [unattested] Iranian). Also somewhat doubtful is the Latin-Indic isogloss that gives us **skauros* (Lat *scaurus* 'clubfooted', Skt *khora-* 'lame').

There are six words denoting conditions of the skin. A word for 'skin eruption' or 'leprosy' survives in OE *teter* (> NE *tetter*) and Skt *dadrú-* 'skin eruption, a kind of leprosy' to give **dedrús*, apparently derived from **der-* 'split'. A Latin-Indic isogloss (Lat *callus* 'callosity' [> borrowed in NE *callus*], Skt *kíṇa-* 'callosity') yields **kl̥nos* 'callosity' from **kal-* 'hard'. The word for 'wart', **worh*$_x$*do-* (e.g. NE *wart*, NPers *balū* 'wart'), has the same form as the word for 'frog' (see Section 9.3) and indicates that the two have been associated since Proto-Indo-European. Words for 'pimple', 'scabby', and 'ulcer' are found respectively as **wr̥h*$_x$*os* (Lat *varus* 'pimple', Lith *vìras* 'measles', Toch B *yoro* '± pimple'), **kreup-* (e.g. OE *hrēof* 'rough, scabby', Lith *kraupùs* 'rough', Toch B *kärpiye* 'common' [< *'rough']), and **h*$_1$*élk̑es-* (Lat *ulcus* 'ulcer' [> by borrowing NE *ulcer*], Grk *hélkos* 'ulcer', Skt *árśas-* 'haemorrhoids').

The word for 'hernia', **kéuh*$_x$*l̥*, is found in five groups (e.g. OE *hēala*, Lith *kū́las*, Rus *kilá*, Grk *kḗlē*, Oss *k'ullaw*), all of which retain this remarkably specific meaning; the word itself apparently derives from **keuh*$_x$*-* 'be bent (convexly)' (see also **kuh*$_x$*los* 'back', Section 11.3). We retrieve **ster-* 'barren' where it generally refers to an animal, usually a 'barren cow' (Lat *sterilis* 'barren', NIce *stirtla* 'barren cow', Bulg *sterica* 'barren cow', Grk *steîra* 'barren cow', *stériphos* 'barren', Arm *ster* 'barren', Skt *starī̆-* 'barren cow'; there is also Alb *shtjerrë* 'lamb', Toch B *śari* 'kid'). A word **wédhris* 'castrated' yields this meaning in Grk *ethrís* 'eunuch' and Skt *vádhri-* 'castrated', and *wether* in NE, but has a more basic meaning 'strike' in Luvian so it is not entirely certain that 'castration' was the meaning in Proto-Indo-European.

To be included in the vocabulary of violence in Proto-Indo-European are those words referring to a 'wound'. **wol/rno/eh$_a$-* is attested in various vowel-grades (e.g. Lat *volnus* 'wound, injury', Alb *varrë* 'wound, injury, sore', Grk *oulḗ* 'scar', Rus *rána* 'wound', Skt *vraṇá-* 'wound') while **h$_a$éru(s)-* and **peles-* are attested by single isoglosses, Germanic-Indic (ON *ørr* 'scar', Skt *áruṣ-* 'wound') and Greek-Tocharian (Grk *ápelos* '[unhealed] wound', Toch B *pīle* 'wound'), respectively. **swero-* '(suppurating) wound' is found more widely (e.g. NWels *chwarren* 'ulcer', OHG *sweren* 'fester', Rus *khvóryj* 'sick', Av *x^{v}ara-* 'wound').

The vocabulary of death is extensive with many words derived from two verbal roots: **mer-* (e.g. Lat *morior* 'die', Lith *mìrštu* 'die', OCS *mĭrǫ* 'die', dialectal Grk *émorten* 'died', Arm *meṙanim* 'die', Hit *mer-* 'disappear, die off', Av *miryeiti* 'dies', Skt *mriyáte* 'dies') and **neḱ-* (e.g. Lat *necō* 'kill', Av *nasyeiti* 'disappears', Skt *náśyati* 'is lost, disappears, perishes', Toch B *nakṣtär* 'disappears, perishes') which were already nominalized in Proto-Indo-European to indicate 'death' and 'dead person' (e.g. **mr̥tís* 'death' in Lat *mors*, Lith *mirtìs*, Av *mərəti-*; **móros* 'death' in Lith *mãras* 'death', OCS *morŭ* 'plague', Grk *móros* 'fate, doom, death', Skt *māra-* 'death'; **mr̥tós* in Lat *mortuus* 'dead', Grk *brotós* 'person', Skt *mr̥tá-*; **neḱs* 'death' in Lat *nex* 'death', Grk *néktar* 'nectar' [< *'death-conquering']; **néḱus* 'death, dead' in Grk *nékus* 'corpse', Av *nasu-* 'corpse', Toch B *eṅkwe* 'man' [< *'mortal']). Other roots include **wel-*, whence the ON Valhalla, the 'hall of the dead' (cf. also ON *valr* 'one who dies on the battlefield', Latv *velis* 'spirit of the dead', Czech *valěti* 'fight, make war', Toch A *wäl-* 'die', *walu* 'dead'). Those languages attesting **dhg^{w}hei-* nowhere indicate a specific meaning 'die' but rather 'disappear, be destroyed' (Skt *kṣīyáte*), and 'dwindle' (Grk *phthínō*). The word for a 'corpse', **néh$_a$wis*, finds this meaning in the North-Western languages (Goth *naus* 'corpse', OPrus *nowis* 'corpse', ORus *navĭ* 'corpse') but there is a Tocharian cognate indicating 'sick' (Toch A *nwām*). And finally, as another type of 'death' we have **g^{w}es-* 'extinguish' which is attested in Baltic (e.g. Lith *gèsti* 'go out'), Slavic (e.g. OCS *ugasiti* 'extinguish'), Grk *sbénnūmi* 'extinguish', Hit *kist-* 'go out', Skt *jásate* 'be extinguished', and Tocharian (e.g. Toch B *kes-* 'go out'). As to our final reconstruction, Anatolian argues for an initial **g-*, Greek and Indic for **g^w-*; the other languages will allow either.

Regional words from the North-West include **káikos* 'one-eyed, cross-eyed' (see above) although there is a possible Indic cognate. There are a number of

West Central words: **kóh$_a$ilus* 'healthy, whole' (both NE *hale* and *whole*—see above); **yak(k)-* ' ± cure, make well' (Celtic, e.g. OIr *īcc* 'cure, treatment', Grk *ákos* 'cure, treatment'); **bher-* ' ± cure with spells and/or herbs' (with problematic Baltic cognates, e.g. Lith *bùrti* 'cast a charm, spell', and sound Alb *bar* 'grass, herb, drug, medicine', and Grk *phármakon* 'something that brings health or harm, drug, medicine'); **k^{w}ent(h)-* 'suffer' is found in Celtic (e.g. OIr *cēsaid* 'suffers'), Baltic (e.g. Lith *kenčiù* 'suffer'), and Grk *páskhō* 'suffer'; **seug-* 'be sick', is based on a Germanic-Armenian isogloss (e.g. NE *sick*, Arm *hiwcanim* 'sicken'). We have already seen **gol(h$_x$)wos* 'bare, bald' (NE *callow*) as a regionally attested form alongside the more widely distributed **kl̥h$_x$wos*; Germanic, Baltic, Slavic, and Armenian attest **bhosós* 'bare, naked' (e.g. NE *bare*, Lith *bãsas* 'barefoot', OCS *bosŭ* 'barefoot', Arm *bok'* 'barefoot'). The root **lerd-* underlies **lord(sk̂)os* 'crooked of body' (Sgael *lorcach* 'lame', MHG *lërz* 'left', Grk *lordós* 'bent backwards so the front of the body is convex'). A root **g^{w}eidh-* may have meant something akin to 'be foul, purulent' (its attestations range from ON *kveisa* 'boil, whitlow' through OCS *židukŭ* 'sap-filled, juicy [of plants]' to Grk *deîsa* 'slime') while semantically more secure is **púh$_x$es-* 'putrefaction, pus' (Lat *pūs* 'pus' [> by borrowing NE *pus*], Lith *puvẽs(i)ai* 'rotten things', Grk *púos* 'pus', Arm *hu* 'purulent blood') from a root **peu(h$_x$)-* 'stink, rot'. A Baltic-Greek isogloss (e.g. Lith *votìs* 'ulcer, abscess, boil', Grk *ōteilḗ* 'wound') gives **weh$_a$t-* '(suppurating) wound'. The verbal root **dheu-* 'die' (e.g. OIr *dīth* 'death, end', Lat *fūnus* 'burial', Goth *diwans* 'mortal', OCS *daviti* 'strangle', Arm *di* 'corpse') also underlies ON *deyja* whence is borrowed NE *die* (some would see *die* as native rather than borrowed); it is possibly related to **dhwes-* 'breathe' as in 'expire'; we might put here **(s)kerb-~(s)kerbh-* 'shrink, shrivel' with some connotations of 'wasting away', e.g. Lith *skur̃bti* 'suffer a decline, wither; mourn', Rus *skórblyj* 'shrivelled', Grk *kárphō* 'let shrivel, dry out'. Greek-Indo-Iranian cognates include **péh$_1$mn̥* 'misfortune, suffering' (Grk *pêma* 'misfortune, suffering, misery', Av *pāman-* 'dryness, scab', Skt *pāmán-* 'skin disease') and **mórtos* 'person, mortal' (dialectal Grk *mortós* 'person; dead', Av *marəta-* 'person, mortal', Skt *márta-* 'person, mortal'). An Indic-Tocharian isogloss (Skt *klām(y)ati* 'becomes weary, fatigues', Toch B *klänts-* 'sleep') is seen in **kh$_x$m(-s)-*'be fatigued, sleepy'.

11.8 The Lexicon of the Body

In terms of numbers of cognates, terms for the body and bodily functions form the largest semantic category in Proto-Indo-European, and those words pertaining to health and disease constitute the second largest (followed by terms relating to speech and then kinship terms). The primacy or near primacy of body parts is found across most languages and the semantic categories of body and health constitute the single largest semantic category in proto-Uralic as well. The importance of body parts is also indicated in word frequency lists and it is at least interesting if not instructive to compare the frequency of mention of body parts in American English compared with the frequency of cognate terms to occur in each IE subgroup (Table 11.8).

The figure indicates a broad conformity in the relative popularity of certain organs with both PIE and English rating the words for 'foot', 'heart', and 'eye' as either the three most frequently cited or widely attested words. On the other hand, a word like 'knee' would drop to about twentieth position in English although it is as well attested as 'eye' in PIE. In some cases the variance in ranking is due to the fact that we can reconstruct multiple words in PIE to fill out what is generally covered by a single word in English, e.g. the PIE words for 'hair' and 'blood'.

Word frequency lists also remind us that the most popular or most frequently spoken form in PIE need not have been the form in which it is usually cited in the handbooks. In English, for example, the word *eye* occurs in about 700th place while the plural *eyes* is the more frequently cited word and falls about 200th place. Similarly, *ears* is at 1,000th place while *ear* is below at 1,500th place; *arms* is at about 800th place and the singular form is at about

Table 11.8. *Frequency of occurrence of body part names in American English and the number of cognate groups in Proto-Indo-European*

PIE Body Parts	No of cognate groups	English body parts	Rank order
Foot	12	foot	1
Heart	11	heart	3
Eye	10	eye	2
Knee	10	tongue	13
Tooth	9	tooth	8
Tongue	9	bone	11
Finger	9	ear	10
Bone	9	shoulder	12
Eyebrow	8	blood	7
Ear	8	hair	4
Chin/jaw	8	nose	9
Breast	8	skin	5
Shoulder	6	arm	6

1,000th. In all these cases, in PIE we might expect that the more often spoken form was in the dual rather than the nominative singular.

Approaches to the folk taxonomy of the body and disease in the Indo-European vocabulary are very few. We have early texts, for example Luvian, that enumerate the twelve parts of the body, but there does not seem to have been much comparative work to see to what extent we may reconstruct a taxonomy of the IE body purely on textual grounds. On the other hand, widespread traces of an Indo-European creation myth that involved the dismemberment of a giant's body (human or bovine) to create the universe and human society does offer some evidence for potential taxonomies. For example, the *R̥gveda* describes how a primeval giant was dismembered and his mouth became the priest class, his hands the warrior, his thighs the farmers, and his feet the workers and artisans. In other traditions there emerges a general pattern of association with the head as the priests, the torso as the warriors, and the lower part of the body equated with the commoners. In his studies of the physical correlations of mythic anatomy, i.e. the creation of the universe from the body parts of a primeval giant, Bruce Lincoln has found widespread evidence among various IE traditions for the following equations: flesh = earth, bone = stone, hair = plants, blood = water, eyes = sun, mind = moon, brain = clouds, head = heaven, and breath = wind.

The reconstructed vocabulary concerning terms for disease is probably extremely partial. A study of the folk taxonomy of disease among the Eastern Subanun of the southern Philippines uncovered 132 single-word labels for disease (and over a thousand words for plants) and discussion of diseases among the Subanun was regarded as the third most popular topic after litigation and botany. As one might expect, there was a taxonomic system which defined by various levels of specificity, e.g. 'skin disease' comprised 'inflammation', 'sores', and 'ringworm' which in turn might be subdivided. This should perhaps warn us then that the reconstructed detritus that gives us six words for skin disease (**dedrús* 'tetter, skin eruption, leprosy', **k̥l̥nos* 'callosity', **worh$_x$do*-'wart', **wr̥h$_x$os* 'pimple', **kreup*- '±rough, scabby', **h$_1$élk̂es*- '±ulcer') might be a fraction of a far more complex taxonomy of disease. And unlike plant names, diseases by their very nature may be progressive and, consequently, our reconstructed terms may in places only be designating the various stages in the progression of a disease and its symptoms.

As to the varieties of cures, the lexical evidence does suggest several means. The root **med*-, with specifically medicinal connotations only in Latin and Iranian, suggests healing as the result of undertaking a specified series of practices to restore normality. The root **h$_{1/4}$eis*- 'refresh' suggests that this might be accomplished with a liquid; the root **yak*(*k*)- leaves the means of cure unclear, while a possible **bher*- indicates the use of herbs in Albanian and

Greek but spells in Baltic (if the Baltic words are indeed cognate with the Balkan words). A number of early Indo-European traditions distinguish between diseases that can be cured by spells, e.g. blindness, and which are appropriate to the highest social function of the priest; diseases that require surgery with a knife, e.g. wounds, fractures, which are appropriate for the warrior class; and diseases requiring the use of herbs, e.g. fevers, emaciation, which are regarded as most closely associated with the lower food-producing estate. Generally, diseases and their cures are discussed within the context of the tripartite social and mythological system proposed for the early Indo-Europeans (see Chapter 25).

Further Reading

In addition to the handbooks, there is a considerable literature on various body parts, here arranged alphabetically: blood (Hamp 1979*b*, Linke 1985, Parvulescu 1989), body (Stalmaszcy and Witczak 1990), bone (Hamp 1974*b*, 1984*b*), eye (Forssman 1969, Hamp 1973*b*, Dahllöf 1974, Hendriksen 1981, Lindeman 2003), hair (Adams 1985*d*, 1988*b*, Markey 1984*a*), haunch (Huld 1997), head (Hamp 1974*c*, Bernabé 1982, Nussbaum 1986), heart (Szemerényi 1970), limb (Benveniste 1956*a*, Hamp 1970, 1982*b*, Puhvel 1976*b*, Markey 1984*b*, Pedrero 1985, Horowitz 1992, Schwartz 1992), mouth (Lindeman 1967, Wennerberg 1972), nose (Hamp 1960, 1974*a*), penis (Takács 1997), skin (Hilmarsson 1985), spleen (Hamp 2002), teeth (Narten 1965), tongue (Winter 1982, Hilmarsson 1982, Hamp 1989*b*), and wool (Lindeman 1990*b*). Several of the vital functions also have specialist literature: live (Hamp 1976), die (Katz 1983, Barton 1989, Woodhouse 2003), cough (Hamp 1980*b*), breath (Roider 1981).

For the medical vocabulary of the Subanun see Frake (1961); the American word frequency list is based on Carroll (1971); the Uralic data derive from Häkkinen (2001). The relationship between anatomy and mythology is covered by Lincoln (1986).

12

Family and Kinship

12.1 Family and Household

One of the best-attested areas of the reconstructed lexicon pertains to the family and kinship relations.

Words for the two sexes are unevenly distributed with the majority associated with males. There are some distinctions in that when descendants of *wih_x*rós* (OIr *fer* 'man, husband', Lat *vir* 'man, husband', OE *wer* 'man, husband' [NE *werewolf*], Lith *výras* 'man, husband', Av *vīra-* 'man; person [as opposed to animals]', Skt *vīrá-* 'hero; [eminent] man; husband') and *h_a*nḗr* (NWels *nêr* 'hero', Umb *ner-* 'chief', Alb *njerí* 'person', Grk *anḗr* 'man', Arm *ayr* 'man, person', Phryg *anar* 'man', Luv *annara/i-* 'forceful, virile', Av *nar-* 'man', Skt *nár-* 'man, person') are found in the same language, the former usually refers to 'male, husband' or the like while the latter sometimes may indicate a more honorific position such as a 'hero' or 'chief', though there is obviously a good deal of overlap. The former may derive from a word meaning 'young' (e.g. Toch A *wir* 'young fresh' or Alb *ri* 'young', if the latter is from **wri*h_x*os* < **wi*h_x*ros*) while the latter indicates 'power, strength' (e.g. OIr *nert* 'strength, power', Lat *neriōsus* 'firm'), and even 'anger' (OPrus *nertien*). Both words appear to derive from roots originally indicating '(youthful) strength'. Perhaps more conjectural is the derivation of **mVnus*, which rests on a not entirely clear Germanic-Indic isogloss (e.g. NE *man*, Skt *mánu-* 'man, person'),

Table 12.1. *Family and household*

*wih$_x$rós	'man, husband'	Lat *vir*, NE *werewolf*, Skt *vīrá-*
*h$_a$nḗr	'man, person'	Grk *anḗr*, Skt *nár-*
*mVnus	'man'	NE *man*, Skt *mánu-*
*r̥sḗn	'male'	Grk *ársēn*, Skt *r̥ṣabhá-*
*wersēn	'male'	Lat *verrēs*, Skt *vr̥ṣán-*
*ĝerh$_a$-ont-	'old man'	Grk *gérōn*, Skt *járant-*
*g^{w}énh$_a$	'woman'	NE *quean*, Grk *gunḗ*, Skt *gnā́-*
*h$_a$yeu-	'young'	Lat *iuvenis*, Skt *yúvan-*
*h$_a$yuh$_x$-n̥-k̂ós	'youth'	Lat *iuvencus*, NE *young*, Skr *yuvaśá-*
*maghus	'young man'	
*maghwih$_a$-	'young woman'	NE *maiden*
*méryos	'young man'	Lat *marītus*, Grk *meîraks*, Skt *márya-*
*merih$_a$-	'young woman'	
*teknom	'child, offspring'	NE *thane*, Grk *téknon*, Skt *tákman-*
*ĝénh$_1$es-	'family'	Lat *genus*, Grk *génos*, Skt *jánas-*
*dóm(h$_a$)os	'house(hold)'	Lat *domus*, Grk *dómos*, Skt *dáma-*
*wik̂-	'extended family, clan'	Lat *vīcus*, Grk *oikíā*, Skt *viś-*
*prih$_x$ós	'of one's own'	NE *free*, Skt *priyá-*
*k̂éiwos	'belonging to the household'	Lat *cīvis*, Skt *śéva-*
*s(w)ebh-	'lineage'	NE *sib*, Skt *sabhā́-*
*swedh-o-	'lineage'	Lat *sodālis*, Grk *éthos*, Skt *svadhā́-*

which many claim to go back to *men- 'think', presumably under the illusion that man is a cognitive creature. The two words for 'male', *r̥sḗn and *wersēn, are similar in shape but differ somewhat in meaning; the first generally indicates 'male' in opposition to 'female' (e.g. Grk *ársēn* 'male', Av *arəšan-* 'male', Skt *r̥ṣabhá-* 'bull; male animal in general') while the second indicates the 'male as sire' and its meanings may range from Lat *verrēs* 'boar', Latv *versis* 'ox', Av *varəšni* 'ram' (also 'male') to Toch B *kau$_u$rṣe* 'bull'. However, the two words overlap a good deal as well. In Avestan *r̥sḗn is added to words to create a special term for the (adult) male of the species, e.g. *aspa-arəšan-* 'stallion' or *gau-arəšan-* 'bull', while both in Sanskrit and Tocharian it is *wersēn that is so used, e.g. Skt *go-vr̥ṣa-* 'bull' and Toch B *kau$_u$rṣe* 'bull'. A word for 'old man', *ĝerh$_a$-ont-, is found in Greek and Indo-Iranian (Grk *gérōn* 'old man', Oss *zærand* 'old', Skt *járant-* 'old man'). Different PIE formations give Alb *grua* 'old woman' and Toch B *śärā-* 'adult male'.

The closest generic word for 'woman' (there are also words for 'wife') is *g^{w}énh$_a$* with its derivatives (e.g. OIr *ben* 'woman, wife', OE *cwene* 'woman, female serf, prostitute', OPrus *genna* 'wife', OCS *žena* 'wife', Grk *gunḗ* 'woman, wife', Arm *kin* 'wife', Av *gənā-* 'woman, wife', Skt *gnā́-* 'goddess, divine female', Toch B *śana* 'woman'). The development of this word in English shows two poles: the *e*-grade gives ultimately English *quean*, i.e. 'an impudent or disreputable woman' (but, in OE, also (any) 'woman or wife'), while a lengthened grade root (*g^w*ēni-*) gives OE *cwēn* 'woman, wife, consort', NE *queen*.

The vocabulary of 'youth' is very much concerned with the concepts of 'strength' and 'ability'. Both **$h_a$yeu-* (OIr *ōa* 'young', Lat *iuvenis* 'young', NE *young*, Lith *jáunas* 'young', OCS *junŭ* 'young', Av *yvan-* 'youth', Skt *yúvan-* 'young') and the extended form **$h_a$yuh$_x$-n̥-ḱós* (e.g. OIr *ōac* 'youth', Lat *iuvencus* 'young (cow)', Skt *yuvaśá-* 'young') derive from **$h_a$óyus* 'strength' while the masculine and feminine forms, **maghus* and **maghwih$_a$-* respectively (e.g. Corn *maw* 'youth; servant', *mowes* 'young woman', OE *mago* 'son; man; servant', *mæg(e)þ* 'maiden, virgin; girl; wife' [> NE *maiden*], Av *maδava-* 'unmarried'), may come from the semantically similar **magh-* 'be able'. Another masculine and feminine set is seen in **méryos* and **merih$_a$-* (Lat *marītus* 'husband; lover, suitor', Alb *shemër* 'co-wife; concubine; (female) rival', Grk *meîraks* 'young man or woman', Av *mairya-* 'young man', Skt *márya-* 'young man, lover, suitor'). While the base meaning may indicate a 'youth', many of the languages reveal extended meanings to include 'warrior', i.e. generalized presumably from 'young warriors' (cf. the use in American English of 'our boys' in reference to soldiers overseas). A 'child' without reference to its sex may have been indicated by the neuter noun **teknom* (e.g. Grk *téknon* 'child') from a root **tek-* 'beget', hence more properly 'offspring'. The range of meanings for this word includes a Germanic series all pertaining to servants of a king or followers (e.g. NE *thane*).

The concept of the 'family' or 'household' is found in **ĝénh$_1$es-* (e.g. Lat *genus* 'family', Grk *génos* 'family', Arm *cin* 'birth', Skt *jánas-* 'family') which derives from **ĝenh$_1$-* 'be born' and **dóm(h$_a$)os* (e.g. Lat *domus* 'house', Lith *nãmas* 'house' (with nasal assimilation of the initial consonant to the second), OCS *domŭ* house', Grk *dómos* 'house', Skt *dáma-* 'house') which is ultimately derived from **dem(h$_a$)-* 'build' on which is formed the noun for 'house(hold)'; Latin also shows the extended form *dominus* 'master of the house'. The **wiḱ-* (e.g. Av *vis-* 'clan', Skt *viś-* 'dwelling; clan', OCS *vĭsĭ* 'village', and with a full-grade **we/oiḱo-* seen underlying Lat *vīcus* 'village', Gothic *weihs* 'village', Grk *oikíā* 'house, household', Toch B *īke* 'place') indicates a residence unit larger than the nuclear family and is generally translated as 'extended family' or 'clan' (see Section 13.1).

Two words are associated with 'friendship' although neither specifically means 'friend'. Four groups attest **prih$_x$ós*; in Celtic and Germanic the cognates indicate one who is 'free' while the Indo-Iranian cognates suggest one who is 'dear' (NWels *rhydd* 'free', NE *free*, Av *frya-* 'dear', Skt *priyá-* 'dear').

Some have seen this word as derived from a (controversial) root *_per-_ 'house', i.e. 'those who belong to one's own household'. Such is also the underlying meaning suggested for *_k̂éiwos_ where the semantics range from 'citizen' (Lat _cīvis_, Oscan _ceus_) to 'household' (Germanic, e.g. OE _hīwan_ 'household'), 'wife' (Baltic, i.e. Latv _sieva_), and 'dear' (Indic, e.g. Skt _śivá-_ 'kind, auspicious, dear', whence also the god Shiva); some derive this word from *_k̂éi-_ 'lie', i.e. either 'those who lie together (in sleep)' or 'those who depend on one another'. The words for 'lineage', *_s(w)ebh-_ (e.g. NE _sib_, perhaps Lat _sodālis_ 'associate', OCS _svobodĭ_ 'free', Skt _sabhā́-_ 'assembly') and *_swedh-o-_ (e.g. perhaps Lat _sodālis_ 'associate', Grk _éthos_ 'custom, habit', Skt _svadhā́_ 'homestead; kindred group'), are both built on the reflexive pronoun 'self'.

Regionally attested vocabulary from the North-West includes *_dhĝhm̥-on-_ 'man' (Lat _homō_ 'person'), which derives from *_dhĝhom-_ 'earth' (see Section 8.1); it is found in Celtic (OIr _duine_ 'human'), Italic, Germanic (OE _guma_ 'man'), and Baltic (Lith _žmuõ_ 'person') and survives in NE _bride<u>groom</u>_ where the element 'groom' derives from OE _guma_ 'man' which was changed to 'groom' by way of (erroneous) folk etymology. The North-West also offers a superb example of how far semantics might diverge between the different Indo-European groups. A *_keh_$_a$_ros_ (originally) 'friendly' is attested in Celtic, Italic, Germanic, and Baltic: in Celtic (OIr _cara_) and Italic (Lat _cārus_) it means 'friend' whereas in Germanic it takes on a different connotation (NE _whore_); in Baltic, on the other hand, it means 'greedy' (Latv _kārs_). From the West Central region both Germanic, e.g. Goth _samkunja_ 'of the same lineage' (NE –_kin_), and Grk _homógnios_ 'of the same lineage' provide possible evidence of *_somo-ĝn̥h_$_1$_-yo-s_ 'same (kinship) line' although these words may be independently formed in the two groups.

The Central European region provides another word for 'man' or 'mortal' built on the root 'to die', i.e. *_mórtos_ 'man, mortal' (see Section 11.7); this may have been independently derived in Grk _mortós_ 'man, mortal' in Hesychius, Arm _mard_ 'man', and Skt _márta-_ 'mortal'. Also of possible independent derivation in Armenian and Iranian is *_ĝerh_$_a$_-o-s_ 'old man' (i.e. Arm _cer_, NPers _zar_). This region also attests the use of *_dṓm_ 'house(hold), nuclear family' (Grk _dô_, Arm _tun_, Av _dam-_, Skt _dā́m_, all 'house') where the structure and the social unit of the house are combined under a single term.

12.2 Marriage

There are two possible words for 'marry', both from the male point of view. As a verb, *_ĝemh_$_x$_-_ only indicates 'marry' in Grk _gaméō_ but derivatives indicate 'son-in-law' (Lat _gener_, Grk _gambrós_, Av _zāmātar-_, Skt _jāmātar-_) and 'suitor'

Table 12.2. *Marriage*

*$\hat{g}emh_x$-	'marry'	Grk *gaméō*
*$h_2wed(h_2)$-	'lead in marriage, marry'	NE *wed*, Skt *vadhū́-*
**pótis*	'husband'	Lat *hospēs*, Grk *pósis*, Skt *páti-*
*pot-nih_a-	'mistress, lady'	Grk *pótnia*, Skt *pátnī-*
*dom(h_a)u-no-s	'master'	Lat *dominus*, Skt *dámuna-*
*$h_1esh_2$ós	'master'	Lat *erus*
*h_1esh_2éh_a-	'mistress'	Lat *era*
*prih_xeh_a-	'wife'	Skt *priyā́-*
?*parikeh_a-	'±concubine; wanton woman'	
*widheweh_a-	'widow'	Lat *vidua*, NE *widow*, Skt *vidhávā-*
*$h_{2/3}$orbhos	'orphan, heir'	Lat *orbus*, Grk *orphanós*, Skt *árbha-*
**yemos*	'twin'	Lat *geminus*, Skt *yamá-*

(Alb *dhëndër*, Skt *jārá-*). In later Greek, and perhaps already in earlier Greek, this word was used also of the sexual act by which a marriage was consummated. More solidly attested is *$h_2wed(h_2)$- which means 'marry' in the North-Western group (NWels *dyweddïo* 'marry', NE *wed*, OPrus *weddē* 'marry', Lith *vedù* 'lead, marry [of a man]') and generally 'bride' in Indo-Iranian (Av *vaδū-*, Skt *vadhū́-*). It is a special use of the verb 'lead', indicating that the male led away the woman in the early Indo-European system of marriage, a system whose vocabulary might be later recreated, e.g. Lat *uxōrem dūcere* 'to lead away a wife', i.e. 'marry'. The husband and wife constituted the 'master' and 'mistress' of the household, which might consist of children, grandchildren, and perhaps unrelated slaves or servants. Of course within a given household not every husband and wife, of which there might be several (father and mother, sons and wives), would be 'master' and 'mistress' but only the most senior ones. Indeed, there is some evidence that, should the senior man die, his eldest son would become the master, but the dowager would remain the mistress. The words for 'master' and 'mistress' are **pótis* (attested from Celtic to Tocharian: Bret *ozah* [< **potis stegesos*] 'husband, master of the house', Latv *pats* 'master of the house; self', Rus *gospódĭ* [< **ghost-poti-*] 'host', Alb *zot* [< **wik̂ā-pot-*] 'master of the house', Grk *pósis* 'husband', Hit *pat* 'self', Av *paiti-* 'husband', Skt *páti-* 'husband, master', Toch A *pats* 'husband') and its feminine derivative *pot-nih_a- (e.g. OPrus *waispattin* 'wife, mistress', Grk *pótnia* 'lady, wife', Alb *zonjë* 'lady, wife', Skt *pátnī-* 'lady, wife'). Viewed from the perspective of householders, we also find *$dom(h_a)u$-no-s* 'master', i.e. the 'master of the house' (e.g. Lat *dominus*, Skt *dámuna-*) as the word is a clear derivative of the word for 'house' (cf. *$dom(h_a)os$* above) with the suffix *-no-* which is used to create words 'leader of'. A Latin-Hittite isogloss gives us both *$h_1esh_2$ós* 'master' and *h_1esh_2éh_a-* 'mistress' with no certain root etymology (Lat *erus* 'master of the house, lord, owner', *era* 'mistress, lady, owner', Hit *ishā-* 'master, lord, owner'). Finally there is a Greek-Indo-Iranian isogloss, **dems-pot-* 'master of the house' (e.g. Grk *despótēs*, Skt *dám-pati-*) which is structurally part of the same set that gives us 'master of the clan', i.e. **wiḱ(-ā)-pot-* (in Baltic, Albanian, and Indo-Iranian). The word **prih_xeh_a-* 'wife' is almost a term of endearment as it derives from **pri$h_x$ós* 'be pleasing, one's own' (see above) and it provides the wife of the Germanic god Oðinn with a name, e.g. ON *Frigg* (cf. also ON *frī* 'beloved, wife', OE *frēo* 'woman', Skt *priyā́-* 'wife'). The underlying semantics of *?*parikeh_a-* are difficult; the word is attested only in MIr *airech* '(type of) concubine' and Av *pairikā-* 'demonic courtesan'. Presumably the meaning attested in Irish is the older one while in Iranian 'the other woman' has suffered a loss of social standing.

The word for 'widow' (**widheweh_a-*) is very well attested (nine groups as 'widow', e.g. OIr *fedb*, Lat *vidua*, NE *widow*, OPrus *widdewu*, Rus *vdová*, ?Alb *ve* (if not a loan from Latin), Hit ^{SAL}*u(i)dati-*, Av *viδavā*, Skt *vidhávā-*, and in a derived form in Grk, *ēítheos*, as 'bachelor'). This word is usually taken as a nominal derivative of a verb **wi-dheh_1-*, attested only in Anatolian, meaning 'separate'. A word for 'orphan' (**$h_{2/3}$orbhos*) is reasonably well attested as well (e.g. OIr *orb* 'heir, inheritance', Lat *orbus* 'bereft, childless, orphan', OCS *rabŭ* 'servant', Arm *orb* 'orphan', Skt *árbha-* 'child') and derives from a verbal form which was still preserved in Hit *har(ap)p-* 'change status'. A word for 'twin' (**yemos*) is supported by cognates in Celtic (OIr *emon* 'twins'), Italic (*geminus* 'twin'), and Indo-Iranian (Av *yəma-*, Skt *yamá-*, both 'twin').

There are a few regional terms. A word for 'marry' (**sneubh-*) seen from the wife's point of view is attested in Italic (Lat *nūbere*) with derivatives in Slavic (OCS *snubiti* 'to pander') and Grk *númphē* 'bride' while a Germanic-Slavic-Greek isogloss (OE *witumo*, OCS *věno*, Grk *hédnon* [< **wedmon*]) gives us **wedmo/eh_a-* 'bride-price' (i.e. the price paid by the groom's family to the bride's to compensate the latter for the loss of a worker). On the basis of both our Proto-Indo-European terms and some of our regional terms, Eric Hamp has suggested that we can reconstruct terms for four stages or events in the Indo-European marriage. It begins with the **perḱ-* 'ask, propose a marriage' (see Section 21.2) which is then followed by the **wedmo/eh_a-*, the exchange of the bride-price. The newly wed wife would be literally 'led away', i.e. **$h_2$wed(h_2)-* 'wed', and **ĝemh_x-* would indicate the consummation of the marriage (for the latter two, see above). A regional term for 'wife', found in

Slavic and Greek, is **sm̥-loghos* (SerbCS *sulogŭ* 'wife', Grk *álokhos* 'bed-fellow, spouse'). Literally it means 'bed-fellow'. Finally we have a Graeco-Aryan isogloss where Grk *despótēs* 'master, lord' and Indo-Iranian (e.g. Skt *dám-pati-* 'master' derive from a compound **dems-pot-* 'master of the house'.

12.3 Kinship

Kinship terms in Indo-European tend to be limited over three generations. The word *h_2euh_2os 'grandfather' is well attested in Anatolian, e.g. Hit *hūhhas*, and a number of groups in both Europe and Asia (e.g. Lat *avus*, ON *afi*, Arm *haw*, Toch B *āwe*, all 'grandfather' except Tocharian B which may be 'uncle' instead). There is also an Albanian-Indic correspondence that yields *suh_xsos

Table 12.3. *Kinship*

*h_2euh_2os	'grandfather'	Lat *avus*
*suh_xsos	'grandfather'	Skt *sūṣā́*
**pro-*	third generation marker	Lat *pro-*, Grk *pro-*, Skt *pra-*
*h_4ep-	fourth generation marker	Lat *ab-*, NE *off-*, Grk *apo*, Skt *apa-*
*$p\underset{\circ}{h}_at\acute{e}r$	'father'	Lat *pater*, NE *father*, Grk *patḗr*, Skt *pitár-*
*somo-$p\underset{\circ}{h}_at\bar{o}r$	'of the same father'	Grk *homopátōr*
*$\hat{g}enh_1$- tōr	'father; procreator'	Lat *genitor*, Grk *genétōr*, Skt *janitár-*
**at-*	'father'	Lat *atta*, Grk *atta*
**t-at-*	'father'	Lat *tata*, Grk *tatâ*, Skt *tatá-*
**papa*	'father, papa'	Lat *pāpa*, Grk *páppa*
**putlós*	'son'	Skt *putrá-*
*$suh_xn\acute{u}s$	'son'	NE *son*, Skt *sūnú-*
*$suh_xy\acute{u}s$	'son'	Grk *huyús*
**népōts*	'grandson; (?) nephew'	Lat *nepōs*, Grk *népodes*, Skt *nápāt*
**neptiyos*	'descendant'	Grk *anepsiós*
*h_2en-	'father's mother'	Grk *annís*
*$m\acute{e}h_at\bar{e}r$	'mother'	Lat *māter*, NE *mother*, Grk *mḗtēr*, Skt *mātár-*
*h_4en-	'(old) woman, mother'	Lat *anus*
*n-h_4en-	'mother'	Lat *nonnus*, Grk *nánnē*, Skt *nanā-*
*h_4em-	'mother'	Lat *amma*, Grk *ammás*, Skt *ambā-*
*m-h_4em-	'mother'	Lat *mamma*, Grk *mámmē*
*h_aekkeh_a-	'mother'	Lat *Acca*, Grk *Akkō*, Skt *akkā-*
*$\hat{g}enh_1trih_a$-	'mother, procreatrix'	Lat *genetrīx*, Grk *genéteira*, Skt *jánitrī-*

(*Cont'd*)

Table 12.3 (*Cont'd*)

**dhuĝ*(*h*$_a$)*tḗr*	'daughter'	NE *daughter*, Grk *thugátēr*, Skt *duhitár-*
**neptih*$_a$*-*	'granddaughter; (?) niece'	Lat *neptis*, Grk *anepsiá*, Skt *naptī́-*
**bhréh*$_a$*ter-*	'±brother'	Lat *frāter*, NE *brother*, Grk *phrḗtēr*, Skt *bhrā́tar-*
**bhreh*$_a$*triyom*	'brotherhood'	Grk *phrātríā*, Skt *bhrātryam*
**swésōr*	'sister'	Lat *soror*, NE *sister*, Grk *éor*, Skt *svásar-*
**pḥ̥*$_a$*trōus*	'paternal kinsman'	Grk *pátrōs*
**pḥ̥*$_a$*tr̥wyos*	'father's brother'	Lat *patruus*, Grk *patruiós*, Skt *pitr̥vyá-*
**daih*$_a$*wḗr*	'husband's brother'	Lat *lēvir*, Grk *dāḗr*, Skt *devár-*
?**swēk̂urós*	'wife's brother'	Skt *śvāśura-*
**syō*(*u*)*ros*	'wife's brother'	Skt *syālá-*
**ĝ* (*e*)*m*(*h*$_x$)*ros*	'sister's husband'	Lat *gener*, Grk *gambrós*
**swék̂uros*	'father-in- law'	Lat *socer*, Grk *hekurós*, Skt *śváśura-*
**swek̂rúh*$_a$*s*	'mother-in-law'	Lat *socrus*, Grk *hekurā́*, Skt *śvaśrū́-*
**ĝenh*$_1$*- tōr*	'father; procreator'	Lat *genitor*, Grk *genétōr*, Skt *jánitár-*
**ĝomh*$_x$*-ter-*	'son-in-law'	Skr *jāmatar-*
**snusós*	'son's wife, brother's wife'	Lat *nurus*, Grk *nuós*, Skt *snuṣā́-*
**ĝh*$_3$*- wos-*	'husband's sister'	Lat *glōs*, Grk *gálōs*, Skt *girí-*
**h*$_1$*yenh*$_a$*-ter-*	'husband's brother's wife'	Lat *ianitrīcēs*, Grk *enátēr*, Skt *yātár-*
**swesr*(*iy*)*ós*	'pertaining to a sister, sisterly; sister's son'	Lat *cōnsobrīnus*, Skt *svasrīya*
**bhendhr̥ros*	'±relation'	Grk *pentherós*, Skt *bhándhu-*

'grandfather' (Alb *gjysh* 'grandfather', Skt *sūṣā́* 'paternal grandmother') from **seuh*$_x$*-* 'beget', the same root that gave the words for 'son' below). Other degrees of descent employ basic prepositions. For example, **pro-* provides the third generation marker, e.g. Lat *pro-avus* 'great-grandfather' while **h*$_4$*ep-* forms the fourth generation marker, e.g. Lat *av-avus* 'great-great-grandfather'; these can be, and normally are, also reversed to provide descending generations, e.g. Lat *pro-nepōs* and Skt *prá-napát-* 'great-grandson' and Lat *ab-nepōs* 'great-great-grandson'. We find **h*$_4$*ep-* also in NE *offspring*.

There is a series of words for 'father'. The formal term, attested in eight groups, is **pḥ̥*$_a$*tḗr* (e.g. OIr *athir*, Lat *pater*, NE *father*, Grk *patḗr*, Arm *hayr*, Av *ptā*, Skt *pitár-*, Toch B *pācer*, all 'father') while it also appears in compound form in Germanic, Greek, Iranian, and Toch A as **somo-pḥ̥*$_a$*tōr* 'of the same father' (ON *samfeðra*, Grk *homopátōr*, OPers *hamapitar-*, Toch A *ṣomapācār*). Possibly of Proto-Indo-European date (if not independent creations from the root 'beget'), is **ĝenh*$_1$*-tōr* 'procreator' (Lat *genitor*, Grk *genétōr*, Skt *janitár-*).

The other terms are widely attested children's words, i.e. **at-*, **t-at-*, and **papa* (e.g. from **at-*: OIr *aithe* 'foster-father; teacher', Lat *atta* 'father', Goth *atta* 'father', Rus *otéc* 'father', Alb *atë* 'father', Grk *áttas* 'father', Hit *attas* 'father'; from **tat-*: NWels *tad*, Lat (inscriptional) *tata*, Grk *tatâ*, Luv *tātis*, Skt *tatá-*, all 'father'; from **papa*: Lat *pāpa* 'father' [whence by borrowing NE *pope*], Grk *páppa* 'papa', Pal *pāpa* 'father').

There are two words for 'son', **putlós* (four groups) which is traditionally derived from **p(a)u-* 'small' + the diminutive suffix *-*tlo-*, i.e. the 'small one' (e.g. Osc *puklo-* 'son', Arm *ustr* 'son' [remodelled from the expected **usl* after *dustr* 'daughter'], Av *puθra-* 'son', Skt *putrá-* 'son'), and the more widely attested **suh$_x$nús* (and the semantically identical **suh$_x$yús*) which derives from **seuh$_x$-* 'bear, beget', i.e. the 'begotten' (e.g. from **suh$_x$nús*: NE *son*, OPrus *soūns* 'son', OCS *synŭ* 'son', Av *hūnu-* 'son', Skt *sūnú-* 'son', Toch B *soṃśke* '(young) son'; from **suh$_x$yús:* Grk *huiús* 'son', Toch B *soy* 'son').

The word for 'grandson' (**népōts* which, in a derivative, **neptiyos*, gives a more general word for 'descendant') is one of the most controversial words in the reconstructed lexicon. Formally, the word is attested in Celtic, Germanic, Italic, Baltic, Slavic, Albanian, Greek, and Indo-Iranian; there is no problem reconstructing the shape of the word to Proto-Indo-European. The problem arises when one finds that, in addition to the meaning 'grandson', the word also means 'sister's son (i.e. nephew)' in Celtic (e.g. OIr *nia* 'sister's son, grandson, descendant'), Lat *nepōs* 'grandson, descendant' and in later Imperial Latin also 'nephew', Germanic (e.g. OE *nefa* 'sister's son, grandson'), Baltic (Lith *nepuotìs* 'grandson'), Slavic (OCS *netijĭ* 'nephew'), and Alb *nip* 'grandson, nephew'. Thus some would argue that both meanings, 'grandson' and 'sister's son', should be ascribed to Proto-Indo-European. Others argue that 'sister's son' is a secondary development among some and not all the North-Western Indo-European languages and, therefore, this second meaning cannot be ascribed to Proto-Indo-European itself, since in the east of the Indo-European world only 'grandson' or the like is attested (e.g. Grk *népodes* 'descendants', OPers *napā* 'grandson, descendant', Skt *nápāt* 'grandson, descendant'). Also arguing for a meaning 'grandson' are NWels *kefnder* 'male cousin' (< **kom-nepōt-*) and Grk *anepsiós* '(male) cousin' (< **sm̥-neptiyo-*). Why should anyone care?

The systems by which people organize their kin vary across the world and anthropologists have long studied and defined a series of basic kinship types, generally named after various ethnic groups among whom they were first studied. Anthropologists have found that these systems of kinship terminology correlate, albeit imperfectly, with social and family organization within the group. Therefore, knowing how a reconstructed language handled kinship terminology suggests how its speakers may have organized certain social and family relationships. A modern English speaker basically utilizes an Eskimo kinship system which provides separate words for each member of the nuclear family, 'father', 'mother', 'brother', and 'sister', and uses none of these terms to refer to anyone outside the nuclear family. Thus there are different terms for 'aunt', 'uncle', 'cousin', etc. As has often been noted, such a system with its emphasis on the nuclear family and the clear separation of it from other familial relationships fits contemporary, mobile, nuclear-family-oriented, Anglo-American society well. On the other hand, English speakers developed this Eskimo kinship terminology by 1200 AD or so, at a time when social and family relationships were very different from what they are now and seemingly less appropriate to an Eskimo system—a fact which should give us pause when determining how much of an insight kinship terminology can give us concerning social and family roles. In any case, the Eskimo kinship system is quite unlike the Hawaiian one where every term used for a nuclear family member is also used for kin outside of the nuclear family. Thus the term for 'father' includes, beside the 'male parent', all uncles whether paternal or maternal. Similarly 'mother' includes all aunts on both sides of the family and 'brother' includes all male cousins and 'sister' includes all female cousins. Other kinship systems are in some sense intermediate between the Eskimo and the Hawaiian types, with tendencies to merge certain nuclear family kin types, but not all, with kin types outside the nuclear family. Of these 'intermediate' types, Indo-Europeanists have been most interested in the Omaha system, since some branches of the family at least show Omaha features and the Omaha system is often associated with strong patrilineal social organization, and it certainly is the case that early, historically attested, Indo-European groups show such a patrilineal tendency. In the classic Omaha system (and not all Omaha systems, or any other system for that matter, show all the tendencies imputed to it) the father and paternal uncle have the same designation as do the mother and maternal aunt, while the children of the paternal uncle and maternal aunt (technically 'parallel cousins') are designated with the same terms as one's brother and sister. There is also a tendency in Omaha systems towards a 'skewing of generations' whereby the maternal uncle is equated with the maternal grandfather and the maternal uncle's children with the maternal grandfather's children, and conversely one's 'grandson' will be called by the same term as one's 'sister's son', i.e. 'nephew'. If one ascribes both meanings 'grandson' and 'sister's son' to Proto-Indo-European **népōts,* then this particular conflation of kin types would support the identification of the Proto-Indo-European kinship system as of the Omaha type. However, if the Proto-Indo-European word meant only 'grandson', then much of the evidence for considering Proto-Indo-European's kinship terminology to have been of the Omaha type disappears. The Omaha type would be a regional, post-Indo-European, type of the North-West.

Taking now female relatives, we have first *$h_2$en- 'grandmother', apparently another child's word but a very old one, e.g. OHG *ana* 'grandmother', OPrus *ane* 'female ancestor', OCS *vŭnǫkŭ* 'grandfather', Grk *annís* 'grandmother', Arm *han* 'grandmother', Hit *hannas* 'grandmother', OPers *nyākā* 'grandmother'. As might be expected, there are numerous words for 'mother', many of them from the language of children (and hence renewable in any given language). The formal term, attested in eleven different groups, is *méh$_a$tēr (e.g. OIr *māthair*, Lat *māter*, NE *mother*, OPrus *mothe*, OCS *mati*, Grk *mḗtēr*, Phryg *matar*, Arm *mayr*, Av *mātar-*, Skt *mātár-*, Toch B *mācer*, all 'mother'). A second term, *$h_4$en-, with a different laryngeal from the word for 'grandmother', is kept separate from the 'grandmother' term only in Armenian and Anatolian, e.g. OIr *Ana* 'mother of the gods', Lat *anus* 'old woman', and Hit *annas* 'mother' distinct from *hannas* 'grandmother' where Hittite retains no trace of the *h_4- in the word for mother but does retain *h_2- in the word for grandmother. Other terms appear to be possible reduplications, e.g. *n-$h_4$en- on *$h_4$en- (e.g. NWels *nain* 'grandmother', Late Lat *nonnus* 'nurse', Alb *nëne* 'mother', Rus *njánja* 'nurse', Grk *nánnē* 'female cousin, aunt', NPers *nana* 'mother', Skt *nanā-* 'mother') and *m-$h_4$em- on *$h_4$em- (e.g. NWels *mam* 'mother', Lat *mamma* 'breast; mu/ommy, grandmother', OHG *muoma* 'aunt', Lith *mamà* 'mother', Rus *máma* 'mother', Alb *mëmë* 'mother', Grk *mámmē* 'mother' (later 'grandmother'), Arm *mam* 'grandmother', NPers *mām* 'mother', Skt *mā* 'mother'). In addition to 'mamma/nanna' type words, Proto-Indo-European also attests *$h_a$ekkeh$_a$-, e.g. Lat *Acca* 'mother' (Roman goddess), Grk *Akkō* (nurse of Demeter), Skt *akkā* 'mother'. And as with the male form for 'procreator', there is also an equivalent feminine form, either inherited or independently created in the different languages, *ĝenh$_1$trih$_a$- (Lat *genetrīx*, Grk *genéteira*, Skt *jánitrī-*). For the next generation we have the widely attested *dhuĝ(h$_a$)tḗr 'daughter' (e.g. Gaul *duxtir*, Osc *fuutír*, NE *daughter*, OPrus *duckti*, OCS *dŭšti*, Grk *thugátēr*, Arm *dustr*, Lyc *kbatra*, Av *duγədar-*, Skt *duhitár-*, Toch B *tkācer*, all 'daughter') and then *neptih$_a$- 'granddaughter'. This latter word behaves very much like that for 'grandson' in that the North-Western languages also indicate the meaning 'niece' (e.g. OIr *necht* 'granddaughter, ?niece', Lat *neptis* 'granddaughter, female descendant', and in later Imperial Lat also 'niece', OE *nift* 'niece; granddaughter; stepdaughter', Lith *neptė* 'granddaughter; niece', ORus *nestera* 'niece', Alb *mbesë* 'granddaughter; niece', but Av *naptī-* 'granddaughter', Skt *naptī́-* 'granddaughter'). Though unlike *nepōts, which meant specifically 'sister's son', *neptih$_a$- meant both 'sister's daughter' and 'brother's daughter' in the languages of the North-West. One might note that English has borrowed, via Old French, the Latin descendants of Proto-Indo-European *nepōts and *neptih$_a$- with the meanings of 'nephew' and 'niece' respectively.

Both words for siblings are very strongly attested. The word for 'brother', **bhréh$_a$ter-*, carries the specific meaning 'brother' in all cognate sets except for Greek where it has come to mean 'kinsman', but it also exhibits extended secondary (?) meanings of 'kinsman, cousin' in Celtic and Slavic (e.g. OIr *brāthair*, Lat *frāter*, NE *brother*, OPrus *brāti*, OCS *bratrŭ*, Grk *phrḗtēr*, Arm *ełbayr*, Av *brātar-*, Skt *bhrā́tar-*, Toch B *procer*). Some suspect that it may have had a similarly wider meaning in Proto-Indo-European, cf. English usage of 'brother' to indicate a group of males related by kinship or even by common social affiliation, e.g. 'a band of brothers'. The possibility of a word for 'brotherhood', **bhreh$_a$tríyom*, is supported by apparent cognates in Slavic (OCS *bratrĭja*), Grk *phrātriā*, and Skt *bhrātryam* although at least one if not more of the groups may have innovated. The word for 'sister', **swésōr*, is similarly widespread (e.g. OIr *siur*, Lat *soror*, NE *sister*, OPrus *swestro*, OCS *sestra*, Arm *k'oyr*, Av *x^{v}aŋhar-*, Skt *svásar-*, Toch B *ṣer*, all 'sister'; Grk *éor* 'cousin's daughter') and, like 'brother', absent only in Albanian and Anatolian (Hittite uses the unique forms *nēgna-* and *neka-* respectively for 'brother' and 'sister'). Words that are so basic to any vocabulary have invited interminable speculation as to their 'deeper' meaning. For example, the word for 'sister' has been variously analyzed as a compound **swe-* 'own' + **sōr* 'woman', i.e. a 'woman of one's own family' or, alternatively, as **su-* 'with' + **h$_1$esōr* 'blood', i.e. '(woman of) one's own bloodline'. Neither derivation is widely accepted.

Words pertaining to a vague concept of 'uncle' or general male relative such as the 'brother-in-law' are problematic. **ph̥$_a$trōus* '(male) paternal relative; father's brother' is attested in its basic form only in Grk *pátrōs* 'paternal relative' but it does have derived forms that are found in Italic (Lat *patruus*), Baltic (OLith *strūjus*), Slavic (OCS *stryjĭ*), Arm *yawray*, and Indo-Iranian (Av *tūirya-* and Skt *pitr̥vyá-*) which pretty much confirms both **ph̥$_a$trōus* and its derivative **ph̥$_a$tr̥wyos* to Proto-Indo-European. That the designation for the father's brother is so obviously a derivative of 'father' might be taken as additional evidence that the Proto-Indo-European kinship system was of the Omaha type. (Latin kinship is apparently alone in equating the father's brother's children with the father's, e.g. *frāter* (*germanus*) 'brother' beside *frāter patruelis* 'father's brother's son'). There is no equally secure Proto-Indo-European term for 'mother's brother'. The languages of the North-West show derivatives of 'grandfather', which would reflect the expected Omaha equation of 'grandfather' and 'mother's brother', but then each group shows a different derivation for 'mother's brother', suggesting the Omaha-like equation of 'grandfather' and 'mother's brother' was only a very late Indo-European development or even one that independently emerged after the dissolution of Proto-Indo-European unity. A word for 'husband's brother' seems solidly attested in **daih$_a$wḗr* (e.g. Lat *lēvir* [the unexpected initial may be due to influence from the Sabine dialect], OE *tācor*, Lith *dieverìs*, OCS *děverĭ*, Grk *dāḗr*, Arm *taygr*, Skt *devár-*) while 'wife's brother' may be found in ?**swēk̂urós* although this word may have been independently derived from the word for 'father-in-law' in the language groups in which it occurs (OHG *swāgur*, Skt *śvāśura-*). PIE **syō(u)ros*, attested in Slavic, Armenian, and Indic, also indicates 'wife's brother' (OCS *šurĭ* 'wife's brother', Arm *hor* 'son-in-law', Skt *syālá-* 'wife's brother').

A word for 'sister's husband' (**ĝ(e)m(h$_x$)ros*) can be reconstructed from Latin and Greek but the same root, rebuilt with a different suffix as **ĝ(e)m(h$_x$)-tēr*, is found in other Indo-European languages of the East (see the discussion under 'marry' above).

The words for both 'father-in-law' (**swék̂uros*) and 'mother-in-law' (**swek̂rúh$_a$s*) are widely attested (e.g. NWels *chwegrwn* 'father-in-law', Lat *socer* 'father-in-law', OE *swēor* 'father-in-law', Lith *šẽšuras* 'husband's father', OCS *svekrŭ* 'husband's father', Alb *vjehërr* 'father-in-law', Grk *hekurós* 'wife's father', Av *x^{v}asur* 'father-in-law', Skt *śváśura-* 'father-in-law'; and NWels *chwegr* 'mother-in-law', Lat *socrus* 'mother-in-law', OE *sweger* 'mother-in-law', OCS *svekry* 'husband's mother', Alb *vjehërr* 'mother-in-law', Grk *hekurā́* 'husband's mother', Arm *skesur* 'husband's mother', Skt *śvaśrū́-* 'mother-in-law'). The word for 'mother-in-law' is clearly derived from the masculine. There is an interesting problem in reconstructing the original semantics of the words. For example, a number of Indo-European groups (Balto-Slavic, Greek, Armenian) use this Proto-Indo-European word for 'father-in-law' to indicate exclusively the 'husband's mother', i.e. the word is used solely from the perspective of the wife and not from that of the husband. Consequently, Oswald Szemerényi suggested that the deeper etymology of the word should be **swé-* 'own' + *k̂oru-* 'head', i.e. 'head of the joint family', a term which would only make sense from the wife's point of view in a patrilineal society. But other Indo-European groups utilize the word from both the husband's and wife's perspective and it has been suggested that this more general meaning was the original meaning which became more specific in some central Indo-European groups.

Cognates in Albanian and Indo-Iranian suggest the existence of **ĝomh$_x$-ter-* 'son-in-law' (see above under 'marry') which derives from **ĝemh$_x$-* 'marry' or, perhaps more specifically, 'to pay the bride-price'. Other relations by marriage include the 'daughter-in-law', **snusós* (e.g. Lat *snurus* 'son's/grandson's wife', OE *snoru* 'son's wife', Rus *snokhá* 'son's wife; bride', Grk *nuós* 'son's wife; bride', Arm *nu* 'son's wife', Skt *snuṣā́-*'son's wife'), and the 'sister-in-law', **ĝl̥h$_3$-wos-* (e.g. Lat *glōs* 'sister-in-law', OCS *zŭlŭva* 'husband's sister', Grk *gálōs* 'sister-in-law', Arm *tal* 'husband's sister', Skt *girí-* 'brother's wife'), here more specifically the 'husband's sister' (the wife's sister is attested in a more restrictedly distributed form). A Proto-Indo-European *$h_1$yenh$_a$-ter-* appears to refer to the 'husband's brother's wife' (e.g. Lat *ianitrīcēs* 'brothers' wives', Lith *jéntė* 'husband's brother's wife', OCS *jętry* 'husband's brother's wife', Grk *enátēr* 'husband's brother's wife', Arm *ner* 'husband's brother's wife', Skt *yātár-* 'husband's brother's wife'). So apparently specific a word makes sense if the usual social unit was an extended family of parents and married sons. The daughter-in-law in such a situation would be in need of a term to refer to her husband's brothers' wives.

The concept of 'nephew', as we have seen, is critical to the identification of the Proto-Indo-European kinship system being of the Omaha type. In addition to the word that also (if not originally) meant 'grandson', i.e. **népōts* (see above), there is also **swesr(iy)ós* 'sister's son' (e.g. OSwed *swiri* 'mother's sister's son', Sanglechi [an Iranian language of the Pamirs] *xīr* 'sister's son', Skt *svasrīya-* 'sister's son'; literally something like 'he of the sister', feminine forms in some languages also indicate 'sister's daughter'). Finally, a weakly attested **bhendhr̥ros* with meanings such as Lith *beñdras* 'companion', Grk *pentherós* 'father-in-law', and Skt *bándhu-* 'relative' defies more precise semantic reconstruction although it is generally presumed to derive from **bhendh-* 'join, tie', i.e. someone connected through marriage or other social bond.

There is an abundance of regionally attested kinship terms although few are specifically from the North-West. Here we find **seno-meh$_a$tḗr* 'grandmother' (literally 'old mother') in Celtic and Baltic (OIr *senmāthair*, Lith *senmotė*—possibly independent creations) and **swesrih$_x$nos* 'sister's son' (Lat *cōnsobrīnus* 'mother's sister's son; (any) cousin', Lith *seserė́nas* 'sister's son') probably originally meant 'pertaining to the sister'; and the **h$_2$éuh$_2$-* which certainly indicates the 'grandfather' also underlies a number of derivations in the North-West that indicate also the 'mother's brother', e.g. Lat *avunculus*. Words spanning the West Central region are far more numerous: a feminized form of the word for 'grandfather', **h$_2$euh$_2$ih$_a$-* 'grandmother', is found in Italic (Lat *avia*), Alb *joshë*, and Grk *aîa*. We have a parallel to 'paternal kinsman' (see above) in **méh$_a$trōus* 'maternal kinsman; maternal uncle', occurring only in Grk *mḗtrōs*. The adjective derived from 'sister', **swes(ri)yós* 'pertaining to a sister, sisterly', might refer specifically to 'sister's son' (see above) or 'mother's brother' (Arm *k'eṙi*). There is a very uncertain cognate set (Baltic [e.g. Lith *dė̃dė* 'uncle'], Slavic [Rus *djádja* 'maternal uncle'], Grk *theîos* 'uncle') perhaps reflecting a **dheh$_1$-* 'uncle'. A Norse-Greek isogloss indicates a word **sweliyon-* 'wife's sister's husband' (ON *svili*, Grk *eilíones* [pl.]). As noted above, the verb **ĝemh$_x$-* 'marry' gives **ĝm̥h$_x$-ro-s* 'son-in-law' in Celtic, Italic, and Greek. A word for 'aunt' is seen in **meh$_a$truh$_a$-* 'mother's sister' or perhaps just 'motherly one' (e.g. OE *mōdrige* 'mother's sister', Grk *mētruiá* 'stepmother', Arm *mawru* 'stepmother, mother-in-law') while *$swoiniyeh_a$- gives us 'wife's sister', i.e. 'sister-in-law' (Lith *sváinė* 'sister-in-law', Latv *svaîne* 'wife's sister', Arm *k'eni* 'wife's sister'). In the West Central area the word for 'granddaughter', *$neptih_a$-, also carries the meaning 'niece' as we have seen above. Possible central European isoglosses include the Albanian-Indic correspondence that yields *$suh_x sos$ 'grandfather' (Alb *gjysh* 'grandfather', Skt *sūṣā́* 'paternal grandmother') from *$seuh_x$- 'beget', the same root that gave the words for 'son' above) while *syō̆(u)ros*, attested in Slavic, Armenian, and Indic, indicates 'wife's brother' (OCS *šurĭ* 'wife's brother', Arm *hor* 'son-in-law', Skt *syālá*- 'wife's brother'). A 'family tree' of the terminology for blood relatives and those in-laws acquired, as it were, by their marrying into the family is found in Figures. 12.1–3.

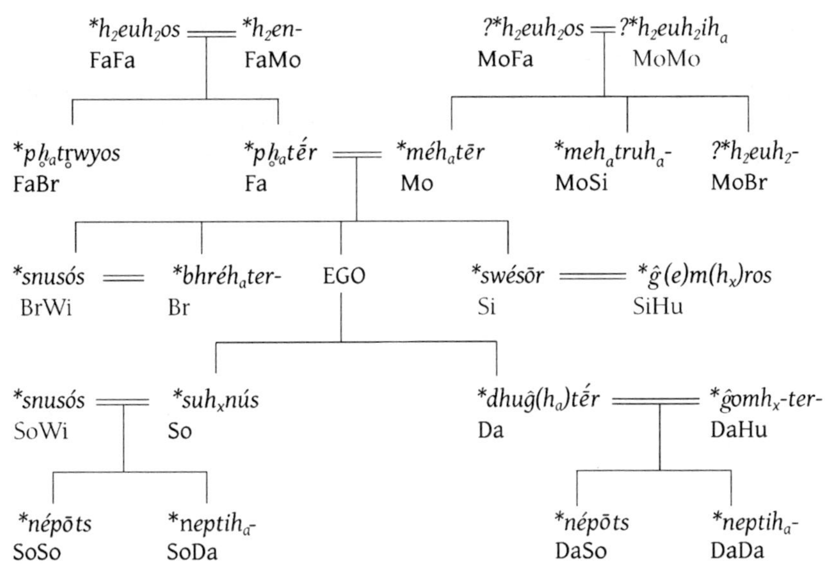

Figure 12.1. Reconstructucted PIE Kinship Terms for Blood Relatives

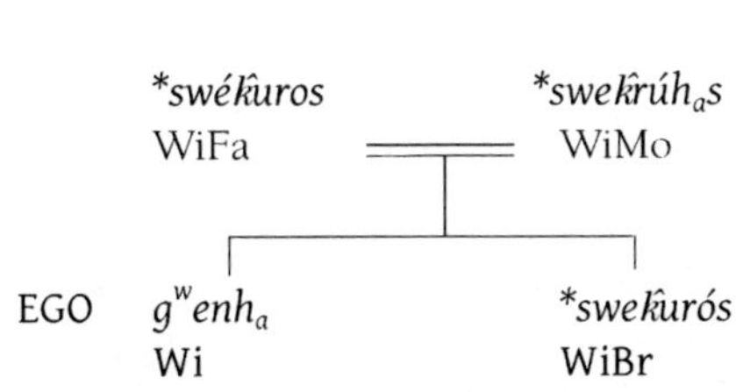

Figure 12.2. In-Law Terminology (for the husband)

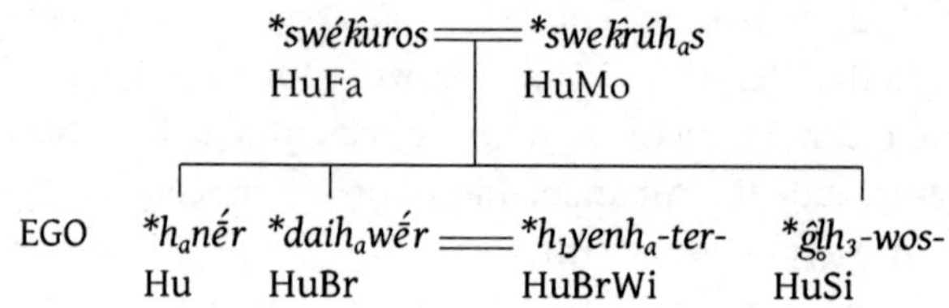

Figure 12.3. In-Law Terminology (for the wife)

Further Reading

General surveys of the IE kinship system have appeared since the nineteenth century, e.g. Delbrück (1889). Among the more important surveys to appear there is Hetterich (1985), Szemerényi (1977), Benveniste (1973*a*), Gates (1971), Wordick (1970), and Friedrich (1966). The terms for marriage are treated in Hamp (1988). The question of mother's brother is discussed in Beekes (1976) and Bremmer (1976). Recent examples of attempts to reduce the kinship terms to their 'basic' meaning can be found in Blažek (2001), Carruba (1995). Other works of interest are Beekes (1992), Bush (1987), Huld (1981), Parvulescu (1989, 1993*a*, 1996), Starke (1987), Wolfe (1993).

13

Hearth and Home

13.1 Dwelling

Architectural terms constitute a significant category of the Proto-Indo-European lexicon although, as we will see below, most of the vocabulary is so general that it can hardly be diagnostic in relating the linguistic evidence to the archaeological evidence of Eurasia. The main terms associated with dwelling and settlement are provided in Table 13.1.

Although we have a regional term that indicates 'settle, dwell' a strongly attested word for 'dwell' eludes us and we have only *$h_2$wes-* 'dwell, stay, pass the night'. The more limited connotations of 'passing the night' are included in Celtic (OIr *foaid*), Grk (*núkta*) *á*(*w*)*esa*, Arm *goy*, and Skt *vásati* but some of these languages (Old Irish, Sanskrit) as well as others, e.g. Goth *wisan*, Hit *hues-*, Av *vaŋhaiti*, and Toch B *wäs-*, indicate a meaning 'live' or 'dwell'. The word probably meant originally 'to spend time' (a Hittite derivative *huski-* means 'wait for, linger') and subsequently developed into meaning 'dwell'. To this we may add **men-* 'stay, remain' although it is a bit diffuse semantically in its various cognates that can be found in Celtic (e.g. OIr *ainmne* 'duty'), Lat *maneō* 'remain', Grk *ménō* 'stand fast, remain', Arm *mnam* 'remain, expect', possibly Hit *mimma-* 'refuse', Skt *man-* 'delay', Toch AB *mäsk-* 'become'.

There are two word for 'build', i.e. **dem*(h_a)- and *k^wei-*. The first yields the meaning 'build' in Grk *démō* and HierLuv *tama-* but more general meanings in

Table 13.1. *Terms for dwelling*

*h$_2$wes-	'dwell, pass the night, stay'	NE *was/were*, Skt *vásati*
*men-	'remain, stay'	Lat *maneō*, Grk *ménō*, Skt *man-*
*dem(h$_a$)-	'build (up)'	NE *timber*, Grk *démō*
*k^{w}ei-	'pile up, build'	Grk *poiéō*, Skt *cinóti*
*teḱs-	'hew, fabricate'	Lat *texō*, Grk *téktōn*, Skt *tákṣati*
*ghórdhos	'fence, hedge; enclosure, pen, fold'	Lat *hortus*, NE *yard*, Grk *khórtos*, Skt *gr̥há-*
*worPo-	'enclosure'	
*wr̥to/eh$_a$-	'enclosure'	NE *-worth*, Skt *vr̥ti-*
*pelh$_x$-	'fort, fortified place'	Grk *pólis*, Skt *pū́r*
*wriyo/eh$_a$-	'fort'	Grk *hríon*
*ḱéiwos	'belonging to the household'	Lat *cīvis*, Skt *śéva-*
*wiḱs	'(social unit of) settlement, extended family group'	Skt *viś-*
*dṓm	'house'	Grk *dô*, Skt *dā́m*
*dóm(h$_a$)os	'house'	Lat *domus*, Grk *dómos*, Skt *dáma-*
*h$_2$wóstu	'dwelling'	Grk *ástu*, Skt *vā́stu*
*kus-	'dwelling'	NE *house*
*ḱēls	'(store)room'	Lat *cella*, NE *hall*, Grk *kalīā́*, Skt *śā́la-*
*ket-	'room'	
*gubho/eh$_a$-	'(store)room, alcove'	NE *cove*
?*pḗr	'house'	
*h$_2$elwos	'elongated cavity, hollow'	Lat *alvus*, Grk *aulós*
*ĝhh̥$_a$wos	'gaping hole'	Grk *kháos*
*h$_2$éryos	'cavity'	
*ḱóuh$_x$r̥	'hole, opening'	Lat *caverna*, Grk *kúar*, Skt *śū́na-*
*ḱoiw-is	'±tube'	

Germanic (e.g. OHG *zeman* 'be fitting' but derived forms in Germanic include NE *timber*), Khot *pa-dīm-* 'make', and Toch AB *tsäm-* 'increase, grow'. The second root, found in Slavic (OCS *činĭ* 'order'), Grk *poiéō* 'pile up, make', and Indo-Iranian (Skt *cinṓti* 'pile up'), suggests an underlying meaning of 'pile up, build'. Along with these construction words we might add **teḱs-* 'hew, fabricate' with its extensive representation, e.g. Lat *texō* 'weave, intertwine, put together, construct', Lith *tašýti* 'hew, trim', OCS *tesati* 'hew', Skt *tákṣati* 'fashions, creates; carpenters, cuts', with a significant set of nominal derivatives: Grk *téktōn* 'architect', *tékhnē* 'art, technique', Skt *tákṣan-* 'carpenter', Hit *taksan-* 'joint', OHG *dehsa* 'axe'.

In terms of construction, there are several words for some form of 'enclosure'. The word **ghórdhos* or **ghórtos* is widely attested with meanings that vary from NWels *garth* 'pen, fold' to Rus *górod* 'town' or Hit *gurtas* 'citadel'. It originally derives from a verbal root **gherdh-* 'gird' (and from which we have NE *gird*) and seems to have indicated some form of hedge or fence that surrounded an area such as a yard or an entire settlement. A Hittite (i.e. Hit *warpa* 'enclosures')- Tocharian (Toch A *warp* 'enclosure') isogloss gives us **worPo-* (where the *-P-* indicates any bilabial, i.e. **b*, **bh*, or **p*) which could probably be extended by Lat *urbs* 'city' (< *'ritual enclosure'). A possible PIE **wr̥to/ehₐ-* or **worto/ehₐ-*, attested in Germanic (e.g. OE *worþ* 'court, courtyard, farm' which remains in many English place names ending in *-worth*), Baltic (e.g. Lith *var̃tai* 'gate, gateway'), Slavic (OCS *rata* 'gate'), Indo-Iranian (e.g. Skt *vr̥ti-* 'enclosure'), and Tocharian (e.g. Toch B *warto* 'forest' if from *'sacred grove' < *'sacred enclosure'), may reflect independent creations in these various groups, all derived from the root **wer-* 'cover, enclose, protect'.

The existence of a fortified site is indicated by two PIE words. Baltic (Lith *pilìs* 'fort, castle'), Grk *pólis* 'city' citadel', and Indic (Skt *pū́r* 'wall, rampart, palisade' and the second member of many place names, e.g. Nagpur, Singapore) (possibly also Arm *k'alak'*) indicate the existence of **pelhₓ-* 'fort'. The second word is **wriyo/ehₐ-*, attested in Thrac *bría* 'city, town built on a hill', Messapic (the city name *Uria*), various Celtic place names such as the British names lying behind English Wrekin and Wroxeter, and Tocharian (e.g. Toch B *rīye* 'city'); both the specific Thracian meaning and the fact that the Greek cognate *hríon* means 'promontory' suggests an original meaning of 'acropolis' in those IE traditions where the word came to mean 'city' and a derivative from **wer-* 'high'.

Words for a 'settlement' tend to be based on social organization rather than architecture. The root **k̂éiwos* indicates the concept of 'citizen' in Italic (Lat *cīvis*), 'member of the household' in Germanic (e.g. OE *hīwan*) and even more abstract concepts such as 'friendly' or 'dear' in Indic (Skt *śivá-*). The **wik̂s* is similarly seen as a social term although it tends to have a more specific 'architectural' meaning, e.g. 'village' in Slavic (OCS *vĭsĭ*) and Av *vīs-*, but 'tribe' or 'clan' in Doric Grk *-(w)ikes* 'tribes'. It also yields derived forms, e.g. **weik̂s-* which gives us Lat *vīlla* (< **weik̂s-lehₐ-*) 'country-house, country estate' and **woik̂os* which underlies Lat *vīcus* 'village, hamlet; quarter of a city' and Grk *(w)oîkos* 'household' (the source of NE *economy*).

There are a number of words pertaining to the house and rooms of the Proto-Indo-Europeans. Although the distribution of **dṓm* 'house' is limited to Grk *dô*, Arm *tun*, and Indo-Iranian (e.g. Skt *dā́m*), it retains an archaic formation (the genitive is **déms*) that suggests PIE status. It may also provide the basis of **dóm(hₐ)os* 'house', if this latter word is not derived directly from the verbal root **dem(h_a)-* 'build'. The verbal root **$h_2$wes-* 'dwell, spend the night' might underlie **$h_2$wóstu* 'dwelling' (reflected in, e.g., Grk *ástu* 'city' and Skt *vā́stu* 'place, seat' and with slightly different underlying forms in NWels *gwas* 'abode', and Toch B *ost* 'house'). Something smaller than a house may be indicated by **k̂ēls* where it indicates a 'storeroom' in Lat *cella*, a 'hut' in Grk *kalīá*; a derivative gives us NE *hall* and it would appear to derive from **k̂el-* 'protect, conceal'. The root **ket-* (e.g. OE *heaðor* 'enclosure, prison', OCS *kotĭcĭ* 'chamber', Av *kata-* 'chamber') similarly refers to a single chamber and was borrowed into the Uralic languages, e.g. Finnish *kota* 'dwelling, tent, hut'. Since **ket-* shows up elsewhere in Indo-European languages with a meaning 'hole' (e.g. Av *čāiti* 'in a hole', Skt *cā́tvāla-* 'hole for the sacrificial fire', Toch B *kotai-* 'hole'), it may be that the 'chamber' was originally something like a 'storage pit'. Another term with 'subterranean' connections is **k(o)us-* which appears in the Germanic words for 'house', e.g. NE *house*, the Tocharian words for 'village' (i.e. a collection of houses), e.g. Toch B *kwaṣai-*, and Arm *xuc'* 'room' and *xul* 'hut'. These would all appear to be derivatives of **keus-* 'hollow out', and the use of this root for 'dwelling' words presumably reflects structures that were at least once semi-subterranean. Another word for 'chamber' is **gubho/eh_a-* where OE *cova* 'bedchamber' gives us NE *cove*; the only non-Germanic cognate is from Bajui, an Iranian language of the Pamirs, where we have *bidyāǰ* 'lower part of a storeroom'. More controversial is a root **pḗr* which is only certainly attested in Anatolian (e.g. Hit nominative *pēr*, genitive *parnas*), and its ascription to Proto-Indo-European is largely dependent on seeing it as the underlying concept behind PIE **pri$h_x$ós* 'dear, beloved', i.e. 'of the same household' and its archaic morphology reflecting a PIE **pḗr* (< **pérr̥*), genitive **pr̥nós*; against such an ascription is the fact that there are similar words for 'house' in non-IE languages of the Near East, e.g. Egyptian *pr* 'house', and thus some would see the Anatolian words as a borrowing from another language.

Before reviewing the evidence for the concrete elements of construction, there are a number of more abstract terms that suggest the concept of a 'cavity' of some sort. **$h_2$elwos* indicates a 'cavity' or 'tube' and carries meanings (some derived) that range from the 'leg of a boot' (Lith *aũlas*) to a 'street' (Rus *úlica*) and a 'beehive' (Lat *alv(e)ārium*). The verbal root **ĝheh_aw-* 'gape, yawn' gives us **ĝh$h̥_a$wos* which yields, among other words, Grk *kháos* 'chaos' and Toch A *ko* 'mouth'. **$h_2$érwo-* is limited to Hit *hariya-* 'valley, dale' and Arm *ayr* 'cave' but there is a related form in Lith *armuõ* 'abyss'. PIE **k̂óuh_xr̥*, a heteroclitic (with an original genitive **k̂u$h_x$nós*), indicates a 'cave' in Lat *caverna*, 'eye of the needle, opening of the ear' in Grk *kúar*, 'lack' in Skt *śū́na-*, 'throat' in Toch B *kor*, and occurs in derived forms in Celtic although its underlying meaning may have been more abstract. Finally, **k̂oiw-is* gives us a word for a 'tube-shaped object' such as a 'spool' (e.g. Lith *šeivà*).

There is a fairly extensive regional vocabulary associated with dwellings. We begin with the North-West set. Celtic, Italic (if Lat *caul(l)ae* 'hole, opening' belongs here), and Germanic (NE *haw* and *hedge*) all derive ultimately from **kagh-* 'hedge, enclosure' from a verbal root **kagh-* 'catch, seize'. There is a regional term for 'fort' **dhūnos* (or **dhuh$_x$nos*?) based on cognates in Celtic (*dun* is a familiar place name element in Ireland and Scotland) and Germanic (NE *down(s)*); the word was also borrowed into Germanic from Celtic (where its Proto-Germanic form was **tūna-*) and it yielded among other things NE *town*. There is a general term **solo/eh$_a$-* or **selo-* 'dwelling, settlement' (Germanic, e.g. OE *sæl* 'room, hall, castle', Baltic, e.g. Lith *salà* 'village', Slavic, e.g. Rus *seló* 'village').

The West Central area also has a good number of cognate sets. These include **bherĝh-* 'height = fort', a problematic set with good Germanic cognates, e.g. OHG *burg* 'fortress' but Greek and Armenian cognates with unexpected forms, e.g. Grk *púrgos* (and not the expected ***párkhos*) which some suggest may derive from a Near Eastern word, e.g. Urartian *burgana-* 'fortress', or others suggest may come from some other Indo-European language that may have preceded Greek into the Aegean area but whose population was subsequently assimilated to Greek. The word **k̂óimos* 'household, village' (NE *home*) is related to Lat *cīvis* 'citizen' and words that mean 'dear' in Sanskrit. Well attested in Celtic, Italic, Germanic, Baltic, and Greek is **trēbs* 'dwelling' (e.g. OIr *treb* 'habitation', Lat *trabs* 'wooden beam', ON *þorp* 'farm, estate' [whence NE place names in *-thorp*], Lith *trobà* 'house, building', Grk *téramna* ~ *téremna* 'house, dwelling').

Finally, from the Greek and Indo-Iranian region we have **mand-* 'enclosure, stall' (also found in Thracian); **tk̂ei-* 'settle, dwell' and its derivative **tk̂ítis* 'settlement' (Grk *ktísis* 'settlement', Av *šiti-* 'settlement', Skt *kṣití-* 'settlement'). A natural physical feature is seen in **káiwr̥(t)* 'cave, fissure (in the earth)' possible seen in (dialectal) Grk *kaíatas* 'ditches, fissures in the ground opened by earthquakes' and Skt *kéraṭa-* 'cave, hollow'. Limited and questionable is **kamareh$_a$* 'vault' which means 'belt' in Avestan; this word was loaned from Grk *kamará* into Lat *camera* and then into French *chambre* and on into English (*chamber*).

13.2 Construction

There is no clear word for the 'wall' of a house in Proto-Indo-European; rather, we have a word that indicates an 'enclosing wall' of a fortification, i.e. **dhíĝhs*, seen most directly in OPers *didā* '(town) wall, fortification' and Skt

Table 13.2. *Construction and furnishing*

**dhiĝhs*	'wall, fortification'	Grk *teîkhos*, Skt *dehī-*
**serk-*	'to construct/repair a wall'	Lat *sarciō*, Grk *hérkos*
**$h_a$énh$_x$t(e)h_a*	'doorjamb'	Lat *antae*, Skt *ā́tā-*
**dhwṓr*	'door, gate'	Lat *foris*, NE *door*, Grk *thúrā*, Skt *dvā́rau*
**telh$_x$-om*	'floor (of planks)?'	Lat *tellūs*, Skt *tala-*
**bhudhnó-*	'bottom'	Lat *fundus*, NE *bottom*, Grk *puthmḗn*, Skt *budhná-*
**dhĝh(e)m-en*	'on(to) the ground'	Lat *humī*, Grk *khamaí*, Skt *jmán* ~ *kṣamā*
**$h_1$rebh-*	'cover with a roof'	NE *rafter*, Grk *eréphō*
**k̂red-*	'framework, beams'	NE *roost*
**k̂líts*	'post, trimmed log'	Grk *klíta*, Skt *śrít-*
**míts*	'stake, post'	Skt *mít-*
**stéh$_2$ur*	'post'	Grk *staurós*, Skt *sthū́ṇā-*
**swer-*	'post, rod'	Lat *surus*, Grk *hérma*, Skt *sváru-*
**pin-*	'±shaped wood'	Grk *pínaks*, Skt *pínāka-*
**stup-*	'±offcut, piece of wood'	NE *stump*, Grk *stúpos*
**k̂ókolos*	'splinter'	Skt *śákala-*
**$h_2$eh$_x$-seh$_a$-*	'hearth'	Lat *āra*
**sedes-*	'seat'	Grk *hédos*, Skt *sádas-*
**nisdos*	'nest'	Lat *nīdus*, NE *nest*, Skt *nīḍá-*
**léghes-*	'place for lying, bed, couch'	Grk *lékhos*
**ster(h_3)mn̥*	'strewn place, ?bed'	Lat *strāmen*, Grk *strôma*, Skt *stáriman-*

sa-dih- 'mound, heap, wall', which has a number of derived forms, e.g. the Av *pairi-daēza-* 'enclosure' which was borrowed into Greek as *parádeisos* 'garden' and then borrowed into English as *paradise*, or Grk *teîkhos* ~ *toîkhos* 'wall', Skt *dehī-* 'wall, bank'. In the North-West languages it refers to claylike substances, e.g. NE *dough*, and suggests that the original concept relates to an 'earthen bank'. It is possible that **serk-* supplies the root for repairing an enclosure or, perhaps better, completing a circle, e.g. Lat *sarciō* 'mend, repair', Grk *hérkos* 'fence, enclosure', Hit *sark-* 'make restitution' (with a meaning adapted to the legal system).

We fare much better with the concept of 'door' as we can reconstruct both **$h_a$énh$_x$t(e)h_a* 'doorjamb' (e.g. Lat *antae* 'pillars framing a door', ON *ǫnd* 'foreroom', Arm *dr-and* 'door-posts', Skt *ā́tā* 'door-posts', and **dhwōr* 'door', the latter with cognates in all major groups (OIr *dorus*, Lat *foris*, NE *door*, Lith *dùrys*, OCS *dvĭrĭ*, Alb *derë*, Grk *thúrā*, Arm *dur-k'*, Skt *dvā́ras*, Toch B *twere*, all 'door(s)' and Hit *andurza* 'within' (literally 'in-doors'). Often the word for 'door' occurs in the dual and indicates two leaves of a door.

The lower and upper extremities of the house are less well established. There is no certain word for the 'floor' of the house. The closest word to fit would be **telh$_x$-om* 'floor' but it only exhibits this meaning in Germanic, e.g. OE *þel* 'floor', *þille* 'plank of floor', and Baltic (e.g. Lith *tìles* 'planks at the bottom of a ship'), but in Celtic, Italic, and Slavic it means 'earth' or 'ground' (e.g. OIr *talam* 'earth, ground', Lat *tellūs* 'earth', Rus *tlo* 'bottom'); its status as Proto-Indo-European rests on whether one accepts as cognate Skt *tala-* 'surface, bottom'. We also have a generic word for 'bottom', i.e. **bhudhnó-* (e.g. MIr *bonn* 'sole of foot', Lat *fundus* 'bottom', OE *botm* [> NE *bottom*], Grk *puthmḗn*, Skt *budhná-* 'bottom, foot') which is extended to mean 'ground' (e.g. Av *bū̆na-*) but not in the sense of the floor of a house. (In the south-east of the Indo-European world derivatives of this word are used to name the archetypical monster, i.e. the Greek *Pūthṓ* and Sanskrit *áhir bhudhnyás* 'snake of the deep'.) There is also an adverb, **dhĝh(e)m-en* 'on the ground', which has been formed from the noun **dhĝhem-* 'earth' (see Section 8.1). There is only one word associated with 'roof' which is widely enough attested to (perhaps) claim PIE status. The verb **h$_1$rebh-* 'cover with a roof' is found in Grk *eréphō* 'cover with a roof' and *orópʰē* 'roof' and possibly in Khufi (an Iranian language of the Pamirs) *rawū̆ǰ* 'plank'; an *o*-grade derivative in Germanic **h$_1$robh-tro-* gives us NE *rafter* (and by way of borrowing from ON we have NE *reef*).

There are a number of words associated with timber construction. A root **k̂red-* 'framework, beams' is attested in Germanic (e.g. NE *roost*), possibly Slavic (e.g. OCS *krada* 'funeral pile', though the initial consonant is phonologically irregular), and Shughni (another Iranian language of the Pamirs) where it means a 'summer pen for cattle' (*χā̆δ*). The underlying meaning of **k̂líts* 'post, trimmed log' depends on its meanings in Celtic (e.g. OIr *clī* 'housepost'), Germanic (e.g. OE *gehlid* 'fence' [< *'string of posts']), and Greek (e.g. *klíta* 'cloister' [< *'arcade' < *'series of posts']) while it tends to indicate a 'ladder' in Indo-Iranian (e.g. Skt *śrit-*). The word **míts* 'stake, post' (e.g. Skt *mit-* 'pillar, post') does indicate an upright post or pillar and there is an underlying verb **mei-* 'fix a post in the ground'. The verb **stéh$_2$-* 'stand' is the basis for **stéh$_2$ur* 'post' (e.g. Grk *staurós* 'cross', Skt *sthū́ṇā-* 'post'; a derivative gives NE *steer*) while some form of 'post' or 'rod' is indicated by **swer-* (e.g. Lat *surus* 'twig, short stalk', Grk *hérma* 'support', Skt *sváru-* 'sacrificial post, stake'). Far more ambiguous is **pin-* '± shaped wood', a proto-sememe of desperation generated by such meanings as 'heap of wood' (Germanic, i.e. OHG *witu-fīna*), 'tree trunk' (Slavic, i.e. OCS *pĭnĭ*), 'plank' (Grk, i.e. *pínaks*), and 'staff, bow' (Indic, i.e. Skt *pinā̆ka-*). A root **stup-* also has a wide set of meanings, e.g. 'stump', 'broom', 'club', and appears to derive from the verbal root **steup-* 'strike' (e.g. Grk *stúpos* 'stick, post, pole', NE *stump*, Toch A *ṣtop* 'club'). Some form of 'splinter' or 'wood-chip' is indicated by the Baltic-Indic isogloss that derives from **k̂ókolos* (i.e. Lith *šakalỹs* 'splinter', Skt *śákala-* 'splinter').

There are few reliably attested words for internal arrangements or furniture. Within the house we are certain that we would find a ***h_2eh_x*-seh*$_a$*-* 'hearth' as in Lat *āra* and Hit *hāssa-*, a derivative of the verbal root ***h_2eh_x*-* 'burn' (it also provides the base for NE *ash*). Although we can reconstruct a word **sedes-* 'seat', this is a fairly transparent nominalization of **sed-* 'sit', and may have been independently created in Celtic (NWels *sedd* 'seat'), Grk *hédos* 'seat', and Indo-Iranian (Av *hadiš-* 'home', Skt *sádas-* 'place'). The same verbal root also gives us **nisdos* 'nest' (e.g. NE *nest*, Lat *nīdus* 'nest', and Skt *nīḍá-* 'nest'), which is literally a 'sit-down place, i.e. **ni-* 'down' + *sed-* 'sit'. Both words pertaining to the concept of 'bed' are obviously derived from verbal roots and may be independent formations in various groups. These comprise **léghes-* (e.g. Grk *lékhos* 'bed, bier') and also **lóghos* (e.g. Grk *lókhos* 'place for lying, ambush', Toch B *leke* 'bed, resting place') from **legh-* 'lie down' and **ster(*h_3*)mn̥* 'strewing, something strewn, strewn place' (in Greek and Sansrikt it does mean 'bed') which derives from **ster(*h_3*)-* 'strew' (Lat *strāmen* 'straw', Grk *strôma* 'straw, bed', Skt *stáriman-* 'act of spreading out; bed, couch').

North-Western terms associated with carpentry include **plut-* 'plank' (e.g. Lat *pluteus* 'movable penthouse, shed', Lith *plaũtas* 'plank'); **masdos* 'post' (e.g. Lat *mālus* 'mast; upright in building a tower', NE *mast*); **perg-* 'pole, post' (e.g. Lat *pergula* 'balcony; outhouse used for various purposes', ON *forkr* 'pole', Rus *poróg* 'threshold'); **reh*$_1$*t-* 'post, pole' (e.g. Lat *rētae* 'trees growing along the bank or in the bed of a stream', NE *rood*); **sth*$_2$*bho/eh*$_a$*-* 'post, pillar' (e.g. NE *staff*, Lith *stãbas* 'post') from the root **steh*$_2$*-* 'stand'; and **ĝhasdhos* 'rod, staff' (Lat *hasta* 'spear'), which yields OE *gierd* 'staff, measuring pole' which explains the basis of NE *yard*. Germanic and Slavic attest a meaning 'roof' for **k̂rópos* 'roof' (NE *roof*, OCS *stropŭ* 'roof') while its only Celtic cognate attests a meaning 'hovel, stall' (MIr *crō*).

From the West Central region we have a Germanic-Greek isogloss from **dm̥pedom* 'floor' (ON *topt* 'place for building', Grk *dápedon* 'floor'), a compound derived from **dem-* 'build' and **ped-* 'foot'. The root **(s)teg-* 'cover' underlies the Celtic-Greek isogloss of **(s)téges-* 'roof' (with derivatives such as OIr *tech* 'house', Lat *tectum* 'roof, ceiling', *tēgula* 'roof-tile', NE *thatch*, Grk *(s)tégos* 'roof, house'). The array of construction terms comprises **bhélh*$_a$*ĝs* 'plank, beam' (e.g. NE *balk*; cf. also Lat *fulciō* 'prop up, support'); **kl̥h*$_x$*-ro-s* 'plank' from **(s)kel-* 'strike, hew' (e.g. OIr *clār* 'plank', Grk *klêros* 'piece of wood used for casting lots') and from the same root we also have **(s)kōlos* 'stake' (e.g. Grk *skôlos* 'pointed stake'); **sph$_a$en-* 'flat-shaped piece of wood' (e.g. Lat *sponda* 'frame of a bed, bedstead', NE *spoon*, and in derived form NE *spade*); **swel-* ~ **sel-* 'plank, board' (e.g. NE *sill*, Grk *hélmata* 'planing, decking'); **k̂súlom* 'worked, shaped wood; post, stake' (e.g. Grk *ksúlom* 'wood', OHG *sūl* 'pillar', Lith *šùlas* 'wooden post, stake'); **kroku-* ~ **kró-kyeh$_a$-* 'post' (Rus *krókva* 'stake', Grk *króssai* 'crenellation'); *(*s*)*teg-* 'pole, post' (e.g. Lat *tignum* 'wooden beam', NE *stake*) where we may expect a shift from 'cover', the meaning of the verbal root, to 'cover with poles' > 'poles', **stl̥neh$_a$-* 'post, support' from **stel-* 'stand' (e.g. OHG *stollo* 'support', Grk *stḗlē* 'pillar'); **wálsos* 'stake' (e.g. Lat *vallus* 'post, stake', NE *wale* 'stripe left on the skin by a blow') may be older if one accepts a potential Indic cognate (Skt *vala-* 'pole, beam'); **ĝhalgheh$_a$-* 'pole, stake' (e.g. NE *gallows*, Lith *žalgà* 'long thin pole'). The root 'to burn' also underlies a West Central isogloss for 'hearth', **h$_2$eh$_x$-tr-eh$_a$-* (e.g. Lat *ātrium* 'hall or entrance way' [< *'large open space above the central fire for the escape of smoke'], Rus *vatra* 'hearth') while the verb 'sit' yields both **sedlom* and **sedros* 'seat, chairlike object' (Lat *sella* 'seat, chair', *sedīle* 'seat', NE *settle*). A Greek-Armenian isogloss gives us **k̂ih$_x$won-* 'pillar, post' (Grk *kī́ōn*, Arm *siwn*).

13.3 Proto-Indo-European Settlement

The reconstructed lexicon provides a very general picture of the residences and architecture of the Proto-Indo-Europeans. Nevertheless, we can at least make an attempt at translating some of the vocabulary into features that might be recoverable from the archaeological record. To begin with, it seems fairly clear that the Proto-Indo-Europeans occupied substantial houses rather than flimsier shelters. For example, among the fourteen terms for dwelling or settlement reconstructed to the largely mobile hunter-fishers of the Uralic language family, we find terms such as the **śarma* 'smokehole of a tent', **ude-me* 'sleeping tent', and even the IE loanword **ket-* 'room' yields the Uralic **kota* 'tent, hut, house'. In contrast, Proto-Indo-European possesses sufficient terms for house, room, and upright timber constructions to suggest a more solid dwelling structure.

The reconstructed lexicon also indicates some form of nucleated settlement, i.e. a group of houses, rather than the type of dispersed settlement that one often encounters on the western periphery of Europe during the Neolithic. We have a series of words for some form of enclosure (**ghórdhos*, **worPo-*, **wr̥to/eh$_a$-*, **pelh$_x$-*, **wriyo/eh$_a$-*) and the extensions of a term for a social unit (**wiḱs*) to indicate a village. Without a precise date and location for the Proto-Indo-Europeans it is difficult to make much archaeologically out of such terms, as broad areas of Europe saw evidence for some form of enclosure from the Early Neolithic onwards, e.g. ditched enclosures around southern Italian Neolithic sites, ditched enclosures around central and west European (Danubian) Neolithic sites, causewayed enclosures in Britain, timber palisade around Balkan tell sites. Moreover, evidence for truly defensive enclosures increases as one enters the Eneolithic and Early Bronze Age, especially in eastern Europe (the steppelands, the Balkans) and Anatolia (e.g. Troy). Regarding the **wiḱs*, we do not appear to have an obvious designation for a settlement unit much larger than a clan, i.e. there is no suggestion in the reconstructed vocabulary for the type of proto-urbanism that one encounters in South-West Asia, Central Asia, India, or Anatolia during the Neolithic.

As to actual house structure, it is certainly easiest to imagine some form of timber-built structure given the abundance of words for post (**ḱred-*, **ḱlíts*, **míts*, *$*st\acute{e}h_2ur$*, **swer-*) and perhaps the word for floor ($*telh_x$*-om*) if timber planks are really implicit in our reconstruction. The word **dhiǵhs* is critical if one wishes to imagine some form of clay daub being employed in wall construction. In this case, we might well imagine that the walls involved wattle and daub, especially as there is very good evidence (see Chapter 14) for words for interweaving or wattling, including that concerned with house construction, e.g. $*wei(h_x)$- 'plait, wattle' which gives ON *veggr* 'wall'. The existence of several rooms for 'chambers' (**ḱēls*, **ket-*, $*gubho/eh_a$-) suggests the presence of either multi-room constructions or specialized outbuildings for storage and other purposes.

Negative evidence is seldom particularly compelling but the reconstructed lexicon not only does not indicate a word for 'brick' but where it does occur among Indo-Europeans who employed bricks in construction, as in Proto-Indo-Iranian **išt(y)a-* 'brick' (>Av *ištiia-*, Skt *iṣṭakā-*), it is commonly explained as a loanword from a non-Indo-European language, but may be an internal Indo-Iranian derivative of $*h_aeis$- 'burn' (Toch B shows a different derivative, *aise* <$*h_aoiso$- in the meaning 'pot'). Bricks were made of sun-dried (and later fired) mud/clay and are the diagnostic building technique of the Neolithic (and later periods) in Anatolia, South-West Asia, and central Asia with some evidence from Neolithic Greece, but beyond Macedonia they are essentially unknown during the Neolithic. In short, the evidence for architectural terms in Proto-Indo-European is most consistent with an architectural tradition somewhere in temperate Eurasia where houses were exclusively built of timber rather than brick.

Further Reading

For general discussion see Knobloch (1980), Lejeune (1977); for enclosures see Della Volpe (1986), Driessen (2001), Makkay (1986), and Rau (1973); the hearth is treated in Della Volpe (1990) and Nagy (1974*b*); the bed in Hamp (1987*c*) and Maher (1981).

14

Clothing and Textiles

14.1 Textiles

Among the obvious domestic pursuits in any society, at least one inhabiting the temperate regions of Eurasia, is the production of textiles and clothing. The reconstructed lexicon has a considerable number of items pertaining to these activities although they fall far short of providing us with an image of Indo-European fashion. We have already seen that the Indo-European vocabulary includes a very well attested word for 'wool' (Section 11.2), a word for 'linen' (Section 10.3) is found in the West Central region (as far east as Greece but no further), and there are several words for animal skins, all of which were potentially manufactured into clothes and containers. Table 14.1 presents a list of the basic terms pertaining to textiles.

The word for a skin container, **bhólĝhis*, is well attested and the element 'skin' or 'belly' is widely found in Celtic (e.g. OIr *bolgr* 'sack', Gaul *bulga* 'leather sack') and Germanic (OE *bel(i)g* 'bag' [> NE *belly*], OHG *balg* 'skin') while other groups indicate simply 'pillow' (Slovenian uses the word *blazína* for a 'feather bed') or 'bolster' (Indo-Iranian, e.g. Av *bərəziš* 'bolster, cushion', Skt *upa-bárhanī-* 'cover, bolster'). It derives from the verbal root **bhelĝh-* 'swell'. The word for 'net', *$h_1$ekt-*, is found in Greek, Anatolian (e.g. Hit *ēkt-*), and Indic (e.g. Skt *ákṣu-*); the Greek forms (Myc *dektu-*, Grk *díktuon*) show a prefix (**d-*) of uncertain origin which also occurs in some other words, e.g. Grk *dákru* 'tear' from *h_2éḱru*.

Table 14.1. *Textile terms*

*_bhólĝhis_	'(skin) bag; bolster'	NE _belly_, Skt _upa-bárhanī-_
*h_1_ekt-_	'net'	Grk _díktuon_, Skt _ákṣu-_
*h_1_eu-_	'put on clothes, cover'	Lat _induō, exuō_
*_wes-_	'be dressed'	Grk _énnūmi_, Skt _váste_
*_wospo/eh_$_a$-	'garment'	Lat _vespa_
*_drap-_ ~ *_drop-_	'clothes, cloak'	Skt _drāpí-_
*_yéh_$_3$_s-_	'gird'	Grk _zṓnnūmi_
*_gherdh-_	'gird, surround'	NE _gird, girdle_
*_kenk-_	'gird, wrap around'	Lat _cingō_, Skt _káñcate_
*_dek̂-_	'thread, hair'	Skt _daśā-_
*_los-_	'cloth'	Skt _las-pūjanī-_
*_p(e)h_$_2$_no/eh_$_a$-	'cloth'	Lat _pannus_, NE _fane_, Grk _pḗnē_
*_pek̂-_	'pull out [wool]'	Lat _pectō_, Grk _pékō_
*_reu(h_$_x$)-	'pull out [wool]'	Skt _róman-_
*_kars-_	'scratch; comb (wool)'	Lat _carrō, carmen_
*_kes-_	'comb'	
*_nak-_	'press, squeeze'	Lat _naccae_
*_plek̂-_	'braid, plait'	Lat _plectō_, Grk _plékō_, Skt _praśna-_
*_resg-_	'plait, wattle'	Lat _restis_, NE _rush_, Skt _rájju-_
*_wei(h_$_1$)-	'plait, wattle'	Lat _vieō_, Skt _váyati_
*_kert-_	'plait, twine'	Lat _crātis_, NE _hurdle_, Grk _kurtía_
*_mesg-_	'intertwine'	NE _mesh_
*_(s)neh_$_1$_(i)-_	'twist fibres into thread'	Lat _neō_, Grk _néō_, Skt _snā́yu-_
*_sneh_$_1$_u-_	'twist fibres into thread'	Lat _nervus_, Grk _neûron_
*_(s)pen-_	'draw, spin'	NE _spin_, Grk _pénomai_
*_terk(w)-_	'twist' (< 'spin')	Lat _torqueō_, Grk _átraktos_, Skt _tarkú-_
*$h_{2/3}$_eu-_	'weave'	NE _weeds_, Skt _u-_
*$h_{2/3}$_webh-_	'weave'	NE _weave_, Grk _huphaínō_, Skt _ubhnā́ti_
*_weg-_	'plait, weave'	Lat _vēlum_, NE _wick_
*_melk-_	'plait, spin'	
*_syuh_$_1$-	'sew'	Lat _suō_, NE _sew_, Grk _kassúō_, Skt _sī́vyati_
*_(s)ner-_	'fasten with thread or cord'	
*_ned-_	'knot'	Lat _nectō_, NE _net_

There are two words associated with getting dressed (with some wide semantic variation). Although *h_1_eu-_ 'put on clothes, cover' is limited to Italic (Lat _induō_ 'put on [clothes]', _exuō_ 'take off [clothes]'), Baltic (e.g. Lith _aũti_ 'put on shoes'), Slavic (OCS _obują_ 'put on shoes', _izują_ 'take off shoes'), and Arm _aganim_ 'dress', there are also nominal derivatives from this verb in Celtic (e.g. OIr *fūan* 'tunic') and Tocharian (Toch B *ewe* 'inner skin'). As we can see, in Baltic and Slavic it specifically pertains to the wearing or putting on of shoes. More widespread is **wes*- 'be dressed' (e.g. Grk *énnūmi* 'get dressed', Arm *z-genum* 'get dressed', Hit *wess*- 'be dressed', Skt *váste* 'wear', Toch B *wäs*- 'be dressed') with abundant nominal derivations, e.g. Lat *vestis* 'clothes'. Among the nouns formed from this verb are **wospo/eh*$_a$- which is found both in Italic and Anatolian where it refers to a specific garment; in Anatolian it means a 'shroud' (Hit *was(sa)pa*- 'garment, shroud', Luv *waspant* 'wearing funeral shrouds') and in Latin the derived *vespa* indicates 'one who steals clothes from the dead'. The second term **drap*- or **drop*- (e.g. Gallo-Roman *drappus* 'clothes', Lith *drãpanos* [pl.] 'clothes', Skt *drāpí*- 'cloak') and may come from **drep*- 'split off', i.e. it originally indicated a skin garment.

Some form of belt is indicated by several terms. The verb **yéh*$_3$*s*- 'gird' (e.g. Lith *júosiu* 'gird, girdle, buckle on [a sword]', OCS *po-jašǫ* 'gird', Alb *n-gjesh* 'gird, buckle on', Grk *zṓnnūmi* 'gird', Av *yāh*- 'gird') not only supplies a word for girding on a belt but also a number of nominal formations indicating the 'belt' itself, e.g. Grk *zṓnē* 'belt', whence via Latin we get NE *zone*. Only Germanic retains the verbal root **gherdh*- 'gird' (e.g. NE *gird*) but this verb appears to underlie all those words associated with a 'fence, enclosure', i.e. **ghórdhs*, which is of Proto-Indo-European date (see Section 13.1). A general verb to 'gird' or 'wrap around' is found in **kenk*- (e.g. Lat *cingō* 'gird, surround', Lith *kinkaũ* 'bridle, harness [a horse]', Skt *káñcate* 'bind' *kāñcī*- 'girdle').

The basic unit of textile manufacture, the 'thread', is attested as **dek̂*- in Germanic (e.g. ON *tāg* 'fibre') and Indo-Iranian (e.g. Khot *dasa*- 'thread', Skt *daśā*- 'fringe'); extended forms tend to mean 'hair', e.g. **dok̂-lo*- give NE *tail* (also OIr *dūal* 'lock of hair'). Other words for 'thread' are regional isoglosses. There are two general words for 'cloth': **los*- carries meanings such as 'rags' in Germanic (e.g. MHG *lasche*), Baltic (e.g. Lith *lãskana*), and Slavic (e.g. Rus *lóskut*) and 'cloth' in Indo-Iranian (e.g. Khot *r(r)aha*- 'cloth', Skt *las-pūjanī*- 'large needle' [< *'cloth piercer'?]—presuming that all these words go together) while **p(e)h*$_2$*no/eh*$_a$- exhibits wide semantic variance from 'linen cloth' (MIr *anan*), 'piece of cloth, garment' (Lat *pannus*), 'thread on the shuttle' (Grk *pḗne*) to 'sheepskin coat' (Roshani *warbōn* [< **vara(h)-pāna*- 'sheep(skin)-coat']); also belonging here is NE *fane* from OE *fana* 'banner, standard', an archaic term for 'flag' in NE where a dialectal term survives better in NE *vane*.

In the preparation of textiles we can begin with the concept of 'pulling out' the wool or fibres which is indicated in Proto-Indo-European by **pek̂*- 'pull out (e.g. wool), comb out (e.g. wool)', e.g. Lat *pectō* 'comb' [verb], *pecten* 'comb' [noun], Lith *pešù* 'pull, tear out, pluck [fowl]', Grk *pékō* 'comb, shear', *pékos* '(raw) wool, fleece', OE *feax* '(head) hair', Toch B *päk*- '±comb out [wool], shear'. The original meaning must have been something like 'harvest wool [by plucking]' and came to mean successively 'harvest wool [by combing]' and 'harvest wool [by shearing]' as the technology of wool-gathering evolved. The meaning became 'fossilized' at one semantic stage or another in the various Indo-European groups. Another verb with much the same meaning is **reu(h_x)-*. The sense of 'pluck wool' exists only in ON *rȳja* (also Norw *ru* 'winter wool') but there are numerous nominal forms such as 'horse's mane' (OIr *rōn*), 'fleece' (Slavic, e.g. Rus *runó*), 'hair' (Indo-Iranian, e.g. NPers *rōm* 'pubic hair', Skt *lóman-* ~ *róman-* 'body hair of men and animals') so that it suggests that the original meaning did involve plucking hairs or wool. There are two words associated with 'combing': **kars-* carries the specific meaning 'comb wool' in Italic (Lat *car(r)ō* 'comb wool', *carmen* 'comb for wool') and Baltic (e.g. Lith *karšiù* 'comb/card wool'); elsewhere it means 'scratch'. The verb **kes-* 'comb' is generally but not exclusively applied to combing human hair (e.g. MIr *cīr* 'comb', Lith *kasà* 'braid', OCS *kosa* 'hair', Hit *kiss-* ~ *kisā(i)-* 'comb') but could be extended to combing either wool (e.g. Grk *ksaínō* 'scrape, comb [hair or wool], full [cloth]') or flax (OE *heordan* [pl.] 'hards [of flax], tow').

One of the most basic methods of producing cloth is through 'felting' and there is one verb, **nak-*, that may have expressed this concept in Proto-Indo-European. It provides us with the Latin word *naccae* for 'cloth-fullers' (if the latter is not a Greek loanword, related in some fashion to [dialectal] Grk *naktá* [pl.] 'felt shoes') and we have the root employed in Greek 'felt shoes', but in Hittite it only means 'weighty, important' (*nakki-*) which takes us closer to the basic verbal root meaning 'press', i.e. 'pressing'. If it only meant 'press' in Proto-Indo-European (or Proto-Indo-Hittite), the meaning 'felt' may have been a later and secondary development.

There are a number of words for 'plaiting'. PIE **plek̂-* is well attested (e.g. Lat *plectō* 'plait, interweave', OE *fleohtan* 'braid, plait', OCS *pleto* 'braid, plait', Grk *plékō* 'braid, plait', Skt *praśna-* 'braiding, basketwork, turban') and in derived form (**plok-so-*) it gives us NE *flax*. Another root, **resg-*, seems to have included coarser plaiting, i.e. wattling (e.g. Lat *restis* 'rope, cord', NE *rush*, Lith *rezg(i)ù* 'knit, do network', OCS *rozga* 'root, branch', NPers *raγza* 'woollen cloth', Skt *rájju-* 'cord, rope'). A root **wei(h_1)-* (cf. Lat *vieō* 'bind, interweave', Skt *váyati* 'weaves') was highly productive in providing nouns, e.g. NE *withy*, Lat *vītis* 'vine', many of which are associated better with the wattling of a house wall (e.g. ON *veggr* 'wall'). Some form of wickerwork attends many of the meanings associated with **kert-* (e.g. Lat *crātis* 'wickerwork, hurdle, honey-comb', NE *hurdle*, OPrus *corto* 'hedge', Grk *kártallos* 'basket', *kurtía* 'wattle') while 'intertwining' is indicated by **mesg-* (e.g. ON *mǫskvi* 'mesh', Lith *mezgù* 'knit', *mãzgas* 'knot', Toch B *meske* 'joint, knot'); one of the cognate forms, MDutch *maesche*, gives us NE *mesh*.

Twisting the fibres into thread is also well attested with several roots. Both *(*s*)*neh*$_1$(*i*)- and **sneh*$_1$*u*- supply not only a series of verbs (e.g. MIr *snīid* 'twists, binds', Lat *neō* 'spin', OHG *nā*(*w*)*en* 'sew, stitch', Latv *snāju* 'twist loosely together, spin', Grk *néō* 'spin') but also nominal forms. For example, the *o*-grade of *(*s*)*neh*$_1$(*i*)- with the suffix *-*teh*$_a$- supplies NE *snood* (and OIr *snāth* 'thread', Latv *snāte* 'linen shawl, cape') while the root without the initial *s*-mobile coupled with the instrumental suffix -**tleh*$_a$- gives NE *needle*. The second verbal form underlies Lat *nervus* 'sinew, tendon' (metathesized form **neuros*) and Grk *neûron* 'sinew, tendon'. A root *(*s*)*pen*- yields meanings such as 'spin' and 'weave' (e.g. NE *spin*, Lith *pinù* 'weave', OCS *pьnǫ* 'tighten, strain', Alb *pe* 'thread', Grk *pénomai* 'toil [at household tasks]', Arm *hanum* ~ *henum* 'weave', Toch B *pänn*- 'draw [out], stretch'). A widely dispersed root **terk*(*w*)- means 'twist' and in a number of languages specifically 'spin' or, nominalized, 'spindle' (e.g. Lat *torqueō* 'twist, wind; torment', Alb *tjerr* 'spin', Grk *átraktos* 'spindle', Skt *tarkú*- 'spindle').

Verbs indicating 'weaving' are several. The most basic is **h*$_{2/3}$*eu*- where we have the NE cognate *weeds* as in 'widow's weeds' (cf. Skt *u*- 'weave', Rus *usló* 'weaving') and a derived form **h*$_{2/3}$*webh*- (e.g. NE *weave*, Alb *vej* 'weave', Grk *huphaínō* 'weave', Hit *huppai*- 'entangle, ensnare', Skt *ubhnā́ti* 'ties together', Toch B *wāp*- 'weave') where we not only find 'weave' but also 'web' and even 'spider' (i.e. Skt *ūrṇa-vābhi*-, literally 'wool-weaver'). Another possibility is **weg*- (e.g. OIr *figid* 'weaves', Lat *vēlum* 'sail, cloth', NE *wick*) although the semantic distance of some of the cognates, e.g. Skt *vāgurā*- 'net for catching animals', may suggests something plaited rather than woven. A similar semantic distance is seen among the derivatives of **melk*-; in Hittite we have *malk*- 'spin, entwine', Tocharian has *mälk*- 'joint together, insert', and OHG *malha* 'bag'.

'Sewing' is indicated with the root **syuh*$_1$- which is both geographically and semantically robust across the Indo-European languages (e.g. Lat *suō*, NE *sew*, Lith *siuvù*, OCS *šijǫ*, Grk *kassúō*, Skt *sī́vyati*, all 'sew'). The root *(*s*)*ner*- supplies a meaning of 'fasten with thread/cord' in Lith *nerìù* 'thread (a needle)', Toch B *ñare* 'thread' (it gave the OE *snēr* 'harpstring' and in its meaning 'bind close together' it may have supplied the basis of NE *narrow*).

Finally we have **ned*- 'knot, bind' (both verbally and also nominal derivatives, e.g. OIr *naiscid* 'binds', Lat *nectō* 'knot, bind' [whose shape has been influenced by *pectere* 'comb wool'], *nōdus* 'knot', NE *net*, Av *naska*- 'bundle') and probably also a series of words in Germanic and Greek (i.e. *adíkē* 'nettle') cognate with NE *nettle*, and there is also a **nedskéh*$_a$- 'tie, ring' from the same root in Celtic (OIr *nasc* 'fastening tie, ring') and Germanic (OHG *nuska* 'metal clasp').

The North-West region exhibits a number of cognate terms related to textiles. Italic (Lat *quālus* 'wicker-basket', *quasillus* 'small basket') and Slavic (e.g. OCS *koši* 'basket') both share *k^was-* '(wicker-) basket'; Germanic (e.g. ON *hrip* 'packbasket') and Baltic (e.g. Lith *krẽpšas* 'large satchel, backpack') both attest a **kreb-* 'basket' which has cognate sets in other languages in its *o*-grade form, e.g. Lat *corbis*, Lith *karbas*, Rus *kórob*, all 'basket'. Celtic and Germanic share a number of terms such as some form of 'cloak' or 'tunic' in **ruk-* 'over-garment' (e.g. OIr *rucht* 'tunic', OE *rocc* 'over-garment, rochet'); **dhelg-* 'pin' (e.g. OIr *delg* 'thorn, pin, brooch', OE *dalc* 'bracelet, brooch'); and a word for 'thread', *pe/oth$_a$mo-* (e.g. OWels *etem* 'thread, yarn', OHG *fadm* 'thread'). This word is derived from **pet-* 'stretch out', i.e. stretch out the arms while preparing yarn from thread, and in the various languages it means either 'thread' or a 'measure of outstretched arms', hence the cognate NE *fathom*. There is also a rare Celtic-Slavic isogloss in **kerd-* 'belt' (e.g. OIr *cris* 'belt', Rus *čéres* 'leather belt'). Finally, there is an Italic (Lat *plūma* 'the downy part of a feather'), Germanic (e.g. NE *fleece*), and Baltic (e.g. Lith *plùskos* [pl.] 'hair') isogloss of **pleus-* '(pluck) fleece, feathers'.

The West Central area provides us with **bhr̥w-* '(bolt of) cloth', a Balto-Greek isogloss (e.g. Lith *bùrva* 'piece of cloth', Grk *phâros* '[bolt of] cloth') which suggests that it derived from a verbal root such as **bher-* 'weave, twine'; Germanic and Greek attest a *baitéh$_a$-* 'cloak' (e.g. Goth *paida* 'tunic, shirt', Grk *baítē* 'shepherd's cloak of skins') which, with its very rare initial **b-*, has suggested to some a loanword from a non-IE language; Italic-Germanic-Greek and Armenian yield **kéntr/n-* '± patch, patched garment' (e.g. Lat *centō* 'patchwork clothes', OHG *hadara* 'patches', Grk *kéntrōn* 'patched clothes', Arm *k'ot'anak* 'clothes') and Germanic-Baltic-Slavic-Greek show a **lōp-* '± strip of cloth, bast, or hide used for clothing' (e.g. OE *lōf* 'headband', Lith *lõpas* 'patch', Rus *lápotĭ* 'bast shoe', Grk *lôpos* 'clothes made from skins'), derived from **lep-* 'strip (off)'. A word for a 'strap' or 'sling' is found in the Italic (Lat *funda* 'sling') and Grk *sphendónē* 'sling' isogloss in *(s)bhond-neh$_a$* from **bhendh-* 'bind'. While we cannot with confidence reconstruct a Proto-Indo-European 'shoe' we do have this word from Celtic (e.g. OIr *cairem* 'shoe-maker'), Baltic (e.g. Lith *kùrpe* 'shoe'), Slavic (e.g. SC *krplje* 'snowshoe'), and Grk *krēpís* 'shoe' and possibly Germanic (e.g. ON *hriflingr* 'shoe') and less certainly Italic (Late Lat *carpisculum* 'little shoe' is surely related but may well be a borrowing from some other Indo-European group) in the form of *kr̥h$_1$pís* which is usually derived from *(s)ker-* 'cut', i.e. a shoe cut out from leather. In terms of textile preparation we have *g^whih$_x$(slo)-* '± sinew, thread' (e.g. NWels *gïau* [pl.] 'nerves, sinews', Lat *fīlum* 'thread', Lith *gijà* 'thread (in a warp), skein', OCS *žica* 'sinew', Lith *gýsla* 'vein', Arm *ǰil* 'cord') where the focus is on something fashioned from animal sinew rather than twisted fibres. Both OE *þrum* (NE *thrum*) and Grk *termióeis* 'be-thrummed' employ **termn-* 'end' in the form of **t(e)rm-* to designate the 'thread-end'. The word for 'a single hair', **pilos*, provides the basis for **pil-so-* or **pil-do-* or, as recently suggested **peld-* 'felt' (Lat *pilleus* 'felt' [adj.], NE *felt*, OCS *plŭstĭ*, Alb *plis*, Grk *pîlos*). In a number of West Central languages, Germanic (e.g. NE *reel*), Baltic (e.g. Lith *krẽklės* 'ragged clothing'), and Greek (e.g. *krékō* 'strike (the web), weave, pluck a stringed instrument', *króks* 'warp') give us **krek-* 'beat the weft with a stick'. The West Central root **knab(h)-* 'pick at, tease out' (e.g. NWels *cnaif* 'fleece', Lith *knabénti* 'to pick/peck at', MDutch *noppe* 'nap, pile' [borrowed into NE as *nap*], Grk *knáphō* 'full (cloth)') is our only possible linguistic attestation of the concept of 'fulling' wool, i.e. felting an already woven fabric. Germanic (NE *string*) and Grk *straggós* 'drawn through a small opening', possibly Celtic (MIr *sreng* 'string, cord' [if not an ON loanword]), give us **strenk-* 'string, to pull (tight)'. Our only two words for some type of headband are confined to Graeco-Aryan correspondences: **puḱ-* 'headband' (Grk *ámpuks* '(metal) headband', Av *pusā-* 'diadem') and **déh₁mn̥* 'band' (Grk *diádēma* 'diadem', Skt *dā́man-* 'band'), the latter from **deh₁-* 'bind'. Finally, our word for 'dye', **reg-*, is attested in Grk *hrézō* 'dye' and Indo-Iranian, in the latter generally indicating a reddish colour (e.g. NPers *rang* 'colour', Skt *rájyati* ~ *rājyate* 'is coloured; reddens').

14.2 Proto-Indo-European Textile Production

It is obvious that we are not able to reconstruct a very elaborate 'wardrobe' for Proto-Indo-European speakers. We are essentially left with a very nondescript development of the verb **wes-* and possibly some form of skin-made garment in **drap-*. The cognate terms supporting a PIE **wospo-* certainly appear to support the notion of some form of blanket rap. This could then be fastend with the help of a **yéh₃s-* 'belt'. Elizabeth Barber reminds us how versatile a simple blanket wrap can be as it may vary in size from a kilt to a cloak to, and as we see in **wospo-*, a shroud. We also have a regional (West Central) word for 'shoe' (**kr̥h₁pís*). This word is usally derived from **(s)ker-* 'cut' which supports the notion of a leather shoe. The Tyrolean 'Iceman', Ötzi, who lived *c.* 3300 BC, wore leather soles and fur uppers. Neolithic shoes were also made of bast (cf. **lōp-* > Rus *lápotĭ* 'bast shoe' above). The northern neighbours of the Indo-Europeans, the Proto-Uralics, were no better blessed with clothing terms. Their reconstructed lexicon yields only eight terms, including some form of shirtlike clothing, two words for belt, and one word for glove (but no word for shoe).

We are, however, able to reconstruct a fairly elaborate vocabulary for textile manufacture, beginning with the harvest of a sheep's wool (by plucking or combing, e.g. **peḱ-*, **reu(hₓ)-*, **kars-*, **kes-*) and proceeding through spinning (**(s)neh₁(i)-*, **sneh₁u-*, **(s)pen-*, **terk(w)-*), weaving (**h₂/₃eu-*, **h₂/₃webh-*, **weg-*), and sewing (**syuh₁-*), with stops along the way, so to speak, for felting (**nak-*), plaiting (**pleḱ-*, **resg-*, **wei(hₓ)-*, **kert-*), fulling (regional **knab(h)-*), and dyeing (regional **reg-*). It seems clear that, in addition to animal skins (**bhólǵhis*, perhaps **drap-* or **drop-*), Proto-Indo-European dress was largely of woollen (**wl̥̄h₂nehₐ-*) manufacture with a lesser role played by plant materials such as flax (**linom*).

The material of textile manufacture has been seen to be an important diacritic of the period or place of the Proto-Indo-Europeans. Naturally, skin garments have been employed since long before the existence of Proto-Indo-European and remain in use to this day. The spread of flax (and to a lesser extent hemp) was a product of the Neolithic where it has been attested since about the seventh millennium BC. The production of flax or linen garments predominated during the Neolithic, roughly in the period *c.*7000–3500 BC, and the recovery of textiles from archaeological sites in Europe during this period is exclusively of linen or some other plant material. Our single cognate term for 'flax' (**linom*) appears to be restricted to the West Central region and there is some question of a loan (Latin into Germanic) here as well. Theoretically, flax could date from the beginnings of the Neolithic onwards; however, in peripheral areas of the Indo-European world, e.g. Ireland and India, it does not appear earlier than the Bronze Age. Moreover, the words for a white linen garment in several Indo-European languages, i.e. Grk *khitṓn*, Lat *tunica* (<**ktunika*), and probably Hit *kattanipu-*, all appear to be borrowed from Semitic, e.g. Akkadian *kitinnu-*; this item being one of the linguistic consequences of what has been called the Bronze Age 'international garment industry'. In short, although the Proto-Indo-Europeans may well have worn linen garments, it is by no means certain that we can recover their original word for this term. What also is apparent is that their textile industry seems to have been more narrowly focused on wool.

The earliest domestic sheep lacked a woolly fleece and were rather covered with coarse hairs or kemps. The earliest evidence for a woolly sheep so far (the depiction of clumps of wool on the figurine of a sheep) derives from Iran and dates to the seventh millennium BC. But actually solid evidence for woolly sheep or woollen textiles outside this area does not appear until about the fourth millennium BC when we have evidence from Mesopotamia, Egypt, and the Caucasus; among the criteria for identifying woolly sheep is the appearance of a significantly taller variety and thus height is sometimes employed as proxy evidence for the spread of woolly sheep. Such taller sheep appear in the steppelands by about the fifth and certainly the fourth millennia BC. The importance of these considerations is that by and large, our evidence for woollen textiles or the exploitation of woolly sheep does not in general date before the fourth millennium BC. We have already seen in Chapter 11 that we have a PIE word for 'wool' (**wĺ̥*h_2*neh*$_a$-), which is unambiguously attested with this meaning in nine IE groups, including Hittite, and there is sufficient corollary evidence in the terms for textile manufacture, e.g. **pek̂-*, **reu*(h_x)-, that the exploitation of woollen textiles should be reconstructed to the speakers of the proto-language. This has been a substantial argument for those who suggest that the Proto-Indo-Europeans had not experienced serious linguistic divergence much prior to the fourth millennium BC, i.e. the Proto-Indo-Europeans are 'post-wool'.

Elizabeth Barber has also attempted to provide some further geographical dimension to Indo-European textile terminology by observing that the reconstructed lexicon attests nothing more than the simple band loom, and where different IE groups such as the Greeks or Latins required terminology for the more sophisticated warp weighted loom, they had to borrow the terminology from other languages. As the warp weighted loom was typical for western and central Anatolia, Greece, the Balkans, and throughout central Europe during the Neolithic, this suggests to Barber that the Proto-Indo-Europeans should have been located somewhere outside this zone.

Further Reading

Other than the encyclopedic entry in Mallory and Adams (1997), the main works on IE textiles are to be found in Barber (1975, 1991, 2001); see also Knobloch (1987*b*, 1992), Watkins (1969), and Driessen (2004).

15

Material Culture

15.1 Containers

In addition to textiles and clothing, there is considerable reconstructable vocabulary pertaining to the rest of material culture. While skin, plant fibres, or wool might be fashioned into containers, there were a variety of other materials—wood, ceramics, and possibly metal—that were also employed to contain materials and these are listed in Table 15.1.

A possible word for 'case' is **welutrom* (it means 'case' in Lat *involūcrum* and Grk *élutron* but 'cloak' in Skt *varútra-*) and as a derivative from *?*wel-* 'wind, turn', it may have been independently formed in some or all the languages. The root **$h_2$em-*'hold, contain' provides a series of words for 'container' in Grk *ámē* 'water bucket, pail', Arm *aman* 'container', and Indo-Iranian (Khot *handra-* 'jar, pot', Skt *ámatram* 'large vessel') although these may be independently formed as well. Much solider are the correspondences that suggest **kumbho/eh$_a$-* 'bowl' (e.g. OIr *coim* 'pot', Grk *kúmbē* 'bowl', Av *xumba-*'pot', Skt *kumbhá-*'pot') which are found from Ireland to India although its derivation, either from **keu-* 'bend' or possibly a loanword into Proto-Indo-European, is disputed. A large 'vessel' or 'cauldron' is indicated by **k^werus* or derivatives, again from Ireland (OIr *coire* 'cauldron') to India (Skt *carú-* 'cauldron'), via Germanic (e.g. OE *hwer* 'pot, bowl, kettle, cauldron'). Toch B *keru* 'drum' might be historically another derivative. The **pēl(h_1)ewis* is some form of

Table 15.1. *Containers*

**welutrom*	'case'	Lat *involūcrum*, Grk *élutron*, Skt *varútra-*
*h_2*em-*	'hold on to, contain'	Grk *ámē*, Skt *ámatram*
**kumbho/eh*$_a$-	'bowl, small vessel'	Grk *kúmbē*, Skt *kumbhá-*
*k^w*erus*	'large cooking pot, cauldron'	Skr *carú-*
**pēlh*$_1$*ewis*	'container'	Lat *pēlvis*, Grk *pélla*, Skt *pālavi-*
**póth*$_a$*r̥*	'shallow dish'	Grk *patánē*
**tek̂steh*$_a$-	'plate, bowl'	Lat *testa*
*$h_{2/3}$*uk*^{w}*/p-*	'cooking vessel'	NE *oven*, Grk *ipnós*, Skt *ukhá-*
**kVlVk̂-*	'cup, drinking vessel'	Lat *calix*, Grk *kúliks*, Skt *kaláśa-*
**poh*$_3$*tlom*	'drinking vessel'	Lat *pōculum*, Skt *pātra-*

'container' whose semantics range from 'goblet' to 'milk-can' and it has usually been derived from **pelh*$_1$- 'fill' (e.g. Lat *pēlvis* 'basin' [whence medical Latin and English *pelvis*], OE *full* 'goblet', Grk *pélla* 'milk-can', Skt *pālavi-* 'pot'). Both Grk *patánē* 'bowl, flat dish' and Hit *pattar* 'dish' suggest that the **póth*$_a$*r̥* was something rather shallow such as a 'dish' or 'low bowl' (though there is also OIr *ān* 'drinking vessel') which is supported by its presumed derivation from **peth*$_a$- 'spread out'. Derived from **tek̂-s-* 'hew, fashion', one might presume that **tek̂steh*$_a$- (Lat *testa* 'plate, pot', Av *tašta* 'cup') originally indicated a wooden vessel. Many of the cognates of *$h_{2/3}$*uk*^{w}*/p-* (Lat *aulla* 'pot', OE *ofen* 'furnace' [> NE *oven*], OPrus *wumpnis* 'bake-oven', Grk *ipnós* 'oven', Hit *hūppar*(*a*)- 'bowl, pot', Skt *ukhá-* 'cooking-pot') suggest an association with cooking and so it may be presumed that this particular vessel was so employed (although in Hittite it may also indicate a 'unit of measure'). The vowels that one reconstructs for **kVlVk̂-* 'cup' are uncertain, and as the distribution is limited to Lat *calix* 'cup, goblet' [> NE *chalice*], Grk *kúliks* 'cup', and Skt *kaláśa-* 'pot, pitcher', some suggest we may be dealing with a Near Eastern loanword. The Italic-Indic isogloss of **poh*$_3$*tlom* 'drinking vessel' (Lat *pōculum* 'cup', Skt *pātra-* 'drinking vessel') derives from **peh*$_3$- 'drink' and may be banal independent formations, i.e. 'an instrument for drinking'.

From the North-West we have **bhidh-* 'large pot' (Lat *fidēlia* 'earthenware pot', Icelandic *biða* 'small tub'), possibly from an otherwise unattested **bheidh-* 'bend' (from either coil-built pottery or basketry), and **h*$_a$*enseh*$_a$- 'handle' (Lat *ānsa*, MHG *ōse* 'ring, loop', Lith *ąsà* 'pot handle') which refers to a pot handle in Italic and Baltic. From the West Central region there is **louh*$_1$*trom* '(wash-) basin' (OIr *lōthar* 'tub, basin', Lat *pō-lūbrum* 'wash-basin', Grk *loetrón* 'bath') from **louh*$_1$- (also reconstructed as **leuh*$_3$-) 'wash'; **kuh*$_x$*p-* 'water vessel' (e.g. Lat *cūpa*, NE *hive*, Grk *kúpellon* 'cup') from **keu*(*h*$_x$)- 'curve'; **kelp-* 'jug, pot' (OIr *cilorn* 'pitcher', Grk *kálpis* 'jug, [water] pitcher'—there is a possibility of an

Indic cognate in Skt *karpara*-'cup, pot'); *(s)pondh(n)os 'wooden vessel' (e.g. ON *spann* 'pail', Lith *spandis* 'pail', OCS *spǫdŭ* 'measure [of grain]', Arm *p'und* 'pot'—the German cognates are uncertain). The Central area (Thracian-Greek) suggests the possibility of a *ĝh(e)utreh$_a$- '±pot' (Thrac *zetraía* 'pot', Grk *khútra* 'pot') but again they may be independent developments.

15.2 Metals

The rather limited vocabulary pertaining to metallurgy in Proto-Indo-European is listed in Table 15.2.

The basic word for 'metal' in Proto-Indo-European is *$h_a$ey-es- (e.g. Lat *aes* 'copper, bronze', NE *ore*, Av *ayah*- 'metal (probably bronze)', Skt *áyas*- [earlier] 'copper', [later] 'iron') and it is generally presumed to mean 'copper' or the copper-tin alloy of 'bronze' although it has come to mean 'iron' in some of the Indo-European languages, e.g. Indo-Iranian; however, there is clear evidence that it earlier meant 'copper' or 'bronze'. In the Germanic languages it tends to mean 'ore' and it is possible it simply meant 'metal' rather than a specific type of metal. The second term, *$h_1$roudhós, is widely enough attested (e.g. ON *rauði* 'red iron ore', OCS *ruda* 'ore; metal', NPers *rōd* 'copper', Skt *lohá*- 'copper') but it is such a banal derivative of *$h_1$reudh- 'red', i.e. the 'red metal' or 'copper', that it probably represents independent developments in different Indo-European groups.

There are two potential words for 'gold'. The more reliably attested is *$h_a$eusom ~ *$h_a$weseh$_a$- (e.g. Lat *aurum*, OPrus *ausis*, Toch B *yasa*, all 'gold'), a noun ultimately derived from the root *$h_a$ewes- 'shine' which also underlies the word for 'dawn', *$h_a$éusōs (see Section 18.6). It has been plausibly suggested that an Indo-European form similar to the one ancestral to Tocharian has been widely borrowed into the Uralic languages, e.g. Proto-Balto-Finnic-Lapp-Mordvin *waśke 'copper, brass', Proto-Ugric *waś 'metal, iron', Proto-Samoyed *wesä 'metal, iron'. The second word, ?*ĝhel-, is a colour word 'yellow' which is often used to supply a word for 'gold', and although the

Table 15.2. *Metals*

*$h_a$ey-es-	'metal > copper > bronze'	Lat *aes*, NE *ore*, Skt *áyas*-
?*$h_1$roudhós	'the red metal, i.e. copper'	Skt *lohá*-
*$h_a$eusom	'gold'	Lat *aurum*
?*ĝhel-	'yellow'	NE *gold*
*$h_2$erĝ-n̥t-om	'white (metal), silver'	Lat *argentum*, Skt *rajatám*

same root is shared across Germanic-Baltic-Slavic, and Indo-Iranian, the differing ablaut grades and suffixes suggest post-Proto-Indo-European formation (e.g. NE *gold*, Latv *zèlts*, Rus *zóloto*, Av *zaranyam*, Skt *híraṇyam*, all 'gold'). In addition to the 'red metal' (copper) and the 'yellow metal' (gold) we have the 'white metal' (silver), *$h_2$erĝ-n̥t-om ~ *$h_2$reĝ-n̥t-om (e.g. OIr *argat*, Lat *argentum*, Arm *arcat'*, Av *ərəzatəm*, Skt *rajatám*, Toch B *ñkante* [with *r ... n assimilated to *n ... n], all 'silver'). Formed like our first word for 'gold', this suggests the use of an adjective (perhaps *$h_2$érĝ-n̥t, genitive *h_2r̥ĝ-n̥t-ós, which was subsequently made thematic) before some noun such as *$h_a$ey-es-, i.e. 'silver-metal'.

The North-West region provides evidence of an early *Wanderwort* in *silVbVr- 'silver' which occurs in Ibero-Celtic (alone of the Celtic languages) *śilaPur*, Germanic (e.g. NE *silver*), Baltic (e.g. Lith *sidãbras*), and Slavic (e.g. Rus *serebró*) and its doubtful vowels and various outcomes of the consonants suggest that it has been borrowed from some non-Indo-European source.

15.3 Tools

The evidence for basic agricultural and woodworking tools is indicated in Table 15.3.

There are four words associated with tillage. The verb 'to plough' is attested as *$h_2$érh$_3$ye/o- (e.g. MIr *airid* 'ploughs', Lat *arō* 'plough', Goth *arjan* 'plough', Lith *ariù* 'plough', OCS *orjǫ* 'plough', Grk *aróō* 'plough',

Table 15.3. *Tools*

*$h_2$érh$_3$ye/o-	'plough'	Lat *arō*, NE *ear*, Grk *aróō*
*mat-	'hoe, plough'	Lat *mateola*, Skt *matyá-*
*$h_{1/4}$okéteh$_a$-	'harrow, rake'	Lat *occa*
*ĝhel-	'plough'	Skt *halá-*
*sr̥po/eh$_a$-	'sickle'	Grk *hárpē*
*g^{w}réh$_x$-w-on-	'quern'	NE *quern*, Skt *grā́van-*
*$h_4$edhés-	'axe, adze'	NE *adze*
*pelek̂us	'axe'	Grk *pélekus*, Skt *paraśú-*
?*tek̂so/eh$_a$-	'axe, adze'	
*$h_x$óleh$_a$-	'awl'	NE *awl*, Skt *ā́rā-*
*k̂oh$_x$nos	'whetstone, hone'	Lat *cōs*, NE *hone*, Skt *śā́ṇa-*
*ko(n)gos	'hook'	NE *hook*
*$h_2$ónkos	'something bent, hook'	Lat *uncus*, Skt *anká-*,Grk *ógkos*
*k^{w}r̥wis	'±tool'	Skt *kr̥vi-*

and perhaps Toch A *āre* if it means 'a plough', Hit *hars* -~ *harsiya*- 'till the earth'—assuming the Hittite word belongs here, the initial has been specified as *h_2) and the nominal derivative, *h_2*érh*$_3$*trom* 'plough', is also widely found (e.g. MIr *arathar*, Lat *arātrum*, ON *arðr*, Lith *árklas*, Grk *árotron*, Arm *arawr*, all 'plough'). The NE cognate *ear* (from OE *erian*) meaning 'to plough' survives only dialectally. That the Proto-Indo-European plough was a fairly primitive one may be indicated by OHG *huohhili* 'wooden hook plough made from a curved branch' and OCS *sokha* '(primitive) wooden plough' which are both derivatives of a Proto-Indo-European word for 'branch' (see Section 10.1). Of course it would not be surprising if the Proto-Indo-European plough were a curved and forked branch since such ploughs are attested well into the Middle Ages. A word 'hoe, plough' or perhaps better 'mattock' is attested by **mat*- (e.g. Lat *mateola* 'hoe', OHG *medela* 'plough', OCS *motyka* 'hoe, mattock', Skt *matyá*- 'harrow'; NE *mattock* is generally derived from a Late Latin form of this word). Words for 'harrow' or 'rake' (or 'furrow') derive from *$h_{1/4}$*okéteh*$_a$- which is widely found among the Indo-European languages (e.g. NWels *oged* 'harrow', Lat *occa* 'harrow', OE *eg(e)ðe* 'harrow, rake', Lith *akė̃čios* [pl.] 'harrow', Oss *adæg* [< **agæd*] 'furrow'). Finally, **ĝhel*- 'plough' is attested in Baltic, Armenian, and Indic (Lith *žúolis* 'sleeper, tie', Arm *jlem* 'plough', Skt *halá*- 'a plough'). The 'sickle', **sr̥po/eh*$_a$-, is attested in Anatolian (Hit *sarpa*- 'agricultural tool [used in ritual along with a plough]') as well as Baltic (Latv *sirpis* 'sickle'), Slavic (e.g. Rus *serp* 'sickle'), Grk *hárpē* 'sickle', and Iranian (Oss *æxsyrf* 'sickle'); Lat *sarpō* 'cut away, prune' supplies a verbal form while the word was borrowed from Baltic into Finnish as *sirppi* 'sickle'. The root *g^wr(e)h_a(-u) 'heavy' provides the basis for *g^w*réh*$_x$*-w-on*- and several other formations that indicate a 'quern' (e.g. OIr *brāu* 'quern', NE *quern*, Lith *gìrna* 'millstone', *gìrnos* [pl.] 'quern', OCS *žrŭny* 'quern', Arm *erkan* 'quern', and perhaps Skt *grā́van*- if it does indicate a 'stone for pressing soma' and Toch B *kärweñe* 'stone' [if <*'millstone']).

There are three words that fill out the semantic field of 'axe' or 'adze'. One is supported by an English (OE *adesa* > NE *adze*) and Hit *ates*- and *atessa*- isogloss, i.e. *h_4*edhés*-. The second is the much discussed **pelek̂us* 'axe'. We find cognates in Grk *pélekus*, Oss *færæt*, and Skt *paraśú*-, and the proto-form is often compared with Semitic forms, e.g. Akkadian *pilakku* which some translate as 'axe' but others translate as 'spindle', which is semantically very distant from 'axe'. Generally, the Proto-Indo-European word is treated as a *Wanderwort*, a loanword that crossed a number of different languages or language families. Finally, the verb **tek̂s*- 'fabricate' provides the basis of **tek̂so/eh*$_a$- 'axe, adze' and several other formations (e.g. OHG *dehsa* 'axe, hatchet', Av *taša*- 'axe', and with a derivative in **-lo/eh*$_a$-, OIr *tāl* 'axe', OHG *dehsala* 'adze, hatchet', Russian Church Slavonic *tesla* 'axe') that may have been independently created in a number of Indo-European groups but might also have some form of late Proto-Indo-European antiquity.

For working leather or drilling wood, we have the **$h_x$óleh$_a$*- 'awl' which is attested in Germanic (e.g. NE *awl*), Khot *aiysna-*, and Skt *ā́rā-*. An instrument for sharpening, the 'whetstone' or 'hone', is indicated by **k̂oh$_x$nos* and various other formatives built on a verb **k̂eh$_x$(i)*- 'sharpen' (e.g. Lat *cōs* [genitive *cōtis*] 'whetstone', NE [a] *hone*, NPers *san* 'whetstone', Skt *śā́ṇa-* 'whetstone').

Some form of 'hook' is attested by **ko(n)gos* (e.g. MIr *alchaing* 'weapon rack', NE *hook*, Rus *kógotĭ* 'claw', Hit *kagas* 'tooth') and **$h_2$ónkos* (e.g. OIr *ēcath* 'fishhook', Lat *uncus* 'hook, barb', OHG *ango* 'fishhook', Lith *ánka* 'knot', OCS *ǫkotĭ* 'hook', Grk *ógkos* 'barb [of an arrow]', Av *aka-* 'hook', Skt *anká-* 'curve; hook'), the latter from **$h_2$enk-* 'bend'. It is almost anyone's guess as to the underlying meaning of **k^{w}r̥wis* which gives us Lith *kir̃vis* 'axe', Rus *cervĭ* 'sickel', and Skt *kr̥vi-* 'weaving instrument', perhaps something like 'tool' in general being derived from **k^{w}er-* 'do, make'.

The North-West yields **sekūr-* 'axe' (Lat *secūris*, OCS *sěkyra*, both 'axe') from **sek-* 'cut'; and **kreidhrom* 'sieve' (e.g. OIr *crīathar* 'sieve', Lat *crībrum* 'sieve', OE *hrīder* ~ *hridder* 'coarse sieve' [> NE *ridder*]) from *(*s*)*ker-* 'cut'. From the West Central region: **$h_a$egwisy(e)h$_a$*- 'axe' (Lat *ascia* 'adze of carpenters and masons', NE *axe*, Grk *aksī́nē* 'axe'); **wog^{w}hnis* 'ploughshare' (Lat *vōmis* 'ploughshare', OHG *waganso* 'ploughshare', OPrus *wagnis* 'coulter', Grk *ophnís* 'ploughshare'); **seh$_1$(i)*- 'sift' which provides the basis for a number of formations that indicate 'sieve' (e.g. NWels *hidl*, ON *sādl*, Lith *síetas*, OCS *sito*, Alb *shosh*); **térh$_1$trom* ~ **térh$_1$dhrom* 'auger' (e.g. OIr *tarathar* 'auger', Lat *terebra* 'auger', Grk *téretron* 'borer, gimlet') from **terh$_1$*- 'pierce'; **kleh$_a$wis* 'bolt, bar; (wooden) hook' (Lat *clāvis* 'bolt, key', Grk *kleís* 'bar, bolt'); **ĝhwáks* 'torch' (Lat *fax* 'torch', Lith *žvãkė* 'candle'); and possibly **dhúbhos* 'wedge, peg' (NE *dowel*, dialectal Grk *túphos* 'wedge'). A Greek-Indic isogloss (Grk *ksurón*, Skt *kṣurá-*) gives us **ksuróm* 'razor' from **kseu-* 'rub, whet'.

15.4 Weapons

Although the Indo-Europeans have been cast often enough as warlike conquerors, their reconstructed arsenal is not particularly extensive. In addition to the 'axe' which we have treated under tools but might also indicate 'battle-axe', we have the weapons indicated in Table 15.4.

There are four words associated with the 'spear'. The **g^{w}éru* means 'spear' or 'spit' in both Celtic (e.g. OIr *biur*) and Italic (e.g. Lat *verū*) but 'staff' in Iranian

Table 15.4. *Weapons*

g^wéru	'spear, spit'	Lat *verū*
**ḱúh$_x$los*	'spear, spit'	Skt *śū́la-*
**ḱel(h$_x$)-*	'± (spear)point'	Grk *kêla*, Skt *śalyá-*
**ĝhai-só-s*	'throwing spear'	NE *garlic*, Grk *khaîos*, Skt *héṣas-*
**wēben*	'cutting weapon, knife'	NE *weapon*
**h$_{2/3}$n̥sis*	'large (offensive) knife'	Lat *ēnsis*, Skt *así-*
*?*ḱos -trom/dhrom*	'knife'	Lat *castrō*, Skt *śástra-*
*?*kl̥tḗr*	'knife'	Lat *culter*, Skt *kuṭhāra-*
**spelo/eh$_a$-*	'shield'	Skt *phálakam*

(e.g. Av *grava-*). An Armenian-Indo-Iranian isogloss gives us **ḱúh$_x$los* (Arm *slak‘* 'pike, spear, dagger, arrow', MPers *swl'ck* 'grill' [< *'complex of spits'], Skt *śū́la-* 'pike, spit, javelin') which does return a meaning 'spear' while **ḱel(h$_x$)-* can mean anything from 'spear' to 'arrow' to 'staff' (e.g. ON *hali* 'point of shaft, tail', OPrus *kelian* 'spear', Alb *thel* 'big nail, spike', Grk *kêla* [pl.] 'arrowshafts', Skt *śalyá-* 'spear, arrowhead'). Although Greek shows 'herdsman's staff' (*khaîos*) for **ĝhai-sós*, Celtic (e.g. OIr *gae* 'spear'), Germanic (e.g. OE *gār* 'spear' [cf. *gār* + *lēac* 'leek' > NE *garlic*]), and Indic (Skt *héṣas-* 'missile') all indicate a 'spear' or some other form of missile and it would appear to be from **ĝhi-* 'throw'. A Germanic (NE *weapon*)-TocharianAB (*yepe* 'weapon, knife') isogloss suggests a PIE **wēben* 'knife'. Of considerable interest is the word **h$_{2/3}$n̥sis* as it means 'sword' in Lat *ēnsis*, Av *ahū-*, and Skt *así-*; it can also mean 'slaughtering knife'. These attested meanings might at first seem to favour a reconstruction as 'sword' but the word would generally be regarded as semantically incongruent with any date before *c.* 2000–1500 BC when the earliest swords began to appear in the archaeological record (there are a very few exceptions). The presumption then is that the word may have originally indicated a 'dagger' or 'knife' (as it seems to do in the earlier Vedic literature) and that it developed the meaning 'sword' independently in each of the language groups in which it is found. Some support for this comes from the fact that there is also a Palaic cognate (*hasīra-*) which gives us our earliest citation of this word and here it means 'dagger'. Other words for 'knife' are of dubious antiquity. A PIE **ḱos-trom/dhrom* is attested with a denominative verb in Lat *castrō* 'I prune', Alb *thadër* 'adze', and Skt *śástra-* 'knife, dagger', all possibly independent creations from **ḱes-* 'cut' and the instrumental suffix. In the case of a potential **kl̥tḗr* 'knife', it is uncertain whether the Lat *culter* '(butcher's) knife' and Skt *kuṭhāra-* 'axe' are cognate as some take the Indic form to have been borrowed from Dravidian.

Shields are also a more recent item of defensive armament, at least in the archaeological record, and while **spelo/eh$_a$-* does yield meanings of 'shield' in

Indo-Iranian (e.g. MPers *ispar* 'shield', Skt *phálakam* 'shield, board'), its Germanic cognate means 'board' (ON *fjǫl*) and the possible Luvian cognate (*palahsa-*) means 'blanket' or 'coat' so that it may have only developed the meaning 'shield' in Indo-Iranian. It is commonly derived from **(s)p(h)el-* 'strip, tear off', suggestive of a wooden or leather shield (see Section 22.1).

The North-West provides evidence of *$*h_aérk^wos$ 'bow and/or arrow' (Lat *arcus*, NE *arrow*); **skéits* 'shield, board' (e.g. OIr *scīath* 'shield', OE *scīd* 'thin piece of wood, shingle', OCS *štitŭ* 'shield', and with an *o*-grade in Lat *scūtum* 'large leather-covered shield'); and possibly *$*lorgeh_a$-* 'club' (e.g. OIr *lorg* 'club', ON *lurkr*, if Germanic has not actually borrowed the word from Celtic). A more widely distributed (West Central) root for 'club' is **bak-* (e.g. OIr *bacc* 'staff', Lat *baculum* 'staff', Grk *báktron* 'staff'; a Middle Dutch cognate *pegge* supplies NE *peg*); the initial **b-* has been explained either as the mark of a 'popular word' (i.e. one apparently used only in informal contexts and subject to the possibility of special phonological changes) or a loanword from some non-Indo-European language. A word for 'spear' or 'spit' is seen in *$*h_aei\hat{k}smo/eh_a$-* 'spear, pointed stick' (e.g. Lith *iẽšmis* 'spit, spear', Grk *aikhmḗ* 'point of spear, arrow, spear'). An Old Norse-Thracian isogloss attests a *$*skolmeh_a$-* 'sword' (ON *skǫlm*, Thrac *skálmē*).

Graeco-Aryan isoglosses include several words pertaining to archery. We have *$*g^w(i)yēh_a$* (e.g. Grk *biós* 'bow', Av *ǰyā́* 'bowstring', Skt *jyā́* 'bowstring'). This word has cognates in Baltic (Lith *gijà* 'warp threads') and Slavic (e.g. OCS *žica* 'thread') but here they refer exclusively to 'thread' and it seems more probable that the underlying PIE meaning simply referred to a 'taut thread' and was specialized to bowstring in Greek and Indo-Iranian. There is also *$*h_1ísus$* 'arrow' (Grk *iós*, Av *išu-*, Skt *íṣu-*); **tóksom* 'bow' (Grk *tókson*, which must go back to the Bronze Age at least as it is attested in Mycenaean *to-ko-so-wo-ko* 'bow-makers', Scyth *taxša-*); and **wáĝros* 'cudgel'. The latter gives us the mythical *vájra-* 'cudgel' of the Indic god Indra where it also indicates the 'thunderbolt' (cf. also Av *vazra-* 'mace, cudgel' [whence Finnish *vasara* 'hammer']); in Greek it occurs in the personal name of *Meleāgros* which means 'caring for the cudgel'. There is also a possible Eastern isogloss in **kert-* 'knife' with cognates in Indo-Iranian (Skt *kr̥tí-* and Av *kərəti* both 'knife') and possibly Toch B *kertte* 'sword' although the latter could have been borrowed from Iranian.

15.5 Ornament

Terms for ornament are extremely few in Indo-European and are largely limited to regional isoglosses. We have already seen the two regional words for 'headband' in Section 14.1. From the West Central area we have **ānos* 'circle, ring' which is attested in OIr *āinne*, Lat *ānus*, and possibly Arm *anur*, all 'ring'. The only possibility of an ornament with PIE distribution may be found in **moni-* 'necklace' where cognates may be claimed for Celtic (OWels *minci* 'collar'), Lat *monīle* 'necklace', Germanic (OE *mene* 'necklace'), Slavic (OCS *monisto* 'necklace'), and Indo-Iranian (e.g. Skt *maṇi-grīvá-* 'carrying a neck ornament'). The word clearly derives from **mono-* 'neck' but the consistently different stem form (i.e. **-i-* rather than **-o-*) suggests that 'necklace' is not just a metaphorical extension of 'neck'.

15.6 Transport

Words associated with vehicles and boats are listed in Table 15.5.

There are two words that indicate a 'wagon'. The first is **weĝhnos* from the verbal root **weĝh-* 'ride in a vehicle' and the word is found in the *e*-grade in Celtic and Tocharian (e.g. OIr *fēn*, Toch B *yakne* 'way, manner') and the *o*-grade in Germanic (e.g. OE *wægn* > NE *wain*; NE *wagon* is a loanword from Middle Dutch) and with a different suffix **weĝhitlom* as Lat *vehiculum* and Skt *vahítram*; still another formation gives us Slavic (e.g. OCS *vozŭ* 'wagon') and Grk *ókhos* 'chariot', including Mycenaean *wo-ka* 'chariot'.

Table 15.5. *Transport*

**weĝhnos*	'wagon'	NE *wagon*
?**h*$_2$*em-h*$_a$*eḱs-ih*$_a$	'wagon-chassis'	Grk *ámaksa*
**k*^{w}*ek*^{w}*lóm*	'wheel'	NE *wheel*, Grk *kúklos*, Skt *cakrá-*
**h*$_{2/3}$*r̥gi-*	'wheel'	
**róth*$_2$*o/eh*$_a$*-*	'wheel'	Lat *rota*, Skt *rátha-*
**yugóm*	'yoke'	Lat *iugum*, NE *yoke*, Skt *yugám*
**dhwerh*$_x$*-*	'yoke'	Grk *théraps*, Skt *dhū́r*
**h*$_a$*eḱs-*	'axle'	Lat *axis*, Grk *áksōn*, Skt *ákṣa-*
**h*$_2$*nobh-*	'navel; nave'	NE *nave*
**h*$_2$*ensiyo/eh*$_a$*-*	'reins'	Grk *ēníā*
**h*$_{2/3}$*éih*$_1$*os*	'shaft (of a cart or wagon)'	NE *oar*, Grk *oiḗïon*, Skt *īṣā-*
**néh*$_a$*us*	'boat'	Lat *nāvis*, Grk *naûs*, Skt *nau-*
**h*$_x$*oldhu-*	'(dugout) canoe, trough'	
*(*s*)*kolmo/eh*$_a$*-*	'boat'	
**h*$_1$*erh*$_1$*trom*	'oar, paddle'	Skt *arítra-*

A Greek-Tocharian isogloss (Grk *ámaksa* '[framework or chassis of] a four-wheeled wagon', Toch A *amäkṣ-pänte* 'wagon-master') gives us *$h_2$em-h_aeḱs-ih_a* which has been explained as a compound of *$h_2$em-* 'hold on to' and *h_aeḱs-* 'axle', i.e. the chassis of a wagon that holds the axle.

There are three words that indicate the 'wheel': **kʷekʷlóm*, **$h_{2/3}$wr̥gi-*, and **róth$_2$o/eh_a-*. The first indicates the 'wheel' in Germanic (e.g. NE *wheel*), Phrygian (*kíklēn* 'Ursa Major', i.e. 'the chariot'), and Indo-Iranian (e.g. Av *čaxra-* 'wheel', Skt *cakrá-* 'wheel; sun-disc'); a form **kʷókʷlos* is found in Grk *kúklos* and Tocharian (e.g. Toch B *kokale*, where it means 'wagon'). The word is derived from **kʷel-* 'turn' after reduplication; in some languages we find it without the reduplication, e.g. **kʷólos* underlies OIr *cul* 'wagon' while **kʷóles-* yields OCS *kolo* 'wagon'. An Anatolian-Tocharian isogloss gives us **$h_{2/3}$wr̥gi-* 'wheel' (e.g. Hit *hurki-* 'wheel', Toch A *wärkänt* 'wheel') while the meanings of the various languages that yield Proto-Indo-European **róth$_2$o/eh_a-* are as likely to indicate 'wagon' (e.g. Lat *rota* 'wagon', Lith *rãtai* [pl.] 'wagon', Av *raθa-* 'wagon, chariot', Skt *rátha-* 'wagon, chariot') as they do 'wheel' (e.g. OIr *roth* 'wheel, circle', Lat *rota* [again] 'wheel', OHG *rad* 'wheel', Lith *rãtas* [sg.] 'wheel') and show the easy transference of the concept, comparable to English slang where 'having wheels' means having a car. A derivative, **róth$_2$ikos*, gives Alb *rreth* 'ring, hoop, tyre (for carriages)' and the Tocharian word (Toch B *retke*) for 'army' (< *'chariotry').

One word for 'yoke', **yugóm*, is widespread (e.g. OWels *iou*, Lat *yugum*, NE *yoke*, Lith *jùngas*, Grk *zugón*, Arm *luc*, Hit *yukan*, Av *yugam*, Skt *yugám*, all 'yoke') and derives from **yeug-* 'join, harness' (see Section 22.5). There is also **dhwerh_x-* 'yoke' seen in Hit *tūriye-* 'harness', Skt *dhū́r* 'yoke', *dhúriya-* 'draft animal', Toch B *trusk-* 'harness', probably also *pyorye* 'yoke' (if Proto-Tocharian **twyoruyen-* < **dhwērh_xu$h_1$en-*) and Grk *théraps* 'comrade; servant' (if < **dhwerh_x-$h_2$ep-* 'yoke-joined') and thus the whole family in English of *therapy*, etc. This looks like a basic root-noun with no verbal antecedents (the verbs in Anatolian and Tocharian are clearly derived from the noun) and may well be older than **yugóm*.

The 'axle' was **h_aeḱs-* (e.g. Lat *axis*, OE *eax*, Lith *ašìs*, OCS *osĭ*, Grk *áksōn*, Skt *ákṣa-*, all 'axle, axis'; NE *axle* is a Norse loanword and derivative of this word) while the root **$h_2$nobh-* supplies meanings of both 'nave' and 'navel' (e.g. NE *nave*, *navel*, OPrus *nabis* 'nave, navel', Skt *nábhya-* 'nave'). Incidentally, the Germanic word for an 'auger' was a 'nave-piercer', i.e. **naba-gaizaz*, e.g. OE *nafo-gar*. With the indefinite article, i.e. **a nauger*, this was falsely analysed as **an auger* and hence NE *auger*. The word for 'reins', **$h_2$ensiyo/eh_a-*, is based on an Irish-Greek isogloss (OIr *ēis(s)e*, Grk *ēniā*, both 'reins') with the possibility of an Indic cognate (Skt *nāsyam* 'nose cord [of a draft-ox, etc.]' where the form, *nā-* instead of the expected **ān-* may reflect the influence of the word for 'nose').

The 'shaft of a wagon' is indicated by *$h_{2/3}éih_1os$ and similar forms; it means 'pole' or 'shaft' in Slavic (e.g. Rus _vojë_), Anatolian (Hit _hissa-_ 'pole, shaft, thill [for harnessing draft animal to a cart]'), and Indo-Iranian (Av _aēša-_ '[pole-]plough, pair of shafts', Skt _īṣā-_ 'pole, shaft') but has shifted to nautical terminology in Germanic, e.g. NE 'oar', and Grk _oiḗïon_ 'tiller, helm, rudderpost'.

From the reconstructable words it is clear the Proto-Indo-European community were familiar with wheeled vehicles and had the necessary terminology for wheels, axles, shafts, and yokes. It may be significant that the words we can reconstruct for this semantic field are both semantically and morphologically transparent, e.g. *k^wek^wlo- 'wheel' (< *'turner, roller') or *$róth_2os$ 'wheel' (< *'runner'). That may suggest that, while well established in late Proto-Indo-European, this terminology (and the objects they represent?) was not particularly ancient in the language. The earliest attested wheels are solid, tripartite disc wheels, i.e. wheels made of three planks joined together by mortise and tenon with their outer edges trimmed to a circle. The invention of the spoke, which made wheels much lighter and therefore transportation much swifter, was considerably later and it may be significant that we can reconstruct no word for 'spoke', even on a regional basis (unless Toch B _pwenta_ 'spokes' and Skt _paví-_ 'wheelband' go together). It is probable that the invention of the spoked wheel (_c._ 2500–2000 BC) may post-date the time of Proto-Indo-European unity.

Water transport is indicated by four words. The basic word for 'boat' appears to be the widely attested *$néh_aus$ from *(s)$néh_a$- 'swim' (e.g. OIr _nāu_, Lat _nāvis_ [> NE _nave_ (of a church)], Grk _naûs_, Oss _naw_, Skt _nau-_, all 'boat'). Because *h_xoldhu- preserves meanings such as Germanic (e.g. OE _ealdoþ_) 'trough' beside 'boat' in other language groups (e.g. Lith _aldijà_ 'boat', Rus _lódka_ 'boat', Toch B _olyi_ 'boat'), it suggests that the original referent may have been a dugout boat of some sort. A Germanic-Tocharian isogloss (e.g. OHG _skalm_, Toch B _kolmo_, both 'boat') secures *(s)$kolmo/eh_a$- which is derived from *(_s_)_kel-_ 'cut'. Baltic and Indic attest a *h_1erh_1trom 'oar, paddle' from *h_1erh_1- 'row' (Lith _ìrklas_, Skt _arítra-_). Other formations from the same root include Lat _rēmus_ 'oar' and OE _rōðor_ 'steering-oar' whence NE _rudder_. None of the reconstructable terminology for boats suggests anything more than canoes or other small craft suitable for crossing rivers or lakes.

Regional transport terms comprise (from the North-West) *_k̂r̥sos_ 'wagon' (Lat _currus_ 'chariot, wagon', MWels _carr_ 'wagon' [> by borrowing NE _car_]) from *_k̂ers-_ 'run' and *_tengh-s-_ 'pole' (e.g. Lat _temō_, OE _þīsl_ 'wagon-pole, shaft') from *_ten-_ pull, stretch'. The root *_dhregh-_ 'run' supplies the basis for the noun *_dhroghós_ 'wheel' in Celtic (OIr _droch_), Grk _trokhós_, and Arm _durgn_ 'potter's wheel' although this nominalization may have been independently formed.

15.7 Roads

Most words for 'path' or 'road' tend to be transparent derivations from verbal forms 'go'. For example, the verbal root *h_1_ei-_ 'go' yields an extended (and heteroclitic) noun *h_1_éitr̥_ (genitive *h_1_itnós_) 'way, road' which is seen in Lat _iter_ 'a going, walk, way', Hit _itar_ 'a going', and Tocharian (e.g. Toch B _ytārye_ 'road, way'). The root *_pent-_ 'find one's way' provides the base of *_póntō_h_2_s_ '(untraced) path' seen in Celtic (e.g. OIr _āitt_ 'place', Lat _pōns_ 'bridge', OPrus _pintis_ 'way', OCS _potĭ_ 'way', Grk _póntos_ 'sea' (< 'path through the sea') and _pátos_ 'path', Arm _hun_ 'ford', and Indo-Iranian (e.g. Skt _pánthās_ 'path'); an Iranian form was borrowed into Germanic to give us NE _path_. PIE *_per-_ 'go across' gave *_pértus_ 'passage, way' which is known from Celtic (e.g. Gaul _ritu-_ 'ford'), Lat _portus_ 'harbour', Germanic (e.g. NE _ford_), and Iranian (e.g. Av _pərətu-_ 'ford, bridge'). And if not independently formed from *_sent-_ 'go', we may have in *_sentos_ 'way, passage' another word of IE antiquity with cognates in Celtic (e.g. OIr _sēt_ 'road'), Germanic (e.g. OE _sīþ_ 'way'), Arm _ənt'ac'_ 'way, passage', and Toch A _ṣont_ 'street'. Finally, from the noun *_ped-_ 'foot', we have *_pedom_ 'footprint, track', attested in Celtic (MIr _inad_ < *_eni-pedo-_ 'position, place'), Lat _peda_ 'sole, footprint', Germanic (ON _fet_ 'step'), Baltic (e.g. Lith _pėdà_ 'footprint'), OCS _podŭ_ 'ground', Grk _pédon_ 'ground', Arm _het_ 'footprint, track', Hit _pēdan_ 'place', Indo-Iranian (e.g. Skt _padám_ 'track'), and perhaps Tocharian (e.g. Toch B _pätsa_ 'bottom').

Regionally, we have from the North-West a possible Latin-Baltic isogloss in Lat _via_ 'way, road', Latv _veža_ 'track' (or merely independent derivations from *_weĝh-_ 'move' that also yields a series of other similar nominalizations, e.g. *_weĝhos_ > NE _way_). From the West Central region we have *_stíghs_

Table 15.6. _Roads_

*h_1_éitr̥_	'way, road'	Lat _iter_
*_póntō_h_2_s_	'(untraced) path'	Lat _pōns_, Grk _póntos_, Skt _pánthās_
*_pértus_	'passage, way'	Lat _portus_, NE _ford_
?*_sentos_	'way, passage'	
*_pedom_	'footprint, track'	Lat _peda_, Grk _pédon_, Skt _padám_

'path' with cognates in Germanic (ON *stig* 'step'), Slavic (OCS *stĭdza* 'step'), and Grk *stíkhos* 'row, line'; it derives from the verbal root **steigh-* 'step, go'.

15.8 Proto-Indo-European Material Culture

The reconstructed lexicon provides broad categories of PIE material culture that can be compared with the archaeological record. Some of the terms for containers, e.g. **welutrom*, *$h_2$em-*, **poh$_3$tlom*, may be independent creations; others may suggest vessels made of wood (**tek̂steh$_a$-*) or perhaps skin (**pēl (h$_1$)ewis*). Nevertheless, there are also words such as **k^{w}erus* that suggest the existence of an originally ceramic container which, over time and space, was transferred to later metal containers such as cauldrons. Another probable ceramic vessel would have been the **h$_{2/3}$uk^w-* and, regardless of the etymological force of some of the other words, e.g. **kumbho/eh$_a$-*, they are often described as ceramic. Other terms for the manipulation of clay and the extensive evidence for domestic cereals clearly indicate that the Proto-Indo-Europeans possessed a ceramic inventory. Our failure to reconstruct more terms is probably due to the instability of a semantic category which was so prone to change because the ceramic forms of the Indo-Europeans in their expansions frequently changed so much that many original terms were probably replaced over time (this stylistic instability can be compared with many traditional Chinese vessels whose forms can be traced back to the Neolithic).

The vocabulary associated with metallurgy is very restricted and at best we can attest the existence of copper/bronze, gold, and silver; words associated with later technologies such as 'iron' escape reconstruction to any great antiquity. Copper has considerable antiquity and appears from the Early Neolithic in restricted areas of Eurasia (South-West Asia, Anatolia, the Balkans), and by the fourth millennium BC it was widely found over much of Europe. It may be significant that we cannot reconstruct a word for 'tin' to any degree of antiquity and so the original meaning of the word was more likely 'copper' than the 'copper-tin' alloy, i.e. 'bronze'. Gold is temporally a little more diagnostic in that it does not appear anywhere in quantity until the fifth millennium BC when it is found in abundance, particularly in south-eastern Europe, and by the fourth millennium BC it spread over a substantial area of Eurasia. Silver is the most diagnostic metal in that it does not appear anywhere earlier than about the mid fourth millennium BC when we can find it from eastern Europe to the Yenisei; it appears somewhat later in the Aegean and the rest of Europe. For this reason, acceptance of a metallurgical package that includes copper, gold, and silver suggests a horizon for Proto-Indo-European in the later Neolithic to Early Bronze Age.

Three of the names for metals are associated with colour terms (see Section 20.4) and it has been argued that such colour terms, i.e. *_$h_1$roudhós_ 'red metal', *_ĝhel-_ 'yellow metal', and *_$h_2$erĝ-n̥t-om_ 'silver metal', are more likely to have been formed on the basis of the metals rather than the reverse, e.g. the plant names 'rose' and 'orange' give us colour words, the turquoise shell gives the colour 'turquoise'. Some have claimed that *_$h_1$roudhós_ derives from Sumerian _urudu_ 'copper', hence, the 'copper colour'. But *_$h_a$eusom_ 'gold' from a root 'shine' indicates that the reverse process might also have obtained in Proto-Indo-European.

Of the terminology for tools, the most diagnostic are those associated with ploughing (*_$h_a$érh$_3$ye/o-_,*_ĝhel-_, *_mat-_). The earliest evidence for the plough anywhere is about the sixth millennium BC (Near East) and solid evidence for ploughs or ploughing (archaeologists can occasionally uncover the scratch marks of early ploughs) in Europe dates to about 3500 BC with some potential evidence that might place it a millennium earlier. Cultivation during the Early Neolithic is generally associated with digging sticks and hence the attribution of the plough to the proto-lexicon provides further support for those who believe that Indo-European 'unity' existed until the later Neolithic.

Most of the remaining tools refer to fairly generic implement types. Axes, for example, have existed since the Lower Palaeolithic (in stone), and while it is perhaps somewhat more likely that the Proto-Indo-European terms referred (at least initially) to stone axes (either chipped flint or polished stone), copper axes are also fairly widespread by the fourth millennium BC.

The reconstructed Indo-European arsenal is not extensive. In the strict sense the lexical evidence for archery is limited to Greece and the Indo-Iranian world. Since the bow and arrow was ubiquitous across Eurasia during the Mesolithic and Neolithic, there is no doubt that the Proto-Indo-Europeans possessed archery and that the lexicon suffered severe attrition; one major cause of loss was the downgrading (in some cases total abandonment) of archery during the Bronze and Iron ages in some regions of Europe. Spears have an even longer pedigree (extending well back into the Palaeolithic) and may again have suffered lexical attrition due to the proliferation of later bronze and iron spearhead types. The tendency for the reflexes of *_$h_{2/3}$n̥sis_ to mean 'sword' makes it attractive to imagine its proto-referent to have been a metal dagger; such daggers, made in copper or bronze, appear during the fourth millennium BC.

The vocabulary concerning wheeled transport has often been regarded as one of the most diagnostic semantic fields in the reconstructed lexicon. The existence of wheeled vehicles in Proto-Indo-European appears unassailable given the number of terms for the vehicle (*$weĝhnos$, *h_2em-h_aeks-ih_a), wheel (*$k^wek^wlóm$, *$h_{2/3}r̥gi$-, *$róth_2o/eh_a$-), axle (*h_aeks-), shaft (*$h_{2/3}éih_ios$), and probably the nave (*h_2nobh-) and reins (*$h_2ensiyo/eh_a$-). The participation of Hittite in this semantic sphere is admittedly weak: it lacks a specifically IE word for the actual wagon (Hittite employs the word *tiyarit-* and *huluganni-* for wheeled vehicles) and the Hittite-Tocharian isogloss *$h_{2/3}r̥gis$ for 'wheel' is contested by some; this leaves *$h_{2/3}éih_ios$ 'shaft' and *$dhwerh_x$- or **yugóm*, both 'yoke', which, some have suggested, might be extended to the pulling of ploughs and not necessarily vehicles. Others would not read this evidence so negatively and would accept that Anatolian also received some of the PIE vocabulary relating to vehicles (and did not separate itself prior to the invention of wheeled vehicles). The earliest evidence for wheeled vehicles, in this case heavy four-wheeled wagons, dates to the fourth millennium BC both in Mesopotamia and in central and eastern Europe, including the north Caucasus.

Further Reading

The basic encyclopedias such as Schrader–Nehring (1917–28) and Mallory–Adams (1997) cover material culture in considerable detail. Other readings include tools (Hamp 1975, Puhvel 1964, Thomson 2001, Wüst 1956); ornament (Mayrhofer 1974); weapons (Huld 1993, Maher 1986, Watkins 1986*a*, Schlerath 1997, Schrijver 2004); transport (Darden 2001, Raulwing 2000), roads (Benveniste 1954, Kololiec 1984), and metals such as 'gold' (Witczak 1994*b*, Driessen 2003) and 'silver' (Mallory and Huld 1984, Untermann 1989).

16

Food and Drink

16.1 Eat and Drink

The topic of this chapter is hunger, the preparation and ingestion of food, and the limited evidence there is in Proto-Indo-European for various foods and drinks. Table 16.1 lists the vocabulary associated with hunger and the ingestion of food.

There is only one word reconstructed to Proto-Indo-European that means 'hunger' (a Hittite-Tocharian isogloss) and even this is problematic in that a comparison between Hit *kāst-* 'hunger' and Toch B *kest* 'hunger' still only yields a PIE **Kos-t-*, i.e. we can only say that the word begins with a velar but must be uncertain which velar that is (it could be **ges-*, for example) since in both Anatolian and Toch A an initial stop will always be voiceless, whatever voicing or aspiration it may have had in Proto-Indo-European.

Many languages distinguish the consumption of foods by animals from that of humans (e.g. NHG *essen* 'to eat' but *fressen* 'to eat like an animal') and a number of the verbs listed here may originally have applied exclusively to one or the other. The most widely attested, apparently the basic, word for 'eat' is *h_1*édmi* which is found in every major IE group save Albanian (e.g. OIr *ithid* 'eats', Lat *edō*, NE *eat*, Lith *ė́du* 'eat', Grk *édō* 'eat (up), devour', Arm *utem* 'eat', Hit *ētmi* 'eat', Av *aδāiti* 'let eat', Skt *ádmi* 'eat', Toch A *nätsw-* 'starve' < *'not-eat'). Albanian does share a cognate with Indic words that

Table 16.1. *Hunger, eating, and drinking*

**Kos-t-*	'hunger'	
*h_1*édmi*	'eat'	Lat *edō*, NE *eat*, Grk *édō*, Skt *ádmi*
*h_4*eu-*	'eat'	Skt *āvayati*
**gras-*	'eat, graze'	Lat *grāmen*, Grk *gráō*, Skt *grásate*
**ĝeP-*	'± eat, masticate'	NE *jowl*
**ĝyeuh*$_x$-	'chew'	NE *chew*
**treg-*	'gnaw'	Grk *trṓgō*
**g*^{w}*erh*$_3$-	'swallow'	Lat *vorō*, Grk *borá*, Skt *giráti*
**k*^{w}*em-*	'swallow'	Skt *cā́mati*
**srebh-*	'gulp, ingest noisily'	Lat *sorbeō*, Grk *hrophéō*
*h_1*ēg*^{w}*hmi*	'drink'	Lat *ēbrius*
**peh*$_3$(*i*)-	'swallow' > 'drink'	Lat *bibō*, Grk *pī́nō*, Skt *píbati*
**leiĝh-*	'lick'	Lat *lingō*, NE *lick*
**ĝeus-*	'taste, enjoy'	Lat *gustō*, NE *choose*, Grk *geúomai*, Skt *juṣáte*
**sweh*$_a$*de/o-*	'be tasty, please'	Grk *hḗdomai*, Skt *svādate*
**dheh*$_1$-	'suck'	Lat *fēlō*, Grk *thḗsato*, Skt *dháyati*
*h_1*edonom*	'food'	Grk *edanón*, Skt *ádanam*
**wór*(h_x)*ĝs*	'nourishment, strength'	Grk *orgḗ*, Skt *ūrjá-*
**dhap-*	'apportion'	Lat *daps*, Grk *dapánē*
**tolko/eh*$_a$-	'sacrifice, sacrificial meal'	
**peh*$_2$-	'guard, cause to graze'	Lat *pāscō*, NE *fodder*, Skt *pā́ti*
**wes-*	'graze'	
**pen-*	'feed, fatten'	Lat *penus*

attest *h_4*eu-* 'eat' (e.g. Alb *ha* 'eat', Skt *āvayati* 'eats, consumes'). This *h_4*eu-* may be the same as the root reconstructed as *h_a*eu-* 'favour, enjoy' (see Section 20.6). The verb **gras-* generally means 'eat, swallow' (e.g. ON *krās* 'delicacy', Grk *gráō* 'gnaw, eat', Skt *grásate* 'swallows, consumes') but as it also yields the word for 'grass' in Lat *grāmen*, it is possible that it may have originally referred to herbivores (or Latin transferred the word to herbivores). Variation in the final (ambiguous) labial in **ĝeP-* has suggested that it might have been a popular word (and therefore frequently altered); in Celtic and Germanic it is represented as nouns pertaining to the 'orifice', e.g. 'mouth, beak, jaw, snout' (OIr *gop* 'muzzle, snout, beak', OE *ceafl* 'jaw, jowl' [> NE *jowl*]) but it appears in verbal form in Baltic and Slavic (e.g. Lith *žebiù* 'masticate, eat slowly', Rus *zobátĭ* 'eat'); in Avestan a nominal derivative *zafar-* ~ *zafan-* refers exclusively to the 'mouth of a demonic being', the *Avesta* often distinguishing words applied to demons from those applied to gods or humans. The verb 'chew' is found in **ĝyeuh*$_x$- (e.g. NE *chew*, Rus *žujú* 'chew', NPers *jāvīdan* 'chew', Toch AB *śuwā-* 'eat') and perhaps also as **treg-* (Grk *trṓgō* 'gnaw [particularly raw fruit]', Arm *t'urc* 'jaw', Toch B *tresk-* 'chew') which may also mean 'gnaw'. There are three verbs associated with 'swallowing'. The best attested is *$g^w erh_3$- (e.g. Lat *vorō* 'swallow [up], devour', Av *jaraiti* 'swallows', Skt *giráti* 'swallows'; some of the cognates indicate swallowing a liquid, e.g. Lith *geriù* 'drink', while others are clearly associated with devouring meat, e.g. Grk *borá* 'meat, food of a predator'. There are fewer distinctions in the meanings descended from *$k^w em$- 'swallow' (e.g. Icelandic *hvōma* 'swallow', Arm *k'imk'* 'throat', Av *a-šam-* 'sip', Skt *cā́mati* 'swallows'), while **srebh-* (e.g. Lat *sorbeō* 'sup, swallow, absorb', Alb *gjerb* 'sip, tipple', Grk *hrophéō* 'gulp down', Arm *arbi* 'drink', Hit *s(a)rap-* 'gulp') often means 'slurp' (in Germanic, e.g. MHG *sürpfeln*, Baltic, e.g. Latv *strebju* 'slurp, spoon', Slavic, e.g. OCS *srŭbati* 'drink noisily') and suggests onomatopoeia, i.e. the sound (to a Proto-Indo-European speaker) of one gulping down food; curiously enough, the Toch B cognate (*särp-*) indicates the 'beating of the heart' (because of the 'lub-dub' noise of the beating heart).

There are two words for 'drink'. Anatolian retains evidence of *$h_1 \bar{e} g^w hmi$, e.g. Hit *ekumi* 'I drink', and this is probably the earlier word, found in Italic (Lat *ēbrius* 'having drunk one's fill, drunk'), Grk *nḗphō* 'am sober' (< *ne-$h_1 \bar{e} g^w h\bar{o}$ 'not drink'), and Tocharian (Toch AB *yok-* 'drink'), which was subsequently replaced (by semantic shift) by *$peh_3(i)$- 'drink', originally indicating 'swallow' (e.g. OIr *ibid*, Lat *bibō*, OPrus *poieiti*, OCS *pijǫ*, Alb *pi*, Grk *pī́nō*, Arm *əmpem*, Skt *píbati*, all 'drink', but Hit *pāsi* ~ *paszi* 'swallows'). This last example is sometimes taken as lexical evidence for the Indo-Hittite hypothesis: the semantic change from 'swallow' to 'drink' happened to the residual Indo-European community after the Anatolian branch had separated from it.

Other oral activities would include the widespread attested **leiĝh-* 'lick' (e.g. OIr *ligid*, Lat *lingō*, NE *lick*, Lith *liežiù*, OCS *lizati*, Grk *leíkhō*, Arm *lizem*, Av *raēza-*, Skt *leh-*, all 'lick'). The concept of 'taste' was closely bound to ideas of 'enjoy, please' and there are two terms in Proto-Indo-European for this. The root **ĝeus-* is widespread and the semantics range from 'taste' to 'test' to 'that which is pleasing' (e.g. OIr *do-goa* 'choose', Lat *dēgunō* and *gustō* 'taste', NE *choose*, Grk *geúomai* 'taste', Av *zaoš-* 'be pleased', Skt *juṣáte* ~ *jóṣati* 'enjoys'). The Graeco-Aryan isogloss *$sweh_a de/o$- (e.g. Grk *hḗdomai* 'rejoice', Skt *svādate* 'becomes savoury') is limited in area but underlies the derived adjective found widely in Proto-Indo-European that indicates 'sweet' (*$sweh_a dús$). The verb 'suck' is well in evidence as *$dheh_1$- (e.g. OIr *denid* 'sucks', Lat *fēlō* 'suck', OHG *tāju* 'suck', Latv *dêju* 'suck', OCS *dojǫ* 'suckle', Grk *thḗsato* 'sucked', Arm *diem* 'suck', Skt *dháyati* 'sucks, suckles').

Words for 'food' in general are uncertain. Grk *edanón*, Anatolian (Hit *adanna-*), and Skt *ádanam* all attest a noun which both etymologically and colloquially could be translated as 'eats', i.e. *$h_1 edonom$ from *$h_1 ed$- 'eat' but the formation is so banal that the (approximately) same word may have been created independently in the various groups. A word for 'nourishment, strength' is seen in *$*wór(h_x)ĝs$* but only in Hit *wargant-* does it mean 'fat' while the other cognates all attest more abstract meanings, e.g. 'anger' (Grk *orgḗ* 'natural impulse, mood, anger'), 'power' (e.g. Av *varəz-* 'power', Skt *ūrj-* ~ *ūrjá-* 'strength, nourishment').

We cannot reconstruct a word for 'meal' outside a ritual context where we have two words: **dapnom* (cf. Lat *daps* 'sacrificial meal', ON *tafn* 'sacrificial animal', Grk *dapánē* 'ostentatious expenditure, consumption', Arm *tawn* 'feast', Hit *tappala-* 'person responsible for court cooking', Toch A *tāp-* 'eat') which derives from **dap-* 'apportion', i.e. share out food in the context of a communal feast, and *$*tolko/eh_a$-* which indicates an 'afterwork feast' in Baltic and Slavic (e.g. Lith *talkà* 'collective assistance; feast after such a work', Rus *toloká* 'afterwork feast') and 'sacrifice' in Tocharian (e.g. Toch B *telki*).

Finally, there are three terms that are probably confined in their proto-meanings to livestock. The verb *$*peh_2$-* generally indicates what a herdsman does, i.e. 'guard, graze' the livestock (e.g. Lat *pāscō* 'feed, lead to pasture; nourish', OCS *pas-* 'protect, guard', Hit *pah(ha)s-* 'protect', Av *pāiti* 'guards', Skt *pā́ti* 'guards', Toch B *pāsk-* 'guard, protect'), or associated concepts such as 'meadow' (NWels *pawr*) or 'fodder' (e.g. NE *fodder*; OIr *aīnches* shifts the meaning to 'bread basket'). As opposed to the transitive activities of what a herdsman does to his herds or flocks, the root **wes-* 'graze' indicates what the animals do themselves (e.g. OIr *fess* 'food', OE *wesan* 'feast, cause to graze', Hit *wesi-* 'pasture', *wesiya-* 'graze', Av *vāstar-* 'herdsman', Toch A *wäsri* 'grassy area, pasture'). The root **pen-* suggests the 'fattening up' of an animal (e.g. Lat *penus* 'store of food', Lith *penù* 'fatten', Pal *bānnu* 'liver' ([<*'the fattened one']).

North-Western words include **smeg-* 'taste (good)' (e.g. OE *smæc* 'taste', Lith *smaguriáuti* 'delight in, nibble on, have a sweet tooth'); **seug/k-* 'suck' (e.g. Lat *sūgō*, NE *suck*, Latv *sùzu* 'suck', OCS *sŭsǫ* 'suck'); and possibly **pitus* if the Celtic (OIr *ith* 'grain'), Baltic (Lith *piẽtūs* 'meal'), and Slavic (OCS *pišta* 'meal') words are not independent creations from an unattested verbal root *$*peih_x$-* 'be fat/swollen' (for other derivatives of this putative root see Section 16.3). The West Central region evidences **kenk-* 'hunger' (e.g. NE *hunger*, Lith *kankà* 'pain, torment', dialectal Grk *kégkei* 'is hungry'; *$*dórk^wom$* 'evening meal' (e.g. Alb *darkë*, Grk *dórpon*, cf. also Alb *drekë* 'breakfast', Bret *dibri* 'lunch'); **mandh-* or **mant-* 'chew' (e.g. Lat *mandō*, OIr *mētal* 'belly', OHG *mindil* 'bite', dialectal Grk *máthuiai* 'jaws') with phonological reshaping suggestive of a 'popular' word; **lab-* 'lick' (e.g. Lat *lambō*, NE *lap*, Grk *láptō* 'slurp, drink', Arm *lap'el* 'lick') and **lak-* 'lick' (e.g. Lith *lakù* 'lap up', OCS *ločŭ* 'lick', Arm *lakem* 'lick'), both 'popular words', the first with both uncharacteristic *_a_ and *_b_, and *_sap-_ or *_sep-_ ' ± taste, come to know' (e.g. OE _sefa_ 'understanding', Osc _sipus_ 'knowing'), difficult because the Armenian cognate (_ham_ 'taste, juice' [< *_sapno-_?]) is uncertain; Lat _sapiō_ 'taste' provides a basis for _sapiēns_ 'wisdom'.

16.2 Preparation

There are a number of verbs that may be grouped under a general concept of 'food or drink preparation'. These are listed in Table 16.2.

There are two words for 'drawing water'. The first is *h_2_eu_(h_x)_s-_ which means 'draw water' or 'pour' in Italic (Lat _hauriō_ 'draw water'), Germanic (ON _ausa_ 'draw water'), and Anatolian (Pal _hussiya-_ 'pour') but the Greek cognate (_aúō_) shows a remarkable semantic shift to 'take fire to'. The second word, *h_2_en-_, has cognates in Grk _ántlon_ 'bilge-water', Arm _hanem_ 'draw out, remove', and Anatolian (Hit _han-_ ~ _haniya-_ 'draw [liquids]'). The concept of 'mixing' boasts no less than three possible Proto-Indo-European words. The root *_yeuh_$_x$- appears to be primarily associated with mixing something moist (e.g. Latv _yàut_ 'mix, mix dough', Skt _yáuti_ 'binds, unites') in that it also yields nominal

Table 16.2. _Food preparation_

*h_2_eu_(h_x)_s-_	'draw water'	Lat _hauriō_, Grk _aúō_
*h_2_en-_	'draw (liquids)'	Grk _ántlon_
*_yeuh_$_x$-	'mix something moist'	Lat _iūs_, Grk _zúmē_, Skt _yáuti_
*_k̂erh_$_x$-	'mix'	Grk _kírnēmi_, Skt _śrīṇā́ti_
*_meik̂-_	'mix'	Lat _misceō_, NE _mix_, Grk _mísgō_, Skt _mekṣayati_
*_menth_$_2$-	'stir'	Skt _ma(n)th-_
*_yeuĝ-_	'stir up, incite; be unquiet'	
*_bher-_	'seethe, bubble'	Lat _fermentum_, Grk _porphū́rō_, Skt _bhuráti_
*_bhreu-_	'seethe'	Lat _ferveō_, NE _brew_, Skt _bhurváti-_
*_seu-_	'boil (something)'	NE _seethe_
*_yes-_	'boil'	NE _yeast_, Grk _zéō_, Skt _yásyati_
*_sret-_	'boil, be agitated, move noisily'	Grk _hróthos_
*_kwat-_	'ferment'	Lat _cāseus_, Skt _kváthati_
*_bhr̥g-_	'roast'	Lat _frīgō_, Grk _phrū́gō_, Skt _bhr̥jjáti_
*_pek_^{w}-	'cook, bake'	Lat _coquō_, Grk _péssō_, Skt _pácati_
*_wer-_	'boil, cook'	
*h_2_omós_	'raw, uncooked'	Grk _ōmós_, Skt _āmá-_

forms meaning 'pottage' and 'soup' (see Section 16.3). The other two roots, **k̂erhₓ*- (e.g. OE *hrēran* 'move, stir', Grk *kírnēmi* 'mix', Av *sar*- 'associate with, mix with', Skt *śrīṇā́ti* 'mixes, mingles') and **meik̂*- (e.g. OIr *mescaid* 'mixes, agitates, troubles', Lat *misceō* 'mix', NE *mix*, Lith *miẽšti* 'mix', OCS *měsiti* 'mix', Grk *mísgō* 'mix', Av *minašti* 'mixes', Skt *mekṣayati* 'mixes, stirs'), mean 'mix' and 'stir (up)'. The act of 'stirring' is found in both **menth₂*- (e.g. ON *mǫndull* 'handle on a pestle', Lith *mę̃sti* 'stir, agitate', OCS *męsti* 'disturb, molest', Skt *má(n)th*- 'stir, whirl, churn, hurt, destroy', Toch B *mänt*- 'remove, destroy, pour out') and **yeuĝ*- (e.g. Goth *jiukan* 'fight, struggle', Av *yaozaiti* 'stirs oneself up', Toch B *yuk*- 'overcome, surpass'). Obviously, these roots can also mean 'stir up', i.e. 'agitate', but the first does show occasional culinary contexts.

There are a number of terms employed to indicate 'boiling'. The root **bher*- shows considerable semantic variation, e.g. 'well', 'yeast', 'bubble', 'move quickly' (e.g. MIr *fobar* 'well', Lat *fermentum* 'ferment, leaven', OE *beorma* 'yeast, leaven', Grk *porphū́rō* 'bubble', Skt *bhuráti* 'moves rapidly, quivers') so its underlying meaning is somewhat conjectural. However, in its extended form as **bhreu*- it is clearly associated with 'boiling' or more specifically with 'brewing' in its European cognates (e.g. OIr *berbaid* 'boils, seethes', Lat *ferveō* 'boil', NE *brew*, Alb *brumë* 'dough', Skt *bhurváṇi*- 'restless, excited'). The meaning 'brew' is found only in the Germanic outcomes of **bhreu*- but there are nominal forms in Italic (Lat *dēfrutum*) and Thracian *brûtos* 'a kind of beer' that indicate an alcoholic drink. The root **seu*- has both concrete meanings, e.g. 'boil' (e.g. NE *seethe*) or 'stew' (Av *hāvayeiti*), and more abstract 'joke around with' (Rus *šutítĭ*). More clearly associated with food preparation is **yes*- (e.g. NWels *ias* 'boiling', OE *gist* 'foam, yeast' [> NE *yeast*], Grk *zéō* 'boil, cook', Av *yaēšya*- 'boil', Skt *yásyati* 'boils', Toch A *yäs*- 'boil', Toch B *yās*- 'excite, ravish' [< *'make boil']) which generally does mean 'boil' (in Hittite the derivative *is(s)na*- means 'dough') while **sret*- or **sredh*- can mean 'boil' but also it can mean 'be agitated' (e.g. MIr *srithit* 'spurt of milk or blood', OHG *stredan* 'effervesce, whirl, boil', Grk *hróthos* 'rushing noise, roar of waves, clash of oars', Toch B *ṣärtt*- 'incite, instigate'). A meaning more akin to 'ferment' may be suggested for **kwat*- which has meanings ranging from 'cheese' (Lat *cāseus*) to 'leaven, sour drink' (OCS *kvasŭ*) and 'boil' (Skt *kváthati*), or 'foam up' (Goth *ƕaþjan*).

Words specifically indicating the 'cooking' of food are several. An extension of a root **bher*-, i.e. **bhr̥g*-, may underlie cognate terms for 'cook' in Lat *frīgō* 'roast, bake, fry' (> NE *fry*), Grk *phrū́gō* 'roast', and Indo-Iranian (e.g. Skt *bhr̥jjáti* 'roasts'). More strongly attested and more productive is **pekʷ*- which not only provides a word for 'cook' in nine groups (e.g. NWels *pobiaf* 'bake', Lat *coquō* 'cook' [> NE *cook*], Lith *kepù* 'bake', OCS *pek* 'bake, roast', Alb *pjek* 'bake', Grk *péssō* 'make ripen, cook', Av *pačaiti* 'cooks', Skt *pácati* 'cooks', Toch AB *päk-* 'become ready for eating [i.e. ripen, be cooked]') but also yields nominal forms, *$pek^{w}tis$* 'cooking' in five and even a possible agent noun, *$pek^{w}ter$-* 'cook', in three groups. There is **wer-* which also returns a meaning 'cook' or 'boil' across a number of Indo-European groups (e.g. Lith *vérdu* 'cook, boil', OCS *vĭrjǫ* 'cook, boil', Hit *war-* 'burn', Toch A *wrātk-* 'cook'). Finally, five groups share a common Proto-Indo-European word for 'raw' or 'uncooked', i.e. *$h_2$omós* (e.g. OIr *om*, Grk *ōmós*, Arm *hum*, NPers *xām*, Skt *āmá-*, all 'raw').

The West Central region provides **sem-* 'draw water' (Lat *sen-tīna* 'bilge-water') if one accepts some questionable Greek cognates (e.g. *ámē* 'bucket') to go with the Celtic (OIr *do-essim* 'pours'), Italic, and Baltic (Lith *sémti* 'draw water'). More secure is **bhōg-* 'bake, roast' (e.g. NE *bake*, Grk *phṓgō* 'roast, toast, parch').

16.3 Foods and Meals

The reconstructed menu of the Proto-Indo-Europeans is limited to the list of cognates indicated in Table 16.3.

Table 16.3. *Foods*

**mḗ(m)s*	'meat'	Lat *membrum*, Grk *mênigks*, Skt *mās-*
$píh_xw\mathring{r}$	'fat(ness)'	Grk *pîar*, Skt *pī́vas-*
**sélpes-*	'oil, fat, grease'	Grk *élpos*, Skt *sarpí-*
**sméru-*	'oil, grease'	NE *smear*
$h_1$opús	'(animal) fat'	Lat *ad-eps*
seh_a-(e)l-	'salt'	Lat *sāl*, NE *salt*, Grk *háls*, Skt *salilá-*
$h_a$melĝ-	'to milk'	NE *milk*, Lat *mulgeō*
**ĝ(l̥)lákt*	'milk'	Lat *lac*, Grk *gála*
**dhédhh1i*	'± coagulated (sour) milk'	Skt *dádhi*
$pipih_xusih_a$	'rich in milk'	Skt *pipyúṣī-*
?**(k)sweid-*	'milk'	
$ksih_x$róm	'± (skim) milk, whey'	Skt *kṣīrám*
**ténkl̥*	'buttermilk'	Skt *takrá-*
?**réughmen-*	'cream'	NE *ream*
$twóh_x\mathring{r}$	'curds, curdled milk'	Grk *tūrós*
**mélit*	'honey'	Lat *mel*, NE *mildew*, Grk *méli*

(*Cont'd*)

Table 16.3. (*Cont'd*)

**médhu*	'mead'	NE *mead*, Grk *méthu*, Skt *mádhu*
**kh$_a$ónks*	'honey-coloured, golden'	Lat *canicae*, NE *honey*, Grk *knēkós*, Skt *kánaka-*
**kóh$_a$-r̥*	'wax'	Grk *kērós*
**h$_a$elut-*	'beer'	NE *ale*
**súleh$_a$-*	'± (fermented) juice'	Skt *súrā-*
**medhwih$_a$-*	'intoxicator'	Skt *Mādhavī-*
**spend-*	'make an offering'	Lat *spondeō*, Grk *spéndō*
**yúh$_x$s-*	'broth'	Lat *iūs*
?**korm-*	'broth, mash?'	Lat *cremor*, Skt *karambhá-*
**wíss*	'poison'	Lat *vīrus*, Grk *iós*, Skt *viṣá-*

Widely and solidly attested, almost invariably with the same meaning of 'meat' across eight groups, is **mḗ(m)s* (e.g. Goth *mimz*, Lith *mėsà*, OCS *męso*, Alb *mish*, Arm *mis*, Skt *mās-* ~ *māsá-*, Toch B *mīsa* [pl.], all 'meat') which also has derived forms such as Lat *membrum* 'member' (which originally indicated a part of a carcass), Grk *mênigks* 'skin, meninges', OIr *mīr* 'bit [< *bit of meat], portion, share', Rus *mjazdrá* 'meat side of skin'. There are a number of words associated with 'fat'. A Greek-Indic isogloss guarantees **píh$_x$wr̥* (Grk *pîar* 'fat, tallow', Skt *pī́vas-* 'fat') but it is suggested that it also has Celtic cognates including the name of 'Ireland' itself, i.e. both the goddess *Eriu* and the name of the island is 'fertile' (< **píh$_x$weryōn*), i.e. fertile land (one might compare the name of a district in Thessaly, *Pīeríā*, and the Homeric phrase *pī́eiran árouran* 'fertile land'). The *o*-grade of **sélpes-* is found in Germanic where it yields NE *salve* and perhaps in Alb *gjalpë* 'butter'. The *e*-grade is to be seen, for example, in Grk *élpos* 'oil, fat, grease', Skt *sarpí-* 'melted butter', Toch B *ṣalype* 'unguent, fat' (and possibly Alb *gjalpë*). The Germanic and Tocharian reflexes of **sméru-* indicate 'oil' or 'grease' (e.g. NE *smear*, Toch B *ṣmare* 'oily, greasy') while the Celtic mean 'marrow' (e.g. OIr *miur*). A well-attested series indicates a word for 'animal fat', i.e. **h$_1$opús* (e.g. Lat *ad-eps* 'lard, suet', Hit *apuzzi* 'animal fat, tallow', Roshani *aδawoǰ* (< **ad-op-eko-*) 'piece of lard', Toch B *op* '± fatness', and probably Arm *atoc'* 'abundant, fertile'). The preservation of meat was effected through the use of 'salt', **seh$_a$-(e)l-*, a word attested in no less than ten groups (e.g. OIr *salann*, Lat *sāl*, NE *salt*, Latv *sāls*, OCS *solĭ*, Grk *háls*, Arm *al*, Toch B *salyiye*, all 'salt', Lith *sólymas* 'brine', Alb *ngjelmët* 'salty', Skt *salilá-* 'sea, flood').

The dairy vocabulary of the Indo-Europeans is impressively extensive. The verb 'milk', **h$_a$melĝ-*, is widely attested (although not in Indo-Iranian) and also serves as the basis for a series of nominalizations (e.g. for the verb: OIr *bligid* ~ *bluigid*, NE *milk*, Lith *mélžu*, ORus *mŭlzu*, Grk *amélgō*, Lat *mulgeō*, Toch A *mālk-*; and, e.g., for the noun: OIr *mlicht*, Rus *molokó*, Alb *mjel*, Toch B *malkwer*). Another noun for milk, **ĝ(l̥)lákt*, is attested in Hittite as *galaktar*, a 'milky fluid from trees and plants' or, perhaps more generally, 'soothing substance, balm, nutriment' and in Grk *gála* 'milk', Lat *lac* 'milk', and in Nūristāni languages such as Waigali *zōr* 'milk'. The underlying verb is present only in Hit *kala(n)k-* 'soothe, satisfy'. The more general meaning in Anatolian as opposed to the more specific 'milk' of the rest of Indo-European may be another instance of an 'Indo-Hittite isogloss' where residual Indo-European, after the separation from the Anatolian branch (or the reverse), underwent a specific lexical innovation not shared by Anatolian. A 'sour milk' is suggested by a noun, **dhédhh₁i* (e.g. OPrus *dadan* 'milk', Alb *djathë* 'cheese', Skt *dádhi* 'coagulated milk, thick sour milk, curds and whey'), formed from **dheh₁(i)-* 'suckle'. Both Baltic and Indic share a participial form of **peih$_x$-* 'be fat/ swollen', **pipih$_x$usih$_a$*, which means 'rich (overflowing) in milk' (e.g. Lith *papìjusi* 'cow which produces milk', Skt *pipyúṣī-* 'rich in milk'). A possible Baltic-Iranian isogloss (e.g. Lith *svíestas* 'butter', Av *xšvīd-* 'milk') yields **(k)sweid-* 'milk' while Albanian provides the sole European example of an otherwise Asiatic **ksih$_x$róm* 'milk' (e.g. Alb *hirrë* 'whey', NPers *šīr* 'milk', Skt *kṣīrám* '[thickened] milk'). The verbal root **tenk-* 'become firm, curdle' yields a noun **ténkl̥* 'buttermilk' (e.g. ON *þēl* 'buttermilk', Skt *takrám* 'buttermilk mixed with water'). A possible Germanic-Iranian isogloss also suggests a word for 'cream', **réughmen-*, which survives in the British dialectal term *ream* (cf. also Av *raoγna-* 'butter'). A word for 'curdled milk' is also indicated by a Slavic-Greek-Iranian isogloss, **twóh$_x$r̥*. In Greek this word is reflected in *tūrós* 'cheese' and *boútūros* literally 'cow-cheese', i.e. 'butter', which was borrowed into Lat *būtȳrum* - *būtūrum* and then into English as *butter*; in Slavic we have for instance Rus *toróg* 'curds, soft cheese', in Iranian we have Av *tūiri-* 'curdled milk, whey'. Finally, the verbal root **ser-* 'flow' has given rise to a number of words for 'whey' or 'cheese', i.e. Lat *serum* 'whey, serum', Alb *gjizë* 'cottage cheese', Grk *orós* 'whey', Toch B *ṣarwiye* 'cheese'.

Another semantic field with very good attestation is that of 'honey'. The noun **mélit* is found widely in the West and Centre (e.g. OIr *mil* 'honey', Lat *mel* 'honey', NE *mildew* [< *'sweet sap'], Alb *bletë* 'honey-bee', Grk *méli* 'honey', *mélissa* 'honey-bee', Arm *melr* 'honey', including Anatolian, e.g. Hit *militt-* 'honey') and has one Iranian cognate in the form of a reference to *melítion*, a drink of the Scythians. The fermented drink made from honey, 'mead', is **médhu* (OIr *mid* 'mead', NE *mead*, Latv *medus* 'honey; mead', OCS *medŭ* 'honey; wine', Grk *méthu* 'wine', Av *maθu* 'berry wine', Skt *mádhu* 'honey; wine', Toch B *mit* 'honey', *mot* [< **mēdhu-*] 'alcoholic drink'). The Proto-Tocharian antecedent of *mit* 'honey' was borrowed into Chinese and appears in contemporary Chinese as *mì* 'honey'. Although **kh$_a$ónks* 'honey-coloured' is basically a reference to a golden colour (e.g. Lat *canicae* [pl.] 'bran', Grk *knēkós* 'pale yellow', Skt *kánaka-* 'gold'), it does yield the meaning 'honey' in Germanic (e.g. NE *honey*) and 'bee' in Tocharian (Toch B *kronkśe*). The related **kóh$_a$-r̥* gives us the word for 'wax' or 'honeycomb' (e.g. Lith *korỹs* 'honeycomb', Grk *kēríon* 'honeycomb', *kērós* 'wax'). We have already seen that it is possible to reconstruct a word for 'wine' (cf. Section 10.3) and to this we can tentatively meet our criteria for positing a Proto-Indo-European 'beer', **h$_a$elut-*, if we add to the North-Western forms (e.g. NE *ale*, OPrus *alu* 'mead', Lith *alùs* 'beer', OCS *olŭ* 'beer') an Iranian (Ossetic) cognate *ælūton* 'beer'. Some form of intoxicating drink is suggested by **súleh$_a$-* with meanings ranging from 'curdled milk' (OPrus *sulo*) and 'kumiss' (Av *hurā*) to '(birch) sap' (Latv *sula*) and an unspecified 'intoxicating drink' (Skt *súrā-*; perhaps the word originally designated fermented [birch] sap). In addition to intoxicating beverages, one might also find the possible Celtic-Indic cognate **medhwih$_a$-*, 'intoxicator' (OIr Medb, the queen of Connacht, Skt Mādhavī, a daughter of Yayāti), which is employed as the name of a deity. Within a religious context, the verb **spend-* means 'pour a libation' in both Greek and Hittite (Grk *spéndō*, Hit *sippand-* ~ *ispant-*).

A 'broth' of some sort is clearly indicated by **yúh$_x$s-* (e.g. Lat *iūs* 'broth, sauce, juice' [> NE *juice*], Lith *jū̃še* 'fish soup', Rus *ukhá* 'broth, fish soup', Grk *zúmē* 'leaven', Skt *yūṣ-* 'soup, broth, water in which pulses of various kinds have been boiled') from the root **yeuh$_x$-* 'mix together' and less certainly by **korm-* which may be a 'broth' in Italic (Lat *cremor* 'broth, pap') and Indic (Skt *karam-bhá-* 'barley porridge, soup') but is resolutely consumed as an 'alcoholic drink' in the different Celtic languages (e.g. OIr *cuirm* 'beer').

Finally, the noun 'poison', **wíss*, is unambiguously attested from Celtic to Tocharian (e.g. MIr *fī* 'poison', Lat *vīrus* 'potent liquid, poison, venom', Grk *iós* '[organic fluid] poison; stagnant smell and taste', Av *viš(a)-* 'poison', Skt *viṣá-* 'poison', Toch B *wase* 'poison') and derives from **weis-* 'flow (slowly)'.

From the West Central we have a word for 'butter', **h$_3$éng^{w}n̥* (e.g. OIr *imb* 'butter', Lat *unguen* 'fat, grease', OHG *ancho* 'butter', OPrus *anctan* 'butter') from **h$_3$eng^w-* 'anoint'. A word **polt-* 'pap, porridge' (e.g. OIr *littiu* 'porridge, gruel', Lat *puls* 'pap, porridge, mash', Grk *póltos* 'pap, porridge') is found in Celtic, Italic, and Greek; **dhrogh-* 'dregs' is attested in the West and Albanian (e.g. ON *dregg*, Lith *drãgės* [pl.], OCS *droždĭje*, Alb *dra*, and probably also Lat *fracēs* [pl.], though the phonological development is not altogether regular, all 'dregs'; NE *dregs* is a Norse loanword). An Italic-Greek isogloss yields **leib-* 'pour, make a libation' (Lat *lībāre*, Grk *leíbō* 'pour out [drop by drop]') while the root **ĝheu-* 'pour' provides the basis for the nominal **ĝheumn-* 'libation' in Grk *kheûma* 'that which is poured', Phryg *zeumán* 'libation', and Skt *hóman-* 'libation'. Finally, the Greek food of the gods, *ambrosíā*, finds an Indo-Iranian cognate in the epithet (Av *aməša-*) or name of a diety (Skt *Amṛ́ta-*) and indicates a regionally attested **n̥-mr̥-tós* 'undying' as an epithet for a sacred drink.

Given the strong evidence for cereal-growing (cf. Section 10.3) in the Proto-Indo-European community, it is a bit surprising that there is no unequivocal word for 'bread' (although there are terms for processed cereals). There is, however, a West Central word for 'dough', **(s)teh$_2$ist* (e.g. OIr *taīs* 'dough', OE *þǣsma* 'leaven', OCS *těsto* 'dough', Grk *staîs* 'dough of spelt flour'). This is a neuter noun of a very archaic shape and that archaic shape might argue for a greater antiquity for the concept 'dough', and hence bread-making in general, than its restriction to the West Central groups might otherwise suggest. That it would appear to be derivative of **(s)teh$_2$-* 'stand' suggests that we may well be reconstructing a term originally meaning 'leavened dough' rather than 'dough' in general. Words such as NE *bread* and Albanian *brumë* 'dough' from **bhreu-* 'boil, brew' also suggest leavened bread but it is the archaic nature of **(s)teh$_2$-ist* that suggests a PIE antiquity for leavened bread.

16.4 Proto-Indo-European Diet

The proto-lexicon emphasizes a diet that included meat, broth, salt, dairy products, the consumption of alcoholic beverages (beer, mead, possibly wine); the reconstructed lexicon of plant remains (Chapter 10) suggests the range of vegetables that may have been consumed. While much of this vocabulary is fairly generic (Proto-Uralic attests the existence of animal fat and broths; its word for honey (**mete*) is, as in the case of Chinese, a loan from Indo-European), some of the reconstructed food terminology is of more specific interest. The word for 'salt' (**seh$_a$-(e)l-*), for example, was a major issue of discussion among linguists of the nineteenth century because it was regarded as diacritical in locating the homeland near a natural source of salt such as the Black Sea or Aegean. In reality, salt springs and later salt mines were exploited over many areas of Eurasia since the Neolithic shift in diet that required salt both for dietary reasons (increasing consumption of cereals resulted in a reduction of salt intake from a meat diet) and for the preservation of meat.

Of greater interest is the abundance of terms associated with milk products, i.e. **h$_a$melĝ-*, **ĝ(l̥)lákt*, **dhédhh$_1$i*, **pipih$_x$usih$_a$*, **(k)sweid-*, **ksih$_x$róm*, **ténkl̥*, **réughmen-*, **twóh$_x$r̥*, which clearly indicates the exploitation of livestock for secondary products. Although both sheep and goats can be milked, the abundance of terms for dairy products in the proto-lexicon suggests the more intensive exploitation of cattle for milk. The chronological significance of dairying is mitigated by our inability to establish the date by which milking was developed in Eurasia. Some would suggest that dairying belongs to the same horizon as other secondary products such as the plough and wheeled vehicles, i.e. the fourth millennium BC, while others would employ either age-slaughter patterns of cattle or the evidence of possible ceramic (milk) strainers to suggest an earlier date. The consumption of milk by adults also has genetic implications in that many people become lactose intolerant after childhood, i.e. become ill when they consume milk. This situation is particularly prevalent in the Mediterranean while lactose tolerance increases as one moves northwards. The ability to consume milk has been seen as a selective advantage among northern Europeans in that it helps replace the necessary quantities of vitamin D which is reduced in regions of poor sunlight. The processing of milk into butter or cheese reduces the ill effects of lactose intolerance.

The different alcoholic beverages also merit brief discussion. The word for 'mead' (*médhu) is well attested phonologically although it has seen some semantic shift in some of the Asiatic languages, e.g. Av *madu-* 'berry wine' (the Ossetic cognate *myd*, however, continues a base meaning 'honey'). There is archaeological evidence for mead from the third millennium BC but it may be considerably older. Beer (*$h_a$elut-) is earliest attested, about the mid fourth millennium BC (Iran and Egypt), but it too may be older. The proliferation of drinking cups that is seen in central and eastern Europe about 3500 BC has been associated with the spread of alcoholic beverages and, possibly, special drinking cults.

Further Reading

Other than handbooks, see for 'eat and drink' (Hamp 1981*b*, Poetto 1974, Kim 2000, Bader 1992, Benveniste 1973*a*: 470–80), 'beer' (Polomé 1996, Kowal 1984); 'milk' (Szemerényi 1958), 'food' (Starke 1985); salt (Thieme 1961); for the archaeological evidence for 'secondary products' see Sherratt (1981) and for the evidence of alcoholic drinks see Sherratt (1987).

17

Proto-Indo-European Society

17.1 Social Organization

There is a large number of words or roots that pertain to the general spheres of society, law, exchange, and warfare that can be reconstructed to various levels of Indo-European. Interpreting these semantic fields in very broad terms, we can indicate those that relate to society and social organization in Table 17.1.

The most loaded term in the reconstructed lexicon is *h_4*erós* or *h_4*eryós* 'member of one's own group' which in Indo-Iranian is generally represented as 'Aryan'. From *h_4*erós* we have Anatolian, e.g. Hit *arā-* 'member of one's own group, peer, friend', Lyc *arus-* 'citizens', while *h_4*eryós* yields (perhaps) OIr *aire* 'freeman', more certainly Av *airya-* 'Aryan', Skt *aryá-* 'kind', *ā́rya-* 'Aryan' (cf. *arí-* 'faithful'). The evidence suggests that the word was, at least initially, one that denoted one who belongs to the community in contrast to an outsider; a derivative of the word is found in Hit *āra* '(what is) fitting' and *natta āra* 'not right', cf. the use of *kosher* which originally meant (in Hebrew) 'what is fitting'. Although in Indo-Iranian the word takes on an ethnic meaning, there are no grounds for ascribing this semantic use to Proto-Indo-European, i.e. there is no evidence that the speakers of the proto-language referred to themselves explicitly as 'Aryans'. Another word for 'people', *h_1*leudhos*, is largely confined to the West (e.g. OE *lēod* 'people, nation', NHG *Leute* 'people', Lith *liáudis* 'people', OCS *ljudĭje* [pl.] 'people') but also has an Iranian cognate in Khowar

Table 17.1. *Society and social organization*

*$h_4$erós	'member of one's own group'	Skt *ā́rya-*
*$h_1$leudhos	'people, freeman'	
**s*(*w*)*edh-*	'custom, characteristic'	Lat *sodālis*, Grk *éthos*, Skt *svadhā́*
*$h_1$euk-	'become accustomed'	Skt *úcyati*
**kr*(*e*)*u-bh-*	'gather, amass'	Grk *krúptō*
*$sók^w$-h_2-ōi	'follower, companion'	Lat *socius*, Grk *aosséō*, Skt *sákhā-*
*h_aeĝmen-	'troop'	Lat *agmen*, Skt *ájman-*
*$pl̥th_2w$-ih_a-	'country, land'	Skt *pr̥thivī́-*
**w*(*n̥*)*nákts*	'leader, lord'	Grk (*w*)*ánaks*
*h_3rḗĝs	'ruler, king'	Lat *rēx*, Skt *rāj-*
**tagós*	'leader'	Grk *tāgós*
**wiḱpots*	'master of the clan'	Skt *viśpáti-*
**pótyetoi*	'rules, is master'	Lat *potior*, Skt *pátyati*
**wal-*	'be strong, rule'	NE *wield*, Lat *valeō*
*$h_2$entbhi-k^wolos	'servant'	Lat *anculus*, Grk *amphípolos*, Skt *abhicara-*
*$h_4$upo-sth_2-i/o-	'servant'	Skt *úpasti-*

roi 'people; man, person'; it derives from the verbal root *$h_1$leudh- 'grow, increase', which in other forms is found, for example, in Lat *līberī* 'children'.

The concept of 'custom' appears in **s*(*w*)*edh-* (e.g. Lat *sodālis* 'companion' [< *'member of a group'], OE *sidu* 'custom', Grk *éthos* 'custom, habit', Skt *svadhā́* 'character, peculiarity, custom', Toch B *ṣotri* 'sign, characteristic') which has been analysed as a compound of **s*(*w*)*e* 'own' and *dh(e)h_1- 'set, establish'. The verb 'to become accustomed' was expressed with *$h_1$euk- (e.g. OIr *do-ucci* 'understands', Goth *bi-ūhts* 'used to', Lith *jùnkstu* 'become accustomed to', OCS *učiti* 'teach', *vyknǫti* 'become accustomed', Arm *usanim* 'learn, be used to', Skt *úcyati* 'is accustomed to'). There is no word for 'assemble'; the closest is 'gather', **kr*(*e*)*u-bh-*, which can mean 'herd together' but does not really indicate a human assemblage (e.g. Grk *krúptō* 'hide', Toch B *kraup-* 'gather, amass; herd').

A 'companion' was quite literally a 'follower', i.e. *$sók^w$-h_2-ōi, from the verbal root *sek^w- 'follow', and in Germanic explicitly indicates those who follow a leader into battle; Latin and Indo-Iranian tend to denote 'friend, companion' (Lat *socius* 'partner, companion', OE *secg* 'follower', Grk *aosséō* 'help', Av *haxā-* 'friend, companion', Skt *sákhā-* 'friend, companion'). Another transparent derivative is *h_aeĝmen- 'troop' from *h_aéĝ- 'drive' which is found in Lat *agmen* 'troop, train' and Skt *ájman-* 'train'.

There is one word preserved that designates 'country' as a landmass, i.e., **pl̥t(hₓ)-h₂w-ihₐ-* which derives from **pleth₂-* 'broad, flat', i.e. the 'broad one' (e.g. OE *folde* 'land', Arm *hol* 'earth, country', Skt *pr̥thivī́-* 'earth'). The Celtic languages retain the word to designate Brittany (e.g. MIr *Letha*, NWels *Llydaw*) while the Greeks similarly used it as a place name, i.e. *Plátaia*; both Celtic and Indic also deified the concept as an '(earth) goddess' (Skt *Pr̥thivī́-* and Gaul *Litavi(s)*).

There are several words associated with leadership positions. A Greek-Tocharian isogloss secures **w(n̥)nákts* which means 'lord' in both groups (Grk *(w)ánaks* 'ruler, lord, prince', Toch A *nätäk* 'lord'). This correspondence is actually a double one since both Greek and Tocharian also reflect the derived feminine equivalent **wnáktihₐ* (Grk *(w)ánassa* 'queen', Toch A *nāśi* 'lady'). The far more widely discussed **h₃rḗĝs* is taken to mean 'king' as it does carry this meaning in Celtic (e.g. OIr *rī* 'king'), Italic (e.g. Lat *rēx* 'king'), and Indo-Iranian (e.g. Av *bərəzi-rāz-* 'ruling in the heights', Skt *rāj-* 'king') and it is also associated with verbs 'to rule'. However, it appears not to have been exclusively political in its meaning but rather to have referred to a person who also had religious functions. Indeed in those situations where the monarchy itself disappeared, as in Rome or Athens, the title of 'king' remained in its priestly function (e.g. the Roman *rēx sacrōrum*). This word too has beside it a widespread feminine derivative (e.g. OIr *rīgain*, Lat *rēgīna*, Khot *rrīṇa*, Skt *rā́jñī-*, all 'queen'), though the details of the formation differ a bit in the various branches. The deeper etymology of this word has been frequently discussed; it is usually explained as an agent noun of **h₃reĝ-* 'stretch out the arm, direct' with some arguing that the word derives from the concept of a king who stretches out his arms in rituals, especially those laying out a precinct, or perhaps a more direct semantic development from 'direct' to 'rule'. Another Greek-Tocharian isogloss is **tagós* which indicates a 'leader' in both groups (e.g. Grk *tāgós* 'leader', Toch A *täśśi* [pl.] 'leaders', and derives from **tăg-* 'put in order, arrange') while the 'master of the clan' is indicated by **wiḱpots* (e.g., Lith *viẽšpatis* 'master', Av *vispaiti-* 'master of the clan', Skt *viśpáti-* 'head of the household'). The verbal expressions of leadership are found in **pótyetoi* (e.g. Lat *potior* 'I am master', Av *paiθyeiti* 'rules', Skt *pátyati* 'rules'; a denominative verb derived from **pótis* 'head of house'; cf. Section 12.2) and **wal-* which is widespread (e.g. Lat *valeō* 'am strong', OE *wieldan* 'govern' [> NE *wield*], Lith *valdýti* 'rule', OCS *vladǫ* 'rule') and means generally 'rule' except where it has been nominalized in Tocharian to mean 'king' (e.g. Toch B *walo*).

There are two compound nouns, both from verbal roots, to indicate 'servant'. Latin, Greek, and Indic all attest **h₂entbhi-kʷolos* (Lat *anculus* 'servant', Grk *amphípolos* 'servant, priest', Skt *abhicara-* 'servant'), literally one who 'moves about on both sides' while Celtic (e.g. MIr _foss_ 'servant') and Indic (e.g. Skt _úpasti-_ 'subordinate, servant') show evidence of having inherited (or perhaps independently created) *_h_$_4$_upo-sth_$_2$_-i/o-_ 'servant' (literally 'one standing below'); a Celtic loan into Latin gives us the Late Lat _vassus_ or _vassalus_, whence NE _vassal_.

The North-Western region provides evidence of *_dhroughós_ 'companion, comrade' (e.g. OE _ge-drēag_ 'troop', Lith _draũgas_ 'friend', OCS _drugŭ_ 'friend, companion'); *_ghostis_ 'guest; stranger, enemy' (e.g. Lat _hostis_ 'stranger, enemy', _hospēs_ 'foreigner, guest; host' [< *_ghosti-pot-_ 'guest-master'], OE _giest_ 'stranger, guest' [the related NE _guest_ is a loanword from ON], OCS _gostĭ_ 'guest', _gospodĭ_ 'master'); *_slóugos_ 'servant' (e.g. OIr _slōg_ 'army, host; crowd, company', Lith _slaugà_ 'service', Rus _slug_ 'servant'). More words derive from the West Central area: *_déh_$_a$_mos_ '(segment of) people' (e.g. OIr _dām_ 'troop, company, retinue', Grk _dêmos_ 'people') from the verbal root *_deh_$_a$- 'cut, divide'; *_pleh_$_1$_dhwéh_$_1$_s_ '(the mass of) people' (Lat _plēbēs_ 'plebeians [as opposed to the patricians]', Grk _plēthūs_ 'throng, crowd; [common] people') whose root also supplies NE _folk_; and *_teutéh_$_a$- 'the people (?under arms)' (e.g. OIr _tūath_ 'a people, nation; [common] people', Oscan _touto_ 'community', OE _þēod_ 'folk', Lith _tautà_ 'people'). The last and much discussed word may be Proto-Indo-European (if one accepts Hit _tuzzi-_ 'army' as cognate) and was also employed in tribal and personal names, e.g. it provides NHG _Deutsch_ (from OHG _diutisk_ 'belonging to the people'). A verb for meeting is seen in *_mōd-_ 'meet' (NE _meet_) while a nominal form *_ger-_ 'herd, crowd' also suggests the meaning 'gather' (e.g. MIr _graig_ 'horse herd', Lat _grex_ 'herd, company', Grk _gárgara_ 'crowd'). A 'leader', here specifically military, is seen in *_koryonos_ 'leader' from *_koryos_ 'army' (see Section 17.5). The verbal root *_h_$_a$_eĝ-_ 'drive' is at the basis of *_h_$_a$_eĝós_ 'leader' (e.g. Grk _agós_ 'leader', Skt _ajá-_ 'driver'). Among the Graeco-Aryan isoglosses we find *_h_$_x$_ēpis_ 'confederate' (e.g. Grk _ēpios_ 'gentle, kind, soothing, friendly', Skt _āpí-_ 'ally, friend, acquaintance', _āpyam_ 'confederation, alliance, friendship'), possibly from *_h_$_2$_ep-_ 'join'; a possible *_des-_ 'enemy' exists if one wishes to accept a questionable Greek cognate (_doûlos_ 'slave' [< *_dos-e-lo-_], the semantic shift would result from the pragmatic fact that the source of most slaves was captured enemies); otherwise the word exists only in Indo-Iranian (e.g. Av _dahyu-_ 'region', Skt _dāsá-_ 'demon, enemy; barbarian; slave', _dásyu-_ 'demon, enemy of the gods, impious man') and has also been explained as a central Asian loanword into Indo-Iranian. Finally, we also have *_tkeh_$_1$- 'rule' (e.g. Grk _ktáomai_ 'procure', Av _xšayati_ 'has power', Skt _kṣáyati_ 'possesses, rules') which also supplies nominal derivatives, e.g. OPers _xāyaθiya_ 'king' > NPers _šāh_ 'king, shah' (> by borrowing NE _shah_ and by a long route into NE _checkmate_ in the game of chess [MPers _šāh mat_ 'the king [is] dead']).

17.2 Give and Take

The verbal expressions of 'giving' and 'taking' are heavily weighted toward the latter as there are only three words that appear to be specifically 'give'. The root *$h_a$ei- yields 'give' in Anatolian and Tocharian (e.g. Hit *pai-* 'give' [< **pe-ai-*], Toch B *ai-* 'give') but 'take' in Grk *aínumai* 'take, seize', a situation that we see does have quite a few parallels in that the action requires a 'giver' and a 'taker' and either side may become the focal point of the word (cf. NE *take to* but also *take from*). The Latin word (*aemulus* 'emulator, rival') is not entirely secure here. A far better attested word is *deh$_3$- (e.g. Lat *dō* 'give', Lith *dúoti* 'give', OCS *dati* 'give', Arm *tam* 'give', Hit *dā-* 'take') which is found in the reduplicated present form in Grk *dídōmi* 'give' and Indo-Iranian (e.g. Av *dadāiti* 'gives', Skt *dádāti* 'gives'), and Italic (e.g. Lat *reddō* [< **re-didō*] 'give back'). Only Hittite preserves the verbal form of *$h_{2/3}$enḱ- (*henkzi* 'bestows') but there are nominal forms in Grk *ógkos* 'burden', Arm *hunjk'* [pl.] 'harvest', and Indo-Iranian (Av *ąsa-* 'group of followers', Skt *áṃśa-* 'portion, share') that show the root was once more widely attested.

Table 17.2. *Give and take*

*$h_a$ei-	'give'	Lat *aemulus*, Grk *aínumai*
*deh$_3$-	'give'	Lat *dō*, Grk *dídōmi*, Skt *dádāti*
*$h_{2/3}$enḱ-	'bestow'	Grk *ógkos*, Skt *áṃśa-*
*$h_1$ep-	'take, seize'	Skt *āpnóti*
*kap-	'seize'	Lat *capiō*, NE *have*, Skt *kapaṭī*
*ghabh-	'take, seize'	Lat *habeō*, Skt *gábhastin-*
*ghrebh-	'grasp, take, enclose'	Skt *gṛbhnā́ti*
*la(m)bh-	'seize'	Grk *lambánō*, Skt *lá(m)bhate*
*nem-	'take/accept legally'	Grk *némō*
*deḱ-	'take, accept'	Lat *decet*, Grk *dék(h)omai*, Skt *dāśnóti*
*deḱes-	'honour'	Lat *decus*, Grk *dékomai*, Skt *daśayáti*
*$h_2$erk-	'hold back'	Lat *arceō*, Grk *arkéō*
*dher-	'be immobile; support'	Lat *firmus*, Skt *dhāráyati*
*$h_a$eiḱ-	'possess'	Skt *ī́śe*
*skabh-	'hold up'	Lat *scamnum*, Skt *skabhnā́ti*

There are more words for 'take'. Perhaps the oldest word is **h₁ep*-which is found in Anatolian and five other groups (e.g. Alb *jap* 'give', Arm *unim* 'possess', Hit *epzi* 'takes', Av *apayeiti* 'obtains', Skt *āpnóti* 'obtains', Toch B *yapoy* 'land' [< *'± dominion']); the o-grade verb *$h_1$op-* 'desire' (Lat *optō* 'wish', OCS *za-(j)apŭ* 'presumption, suspicion', Grk *epi-ópsomai* 'choose') would appear to be a derivative. Also widespread is **kap-* which means 'have' in Germanic but tends to mean 'seize' in Baltic and Albanian (e.g. OIr *cāin* 'law, tribute', Lat *capiō* 'take', NE *have*, Latv *kàmpju* 'seize', Alb *kap* 'catch, grab, seize', Grk *káptō* 'gulp down', Skt *kapaṭī* [dual] 'two handfuls'). Although **ghabh-* is primarily attested in the West (e.g. OIr *gaibid* 'takes', Lat *habeō* 'have', Lith *gabenù* 'present', Pol *gabać* 'seize'), it provides one of the Sanskrit words for 'hand' (*gábhastin-*). A verb 'grasp' is seen in **ghrebh-* (Middle Dutch and MHG *grabben* 'seize', Latv *grebju* 'seize', OCS *grabiti* 'snatch up', Hit *k(a)rap-* 'devour', Av *gərəwnāiti* 'takes', Skt *gr̥bhnā́ti* 'grabs'); the NE *grab* is also related but is a loanword, probably from Middle Dutch. The root **la(m)bh-* is generally found to underlie words for 'goods, possessions' but still retains a verbal meaning 'seize' in Indic (e.g. Lith *lõbis* 'possessions, riches', Grk *lambánō* 'seize, take', Skt *lá(m)bhate* 'seizes, takes'). The verb **nem-* yields 'gift' in OIr *nem*, 'rent' in Baltic (e.g. Lith *núoma*), 'loan' in Av *namah-*, 'harvest' in Toch B *ñemek* but 'distribute, possess' in Grk *némō* and 'take' in Germanic (e.g. NHG *nehmen*), again showing the bipolar nature of giving and taking. The root **dek̂-* is associated with the concepts of 'order' and 'proper behaviour' which suggests that it originally meant 'accept properly or graciously' (e.g. Lat *decet* 'it is proper', *doceō* 'seem, appear', OE *teohhian* 'determine, consider; think, propose', ORus *dositi* 'find', Grk *dék(h)omai* 'take, accept; receive graciously; expect', Hit *takki* 'is the same as', Skt *dāśnóti* 'brings an offering'). An extended form **dek̂es-* gives us the notion of 'honour', e.g. Lat *decus* 'honour', Av *dasəma-* 'defence, respect', Skt *daśasyáti* 'serves, obliges'; it also gives OIr *dech* 'best'.

The concept of 'hold, possess' sometimes crosses with 'hold up, support' and we include both meanings here. The first meaning is clearly seen in *$h_2$erk-* which means 'hold, have' in Hittite and some other groups (e.g. Lat *arceō* 'shut in; keep at a distance, prevent', Grk *arkéō* 'ward off, defend; assist', Arm *argelum* 'hinder, restrain, hold back', Hit *hark-* 'hold, have', possibly Toch B *ārk-* 'be obliged to' [if with a semantic development like NE *have to*]) while possession is also indicated in *$h_a$eik̂-* (e.g. OE *āgan* 'possess' [whence NE *own*], Av *ise* 'is lord of', Skt *ī́śe* 'owns, possesses', Toch B *aik-* 'know'). The root **dher-*, on the other hand, may have originally meant something like 'immobile' (e.g. Lat *firmus* 'solid, firm', OE *darian* 'lie motionless, lurk') then 'hold fast' (e.g. Av *dārayat* 'holds fast') and finally 'holds' (as in Skt *dhāráyati*) while the semantic field of **skabh-* also seems to mean 'hold up' (e.g. Lat *scamnum* 'stool, bench', Av *upa-skambəm* 'support, prop', Skt *skabhnā́ti* 'supports, fixes').

There are two North-Western regional terms for 'take': **ghreib-* 'grip, grasp' (e.g. NE *grip, gripe*, and *grope*, Lith *griẽbti* 'seize'), and **h₁em-* 'take, distribute' (e.g. Lat *emō* 'take', Lith *imù* 'take', OCS *imǫ* 'take'). Verbal roots from the West Central region are plentiful: **h₁rep-* 'snatch, pluck' (e.g. Lat *rapō* 'snatch away, carry off, plunder', Lith *ap-rẽpti* 'seize, embrace', Alb *rjep* ~ *rrjep* 'flay, rob', Grk *eréptomai* 'browse on, feed on' [< *'pluck']); **ghe(n)dh-* 'seize, take in' (e.g. OIr *ro-geinn* 'finds a place in', Lat *pre(he)ndō* 'grasp', NE *forget, begin*, Lith *godóti* 'guess, suppose', OCS *gadati* 'imagine, guess', Alb *gjej* 'find, obtain', Grk *khandánō* 'take in, comprise'); **kagh-* 'catch, grasp' (e.g. NWels *cau* 'close, clasp', Lat *cōlō* 'tend, take care of', OE *haga* 'hedge', Alb *ke* 'has, holds'); **sel-* 'seize, take possession of' (e.g. OIr *selb* 'possession', OE *sellan* 'hand over' [> NE *sell*], Grk *heleîn* 'take'); **twer-* 'take, hold' (e.g. Lith *tveriù* 'seize, take hold of', *turiù* 'have, hold', OCS *tvoriti* 'shape, make', Grk *seirá* 'band, bond'); possibly **dergh-* 'grasp' (e.g. MIr *dremm* 'troop, band of people', ON *targa* 'shield', NE *targ*, Grk *drássomai* 'lay hold of, grasp with the hand', Arm *trc'ak* 'bundle of brushwood'); **(s)lag^w-* 'take, hold' (NE *latch*, Grk *lázomai* 'take, hold'); and **wer-* which means 'find' but in extended form also 'take' (e.g. Arm *gerem* 'take prisoner', Lith *su-resti* 'catch').

17.3 Exchange and Property

There are a number of terms specifically associated with the activities involved in exchange (Table 17.3), a better word than 'trade' when dealing with the level of social complexity probably obtaining among the Proto-Indo-Europeans.

The basic root indicating 'exchange' is **mei-* which underlies verbal forms in Baltic (Latv *míju* 'exchange'), Indo-Iranian (e.g. Av *fra-mita-* 'changed', Skt *máyate* 'exchanges', *minā́ti* 'exchanges, deceives'), and Tocharian (Toch B *mäsk-* 'exchange') but also a number of nominal forms with meanings ranging from 'treasure' (OIr *mōin*) to 'punishment' (Av *maēni-*); NE *mean* is included here, originally from a meaning 'common' in Germanic. One should also compare Lat *commūnis* 'common' (whence, via Old French, comes NE *common*). We also have the root in an extended version, **meit-* (e.g. Lat *mūtō* 'change', Goth *maidjan* 'exchange', Latv *mietuôt* 'exchange', Skt *méthati* ~ *mitháti* 'exchanges'), which underlies the name of the Indo-Iranian Mitra/Mithra, the god in charge of contractual relationships. The concept of 'purchase' is found in **wes-no-* (e.g. Lat *vēnum* 'that which is sold', OCS *věno* 'bride-price', Arm *gin* 'price', Skt *vasná-* 'price', and, with a different ablaut grade, Grk *ônos* 'price [usually of a

Table 17.3. *Exchange and property*

*mei-	'exchange'	Skt *máyate*
*meit-	'exchange'	Lat *mūtō*, Skt *méthati*
*wes-no-	'purchase'	Lat *vēnum*, Grk *ônos*, Skt *vasná-*
$*k^{w}rei(h_a)$-	'pay'	Grk *príamai*, Skt *krīṇā́ti*
*per-	'exchange, barter'	Lat *inter-pres*, Grk *pérnēmi*
*pel-	'± sell'	Grk *pōléō*, Skt *páṇate*
$*kuh_xs$-	'hire'	NE *hire*
*deu(s)-	'be lacking'	NE *tire*,Grk *déomai*, Skt *doṣa-*
$*h_1eg$-	'be in need, lack'	Lat *egeō*
*menk-	'lack'	Lat *mancus*, Skt *mankú-*
*das-	'lack'	Skt *dásyati*
$*déh_3r/n$-	'gift'	Lat *dōnum*, Grk *dôron*, Skt *dāna-*
$*h_{2/3}ón\hat{k}os$	'what is bestowed'	Grk *ógkos*, Skt *áṃśa-*
$*p\mathring{r}(h_3)tis$	'what is distributed'	Lat *pars*, *portiō*, Skt *pūrtá-*
*bhag-	'apportion'	Skt *bhága-*
$*h_2elg^{w}ho/eh_a$-	'payment, prize'	Grk *alphḗ*, Skt *arghá-*
*misdhós	'reward, prize'	Grk *misthós*, Skt *mīḍhá-*
$*h_2ó/ép(e)n$-	'goods, wealth'	Lat *opulentus*, Grk *áphenos*, Skt *ápnas-*
$*réh_1is$	'possessions'	Lat *rēs*, Skt *rayí-*
$*lóik^{w}nes$-	'(inherited) possessions'	NE *loan*, Skt *rékṇas-*
*wósu	'goods'	Skt *vásu-*
$*h_1ónh_xes$-	'burden'	Lat *onus*, Skt *ána-*
*soru	'booty'	Lat *servus*?
$*speh_1(i)$-	'be sated, prosper'	Lat *spēs*, Skt *sphā́yate*
$*(s)teh_4$-	'steal'	Grk *tētáomai*, Skt *(s)tāyú-*
*mus-	'steal'	Skt *muṣṇā́ti*
*teubh-	'steal'	NE *thief*

captive]') which derives from *_wes-_ 'buy' (e.g. Hit *wasi* 'buys') while $*k^{w}rei(h_a)$- 'pay' (e.g. OIr *crenaid* 'buys', ORus *krĭnuti* 'buy', Grk *príamai* 'buy', Skt *krīṇā́ti* 'buys', Toch B *käry-* 'buy') has adopted the specific meaning of 'bride-price' in Celtic (OIr *tinnscra*) and Baltic (Lith *krieno*) derivatives. Another word for 'exchange' is also seen in *_per-_ (e.g. OIr *renaid* 'sells, barters, exchanges', Lat *interpres* 'go-between', *pretium* 'price', Grk *pérnēmi* 'sell', Av *pairyante* 'they compared'; the Lat *pretium* via French gives NE *price* and *interpres* provides the base of NE *interpret*). The root *_pel-_ is Proto-Indo-European if one accepts a potential Indic cognate (e.g. ON *falr* 'to be sold', Lith *pelnas* 'profit', Rus *polón* 'booty', Grk *pōléō* 'sell', Skt *páṇate* 'bargains, haggles'). A very particular economic term, **kuh$_x$s-*, 'to hire (goods or services)', is preserved in a Germanic-Hittite correspondence (e.g. NE *hire*, Hit *kuss-* 'hire').

A number of words indicate 'lack, want of'. Although **deu(s)-* indicates lack of energy or colour in OE *tēorian* 'faint, grow weary; fade [of colurs]' > NE *tire*, it indicates a more general 'lack' in Grk *déomai* and not only 'want' but also 'crime' in Indic (Skt *doṣa-*). A wider semantic variability is found in those words that may derive from **h$_1$eg-* (e.g. Lat *egeō* 'need', ON *ekla* 'lack', Hit *aki* 'dies', Toch AB *yäk-* 'neglect, be careless about' [<*'be lacking with regard to']). Semantically more secure is **menk-* which does generally mean 'lack' from Latin to Tocharian (e.g. Lat *mancus* 'maimed', OHG *mengen* 'be lacking', Lith *meñkas* 'feeble, weak; scanty; insignificant', Skt *maṅkú-* 'wobbly', Toch AB *mänk-* 'be deprived of; lack'). The root **das-* yields a very specific meaning in Hittite, i.e. *das(u)want-* 'blind' (cf. dialectal Norw *tasa* 'unravel', Skt *dásyati* 'suffers want, becomes exhausted').

There are quite a few words to indicate 'possessions' of some sort or another. The verbal root **deh$_3$-* 'give' provides the basis for the well-attested **déh$_3$r/n-* 'gift' (e.g. OIr *dān*, Lat *dōnum*, Lith *duonìs*, OCS *danĭ*, *darŭ*, Grk *dôron*, Arm *tur*, Skt *dāna-*, all 'gift'). Other products of giving are **h$_{2/3}$ónkôs* 'what is bestowed' (e.g. Grk *ógkos* 'burden', Arm *hunjk'* [pl.] 'harvest', Hit *henkan-* 'fate, death', Skt *áṃśa-* 'portion, share'), a noun formed from the verb **h$_{2/3}$enk̂-* 'bestow'; and **pr̥(h$_3$)tis* 'what is distributed' if the putative cognates (in Latin *pars* 'part', *portiō* 'portion', and Skt *pūrtá-* 'gift, granting, reward') are not independent creations from **per(h$_3$)-* 'sell, distribute'. The concept of 'apportion', **bhag-*, has religious associations in Phrygian where *Bagaîos* is an epithet of Zeus, and the Skt *bhága-* 'apportion' was deified as one of the Vedic gods; an Iranian cognate (e.g. Av *baga-* 'good fortune') was borrowed into Slavic to give the word for 'god', *bogŭ*; in Tocharian (e.g. Toch B *pāke*) the word retains the meaning 'share' (see Chapter 22). The word **h$_2$elg^{w}ho/eh$_a$-* 'payment, prize' (e.g. Lith *algà* 'payment, salary', Grk *alphḗ* 'earnings', Hit *halkuessar* 'produce, supplies [for cultic use]', Av *arəǰah-* 'value, price', Skt *arghá-* 'value, price') was borrowed from early Indo-Iranian into Uralic, e.g. Finnish *arvo* 'prize', while **misdhós* seems to indicate a similar meaning (e.g. OE *meord* 'reward, pay', OCS *mĭzda* 'reward, wages', Grk *misthós* 'reward, wages', Av *mīžda-* 'reward, gift', Skt *mīḍhá-* 'competition, contest, prize'); both terms range in their meanings from 'prize' to 'wages'. Goods in terms of 'wealth' is clearly seen in **h$_2$ó/ép(e)n-* (e.g. Lat *opulentus* 'rich, wealthy; opulent', *Ops* 'deity of abundance', Grk *áphenos* 'wealth', Hit *happina(nt)-* 'rich', Av *afnah-vant-* 'wealthy', Skt *ápnas-* 'wealth') although its root derivation is disputed: both **h$_3$ep-* which underlies a set of Anatolian words relating to 'business' and **h$_2$op-* 'work' have been suggested and here we have followed the latter suggestion. The concept of 'possessions' is also found in *$réh_1is$ (e.g. Lat *rēs* 'thing, affair, circumstance; possessions, wealth; business matter; law-suit', Av *raēvant-* 'rich, splendid, ostentatious', Skt *rayí-* 'possession, wealth'). Possessions in terms of 'leavings', i.e. inherited possessions, was indicated by *$lóik^wnes$- from *$leik^w$- 'leave'; it retains the meaning 'inheritance' in Indo-Iranian (e.g. Av *raēxnah-* 'inheritance, goods', Skt *réknas-* 'inherited possessions') but tends to mean a 'loan' in Germanic (e.g. OE *lǣn* 'loan, lease, grant, leased land'; NE *loan* is borrowed from Old Norse). The underlying word 'good' is found nominalized in both Anatolian (Luv *wāsu* 'goods') and Indic (Skt *vásu-* 'wealth, goods, riches, prosperity') which at least suggests the possibility of a PIE **wósu* 'goods' if these are not independent creations (cf. the same semantic development in NE *goods*). Possessions as a 'burden' is indicated by the Italic-Indic isogloss that yields *$h_1ónh_xes$- (Lat *onus* 'burden', Skt *ánas-* 'wagon-load'). Goods in terms of the spoils of war, i.e. 'booty', may be attested in **soru* which exists only in Anatolian (Hit *sāru* 'booty [particularly captured men, cattle, and sheep]') but there are derived forms in Celtic that indicate 'raiding' (perhaps MIr *serb* 'theft', NWels *herw* 'raid [whose principal goal was usually cattle]; outlawry') which strengthen the reconstruction; possibly Lat *servus* 'slave' is to be placed here if slaves are seen as booty (cf. the possible history of Grk *doûlos* 'slave' in Section 17.1). Those with the 'wealth', one might expect, would be *$speh_1(i)$- 'be satisfied, successful' (e.g. Lat *spēs* 'hope', OE *spōwan* 'thrive, succeed', Lith *spė́ju* 'have free time', OCS *spěti* 'be successful, prosper', Hit *ispā(i)-* 'get full, be filled, be satiated', Skt *sphā́yate* 'grows fat', Toch B *spāw-* 'spread out'; see Section 20.7).

For those without wealth who wish to acquire it illegally, there are three words for 'steal'. The first, *$(s)teh_4$-, is closely associated with derivatives meaning 'secret' and hence this indicates stealth (e.g. OIr *tāid* 'thief', OCS *tają* 'hide', Grk *tētáomai* 'deprive, rob', Hit *tāyezzi* 'steals', Av *tāyu-* 'thief', Skt *(s)tāyú-* 'thief', Toch B *ene-stai* 'in secret'); no such connotations are indicated by **mus-* which may have originally meant 'move aside' (e.g. OHG [*Lex Salica*] *chrēo-mōsido* 'grave-robbery', Skt *muṣṇā́ti* 'steals', Toch B *mus-* 'steal', Toch AB *mus-* 'lift, move aside'), perhaps a concept not far removed from modern NE *lift* for 'steal'. A Germanic-Tocharian isogloss supplies us with **teubh-* 'steal' (e.g. NE *thief*, Toch B *cowai* 'theft').

In the North-West the verbal root **kob-* 'suit, fit' yields a nominal **kobom* 'success' (e.g. OIr *cob* 'victory', ON *happ* 'luck' [NE *hap*, whence the adjective *happy*, is related but is a loanword from ON], OCS *kobĭ* 'divination'); **lau-* 'benefit, prize' (e.g. OIr *lōg* 'reward, prize', Lat *lucrum* 'gain, benefit' [slightly pejorative, whence NE *filthy lucre*], OE *lēan* 'reward, recompense'). The West Central region offers **ster-* 'steal' (e.g. perhaps OIr *serb* 'thief', Grk *steréō* 'deprive, rob') which, in Germanic, reveals itself as **stel-* (e.g. NE *steal*). To be 'rich' is indicated in (the poetic language) of Greek and Indic as *h_1*su-dh*h_1*-énos* 'rich, well-off', literally 'well-placed' (Grk *eutheneō̃* 'thrive, flourish', Skt *su-dhána-* 'rich'). And a far eastern isogloss (Indo-Iranian-Tocharian) is seen in **yem-* 'hold' (e.g. Av *yam-* 'hold', Skt *yam-* 'hold, sustain, offer, grant', Toch B *yäm-* 'achieve, obtain; reach' [< * 'come to hold' or the like], *yām-* 'do, make, effect').

17.4 Law and Order

The vocabulary of law (Table 17.4) is not extensive in Proto-Indo-European and much of the concept of 'law' derives from that of 'order' or 'what is fitting'. For example, we have *h_a*értus* from the root *h_a*er-* 'fit' which had already shifted to an association with cosmic order by the time of Indo-Iranian (e.g. Lat *artus* 'joint', MHG *art* 'innate feature, nature, fashion', dialectal Grk *artús* 'arranging, arrangement', Arm *ard* 'ornament, shape', Av *arəta-* 'order', Skt *r̥tú-* 'right time, order, rule', Toch B *ārtt-* 'love, praise'). More closely associated with ritual propriety is the Italic-Indo-Iranian isogloss that yields **yew(e)s-* (Lat *iūs* 'law, right, justice, duty', Av *yaož-dā-* 'make ritually pure', Skt *śáṃca yóśca* 'health and happiness') with a derived adjective **yust(iy)os* seen certainly in OIr *uissse* 'just right, fitting' and possibly OCS *istŭ* 'actual, true'. 'Law' itself, **dhéh*$_1$*-men-/i-*, is 'that which is established' and derives from **dhéh*$_1$*-* 'put, establish' but occurs in that meaning only in Grk *thémis* 'law' and Skt *dhā́man-* 'law' (we also have **dhéh*$_1$*tis* [e.g. Lat *conditiō* 'basis', NE *deed*, Grk *thésis* 'order', and Skt *-dhiti-* 'position']) though the same kind of semantic development is seen in Germanic (e.g. NE *law*) and Italic (e.g. Lat *lex*

Table 17.4. *Law and order*

*h_a*értus*	'fitting, order'	Lat *artus*, Grk *artús*, Skt *r̥tú-*
**yew(e)s-*	'order'	Lat *iūs*, Skt *yóśca*
**dhéh*$_1$*mi-/men-*	'what is established, law'	Grk *thémis*, Skt *dhā́man-*
**dhéh*$_1$ *tis*	'what is established'	Lat *con-diti-ō*, Grk *thésis*, Skt – *dhiti-*
*$h_{2/3}$*wergh-*	'± commit a crime'	
*h_1*lengh-*	'blame, reproach'	Grk *elégkhō*
*h_1*óitos*	'a going; oath'	NE *oath*, Grk *oĩtos*
**k*^{w}*oineh*$_a$*-*	'compensation'	Grk *poinḗ*
**k*^{w}*ei-*	'pay, compensate'	Grk *tínō*, Skt *cáyati*
**serk-*	'make restitution'	Lat *sarciō*

'law'), both from **legh-* 'lie', i.e. 'that which is laid out', and thus the concept is pan-Indo-European. We have **$h_{2/3}$wergh-* ' ± commit a crime' (e.g. ON *vargr* 'felon, criminal; wolf', OPrus *wargs* 'evil', Rus *vórog* 'enemy, devil', with different formations in Anatolian [Hit *hurkil* 'sin, sexual perversion'] and Tocharian [Toch B *wārṣṣe* 'highwayman, bandit']) which has taken on the secondary meaning 'wolf' in ON. A word for 'blame' possibly underlies the Greek-Anatolian isogloss **$h_1$lengh-* where 'blame' is found in Grk *elégkhō* but 'swear' in Anatolian, e.g. Hit *li(n)k-* where it is taken to indicate the practice of calling down a curse on oneself if one violated an oath. The word for 'oath', **$h_1$óitos*, is found in Celtic (e.g. OIr *oeth* 'oath'), Germanic (e.g. NE *oath*), Grk *oĩtos* 'course, fate', and Tocharian (Toch B *aittaṅka* 'directed towards') but it only carries the meaning 'oath' in the two Western language groups. It is commonly derived from the verb **$h_1$ei-* 'go' which has been explained by a practice of walking between slaughtered animals as part of taking an oath (see Section 20.1).

The making of 'restitution' is indicated by two roots: **k^woineh$_a$-* (e.g. Lith *káina* 'price', OCS *cěna* 'price', Grk *poinḗ* 'compensation for a crime, blood-price', Av *kaēna-* 'vengeance, hatred') from the root **k^wei-* 'pay, compensate' seen in OPrus *er-kīnint* 'freed from the devil', Grk *tínō* 'make someone pay (a debt, ransom, fine)', Lyc *tti-* 'pay, requite', Av *kāy-* 'pay, compensate', Skt *cáyati* 'pay, compensate' (compare another derivative from this verb, MIr *cin* 'guilt, crime, payment due') and **serk-* which is a semantic extension of 'make a circle, complete', perhaps in the sense of restoring the integrity of the system (e.g. Lat *sarciō* 'make restitution; make whole [i.e. repair]', Hit *sarnikzi* 'makes restitution', Toch B *serke* 'circle'; see Section 13.2).

From the North-West is **dhl̥gh-* 'debt' (e.g. OIr *dligid* 'is entitled to, is owed', Goth *dulgs* 'debt', OCS *dlŭgŭ* 'debt'). The West Central region supplies **$h_a$eig^{w}hes-* 'shame' (e.g. Goth *aiwiski* 'shame', Grk *aĩskhos* 'shame'). Greek-Indic cognates include **h_aēgos* 'shame' (Grk *ágos* 'guilt, pollution', Skt *āgas* 'guilt, sin') and **$h_a$emh$_3$-* 'lays hold, grasps; swears' (Grk *ómnūmi* 'swear', Skt *ámīti* 'lays hold of, grasps; swears'); the meaning 'swears' may be a late development in the groups involved and reflects the custom of grasping some sacred object while one makes an oath (cf. the practice of swearing with one's hand on the Bible in a contemporary court).

17.5 Strife and Warfare

The Indo-Europeans are often stereotyped as warriors, and it must be admitted that they did possess a rich vocabulary relating to strife and conflict (Table 17.5)

Table 17.5. *Strife and warfare*

**h_3enh_2-*	'contend, quarrel'	Grk *ónomai*
**mel-*	'argue, contend'	Grk *mōléō*
**reus-*	'± contend with, be angry at'	Skt *róṣati*
**h_4erg^w-*	'argue, assert'	Lat *arguō*
**$peh_1(i)$-*	'harm'	Lat *patior*, Grk *pêma*, Skt *pī́yati*
**dhebh-*	'harm'	Skt *dabhnóti*
**mel-*	'harm'	
**$dhwerh_x$-*	'harm'	Skt *dhvárati*
**keh_au-*	'strike, hew'	NE *hew*
**k̂er-*	'decay'	Lat *cariēs*, Grk *keraḯzō*, Skt *śī́ryate*
**h_aei-*	'assail, afflict'	Skt *énas-*
**g^when-*	'strike'	Lat *dēfendō*, Grk *theínō*, Skt *hánti*
**wen-*	'strike, wound'	NE *wound*
**bher-*	'strike (through), split'	Lat *feriō*, NE *bore*, Grk *pharóō*, Skt *bhr̥ṇā́ti*
**wedh-*	'push, strike'	Grk *éthei*, Skt *vadh-*
**(s)peud-*	'push, repulse'	Lat *pudet*, Grk *speúdō*
**per-*	'strike'	Skt *pr̥t-*
**kreu(-s)-*	'strike'	NE *rue*, Grk *kroúō*
**pyek-*	'strike'	NE *fight*
**$temh_x$-*	'be struck, be exhausted'	Lat *tēmētum*, Skt *tā́myati*
**$bheih_a$-*	'strike'	Lat *perfinō*
**$h_aeĝ$-*	'fight'	Grk *agṓn*, Skt *ājí-*
**yeudh-*	'moved, stirred up; fight'	Lat *iubeō*, Grk *husmī́nē*, Skt *yúdhyati*
**dhg^whei-*	'destroy'	Grk *phthínō*, Skt *kṣiṇā́ti*
**h_3elh_1-*	'destroy'	Lat *ab-oleō*, Grk *óllūmi*
**h_2erk-*	'rend, destroy'	
**h_2erh_x-*	'destroy'	
**$bhreh_xi$-*	'destroy, cut to pieces'	Lat *friō*, Skt *bhrīṇánti*
**seĝh-*	'hold fast, conquer'	Grk *ékhō*, Skt *sáhas-*
**g^wyeh_a-*	'physical power; overcome'	Grk *bíā*, Skt *jyā́*
**h_aeuges-*	'strength'	Lat *augustus*, Skt *ójas-*
**$weih_xs$*	'vital force'	Lat *vīs*
**h_alek-*	'defend, protect'	Grk *aléksō*, Skt *rákṣati*
**ser-*	'protect'	Lat *servō*
**gheuĝh-*	'protect, hide'	Skt *gū́hati*
**k̂eudh-*	'hide'	NE *hide*, Grk *keúthō*
**dhers-*	'brave'	NE *dare*, Grk *thérsos*, Skt *dhr̥ṣṇóti*
**$leh_2wós$*	'people (under arms)'	Grk *lā́(w)ós*
**koryos*	'people (under arms)'	Grk *koíranos*

although many of the verbal roots listed below may also have been associated with non-aggressive physical acts (see Section 22.3).

The vocabulary of the quarrel includes at least four verbs. A Celtic-Greek-Anatolian isogloss secures *$h_3$enh$_2$- which takes on the meaning of 'sue' in Hit *hann(a)*- 'contend against, contest, take legal action [against], sue' and Grk *ónomai* 'impugn, quarrel with' but OIr *on* 'shame, disgrace, dishonour'. There are also legal aspects to some of the German and Greek cognates derived from **mel*- while the Tocharian means 'argue, contest' (ON *māl* 'speech, legal dispute', Grk *mōléō* 'contend, bring an action in a suit', Toch B *mäl*- 'argue, contest'). The verb **reus*- indicates the notion of anger or rage in its Germanic and Indic forms (e.g. MHG *rūn* 'make a noise, uproar; bluster, rave, rage', Skt *roṣ*- 'displeases, takes offence at', Toch B *räs*- 'criticize, accuse, object to') while the meanings indicated in Lat *arguō* 'assert, prove, accuse' and Hit *arkuwai*- 'plead, argue, make excuses') suggest that we reconstruct 'argue, assert' for *$h_4$erg^w-.

Verbs indicating 'harm' are several. Although the Lat *patior* is not entirely secure here (it may be *p$\mathring{h}_1$-t-, but it need not), there is still enough evidence to postulate *peh$_1$(i)- 'harm' (e.g. Goth *fijan* 'hate', Grk *pêma* 'suffering, misfortune', Skt *pī́yati* 'blames, reviles'). The precise underlying semantics of **dhebh*- are somewhat obscure as meanings range from 'hit' (Baltic, e.g. Lith *dobiù* 'beat, hit, kill'), 'harm' [in general] (Indic, e.g. Skt *dabhnóti* 'hurts, injures; deceives; abandons'), 'belittle' (Anatolian, e.g. Hit *tepnu*-), and 'deceives' (Av *dab*-). A rare Celtic-Tocharian isogloss supports **mel*- (OIr *millid* 'harms', Toch B *mäl*- 'wound, damage') which is perhaps related to the verb *melh$_2$- 'grind', while **dhwer*- 'pierce' may underlie *dhwerh$_x$- 'harm' which does involve physical damage (e.g. Hit *duwarnai*- 'break, shatter', Skt *dhvárati* 'bends, cause to fall, hurts'). Although **k̂er*- carries an intransitive meaning 'decay' (e.g. OIr *ara-chrin* 'decays', Lat *cariēs* 'decay', Skt *śī́ryate* 'decays'), it also furnishes transitive verbs 'harm, injure' (e.g. Alb *ther* 'slaughter, stab, goad', Grk *keraḯzō* 'devastate, kill', Av *a-sarəta*- 'unbroken'). A possible Anatolian-Indo-Iranian isogloss underlies *$h_a$ei- 'assail' (e.g. Hit *inan*- 'illness', Av *aēnah*- 'violence, damage', Skt *énas*- 'sin, guilt'; also perhaps dialectal Grk *zētrós* 'executioner', and Skt *yātár*- 'avenger' if from a derivative *h_ay-eh$_a$-).

The verbal act of striking is very well represented although the semantic differences among the various terms are unclear. The best-attested root is *g^{w}hen- which is found in eleven different groups (OIr *gonaid* 'wounds, strikes', Lat *dēfendō* 'protect', ON *gunnr* 'combat', Lith *genù* 'drive cattle; hunt', Rus *gon* 'a drive, a hunt', Grk *theínō* 'strike', *phónos* 'murder', Arm *ganem* 'strike', Hit *kuēnzi* 'strikes', Av *jainti* 'strikes, Skt *hánti* 'strikes', Toch B *käsk*- 'scatter [violently]'); this is the predominant verb used in the 'hero slays a serpent' motif which plays an important role in Indo-European mythology (see Section 25.5).

The root ***wen-* means 'wound' in general but the semantics of NWels *gweint* 'bored through' and Hit *wen-* 'copulate with' suggest a piercing motion (cf. also NE *wound*, Arm *vandem* 'destroy'). An action involving a boring motion can also be seen in **bher-* (MIr *bern* 'gap, chasm', Lat *feriō* 'strike, pound', NE *bore*, Lith *bar(i)ù* 'revile, abuse', Rus *borjú* 'subdue, throw down', Grk *pharóō* 'plough', Arm *brem* 'dig up, hollow out, bore', NPers *burrad* 'cuts', Skt *bṛṇā́ti* 'wounds'). The root **keh$_a$u-* is associated with both striking down and forging (e.g. NE *hew*, Lith *káuja* 'strikes, forges', OCS *kovǫ* 'forge', Toch B *kau-* 'strike down, kill, destroy'). Although the root **wedh-* 'push, strike' may indicate a meaning 'press' in some of its cognate sets, it also carries the connotation of strike (with a weapon or tool) in many others: Celtic (OIr *fāiscid* 'presses' but *fodb* 'weapon'), Baltic (e.g. Lith *vedegà* 'a kind of axe'), Grk *éthei* 'destroys', Anatolian (e.g. Hit *wezz-* 'strike, urge'), Indo-Iranian (e.g. Skt *vadh-* 'strikes, pushes, slays'), Tocharian (e.g. Toch B *wät-* 'fight'). The derivative **wedhris* 'castrated' (Grk *ethrís*, Skt *vádhri-*) certainly suggests a striking blow. Another word for 'push' or something similar (the semantic range of the cognates is wide) is indicated by **(s)peud-* which underlies Lat *pudet* 'shames' and *repudium* 'casting off; divorce', Baltic (Lith *spáudiu* 'press, squeeze'), Alb *punë* 'work', Grk *speúdō* 'urge on, hasten', Arm *p'oyt'* 'zeal', and NPers *poy* 'haste, speed'.

Beating and battle are concepts associated with **per-* (e.g. Lith *periù* 'beat with brushwood, flog', Rus *pru* 'press, oppress', Alb *pres* 'cut down, cut off, split', Arm *hari* 'struck', Av *pərət-* 'battle, strife', Skt *pṛt-* 'battle, strife'). With or without the *s*-extension, the root **kreu(-s)-* indicates 'strike' (e.g. NE *rue*, Grk *kroaínō* 'stamp, strike with the hoof [of a horse]', Toch AB *kärn-* 'strike, afflict'; ON *hrosti* 'mashed malt', Lith *krušù* 'smash, crash; grind', OCS *sukrušiti* 'shatter', Grk *kroúō* 'strike [together], strike a stringed instrument with a plectrum, knock [at the door]'). Germanic develops the idea of 'fight' (e.g. NE *fight*) from **pyek-* which otherwise means 'strike' (e.g. Alb *për-pjek* 'strike', Toch B *pyāk-* 'strike [downward], batter, beat [of a drum], penetrate [as the result of a downward blow]'). Only Slavic exhibits the active meaning 'torture' for **temh$_x$-* (OCS *tomiti* 'torture, harass, tire'); the other cognates indicate the state of being struck down (by disease, drink, exhaustion) (e.g. MIr *tām* 'sickness, death', Lat *tēmētum* 'any intoxicating drink', NHG *damisch* 'foolish, silly', Skt *tā́myati* 'gasps for breath, is faint, stunned, exhausted'). The root **bheih$_a$-* uniformly supplies meanings of 'strike' (e.g. OIr *benaid* 'strikes', Lat *perfinō* 'break through, shatter', OCS *bijǫ* 'strike', Av *byente* 'they struggle, strike'). The verb to 'fight' is also indicated through the use of **h$_a$eĝ-* 'drive' which was already extended in Proto-Indo-European times to mean 'combative activity' (e.g. Grk *agṓn* 'athletic contest', Skt *ájman-* 'career, passage, battle', *ājí-* 'race, fight', OIr *tāin* [< **to-ag-no-*] 'raid'). A meaning of 'fight' survives in

Celtic, Greek, and Indo-Iranian to reconstruct **yeudh-* (e.g. Lat *iubeō* 'order, command', Lith *judù* 'move, stir', Grk *husmī́nē* 'battle', Av *yūiδyeiti* 'fights', Skt *yúdhyati* 'fights', Toch A *yutk-* 'be anxious').

Increasing the effect of the violence, we can move to 'destroy' which includes **dhg^{w}hei-* with a secure Greek-Indo-Iranian correspondence (Grk *phthínō* 'destroy', Av *dəǰīt.arəta-* 'destroying Arta', Skt *kṣiṇā́ti* 'destroys') and less secure cognates from Celtic (OIr *tinaid* 'vanishes') and Italic (Lat *situs* 'abandonment'). Along with Latin and Greek we can also include Anatolian to support the reconstruction of **h$_3$elh$_1$-* 'destroy' (e.g. Lat *ab-oleō* 'destroys', Grk *óllūmi* 'destroy', Hit *hullā(i)-* 'combat, fight'). Hittite and other correspondences secure both **h$_2$erk-* (e.g. OIr *oirgid* 'slays', Arm *harkanem* 'split, fell', Hit *harkzi* 'is destroyed') and **h$_2$erh$_x$-* (e.g. Lith *ìrti* 'dissolve, go asunder', OCS *oriti* 'destroy', Hit *harra-* 'destroy') to this semantic set. More questionable is **bhreh$_x$i-* (e.g. Lat *friō* 'tear apart', Rus *britĭ* 'shave', Skt *bhrīṇánti* 'injure, hurt') with a doubtful Celtic cognate (OIr *ro-bria* [subj.] 'may spoil, destroy'). To conquer one's enemy is indicated by **seĝh-* and its derivatives which mean 'conquer', 'victory' (e.g. OIr *seg* 'strong', NHG *Sieg* 'victory', Grk *ekhurós* 'firm, strong', Hit *sakkuriya-* 'overcome', Skt *sáhas-* 'victory', *sáhuri-* 'victorious'), and 'hold fast' (it supplies the basic Greek verb *ékhō* 'hold'). The word was also a popular element in personal names among the Celts (e.g. Gaulish *Sego-marus*) and Germans (ON *Sigurðr*). Probably originally a nominal root, **g^{w}yeh$_a$-* which means 'physical force' in both Greek and Indic can also mean 'overcome' (e.g. ON *kveita* 'make an end to, kill', Grk *bíā* 'physical force, violence', Skt *jyā́* 'force, violence', *jinā́ti* 'overpowers, suppresses'). Other words indicating 'physical strength' include **h$_a$euges-* (e.g. Lat *augustus* 'sacred', Av *aojah-* 'strength', Skt *ójas-* 'strength'), which has generally been linked to the type of strength required of a warrior. The word **weih$_x$s* 'strength' (e.g. Lat *vīs*, Grk *ī́s* both 'strength') seems to be a 'vital force' and has been linked with one of the words for 'man', **wih$_x$rós* (see Section 12.1).

There are several words for 'protect' or 'defend'. A verbal root **h$_a$lek-* is attested in Germanic (OE *ealgian* 'protect'), Grk *aléksō* 'defend', Arm *aracel* 'tend', and Skt *rákṣati* 'protect'; in Germanic and Baltic this root was extended to include temples and sacred groves, e.g. OE *ealh* 'temple', Lith *al̃kas* 'sacred grove'. Three groups attest a root **ser-* 'protect' (Lat *servō* 'guard', Lydian *sarẽta* 'protector', and Av *haraiti* 'defends'). A root **gheuĝh-* 'protect, hide' is attested in Baltic (Lith *gũžti* 'cover with something warm') and Indo-Iranian (e.g. Av *gūzra-* 'hidden, secret', Skt *gū́hati* 'conceals'). Another root, **k̂eudh-* 'hide', appears in Germanic (e.g. NE *hide*), Grk *keúthō* 'hide', and Arm *suzanem* 'hide' and then, after metathesis into **dheuk̂-*, in Germanic (e.g. for Tolkien fans OE *dēagol* 'secret, hidden') and Tocharian (Toch B *tuk-* 'be hidden'). And the quality associated with warriors is suggested by a PIE

**dhers-* 'brave' with cognates in Germanic (e.g. NE *dare*), Baltic (e.g. Lith *drįsù* 'dare'), Grk *thérsos* 'bravery', and Indo-Iranian (e.g. Skt *dhr̥ṣṇóti* 'is bold, dares').

A Proto-Indo-European word for 'army' remains illusive with the best candidate being *$*leh_2wós$* from a root *$*leh_2$-* 'military action'. It is attested in Grk *lā́(w)ós* 'people', [pl.] 'army', Doric Grk *lāgétās* 'leader of the people', and Phryg *lawagtei* 'military leader' in terms of a military leader or his unit; only Hit *lahha-* 'campaign' increases the number of cognates but the Hittite word does not actually indicate a military unit, but rather military action. A second and similar word **koros* appears as OPers *kāra-* 'people, army' and Lith *kãras* 'war' and in derived form, **koryos* 'army, war-band, unit of warriors', in MIr *cuire* 'troop, host', OE *here* 'army', Lith *kãrias* 'army', Grk *koíranos* 'army leader' (see Section 17.1).

The North-West region yields evidence of **katu-* 'fight' (e.g. OIr *cath* 'battle', OHG *hadu-* 'fight', OCS *kotora* 'fight'; also widely employed in Celtic [e.g. Gaul *Catu-rīx*] and Germanic [e.g. OHG *Hadubrant*] personal names); **weik-* 'fight' (e.g. OIr *fichid* 'fights', Lat *vincō* 'conquer', OE *gewegan* 'fight', Lith *apveikiù* 'defeat', Rus *vek* 'force'); the noun **nant-* 'combat, fight' (OIr *nēit* 'battle, combat', ON *nenna* 'strive'); **bheud-* 'strike, beat' (e.g. OIr *bibdu* 'guilty; enemy', Lat *fūstis* 'cane, cudgel', NE *beat*); **bhlaĝ-* 'strike' (Lat *flagrum* 'whip', ON *blekkja* 'strike', Lith *blaškaũ* 'throw, fling'); **slak-* 'strike' (e.g. MIr *slacc* 'sword', NE *slay*), and the participle from **kap-* 'seize', **kaptos* 'captive' (e.g. Lat *captus* 'captive', NE *haft*); **bhergh-* 'keep, protect' in Germanic (e.g. OE *beorgan* 'keep'), Baltic (Lith *bìrginti* 'be parsimonious') and Slavic OCS *brěšti* 'care for'; and possibly **wreg-* 'press, oppress' if Lat *urgeō* 'press, oppress' is indeed cognate with a Germanic series (e.g. ON *reka* 'avenge, punish', OE *wrecan* 'avenge, punish' > NE *wreak*). The West Central area shows **sket(h)-* 'injure, harm' (e.g. OIr *scīth* 'tired', OE *skaðian* 'injure' [NE *scathe* is related but a Norse loanword], Grk *askēthḗs* 'uninjured'), and to add to the number of words for 'strike' we have *$*pleh_ak/g$-* 'strike, strike one's breasts' (e.g. in various forms seen as Lat *plectō* 'strike, punish' and *plangō* 'strike, strike one's breast in lamentations, bewail', OE *flōcan* 'strike, clap', Lith *plàkti* 'strike', OCS *plakati sę* 'weep, be sorrowful', Grk *plā́ssō* 'strike'); *$*g^wel$-* 'strike, stab' (e.g. NWels *ballu* 'die', NE *kill* and *quell*, OPrus *gallan* 'death', Lith *gélti* 'sting', ache', Arm *kelem* 'torture'), a word that also provides the base for an 'insect's stinger', i.e. *$*g^welōn$* (Lith *geluõ* 'insect's stinger', dialectal Grk *déllithes* [pl.] 'wasps'); another verb *$*kelh_1$-* 'strike' (e.g. Lat *calamitās* 'loss, injury, damage, misfortune' [> by borrowing NE *calamity*], Lith *kalù* 'strike, forge', OCS *koljǫ* 'stab, slaughter', Grk *keleós* 'green woodpecker'); *$*bhlih_x\hat{g}$-* 'strike' (e.g. Lat *fligō* 'strike', Latv *blaizît* 'crush, strike', Grk *phlī́bō* 'press'), and a Serbo-Croatian-Armenian isogloss *$*deph_x$-* 'strike' (SC *depiti* 'strike', Arm *top'em* 'strike'. Baltic and Greek provide *$*yeh_1g^weh_a$-* 'power, youthful vigour' (e.g. Lith *jegà* 'strength, power', Grk *hḗbē* 'youth, vigour, puberty'). The Graeco-Aryan isoglosses comprise **tk̂en-* 'strike' (Grk *kteínō* 'kill', Skt *kṣaṇóti* 'hurts, injures, wounds') and **dusmenēs* 'hostile', literally 'bad-thought' (Grk *dusmenḗs* 'hostile', Av *dušmanah-* 'hostile', Skt *durmanās* 'sad').

17.6 Occupations

The creation of agent nouns in the different Indo-European languages is so productive that there are few words for occupations that can be attributed to Proto-Indo-European with any degree of certainty. The lack of reconstructable occupational terms may also suggest that Proto-Indo-European society was not one with much occupational specialization.

A word **tek̂s-(t)or/n-* can be reconstructed from Italic, Greek, and Indo-Iranian; the meanings range from 'weaver' (Lat *textor*) to 'carpenter' (Grk *téktōn*, Skt *tákṣan-*) to 'creator' (Av *tašan-*). It derives from the verbal root **tek̂s-* 'fabricate', and the semantic divergence may be due either to the fact that the verbal root itself is ambiguous or the fact that the craft of the carpenter also included the construction of wattled ('woven') walls. The herdsman, **wéstor-*, is reconstructed from Hit *westara-* 'herdsman' and Av *vāstar-* 'herdsman' and derives from the verbal root **wes-* 'graze'. The verb **yeudh-* 'fight' underlies **yudhmós* 'fighter' which is attested in Slavic (OCS *o-jĭminŭ* 'warrior') and Indic (Skt *yudhmá-*).

Regionally attested occupations are from the West Central region and comprise a word for 'craft', **kérdos*, attested in Celtic (OIr *cerd* 'craftsman', NWels *cerdd* 'song, poem; craft') and Greek (*kérdos* 'profit' but in the plural it means 'cunning arts; craft'); **dhabhros* 'craftsman' (Lat *faber* 'workman, artificer, smith', Arm *darbin* 'smith') from the root **dhabh-* 'put together' and two words for 'herdsman', **g*^{w}*ou-k*^{w}*olos* 'cowherd', literally 'one who turns/ moves cows' (e.g. MIr *búachail* 'cowherd', Grk *boukólos* 'cowherd'), and **poh*$_2$*imén-* 'herdsman' (Lith *piemuõ* 'herdsman', Grk *poimḗn* 'herdsman') from **poh*$_2$*(i)-* 'watch (cows)'.

Table 17.6. *Occupations*

**tek̂s-(t)or/n-*	'one who fabricates'	Lat *textor*, Grk *téktōn*, Skt *tákṣan-*
**wéstor-*	'herdsman'	
**yeudhmós*	'fighter'	Skt *yudhmá-*

17.7 Proto-Indo-European Society

The degree of social complexity generally correlates with the size of the social aggregates and the nature of the economic system involved. Although there are always exceptions to the rule, hunter-gatherer societies are most often egalitarian, lacking strong positions of leadership and social ranking; moreover, they tend to be organized into relatively small social aggregates—families, bands, possibly small tribes. A presumably hunter-gathering society such as Proto-Uralic reveals little more than a word for 'lord' which is itself a loanword from Indo-Iranian. The Proto-Indo-Europeans with their clear evidence for an economy based on domesticated plants and animals, settled life, metallurgy, and the more advanced technology (plough, wheeled vehicles) of the so-called Secondary Products Revolution would suggest that we might find a larger semantic field for social institutions. And this, indeed, is precisely what we do find although we must always beware of attempting to reconstruct an entire social system from the residue of the lexical debris that has survived.

Proto-Indo-European seems to have had some form of social ranking with various degrees of social status. Leadership positions would include the *_w(n̥)nákts_ 'leader, lord', *_h_3rḗĝs_ 'ruler, king', *_tagós_ 'leader', and *_wiḱpots_ 'master of the clan' and there are even verbal expressions of authority seen in *_pótyetoi_ 'rules, is master', *_wal-_ 'be strong, rule', and possibly *_h_3rḗĝti_ 'rules'. The nature of leadership probably involved a sacerdotal element if we can correctly recover the etymological nuances of *_h_3rḗĝs_. But terms such as *_tagós_ 'leader', i.e. 'the one who puts in order', and *_sók^{w}-h_2-ōi_ 'follower, companion' suggest at least the image of leaders in warfare as well, and this possibility is greatly enhanced by the recovery of other names for warrior sodalities i.e. *_leh$_2$wós_ 'people (under arms)', *_h_aeĝmen-_ 'troop', and *_koryos_ 'people (under arms)' with its own West Central designation *_koryonos_ 'leader (of the _koryos_)'. To what extent the realia of these institutions can be painted in with later ethnographic evidence of war-bands from Ireland to India is not entirely clear but it is difficult to deny the existence of such institutions. Moreover, the vocabulary of strife, as we have seen, is fairly extensive (at least twenty-seven verbs) and while a number may be dismissed as purely expressions of the general application of physical force, e.g. striking an object, others such as *_seĝh-_ 'hold fast, conquer' certainly make better sense in a military context. For some time Indo-European homeland research has found itself all too often cast in the form of an insidious dichotomy: did the Indo-Europeans expand as peaceful farmers or warlike herdsmen? That farmers may also be aggressive and belligerent is well known to anyone who has encountered, for example, agricultural African societies; conversely, pastoralists need not be painted in the same terms as the Golden Horde. In any event, there does seem to be sufficient retention of the vocabulary of strife and warfare in the reconstructed lexicon to suggest at least that those who wish to portray the Proto-Indo-Europeans as some form of New Age agrarian movement are strongly contradicted by the lexical evidence.

Our recovery of legal institutions, at least on the basis of the reconstructed lexicon, is meagre. There seems to be an acceptance of a concept of *$h_a$értus* 'what is fitting', i.e. the cosmic order that must be maintained. This should be done by adhering to **dhéh$_1$mi-/men-* 'what is established, law', here generally taken (on the basis of Greek and Indo-Iranian comparative studies) to be the law that has been established (**dhéh$_1$-*) by the gods for humans. The other term, **yew(e)s-*, 'law, ritual norm', has been seen to express the notion of ritual prescriptions, the recitation of which led to the establishment (or re-establishment) of order. Punishment for violation of the law such as murder or failure to abide by an oath required some form of compensation seen in both **k^{w}oineh$_a$-* and **serk-* 'make restitution'.

The range of vocabulary concerned with exchange and wealth is reasonably extensive and supports the hypothesis that the Proto-Indo-Europeans were involved in some degree of social ranking. If we read the nuances of the terms rightly, then both **mei-* and **meit-* 'exchange' are terms concerned with the concept of balanced reciprocity, i.e. an exchange relationship where neither side seeks an advantage. This is the type of exchange that one might expect to operate within families, clans, or perhaps at the tribal level. The exchange might have involved material goods (**wes-no-*) but possibly also the payment of a bride-price (**k^{w}rei(h$_a$)-*). More distant exchange is suggested by **per-* 'exchange, barter' which may have derived from the concept of 'transport across' and is employed so in Homeric Greek where it designates the sale of slaves overseas. Exchange outside one's group might lead to negative reciprocity where each side seeks a more advantageous recovery from the transaction.

There are a series of terms for lack or poverty (**deu(s)-* 'be lacking', **h$_1$eg-* 'be in need, lack', **menk-* 'lack', **das-* 'lack'), as well as words for wealth (e.g. **h$_2$ó/ép(e)n-* 'goods, wealth', **réh$_1$is* 'possessions', **wósu* 'goods'). These may have been acquired through a lifetime but also they may have been inherited (**lóik^{w}nes-*). The context of use in both Greek and Indic derivatives of **h$_2$elg-^{w}ho/eh$_a$-* 'payment, prize' supports the notion that human chattels were a Proto-Indo-European commodity. The noun **soru* 'booty' also suggests wealth in the forms of captured men or livestock and this is supported by expressions built on **h$_a$eĝ-* 'drive', e.g. OIr *tāin bō* 'cattle-raid', Lat *bovēs agere* 'raid for cattle', Av *gąm varətąm ąz-* 'drive off cattle as booty', and, the widespread practice of cattle-raiding attested in the earliest Indo-European literature from Ireland to

India. This manner of gaining wealth should probably be set outside the semantic ramifications of *(*s*)*teh*$_4$-, **mus*-, and **teubh*-, all 'steal' in a presumably culturally unsanctioned manner.

Further Reading

On the problem of 'Aryan' see the Thieme–Dumézil debate in Thieme (1938, 1957), Dumézil (1941, 1958); also Thurneysen (1936), Bailey (1959, 1960), Szemerényi (1977), Cohen (2002). The Indo-European 'king' is discussed in Gonda (1955*b*), Sihler (1977), Scharfe (1985), Strunk (1987), Watkins (1995); other aspects of social organization can be found in Benveniste (1973*a*), Buti (1987), Della Volpe (1993), Duhoux (1973), Ivanov (1960), Losada Badia (1992), Nagy (1987), Scheller (1959), Schlerath (1987), Winter (1970), Zimmer (1987). Exchange is discussed in Benveniste (1973*a*), Markey (1990), Parvulescu (1988*b*), and Ramat (1983) and law in Palmer (1956), Watkins (1970*a*, 1986*b*), Puhvel (1971), and the collected readings in Puhvel (1970). The IE war-band has been much discussed from the seminal Wikander (1938) through Crevatin (1979), McKone (1987), Weitenberg (1991), and most recently in a conference edited by Das and Meiser (2002); for PIE 'booty' see Watkins (1975).

18

Space and Time

18.1 Space

The semantic categories of space and time are so fundamental to any language that there is an impressive degree of retention of a range of words, particularly those relating to position. The general terms for space are listed in Table 18.1.

The concept of an 'open space' is found in **réuh$_x$es-* which indicates 'open fields' in Celtic (e.g. OIr *rōi* 'field, open land') and Italic (e.g. Lat *rūs* 'country-side, open fields') and 'space' in Av *ravah-*. The same root with a different extension gives us NE *room*. The underlying verb (**reuh$_x$-*) is preserved only in Toch AB *ru-* 'be open'. Semantically more opaque is **ĝhóh$_1$ros* which is a 'free space, area between, land' in Grk *khō̂ros* but a 'pit, hole' in Tocharian (e.g. Toch B *kāre*); an *e*-grade gives a Greek word for 'widow' (*khḗrā*). The verbal concept of 'have room' is found in **telp-* (e.g. OIr *-tella* 'have room for something', Lith *telpù* 'find or have room enough; enter', Skt *tálpa-* 'bed', Toch B *tälp-* 'be emptied of, purge'). General words for a 'place' are built on the verbal root **steh$_2$-* 'stand', hence we have **stéh$_2$tis* (e.g. Lat *statiō* 'position, station', NE *stead*, Lith *stãčias* 'standing', Grk *stásis* 'place, setting, standing, stature', Av *stāiti-* 'station', Skt *sthíti-* 'position') and **stéh$_2$mōn* (e.g. Lat *stāmen* 'warp', NE *stem*, Lith *stomuõ* 'stature', Grk *stḗmōn* 'warp', Skt *sthā́man-* 'position', Toch B *stām* 'tree'). As we can see, the first generally does indicate a 'place' or 'station' while the range of meanings of the second word is

Table 18.1. *Space*

**réuh$_x$es-*	'open space'	Lat *rūs*
**ĝhóh$_1$ros*	'gap, empty space'	Grk *khôros*
**telp-*	'have room'	Skt *tálpa-*
**stéh$_2$tis*	'place'	Lat *statiō*, NE *stead*, Grk *stásis*, Skt *sthíti-*
**stéh$_2$mōn*	'what stands, stature'	Lat *stāmen*, NE *stem*, Grk *stḗmōn*, Skt *sthā́man-*
**h$_4$erh$_2$os*	'border, line, limit'	Lat *ōra*
**morĝ-*	'border'	Lat *margō*
**térmn̥*	'border'	Lat *termen*, Grk *térma*, Skt *tárman-*

much wider, e.g. 'warp' of a loom (Latin, Greek), 'stem' (Germanic), and 'tree' (Tocharian).

There are three words that indicate 'border'. Hit *arha-* 'line, boundary' preserves PIE **h$_4$erh$_2$os* while derivatives may be found in Italic (Lat *ōra* 'brim, edge, boundary, region'), Germanic (e.g. OE *ōra* 'border, bank, shore'), and Baltic (e.g. Latv *âra* 'border, boundary; country; limit'). Another word, **morĝ-*, indicated a 'border' or 'district' from Celtic to Avestan (e.g. OIr *mruig* 'district', Lat *margō* 'edge' [> by borrowing NE *margin*], OE *mearc* 'border, district' [NE *marches* is from Old French, in turn from Germanic], Av *marəza-* 'border country'). The root **ter-* 'cross over' underlies the third word, **térmn̥* (e.g. Lat *termen* 'border', Grk *térma* 'border, goal, end point', Arm *t'arm* 'end', Hit *tarma-* 'stake', Skt *tárman-* 'point of sacrificial post'); both Hittite and Indic provide a concrete meaning here, i.e. 'post, stake', a device employed to mark the limit of something.

18.2 Position

Words indicating position, with respect to both space or time, include the adpreps, i.e. adverbs and prepositions, which are both basic and well preserved in the Indo-European languages. The rather extensive list is indicated in Table 18.2.

There are four words to indicate position 'before' or 'in front'. The first, **h$_2$enti* (e.g. Lat *ante* 'in front of', Lith *añt* 'on, upon; at', Grk *antí* 'instead of, for', Arm *ənd* 'for', Hit *anti* 'facing, frontally; opposite, against', *hanza* 'in front of', Skt *ánti* 'opposite'), is in fact a frozen case form of **h$_2$ent* 'face, forehead' (cf. Lith *añtis* 'breast(s)', Hit *hant-* 'forehead, front', Toch B *ānte* 'brow'). The other three are all derived ultimately from the preposition **per* 'through', here in the extended meanings 'through, beyond, in front of'. These are **pr̥h$_a$éh$_1$*

Table 18.2. *Position*

**$h_2$enti*	'in front'	Lat *ante*, Grk *antí*, Skt *ánti*
**pr̥h_aéh_1*	'in front of; before (of time)'	NE *fore*, Grk *pará*, Skt *purā*
**pr̥$h_a$éi*	'in front of; before (of time)'	Lat *prae*, Skt *paré*
**pro*	'forward, ahead, away'	Lat *prō*, Grk *pró*, Skt *prá-*
**terh_2-*	'across, through, above'	Lat *trāns*, NE *through*, Skt *tirás*
**proti*	'against, up to'	Grk *protí*, Skt *práti*
**$h_1$entér*	'into, between'	Lat *inter*, Skt *antár*
**(s)me*	'middle, among'	Grk *metá*, Skt *smat*
**per*	'over, through, about'	Lat *per*
**$h_1$en(i)*	'in, into'	Lat *in*, NE *in*, Grk *en*
**$h_1$én-do*	'into'	Lat *endo*, Grk *éndon*
**$h_a$ed*	'at, to'	Lat *ad*, NE *at*
**do* ~ **de*	'to, toward'	Lat *dō-nec*, NE *to*, Grk *-de*
**ko(m)*	'with, side by side'	Lat *cum*, Skt *kám*
**sek^{w}o-*	'following'	Lat *secus*, Skt *sácā*
**som-*	'(together) with'	Skt *sam-*
**$h_1$énh_1u*	'without'	NHG *ohne*, Grk *áneu*
**b(h)eĝh*	'without'	Skt *bahí-*
**sen-i-/u-*	'apart'	Lat *sine*, Skt *sanitúr*
**wi-*	'apart, in two, asunder'	Lat *vitium*, Skt *vi-*
**$h_4$eu*	'away (from)'	Lat *au-ferō*, Skt *áva*
**$h_a$et*	'away, beyond'	Lat *at*, Grk *atár*, Skt *átas*
**$h_4$épo*	'back, behind'	Lat *ab*, Grk *apó*, Skt *ápa*
**$h_4$ep-ér-*	'back, behind'	Skt *ápara-*
**posti*	'after'	Lat *post(e)*
**po-sk^{w}o-*	'behind'	Skt *páścāt*
**witeros*	'far'	NE *withershins*, Skt *vitarám*
**$h_2$entbhi-*	'around, on both sides'	Lat *ambi-*, Grk *amphí*, Skt *abhíta-*
**$h_4$upó*	'up (from underneath)'	NE *up*, Grk *hupó*, Skt *úpa*
**ūd*	'upward, out (from under)'	NE *out*, Skt *ud-*
**$h_a$en-h_ae*	'up (onto), upwards, along'	NE *on*, Grk *aná*
**$h_1$epi* ~ **$h_1$opi*	'near, on'	Lat *ob*, Grk *epí*, Skt *ápi*
**(s-)$h_4$upér(i)*	'over'	Lat *s-uper*, NE *over*, Grk *hupér*, Skt *upári*
**bhr̥ĝhús* ~ **bhr̥ĝhént-*	'high'	Skt *br̥hánt-*
**$h_2$erdus*	'high, lofty'	Lat *arduus*
**wor$h_x$dhus*	'upright, high'	Grk *(w)orthós*, Skt *ūrdhvá-*
**wers-*	'peak'	Lat *verrūca*, Grk *hérma*, Skt *várṣman-*
**ni*	'downwards'	NE *nether*, Skt *ní*

(*Cont'd*)

Table 18.2. (*Cont'd*)

$*kat\text{-}h_ae$	'down'	Grk *katá*
**dheub-*	'deep'	NE *deep*
**n̥dhés* ~ **n̥dhero-*	'under, low'	NE *under*, Skt *ádhara-*
**ner*	'under'	NE *north*, Grk *nérthen*
$*s\text{-}h_4upó$	'underneath'	Lat *sub*

(e.g. NE *fore*, Grk *pará* 'by, near, alongside of, beyond', Arm *ar* 'near, at', Av *parə* 'before', Skt *purā* 'formerly'), $*pr̥h_aéi$ (e.g. Gaul *are-* 'before, by; east' ['east' is in front of anyone who orients him- or herself by the sun which appears to have been the Proto-Indo-European custom], Lat *prae* 'before', Lith *priẽ* 'by, at, near; in the time of', Grk *paraí* 'before', Skt *paré* 'thereupon') and **pro* (e.g. Lat *prō* ~ *pro* 'before, in front of, before', OHG *fir-* 'before', OPrus *pra* 'through', Grk *pró* 'in front of; before [of time]', Hit *parā* 'forward, further', Av *frā* 'in front of', Skt *prá-* 'before'). The equivalent of 'across' is seen in $*terh_2$- which includes among its NE forms both *through* and *thorough* (cf. also OIr *tar* 'across, above', Lat *trāns* 'across', Av *tarō* 'over, to', Skt *tirás* 'over, across, apart'). 'Against' is **proti* which is formed from **pro* + an adverbial suffix **ti* (e.g. Latv *pretī* 'against', OCS *protivŭ* 'towards', Grk *protí* 'at, in front of, looking towards', Skt *práti* 'against'). The word for 'between', $*h_1entér$ (e.g. OIr *eter* 'into, between', Lat *inter* 'between', OHG *untar(i)* 'between', OCS *ǫtrĭ* 'inside', Alb *ndër* 'between, among', Av *antarə* 'within, between', Skt *antár* 'between'), is derived from $*h_1en$ 'in'. The word for 'middle' was $*(s)me(\text{-}th_a)$ (e.g. OE *mid* 'with', Alb *me* 'with', Grk *metá* 'with, among', Av *mat* '(together) with', Skt *smat* 'with') but was extended in a series of widespread derivatives, e.g. **medhyos* underlies both Lat *medius* and NE *mid* (cf. also MIr *mide* 'middle', OPrus *median* 'forest' [< 'that which lies between (settlements)'], Rus *mežá* 'border', Alb *mjesditë* 'noon', Grk *mésos* 'middle', Arm *mēǰ* 'middle', Av *maiδya-* 'middle', Skt *mádhya-* 'middle').

The preposition 'in' is indicated by $*h_1en(i)$ and $*h_1én\text{-}do$ (e.g. OIr *in* 'in(to)', Lat *in* 'in(to)', NE *in*, Lith *iñ* 'in', Alb *inj* 'up to', Grk *en* 'in', Arm *i* 'in',Toch AB *y(n)-* 'in, among'; and Lat *endo* 'in', Alb *ndë* 'in', Grk *éndon* 'within', Hit *anda(n)* 'in'). The widespread $*h_aed$ meant 'to' (e.g. Irish *ad-* 'to', Lat *ad* 'to, at', NE *at*, Phryg *ad-* 'to') as did **do* or **de* (e.g. OIr *do*, Lat *dō-nec* 'up to', NE *to*, Lith *da* 'up to', OCS *do* 'up to', Grk *-de* 'toward', Av *-da* 'to'). The concept of accompaniment is indicated by three words meaning 'with'. The first, **ko(m)* (e.g. OIr *com-* 'with', Lat *cum* 'with', OCS *kŭ* 'toward', Skt *kám* 'toward'), is widespread and old while $*sek^wo$- indicates the 'following' (e.g. OIr *sech* 'past, beyond', Lat *secus* 'after, beside, otherwise', Latv *secen* 'by, along', Av *hačā* 'from, out of; in accordance with', Skt *sácā* 'together with', *sakám* 'with') and derives from the verbal root *$*sek^w$*- 'follow'. The third, **som-* (e.g. OHG *samn* 'together', Lith *sam-* 'with', OCS *so-* 'with', Av *ha(m)-* 'together', Skt *sam-* 'with'), is an *o*-grade derivative of **sem-* 'one'. There are two words to indicate 'without': *$*h_1énh_1u$* and **b(h)eĝh* (e.g. NHG *ohne* 'without', Grk *áneu* 'without', Oss *ænæ* 'without'; and Lith *bè* 'without; but', OCS *bez* 'without', Skt *bahí-* 'outside'). Separation is also indicated by two words meaning 'apart', i.e. **sen-i-/u-* (e.g. OIr *sain* 'especially', Lat *sine* 'without', Hit *sanizzis* 'excellent', Av *hanarə* 'except, without', Skt *sanitúr* 'apart from', Toch B *snai* 'without'; a derived form gives us NE *sunder*) and **wi-* (e.g. Av *vi-* 'apart, off', Skt *vi-* 'asunder', and derivatives in Lat *vitium* 'defect' [> by borrowing NE *vice*], NHG *wider*).

Those words indicating distance or 'back' are relatively numerous. The word 'away' was conveyed by *$*h_4eu$* (e.g. OIr *ō* 'from', Lat *au-ferō* 'carry away', Lith *au-* 'away', OCS *u-* 'away', Hit *awan* 'away', *u-* 'hither', Av *ava* 'down, off', Skt *áva* 'from') and *$*h_aet$* (e.g. OIr *aith-* 'back, out of', Lat *at* 'but', Goth *aþ-þan* 'however', Lith *ato-* 'back, away', OCS *ot-* 'away, out', Grk *atár* 'however', Skt *átas* 'from there', Toch B *ate* 'away'). The terms 'back' and 'behind' have at least four reconstructable words. The first *$*h_4épo$* (e.g. Lat *ab* 'from', Goth *af* 'from, since', Grk *apó* 'from', Hit *āppa* 'behind', Av *apa* 'away from', Skt *ápa* 'away, forth') also has a shortened version *$*(h_4)po$* which is used as a verbal prefix in Baltic (e.g. Lith *pa-*) and Slavic (e.g. OCS *pa-*), Av (*pa-*), and can also be seen in Lat *po-situs* 'situated', and perhaps Alb *pa* 'without'. Another derived form is *$*h_4 ep-ér-$* (e.g. Goth *afar* 'after', Av *apara-* 'behind, following, other', Skt *ápara-* 'later') which, with a different extension, gives us NE *after*. The third word, **posti* (e.g. Lat *post(e)* 'after', Arm *əst* 'after', Toch B *postäṃ* 'after'), is derived from **pos* (e.g. Lat *posterus* 'behind', Lith *pàs* 'at, with', *pãstaras* 'last, furthest behind', OCS *po* 'after', dialectal Grk *pós* 'near, by', and perhaps Alb *pa* 'without') which may itself derive (as the genitive form) from either *$*h_1ep-$* 'near' or *$*h_4ep-$* 'back'. The final form (*$*po-sk^wo-$*, cf. Lith *paskuĩ* 'behind; after that, later on', Alb *pas* 'after', Av *paskāt* ~ *pasča* 'behind', Skt *páścāt* ~ *paścā* 'behind, westerly' [because the west is to one's back when oriented to the rising sun]) is a compound of **po* 'back' and *$*sek^w$*- 'follow'. The original meaning of **witeros* (e.g. NE *withershins*, Av *vītara-* 'a further one', Skt *vitarám* 'far away') is not entirely clear but may have been 'far' (as in Indo-Iranian, although it is 'against' in Germanic); it is a compound of **wi-* 'apart, in two' and *-*tero-*, the comparative suffix.

A derivative of *$*h_2ent-$* 'face' provides a word for 'around, on both sides'; i.e. *$*h_2(e)nt-bh-i$* (e.g. OIr *imm-* ~ *imb-* 'about, mutually', Lat *ambi-* 'on each side of, around, about', OHG *umbi* 'about', Alb *mbi* 'over', Grk *amphí* 'about, near', Arm *amb-olǰ* 'complete', Av *aiwitō* 'on both sides', Skt *abhíta-* 'on both sides').

A number of words can be reconstructed to mean 'up'. The oldest is perhaps *$h_4$upó (e.g. OWels *gwo-* [preverb], OE *ufe-* 'on', and with doubled consonant, OE *upp(e)* 'up' [> NE *up*], Grk *hupó* '(to) under, by, towards', Av *upa* 'towards', Skt *úpa* 'upwards, towards') which has an underlying verbal root *$h_4$up- that means 'go up, rise' (e.g. Hit *ūpzi* '[the sun] rises', Alb *hypem* 'go up'). A good example of how prepositions may alter their meaning in various languages is seen in the fact that the other two words for Proto-Indo-European 'up', **ūd* and *h_a en-h_ae, yield the NE prepositions 'out' and 'on' respectively (cf. also dialectal Grk *hu-* 'on', Skt *ud-* 'out'; Grk *aná* 'up on, up along, over, through, among', Av *ana* 'onto'). The widespread (ten groups) *$h_1$epi indicates a meaning of 'near' or 'on' (e.g. OIr *iar* 'after', Lat *ob* 'towards', Lith *ap-* 'about', OCS *ob* 'on', Grk *epí* 'on, upon, on top of', *ópisthen* 'behind', Arm *ev* 'and, also', Av *aipi* 'upon', Skt *ápi* 'also, in addition'). Also widespread are descendants of *(s-)$h_4$upér(i) 'over' (e.g. OIr *for-* 'over', Lat *super* 'over', NE *over*, Grk *hupér* 'over; beyond', Av *upairi* 'over', Skt *upári* 'over'). The adjective 'high' is indicated by **bhr̥ĝhús* (Arm *barjr* 'high', Anatolian, e.g. Hit *parku-* 'high', Toch B *pärkare* 'long' [with a change to a horizontal perspective from the original vertical one]) or **bhr̥ĝhént-* (Celtic, e.g. OIr *Brigit* [proper name], Germanic, e.g. ON *Borgundarholmr* 'Bornholm' [an island that rises high out of the sea], Indo-Iranian, e.g. Av *bərəzant-* 'high', Skt *bṛhánt-* 'high, great'). Among other derived forms is Lat *for(c)tis* 'strong'. A nominal form **bherĝhs* gives both NE *barrow* and *borough* (as well as NHG *Berg* 'mountain' and *Burg* 'fortress' and Av *barš* 'height'). Another adjective for 'high' is seen in *$h_2$erdus (e.g. OIr *ard* 'high', Lat *arduus* 'steep, lofty; difficult', ON *ǫrðugr* 'steep', Hit *harduppi-* 'high'). A PIE *worh$_x$dhus 'upright, high' is seen in Grk *(w)orthós* 'upright, standing', Indo-Iranian (e.g. Skt *ūrdhvá-* 'upright; high'), and Toch A *orto* 'from above'. The word for 'peak' was **wers-* (e.g. OIr *ferr* 'better' [< *'higher'], Lat *verrūca* 'varus, pimple', OE *wearr* 'sill', Lith *viršùs* 'highest point', Rus *verkh* 'peak', Grk *hérma* 'point, top', Skt *várṣman-* 'height, peak'). The Greek word for 'heaven', *ouranós*, may belong here as well if, as has been suggested, it comes from **worsm̥nó-*.

In the opposite direction we have **ni* (e.g. OIr *ne* 'down', NE *nether*, OCS *nizŭ* 'down', Arm *ni-* 'down, back, into', Skt *ní* 'down') and *kat-h_ae (e.g. Grk *káta* ~ *katá* 'down; through, among; according to', Hit *katta* 'down, by, with, under', *katkattiya-* 'kneel, go down', Toch B *kätk-* 'lower'), both 'down(-wards)'. The word for 'deep', **dheub-*, is attested in Celtic (possibly, e.g. NWels *dufn* 'deep'), Germanic (e.g. NE *deep*), Baltic (e.g. Lith *dubùs* 'deep'), Slavic (e.g. OCS *dŭno* 'ground, floor' *dŭbrŭ* 'ravine, valley'), Alb *det* 'sea', and, with a radical shift in meaning to 'high', also Tocharian (e.g. Toch B *tapre*; for the semantic change we might compare NE 'high seas'). It is a much discussed word since it offers evidence for the elusive (and very rare)

Proto-Indo-European **b-*; otherwise, if the Tocharian and Albanian forms are not accepted, it has been seen as a north-west European substrate term, borrowed possibly from a non-Indo-European language. The word 'under' or 'low' is seen in **n̥dhés* (e.g. ON *und* 'under', Arm *ənd* 'under', Lyc *ẽti* 'down, below', Skt *adhás* 'under', Toch B *ette* 'downward, under') or with the comparative suffix (i.e. 'lower') **n̥dhero-* (e.g. Lat *īnfernus* 'lower', NE *under*, Goth *anderas* 'lower'. Lycian *ẽtre/i-* 'lower', Av *aδara-* 'the lower', Skt *ádhara-* 'lower'). The peculiar semantic development of **ner* 'under' (e.g. NE *north*, Grk *nérthen* 'from below', Tocharian *ñor* 'below, beneath, under') to Germanic 'north' is explained by the Indo-European system of orientation which involves facing the sun so that straight ahead is east and the left or north is 'low' compared with the right or south where the sun will be high. The underlying verbal meaning is preserved in Lith *neriù* 'plunge, dive into'. We have already seen how **$h_4$upó* meant 'up' or, in its verbal form, 'going up'; the activity suggests 'rising from underneath' and the meaning of the related form **s-$h_4$upó* is exclusively 'underneath' (e.g. Lat *sub* 'underneath', *animālia suppa* 'animals [on all fours]', Arm *hup* 'near', Hit *suppala-* 'animal', Toch B *spe* 'near').

Regional terms for position included from the North-West **$h_a$elnos* 'beyond, yonder' (e.g. OIr *oll* 'ample', Lat *uls* 'beyond', NE *all*, OCS *lani* 'last year') which is based on the same root that gives Proto-Indo-European 'other'; **dē* 'away (from)' (e.g. OIr *di* 'away', Lat *dē* 'away'). From the West Central region are **dis-* 'apart, asunder' (Lat *dis-* 'asunder', Goth *dis-* 'apart', Alb *sh-* 'apart', Grk *diá* 'through, on account of') from the numeral 'two'; **$h_a$ed* 'at, to' which is found in the North-West and Phrygian (e.g. OIr *ad-* [preverb], Lat *ad* 'to, at', NE *at*, Phryg *ad-* 'to'); **ksun* 'with' (Lith *sù* 'with', Rus *s*(*o*) 'with', Grk *ksún* ~ *sun* 'with'); **pos* 'immediately adjacent; behind, following' (Lat *posterus*) which we have already seen in extended form in Proto-Indo-European; **ĝhō-* 'behind' (Lith *až*(*ù*) 'behind', Rus *za* 'by, to', Arm *z-* 'with regard to'); **h_1eĝhs* 'out (of)' (e.g. OIr *ess-* 'out', Lat *ex* 'out (of)', Latv *iz* 'out', OCS *iz* 'out', Grk *eks* 'from, out of'). A Greek-Indo-Iranian isogloss is seen in **dl̥h_3ĝhmós* 'aslant' (e.g. Grk *dokhmós* 'slanting, oblique', Skt *jihmá-* 'athwart, oblique') and an 'easternism', i.e. Indo-Iranian-Tocharian isogloss, is **$h_a$en-u* 'up (onto), upwards, along' (e.g. Av *anu* 'after, corresponding to, towards', Skt *ánu* 'after, along, over, near', Toch B *oṃṣmeṃ* 'from above').

18.3 Direction

There are a handful of terms in Proto-Indo-European concerned with 'direction', which, as we will see, plays a significant role in Indo-European conceptualization of their world. The words are listed in Table 18.3.

Table 18.3. *Direction*

**deiḱ-*	'rule, canon, measure'	Grk *díkē*, Skt *diś-*
**déḱsinos*	'right'	Lat *dexter*, Grk *deksiós*, Skt *dákṣina-*
**h₃reĝtos*	'right'	Lat *rēctus*, NE *right*, Grk *orektós*
**laiwós*	'left'	Lat *laevus*, Grk *laiós*
**seuyós*	'left'	Skt *savyá-*
**hₐeust(e)ro-*	'east'	Lat *auster*, NE *eastern*

There is no word specifically for 'direction' that we can reconstruct although the concept would fit broadly into the meanings one might ascribe to **deiḱ-* which does mean 'direction' in Indic (e.g. Skt *diś-* ~ *diśā-*) but 'justice' in Grk *díkē*. An *o*-grade form gives meanings as varied as 'plot of land' (ON *teigr*) and 'direction' (e.g. OHG *zeiga* 'directions', Skt *deśá-* 'direction, region') and the base meaning of the word has been explained as 'norm' or 'fixed point' which might then develop into meaning 'direction', a 'fixed area' such as a plot of land, etc.

There are two words for 'right': **déḱsinos* and related formations that are found in nine groups (e.g. OIr *dess*, Lat *dexter*, OHG *zeso*, Lith *dẽšinas*, OCS *desnŭ*, Alb *djathtë*, Grk *deksiós*, Av *dašina-*, all 'right', Skt *dákṣina-* 'right, south') and **h₃reĝtos* which derives from **h₃reĝ-* 'stretch out' (e.g. OIr *recht* 'law, authority', Lat *rēctus* 'right', NE *right*, Grk *orektós* 'stretched out', Av *rašta-* 'right, straight'), the same root that underlies the word for 'king' (cf. Section 17.1). There are also two Proto-Indo-European words (at least) for 'left': **laiwós* (Lat *laevus*, OCS *lěvŭ*, Grk *laiós*, all 'left', Toch B *laiwo* 'lassitude') and **seuyós* (OCS *šujĭ*, Av *haoya-*, Skt *savyá-*), neither of which has any certain root connection.

Only one cardinal direction can be reconstructed. The word for 'east', **hₐeust(e)ro-*, (e.g. Lat *auster* 'south wind; south country', NE *eastern*, Latv *àustrums* 'east', OCS *ustrŭ* 'summer', Av *ušatara-* 'east') is a transparent derivative from **hₐeus-* 'dawn', i.e. the direction of the rising sun. However, the evidence is good that the corresponding cardinal direction, i.e. 'west', could also be denominated by reference to the sun, more particularly by reference to the evening (e.g. NE *west*) or the setting of the sun though no particular Proto-Indo-European word is reconstructable. A competing system of orientation in Proto-Indo-European was one that presumed the speaker was facing the rising sun. 'East' was then 'forward', 'west' was 'behind', etc. (cf. the discussions of **po-sekʷo-*, **ner*, and **déḱsinos* above). Nevertheless, while this system itself is reconstructable, the individual manifestations of the system are all creations of the individual stocks.

We can add a regional term from the West Central languages: **skaiwós* 'left' (Lat *scaevus*, Grk *skaiós*), a rhyme word of **laiwós*.

18.4 Placement (Verbs)

Among the more fundamental verbs in any language are those that indicate the positioning of an object and this is no less so with respect to Indo-European. The verbal expressions of putting, standing, lying, setting, etc. are indicated in Table 18.4.

The primary verb for putting something into place is **dheh₁-* which forms a reduplicated present (in Greek, Hittite, Indo-Iranian, and Tocharian), i.e. Grk *títhēmi* 'I set', Hit *tittiya-* 'establish', Av *dadāiti* 'puts, brings', Skt *dádhāti* 'puts, places, lays', Toch B *tattaṃ* 'will put', or new formations in other groups (e.g. Lat *facere*, NE *do*, Lith *dėti* 'lay', OCS *děti* 'lay', Arm *dnem* 'put, place', Hit *dāi* 'puts, places', *tēzzi* 'says', Toch AB *tās-* ~ *täs-* 'put, lay'). To put into a standing position we have **stel-* (e.g. NE *stall*, NHG *stellen* 'put, place', OPrus *stallit* 'stand', Alb *shtjell* 'fling, toss, hurl', Grk *stéllō* 'make ready; send', Skt *sthálam* 'eminence, tableland; dry land, earth'). To 'set in place' is indicated by **tāg-* with meanings as varied as 'get married' (Baltic, e.g. Lith *sutógti* 'get married;

Table 18.4. *Placement (verbs)*

**dheh₁-*	'put, place'	Lat *facere*, NE *do*, Grk *títhēmi*, Skt *dádhāti*
**stel-*	'put in place, (make) stand'	NE *stall*, Grk *stéllō*, Skt *sthálam*
**tăg-*	'set in place, arrange'	Grk *tāgós*
**yet-*	'put in the right place'	Skt *yátati*
**k̂ei-*	'lie'	Grk *keîmai*, Skt *śáye*
**legh-*	'lie'	Lat *lectus*, NE *lie*, Grk *lékhetai*
**h₁ēs-*	'sit'	Grk *êsthai*, Skt *āste*
**sed-*	'sit (down)'	Lat *sīdō*, NE *sit*, Grk *hízdō*, Skt *sī́dati*
**sed-*	'set'	NE *set*
**(s)teh₂-*	'stand (up)'	Lat *sistō*, Grk *hístēmi*, Skt *tíṣṭhati*
**stembh-*	'make stand, prop up'	Grk *astemphḗs*, Skt *stámbhate*
**k̂lei-*	'lean'	Lat *clīvus*, NE *lean*, Grk *klī́nō*, Skt *śráyate*
**reh₁-*	'put in order'	Lat *reor*?, Skt *rādhnóti*
**sem-*	'put in order/together'	Skt *samayati*
**ser-*	'line up'	Lat *serō*, Grk *eírō*, Skt *sarat-*
**reik-*	'scratch; line'	NE *row*, Grk *ereíkō*?, Skt *rekhā́* ~ *lekhā́*
**wórghs*	'chain, row, series'	Grk *órkhos*

ally oneself with') and the actions of a military 'commander' (Thessalian Grk *tāgós* 'military leader', Iranian, i.e. Parth *tgmdr* '± commander', Tocharian, e.g. Toch B *tāś* 'commander'). Very wide semantic variation attends the root **yet-* which might be taken to mean 'put in the right place' (e.g. NWels *addiad* 'longing', SC *jatiti se* 'flock together', Av *yataiti* ~ *yatayeiti* 'puts oneself in the right or natural place', Skt *yátati* 'puts oneself in the right or natural place', Toch AB *yät-* 'adorn', *yāt-* 'be capable of [intr.]; have power over; tame').

Other verbs place an object or find an object in a particular position. There are, for example, two verbs for 'lie'. The root **k̂ei-* (e.g. Grk *keîmai* 'lie', Hit *kittari* 'lies', Av *saēte* 'lies, rests', Skt *śáye* 'lies') is conjugated in the middle rather than the active voice and in poetic language the word is also used to indicate the position of the deceased (e.g. Homeric Grk *keîtai Pátroklos* '[here] lies Patroclus'). The other root **legh-* not only supplies NE *lie* but in derived forms also *law*, i.e. what is laid down, and *low*, i.e. lying down flat (cf. also MIr *laigid* 'lies', Lat *lectus* 'bed', OCS *lěžati* 'lie', Grk *lékhetai* 'lies', Hit *lāki* 'lays aslant', Toch B *lyäk-* 'lie'). There are two verbs for 'sit'. Greek, Anatolian, and Indo-Iranian attest ***h_1*ēs-* (e.g. Grk *êsthai* 'sit', Hit *ēsa* 'sits', *āszi* 'stays, remains, is left', Av *āste* 'sits', Skt *āste* 'sits') which appears to be an intensive of ***h_1*es-* 'be' (one might note that Spanish employs both the original verbs 'be' and 'sit' in its paradigm for 'be'). Nine groups attest **sed-* 'sit' (e.g. OIr *saidid* 'sits', Lat *sīdō* 'sit down', *sedeō* 'sit, be sitting', NE *sit*, Lith *sė̃du* 'sit down', OCS *sěsti* 'sit down', Grk *hízdō* 'sit', Arm *nstim* 'sit', Av *hiδaiti* 'sits', Skt *sī́dati* 'sits') and this also supplies a causative **sodye/o-* 'set'. The basic verb for 'stand' is seen in **(s)teh*$_2$*-* which indicates a reduplicated present (e.g. OIr *-sissedar* 'stands', Lat *sistō* 'stand up', Grk *hístēmi* 'stand', Av *hištaiti* 'stands', Skt *tíṣṭhati* 'stands'). Other formations exist, however, and yield Lat *stō* 'stand' and NE *stand*. The same root also underlies **stembh-* 'make stand' (e.g. Lith *stem̃bti* 'produce a stalk [of plants]', Grk *astemphḗs* 'imperturbable, firm', Av *stəmbana-* 'support', Skt *stámbhate* 'prop, support; hinder, restrain', Toch AB *stäm-* 'stand'). The verb **k̂lei-* 'lean' (e.g. Lat *clīvus* 'slope', NE *lean*, Lith *šliẽti* 'lean against', Rus *sloj* 'layer, level', Grk *klī́nō* 'cause to lean', Av *sray-* 'lean', Skt *śráyate* 'clings to, leans on', Toch B *kläsk-* 'set [of sun]') has developed secondary meanings in Celtic and Italic for 'left' (e.g. OIr *clē*) and 'inauspicious' (e.g. Lat *clīvis*) along the same lines as we have already seen for 'bent', i.e. 'what is not straight'.

Placement in order is indicated by a series of words. PIE **reh*$_1$*-* 'put in order' maintains a strongly verbal connotation in the West, e.g. OIr *rād-* 'say', Goth *rōdjan* 'talk', OCS *raditi* 'take care of'; but it means 'prepare' in Indo-Iranian, e.g. Skt *rādhnóti*; there is a potential Latin cognate in *reor* 'count, calculate' that is not universally accepted. There is also a denominative **sem-* 'put in order/together' from **sem-* 'one, unity' with cognates in Germanic

(ON *semja* 'put together'), Indic (Skt *samayati* 'puts in order'), and Tocharian (Toch B *ṣäṃs-* 'count'). The more specific meaning of 'line up' is found in **ser-* with OIr *sernaid* 'arranges', Lat *serō* 'line up, join, link', Lith *sėris* 'thread', Grk *eirō* 'line up', Hit *sarra-* 'break', and Skt *sarat-* 'thread' with more than a hint that this term derives from the world of textiles. An extended form of **rei-* 'scratch' gives us **reik-* 'scratch, line' with cognates in Celtic (NWels *rhwyg* 'break'), Germanic (e.g. NE *row*), Baltic (Lith *riekė̃* 'slice [of bread]'), possibly Grk *ereíkō* 'bend, bruise', and Skt *rekhā́* ~ *lekhā́* 'line'. There is also a *wórghs* 'chain, row, series' based on Alb *varg* 'chain, row, string, strand', Grk *órkhos* 'row of vines', and Toch B *warke* 'chain, garland'.

There are two North-West isoglosses: possibly **dheig^{w}-* 'stick, set up' (if one can live with comparing Lat *fīgō* 'fasten' and if one accepts the possible Germanic cognates, NE *dike*; cf. also Lith *díegiu* 'prick; plant, sow'); and **knei-g^{w}h-* 'lean' (Lat *cōnīveō* 'blink' which is borrowed as NE *connive*; cf. also Goth *hneiwan* 'bow').

18.5 Shape

The words describing shapes or forms are indicated in Table 18.5.

Several words are associated with circularity. We have already seen (Section 17.4) **serk-* which is associated with 'restitution' in the sense of 'completing a circle'. There is also **h$_3$érbhis* 'circle, disc' in both Latin and Tocharian (e.g. Lat *orbis* 'ring, circle, cycle; disc, world, orb', Toch B *yerpe* 'disc, orb'). A meaning something like 'crooked' may be suggested for **(s)keng-* that means 'limp' in a number of language groups (e.g. OIr *scingim* 'spring', ON *skakkr* 'skewed, distorted', OHG *hinken* 'go lame', Grk *skázō* 'limp, go lame', Skt *khañjati* 'limps'). The concept 'broad' is reconstructed as **pl̥th$_2$ús* (e.g. Lith *platùs* 'broad', Grk *platús* 'broad', Av *pərəθu-* 'broad, wide', Skt *pr̥thú-* 'broad, wide') which is derived from **pleth$_2$-* 'spread'. Related is **pelh$_a$k-* 'spread out flat' (e.g. OE *flōh* 'flagstone', Lith *plãkanas* 'flat', Grk *pláks* 'flat surface') whose Latin (*placeō* 'please, be acceptable to', *plācō* 'soothe, calm') and Tocharian (Toch AB *plāk-* 'be in agreement') attestations tend to mean 'please, be agreeable', i.e. 'be level, even' (see Section 20.6). What might be otherwise a Graeco-Aryan isogloss, i.e. **wérh$_x$us* 'broad, wide' (e.g. Grk *eurús* 'broad, wide', Av *vouru-* 'broad, wide', Skt *urú-* 'broad, wide'), may be extended by Toch B *wartse* 'wide' and indicate a word of PIE date.

'Narrow' is indicated by **h$_a$enĝhus* (e.g. OIr *cum-ung* 'narrow, restricted', Lat *angi-portus* 'narrow street, cul de sac', OE *enge* 'narrow', Lith *añkštas* 'narrow', MPers *hnzwg-* 'narrow', Skt *aṃhú-* 'narrow').

Table 18.5. *Shape*

*serk-	'make a circle, complete'	Lat _sarciō_, Grk _hérkos_
_*h$_3$érbhis_	'circle, orb'	Lat _orbis_
*(s)keng-	'crooked'	Grk _skázō_, Skt _kháñjati_
_*pl̥th$_2$ús_	'broad, wide'	Grk _platús_, Skt _pr̥thú-_
*pelh$_a$k-	'spread out flat'	Lat _placeō_, Grk _pláks_
*wérh$_x$us	'broad, wide'	Grk _eurús_, Skt _urú-_
_*h$_a$enĝhu-_	'narrow'	Lat _angi-portus_, Skt _aṃhú-_
_*h$_a$érdhis_	'point'	Grk _árdis_, Skt _ali-_
*bhr̥stís	'point'	Lat _fastīgō_, NE _bristle_, Skt _bhr̥ṣṭí-_
_*h$_a$eḱ-_	'sharp, pointed'	Lat _ācer_, Grk _akḗ_, Skt _áśri-_
*ḱent-	'sharp'	Grk _kentéō_
*men-	'project'	Lat _mentum_
*dheb-	'thick, packed'	NE _dapper_
*tegus	'thick, fat'	NE _thick_
*ténus	'thin, long'	Lat _tennuis_, NE _thin_, Grk _tanaós_, Skt _tanú-_
*kr̥ḱós	'thin'	Skt _karś-_
*makros	'thin, long'	Lat _macer_, Grk _makrós_
*duh$_a$ros ~ dweh$_a$ros	'long (of time, space)'	Lat _dūrāre_, Grk _dērós_, Skt _dūrá-_
_*dl̥h$_1$ghós_	'long'	Lat _in-dulgeō_, Grk _dolikhós_, Skt _dīrghá-_
*dlonghos	'long'	Lat _longus_, NE _long_

A 'point' or 'pointed' shape is indicated by several words. Both _*h$_a$érdhis_ (e.g. OIr _aird_ 'point; direction', ON _erta_ 'to goad', Grk _árdis_ 'arrowhead', Skt _ali-_ 'bee') and _*bhr̥stís_ (e.g. OIr _barr_ 'point, tip', Lat _fastīgō_ 'make pointed, bring to a point', NE _bristle_, Rus _boršč_ 'hogweed', Skt _bhr̥ṣṭí-_ 'point') mean a 'point' while 'sharp' or 'pointed' is attested by _*h$_a$eḱ-_ (e.g. NWels _hogi_ 'to sharpen', Lat _ācer_ 'sharp; pungent, sour', _acus_ 'needle', Lith _aš(t)rùs_ 'sharp', OCS _ostrŭs_ 'sharp', Alb _athët_ 'sour', Grk _akḗ_ 'point', Arm _aseln_ 'needle', NPers _ās_ 'grinding stone', Skt _áśri-_ '[sharp] edge') and _*ḱent-_ (e.g. Goth _handugs_ 'wise', Latv _sīts_ 'hunting spear', Grk _kentéō_ 'prick'). A verbal root _*men-_ 'project' is suggested by several cognates for jutting parts of the face or projections, e.g. NWels _mant_ 'mouth, lip', Lat _mentum_ 'chin', _prō-mineō_ 'project', Hit _mēni-_ 'face, cheek', Av _fra-manyente_ 'gain prominence'.

Both words for 'thick' are placed in the category of Proto-Indo-European because of Anatolian cognates (otherwise they are confined to the North-West). The root _*dheb-_ has meanings such as 'thick' and 'strong' (e.g. OHG _tapfar_ 'weighty, strong', OPrus _debīkan_ 'large', Rus _debëlyj_ 'strong') and it is the latter which supplies the underlying semantics to the Hittite cognate *tabarna-* 'ruler' (cf. Luvian *tapar-*'rule'). A Middle Dutch cognate supplies NE with *dapper*. The other root, **tegus*, is otherwise confined to Celtic (e.g. OIr *tiug* 'thick') and Germanic (e.g. NE *thick*) but Hit *tagu-* 'fat, swollen' is a plausible candidate as well. There are three words for 'thin'. The verbal root **ten-* 'extend, stretch' provides the basis for **tn̥nus* 'thin' (e.g. OIr *tanae* 'thin', Lat *tenuis* 'thin, fine', NE *thin*, Lith *tęvas* ' thin, slim', OCS *tĭnŭkŭ* 'slender, thin', Grk *tanaós* 'long, elongated', MPers *tanuk* 'thin, weak', Skt *tanú-* 'thin, slender, small'), in this case, 'that which is stretched'. The meaning 'thin' found in **kr̥ḱós* would appear to come originally from a verb 'be thin, emaciated' and may mean anything from a 'shrivelled tree' (Czech *krs*) to 'lean cows' (Indo-Iranian, e.g. Av *kərəsa-gu-*, Skt *kr̥śa-gu-* 'having lean cows'); one should compare also ON *horr* 'thinness', Czech *krsati* 'lose weight, wane', Lith *káršti* 'be aged or decrepit', Skt *karś-* 'grow/be thin or lean'. A third word for 'thin', **makrós* 'thin, long' (e.g. Lat *macer* 'lean, meagre, thin' [which via French is borrowed into English as *meagre*], ON *magr* 'thin', Grk *makrós* 'long, big, high; deep, long-lasting') is found in this form only in the Centre and West of the Indo-European world, but related are Hit *maklant-* 'thin' and Av *mas-* 'long' in the East.

There are several words to express 'length'. A PIE **duh$_a$ros* ~ *dweh$_a$ros* which could express both 'a long time' and physical length is attested in Lat *dūrāre* 'to last', Grk *dērós* 'long', Arm *erkar* 'long', Av *dūire* 'far', and Skt *dūrá-* 'far', and with a different suffix we have Hit *tūwa-* 'far, distant'. We also have **dl̥h$_1$ghós* 'long' found in Lat *in-dulgeō* 'long-suffering', Goth *tulgus* 'firm', Lith *ìlgas*, OCS *dlŭgŭ*, Alb *gjatë*, Grk *dolikhós*, Hit *daluki-*, Skt *dīrghá-*, all 'long', and **dlonghos* 'long' seen in Lat *longus*, NE *long*, and MPers *derang*, all 'long'.

There are some regionally attested words. From the North-West comes **pandos* 'curved' (Lat *pandus* 'curved, bent', ON *fattr* 'bent back') and **g^{w}ret-sos* 'thick' (e.g. MIr *bres* 'large, thick', Lat *grossus* 'thick'); **bhar-* 'projection' which appears to underlie several derived forms such as **bharko-* (MIr *barc* 'spear shaft', SC *br̂k* 'point') and the word for 'barley' (**bhárs-* > OIr *bairgen* 'bread', Lat *fār* 'spelt, grain', NE *barley*) and words for 'beard' (Section 10.1); and **seh$_1$ros* 'long' (OIr *sīr* 'long lasting', Lat *sērus* 'late', OE *sīd* 'long'. From the West Central region are: **(s)kel-* 'crooked' (e.g. OE *scēolh* 'crooked', OPrus *culczi* 'thigh', Bulg *kúlka* 'thigh', Alb *çalë* 'lame', Grk *skélos* 'thigh'); **(s)kamb-* 'curve' (e.g. OIr *camm* 'curve', Grk *skambós* 'curve'); **kan-t(h)o-* 'corner, a bending' (e.g. NWels *cant* 'tyre' [Lat *canthus* or *cantus* 'wheel rim' comes from Gaul], Rus *kut* 'angle', Grk *kanthós* 'corner of the eye'); possibly a Germanic-Greek isogloss **sten-* 'narrow' (e.g. ON *stinnr* 'stiff, hard', Grk *stenós* 'narrow') but the semantic difference is great; **skidrós* 'thin' (OHG *sceter* 'thin', Latv *šķidrs* 'thin', dialectal Grk *skidarós* 'thin, slender').

18.6 Time

The reconstructed vocabulary relating to time is listed in Table 18.6.

There is one word in Proto-Indo-European that can be reconstructed to indicate (some) 'period of time', i.e. *prest-; it means a 'period of time' in Germanic (e.g. ON *frest* 'period of time, interval', OHG *frist* 'period of time, interval') and a more general 'time, occasion; season' in Tocharian (e.g. Toch A *praṣt*). The word for 'now', *nu-, is a good example of one of those small words that is phonetically stable and, with either a short or long vowel, it is attested as *nu* in no less than nine Indo-European groups (e.g. Lat *num*, NE *now*, Lith *nù*, OCS *nŭ*, Grk *nŭ(n)*, Hit *nu*, Av *nū*, Skt *nú*, Toch B *no*, all 'now'); it is related in some way to the adjective *néwos 'new' (see below). The word 'soon' was indicated by *mok̂s (e.g. OIr *mō* 'soon', Lat *mox* 'soon', Av *mošu* 'as soon as', Skt *makṣú* 'soon').

Table 18.6. *Time*

*prest-	'(period of) time'	
*nu-	'now'	Lat *num*, NE *now*, Grk *nū̆(n)*, Skt *nú*
*mok̂s	'soon'	Lat *mox*, Skt *makṣú*
*h$_a$eyer-	'early'	Grk *ēérios*
*prō-	'early, morning'	Grk *prōí*, Skt *prātár*
*h$_a$éusōs	'dawn'	Lat *aurōra*, NE *Easter*, Grk *héōs*, Skt *uṣā́-*
*h$_a$(e)us-sk̂eti	'it lights up, dawns'	Skt *ucchàti*
*h$_a$éĝhr̥	'day'	NE *day*?, Skt *áhar-*
*deino-	'day'	Lat *nundinae*, Skt *dínam*
*dye(u)-	'day'	Lat *diēs*, Grk *éndīos*, Skt *divasá-*
*(dh)ĝhyes	'yesterday'	Lat *herī*, NE *yester*, Grk *khthés*, Skt *hyá-*
*nek^{w}t-	'night'	Lat *nox*, NE *night*, Grk *núks*, Skt *nákt-*
*n̥k^{w}tus	'end of the night'	Grk *aktís*, Skt *aktú-*
*k^{w}sep-	'night'	Grk *pséphas*, Skt *kṣáp-*
*wésr̥	'spring'	Lat *vēr*, Grk *éar*, Skt *vasantá-*
*sem-	'summer'	NE *summer*, Skt *sámā*
*h$_1$es-en-	'autumn'	Grk *op-ōrē*
*ĝheim-	'winter, snow'	Lat *hiems*, Grk *kheîma*, Skt *héman*
*wet-	'year'	Lat *vetus*, NE *wether*, Grk *étos*, Skt *vatsá-*
*(h$_1$)yēro/eh$_a$-	'year, new season'	Lat *hōrnus*, NE *year*, Grk *hôros*
*perut-	'last year'	Grk *pérusi*, Skt *parút*
*h$_x$ōk̂-us	'fast'	Lat *ōcior*, Grk *ōkús*, Skt *āśú-*
*h$_a$eĝilos	'fast'	Lat *agilis*, Skt *ajirá-*
*néwos	'new'	Lat *novus*, NE *new*, Grk *néos*, Skt *náv(y)a-*
*sénos	'old'	Lat *senex*, Grk *hénos*, Skt *sána-*

If we begin concretely with the beginning of the day, we can start with those expressions for 'early', **h_aeyer-* and **prō-*. The first means 'early' in Germanic (e.g. OHG *ēr*), 'morning meal' in Grk *ắriston*, cf. also *ēérios* 'of the morning, in the morning' and 'day' in Av *ayarə*. The second shows a similar variation in meanings from 'early' to 'morning' (e.g. OHG *fruo* 'early', Grk *prōí* 'early, in the morning', Skt *prātár* 'early') and appears to have been a lengthened grade of a form ultimately based on **per-* 'forward, through'. The word 'dawn' and its derived verbal form are **h_aéusōs* (cf. above and e.g. OIr *fāir* 'sunrise', Lat *aurōra* 'dawn', OE *ēastre* 'goddess of springtime' [> NE *Easter*], Lith *aušrà* 'dawn', OCS *ustra* 'morning', Grk *héōs* 'dawn', Av *ušā-* 'dawn', Skt *uṣā́-* 'dawn') and **h_a(e)us-sk̂eti* (e.g. Lith *aũšta* 'it dawns', Av *usaiti* 'it dawns', Skt *uccháti* 'it dawns'), formed from the verbal root **h_aewes-* 'shine' (Section 18.3) which also underlies the word for 'gold' (see Section 15.2). As we have seen above, this word also provided the basis for 'east' in many Indo-European traditions (e.g. NE *east*) and in others it was the dawn which provided the *orientation* (cf. Lat *oriēns* 'east') to the cardinal directions; in both Celtic and Sanskrit the east is the 'forward direction' and the west 'the behind direction' (though in Iranian it is the south and north which are 'forward' and 'behind' which probably tells us something interesting about the history of Proto-Iranian or Proto-Iranians if we only knew what). The 'dawn' was also deified as a goddess in Proto-Indo-European culture (see Section 23.1).

There are three words reconstructable for 'day'. The first of these, **h_aéĝhr̥*, is problematic in that it is supported only by Germanic (e.g. NE *day*) and Indo-Iranian (e.g. Av *azan-* 'day', Skt *áhar-* 'day') and all the Germanic forms show the result of an initial **d-* which has been variously explained (away) as having crossed with the Proto-Germanic **dāʒwaz* 'warm time of the year' ([< **dhōg^who-* 'burning'] or from the false division of an expression such as **tod h_aéĝhr̥* 'that day' into **to(d) dh_aéĝhr̥*. Neither explanation has inspired much confidence. The other two words, **deino-* ~ **dino-* (e.g. with the full-grade: Goth *sinteins* 'daily', Lith *dienà* 'day'; and with the zero-grade: OIr *trēdenus* 'three-day period', Lat *nundinae* 'the ninth [market] day', OCS *dĭnĭ* 'day', Skt *dínam* 'day') and **dye(u)-* (e.g. OIr *dīa* 'day', Lat *diēs* 'day', Grk *éndīos* 'at mid-day', Arm *tiw* 'day', Hit *sīwatt-* 'day', Skt *divasá-* 'day'), both derive from **dei-* 'shine'. The latter **dyeu-* has also furnished derivatives meaning 'sky' (see Section 8.4), 'heaven', 'god' (see Section 23.1). The word for 'yesterday', reconstructed from seven groups, was **(dh)ĝhyes* (e.g. OIr *indē* 'yesterday', Lat *herī* 'yesterday', NE *yester-*, Alb *dje* 'yesterday', Grk *khthés* 'yesterday', Av *zyō* 'yesterday', Skt *hyá-* 'yesterday'). So far as we can tell, for the Proto-Indo-Europeans there was no 'tomorrow'.

For 'night' we have the root **nek^wt-* which is found in ten groups and clearly means 'night' in all of them (e.g. OIr *innocht* 'at night', Lat *nox* 'night',

NE *night*, Lith *naktìs* 'night', OCS *noštĭ* 'night', Alb *natë* 'night', Grk *núks* 'night', Hit *nekuz* 'at night', Skt *nákt-* 'night', Toch A *nokte* 'at night'). Perhaps more interesting is *$\text{\textit{n̥k}}^{w}$*tus*, apparently a zero-grade of the former root, which means 'early morning' (Germanic, e.g. OE *ūhte*), 'ray of sunlight' (Grk *aktís*) and 'night' (Skt *aktú-*). Indic also retains a meaning 'end of night' and given the derivation and the semantics of the cognate forms in the daughter languages, this would appear to be the earliest meaning. Emphasis on 'darkness' is found in **k*^{w}*sep-* where both Greek and Avestan mean 'darkness' (Grk *pséphas*, Av *xšap-*) while Hittite and Indic indicate the 'night' (Hit *ispant-*, Skt *kṣáp-*).

The names of four seasons are reconstructable to Proto-Indo-European. The word for 'spring', **wésr̥*, is a heteroclitic, e.g. Lith *vãsara* but Skt *vasantá-* (cf. also OIr *errach*, Lat *vēr*, OCS *vesna*, Grk *éar*, Arm *garun*, all 'spring', Av *vaŋri* 'in spring'). We may be able to add Tocharian to the list of languages attesting **wes-* 'spring' if, as has been suggested, the Tocharian word for 'grain' (e.g. Toch B *ysāre*) is from a derivative, **wes-eh*$_a$*-ro-*, originally 'spring wheat'. 'Summer' was **sem-* (e.g. OIr *sam* 'summer', NE *summer*, Arm *am* 'year', Av *ham-* 'summer', Skt *sámā* 'season, year', Toch A *ṣme* 'summer'). A word for 'autumn' or 'harvest time', **h*$_1$*es-en-*, is attested in five groups, including Anatolian (e.g. Goth *asans* 'summer, harvest time', OPrus *assanis* 'harvest', OCS *jesenĭ* 'autumn', Grk *op-ṓrē* 'end of summer harvest time' (< **op-osar-ā*), Hit *zena*(*nt*)- 'autumn') but it is the only season for which we do not find a reflex in Indo-Iranian. No such problem with **ĝheim-* 'winter' which is certainly attested in ten groups and is probably to be seen in the eleventh, Germanic, as well (e.g. Gaul *Giamonios* [name of a winter month], Lat *hiems* 'winter', Lith *žiemà* 'winter', OCS *zima* 'winter', Alb *dimër* 'winter', Grk *kheîma* 'winter', Arm *jiwn* 'snow', Hit *gimmant-* 'winter', Av *zyām-* 'winter', Skt *héman* 'in winter'; in Germanic we have ON *gymbr* 'ewe lamb one year old' [whence by borrowing dialectal English *gimmer* 'ewe between the first and second shearing']). The word for the entire 'year' was **wet-* (e.g., Grk *étos* 'year', Hit *witt-* 'year', Skt *vatsá-* 'year') which often takes on the derived meaning of 'yearling', e.g. Celtic 'sow' (OIr *feis*), Germanic (e.g. NE *wether*), and with the addition of *-*u*(*so*)- we have the meaning 'old' (e.g. Lat *vetus*, Lith *vẽtušas*, OCS *vetŭchŭ*, Sogdian *wtšnyy*, all 'old'), presumably from the notion of 'having [many] years'. The zero-grade of **wet-* can be found in the compound **perut-*, i.e. **per* + **wet-* 'last year' (e.g. ON *fjọrð* 'last year', Grk *pérusi* 'last year', Arm *heru* 'last year', Skt *parút* 'in past years'). Another word for 'year' was *(*h*$_1$)*yēro/eh*$_a$- (e.g. Lat *hōrnus* 'of this year', NE *year*, OCS *jara* 'spring', Grk *hôros* 'time, year', Luv *āra/i-* 'time', Av *yārə* 'year') which overlaps both the notion of 'time' in general and that of 'new season'.

Finally, we have several adjectives. The concept of velocity is seen in *h_x_ōḱus_ 'fast' (e.g. OIr _di-auc_ 'not-fast', Lat _ōcior_ 'faster', Grk _ōkús_ 'fast', Av _āsu-_ 'fast', Skt _āśú-_ 'fast') which is apparently derived from *h_x_eḱ-_ 'sharp'. The Latin-Indic isogloss *h_a_eĝilos_ 'fast' (Lat _agilis_ 'quick', Skt _ajirá-_ 'quick, agile') may be independent formations built on the verbal root *h_a_eĝ-_ 'drive'. The word for 'new', *_néwos_, is found across the Indo-European languages (e.g. Lat _novus_, OCS _novŭ_, Grk _néos_, Hit _nēwas_, Av _nava-_, Skt _náva-_, Toch B _ñuwe_, all 'new'); an extended form, *_néwyos_, gives us e.g. NE _new_, Lith _naũjas_, Ionic Grk _neîos_, Skt _návya-_, all 'new'. Both *_néwos_ and *_néwyos_ are related to *_nu_ 'now' (cf. above). Also widespread are the descendants of *_sénos_ 'old' (e.g. OIr _sen_ 'old', Lat _senex_ 'old', Goth _sinista_ 'eldest', Lith _sẽnas_ 'old', Grk _hénos_ 'last year's', Arm _hin_ 'old', Av _hana-_ 'old', Skt _sána-_ 'old').

Regional words include (from the North-West): *_yam/yau_ 'now, already' (e.g. Lat _iam_ 'now, already', OHG _ju_ 'already', Lith _jaũ_ 'already', OCS _ju_ 'already'); *h_a_etnos_ 'year' (e.g. Lat _annus_ 'year', Goth _aþna-_ 'year'), from the verbal root *h_a_et-_ 'go' (i.e. 'what's gone'); *h_2_ē_h_x_trōó-_ 'quick, fast' (e.g. OHG _ātar_ 'quick', Lith _otrùs_ 'lively'; from *h_2_e_h_x- 'burn'); *_ḱeigh-_ 'fast' (e.g. OE _hīgian_ 'hasten' [> obsolete or archaic NE _hie_], Rus _sigátĭ_ 'spring', with a possible but uncertain Indic cognate, i.e. Skt _sīghrá-_ 'quick, fast'); and a problematic *_bhris-_ ~ *_bhers-_ 'fast' (e.g. NWels _brys_ 'haste, speed', Lat _festinō_ 'hurry oneself', Lith _burzdùs_ 'fast', Rus _borzój_ 'fast'). From the West Central area we have *_kēs(ḱ)eh_$_a$- 'time' (a Slavic-Albanian isogloss), e.g. OCS _časŭ_ 'time', Alb _kohë_ 'time, period, epoch; weather'; *_wésperos_ ~ *_wékeros_ 'evening' (e.g. Lat _vesper_, Lith _vãkaras_, OCS _večerŭ_, Grk _hésperos_, Arm _gišer_, all 'evening') whose root lies at the base of the Germanic words for 'west' (NE _west_), i.e. the direction of sunset (cf. the discussion of the cardinal directions above); *h_1_en-_ 'year' (e.g. Grk _énos_ 'year', and derivatives in Lith _pér-n-ai_ 'in the last year', dialectal Rus _lo-ni_ 'of last year'). A Greek-Armenian isogloss for 'day' is *h_2_e_h_x_-mer-_, a derivative of *h_2_e_h_x- 'burn' (i.e. Grk _ēmérā_, Arm _awr_), and both Greek and Indic extend the meaning of the colour term 'white' to also include 'fast', e.g. 'flashing' in *h_a_r̥ĝ-rós_ which is used to describe fast dogs and horses (Grk _agrós_, Skt _r̥jrá-_).

18.7 Proto-Indo-European Space and Time

It has been commonly accepted that the concepts of space and ownership would have been altered by the shift from hunting-gathering to agriculture. Rigid definitions of territorial ownership were likely to be weak among seasonally mobile populations except for those who attempted to defend fixed year-round resources such as fishing rights to particular tracts of waterway or coast. On the other hand, the transition to sedentary society would have seen not only the emergence of the concept of material wealth but also territorial possession. Moreover, the production of stable upstanding structures, it is argued, would have resulted in the creation of abstract geometric terms that would not have existed in what anthropologists might term a previously 'uncarpentered' world.

When we review the spatial terminology of Proto-Indo-European we find evidence enough for the concept of territorial boundaries or regional entities seen, for example, in words such as *$h_4$erh$_2$o-*, **morĝ-*, and **térmn̥*, all 'border'. The last suggests the use of physical markers such as posts to define a precinct or territory while **morĝ-* displays a remarkably stable meaning of 'district, region' from one end of the Indo-European world to the other. With respect to the concept of 'place' the use of derivatives of **steh$_2$-* 'stand' correlates well enough with the concept of the erection of structures.

The expression of position is accomplished through the use of adpreps, i.e. words that function as both an adverb and preposition. Although Indo-European could express position through its nominal case endings, clearly there was a need to employ individual words as well to indicate the precise nuances of location. Some of these words clearly reveal the specialized use of nominal case forms, e.g. **h$_2$ent-* 'face' > **h$_2$enti* 'in front'. The adpreps were often employed with verbs and fused with them to form single words in many IE groups, e.g. NE *understand, undertake, undercut, underline*; Early Irish seems to have delighted in compounding prepositions before verbs, e.g. *do-opir* 'takes away' <**dī+uss+ber-*, i.e. 'from-away-carry'.

Geometric shapes have been the subject of taxonomic research where H. W. Burris's study of seventy-two languages has revealed an evolution of geometric terms. The simplest, stage 1, possess no geometric terms; at stage 2 there are terms for circle or curve; at stage 3 the concept of the square or angularity is added to the circle; stage 4 adds the triangle and stage 5 also reveals a word for rectangle. It has been claimed that Proto-Indo-European belonged with the nine languages of stage 1 in that it lacked any terms for geometric shapes. Nevertheless, there are two potential candidates: **serk-* if we can presume that the original meaning was 'make a circle' and then its more common meaning 'make restitution' is merely a metaphorical extension of the geometric term, and **h$_3$érbhis* 'circle, orb' on the basis of a Latin-Tocharian isogloss. We should not be surprised if a language that possessed the terminology of wheeled vehicles (and had at least three words for 'wheel') also possessed a term for 'circle', and if the evolutionary scale has any validity, then Proto-Indo-European should probably be placed at stage 2 rather than stage 1.

The Proto-Indo-Europeans appear to have employed two systems of establishing and naming directions. One was based on a literal 'orientation', i.e. facing east so that there would be a series of equations: east = front, west = back, north = left (unpropitious, female), south = right (propitious, male). Residues of this can be found in various IE languages, e.g. **dék̂sinos* yields OIr *dess*, Av *dašina-*, and Skt *dákṣina-*, all both 'right' and 'south'; OIr *clē* 'left' underlies OIr *fochla* 'north' while the words for north in Germanic (e.g. NE *north*) are cognate with Umbrian *nertru* 'left'. The polar opposition is also seen to embody a sexual opposition and a contrast between the propitious right/south and the unpropitious left/south. For example, OIr *clē* not only means 'left' but also 'inauspicious, bad' while in Latin loanwords English still preserves the contrast between *dexter* 'right' (*dexterous*) and *sinister* 'left, wrong, perverse'

The second system is keyed to sunrise so that east or south, for example, is associated with the dawn, e.g. PIE **$h_a$éusōs* 'dawn' underlies Lat *auster* 'south wind' and OE *ēaste* 'east'.

Time reckoning in Proto-Indo-European involves a number of areas that might involve folk taxonomies of which we might want to know far more. As any traveller who has grasped a phrase book of useful expression knows, different cultures have varying concepts as to what parts of the day are most appropriate for a 'good afternoon' or 'good evening' (consider the contextual meaning of 'good night' which may suggest either spending a 'good night' out or the finality of going to bed). The multiplicity of terms for the parts of the day suggest that PIE may have had more diverse nuances than our reconstructed meanings indicate. For example, did the day begin with **$h_a$éusōs* 'dawn' when the sun began to shine (and hence *deino-* and **dye(u)-*, both 'day' and derived from **dei-* 'shine') or at **n̥k*^{w}*tus* 'night, end of night', the latter probably a zero-grade derivative of **nek*^{w}*t-* 'night' but with meanings attested such as OE *ūhte* 'early morning', and Grk *aktís* 'ray of sunlight'? What, if any, was the distinction between **nek*^{w}*t-* and **k*^{w}*sep-*, both 'night'?

The seasons of the year are also an area of folk taxonomy. It has been suggested, for example, that Old English (and other Germanic languages) shows evidence of a two-seasonal system (*sumer*, *winter*) recently crossed with a four-seasonal (*lencten* 'Lent', *hærfest* 'harvest') system, and a two-season system has also been attributed by some to the Proto-Indo-Europeans. This seems to be contradicted by the lexical evidence that strongly attests (at least) a **wésr̥* 'spring', **sem-* 'summer' and **ĝheim-* 'winter, snow'; if the set for **$h_1$es-en-* 'autumn' is secure with cognates in the North-West (Germanic, Baltic, Slavic), the Central region (Greek), and Anatolian, then it can hardly be denied to the Proto-Indo-Europeans. Moreover, the terms for spring, autumn, and winter are all heteroclitics which is generally an additional argument for antiquity.

Further Reading

The concept of borders in IE is treated in Della Volpe (1992); PIE adpreps are discussed in Friedrich (1987); direction is treated in Hamp (1974*d*), Markey (1982), Meid (1987), Parvulescu (1985), Van Leeuwen-Turnovcová (1990), and Winter (1988); the 'evolutionary' pattern of shapes is provided in Burris 1979, the folk taxonomy of the Indo-European seasons is covered in Anderson (2003); for aspects of time see Puhvel (1987*b*), Szemerényi (1959), and for size, see Winter (1980).

19

Number and Quantity

19.0 Numerical Systems

The numerical system of Indo-European is one of its more stable elements, but even here there has been considerable remodelling of words although the roots have often been retained. Some of the remodelling is due to the fact that numbers are often recited in series which enhances the chances of a preceding number affecting a later number in the sequence or the latter affecting an earlier one by anticipation, e.g. the expected outcome of the numeral 'nine' in Latin (under one hypothesis) should have been ***noven* but the ending was altered to *novem* on the analogy of the preceding 'seven', *septem*, and the following 'ten', *decem*. Another, more certain example is provided by Skt *aṣṭamá-* 'eighth' and possibly *navamá-* 'ninth' which owe their ordinal suffix *-má-* (rather than the expected *-vá-* and possibly *-ná-* respectively) to the combined influence of *saptamá-* 'seventh' and *daśamá-* 'tenth'. Also, since counting systems were evolutionary, i.e. began quite simple, often based on finger counting, linguists have often sought an underlying system of complexity through composition, i.e. joining previous numbers together to make larger ones, and hence there has been quite a lot of etymological speculation as to the underlying meaning or formation of many of the numerals. However, while it is almost certainly the case that the Proto-Indo-European system of numbers was built up over a long period of time, that period of building is likely to have been so long in the past that the constituent elements of the numbers are beyond etymological recovery. Since all known cultures which herd animals have fully formed counting systems (one might assume from sheer economic necessity in keeping track of sheep, goats, etc.) and since the archaeological evidence is strong that Proto-Indo-Europeans, whoever they were exactly, had a long familiarity with domestic animals, it is almost certain that the system of numbers we can reconstruct for Proto-Indo-European had a long history in pre-Proto-Indo-European.

19.1 Basic Numerals

The basic cardinal and ordinal numbers plus some additional forms are provided in Table 19.1. Here the great variation in reconstructed forms has been simplified and many of the alternatives suggested by different language groups

Table 19.1. *Basic numbers*

	Cardinal	
1	*h_1*oi-no-s*	Lat *ūnus*, NE *one*, Grk *oínē*
	**sem-s* 'united as one, one together'	Grk *heîs*
2	**dwé*h_3(*u*)	Lat *duo*, NE *two*, Grk *dúō*, Skt *dvā́*
3	**tréyes*	Lat *trēs*, NE *three*, Grk *treîs*, Skt *tráyas*
4	*k^w*etwóres*	Lat *quattuor*, NE *four*, Grk *téssares*, Skt *catvā́ras*
5	**pénk*^{w}*e*	Lat *quīnque*, NE *five*, Grk *pénte*, Skt *páñca*
6	**kswek̂s*	Lat *sex*, NE *six*, Grk *héks*, Skt *ṣáṣ*
7	**septḿ̥*	Lat *septem*, NE *seven*, Grk *heptá*, Skt *saptá*
8	*h_x*ok̂tṓ*(*u*)	Lat *octō*, NE *eight*, Grk *oktṓ*, Skt *aṣṭā́*
9	*h_1*newh*$_1$*m̥* (*h_1*néwh*$_1$*n̥*?)	Lat *novem*, NE *nine*, Grk *ennéa*, Skt *náva*
10	**dék̂m̥*(*t*)	Lat *decem*, NE *ten*, Grk *déka*, Skt *dáśa*
12	**dwō dek̂m̥*(*t*)	Lat *duodecim*, Grk *dṓdeka*, Skt *dvādaśá*
15	**penk*^{w}*e dek̂m̥*(*t*)	Lat *quīndecim*, Skt *páñcadaśa*
20	**wīkitih*$_1$	Lat *vīgintī*, Grk *eíkosi*, Skt *vim̥śatí*
30	**trī-k̂omt*(h_a)	Lat *trīgintā*, Grk *triā́konta*, Skt *trim̥śát*

(*Cont'd*)

Table 19.1. (*Cont'd*)

50	**penk*^{w}*ē-k̂omt*(h_a)	Lat *quīnquāgintā*, Grk *pentḗkonta*, Skt *pañcāśát*
60	**kswek̂s-k̂omt*(h_a)	Lat *sexāgintā*, Grk *heksḗkonta*
100	**k̂m̥tóm*	Lat *centum*, NE *hundred*, Grk *hekatón*, Skt *śatá-*
	Ordinals	
1	**per*(h_x) -	Lat *prīmus*, NE *first*, Grk *prôtos*, Skt *pū́rva-*
2	**dwi-yos* ~ **dwi-tos*	Skt *dvitī́ya-*
3	**triy-os*	
4	**k*^{w}*tur-yós* ~ **k*^{w}*etwor-to-*	Lat *quārtus*, NE *fourth*, Grk *tétartos*, Skt *turī́ya-*
5	**pn̥k*^{w}*-tós*	Lat *quīntus*, NE *fifth*, Grk *pémptos*, Skt *pakthá-*
6	**kswek̂s-os*	Lat *sextus*, NE *sixth*, Grk *héktos*, Skt *śaṣṭhá-*
7	**septm̥-mós*	Lat *septimus*, NE *seventh*, Grk *hébdomos*, Skt *saptamá-*
8	***h_x*ok̂to-wós*	Lat *octāvus*, NE *eighth*, Grk *ógdoos*, Skt *aṣṭamá-*
9	***h_1*newh*$_1$*m̥/n̥-mos*	Lat *nōnus*, NE *ninth*, Grk *énatos*, Skt *navamá-*
10	**dek̂m̥(t)-os*	Lat *decimus*, NE *tenth*, Grk *dékatos*, Skt *daśamá-*
	**dwoi-* 'two, group of two'	
	**dwi-* 'bi-'	Lat *bi*, NE *twi-*, Grk *di-*, Skt *dvíṣ-*
	**dwis* 'twice'	Lat *bis*, Grk *dís*, Skt *dvíṣ*
	**dwoyos* 'double(d), twofold'	Grk *doiós*, Skt *dvayá-*
	**dw(e)i-plos* 'double, twofold'	Lat *duplus*, Grk *diplós*
	**bhōu* 'both'	Lat *ambō*, NE *both*, Grk *ámphō*, Skt *ubháu*
	**tris* 'thrice'	Lat *ter*, Skt *tríṣ*

have been omitted. There follows a discussion of the various basic numbers, one by one, with attention paid to the etymological speculations that have been offered. And they are speculative indeed, in many cases more revealing of the ingenuity of etymologists than the actual history of Proto-Indo-European.

The basic numeral 'one' is ***h_1*oi-* followed by the suffix *-no-* in Celtic (e.g. OIr *oīn* 'only one, single'), Lat *ūnus* 'one', Germanic (e.g. NE *one*), Baltic (e.g. Lith *víenas* 'one'), Slavic (e.g. OCS *ino-* 'one-' [as a prefix], *jed-in-* 'one'), perhaps Alb _një_ 'one', Grk _oínē_ 'ace on a die', or _-wo-_ (Grk _oîos_ 'single, alone', Av _aēva-_ 'one'), or _-ko-_ (Skt _éka-_ 'one'). The root etymology is generally presumed to be the anaphoric pronoun, i.e. _*$h_1$ei-_, cf. NE _one_ in the sense 'One does what one's told'. Although there are a number of other theories, this etymology is one of the few thought up for any of the numbers that is at all likely to be correct. Because _*$h_1$oinos_ (etc.) is etymologically transparent it is probably a relatively recent addition to the number system. The variation in suffixes (_*-no-_, _-*wo-_, _*-ko-_) in the various stocks also suggests the form of this number was still somewhat plastic at the time that Proto-Indo-European unity was dissolving. Another way of expressing 'one' is _*sem-s_ (again with different suffixes and grades) which probably originally indicated 'one united together' (e.g. perhaps Alb _një_ 'one', certainly Grk _heîs_ [m.], _mía_ [f.], _hén_ [nt.] 'one', Arm _mi_ 'one', Toch B _ṣe_ [m.], _sana_ [f.] 'one'). The ordinal 'first' is derived in a variety of forms from the root _*per(h_x)-_ or _*pro-_, e.g. Lat _prīmus_ which is _*pri-is-_ + the superlative suffix _-mo-_, Alb _parë_ 'first', Av _paurva-_ 'prior', Skt _pū́rva-_ 'first', Toch B _parwe_ 'first', all from _*pr̥h_x-wo-_, OE _frum_ 'primal, original, first', Lith _pìrmas_ 'first', both from _*pr̥h_x-mo-_, NE _first_ from _*pr̥h_x-isto-_.

The number 'two' was _*dwoh_3(u)_ (neuter: _*dwoih_1_) which may have originally been _*du_ but was progressively extended by suffixes to indicate 'duality', i.e. a dual ending, and markers to indicate gender distinctions as it was declined (e.g. OIr _dāu_ [m.], _dī_ [f.], _dā_ [nt.], Lat _duo_ [m./nt.], _duae_ [f.], NE _two_, Lith _dù_ [m.], _dvì_ [f.], OCS _dŭva_ [m.], _dŭvě_ [f./nt.], Alb _dy_, Grk _dúō_, Arm _erku_, Av _dva_ [m.], _baē_ [f./nt.], Skt _dvā́_ [m.], _dvé_ [f./nt.], Toch A _wu_ [m.], _we_ [f.]) The ordinal shows both _*dwi-to-_ and _*dwi-t(i)yo-_ (e.g. Alb _dytë_, Av _daibitya-_ ~ _bitya-_ [< pre-Av _*dwitya-_], Skt _dvitī́ya-_ [cf. also _dvitā́_ 'doubly so'], Toch B _wate_). An even older form, _*dwiy-o-_, is probably reflected in Hit _duyanalli-_ '± second officer' (a particular functionary in the Hittite court). The same numerical root also supplies a series of other words associated with duality. _*dwoi-_ indicated a 'twosome' (cf. OIr _dīas_ 'couple', Hit _tān_ 'for the second time'), while _*dwi-_ was employed as a prefix 'bi-' (e.g. Lat _bi-_, NE _twi-_, Grk _di-_, Av _bi-_, Skt _dvi-_). The multiplicative 'twice' was indicated with _*dwis_ (e.g. OIr _fo di_, Lat _bis_, NE _twice_, Grk _dís_, Av _biš_) while both _*dwoyos_ (e.g. Grk _doiós_ 'doubled', Skt _dvayá-_ 'duplicity') and _*dw(e)i-plos_ (e.g. OIr _dīabul_, Lat _duplus_, Grk _diplós_) meant 'twofold'. The root etymology has often been taken as a demonstrative pronoun indicating 'that one further away' that developed into a cardinal number; alternatively, it has been suggested that the reverse process makes better sense. Neither suggestion seems at all likely. A different root, _*bhōu_, was employed, almost always with various intensifying prefixes, to indicate 'both' (e.g. Lat _ambō_ 'both', OE _bēgen_ 'both' [NE _both_ is an Old Norse loanword], Lith _abù_ 'both', OCS _oba_ 'both', Grk _ámphō_ 'both', Av _uba-_ 'both', Skt _ubháu_ 'both', Toch B _antapi_).

The number 'three', **tréyes* (neuter: *$*trih_a$*), is also marked by different forms for the different genders and was declined as an *i*-stem plural (e.g. OIr *trī*, Lat *trēs*, NE *three*, Lith *trỹs*, OCS *trije* [m.], *tri* [f./nt.], Alb *tre* [m.], *tri* [f.], Grk *treîs*, Arm *erek'*, Hit *tēri-*, Av *θrayō* [m./f.], *θri* [nt.], Skt *tráyas* [m./f.], *trī* [nt.], Toch B *trai* [m.], *tarya* [f.]). In some languages we have reflections of a very unusual feminine form, **t(r)is(o)res*, i.e. OIr *teōir*, Av *tišrō*, Skt *tisrás*. The underlying derivation of **tréyes* is generally sought in either **ter* 'further', i.e. the number beyond 'two', or from a **ter-* 'middle, top, protruding', i.e. the middle finger, assuming one counted on one's fingers in Proto-Indo-European. Again, the probability that either suggestion is correct is very low. The ordinal number is indicated by a variety of forms similar to **triy-o* (e.g. Arm *eri* 'third', Hit *teriyan* 'third', *tariyanalli-* '± third officer'), or **tri-to-* (e.g. Alb *tretë*, Grk *trítos*, Skt *tritá-*, Toch B *trite*), or finally **t(e)r(e)tiyo-* (e.g. NWels *tryddyd*, Lat *tertius*, NE *third*, Lith *trẽčias*, Rus *trétij*, Av *θritiya-*, Skt *tr̥tíya-*) which is presumably a conflation of sorts, in various ways, of the previous two while **tris* supplies the multiplicative (e.g. Lat *ter*, Grk *trís*, Av *θriš*, Skt *tríṣ*; despite its apparent phonetic similarity, NE *thrice* is of a different origin).

'Four' is indicated by *$*k^w etwóres$* (neuter: *$*k^w etwórh_a$*) and is found in all the major groups (e.g. OIr *cethair* [m.], Lat *quattuor*, NE *four*, Lith *keturì*, OCS *četyre* [m.], *četyri* [f./nt.], Alb *katër*, Grk *téssares* [m./f.], *téssara* [nt.], Arm *č'ork'*, Av *čaθwārō* [m.], Skt *catvā́ras* [m./f.], *catvā́ri* [nt.], Toch B *śtwer* [m.], *śtwāra* [f.]) except for Anatolian which employs **mei-wos* (Hit *meyu-*, Luv *māwa*). Some languages reflect the presence, as with 'three', of a morphologically very unusual feminine form, *$*k^w etes(o)res$*, i.e. OIr *cethēoir*, Av *čataŋrō*, Skt *cátasras*. In Germanic, the influence of the following *$*pénk^w e$* explains the aberrant initial **f-*, e.g. OE *fēower* (NE *four*), OHG *fior*, rather than the expected **hw-*. There has been a host of attempts to etymologize *$*k^w etwóres$*, with two of the most popular (among many) being some relationship to the concept of either little finger or span of four fingers (where *$*k^w et\text{-}wor$* would be a derivative of *$*k^w et\text{-}$* 'stretch' found otherwise only certainly in the Baltic languages, e.g. Lith *ket-*), or the word has been analysed as the enclitic *$*k^w e$* 'and' + **tur-* (derived from **tur-* 'three'), i.e. 'after three' = 'four' (though of course the attested forms of 'three' are unanimous in demanding a reconstruction **ter-* or *trei-*, not **tur-*). The Anatolian form has been derived from **mei-* 'be small' and hence reference either to the 'little finger' or to a subtractive basis, i.e. 'five minus one' (as one does with the Roman numeral IV); alternatively, the opposite meaning 'large', associated with *$*meh_1\text{-}$* 'large', has also been suggested, hence 'the large span'. And both of these have been combined into a single expression, alternatively, *$*meh_1u\text{-}$* *$*k^w etwor$* 'big span' or **meyu-* *$*k^w etwor$* 'little finger', with Anatolian preserving the first element and the rest of Proto-Indo-European the second. Neither (highly unlikely) suggestion explains the universal morphological plural of the attested forms for 'four', nor offers an explanation for the strange feminine form. The ordinal is *k^wetw(o)r-to-s (e.g. Lat *quārtus*, NE *fourth*, Lith *ketvir̃tas*, Rus *četvërtyj*, Alb *katërt*, Grk *tétartos*, Av *čaθru-*, Skt *caturthá-*, Toch B *śarte*). Though geographically restricted in its attestation, a zero-grade *k^wturyos (e.g. Hit *kutruwa(n)-* 'witness' [i.e. 'fourth party to a transaction' (after the two originals and the judge/arbiter/recorder)] from a pre-Hit *k^wtruyos, itself by metathesis from *k^wturyós, Av *tūirya-* 'fourth', Skt *turī́ya-* 'fourth'), is probably older. (One can at least imagine that the Hittite butchers' term, *kudur* 'leg of beef, sheep, etc.', might have originally meant 'quarter' [as in the English butchers' term] and reflect an even older Proto-Indo-European form, *k^wturóm 'fourth'.)

The numeral 'five', *pénk^{w}e (e.g. OIr *cōic*, Lat *quīnque*, NE *five*, Lith *penkì*, Grk *pénte*, Arm *hing*, Av *panča*, Skt *páñca*, Toch B *piś*), is, like all the other higher numbers to 'ten', uninflected for number or gender. There is also evidence of a derivative *pénk^{w}ti- (e.g. OCS *pętĭ* 'five', Alb *pesë* 'five', Skt *pánkti-* 'group of five'). Celtic and Italic show the regular assimilation of Proto-Indo-European *p...k^w to *k^w...k^w, hence Lat *quīnque* rather than the otherwise expected *pīnque, while the Germanic forms show an irregular assimilation of *p...k^w to *p...p, giving a Proto-Germanic *fimfi. NWels *pimp* looks as if it has undergone the assimilation we see in Germanic but actually it is a regular descendant of Proto-Celtic *k^wenk^{w}e, since in the branch of Celtic to which Welsh belongs all Proto-Celtic *k^w become *p*. Thus the apparent agreement of NWels *pimp* and Proto-Germanic *fimfi illustrates the possibility of a single result being the product of very different processes and histories. The ordinal was *pn̥k^{w}tós (e.g. Av *puxδa-*, Skt *pakthá-*). Most stocks show a presumably later, and independently created full-grade, form, *pénk^w-tos (e.g. Lat *quīntus*, NE *fifth*, Lith *peñktas*, OCS *pętŭ*, Alb *pestë*, Grk *pémptos*, Toch B *piṅkte*).

The number *penk^{w}e has plausibly been connected etymologically with *pn̥(k^w)stí- 'fist' (e.g. NE *fist*, Lith *kùmstė* [< *punkstė] 'fist', OCS *pęstĭ* 'fist'). Presumably the latter was originally then 'group of five [fingers]' or the like though it has been suggested that the derivation went the other way and that the basic word for 'hand' or 'fist' came to be the ordinary word for 'five' and was replaced in its originally primary meaning of 'hand' by other words. The Germanic words for 'finger', e.g. NE *finger*, have also been made part of the equation, assuming that they are to be derived from a Proto-Indo-European *penk^{w}rós 'one of five' or the like (one might compare Arm *hinger-ord* 'fifth'). However, the absence of any nominal inflection on the word for 'five' makes a nominal origin 'hand' for it most unlikely, though there is no bar to seeing 'fist' and 'finger' as nominal derivatives of the numeral 'five' (Section 11.3). *penk^{w}e has also been linked to Hit *panku-* 'all, totality', hence the numeral would have originally meant something like 'completing the count of all fingers of the hand'. The supposed semantic development is hardly compelling and, in any case, the Hittite word is more plausibly taken as representing **bhonĝhu-* 'thickness' (see Section 19.2).

The only external comparison for **penk^{w}e* that has any plausibility is the comparison with Proto-Uralic 'palm of the hand' (cf. Finnish *pivo* 'palm') but here again both the phonological and semantic equations are pretty loose and not very convincing.

The word for 'six' shows a multiplicity of reconstructions. Phonologically most complex, and probably the oldest, is **ksweks̑* which lies behind Av *xšvaš*. Other languages show some sort of simplification of the initial consonant cluster. From **kseks̑* we have Lith *šeši*, OCS *šestĭ*, dialectal Grk *ksέstriks krithḗ* 'six-rowed barley', and Skt *ṣáṣ*. From **(s)weks̑* we have OIr *sē*, NWels *chwech*, and possibly Grk *héks* (dialectal Grk *wéks*), Arm *vec'*, Toch B *ṣkas*. From **seks̑* we have Lat *sex*, NE *six*, Alb *gjashtë*, and possibly Toch B *ṣkas*. Finally, from **weks̑* we have possibly Grk *héks*, Arm *vec'*. We lack evidence from Anatolian as in Hittite 'six' is always represented symbolically rather than being written out. The ordinal shows similar phonological diversity combined with the morphological divergence between those forms expanded by **-o-* (only in Gaul *suexos*, and that has sometimes been taken as an engraver's mistake for **suextos*) and those expanded by **-to-* (e.g. OIr *seissed*, Lat *sextus*, NE *sixth*, OPrus *usts* ~ *uschts*, Lith *šẽštas*, Bulg *šésti*, Alb *gjashtë*, Grk *héktos*, Av *xštva-* (< *Proto-Iranian **xšušta-*?), Skt *ṣaṣṭhá-*, Toch B *ṣkaste*).

The most complex 'home-grown' etymological explanation would involve the reduction of a compound involving **ĝhés-r-* 'hand' + **h$_a$eug-* 'increase, grow' > **ĝhs-weks̑* > **ksweks̑*. which would have meant 'hand-overgrowing', i.e. having to shift your finger count to the second hand. However, such an explanation can be charitably called strained from both the phonological and morphological point of view. The complex, and otherwise unexampled, initial consonant cluster **ksw-* has suggested to several investigators that we may be looking at a word that was originally borrowed from some non-Indo-European source. Foreign parallels to the Proto-Indo-European forms have been noted since the time of Franz Bopp who compared the Proto-Indo-European form with Proto-Kartvelian (a language group of the Caucasus composed of Georgian and closely related languages) **ekšw-* 'six'; other comparisons are Hurrian (an extinct language of eastern Anatolia) *šeeže*, Akkadian *ši/eššum* (the form used to modify definite feminine nouns) 'six'. These are variously explained as borrowing into or from (in the Kartvelian case) Proto-Indo-European. However, with the exception of the Kartvelian forms, the proposed models for the Proto-Indo-European word are only vaguely similar phonetically and there is no good reason why a foreign *š-* or the like should generate a Proto-Indo-European **ksw-*. One might also note that the attested Akkadian form is far too late to have been the model for Proto-Indo-European borrowing, no matter where the Proto-Indo-Europeans may have been located, and the earlier Proto-Semitic form of 'six', **šidṯ(at)*, looks even less promising as a model for **ksweḱs*.

The word for 'seven', **septḿ̥*, is attested in almost all Indo-European groups and is firmly reconstructable to Proto-Indo-European (e.g. OIr *secht*, Lat *septem*, NE *seven*, Lith *septynì*, OCS *sedmĭ*, Alb *shtatë*, Grk *heptá*, Arm *ewt'n*, Av *hapta*, Skt *saptá*, Toch A *ṣpät*), as is its ordinal counterpart (e.g. OIr *sechtmad*, Lat *septimus*, NE *seventh*, Lith *sẽkmas* ~ [analogical] *septiñtas*, OCS *sedmŭ*, Alb *shtatë*, Grk *hébdomos*, Av *haptaθa-*, Skt *saptamá-* ~ [analogical] *saptátha-*, Toch A *ṣäptänt*). How it arrived in Proto-Indo-European has been a subject of long discussion. Generally, the fact that many other language families in the surrounding region possess a similar word for 'seven' has argued for borrowing. Generally, the source is taken to be from pre-Akkadian **sabá-tum* (the form used to modify masculine definite nouns) 'seven'. However, as was the case with 'six', the pre-Akkadian form would be too late to serve as a model for the Proto-Indo-European word and the Proto-Semitic **šab'(at)* looks considerably less helpful.

The reconstruction of the numeral 'eight', **h_xoḱtoh$_3$(u)*(e.g. OIr *ocht*, Lat *octō*, NE *eight*, Lith *aštuonì*, OCS *osmĭ*, Alb *tetë*, Grk *oktō*, Arm *ut'*, Lycian *ait-*, Av *ašta*, Skt *aṣṭā(u)*, Toch B *okt*), is, in form, the dual of the *o*-stem. The ordinals are formed regularly (e.g. OIr *ochtmad*, Lat *octāvus*, NE *eighth*, Lith *ãšmas* ~ *aštuñtas*, OCS *osmŭ*, Alb *tetë*, Grk *ógdo(w)os*, Av *aštəma-*, Skt *aṣṭamá-*, Toch B *oktante*). The dual morphology suggests that 'eight' consists of two **h_xoḱto-* which simple arithmetic would suggest meant 'four', yet we have already seen that the word for 'four' in Proto-Indo-European was not **h_xoḱto-*. A way around this problem has been to see the basic root here as **h_aeḱ-* 'sharp, pointed' and the semantic development to involve the fingers as the 'pointed' sticking-out parts of the hand. In this way the numeral 'eight' would be ultimately **h_aoḱtoh$_1$(u)* 'two sets of points (fingers) of a hand'. Though a **h_xoḱto-* 'foursome [of fingers]' is otherwise unattested in Indo-European, such a Proto-Indo-European word may lurk in the form of a borrowing into Proto-Kartvelian in the form of **otxo-* 'four' in that language. It has also been suggested that an *i*-stem version of **h_xoḱto-* might be attested in the Av *ašti-* 'four-fingers' breadth' though the Avestan word has also plausibly been taken as an Iranian semantic development of a Proto-Indo-Iranian word meaning 'reaching' seen otherwise in Skt *áṣṭi-* 'reaching'.

As with 'six', the reconstructed shape of 'nine' presents several problems which might be summed up in two questions: does the number begin with **h_1(e)n-* or just **n-* and does it end in **-m̥* or **-n̥*? The forms are, e.g., OIr *noí*,

Lat *novem*, NE *nine*, Lith *devynì*, OCS *devętĭ* (the Baltic and Slavic initial consonant influenced by that of 'ten'), Alb *nëndë*, Grk *ennéa* (with difficult *-nn-* instead of *-n-*), Arm *inn*, Av *nava*, Skt *náva*, Toch AB *ñu*. The ordinal forms are similar: OIr *nōmad*, Lat *nōnus*, NE *ninth*, Lith *deviñtas*, OCS *devętŭ*, Alb *nëndë*, Grk *énatos*, Av *naoma-*, Skt *navamá-*, Toch B *ñunte*. The evidence for *h_1(e)n- is limited to Greek and Armenian, but if the actual initial was *h_1n-, those would be the only two Indo-European branches to show any trace of the laryngeal anyway. Lat *nōnus* would be much simpler to explain if the Proto-Indo-European original ended in *-n̥, whereas OIr *nōmad*, Skt *navamá-* are harder, and Toch B *ñmuk* '90' almost impossible, to explain unless we start from *-m̥. The evidence of Baltic and Germanic would seem to favour *-n̥ except we know that all final *m*'s became *n* in the histories of those branches, so they really give no evidence one way or another.

Etymologically, the reconstructed form has been variously explained as derived from *néwos 'new' (see Section 18.6), hence the 'new number' (after 'eight'), or from *$h_1$énh_1u 'without'. The first explanation has only the phonological similarity of 'nine' and 'new' going for it. If the latter, it would be another example of a subtractive formation where the number 'nine' would then be explained as 'ten without (= less) one'. Such an explanation is strengthened by undoubted examples in Indo-European of 'eleven' being '[ten] with one left over'. Thus the most likely reconstruction for Proto-Indo-European 'nine' is *$h_1$néwh_1m̥ (an accusative to a consonant stem?), with *$h_1$néwh_1n̥ (an old locative to an *n*-stem?) also a strong contender.

Proto-Indo-European was a decimal-based system (other systems cannot be entirely excluded) whose indeclinable "cornerstone" form was *dék̂m̥ or *dék̂m̥t (e.g. OIr *deich*, Lat *decem*, NE *ten*, Lith *dešimtìs*, OCS *desętĭ*, Alb *dhjetë*, Grk *déka*, Arm *tasn*, Av *dasa*, Skt *dáśa*, Toch B *śak*). The form with a final *-t appears most clearly in the formation of the decades and of the word for 'hundred'. It is probably the original form from which the shorter variant was created by the loss of the final *-t in the otherwise very rare cluster *-m̥t. The oldest reconstructable formation of the ordinal numbers would appear to involve the addition of the inflectible suffix *-o- to the cardinal number (hence *triyós 'third', *kswek̂sos 'sixth', *septmós, *$h_x$ok̂towós 'eighth', *$h_1$néwh_1m̥mós 'ninth', and *d(e)k̂m̥tós 'tenth'). The loss of the final *-t, if such it was, in the word for 'ten' created the basis of a morphological reanalysis in *dek̂m̥tos 'tenth' from *dek̂m̥t-os to *dek̂m̥-tos or the creation of a new ordinal *dek̂m̥m-os. The new *-to- was extended as an ordinal-deriving ending even in Proto-Indo-European times (witness *pn̥k^wtós 'fifth') and continued its extension to other numbers in the individual stocks. In any case, both *dek̂m̥tos and *dek̂m̥mos are reflected in the cardinal forms found in the various branches (e.g. OIr *dechmad*, Lat *decimus*, NE *tenth*, Lith *dešim̃tas*,

OCS *desętĭ*, Alb *dhjetë*, Grk *dékatos*, Av *dasəma-*, Skt *daśamá-*, Toch B *śkante*). Among the numerous etymological speculations, three are particularly popular. Some analyse the word as **de-* 'two' + *k̂omt-* 'hand', i.e. the numeral 'ten' is the result of counting all the fingers on both hands. Among the more notable problems with this theory is that it is not all that clear why **dwéh*$_3$*(u)* 'two' should give **de*, and the 'hand' word which forms the second half of the putative compound is limited to several groups at best. Moreover, we do not find the expected dual form as in 'eight' if the first element really was 'two'. It has also been analysed as **dek̂-* 'right' + *k̂omt-* 'hand', i.e. presuming that one began with the left hand, the numeral 'ten' was what one completed with the right hand. Alternatively, the root has been interpreted as **dek̂-* 'reach', i.e. what has been reached, the end, the last number of the basic counting system. None of these proposals is at all persuasive.

The unit 'ten' is employed in forming the teens, e.g. **dwō dek̂m̥* 'twelve (two-ten)' (e.g. NWels *deuddeg*, Lat *duodecim*, Grk *dṓdeka*, Arm *erkotasan*, Av *dvadasa*, Skt *d(u)vādaśá*), **penk*^{w}*e dek̂m̥* 'fifteen (five-ten)' (e.g. Lat *quīndecim*, NE *fifteen*, Arm *hingetasan*, Av *pančadasa*, Skt *páñcadaśa*). For the decades, we find that the word for 'twenty', **wīk̂m̥tih*$_1$ (e.g. OIr *fiche*, Lat *vīginti*, Alb *njëzet* [*një-* is 'one'], Grk *eíkosi*, Arm *k'san*, Av *vīsaiti*, Skt *viṃśatí*, Toch B *ikäṃ*), is easily analysable as **dwī-* 'two' + **k̂m̥tih*$_1$ 'tens' while the other decades are formed on the full-grade, e.g. **trī-k̂omt(h*$_a$*)* 'thirty' (e.g. OIr *trīcho*, Lat *trīgintā*, Grk *triā́konta*, Arm *eresun*, Av *θrisa(n)t-*, Skt *triśát*, Toch B *täryāka*); **penk*^{w}*ē-k̂omt(h*$_a$*)* 'fifty' (e.g. OIr *coīca*, Lat *quīnquāgintā*, Grk *pentḗkonta*, Arm *yisun*, Av *pančāsatəm*, Skt *pañcāśát*, Toch B *piśāka*), **(k)s(w)ek̂s-k̂omt(h*$_a$*)* 'sixty' (e.g. OIr *sesca*, Lat *sexāgintā*, Grk *eksḗkonta* [both Latin and Greek with an analogical medial vowel], Arm *vat'sun*, Toch B *ṣkaska*). The length of the vowel in **wīk̂m̥tih*$_1$, **trī-k̂omt(h*$_a$*)*, etc., almost surely reflects the simplification of an earlier cluster **dk̂-* with concomitant lengthening of the preceding vowel.

The word for 'ten' is obviously related to the word for 'hundred', **k̂m̥tóm* (e.g. OIr *cēt*, Lat *centum*, NE *hundred*, Lith *šim̃tas*, OCS *sŭto*, Grk *hekatón*, Av *satəm*, Skt *śatám*, Toch B *kante*) and is generally explained as a shortened version of **dk̂m̥tóm*, itself a shortening of **dk̂m̥t dk̂m̥tóm* 'ten tens' or 'tenth ten'.

To sum up the etymological discussion, it would seem that two of the basic numbers, one of the words for 'one' (**h*$_1$*oinos* [etc.]) and the word for 'hundred', have excellent etymologies while two more, 'eight' and 'nine', have plausible ones. The rest remain mysterious.

Regional terms for numerals are few and both the reconstructed words for 'thousand' have limited distributions. The North-West yields **tuh*$_a$*s-k̂m̥tyós* (e.g. NE *thousand*, Lith *túkstantis*, OCS *tysęsti*) which is literally a 'swollen (or 'strong') hundred', while a Greek-Indo-Iranian isogloss is seen in **ĝhesl(iy)os* (e.g. Grk *khī́lioi* [pl.], Av *hazaŋra-*, Skt *sa-hásram*) where the initial element *ĝhes- is probably related to the word for 'hand' (see Section 11.3) and the number is possibly an expression of a handful or two handfuls of grain.

19.2 Measure and Quantity

In addition to the numerical system we can also reconstruct a vocabulary associated with the measurement of articles and expressions of quantification. Those assigned to Proto-Indo-European are listed in Table 19.2.

The verbal root *meh$_1$- (e.g. Alb *mat* 'measure', Av *mā-* 'measure', Skt *mímāti* 'measures') provides the basis for the noun *méh$_1$tis 'measure' (e.g. Lat *mētior*

Table 19.2. *Measure and quantity*

*méh$_1$tis	'measure'	Lat *mētior*, Grk *mē̂tis*, Skt *mā́ti-*
*med-	'measure, weigh'	Lat *meditor*, NE *mete*, Grk *médomai*
*wi-dhh$_1$-	'put asunder'	Lat *dīvidō*, Skt *vidhā́-*
*deh$_a$(i)-	'cut up; divide'	NE *tide*, Grk *daíomai*, Skt *dā́ti*
*bhag-	'divide, distribute'	Grk *phageîn*, Skt *bhájati*
*kaiwelos	'alone'	Lat *cae-lebs*, Skt *kévala-*
*sem-go-(lo)s	'single one'	Lat *singulī*
*sem-	'at one time, once'	Lat *semper*, *semplex*, Grk *haploûs*
*somos	'same'	NE *same*, Grk *homós*, Skt *samá-*
*sm̥mós	'some, any'	NE *some*, Grk *hamós*, Skt *samá-*
*sēmis	'half'	Lat *sēmi*, Grk *hēmi-*, Skt *sāmí-*
*h$_a$élyos	'other'	Lat *alius*, NE *else*, Grk *állos*
*pelh$_1$-	'fill'	Lat *pleō*, Grk *pímplēmi*, Skt *píparti*
*pl̥h$_1$nós	'full'	Lat *plēnus*, NE *full*, Skt *pūrá-*
*pélh$_1$us	'much'	Grk *polús*, Skt *purú-*
*bhénĝhus	'thick, abundant'	Lat *pinguis*, Grk *pakhús*, Skt *bahú-*
*g^{w}honós	'± thick, sufficient'	Grl *eutheneō*, Skt *ghaná-*
*sph̥$_1$rós	'± fat, rich'	Lat *prosper*, NE *spare*, Skt *sphirá-*
*meĝh$_a$-	'large, great'	Lat *magnus*, Grk *mégas*, Skt *máhi-*
*h$_1$eu(h$_a$)-	'empty, wanting'	Lat *vānus*, NE *wan*, *wane*, Grk *eûnis*, Skt *ūná-*
*wak-	'be empty'	Lat *vacō*
*tusk̂yos	'empty'	Skt *tucchyá-*
*mei-	'less'	Lat *minus*, Grk *minuṓrios*
*mr̥ĝhus	'short'	Lat *brevis*, NE *merry*, Grk *brakhús*, Skt *múhu-*
*menus/menwos	'thin (in density)'	Grk *mánu*, Skt *manā́k*
*tenk-	'become firm, thicken; shrink'	Skt *tanákti*
*reuk/g-	'shrink, wrinkle up'	Lat *rūga*

'measure', OE *mǣþ* 'measure', Alb *mot* 'season; rainstorm', Grk *mêtis* 'plan, Skt *mā́ti-* 'measure') and other derivatives, e.g. NE *meal* which in OE *mǣl* meant 'measure, mark, appointed time', which then specialized to 'meal time', and Hit *mēhur* 'time'. The root **med-* also meant 'measure' (e.g. OIr *midithir* 'judges', Lat *meditor* 'meditate', OE *metan* 'measure, mete out' [> NE *mete*], Grk *médomai* 'provide for, be mindful of', *mḗdomai* 'intend; plot', Arm *mit* 'thought, reason') and in Latin (*medeor* 'cure', *medicus* 'doctor), Greek (Mēdos, god of medicine), and Avestan (*vi-madaya* 'act as a healer'), it took on special medical connotations.

Another way of measuring out is through division for which there are several words in Proto-Indo-European. The meanings for **wi-dhh*$_1$*-* are fairly wide-ranging, e.g. 'divide' (Lat *dīvidō*), 'interior' (Baltic, e.g. Latv *vidus*), 'bring' (Hit *widā(i)-*), and 'distribute' (Skt *vi-dhā-*), but the nominal derivative **widh-h*$_1$*eweh*$_a$*-*, 'widow' (see Section 12.2), helps secure the proto-meaning as 'put asunder'. The verbal root **deh*$_a$*(i)-* means 'divide' in most languages (e.g. Alb *për-daj* 'distribute, divide, scatter', Grk *daíomai* 'divide; feast on', Skt *dā́ti* 'cuts up, divides') or indicates a portion of what has been divided up, e.g. OIr *dām* 'host, retinue' or Grk *dêmos* 'people' and 'tide' (as in a time of year) in Germanic (e.g. NE *tide* and *time*) and Arm *ti* 'age, time'. The root **bhag-* is similarly attested in verbal form as 'divide, apportion' (e.g. Grk *phageîn* 'eat', Av *bag-* 'distribute', Skt *bhájati* 'divides, distributes, enjoys') and nominal, i.e. 'portion' (e.g. Rus *bog* 'god', Av *baγa-* 'god', Skt *bhága-* 'lord', Toch B *pāke* 'share, portion'), and underlies the name of a deity (see Section 17.1, 23.1).

Other than the numeral 'one', **h*$_1$*oinos*, there are other singulatives (with the extension **-ko-*, e.g. **h*$_1$*oinoko-*, we have NE *any*). A Latin-Sanskrit (and possibly Baltic) isogloss gives us **kaiwelos* (Lat *caelebs* 'living alone, celibate', Skt *kévala-* 'alone') while the much used **sem-* appears in **sem-go-(lo)s* 'single one' (Lat *singulī* 'single, individual'). It also provides the basis for the multiplicative of 'one', i.e. 'once', **sem-* (Lat *sem-per* 'always', *sim-plex* 'single', Grk *haploûs* 'singly, in one way') or **semlo-m* (OIr *samlith* 'like, as', Lat *simul* 'simultaneously, together, at the same time', OE *simbel(s)* 'always'). An *o*-grade nominal form **somos* gives us the meaning 'same' (e.g. OIr *-som* 'self; that one', NE *same*, OCS *samŭ* 'himself', Grk *homós* 'similar, same', Arm *omn* 'some, certain, any', Av *hama-* 'same', Skt *samá-* 'equal, like, same', Toch AB *sam* 'like, even') while a zero-grade **sm̥mós* meant 'some, any' (e.g. NE *some*, Grk *hamós* 'anyone', Arm *amen(ain)* 'all, each', Av *hama-* 'anyone', Skt *samá-* 'anyone'). Less certain is the word for 'half', **sēmis* (or **seh*$_1$*mis*?; e.g. Lat *sēmi-* 'half-', OHG *sāmi-* 'half-', Grk *hēmi-* 'half-', Skt *sāmí-* 'half-'), which has been variously interpreted as a lengthened grade of **sem-* 'one' or derived from the verbal root **seh*$_1$*-* 'separate'; certainly the latter makes more sense semantically. The Proto-Indo-European word for 'other' was **h*$_a$*élyos* (e.g. OIr *aile*, Lat *alius*, NE *else*, Grk *állos*, Arm *ayl*, Toch B *alyek*).

The verb *$pelh_1$- 'fill' is conjugated as a reduplicated present in Grk *pímplēmi* and Skt *píparti* and it is attested in other formations elsewhere (e.g. OIr *līnaid* 'fills', Lat *pleō* 'fill', Arm *helum* 'pour', Av *par*- 'fill'). It also provides the basis for the adjective *$p̥lh_1nós$ (e.g. OIr *lān*, NE *full*, Lith *pìlnas*, OCS *plŭnŭ*, Av *pərəna*- 'filled', Skt *pūrṇá*- 'full', Toch B *pällew* 'full [of the moon]'; Lat *plēnus* is from the full-grade) and the word for 'much', *$pélh_1us$ (e.g. OIr *il*, OE *fela*, Grk *polús*, Av *pouru*-, Skt *purú*-, all 'much'); the comparative form *$pleh_1yos$ is the basis of Lat *plūs* 'more' and likewise OIr *līa* 'more', Av *frāyah*- 'more', and Skt *prāyá*- 'mostly, commonly'. Other expressions of 'abundance' were **bhéng̑hus* (e.g. Lat *pinguis* 'fat' [with mysterious initial *p*-], OHG *bungo* 'bump', Latv *bìezs* 'thick', Grk *pakhús* 'thick, compact', probably Hit *panku*- 'total, entire, general' [see also above], Skt *bahú*- 'much, many; numerous, compact; abounding in') which has a basic meaning of 'thick' and derives from the verbal root (attested only in Skt *báhate* 'increases') **bheng̑h*- 'grow, increase'. The concepts of 'thickness' and 'fullness' also lie behind *g^whonós (e.g. Lith *ganà* 'enough', OCS *gonĕti* 'suffice', perhaps Grk *eutheneō* 'flourish', Arm *y-ogn* 'much', certainly again OPers *āganiš* 'full', Skt *ghaná*- 'thick'). The verbal root *$speh_1(i)$- 'flourish' yielded *$sph̥_1rós$ 'fat, rich' (e.g. Lat *prosper* 'lucky', NE *spare*, OCS *sporŭ* 'rich', Skt *sphirá*- 'fat'). Finally, the adjective 'large, great', *$meĝh_a$-, is well attested in ten groups (e.g. OIr *maige* 'great, large', Lat *magnus* 'large', OE *micel* 'large', Alb *madh* 'large', Grk *mégas* 'large', Arm *mec* 'large', Hit *mēkkis* 'much, many, numerous', Av *maz*- 'large', Skt *máhi*- 'large', Toch B *māka* 'many'); only *much* (with unexpected loss, dating to Middle English, of the final -*l*) and the dialectal *mickle* (corresponding in form to Grk *megálos*) survive as direct descendants in English, although the Greek-derived prefix *mega*- is quite productive in modern English.

There are also words to indicate 'emptiness' or 'lack'. Widespread is *$h_1eu(h_a)$- with consistent meanings across six groups (e.g. Grk *eûnis* 'deprived', Arm *unayn* 'empty', Lat *vānus* 'empty', NE *wan*, *wane*, Av *ūna*- 'wanting', Skt *ūná*- 'lacking'). A Latin-Hittite isogloss attests **wak*- (Lat *vacō* 'am empty', Hit *wakk*- 'fail, be lacking') while the verbal root **teus*- 'to empty' (Av *taošayeiti* 'lets fall, lets go') supplies **tusk̑yos* which is attested in Balto-Slavic (e.g. Lith *tùščias* 'empty, poor', Rus *tóščyj* 'empty') and Indo-Iranian (e.g. NPers *tuhī* 'empty', Skt *tucchyá*- 'empty'). A root **mei*- 'less' supplies both the adjective **minus* (Lat *minus* 'small', Goth *minnists* 'smallest', Grk *minuṓrios* 'short-lived') and a verb **minéuti* (e.g. Corn *minow* 'lessen', Lat *minuō* 'lessen', Grk *minúthō* 'lessen, decrease', Skt *minóti* 'lessens'). The meaning 'short', with respect to both time and space, is indicated by **mr̥ĝhus* (e.g. Lat *brevis* 'short', NE *merry*, Grk *brakhús* 'short [of time or space]', Av *mərəzu*- 'short', Skt *múhu*- 'short') where the Lat *brevis* and Grk *brakhús* are presumed to involve a change of **mr*- > *br*-. Another expression of smallness is seen in **menus/menwos* 'thin, sparse, fine' (e.g. OIr *menb* 'small, tiny', Grk *mánu* 'small', Arm *manr* 'small, fine', Skt *manāk* a little, slightly'). A root *tenk- covers a semantic bundle that includes 'shrink' and 'make thick/compact' which suggests that the original referent concerned the behaviour of congealing dairy products. It is found in Celtic (OIr *tēcht* 'coagulated'), Germanic (ON *þēl* 'buttermilk'), Baltic (Lith *tánkus* 'thick, copious'), Indo-Iranian (Skt *tanákti* 'pulls together', *takrám* 'buttermilk'), and Tocharian (e.g. Toch B *tañki* 'very, fully; full'). A Latin-Baltic-Tocharian isogloss secures *reuk/g- 'shrink, wrinkle up' (Lat *rūga* 'wrinkle', Lith *runkù* 'shrivel up', Toch B *ruk-* 'grow lean (with hunger)'.

From the North-West we have *$h_1$ónteros 'other' (e.g. NE *other*, Lith *añtras* 'other, second', OCS *vŭtorŭ* 'second'); *w(e)$h_a$stos 'empty' (e.g. OIr *fās* 'empty', Lat *vastus* 'empty, unoccupied', NE *waste*) which may be an enlargement of the PIE *$h_1$eu(h_a)- 'empty'; *(s)keup- 'bundle' (e.g. NE *sheaf*, Rus *čup* 'tuft, head of hair, crest'); *menegh- 'abundant' (e.g. OIr *meinic(c)* 'abundant', NE *many*, OCS *mŭnogŭ* 'abundant'), possibly Proto-Indo-European if one accepts Skt *maghá-* 'gift, reward, wealth' as cognate; and *kerdheh$_a$- 'herd, series' (e.g. NE *herd*, Lith *(s)kerdžius* 'herdsman', OCS *črěda* 'herd, series'). From the West Central region we have *meh$_1$ro- ~ *moh$_1$ro- 'large' (e.g. OIr *mār* 'large', ON *mærr* 'known, famous, great', OCS *Vladi-mĕrŭ* [personal name], Grk *egkhesí-mōros* 'mighty with a spear') from *meh$_1$- 'grow'; *pau- 'little, few' (e.g. Lat *pauper* 'poor', *paucus* 'few', *parvus* 'small', NE *few*, Grk *paũros* 'little'); *sm̥teros 'one or the other of two' (e.g. NWels *hanner* 'half', Grk *héteros* 'one or the other of two'); possibly *méuh$_x$kō(n) 'heap' (e.g. NE *hay-mow*, dialectal Grk *múkōn* 'heap'); *$h_a$rei(h_x)- 'number, count (out)' (e.g. OIr *āram* 'number', *rīm* 'number, computation', NE *rhyme* [with unetymological, Greek-influenced spelling], Grk *arithmós* 'number') and with extensions we have Lat *ratiō* 'calculation, reckoning' and the element *-red* in NE *hundred*; *del- 'aim, compute' (e.g. NE *tell*, Grk *dólos* 'guile, bait', Arm *tol* 'row'). A Greek-Armenian isogloss is seen in *k̂enós 'empty' (Grk *kenós* 'empty', Arm *sin* 'empty') and a Greek-Indic isogloss is *$h_1$er(h_1)- 'separate' (i.e. Grk *erẽmos* 'desolate, lonely, solitary', Skt *r̥té* 'except, without' [it is interesting that there is apparently no relationship between *$h_a$rei(h_x)- 'count out' and *$h_1$er(h_1)- 'separate']).

Further Reading

There have been recent surveys of the IE numerical system. The most extensive is Gvozdanivic (1992); see also Blažek (1999*a*), Schmidt (1992), Schmid (1989), Justus (1988), and Szemerényi (1960); the root for 'measure' is discussed in Haudry (1992), 'size' in Winter (1980), and 'weight' in Peeters (1974).

20

Mind, Emotions, and Sense Perception

20.1 Knowledge and Thought

There is a rich reconstructable vocabulary in Indo-European pertaining to the mental and sensory processes. Those words specifically concerned with knowing and thinking are indicated in Table 20.1.

There are two widely attested verbs for 'know' in Proto-Indo-European. The first, *ĝneh$_3$-, with its many derivatives, denotes becoming acquainted with, i.e. knowing (a person), recognizing. The present may either be *ĝn̥h$_3$-neh$_a$- (e.g. OIr _ad-gnin_ 'recognizes', OE _cunnan_ 'know, be able to', Lith _žinóti_ 'known', Av _zānāiti_ 'knows', Skt _jānā́ti_ 'knows, recognizes', Toch A _knānā-_ 'know'), or formed with the suffix *-sk̂e/o-, (e.g. Lat _(g)nōscō_ 'know', Alb _njoh_ 'know', Grk _gignṓskō_ 'know'). The same root also provides a series of deverbatives, e.g. *ĝneh$_3$tis 'knowledge' (e.g. Lat _nōtiō_ 'a becoming acquainted, investigation; conception', Rus _znatĭ_ '[circle of] acquaintances', Grk _gnôsis_ 'knowledge', Skt _pra-jñāti-_ 'knowledge'), *ĝn(e)h$_3$tēr 'knower' (e.g. Lat _nōtor_, Grk _gnōstḗr_ (with analogical _–s-_), Av _žnātar-_, Skt _jñātár-_, all 'knower'), and *ĝn̥h$_3$tós 'known' (e.g. OIr _gnāth_ 'used to, known', Lat _nōtus_ 'known', Grk _gnōtós_ 'known', Skt _jñātá-_ 'known'). The second root, *weid-, indicates 'seeing' or 'knowing as a

Table 20.1. *Knowledge and thought*

**ĝneh₃-*	'know, be acquainted with'	Lat *gnōscō*, NE *can*, Grk *gignṓskō*, Skt *jānā́ti*;
**weid-*	'see, know (as a fact)'	Lat *videō*, NE *wit*, Grk *oîda*, Skt *véda*
**men-*	'think, consider'	Lat *meminī*, Grk *mémona*, Skt *mamné*
**ménmn̥*	'thought'	Skt *mánman-*
**méntis*	'thought'	Lat *mēns*, NE *mind*, Skt *matí-*
**meino-*	'opinion'	NE *mean*, *bemoan*
**teng-*	'think, feel'	Lat *tongeō*, NE *think, thank*
**men(s)-dh(e)h₁-*	'learn'	Grk *manthánō*, Skt *medhā́*
**(s)mer-*	'remember, be concerned about'	NE *mourn*, Grk *mérimna, mártus*, Skt *smárati*
**mers-*	'forget'	NE *mar*, Skt *mṛ́ṣyate*
**k̂red-dheh₁-*	'believe'	Lat *crēdō*, Skt *śrád-dhāti*
**h₂/₃ehₓ-*	'trust in, believe'	Lat *ōmen*
**h₁ger-*	'awake'	Grk *egrḗgora*, Skt *jāgárti*
**der-*	'sleep'	Lat *dormiō*, Grk *édrasthon*, Skt *drā́ti*
**ses-*	'rest, sleep, keep quiet'	Skt *sásti*
**swep-*	'sleep, dream' (vb)	Lat *sōpiō*, Skt *svápiti*
**swópnos*	'sleep, dream' (noun)	Lat *somnus*
**swópniyom*	'dream'	Lat *somnium*, Grk *enúpnion*, Skt *svápniyam*

fact' rather than recognizing a person. It was essentially a perfect, **wóide* 'have seen', that was reinterpreted as a present 'know' (e.g. OIr *ro-fetar* 'knows', Lat *videō* 'see', OE *witan* 'know' [cf. NE *wit*], Lith *véizdmi* 'see', OCS *vědě* 'know', Grk *oîda* 'know', Arm *gitem* 'know', Av *vaēδa* 'know[s], see[s]', Skt *véda* 'know[s]'). It too supplies a number of other words, e.g. **widmén-* 'knowledge' (e.g. Grk *ídmōn* 'skilled', Skt *vidmán-* 'wisdom', Toch B *ime* 'consciousness, awareness, thought'), **weides-* 'what is seen' (e.g. MIr *fīad* 'face to face', NE *-wise* as in 'lengthwise', Lith *véidas* 'face', OCS *vidŭ* 'appearance', Grk *eîdos* 'appearance', Skt *védas-* 'knowledge').

The verb to 'think' is also evidenced by two verbs. The most productive is **men-* which also took a perfect **memónh₂e* 'think, remember' (e.g. Lat *meminī* 'remember', Grk *mémona* 'yearn', Skt *mamné* 'thinks') and two different presents, i.e. **mn̥yétor* seen in Celtic (OIr *do-moinethar* 'believes'), Baltic (Lith *miniù* 'remember'), Slavic (OCS *mĭnjǫ* 'think'), Grk *maínomai* 'rage, be mad',

Indo-Iranian (Av *mainyeite* 'thinks', Skt *mányate* 'thinks') and **mnéh$_a$ti* (Grk *mnêma* 'remembrance', Luv *m(a)nā-* 'see, look upon'). From this root we also have **ménmn̥* (e.g. OIr *menma* 'spirit, sense', Skt *mánman-* 'mind, perception') and **méntis* (e.g. Lat *mēns* 'thought', NE *mind*, Lith *mintìs* 'thought', OCS *pamętĭ* 'thought', Av *-maiti-* 'thought', Skt *matí-* 'thought'), both centring on the notion 'thought'. Semantically different is **meino-* 'opinion' (e.g. OIr *mīan* 'wish, desire', NE *mean, bemoan*, OCS *měnję* 'mention', Toch B *onmiṃ* 'remorse'). The verb 'learn' is formed with a compound of the root, i.e. **men(s)-dh(e)h$_1$-* 'mind-place/put' (e.g. NWels *mynnu* 'wish', OHG *mendōn* 'rejoice', *munter* 'lively', Lith *mañdras* 'lively, awake', OCS *mądrą* 'wise', Alb *mund* 'be able', Grk *manthánō* 'learn', Av *mąz-dā-* 'stamp in the memory', *mazdā* 'wisdom', Skt *medhā́* 'wisdom'). The sense of 'think' as 'to be of the opinion, feel' seems to have been indicated by **teng-* where the concept of 'feel' is seen in Germanic (e.g. NE 'thank' as well as 'think') and Tocharian (Toch B *taṅkw* 'love' as well as *cäṅk-* 'please') while Albanian clearly took a negative emotional turn to yield *tëngë* 'resentment, grudge'; more purely cognitive in meaning is Lat *tongeō* 'know'.

The verb to 'remember' was **(s)mer-* (e.g. NE *mourn*, Lith *merëti* 'worry about', Grk *mérimna* 'thought, care, anxiety', *mártus* 'witness' [> by borrowing NE *martyr*], Av *maraiti* 'observes', Skt *smárati* 'remembers, longs for') which also appears in reduplicated form, e.g. Lat *memoria* 'remembrance', OE *mimorian* 'remember', Arm *mormok'* 'care'. It is interesting that the two antonymic verbs 'remember' and 'forget' should resemble each other so closely in form. PIE **mers-* indicates 'forget' in Baltic (e.g. Lith *mirštù* 'forget, overlook'), Arm *moṙanam* 'forget', Skt *mr̥ṣyate* 'forgets, neglects', and Toch AB *märs-* 'forget' but shows a different set of meanings in Germanic (e.g. OE *mierran* 'disturb, confuse, hinder' [> NE *mar*]) which has led to some doubt that the Germanic set belongs here.

Belief was indicated by a compound **k̂red-dheh$_1$-* (e.g. OIr *creitid* 'believes', Lat *crēdō* 'believe', Av *zrazdā-* 'believing', Skt *śrád-dhāti* 'believes, has trust in', *śrad-dhā́-* 'faith'). Although there are problematic forms involved in Iranian, this compound is traditionally explained as 'heart-put/place' and it is surely old in Indo-European as it occurs as an uncompounded expression in Hit, i.e. *k(a)ratan dai-* 'place the heart'. There is a possible Irish-Parthian (an Iranian language) isogloss (OIr *iress* 'belief', Parth *parast* 'ardor') indicating **peri-steh$_2$-* 'stand before' > 'belief' although it is just as likely that these are independent creations in the two languages. Another root is supplied by **h$_{2/3}$eh$_x$-* (e.g. Lat *ōmen* 'sign, omen', Hit *hā(i)-* 'believe, take as truth') with which some would also include the Celtic (e.g. OIr *oeth*) and Germanic words for 'oath' (including NE *oath*)(see Section 17.4).

We have at least one root indicating 'awake', *$h_1$ger-, found in Alb *ngre* 'awake, raise up, lift', Grk *egrḗgora* 'was awake', and Indo-Iranian (Av *jagāra* 'was awake', Skt *jāgárti* 'is awake, awakes') but also perhaps in Lat *expergō* 'I waken' (if from *ex-per-gr-). There are more words associated with 'sleep'. A series of enlargements of a root *der- gives us verbs to 'sleep' in Italic (Lat *dormiō* 'sleep'), Slavic (OCS *dremljǫ* 'doze'), Grk *édrasthon* 'slept', and Skt *drā́ti* 'sleeps' but there is no clear survival of the original unenlarged verbal form. An Anatolian-Indo-Iranian isogloss gives us *ses- 'sleep' (e.g. Hit *sess-* 'sleep', *sessnu-* 'put to bed', Av *hah-* 'sleep', Skt *sásti* 'sleeps') which may be onomatopoeic if Proto-Indo-Europeans counted *s*'s rather than *z*'s when they snored. The verbal root *swep- supplied two presents: *swépti 'sleeps, dreams' (e.g. OE *swefan*, OCS *sŭpati*, Hit *supp-*, Av x^v*ap-*, Skt *svápiti*, all 'sleep') and a causative *swopéyeti ~ *swōpéyeti 'puts to sleep' (Lat *sōpiō* 'lull to sleep', OE *swebban* 'lull to sleep, kill', Skt *svapáyati* ~ *svāpáyati* 'lulls to sleep'). In addition there is the derived noun *swópnos ~ *swépnos 'sleep, dream' (e.g. Lat *somnus* 'sleep', Lith *sãpnas* 'dream', OE *swefn* 'sleep', Grk *húpnos* 'sleep', Av h^v*afna-* 'sleep', Skt *svápna-* 'sleep', Toch B *ṣpane* 'sleep, dream'). Similar is the *supnós that lies behind OCS *sŭnŭ* 'sleep', Alb *gjumë* 'sleep', and Arm *k'un* 'sleep'. When we add to this mix Lat *sopor* 'overpowering sleep', Grk *húpar* 'true dream, vision; walking reverie', Hit *suppariya-* 'dream', it would appear that early Proto-Indo-European had a noun *swópr̥ ~ *swépōr (genitive *supnós) that was morphologically rebuilt in various ways to give all of these various reflexes. The two concepts of 'sleep' and 'dream' regularly fall together in many Indo-European languages and there does not seem to be a set of different roots to distinguish the two activities in Proto-Indo-European. The closest we can come to a Proto-Indo-European 'dream' is *swópniyom seen in Lat *somnium* 'dream', Baltic (Lith *sapnỹs* 'sleep, dream'), perhaps Grk *enúpnion* 'dream', Skt *svápnyam* 'vision in a dream'; similar is the *supn(iy)om of Slavic (OCS *sŭnije* 'dream'), Tocharian (Toch B *sänmetse* 'in a trance'), and perhaps Grk *enúpnion* 'dream' but the different groups may have independently created these words from *swep-.

From the North-West we have *sent- 'perceive, think' (e.g. Lat *sentiō* 'feel', *sēnsus* 'feeling, meaning', NHG *Sinn* 'meaning', Lith *sentė́ti* 'think', OCS *sęštĭ* 'wise'). From the West Central region there is *ghou- 'perceive, pay heed to' (e.g. Lat *faveō* 'favour', ON *gā* 'pay attention to', OCS *govějǫ* 'honour', Arm *govem* 'praise'); *g^whren- 'think' (a Germanic-Greek isogloss): on the Germanic side we have ON *grunr* 'suspicion' and *grundr* 'meditation' while the Greek cognates include both *phronéō* 'think' and *phrḗn* 'midriff; spirit', suggesting that the Greeks or their ancestors once placed the organ of knowledge in the chest and not the head; an Albanian-Greek-Armenian isogloss gives *$h_3$énr̥ 'dream' (Alb *ëndërr*, Grk *ónar*, Arm *anur*). There are several Graeco-Aryan isoglosses:

from the root **men-* 'think' comes **ménes-* 'thought' (i.e. Grk *ménos*, Av *manah-*, Skt *mánas-*), and several shared formations are built on **dens-* 'teach, inculcate a skill' (e.g. Grk *didáskō* 'teach', Av *dīdaiŋhē* 'am instructed').

20.2 Sight

In terms of the five senses, sight provides far more reconstructable items of vocabulary than any of the other senses. The basic Proto-Indo-European vocabulary associated with vision is indicated in Table 20.2.

There are several terms for 'appear'. We can supply 'appear' as the tentative meaning to **k^{w}ek̂/ĝ-* whose range of meanings comprises 'show' (OCS *kažǫ*), 'sign' (Grk *tékmar*), 'teaches' (Av *čašte*), and 'appears' (Skt *cáṣṭe* 'sees,

Table 20.2. *Sight*

**k^{w}ek̂/ĝ-*	'appear'	Grk *tékmar*, Skt *cáṣṭe*
**weik-*	'appear'	Grk *eikṓn*, Skt *viśati*
**derk̂-*	'glance at'	Grk *dérkomai*, Skt *dṛ́ṣṭi-*
**leuk-*	'see'	Grk *leússō*, Skr *lókate*
**(s)pek̂-*	'observe'	Lat *speciō*, Grk *sképtomai*, Skt *páśyati*
**sek^w-*	'see'	NE *see*
**wel-*	'see'	Lat *voltus*
**leĝ-*	'see'	Lat *legō*, NE *look*
**bheudh-*	'pay attention, be observant'	Grk *peúthomai*, Skt *bódhati*
**bhoudhéye/o-*	'waken, point out'	Skt *bodháyati*
**swerh$_x$K-*	'watch over, be concerned about'	NE *sorrow*
**wer-*	'perceive, give attention to'	Lat *vereor*, NE *ware, wary*, Grk *oráō*
**wet-*	'see (truly)'	Lat *vātēs*, Skt *vatati*
**wer-b(h)-*	'oversee, protect'	
**h$_3$eu-*	'perceive'	Lat *audiō*, Grk *aisthánomai*, Skt *uvé*
**k^{w}ei-*	'perceive'	Grk *atízō*, Skt *cikéti*
**(s)keuh$_1$-*	'perceive'	Lat *caveō*, Grk *koéō*
**seh$_a$g-*	'perceive acutely, seek out'	Lat *sāgiō*, NE *seek*, Grk *hēgéomai*
**h$_3$ēwis*	'obvious'	
**meigh-* ~ **meik-*	'close the eyes'	Lat *micō*

appears', *kāśate* 'appears, is brilliant, shines'). Another root, **weik*-, is sometimes associated with the concept of 'appear, come into sight' (e.g. Lith *vỹkti* 'come, go', Grk *eĩke* 'it appeared good', Av *visaiti* 'presents itself', Skt *viśati* 'enters') but also has nominal forms indicating 'image' in both Germanic and Greek (e.g. OE *wīh* ~ *wēoh* 'image, idol', Grk *eikṓn* 'image, likeness' (our NE *icon* is a loanword from Greek).

There are a series of words meaning 'see'; some of these are independent roots and others involve ancient semantic shifts from other verbs. To the former belong **derḱ*- (e.g. OIr *ad-con-darc* 'have seen', Goth *ga-tarhjan* 'distinguish, note', Alb *dritë* 'light', Grk *dérkomai* 'see', Skt *dṛ́ṣṭi*- 'sight') with its textbook reduplicated perfects in Grk *dédorka*, Av *dādarəsa*, and Skt *dadárśa*. This verb may have been the expression *par excellence* of the baleful look of the dragon or monster of Proto-Indo-European mythology. Both Greek (*drákōn* whence, via Latin, NE *dragon*) and OIr (*muirdris* '± sea-dragon') have derivatives of this root as the word for 'dragon' (though the formations are different and independent: **dr̥ḱónt*- and **dr̥ḱsi*- respectively). The root *(*s*)*peḱ*- is similarly widespread (e.g. Lat *speciō* 'see', OHG *spehōn* 'spy', Grk *sképtomai* 'look at', Av *spasyeiti* 'spies', Skt *páśyati* 'sees', Toch AB *päk*- 'intend') while **wel*- is limited to Celtic (e.g. NWels *gweled* 'see') and Tocharian (Toch B *yel*- 'examine, investigate') but there are derived forms in Italic (Lat *voltus* 'facial expression, appearance, form') and Germanic (e.g. OE *wuldor* 'fame'). Those verbs where there has been semantic specialization include **leuk*- which generally means 'see' in most groups (e.g. NWels *amlwg* 'evident', OPrus *laukīt* 'seek', OCS *lučiti* 'meet someone', Grk *leússō* 'see', Skt *lókate* 'perceives') but can hardly be separated from **leuk*- in the sense of 'shine' (see Section 20.3). The verb 'follow', **sek*^{w}-, also yields 'see' in many languages in the sense of 'follow with the eyes' (e.g. NE *see*, Lith *sekù* 'follow, keep an eye on', Alb *shoh* 'see'); it is an ancient metaphoric shift and is found in Anatolian where Hittite attests *sākuwa* 'eye' and Lydian *saw*- 'see'. Finally, the verb 'gather', **leǵ*-, gives us 'see' in Italic (e.g. Lat *legō* 'gather; read'), Germanic (e.g. NE *look*), and Tocharian (AB *läk*- 'see').

To these verbs for 'see' we can add a series of words that hover around 'perception', sometimes visible. For example, **bheudh*- carries the meaning 'observe' in Slavic, Greek, and Indo-Iranian (e.g. Rus *bljudú* 'observe, pay attention to', Grk *peúthomai* 'examine, experience', Av *baoδaiti* 'notices, observes', Skt *bódhati* 'is awake, wakes up; observes, understands'; a buddha is someone who is 'awake', i.e. understands how the world works); in Germanic it has shifted to 'ask, offer' (e.g. OE *bēodan*, NE *bid*). The root supplies a causative **bhoudhéye/o*- 'waken, point out' (e.g. Lith *baudžiù* 'waken', OCS *buditi* 'waken', Av *baoδayeiti* 'indicates', Skt *bodháyati* 'wakens'). To 'watch over' or 'be concerned about' underlies **swerh*$_x$*K*- where it generally denotes something closer to 'guarding' than actually employing a visual sense (e.g. OE *sorgian* 'grieve, be sorry for, be anxious about', Lith *sérgti* 'keeps watch over', Skt *sū́rkṣati* 'takes care of'). The English 'wary' or 'beware' probably provides a reasonable approximation of the underlying meaning of **wer-* (e.g. Lat *vereor* 'honour, fear', NE *ware* and *wary*, Latv *vērt* 'look, gaze, notice', Grk *oûros* 'guard', *oráō* 'see', Hit *werite-* 'put one's attention', Toch AB *wär-* 'smell'). The extended form **wer-b(h)-* involves a Baltic-Tocharian isogloss, again with meanings 'guard' as well as 'observe' (OPrus *warbo* 'protects', Toch AB *yärp-* 'oversee, observe, take care of'). A specialized, possibly sacred vision is to be found in **wet-* 'see (truly)' with cognates in Celtic (OIr *fethid* 'sees, pays attention to'), Lat *vātēs* 'seer, prophet', and Skt *ápi vatati* 'is familiar with, is aware of'; derived forms include **wṓto-* '(true) knowledge, shamanic wisdom' (OIr *fāth* 'prophetic wisdom', OE *wōþ* 'song, poetry', **wōtó-* 'having (true) knowledge' > OE *wōd* 'furious, frenzied' (> archaic NE *wood* 'mad') and **wōtonó* 'who incarnates' **wṓto-* seen in the Germanic divine names of OE *Woden*, ON *Oðinn* (see Section 23.2). The root **$h_3$eu-* does mean 'see' in Anatolian (Hit *ūhhi* 'see') and Indic (Skt *uvé* 'I see) but the extended form **$h_3$ewis-* gives 'hear' in Italic (Lat *audiō*) and 'perceive' in Grk *aisthánomai*; the derived causative means 'show, reveal' (i.e. 'make see') in OCS (*aviti*). An extended form **h_3ēwis* gives us a Slavic-Iranian isogloss that means 'obvious' in both groups (OCS *(j)avě*, Av *āviš*). Enlarged forms of **k^wei-* 'perceive' yield the meaning 'see' in Celtic and 'read' in Baltic-Slavic (e.g. OIr *ad-ci* 'sees', Lith *skaitaũ* 'count, read', OCS *čĭtǫ* 'count, reckon, read'); the unextended root is found in Grk *a-tízō* 'pay no attention' and Skt *cinóti* ~ *cikéti* 'perceives'. Another root rendering two different senses is **keuh$_1$-* whose outcomes include 'see', 'seer' (Lyd *kaweś* 'priest', Av *kavā* 'seer', Skt *kaví-* 'wise, seer') but also (in extended form) NE *hear*, Grk *akoúō* 'hear', Lat *custōs* 'watchman', and, with *s*-mobile, NE *show* and Arm *c'uc'anem* 'show' (cf. also Lat *caveō* 'take heed', OE *hāwian* 'look at', OCS *čujǫ* 'note', Grk *koéō* 'note'). A PIE **seh$_a$g-* 'perceive acutely, seek out' is attested in Celtic (e.g. OIr *saigid* 'seeks out', Italic (Lat *sāgiō* 'perceive acutely', *sāga* 'fortune-teller'), Germanic (e.g. NE *seek*), Grk *hēgéomai* 'direct, lead', and Anatolian (Hit *sākiya-* 'make known').

A root **meigh-* or **meik-* (the evidence is ambivalent about the ending) is reconstructed to mean 'close the eyes' (Toch B *mik-*) either as 'fall sleep' (Baltic, e.g. Lith *(už-)mìgti*) or merely as 'blink' (Slavic, e.g. Rus *mžatĭ*; and metaphorically in Italic, e.g. Lat *micō* 'move quickly, flash').

The West Central area gives **prep-* 'appear' (e.g. OIr *richt* 'form', Grk *prépō* 'appear', Arm *erewim* 'am evident, appear') and a nominal derivative of **ĝnéh$_3$-* 'know', i.e. **ĝnéh$_3$mn̥* (Lat *cognōmen* 'surname', Rus *znamja* 'sign, mark', Grk *gnôma* 'distinctive mark'); in both Grk *ópōpa* 'have seen', *opīpeúō* 'stare at', and Indic (Skt *ī́ksate* 'sees') one could literally 'eye' something, i.e. 'see' (**h_3ek^w-*), a unique verbal use of the word for 'eye'. Again in Greek and Indic, either inherited or independently created, we find from **derḱ-* 'see' an adjective (from the participle) **derḱetos* 'visible' (Grk *-dérketos*, Skt *darśatá-*).

20.3 Bright and Dark

There is an extensive reconstructed vocabulary relating to brightness, so much so that a perusal of some etymological dictionaries gives one the impression that the central concepts of the Indo-Europeans might be reduced to 'bright' and 'swell'. Darkness has a much more limited vocabulary associated with it. The relevant forms are indicated in Table 20.3.

The verbal root **leuk-* 'shine' was highly productive in Indo-European (e.g. Lat *lūceō* 'shine', Hit *lukke-* 'shine', Skt *rócate* 'shines', Toch AB *luk-* 'shine'; Lat *lūceō* 'kindle', Hit *lukke-* 'kindle', Av *raočayeiti* 'makes shine', Skt *rocáyati* 'makes shine') and underlies the noun **lóuk(es)-* 'light' (e.g. Lat *lūx*, Arm *loys*, Av *raočah-*, Skt *rocí-*, Toch B *lyuke*, all 'light') and the *o*-stem adjective **leukós*

Table 20.3. *Bright and dark*

**leuk-*	'shine'	Lat *lūceō*
**lóuk(es)-*	'light'	Lat *lūx*, Skt *rocí-*
**leukós*	'light, bright, clear'	Grk *leukós*, Skt *rocá-*
**dei-*	'shine, be bright'	Grk *déato*, Skt *dīdeti*
**lap-*	'shine'	Grk *lámpō*
**bheh$_2$-*	'shine'	Grk *phaínō*, Skt *bhā́ti*
**bhleg-*	'burn, shine'	Lat *fulgō*, NE *black*, Grk *phlégō*, Skt *bhrā́jate*
**bherh$_x$ĝ-*	'shine, gleam'	NE *bright*
**(s)kand-*	'shine, glitter'	Lat *candeō*, Grk *kándaros*, Skt *cándati*
**sweid-*	'shine'	Lat *sīdus*
**mer-*	'shine, shimmer'	Lat *merus*, Grk *marmaírō*, Skt *márīci-*
**ḱeuk-*	'shine, burn'	Grk *kúknos*, Skt *śócate*
?(s)plend-*	'shine'	Lat *splendeō*
**(s)koitrós*	'bright, clear'	Skt *citrá-*
**dh(o)ngu-*	'dark'	
**tómh$_x$es-*	'dark'	Lat *temere*, Skt *támas-*
**h$_1$reg^w-es-*	'(place of) darkness'	
**swer-*	'darken'	Lat *sordēs*
**sḱóyh$_a$*	'shade'	Grk *skiā́*, Skt *chāyā́-*

'bright' (e.g. OIr *lōch* 'glowing white', Lith *laũkas* 'blazed, with a white spot on the forehead [of animals]', Grk *leukós* 'light, bright, clear', Skt *rocá-* 'shining, radiant'). Another root **dei-* (e.g. ON *teitr* 'glad', Grk *déato* 'is seen', Skt *dī́deti* 'shines is bright') may have been primarily concerned with the brightness of the sky as it provides the basis of the name of the Indo-European sky deity (**d(i)yēus* 'sky god', **deiwós* 'god', see Section 23.1). A third root **lap-* also means 'shine' (cf. NWels *llachar* 'shining', Grk *lámpō* 'give light, shine') but its connections with fire, e.g. 'flames' (OIr *lasaid*), 'torch' (Baltic, e.g. Lith *lópė*), and 'glows' (Hit *lāpzi*), suggest that it may have been specifically related to the brightness of fire. The root **bheh*$_2$*-* also means 'shine' and it is difficult to discern any more specific semantic connotation (e.g. OIr *bān* 'white', OE *bōnian* 'ornament, polish', Alb *bej* 'do' [< *'bring to light'], Grk *phaínō* 'bring to light', Luv *piha-* 'splendur', Av *bā-* 'shine', Skt *bhā́ti* 'shines', *bhā́s-* 'light, splendour'). A fifth root **bhleg-* yields meanings associated with burning in Lat *flamma* 'flame', *fulmen* 'lightning', NE *black*, i.e. 'burned', and Greek and elsewhere (e.g. Grk *phlégō* 'burn', Av *brāzaiti* 'gleams, shines', Skt *bhrā́jate* 'gleams, shines, glitters', Toch AB *pälk-* 'shine'), which may suggest again an association with the brightness of fire. The root **bherh*$_x$*ĝ-* means 'shine' (e.g. NWels *berth* 'shiny', NE *bright*, Lith *brė̃kšta* 'dawns', Pol *brzask* 'dawn', Alb *bardhë* 'white') and underlies the Proto-Indo-European word for the 'birch' because of its shiny white or silver bark (see Section 10.1). A seventh root **(s)kand-* 'shine' (e.g. NWels *cann* 'white, bright', Lat *candeō* 'glitter, shine', Skt *cándati* 'shines, is bright') has reflexes in Albanian and Indic that indicate the 'moon' (Alb *hënë*, Skt *candrá-* 'shining; moon'); in dialectal Greek the reflex means 'coal' (*kándaros* [< presumably from *'glowing']). Among the Latin cognates are *candidātus* 'candidate for office' because of the white toga which was worn. The root **sweid-* 'shine' (e.g. OE *switol* 'distinct, clear', Lith *svidù* 'shine, am glossy', Av x^v*aēna-* 'glowing') not only gives us a Latin word for 'star' (*sīdus*) but also *consīderō* 'consider' which literally meant 'consult the stars'. Another Proto-Indo-European word for 'shine' is **mer-* (e.g. Lat *merus* 'pure, bare', OE *āmerian* 'test, examine; purify', Rus *mar* 'blaze of the sun', Grk *marmaírō* 'shimmer', Skt *márīci-* 'shining beam') and a tenth root is **k̂euk-*, which also carries meanings relating to burning in Indo-Iranian and Tocharian (e.g. Av *suč-* 'burn, flame', Skt *śócate* 'shines, glows, burns', Toch B *śukye* 'shining') but *kúknos* 'swan' in Greek. Another possible root is ?**(s)plend-* 'shine' (e.g. OIr *lēs* 'light', Lat *splendeō* 'shine, glitter', Lith *spléndžiu* 'light'); its Asian attestation depends on the acceptance of Tocharian *plāntā-* 'rejoice, be glad' as cognate, i.e. 'be shining' (cf. such an English sentence as, 'She was positively glowing'). An adjective 'bright' **(s)koitrós* is attested on the one hand by a Germanic-Baltic isogloss (e.g. OE *hādor* 'clear', Lith *skaidrùs* 'bright, clear [of weather], limpid [of water]') and a related Indo-Iranian (Av *čiθra-* 'clear', Skt *citrá-* 'excellent, bright') that may all derive from an otherwise unattested noun **(s)kóit-*.

There are four roots assignable to Proto-Indo-European that convey 'darkness'. A Hit *dankuis* 'dark' secures the antiquity of **dh(o)ngu-* (otherwise limited to Celtic, e.g. NWels *dew* 'mist, smoke', and Germanic, NHG *dunkel* 'dark'). The root **tómh$_x$es-* (e.g. Lith *tamsà*, Av *təmah-*, Skt *támas-*, all 'darkness') would appear to be a deverbative (the underlying verb being preserved in Lith *témti* 'become dark'); the Latin cognate *temere* 'by chance' derives its meaning from being 'in the dark'. A 'place of darkness' is suggested by **h$_1$reg^w-es-* (Goth *riqis* 'darkness', Toch B *orkamo* 'dark') which means 'evening' (Arm *erek*), 'night' (Skt *rájas-*) but also supplies the word for the Greek underworld *érebos*. The darkening of a surface was indicated with **swer-* or an extended form such as **swerd-*, e.g. Lat *sordēs* 'dirt, soil, uncleanliness', NE *swart* (the underlying verb is preserved only in Iranian, e.g. Oss *xuarun* 'to colour'). Finally, the word for 'shade' or 'shadow' was **sḱóyh$_a$* (e.g. Latv *seja* 'shadow; ghost', Rus *sen* 'shade, shadow', Alb *hie* 'shade, shadow; ghost, spectre', Grk *skiā́* 'shade, shadow; reflection, image; ghost, spectre', Av *asaya-* 'who throws no shadow', Skt *chāyā́-* 'shade, shadow', Toch B *skiyo* 'shadow').

There are a considerable number of regionally restricted words for light and dark. From the North-west region we have **ĝher-* 'shine, glow' (e.g. NE *grey*, Lith *žeriù* 'shine', OCS *zĭrjǫ* 'glance, see'); **leip-* 'light, cause to shine' (e.g. ON *leiptr* 'lightning', Lith *liepsnà* 'flame, blaze'); **bhlendh-* 'be/make cloudy' (e.g. NE *blind, blunder*, Lith *blandùs* 'unclean', Rus *blud* 'unchastity, lewdness'); and **merk-* '± darken' (e.g. OIr *mrecht-* 'variegated', NE *morn*, Lith *mérkiu* 'close one's eyes, wink', OCS *mrakŭ* 'dark'). From the West Central region: **g^{w}haidrós* 'bright, shining' (e.g. Lith *gaidrùs* 'fine, clear [of weather], bright, limpid [of water]', Grk *phaidrós* 'beaming [with joy], cheerful'); **(h$_a$)merh$_x$g^w-* 'dark' (e.g. ON *myrkr* 'darkness' [which was borrowed as NE *murk*], Lith *márgas* 'variegated', Alb *murg* 'black', Grk *amorbós* 'dark'); **(h$_a$)mauros* 'dark' (Rus *(s)muryj* 'dark grey', Grk *amaurós* 'dim, faint'); and **skótos* 'shadow, shade' (e.g. OIr *scāth* 'shadow, reflection; ghost, spectre', NE *shadow*, Grk *skótos* 'darkness, gloom; shadow'). The Central (Albanian-Greek) region offers **h$_2$eug-* 'shine, become bright' (Alb *agon* 'dawns', Grk *augḗ* 'beam of light'). Graeco-Aryan isoglosses include **kal-* 'beautiful' (e.g. Grk *kalós* 'beautiful', Skt *kalya-* 'healthy, prepared for, clever', *kalyāṇa-* 'beautiful'); from **bheh$_2$-* 'shine' both **bhéh$_2$(e)s-* 'light' (e.g. Grk *phōs*, Skt *bhās-* 'light') and **bhéh$_2$tis* 'light' (e.g. Grk *phásis* 'star rise', Skt *bhā́ti-* 'splendour'); and **dhwenh$_2$-* 'cover over, darken' (e.g. Skt *dhvāntá-* 'covered, veiled, dark; darkness, night'; the Grk cognates have shifted to 'die' [*thnḗskō*], 'mortal' [*thnētós*], and 'death' [*thánatos*]).

20.4 Colour

Words pertaining to colours reconstructable to Proto-Indo-European are indicated in Table 20.4.

A widely attested **peiḱ-* provides a word for 'paint, colour' in Indo-European (e.g. Lat *pingō* 'paint, colour', OE *fāh* 'coloured', Lith *piẽšti* 'draw, write', OCS *pisati* 'write', Grk *poikílos* 'coloured', Av *paēsa-* 'colour', Skt *piṃśáti* 'colours, paints', Toch AB *pik-* 'write, paint').

There are two words reconstructiable to Proto-Indo-European for 'black'. The one with the greatest distribution is **mel-n-* (e.g. Latv *melns* 'black', Grk *mélās* 'black', Skt *maliná-* 'dirty, black') which, in addition to 'black', yields 'yellow' (NWels *melyn*), 'reddish' (Lat *mulleus*), and 'blue' (OPrus *melne* 'blue spot', Lith *mẽlas* 'dark blue', *mélynas* 'blue' but 'black' in Latvian). The range

Table 20.4. *Colours*

**peiḱ-*	'paint, mark'	Lat *pingō*, Grk *poikílos*, Skt *piṃśáti*
**mel-n-*	'dull or brownish black'	Lat *mulleus*, Grk *mélās*, Skt *maliná-*
**kʷr̥snós*	'black'	Skt *kr̥ṣṇá-*
**h*$_2$*r̥ĝ(u)*	'white'	Lat *argentum*, Grk *árguros*, Skt *árjuna-*
**h*$_4$*elbhós*	'white'	Lat *albus*, Grk *alphós*
**bhelh*$_1$*-*	'white'	NE *ball*
**ḱweitos*	'white'	NE *white*, Skt *śvetá-*
**bhelh*$_1$*-*	'white'	Lat *flāvus*, Skt *bhālam*
**bhrodhnós*	'± pale'	Skt *bradhná-*
**h*$_1$*reudh-*	'(bright) red'	Lat *rūfus*, NE *red*, Grk *eruthrós*, Skt *rudhirá-*
**h*$_1$*elu-*	'dull red'	Skt *aruṣá-*
**ḱóunos*	'red'	Skt *śóṇa-*
**ḱyeh*$_1$*-*	'deep intense shade, ± green'	NE *hue*, Skt *śyāvá-*
**ḱer-* ~ **ḱr̥-wos*	'greyish blue, greyish green'	Skt *śārá-*
**modheros*	'blue/green'	NE *madder*
**ĝhel-* ~ **ghel-*	'yellow'	Lat *helvus*, NE *yellow*, Skt *hári-*
**bher-*	'brown'	NE *brown*, Grk *phrūnos*, Skt *babhrú-*
**ḱas-*	'grey'	Lat *cānus*, NE *hare*, Skt *śaśá-*
**pl̥h*$_x$*-*	'grey, pale'	Lat *pallidus*, NE *fallow*, Grk *poliós*, Skt *palitá-*
**perḱ-*	'speckled'	Lat *pulcher*, Grk *perknós*, Skt *pr̥ṣní-*

has suggested a 'dull or brownish black'. Still, while '(dark) blue' and 'black' seem a natural enough combination, the words for 'yellow' and 'reddish' are semantically rather difficult. A Baltic-Slavic-Indic isogloss yields *k^{w}r̥snós (e.g. OPrus *kirsnan* 'black', OCS *črŭnŭ* 'black', Skt *kr̥ṣṇá-* 'black') with a derived form in Alb *sorrë* meaning 'crow'. This may be a somewhat later word and indicate a 'shiny black' (cf. also Lith *kéršas* 'black and white, piebald').

As with roots indicating 'shine, bright', there are also a number of words for 'white'. The most widespread and productive root is *h_2r̥ĝ(u)- (e.g. Hit *harkis* 'white'; and a *u*-stem in Grk *árguros* 'silver', Skt *árjuṇa-* 'light, white', Toch B *ārkwi* 'white') which also gives a full-grade *$h_2$erĝ-n̥t-om 'silver' (e.g. OIr *argat*, Lat *argentum*, Arm *arcat'*, Av *ərəzatəm*, Toch B *ñkante* [with assimilation at some point of *r...n to *n...n]) and an *s*-stem adjective *h_2r̥ĝ-es- 'white' (i.e. Grk *argḗs*). A whitish colour is also denoted by *$h_4$elbhós which yields 'swan' in OHG *albiz* and OCS *lebedĭ* and 'cloud' in Hit *alpā-*; otherwise it means 'white' (e.g. Lat *albus* 'white', Grk *alphós* 'white leprosy'). Baltic, Slavic, and Indo-Iranian all attest *k̂woitós ~ *k̂witrós 'white' (e.g. Lith *švitrùs* 'bright', OCS *svĭtĭ* 'light', Av *spaēta-* 'white', Skt *śvetá-* 'white, bright', *śvitrá-* 'whitish, white'). The Germanic family represented by NE *white* must also belong here, though it seems to presuppose a related *k̂weidos (cf. also the Germanic family represented by NE *wheat*, from *k̂woidis, i.e. 'the white/light [grain]'). Another widespread word is *bhelh$_1$- 'white' (e.g. NWels *bal* 'white', Lith *bãlas* 'white', Grk *phalós* 'white', OCS *bělŭ* 'white') with a host of derived forms including Lat *flāvus* 'blond', NE *ball* (= horse with white blaze), Skt *bhālam* 'gleam, forehead'. The underlying verb appears in Lith *bálti* 'grow white, pale'. More ambiguous is *bhrodhnós which may fall between 'white' in Slavic (e.g. OCS *bronŭ* 'white, variegated [of horses]') and 'pale red' in Indic (i.e. Skt *bradhná-* 'pale red, yellowish, bay [of horses]', Kashmiri *bodur^u* 'tawny bull'). It is noteworthy that the two traditions that reflect this word largely restrict it to animals.

There are three words for 'red'. The most secure is *$h_1$reudh- which is generally represented in most languages as an *o*-grade adjective, i.e. *$h_1$roudhós (*e.g. OIr rūad* 'red', Lat *rūfus* 'red', NE *red*, Lith *raũdas*, Rus *rúdyj* 'blood-red, red-haired', Av *raoidita-* 'red', Skt *róhita-* 'red', *lohá-* 'reddish'). A second widely found form is *$h_1$rudhrós (e.g. Lat *ruber* 'red', Grk *eruthrós* 'red', Skt *rudhirá-* 'red', Toch B *ratre* 'red'). The second root, *$h_1$elu-, shows considerable semantic deviation, e.g. 'yellow' (Germanic, e.g. OHG *elo*), 'white' (Av *auruša-*), but 'reddish' (Indic, i.e. Skt *aruṣá-* and *aruṇá-* 'reddish, golden'). It has often been supposed that the *$h_1$el- of *$h_1$elu- is the base of the designation of the red deer (cf. Chapter 9.1). Perhaps the difference between *$h_1$reudh- and *$h_1$elu- is between 'high-intensity red' and 'low-intensity red', a kind of distinction that is not unknown in other languages. A Slavic-Indic isogloss secures

**ḱóunos* 'red' (e.g. Rus *suníca* 'wild strawberry', Skt *śóṇa-* 'red') and may be extended to Celtic if we accept 'lovely' as an acceptable semantic shift (seen in MIr *cūanna* and NWels *cun*).

The perceptual variation between 'blue' and 'green' is often ambiguous between different languages and this ambiguity is strikingly obvious in the reconstructed Proto-Indo-European lexicon. We have, for example, **ḱyeh*$_1$*-*, from which we have OE *hǣwen* 'blue, purple, green, azure, grey' (and OE *hīw* 'colour', giving NE *hue*) and the range of meanings across the other Indo-European cognates is similarly impressive, e.g. '(light/dark) grey' (Lith *šývas* 'light grey', OPrus *sywan* 'grey', OCS *sivŭ* 'dark grey', Alb *thinjë* 'grey', Lith *šẽmas* 'blue-grey'), 'sea green' (Serbo-Croatian *sinji*), '(dark) brown, dark green' (Skt *śyāmá-* 'dark brown, dark green', *śyāvá-* 'brown'), 'black, dark grey' (Sogdian *š'w* 'dark-coloured', Toch B *kwele* 'black, dark grey'). The root **ḱer-* yields meanings suggesting a 'greyish blue/green' (e.g. Lith *širvas* ~ *širmas* 'blue-grey' [cf. *širvìs* 'hare'], Alb *thjermë* '(blue-)grey', *surmë* 'dark grey, black', Skt *śārá-* 'coloured'). Somewhat tighter in terms of semantics are the Germanic, Slavic, Anatolian, and Tocharian reflecting PIE **m(o)dhro-* (e.g. NE *madder*, SC *modar* 'blue' [the Germanic and Slavic reflect Proto-Indo-European **modhrós*], Hit *āntara-* 'blue' [< **m̥dhrós*], Toch B *motartse* 'green' [< **modr̥-tyo-*]). This word would be the best candidate for a Proto-Indo-European word for 'blue' or at least 'blue/green'. The association of the Germanic words for 'red' arises from the use of the madder root as a red dye. The current use of madder and its cognates in Germanic to designate the plant *Rubia tinctorum* is itself a secondary transfer, on the basis of the root's use in dyeing, from an earlier reference to the bedstraws, some of whose species also have roots used to produce red dye. The bedstraws, however, may have been called **modhrós* because of their characteristic yellow-green flowers.

There is one root reconstructed for 'yellow', **ĝhel-* ~**ghel-*. Meanings generally fall around 'yellow' or 'gold' (e.g. OIr *gel* 'white', NWels *gell* 'yellow', Lat *helvus* 'honey yellow', NE *yellow*, Lith *geltas* 'yellow', *želvas* 'golden', Av *zairi-* 'yellow', and Skt *hári-* combines both 'yellow' and 'green') but as we see we also find that this root provided a base for 'green' in Slavic and Greek, e.g. OCS *zelenĭ* 'green', Grk *khlōrós* 'green', and Skt *hári-* 'yellow, green'. That its original meaning was indeed 'yellow' is indicated by the number of words for 'gold' (i.e. 'the yellow [metal]') built on this root (e.g. NE *gold*, Latv *zèlts*, OCS *zlato*, Av *zaranyam*, Skt *hiraṇyam*).

A root **bher-* meant 'brown' and was quite productive in that it underlies the Proto-Indo-European word for 'beaver' (Section 9.1) and the Germanic words for 'bear' (Section 9.1); it also renders 'toad' in Greek and is a horse colour in Mitanni. The colour words from this root come in many different formal shapes. We have **bhruh*$_x$*nos* in NE *brown* and Grk *phrûnos* 'toad' [<'the brown one'], **bhebhru-* in Mitanni *papru-* 'brown [of horses]', Skt *babhrú-* 'reddish brown' (and in the Proto-Indo-European word for 'beaver'), and **bhēro-* in Lith *bė̃ras* 'bay [of horses]'.

There are also two roots for 'grey' in addition to the 'blue/grey' above. The first is **ḱas-*, and although it can mean 'grey' in Lat *cānus* and ON *hǫss* (or 'old' in Osc *casnar*), it generally means 'hare' (e.g. NWels *ceinach*, NE *hare*, OPrus *sasins*, Khot *saha-*, Skt *śaśá-*) and shows that this animal was originally 'the grey one' (Section 9.1). The second is **pl̥h$_x$-*; it means 'grey' in Celtic (e.g. MIr *līath*), Baltic (Lith *pìlkas*), Grk *pelitnós, poliós*, Indo-Iranian (Av *pouruša-*, Skt *palitá-*), 'pale' in Lat *pallidus*, 'fallow' in Germanic, e.g. NE *fallow*, 'old man' in Alb *plak*, but 'white' in Arm *alik'*; this root is probably the basis for **pél(h$_x$)us* 'mouse' which would be then another 'grey one' (Section 9.1).

Finally, **perḱ-* renders 'speckled' across most languages in which it is preserved (MIr *erc*, Grk *perknós*, Skt *pr̥ṣṇí-*); Latin has shifted in meaning to 'beautiful' (*pulcher*, and with dissimilation of **r ... r* to *l ... r*) and in Germanic, e.g. NHG *Farbe*, to 'colour' in general.

There are a few regionally attested colour terms. From the North-West we have **slih$_x$u-* 'plum-coloured' (e.g. OIr *lī* 'colour', Lat *līvor* 'bluish colour', NE *sloe*, Rus *slíva* 'plum'); and **rei-* 'striped, spotted' (e.g. OIr *rīabach* 'streaked, striped', Latv *ràibs* 'spotted', Rus *ríbyj* 'variegated' and perhaps NE *roe*); and a Celtic-Italic isogloss **badyos* '(yellow) brown' (OIr *buide* 'yellow', Lat *badius* 'bay (of a horse)'; from the West Central region is **ḱeir-* 'dull or brownish black' (e.g. OIr *cīar* 'dark brown', NE *hoar*, OCS *sěru* 'grey', Alb *thirr* 'soot', Grk *kíraphos* 'fox', *kirrós* 'orangy'). A Greek-Indic isogloss is seen in the expression **pl̥h$_1$u-poik/ḱos* 'many-coloured, variegated' (Grk *polupoíkilos*, Skt *puru-péśa-*); a possible Gothic cognate *filu-faihs* 'very diverse' is somewhat doubtful as it may have been created purely to resemble the Greek cognate which it was translating (although it would provide a nearly irresistible though egregiously false etymology for NE *filofax*).

20.5 Hearing, Smell, Touch, and Taste

Words directly describing the other four senses are far more sparsely reconstructed than sight (see Table 20.5). This observation is not meant to suggest any particular insight into the Proto-Indo-European mind as the vocabulary associated with 'what is audible', i.e. speech, is enormous and is handled elsewhere in Chapter 21. And if we extend the general meaning of 'touch' to all those activities involving the manipulation of objects, we will see that the associated vocabulary, here reviewed in Chapter 22, is also very extensive.

Table 20.5. *Hearing, smell, touch, and taste*

**k̂leu-*	'hear'	Lat *clueō*, Grk *kléō*, Skt *śr̥ṇóti*
**k̂leus-*	'hear'	NE *listen*, Skt *śróṣati*
pū-* (puh*$_x$-?)	'stink'	Lat *pūteō*, Grk *púthō*, Skt *pū́yati*
**deg-*	'touch'	
**ml̥k̂-*	'touch lightly'	Lat *mulceō*, Skt *mr̥śáti*
**klep-*	'± lay hand to'	NE *helm*, *halter*, Grk *kléptō*
**sweh*$_a$*dús*	'sweet'	Lat *suādus*, NE *sweet*, Grk *hēdús*, Skt *svādhú-*
**h*$_2$*em-ro-s*	'bitter, sour'	Lat *amārus*, Skt *amlá-*

There is only one root for 'hear', **k̂leu-* (e.g. OIr *ro-cluinethar* 'hears', Lat *clueō* 'am called', Goth *hliuma* 'hearing', OCS *sluti* 'be called', Alb *quaj* 'call, name; consider', Grk *kléō* 'tell of, make famous', Arm *lsem* 'hear', Av *surunaoiti* 'hears', Skt *śr̥ṇóti* 'hears', Toch B *klautso* 'ear'), which also appears extended as **k̂leus-* (e.g. OIr *clūas* 'ear', NE *listen*, Lith *klausaũ* 'I hear', OCS *slyšati* 'hear', Messapic *klaohi* 'hear!', Skt *śróṣati* 'hears', Toch B *klyaus-* 'hear'). The root is ubiquitous and also appears in a number of derived forms, e.g. **k̂lutós* 'what is heard', i.e. 'fame', a central concept of the Indo-European poetic heritage (e.g. OIr *cloth* 'fame', Lat *inclutus* 'famous', Grk *klutós* 'famous', Arm *lu* 'known', Skt *śrutá-* 'famous'; see Section 21.5); a lengthened grade e.g. **k̂lūtós* in Germanic gives us NE *loud*.

There is no word reconstructable to Proto-Indo-European for 'to smell', i.e. perceive the odour of something, as opposed to smell = stink. The latter concept can be expressed with **pū-* (**puh*$_x$-?) which is recovered from Italic (Lat *pūteō* 'stink'), Baltic (e.g. Lith *púdau* 'rot'), Grk *púthō* 'become rotten', and Indo-Iranian (Av *puyeiti* 'rots', Skt *pū́yati* 'stinks') and which is believed to be the equivalent of NE interjection *pew!* and hence of onomatopoeic origin.

There are at least three words that broadly indicate 'touch'. A Germanic-Tocharian isogloss (ON *taka* 'touch': Toch B *täk-* 'touch') indicates a root **deg-* 'touch'. A Latin-Indic isogloss of **ml̥k̂-* 'touch lightly' is based on meanings of 'stroke' in both languages (Lat *mulceō* 'stroke, touch lightly, fondle', Skt *mr̥śáti* 'strokes, touches'). A more general (or sinister) 'lay hand to' would seem to be the meaning of **klep-* (e.g. NE *helm*, *halter*, OPrus *anklipts* 'concealed', Toch AB *kälp-* 'find, get, achieve, obtain', Toch B *klep-* 'touch with the hands, investigate, test'). Verbal forms in Gothic, Greek, and Tocharian means 'steal' (Goth *hlifan*, Grk *kléptō*, Toch B *kälyp-*).

Finally, taste is expressed in a well-attested **sweh*$_a$*dús* 'pleasing to the senses, tasty' where a specific meaning of 'sweet' is suggested in Germanic (e.g. NE *sweet*), Skt *svādhú-* 'sweet', and Toch B *swāre* 'sweet', while a zero-grade gives us Lith *sū́dyti* 'to salt'; Lat *suāvis* 'pleasing to the senses', and Grk *hēdús* 'what is pleasing to the senses' carries a more general meaning while the Celtic examples are retained only in Gaulish personal names, e.g. *Suadu-rīx*. Other examples relating to taste may be found in Chapter 16. Finally, a word for 'bitter' *$*h_2$em-ro-s*, from a root *$*h_2$em-* 'raw, bitter', is also widely attested (e.g. Lat *amārus* 'bitter', OE *ampre* 'sorrel, dock', Skt *amlá-* 'bitter') though not without curious semantic inversions, e.g. Arm *amok'* 'sweet', Alb *ëmbël* 'sweet'.

To these we may add a few regional terms from the West Central area: *$*h_3$ed-* 'give off a smell' (e.g. Lat *oleō* 'smell, stink', Lith *úodžiu* 'smell', OCzech *jadati* 'sniff out, investigate', Grk *ózō* 'smell', Arm *hotim* 'smell'); **tag-* 'touch' (e.g. Lat *tangō* 'touch' OE *þaccian* 'touch lightly, stroke', Grk *tetagōn* 'seizing'); and **ghrei-* 'touch lightly' (e.g. Lith *gr(i)ejù* 'skim [cream]', Grk *khríō* 'touch the surface of a body lightly, graze; [hence] rub or anoint with oil, coat with colour' [the past participle of this verb, *khristós*, was used to translate the Hebrew *Messiah*, whence, by borrowing, NE *Christ*]).

20.6 The Good, Bad, and the Ugly

Here we have grouped together what are largely adjectives and some verbs indicating major positive and negative qualities (Table 20.6*a*).

Table 20.6*a*. *Positive qualities*

**wesu-*	'excellent, noble'	Lat *Vesuna*, Skt *vásu-*
$*h_1$(e)su-	'good'	Grk *eű̃s*
$*(h_1)$su-	'good'	Grk *eu-*, Skt *su-*
$*h_1$sónt-	'real, true'	Lat *sōns*, NE *sooth*, Skt *satyá-*
**mel-*	'good'	Lat *melior*
$*h_a$eu-	'favour'	Lat *aveō*, Skt *ávati*
$*h_1$erh_as-	'be well disposed to someone'	Grk *éramai*
**teu-*	'look on with favour'	Lat *tueor*
**teus-*	'be happy'	Skt *túṣyati*
?$*h_3$ens-	'be gracious to, show favour'	Grk *prosēnḗs*
$*$pleh$_a$k-	'please'	Lat *placeō*
$*$geh$_a$u-	'rejoice'	Lat *gaudeō*, Grk *gánumai*
$*$geh$_a$dh-	'rejoice'	Grk *gēthéō*
**meud-*	'be merry'	Skt *módate*

There are four words or roots indicating 'good' attributable to Proto-Indo-European. The root **wesu-* (e.g. OIr *feib* 'in excellence', Luv *wāsu* 'good', Av *vohu-* 'good', Skt *vásu-* 'good') not only means 'good' but frequently appears in personal or tribal names among different Indo-European groups, e.g. Gaul *Vesu-avus*, Lat *Vesuna* (name of a goddess), the Germanic tribal name *Wisi* (e.g. the Visigoths). The rhyming **h_1(e)su-* yields 'good' in Greek and Anatolian (e.g. Grk *eṻs* 'good, useful', Hit *āssu-* 'good') and may also be seen in Lat *erus* 'master' and the Celtic divine name *Esus*, though both the Latin and Celtic have other possible etymologies. As a prefix **(h_1)su-* is even more widespread (e.g. OIr *so-* 'good', OCS *sŭ-dravŭ* 'healthy', Grk *hu-giḗs* 'healthy', *eu-* 'good', Av *hu-* 'good', Skt *su-* 'good', Toch B *saswe* 'lord' [< **$h_1$su-suh$_x$ó-* 'well-born']). This entire complex is usually derived from **$h_1$es-* 'to be'. The same verb provides the basis for a word for 'true', **$h_1$sónt-*, the participial of **$h_1$es-* 'be', with certain legal connotations in Lat *sōns* 'guilty', Germanic (e.g. OE *sōðian* 'bear witness, prove true' > NE *soothe* and also NE *soothsayer*), and also Hit *asānt-* 'being, existing' but also *asān-at iyanun-at* "it (is) true, I did it". It also indicates 'true' in Indo-Iranian (e.g. Skt *satyá-*). An Italic-Baltic-Anatolian isogloss gives us **mel-* 'good' (e.g. Lat *melior* 'better', Lith *malonùs* 'pleasant', Hit *malā(i)-* 'approve, be favourable').

Words indicating something akin to 'favour' include **$h_a$eu-* (e.g. OIr *con-ōi* 'guards', Lat *aveō* 'desire strongly', Runic *auja* 'good fortune', Doric Grk *aïtas* 'friend', Av *avaiti* 'cares for, helps', Skt *ávati* 'is pleased, promotes'). If Alb *ha* 'eat' belongs here (< * 'enjoy [food]'), then the PIE root is **$h_4$eu-*. A second 'favour' word is manifested in the Greek-Tocharian isogloss **$h_1$erh$_a$s-* (e.g. Grk *éramai* 'love', Toch AB *yärs-* 'be deferential, respectful'). Another root for 'look on with favour' is **teu-* (e.g. OIr *tūath* 'north', Lat *tueor* 'observe, protect', OE *þēaw* 'custom') which requires acceptance of a potential Luvian cognate *tāwa/i-* 'eye' to broaden the distribution of cognates beyond the North-West. The underlying logic here is 'look on with favour' > 'look/observe' > 'eye'. The Old Irish cognate is the direction word *tūath* 'north, left' which is normally the unfavourable direction in Indo-European, hence it is presumed that here 'favour' is being used euphemistically. A fourth possible root is **$h_{1/4}$ens-* which involves a Germanic-Greek-Hittite isogloss (e.g. OHG *anst* 'favour', Grk *prosēnḗs* 'gentle, kind, soft', Hit *ass-* ~ *assiya-* 'be favoured, be dear, be good'). A Latin-Tocharian isogloss gives us **pleh$_a$k-* 'please', a verb derived from the adjective **pleh$_a$k-* 'flat', i.e. 'make level, smooth' as in Lat *plācō* 'smooth, calm', the source of NE *placate* and *placeō* 'please' (through Old French) *please*, and Toch AB *plāk-* 'be in agreement' (see Section 18.5). A Proto-Indo-European **teus-* 'be happy' (arguably an extended form of **teu-* favour') is indicated by a Hittite-Indic isogloss (Hit *duski-* 'be happy', Skt *túṣyati* 'is delighted with'). A Greek-Tocharian isogloss yields **geh$_a$dh-* rejoice' (e.g. Grk *gēthéō* 'am happy, rejoice', Toch AB *kātk-* 'rejoice'); another form derived from the same (unattested) root (*geh_a-) is *$geh_a u$- 'rejoice, swell with joy' (e.g. OIr *gūaire* 'noble', Lat *gaudeō* 'am happy, rejoice', Lith *džiaugúos* (<*gaudžiúos*) 'am happy', Grk *gánumai* 'rejoice', *gaûros* 'proud') which is restricted to the West Central region. The root **meud-* 'be merry' is found in Indo-Iranian (Av *maoδanō-kara-* 'lust-inducing', Skt *módate* 'is cheerful', *mudrá-* 'merry, cheerful') and in derived form also in Baltic (e.g. Lith *mudrùs* 'cheerful, lively').

The other regional terms are (from the North-West): *$meh_a(t)$- 'good' (e.g. OIr *maith* 'good', Lat *mānis* 'good'); *weh_1ros (or **wēros*) 'true' in Celtic (OIr *fīr*), Lat *vērus*, Germanic (OHG *wār*), all 'true' and possibly OCS *věru* 'belief' if it is not a borrowing from Germanic; the West Central area: **ghleu-* 'revel' (e.g. NE *glee*, Lith *gláudoti* 'joke', Rus *glum* 'joke', Grk *khleúē* 'joke'); **loid-* 'play, jest' (e.g. Lat *lūdō* 'play', Grk *lízei* 'plays'); Greek and Indic preserve or have independently created the compound *h_1*su-menes-ye/o-* 'be well disposed to', i.e. 'good' + 'thought' + verbal suffix (Grk *eumenéō* 'am gracious', Skt *sumanasyáte* 'is favourable').

A possible word *h_a*egh-lo-* from a root *h_a*egh-* 'unpleasant' may be attested between the North-Western languages and Indo-Iranian (e.g. MIr *ālad*

Table 20.6*b*. *Negative qualities*

*h_a*egh-los*	'unpleasant'	Skt *aghalá-*
**dus-*	'bad' (as prefix)	Grk *dus-*, Skt *duṣ-*
**ĝhalh$_x$ros*	'evil, unpleasant, unhealthy'	NE *gall*
*$h_{2/3}$*wop-*	'treat badly'	NE *evil*
**rabh-*	'± ferocity'	Lat *rabiēs*, Skt *rábhas-*
**bhibhóih$_x$e*	'is afraid'	NHG *beben*, Skt *bibhā́ya*
**dwei-*	'fear'	Grk *deídō*, Skt *dvéṣṭi*
*neh_2-	'be timid'	
*$k^w eh_1(i)$-	'fear, revere'	Grk *tíō*, Skt *cā́yati*
**perk-*	'fear'	NE *fright*
**tres-*	'tremble, fear'	Lat *terreō*, Grk *tréō*, Skt *trásati*
**ĝheis-*	'frighten'	NE *ghost*, Skt *héḍa-*
*$terg^w$-	'scare'	Lat *torvus*, Grk *tarbéō*, Skt *tárjati*
**ghres-*	'± threaten, torment'	
**sker-*	'± threaten'	
**dhreugh-*	'deceive'	Skt *drúhyati*
*(*s*)*weig-*	'deceive'	
*(*s*)*mel-*	'deceive'	
*meh_a-	'wave/trick (with the hand)'	Skt *māyā́*
**meng-*	'± charm, deceive'	Grk *mágganon*

'wound', OE *egle* 'disagreeable, loathsome', Av *aγō-* 'bad', Skt *aghá-* 'bad', *aghalá-* 'terrible'); alternatively, the **-lo-* suffix may have been added independently in the two regions. The prefix **dus-* 'bad' or, in English terms, 'un-' or 'ill-', is well attested across the Indo-European world (e.g. OIr *do-* 'bad, mis-', OE *tor-* 'un-', NHG *zer-* [verbal prefix], Grk *dus-* 'bad, mis-', Av *duš-* 'bad, mis-', Skt *duṣ-* 'bad, mis-'); Lat *dif-* may be cognate here. It occurs residually in Slavic, e.g. in Rus *doždĭ* 'rain, bad weather', originally 'bad-sky'. An OIr *galar* 'sickness, distress': Hit *kallara-* 'something unpleasant' isogloss is the basis for the reconstruction of **ĝhalh$_x$ros* 'evil, unpleasant' although there are related forms in some other groups (e.g. NE *gall* [on the skin], Lith *žalà* 'damage, loss; injury; wrong', Ukrainian *zolok* 'painful place of a wound'). A verbal root **h$_{2/3}$wop-* 'treat badly' is recovered from Celtic (OIr *fel* 'bad'), Germanic (e.g. NE *evil*), and Anatolian (*huwappi* ~ *huwapzi* 'ill-treats, despoils'). A possible root **rabh-* underlies an Italic-Indic isogloss (Lat *rabiēs* 'violence', Skt *rábhas-* 'ferocity') to mean something like 'ferocity'.

The semantic field of 'fear' is well represented in the reconstructed lexicon. Germanic (e.g. OE *beofian* 'tremble', NHG *beben* 'tremble') and Indic (Skt *bibhā́ya* 'is afraid') attest an old perfect (rebuilt in Germanic with present endings) **bhibhóih$_x$e* 'is afraid'. The verb **dwei-* is variously recovered meaning 'fear' and 'frighten' (e.g. Grk *deidō* 'fear', Arm *erknč'im'* 'frighten', perhaps Luv *kuwaya-* 'fear', Av *dvaēš-* 'be hostile, provoke', Skt *dvéṣṭi* 'hates, is hostile', Toch A *wi-* 'be frightened'); it appears to derive from the numeral **dwi-* 'two' and its etymology may have been something like 'be of two minds' or, in the hindsight of modern psychological theory, express the natural decision-making process between 'fight and flight' when confronted with a danger. A MIr *nār* 'modest': Hit *nāh-* 'be afraid' isogloss furnishes **neh$_2$-* 'be timid'. The concept of devotional 'fear' or 'reverence' is found in **k^{w}eh$_1$(i)-* (e.g. OCS *čajǫ* '(a)wait, hope', Grk *tíō* 'honour, revere', perhaps Luv *kuwaya-* 'fear', Skt *cā́yati* 'reveres, pays attention to'). The root **perk-* 'fear' is based on a Germanic-Tocharian isogloss (e.g. NE *fright*, Toch AB *pärsk-* 'be afraid'). The physical manifestation of fear is found in **tres-* 'tremble, fear' (e.g. MIr *tarrach* 'fearful', Lat *terror* 'terror', Lith *trišù* 'tremble', Grk *tréō* 'tremble, flee', Av *tərəsaiti* 'fears', Skt *trásati* 'trembles, is afraid'; see also Section 22.4). To 'frighten' or 'scare' is also indicated by various words. The verbal root **ĝheis-* 'frighten' also occurs as an *o*-grade in Germanic to give us NE *ghost* (cf. also ON *geiska-fullr* 'full of fear', Av *zaēša-* 'horrible', Skt *héḍa-* 'anger'). Something on the order of 'scare' or 'threaten' lies behind **terg^w-* (e.g. NWels *tarfu* 'hunt', Lat *torvus* 'piercing wild [of the eyes]', OE *þracian* 'fear, feel dread, shudder', Grk *tarbéō* 'scare', Skt *tárjati* 'threatens, scolds'). Two isoglosses involving Tocharian provide us with two roots for 'threaten': **ghres-* (Toch AB *krās-* 'vex, torment' with Baltic, e.g.

Lith *gresiù* 'threaten, menace') and **sker-* (Toch B *skär-* 'speak hostilely, threaten; reproach' with Germanic, e.g. MLG *scheren* 'ridicule').

The Proto-Indo-Europeans had a vocabulary of deception. The root **dhreugh-* 'deceive' is attested in both verbal forms, e.g. OHG *triogan* 'deceives', Skt *drúhyati* 'harms, is hostile to', and also provides nominal forms indicating spectres in the West (e.g. MIr *aur-fraich* 'ghost', ON *draugr* 'ghost' and abstracts in Indo-Iranian (e.g. Av *draoga-* 'lie'); it also underlies the Germanic words for dream (as a false vision), e.g. ON *draumr* 'dream'. A Germanic (e.g. OE *swīcan* 'betray') -Tocharian (Toch A *wek-* 'to lie') isogloss secures the root **(s)weig-* 'deceive'. A PIE **(s)mel-* 'deceive' is based on cognates in Baltic (e.g. Lith *mẽlas* 'lie'), Arm *mel* 'sin', Iranian (Av *mairya-* 'deceitful'), and Tocharian (Toch A *smale* 'lie'). A physical dimension to deception is suggested by PIE *meh$_a$-* 'wave/trick (with the hand)' where the Baltic cognates suggest a simple motion, e.g. Lith *móju* 'wave, signal with the hand', but the other cognate groups indicate an element of deception, e.g. Rus *ob-manútĭ* 'trick, deceive', Skt *māyā́* 'trick, illusion', Toch A *māsk-* 'switch, juggle'. Finally, there is the somewhat questionable equation of MIr *meng* 'deceit, guile', Grk *mágganon* 'charm, philtre', Oss *mæng* 'deceit' to propose a PIE **meng-* '± charm, deceive'.

From the North-West we have **leud-* 'act hypocritically, badly' (e.g. OE *lot* 'deception', OPrus *laustinti* 'humble, abase', OCS *ludŭ* 'foolish'); **saiwos* 'hard, sharp, rude' (e.g. Lat *saevus* 'hot-headed, raging, furious', Latv *sievs* 'hard, curt'); and **meug-* '± cheat, deceive' (e.g. OIr *formūchtha* 'smothered, concealed', Lat *muger* 'dice cheat', and NE *meecher*). From the West Central region **bhorg^{w}o-* 'angry, violent' (e.g. OIr *borb* 'stupid, violent', Latv *bar̃gs* 'hard, unfriendly', Arm *bark* 'angry, violent'); **h$_1$óistro/eh$_a$-* 'anger, any strong feeling' (e.g. Lith *aistrà* 'passion', Grk *oîstros* 'gadfly, sting, anger'; from **h$_1$eis-* 'set in motion'; *oîstros* is borrowed, via Latin, in NE *estrus*); **h$_a$egh-* 'be afraid, be downcast' (e.g. OIr *ad-āgathar* 'fears', ON *agi* 'terror', Grk *ákhos* 'mental pain or distress'); **garĝos* 'frightening, threatening' (e.g. OIr *garg* 'rough', OCS *groza* 'shudder, horror', Arm *karcr* 'hard', Grk *gorgós* 'terrible, frightful, savage'); and **kel-* 'deceive' (Lat *calvor* ~ *calvō* 'deceive', OE *hōl* 'slander', Grk *kēléō* 'bewitch, deceive'). A possible Greek-Indic isogloss is seen in **k̂et-* 'be angry' (Grk *kótos* 'spite, anger', Skt *śátru-* 'enemy').

20.7 Desire

Expressing a wish or desire in Indo-European could be accomplished both by the optative mood of the verb and by a relatively extensive vocabulary associated with the concept of 'desire'.

Table 20.7. *Desire*

$*wenh_x$-	'desire, strive to obtain'	Lat *venus*, Skt *vánas-*
**ĝhor(ye/o)-*	'desire'	Lat *horior*, NE *yearn*, Skt *háryati*
**gheldh-*	'desire'	Skt *gṛ́dhyati*
$*h_xih_xiĝh$-(e/o)-	'desire (strongly)'	Grk *ī́khar*, Skt *ī́hate*
**?moud-*	'desire strongly'	
**weḱ-*	'wish, want'	Grk *hekṓn*, Skt *váśmi*
**wel-*	'wish, want'	Lat *volō*, NE *will*, Skt *vṛṇīté*
$*h_aeis$-	'wish for, seek out'	Lat *aeruscāre*, NE *ask*, Skt *icchá́ti*
**las-*	'be greedy, lascivious'	Lat *lascīvus*, NE *lust*, Grk *lilaíomai*, Skt *lasati*
$*seh_2(i)$-	'satisfy, fill up'	Grk *ā́menai*, Skt *asinvá-*
**terp-*	'take (to oneself), satisfy oneself'	Grk *térpomai*, Skt *tṛ́pyati*
$*speh_1$-	'be satisfied, be filled, thrive'	Lat *spēs*, Skt *sphā́yate*

The verbal root *$*wenh_x$-* yields a variety of meanings ranging from the relatively tame, e.g. ON *vinr* 'friend' or Av *vantā* 'wife', across 'lust' (Lat *venus*, Skt *vánas-*) and possibly as far as Hit *wen-* 'copulate' if it is not from **wen-* 'strike' (cf. also Toch B *wīna* 'pleasure'). An **-sk-* suffixed form gives NE *wish* and Skt *vā́ñchati* 'wishes, desires'. 'Desire' is also the meaning of the widely attested **ĝhor(ye/o)-* where some groups retain the emphasis on striving and yearning, e.g. Italic and Germanic (e.g. Lat *horior* 'exhort, incite', NE *yearn*), while others emphasize completion of desire, e.g. Grk *khaírō* 'rejoice', Skt *háryati* 'finds pleasure in, desires', and Toch B *ker(y)-* 'laugh'. A Slavic-Indic isogloss gives us **gheldh-* 'desire' (e.g. OCS *žlĭděti* 'desire', *gladŭ* 'hunger', Skt *gṛ́dhyati* 'is envious', *gardha-* 'envy'), while perhaps a stronger yearning is to be found in *$*h_xih_xiĝh$ -(e/o)-* (e.g. Grk *ī́khar* 'violent desire', Av *īžā-* 'desire', Skt *ī́hate* 'strives for, wants', Toch B *ykāsse* 'concupiscence'). Baltic-Slavic and Tocharian provide evidence for **moud-* 'desire strongly' (e.g. Lith *maudžiù* 'desire passionately', Czech *mdlíti* 'desire', Toch B *maune* 'avarice, avidity').

There are several verbs that seem to express 'wish'. Hittite and Indo-Iranian all attest **weḱ-* (e.g. Hit *wēkmi* 'I wish', Av *vasəmi* 'I wish', Skt *váśmi* 'I wish') while the Greek cognate, *hekṓn*, means 'willingly'. There is no clear semantic distinction between this and *$*wel(h_x)$-* 'wish' (e.g. MWels *gwell* 'better', Lat *volō* 'want', NE *will*, Lith *pa-vélmi* 'wish', OCS *veljǫ* 'wish', Arm *gel* 'beauty', Av *var-* 'choose, wish', Skt *vṛṇīté* 'chooses'). On the other hand there is a strong sense of 'seek out' to be found in *$*h_aeis$-* where this is the meaning exhibited in Baltic (e.g. Lith *íeškau* 'seek') and Indo-Iranian (Av *isaiti* 'seeks, wishes', Skt *éṣati* 'seeks', *iccháti* 'wishes, seeks'); Lat *aeruscō* and Germanic (e.g. NE *ask*) tend to mean 'ask'. Finally, desire is also expressed in the widely found outcomes of **las-* 'be greedy' (e.g. OIr *lainn* 'eager, greedy', Lat *lascīvus* 'lascivious', NE *lust*, Lith *lokšnùs* 'loving, amorous, tender', OCS *laskati* 'flatter', Grk *lilaíomai* 'desire', dialectal Grk *lástē* 'courtesan', Skt *lasati* 'strives, plays, is delighted').

There were several different ways to indicate 'satisfy'. A verbal root **seh*$_2$*(i)-* 'satisfy' (e.g. Grk *ắmenai* 'satisfy oneself', Arm *hač* 'contented', Hit *sāh-* 'stuff full, clog up', Skt *asinvá-* 'unsatisfied', TochA *si-* 'be satisfied') provides a noun **séh*$_2$*tis* 'satisfaction' (e.g. OIr *saith* 'satisfaction', Lat *satis* 'enough', Lith *sótis* 'satiety'). An adjective **sh̥*$_a$*tós* 'satisfied' (e.g. OHG *sat* 'satisfied' Grk *áatos* 'insatiable') underwent an interesting semantic development in English: OE *sæd* 'satisfied' came to mean 'heavy' (as if one were full) which ultimately yields NE *sad*. The semantic range of **terp-* is rather wide in that Germanic indicates 'need' (e.g. OE *þurfan* 'need, lack'), Av 'steal' (*tarəp-*, presumably the meaning developed from a euphemistic extension of 'satisfy oneself'; cf. also Skt *paśu-tr̥p-* 'cattle stealing'), while Greek and Indic indicate the basic meaning 'satisfy' (e.g. Grk *térpomai* 'satisfy myself', Skt *tŕ̥pyati* 'be sated'; cf. also Lith *tarpstù* 'flourish', OCS *trŭpěti* 'suffer, endure', Toch A *tsārwā-* 'be confident, rejoice'); it also exists in a widespread derived form **térptis* (gen. **tr̥ptéis*) 'satisfaction' found in Germanic (ON *þurft* 'need'), Grk *térpsis* 'satisfaction', Skt *tŕ̥pti-* satisfaction'. While the Latin reflex of **speh*$_1$*-* (e.g. OE *spōwan* 'thrive, succeed', Lith *spė̃ju* 'have free time', OCS *spěti* 'be successful, prosper', Toch B *spāw-* '± spread out'), i.e. *spēs*, only means 'hope', the Indic indicates completion of the desire in the meaning 'grows fat' (Skt *sphā́yate*) and the root is the basis for one of the words for 'fat', **sph̥*$_1$*rós* (see Section 17.3).

The few regionally restricted words are (from the West Central region) **h*$_1$*op-* 'desire' (e.g. Lat *optō* 'wish', OCS *za-(j)apŭ* 'presumption, suspicion', Grk *epiópsomai* 'choose'), perhaps from **h*$_1$*ep-* 'grasp'; **g*^{w}*hel-* 'wish, want' (e.g. OCS *želěti* 'wish', Grk *thélō* 'wish'); an Avestan-Tocharian isogloss yields **k*^{w}*lep-* 'desire' (Av *xrap-* 'desire', Toch AB *kulyp-* 'desire').

20.8 Love and Hate

Frequently, roots for 'desire' or 'want' also yield meanings 'love' but there are a series of words that are more specifically associated with the vocabulary of 'love' and 'hate'.

The verbal root **keh*$_a$*-* is only found as such in Indo-Iranian (e.g. Av *kā-* 'long for', Skt *kāyamāna-* 'liking') but in derived form **keh*$_a$*-ro-* we find it

Table 20.8. *Love and hate*

**keh*$_a$*-*	'love'	Lat *cārus*, NE *whore*
**kem-*	'love'	Skt *kāmáyati*
**ken-*	'love'	Skt *cánas-*
**prih*$_x$*-eh*$_a$*-*	'love'	NE *friend*, Skt *priyāyáte*
**leubh-*	'love, desire'	Lat *lubet*, NE *love*, Skt *lúbhyati*
**h*$_x$*leh*$_a$*d-*	'dear'	
**kus-*	'kiss'	NE *kiss*, Grk *kunéō*
**h*$_3$*ed-*	'hate'	Lat *ōdī*, *odium*, Grk *odúsasthai*
**k̂eh*$_a$*des-*	'±concern; hate'	NE *hate*, Grk *kêdos*
**peik/k̂-*	'be hostile, hate'	NE *foe*, Skt *píśuna-*
**(h*$_x$*)neid-*	'insult'	Grk *oneidízō*, Skt *nindati*
**pih*$_x$*(y)-*	'revile'	Skt *pī́yati*

providing words for endearment in Celtic (e.g. OIr *cara* 'friend', *caraid* 'loves') and Italic (Lat *cārus* 'dear') while it shifted to 'adulterer' and 'whore' in Germanic (e.g. NE *whore*). Probably related to this root are two others beginning with the same velar, **kem-* (e.g. Lith *kamaros* [pl.] 'lasciviousness', Skt *kāmáyati* 'longs for, is in love with, copulates with', Toch B *kāñm-* 'play') and **ken-* (e.g. MIr *cin* 'love, tendency', Av *čanah-* 'demand, request', Skt *cánas-* 'pleasure'), both of which can be given a proto-meaning of 'love'. The root **prih*$_x$*-eh*$_a$*-*, found from Germanic to Indic (e.g. Goth *frijōn* 'love', *frijōnds* 'friend', OCS *prijajǫ* 'am favourable', Skt *priyāyáte* 'befriends'), tends to give verbal meanings of 'love', as in OE *frīgan* 'love', and nominal meanings of 'friend'. This **prih*$_x$*-eh*$_a$*-* is a verbal derivative of **prih*$_x$*-ós* 'of one's own' (e.g. ON *frī* 'beloved, spouse', Av *frya-* 'dear', Skt *priyá-* 'dear', and, significantly, NE *free*, NWels *rhydd* 'free'). In turn, this **prih*$_x$*ós* may be an adjectival derivative of **pēr* 'house' (if this word is truly Proto-Indo-European, cf. Sections 12.1, 13.1) originally 'of one's own household'. Meanings of both 'desire' and 'love' can be credited to **leubh-* (e.g. Lat *lubet* ~ *libet* 'pleases', *lubīdō* ~ *libīdō* 'desire, pleasure', NE *love*, Lith *liaupsẽ* 'glorification', OCS *lyuby* 'love', Alb *laps* 'wish', dialectal Grk *luptá* 'courtesan', Skt *lúbhyati* 'desires ardently'). A derivative in the North-West gives us a standard word for 'dear' (e.g. OE *lēof* 'dear' [> (archaic) NE *lief*], OCS *ljubŭ* 'dear'; cf. also the corresponding noun in Skt *lóbha-* 'desire'). The root **h*$_x$*leh*$_a$*d-* supplies words for 'dear' in Slavic (e.g. Rus *ládyj* 'dear') and Tocharian (e.g. Toch B *lāre* 'dear'), 'love, caress' in Arm *alalem* and 'desires' in Skt *lāḍayate* (*-ḍ-* < **-dr-*) while in Lycian it yields *lada-* 'wife' (cf. also Rus *láda* 'wife'). A verbal root **kus-* 'kiss' is reconstructed on the basis of Grk *kunéō* 'kiss', Hit *kuwaszi* 'kisses', and possibly Germanic; doubt exists for the Germanic words, e.g.

ON *kyssa*, OHG *kussen*, NE *kiss*, because Proto-Indo-European **k* should give Germanic **h* and not **k* unless the *k* was employed for some sound-symbolic reason, i.e. somehow a hard *k*-sound was thought to be appropriate for a kissing noise among the speakers of Proto-Germanic.

There are several words for 'hate'. The root **h₃ed-* tends to mean either 'hate' or 'fearsome' (e.g. Lat *ōdī* 'hate' [verb], *odium* 'hate' [noun], OE *atol* 'atrocious', Grk *odúsasthai* 'be angry at, hate', Arm *ateam* 'hate', Hit *hatukzi* 'is terrible') and underlies the name of the Greek hero *Odysseus*. There seems to be a semantic divergence in the meaning of **ḱeh$_a$des-* which indicates 'hate' in the West (Celtic, e.g. MIr *cais* 'hate', and Germanic, e.g. NE *hate*) but 'care for' in Grk *kêdos* 'care, concern, sorrow' and Indo-Iranian (Av *sādra-* 'grief' and perhaps Skt *ri-śādas-* if the latter means 'caring for a stranger'). Hostility of some sort is more uniform across the cognates derived from **peik/ḱ-* 'hate' (e.g. NE *foe*, Lith *peĩkti* 'blame, rebuke, censure', Arm *hēk'* 'unfortunate, suffering', Skt *píśuna-* 'backbiting, wicked'). One can actively implement one's hostility through two verbs for 'insult' or 'revile'. Six groups evidence *(*h$_x$*)*neid-* 'insult, despise, curse' (e.g. Goth *ga-naitjan* 'treat shamefully', Lith *niedėti* 'despise', Grk *oneidízō* 'revile', Arm *anēc* 'curse', Av *naēd-* 'insult', Skt *níndati* 'insults') while a verbal **pih$_x$(y)-* 'revile' (e.g. OE *fēon* 'hate', NE *fiend*, Skt *pī́yati* 'insults') would appear to derive from **peh$_x$-* 'misfortune' (e.g. Grk *pêma* 'suffering, misfortune').

To these we can add the regional (West Central) form **h$_a$leit-* '± do something hateful or abhorrent' (e.g. OIr *lius* 'abhorrence', NE *loath*, Grk *alitaínō* 'trespass, sin') and **kaunos* 'humble, lowly', despised' seen in Germanic (OE *hēan* 'lowly, despised'), Baltic (Latv *kàuns* 'shame, disgrace'), and Grk *kaunós* 'bad, evil'.

20.9 Hot, Cold, and other Qualities

In Table 20.9 we gather together a series of words that describe basic perceptions such as hot, cold, wet, dry, heavy, light, etc.

The root **g^{w}her-* 'warm' reveals several derived forms such as **g^{w}hermós* 'warm' which is almost ubiquitous (nine groups: e.g. Lat *formus* 'warm', NE *warm*, OPrus *gorme* 'heat', Thrac *germo-* 'warm', Alb *zjarm* 'fire', Grk *thermós* 'warm', Arm *jerm* 'warm', Av *garəma-* 'hot', Skt *gharmá-* 'heat, glow') and the more limited Celtic-Indic isogloss **g^{w}hrensós* 'warm' (e.g. OIr *grīs* 'heat, fire', Skt *ghraṃsá-* 'heat of the sun'). The semantic temperature of **tep-* may have been hotter than the two previous words, while it is 'lukewarm' in Lat *tepeō* 'be lukewarm', it is 'hot' otherwise (e.g. OIr *te* 'hot', Umb *tefru* 'burnt sacrifice', OE *þefian* 'gasp, pant', Rus *topitĭ* 'heat', Grk *téphrā* 'ashes', Hit *tapissa-* 'fever, heat',

Table 20.9. _Qualities_

*_g^{w}hermós_	'warm'	Lat _formus_, NE _warm_, Grk _thermós_, Skt _gharmá-_
*_g^{w}hrensós_	'warm'	Skt _ghraṃsá-_
*_tep-_	'hot'	Lat _tepeō_, Grk _téphra_, Skt _tápati_
*_k̂elto-_	'cold'	Lat _calidus_
*_k^{w}rustēn_	'(freezing) cold'	Lat _crusta_, Grk _krustaínomai_
*_h$_2$es-_	'be/become dry'	Lat _āreō_
*_sausos_	'dry'	Lat _sūdus_, NE _sear_
*_ters-_	'dry'	Lat _torreō_, Grk _térsomai_, Skt _tṛ́ṣyati_
*_siskus_	'dry'	Lat _siccus_
*_se(n)k-_	'cease to flow, dry up'	Skt _ásakra-_
*_h$_1$res-_ ~ *_h$_1$ers-_	'liquid, moisture'	Lat _rōs_, Skt _rása-_
*_m(e)h$_a$d-_	'become wet, moist, fat'	Lat _madeō_, NE _meat_, Grk _madáō_, Skt _máda-_
*_g^{w}reh$_x$-u-_	'heavy'	Lat _gravis_, Grk _barús_, Skt _gurú-_
*_tengh-_	'be heavy, difficult'	
*_h$_1$le(n)g^{w}h-_	'light (of weight)'	Lat _levis_, NE _light_, Grk _elakhós_, Skt _laghú-_
*_kreup-_	'rough'	NE _rough_
*_pastos_	'firm'	NE _fast_, Skt _pastyám_
*_ĝhers-_	'stiffen (of hair), bristle'	Lat _horreō_, NE _gorse_, Skt _hárṣati_
*_(s)terh$_1$-_	'stiff'	NE _stare_, Grk _stereós_
*_sth$_2$ei-_	'become hard, fixed'	Lat _stīria_, Skt _styā́yate_
*_st(h$_2$)eug-_	'stiff'	
*_mel(h$_1$)-_	'soft'	Lat _mollis_, Grk _bladús_, Skt _mṛdú-_
*_(s)lag-_	'slack'	Lat _laxus_, NE _slack_, Grk _lagarós_
*_(s)lei-_	'sticky, slimy, slippery'	Lat _līmus_, NE _slime_, Grk _leímaks_, Skt _limpáti_

Av _tāpaiti_ 'be warm', Skt _tápati_ 'warms, burns'. That derivatives tend to be hotter than just warm suggests that the underlying meaning was 'hot'. The Albanian cognate is _ftoh_ 'make cold', which seems surprising semantically but is understandable once one realizes that the initial _f-_ reflects a PIE *_h$_2$eps-_ 'from' and thus _ftoh_ is originally 'make from-heat' or the like. That temperatures may have been experienced among the Indo-Europeans according to intensity rather than degrees is seen in *_k̂elto-_ 'cold' whose Latin and Welsh cognates are _calidus_ 'warm, hot' and _clyd_ 'sheltered, warm, snug' respectively (but 'cold' in Baltic, e.g. Lith _šáltas_, Iranian, e.g. Av _sarəta-_, and in some of its derived forms such as Skt _śíśira-_ 'cold season'). Really 'freezing cold' is indicated by a Greek-Tocharian isogloss that gives *_k^{w}rustēn_ (e.g. Grk _krustaínomai_ 'am congealed with cold, freeze', *krūmós* 'icy cold, frost', Toch B *krośce* 'cold'); Grk cognates include *krustállos* 'ice; crystal'. Derived forms also include Lat *crusta* 'crust', OHG *hroso* 'ice, crust', and Latv *kruvesis* 'frozen mud'.

There are at least four Proto-Indo-European words for 'dry', some verbal and some adjectival. The root *$h_a$es- means 'be(come) dry' (e.g. Lat *āreō* 'be dry', *āridus* 'dry', Czech *ozditi* 'dry malt', Grk *ázomai* 'become dry', Toch AB *ās-* 'become dry'). Sometimes connected here are words for ash and hearth (e.g. NE *ash*, Lat *āra* 'hearth') but they are probably better connected with *h_2eh_x- 'burn'. The adjectival **sus-* ~ **sausos* is widespread (e.g. Lat *sūdus* 'dry, without rain', Alb *thaj* 'dry up', Av *haoš-* 'wither away', Skt *śuṣ-* 'become dry'; OE *sēar* [> NE *sere*], Lith *saũsas*, OCS *suchŭ*, Grk *aũos*, all 'dry'). Another word **ters-* 'dry' (e.g. Lat *torreō* 'dry', ON *þerra* 'dry', Alb *ter* 'dry off', Grk *térsomai* 'become dry', Arm *t'aṙamim* 'wilt, fade', Skt *tṛ́ṣyati* 'thirsts') also yields an extended form **tr̥sus/*tr̥stos* 'dry' (e.g. Lat *torrus* 'dried out', ON *þurr* 'parched', Av *taršu-* 'dry', Skt *tr̥ṣú-* 'greedy, desirous, vehement') which is semantically consistent except for Skt *tr̥ṣú-* 'greedy, vehement'. Another term for 'dry up', **se(n)k-*, seems to have specifically referred to the drying up, i.e. the ceasing to flow, of streams or the like (e.g. NE *singe*, Lith *senkù* 'ebb, drain away, dry up [of water]', OCS *i-sęknǫti* 'dry up [of water]', Skt *ásakra-* 'not drying up') and it yields a reduplicated form **siskus* 'dry' (e.g. NWels *hysb*, Lat *siccus*, Av *hišku-*, all 'dry'); in Old Irish this word (*sesc*) has shifted semantically to 'sterile' (of livestock).

There are numerous regional terms for 'wet' but a few may be assigned to Proto-Indo-European. A root *$h_1$res- or *$h_1$ers- means 'dew' in Lat *rōs*, Baltic (e.g. Lith *rasà*), and Slavic (e.g, OCS *rosa*) but it tends to mean something moister in the other languages (in Avestan it supplies the name of the river Volga, *Raŋha*, while in Sanskrit it provides *rása-* 'liquid, moisture', and in Albanian it gives *resh* 'rains'). More semantically divergent are the outcomes of **mad-* which seem to include 'become wet' but also 'become fat' (e.g. OIr *maidid* 'breaks, bursts forth, gushes', Lat *madeō* 'am moist, drip', Alb *maj* 'feed, fatten [of animals]', Grk *madáō* 'am damaged by wetness or humidity, drip'); in Indo-Iranian it yields 'alcoholic drink' (i.e. Av *maδa-*, Skt *máda-*) but in Germanic 'meal' (NE *meat* is an even more specific use of OE *mete* 'food').

There are two words for 'heavy'. The basic sense of weight was conveyed by *$g^w reh_x$-u- which gives us Grk *barús* (see the loan in NE *barometer*; cf. also MIr *bair* '± heavy', Lat *gravis* 'heavy', Latv *grūts* 'heavy', Toch B *krāmär* 'weight, heaviness'); the Sanskrit cognate *gurú-* 'heavy' also gives us the name of an Indian sage. Heavy in the sense of 'difficult' seems to have been conveyed by **tengh-* (e.g. ON *þungr* 'heavy, difficult, unfriendly', Lith *tingùs* 'idle, lazy, sluggish', OCS *o-tęžati* 'become heavy, loaded', Toch B *täṅk-* 'hinder, obstruct'). There is one word for 'light of weight', *$h_1le(n)g^wh$- (e.g. OIr *laigiu* 'lighter, poorer', Lat *levis* 'light', NE *light*, Lith *leñgvas* 'light, easy, slight', OCS *lĭgŭkŭ* 'light', Alb *lehtë* 'light, soft, slight, nimble', Grk *elakhós* 'small, little', Oss *ræwæg* 'light', Toch B *lank$_u$tse* 'light') which, in some languages (Germanic, Greek, Indic), shifted to mean 'rapid', i.e. light of foot (e.g. OHG *lungar* 'rapid', Grk *elaphrós* 'light, fast', Skt *laghú-* 'fleet, fast').

The concept of 'rough' was indicated by **kreup-*, an isogloss of Germanic (e.g. NE *rough*), Baltic (Lith *kraupùs* 'dreadful, rough; timid'), and Tocharian (e.g. Toch B *kärpiye* 'common, raw, rough'). A word **pastos* 'firm' may be considered Proto-Indo-European if one accepts Skt *pastyám* 'habitation' as cognate with the Germanic (e.g. NE *fast* [as in 'stand fast']) and Arm *hast* words for 'firm'. There are four words to convey 'stiff'. The root **ĝhers-* (e.g. NE *gorse*, Lat *horreō* 'bristle', Av *zaršayamna-* 'feathers upright', Skt *hárṣati* 'bristles, becomes erect or rigid; becomes sexually excited') is certainly to be associated with **ĝher-* 'hedgehog' (see Section 9.2) and possibly **ĝhor-* 'young pig' (see Section 9.2; perhaps from the bristles of the pig). A **(s)terh$_1$-* is well attested in the North-West (e.g. NE *stare*, Lith *starinù* 'tighten, stretch, make stiff', OCS *strada* 'hard work') but also has Greek and Tocharian cognates (e.g. Grk *stereós* 'stiff, firm', Toch B *ścire* 'hard, rough'). The basic verbal root **steh$_2$-* 'stand' provides the basis for two other words: **sth$_2$ei-* 'become hard, fixed' (e.g. Lat *stīria* 'icicle', Frisian *stīr* 'stiff', Lith *stóras* 'stiff', Skt *styā́yate* 'becomes fixed, coagulated, hardens', Toch B *stināsk-* 'be silent') and **st(h$_2$)eug-* 'stiff' (e.g. Lith *stúkti* 'stand tall', Rus *stúgnuti* 'freeze', Toch B *staukk-* 'swell, bloat').

The root **mel(h$_1$)-* 'soft' is found in a number of derived forms, e.g. **ml̥dus* (e.g. Lat *mollis* 'soft', OPrus *maldai* 'young', OCS *mladŭ* 'young, soft', Grk *bladús* 'slack', Arm *melk'* 'soft, limp', Skt *mr̥dú-* 'soft, tender, mild'), that secure its assignment to Proto-Indo-European. 'Slimy' was indicated by **(s)lei-*, often found in extended form **leip-* (e.g. OIr *as-lena* 'pollute', Lat *linō* 'anoint', OCS *slina* 'spit', Grk *alínō* 'anoint'; OIr *slemon* 'slippery, slick, polished', Lat *līmus* 'mud', *līmax* 'slug', NE *slime*, Rus *slimák* 'slug', Grk *leímaks* 'slug, snail'; NHG *bleiben* 'remain, stay', Lith *lìpti* 'stick, be sticky', OCS *pri-lĭpją* 'stick on/to', *Skt limpáti* 'smears', Toch A *lip-* 'remain') (see Section 22.5).

There are numerous regionally attested words to be added here. From the North-West come **keh$_x$i-* 'hot' (e.g. NE *hot*, Lith *kaĩsti* 'heat, become hot'); **gel-* 'cold, to freeze' (e.g. Lat *gelū* 'cold, frost', NE *cold*); **leh$_a$t-* 'wet, moist' (e.g. MIr *lathach* 'mud', OHG *letto* 'clay', Grk *látaks* 'drops', and various Baltic river names); **welk-* or **welg-* 'wet' (e.g. OIr *folc* 'heavy rain', OHG *welk* 'wet, moist, mild', Lith *vìlgau* 'moisten', OCS *vlaga* 'moisture juice of plants'); **h$_1$wes-* 'moist, especially of the ground or plants' (e.g. Umb *vestikatu* 'offer a libation', OE *wōs* 'juice, broth', Latv *vasa* 'forest with wet ground and blue clay'); **senh$_x$dhr-* 'congealed moisture, slag' (e.g. NE *cinder*, RusCS *sjadry* 'clotted blood'); *$*ghleh_xdh-(ro)-*$ 'smooth' (Lat *glaber* 'smooth', NE *glad*, Lith *glodùs* 'smooth(ed)', OCS *gladiti* 'to smooth') from the root **ghel-* 'shine'; **l(e)nto-* 'soft' (NWels *llathr* 'smooth', Lat *lentus* 'soft, tender', NE *lithe*, Lith *leñtas* 'quiet, calm'); and *$*suh_x$-ros* 'sour, acid' (NE *sour*, Lith *sū́ras* 'salty', OCS *syrŭ* 'wet'). From the West Central region: **wel-* 'warm, heat' (e.g. NE *well* as 'well up' [from *'boil'], Alb *valë* 'heat, boiling', Arm *gol* 'heat'); *$*h_3$eug-* 'cold' (e.g. OIr *ūacht* 'cold', Lith *áušti* 'become cold', Arm *oyc* 'cold'); **srīges-* (or *$*srih_x$ges-*) 'cold, frost' (Lat *frīgus* 'cold, frost', Grk *rhîgos* 'frost, cold'); **teng-* 'to moisten, soak' (Lat *tingō* 'moisten', OHG *thunkōn* 'dunk', Grk *téggō* 'moisten'); **reĝ-* or **rek-nos* 'moist, make wet' (e.g. Lat *(ir)rigāre* 'water, irrigate', NE *rain*, Lith *rõkia* 'drizzles', Alb *rrjedh* 'flow, pour'); *$*weg^w$-* 'wet' (e.g. Lat *ūvidus* 'wet', ON *vǫkr* 'wet, moist', Grk *hugrós* 'liquid, fluid'); **(s)meug-* ~ **(s)meuk-* 'slick, slippery' (e.g. OIr *mocht* 'soft, tender', Lat *mungō* 'blow the nose', ON *mjūkr* 'soft, malleable', Grk *mússomai* 'blow the nose')—the verbal forms indicate 'blow the nose', cf. Lat *mūcus* 'mucus', and this set has been related to a larger (potentially PIE) group of words meaning 'to run away', e.g. Lith *mùkti* 'slip away from', Skt *muñcáti* 'looses, frees', Toch B *mauk-* 'to let go'; and just possibly **swombhos* 'spongy' (e.g. OE *swamm* 'mushroom', Grk *somphós* 'spongy'). There is somewhat disputable evidence for **menkus* 'soft' seen in a Baltic-Slavic-Albanian isogloss (Latv *mîkst* 'soft', OCS *mękŭkŭ* 'soft', Alb (Gheg) *mekan* 'weak'. An adjective 'slack' is indicated by **slag-* with cognates in Celtic (OIr *lac* 'slack, weak'), Lat *laxus* 'slack, loose', Germanic (e.g. NE *slack*), Baltic (Latv *legans* 'slack, soft'), and Grk *lagarós* 'slack' (there are also quite disputable cognates in both Indic and Tocharian). There is one Greek-Indic correspondence (Grk *ksērós* 'dry, dried up', Skt *kṣārá-* 'caustic, burning') in **k̂sēros* 'dry (of weather or land)', a lengthened grade derivative of **k̂seros* seen in cognates in other groups (e.g. Lat *serēnus* 'dry, clean', OHG *serawēn* 'become weak', Arm *č'or* 'dry').

20.10 Proto-Indo-European Perception

The sensual perception of the Proto-Indo-European lexicon is another area that may be appropriately analysed from the point of folk taxonomy. Although we customarily list five senses for ourselves: sight, hearing, taste, smell, and touch, Aristotle counted only four (taste was merely a form of touching). As Earl Anderson reminds us in his *Folk-Taxonomies in Early English*: "the five senses are a linguistic construct and a cultural convention." The Classical and Christian worlds tended to rank the senses with taste and touch at the bottom as they are shared by all animals; the logic of this may escape us but we are told by Aulus Gellius that humans are the ones who are best delighted through sight and hearing. Even a fairly parsimonious acceptance of the numerous words for 'see' would result in at least about half a dozen verbs: **derḱ-* 'glance at', **leuk-* 'see', **(s)peḱ-* 'observe', **sek^w-* 'see', **wel-* 'see', **leĝ-* 'see', whereas only one root serves for 'hear' (**ḱleu-*). This apparent focus on 'sight' among the senses is hardly unique as sight was regarded by Plato as the most important of the senses and this theory has been echoed since in western tradition. The concept of 'touch' is perhaps more ambiguous to localize within the several words which cover this semantic field, i.e. **deg-*, **ml̥ḱ-*, and probably more remotely **klep-*. 'Smell' as a sense is lacking although **pū-* 'stink' indicates its cognitive existence and there is no evidence for the lexicalization of 'taste' although again there is certainly enough evidence that the Proto-Indo-Europeans experienced the differences between 'sweet' and 'bitter'.

Proto-Indo-European cognition is another area where our lexical evidence hints at various levels of perception that invite our attention. We have seen how one of the main means of expressing knowledge is through a verb associated with sight, i.e. **weid-*, and that 'thinking' is handled by a different root, **men-*, a split in the cognitive process that we would share today (in many languages this can also be handled by different verbal systems). It is interesting then that the concept of belief is expressed through a frozen expression 'to put heart' (**ḱred-dheh$_1$-*) which would lead one to suspect either that the cognitive organ was the heart and not the brain in Proto-Indo-European or that belief was not strictly a cognitive process but more an act of faith.

One area that has seen considerable discussion is that of colour categories, especially since the publication of Berlin and Kay's influential works on colour terms. They proposed a seven-stage evolutionary system whereby primary colours have been lexicalized. By primary colour terms we mean words that cannot be further analysed nor seen to be subsets of another colour term (as 'scarlet' is a type of 'red') nor employed for a restricted range of objects, e.g. 'blond', 'brunette' for hair colours or 'bay and 'roan' for horses. The ultimate test is the native perception of the speaker of a language which, of course, is denied to us when we must work with a reconstructed lexicon. In the evolutionary system of Berlin and Kay, stage 1 is marked by distinctions for only WHITE and BLACK; stage 2 adds ROW, a category that embraces what we might regard as 'red' and 'yellow'; stage 3 adds a fourth colour (WHITE, BLACK, RED, YELLOW or WHITE, BLACK, ROW, and GRUE [a category that combines our 'green' and 'blue']); stage 4 adds one further category by deconstructing ROW into RED and YELLOW and possessing GRUE; in the next stage GRUE is deconstructed into its components, i.e. separate words for BLUE and GREEN are not expected until all the other categories have been filled out. Later categories see the introduction of BROWN, PINK, PURPLE, ORANGE, and GREY. One has generally presumed that one can move up through the stages but it would be unusual to move down, i.e. lose colour terms or combine them, though development in the latter direction is exemplified. So when we find that Homeric Greek is classified as a stage 3 or even stage 2 language, then how do we reconcile our list of no less than eight potential colour categories in PIE, i.e. BLACK (*mel-n-, *k^wr̥snós), WHITE (*h_2r̥ĝ(u), *$h_4$elbhós, *bhelh_1-, *k̂weitos), RED (*$h_1$reudh-, *$h_1$elu-, *k̂óu-nos), GREEN (*k̂yeh_1-, *k̂er- ~ *k̂r̥-wo-?), BLUE (*modhr-?), YELLOW (*ĝhel- ~ *ghel-), BROWN (*bher-), and GREY (*k̂as-)?

First, it is evident that our reconstructed proto-meanings are not necessarily the precise colour categories required in 'yellow' (Celtic), 'red' (Italic), 'blue' (Baltic), 'black' (Baltic, Greek, Indic). *k^wr̥snós is at least semantically consistent as 'black' but it is confined to Balto-Slavic and Indic. In any event, there is no one who would dispute our ability to reconstruct the categories WHITE, BLACK, and RED to Proto-Indo-European. Now do we really have RED or only ROW? If we only had the evidence of *$h_1$elu- which returns meanings of 'yellow' (Germanic), 'gold' (Indic), 'white' (Iranian), and 'red' (Indic) we might well regard this as reflecting the different potential outcome of an original ROW. But we also have PIE *$h_1$reudh- which is the best-attested colour term in Indo-European and bears the meaning 'red' in the nine different groups in which it survives. As for YELLOW, we have *ĝhel- or *ghel- which tends to mean 'yellow' or 'golden' across seven language groups; where it attests a different meaning, it is noteworthy that it is 'white' (Celtic), 'brown' (Celtic), or 'green' (Slavic, Greek) but never 'red'. If the stadial system has any validity, we might then expect GRUE or, if more advanced, separate categories for GREEN and BLUE. PIE *k̂yeh_1- behaves with all the semantic variability that one might expect at this end of the colour scale. It can mean 'green' (Slavic, Indic), 'grey' (Germanic, Baltic, Slavic, Albanian, Tocharian), 'blue' (Germanic, Slavic), and 'black' or 'dark' (Iranian, Indic, Tocharian). PIE *k̂er- offers a similar disparate range of meanings. The word for 'blue' (*modhr-?) is consistent in its meaning in Germanic, Slavic, and Hittite but its Germanic meaning is consistently 'madder', the plant that provides a reddish dye, and hence there is reason to suspect that it is not a primary colour term. Similarly, the words for BROWN (*bher-), are so frequently associated with animals, e.g. the bear (Germanic), toad (Greek), horses (Baltic, Indic), and the word for GREY (*k̂as-) with the meaning 'hare' in Celtic, Germanic, Baltic, and Indo-Iranian, that we have good reasons to doubt their status as primary terms in Proto-Indo-European. This would all suggest that our primary colours in Proto-Indo-European were probably confined to BLACK, WHITE, RED, YELLOW, and perhaps GRUE, thus indicating at least a stage 3 if not stage 4 language in terms of colour terminology.

Further Reading

Colour perception is discussed in Berlin and Kay (1969), Kay and McDaniel (1978), Anderson (2003), Shields (1979), Wescott (1975); more specific language studies are to be found in Lazar-Meyn (1994), Moonwomon (1994), and Lerner (1951); other aspects are in Bader (1986), Crepajac (1967), and Hamp (1971*b*). For 'good–bad' see Costa (1990). There are a number of articles on 'sleep' and 'dream': Barton (1985), Jamison (1982–3), Schindler (1966), Watkins (1972*a*); 'seeing/knowing' is treated in Hamp (1987*d*), Jassanoff (1988), Lindeman (2003), Porzio Gernia (1989). Seebold (1973); for 'shine' see Mazjulis (1986); for 'sweet/taste' see Lindeman (1975), Stang (1974); 'hearing' is treated in Frisk (1950).

21

Speech and Sound

21.0 Speech and Sounds

There is a rich vocabulary pertaining to speech and sound that may be reconstructed to Proto-Indo-European. Below we briefly review the evidence, first of 'speech' in its more general aspect and then at higher registers, e.g. the language of poets, and finally in terms of the various sounds that might be emitted by either a human or animal. Because of the very nature of this latter semantic sphere, many roots or words will be by their very nature onomatopoeic and there will be frequent instances where it is simply impossible to determine whether the root in question was inherited, borrowed, or independently created.

21.1 Speech

The primary roots and words concerned with speaking or calling out are listed in Table 21.1.

There were at least two basic words for 'speak'. The root *wek^w- with its o-grade present formation *$wok^w ti$ is widespread and old in Indo-European (e.g. OIr *focal* 'word', Lat *vocō* 'call', OHG *giwahanem* 'recall', OPrus *wackitwei* 'entice', Grk *eîpon* 'spoke', Arm *gočem* 'call', Av *vak*- 'say', Skt *vívakti* 'speaks,

Table 21.1. *Speech*

$*wek^{w}$-	'speak'	Lat *vocō*, Grk *eîpon*, Skt *vívakti*
**(s)wer-*	'say, speak'	Lat *sermō*, NE *swear*, Grk *eírō*
$*h_1eĝ$-	'say'	Lat *aiō*, Grk *ê*
**ter-*	'± speak out'	
**wed-*	'raise one's voice'	Skt *vádati*
$*mleuh_x$-	'speak'	Skt *bráviti*
**rek-*	'speak'	
$?*g^{w}et$-	'say'	NE *quoth*, Skt *gádati*
**gal-*	'call out, speak'	Lat *gallus*, NE *call*
**ĝar-*	'shout, call'	Lat *garriō*, NE *care*, Grk *gêrus*
**neu-*	'± cry out'	Lat *nūntius*, Skt *návate*
$*ĝheu(h_x)$-	'call to, invite, invoke'	NE *god*, Skt *hávate*
$*kelh_1$-	'call out to'	Lat *calō*, Grk *kaléō*, Skt *uṣā-kala-*
**k̂euk-*	'cry out (to)'	
**deik̂-*	'show'	Lat *dīcō*, Grk *deíknumi*, Skt *diśáti*
$*d(h)ek^{w}$-s-	'show'	
$*t(e)h_2u$-s-	'be silent'	Skt *tūṣṇī́m*
$*h_1erh_1$-	'quiet, at rest'	Grk *erêmos*, Skt *rámate*
$*k^{w}eih_1$-	'rest, quiet'	Lat *quiēs*

says', Toch B *wesk-* 'speak, say'). Equally widespread is **(s)wer-* 'say, speak' (e.g. OPrus *wertemmai* 'we swear', Rus *vru* 'lie', Grk *eírō* 'say', Hit *wer(i)ye-* 'call, summon'; Lat *sermō* 'conversation, lecture' [> by borrowing NE *sermon*], NE *swear*, OCS *svariti* 'despise; battle', Lyd *śfarwa-* '± oath', Toch B *ṣarm* 'origin') with no clearly discernible distinction between it and the preceding word. Greek employs **(s)wer-*, i.e. Grk *eírō*, in the present and $*wek^{w}$-, i.e. Grk *eîpon*, in the aorist and it is possible that such a paradigm from two different roots derived from a still earlier period. In derived form, **(s)wer-* also yields NE *word* (cf. also Lat *verbum* 'word' and Lith *var̃das* 'name'). A root $*h_1eĝ$- 'say' is found in Lat *aiō* 'say', Grk *ê* 'said', Arm *asem* 'say', and Toch AB *āks-* 'announce, proclaim, instruct' and is clearly of Proto-Indo-European age. A root **ter-* probably had some semantic specialization in Proto-Indo-European; in Hit *tar-* and Lith *tariù* it renders 'say' but in other languages we find 'noise', e.g. Celtic (MIr *to(i)rm* 'noise, din, uproar'), Baltic (OPrus *tārin* 'noise'), Slavic (Rus *torotóritĭ* 'chatter, prattle'), in Luvian it means 'curse' (*tātariya-*) and in Tocharian 'implore' (Toch B *tär-*). The root **wed-* 'raise one's voice' also has meanings that connote at least a loud or solemn sound (e.g. OHG *far-wāzan* 'deny, disavow', Lith *vadinù* 'call, name', OCS *vaditi* 'accuse', dialectal Grk *wodáō* 'lament', Skt *vádati* 'speaks, says; raises one's voice, sings'). A Slavic-Indo-Iranian-Tocharian isogloss gives us *$mleuh_x$- 'speak' (e.g. OCS *mlŭvati* 'create a disturbance', Av *mraoiti* 'says, recites', Skt *bráviti* 'says', Toch B *pälw-* 'mourn') while **rek-* is attested only in Slavic and Tocharian (e.g. OCS *rešti* 'say', Toch B *reki* 'word'). A possible root *g^wet*- 'say' (there is some doubt about the status of some of the proposed cognates) is based on Germanic, Armenian, and Indo-Iranian (e.g. OE *cweðan* 'say' [whose past tense is reflected in (archaic) NE *quoth*], Arm *koč'em* 'call', Sogdian *žut* 'says', Skt *gádati* 'says').

Other words broadly meaning 'call (out)' include **gal-*, a word largely of the North-West but extended by an Ossetic cognate (e.g. OIr *gall* 'swan', NWels *galw* 'call', Lat *gallus* 'cock', OE *ceallian* 'call' [NE *call* is not directly from Old English but rather borrowed from the latter's ON cognate *kalla*], Lith *gal̃sas* 'echo', OCS *glasŭ* 'voice', Oss *γalas* 'sound'). The root **ĝar-* (e.g. OIr *do-gair* 'call', Lat *garriō* 'chatter, prattle', OE *cearu* 'care, sorrow, mourning' [> NE *care*], Grk *gêrus* 'voice, call') is similarly extended in its distribution to Asia by virtue of an Ossetic cognate (*zarun* 'sing'); its meanings generally indicate a calling out or 'shout' (in Armenian we again find it forming bird names, *cicaṙn* 'swallow', *cicaṙnuk* 'nightingale'). The Germanic meaning 'mourn' may give some indication of Proto-Indo-European, or at least Pre-Germanic, mourning customs involving wailing by the mourners. A loud 'call' or 'cry' is also indicated by the semantic range of **neu-* (e.g. OIr *nūall* 'cry, noise', Lat *nūntius* 'message; messenger', Latv *nauju* 'cry', NPers *navīdan* 'cry', Skt *návate* 'shouts cries', Toch AB *nu-* 'roar'). The connotation of 'invoke' seems to lie behind some of the cognates derived from *$\hat{g}heu(h_x)$- (e.g. OIr *guth* 'voice', OCS *zovǫ* 'call', Av *zavaiti* 'calls', Skt *hávate* 'calls, invokes', Toch B *kuwā-* 'call, invite'); it supplies the Germanic word for 'god' as 'what is invoked' (**ĝhutóm*) and probably also in Tocharian (e.g. Toch B *ñakte* 'god' < **ní-ĝhuto-* i.e. 'the one invoked downward') and, as we have seen, it may carry the meaning 'invoke' also in Indic. Another noisy 'call' is seen in *$kelh_1$- which gives the 'cock' in Celtic and Indic (e.g. OIr *cailech*, Skt *uṣā-kala-* < *'dawn-singer') and more formal acts of announcement, e.g. Lat *calendae* 'the first days of the month on which the ides and nones were announced', the ultimate origin of NE *calendar*, and Grk *kaléō* 'call', *kalḗtōr* 'herald' (cf. also ON *hjala* 'chatter, talk', Latv *kaļuôt* 'chatter', Hit *kalless-* 'call'). A Baltic-Tocharian correspondence gives us **k̂euk-* 'cry out' (e.g. Lith *šaukiù* 'call, cry, shout; summon', Toch B *kuk-* 'call out to').

What we would translate as 'show' indicates a strong if not primary verbal component. The widely attested **deik̂-* may mean 'say', 'accuse', 'announce', as well as 'show' in the various languages where it is attested (e.g. Lat *dīcō* 'say', OE *tēon* 'accuse', Grk *deíknumi* 'show', Av *disyeiti* ~ *daēsayeiti* 'shows', Skt *diśáti* ~ *deśayati* 'shows'). A Hittite-Avestan isogloss supports the reconstruction of *$d(h)ek^w$-s*- 'show' (Hit *tekkussa-* 'show', Av *daxša-* 'teach, show').

The most widely attested word for 'be silent' is **t(e)h₂us-* (e.g. OPrus *tusnan* 'quiet', Hit *tuhussi(i)ye-* 'keep quiet, acquiesce', Av *tušni-* 'sitting quietly', Skt *tūṣṇīm* 'quiet, silent'). To this we might add words for 'quiet' such as **$h_1$erh$_1$-* 'quiet, at rest' with cognates in Celtic (e.g. NWels *araf* 'quiet, calm', Gothic *rimis* 'rest', Baltic (e.g. Lith *rìmti* 'to be calm', Grk *erêmos* 'lonely', and Indo-Iranian (e.g. Skt *rámate* 'stays still, calms down'). We might also add **k^weih$_1$-* 'rest, quiet' seen in Lat *quiēs* 'quiet', OE *hwīl* 'while, time' (> NE *while*), OCS *pokojĭ* 'peace, quiet, rest', Arm *han-gist* 'rest, quiet', OPers *šiyāti* 'comfort' (note also Lat *quiētus* 'quiet', Av *šyāta-* 'happy').

Regionally attested cognates comprise (from the North-West) **tolk^w-* 'speak' (e.g. OIr *ad-tluichetar* 'gives thanks, rejoices', Lat *loquor* [<**tloquor*] 'speak', OCS *tlŭkŭ* 'meaning, explanation'); **(s)trep-* '± cry out, dispute' (e.g. Lat *strepō* 'cry loudly, make noise', OE *þrafian* 'restrain, reprove; urge, demand'); **weh$_a$b-* 'cry, scream' (NE *weep*, Lith *võbyti* 'summon at court', OCS *vabljǫ* 'cry'); **leugh-* 'lie, tell a lie' which yields 'lie' in Germanic (e.g. NE *lie*) and Slavic (e.g. OCS *lŭžǫ* 'lie') but 'ask' in Baltic (e.g. Lith *lūgóti* 'ask'); **tak-* 'be silent' (e.g. OIr *tachtaid* 'chokes, stifles', Lat *taceō* 'am silent', ON *þegja* 'be silent'); and **(s)tel-* 'be still, quiet' may involve the absence of speech in some of its cognates in Celtic (OIr *tuilid* 'sleeps'), Germanic (e.g. NE *still*), Baltic (e.g. Lith *tylà* 'quiet person'). From the West Central region: **bheh$_a$-* 'speak' (e.g. Lat *for* 'speak', NE *ban*, Rus *báju* 'relate', Grk *phēmí* 'say', Arm *bay* 'says') with derived **bheh$_a$meh$_a$-* 'saying' (Lat *fāma* 'talk, reputation, fame', Grk *phḗmē* 'saying, speech'); **(s)preg-* 'speak' (e.g. NE *speak*, Alb *shpreg* 'express, voice, utter'); **ghel-* 'cry out, sing' (e.g. NE *yell*, Rus *na-gáliti* 'cry, sing', Grk *khelīdṓn* 'swallow' [the bird]); **(s)weh$_a$gh-* '± cry out; resound' (e.g. Lat *vāgiō* 'cry, squall [of babies], scream', NE *sough*, Lith *svagė́ti* 'sound', Grk *ēkhḗ* 'noise', *ēkhéō* 'sound, ring'); **bheidh-* 'persuade, compel, confide' (Lat *fīdō*, OE *bædan* 'urge', OCS *běditi* 'constrain', Alb *be* 'oath', Grk *peíthō* 'persuade'; **swīg/k-* 'be silent, hush' with a possible onomatopoeic origin (e.g. OE *swīgian* 'be silent', Grk *sīgáō*); and **neu-* 'nod' (Lat *ad-nuō* 'agree by nodding', Grk *neúō* 'nod') which does have a putative but semantically distant and therefore unsecure Indic cognate (Skt *návate* 'goes, moves').

21.2 Elevated Speech

While it is not always possible to distinguish the register associated with different words, we can attempt a rough division between those words that simply convey the act of speech and those which carry a more formal nuance, e.g. the distinction between 'say' and 'proclaim'. In Table 21.2 we have

Table 21.2. *Elevated speech and song*

**k̂eh$_1$-*	'declare solemnly'	
**k̂e(n)s-*	'declare solemnly'	Lat *cēnseō*, Skt *śáṃsati*
**h$_{1/4}$ōr-*	'speak a ritual formula'	Lat *ōrō*, Grk *arā́*, Skt *ā́ryati*
**(s)pel-*	'say aloud, recite'	NE *spell*, Grk *apeiléō*
**yek-*	'± express, avow'	Lat *iocus*, Skt *yā́cati*
**h$_1$erk^w-*	'praise'	Skt *árcati*
**h$_1$eug^wh-*	'speak solemnly'	Grk *eúkhomai*, Skt *ójate*
**weg^wh-*	'speak solemnly'	Lat *voveō*, Skt *vāghát-*
**g^{w}erh$_x$-*	'praise'	Lat *grātēs*, Skt *gṛṇā́ti*
**kar-*	'praise loudly'	Skt *carkarti*
**seng^wh-*	'sing, make an incantation'	NE *sing*, Grk *omphḗ*
**geh$_1$(i)-*	'sing'	Skt *gā́ti*
**pei-*	'sing'	
**sh$_2$ómen-*	'song'	Grk *húmnos*, Skt *sā́man-*
**k̂léwes-*	'fame'	Lat *cluor*, Grk *kléos*, Skt *śrávas-*
**h$_1$nómn̥*	'name'	Lat *nōmen*, NE *name*, Grk *ónoma*, Skt *nā́ma*
**meldh-*	'pray, speak words to a deity'	NE *meld*
**g^whedh-*	'ask, pray'	NE *bid*, Grk *théssasthai*
**h$_2$eru-*	'± pray, curse'	Grk *aráomai*
**telh$_x$-*	'± pray'	
**perk̂-*	'ask, ask for (in marriage)'	Lat *poscō*, Skt *pṛccháti*
**kreuk̂-*	'cry out, raise the hue and cry'	Skt *króśati*

assembled those words which we might associate with a higher register or more formally specialized area of speech.

A verbal root **k̂eh$_1$-* with a present **k̂éh$_1$ti* (e.g. Alb *thotë* 'says', OPers *θātiy* 'says, proclaims') conveys a more formal manner of speaking in Indo-Iranian and may be translated as 'declare solemnly'. More certain of its formal connotations is **k̂e(n)s-* whose meanings range from 'proclaim solemnly' to 'praise', i.e. in both judicial and religious spheres (e.g. Lat *cēnseō* 'proclaim solemnly, judge, assess, estimate, tax', OE *herian* 'praise', Av *sənghaiti* 'proclaims', Skt *śáṃsati* 'recites, praises, declares, vows'); see also below. The root **h$_{1/4}$ōr-* 'speak a ritual formula' underlies the Latin word (*ōrō*) for 'address the gods' and *ōrāculum* 'oracle', a Greek word (*arā́*) for 'prayer' and Hit *ariya-* 'consult an omen' (cf. also Rus *orú* 'cry out', Skt *ā́ryati* 'acknowledges, praises'). The root **(s)pel-* is sometimes associated with formal recitation, e.g. NE *spell* (as in *gospel*, i.e. good-story, but also *spell* as 'incantation' and the derived verb *to spell*), Alb *fjalë* 'tale' (also 'word, statement'), and Arm *aṙa-spel* 'saying, riddle' (cf. also Latv *pel̃t* 'revile, slander', Grk *apeiléō* 'hold out in promise or in threat', Toch AB *päl-* 'praise'). More ambiguous is **yek-* where the range of meanings is disparate, e.g. Lat *iocus* 'joke' but Umb *iuka* 'prayers' (cf. also MWels *ieith* 'speech', OHG *jëhan* 'express, explain', Skt *yā́cati* 'asks, solicits, entreats'); about the only thing we can say is that it meant some form of verbal expression.

Among the formal expressions, those that comprise the concept of 'praise' are well represented in Indo-European. We have both the verbal root *h_1erk^w- 'praise' (e.g. Hit *arkuwai-* 'explain, answer', Skt *árcati* 'praises') and a nominal derivative *h_1erk^wós 'song of praise' (e.g. OIr *erc* 'heaven', Arm *erg* 'song', Oss *arγaw* 'tale', Skt *arká-* 'song', Toch B *yarke* 'honour'). The verbal root *h_1eug^wh- 'praise' takes a present *$h_1$éug^{w}hetor and renders 'praises' and 'proclaims' (e.g. Grk *eúkhomai* 'pray [for], vaunt', Lyd *ow-* '± proclaim', Av *aojaite* 'says, pronounces', Skt *ójate* 'they praise'). Probably related to it is *weg^{w}h- which returns meanings of 'vow, promise solemnly, consecrate' in Lat *voveō* and 'sacrificer, supplicant, institutor of a sacrifice' in Skt *vāghát-*, as well as the more mundane Arm *gog* 'say'. The root *g^werh_x- 'praise' (e.g. OPrus *girtwei* 'praise', Alb *gërshas* 'invite to a marriage', Av *gar-* 'praise', Skt *gr̥ṇā́ti* 'sings, praises') gives us the Irish and Welsh words for *bard* (*bardd* in Welsh, on which see further below); a derivative is Lat *grātēs* [pl.] 'thanks' (i.e. 'praisings'). The root **kar-* indicates 'praise' in Indo-Iranian (Av *čarəkərə-* 'praise', Skt *carkarti* 'praises') and 'fame' (e.g. OE *hrēþ*) and 'report' (e.g. ON *herma*) in Germanic.

There are several words associated with singing. Ascription of *seng^{w}h- 'sing' to Proto-Indo-European rests on whether one accepts Prakrit *saṃghaï* 'say, honour' as cognate with a series of Celtic, Germanic, and Greek words (e.g. MWels *dehongli* 'explain', NE *sing*, *song*, Grk *omphḗ* 'divine voice, prophecy'). The root *$geh_1(i)$- 'sing' is restricted to Baltic, Slavic, and Indo-Iranian (e.g. Lith *giedóti* 'sing [hymns]', ORus *gajati* 'crow', Av *gāθā-* 'metre, line of poetry', Skt *gā́ti* ~ *gā́yati* 'sings', *gāthā-* 'song'); the Av *gāθā-* 'metre', is also the name of the earliest section of the *Avesta*. A Slavic-Tocharian isogloss gives us **pei-* 'sing' (e.g. OCS *pěti* 'sing', Toch B *pi-* 'sing'). Another possible Proto-Indo-European word for 'sing' is **kan-*, on which see below. The Proto-Indo-European word for 'song' was *sh_2ómen-, e.g. Grk *húmnos* 'song, festival song (of praise in honour of gods and heroes)' (borrowed into NE as *hymn*), Hit *ishamai-* 'song, melody', Skt *sā́man-* 'song, chant').

As we have already seen, acts of 'praising' and 'singing' would have been closely associated with the concept of 'fame'. Proto-Indo-European **k̂léwes-* 'fame' (e.g. OIr *clū* 'fame', Lat *cluor* 'glory', OCS *slovo* 'word', Grk *kléos* 'fame', Av *sravah-* 'word', Skt *śrávas-* 'fame', Toch B *-kälywe* 'fame') is from **k̂leu-* 'hear' (see also Section 20.5), i.e. 'what is heard', a central feature of the Indo-European poetic tradition. As one's fame attaches to one's name, we should add here *$h_1$nómn̥ 'name' which is attested in all major Indo-European groups (e.g. OIr *ainm*, Lat *nōmen*, NE *name*, OPrus *emens*, OCS *imę*, Alb *emër*, Grk *ónoma*, Arm *anum*, Hit *lāman*, Av Skt *nā́ma*, Toch B *ñem*, all 'name'). The actual expression for giving a name was *$^*h_1$nómn̥ dheh$_1$-* 'name-put' which is seen in OCzech *dieti jmě*, Hit *lāman dā-*, Skt *nā́ma dhā-* and as a noun in Grk *onomatothétēs* 'name-giver'. Although there are regionally attested words for the 'poet', there is no single well-attested form for Proto-Indo-European. As we have seen, the Celtic word for 'bard' (OIr *bard*, NWels *bardd*) was based on the verbal root *$^*g^w$erh$_x$-* 'praise'. It is actually from a nominal compound *$^*g^w$r̥h$_x$-dhh$_1$-ó-s* which itself derives from the verbal compound *$^*g^w$r̥h$_x$-dheh$_1$-* 'praise-put'. This collocation exists as an uncompounded expression in Indo-Iranian, i.e. Av *garəm dā-*: Skt *giram dhā-* 'give praise' but the Indo-Iranian and Celtic evidence is insufficient to allow us to reconstruct 'praise-put' to Proto-Indo-European; the phrase may well have been independently created at either end of the Indo-European world.

In addition to some of the words for 'praise' or 'speak solemnly', which may also be translated as 'pray', we have several more words that can be simply rendered 'pray'. Although the Germanic cognates of **meldh-* do not have obviously religious connotations (e.g. OE *meld(i)an* 'announce, declare, proclaim, reveal'; NE *meld* 'show a combination of cards in a game' is a loan borrowed from German [cf. OHG *meldōn* 'report']), the other cognates in Baltic (e.g. Lith *meldžiù*), Slavic (e.g. OCS *moljǫ*), Arm *malt'em*, and, most significantly, Hit *maldā(i)-*, all mean 'pray'. Those words derived from *$^*g^w$hedh-* rather consistently mean 'pray' (OIr *guidid* 'asks, prays', Lith *gedáuju* 'desire', OCS *žęždǫ* 'desire', dialectal Grk *théssasthai* 'ask, pray', Av *jaiδyemi* 'ask, pray'); to these we might add NE *bid.* A Greek-Luvian correspondence gives *$^*h_2$eru-* which can mean both 'pray' and 'call down a curse' (Grk *aráomai* 'pray, vow; call down a curse', Luv *hīrūt-* 'curse'). A Germanic-Hittite isogloss yields **telh$_x$-* 'pray' (e.g. ON *þulr* 'wiseman, sage, sayer of sacred rituals', Hit *talliya-* 'appeal to a god for help').

Although **perḱ-* 'ask' (e.g. OIr *arcu* 'ask', Lat *poscō* 'ask', *precor* 'ask for', OHG *forscōn* 'ask, examine', Lith *prašaũ* 'request', OCS *prositi* 'ask', Arm *harc'anem* 'ask', Av *pərəsaiti* 'asks', Skt *pr̥ccháti* 'asks', Toch AB *pärk-* 'ask') may carry a general meaning it is also the best candidate we have in Proto-Indo-European for 'to ask for someone in marriage' (cf. particularly Lat *procus* 'wooer', Lith *peršù* 'ask in marriage', Arm *harsn* 'bride'; see Section 12.2). Finally, a judicial connotation adheres to **kreuḱ-* which has both Germanic and Indic cognates that mean 'raise a hue and cry' (OE *hrēam* '[judicial] outcry', Av *xraos-* 'call', Skt [*ánu*] *króśati* 'cries out, raises the hue and cry').

From the West Central region: **kan-* 'sing' (e.g. OIr *canaid* 'sings', Lat *canō* 'sing', *carmen* 'song, prophecy, form of incantation' OHG *hano* 'cock', Grk *ēi-kanós* 'cock' [literally 'dawn-singer' just as in Skt *uṣā-kala-*], and probably

Toch B *kene* 'song, tune', in which case we have a general Proto-Indo-European word rather than a regionalism) and **sek*^{w}- 'say, recount publicly' (e.g. OIr *insce* 'discourse', Lat *īnseque* 'say!', NE *say*, Lith *sakaũ* ~ *sekù* 'say', OCS *sočiti* 'indicate', Grk *ennépō* 'say'). Greek-Indo-Iranian correspondences (Grk *kḗruks* 'herald', Skt *kārú-* 'one who sings or praises, poet') comprise **kāru-* 'poet' (from **kar-* 'praise' although the Indo-European status of the Greek word has been challenged) and **steu-* 'praise' (Grk *steûtai* 'make a gesture of or show of [doing something], promise, engage oneself, or threaten [to do something]', Av *staoiti* 'praises', Skt *stáuti* 'praises'). Indo-Iranian and Tocharian share a regional development of **k̂eh*$_1$- 'declare solemnly' as **k̂eh*$_1$*s-* 'instruct' (Av *sāh-* 'say instruct, call', Skt *śāsti* 'punishes, controls, commands, instructs', Toch A *kās-* 'chide, reprimand') and a common root **yeh*$_a$- 'ask for, beg' (e.g. Skt *yā-* 'beg, entreat', Toch B *yāsk-* 'beg').

21.3 Interjections and Human Sounds

Here we have gathered together in Table 21.3 those words which may be described as interjections or describe the type of noises that might issue from a human (laugh, babble, moan, etc.); animal noises will be treated separately in Section 21.4 although there will be some crossing between these two spheres, e.g. both people and wolves 'howl' in English. Obviously, when dealing with words that may be sound symbolic, there may be independent onomatopoeia involved rather than genetic inheritance.

The instrument responsible for making the following noises is the **wōk*^{w}*s* 'voice' (e.g. Lat *vōx*, Grk [acc.] *ópa*, Av *vāxš*, Skt *vāk*, Toch B *wek*, all 'voice'), a nominal derivative from **wek*^{w}- 'speak'. The standard vocative particle in Proto-Indo-European was **ō* where it meets this formal use in Celtic (e.g. OIr *ā*), Germanic (MHG *ā*, NE *O*), Baltic (Lith *ō*), Slavic (OCS *o*), Grk (*ō̂*), and Indic (Skt *ā*). In Lat *ō* it is a cry (as it may also be in Greek) and in Goth *ō* it means 'alas'. The expression of grief seen in **wai* 'alas' has undergone irregular phonological developments but would seem to be strongly reconstructed nevertheless (e.g. OIr *fae*, Lat *vae*, OE *wā*, Lith *va*, Grk *ouaí*, Av *vayōi*, all 'alas', and NE *woe*, Alb *vaj* 'lament', Arm *vay* 'woe, misfortune'–compare also Yiddish, and now English, *oy veh*).

The word for 'laugh' in Proto-Indo-European was obviously onomatopoeic and although it is provided a root reconstruction, i.e. **kha-*, it is generally found in reduplicated form, e.g. in addition to the Lat *cachinnō* 'laugh' we have OE *ceahhettan*, OCS *chochotati*, Grk *ka(g)kházō*, Arm *xaxank*, Skt *kákhati* ~ *khákkhati*, all 'laugh', suggesting that one might have laughed **kha kha!* in

Table 21.3. *Human noises*

$*wōk^ws$	'voice'	Lat *vōx*, Grk *ópa*, Skt *vāk*
**ō*	'O'	Lat *ō*, NE *O*, Skt *ā*
**wai*	'alas'	Lat *vae*, NE *woe*, Grk *ouaí*
**kha-*	'laugh'	Lat *cachinnō*, Grk *ka(g)kházō*, Skt *ká(k)kati*
**ha ha*	(laughing sound)	Lat *hahae*, Grk *hà há*, Skt *ha ha*
**ha*	(sound of surprise)	Lat *hā*, Grk *hā*, Skt *ha*
**smei-*	'smile, laugh'	NE *smile*, Grk *meidiáō*, Skt *smáyate*
**baba-*	'babble'	Lat *babit*, NE *baby, babble*, Grk *babázō*, Skt *bababā-karóti*
**balba-*	'± stammer'	Lat *balbus*, NE *babble*
**lal-*	'babble'	Lat *lallō*, NE *lullaby*, Grk *laléō*, Skt *lalallā-*
$*reudh_a$-	'mourn, lament'	Lat *rudō*, Skt *róditi*
**glaĝh-*	'cry out, lament'	Skt *gr̥háti*
**leug-*	'grieve, be pained'	Lat *lūgeō*, Grk *lugrós*
**sten-*	'moan'	Grk *stónos*, Skt *stánati*
**murmur-*	'murmur'	Lat *murmurō*, Grk *mormúrō*, Skt *marmar-*
**mug-*	'± make a (low) noise'	Lat *mūgiō*, Grk *múzō*, Skt *múñjati*
$*(s)pr̥h_xg$-	'crackle, sputter'	Grk *spharagéomai*, Skt *sphū́rjati*
$*meh_1(i)$-	'± mumble'	Grk *mimikhmós*, Skt *mímāti*
**dhren-*	'± rumble, drone'	Lat *drēnsō*, NE *drone*, Grk *thrênos*, Skt *dhráṇati*
$*\hat{k}wesh_x$-	'± breathe; sigh, groan'	Lat *queror*, NE *wheeze*, Skt *śvásiti*
$*\hat{g}h(h_1)iy\text{-}eh_a$-	'yawn'	Lat *hiāre*, NE *yawn*
**dhwen-*	'sound'	NE *din*, Skt *dhvánati*
$*swenh_x$-	'(re)sound'	Lat *sonō*, NE *swan*, Skt *svánati*
**klun-*	'resound'	
**gerg-*	'± crack, resound'	NE *crack*, Skt *gárjati*
**ĝhwonos*	'a sound, voice'	
**k̂léutrom*	'a sound'	Skt *śrótra-*

Proto-Indo-European. Alternatively, we have the more familiar **ha ha* (Lat *hahae*, Grk *hà há*, Skt *ha ha*). A single **ha* tended to indicate surprise (Lat *hā*, Grk *hā*, Skt *ha*). The root **smei-* means 'smile' in ME and NE *smile*, Grk *meidiáō* and Indic *smáyate* but 'laugh' in Norw *smila*, Baltic (Latv *smeju*), Slavic (OCS *smějǫ*), and Tocharian (Toch B *smi-*).

Words for 'babble' are so clearly onomatopoeic that certainty of reconstruction is impossible. There are three widespread words or, perhaps more accurately, sounds: **baba-* (e.g. Lat *babit* 'bears himself proudly, prances', *babiger* 'foolish, simple', NE *baby, babble*, Lith *bóba* 'old woman', OCS *baba* 'old woman', Alb *bebe* 'newborn child', Grk *babázō* 'babble', Skt *bababā-karóti* 'crackles [of a fire]'); **balba-* (and **balbal-* and **barbar-*), e.g. Lat *balbus* 'stammer', NE *babble*, Lith *blebénti* 'stammer', Czech *beblati* 'stammer'; Grk *bárbaros* 'non-Greek speaker' [whence via Latin to NE *barbarian*], Skt *barbara-* 'stammerer, non-Indic speaker'); and **lal-* (e.g. Lat *lallō* 'sing to sleep', NE *lullaby*, NHG *lallen* 'stammer, babble, speak indistinctly', Lith *lalúoti* 'stammer', Rus *lál* 'babbler', Grk *lálos* 'babbling, loquacious', *laléō* 'talk, chat, prattle', Hit *lala-* 'tongue', Skt *lalallā-* 'indistinct or lisping utterance'). The first exhibits the meaning 'babble', e.g. Grk *babázō* 'babble' or, in Indic, 'crackle' but is also associated with infants and shows a two-way semantic development such that we have a meaning 'baby' in English and Albanian but a reversed perspective in Middle High German, Lithuanian, and Old Church Slavonic where we find 'old woman' or 'mother'. Clearly related are those that close the initial syllable with an **-l-* or **-r-*. The meaning of these extended forms seems to have also included a pejorative for 'speak in a foreign way'. Hence both Grk *bárbaros* and its Skt equivalent *barbara-* could refer to one who did not speak the respective language concerned, i.e. a barbarian was literally someone whose speech sounded like *bar-bar*. The third word generally means 'babble' but in Hit *lala-* means 'tongue'.

A number of words fill out the vocabulary of 'grief'. The verbal root **reudh*$_a$- (with a present **réudh*$_a$*ti*) 'mourn' (Lat *rudō* 'roar, bellow, bray', ON *rauta* 'roar' [whence by borrowing NE *root* (for someone)], OE *rēotan* 'moan', Lith *raumi* 'mourn, lament', Slov *rydati* 'weep, cry, sob', Av *raod-* 'lament, mourn', Skt *róditi* 'weeps, roars') also yields a derivative **roudh*$_a$*os* 'cry' (OHG *rōz*, Lith *graudà*, Skt *róda-*, all 'cry'). There is also **glaĝh-* 'cry out' (e.g. OHG *klagōn* 'bewail, complain about', Av *gərəzaiti* 'laments, cries', Skt *gr̥háte* 'lament'). Latin, Greek, and Tocharian all point to a **leug-* 'weep' (Lat *lūgeō* 'mourn, lament', Grk *leugaléos* 'sad, horrible', *lugrós* 'baneful, mournful', Toch B *lakle* 'pain, suffering'). A 'moan' was conveyed by **sten-* (e.g. OE *stenan*, Lith *stenù*, OCS *stenjǫ*, all 'moan', Grk *sténō* 'roar', *stónos* 'moaning', Skt *stánati* 'thunders') which is probably related to **(s)tenh*$_x$- 'thunder' (see Section 8.4).

Another reduplicated form is **murmur-* 'murmur', e.g. Lat *murmurō* [whence by borrowing NE *murmur*], Lith *murménti*, Grk *mormúrō*, Arm *mrmrm*, all 'murmur', and Skt *marmar-* 'roaring'. There are a series of sounds that defy easy semantic reconstruction. Probably the clearest is **mug-* whose meanings run from Hit *mugā(i)-* 'entreat' to low moaning sounds (e.g. Lat *mūgiō* 'low, bellow', OHG *muckazen* 'grumble', Grk *múzō* 'mutter, moan, growl', Skt *múñjati* 'makes a noise'); it would appear to be an enlargement of **mu-* a low sound of some sort (in Czech it does mean to 'moo' like a cow). Germanic, Baltic, and Greek agree that their derivatives from **(s)pr̥h*$_x$*g-* mean 'crackle' (e.g. ON *spraka*, Lith *spragėti*, Grk *spharagéomai*); the Indic cognate means 'thunders' (Skt *sphū́rjati* 'thunders, rumbles'). The sound indicated by **meh₁(i)-* is difficult to ascertain as it means 'stammer' in OCS *mŭmati*, 'neigh' in Grk *mimikhmós*, 'bleat' in Armenian and Indic (*mayem* and *mímāti* respectively), but 'speak' in the oldest attested language, Hit *memma-*. The sound made in **dhren-*, if Germanic, Lithuanian, and Greek are anything to go by, should approximate that of a bee as it does produce the word 'drone' in these different groups (e.g. NE *drone*, Lith *trãnas*, Grk *thrōnaks*; cf. also MIr *dresacht* 'creaking noise', Lat *drēnsō* 'cry [of a swarm]', Grk *thrênos* 'funeral lamentation', Arm *drnč'im* 'toot, resound', Skt *dhráṇati* 'resounds', and perhaps Toch B *treṅk-* 'speak'). A 'sigh' or some other breathing sound is associated with **k̂wesh$_x$-*; it can mean 'lament' in Lat *queror* and Toch B *kwäs-* but in Germanic and Indic we have 'cough' (OE *hwōsan*), 'snort', 'hiss', etc., Skt *śvásiti*; NE *wheeze* is a loanword from Old Norse. The concept of 'yawn' or 'open the mouth wide' is provided by various forms related to **ĝh(h₁)iy-eh$_a$-* which provide the North-Western words (Lat *hiāre*, OHG *gīēn*, NE *yawn*, Lith *žióju*, Rus *zijátĭ*, all 'yawn') but with an o-grade we have Toch B *kāyā-* 'yawn, gape'.

There is a series of totally ambiguous sounds. A Germanic-Baltic-Indic isogloss delivers **dhwen-* which seems to be some form of 'loud noise' (e.g. NE *din*, Lith *dunděti* 'rumble, roar, thunder', Skt *dhvánati* 'sounds, roars'). Although the Sanskrit word derived from **swenh$_x$-*, *svánati*, means 'roars, makes sound', the fact that the word means 'resound' in other languages (e.g. Lat *sonō*, Latv *sanēt*), 'sing' in OE *swinsian*, and 'play a musical instrument' in OIr *seinnid* suggests a meaning 'resound' or something less noisy; derivatives of the verbal root include Lat *sonus* 'sound' and NE *swan* (< *'singer'). A Germanic-Tocharian isogloss preserves **klun-* 'resound' (e.g. OE *hlynn* 'sound, noise, roaring stream', Toch AB *käln-* 'resound'). The root **gerg-* is regarded as onomatopoeic but it is by no means clear what that sound signifies; it means 'creak' and 'crack' in Germanic and Baltic (e.g. OE *cearcian* 'creak, gnash', NE *crack*, Lith *gìrgždžiu* 'creak') but 'roars, howls' in Indic (Skt *gárjati*) and simply 'noise' in Arm *karkač*. The verbal root **ĝheu(h$_x$)-* 'call' yields the derivative **ĝhwonos* 'sound, voice' (OCS *zvonŭ* 'noise', Alb *zë* 'voice', Arm *jayn* 'voice') while from the the root **k̂leu-* 'hear' (see also Section 20.5) regularly (and perhaps independently) derived **k̂léutrom* 'a sound' (e.g. OE *hlēodor* 'sound', Av *sraoθram* 'song', Skt *śrótra-* 'tone').

Regional correspondences are all from the West Central region and offer frequent question marks over the solidity of their reconstruction (so many are onomatopoeic). We have **gag-* 'cackle' (e.g. NE *cackle*, Lith *gagù*, Rus *gogolátĭ*, Arm *kakač'em*, all 'cackle') and a possible Welsh-Greek isogloss **sward-* 'laugh' (NWels *chwarddiad* 'laugh', Grk *sardánios* '(bitter) laughter', *sardázō* 'scoff, jeer' [whence by borrowing NE *sardonic*]); **leh$_a$-* 'complain, cry out' (e.g. OIr *liïd* 'complains', Lat *lāmenta* 'lamentation', dialectal Grk *laíō*

'± make a sound', Arm *lam* 'cry, weep') which might be the same as *$*leh_a$-* 'bark' (see Section 21.4); **ĝem-* 'weep, lament, moan' (e.g. NIr *geamh* 'prattle', Lat *gemō* 'sigh, moan, lament, groan', Arm *cmrim* 'grieve'); **yu-* '± shout (for joy)' (e.g. MIr *ilach* 'victory cry', Lat *iūbilō* 'shout', NE *yowl*, Grk *iúzō* 'shout'); **sner-* '± rattle, growl' (e.g. NE *snore, snarl*, Lith *niùrniu* 'growl, grumble', dialectal Grk *énuren* '± cried out'); **ger-* '± hiss, howl' (e.g. OE *ceorran* 'creak', Lith *gùrti* 'yell', Alb *nguron* 'howls [of the wind]'); **srenk-* 'snore' (OIr *sreinnid* 'snores', Grk *hrégkō* 'snore'); and *$*gheh_a$-* 'yawn' (ON *gan* 'yawn', Grk *kháskō* 'yawn').

21.4 Animal Sounds

We have already seen that the words for the names of birds are often onomatopoeic and in addition to these there are a number of other words associated with the speech of animals. That the language of animals is specific to one's individual language is easily illustrated by the fact that an English-, German- and Greek-speaking dog all bark slightly differently, i.e. NE *bow-wow*, NHG *wau-wau*, and Grk *baubau*. Noises associated with animals are listed in Table 21.4.

The root **bhrem-* would seem to involve some sort of buzzing or roaring sound and it tends to mean 'roar' in Germanic (e.g. OE *bremman*) but returns a Sanskrit word for 'bee' (*bhramará-*); cf. also Lat *fremō* 'growl, roar', NHG *brummen* 'growl, grumble, hum', Pol *brzmieć* 'resound'). A Proto-Indo-European dog was said to *$*leh_a$-* 'bark' (e.g. Lat *lātrō* 'bark [at]; rant, roar', Lith *lóju* 'bark', OCS *lają* 'bark', Alb *leh* 'bark', Oss *ræjun* 'bark', Skt *rāyati* 'barks') or **bhels-* 'howl' (e.g. OE *bellan* 'roar, howl', Skt *bhaṣati* 'barks, yelps') or **bukk-* 'howl' (SC *búkati* 'howl', Grk *búktēs* 'howling', Av *buxti-* 'howling', Skt *bukkati*

Table 21.4. *Animal sounds*

**bhrem-*	'± make a noise (of animals)'	Lat *fremō*, Skt *bhramará-*
$*leh_a$-	'bark'	Lat *lātrō*, Skt *rāyati*
**bhels-*	'yelp, howl'	Skt *bhaṣati*
**kau(k)-*	'cry out; cry out as a bird'	Lat *cavannus*, Grk *kḗks*, Skt *kóka-*
**ker-*	'± caw'	Lat *corvus*, Grk *kóraks*, Skt *karaṭa-*
**ul-*	'± howl, hoot'	Lat *ululāre*, Grk *huláō*, Skt *ulūlú-*
**gher-*	'± cry (of animals or birds)'	Lat *hirrīre*, Skt *ghā́rghara-*
**bukk-*	'howl'	Grk *búktēs*, Skt *bukkati*
**reu-*	'roar, howl'	Lat *rūmor*, Grk *ōrū́omai*, Skt *ruváti*

'barks'). The first word means 'bark' in the six groups in which it is attested and it is not obviously onomatopoeic but seems to be firmly inherited from Proto-Indo-European. It is also curious that the other two roots do not themselves appear to be onomatopoeic or, at least, if **bukk-* is, it does not reflect a sound that an English speaker would intuitively regard as a 'howling noise'.

There are several words for 'bird cry'. The raucous-sounding **kau(k)-* (e.g. Skt *káuti* 'cries out', Lith *kaukiù* 'howl', Grk *kōkúō* 'cry, lament' Arm *k'uk'* 'sighing, groaning', Skt *kokūyate* 'cries out') has been associated with the word for 'owl': Celtic (NWels *cuan* 'nightowl'), Italic (Lat *cavannus* 'nightowl'), Germanic (OHG *hūwo*); the 'tern' (Grk *kḗks*), and the 'goose' (Skt *kóka-* 'kind of goose'). Lat *corvus* and Grk *kóraks* return 'raven' as a derivative of **ker-* while the Indic cognate (Skt *karaṭa-*) means 'crow' (cf. also Czech *krákorati* 'cackle', Grk *skorakízō* 'dismiss contemptuously'). Both Latin and Indic mean 'owl' (Lat *uluc(c)us* '[screech] owl', Skt *úlūka-*) as a name built on **ul-* although this can also mean 'howl' (Grk *huláō*, Lat *ululāre*), 'ululate' (Skt *ulūlú-* 'ululating'), and even 'shout hello' (Lith *ulūlóti*). A more general 'animal cry' was **gher-* which may be independently invented over a number of its putative cognate languages (e.g. Lat *hirrīre* 'howl like a rabid dog', ON *garpr* 'warlike man', RusCS *gŭrkati* 'coo', Skt *gharghara-* 'gurgling'). Certainly the semantic disparities seen in this group would seem to favour the notion of independent creation rather than inheritance.

Finally, **reu-* 'roar, howl' can be found with this meaning in Germanic (e.g. ON *rymja* 'roar'), Slavic (e.g. OCS *rovǫ* 'roar'), Grk (*ōrúomai* 'howl'), and Indic (Skt *ruváti* 'roars, bellows'); in Lat *rūmor* it has come to mean 'rumour, common talk'.

Regional words from the North-west comprise **kem-* 'hum' (e.g. NE *hum*, Latv *kamines* 'bee, bumble-bee', Rus *cmelĭ* 'bumble-bee') returning 'bee' in Baltic and Slavic; **bherg-* '± bark, growl' (e.g. NE *bark*, Lith *burgė́ti* 'spurt, splash, splutter, howl'); and **bhleh₁-* 'bleat' (e.g. Lat *fleō* 'weep, cry, lament; shed tears', MHG *blæjen* 'bleat', Latv *blêju* 'bleat', Rus *bléju* 'bleat'). From the West Central region: **baub-* 'bark, low' (Lat *baubor* 'bark', Lith *baũbti* 'low [of cows]', Grk *baüzō* 'bark') with 'bark' in Latin and Greek but 'low (of cattle)' in Lithuanian; **kla(n)g-* 'scream (of birds)' (Lat *clangō* 'cry [of birds]', ON *hlakka* 'cry [of an eagle]', Lith *klagė́ti* 'cackle', Grk *klázō* 'resound', *klaggṓdēs* 'shouting, screaming [of people and birds], barking or baying [of dogs]'); **g(h)ru(n)(d)-* 'grunt' (e.g. Lat *grunniō* ~ *grundiō* 'grunt', NE *grunt*, Grk *grúzō* 'grunt'); and **b(h)(o)mb(h)-* '± muffled noise' (e.g. ON *bumba* 'drum', Lith *bambė́ti* 'roar', Rus *búben* 'drum', Alb *bumbullit* 'it thunders', Grk *bómbos* 'muffled noise') with related words for 'bee' in Lith *bam̃balas*, Grk *bombúlē*, and Skt *bambhara-*.

21.5 Proto-Indo-European Speech

In their typological distinctions between humans and beasts, Gamkrelidze and Ivanov emphasize speech as a major defining characteristic of humans (a feature also found in many non-IE traditions) and in Old English we find *reordberend* 'speech-bearers' as a kenning for human beings. The category of speech in Indo-European is one of its larger semantic fields. If these are divided into twenty-five categories, speech trails only after words concerning the body and health and the large variety of action verbs. Interestingly enough, if the same semantic fields are superimposed on Proto-Uralic, speech is one of the least represented categories and ties for twentieth place. What this says about the loquaciousness of Indo-Europeans vis-à-vis Uralics is anyone's guess.

Among the variety of words for speech reconstructed to Proto-Indo-European is fairly convincing evidence of different registers. In English we can 'utter', 'declare', 'pronounce', 'asseverate', or, dropping a level, we can 'talk' and 'say', and now in free fall, 'yak', 'gab', and 'yap', and ultimately enter a world where we are unsure whether it is humans or animals making the noises, e.g. 'growl', 'grunt', 'yelp'. A similar range of expression seems to have been open to the Proto-Indo-Europeans. Words based on **k̂e(n)s-* and *$h_{1/4}$*ōr-*, for, example, appear to fill out special formal contexts of speech associated with religion or the law. It is likely that the less nuanced expressions of speech include the more widely attested forms such as **wek*^{w}- and *(*s*)*wer-* while at the bottom we might have some of the expressions associated with children or foreigners, e.g. **lal-*, **baba-*.

Among the key functions of speech was prayer. Words for 'pray' are well attested in Proto-Indo-European, e.g. **meldh-*, **g*^{w}*hedh-*, and the structure of the earliest IE prayers appears to follow a basic pattern of invocation to the deity, statement of why the deity should assist one or be honoured, and then the actual request, often with an imperative verb. In some IE traditions, e.g. Phrygian, Italic, we have abundant evidence for curses as well as prayers, especially in the context of protecting graves from defilement, and this is further supported by the evidence in Greek and Anatolian for *h_2*eru-* '± pray, curse'. We have also seen the specialized use of the verb **perk̂-* 'ask' to indicate a marriage proposal.

In addition to the verbs listed above that indicate recite or sing, e.g. *(*s*)*pel-*, **seng*^{w}*h-*, there are a number of isoglosses, generally involving Greek and Indo-Iranian, that suggest specific collocations associated with the art of poetry. For example, the standard verb for 'make' (**tek̂s-*) is found associated with 'speech' (**wék*^{w}*os*) in Grk *epéōn téktones*, Av *vačastašti-*, and Skt *vácas takṣ-* to suggest a PIE 'fashion speech'. Another technical verb that enters the realm of poetry is

**webh-* 'weave' where we find that words can be woven in OE *wordcræft wæf* 'he wove poetry', Grk *mū́thous kaì mḗdea pâsin húphainon* 'they have woven words and thoughts for all', and Avestan where *vaf* can mean both 'weave' and 'praise'.

Recitation of poetry and the fame of heroes appears in almost all IE traditions and the entire vocabulary of 'fame everlasting' (**k̂léwos n̥dhgʷhitom*) has already been mentioned in Section 20.5 and we have listed some of the reconstructed poetic phrases in Table 7.9. These examples of poetic diction are unfortunately the closest we can get to reconstructing Proto-Indo-European poetry although comparisons between the different Indo-European traditions permit us to suggest some of the general features of the verse. For example, there are widespread examples in a number of poetic traditions for what Martin West terms the 'Augmented Triad'. This involves a verse line where three names are indicated and the last is marked by some form of epithet, e.g. in the *R̥gveda* we have *Indrāṇī́, Agnā́yi, Aśvíni rā́t* 'Indrāni, Agnāyī, Aśvinī the queen', in Homer one finds *ē Aías ē Idomeneùs ē dîos Odusseús* 'Ajax and Idomeneus or lordly Odysseus', in Beowulf an example would be *Heorogār ond Hrōðgar ond Hālga til* 'Heorogar, Hrothgar, and Halga the good'. To go further and reconstruct the actual metrical system of the Proto-Indo-Europeans has been attempted a number of times and there is no doubt that there are striking similarities between some of the earliest poetic traditions, especially Greek and Indic, e.g. both offer examples of lines that are twelve, eleven, or eight lines long. But the only concrete observation that includes all the relevant evidence indicates that the Proto-Indo-Europeans probably had a variety of metres with stable patterns of long and short syllables and numbers of syllables per line.

A number of IE traditions recognize a distinction between the language of gods and that of humans. In Norse poetry we find a series of pairs where the first is the divine word and the second is that of humans, e.g. *fold/jorð* 'earth', *sunna/sōl* 'sun', *mȳlinn/māni* 'moon'. Other traces derive from Greek, e.g. *khalkis/kúmindis* 'some type of bird', Skt, e.g. *háya-/áśva-* 'horse', and, especially, in Avestan where certain words are only associated with the demons of Zarathustra's religion.

Finally, is there any evidence for Proto-Indo-European personal names? Probably, if some of the examples of poetic diction are truly evidence of cognate personal names, e.g. Illyr *Vescleves-*, Grk *Eukleḗs*, and Skt *Suśráva-* all derive from PIE **k̂léwos wésu* ~ **k̂léwos h₁esu-* 'possessing good fame'. The other area where we may suspect the retention of ancient Proto-Indo-European names (though find it difficult to prove) is the use of cognate animal names or numerals as a personal name among various Indo-European groups, e.g. OIr *Olc*, OE *Wulf*, Grk *Lúkos*, Skt *Vŕ̥ka-*, all from PIE **wl̥̂kʷos* 'wolf'; Lat *Quārta*, Lith *Keturai*, Rus *Četvertoj*, Grk *Tetartíōn*, all 'Fourth'.

Further Reading

The word for 'name' and possible Indo-European names can be found in Beekes (1987*b*), Markey (1981), Pinault (1982), Schmitt (1973), and Watkins (1970*a*). Indo-European verse has been frequently discussed and the reader is directed to just some of the works: Bader (1989), Campanile (1977, 1990), Kurłyowicz (1975), Meid (1978, 1990), Nagy (1974*c*), Schmitt (1967), Watkins (1995), West (1973, 2004). For 'speech' see Turcan (1982); against a PIE **kāru-* see Beekes (2003); the interjections were treated long ago in Schwenter (1924); for the 'language of gods and men' see Watkins (1970*b*).

22

Activities

22.1 Existence, Ability and Attempt

Verbs associated with 'being' and 'doing' are obviously a fundamental concept in any vocabulary and such words are often very strongly reconstructable to Proto-Indo-European. A list of the basic verbs is provided in Table 22.1.

The basic verb 'to be', **$h_1$es-*, is reconstructed in its principal parts which may be displayed in tabular form (Table 22.2).

The origin of the verb is often associated with **h_1ēs-* 'sit', which looks like a lengthened grade derivative of **$h_1$es-*. One might compare the paradigm of Spanish *ser* 'be' which historically is a mixture of the Latin words for 'be' and 'sit'. The English verb 'to be' (also, e.g., OIr *-bīu* 'become', Lat *fīō* 'become', Lith *bū́ti* 'be', OCS *byti* 'be') derives from our second form, **bheu(h_x)-* 'come into being', and this form tends to supply the aorist forms in a number of Indo-European groups (e.g. Grk *éphūn* 'would be', Skt *ábhūt* 'was', and perhaps Lat *fuī* 'was, have been', OCS *by* 'was'). It also exhibits nominal derivatives such as **bhuto-* 'dwelling' (e.g. OIr *both* 'hut', NWels *bod* 'dwelling', OPrus *buttan* 'house', Lith *bùtas* 'house').

Table 22.1. *Existence, doing, and making*

**$h_1$es-*	'be'	Lat *est*, NE *is*, Grk *estí*, Skt *ásti*
**bheu(h_x)-*	'come into being, be; grow'	Lat *fīō*, NE *be*, Skt *bhávati*
**magh-*	'be able'	NE *may*, Skt *maga-* [?]
**sen(h_a)-*	'seek, accomplish'	Grk *ánūmi*, Skt *sanóti*
**dhers-*	'venture, be bold; undertake'	Skt *dhr̥ṣṇóti*
**k^wer-*	'do, make, build'	Skt *karóti*
**yeh_1-*	'do, make; act vigorously'	Grk *hḗrōs*, Skt *yātú-*
**kon-*	'do, make'	Lat *cōnor*
**$h_a$er-*	'prepare, put together'	Lat *ars*, Grk *araríshō*, Skt *ará-*
**sep-*	'handle (skilfully), hold (reverently)'	Lat *sepeliō*, Skt *sápati*
**dheuĝh-*	'be useful, produce something useful'	Grk *teúkhō*, Skt *doháti*
**bheug-*	'use'	Lat *fungor*, Skt *bhunákti*
**werĝ-*	'work'	NE *work*, Grk *hrézō*
**$h_x$ópes-* (noun)	'work'	Lat *opus*, Skt *ápas-*
**dheiĝh-*	'work clay; build up'	Lat *fingō*, NE *dough*, Skt *déhmi*

A verb 'be able', **magh-*, is widespread within the West and Centre of the Indo-European world (e.g. NE *may*, Lith *magė́ti* 'please, be agreeable', OCS *mogǫ* 'am able') but it lacks clear cognates in the East unless one accepts a number of potentially derived forms such as Av *moγu-* (whence ultimately Lat *magus*, plural *magi*) and Skt *maga-* 'magician', i.e. 'one who has power' (though the *-g-* of Sanskrit rather than the expected **-gh-* is difficult). The verb 'accomplish' or 'seek to accomplish' is seen in **sen(h_a)-* where the meanings run from 'strive' to 'win' (e.g. OIr *do-seinn* 'pursues, strives', Grk *ánūmi* 'accomplish, get [somewhere, something]', Hit *sanhzi* 'seeks, plans, demands', Av *han-* 'gain, obtain', Skt *sanóti* 'wins, gets; grants'). Another verb 'attempt', **dhers-* (e.g. Lith *drę̃sù* 'dare', Skt *dhr̥ṣṇóti* 'is bold, dares'), also yields adjectival formations, e.g. Germanic **dorso-* > NE *dare* and words for 'brave' in Grk *thérsos* 'bravery' and Iranian (Av *daršì-* 'brave').

Table 22.2. *The verb 'to be' in selected IE languages*

PIE	OIr	Lat	OE	Lith	Grk	Hit	Skt
**$h_1$ésmi*	*am*	*sum*	*eom*	*esmì*	*eimí*	*ēsmi*	*ásmi* ('I am')
**$h_1$ésti*	*is*	*es*	*is*	*ẽsti*	*estí*	*ēszi*	*ásti* ('she/he is')
**$h_1$sénti*	*it*	*sunt*	*sind*	—	*entí*	*asanzi*	*sánti* ('they are')

The actual 'doing' or 'making' was conveyed by a number of different verbs. Hittite and Tocharian alone preserve the underlying verb form **yeh*$_1$*-*, i.e. Hit *iēzi* 'does, makes', Toch A *ya-* 'do, make', but nominal derivatives are widely found including Grk *hḗrōs* 'hero' and the name of the goddess *Hḗrā*; here Indo-Iranian has shifted the meaning to the occult, e.g. Skt *yātú-* 'witchcraft'. A similar partial shift to magic is seen in the descendants of **k*^{w}*er-* (e.g. OIr *cruth* 'form', Lith *kuriù* 'make, build, create', OCS *kručĭjĭ* 'smith', Av *kərənaoiti* 'does, makes', Skt *kr̥ṇóti* 'does, makes, performs; executes, builds'; but Lith *kẽras* 'magician', Rus *čáry* 'sorcery'). An Ossetic cognate (*kæn-* 'make') of what is otherwise a Western and Central distribution of **kon-* (e.g. OWels *di-goni* 'makes, does', Lat *cōnor* 'put myself in motion, attempt', Czech *konat* 'do, achieve') secures its Proto-Indo-European antiquity; the root is preserved in NE *deacon* which is borrowed from Grk *diā́konos*. A primarily south-eastern distribution (e.g. Grk *araríṡkō* 'put together', Arm *aṙnem* 'make', Av *arānte* 'they set themselves, remain') is associated with **h*$_a$*er-* (our Skt cognate *ará-* means 'spoke [of a wheel]') but it also has more widespread nominal derivatives such as Lat *ars* 'art', Arm *ard* 'structure, ornament', Skt *r̥tú-* 'fixed time, time appointed for some purpose'). Semantically more distant (and also difficult in terms of establishing a more precise proto-meaning) is **sep-* which conveys such concepts as 'touch, serve, prepare' (in Grk *hépō* 'serve, prepare', Av *hap-* 'hold', Skt *sápati* 'touches, handles, caresses; venerates', and the Latin derivative *sepeliō* 'bury', i.e. 'prepare a body', which is the formal equivalent of Skt *saparyáti* 'honours, upholds') and is associated with the management of horses in both Greek and Sanskrit (Grk *methépō* ~ *ephépō* 'manage [horses]', Skt *sápti-* 'team of horses').

There are two verbs to 'use' indicated for Proto-Indo-European. The most widely attested is **dheuĝh-* whose meanings fluctuate around 'use', 'be fitting', 'succeed' in most of its Western and Central cognates (e.g. OIr *dūal* 'fitting', OE *dugan* 'be useful', NE *doughty*, Rus *dúžyj* 'strong, healthy', Grk *teúkhō* 'prepare') but is associated with the act of 'milking' in Skt *dóhati* 'extracts, milks'; both this semantic shift and its implications for a more precise reconstruction of the proto-meaning have been widely discussed (most recently it has been interpreted as 'be strong, have force'). A root **bheug-* 'use' is based on a Latin-Sanskrit isogloss (Lat *fungor* 'am engaged in, perform', Skt *bhunákti* 'aids, serves, protects', *bhuṅkté* 'enjoys, uses, consumes').

There are a number of words for 'work'. Widespread are the forms attesting **werĝ-* 'work' which are semantically consistent except for Tocharian where the meaning is 'strength, power' (e.g. NE *work*, Grk *hrézō* 'do', Av *vərəzyeiti* 'works', Toch B *warkṣäl* 'power, strength, energy'). A noun 'work' is attested as **h*$_x$*ópes-* (e.g. Lat *opus* 'work', OE *æfnan* 'to work, make', Av *-apah-* 'work', Skt *ápas-* 'work') which may be related (by way of an early avatar of the 'Protestant work ethic'?) to **h*$_2$*op-* 'wealth' (e.g. Lat *opēs* [pl.] 'possessions, abundance, wealth', Grk *áphenos* 'wealth', Hit *happina(nt)-* 'rich', Av *afnahvant-* 'wealthy', Skt *ápnas-* 'wealth'). The underlying semantics of **dheiĝh-* indicate that it was specifically associated with the working of clay (e.g. Lat *fingō* 'fashion', Skt *déhmi* 'smear, anoint', Toch AB *tsik-* 'fashion [pots, etc.]'), hence the English cognate *dough*; in Greek and Indo-Iranian it is also associated with building walls, e.g. Av *pairi-daēzayeiti* 'build a wall around' which, via Greek then Latin then French, gives us NE *paradise*, but there are also cognates of more general meaning, e.g. OIr *con-utainc* 'builds', Lith *díežti* 'whip, beat', Arm *dizanem* 'heap up'.

From the North-West we have **gal-* 'be physically able' in Celtic (e.g. NWels *gallu* 'is able') and Baltic (e.g. Lith *galiù* 'am able'); **kob-* 'fit, suit, accomplish' from Celtic (OIr *cob* 'victory'), Germanic (ON *happ* 'chance, luck', whence by borrowing NE *happy*), and Slavic (OCS *kobĭ* 'divination'); and two roots confined to Germanic and Baltic: **k̂elb-* 'help' (e.g. NE *help*, Lith *šelpiù* 'help, support') and **neud-* 'use, enjoy' (e.g. OE *nēotan* 'use, enjoy' [where the NE cognate *neat* 'work animal, cattle' is now rarely heard, although one can still buy neat's foot oil], Lith *naudà* 'use, property'). From the West Central area we have **per-* 'trial, attempt', found in Lat *experior* 'attempt', Grk *peĩra* 'attempt', and Arm *p'orj* 'test, proof'; and a Baltic-Greek isogloss **derh$_a$-* 'work' (e.g. Lith *dar(i)aũ* 'do, make', Grk *dráō* 'make, do'). A Greek-Indic isogloss (Grk *-kmētós* 'made, worked', Skt *śamitá-* 'prepared') furnishes us with **k̂meh$_a$-* 'made, prepared' from **k̂emh$_a$-* whose transitive meaning is 'work' and intransitive is 'become tired'.

22.2 Reductive Activities

In this general category we have assembled all those words that relate to reducing material in some way by breaking, crushing, grinding, cutting, or carving. The vocabulary, as one can see in Table 22.3, is fairly extensive and could obviously be augmented if we were to include the verbs of aggressive action listed in Table 17.5 and some of the verbs associated with construction in Section 13.1.

A number of roots express the concept of breaking or crushing. The meaning 'break' is associated with the Irish, Armenian, and Indic descendants of **bheg-* (e.g. OIr *boingid*, Arm *bekanem*, Skt *bhanákti*); the Baltic cognates (e.g. Lith *beñgti*) indicate 'finish, end', perhaps from 'breaking off'. The semantic range attested under **leuĝ-* is even wider with 'break' in Baltic (Lith *láužti*) and Skt *rujáti* but Latin and Tocharian indicate 'pain' (Lat *lūgeō* 'mourn', Toch B *lakle* 'pain, suffering') while the Celtic cognates (e.g. OIr *lucht* 'load, cargo') mean 'burden'. The putative Sanskrit cognate, *rúpyati*, from **reup-* 'break' has been challenged

Table 22.3. *Reductive activities*

**bheg-*	'break'	Skt *bhanákti*
**leuĝ-*	'break, break off'	Lat *lūgeō*, Skt *rujáti*
**reup-*	'break'	Lat *rumpō*, NE *rift*, ?Skt *rúpyati*
**mer-*	'crush, pulverize'	Grk *maraínō*, Skt *mr̥ṇā́ti*
**wes-*	'crush, grind, pound, wear out; wither'	
*(*s*)*terĝh-*	'± crush'	Skt *tr̥ṇéḍhi*
**weld-*	'crush, grind, wear out'	NE *wilt*
**del-*	'carve, split, cut'	Lat *dolō*, Grk *daidállō*, Skt *dálati*
*(*s*)*ker-*	'cut apart, cut off'	NE *shear*, Grk *keírō*, Skt *kr̥ṇā́ti*
**skeh$_1$i*(*-d*)-	'cut'	Lat *scindō*, NE *shit*, Grk *skhízō*, Skt *chyáti*
**sek-*	'cut'	Lat *secō*
**k^{w}er-*	'cut'	Skt *-kr̥t*
**put-*	'cut'	Lat *putāre*
**bheid-*	'split'	Lat *findō*, NE *bite*, Grk *pheídomai*, Skt *bhinádmi*
**waĝ-*	'split'	Lat *vāgīna*, Grk *ágnūmi*, Skt *vájra-*
*(*s*)*kel-*	'split (apart), cut'	NE *skill*, Grk *skállō*
**bher-*	'strike (through), split'	Lat *feriō*, NE *bore*, Grk *pharáō*, Skt *bhr̥ṇā́ti*
**wel*(*h$_2$*)-	'strike, tear at'	Lat *vellō*, Grk *oulḗ*
**der-*	'tear off, flay'	NE *tear*, Grk *dérō*, Skt *dr̥ṇā́ti*
**drep-*	'scratch, tear'	Grk *drépō*
**rendh-*	'rend, tear open'	NE *rend*, Skt *rándhram*
**reu*(*h$_x$*)-	'tear out, pluck'	Lat *ruō*
**h$_1$reik-*	'tear (off)'	Grk *ereíkō*, Skt *rikháti*
*(*s*)*pel-*	'tear off, split'	Lat *spolium*, Grk *spólia*, Skt *phā́la-*
*(*s*)*pelt-*	'split'	NHG *spalten*, Skt *pā́ṭati*
**leup-*	'peel'	Skt *lumpáti*
**bhedh-*	'dig, burrow'	Lat *fodiō*
**h$_3$reuk-*	'dig up'	Lat *runcō*, Grk *orússō*, Skt *lúñcati*
**k̂euh$_x$-*	'hollow out'	Lat *cavus*, Grk *kúar*, Skt *śū́nya-*
**keh$_a$u-*	'hollow out'	Lat *cūpa*, Grk *kū́pē*, Skt *kū́pa-*
**keus-*	'hollow out'	Skt *kóṣa-*
**terh$_1$-*	'pierce by rubbing'	Lat *terō*, Grk *teírō*, Skt *tārá-*
**h$_{2/3}$weg*(*h*)-	'pierce'	
**dhwer-* ?	'pierce'	Grk *túrkhē*
**steig-*	'prick'	Lat *īn-stīgō*, NE *stick*, Grk *stízō*, Skt *téjate*
**kel-*	'prick'	NE *holly*, Skt *kaṭamba-*

(*Cont'd*)

Table 22.3. (*Cont'd*)

**red-*	'gnaw, scrape'	Lat *rōdō*, NE *rat*, Skt *rádati*
**bhes-*	'rub'	Grk *psáō*, Skt *bábhasti*
**merd-*	'± rub, scrape'	Lat *mordeō*, Skt *mr̥dnā́ti*
**ḱehₓ(i)-*	'sharpen, hone'	Lat *catus*, NE *hone*, Skt *śíśāti*
**kseu-*	'rub, whet'	Grk *ksúō*, Skt *kṣṇáuti*

as it means 'suffer racking pain'. However, if it is accepted, then the distribution is Proto-Indo-European (cf. also Lat *rumpō* 'break', NE *rift*, Lith *rūpė́ti* 'grieve, afflict'). The meaning 'crush' is found in four more roots. The active meaning behind **mer-* 'crush' is preserved only in Greek, Hittite, and Sanskrit (Grk *maraínō* 'extinguish [a fire]', Hit *mariyattari* 'is smashed', Skt *mr̥ṇā́ti* 'crushes, grinds') while the other cognates yield the results, e.g. OIr *meirb* 'lifeless', OE *mearu* 'soft'. Hittite preserves a meaning 'press' from **wes-* (*wesuriya-* 'press, oppress') while the Germanic and Albanian cognates mean 'wither' (e.g. OE *wisnian* 'dry up, wither, waste away', Alb *veshk* 'wither, shrivel, wilt'). A PIE *(*s*)*terĝh-* '± crush' rests on a Hittite-Indic isogloss where both exhibit a rare and presumably archaic *ne*-present, i.e. *(*s*)*tr̥-né-ĝh-ti* (Hit *istarninkzi* 'afflicts', Skt *tr̥ṇéḍhi* 'crushes, bruises'). Although there are few cognate sets for **weld-*, i.e. NWels *gwlydd* 'mild, soft, tender', NE *wilt*, and Tocharian (Toch B *wālts-* 'crush, grind'), their distribution indicates Proto-Indo-European status.

The concept of 'cut' is well represented in Proto- Indo-European. A root **del-* 'cut' is widely found in Europe (e.g. OIr *dello* 'form', Lat *dolō* 'hew', ON *telgja* 'carve', Lith *dalti* 'divide', Alb *dalloj* 'cut', Grk *daidállō* 'work cunningly') and its ascription to Proto-Indo-European depends on acceptance of a potential late Indic cognate (Skt *dálati* 'bursts, cracks'); as we see, it means 'cut' in Germanic, 'divide' in Baltic, but shows extended meanings associated with manufacture in Greek (cf. Daedalus who invents wings for himself and his too high-flying son Icarus) and in Celtic 'form'. The meaning 'cut apart/off' appears to underlie the widely attested *(*s*)*ker-*, e.g. Hit *karsmi* 'cut off, castrate' (and also OIr *scaraid* 'separates, divides', NE *shear*, Lith *skiriù* 'separate, divide', Rus *krojú* 'cut', Alb *shqerr* 'tear apart', Grk *keírō* 'cut', Arm *k'erem* 'scrape off, scratch off', Skt *kr̥ṇā́ti* 'wounds, kills'). It also exists in an extended form *(*s*)*kert-* (e.g. Lith *kertù* 'hew', Arm *k'ert'em* 'skin', Hit *kartai-* 'cut off', Av *kərəntaiti* 'cuts', Skt *kr̥ntáti* 'cuts') and the word underlies ON *skor* 'notch' (i.e. 'what has been cut') which is borrowed into English to gives us *score*. A word **skeh₁i-d-* generally yields meanings of 'cut' or 'split' (e.g. Lat *scindō* 'cut', Lith *skíedžiu* 'separate', OCS *čěditi* 'filter, strain', Grk *skhízō* 'split, tear') but in Germanic it gives us 'defecate', e.g. OE *be-scītan* > NE *shit*. An unextended **skeh₁i-* gives Skt *chyáti* 'cuts'. The even more fundamental root

**sek*- 'cut' (e.g. MIr *eiscid* 'cuts off', Lat *secō* 'cut', Lith *į-sė́kti* 'dig', OCS *sěkǫ* 'cut') also gives us Lat *sciō* 'know' and Hit *sakk*- 'know'. The semantic change from *'cut' to 'know' is not, admittedly, an obvious one, but it is confirmed by the same change in the history of **ker-s*-, another enlargement of **ker*- (above) which means 'cut' in Hit *karsmi*, as we would expect, but 'know' in Tocharian (AB *kärs*-). The root **kʷer*- retains its original verbal meaning 'cut' in Anatolian (e.g. Hit *kuerzi* 'cuts') but NWels *pryd* 'time', Osc *-pert* '... time[s]', and Skt *-kr̥t* '... time[s]' all employ this root also to mean 'time(s)', i.e. a 'slice of time'. A Latin-Tocharian isogloss supports a PIE **put*- 'cut' (Lat *putō* 'prune', Toch AB *putk*- 'divide, share, separate'). To these we may add the words for 'split'. A PIE **bheid*- 'split' (e.g. Lat *findō* 'split', Skt *bhinádmi* 'bite') supplies the Germanic words for 'bite' and the Grk cognate *pheídomai* 'spare' develops from the idea of 'separating oneself from' something. The root **waĝ*- retains verbal meaning 'split' in Grk *ágnūmai* 'break apart, snap, crush', Anatolian (Hit *wāki* 'bites'), and Tocharian (Toch AB *wāk*- 'split open, separate but remain attached; bloom') but reveals nominal forms in Latin (where we have *vāgīna* 'sheath, scabbard', the encasement of a weapon), and in India the mythical *vájra*-, the 'club' or 'splitter' of the god Indra. Another verb, *(*s*)*kel*-, 'split' (e.g. Grk *skállō* 'hoe, stir up', Arm *skalim* 'split, be splintered', Hit *iskalla*- 'slit, slash, tear') or 'chip' in Celtic and Baltic (e.g. MIr *scoiltid* 'chips', Lith *skeliù* 'chip'), develops a secondary meaning of 'that which is apart, distinguished' in Germanic, hence ON *skil* 'distinction' which is borrowed into English as *skill*. Finally, we have **bher*- 'strike (through), split' with cognates in Lat *feriō* 'strike, pound', OE *borian* > NE *bore*, Lith *bar(i)ù* 'revile, abuse', OCS *borjǫ* 'fight, struggle', Grk *pharáō* 'plough', Skt *bhr̥ṇā́ti* 'wounds'.

Words that suggest the concept of 'tearing' include **wel*(h_2)- with meanings of 'strike', e.g. Hit *walh*- 'strike, attack' as well as 'pluck, tear' (e.g. Lat *vellō*); in Hieroglyphic Luvian (*wal*(*a*)-) and Tocharian (Toch A *wäl*-) it means 'die' and in Germanic it is employed to denote either a 'corpse on a battlefield', e.g. ON *valr* (whence we have both *Valhalla* and *Valkyrie*), or the 'battlefield' itself. The root **der*- is more properly 'tear' or 'flay' as in NE *tear*, Lith *diriù* 'flay', OCS *derǫ* 'flay', Grk *dérō* 'skin, flay', Arm *teřem* 'flay, strip bark', Av *darədar*- 'split', Skt *dr̥ṇā́ti* 'causes to burst, tears', Toch AB *tsär*- 'separate'. An extended form, **drep*- 'scratch, tear', is widely found (e.g. Rus *drjápati* 'scratch, tear', Grk *drépō* 'pluck'); the possible Tocharian cognates (Toch A *räp*-, Toch B *rāp*-) show the meaning 'dig', and the possible Anatolian cognates show the meaning 'plough' (e.g. Hit *tēripzi* 'ploughs'). A Germanic-Indic isogloss secures **rendh*- 'rend' (e.g. NE *rend*, Skt *rándhram* 'opening, split, hole'). A meaning 'tear out' or 'pluck' is seen in **reu*(h_x)- (e.g. MIr *rūam* 'spade', Lat *ruō* 'tear off; fall violently', ON *rȳja* 'pluck wool from a sheep', Lith *ráuju* 'pull out, weed', OCS *rŭvǫ* 'pull out', Toch AB *ruwā*- 'pull out [from below the surface with violence]'). Both the

Welsh and Greek cognates derived from *$h_1$reik- mean 'tear' (NWels *rhygo*, Grk *ereíkō*) while other cognates yield meanings of 'pull a thread' (OHG *rīhan*), 'cut bread' (Lith *riekiù*), and 'scratch' (Skt *rikháti*). As a verb *(s)pel- is only attested in Skt *phálati* 'bursts, splits in two' with its derivative *phā́la-* 'ploughshare' (< *'splitter'), but there is a widespread PIE derivative *spolih$_x$om 'something torn or split off' in Lat *spolium* 'hide stripped from an animal; booty, spoils', dialectal Grk *spólia* [pl.] 'wool plucked from the legs of sheep', Lith *spãliai* [pl.] 'refuse of hemp and flax', as well as other derivatives meaning 'hide, skin' (see Section 11.3). An enlarged *(s)pelt- 'split' is more widespread as a verb (e.g. OHG *spalten*, OCS *ras-platiti*, Skt *sphá̱ṭati*, all 'split', and Skt *páṭati* 'splits, apart, bursts'). Other, less widespread, enlargements of *(s)pel- are common (e.g. NE *split*). A Balto-Slavic-Indic isogloss gives us *leup- 'peel' (e.g. Lith *lupù* 'peel', Skt *lumpáti* 'break, violate, hurt').

Although we find 'dig' in some of the daughter languages, there are several more specific forms reconstructed to Proto-Indo-European. The underlying meaning of *bhedh- is clearly 'dig' (Lat *fodiō*, Hit *padda-* ~ *pidda-*) with obviously derived meanings in other language groups, e.g. 'grave' (NWels *bedd*), 'plough' (Toch A *pāt-*). There have been attempts to place the Germanic set that includes NE *bed* here under the reasoning that the Proto-Germans once slept in hollows in the ground like animals but this set is far more likely to derive from a homophonous *bhedh- 'bend' which yields 'cushion'. The verb *$h_1$reuk- means 'dig' in Baltic and Greek (Latv *rūkīt*, Grk *orússō*, and indirectly in Celtic, i.e. OIr *rucht* 'pig' [i.e. *'one who digs up']) but the idea of 'plucks' appears in Latin (where the cognate *runcō* means 'weeds') and Skt *lúñcati* 'tears, plucks'.

The notion of 'hollowing out' is seen in three roots with largely nominal derivatives. The first, *k̂euh$_x$-, is to be seen in MIr *cūa* 'hollow', Lat *cavus* (Early Lat *covus*) 'cave', Alb *thellë* 'deep', Grk *kúar* 'eye of a needle' *koîlos* 'hollow, deep', Arm *soyl* 'hole', Skt *śūnya-* 'empty, hollow', Toch B *kor* 'throat'. The second, *keh$_a$u-, appears enlarged with a *-p- in Lat *cūpa* 'cask', Grk (Hesychius) *kū́pē* 'cave', Skt *kū́pa-* 'hole, hollow, cave'. Enlarged with *-l- we have, e.g. Lat *caulis* 'stalk', NE *hollow*, Grk *kaulós* 'stalk', Lith *káulas* 'bone', Skt *kúlyam* 'bone', and perhaps Hit *gullant-* if, as seems likely, it means 'hollow'. Finally, we have *keus- in the Lithuanian verb *kaũšti* 'hollow out' and various nominal derivatives, e.g. ON *hauss* 'skull', Lith *káušas* 'skull, ladle', Skt *koṣa-* 'vessel', and various words for 'dwelling' of some sort, e.g. NE *house*, Arm *xuc'* 'room', Khot *kūṣda-* 'mansion', Toch B *kuṣā-* 'village' [< *'collection of dwellings'], all suggesting that one type of Proto-Indo-European dwelling was at least partially dug below ground level (see Section 13.1).

There are several terms for 'pierce'. The first, *terh$_1$- might be glossed as 'pierce by rubbing' and is widely attested, e.g. in OIr *tarathar* 'instrument for drilling', Lat *terō* 'rub, wear away', Lith *trinù* 'rub', OCS *tĭrǫ* 'rub', Alb *tjerr* 'spin' [< *'rub yarn back and forth'], Grk *teírō* 'pierce', Skt *tārá-* 'piercing' (see Section 15.3). The other two verbs of piercing are much less abundantly seen. The first, *$h_{2/3}$*weg(h)*-, is found in both Hit *hwek-* 'slaughter, butcher, slay', and OPers *vag-* 'pierce'. The second, **dhwer-*, shows up in Lith *duriù* 'thrust, stab', Grk *túrkhē* 'two-pronged fork', Arm *dur* 'tool, gimlet'; an enlarged **dhwerh*$_x$- may appear in Hit *dwarnai-* 'break, shatter', Skt *dhvárati* 'bends, causes to fall, shatters'.

There are two verbs for 'prick'. A root **steig-* is both widely attested and semantically reasonably congruent across the various Indo-European groups (e.g. Lat *īnstīgō* 'goad', NE *stick* and *stitch*, Grk *stízō* 'prick, tattoo', Av *bi-taēγa-* 'having two edges', Skt *téjate* 'is sharp, makes sharp'). A second root, **kel-*, has a verbal meaning but no verbs: here we have a set of nouns, e.g. 'holly' (Celtic, Germanic), 'ear of grain' (Slavic, e.g. OCS *klasŭ*), 'barley meal' (Toch B *klese*), 'straw, chaff' (Alb *kallí*), and 'arrow' (Skt *kaṭamba-*), from which we presume an underlying verbal root for something 'sharp' or 'prickly'. It may be related to the homophonous root **kel-* 'cut'. The English *rat* takes its name from **red-* 'gnaw, scrape' (cf. also Lat *rōdō* 'gnaw', MPers *randītan* 'scrape, smooth', Skt *rádati* 'bites, gnaws, cuts, makes way, opens').

For 'rubbing' we have two Proto-Indo-European terms, **bhes-* and **merd-*. The former occurs in Alb *fshij* 'sweep, wipe, brush', Grk *psáō* 'rub', Skt *bábhasti* 'chews thoroughly, devours', *psā́ti* 'chews, swallows'. The latter also shows a connection with oral activities in Lat *mordeō* 'bite', but Skt *mr̥dnā́ti* 'rubs', Toch B *märtk-* 'shave [hair]'.

Two words appear to be reconstructable for 'sharpen, hone'. The first, **k̂eh*$_x$*(i)*-, appears as a verb only in Indic, i.e. in Skt *śíśāti* ~ *śyáti* 'sharpens, whets', but much more widely in a number of old derivatives (e.g. Lat *catus* 'wise', perhaps Grk *kōnos* 'pinecone, fircone; peak of a helmet' [if < *'sharp(ened) object'], Skt *śā́ṇa-* 'whetstone', Toch B *kāntsā-* 'sharpen', Arm *srem* 'sharpen', NE *hone*). The second, **kseu-*, appears in Lat *novācula* (< **ksnewā-tlā-*) 'razor', Grk *ksúō* 'sharpen', *ksurón* 'razor', Av *hu-xšnuta-* 'well-sharpened', Skt *kṣṇáuti* 'sharpens, whets', *kṣurá-* 'razor'.

There are many regional terms for breaking, cutting, and other reductive activities. From the North-West we have **bhreĝ-* 'break' (e.g. Lat *frangō* 'break', NE *break*); **dhelbh-* 'dig' (e.g. NE *delve*, Lith *dálba* 'crowbar'); **ghrebh-* 'dig' (e.g. NE *grave*, Lith *grė̃bti* 'rake', OCS *pogrebǫ* 'bury'); **dhelg-* 'sting, pierce' (e.g. OIr *delg* 'needle, pin', Lat *falx* 'curved blade', OE *dalc* 'bracelet, brooch', Lith *dilgùs* 'stinging, smart'); **skebh-* 'scratch, shave' (e.g. Lat *scabō* 'shave, scratch', NE *shave*, Lith *skabùs* 'sharp', OCS *skoblĭ* 'scraping knife'); and **k*^{w}*ed-* 'whet, sharpen' (Lat *triquetrus* 'having three corners', NE *whet*).

From the West Central region there is **bhreus-* 'break, smash to pieces' (e.g. OIr *bruid* 'breaks, crashes', Lat *frustum* 'piece', NE *bruise*, Alb *breshër* 'hail'), perhaps an enlargement of *_bher-_ 'strike (through), split'; *_$h_3$lem-_ 'break' (e.g. OIr _ro-laimethar_ 'dares, ventures', NE _lame_ [<*'broken'], Latv _lemesis_ 'ploughshare', OCS _lomljǫ_ 'break', Alb _lemë_ 'threshing floor', Grk _nōlemés_ 'without a break, unceasingly'); *_wreh$_1$ĝ-_ 'break, tear to pieces' (e.g. Lith _rė̃žti_ 'cut, scratch', OCS _rězati_ 'cut, hew', Grk _rhḗgnūmi_ 'break'); *_gleubh-_ 'cut off, cut out' (e.g. Lat _glūbō_ 'peel', NE _cleave_, Grk _glúphō_ 'carve out' whence _glyph_); *_(s)grebh-_ 'scratch, cut' (e.g. NE _carve_ [NE _scrape_ is borrowed from ON _skrapa_], OPrus _gīrbin_ 'number', OCS _žrěbŭ_ 'lot', Grk _gráphō_ 'scratch'); *_kerd-_ 'cut into, carve' (e.g. OIr _cerd_ 'art, handicraft', Grk _kérdos_ 'profit'); *_$h_1$reip-_ 'tear' (e.g. Lat _rīpa_ 'river bank', ON _rīfa_ 'tear out', Grk _erípnai_ [pl.] 'broken cliff') is an extended form of the unextended, and unattested, *_$h_1$rei-_ also seen in the more widely attested *_$h_1$reik-_ (above); *_plek̂-_ '± break, tear off' (e.g. NE _flay_, Lith _plė̃šiù_ 'tear off', Alb _plas_ 'burst, break'); *_lak-_ 'rend, tear' (Lat _lacer_ 'worn out', Alb _lakur_ 'naked', Grk _lakízō_ 'tear'); *_lep-_ 'peel' (Grk _lépō_ 'peel' and nominal derivatives in other groups, e.g. OE _lōf_ 'headband', Lith _lãpas_ 'leaf', Rus _lápotĭ_ 'bast-shoe', Alb _lapë_ 'dewlap of an ox'); *_g^wel-_ 'sting, pierce' (e.g. Lith _gélti_ 'sting [as a bee]', Grk _belónē_ 'needle'); *_geid-_ 'tickle', a Germanic-Armenian isogloss, both with the same meaning (e.g. OE _citelian_, Arm _kcem_); *_peug-_ 'prick, poke' (Lat _pungō_ 'prick', Grk _pugmḗ_ 'fist'); *_ter(i)-_ 'rub, turn' (e.g. Lat _terō_ 'rub', Lith _trinù_ 'rub', OCS _tĭrǫ_ 'rub', Grk _teírō_ 'rub'); *_treu(h_x)_ - 'rub away, wear away' (e.g. NE _throw_, OCS _tryjǫ_ 'rub', Grk _trúō_ 'rub down'), an enlargement of *_ter(i)-_. A Greek-Indo-Iranian isogloss attests *_$h_3$merĝ-_ 'wipe off' (Grk _omórgnūmai_ 'wipe off', Av _marəzaiti_ 'strokes', Skt _mr̥ṇákti_ 'wipes off'). Finally, there is *_(s)kerbh-_ ~ *_(s)kerbh-_ 'shrink, shrivel' with the following cognates: ON _skorpna_ 'shrivel', Lith _skur̃bti_ 'suffer a decline, wither; mourn', Rus _skórblyj_ 'shrivelled', Grk _kárphō_ 'let shrivel, dry out'.

22.3 Rotary and Lateral Motion

Grouped here are verbal activities involving twisting, turning, shaking, and covering over.

A verb 'turn' is well attested in Proto-Indo-European. The root *_k^wel-_ and its extended form *_k^wleu-_ both mean 'turn' and arguably suggest rotary or circular motion. The evidence for rotary motion is suggested by its association with wheels (one of the nominal forms for 'wheel', *_k^wek^wlóm_ or *_k^wek^wlós_, is a reduplicated form of this verb and the Old Irish cognate of the unreduplicated verbal form is _cul_ 'wagon' while Greek also provides a nominal derivative _pólos_ 'axle'). The other cognate forms are all verbs with more generalized meanings, e.g. Indo-Iranian 'circulate, wander' (Av _čaraiti_ 'circulates', Skt _cárati_ 'moves, wanders, drives'), possibly suggesting the type of cyclic movements attributed

Table 22.4. *Rotary and lateral activities*

_*k^{w}el-_	'turn'	Lat *colō*, Grk *pélō*, Skt *cárati*
*k^{w}leu-	'turn'	
*trep-	'turn'	Lat *trepit*, Grk *trépō*, Skt *trápate*
*wert-	'turn'	Lat *vertō*, Grk *bratánon*, Skt *vártate*
*weig/k-	'± turn, yield'	Grk *eíkō*, Skt *vijáte*
*wendh-	'wind, twist'	NE *wind*, Grk *kánnathron*, Skt *vandhúra-*
*derbh-	'turn, twist'	Skt *dr̥bháti*
*k^{w}erp-	'turn'	NE *wharve*, Grk *karpós*
*twer-	'stir, agitate'	Lat *trua*, Grk *otrū́nō*, Skt *tvárate*
*weip- ~ _*weib-_	'turn'	Lat *vibrāre*, NE *wave*, *wipe*, Skt *vépate*
*wel-	'turn, wind, roll'	Lat *volvō*, Grk *eiléō*, Skt *válati*
?*(w)rep-	'turn, incline'	Grk *rhépō*
*(s)pre(n)g-	'wrap up, constrict'	Grk *spárgō*
*weis-	'twist, wind around'	NE *ware*, Skt *véṣa-*
_*k̂em-_	'cover'	Skt *śāmūla-*
*(s)keu(h$_x$) -	'cover, wrap'	Lat *ob-scūrus*, Grk *skúlos*, Skt *skunā́ti*
*trem-	'shake, tremble (in fear)'	Lat *tremō*, Grk *trémō*
*tres-	'tremble, shake with fear'	Lat *terrēre*, Grk *tréō*, Skt *trásati*
*rei-	'tremble, be unsteady'	Skt *lelḗya*
*kseubh-	'shake'	Skt *kṣúbhyati*
*wer-	'surround, cover, contain'	Lat *aperio*, Grk *érumai*, Skt *vr̥ṇóti*

to pastoralists (cf. also Alb *sjell* 'turn around', *qell* 'carry', Grk *pélō* 'be in motion; be'). The Latin cognate *colō* can mean 'till; dwell; care for'. That the first meaning may have been original, i.e. 'turn the earth over', is perhaps suggested by _*trep-_ 'turn' whose potential Hittite cognate is *tēripp-* 'plough' (if, indeed, this word belongs here and not with _*drep-_ in Section 22.3); the other cognate forms indicate simply 'turn' (Lat *trepit* 'turns', Grk *trépō* 'turn') except for Skt *trápate* 'becomes perplexed'. A root _*wert-_ also indicates 'turn' (e.g. OIr *do-fortad* 'pour out', Lat *vertō* 'turn', Lith *verčiù* 'turn', OCS *vrĭtěti sę* 'draw around', dialectal Grk *bratánon* 'ladle', Av *varət-* 'turn', Skt *vártate* 'turns', Toch A *wärt-* 'throw') and in Indo-Iranian has specific associations with chariotry, e.g. Sog *wrtn* 'chariot' or Mitanni *-wartanna* 'lap around a horse track'. This root supplies the Germanic languages with their verb 'become', e.g. OE *weorþan* 'become', OHG *werdan* 'become'. Semantically more vague is _*weig/k-_ which does yield the meaning 'turn' in ON (*vīkja* ~ *vīkva*), but also 'yield' in the other Germanic languages and Greek (e.g. OE *wīcan*, Grk *eíkō*), 'throw' in Av *vaēg-*, and 'disappear' in Toch AB *wik-*.

The related concept of 'wind' or 'twist' can be seen in _*wendh-_ whose reflexes are both verbs, e.g. NE *wind*, and nominal forms that suggest any object produced by twisting flexible branches or osiers, e.g. Grk *kánnathron* 'basket-carriage' or Skt *vandhúra-* 'wicker carriage' (cf. also Umbrian *pre-uendu* 'turn', Arm *gind* 'ring', Toch AB *wänt-* '± cover, envelop'). Similarly, **derbh-* can mean simply 'turn' in Germanic (e.g. OE *tearflian* 'turn, roll, wallow') but it indicates something bound by twisting in Armenian and Indo-Iranian (Arm *toṙn* 'cord', Av *dərəβδa-* 'bundle of muscles', Skt *dr̥bháti* 'knots, ties'). Germanic also preserves a basic meaning 'turn' for **kʷerp-* (e.g. OE *hweorfan* 'turn, change') which gives us nominal forms such as Grk *karpós* 'wrist' and words for 'spear' in Celtic (MIr *carr*, NWels *pâr*) and, by metaphorical extension, 'be concerned with' (<*'turn onself toward') in Toch AB *kurp-*. To 'turn' in the sense to 'stir' is suggested by **twer-* which means both 'stir' and 'agitate, stir up' (e.g. Lat *trua* 'scoop, ladle', OE *þweran* 'stir, churn, agitate', Grk *otrū́nō* 'drive, agitate', Skt *tvárate* 'hurry')(see also Section 16.2 for terms associated with food preparation). A possible Greek-Tocharian isogloss suggests **(w)rep-* 'turn, incline' (Grk *hrépō* 'incline oneself, be inclined to', Toch A *rapuñe* 'desire, cupidity').

More distant concepts are 'wrap up, constrict' seen in **(s)pre(n)g-* whose outcomes suggest a meaning 'wind around' (for Greek 'swaddle' in *spárgō*) or Baltic 'constrict' (e.g. Lith *springstù* 'choke, become choked or constricted'), cf. also MHG *phrengen* 'oppress', Toch AB *präṅk-* 'restrain oneself, hold back'. Surviving in English only dialectally is *ware* in the meaning of 'seaweed' which is derived from **weis-* 'twist, wind around' and attests just one of the ways this verbal concept was preserved in different Indo-European groups; others include Lith *výstyti* 'swaddle' and Skt *véṣa-* 'dress', Rus *víkh(o)rĭ* 'whirlwind', and Arm *gi* 'juniper'.

There are several words for 'cover' which often take nominal formations. Proto-Indo-European **k̂em-* 'cover' gives us words for clothing in Late Lat *camīsia* 'linen shirt, nightgown' (perhaps borrowed from Gaulish), Germanic (e.g. OE *hama* 'dress, covering'), and Skt *śāmūla-* 'thick woollen shirt' while **(s)keu(h_x)* - preserves its original meaning in Lat *ob-scūrus* 'dark, obscure', i.e. 'covered', and Indic (i.e. Skt *skunā́ti* 'covers') or in words for 'hide' (NE *hide* is derived from this root with a *t*-extension while Grk *skúlos* 'pelt, skin' shows an **-l-*) or 'leather' (Grk *skûtos*).

The lateral motion of shaking or, by extension, trembling is indicated by four words. A Proto-Indo-European **trem-* 'shake, tremble' is well attested in five groups (e.g. Lat *tremō* 'shake', Lith *trìmti* 'shake', Alb *tremb* 'scare, startle, shock', Grk *trémō* 'shake', Toch A *träm-* 'be enraged'); NE *tremble* is ultimately borrowed from Late Latin. The semantic range of **tres-* includes both 'shaking' and 'fear' itself (e.g. MIr *tarrach* 'fearful', Lat *terrēre* 'terrify', *terror* 'terror', Lith *trišù* 'tremble', OCS *tręsǫ* 'tremble', Grk *tréō* 'tremble, flee', Av *tərəsaiti* 'fears', Skt *trásati* 'trembles, is afraid'; see also Section 20.6) and both

**trem-* and **tres-* may derive from a common though unattested verbal root ***ter-*. A PIE **rei-* rests entirely on a Gothic-Sanskrit correspondence (Goth *reiran* 'tremble, shake', Skt *leláyati* 'swings, is unsteady') and there is a Polish-Indo-Iranian isogloss that gives us **kseubh-* 'shake' (Polish *chybnąć* 'shake', Av *xšaob-* 'agitate', Skt *kṣúbhyati* 'shakes').

From the North-West there is **kret-* 'shake' (e.g. MIr *crothaid* 'shakes', OE *hraðe* 'quick', Lith *krečiù* 'shake, jolt; strew by shaking'); **(s)ku(n)t-* 'shake, jolt' (e.g. NE *shudder*, Lith *kuntù* 'recover, get better' [i.e. 'shake something off'], OCS *skytati sę* 'wander'); **kreut-* '± shake' (e.g. ON *hraustr* 'quick', Lith *krutù* 'move, stir'); **slenk-* 'turn, twist (like a snake)' (e.g. NWels *llyngyr* 'worms', NE *sling*, Lith *slenkù* 'crawl [like a snake]'); **swerbh-* 'turn, move in a twirling motion' (e.g. NWels *chwerfan* 'spindlewhorl', OE *sweorfan* 'wipe, rub', Latv *svārpstît* 'bore', OCS *svrabŭ* 'scabies'). The West Central region offers a possible **k^{w}at-* 'shake', a Latin (*quatiō* 'shake')-Greek (*pássō* 'strew') isogloss; **sper-* 'wrap around', a Baltic (Lith *spartas* 'band, ribbon')-Greek (*speîra* 'coils')-Armenian (*p'arem* 'enclose, surround') isogloss; **k̂el-* 'conceal, cover' (e.g. OIr *ceilid* 'conceals, dissembles', Lat *cēlō* 'conceal', OE *helan* 'conceal', Grk *kalúptō* 'cover'); **(s)teg-* 'cover' (e.g. Lat *tegō* 'cover', NE *thatch*, Lith *stíegiu* 'put on a thatch roof', Grk *stégō* 'cover'), which has a possible Sanskrit cognate in *sthagayati* 'covers' which, if accepted (the *-th-* suggests to some a non-Indo-European origin for the word in Indic), would point to Proto-Indo-European status. There is a Greek-Indo-Iranian isogloss in **tweis-* 'shake' (Grk *seíō* 'shake', Av *θwaēšah-* 'fear, anxiety', Skt *tvéṣate* 'is excited').

22.4 Bind, Stick, and Smear

The concept of attachment, both natural and artificial, is reflected in a series of roots, largely verbal, to describe the act of binding, both metaphorically and through the use of an instrument, sticking, and smearing. These are listed in Table 22.5.

The root **bhendh-* 'bind' exhibits verbal reflexes in Germanic and Indo-Iranian, e.g. NE *bind*, Av *bandayeiti* 'binds', Skt *badhnáti* 'binds', but is also reflected in nominal forms in Grk *peîsma* 'rope' and, evidently in an extended sense to indicate a social binding, as kinship terms such as 'companion' or 'father-in-law' in Baltic (Lith *beñdras* 'companion'), Grk *pentherós* 'father-in-law', and Skt *bándhu-* 'kinsman; connection, kinship' (see Section 12.3). A small group of correspondences (Albanian-Greek-Sanskrit) indicates **deh$_1$-* 'bind' (the Alb *duaj* is nominal 'sheaves', but Grk *déō* and Skt *dyáti* are verbal 'bind'). A root **h$_2$ep-* is attested in Latin, Anatolian, and Tocharian (e.g. Lat *aptus*

Table 22.5. *Binding*

**bhendh-*	'bind'	NE *bind*, Grk *peîsma*, Skt *badhnā́ti*
**deh₁-*	'bind'	Grk *déō*, Skt *dyáti*
**h₂ep-*	'fasten, join'	Lat *aptus*
**ghedh-*	'join, fit together'	NE *together*, Skt *gádhya-*
**yeu-*	'bind, join together'	Skt *yáuti*
**h₂emĝh-*	'tie, constrain'	Lat *angō*, Grk *ágkhō*
**dherĝh-*	'bind fast'	Skt *dṛ́hyati*
pehₐĝ-*~pehₐk̂-*	'fasten securely'	Lat *pangō*, Grk *pḗgnūmi*, Skt *pāśáyati*
**seg-*	'fasten'	Skt *sájati*
**kergh-*	'bind'	
**h₃engʷ-*	'anoint (with salve), (be)smear'	Lat *unguō*, Skt *anákti*
**leip-*	'adhere, stick; smear'	Skt *limpáti*
**hₐlei-*	'smear'	Lat *linō*, Grk *alínō*, Skt *linā́ti*

'fitted to; appropriate, fitting' [> by borrowing NE *apt*], Hit *happ-* 'join, attach', Toch A *āpsā* [pl.] 'limbs') and like **bhendh-* it may underlie words with extended social meanings such as Skt *āpí-* 'ally'. The root **ghedh-* 'join, fit together' (e.g. NE *together*, Lith *guõdas* 'honour, respect', OCS *godŭ* 'appointed time', Skt *gádhya-* 'what really holds fast, what suits one') also means 'fitting' and yields an *o*-grade **ghōdho-* in Germanic whence we have NE *good*. The basic root **yeu-* 'bind, join together' (e.g. Lith *jáutis* 'ox, steer' [<*'that which is yoked'], Skt *yáuti* 'binds, unites') is more widely found in the extended form **yeu-g-* 'yokes' and yields that meaning in Italic (Lat *iungō*), Baltic (Lith *jùngti*), Grk *zeúgnūmi*, and Skt *yunákti* (see also Section 15.5). The meaning 'constrain' as well as simply 'tie' is suggested in **h₂emĝh-* where Lat *angō* can mean anything from 'tie' to 'throttle' while Slavic (e.g. OCS *ǫžǫ*) and Av *ąz-* indicate 'constrain'; the Hittite cognate *hammenk-* can mean 'tie' or 'betroth'. Constraint is also suggested in **dherĝh-* where we find a Baltic nominal form meaning 'belt' (Lith *dir̃ža*) and Av *darəzayeiti* 'fetters'. The semantic range of **pehₐĝ-* ~ **pehₐk̂-* suggests a meaning such as 'fasten securely' as many of the Germanic cognates indicate 'capture' (e.g. Goth *fahan*) while Grk *pḗgnūmi* means 'plant, make solid' (cf. also Lat *pangō* 'drive in', Skt *pāśáyati* 'binds'). It may be that Lat *pāx* 'peace' [> via Old French NE *peace*] also belongs here as *'a binding together by treaty'. A root **seg-* 'fasten' is found from Ireland (where it is nominalized as OIr *sūainem* 'cord') to India (Lith *sègti* 'fasten, buckle', OCS *sęgnǫti* 'take, grab', Skt *sájati* 'fastens'). A Baltic-Tocharian isogloss secures **kergh-* 'bind' (Lith *ker̃gti* 'tie, bind', Toch AB *kärk-* 'bind').

A root *h_3eng^w- supplies the basis for both a verb 'anoint, smear' (e.g. Lat *ung(u)ō* '(be)smear, anoint', Arm *awcanem* 'anoint', Skt *anákti* 'anoints') and nominal derivatives that indicate either 'butter' in the West (e.g. OIr *imb*, OHG *ancho*, OPrus *anctan*) or 'salve' in the East, e.g. Skt *áñjas*-. The semantic field of **leip*- suggests a proto-meaning of 'smear' (as in Hit *lipp*-) or 'adhere' (as in Baltic and Slavic, e.g. Lith *limpù*, OCS *pri-lĭpją* 'stick on') which also developed into 'remain' or 'be left over' (still attached?) in Germanic and Tocharian (e.g. OE *bilīfan*, Toch AB *lip*-). Related is Grk *liparós* 'fat, anointed' (see Section 20.10). Meanings of 'smear' or 'stick' are fairly uniform across those cognates that derive from *$h_a$lei*- 'smear' (e.g. OIr *as-lena* 'stain', Lat *linō* 'smear', Lith *laistaũ* 'smear', Grk *alínō* 'spread, smear', Skt *linā́ti* 'pastes', Toch B *linā*- 'stick, place').

West Central words comprise **mer*- 'braid, bind' (e.g. NE *moor* [a boat] [<MLG *mōren*], Grk *mérmīs* 'cord'); **(h_2)wer*- '± attach' (a Balto-Slavic-Albanian isogloss [e.g. Lith *vérti* 'thread a needle', Rus *veráti* 'prick', Alb *vjerr* 'hang up'] though one might possibly include Grk *aeírō* 'attach' here); **kol*- 'glue' (e.g. MLG/MDutch *hêlen* 'stick', Grk *kólla* 'glue'), and possibly **smeid*- 'smear' if one can accept Arm *mic* 'dirt' as cognate with various German words (e.g. Goth *ge-smeitan* 'smear').

22.5 Bend and Press

The vocabulary associated with bending, pressing, and folding is indicated in Table 22.6.

The vocabulary associated with the concept 'bend' is fairly large and we are in some instances able to suggest specific differences in meaning between the different words. The semantics of **$h_2$enk*- 'bend' suggests that this word was used to describe an object that held a bent shape; the meaning 'hook' or 'barb' can be found in Celtic (OIr *ēcath*), Germanic (OHG *ango* 'fishhook'), Slavic (OCS *ąkotĭ*), Grk *ógkos* 'barb', and Iranian (Av *aka*-). The underlying verb is only certainly found in MPers *ančītan* 'bend', but may also be seen in Hit *hinkzi* 'bows (reverentially), curtsies' though there are phonological difficulties. The object bent in **bhedh*- seems to have been the human body, e.g. Toch B *pauto* 'honour', i.e. bend one's knees; the Germanic cognates that have been sometimes placed here are all associated with the concept of 'ask', i.e. 'request on bended knee' (NE *bid*), while Alb *bind* means 'convince'. Less clear is **bheug*- 'bend' which yields meanings of both 'bend' (OHG *biogan*, Skt *bhujáti*) and 'break' (Goth *biugan*) or survives merely in terms of a curved shape (Latv *bauga* 'hill').

Two roots provide interesting case studies. The root **geu*- is treated as a verbal root which only survives in a number of nominal forms, e.g. **gudom*

Table 22.6. *Bend and press*

*$^*h_2enk$-	'bend'	Lat *uncus*, Grk *ógkos*, Skt *áñcati*
**bhedh-*	'bend (one's body)'	NE *bid*, Skt *bā́dhate*
**bheug-*	'bend (an object)'	Skt *bhujáti*
**geu-*	'curve'	
**keu-k-*	'curve'	NE *high*, Skt *kucáti*
**kleng-*	'bend, turn'	Lat *clingō*, NE *link*
**leng-*	'bend'	Skt *ráṅgati*
**lenk-*	'bend; traverse, divide'	
**nem-*	'bend'	Skt *námati*
**pel-*	'fold'	Lat *duplus*, Grk *diplóos*
**swe(n)g-*	'bend, swing'	NE *swing*, Skt *svájate*
**weng-*	'bend'	NE *wink*, Skt *váṅgati*
**prem-*	'press down or back'	Lat *premere*
**menk-*	'press'	Grk *mássō*, Skt *mácate*
**bhrak-*	'squeeze together'	Lat *farciō*, Grk *frássō*
**puḱ-*	'press together'	Grk *ámpuks*

'intestines', **gu-ro-s* 'lock of hair', **gu-r-nos* 'back', all presumably derived from a no longer extant (or at least recoverable) verbal form. The wide semantic range of the meanings associated with the cognate forms derived from **keu-k-* 'curve' are truly daunting. Skt *kucáti* 'bends, curves' provides a base verbal meaning which is also seen in nominal form as *kuca-* 'breast' which takes us into the realm of anything 'curved', e.g. OIr *cūar* 'curved' which may include a 'hill', e.g. Lith *kaũkaras*, and then on to the abstract meaning 'high', e.g. NE *high*, Toch B *kauc* 'high'; Baltic words for 'devil' (OPrus *cawx*) or 'goblin' (Lith *kaũks*) are explained either by the fact that goblins are covered with warts, boils, have crooked backs or noses (cf. OCS *kukonosŭ* 'curve-nosed'), or, alternatively, such creatures live in or under hills.

A root **kleng-* 'bend' is attested in the North-West with meanings such as 'gird' (Lat *clingō*) and 'chain' (NE *link*) while the Tocharian cognates indicate a 'vehicle/way of arriving at knowledge' (Toch B *kleṅke*) and 'doubt' (Toch B *kläṅk-*). Two similar roots, **leng-* and **lenk-*, both mean 'bend'; Lithuanian preserves both of these words in *lingúoti* 'soar' and *leñkti* 'tilts, bends' respectively (cf. also Slov *lągāc* 'bend', OCS *raz-lęciti* 'separate, divide', Alb *lëngor* 'flexible', Skt *ráṅgati* 'moves here and there', Toch AB *läṅk-* 'hang' [<*'dangle']), Toch B *leṅke* 'valley, cleft'). We have seen how 'bend' > 'curve' > 'hill' above in the discussion of **keu-k*; the example of Toch B *leṅke* shows that semantic evolution might also lead to a concave shape such as a 'valley', also seen in NWels *nant* or Gaul *nanto*, both derived from **nem-* 'bend'. Some would assign to this root a series of words indicating a 'sacred grove', e.g. OIr *neimed*, Lat *nemus*, Fris *nimidas*, Grk *némos*, on the supposition that we have 'bend' > 'bow in reverence' > 'place where one honours the gods'. The verb itself is to be seen in Av *nəmaiti* 'bends', Skt *námati* 'bends, bows, submits oneself to', Toch AB *näm-* 'bend'. A root **pel-* indicates 'fold', both in the literal sense, e.g. NE *fold* as in to fold a piece of cloth (similarly Alb *palë* 'fold') or Grk *péplos* 'garment that falls in folds' to the more abstract multiplicative, e.g. OIr *dīabul*, Lat *duplus*, Grk *diplóos* 'double', i.e. 'twofold'. Of less certain status is **swe(n)g-* with cognates in the West in Celtic and Germanic, e.g. NE *swing*, and a possible cognate in Skt *svájate* 'embraces' and possibly Toch B *suk-* 'hand over'. Similarly, the status of a PIE **weng-* 'bend' (NE *wink*, Lith *véngti* 'try to avoid', Alb *vang* 'felloe') depends on acceptance of the existence of a Skt *váṅgati* 'limps' which occurs in medieval dictionaries but nowhere in texts.

The meaning 'press' or 'squeeze' is found in three possible Proto-Indo-European roots. A Latin-Tocharian isogloss secures **prem-* where Lat *premere* 'press down' is compared with Toch B *prām-* 'restrain'. More widely attested is **menk-* which gives us a Greek word for 'knead', i.e. *mássō*, and Skt *mácate* 'crushes', as well as Germanic, e.g. OE *mengan* 'mix', Lith *mìnkyti* 'knead, touch', OCS *mękŭkŭ* 'soft, delicate'. The underlying meaning of **bhrak-* is more difficult; Grk *phrássō* can mean 'push together' and the root may also have indicated that this resulted in making something firm, e.g. Toch B *prākre* 'firm' and Lat *fartus* 'thick'; to this series is also added the far more semantically opaque OIr *barc* 'storm, fury' (perhaps indicating that one is in the 'thick' of things). Finally, **puk̂-* 'press together' provides the base for both the Greek and Iranian words for a 'headband' (Grk *ámpuks*, Av *pusā-*) as well as Alb *puth* 'kiss'.

Regional words from the North-West include **māk-* 'press' (e.g. Lat *mācerō* 'tenderize by marination', Latv *màkt* 'oppress, depress', Czech *mačkati* 'press, squeeze') and **greut-* '± compress', an Irish (OIr *gruth* 'cheese')-English (NE *crowd*) isogloss. Far more words derive from the West Central area: **kam-p-* 'bend (of terrain)' (e.g. Lat *campus* 'field', Goth *hamfs* 'maimed', Lith *kam̃pas* 'corner; region', Grk *kampḗ* 'bend of river'); **kʷelp-* 'arch', a Germanic-Greek (e.g. OE *hwealf* 'vault', Grk *kólpos* 'fold, hollow') isogloss; **lerd-* '± crooked' (Scots Gaelic *lorcach* 'lame', Grk *lordós* 'stooped', Arm *lorc'k'* 'twisted bodies'); **leug-* 'bend; bend together, entwine' (e.g. OIr *fo-long-* 'sustains, supports', Lat *luctō* 'struggle', NE *lock* (of hair) and *lock* of door (a bending together), Lith *lùgnas* 'flexible, pliable', Grk *lugízō* 'fold, bend'); **gem-* 'press, squeeze together, squeeze' (e.g. MIr *gemel* 'fetters', Umb *gomia* 'pregnant', OE *cuml* 'swelling, wound', Lith *gùmstu* 'seize, grasp', OCS *žimǫ* 'press', Grk *gémō* 'am full', Arm *čmlem* 'press together'); **treud-* 'thrust, press' (e.g. OIr *trom* 'oppressive', Lat *trūdō* 'thrust', Goth *us-þriutan* 'bother, persecute', OCS *truditi* *sę* 'exert oneself', Alb *tredh* 'castrate'); **kem-* '± press together' (e.g. NE *hamper*, Lith *kamúoti* 'press together', Rus *komítĭ* 'press into a ball', Grk *kômos* 'band of revellers (= crowd)', Arm *k'amel* 'press, squeeze, filter'); **gen-* '± compress' which underlies many extended forms, e.g. NE *knock*, *knife*, dialectal Grk *knuzóō* 'draw together'. A Greek-Indic isogloss is seen in **pisd-* 'press' (Grk *piézō* 'press', Skt *pīḍáyati* 'presses').

22.6 Inflation

The vocabulary associated with swelling and blowing is rich in Proto-Indo-European and is listed below in Table 22.7.

The semantic field of the derivatives of **bhleu-* 'swell, overflow' is rather varied and none specifically means 'swell' but rather 'roar' (Baltic, e.g. Lith *bljaúju*), 'spew' (Slavic, e.g. OCS *bljujǫ*), and 'gush, teem, overflow' (Grk *phléō*). Extended forms in **-d*, however, include Toch B *plutk-* 'swell' and Grk *phludáō* 'have an excess of moisture'; an extended form in **-g-* yields Lat *fluō* 'flow' and *flūmen* 'river', Grk *phlúzō* 'boil up, boil over'. The meaning 'swell' is better attested in **bhelĝh-*, e.g. OIr *bolgaid* 'swells', OHG *belgan* 'swell up', and it underlies the widespread PIE **bhólĝhis* 'bag'. A metaphorical use of 'swell' is to be found in **k̂euh$_1$-* whose semantics may either focus on pregnancy, e.g. Lat *inciēns* 'pregnant', Grk *kuéō* 'am pregnant', or the concept of 'swells with power, be powerful', e.g. Skt *śváyati* 'swells, becomes powerful' which in derived forms yields NWels *cawr* 'giant', Grk *kū́rios* 'lord', and 'powerful' in Indo-Iranian (e.g. Av *sū́ra-*, Skt *śū́ra-*). Similarly, **teuh$_a$-* 'swell' also means

Table 22.7. *Inflation*

**bhleu-*	'swell, overflow'	Grk *phléō*
**bhelĝh-*	'swell'	
**k̂euh$_1$-*	'swell, grow great with child'	Lat *inciēns*, Grk *kuéō*, Skt *śváyati*
**teuh$_a$-*	'swell (with power), grow fat'	Grk *sáos*, Skt *távīti*
**h$_2$weh$_1$-*	'blow'	Grk *áēsi*, Skt *vā́ti*
**bhel-*	'blow, blow up, swell'	Lat *flō*, NE *blow*, Grk *phallós*, Skt *bhāṇa-*
**peis-*	'blow to make a noise'	Lat *spīrō*, Skt *picchorā*
**swei-*	'blow to hiss or buzz'	Grk *sízō*, Skt *kṣvédati*
**p(h)eu-*	'blow, swell'	Lat *pustula*, Grk *phûsa*, Skt *púṣyati*
**per-*	'blow (on a fire)'	Grk *prḗthō*
**bhes-*	'blow'	Grk *psū́khō*, Skt *bábhasti*

'powerful' or 'strong' (e.g. Av *tav-* 'be capable of', Skt *távīti* 'is strong, powerful'). This word may take a literal meaning of 'fat' as well (rather than pregnant) with the interesting contrast in meanings between ORus *tyju* 'become fat' and Grk *sáos* 'healthy'. The *$*tuh_a s$-$\hat{k}\mathring{m}$to-* 'fat-hundred' is the basis for 'thousand' (see Section 19.1) in Germanic (e.g. NE *thousand*), Baltic (Lith *túkstantis*), and Slavic (OCS *tysęšta*) and Tocharian 'ten thousand' (e.g. Toch B *tumane*).

The clearest root designating 'blow' is *$*h_2weh_1$-* with derivatives (including extended forms) in nine Indo-European groups (e.g. OE *wāwan* blow', OCS *věžjati* 'blow', Grk *áēsi* 'blows', Av *vāiti* 'blows', Skt *vā́ti* 'blows'). The verbal form universally means 'blow' while the nominalized participle *$*h_2weh_1$-ntos* gives us our Proto-Indo-European word for 'wind', e.g. NWels *gwynt*, Lat *ventus*, NE *wind*, Hit *huwant-*, Skt *vā́ta-*, Toch B *yente*. The verb 'blow' is also attested by **bhel-* although only Germanic and Italic (e.g. NE *blow*, Lat *flō* 'blow') retain the verbal sense while other groups have nominalized the root, e.g. Lat *follis* 'leather sack inflated with air'; two groups (OIr *ball ferda* and Grk *phallós*) employ the root to form their words for 'penis'. In Indic we have a different kind of metaphorical transfer in Skt *bhāṇḍa-* 'pot'. To 'blow to make a noise' is indicated by **peis-* which means 'to whistle' in OCS *piskati* and 'flute' in Skt *picchorā*; more prosaically we have OE *fisting* 'fart', but a simple 'blow' in Lat *spīrō* and 'blow an instrument' in Toch A *pis-*. Another musical 'blow' is to be seen in **(k)swei-*, e.g. OIr *sēitid* 'blows', OCS *svistati* 'whistle', Grk *sízō* 'crackle', Skt *kṣvédati* 'buzzes, hums, murmurs', and the extended form in Goth *swiglōn* 'play the flute'. A root **p(h)eu-*, surely onomatopoeic in origin, and its extended forms may have originally meant 'swell' or 'blow'; literal meanings such as Grk *phûsa* 'wind, blast' exist alongside other cognates that indicate an inflated shape, e.g. both OPrus *pounian* and Grk *pugḗ* mean 'buttocks', Rus *púlja* means 'ball', and MIr *ūan* mean 'foam'. Associations with burning or smoke in OCS and Greek suggest that **per-* might have meant 'blow on a fire' (e.g. OCS *para* 'steam, smoke', Grk *prḗthō* 'blow, *pímprēmi* 'burn', Hit *p(a)rāi-* 'breathe, blow'). A Greek-Indic-Tocharian isogloss has been suggested to support **bhes-* 'blow' (Grk *psū́khō* 'cool off' [<*'cool off by blowing'?], Skt *bábhasti* 'blows', Toch B *pās-* 'whisper').

There are few regional terms. From the North-West comes **bhreus-* 'swell' (e.g. OIr *brū* 'belly, breast', NE *breast*, Rus *brostĭ* 'bud') and from the West Central region: **bhlei-* '± become inflated' (Latv *blîstu* 'become thick', Grk *phlidáō* 'overflow of moisture'), an enlargement on Proto-Indo-European *bhel-* 'blow'; *$*h_a eid$-* 'swell' (e.g. OHG *eiz* 'abscess', Lat *aemidus* 'swollen', Grk *oidéō* 'swell', *Oidípous* 'Oedipus' [literally 'swollen-foot'], Arm *aytnum* 'swell').

22.7 Extend

A number of words, grouped together under the general meaning of 'extend', 'stretch', or 'hang', are listed in Table 22.8.

Nine groups provide evidence for a PIE _*$h_3$reĝ-_ 'extend' which provides the base for two other important concepts: 'correct' and 'king'. The semantic field normally covered by the cognate forms is 'extend' or 'stretch' (e.g. OIr _rigid_ 'stretches', OE _reccan_ 'stretch out; be concerned about' [> NE _reck_], Lith _rę́žti_ 'stretch', Grk _orégō_ 'stretch', Skt _ṛñjáti_ 'stretches') but in Lat _regō_ 'direct in a straight line' and Av _rāzayeiti_ 'adjusts, arranges', we find the notion of 'order' which provides the semantic link to _*$h_3$reĝtos_ 'right, correct', i.e. 'ordered', and _*h_3rḗĝs_ 'ruler, king', perhaps 'one who puts/keeps things in order' (see Section 17.1). A root _*ten-_ 'stretch' is well attested, both in its root form and with various extensions (e.g. Lat _tendō_ 'stretch', OE _þenian_ 'stretch', Lith _tìnti_ 'swell', Alb _ndej_ 'extend, stretch, spread', Grk _tanúō_ 'stretch', Skt _tanóti_ 'expands, stretches'). It yields such derivatives as Lat _tenuis_ 'thin' and NE _thin_, as well as a participial form _*tn̥-tó-s_ which is reflected perfectly in Lat _tentus_, Grk _tatós_, and Skt _tatá-_ 'stretched'. The same root with an _s_-extension, _*ten-s-_, yields 'pull' if the Germanic and Baltic cognates in the West (e.g. OHG _dinsan_ 'pull', Lith _tę́sti_ 'stretch, pull') and the corresponding Indic word (Skt _taṃsayati_ 'draws to and fro') are not independent creations. Also meaning 'pull' is _*teng(h)-_ where the verbal meaning is retained in Slavic and Iranian (OCS _ras-tęgǫ_ 'pull apart', Av _θang-_ 'pull') but the word has been nominalized in both Latin and Germanic to refer to the 'pole' on a vehicle (e.g. Lat _tēmō_ 'chariot pole', OE _þīxl_ 'wagon-pole, shaft'). The set of cognates that suggests a _*ten-p-_, which through assimilation is reconstructed as _*temp-_ 'stretch', shows such wide semantic variation that the status of some of the cognate forms is not

Table 22.8. _Extend_

_*$h_3$reĝ-_	'extend, stretch'	Lat _regō_, NE _reck_, Grk _orégō_, Skt _ṛñjáti_
*ten-	'stretch'	Lat _tendō_, Grk _tanúō_, Skt _tanóti_
*temp-	'stretch'	Lat _tempus?_
*teng(h)-	'pull'	Lat _tēmō_
*ten-s-	'pull'	Skt _taṃsayati_
*seik-	'reach for'	Grk _híkō_
*pleth₂-	'spread out'	Lat _plantō_, Skt _práthati_
*ster-	'spread out'	Lat _struō_, NE _strew_, Grk _stórnūmi_, Skt _stṛṇóti_
*k̂onk̂-	'hang'	Lat _cunctor_, NE _hang_, Skt _śáṅkate_
*lemb- ~ _*remb-_	'hang down'	Lat _limbus_, Skt _rámbate_

entirely secure. Baltic (e.g. Lith *tem̃pti* 'stretch out, pull out') shows the meaning 'stretch' while Germanic (ON *þambr*) and Slavic (OCS *tǫpŭ*) show 'thick' (and not 'thin'!). The Tocharian cognate, e.g. Toch A *tampe*, means 'power' (and Toch AB *cämp-* 'be able to') while Lat *tempus* 'time' which is set here by some suggests conceiving of time as a linear object, a concept that we have no problem with today but which raises problems when extrapolated into antiquity. A root **seik-* 'reach for' can mean 'reach with the hands' as in Lith *síekti* 'reach for something', but Toch B *sik-* 'set foot', i.e. 'reach out the foot', indicates that the lower limbs may be also envisaged; the latter would also seem to be the case with Grk *híkō* 'arrive, reach'. A root **pleth*$_2$- 'spread out' (e.g. OIr *lethaid* 'extends, expands', Lat *plantō* 'plant', Lith *plečiù* 'widen, spread out', Skt *práthati* 'spreads out') also yields the widespread adjectival form **pl̥th*$_2$*ús* 'broad, wide' (see Section 18.5). A productive root **ster-* occurs with several enlargements, e.g. Lat *struō* 'build up' and *sternō* 'spread out', NE *strew*, Alb *shtrij* 'stretch', Grk *stórnūmi* 'spread out', Av *stərənaoiti* ~ *stərənāiti* 'spreads out', Skt *str̥ṇóti* ~ *str̥ṇāti* 'spreads out').

There are two forms for 'hang'. A root **k̂onk-* is well attested in this meaning in Germanic (e.g. NE *hang*) and Hit *kank-* 'hang' but has undergone a shift to an emotional state in Indic, e.g. Skt *śáṇkate* 'doubts, fears' (as in 'left hanging'), while Lat *cunctor* 'delay' would seem to be 'hang about'. A word **lemb-* or **remb-* 'hang down' retains this meaning in Skt *rámbate* 'hangs down' and is nominalized in Lat *limbus* 'hem, border'.

From the North-West we have **reiĝ-* 'extend, stretch out (a body part)' (e.g. OIr *ringid* 'twists, tortures', NE *reach*, Lith *réižti* 'stretch, tighten') and **kleh*$_a$- 'spread out flat' (e.g. Lith *klóju* 'spread out', and with extensions NE *lade*, OCS *kladǫ* 'load, lay'); and from the West Central region: **peth*$_a$- 'spread out (the arms)' (Lat *pandō* 'spread out', NE *fathom*, Grk *pítnēmi* 'spread out') where not only Germanic but also Celtic, e.g. OWels *etem* 'fathom', and Lat *passus* 'step, fathom', all employ the root as a unit of measurement, the 'fathom'.

22.8 Throw

Words indicating 'throw' are listed in Table 22.9.

A verb *(*s*)*keud-* 'throw' is attested by cognates in Germanic (e.g. NE *shoot*), Slavic (e.g. Rus *kidátĭ* 'throw'), and Alb *hedh* which all mean 'throw' and, in the East, Skt *códati* 'incites' and Tocharian. The Tocharian cognates, e.g. Toch B *kaume*, indicate the 'shoot of a plant', a semantic development paralleled in English where the same part of a plant derives ultimately from the Middle English verb *shooten* 'throw'. An alternative root with the same meaning is **h*$_1$*es-* 'throw'

Table 22.9. *Throw*

*(*s*)*keud-*	'throw, shoot'	NE *shoot*, Skt *códati*
**h₁es-*	'throw, hurl'	Skt *ásyati*
**gʷelh₁-*	'throw'	Grk *bállō*
**swep-*	'throw, sweep'	Lat *supō*, NE *sweep*, Skt *svapū́*
**smeit-*	'throw'	Lat *mittō*
**pers-*	'sprinkle'	Skt *pŕ̥ṣat-*
**sper-*	'strew, sow'	Grk *speírō*
*(*s*)*ked-*	'scatter'	NE *scatter*, Grk *skídnēmi*

which is attested in Hittite and Indo-Iranian (e.g. Hit *siyēzi* 'throws, hurls', Av *as-* 'throw', Skt *ásyati* 'throws, hurls'). The root **gʷelh₁-* 'throw' supplies the same meaning again (e.g. NWels *blif* 'catapult', Grk *bállō* 'throw', Av *ni-γar-* 'be thrown down'). Although **swep-* 'throw' retains its verbal meanings in Latin (e.g. *supō* 'throw') and Slavic (e.g. OCS *sŭpǫ* 'strew, pour about'), it is often nominalized into an object that is either thrown or might make a sweeping motion, e.g. ON *svāf* 'spear' and *sōfl* 'broom', Skt *svapū́* 'broom', and Toch B *sopi* 'net, snare, throwing net'. A possible Latin-Avestan isogloss suggests **smeit-* 'throw' (Lat *mittō* 'let go, send', Av *maēθ-* 'throw').

Semantically more distant are words for 'sprinkle' and 'scatter'. A root **pers-* 'sprinkle' indicates either the verbal action, e.g. Hit *pappars-* and Toch AB *pärs-*, both 'sprinkle', or the type of material that might be sprinkled, e.g. Skt *pŕ̥ṣat-* 'drop', OCS *prachŭ* 'dust', or from which one might be sprinkled, e.g. ON *fors* 'waterfall'. The alternation between verbal form and nominalization is also seen in **sper-* 'strew, sow' where both Grk *speírō* and Hit *ispāri* retains the verbal forms and OHG *sprāt* 'scattering' the underlying meaning, but we also have Alb *farë* and Grk *spérma*, both 'seed', and more distantly, OIr *sreb* 'stream'. Another word for 'scatter' is *(*s*)*ked-* with cognates in Germanic, Baltic, Greek, and Tocharian (e.g. NE *scatter*, Lith *kedě́ti* 'burst', Grk *skídnēmi* 'scatter, strew, sprinkle', Toch AB *kätnā-* 'scatter, strew, sow').

From the North-West: **sperhₓg-* 'strew, sprinkle' (Lat *spargō* 'strew', NE *spark* and *sprinkle*); from the West Central area we have a Latin (*iaciō*)-Greek (*híēmi*) correspondence that attests a **yeh₁-* 'throw'.

22.9 Clean

There are four words associated with 'cleaning' or 'washing' that may be attributed to Proto-Indo-European.

Widespread are cognates derived from *$neig^{w}$-* 'wash' which carries that meaning in Celtic (OIr *nigid*), Grk *nízō*, and Indo-Iranian (Av *naēnižaiti* 'washes', Skt *nénekti* 'washes') although there are problems with the Irish form (as Proto-Indo-European *g^{w} > Celtic *b* and not *g*). Tocharian *lik-* 'wash' may belong here too, if the initial *l-* can be explained as resulting from the contamination of some other root (e.g. *$leuh_1$-* 'wash'). PIE *$neig^{w}$-* also exhibits a derived form *nig^{w}-tos* 'washed', seen in OIr *necht*, Grk *ániptos* 'unwashed', and Skt *niktá-*. In Germanic the root is nominalized to designate a 'water spirit', e.g. NE *nix* ~ *nixie*. An Anatolian (Hit *ārr(a)-*)-Tocharian (Toch A *yär-*) isogloss secures *h_1erh_x-* 'wash'. The precise semantics of *$m(e)uh_x$-* 'wash' presents an interesting puzzle. In Baltic (e.g. OPrus *amūsnan*), Slavic (OCS *myjǫ*), and Cypriot Grk *mulásasthai*, the cognates all mean 'wash'; however, in both MIr *mūm* and Skt *mū́tra-* the meaning of the nominal derivatives found in those languages is 'urine'. Some have suggested that the meaning here has shifted from 'wash' to 'dirt' although it should be noted that urine was employed by the Romans as a mouthwash and was a component of toothpastes and mouthwashes up the eighteenth century; in India, the walls of a room might be washed in cow's urine to honour a guest, so there is some evidence that the notion of urine as a cleanser is of Proto-Indo-European age. A verbal root *$peuh_x$-* 'clean' is found in both Germanic (OHG *fowen* 'sieve, clean grain') and Skt *paváyati* 'cleanses' and in various derivatives, e.g. *puh_x-to-s* 'cleaned' (e.g. Lat *putus* 'clean', Av *pūtika-* 'serving as purification', Skt *pūtá-* 'clean') and *puh_x-ro-s* 'clean' (e.g. OIr *ūr* 'new, fresh', Lat *pūrus* 'pure').

There are two West Central regional words: **k̂leu-* 'clean' (OLat *cloāca* 'gutter', OE *hlūttor* 'clean', Lith *šlúoju* 'sweep', Grk *klúzō* 'wash') and *$leuh_1$-* 'wash, bathe', (Lat *lavō* 'wash', Grk *loúō* 'wash', Arm *loganam* 'bathe, wash myself'). There is also a Greek-Indic isogloss in *$h_aidhrós$* 'pure' (Grk *itharós* 'glad; pure', Skt *vīdhrá-* [< *$wi-h_aidhro$-* 'burned away'] 'clean, pure' which derives from *h_aeidh-* 'burn' and may either be inherited or independent developments).

22.10 Movement

There are a considerable number of roots that have been reconstructed with the general semantic field of 'set in motion' or 'move'. In some cases, the recon-

Table 22.10. *Clean*

*$neig^{w}$-	'wash'	Grk *nízō*, Skt *nénekti*
*h_1erh_x-	'wash'	
*$m(e)uh_x$-	'wash (in urine?)'	Grk *mulásasthai*, Skt *mū́tra-*
*$peuh_x$-	'clean'	Skt *paváyati*

structed meanings are reasonably justified by the evidence from the various Indo-European groups while in other cases they reflect an act of semantic desperation to attempt to find a common core that might account for a wide range of meanings that have something vaguely to do with motion. The list of movement words is found in Table 22.11.

Both *$h_1$er-* 'set in motion (horizontally)' and *$h_3$er-* 'set in motion (vertically)' seem assured for Proto-Indo-European but their similarity in meaning made them liable to confusion, probably even before the loss of laryngeals made them largely homophonous. Surely belonging to the first are Grk *érkhomai* 'set out; come; got' and Skt *r̥ccháti* 'goes towards, reaches'; while surely belonging to the second is Lat *orior* 'rise' (whence NE *orient*). There is a set of forms with a **neu*-present, i.e. Skt *r̥nóti* 'sets in motion', Av *ərənaoiti* 'sets in motion', Grk *ornūmi* 'stir up', and Arm *y-arnem* 'stand up' which would seem to have both meanings. Finally there is Hit *arta* 'stands, is present, occurs' which must reflect **$h_1$er-* but which is semantically compatible only with **$h_3$er-*.

For the root **$h_1$eis-* the Indo-Iranian cognates, e.g. Skt *iṣṇā́ti* and Av *aēš-*, do indicate 'set in motion' while other cognates indicate slightly different activities, e.g. ON *eisa* 'go dashing' or, further removed, Grk *ináō* 'pour'. The derivatives of a root **kei-* also generally indicate 'set in motion' (e.g. Lat *cieō* 'set in motion', Grk *seúō* 'set in motion', Arm *c'vem* 'set off', Av

Table 22.11. *Movement*

**$h_1$er-*	'set in motion (horizontally)'	Grk *érkhomai*, Skt *r̥ccháti*
**$h_3$er-*	'set in motion (vertically)'	Lat *orior*
**$h_1$eis-*	'set in motion'	Grk *ináō*, Skt *iṣṇā́ti*
**kei-*	'set in motion'	Lat *cieō*, Grk *seúō*, Skt *cyávate*
**$h_2$lei-*	'set in motion'	Grk *áleison*
**yeudh-*	'set in motion, stir up'	Lat *iubeō*, Grk *husmī́nē*, Skt *yúdhyate*
wegh-* (weĝh-?*)	'shake, set in motion'	Lat *vexāre*, NE *wag*, Grk *gaiḗ-okhos*
**seuh₃-*	'set in motion'	Skt *suváti*
**neik-*	'begin'	
**meu(h_x)-*	'move'	Lat *moveō*, Grk *ameúsasthai*, Skt *mī́vati*
**meus-*	'move; remove'	Skt *muṣṇā́ti*
**dheu(h_x)-*	'be in (com)motion'	Lat *suf-fiō*, Grk *thúō*, Skt *dhūnóti*
**$h_1$rei-*	'move'	NE *run*, Grk *orī́nō*, Skt *ríṇvati*
**$h_1$eig-*	'move'	Grk *epeígō*, Skt *éjati*
**selĝ-*	'release, send out'	Skt *sr̥játi*
**TerK-*	'release, allow'	

š(y)avaite 'sets off', Skt *cyávate* 'goes forth'; Alb *qoj* means 'wake'). The root *$h_2$lei-*, however, retains 'set in motion' only in Anatolian (e.g. Hit *halā(i)-*) but elsewhere is associated with liquids, either in a verbal sense, e.g. Lith *lẽju* 'pour', OCS *lějǫ* 'pour', or nominalized into some form of liquid, e.g. OHG *līth* 'fruit wine', OIr *lie* 'sea', or something associated with liquids, e.g. Lat *lītus* 'beach' Grk *áleison* 'cup'. The semantic field of **yeudh-* 'set in motion' (e.g. Lat *iubeō* 'order', Lith *judù* move oneself, stir', Pol *judzić* 'incite', Av *yaozaiti* 'becomes agitated [of water and emotions]', Toch A *yutk-* 'become upset, worry') also includes specialized developments assocated with combat, e.g. Grk *husmī́nē* 'combat', Skt *yúdhyate* 'fights'. A 'shaking motion' lies behind a number of the cognates derived from **wegh-* or **weĝh-*, e.g. Lat *vexāre* 'shake, vex', Goth *wagjan* 'shake', and Grk *gaiḗ-okhos* 'earth-shaking' (cf. also Tocharian *wāsk-/wäsk-* 'move, budge, have motion [intr.]; move [tr.]'). A root **seuh_3-* 'set in motion' retains this precise meaning in Skt *suváti* (*cf. also OIr soïd* 'twists, turns', Hit *suwāi-* 'push, urge', Av *hunāiti* 'seeks to create; drives forward', Toch B *ṣewi* 'pretext, excuse'); in Anatolian we have both Hit *sunna-* 'fill' and Palaic *sūnat* 'poured out', which suggests again an association with liquids. We also have **neik-* 'begin' attested in Baltic (e.g. Lith *u-ninkù* 'begin'), OCS *vŭz-nīknoti* 'regain consciousness', and Hit *nini(n)k-* 'start up, mobilize'.

We can reconstruct a meaning 'move' for at least three roots. A widespread root is **meu(h_x)-* (e.g. Lat *moveō* 'set in motion', Lith *máuju* 'put on or off', Grk *ameúsasthai* 'surpass, outstrip; pass over', Hit *mauszi* 'falls', Av *ava-mīva-* 'take away', Skt *mī́vati* 'shoves, moves, sets in motion', to Toch B *miw-* 'shake' which also appears in an old enlarged form **meus-* where the semantics suggests not so much 'move' as 'remove', e.g. OHG *chrēo-mōsido* 'grave-robbers', Khot *muśśa* 'robbers', Skt *muṣṇā́ti* 'steals', Toch AB *musnā-* 'lift, move [aside]', *musk-* 'disappear', *mäs-* 'go'; the verb would appear to underlie the root noun **mū́s* 'mouse', i.e. the 'stealer' (see Section 9.1). A root **dheu(h_x)-* indicates movement in the sense of 'being stirred up (like dust or smoke), e.g. Lat *suf-fiō* 'smoke', ON *dȳja* 'shake', Goth *dauns* 'dust, smoke', Lith *dujà* 'dust', OCS *dunǫ* 'blow', Alb *deh* 'intoxicate, make drunk', Grk *thúō* 'rush on', Arm *dedevim* 'shake', Av *dvažaiti* 'flutters', Skt *dhūnóti* 'shakes, moves about; kindles a flame', *dhūli-* 'dust', Toch B *tweye* 'dust'. The movement indicated by **$h_1$rei-* often suggests both 'run' and 'flow', e.g. NE *run*, OCS *vy-rinoti* 'thrust out', Skt *rínvati* 'lets flow'; Greek shows semantic extensions, e.g. Grk *orī́nō* 'stir', *erīnúō* 'be angry with', i.e. 'be stirred up', Toch AB *rin-* 'renounce'. A possible root **$h_1$eig-* 'move' is based on ON *eikinn* 'furious', OCS *igrati* 'play', Grk *ep-eígō* 'drive on', and Skt *éjati* 'stirs'. PIE **selĝ-* 'release, send out' can be found in Celtic where it is associated with hunting, i.e. releasing hunting dogs? (OIr *selg* 'hunt'), Germanic (e.g. MHG *silken* 'drip'), and Indo-Iranian (Av *hərəzaiti*, Skt *sr̥játi*, both 'releases'). And, finally, a Hittite (*tarna-* 'let, release')-Tocharian (Toch AB *tärk-* 'let go, allow') isogloss suggests a PIE *TerK- 'release'. Both languages reflect a PIE present stem *T̥rK-neh$_a$-.

From the North-West (a Celtic-Italic isogloss) we have *pelh$_a$- 'set in motion' (e.g. OIr *ad-ella* 'seeks', Lat *pellō* 'push'). Indo-Iranian and Tocharian offer two isoglosses: *kerh$_x$- 'propel' (Skt *kiráti* 'pour out, throw', Toch B *kärsk-* 'propel') and *weip- 'set in motion, agitate' (e.g. Av *vip-* 'throw, ejaculate', Skt *vépati* 'trembles', Toch B *wip-* 'shake').

22.11 Pour and Flow

Gathered here in Table 22.12 are those words that are specifically concerned with the movement of liquids, either transitively, i.e. 'pour', or intransitively, i.e. 'flow'.

The meaning 'pour' is clearly reconstructed for *ĝheu- where its reflexes either appear in the verbal form, e.g. Grk *khé(w)ō* 'pour', Toch AB *ku-* 'pour', or nominalized either as the object from which something is poured, e.g. Lat *fūtis* 'pitcher', Av *zaoθra-* 'libation', or the one who does the pouring, e.g. Skt *hótar-* 'priest' who *juhóti* 'pours out the sacrificial libation'. We also have *seik- 'pour' where it means 'strain' in Grk *ikmázō* and 'sprinkles' in Indo-Iranian, e.g. Av *hičaiti*, Skt *siñcáti*; and 'overflow' in Toch A *sik-*; the now obsolete NE *sye* 'sink' belongs here and probably also Lat *siat* 'urinates' (in baby talk). Only Hittite retains the verbal meaning of *leh$_2$- 'pour, make flow', i.e. *lahhuzi* 'overflows, pours' (and also *lahni-* 'bottle, pitcher'); elsewhere we only have nominalizations, e.g. Lat *lāma* 'bog', Grk *lēnós* 'tub', Toch B *lāñe* 'flood'.

Table 22.12. *Pour and flow*

*ĝheu-	'pour'	Lat *fūtis*, Grk *khé(w)ō*, Skt *juhóti*
*seik-	'pour out; overflow'	Lat *siat*, NE *sye*, Grk *ikmázō*, Skt *siñcáti*
*leh$_2$-	'pour, wet, make flow'	Lat *lāma*, Grk *lēnós*
*h$_1$ers-	'flow'	Lat *errō*, Grk *aperáō* Skt *árṣati*
*h$_1$reih$_x$-	'move'	Skt *riṇā́ti*
*g^{w}el(s)-	'well up, flow'	Grk *plúō*, Skt *gálati*
*h$_a$el-	'well up, flow'	Skt *árma-*
*sreu-	'flow'	Grk *rhéō*, Skt *srávati*
*weis-	'ooze out'	NE *ooze*, Skt *aveṣan*

Verbal roots for 'move' and 'run' may either have encompassed the movement of liquids as well or have served as the base (with extensions) to form new words for 'flow'. One such possible enlargement is from *$h_1$er- 'move' where we have *$h_1$ers- 'flow'. The original verbal meaning is attested in Hit *arszi* 'flows', Skt *árṣati* 'flows', Grk *aperáō* 'pour out', while in the West the word has come to mean 'go off course', e.g. Lat *errō* 'go astray', OHG *irran* 'confused' (with a somewhat different semantic specialization we have Arm *eṙam* 'seethe, be disquieted'). Another extended form, the verbal root *$h_1$reih$_x$- 'move', has been further extended as *$h_1$rih$_x$tís to give 'waterfall' in Celtic (OIr *rīathor*), Skt *rītí-* 'stream, run', also related is Lat *rīvus* 'brook'. Both the Germanic and Greek reflexes of *g^wel(s)- mean 'well up', e.g. OHG *quellan*, Grk *blúō*, while Skt *gálati* and Toch B *käls-* mean something like 'trickle, ooze'. A root *$h_a$el- 'well up, flow' is based on the connection between Lith *al̃mės* 'serum, pus' on the one hand, and Skt *árma-* and Toch B *ālme*, both 'spring' on the other (cf. also Latv *aluôgs* 'spring'); to these are also added a number of European river names, e.g. *Almus, Alma*. A root **sreu-* 'flow' is attested in its basic verbal form, e.g. Lith *sraviù* 'ooze', Grk *rhéō* 'flow', Arm *aṙoganem* 'moisten', *srávati* 'flows', or in extended forms, e.g. NE *stream*. The verbal root **weis-* survives only in Skt *aveṣan* 'they flowed' but it underlies the noun **wis-* 'poison', NE *ooze*, and a number of European river names, e.g. *Weser, Vistula*.

In the North-West we find **ĝheud-*, an enlargement of **ĝheu-* 'pour', in Italic (e.g. Lat *fundō* 'pour') and Germanic (e.g. NHG *giessen*). In the West Central area is **del-* 'flow' (e.g. NE *tallow*), **ser-* 'flow' (which underlies **sreu-* above), seen in verbal form solely in MIr *sirid* 'wanders through' but nominalized elsewhere, e.g. Lat *serum* 'whey', Alb *gjizë* 'whey, cheese', Grk *orós* 'whey', Toch B *ṣarwiye* 'cheese'; **leg-* 'drip, trickle' (e.g. OIr *legaid* 'perishes, melts', NE *leach*, Arm *lič* 'bog') and **stag-* 'seep, drip' (e.g. Lat *stāgnum* 'standing water', Grk *stázō* 'drip'). A Greek-Indo-Iranian isogloss is seen in *dhg^{w}her- 'flow (away)', e.g. Grk *phtheírō* 'ruin, waste', Av *γzaraiti* 'flows', Skt *kṣárati* 'flows, perishes'.

22.12 Come and Go

The concepts of 'come' and 'go' are so basic that we are hardly surprised that there are a large number of roots associated with these concepts. They are listed in Table 22.13.

There are two variants of the basic root 'come', *g^wem- (Lat *veniō* 'come', NE *come*, Grk *baínō* 'come', Skt *gácchati* 'goes', Toch B *käm-* 'come'; in Baltic there has been a semantic specialization to 'come into the world', e.g. Lith *gimù* 'am

Table 22.13. *Come and go*

$*g^{w}em$-	'come'	Lat *veniō*, NE *come*, Grk *baínō*, Skt *gácchati*
$*g^{w}eh_a$-	'come'	Grk *bibánti*, Skt *jígāti*
$*h_1ei$-	'go'	Lat *eō*, Grk *eîmi*, Skt *éti*
$*h_aet$-	'go'	Lat *annus*, Skt *átati*
**sed-*	'go'	Skt *ā-sad-*
**sent-*	'go'	NE *send*
$*yeh_a$-	'go, travel'	Skt *yā́ti*
$*leit(h_x)$-	'go away, go forth'	NE *lead*, Grk *loiteúō*
$*h_1leudh$-	'go (out)'	Grk *ḗluthon*
$*seh_1(i)$-	'go forward, advance'	Grk *īthúō*, Skt *sádhate*
**per-*	'pass through'	Lat *portāre*, NE *fare*, Grk *peráō*, Skt *píparti*
$*terh_2$-	'bring across; overcome'	Lat *intrāre*, Grk *trānḗs*, Skt *tárati*
**tem-*	'reach, attain'	Grk *témei*
$*h_1enek̂$-	'attain'	Lat *nanciō*, Grk *enegkeîn*, Skt *aśnóti* – *náśati*
**serK-*	'pass, surpass'	
*?*ked-*	'± pass through'	Lat *cēdō*
**steigh-*	'step (up), go'	Grk *steíkhō*, Skt *stighnóti*
**ĝhengh-*	'step, walk'	Skt *jáṃhas-*
**ghredh-*	'step, go'	Lat *gradior*
**spleiĝh-*	'step, go'	Grk *plíssomai*, Skt *pléhate*

born'). Related in root but less clearly indicating motion towards the speaker is *$*g^{w}eh_a$-*, e.g. OIr *baid* 'dies', Latv *gãju* 'go', dialectal Grk *bibánti* 'they stride', Skt *jígāti* 'goes'. This alteration *$*g^{w}em$-*: *$*g^{w}eh_a$-* is paralleled in the verbal root 'to run', i.e. *drem-* : *$*dreh_a$-* (see Section 22.14).

The basic (or at least most widely attested) verb for 'go' is *$*h_1ei$-* which is found in all major groups save Albanian and Armenian (e.g. Lat *eō* 'go', Goth *iddja* 'went', Lith *eimì* 'go', OCS *iti* 'go', Grk *eîmi* 'will go', Hit *yanzi* 'they go', Av *aēiti* 'goes', Skt *éti* 'goes', Toch AB *i-* 'go'). The semantics are regularly 'go', e.g. Lat *eō* 'go', Grk *eîmi* 'go', except for Celtic where it appears as NWels *wyf* 'am'. Skt *átati* 'goes' alone preserves the verbal meaning of *$*h_aet$-* 'go' which otherwise we find meaning 'year', e.g. Lat *annus*, Goth *aþn*. Here the presumed semantic development runs 'go' > 'cycle' > 'year'. A root **sed-* 'go' would be problematic in that it is homophonous with the basic verb 'sit'. It is preserved as such only in Indo-Iranian and there only with a prefix, e.g. Av *āsnaoiti* 'approaches', Skt *ā-sad-* 'enter', but is found elsewhere in derived form, e.g. the Greek *o*-grade noun *hodós* 'way', OCS *chodŭ* 'walk'. A verbal root **sent-* 'go' underlies the Germanic and Baltic words for 'send' (e.g. NE *send*, Lith *suntù* 'send') but a more general meaning survives in OHG *sinnan* 'go', Av *hant-* 'arrive', and in nominal derivatives such as OIr *sēt* 'way', OHG *sind* 'way, side',

Arm *ənt'ac'* 'way, passage', Toch A *ṣont* 'street'. A verb **yeh$_a$-*, possibly an iterative-intensive derivative of **h$_1$ei-*, i.e. **h$_1$y-eh$_a$-*, means 'ride' in Baltic and Slavic, e.g. Lith *jóju* 'ride', OCS *jadǫ* 'ride', but simply 'go' in Indo-Iranian (Av *yā-* 'go', Skt *yā́ti* 'goes, travels') and Tocharian (AB *yā-* 'go, travel').

Other verbs suggest motion in a particular direction. For example, **h$_1$leudh-* 'go (out)' appears in the form of the same thematic aorist (**h$_1$leudhét*) in OIr *lod* 'went', Grk *ḗluthon* 'went', and Toch AB *lac-* 'went out'. The meaning of **leit(h$_x$)-* would also appear to include 'go away', e.g. Toch B *lit-* 'pass on' (cf. also OE *līðan* 'go, travel', NE *lead*); three groups all suggest an association with death, i.e. Germanic (OHG *beleite* 'burial'), Grk *loiteúō* 'bury', and Iranian (Av *raēθ-* die'), suggesting that this verb may also have indicated 'pass away'. Movement that is forward or, perhaps better, 'straight on' seems to have been indicated by **seh$_1$(i)-* where we have Grk *īthúō* 'press forward', Phryg *sideto* 'succeeded, achieved', and Skt *sádhate* 'suceeds'; Hit *zāi-* means 'cross over'. To 'go beyond' was **per-*, a verbalization of the preposition **per* 'through'. It is widely attested both as a verbal form, e.g. Lat *portāre* 'lead', NE *fare*, OCS *na-perjǫ* 'bore through', *perǫ* 'fly', Alb *sh-pie* 'send, carry, take to, lead', Grk *peráō* 'pass through', *peírō* 'pierce, bore through', Arm *hordan* 'go away', Av *-par-* 'convey across', Skt *píparti* 'conveys across; saves', and in derived form as the nouns **pértus* 'passage way', e.g. Lat *portus* 'harbour', ON *fjǫrðr* 'estuary' [whence by borrowing NE *fjord*], NE *ford*, Av *pərətu-* 'bridge'. Another preposition similarly verbalized into a motion was **ter* 'through' which yields **terh$_2$-* 'bring across; overcome', the second meaning seen in Hit *tarhzi* 'defeats', Skt *tárati* 'overcomes'; we also have Lat *intrāre* 'enter' (cf. also Skt *trā́yati* 'protects, shelters', Grk *trānós* 'penetrating, clear'). A Greek (*témei* 'arrives, reaches')–Tocharian (Toch AB *täm-* 'be born') isogloss secures a PIE **tem-* 'reach, attain'; the notion of birth in Tocharian can be compared with the development of PIE **g^{w}em-* 'come' which yields 'be born' (e.g. Lith *gemù*) in Baltic. A more widely distributed word with the meaning 'attain' is **h$_1$enek̂-* which is found in OIr *ro-icc* 'reaches', Lat *nanciō* 'attain', OE *geneah* 'is adequate' (cf. NE *enough*), Lith *nešù* 'carry', OCS *nesǫ* 'carry', Grk *enegkeîn* 'to carry', Arm *hasanem* 'arrive', Skt *aśnóti* ~ *náśati* 'gains', and Toch A *ents-* 'take, grasp, seize'. A Hittite-Tocharian isogloss indicates **serK-* 'pass' (Hit *sarku-* 'projecting, immense, powerful', Toch B *ṣärk-* 'pass, surpass, go beyond') while a Latin-Tocharian isogloss gives us **ked-* 'pass through' seen in Lat *cēdō* 'go from', Toch AB *kätk-* cross over'.

The original semantics of **steigh-* 'step, go' are imprecise: we have 'stride' in Celtic (OIr *tīagu*), 'climb' in Germanic (e.g. OHG *stīgan*) and Indic (Skt *stighnóti*), 'hurry' in Baltic (e.g. Lith *steigiù*), 'step, go' in Grk *steíkhō*, and simple 'come' in OCS *stignǫ*. It provides the basis for several widespread derivatives such as **stíghs* 'step' (e.g. ON *stig* 'step', OCS *stĭdza* 'footstep;

street', Grk *stíkhos* 'row, line') and **stóigho/eh$_a$*- 'way' (e.g. OHG *steiga* 'step, way', Alb *shteg* 'path', Grk *stoîkhos* 'row, line'). There are several other words that indicate 'step'. Verbal forms of **ĝhengh*- 'step are preserved in Celtic, e.g. OIr *cingid* 'steps', Germanic, e.g. OE *gangan* 'go', Baltic, e.g. Lith *žengiù* 'stride, step', or in nominalized forms, e.g. Av *zanga*- 'ankle', Skt *jáṃhas*- 'step, wing-beat'. Also reasonably widespread is **ghredh*- 'step, go', seen in, for example, OIr *in-greinn* 'pursue', Lat *gradior* 'stride', *gradus* 'step' (whence by borrowing NE *grade*), Goth *griþs* 'step', Lith *grìdyju* 'go, wander about', Rus *grjadú* 'go'. Finally, **spleiĝh*- 'step, go' is attested verbally in Greek and Indic (Grk *plísso-mai* 'stride out', Skt *pléhate* 'goes') and also shows some interesting nominalization in Grk *plikhás* 'space between the thighs' and OIr *slīasait* 'thigh'.

From the North-West is **meih$_x$*- 'go', e.g. MWels *mynet* 'go', Lat *meō* 'go, wander', OCS *minǫ* 'pass away, pass by'. From the West Central area we have **h$_1$el*- 'go', e.g. MWels *el* 'may go', Grk *elaúnō* 'drive', Arm *el* 'climbed, came out'. And if not independently formed in Greek and Indo-Iranian, there is evidence for **peri-h$_1$es*- 'surpass', i.e. Grk *períesti* 'comes round', Skt *pary asti* 'surpasses'.

22.13 Run and Jump

The vocabulary of motion also includes a variety of words to indicate more specialized activities such as running, hurrying, jumping, and flying, which are listed in Table 22.14.

There are at least four PIE roots for 'move quickly, hurry'. The verbal reflexes of **speud*-, e.g. Lith *spáusti* 'press', Grk *speúdō* 'hurry', and its *o*-grade derivative **spoudeh$_a$*-, e.g. Lith *spaudà* press', Grk *spoudḗ* 'haste', Arm *p'oyt'* 'zeal', NP *poy* 'haste', indicate swift movement (or, in the case of Armenian, a metaphorical extension) while a derived nominal form in Germanic yields the word for 'spear', e.g. OHG *spioz*, whereas Alb *punë* yields the general term for 'work'. NE *spring* derives from a PIE **sperĝh*- 'move energetically', seen also in Grk *spérkhō* 'drive, press' and with further semantic developments in Indic, e.g. Skt *spṛháyati* 'desires' (cf. Av *ā-spərəza*- 'excited'), and Tocharian, e.g. Toch AB *spärk*- 'disappear, perish'. The root **sel*- 'move quickly' probably has its original meaning preserved in Skt *ucchalati* (< **ud-sal*-) 'hurries forward' (cf. also Toch AB *säl*- 'fly' and *säl*- 'throw [down]') which develops into 'send', Arm *ylem*, OCS *sŭljǫ*, and into 'deliver', e.g. OE *sellan* (NE *sell*); we also have nominalizations of the one delivering, e.g. OCS *sŭlŭ* 'messenger'. A Celtic-Germanic-Tocharian isogloss suggests the existence of **krob*- 'hurry', e.g. OIr *crip* 'quick', ON *hrapa* 'fall, hurry', Toch AB *kārpā*- 'descend, come down, step down'.

Table 22.14. *Run and jump*

**speud-*	'hurry'	Grk *speúdō*
**sperĝh-*	'move energetically'	NE *spring*, *Grk spérkhō*, Skt *spr̥háyati*
**sel-*	'move quickly'	NE *sell* and *sale*, Skt *ucchalati*
*?*krob-*	'hurry'	
**bheg^w-*	'run'	Grk *phébomai*
**dreh$_a$-*	'run'	Grk *édrān*, Skt *drā́ti*
**drem-*	'run'	Grk *drameîn*, Skt *drámati*
**tek-*	'run, flow swiftly'	Skt *tákti*
**reth$_2$-*	'run'	Skt *rátha-*
**dhen-*	'run, flow'	Lat *fōns*, Skt *dhánvati*
**k̂ers-*	'run'	Lat *currō*, Grk *epíkouros*
**preu-*	'jump'	Skt *právate*
**preug-*	'jump'	NE *frog*
**h$_1$leig-*	'jump'	Grk *elelízō*, Skt *réjate*
**lek-*	'jump, scuttle along'	Grk *lēkáō*
**dher-*	'leap, spring'	Grk *thorós*, Skt *dhā́rā*
**skand-*	'jump'	Lat *scandō*, Skt *skándati*
**skek-*	' ± jump'	Skt *khacati*
**pet(h$_a$)-*	'fly'	Lat *petō*, Grk *pétomai*, Skt *pátati*
**dih$_1$-*	'fly; move swiftly'	Grk *díemi*, Skt *dī́yati*

A root **bheg^w-* 'run' is attested in Baltic (e.g. Lith *bė̃gu* 'run, flee'), Slavic (e.g. Rus *begú* 'run, flee'), and Grk *phébomai* 'flee' and finds its Asian cognate preserved solely in modern Indic, i.e. Hindi *bhāgnā* 'flee'. As mentioned above, we have the related pairing of **dreh$_a$-*, (reduplicated) ON *titra* 'tremble', Grk *édrān* 'ran', Skt *drā́ti* 'runs', and **drem-*, e.g. OE *trem* 'footstep', Grk *drameîn* 'run', Skt *drámati* 'runs about'; the Toch B reflex of this root is *rmer* 'swift', originally from **dremor-*. The verbal reflexes of **tek-*, e.g. OIr *teichid* 'flees', Lith *tekù* 'run, flow [of water], rise [of sun]', Rus *tekú* 'flow', Alb *ndjek* 'follow', Skt *tákti* 'hurries', occasion no surprise; in Germanic the root has been nominalized into the *o*-stem **tekwós* 'runner' where it survives as 'servant', e.g. OE *þēow*, OHG *deo*; a semantically very different nominalization appears in Toch B *cake* 'river'.

The basic verbal meaning of **reth$_2$-* 'run' survives only in Celtic, e.g. OIr *reithid* 'runs', NWels *rhedaf* 'run', but it is well known as a deverbative noun **roth$_2$eh$_a$-* or **róth$_2$os* 'wheel', e.g. OIr *roth* 'wheel', Lat *rota* 'wheel', OHG *rad* 'wheel', Lith *rãtas* 'wheel' (and plural *rãtai* 'wagon'), Alb *rreth* 'ring, hoop, tyre', Av *raθa-* 'chariot, wagon', Skt *rátha-* 'chariot, wagon'; the Tocharian word for 'army', e.g. Toch B *retke*, is probably derived from PIE **róth$_2$ikos* 'pertaining to chariot', i.e. the army was originally the 'chariotry'. As with 'go', one might also combine the concept of 'run' with 'flow' as in **dhen-* where Skt *dhanáyati* 'runs, sets in motion' exists alongside *dhánvati* 'runs, flows' (cf. also OPers *danuvatiy* 'flows', Toch AB *tsän-* 'flow'); Lat *fōns* 'spring' is another example of the meaning 'flow'. The root **k̂ers-*, on the other hand, seems exclusively to have meant 'run', e.g. Lat *currō* 'run', MHG *hurren* 'hasten', Grk *epíkouros* 'running for help'; it is also nominalized as in OIr *carr* 'vehicle' (the source of NE *car* is Lat *carrus* which was itself a borrowing from Celtic) and perhaps in the family of NE *horse*.

Several roots served for 'jump' in Proto-Indo-European. Both **preu-* and an extended form **preug-* yield both verbal reflexes, e.g. Skt *právate* 'jumps' and from the extended form we have, e.g., Lith *sprū́gti* 'leave, escape', Rus *prýgnutĭ* 'leap', Toch B *pruk-* 'make a leap', and agree on giving a nominal form 'the jumper' to the 'frog', e.g., NE *frog*, Skt *plava-*. Semantically less clear is **h₁leig-* 'jump' which does retain that meaning in Germanic, e.g. OE *lācan* 'leap, fly' or NPers *ālēxtan* 'jump', but it also means 'tremble' (Skt *réjate*) and 'whirl around' (Grk *elelízō*) or 'run around wildly' (Lith *láigyti*). The root **lek-* can be found in various derived forms to give 'jump', e.g. Grk *lēkáō* 'dance', *likertízō* 'jump', MHG *lecken* 'hop', Latv *lēkāju* 'jump about', or nominalizations such as Lat *lōcusta* 'locust' and NE *lire* that survives in British dialect to refer to the 'calf of the leg' (< OE *līra*). Alongside MIr *dar-* 'spring', Grk *thrṓiskō* 'leap, spring, attack, assault', and Skt *dhā́rā* 'flood', Greek contributes *thorós* 'semen' (presumably with the emphasis on ejaculation rather than the substance) as part of the cognate set from **dher-* 'leap, spring'. The root **skand-* is attested in Celtic (OIr *sceinnid* 'leaps'), Lat *scandō* 'climb', and Skt *skándati* 'jumps'. The semantic fields of the various cognates that derive from **skek-* are not quite so transparent. Lith *skataũ* (where **skak-* has been dissimilated to **skat-*) has 'jump' and OCS *skočiti* 'jump', but Germanic, e.g. ON *skagi* 'point of land sticking out', Indic, e.g. Skt *khacati* 'projects (of teeth)', and Toch AB *skāk-* 'balcony' (as something that projects) all suggests a positional nuance to the original semantics.

The basic root for 'fly' is **pet(h_a)-* which is well attested, e.g. NWels *hedeg* 'fly', Lat *petō* 'fly at, attack', Grk *pétomai* 'fly', Hit *peta-* 'fly', Skt *pátati* 'flies'. The precise action found in **dih₁-* 'flies, moves swiftly' is less clear and while we have Skt *dī́yati* 'flies' we also have Grk *díō* 'run away' and Latv *diêt* 'dance' (and *dīan* 'fast' in OIr).

The North-West provides another example of a base meaning 'run' that yields derivatives 'runner, servant', i.e. **tregh-* 'run', e.g. Goth *þragjan* 'run' but ON *þræll* 'servant'; in Celtic the verbal root has been nominalized to indicate 'foot', e.g. OIr *traig*, NWels *troed*, both 'foot'. Related possibly in some way is the similar **dhregh-* 'run', a West Central word, which yields both verbal meanings, e.g. Latv *drāžu* 'run fast', Grk *trékhō* 'run', and nominalizations, e.g. OIr *droch*,

Grk *trokhós*, Arm *durgn*, all 'wheel'. An Italic-Greek isogloss secures **sel-* 'jump' (Lat *saliō*, Grk *hállomai*, both 'jump'), which may be a local semantic development of **sel-* 'move quickly' (see above), while a Baltic-Greek (i.e. Lith *šókti* 'jump, dance': Grk *kēkíō* 'jump') isogloss attests **ḱeh*$_a$*k-* 'jump'. For **sker-* we attribute some meaning such as '± hop about' because we have Grk *skaírō* 'jump, hop, dance', OHG *scerōn* 'be mischievous', and words for 'locust'; in OE *scere-gescēre* and Lith *skėr̃ys*. Running to some purpose is suggested by the West Central word **bheug-* 'flee', e.g. Lat *fugiō* 'flee', Grk *pheúgō* 'flee'. Greek and Indo-Iranian yield cognate forms derived from **dheu-* 'run' (Grk *théō* 'run', MPers *dawīdan* 'run', Skt *dhávate* 'runs') but the word may be PIE if one accepts possible Germanic cognates such as NE *dew*. A laryngeal extension on the base root 'fly', **pet-*, namely **peth*$_a$*-*, is seen in Grk *petámai* 'fly' and Skt *patiṣyáti* 'will fly'.

22.14 Crawl, Slide, and Fall

In this section we summarize the small number of words associated with crawling, sliding, and falling (see Table 22.15).

The standard term for to 'crawl on one's belly' (rather than on all fours) would appear to have been **serp-* with its textbook series of cognates: Lat *serpō*, Grk *hérpō*, Skt *sárpati*, all 'crawl', and the congeries of its nominal derivatives, i.e. Lat *serpēns*, Alb *gjarpër*, Skt *sarpá-*, all 'snake' (see Section 9.3). A second word, **(t)sel-* 'sneak up on, creep, crawl', generally means precisely this in its various cognates, e.g. Lith *selù* 'sneak, prowl, step softly', Arm *solim* 'crawl', Av *srvant-* 'crawling', Skt *tsárati* 'creeps up on, sneaks'; it also has nominal forms that might indicate the 'snake', e.g. Alb *shligë*, but also the 'turtle' or 'snail' (OIr *selige*). To 'slip' may be at least one of the semantic connotations of **(s)meug-* or **meuk-* which means 'slide, slip' in OE *smūgan* or 'slip away from' in Lith *munkù*; in Lat *ē-mungō* and Grk *apomússō* we have either 'blow' or 'wipe' one's nose (and

Table 22.15. *Crawl, slide, and fall*

**serp-*	'crawl'	Lat *serpō*, Grk *hérpō*, Skt *sárpati*
**(t)sel-*	'sneak up on, crawl up on'	Skt *tsárati*
**(s)meug-* ~ **meuk-*	'slip'	Lat *-mungō*, Grk *apoméussō*, Skt *muñcáti*
**(s)leidh-*	'slide'	NE *slide*, Grk *olisthaínō*, Skt *srédhati*
**ḱad-*	'fall'	Lat *cadō*, Skt *śad-*
**pteh*$_1$*-*	'fall'	Grk *aptḗs*
**ped-*	'fall'	Lat *pessum*, Skt *pádyate*

compare Lat *mūcus* and the NE borrowing of the same spelling and meaning); Skt *muñcáti* indicates 'lets loose, frees' while OCS *mŭčati* 'chase' and Toch B *mäk-* 'run' both have reference to swift motion. NE *slide* derives from *(*s*)*leidh-* 'slide' which generally means 'slip' or 'slide' (cf. also Lith *slýstu* 'slide, slip', OCS *slědŭ* 'track [in the grass]', Grk *olisthaínō* 'slip') except Skt *srédhati*, which is problematic (whether it is a certain cognate), as it means 'fails, errs', perhaps from *'slides off'.

There are three words for 'fall'. Four groups (Celtic, Italic, Armenian, and Indic) attest **k̂ad-* 'fall', e.g. OIr *casar* 'hail', Lat *cadō* 'fall' and the nominalized *cadāver* 'corpse', i.e. the 'fallen', Arm *c'acnum* 'fall', Skt *śad-* 'fall'. The negative Grk *aptḗs* means 'not-falling' and the derived Av *tāta-* 'fallen (of rain)' supports a **pteh$_1$-* 'fall' although the possible Hittite cognate *piddāi-* means 'flees'. The root for 'foot', **ped-*, also serves as a verb 'fall', e.g. Lat *pessum* 'to the ground', OE *gefetan* 'fall', OCS *padǫ* 'fall', Av *paiδyaiti* 'moves down, plunges down', Skt *pádyate* 'falls'.

From the North-West we have **rēp-* 'crawl', e.g. Lat *rēpō* 'crawl, go on all fours', Lith *rėplióti* 'crawl, go on all fours', whose cognates in both Italic and Baltic indicate crawling on all fours; this word then contrasts semantically with the more widely found root **serp-* 'crawl on one's belly' (see above), hence we have (via loanwords from Latin), both NE *serpent* and *reptile*. Another possible North-West word (an Italic-Germanic isogloss) is **sleubh-* 'slide', e.g. Lat *lūbricus* 'slippery, NE *sleeve*. From the West Central region there is **phŏl-* (**ph$_x$ŏl-*?) 'fall', e.g. NE *fall*, Lith *púolu* 'fall', Arm *p'ul* 'fall, crush'.

22.15 Travel

Here we group all of the other words for motion which are either too vague, e.g. 'find one's way', or too specific, e.g. 'hunt', to be placed in the other categories. These are listed in Table 22.16.

The reconstructed meaning of **pent-* comes by a logical but curious (and hardly foolproof) route. Only Germanic offers a verbal form, e.g. NE *find*, which must then be combined with its widespread nominal derivative **póntōh$_2$s* 'path', e.g. Lat *pōns* 'bridge', Grk *pátos* 'path', Skt *pánthās* 'path', hence we have 'find' + 'path', i.e. 'find one's way'. 'Leave' in the sense of 'leave behind' was expressed with **leik^w-* seen in Lat *linquō* 'leave', NE *loan*, Lith *liekù* 'leave', Grk *leípō* 'leave', Arm *lk'anem* 'leave', Av *irinaxti* 'releases', Skt *riṇákti* 'leaves' while 'leave' in the sense of 'go away' is found in **deuh$_4$-*, e.g. Grk *dḗn* 'long, far', Hit *tūwa* 'to a distance', Skt *dávati* 'goes', *dūrá-* 'distant, remote'. The basic verb of motion in English, NE *go*, derives from **ĝheh$_1$-* 'leave', e.g. Grk *kikhā́nō* 'meet with', Av *zizāmi* 'leave off', Skt *jáhāti* 'leaves'. NE *let* comes from **leh₁d-* 'leave' which is limited to the Western and Central regions (e.g. also Lith *léidžiu* 'leave', Alb *lë* 'leave, let, abandon, allow') but has an unextended form in Hit *lā(i)-* 'let go'.

The semantics of **nes-* 'return home' are hardly precise. Grk *néomai* does mean 'return home' and the Iranian cognate Av *asta-* 'house', but in Germanic the word means 'be saved, heal', e.g. OE *ge-nesan* 'be saved' and Skt *násate* means 'unite with'. The verbal root **h$_a$el-* provides more problems since its reflexes in Lat *ambulō* 'take a walk', Baltic (Latv *aluôt(iês)* 'go astray'), and Grk *aléomai* 'go astray' all suggest 'wander' while Greek also offers *aleúomai* 'avoid' and Toch AB *āl-* 'keep off'. Either we have a single verb with divergent semantic histories or two homophonous verbs: 'wander' and 'avoid'.

There are two verbs for 'lead'. The root **neih$_x$-* 'lead' is limited to Anatolian, e.g. Hit *nāi-* 'leads', and Indo-Iranian, e.g. Skt *náyate* 'leads', while the other form **h$_2$wed(h$_x$)-* 'lead' carries the specific meaning of 'take a wife' in the various IE groups except for Anatolian, e.g. Hit *huett(iya)-* 'draw, pull'; this word and its meaning is discussed under kinship and marriage in Section 12.2. For 'follow' we have **sek^w-*, e.g. OIr *sechithir* 'follows', Lat *sequor* 'follow', Lith *sekù* 'follow, keep an eye on', Grk *hépomai*, Skt *sácate* all 'follow(s)' as well as a nominal derivative **sók^{w}h$_2$ōi* 'follower', e.g. ON *seggr* 'follower', Skt *sákhā-* 'friend'. This verb is probably the same as **sek^w-* 'see' (Section 20.2), where 'see' is a development of 'follow with the eyes'. 'Follow' in the sense of 'pursue' is suggested by **wei(h$_x$)-* 'go after', e.g. Lat *vīs* 'thou wantest', Lith *vejù*

Table 22.16. *Travel*

**pent-*	'find one's way'	NE *find*
**leik^w-*	'leave (behind)'	Lat *linquō*, NE *loan*, Grk *leípō*, Skt *riṇákti*
**deuh$_4$-*	'leave, go far away'	Grk *dḗn*, Skt *dávati*
**ĝheh$_1$-*	'leave'	NE *go*, Grk *kikhā́nō*, Skt *jáhāti*
**leh$_1$d-*	'leave'	NE *let*
**nes-*	'return home'	Grk *néomai*, Skt *násate*
**h$_a$el-*	'wander'	Lat *ambulō*, Grk *aléomai*
**neih$_x$-*	'lead'	Skt *náyate*
**sek^w-*	'follow'	Lat *sequor*, Grk *hépomai*, Skt *sácate*
**wei(h$_x$)-*	'go after'	Lat *vīs*, Skt *véti*
**leuh$_x$-*	'hunt'	
**wreg-*	'track, hunt, follow'	Lat *urgēre*, NE *wreak*
**h$_a$eĝreh$_a$-*	'hunt'	Grk *ágrā*

'chase, drive, pursue', Grk *híemai* 'strive', Skt *véti* 'follows, strives', Toch B *wāyā-* 'will drive, lead'. Words more explicitly suggesting hunting include **leuh*$_x$*-* where Slavic retains the verbal meaning, e.g. Rus *lov* 'capture, catch', but the nominal derivative **léuh*$_x$*ōn* 'he of the hunt' is found in Greek and Tocharian (Grk *léōn* 'lion' [< *'the hunter'; whence by borrowing the words for 'lion' in most European languages, including English], Toch B *luwo* 'animal' [< *'the hunted']). The root **wreg-* 'track, hunt' is solidly attested with cognates in Lat *urgēre* 'press', Germanic (NE *wreak*), Anatolian (Hit *ūrki-* 'track'), and Tocharian (Toch B *werke* 'chase, hunt'). The verbal root **h*$_a$*eĝ-* 'drive' provides the basis for **h*$_a$*eĝreh*$_a$*-* 'hunt' which is attested in Celtic, e.g. OIr *ār* 'carnage', Grk *ágrā* 'hunt', and Av *azrō-* 'hunt' (see Section 22.18).

22.16 Swim

There are a small number of words associated with motion through water, i.e. swimming, diving, and bathing, which have been assembled here in Table 22.17.

A verbal root 'dive' is reconstructed for **mesg-* which yields Lat *mergō* 'dip, dive' and *mergānser* 'duck' (literally, *'diving goose' or the like), Lith *mazgóti* 'wash up' (i.e. *'dip repeatedly'), and Skt *májjati* 'sinks'. Another possible root—if one accepts all the potential cognate forms—is **g*^{w}*ādh-* (**gweh*$_a$*dh-*?) 'dive': the Celtic correspondences are without much difficulty, e.g. OIr *bāidid* 'dives, drowns', but the other potential cognates are land forms, i.e. Grk *bēssa* 'valley', Av *vi-gāθa-* 'ravine'. Another possibilty is **g*^{w}*abh-* 'dip' with ON *kafa* 'dive', and Grk *báptō* 'dip in' (whence by borrowing NE *baptism* and related words) which some would relate to the Indo-Iranian words for 'deep', e.g. Skt *ga(m)bhīrá-*. Much more convincing is **sneh*$_a$*-* 'swim' with cognates in Celtic (OIr *snāïd*), Italic (Lat *nō*), Grk *nḗkhō*, Indo-Iranian (Skt *snā́ti*), and Tocharian (Toch B *nāsk-*), all 'bathe, swim' (cf. also Av *snayeiti* 'washes'). Another word

Table 22.17. *Swim*

**mesg-*	'dip under water, dive'	Lat *mergō*, Skt *májjati*
*?*g*^{w}*ādh-*	'dive'	Grk *bēssa*
*?*g*^{w}*abh-*	'dip'	Grk *báptō*
**sneh*$_a$*-*	'swim'	Lat *nō*, Grk *nḗkhō*, Skt *snā́ti*
**pleu-*	'float, swim; wash'	Lat *pluit*, NE *flow*, Grk *plé(w)ō*, Skt *plávate*
**geh*$_x$*ĝh-*	'± enter water, wade'	Skt *gā́hate*
**h*$_1$*erh*$_1$*-*	'row'	NE *row*

for 'swim' is *_pleu-_ where the meaning 'swim' is retained in Grk _plé(w)ō_ and Skt _plávate_, but other cognates include OIr _luïd_ 'moves', Lat _pluit_ 'it rains', NE _flow_, OCS _plovǫ_ 'flow', Arm _luanam_ 'wash', and Toch B _plus-_ 'float'. A Slavic-Indic isogloss suggests *_geh_$_x$_ĝh-_ 'wade, enter water', e.g. Slov _gáziti_ 'wade', Skt _gā̆hate_ 'wade'. Finally, with respect to propelling a boat, we have *_h_$_1$_erh_$_1$_-_ 'row' with the verbal meaning confined to the North-West, e.g. OIr _rāïd_ 'rows', NE _row_, but the derived noun *_h_$_1$_erh_$_1$_tér_ 'rower' also found in Grk _erétēs_ and Skt _aritár-_.

There are two words from the North-West associated with movement in water. A root *_swem-_ 'swim' is built on a Celtic-Germanic isogloss where the Germanic cognates, e.g. NE _swim_, are not problematic but the Celtic words, e.g. OIr _do-seinn_ 'moves', are not specifically related to movement within water. Semantically better supported is *_wadh-_ 'wade', e.g. Lat _vādō_ 'ford a river', NE _wade_, and nominal derivatives that indicate 'ford' or 'water' (e.g. Lat _vadum_ 'ford', OE _gewæd_ 'ford').

22.17 Convey

Our final selection of verbal roots concerns those that involve setting in one way or another something else in motion, either by conveyance, e.g. 'carry', or some other form of propulsion, e.g. 'push', 'pull'. The relevant verbs are indicated in Table 22.18.

Although absent in Anatolian, the root *_bher-_ 'carry' is otherwise a textbook root, whose paradigm frequently graces handbooks of Indo-European linguistics (including ours, see Table 1.5). The meaning in the different groups is fairly uniform as 'carry', e.g. OIr _beirid_, Lat _ferō_, NE _bear_, Alb _bie_, Grk _phérō_, Arm _berem_, Skt _bhárati_, Toch AB _pär-_, or 'take' (in Slavic, e.g. Rus _berú_); only Baltic poses a problem where the phonetic equivalent, e.g. Lith _beriù_, means 'strew'. The root also provides a basis for a series of nominal forms, e.g. *_bhérmn-_ 'load' (OCS _brěmę_ 'load', Grk _férma_ 'fruit', Skt _bhárman-_ 'load'); *_bhr̥tís_ 'carrying' (Lat _fors_ 'luck', NE _birth_, Skt *_bhr̥tí-_ 'carrying'). As in English, this word is often used to indicate 'bear a child'. Also widely attested is *_weĝh-_ 'carry', e.g. Lat _vehō_ 'bear', NE _weigh_ (as in 'weigh anchor'), Lith _vežù_ 'drive', OCS _vezǫ_ 'drive', Alb _vjedh_ 'steal', Grk _(w)ekhéto_ 'he should bring', Skt _váhati_ 'carries'. The difference between the semantics of this root and *_bher-_ is not entirely clear; however, the verbal cognates in Celtic, Latin, Baltic, and Indo-Iranian can also mean 'ride/drive (a vehicle)' and there are nominal derivatives, e.g. *_weĝhitlom_ 'vehicle' (Lat _vehiculum_, Skt _vahítram_). It is possible that the

Table 22.18. *Convey*

**bher-*	'carry'	Lat *ferō*, NE *bear*, Grk *phérō*, Skt *bhárati*
**weĝh-*	'bear, carry also ride'	Lat *vehō*, NE *weigh*, Grk (*w*)*ekhéto*, Skt *váhati*
**deuk-*	'pull'	Lat *dūcō*, NE *tow*, Grk *deúkei*
**selk-*	'pull'	Lat *sulcāre*, NE *sullow*, Grk *hélkō*
**$h_4$welk-*	'pull'	Grk *ṓlka*
**dhreĝ-*	'glide, pull (something) across'	Skt *dhrájati*
**(s)teud-*	'push, thrust'	Lat *tundō*, Skt *tudáti*
**reudh-*	'± push back'	NE *rid*, Skt *rudh-*
**sperh₁-*	'kick, spurn'	Lat *spernō*, NE *spurn*, Grk *spaírō*, Skt *sphurā́ti*
**$telh_2$-*	'lift, raise'	Lat *tollō*, NE *thole*, Grk *talássai*, Skt *tulā́*
**kel(h_x)-*	'lift, raise up'	Lat *ante-cellō*, Grk *keléontes*
**h_aeĝ-*	'drive'	Lat *agō*, Grk *ágō*, Skt *ájati*
**kel-*	'drive'	Lat *celer*, Grk *kéllō*, Skt *kaláyati*

original PIE meaning also contained the concept of 'ride' or 'drive' but we cannot be certain that this meaning was not a secondary development in later Indo-European.

There are at least three roots for 'pull'. The root **deuk-* 'pull' is largely confined to the West and Centre regions but with Toch A *tkā-* 'will stir, consider', it can be assigned to Proto-Indo-European. The groups not only retain the basic verbal meaning, e.g. Lat *dūcō* 'lead', NE *tow*, *tie*, Alb *nduk* 'pull hair out', but also extended meanings where Lat *dūcō* may also mean 'deduce' while the Greek cognate *deúkei* means 'considers' as it does in Tocharian A. Toch B *sälk-* 'pull out' offers the sole Asian cognate from **selk-* 'pull', e.g. Lat *sulcāre* 'to plough', Grk *hélkō* 'pull', and NE *sullow*, which survives as a dialect word for 'plough'. Possibly related to **selk-* as a rhyme word is **$h_4$welk-* 'pull' which is attested in Baltic (e.g. Lith *velkù* 'pull'), Slavic (e.g. OCS *vlěkǫ* 'pull'), Alb *heq* 'pull [out], remove', Grk *ṓlka* 'furrow', and Iranian (Av *frāvarčātiti* 'carries off'). Finally, there is **dhreĝ-* 'glide, pull (something) across' which is attested in ON *drak* 'stripe', Lith *drežóti* 'tear apart', and Skt *dhrájati* 'move'.

Several words served for 'push'. A root **(s)teud-* 'push' can be attested from both the West, e.g. OIr *do-tuit* 'makes to fall', Lat *tundō* 'push, strike' and with the *s-*, *studeō* 'strive' (i.e. 'push oneself'), *studium* 'zeal' (borrowed into NE as *study*), Goth *stautan* 'push', Alb *shtyj* 'push', and the East, e.g. Skt *tudáti* 'pushes, strikes'. To 'push back' seems to have been the underlying meaning of **reudh-* seen in NE *rid*, Skt *rudh-* 'check, restrain', and Toch AB *rutk-* 'move, remove'. Here we might also include 'move with the foot', i.e. 'kick', *$sperh_1$- with derivitives such as Lat *spernō* 'separate; spurn', NE *spurn*, Latv *spert̃* 'kick', Grk *spaírō* 'palpitate, give a start', Skt *sphurā́ti* 'springs, spurns', and Hit *ispar-* 'tread down, destroy'.

There are two verbs for 'raising' or 'lifting': *$telh_2$-, e.g. Lat *tollō* 'lift', NE *thole*, Grk *talássai* 'bear, suffer', Arm *t'ulow* 'let, permit', Skt *tulā́* 'scales'. Both the NE *thole* (which survives in dialect form to mean 'suffer, endure') and Greek suggest that the meaning has been extended to 'hold up' in the metaphorical sense; other cognates, e.g. Toch AB *täl-* 'uphold, raise', preserve the original meaning while MIr *tlenaid* 'takes away' reveals a further semantic shift. The second verb, *kel(h_x)- has cognates such as Lat *ante-cellō* 'surpass', Grk *keléontes* 'vertical beams in an upright loom', augmented by Lith *kélti* 'raise up' and Toch AB *käly-* 'stand'. There are also nominal derivatives to indicate a raised topographical feature, e.g. NE *hill.*

Very well attested is the verb *h_aeĝ- 'drive', e.g. Lat *agō*, Grk *ágō*, Skt *ájati*, all 'drive(s)', also known in Celtic, e.g. OIr *ad-aig* 'drive', Germanic, e.g. ON *aka* 'travel', Arm *acem* 'lead', and Toch AB *āk-* lead'. The explicit context of the verb often indicates that one of its original meanings was probably 'drive cattle' and it occurs in expressions indicating raiding for cattle, e.g. OIr *tāin* (< **to-aĝ-no-*) *bō* 'cattle raid', Lat *bovēs agere* 'to drive or raid for cattle', Av *gąm varətąm az-* 'drive off cattle as booty'. A root **kel-* is seen in Lat *celer* 'swift', Grk *kéllō* 'drive a ship to land', Skt *kaláyati* 'impels'; related are the Germanic words for 'hold', e.g. NE *hold*, which in Gothic is *haldan* 'pasture cattle'; an extended form in Tocharian, i.e. Toch B *kälts-* means 'press, goad, drive'.

A number of regional words are found in the North-West. A root **dhregh-* 'pull, tear (out)', is found in Germanic (e.g. NE *draw*), Baltic (e.g. Latv *dragãju* 'tear'), Slavic (e.g. Rus *dërgatĭ* 'pluck, tear'), and possibly in Lat *trahō* 'pull', though the initial *t-* is problematic; **skeubh-* 'push away, push ahead' is also found in the same three groups, e.g. NE *shove*, Lith *skùbti* 'hurry', OCS *skubǫ* 'pluck, tear off'; **telk-* 'push, thrust' is found in Celtic, Baltic, and Slavic (e.g. OIr *tolc* 'blow', Lith *tìlkti* 'be tame', Rus *tolkátĭ* 'push, shove'); Germanic, e.g. NE *drive* and *drove* (of cattle), and Baltic (e.g. Lith *drimbù* 'slowly drop down') provide evidence for **dhreibh-* 'drive'; both Old Norse and Lithuanian employ this verb to describe the fall of snow. A Celtic-Germanic isogloss gives us **reidh-* 'ride', e.g. MIr *rīadaigid* 'rides', NE *ride*. There is one purely Asiatic isogloss: **neud-* 'push (away)', attested in Skt *nudáti* 'pushes' and Toch B *nätk-* 'thrust, push away'.

Further Reading

The basic assemblage of Indo-European verbs is in (Rix et al. 2001). Other thematic discussions are Vendryès (1932) and Niepokuj (1994); for **sek*^{w}- see Baldi (1974), **bher-* see Hamp (1982*c*), and for a recent interpretation of **dheugh-* see Krasukhin (2000).

23

Religion

23.1 Deities

Approaches to the study of Indo-European religion and mythology differ substantially from those of the other semantic categories. There are several reasons for this difference. First, and obvious, is the paucity of terms for the names of deities reconstructable to Proto-Indo-European; with the exception of a few reconstructions that are found in almost any textbook, a number listed in Table 23.1 are of uncertain or, frankly, doubtful validity. Second, given the very nature of the subject—the ideological content of an ancient culture (here substituting 'culture' for 'reconstructed proto-language')—it has attracted far more attention than many other semantic categories. Finally, unlike most other semantic categories, there exists an entire academic field devoted to the study of comparative religion or mythology that has devised techniques other than strictly philological to reconstruct the deities and ideological content of Proto-Indo-European mythology. This chapter will briefly review the linguistic evidence while other approaches to Indo-European religion will be surveyed in Chapter 25.

The basic word for 'god' in Proto-Indo-European appears to have been **deiwós*, itself an *o*-stem derivative of **dyeu-* 'sky, day' < **dei-* 'shine, be bright' and it is widely attested across the Indo-European groups, e.g. OIr *día*, Lat *deus*, Lith *diẽvas*, Hit *sius*, Skt *devá-*, all 'god' in turn; in both Slavic and Iranian, e.g. Av *daēva-*, the word means 'demon', a result of a religious

Table 23.1. *Deities and mythical personages*

**deiwós*	'god'	Lat *deus*, NE Tuesday, Skt *devá-*
**dhēh₁s*	'god'	Lat *fēriae*, Grk *theós*, Skt *dhiṣā́*
**h_aénsus*	'god, spirit'	Skt *ásu-*
**dyḗus ph̥_atḗr*	'sky father'	Lat *Jūpiter*, Grk *Zeús patḗr*, Skt *dyáuṣ pitā́*
**dhuĝh_atḗr diwós*	'sky daughter'	Grk *thugátēr Diós*, Skt *duhitā́ diváh*
**h_aéusōs*	'dawn goddess'	Lat *Aurōra*, Grk *Ēṓs*, Skt *Uṣā́s-*
**bhr̥ĝhn̥tih_a-*	'high one'	Skt *br̥hatī*
**neptonos* ~ **h₂epōm nepōts*	'grandson of waters'	Lat *Neptūnus*, Skt *Apā́m Nápāt*
wl̥kānos*/wl̥keh_anos*	'smith god'	Lat *Volcānus*
**bhagos*	'apportioner'	Skt *Bhága-*
**perkʷunos*	'thunder god'	?Skt *Parjánya*
??**māwort-*	'god of war'	Lat *Mārs*, Skt *Marutás*
**manu-*	'Man, ancestor of humankind'	Skt *Mánu*
**dhroughós*	'phantom'	Skt *drógha-*
?**h₄(e)l̥bh-*	'elf'	NE *elf*, Skt *r̥bhú-*

reformation that degraded prior deities to demons to make way for the new religion preached by Zarathustra. (The change, which began in Iranian, presumably spread to Slavic during the long period of prehistoric cultural exchange, centered on the south Russian steppes, between Iranian and Slavic.) In Germanic, the word for 'god' survives as the name of the god Tyr, a Germanic war god, e.g. OE *Tīw* and NE *Tuesday*, a specific deity whose name is built on the same word was **dyḗus ph̥_atḗr* 'sky father'. There are both exact cognates of this form, e.g. Lat *Jūpiter*, Illyr *Dei-pátrous*, Grk *Zeús patḗr*, Skt *dyáuṣ pitā́*, and modified reworkings employing other words for 'father', e.g. Pal *tiyaz... pāpaz*. A derived adjective, **diwyós* 'divine', is attested in Lat *dīus*, Grk *dîos*, and Skt *divyá-*.

We also have some evidence for a feminine deity as well, i.e. **dhuĝh_atḗr diwós* 'sky daughter', whose name is preserved in Lith *diẽvo duktė̃* 'Saulytė' who was represented as the 'daughter of the sky', Grk *thugátēr Diós*, Skt *duhitā́ diváh*. This epithet is specifically applied to the 'dawn goddess', **h_aéusōs*, in Baltic, Greek, and Indic tradition. The cognate set is Lat *Aurōra*, Lith *Aušrine*, Latv *Auseklis*, Grk *Ēṓs*, and Skt *Uṣás-*.

The celestial nature of the Proto-Indo-European gods is also supported by the two etymologically unrelated words for 'god' in Germanic and Tocharian. NE *god* and its congeners (e.g. NHG *Gott*) is from Proto-Indo-European **ĝhutóm* 'that which is called/invoked' while in Toch B we have *ñakte* (Toch A *ñkät*) from Proto-Indo-European **ni-ĝhutos* 'he who is invoked downwards (i.e. from the sky)'.

Another word for 'god' is supplied by **dhēh₁s* where the meaning 'god' survives in Grk *theós* and Arm *dikʿ* 'the gods' but is attested otherwise in the remaining cognate forms, e.g. Lat *fēriae* 'festival day', Skt *dhiṣána-* (epithet of various gods) and *dhiṣā́* 'with impetuosity'; the latter's semantic development might be compared with NE *enthusiasm*, ultimately borrowed from Greek and meaning '(having) a god inside'. There is also **$h_a$énsus* 'god, spirit' which is based on a Germanic-Indo-Iranian isogloss. The Germanic forms include ON *ōss* 'god' (in the nominative plural we have the famous *Æsir* of Norse mythology) while in Iranian we have *ahura-* 'god, lord' and *Ahura-mazdāh*, the highest of the gods in the pantheon of Zarathustra, and in Indic there is Skt *ásu-* 'powerful spirit' and the *Asura-*, a special class of Indic deities.

The remaining names of the "special-purpose" deities all pose special problems. One may, for example, propose a **bhr̥ĝhn̥tih$_a$-* 'high one' where Celtic offers the name of a goddess, e.g. OBrit *Brigantia*, Germanic offers a female personal name, e.g. OHG *Burgunt*, and Indic provides a cognate adjective, Skt *br̥hatī* 'high, lofty', but no corresponding deity or myth, leaving it likely that, as a divine name, it is a Celtic innovation. Some propose a **neptonos* or **$h_2$epom nepōts* 'grandson/nephew of waters'. The latter is solidly reconstructed to Indo-Iranian, e.g. Skt *Ap ā́m Nápāt*, but both of the putative Western reflexes, OIr *Nechtain* and Lat *Neptūnus*, have been challenged, in terms of their relationship both with the Indo-Iranian deity and with each other. A PIE **wl̥kānos/*wl̥keh$_a$nos* 'smith god' is also insecure and based on the proposed correspondence between the Roman smith god, Lat *Volcānus* (which is otherwise derived from Etruscan or some Aegean language), and Oss *wærgon*, a smith god. In this case the proposed cognates are desperately few (and the proposed equation suffers by not being attested in an ancient Iranian language), but the phonological relationship would be perfect. The divine nature of a deified **bhagos* 'apportioner' is secure only in Indo-Iranian (Skt *bhága-*, Av *baga-*, the latter of which was borrowed into Slavic to provide the standard word for 'god', *bogŭ*); it also serves as an epithet of Zeus in Phrygian *Bagaîos* but retains its purely etymological meaning (< **bhag-* 'apportion') in Tocharian, e.g. Toch B *pāke* 'share, part' (see Section 17.3). A 'thunder god' is indicated by **perk^{w}unos* which is attested in Germanic, e.g. *Fjǫrgyn*, mother of the Norse thunder god Thor, the Lithuanian thunder god *Perkūnas*, and the Old Russian thunder god *Perúnŭ*; his identification as a Proto-Indo-European deity, rather than a specifically North-Western Indo-European one, depends on whether one accepts that Skt *Parjánya* (presupposing a Proto-Indo-European **perg^{w}enyo-*), a weather god, is also cognate. Even more dubious are attempts to postulate a 'war god', **māwort-*, on the basis of Lat *Mārs* and Skt

Marutás, the companions of the Vedic war god Indra. In these last two cases, and more particularly in the last one, the amount of irregular sound change one has to assume, in the absence of an exact semantic equation, is more than most historical linguists are prepared to accept.

If the individual deities do not fare well (at least in terms of reconstruction), there is more widespread acceptance of the ancestor of humans, **manu-* based on Germanic *Mannus*, the mythological ancestor of the Germans, and the Indo-Iranian ancestor of humanity, e.g. Skt *Mánu*. Another possible reconstruction is **h_4(e)l̥bh-* which is attested in Germanic, e.g. NE *elf*, and Skt *r̥bhú-* 'an artisan deity'. Finally, a 'phantom', **dhroughós*, is suggested on the basis of Celtic (OIr *airdrech* 'phantom', Germanic, e.g. ON *draugr*); as a personalized form it is limited to the North-West but it is cognate with Skt *drógha-* 'deceiving' and derives from **dhreugh-* 'deceive' (see Section 20.6).

Regionally reconstructed deities are neither numerous nor always secure. From the North-West we have a possible **dhwes-* 'spirit' from the verb **dhwes-* 'breathe' found in Celtic (Gaul *dusios* 'type of demon'), MHG *getwās* 'fantom', and Baltic (Lith *dvasià* spirit'). For the West Central region there is OIr *trīath* 'sea' which is phonetically close to and semantically not too distant from the name of the Greek sea god *Trī́tōn*, the son of Poseidon, but a proto-form **trih$_a$tōn* 'watery (one?)' remains highly speculative. Perhaps more probably related are Lat *lemurēs* 'nocturnal spirits who devour the dead' and Grk *lámia* 'a female flesh-eating monster used to scare children with' which might derive from **lem-* '(nocturnal) spirit'. Greek-Indo-Iranian isoglosses comprise several potential cognate deities (and their names). An Indo-European *péh$_2$usōn* 'pastoral god' is predicated on Grk *Pā́n* and Skt *Pūṣā́*; the suggested underlying root, *peh$_2$-* 'protect, feed cattle', is congruent with the fact that both deities are depicted as pastoral gods within their respective pantheons. Similarly, the word *k̂érberos* 'spotted' would seem to underlie the names of both the Greek hound of Hades *Kérberos* and the epithet (*śárvara-*) of one of the dogs of Yama, the Indic god of the dead. There are fewer semantic reasons to link the Greek fury *Erīnū́s* with the Indic goddess *Saraṇyū́*, wife of the Sun, although the phonological correspondence of both their names (**seren(y)uh$_x$s*) does seem sound enough.

23.2 The Sacred

The vocabulary of the sacred (Table 23.2) challenges us to understand the underlying connotations of each of the terms we can reconstruct. On a comparative basis the idea of the sacred is often associated with some form of rite

Table 23.2. *The sacred and sacrifice*

*sakros	'holy'	Lat _sacer_
*weik-	'consecrate'	Lat _victima_, NE _witch_, Skt _vinákti_
*k̂wen(to)-	'holy'	
*noibhos	'holy'	
*seup-	'pure'	
*wōtis	'god-inspired'	NE _Wednesday_, Skt _api-vat-_
*k̂ouh$_1$_ros_	'powerful'	Grk _kū́rios_, Skt _śū́ra-_
_*h_$_a$_euges-_	'strength'	Lat _augustus_, Skt _ójas-_
*kouh$_1$_ēi(s)_	'priest'	Grk _kóēs_, Skt _kaví-_
*bhlaĝhmēn	'priest'	Lat _flāmen_, Skt _brahmán-_
?*pent- + _*dheh_$_1$_-/*k_^{w}_er-_	'priest'	Lat _pontifex_, Skt _pathi-kr̥t-_
?*bhertōr	'priest'	
_*h_$_a$_ed-bher-_	'sacrifice'	cf. Skt _prá-bhartar-_
_*d(h_$_3$_)eu-_	'be favourable to'	Lat _bonus_, Skt _dúvas-_
_*h_$_x$_olu-_	'± spell'	

by which something or someone is separated apart from the secular world. Alternatively, the sacred may be associated with being complete, infused with a special power. PIE _*sakros_, for example, exhibits cognates in Lat _sacer_ 'sacred' and _sacerdōs_ 'priest' and Tocharian, e.g. Toch B _sākre-_ 'happy', with a more distant connection with Hit _saklāi-_ 'rite, custom'; one might then envisage a rite by which something is made sacred and some would derive this form from the verbal root _*sek-_ 'cut', i.e. cut off from the world. The cognates of _*weik-_ 'consecrate' can be both nominal, e.g. Lat _victima_ 'sacrificial victim' and NE _witch_, and verbal where Indo-Iranian suggests that the act of consecration involves setting something or someone apart, e.g. Goth _weihan_ 'consecrate' (and _weihs_ 'holy'; cf. NHG _Weihnachten_ 'Christmas Eve') but Skt _vinákti_ 'select out'. Similarly, the Western cognates of _*wōtis_ 'god-inspired' are nominal, usually names of priests such as OIr _fāith_ 'prophet' or gods, e.g. ON _Ōðinn_ 'Odin', while the verbal forms are found in Indo-Iranian, e.g. Skt _api-vat-_ 'inspires' (see Sections 20.2, 21.2). A verbal origin probably underlies both _*k̂wen(to)-_ 'holy' (e.g. Lith _šveñtas_ 'holy', OCS _svętŭ_ 'holy', Av _spənta_ 'holy') which is derived from _*k̂eu(h_$_1$_)-_ 'swell', hence, 'swollen (with some form of sacred force)' and _*noibhos_ 'holy' (OIr _noīb_, OPers _naiba-_, both 'holy') from _*nei-_ 'be excited', again some form of sacred animation. The first root also provides the basis for _*k̂ouh_$_1$_ros_ 'powerful (i.e. swollen)', although in its derivatives it generally refers to a powerful human, a hero, as in OIr _cora(i)d_, Skt _śū́ra-_; it is also a proper name in Thracian _Soura-_. A division between physical and spiritual strength, however, is far less clear in _*h_$_a$_euges-_ 'strength', where Skt _ójas-_ can refer both to the physical might of a warrior and also the spiritual potential of a deity, and in Latin the semantic sphere is purely sacred, e.g. Lat *augustus* 'sacred' and the related *augur* 'priest, seer'. Only Umb *supa* and Hit *suppa-* provide evidence of a PIE **seup-* 'pure' but both indicate the 'viscera of a sacrificed animal', i.e. something tabu for humans, while Hit *supp-i-* renders 'pure'. Despite the fewness of cognates, the perfect semantic and phonological correspondences would seem to make this a certain Proto-Indo-European word.

Reconstructed words for a Proto-Indo-European 'priest' are insecure but there are at least three candidates. A word for priest, *$kouh_1\bar{e}i(s)$, is found in Grk *kóēs* 'priest', Lyd *kaweś* 'priest', and Skt *kaví-* 'seer', from *$(s)keuh_1$- 'perceive'. A Latin-Messapic-Indo-Iranian isogloss (Lat *flāmen* 'priest', Messapic *blamini* 'priest', OPers *brazman-* 'appropriate form, appearance', Skt *brahmán-* 'priest') indicates a (remote) possibility for **bhlaĝhmēn* 'priest' which is primarily challenged because the *-ĝh-* of the reconstructed form is nowhere evident in the Latin word nor can one find any further evidence of a root **bhlaĝh-* in any of the other Indo-European languages. Even more remote is **pent-* + *$dheh_1$-/*k^wer-, a compound of **pent-* 'path' and either *$dheh_1$- 'put, establish' (in Lat *ponti-fex*) or *k^wer- 'make' in Skt *pathi-kr̥t-* 'path-maker', also a religious title applied to priests. Both suggest the concept of a 'path-maker' which in Latin is exclusively employed in a religious context, i.e. 'one who makes a path to the gods' while the Indic form can be applied to priests. The root **bher-* 'carry' provides the basis for another weakly attested word for 'priest', i.e. **bhertōr* 'one who bears (offerings)' which is found in Umb *ars-fertur* 'priest' and Av *fra-bərətar-* 'priest' which could certainly be the result of independent creation. The same root is found in the compound *$h_a$ed-bher- 'sacrifice', literally 'brings to', that is 'make an offering', which is attested in Celtic (OIr *ad-opair* 'sacrifice), Italic (Umb *arsfetur* 'priest'), and Indo-Iranian, e.g. Skt *prá-bhartar-* 'one who brings'; again assignment to Proto-Indo-European is uncertain as the Indo-Iranian cognates employ a different preposition (*pro-*) from the Western languages.

The semantic sphere of *$d(h_3)$eu- 'be favourable to' (probably from *deh_3- 'give') may extend to the religious idea of 'worship', e.g. the cognate Skt *dúvas-* 'worship', *duvasyáti* 'honours', although its Western cognates may mean 'strong' (OIr *de(i)n*) or 'good', Lat *bonus* from OLat *duenos*). Finally, we have a Germanic-Hittite isogloss to support a vaguely understood *$h_x$olu- or **alu-* '±spell'; the Hit *alwanzatar* means 'witchcraft, spell' while the Germanic forms, e.g. Runic *alu*, may mean 'spell' and are more certainly associated with the supernatural.

We have a Celtic-Germanic isogloss that yields *soito/eh_a- 'sorcery' (NWels *hud* 'magic', ON *seið* 'magic') and a Slavic (OCS *čudo* 'wonder')-Greek (*kûdos* 'renown'), both from **keudes-* 'magic force'. There are several

Greek-Indo-Iranian isoglosses. A root _*yaĝ-_ 'honour, worship' is attested by Grk _házomai_ 'dread' (and _hágios_ 'holy') and Skt _yájati_ 'worships'; here the Greek denotes the fear one feels in the presence of the deities while both the Greek and Indic reflexes of _*tyeg_^{w}- 'give way, pull oneself back (in awe)' suggest such negative connotations (Grk _sébomai_ 'worship, honour', _sobéō_ 'frighten off, drive away', Skt _tyájati_ 'stands back from something'). 'Sacred power', _*ish_$_{1}$_ros_, is indicated by a series of cognates in both Greek, e.g. _hierós_ 'sacred, powerful', and Skt _iṣirá-_ 'powerful', cf. the cognate expression Grk _hieròn ménos_: Skt _iṣiréna mánasā_ 'sacred strength'.

Further Reading

For a general treatment of all the deities see Puhvel (1987_a_). Specific discussions can also be found in Nagy (1974_a_), Polomé (1980), Polomé (1986), Kazanas (2001), Haudry (1987), Motz (1998), Euler (1987), and Seebold (1991).

24

Grammatical Elements

24.0 Pronouns

Generally, along with numerals and some kinship and body terms, the most persistent elements in any language tend to be basic grammatical forms such as pronouns and conjunctions. Indo-European is no exception here and we can reconstruct on a fairly broad basis the various pronouns of Proto-Indo-European.

24.1 Personal and Reflexive Pronouns

Although most modern European-derived languages recognize three personal pronouns, i.e. first person *I* and *we*, second person *you*, and third person *he/she/it* and *they*, there is no evidence for a third person in Proto-Indo-European. Instead, we find well-supported evidence for demonstrative pronouns, e.g. *this* or *that*. Of the first two persons, we find, as we might expect, that these words were in such frequent use in any language that there are variable forms depending on whether the pronoun was merely stated, e.g. *h_1eĝ 'I', emphasized, e.g. *h_1eĝóm 'I myself', or an enclitic, i.e. placed as a particle at the end of another word, e.g. *$h_1$me. The emphatic forms involve the addition of a suffix *-om to the base form. Also, in addition to the singular and plural forms, each of the pronouns also attests the existence of a dual form to express pairs, i.e. 'we two', 'you two'. The primary personal pronouns are indicated in Table 24.1.

The nominative form of the first person pronoun in the various IE groups might be derived from the PIE first person or from the emphatic form or from the accusative. Those drawing directly on the PIE nominative (*h_1eĝ*) include Italic (e.g. Lat *ego* 'I'), Germanic (e.g. OE *ic* 'I' (> NE *I*), Baltic (e.g. Lith *aš* 'I'), Arm *es* 'I'; the emphatic form (*h_1eĝóm*) supplied Slavic (e.g. OCS *(j)azŭ* (< *h_1eĝóm*), Alb *unë*, Grk *egṓ(n)*; and Indo-Iranian (e.g. Skt *ahám* 'I'); the accusative (*$h_1$me*) is found as the base form for Celtic (OIr *mē* 'I'), Anatolian (e.g. Lyc *amu* ~ *ēmu* 'I, me'), and Tocharian (Toch B *ñaś* [< *$h_1$mé-ĝe*]). The first person dual is less widely attested but found in Germanic (e.g. OE *wit* 'we two'), Baltic (Lith *mùdu* 'we two, us two'), Slavic (e.g. OCS *vě* 'we two'), Grk *nṓ* 'we two, us two', Indo-Iranian (e.g. Skt *āvā́m* 'we two, us two'), and Toch B *wene* 'we two, us two'. More widespread is the plural form **wéi* 'we' (emphatic **weyóm*) that is found in Celtic (e.g. OIr *nī* 'we, us'), Italic (e.g. Lat *nōs* 'we, us'), Germanic (e.g. OE *wē* 'we'), Baltic (e.g. Lith *mẽs* 'we'), Slavic (e.g. OCS *my* 'we'), Alb *ne* (< **nōs*) 'we, us', Grk *hēmeîs* 'we', Arm *mek'* 'we', Hit *wēs* 'we', Skt *vayám* 'we', and Tocharian (e.g. Toch B *wes* 'we, us'). Here again there have been shifts from other forms and influences from different numbers seen, for example, in the tendency of Baltic, Slavic, and Armenian to replace the initial **n-* by *m-*, either influenced by the first person singular pronoun or because of the influence of the first person plural verbal endings in *-*m*-, or both.

The second personal pronoun also possessed a nominative *$túh_x$* 'thou', emphatic *$tuh_xóm$*, accusative **téwe,* and enclitic **te* although these were better differentiated in the different IE groups than was the case of the first person. Cognates are found in Celtic (e.g. OIr *tū* 'thou, thee'), Italic (e.g. Lat *tū* 'thou', *tē* 'thee'), Germanic, e.g. OE *þū* 'thou' [> NE *thou*], *þe* [> NE *thee*]), Baltic (e.g. Lith *tù* 'thou', *tavẽ* 'thee'), Slavic (e.g. OCS *ty* 'thou', *tę* 'thee'), Alb *ti* 'thou', *ty* 'thee' (enclitic *të*), Doric Grk *tú* 'thou', Arm *du* 'thou', *z-k'ez* (< **twe-*) 'thee', Anatolian (e.g. Hit *zīg* 'thou' (with a *-g* from the first person)), Indo-Iranian

Table 24.1. *Personal and reflexive pronouns*

*h_1eĝ	'I'	Lat *ego*, NE *I*, Grk *egṓ*, Skt *ahám*
*$nóh_1$	'we two'	Grk *nṓ*, Skt *āvā́m*
*wéi	'we'	Lat *nōs*, NE *we*, Grk *hēmeîs*, Skt *vayám*
*$túh_x$	'thou'	Lat *tū*, NE *thou*, Grk *sú*, Skt *tvám*
*$wóh_1$	'you two'	Skt *yuvā́m*
*yuh_xs, *uswé ~ *swé	'ye'	Lat *vōs*, NE *ye*, Grk *humeîs*, Skt *yūyám*
*séwe	'-self'	Lat *sē*, Grk *heé;*, Skt *svá-*

(e.g. Skt *tvám* thou', *tvā́m* 'thee'), and Tocharian (e.g. Toch B *tuwe* 'thou', *ci* 'thee'). There were two forms for the dual: nominative **wóh₁* 'ye two, you two' and accusative **uh₁wé* 'you two' with cognates in Germanic (e.g. OE *git* 'ye two', *inc* ~ *incit* 'you two'), Baltic (e.g. Lith *jùdu* 'ye/you two'), Slavic (e.g. OCS *va* 'ye/you two'), Indo-Iranian (e.g. Skt *yuvā́m* 'ye/you two'), and Toch B *yene* 'ye/you two'. The second person plural has seen massive rebuilding of its forms, i.e. **yuh$_x$s* 'ye', **uswé* ~ **swé* 'you', and enclitic **wos*, e.g. the accusative serves as the nominative form for Celtic, Italic, Slavic, Albanian, Greek, and Anatolian. The plural forms include Celtic (e.g. OIr *sī* 'ye, you'), Lat *vōs* 'ye, you', Germanic (e.g. OE *gē* 'ye' [> NE *ye*], *ēow* 'you' [> NE *you*]), Baltic (e.g. Lith *jū̃s* 'ye', *jus* 'you'), Slavic (e.g. OCS *vy* 'ye, you'), Alb *ju* 'ye', Grk *humeîs* 'ye', *huméas* 'you', Arm *i-jez* 'you', Anatolian (e.g. Hit *sumēs* 'ye, you'), Indo-Iranian (e.g. Skt *yūyám* 'ye', *yuṣmā́n* 'you', enclitic *vas*), and Tocharian (e.g. Toch B *yes* 'ye, you').

The reflexive pronoun (**séwe*) is well attested across most IE groups such as Italic (e.g. Lat *sē* 'him-/her-/itself'), Germanic (e.g. OHG *sih* 'him-/her-/itself'), Baltic (e.g. Lith *savẽ* '-self'), Slavic (e.g. *sę* '-self'), Alb *u* 'him-/her-/itself', Grk *hé* ~ *heé* 'him-/her-/itself', Indo-Iranian (e.g. Skt *svá-* 'one's own'), and Tocharian (e.g. Toch B *ṣañ* 'one's own').

24.2 Demonstrative Pronouns

To complete the basic paradigm of our modern personal pronoun, PIE employed three genders of one of the demonstrative pronouns. There were two that could have served. The most likely was built on **h₁ei-* 'this (one)', i.e. **h₁éi* (with an emphatic **h₁eyóm*) 'he, this (one)', **h₁ih$_a$-* 'she, this (one)', **h₁id* (emphatic **h₁idóm* ~ **h₁idéh$_a$*) 'it'. Alternatively, Proto-Indo-European also offered a pronoun indicating 'that (one)', i.e. **so* 'that one, he', **seh$_a$* 'that one, she', **tód* 'that one, it'. Most of the other demonstrative pronouns may be derived from these two with the addition of suffixes that will reappear when we examine the interrogative and relative pronouns. The main demonstrative forms are listed in Table 24.2.

The demonstrative pronouns are spottily attested across the entire IE world. The pronoun 'this one', i.e. **h₁éi* / **h₁ih$_a$-* / **h₁id*, designates all three genders (he/she/it) as can be seen in the list of cognates: Lat *is* ~ *īs/eā/id* 'he/she/it', Germanic (e.g. OHG *ir* ~ *er/iz* ~ *ez* 'he/it'), Baltic (e.g. Lith *jìs/jì* 'he/she'), Cypriot Grk *ín* 'him, her', Anatolian (e.g. HierLuv *is* 'this'), and Indo-Iranian (e.g. Skt *ayám/iyám/idám* 'he/she/it;this'). Its corresponding 'that one', **so*/**seh$_a$* /**tód*, is also widely attested in Celtic (e.g. OIr *-so/-d* 'this one'), Lat *is-te/is-ta/is-tud* 'this (one)', Germanic (e.g. OE *sē/sēo/þæt* (> NE *that*) 'the',

Table 24.2. *Demonstrative pronouns*

*h_1*éi* /*h_1*i*h_a- /*h_1*id*	'this one'	Lat *īs/eā/id*, NE *it*, Grk *ín*, Skt *ayám/iyám/idám*
so* /seh*$_a$/**tód*	'that one'	Lat *is-te/is-ta/is-tu*, NE *that*, Grk *ho/hē/tó*, Skt *sá/sā́/tát*
**k̂ís*	'this (one)'	Lat *cis*, NE *he*, Grk *sḗtes*
*h_1*iteros*	'(an)other'	Lat *iterum*, Skt *ítara-*
*h_1*ith*$_a$	'thus'	Lat *item*, Skt *íti*
*h_1*idh*$_a$	'here'	Lat *ibī*, Grk *ithāgenḗs*, Skt *ihá*
**tór*	'there'	NE *there*, Skt *tár-hi*
**todéh*$_a$	'then'	Skt *tadā́*
**téh*$_a$*wot(s)*	'so many, so long'	Grk *téōs*, Skt *(e-)tā́vat*

OHG *der/die/daz* 'the', Goth *sa/sō/þata* 'that (one)', Baltic (Lith *tàs/tà* 'that [one]'), Slavic (e.g. OCS *tŭ/ta/to* 'that [one]'), Alb *ai/ajo* 'he/she', Grk *ho/hē/tó* 'the', Arm *ay-d* 'that', Hit *ta* 'and, then', Indo-Iranian (e.g. Skt *sá/sā́/tát* 'that [one]'), and Toch B *se/sā/te* 'such (a one)'. This pronoun supplies the definite article in Germanic and Greek. Another word for 'this (one')' was **k̂ís* with cognates in Celtic (e.g. OIr *cē* 'here, on this side', Lat *cis* 'on this side of', Germanic (e.g. OE *hē* 'he' [> NE *he*]), Baltic (e.g. Lith *šìs* 'this [one]'), OCS *sĭ* 'this (one)', Alb *sot* (< **k̂yeh*$_a$*-dih*$_x$*tei*) 'today', Grk *sḗtes* (< **k̂yeh*$_a$*-wetes*) 'in this year', and Hit *ki* 'this'.

The pronoun *h_1*iteros* '(an)other' is based on a Latin-Sanskrit isogloss (Lat *iterum* 'again', Skt *ítara-* 'the other, another'). Somewhat more widespread is *h_1*ith*$_a$ 'thus' with cognates in Celtic (e.g. MWels *yt-* (verbal particle), Lat *item* 'also, likewise', *ita* 'so, thus, in this manner', Baltic (e.g. Lith [dial.] *it* 'as'), and Indo-Iranian (e.g. Skt *íti* 'thus, in this manner'). The pronoun *h_1*idh*$_a$ 'here' is attested in Celtic (e.g. OIr *-id-* [infixed particle]), Lat *ibī* 'there', Grk *ithāgenḗs* 'here born', and Indo-Iranian (e.g. Skt *ihá* 'here'). 'There', **tór*, is limited to cognates in Germanic and Indic, i.e. OE *þǣr* 'there' (> NE *there*), Skt *tár-hi* 'at the time, then'. The temporal pronoun **todéh*$_a$ 'then' is also limited to two main groups, Baltic (Lith *tadà* 'then') and Indo-Iranian (Av *taδa* 'then', Skt *tadā́* 'then'). A pronoun **téh*$_a$*wot(s)* 'so many, so long' is found in Grk *téōs* 'so long, meanwhile', Indo-Iranian (e.g. Skt *(e-)tā́vat* 'so much, so many; so great, so far'), and Tocharian (e.g. Toch B *tot* 'so much, so many; so great; so far').

Demonstrative pronouns were relatively productive in the different IE regional groups and we have several isoglosses. From the West Central region we have **tóti* 'so much, many' (Lat *tot* and Grk *tósos* both 'so many'); **teh*$_a$*li* 'of that sort or size' (Lat *tālis* 'of that sort', Lith *tõlei* 'so long', Grk *tēlíkos* 'so old'); **téh*$_a$*mot(s)* 'then, at that place' (Latv *nuo tām* 'from there', OCS *tamo* 'thither',

Grk *tēmos* 'then'); and *$h_a$en- 'that' (OIr *an-d* 'here', Lat *an* 'or; whether', Lith *añs* 'yon', OCS *onŭ* 'he; yon', Alb *a* 'whether', and Grk *án* 'possibly').

24.3 Interrogative Pronouns

Proto-Indo-European interrogative pronouns are built on the stem *k^wo- after which we will often find the same form of extensions, temporal or spatial, that we have encountered in the demonstrative pronouns. This form is well represented across most of the IE groups, e.g. this is the NE *wh-* group (*who, what, which, why?*) which was phonetically more transparent in OE *hw-* or the Latin *qu-* words. The interrogatives formed part of a systemic relationship with the relatives and demonstratives so that many of the terms can be placed into a set, e.g. *k^wóteros 'which (of two)': **yoteros* 'which of the two', *k^wodéh$_a$ 'when': *todéh$_a$ 'then', *k^wór 'where': **tór* 'there'. The main interrogatives reconstructed for PIE are given in Table 24.3.

There is evidence from the various IE groups for the relatively extensive list of interrogative pronouns. PIE *k^wós 'who' is found in Celtic (e.g. OIr *nech* [< *ne-k^wos] 'someone, anyone'), Germanic (e.g. OE *hwā* 'who' [> NE *who*]), Baltic (e.g. Lith *kàs* 'who, what'), Slavic (e.g. OCS *česo* 'whose'), Alb *kë* 'whom', Grk *toû* 'whose', Arm *ov* (< *k^wos/k^wom) 'who', Indo-Iranian (e.g. Skt *kás* [masc.] 'who', [fem.] *kā́* 'who', *kásya* 'whose'). There is also a form *k^wís 'who' which is confined to Lat *quis* 'who, which one', Grk *tís* 'who', Hit *kuis* 'who', and Av *čiš* 'who'. PIE *k^wód 'what' is found in Celtic (OWels *pa* 'what'), Lat *quod* 'in respect to which; that, in that' (conj.), Germanic

Table 24.3. *Interrogative pronouns*

*k^wós	'who'	NE *who*, Grk *toû*, Skt *kás*
*k^wís	'who'	Lat *quis*, Grk *tís*
*k^wód	'what'	Lat *quod*, NE *what*, Skt *kád*
*k^wíd	'what, what one'	Lat *quid*
*k^wóteros	'which (of two)'	Lat *uter*, NE *whether*, Grk *póteros*, Skt *katará-*
*k^wóm	'when'	Lat *cum*
*k^wodéh$_a$	'when'	Skt *kadā́*
*k^wór	'where'	Lat *quōr*, NE *where*, Skt *kárhi*
*k^wu ~ *k^wū́	'where'	Lat *ubi*, Grk *pu-*, Skt *kū́*
*k^wóti ~ *k^wéti	'how much/many'	Lat *quot*, Grk *pósos*, Skt *káti*
*k^woih$_x$os	'pertaining to whom/what'	Lat *cūius*, Grk *poîos*

(e.g. OE *hwæt* 'what' [> NE *what*]), Anatolian (e.g. Pal *-kuwat* [generalizing particle]), and Indo-Iranian (e.g. Skt *kád* 'what'). A PIE *k^w*id* 'what, what one' is attested in Lat *quid* 'what, what one', Slavic (e.g. OCS *čĭto* 'what'), Arm *in-č* 'some', Hit *kuit* 'what' (interrogative), and Iranian (e.g. Av *čit* [generalizing particle]).

To express 'which (of two)', PIE utilized *k^w*óteros* which is found in Lat *uter* 'which', Germanic (e.g. OE *hwæðer* 'which' [> NE *whether*]), Baltic (e.g. Lith *kataràs* ~ *katràs* 'which'), OCS *koteryjĭ* 'which', Grk *póteros* 'which', and Indo-Iranian (e.g. Skt *katará-* 'which'). The initial labiovelar exhibits the expected different treatment in Greek where we find *k^w*i-* > Grk *ti-* but *k^w*o-* or *k^w*u-* > Grk *po-/pu-*.

The temporal interrogative *k^w*óm* 'when', which was a special development of the masculine accusative of *k^w*ós*, is found as a relative pronoun in Lat *cum* 'when', but as interrogatives in Goth *han* 'when', Baltic (e.g. OPrus *kan* 'when'), OCS *ko-gda* 'when', Alb *kë* 'when', and Av *kəm* 'how'. Another expression for 'when' was *k^w*odé*h_a which can be found in Baltic (Lith *kadà* 'when') and Indo-Iranian (Av *kaδa* 'when', Skt *kadā́* 'when').

The spatial interrogative *k^w*ór* 'where' is attested in OLat *quōr* 'why, wherefore', Germanic (e.g. OE *hwǣr* 'where' [> NE *where*]), and Skt *kárhi* 'when, at what time'. There is also *k^w*u* ~ *k^w*ū́* 'where' seen in Celtic (e.g. OIr *co* 'how; where'), Lat *ubi* 'where' (the unexpected loss of the labiovelar in Latin for PIE *k^w*u* is explained by false analysis, i.e. old compounds such as *nē-cubi* 'so that nowhere' were falsely split *nēc-ubi* [negation – where]), Baltic (e.g. OPrus *quei* 'where'), OCS *kŭde* 'where', Alb *kush* 'who', Grk *pu-* 'where', Hit *kuwapi* 'where', Indo-Iranian (e.g. Skt *kū́* 'where'), and Tocharian (e.g. Toch B *$k_u$se* 'who'); from an extended form *k^w*úr* we have Lith *kur̃* 'where', Alb *kur* 'where', and Arm *ur* 'where'.

There are variable forms attesting a PIE *k^w*óti* ~ *k^w*éti* 'how much/many'. The first underlies Lat *quot* 'how many', Grk *pósos* 'how much, how many', and Skt *káti* 'how much, how many' while the latter gives us Bret *pet der* 'how many days' and Av *čaiti* 'how many'. Finally, *k^w*oi*h_x*os* 'pertaining to whom/what' is limited to Lat *cūius* 'whose', and Grk *poîos* 'of what kind'.

There are a few regional terms. From the North-West we may have *k^w*e*h_a*k-* 'of what sort' seen in Celtic (OIr *cāch* 'everyone'), Baltic (Lith *kók(i)s* 'of what sort; any, some; whatever [relative]'), and Slavic (OCS *kakŭ* 'of what sort'). From the West Central region we have *k^w*e*h_a*li* 'of what sort, of what size' seen in Lat *quālis* 'of what sort, of what kind', Baltic (Lith *kõlei* 'how long'), Grk *pēlíkos* 'how old, how large', and from a form *k^w*oli* we have OCS *kolikŭ* 'how large', *kolĭ* 'how much'. There is also a Latin (*quam* 'how, in what way; as')-Armenian (Arm *k'an* 'as', *k'cani* 'how many?') isogloss (*k^w*e*h_a*m*).

24.4 Relative Pronouns

Although interrogative pronouns could develop a relative meaning in the later Indo-European languages (e.g. *Who* ate the apple? It was John *who* ate the apple), the PIE relative was formed on **yo-* with the same suffixes we have already seen in the demonstrative and interrogative pronouns. There are fewer true relatives reconstructable than interrogatives and a number are solely attested in Greek and Indo-Iranian. These are listed in Table 24.4.

The set **yós/*yéh*$_a$*/*yód* is also attested in Celtic (e.g. Gaul *dugiionti-io* 'who serve') and as a suffix in Baltic (e.g. Lith *geràs-is* 'good') and Slavic (e.g. OCS *dobrŭ-jĭ* 'kind, good'). The other **yo-* examples are represented solely by Greek (*hós/hḗ/hó* 'who, what, that') and Indo-Iranian (e.g. Skt *yás/yā́/yád* 'who, what, that'), although their correlative interrogatives and demonstratives may be better attested, e.g. although **yóti* 'as much' lacks any other European examples than Greek, both **k*^{w}*óti* 'how much' and **tóti* 'so much' are also preserved in Latin. Outside this 'system' is another interrogative or relative particle, **me/o-*, which is attested in Celtic (Bret *ma* ~ *may* 'that'), Anatolian (Hit *masi* 'how much'), and Tocharian (Toch A *mänt* 'how').

All other relatives, although clearly part of the same system of suffixes found elsewhere, only survive (or were created?) in Greek and Indo-Iranian. They include **yoteros* 'which of the two' seen in Doric Grk *óteros* 'which of the two', Av *yatāra-* 'which of the two', Skt *yatará-* 'which of the two'; **yóti* 'as much, as many': Grk *hósos* 'as many', Skt *yáti* 'as many as, as often as'; and **yéh*$_a$*wot(s)* 'as many, as long' seen in Grk *héōs* 'as long as', and Skt *yāvat* 'as much, as many; as great, as large; as often, as far'.

24.5 Conjunctions

Such frequent particles of speech as conjunctions have survived reasonably well in the IE languages and are listed below in Table 24.5.

PIE 'and' is attested primarily as an enclitic, i.e. a word attached to or following another word, e.g. the familiar (to any student who survived their first day of Vergil) Latin *arma virumque* 'arms man-and', i.e. 'the arms and the man'. This pattern is evident in both the use of **-k*^{w}*e* 'and' seen in Celtic (e.g.

Table 24.4. *Relative pronouns*

**yós/*yéh*$_a$*/*yód*	'who, what, that'	Grk *hós/hḗ/ho*, Skt *yás/yā́/yád*
**me/o-*	(interrogative/relative)	

Table 24.5. *Conjunctions*

*-k^we	'and'	Lat *-que*, Grk *te*, Hit *-ki*, Skt *ca*
*-yo	'and'	Hit *-ya-*
*$h_1$eti	'and, in addition'	Lat *et*, Grk *héti*, Skt *áti*
*ar	'and, thus'	Grk *ára*
*it-	'thus'	Lat *ita*, Skt *íti*
*ne	'thus'	Lat *nē*, Grk *tóne*, Skt *ná*
*-wē	'or'	Lat *-ve*, Grk *hē-(w)é*, Skt *vā*
*ne	'not'	Lat *ne-fās*, NE *no*, Hit *natta*, Skt *ná*
*mē	'not'	Grk *mḗ*, Skt *mā*

OIr *na-ch* 'not'), Lat *-que* 'and', Germanic (Goth *-h*), Mycenaean Grk *-qe* (Grk *te* 'and'), Arm *-k'* 'and', Hit *-ki* 'and', and Indo-Iranian (e.g. Skt *ca* 'and') and **-yo* 'and' seen in Myc *jo-* 'and', Hit *-ya-* 'and', and Toch A *-yo* 'with'. There is, however, also the word **$h_1$eti* that might convey 'and' as well as 'further, yet' (Gaulish *eti* 'also, further', Lat *et* 'and also', Goth *iþ* 'but', Grk *éti* 'yet, further') or, in Indo-Iranian, 'over' (Skt *áti* 'over, towards'), and **ar* which can indicate 'and, also' in Baltic (e.g. OPrus *ir* 'and, also') and Prākrit (*ira* 'and') but 'now, thus' in Greek *ára*. Other words for 'thus' are found as **it-* with cognates in Celtic (MWels *yt-* [preverb]), Lat *ita* 'thus', Baltic (Lith *ìt* 'very'), and Skt *íti* 'thus', and *nē* which can mean 'as, thus' in Baltic (e.g. Lith *ne*), Slavic (e.g. OCS *neže*), Grk *tóne*, 'like' in Skt *ná*, and appears as an interrogative particle in both Latin (*nē*) and Germanic (e.g. OHG *ne*). The meaning 'or' is universal across the descendants of **-wē* in Celtic (OIr *nō*), Lat *-ve*, Grk *ē-(w)é*, Indo-Iranian (e.g. Skt *vā*), and Tocharian (Toch B *wat*).

There are two negatives, **ne* and **mē*. The first, which is very widely attested in a variety of negative forms, e.g. both 'no, not' and 'un-', appears to be the usual form for expressing negation (e.g. Lat *nōn*, OE *ne*, Lith *ne*, OCS *ne*, Hit *natta*, Skt *ná*), and in a phonologically reduced form **n̥-*, it appears as the ubiquitous Indo-European prefix of negation (e.g. Lat *in-*, Gmc *un-*, Grk-Av-Skt *a-*). On the other hand, **mē*, which does not appear in the North-West, appears to have been employed in marking a prohibition and is attested in Alb *mos*, Grk *mḗ*, Arm *mi*, Skt *mā*, Toch B *mā*, all 'not'.

Further Reading

The Indo-European pronouns have been surveyed in Schmidt (1978) and Katz (2003).

25

Comparative Mythology

25.0 Reconstructing Mythologies

As we have seen in Chapter 23, the reconstructed vocabulary pertaining to religion is somewhat limited, certainly when compared with various other semantic categories such as flora, fauna, and material culture. The problems of reconstructing the names of the deities and other mythological concepts are several.

First, there is the problem of recovering the proper names of deities in the proto-language as they would appear to be highly susceptible to attrition and innovation, as anyone who has ever compared lists of popular given names through time can observe. Moreover, deities, by their very nature, frequently attract numerous epithets or by-names, e.g. 'lord', 'deliverer', 'almighty'; as these will suffer differential survival among sister groups or replace existing names, references to what were once the same deity may well be lost over time.

Second, we have the problematical context of our sources. Most of the evidence from European traditions, e.g. Celtic, Germanic, Baltic, Slavic, provides us evidence only after it has been 'sieved' through a Christian filter (or, in the case of Gaulish, a Roman filter). Other traditions such as Anatolian have clearly crossed with local religious traditions, e.g. Hattic, Hurrian, or in the case of Greek religion, we suspect major interference from an unknown substrate and Near Eastern adstrates. Greek mythology then impacted heavily on Roman myth which, some would argue, went underground into early Roman history. Excluding those traditions which are poorly known or obviously intermixed with non-Indo-European traditions, this leaves only Indo-Iranian mythology, and yet we know that Iranian religion passed through a major religious restructuring under Zarathustra. The assumption that Indo-Aryan mythology as espoused in the Vedas is 'pure' is just that—an assumption—and we might recall that the three main deities worshipped by Hindus, Vishnu, Śiva, and Śākti, were very much minor deities of the *R̥gveda* where most hymns are dedicated to Indra, Agni, and Soma. So there is no assurance that even the earliest Indic religious traditions that we can recover in the Vedas represent something that can be projected back into distant antiquity.

All previous reconstruction of Indo-European semantic categories has relied exclusively on the actual evidence of language. We have not attempted (nor regarded it as a valid approach) to compare, for example, weapons across the Indo-European world to 'reconstruct' the armament of the Proto-Indo-Europeans. Nor would we feel on particularly solid ground examining the comparative evidence for political systems, settlement patterns, or economic strategies as a route to the Proto-Indo-European past. All of these are so heavily influenced by their contemporary environments that it would be nearly impossible to distinguish between what was old and inherited and what was the product of the existing state of technology or the natural environment. Yet the desire to compare mythological systems, irrespective of whether they offer comparable lexical matches between different Indo-European groups, has been sufficient to generate an entire academic discipline—comparative mythology.

The premisses and purposes of comparative mythology vary considerably. Already by the early eighteenth century it was possible to discern striking similarities between some Greek myths and those of some Native American tribes. The reasons for such similarities vary from one school of thought to the next and none is mutually exclusive, i.e. there is no single 'right way' to examine mythology and each approach has something to recommend itself. We will briefly review the major approaches to Indo-European mythology below but first it is useful to describe the three types of results that scholars may uncover when comparing the mythologies of different traditions or languages.

25.0.1 Search for Universals

Some examine mythological systems for universal motifs that might develop independently in different regions throughout the world, e.g. the widespread human tendency to distinguish between four directions and attribute to each a different symbolism, colour, or role in their society or the tendency to associate a cluster of social or gender concepts with the distinction between left and right, e.g. right = male, strong while left = female, weak. Warrior and fertility deities can be found in Europe, Asia, Africa, and the New World. If there is a highly developed metallurgical technology, we often find smith gods. In reviewing the mythologies of the various Indo-European traditions there will always remain a problem in discerning between that which is generic (the tendency for war gods to also double as weather gods, employing bolts of lightning as their weapon) and what may be evidence for a historical connection. Indo-European is just as much (or little) a repository of such widespread beliefs as any other tradition and is often mined for elucidating universal motifs.

25.0.2 Search for Historical Origins

While some myths may well reflect universals, sometimes the correspondence strikes researchers as so close that it seems to require a historical explanation. For example, the Greek myth that a widowed husband (Orpheus) journeys to the Otherworld to retrieve his dead wife can also be found in North America. If one believes that this correspondence is too close and too unusual to be a product of some 'universal', then some form of historical connection is sought. Folklorists have sought and traced the origins of many folktales that have travelled widely across the globe, and mythology, especially when repackaged (some would say 'debased') to a folk narrative, can make the same journey. In some cases, we must be particularly on our guard since we know of historical connections, either between different traditions in general or between the class of society that was likely to preserve and reshape the mythological record. The Romans obviously appreciated, adopted, and reworked Greek mythology, and the Greeks in turn were exposed to the mythologies of non-IE Near East civilizations, and also that of their perennial enemies but linguistic cousins, the Iranians. And for those whose mythology has come through a Christian prism, we may find examples where native tradition has been restructured to satisfy a biblical framework, e.g. in Irish learned tradition the first settler in Ireland was the granddaughter of Noah while the Germans sought their ancestor in Ashkenaz, the grandson of Noah.

25.0.3 *Search for Genetic Connections*

If the similarities are so great that one is forced to assume some connection between two traditions, then we may be dealing with a common genetic origin rather than some historical contact. In this case, the family tree of a linguistic group provides a rough proxy of the group's mythological evolution as well. If the names of the deities can be reconstructed to Proto-Indo-European, then surely there may also be traces of the mythology, the sacred narratives, surrounding the deities. The problem here is that the hard lexical evidence, the names of Proto-Indo-European deities that we have reviewed in Chapter 23, is not particularly abundant nor do they provide much in the way of comparable narratives. From the standpoint of a comparative mythologist, we should not be limited to studying only those deities that offer a lexical correspondence but also examine the broad pattern of characteristics associated with the different deities and narratives concerning them to recover what we can of the ancestral Proto-Indo-European myth from which they are derived. In the end, we may not know the name of the deities but we will be able to recover something of their career, their abilities and function within Proto-Indo-European mythology. This approach is not unique to Indo-European and can be undertaken with any language family.

Finally, the actual sources to reconstruct a Proto-Indo-European mythology vary greatly among the different Indo-European traditions. India offers a vast literature and its hymns and rituals as described in the Vedas provide one of the fundamental sources of Indo-European mythology. In addition, its major epic literature, especially the *Mahābhārata*, provides abundant reworking of mythic elements, and offers further evidence of Indo-Aryan mythology. The reconstruction of Proto-Indo-Iranian religion is hampered by the much smaller residue of Iranian mythology and the fact that it has largely passed through Zarathustra's religious revolution before our earliest texts. It still provides us with some lexical and thematic evidence of the Indo-Iranian pantheon in either different guises (names) or altered characters, e.g. there was a systematic demonization of a number of earlier Indo-Iranian divinities.

Although Greek mythology is often regarded as 'The Mythology', it does not serve this function in Indo-European comparative studies. There appear to be far too many aspects that are more easily explained as the product of extraneous influences, either substrates or adstrates, e.g. the goddess Aphrodite was 'borrowed' from the Near East, and far too little that is directly comparable with other Indo-European mythologies. Here again, epic literature, particularly the works of Homer, can be pressed into comparative service. Although Greek mythology was adopted by the Romans and reworked in primarily literary creations of Virgil and Ovid, original Roman mythology was reinterpreted by the Romans as history and comparativists have been able to use that 'history' as a mainstream of inherited Indo-European mythology. This history, coupled with Roman ritual, provides one of the major props of Indo-European comparative mythology.

In western Europe, Germanic, more specifically Norse, mythology provides a third major source of comparanda. Here we have both works that are explicitly of a mythological nature (the Norse Eddas) and material which probably houses mythic residues (the sagas). To a lesser extent, Celtic offers similar evidence in its tales of the Irish mythological cycle and in the heroic literature of both Ireland and Wales.

The sources of mythology for eastern Europe are much poorer. Much of it consists of the accounts of Christians who wrote of the customs of their pagan neighbours, or snippets that have survived in native folk poetry, e.g. Lithuanian folk songs, or early historical sources, e.g. Russian chronicles. Recent work has also exploited the Armenian epic literature for its mythological residue. Among the poorest sources are Anatolian which has derived so much of its mythology and ritual from its non-Indo-European neighbours and Tocharian whose attested religious content is essentially limited to Buddhism.

25.1 Approaches to Mythology

How one approaches the sacred narrative itself that comprises mythology has varied through time, and from which discipline one comes from to study mythology. The following approaches are the main ones that have been employed to unravel the 'meaning' of Indo-European myths.

25.1.1 Meteorological School

The meteorological (also naturist or solar) school emphasizes natural phenomena as a key to understanding mythology. We have already seen that PIE **deiwós* 'god' derives from the same root (**dyeu-*) that gives us 'sky, day'. To this we can add the similarly derived **dyḗus ph̥ₐtḗr* 'father sky' (at the apex of both Greek and Roman mythology and present in Indic) as well as a **dhuĝh̥ₐtḗr diwós* 'sky daughter' which appears to be an ancient epithet for the 'dawn' (*$h_a$éusōs*), who is deified (we have cognates in India, Greece, Italy, and the Baltic). A solar (female) deity may also be tentatively reconstructed. Some would accept a PIE **perk^{w}unos* as a 'thunder god'. A 'mother earth' is confined

Table 25.1. *The three heavens of the Indo-Europeans after J. Haudry*

Day	Celestial	white
Dawn/twilight	Bridging	red
Night	Night spirits	dark

to east European languages (Baltic, Slavic, Thracian, Phrygian). To these we might add *$*h_4(e)\underset{\circ}{l}bh$-* 'elf' on the basis of Germanic and Sanskrit, a word which apparently derives from *$*h_4elbhós$* 'white', hence the 'shining ones' who, in Vedic tradition, are associated with the New Year. Clearly there is some evidence then for the deification of natural phenomena but the associated narratives that we might expect concerning such deities are extremely meagre and largely limited to their cosmic function. The Dawn, for example, is portrayed in several traditions as a reluctant bringer of day who was punished for her delay in bringing light. The major recent attempts to employ a largely meteorological approach to Indo-European mythology can be found in the works of Jean Haudry who suggests that the Proto-Indo-European cosmos consisted of three 'heavens' along the lines indicated in Table 25.1.

The problem with the meteorological approach is that it is extremely limited: if we get little enough narrative out of the nature divinities that we can reconstruct lexically, it is extremely unlikely that we are going to be able to do much with the vast amount of mythic narrative where meteorological divinities are not apparent. For some, any god that was described as 'shining' or 'bright' was a manifestation of the sun god and every action undertaken by the deity could then be interpreted as the course of the sun through the day or the year. The meteorological school has largely been replaced by other approaches that do not attempt to reduce all deities into natural phenomena.

25.1.2 Ritual School

This school argues that myths are best understood in the context of the rituals which they are employed to explain. If one accepts that the ancient Indo-Europeans made sacrifice to their deities to maintain fertility, order, or to deliver specific services such as wealth or protection, then we may expect a body of mythology to explain how such rituals came into being or what the specific acts of the ritual are meant to represent. For example, Bruce Lincoln has written on the fundamental relationship between the sacrifice of animals in early Indo-European society and the cosmogonic myth that explains the creation of the world from a single sacrifice (see below). In this way, every sacrifice is a re-enactment of the original sacrifice (cf. the Christian concept of communion as a re-enactment of the Last Supper and subsequent sacrifice).

25.1.3 Functionalist School

From the perspective of a functionalist, such as the great anthropologist Emile Durkheim (1858–1917), religion was 'society personified' and the various deities were collective representations of the different classes of society. When one considers the various pantheons of the different Indo-European traditions, we find an assortment of deities who broadly fill out the social roles of the (archaic) societies that worshipped them. The palace intrigues of Near Eastern and Aegean pantheons mirror the social structure of the palace society that created them; these may be contrasted with the Norse pantheon which reflects the warband mentality of the early Germanic peoples. The Christian tradition with its 'Good Shepherd', 'Lamb of God', and church pastors (< Lat *pastor* 'shepherd') provides useful hints of its roots in the pastoral culture of the ancient Jews.

A comparison of social institutions among the different Indo-European traditions from India to western Europe reveals a recurrent pattern of three social 'estates': priests, warriors, and herder-cultivators (Table 25.2), a socio-ideological system that continued into the Middle Ages where we find the same system of *oratores, bellatores*, and *laboratores*, and if one wishes to push it to extreme lengths, to the ideology of the American government which has a judiciary (priests), executive (warriors, e.g. 'Commander-in-chief'), and a Congress ([the representatives of the] assembled masses).

Can these three culturally widespread 'estates' be reconstructed to Proto-Indo-European society? Certainly not, at least on the basis of purely lexical evidence, and even if we could show broad sets of cognates for each 'estate', we would still be hard pressed to define what precisely these different 'estates' actually represented in Proto-Indo-European society. Given what we might

Table 25.2. *Indo-European social classes*

Classes	India (castes)	Iran	Greece (Athens)	Gaul (from Caesar)
priest	*brahman*	*āθravan-*	*hieropoioi*	*druides*
warrior	*kṣatriya*	*raθaēštar*	*phulakes*	*equites*
herder-cult.	*vaiśya*	*vastryō fšuyant-*	*georgoi*	*plēbēs*

expect from their level of socio-economic complexity, it is unlikely that the Proto-Indo-Europeans would have had hard and fast 'classes' such as are found in historical India into which one was born and remained through one's life. Rather, we might expect that these represented general organizing principles or, as Georges Dumézil (1898-1986), the leading exponent of the functional approach to Indo-European mythology, described them, *fonctions*.

Dumézil argued that an analysis of the mythology of the different Indo-European traditions revealed an underlying tripartite structure that constantly replicated or emphasized the three Indo-European 'functions'. This structure could be revealed by the sequence in which the appropriate deities might be mentioned, e.g. the Mitanni treaty lists the Indo-Aryan gods Mitra and Varuna (often joined together in the *R̥gveda* and associated with priests), Indra (the war god), and the Nasatya (twins associated with the lower orders). In Greek tradition we find three deities, each associated with a different divine sphere, offering bribes to Paris: Hera offered kingship, Athena offered military victory, and Aphrodite promised the love of the most beautiful woman, arguably a reference to fertility. As Dumézil argued, the Roman equivalents were reinterpreted as history rather than mythology. This is reflected in Livy's account of the first Roman kings where Romulus and Numa appear to fill the function of priests, Tullus Hostilius excelled as a warrior, and Ancus Martius undertook the type of public works projects that might assign him to the third function.

Over decades of research, Dumézil's system was refined by both himself and others. The first function, rulership, was divided into two different aspects which, according to Dumézil, tended to be represented by two different deities in various Indo-European traditions. In Vedic tradition sovereignty is held by two deities, Varuna and Mitra, which reflected the priestly and juridical aspects of kingship (Mitra was 'contract' personified). Other 'Varunaic' deities include the Roman Jūpiter (revealing that the lexical reflex of the sky god may have a specific function), and Germanic Oðinn while the Mitraic equivalents are Dius Fidius and Tyr respectively.

A number of scholars have proposed an additional fourth function. In some cases this is motivated by explicit statements that indicate an ancient fourth or artisan class division of early Indo-European societies; in other cases a fourth element derives from the practice of quartering mythic landscapes, each of the cardinal directions serving to indicate a single social function, as was the case in early Ireland. For N. Allen, the Fourth Function is the one set outside the other three, an alien otherness that must be incorporated into the mythic scheme, while E. Lyle suggests that an essentially female function was juxtaposed against the other three primarily male-oriented functions.

25.1.4 Structuralist School

The structuralist approach analyses mythology (and phenomena in general) in terms of binary oppositions, e.g. left–right, male–female, black–white. Derived from the structural school in linguistics, this approach was developed by Claude Lévi-Strauss (1908–) for anthropology. It fundamentally argues that the organization of binary opposites is a basic property of the human mind and how we view the world around us. Its application to mythology, which is itself a product of the human attempt to understand our universe, is understandable although its product tends to reflect an approach to mythology that emphasizes universals rather than genetic connections. Nevertheless, refinements of the Dumézilian system which distinguish between opposites within the same function, e.g. the protective but also destructive aspects of the Second Function, indicate where a structural approach may also be useful.

25.2 Deities

Below are summarized the names or types of deities that have generally been reconstructed to Proto-Indo-European as we have seen in Section 23.1. It should be emphasized that the proto-categories are perhaps more abstract that their single name might suggest, i.e. what is meant by a war god may have actually included a number of different deities within the earlier system. In some cases we may find the same individual under two different names, e.g. 'sky daughter' and 'dawn' would appear to be the same deity. In other cases, a single deity from one of the Indo-European traditions may be included under a number of different headings. Just as a screenwriter when working from a literary source will routinely collapse different characters into a single individual to have a manageable cast for his script, so also did the different Indo-European groups juggle with their deities to fill out sometimes multiple roles, e.g. the use of the sky god in Greece and Rome to fulfil roles of the thunder god, war god, and others.

Sky god (**dyḗus ph̥ₐtḗr*). The sky god or 'father sky' is lexically the most secure deity and heads the pantheons of Greece and Rome but apparently receded in importance in Indic tradition to a vague ancestral figure. Here the equivalencies involve either lexical cognates: Skt (Vedic) *dyáuṣ pitā́* = Grk *Zeùs patḗr* = Lat *Jūpiter* = Illyrian *Dei-pátrous* or semantic cognates where there has been replacement of the lexical elements but a retention of the underlying meaning, e.g. Hit *attas Isanus* 'father sun god', Latv *Dievs, Debess tēvs* 'god, father of heaven', and possibly Russian *Stribogŭ* 'father god'. Other than ruling in respective pantheons, and serving as father to several other Indo-European deities, the sky god is also seen (at least in some traditions) to unite with 'mother earth'. A potential functional (though not lexical) correspondence includes the Norse ancestral deity *Heimdalr*.

Sky daughter (**dhuĝh̥ₐtḗr diwós*). The existence of a 'sky daughter', who is also identified as the 'dawn', is supported by the lexical correspondences of Skt *duhitā́ diváh*, Grk *thugátēr Diós*, and Lith *diẽvo duktė̃*.

Dawn goddess (**hₐéusōs*). Identified with the 'sky daughter', the Proto-Indo-European word for 'dawn' is deified in a number of Indo-European traditions: Skt *Uṣā́s-* = Grk *Eōs* = Lat *Aurōra* = Lith *Aušrine*.

Divine twins. There is no convincing lexical set for these 'sons of the sky god' but they are abundantly represented at every level (myth, history, folklore) in the various Indo-European traditions. Here we find the regular association between the two sons of the sky god, depicted as young men and closely associated with horses (or in some case they are represented as horses, e.g. the Greek Kastōr and Polydeukēs, possibly the Anglo-Saxon Hengist and Horsa, the Welsh Bran and Manywydan), who share a sister or consort (Greek Helenēs, Welsh Branwen) who is the daughter of the sun or sky god. Their origin has been sought in a meteorological explanation: the divine twins are the steeds who pull the sun across the sky and by the Bronze Age we find representations of solar chariots. The twin brothers are often differentiated: one is represented as a young warrior while the other is seen as a healer or concerned with domestic duties. Collectively, they are identified as follows: Skt *Aśvin* ~ *Nasatya* = Av *Nāŋhaithya* ~ Grk *Dioskuri* ~ Latv *Dievo suneliai*.

First Function (*juridical*). This marks a deity type who fills out the first (sovereign) function in its juridical aspect, i.e. a deity that oversees the relations between humans and guarantees pacts. Within the various Indo-European pantheons the standard equivalencies are given as: Skt (Vedic) Mitra ~ Skt (*Mahābhārata*) Yudhiṣṭhira ~ Av Mithra ~ Lat Dius Fidius ~ Lat (Livy's history of Rome) Numa Pompilius ~ Lat (Livy) Mucius Scaevola ~ ON Tyr ~ OIr Núadu. The Sanskrit and Iranian evidence indicates a Proto-Indo-Iranian **Mitra*. There is evidence from the Roman and Germanic traditions of a critical false-swearing by this deity who protects oaths with a consequent loss of the left arm. Irish tradition does not offer the motif of a false oath but the equivalent character (Núadu) does lose his arm in battle.

First Function (*sacred*). This deity is primarily in charge of the relationship between humans and sacred order. The equivalencies are Skt (Vedic) Varuna ~ Skt (*Mahābhārata*) Pāṇḍu ~ Av Ahura Mazdāh ~ Lat (Livy) Romulus ~ Lat (Livy) Horatio Cocles ~ ON Oðinn ~ OIr Esus ~ Lith Velinas. Both the Roman Horatio Cocles and the Norse Oðinn are closely associated with the loss of one eye.

Second Function (*warfare*). One cannot retrieve a single name of a Proto-Indo-European war god. A proposed lexical correspondence (that would yield a PIE **māwort-*) between the names of the Latin war god *Mārs* and the Skt *Marutás* is doubtful; the latter are companions of the war god Indra. Rather we have, with the exception of Indo-Iranian, a series of differently named war gods: Skt Indra ~ Skt (*Mahābhārata*) Arjuna ~ Av Indara ~ Lat Mārs ~ Lat (Livy) Tullus ~ ON Thōrr ~ Gaul Taranis ~ OIr Ogma.

The second function can also be viewed in terms of two aspectually contrasting warrior functions—: defensive (good) and offensive (wild, destructive to the community itself)—and this opposition is seen to be played out among some of the pantheons. The more destructive manifestations are seen in the following correspondences: Skt (Vedic) Vāyu (a storm god) ~ Skt (*Mahābhārata*) Bhīma ~ Av Vayu.

Thunder god (**perk^{w}unos*). The lexical set consists of ON *Fjǫrgyn*, Lith *Perkū́nas*, ORus *Perúnŭ*, and perhaps Skt *Parjányа*. The underlying root is probably **per-* 'strike' with different extensions built in different groups. The North-West European set is relatively coherent with associations with the thunder god (*Fjǫrgyn* was the mother of the Norse thunder god Thōrr), hurling lightning, use of the club both in battle but also as a fertility symbol at weddings. The association of the North-Western deities with the Sanskrit deity is not so clear, although the latter is depicted as a rain god in the Vedas.

Third Function. No lexical correspondence here but rather a series of gods who find themselves third in canonical order of deities and who are associated with fertility. These may especially include the divine twins but also single deities such as Lat Quirinus or ON Freyr, Gaul Teutates and OIr Bres.

Transfunctional goddess. There is no lexical evidence for such a deity but the different Indo-European traditions are replete with examples of goddesses whose qualities either comprise or dispense the three functional categories. Such goddesses may be provided with a trifunctional epithet, e.g. the name of the Iranian goddess Arədvi Sūra Anāhitā may be rendered 'moist, strong, and pure' just as Athena is showered with the epithets *pólias*, *nikē*, and *hugíea* 'protectress, victory, well-being' and Juno is *Seispes Māter Regīna* 'safe, mother, queen', in all cases—although not necessarily in canonical order—words suggesting the three Dumézilian functions. We have already seen how the three functions may also be split among three associated goddesses, e.g. the Greek judgement of Paris where Hera promises rulership, Athena military victory and Aphrodite offers the love of the most beautiful woman, or the three semi-divine Machas of early Irish literature.

Aryan god (**h$_4$erós*). A deity in charge of welfare is indicated by a number of lexical correspondences (Skt *Aryaman*, Av *airyaman*, Gaul *Ariomanus*, OIr *Eremon*, and non-cognate functional correspondences, e.g. Vidura in the

Mahābhārata. The Aryaman-type deity is associated with the building and maintenance of roads or pathways, with healing, especially involving a ritual where cattle urine or milk is poured in a furrow, and the institution of marriage. In this sense he is seen as a 'helper' to the First Function deity of the Mitra type.

In addition to these there are a number of deities that have been proposed either on the basis of limited isoglosses (Greek-Sanskrit) or on questionable linguistic evidence.

Pastoral god (**péh₂usōn*). Primarily a Greek (*Pā̃n*)-Sanskrit (*Pūṣā́*) correspondence, possibly from **peh₂-* 'protect, feed (cattle)'. Both deities are pastoral gods and are closely associated with goats. In Greek mythology some of Pan's original characteristics may also have been assimilated by his father Hermes.

Medical god. Both the Indic god Rudra and Greek Apollo inflict disease from afar by their bows and are also known as healers; both are also associated specifically with rodents, Rudra's animal being the '(rat) mole' and Apollo was also known as *Smintheus* 'rat god'.

Decay goddess. This is based on an Indic-Latin isogloss where both traditions indicate a goddess (Skt Nírr̥ti-, Lat Lūa Mater) whose names derive from verbal roots 'decay, rot' and are associated with the decomposition of the human body.

Wild god (**rudlos*). The only certain deity by this name is the Skt *Rudrá-* although there is an ORus *Rŭglŭ* (name of a deity) that might be cognate. Problematic is whether the name derives from **reud-* 'rend, tear apart' as Lat *rullus* 'rustic' or from the root for 'howl'.

River goddess (**deh$_a$nu-*). This is largely a lexical correspondence, e.g. Skt *Dānu*, whose son holds back the heavenly waters, and Irish *Danu*, Wels *Dôn*, both ancestor figures. The same root underlies the names of many of Europe's larger rivers, including the Danube, Don, Dnieper, and Dniester (the latter three as Iranian loans). Other than the deification of the concept of 'river' in Indic tradition, there is really no evidence for a specific river goddess.

Sea god (**trih$_a$tōn*). Even more doubtful is the Celtic-Greek possible correspondence between OIr *trïath* 'sea' and the Greek sea god *Trī́tōn*, the son of Poseidōn. The lexical correspondence is only just possible and with no evidence of a cognate sea god in Irish (there are other sea deities but these are not lexically cognate), there is really no certain evidence of a god of the sea.

Smith god (**wl̥kānos/*wl̥keh$_a$nos*). This is based on a linguistically doubtful comparison of the name of the Latin smith god *Volcānus* and the Ossetic smith god *wærgon*. The problem here lies in the etymology of the Latin name which may be derived from Etruscan or an Aegean loanword. There are no mythological elements, other than those generic to most smith gods, that might unite the Latin and Iranian deities.

25.3 Creation

Although the various Indo-European groups exhibit different creation myths, there appear to be elements of a Proto-Indo-European creation myth preserved either explicitly or as much altered resonances in the traditions of the Celts, Germans, Slavs, Iranians, and Indo-Aryans. These traditions all indicate a proto-myth whereby the universe is created from a primeval giant—either a cow such as the Norse Ymir or a 'man' such as the Vedic Puruṣa—who is sacrificed and dismembered, the various parts of his anatomy serving to provide a different element of nature. The usual associations are that his flesh becomes the earth, his hair grass, his bone yields stone, his blood water, his eyes the sun, his mind the moon, his brain the clouds, his breath the wind, and his head becomes the heavens. This body not only fills out the material world but the dismemberment also provides the social tiers with the head associated with the First (ruling) Function, the arms being equivalent with the warrior function, and the lower torso, with its sexual organs, the fertility function.

As to the identity of the sacrificer we have hints in a related sacrifice that serves as the foundation myth for the Indo-Iranians, Germans, and Romans (with a possible resonance in Celtic). Here we find two beings, twins, one known as 'Man' (with a lexical cognate between Germanic *Mannus* and Skt *Manu*) and his 'Twin' (Germanic *Twisto*, Skt *Yama* with a possible Latin cognate if *Remus*, the brother of Romulus, is derived from **Yemonos* 'twin'). In this myth 'Man', the ancestor of humankind, sacrifices his 'Twin'. The two myths, creation and foundation of a people, find a lexical overlap in the Norse myth where the giant *Ymir* is cognate with Skt *Yama* and also means 'Twin'.

The dismemberment of the primeval giant of the creation myth can be reversed to explain the origins of humans and we find various traditions that derive the various aspects of the human anatomy from the results of the original dismemberment, e.g. grass becomes hair, wind becomes breath.

The creation myth is then essentially a sacrifice that brought about the different elements of the world. Conversely, as Bruce Lincoln has suggested, the act of sacrifice itself is a re-enactment of the original creation. There is evidence in various Indo-European traditions, e.g. Rome, India, that the parts of the sacrificed animal were dispersed according to the prevailing social patterns and, therefore, we may view the act of sacrifice as an attempt to restore the balance of the world. This same notion may be carried also into the burial ritual of at least some of the Indo-European traditions where it was imagined that the deceased disintegrated back into its constituent parts, e.g. in the *R̥gveda*, the eye of the deceased goes back to the sun, his breath to the wind. In a sense then, after the initial creation, life is essentially recycled.

25.4 War of the Foundation

This myth is attested primarily on the basis of Germanic (Norse) and Roman sources but elements of it have also been claimed for Greek and Sanskrit. The myth depicts the forceful incorporation of Dumézil's Third (fertility) Function into a social world run by the first two functions. In Norse mythology, the myth is expressed as a war between the Æsir, the gods of the first two functions, led by Oðinn and Thōrr, against the Vanir who were led by the fertility gods Freyr, his sister Freya, and Njörðr. After a period of warfare the two sides conclude a pact of peace with the three fertility deities coming to live among the Æsir, thus providing representatives of all three functions within a single social group. The Roman parallel is found in the legend of Romulus who, finding Rome lacking in women (fecundity), wars with the Sabines. The Sabine women intercede and bring about peace between the two sides and, again, the incorporation of the Third Function into society. The Trojan War has also been interpreted in such light (the Greeks as the first two functions and the Trojans with Helen as the third). In Indic mythology, the Aśvins, representatives of the Third Function, find their way into the world of the other gods blocked by Indra until he is tricked into letting them in, thus securing a three-function society.

25.5 Hero and Serpent

One of the central myths of the Indo-Europeans involves the slaying of a serpent, often three-headed, by the archetypal hero, either deity or human. Calvert Watkins has argued that this deed has left some lexical evidence in the frozen expression *$(h_1e)g^w$*hént* $h_1$óg^{w}him* 'he killed the serpent', preserved as such in Indo-Iranian with lexical substitutions in Hittite, Greek, and Germanic. The association with three heads or some aspect of triplicity is indicated either by descriptions of the monster, e.g. the three-headed dog

Kérberos who guards the Greek Underworld, the name of the hero, e.g. the Skt *Trita Āptya*, or in some other aspect of triplicity, e.g. Horatio Cocles' defeat of three opponents in early Roman history. Bruce Lincoln has suggested that the context of this slaying is during the first cattle-raid where a monster runs off with the cattle of a hero whom he designates *Tritos 'the third' who then sets off in pursuit, accompanied by *H_anḗr 'Man', kills the serpent, and recovers his cattle. Traces of this myth are seen in Indo-Iranian, Hittite, Greek, and Norse traditions.

25.6 Horse Sacrifice

It is largely the residue of ritual rather than explicit myths that points to the existence of a specific association between the assumption of kingship and the ritual mating with and sacrifice of a horse. The Indic *aśvamedha*, an inauguration ceremony, and the Roman *Equus October* both involve the sacrifice of a horse either to a warrior deity or on behalf of the warrior class; the victim was a stallion that excelled on the right side of the chariot, and the victim was dismembered, different parts of the anatomy going to either different locations or functionally different deities. The medieval inauguration of an Irish king in County Donegal which involved the king-designate bathing in a cauldron with the dismembered pieces of a horse may also be a reflex. The underlying myth, particularly in Indic, suggests some form of mating between the king and the horse (mare), the latter of which behaves as a transfunctional goddess and passes to the king the gifts of the three functions that make up the totality of society.

25.7 King and Virgin

A recurrent theme, though not without considerable modifications (if genetically inherited) or differences, is that of a virgin rescuing a king which is found in Indic, Roman, Scandinavian, and Celtic sources. The basic structure involves a king whose future (including his descendants) is endangered because of his immediate male relatives (sons, uncle, etc.) but is allowed to prevail because of a virgin (often his daughter) who provides the offspring necessary to the king's survival. In the Indic tale, for example, King Yayāti is rescued by four sons born to his daughter (who mated with three kings and a teacher); in Roman tradition King Numitor's line is ensured by the birth of Romulus and Remus because his virgin daughter, Rhea Silvia, was made pregnant by Mārs.

25.8 Fire in Water

This mythic element is postulated on the basis of several disputed divine names and some general mythic elements found in several Indo-European traditions (Celtic, Italic, and Iranian). The lexical argument (Section 23.1) posits a PIE **neptonos* or **$h_2$epōm nepōts* 'grandson/nephew of waters' on the basis of Skt *Apā́m Nápāt*, Av *Apąm Napāt*, and much less securely OIr *Nechtain* and Lat *Neptūnus*. The myth itself depicts a divine being associated with fire who inhabits water (in the Celtic myth there is a sacred well of Nechtain whose fire burns out the eyes of those who approach it, in the *Avesta* the fiery power is the *xvarənah*, the burning essence of kingship, which was placed in Lake Vourusaka) and who can only be approached by someone especially designated for the task. Although there is no corresponding mythic evidence from Germanic, the ON kenning *sævar niðr* 'son of the sea', i.e. 'fire', may provide some linguistic support for the equation.

25.9 Functional Patterns

There are a number of patterns in Indo-European narratives that replicate the three functions. Among the more striking are the motifs known as the 'the sins of the warrior' and the 'threefold death'. The first motif deals with a representative of the Second Function whose downfall involves sins against all three functions, e.g. the Germanic Starkaðr slays a king (violation of the First Function), flees in battle as a coward (violating his Second Function as a warrior), and kills for money (a violation here taken to be against the third estate). Traces of this motif also occur in other Indo-European traditions, e.g. Greek where Hēraklēs manages three comparable sins or the *Mahābhārata* where Śiśupāla commits three similar sins.

The 'threefold death' associates a particular type of death with a particular function or functional deity. For example, classical sources indicate that among the Gauls victims dedicated to the First Function figure (Esus) were hanged; the Second Function (Taranis) received victims who had been burnt; and victims dedicated to the Third Function (Teutates) were drowned. The motif is also found in Germanic where the First Function deity, Oðinn, is known as the 'hanged god' while victims to the fertility (Third Function) deity Nerthus were drowned. These patterns are replicated in the heroic literatures of the Celtic and Germanic peoples although the motif is believed to have been more widespread. Essentially, it establishes a pattern of death which is directly associated with the three functions where the First receives hanging, the Second burning or bloodshed (by sword or other appropriately military weapon), and the Third Function victim is drowned.

25.10 Death and the Otherworld

There is an abundance of evidence for various beliefs concerning death and the afterlife in the different Indo-European traditions but ferreting out an original belief is difficult. Many Indo-European traditions portray death as a journey and in the case of Celtic, Germanic, and Greek, and to a lesser extent Slavic and Indic, this may involve a journey across a river where the deceased is ferried by a **ĝerh$_a$ont-* 'old man'. On this journey they may also encounter a dog who serves either as a guardian of the Otherworld or as a guide. Here we have some linguistic evidence in the cognate names of Greek *Kérberos*, the three-headed dog of Hades, and the Indic *Śárvara*, one of Yima's dogs, both deriving from a PIE **k̂érberos* 'spotted'. Both Greek and Indic traditions also have a river 'washing away' either memories or sins while Germanic and Celtic traditions attest a belief of wisdom-imparting waters; Bruce Lincoln has suggested that these two may be joined together where the memories of the deceased are washed away into a river but others, lucky enough, may drink of such water and gain inspiration. The actual afterlife is attested in so many different ways—as a pleasant meadow, a place of darkness, island, house, walled enclosure—that it is difficult to ascribe any particular belief to Proto-Indo-European. The ruler of the dead, however, may well be the sacrificed twin of the creation myth as suggested by Indo-Iranian tradition and to a lesser degree by Germanic.

25.11 Final Battle

Celtic, Italic, Germanic, Indo-Iranian, Armenian, and Greek all reveal traces of an Indo-European eschatological myth, i.e. a myth that describes the end of the world in terms of a cataclysmic battle, e.g. the Battle of Kurukshetra from the *Mahābhārata*, the Second Battle of Mag Tured in Irish tradition, Ragnarök in Norse tradition, the Battle of Lake Regillus in Roman history, Hesiod's Titanomachy, and the Plain of Ervandavan in Armenian history. In all these traditions the end comes in the form of a major battle in which gods (Norse, Greek), demi-gods (Irish), or major heroes (Roman, Indo-Aryan, Armenian) are slain. The story begins when the major foe, usually depicted as coming from a different (and inimical) paternal line, assumes the position of authority among the host of gods or heroes, e.g. Norse Loki, Roman Tarquin, Irish

Bres. In this position he exploits the labour of the protagonists until he is driven out and returns to his own people. A new leader then springs up among the protagonists (e.g. Irish Lug, Greek Zeus) often the **nepōt-* 'grandson' or 'nephew' of the deposed leader. The two sides then prepare for a major war (in Germanic and Iranian myth there is also a great winter) and the two forces come together and annihilate each other in a cataclysmic battle. Since a new order is called into existence after the battle, the myth may not be eschatological in the strict sense but rather represent a mythic encounter that brought a past golden age to an end.

25.12 Current Trends

Current trends in Indo-European comparative mythology are taking several directions. The evidence for trifunctional (or quadri-functional) patterns is continually being augmented by further examples both from well-researched sources, e.g. Indic, Roman, Norse, and from other traditions such as Greek and Armenian that have seen far less attention. Moreover, an increasing number of scholars have been examining the narrative structure of the earliest literary traditions of the various Indo-European groups to reveal striking parallels between different traditions. For example, N. B. Allen has shown how much of the career of the Greek Odysseus is paralleled by distinct incidents in the lives of Arjuna in the *Mahābhārata*, the Buddha in the earliest Buddhist texts, and CúChulainn in early Irish heroic literature. Other scholars such as Claude Sterckx, Stepan Ahyan, and Armen Petrosyan have uncovered detailed correspondences in other early Indo-European traditions. According to Allen, the close coincidences go beyond both the type of random generic parallels that one might expect between different literary traditions and beyond what we might ascribe to some form of distant diffusion. He argues that such comparisons provides us with at least some of the detritus of the Proto-Indo-European narrative tradition.

Further Reading

The best general treatise is Puhvel (1987*a*); for the core of Dumézil see Dumézil (1968–73) and Littleton (1973); cases for a 'Fourth Function' can be found in Allen (1987), Lyle (1990); the mythic structure of IE medicine is to be found in Benveniste (1945); the "three sins of the warrior" are the subject of Dumézil (1970); representative new approaches within the Dumézilian tradition that seek new patterns of underlying Indo-European narratives include Ahyan (1998), Allen (2000*a*, 2000*b*, 2002), Miller

(2000), Petrosyan (2002), Sterckx (1994); a different approach to IE mythology can be found in Haudry (1987). The topics of creation, sacrifice, death, and the Otherworld can be found in the various works of Lincoln (1980, 1981, 1986, 1991, 1995); various deities are discussed in Dexter (1996), Nagy (1974*a*), Watkins (1995); the divine twins are treated in Ward (1968), Lehmann (1988), Grottanelli (1986), Dubuisson (1992), and York (1995); the subject of sacred vocabulary is handled in York (1993); summaries of the eschatological model are found in O'Brien (1976) and more recently Bray (2000); death beliefs are in Puhvel (1969), Hansen (1980), and Lincoln (1980), while burial is discussed by Jones-Bley (1997).

26

Origins: The Never-Ending Story

26.1 The Homeland Problem

Sir William Jones had hardly postulated the existence of what we now term the Indo-European language family before he set future Indo-European studies its longest and most frustrating problem. In the same lecture (see Section 1.1) in which he described the relationship between the various ancient languages, he also remarked that in a future discourse he would attempt to follow them back to 'some central country'. In his later lectures he argued that the homeland lay in greater Iran. This assertion set off a legacy of debate in which homelands have been set anywhere from the North to the South Poles, from the Atlantic to the Pacific. Before we briefly review the different approaches and solutions to the homeland problem, we should ask ourselves whether this is even a legitimate problem.

Why must the Indo-European languages be derived from a smaller geographical area than that in which we find them when they begin to enter the historical record? Why couldn't they have always been there, at least since the time of *Homo sapiens sapiens?* This is indeed an argument made by a several scholars who locate the Indo-Europeans right across Europe from the beginning of the Upper Palaeolithic onwards, i.e. *c.* 40,000 years ago. The reasons for not making such an assumption are several.

First, from our initial historical records onwards we can see Indo-Europeans expanding centrifugally, at least beyond the periphery of their historical distribution (Maps 1.1, 1.3). Iberia maintains evidence of both prehistoric and current non-Indo-European populations, e.g. Basques, as does Italy (Etruscans). The Iranian language expanded south to absorb the earlier Elamite language of southern Iran and Indo-Aryan languages spread southwards and eastwards to absorb, at least partially, Munda and Dravidian languages. The Anatolian languages are so laced with loanwords from their non-Indo-European neighbours that languages such as Hittite are often seen as having been superimposed on a Hattic substrate.

Second, the reconstructed lexicon, no matter how narrow or broadly we interpret it, makes it abundantly clear that the proto-language possessed a mixed arable agriculture-stockbreeding economy, some metals, ceramic technology, and wheeled transport. As agriculture did not exist in either Europe or India prior to the seventh millennium, it is difficult to sustain an argument that the Indo-Europeans were scattered across Eurasia from the fortieth millennium BC onwards. As a cultural phenomenon, Proto-Indo-European cannot have begun disintegrating until it had already adopted a Neolithic economy and technology.

Third, the greater an area that we assign to a language (whatever continuum of dialects that we might imagine for Proto-Indo-European), the greater the opportunity for language divergence over time. In concrete terms, the larger the area that we imagine for the speakers of what we notionally reconstruct as a proto-language, the more rivers, mountains, seas, variation in economic strategies, social systems, contacts with non-Indo-European substrates, we must imagine contributing to linguistic diversity. While we cannot assign a one-to-one relationship between language change, time, and area, we do know that all of these features are factors. Conversely, if we find a single language over a large area we tend to presume a short period of time for its spread.

There have been periods of broad consensus, e.g. an Asian homeland was the favourite for much of the nineteenth century but a European homeland (where in Europe was another question altogether) has been the primary choice of most scholars since the early twentieth century. Now, the consensus is still probably European but there are a number of scholars who would support Anatolia (Turkey) or other areas of Asia. With so much dispute and with everyone working with the same general body of evidence, we are clearly dealing with profound methodological differences. How do we determine the centre of the spread of a language? Are there universal principles that we can employ to determine the prehistoric location of a language?

The most obvious approach to finding the Indo-European homeland, i.e. selecting a geographical location in time and convincing the rest of the world that one is right, is examining the distribution of languages from their centres in many historically controlled situations so that we can observe the processes and principles involved. The problem with this approach is that there is really nothing suitable. Where we can observe the expansion of a major language group, e.g. Romance or Germanic, it is under historical circumstances that are hardly likely to have obtained at the time of Indo-European expansions. Where we find language families that more closely approximate the social conditions of Proto-Indo-European, e.g. Chinese, Uralic, Algonquian, we find ourselves dealing with other unresolved homeland problems. In short, no language family has provided a suitable laboratory to work out confidently the rules of the game. That is not to say that many solutions do not try to argue from what are posited to be well-established principles, but few if any of such principles can be regarded as wholly compelling from an empirical standpoint.

26.2 Homeland Approaches

The search for the Indo-European homeland is an exercise in logic and the diversity of solutions is primarily due to the variety of approaches that have been taken. Below follows a brief compendium of the type of more serious arguments that have been adduced to locate the original location of the Indo-Europeans.

26.2.1 External Language Relations

Just as adjacent languages may mutually influence each other when in contact so also do adjacent language families. Linguists have discerned loanwords or grammatical loans (or mutual inheritances) between Indo-European on the one hand and Uralic, Afro-Asiatic (here Semitic), and Kartvelian. These presumed contacts have supported homelands set in the steppelands of Eurasia (with the Uralics in the forest zone to the north), in eastern Anatolia (to accommodate an interface between Kartvelian and Semitic), and in central Asia (distant Semitic relations and again with Uralics to the north). The problems with such an approach have been discerning the time depth of the 'contacts', i.e. what have been interpreted as Uralic-Proto-Indo-European loans by some have been seen to be much later contacts between Iranians or Indo-Iranians and Uralics. The nature of the contacts may also be disputed, i.e. where we may find apparent loanwords between two language families, it is presumptive that these must have been in direct contact with one another when the language groups could still have been geographically distant and the lexical connections are *Wanderwörter*, i.e. far-travelled cultural loanwords. Third, it may be disputed whether the relationship reflects a contact relationship between two different language families or whether the evidence points to the retention of shared terms from genetically related language families which share a common origin, i.e. the similarities go back to a time long prior to the formation of the two proto-languages involved. It should also be emphasized that language families are not synchronic, i.e. there is no reason to postulate the same time depths to every language family. Some uniform proto-language may have been spoken over a geographically compact area at the same time when their neighbours had already differentiated into different language groups of an already expanded family.

26.2.2 Centre of Gravity

The distribution of the different language groups, it is argued, should provide important clues as to their origin. In the biological sciences, for example, a map of the different genera and species of a plant or animal often indicates the probable area of origin. This argument generally involves an appeal to maximum diversity to indicate the centre of a language dispersal. The English language is most uniform in areas where it has expanded most recently (Australia, New Zealand) and shows more evidence of regional dialects in areas settled somewhat earlier (North America) and greatest diversity in areas where it has existed longest (England). If we continue this approach, we would argue that as there are far more Germanic languages in north-west Europe it is far more likely that English derived from there rather than the reverse, i.e. that the other Germanic languages spread from England to the Continent. This approach has been a staple of homeland solutions everywhere in the world. It also has a converse principle: where we find the greatest homogeneity of languages, that area is likely to have been most recently occupied. In general, these principles have selected for homelands in or adjacent to the Balkans. Here we can list a series of language groups, e.g. Greek, Albanian, Illyrian, Thracian, Dacian, Slavic, which are portrayed as a central core while on the periphery we find large areas occupied by single language groups (Indo-Iranians in the east and Celtic (here seen in terms of its broad Iron Age distribution) in western and central Europe).

The problem with this approach is that it is extremely difficult to apply at a consistent date or with a suitable control of the actual diversity of the languages involved. We may be able to pack our putative Balkan core with Illyrian, Thracian, and Dacian but we have no idea how different they were from each other or from neighbouring Indo-European groups. Moreover, we have no absolute measure of difference in the first place. Although we tend to use languages as the common unit of measurement, the diversity between languages of the same family is hardly uniform. For example, the major Scandinavian languages of Norwegian, Swedish, and Danish are very broadly mutually intelligible as also are the Eastern Slavic languages of Russian and Byelorussian, more distantly Ukrainian. If we simply count the number of early languages we know and their diversity in specific locations, it is probable that Italy would be judged the winner with its numerous, poorly attested Iron Age languages that shared the peninsula along with Latin. In Italy the linguistic diversity attested by our earliest linguistic records has been replaced with relative linguistic uniformity by the spread of Latin. In Anatolia the linguistic diversity of our earliest records was replaced by the spread of Greek and then, later, by the spread of Turkish. How many other areas where our earliest knowledge is of linguistic uniformity are the products of exactly the same process?

26.2.3 Cladistic Correlation

The family tree of the Indo-European languages has often been seen as a partial proxy to the geographical relationships between the different languages. For example, many if not most linguists would see the separation between Anatolian and the other Indo-European languages as among the earliest 'splits'. For this reason, homeland solutions are devised to accommodate these intrafamily relationships, generally by having the homeland not too distant from the historical seats of the Anatolian languages. Following this line of reasoning, the Proto-Indo-European homeland is placed in Anatolia, requiring all the other Indo-European languages to separate off from Anatolia (either to the east or to the west), or the homeland is placed somewhere not too distant from Anatolia, e.g. the steppelands, so that the future Anatolians might be accounted for by the initial Indo-European expansions. The problems involved with this method are several. First, there are competing family trees to explain the Indo-European languages and the differences will govern the nature of the geographical relationships proposed. Second, it is presumptuous to read geographical co-ordinates into a linguistic relationship. For example, although many trees will suggest reasons for placing the Indo-Iranians linguistically close to the Greeks and Armenians (see Figs. 5.1, 5.2, and 5.3), how do we translate this relationship into a geographical expression of where they may have shared this mutual development (or contact)? It may have been in India, Iran, the steppes, Anatolia, the Balkans, Greece itself, or somewhere outside this broad band.

26.2.4 Onomastics

This approach presumes that the proto-language itself might have left identifiable traces on the named landscape. The primary use of such an approach has been in the area of river names on the assumption that these represent the oldest and lexically least altered component of the landscape. Hence, if one can discern Proto-Indo-European names for rivers, we can presume that we have found an area in which the Proto-Indo-Europeans once lived. Such an approach has thrown up homelands in the Baltic or central and eastern Europe. These hydronymic solutions run into very serious problems. Many would dispute the interpretation of the empirical evidence, i.e. that one can confidently etymologize the names of rivers beyond an existing language system. The systems of ancient river names require appeals not to specific Indo-European languages but to derivations from Proto-Indo-European roots, and there is no way of checking the credibility of assigning river names like 'the bright', 'the runner', etc. One linguist's Indo-European names become another's proto-Basque, or Caucasian or anything else.

There are several other onomastic approaches although these play little part in more recent research. Iranian tradition spoke of an *Airyana vaeja* 'seed of the Aryans' as a particular (but unspecified) geographical location and that tradition set many scholars off to localize it in some particular place. Moreover, it was often assumed by such scholars that the homeland of the 'Aryans' could be assumed, without much further ado, to be the homeland of their ancestors, the Proto-Indo-Europeans, as well. In actuality the *Airyana vaeja* would have been the homeland of (a major branch of) the Iranians alone.

26.2.5 Conservation Principle

One of the recurrent arguments employed to determine the Indo-European homeland on the basis of purely linguistic evidence is the assumption that the homeland is most likely in the area where we find the least altered Indo-European language. This presumption is based on the logic that, if a language has not moved, it will have experienced far less impetus to change, e.g. impact of substrates or contacts with other languages, than those languages that have spread through more distant migration. This principle was initially applied in the nineteenth century when it was assumed that Sanskrit was the closest to the proto-language, but over the course of the next century two other contenders appeared. The archaic nature claimed for Anatolian made it possible to suggest that it was the least moved language, but this conclusion was mitigated by the clear evidence of loanwords from a variety of its neighbours (Semitic, Hattic, Hurrian) and the internal evidence that indicated that Hittite had been adopted by a non-Indo-European substrate. Alternatively, the Baltic languages, particularly Lithuanian, were seen to be remarkably conservative, especially in light of their late attestation. This conservatism provided one of the cornerstones for those who sought an Indo-European homeland on the shores of the Baltic Sea.

The conservation principle suffers from several serious defects. Its application requires one to measure how conservative were the various Indo-European languages, but this comparison cannot be done on a level playing field because the various languages entered the historical record at different times. To compare Sanskrit with a putative date of *c.*1200 BC with Lithuanian at AD 1800 is patently unfair (and assessing the state of Lithuanian at 1200 BC requires a time machine). As it is impossible to compare any more than three language groups at *c.* 1000 BC (Indo-Iranian, Greek, and late Anatolian) one is not comparing the full range of Indo-European languages. If one applies the principle by a time when all the languages can be brought into play, we then find ourselves comparing the modern languages of India (Hindi-Urdu, Bengali, etc.) with the Romance languages (French, Italian, etc.) and we will have to ignore all earlier evidence, including whole language groups (Anatolian, Tocharian) or well-attested earlier stages of the language groups (Sanskrit, Latin). Secondly, there is no empirical measuring device to ascertain in any reliable quantitative manner how conservative or how innovative the Indo-European languages are. There is no commonly agreed scale by which one could compare each language group against a standard (reconstructed Proto-Indo-European). Third, the underlying logic of the exercise is largely based on the assumption that language change is a product of language contact, i.e. the reason that a language spread through migration is likely to experience more change is that it has undergone imperfect learning by substrate populations (or come into contact with foreign languages). While these may influence language change, they are hardly the only reasons for it. Finally, if conservation did indicate lack of movement from a putative homeland we would expect that there would be a corresponding gradient of conservatism running from the homeland to the most travelled language group; in fact, there is no such evidence of a graduated abandonment of the 'mother tongue' over distance.

26.2.6 *Linguistic Palaeontology*

The analysis of the reconstructed proto-lexicon for clues as to the location of a proto-language is a widely employed technique although many prefer a different term, e.g. lexico-cultural analysis, from the original nineteenth-century term, linguistic palaeontology, that led to discredited results. The underlying premiss is that if we can reconstruct the environment and technology known to the Proto-Indo-Europeans, we should be able to determine their location. The main areas of interest are the words for trees, animals, and material culture, all of which may have had restricted distributions in the past. The technique requires an appeal to archaeological and palaeo-environmental evidence to set broad limits on where the proto-language may have been spoken. This exercise is often only intelligible when we also have some idea of *when* Proto-Indo-European was spoken (see Chapter 6) because the distribution of plants, animals, and most especially material culture has varied greatly through time. If one accepts the broad dates provided earlier, i.e. *c*. 4500-2500 BC, for Proto-Indo-European, the lexico-cultural evidence does little to confine the potential area of the homeland. The difficulty is that the more geographically specific the reconstructed item, the less likely it is for the word to have survived once the Indo-Europeans expanded beyond a region where it existed. Or, the word might then be applied to a new species of plant or animal and we will be left with critical uncertainty as to what the proto-lexeme actually meant. We have already seen this in three of the classic Indo-European homeland arguments which required us to determine whether **lóḱs* meant 'Atlantic salmon' or 'salmon trout', **bheh$_a$ĝós* meant the common beech (*Fagus silvatica*) or some other species of beech (*Fagus taurica* or *Fagus orientalis*) or some other tree altogether, and whether **h_1éḱwos* referred to the 'domestic horse' or the 'wild horse' (or both)? There is no cultural item that clinches a homeland in any specific location but it should not be imagined that the lexical cultural evidence is altogether useless. It does provide us with a fairly consistent impression of the time of Proto-Indo-European (Late Neolithic/Eneolithic) and it provides us with evidence that renders some potential homelands much less likely than others, e.g. the absence of the evidence of the horse altogether from both Greece and Italy before the Bronze Age makes it less likely that these were the earliest seats of the Indo-Europeans.

26.2.7 Physical Anthropology

The use of physical anthropological evidence (now the term 'bio-archaeological' is often preferred) emerged as a major technique of the latter nineteenth century but after the excesses of twentieth-century racists it has few supporters, at least within the sphere of Indo-European studies, as this area is precisely where the excesses were inflicted. The assumption here is that human physical type may serve as proxy evidence for the speakers of a language family. There were several approaches. One depended on phenotypic differences, i.e. the outward appearance of different peoples. Scholars mined historical records and literature for descriptions of the earliest Indo-Europeans and then argued whether they were blond or brunette (given the range of meanings of colour terms in ancient literatures this is not always an easy task) and employed such evidence to determine the likely homeland. This method produced arguments of truly staggering illogic as pseudo-scientists sought the epicentre of European blondness under the assumption that only there could one have acquired light hair and only there could have been the homeland. As cloning techniques were unlikely to have been present during the period 4500–2500 BC, it is difficult to see why the phenotype of the original population of so physically disparate speakers as the Indo-Europeans had to be uniformly blond, brunette, or whatever colour one might imagine.

A second approach involved the analysis of skeletal anatomy, primarily the human skull, which was divided into certain 'subracial' categories, e.g. Nordic, Armenian, Mediterranean, or into the broader categories of skull length to breadth ratio, i.e. brachycephalics (brachycranials if it was your skull and not your living head) who had wide heads and dolichocephalics (dolichocranials) with long heads. The problem here is that if children of dolichocephalics could turn out brachycephalic, how could one seriously regard such broad distinctions as meaningful? It has proven difficult to sort out which measurements of the human skull are measuring something that is entirely genetic, i.e. inherited, versus those which may differ either randomly or because of the environment, especially the diet. Those who still measure skulls generally do so within the context of multivariate analysis where a number of different, and presumably more reliable, measurements are analysed statistically in order to determine the direction of gene flow from one population to another. Even this technique is not widely employed simply because many, perhaps most, physical anthropologists have abandoned such analysis.

A third approach is genetic, i.e. either the analysis of the genetic composition of modern populations or the extraction of genetic data (ancient DNA) from skeletal material. This method has proved to be a growth industry in language studies (there is grant money out there to be gained) but the results are still far from reliable. Analysis of modern populations as proxy evidence for past migrations, especially migrations that should have occurred thousands of years earlier, have yielded quite conflicting interpretations. One of the earliest and still discussed is the work of Luca Cavalli-Sforza and his colleagues on the distribution of human genes in European populations where the first principal component, indicated by a genetic path from South-West Asia westwards across Europe, has been interpreted as the result of the expansion of the first farmers in the seventh millennium BC or, alternatively and in no way in association with the spread of Indo-European speech, that of modern *Homo sapiens sapiens* populations *c.* 40,000 BC. The temptation to read every cline on a map of genetic features as a migration and tie it to a putative linguistic movement has led to ostensibly circular reasoning. As for the use of ancient DNA, actually establishing gene flow among ancient populations where there is control for the date of the gene flow, the techniques involved are of a far higher magnitude of difficulty. Ancient DNA is often very poorly preserved, expensive to recover, and without analysis of a large area, valid conclusions cannot be made. The technique may in time become a useful tool but that day is some way off.

Finally, the problem with both genetic and phenetic approaches is that there is an assumed correlation between language and human physical type. Studies of current language boundaries do reveal some correlations but many of these involve natural barriers (seas, mountains) and none can be reliably factored for time, i.e. there is no way to distinguish whether a currently observable border between, say, Romanian (Italic) and Bulgarian (Slavic) is a modern feature or reflective of an earlier border between Dacian and Thracian or a still earlier border. The requirement of a genetic trail could only be accepted if one required that for language shift to occur there must be a constant human vector involved so that there was major directional gene flow. Given the fact that in most cases we are probably speaking of language shift between neighbouring peoples, there is no requirement whatsoever that the trail of language shift should also leave a clearly defined genetic trail as well. Nor for that matter can we assume that if we do find a genetic trail, this necessarily resulted in a language shift favourable for those carrying the gene rather than their absorption by local populations.

26.2.8 Retrospective Archaeology

We have already seen archaeological involvement in the use of linguistic palaeontology but it may be employed in a number of other ways as well. The most obvious is the retrospective method where one examines those archaeological cultures that must have been associated with different Indo-European language groups and attempts to work backwards to the 'proto-culture'. The unit of analysis here is the so-called 'archaeological culture', a classification device employed by archaeologists to deal with similar and geographically confined material culture and behaviour. This method fails to convince for at least two major reasons.

The retrospective technique presumes that one can employ cladistic techniques to provide an archaeological family tree much like a linguistic tree. But this is not at all what one actually does because the archaeologically defined cultures show constant mutual contact in terms of ornamental styles, architecture, metallurgy, or any other phenomenon of cultural life, i.e. there is no single line of 'gene flow' within a continuum of archaeological cultures. Moreover, the definition of the individual units may well vary through time, e.g. in the Neolithic ceramics tend to be critical for distinguishing one culture from another but by the Bronze Age, metallurgical tradition and mortuary practice become more critical elements.

Secondly, even if one were convinced of the underlying logic of the retrospective method, it still falls apart on empirical grounds once one has worked back to *c.*3000 BC (in some cases the retrospective method disappears altogether). Many of the language groups of Europe, i.e. Celtic, Germanic, Baltic, and Slavic, may possibly be traced back to the Corded Ware horizon of northern, central, and eastern Europe that flourished *c.*3200–2300 BC. Some would say that the Iron Age cultures of Italy might also be derived from this cultural tradition. For this reason the Corded Ware culture is frequently discussed as a prime candidate for early Indo-European; in the past it was even suggested as the Proto-Indo-European culture. However, the Corded Ware cannot even remotely explain the Indo-European groups of the Balkans, Greece, Anatolia, nor those of Asia. For the steppeland regions of Eurasia, the retrospective method takes us back through the Bronze Age Andronovo and Timber-grave cultures of the Eurasian steppe to the underlying Yamna culture of *c.*3600–2200 BC. This method can supply us with an archaeological proxy for the Eastern Iranians but that is about all the retrospective method gets us. We may argue that the Yamna culture should minimally reflect the proto-Indo-Iranians if not more; however, we cannot do this by the retrospective method since there is no ancestral culture that territorially underlies the Iranians or Indo-Aryans, i.e. there is no specific culture X that both embraces the historical seats of the Indo-Iranians and can also be traced back to the Yamna culture. Similarly, there is really no solid evidence in the retrospective method in Greece that takes us anywhere that we can confidently tie to one of the other two 'ancestral cultures'; nor Anatolia. Sooner or later the retrospective method leads us to a series of what seem to appear to be independent cultural phenomena that somehow must be associated with one another. In that lies most of the archaeological debate concerning Indo-European origins.

26.2.9 Prospective Archaeology

The opposite method to a retrospective approach is a prospective approach where one starts with a given archaeological phenomenon and tracks its expansion. This approach is largely driven by a theory connected with the mechanism by which the Indo-European languages must have expanded. Here the trajectory need not be the type of family tree that an archaeologist might draw up but rather some other major social phenomenon that can move between cultures. For example, in both the nineteenth century and then again in the later twentieth century, it was proposed that Indo-European expansions were associated with the spread of agriculture. The underlying assumption here is that only the expansion of a new more productive economy and attendant population expansion can explain the widespread expansion of a language family the size of the Indo-European. This theory is most closely associated with a model that derives the Indo-Europeans from Anatolia about the seventh millennium BC from whence they spread into south-eastern Europe and then across Europe in a Neolithic 'wave of advance'. A later alternative mechanism is the spread of more pastoral societies who exploited the horse (and later the chariot) and carried a new language across Europe and Asia from the fourth millennium BC onwards. The underlying assumption here is that the vector of Indo-European language spread depended on a new, more aggressive social organization coupled with a more mobile economy and superior transportation technology. As this theory sets the homeland in the steppelands north of the Black and Caspian seas among different cultures that employed barrows for their burials (Russian *kurgan*), it is generally termed the Kurgan theory.

Although the difference between the Wave of Advance and Kurgan theories is quite marked, they both share the same explanation for the expansion of the Indo-Iranians in Asia (and there are no fundamental differences in either of their difficulties in explaining the Tocharians), i.e. the expansion of mobile pastoralists eastwards and then southwards into Iran and India. Moreover, there is recognition by supporters of the Neolithic theory that the 'wave of advance' did not reach the peripheries of Europe (central and western Mediterranean, Atlantic and northern Europe) but that these regions adopted agriculture from their neighbours rather than being replaced by them.

In short, there is no easy way to locating the Indo-European homeland; there is no certain solution.

26.3 What Does the Homeland Look Like?

One of the problems of homeland research is that often those searching for it are not clear what they are looking for or likely to find. If we consider the problem from first principles, then there is absolutely no reason to imagine that Proto-Indo-European began with the origins of human speech. Once that is accepted, then obviously Proto-Indo-European must have had ancestral stages that pre-date its appearance. In some cases, linguists have attempted to reconstruct Pre-Proto-Indo-European, generally through internal reconstruction. Often the ancestry is traced to earlier proposed linguistic stages, e.g. Proto-Indo-Uralic or Nostratic, but even here one is seldom proposing a language stage earlier than *c.*15,000–10,000 BC. Moreover, as we trace Indo-European along the developmental line of a still longer language tree, our control of time and space becomes increasingly weaker. If one, for example, wished to derive Proto-Indo-European from Nostratic, there is an overwhelming temptation to locate a Nostratic homeland and use this as a proxy homeland for Proto-Indo-European. But once this is done, we exclude from the equation vast tracts of Eurasia whose cultures will then remain linguistically anonymous for they fall outside the geographical area of anyone's Nostratic (generally localized to somewhere in South-West Asia). We are accumulating unknowables at an alarming rate.

The result is that Proto-Indo-European defines that stage in a linguistic continuum retrievable by the comparative method. It was not an 'instant' in the life of a language nor was it a recognizable event to those who spoke it (occasionally in the nineteenth century scholars provided explicit scenarios where the Proto-Indo-Europeans resided in some confined, possibly isolated, territory where they 'perfected' their language). If we must accept that the temporal boundaries of our definition are blurred over many centuries, perhaps on the order of one or two thousand years, then it follows that the territorial boundaries of the proto-language are also very blurred. It is almost inconceivable that the linguistic borders of Proto-Indo-European could have remained static for a millennium or two. The best we can hope for is a dead reckoning of an area at a particular range of time in the hope that it encompasses much of what we believe to have been the ancestral speech of the Indo-Europeans.

26.4 Evaluating Homeland Theories

In a world with so many competing theories, how can we evaluate which are the most probable? Many homeland solutions depend on the reiteration (often in tones of vastly greater confidence than is warranted) of one or two pieces of evidence and selective amnesia concerning all the objections to the theory. Although there is not a single solution that may not be regarded as damaged goods, there are some that seem beyond repair, but we need some explicit guidelines to separate these from the real contenders. The following comprises a partial arsenal of criteria by which one might assess a potential solution.

26.4.1 Temporal Relationship

A solution cannot date after 2000 BC by which time we may expect to find an already differentiated Anatolian as well as Indo-Iranian and probably Greek.

How early a solution is admitted depends on individual decisions regarding the temporally most diagnostic vocabulary. That the vocabulary is clearly one reflecting at least a Neolithic economy and technology, i.e. domesticated plants and animals, ceramics, means that it cannot be set anywhere on this planet prior to *c.* 8000 BC. Although there are still those who propose solutions dating back to the Palaeolithic, these cannot be reconciled with the cultural vocabulary of the Indo-European languages. The later vocabulary of Proto-Indo-European hinges on such items as wheeled vehicles, the plough, wool, which are attested in Proto-Indo-European, including Anatolian. It is unlikely then that words for these items entered the Proto-Indo-European lexicon prior to about 4000 BC. This is not necessarily a date for the expansion of Indo-European since the area of Proto-Indo-European speech could have already been in motion by then and new items with their words might still have passed through the continuum undetected, i.e. treated as inheritances rather than borrowings. All that can be concluded is that if one wishes to propose a homeland earlier than about 4000 BC, the harder it is to explain these items of vocabulary.

26.4.2. Linguistic Relationship

Any solution should accommodate the broad requirements of whatever family tree is being proposed. In general, there is probably some broad although not universal consensus that would see a separation between Anatolian and the other Indo-European languages (see Figs. 5.3 and 5.4). Many have argued that Greek, Armenian, and Indo-Iranian share a number of innovations that suggest that there should have been some form of linguistic continuum between their predecessors. This line of thinking then presupposes various peripheries such as Germanic, Baltic, and Slavic in some form of relationship and possibly Celtic and Italic in another, still related to the north European languages. The position of Tocharian still remains beyond solid consensus other than the fact that it cannot be brought into the same continuum as Indo-Iranian. If a solution to the homeland can avoid totally contradicting these relationships, it can be regarded as a potential model.

26.4.3 External Relationship

There is evidence for loanwords and possibly genetic connections between Proto-Indo-European and other language families, most particularly Uralic and Semitic. The interpretation of the empirical evidence here is not now (nor ever has been) the subject of much consensus and attempts to dead reckon the Proto-Indo-European homeland on a notional idea of its relationship with these other language families have plenty of problems. At best a solution should be able to devise a way by which Proto-Indo-European could have borrowed from and loaned words to these two major groups. It would, however, be a mistake to imagine that these relations can be translated into specific geographic co-ordinates, especially when we do not know the prehistoric location of the other language families any better than Indo-European.

26.4.4 *Total Distribution Principle*

The correct solution to the Indo-European homeland problem explains the origins and distribution of all the Indo-European languages. All too often a solution proceeds from some form of argument for the local continuity of a language in a particular area and then extrapolates this back to the homeland itself. In the nineteenth and first half of the twentieth century, the model of continuity helped drive a north European solution to the homeland problem, i.e. if there is no evidence that anyone brought a new language into northern Europe, then there must have been local continuity in this region and all the other Indo-European languages derive from northern Europe. Today there is an entire school that makes a similar argument for local continuity in northern India and argues that there lies the homeland. In both cases—or any other case for regional continuity—a solution is made for one area and the rest of the Indo-European world is forced to accommodate it, generally without the slightest credible evidence. No solution is valid if it only rests on local continuity; it must provide a viable model for the spread of all the Indo-European languages.

26.4.5 *Plausible Vector Principle*

The expansion of the Indo-European languages was a social phenomenon or many individual phenomena that spanned much of Eurasia. This expansion could not have taken place without a social vector that should have left some trace in the archaeological record (ancient DNA may eventually have some role to play here). Generally, all solutions can be divided into two main models: demographic replacement and language shift. In the first, the primary vector will be a new population speaking some form of Indo-European that swamps or replaces an earlier non-Indo-European-speaking population. The most popular model for demographic replacement is the 'wave of advance' that sees the greater productivity of the farming economy as the factor that drove both farming populations and their expansion through Europe where they carried the Indo-European speech. One might also suggest that there may have been regional migrations where an influx of Indo-European speakers settled an area after a major socio-economic collapse (e.g. there is major cultural change and relocation in the Balkans in the fourth millennium BC, or the collapse of the Indus Valley Civilization in the second millennium BC).

Alternatively, there are language shift models that do not require population replacement but rather the spread of a language, perhaps through a minimum number of individuals, due to a variety of social processes that encouraged local non-Indo-European peoples to shift their language. Identifying the social processes is a major challenge. Generally, language shift models have employed some form of 'elite dominance', i.e. postulated that the Indo-Europeans expanded through military aggression and superimposed themselves on substrates who eventually adopted Indo-European speech. One of the most popular theories, that of Marija Gimbutas, emphasized the role of the horse and horse riding as a key element in the expansion of Indo-European populations off the steppe into south-eastern and central Europe.

26.4.6 Exclusion Principle

Although this is not a hard and fast principle, where we find very early in the historical record evidence for non-Indo-European populations, it is unlikely that we would have reason to set the Proto-Indo-European homeland in the same place. We have written records from the third millennium BC onwards that provide either direct or reasonable inferential evidence as to the location of the Egyptian, Semitic, Sumerian, Hattic, Hurrian, Elamite, and other lesser-known non-Indo-European languages. It is not impossible for the Indo-European homeland to have been located in an area later occupied by a non-Indo-European language, but the earlier our evidence for a non-Indo-European language, the more difficult it becomes to place Indo-Europeans in the same place. Moreover, unless one wishes to explain Indo-European migrations in terms of a refugee model, i.e. the Indo-Europeans were pushed out of their homeland by a more powerful people (and somehow then went on to dominate much of Eurasia), it is difficult to imagine what economic or social process might have given the Indo-Europeans the edge in their expansions. A corollary of this principle is the expectation that if one wishes to place the homeland in the same area or adjacent to a non-Indo-European language (family), one might expect evidence of linguistic contacts between the two.

26.5 Processes of Expansion

A language, certainly a prehistoric language, cannot spread on its own but requires a vector. Essentially there are two vectors: human beings and their social institutions. The most obvious vector is the human vector, i.e. the migration of a population speaking a particular language who carry it beyond its former territory. For much of the history of the Indo-European homeland problem, human vectors have been the most popular. In the nineteenth and early twentieth centuries, one often read of a Proto-Indo-European people who spilled out from their homeland to cover (often conquer) much of Eurasia. Currently, the most popular human vector is that associated with an Anatolian homeland which links the spread of the Indo-Europeans with the expansion of the earliest farmers. The hunter-gatherer economies of Eurasia may be generally characterized as small and occupying certain ecological niches while the introduction of farming permitted larger families, greater population increase, and density and promoted the expansion of farming populations at the expense of local Mesolithic hunter-gatherers. Population movement is also invoked for a number of the Later Bronze Age and Iron Age cultures which may be seen to adumbrate the later mass 'folk wanderings' of the Celts, Germans, and other peoples of early historic Europe.

The second vector is a social one where a language spreads because it is associated with particular social institutions. This is not to deny that there may also be some population movement but the vector most responsible for the spread of a language is seen to be social rather than strictly biological. For a language to spread over previous populations who have not been deliberately exterminated (unlikely in prehistory) or been entirely swamped by a much more fertile immigrant population, this requires some form of language shift. The rules for language shift are not hard and fast, and generalizing from a handful of cases, often drawn from modern societies or population groups vastly different in technologies, may be an unsuitable model for Proto-Indo-European. But there are certain obvious principles that we may expect operated in the time of early Indo-European expansions. The first is that societies do not immediately shift their language but rather experience a period of societal bilingualism before they acquiesce to the full adoption of a new language.

Societal bilingualism requires some form of social impetus. There must be some reason for people to make the effort to learn a new language in addition to their own, and an equally compelling reason for them to ultimately abandon their former language for the new one. A social perspective on language use indicates that it is employed in different social domains. For example, there is the domestic domain, the language spoken at home; there is a religious domain, the language spoken when talking to one's deities or in ceremonial precincts; a domain of exchange, the language of the marketplace. If Indo-European spread through language shift, then we might expect that when its speakers came into contact with non-Indo-European-speaking populations, there was some attraction for them to enter one or more of the social domains of the Indo-Europeans: to do this, they had to learn Indo-European. As time progressed, and we may not be talking about more than two generations for any individual group, the local population came to think of themselves more and more as Indo-European speakers and began abandoning their original language in its other social domains. Generally, the last to go will be the domestic domain where, in the most extreme cases, we are left with the poignant image of a grandparent who cannot converse with his or her grandchildren.

So what might have attracted non-Indo-European speakers to enter the social domains of the Indo-Europeans? As fundamentally logical as this question might seem, answers are remarkably few and conclusions even scarcer. One of the obvious and most frequent models was that of a very brusque elite dominance, i.e. the Indo-European speakers conquered local populations and somehow forced them to adopt the new language. Other models focus on Indo-European religion and perhaps religious institutions that may have attracted local populations. There have certainly been enough examples where religion and the military worked hand in hand, e.g. the expansion of Spanish Catholicism in the Americas, Arabic Islam in North Africa and the Middle East. Exchange systems have also been invoked on occasion with the suggestion that Indo-European was a lingua franca, a trade language that was adopted among many different peoples. Warrior sodalities (war-bands) have also been invoked—not because they in themselves subjected new populations but rather because they would have attracted young males into an acculturizing institution that offered room for advancement in the new system. Finally, we might invoke the Indo-European social system itself with its admittedly limited evidence for kings and tribes which may have attracted new members, especially if their own political systems were in a state of collapse or lacked centralized institutions.

We should avoid a false dichotomy between the population and social vector as if the spread of the Indo-European languages was due purely to one or the other means. It may well have fluctuated from one instance to the next and it is easy to see how populations who have experienced language shift might be the next population to migrate and carry it into a new territory. A number of the cultures most closely associated with current theories of Indo-European expansions, e.g. the Corded Ware culture of northern and central Europe, the BMAC of central Asia and the Indian borderlands, can be variously interpreted as the result of population movements or primarily social phenomena (cults). From an archaeological point of view, it may well be worth distinguishing the two phenomena, but from the standpoint of linguists, either phenomenon may have served as a vector for language shift.

26.6. Where Do They Put it Now?

All too often surveys of the Indo-Europeans eventually conclude with something on the order of 'scholars have concluded that the most likely area of the homeland is... X' with a brief defence of one particular solution (this type of scholarship has been going on since the late nineteenth century). In fact, we not only lack total consensus but where we seem to find something of a major school it is often formed by deference rather than conviction, i.e. linguists or archaeologists indicate agreement with a particular theory that they have not themselves investigated in any depth. This situation means that a small number of advocates—at times, very vigorous advocates—provide an assortment of homeland theories for the rest of their colleagues to comply with passively. The homeland is an interesting question but it is so difficult to resolve (we have over two centuries of dispute to prove that) and requires the application of so many less than robust means of argument that most archaeologists and historical linguists do not find it a worthwhile enterprise, at least for themselves. The last word is, therefore, far from written and in this remaining section we only attempt to prepare the reader to engage the current state of argument critically.

Currently, there are two types of models that enjoy significant international currency (Map 26.1).

There is the Neolithic model that involves a wave of advance from Anatolia *c.* 7000 BC and, at least for south-eastern and central Europe, argues primarily for the importation of a new language by an ever growing population of farmers. This part of the model has reasonable archaeological support in that there is a fair amount of archaeologically informed consensus that derives the earliest farming communities in the Balkans from somewhat earlier farming communities in Anatolia. For the periphery of Europe the means of explanation become less clear, and rather than a language expansion driven primarily by Early Neolithic population expansion, this model now seems to admit of later (Late Neolithic, Bronze, or Iron Age) movements into Mediterranean, Atlantic, and northern Europe. For the steppelands, it envisages the spread of an agricultural economy from the Balkans to the steppes where it was then carried, in the Bronze Age, beyond the Urals and then south into the territories

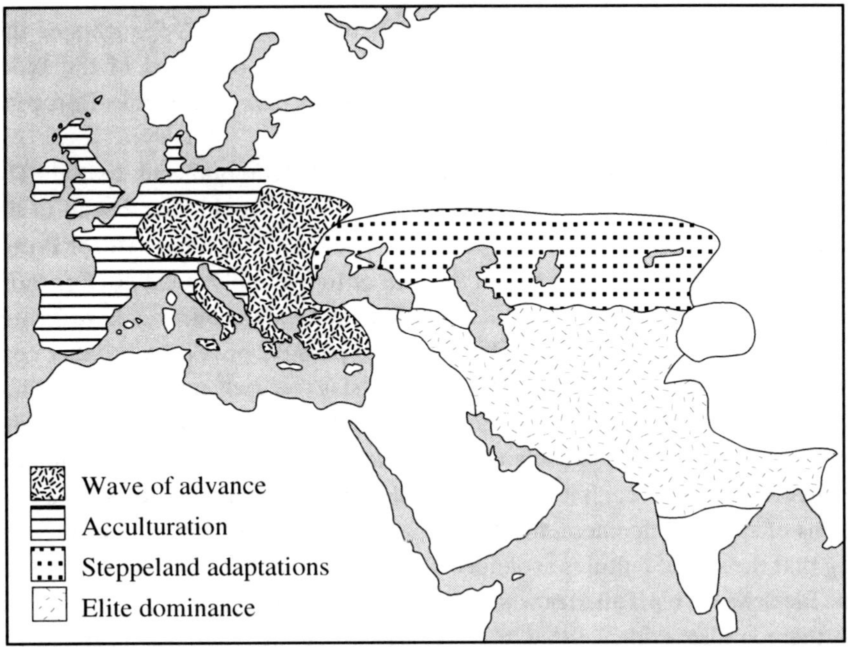

Map 26.1. The Indo-European homeland problem

of the historic Indo-Iranians and Tocharians. Some opponents of this solution admit that the initial archaeological scenario may be true but suggest that the Early Neolithic farmers spoke an unknown non-Indo-European language, possibly related to the historically attested non-Indo-European languages of Anatolia (e.g. Hattic, or possibly one of the Caucasian languages).

Alternatively, there is the steppe or kurgan model which sees the Proto-Indo-Europeans emerging out of local communities in the forest-steppe of the Ukraine and south Russia. Expansion westwards is initiated *c.* 4000 BC by the spread from the forest-steppe of mobile communities who employed the horse and, within the same millennium, wheeled vehicles. These intruded into south-eastern Europe at a time when there was major restructuring of local societies (variously attributed to climatic change, local social evolution, or intrusive steppe populations or a combination of the three). The hard archaeological evidence, i.e. the recurrence of the classic steppe burial type in the Balkans, is reasonably solid as far as the river Tisza. Beyond Hungary, this model relies on far less stringent archaeological evidence. A central component is that it requires some form of genetic derivation of the Corded Ware culture of the north European plain from the steppe cultures (one can talk either of direct derivation or the spread of a symbolic and social system that was initiated in the steppe). As for the Asiatic Indo-Europeans, it offers the model that was adopted later by those who support the Neolithic model. Opponents of this theory would tend to see the steppe cultures as the ancestors of the Indo-Iranians and possibly the Tocharians but not of the entire Indo-European family.

The dispute here is thus one of degree, both temporal and spatial. The Neolithic model implicitly suggests that separation should have begun in the seventh millennium while the steppe theory would set a terminal date for Proto-Indo-European in about the end of the fifth or fourth millennium BC. For those who believe that the most recent technological items reconstructed to Proto-Indo-European, e.g. wheeled vehicles, wool, plough, provide a broadly congruent terminal date, then the Neolithic model is too early unless it is modified to suggest that the Proto-Indo-European territory during the seventh to fifth millennia was still so relatively confined that loanwords of the fourth millennium could pass through it indistinguishable from the inherited vocabulary. In terms of spatial differences, the Neolithic model subsumes the steppe by arguing that the steppe cultures expanded westwards from the south-west corner of the Black Sea. This is an area where there is considerable archaeological dispute as there is also evidence that the Neolithic economy may have entered the steppe region via the Caucasus, which would provide a markedly different origin not only for livestock and cereals but also for the Neolithic vocabulary reconstructed to Proto-Indo-European. In any event, there is really no case for a 'wave of advance' across the Ukraine and south Russia from the Balkans. Another critical spatial issue is raised if we position the Proto-Indo-Europeans in Anatolia and derive the Anatolians from local Neolithic populations (4,000 years earlier). One must reconcile this with the consensus that Anatolian was a superstrate on local non-Indo-European language families. To avoid this issue, either the Proto-Indo-Europeans must be moved to the far west of Anatolia during the Neolithic or the non-Indo-European Hatti must be introduced later to the story, not as the indigenous population but themselves as intrusive.

As both theories explain the Asian Indo-Europeans in the same manner, there is no dispute there although it does militate against one of the most attractive aspects of the "wave of advance". The archaeological evidence for an expansion from the steppelands across historical Iran and India varies from the extremely meagre to total absence: both the Anatolian and the Kurgan theory find it extraordinarily difficult to explain the expansion of the Indo-European languages over a vast area of urbanized Asian populations, approximately the same area as that of Europe. To assert, as some supporters of the 'Wave of Advance' theory do, that only a major change such as agriculture could explain the distribution of the Indo-European languages does seem to be contradicted even by their own models. In terms of the Europeans west of the Black Sea, the Neolithic model provides a larger area for the initial Indo-Europeanization, i.e. both south-east and central Europe. The steppe model is not nearly so secure for explaining central Europe. As for the peripheries of Europe, both confront analogous problems of language shift.

We can speculate what the future might hold for homeland studies. Although much now appears about the relationship between DNA and language, it will remain to be seen how appropriate the techniques of genetics are in unravelling linguistic phenomena. From historical linguistics we may look for greater attention to that part of the vocabulary of various Indo-European groups that is not easily assignable to Proto-Indo-European. This is the area of substrate studies which has often lain on the periphery of Indo-European studies, at least when the substrate was a wholly unknown language, but which may see some useful and credible developments that could suggest what parts of the vocabulary of the different Indo-European groups were absorbed outside the inherited vocabulary. From archaeology we might hope for greater attention to social models that bridge the gap between the phenomenon of language and the material remains and patterns that constitute the archaeological record.

Further Reading

General surveys or assessments are found in Mallory (1989, 1997*a*). The classic Anatolian/Neolithic theory is presented in Renfrew (1987) and then modified in (1996, 1999); variations on an Anatolian homeland can be found in Sherratt and Sherratt (1988), Gamkrelidze and Ivanov (1995), Dolgopolsky (1987), Drews (1988), Zvelebil and Zrelebil (1988); and in opposition Diakonoff and Neroznak (1985). The classic steppe theory is presented in Gimbutas (1991, 1997), Anthony (1991), Mallory (2002); other theories are to be found in Häusler (2002) and Nichols (1997, 1998). Physical anthropology and the Indo-European problem is exhaustively treated in Day (2001), see also Mallory (1995).

Appendix 1
Basic Sound Correspondences between PIE and the Major IE Groups[a]

PIE	Celt OIr	Ital Lat	Gmc OE	Balt Lith	Slav OCS	Alb Alb	Grk Grk	Arm Arm	Anat Hit	Iran Av	Ind Skt	Toch TochB
*p	ø	p	f	p	p	p	p	h ~ ø ~ p‘ ~ y ~ w	p ~ pp	p	p	p
*b	b	b	p	b	b	b	b	p	p	b	b	p
*bh	b	f/b	b	b	b	b	ph	b	p	b	bh	p
*t	t	t	þ	t	t	t	t	t‘ ~ d ~ y	t ~ tt	t	t	t [c]
*d	d	d	t	d	d	d	d	t	t	d	d	t ~ ø [ts]
*dh	d	f/d	d	d	d	d	th	d	t	d	dh	t [ts]
*k̂	c	c	h	š	s	th	k	s ~ j	k ~ kk	s	ś	k [ś]
*ĝ	g	g	c	ž	z	dh	g	c ~ t	k	z	j	k [ś]
*ĝh	g	h	g	ž	z	d	kh	j	k	z	h	k [ś]
*k	c	c	h	k	k [č/c]	k [q]	k	k‘ ~ g	k ~ kk	k [č]	k [c]	k [ś]
*g	g	g	c	g	g [ž/z]	g [gj]	g	k ~ c	k	g [ǰ]	g [ǰ]	
*gh	g	h	g	g	g [ž/z]	g [gj]	kh	?	k	g [ǰ]	gh [h]	k [ś]
*k^w	c	qu	hw	k	k [č/c]	k [s]	p ~ t	k‘ ~ h ~ g [č‘]	ku ~ kku	k [č]	k [c]	k ~ kw [ś]
*g^w	b	v/gu	cw	g	g [ž/z]	g [z]	b ~ d	k	ku	g [ǰ]	g [j]	k ~ kw [ś]
*g^{w}h	g	f/u	w	g	g [ž/z]	g [z]	ph ~ th	g [ǰ]	ku	g [ǰ]	gh [h]	k ~ kw [ś]
*s	s	s	s	s	s	gj ~ sh	h ~ ø ~ s	h ~ ø	s	h ~ s- š	s ~ ṣ	s [ṣ]
*y	ø	i	gi	j	j	gj	h ~ z	z ~ ø	y	y	y	y
*w	w	v	w	v	v	v	ø	g	w	v	v	w [y]
*m	m	m	m	m	m	m	m	m	m	m	m	m
*n	n	n	n	n	n	n	n	n	n	n	n	n [ñ]

(*Cont'd*)

Appendix 1 (*Cont'd.*)

PIE	Celt OIr	Ital Lat	Gmc OE	Balt Lith	Slav OCS	Alb Alb	Grk Grk	Arm Arm	Anat Hit	Iran Av	Ind Skt	Toch TochB
*l	l	l	l	l	l	l	l	l	l	r	l ~ r	l
*r	r	r	r	r	r	r	r	r	r	r	r ~ l	r
*m̥	em	em ~ im	um	im	ę	e	a	am	am	a	a	am/äm
*n̥	en	en ~ in	un	in	ę	e	a	an	an	a	a	an/än
*l̥	li ~ al	ol	ul	il	ĭl	li ~ le	al	al	al	ərə	r̥	al/äl
*r̥	ri ~ ar	or	ur	ir	ĭr	ri ~ re	ar	ar	ar	ərə	r̥	ar/är
*i	i	i	i	i	ĭ	i ~ e	i	i	i	i	i	(y)a/y(ä) ~ a/ä
*ī	ī	ī	ī	y	i	i	ī	i	ī	ī	ī	(y)i
*e	e	e	e	e	e	ja ~ je	e	e ~ (- a)	e (~ a ~ i)	a	a	(y)a/(y)ä
*ē	ī	ē	ǣ	ė	ě	o	ē	i	ē	ā	ā	(y)e
*o	o	o	æ ~ a	a	o	a	o	o ~ u (- a)	a ~ ā	a	a	e
*ō	ā	ō	ō	uo	a	e	ō	u	ā	ā	ā	ā
*a	a	a	æ ~ a	a	o	a	a	a	a	a	a	ā
*ā	ā	ā	ō	o	a	o	ā ~ ē	a	ā	ā	ā	ā
*u	u	u	u	u	ŭ	u	u	u	u	u	u	a/ä
*ū	ū	ū	ū	ū	y	y (- i)	ū	u	ū	ū	ū	o
*h_1	ø	ø	ø	ø	ø	ø	ø	ø	ø	ø	ø	ø
*h_2	ø	ø	ø	ø	ø	ø	ø	ø ~ h	h ~ hh	ø	ø	ø
*h_3	ø	ø	ø	ø	ø	ø	ø	ø ~ h	h	ø	ø	ø
*h_4	ø	ø	ø	ø	ø	h	ø	ø	ø	ø	ø	ø

[a] Only what might be called the 'major' outcomes are listed here. All languages show other outcomes of some of these Proto-Indo-European sounds that are conditioned by special environments. Outcomes enclosed in square brackets are those resulting from palatalization, i.e. when the sound was (originally) followed by a front vowel (ĭ, ĕ).

Appendix 2 Proto-Indo-European to English Wordlist

***a**

**ālu-*	'±esculent root'
**ānos*	'circle, ring'
**ar*	'and, thus'
**at-*	'father'

***b**

**baba-*	'babble'
**badyos* (NW)	'(yellow) brown'
**baitéh$_a$-* (WC)	'cloak'
**bak-* (WC)	'club'
**balba-* ~ *barbar-*	'±stammer'
**baub-* (WC)	'bark, low'
**bélos*	'strong'
**b(e)u-*	'owl'
**bukk-*	'howl'
**bulis*	'±rump'

***bh**

**bhabheh$_a$-* (WC)	'bean'
**bhag-*	'divide, distribute'
bhagos* [bhag-* 'divide']	'apportion(er)'
**bhāĝhus*	'(fore)arm, foreleg'
**bhaḱó/eh$_a$-* (WC)	'bean'
**bhar-* (NW)	'projection'
bhardheh$_a$-* (NW) [bhar-* 'project']	'beard'
bhares-* (NW) [bhar-* 'project']	'barley'
bharko-* (NW) [bhar-* 'project']	'pointed object'
bhárs* (WC?) [bhar-* 'project']	'barley'
bhébhrus* [bher-* 'brown']	'beaver'
**bhedh-*	'bend (one's body)'
**bhedh-*	'dig, burrow'
**bheg-*	'break'
**b(h)eĝh*	'without'

*bheg^w-	'run'
*bheh$_2$-	'shine'
*bhéh$_2$(e)s- (GA)	'light'
*bhéh$_2$tis (GA)	'light'
*bheh$_a$- (WC)	'speak'
*bheh$_a$ĝós (WC)	'beech'
*bheh$_a$meh$_a$- (WC) [*bheh$_a$- 'speak']	'saying'
*bheid-	'split'
*bheidh-	'bend'
*bheidh- (WC)	'persuade, compel, confide'
*bhei(h$_x$)-	'strike'
*bhel-	'blow, blow up, swell'
*bhel-	'bloom, blossom'
*bhel-	'shine'
*bhel- (NW)	'henbane'
*bhel- (NW)	'wildcat; ±marten'
*bhel- (WC)	'coot'
*bhelĝh- [*bhel- 'blow']	'swell'
*bhelh$_1$- [*bhel- 'shine']	'white'
*bhélh$_a$ĝs (WC)	'plank, beam'
*bhels-	'yelp, howl'
*bhendh-	'bind'
*bhendhr̥ros [*bhendh- 'bind']	'±relation'
*bhénĝh-	'draw together, be thick'
*bhénĝhus [*bhénĝh- 'draw together']	'thick, abundant'
*bher-	'brown'
*bher-	'weave, twine'
*bher-	'seethe, bubble; roast'
*bher-	'strike (through), split, cut'
*bher-	'carry'
*bher- (WC?)	'±cure with spells and/or herbs'
*bhére/o- [*bher- 'carry']	'bear (a child)'
*bherg- (NW)	'±bark, growl'
*bhergh- (NW)	'keep, protect'
*bherĝh-	'high; hill'
*bherĝh- (WC) [*bherĝh- 'high']	'height = fort'
*bherh$_x$ĝ-	'shine, gleam'
*bherh$_x$ĝos [*bherh$_x$ĝ- 'shine']	'birch'
*bhertōr [*bher- 'carry']	'priest'
*bherug- (WC)	'gullet'
*bhes-	'blow'
*bhes-	'rub'
*bheud- (NW)	'strike, beat'
*bheudh-	'pay attention, be observant'

*bheug-	'bend (an object)'
*bheug-	'use'
*bheug- (WC)	'flee'
*bheu(h_x)-	'come into being, be; grow'
*bhibhóih$_x$e	'is afraid'
*bhidh- (NW?)	'large pot'
*bhik^{w}ó- (NW) [*bheih$_a$- 'strike']	'bee, stinging insect'
*bhlaĝ- (NW)	'strike'
*bhlaĝhmēn	'priest'
*bhleg-	'burn, shine'
*bhleh$_1$- (NW)	'bleat'
*bhlei- (WC) [*bhel- 'blow']	'±become inflated'
*bhlendh- (NW)	'be/make cloudy'
*bhleu-	'swell, overflow'
*bhlh$_a$d- [*bhel- 'bloom']	'leaf'
*bhlih$_x$ĝ- (WC)	'strike'
*bhloh$_x$dho- (NW) [*bhel- 'bloom']	'flower'
*bhodh$_x$rós	'deaf'
*bhōg- (WC)	'bake, roast'
*bhólĝhis - [*bhel- 'blow']	'(skin) bag; bolster'
*bhóliom- (WC) [*bhel- 'bloom']	'leaf'
*bhólom - [*bhel- 'shine']	'forehead'
*b(h)(o)mb(h)- (WC)	'±muffled noise'
*bhorg^{w}o- (WC)	'angry, violent'
*bhosós (WC)	'bare, naked'
*bhōu	'both'
*bhoudhéye/o- [*bheudh- 'pay attention']	'waken, point out'
*bhrak-	'squeeze together'
*bhreĝ- (NW)	'break'
*bhreh$_1$wr̥ (WC)	'spring'
*bhréh$_a$ter-	'±brother'
*bhreh$_a$tríyom [*bhréh$_a$ter- 'brother']	'brotherhood'
*bhreh$_x$i-	'destroy, cut to pieces'
*bhrem-	'±make a noise (of animals)'
*bhrentós (WC)	'stag'
*bhreu- [*bher- 'seethe']	'seethe'
*bhreu- [*bher- 'strike']	'cut, break up'
*bhreu- (WC)	'boil, brew'
*bhreus- (WC) [*bher- 'strike']	'break, smash to pieces'
*bhreus- (NW)	'swell'
*bhr̥g- [*bher- 'seethe']	'roast'
*bhr̥ĝhn̥tih$_a$- [*bherĝh- 'high']	'high one'
*bhr̥ĝhús ~ *bhr̥ĝhént- [*bherĝh- 'high']	'high'
?*bhris- ~ *bhers- (NW)	'fast'

*bhrodhnós	'±pale'
*bhr̥stís	'point'
*bhrúh$_x$s	'eyebrow'
*bhr̥w- (WC) [*bher- 'weave']	'(bolt of) cloth'
*bhudhnó-	'bottom'
*bhuĝos	'buck, he-goat'

***d**

*daih$_a$wḗr	'husband's brother'
*dap-	'apportion'
*dapnom [*dap- 'apportion']	'sacrificial meal'
*das-	'lack'
*de ~ do	'toward'
*dē (NW) [*de ~ do 'toward']	'away (from)'
*dedrús [*der- 'tear off']	'tetter, skin eruption, leprosy'
*deg-	'touch'
*deh$_1$-	'bind'
*déh$_1$mn̥ (GA) [*deh$_1$- 'bind']	'band'
*deh$_3$-	'give'
*déh$_3$r/n- [*deh$_3$- 'give']	'gift'
*deh$_a$(i)-	'cut up; divide'
*déh$_a$mos (WC) [*deh$_a$(i)- 'cut up']	'(segment of) people'
*deh$_a$nu-	'river'
*deh$_a$u-	'kindle, burn'
*dei-	'shine, be bright'
*deik̂-	'rule, canon, measure'
*deik̂-	'show'
*deino- [*dei- 'shine']	'day'
*deiwós [*dei- 'shine']	'god'
*dek̂-	'thread, hair'
*dek̂-	'take, accept'
*dek̂es- [*dek̂- 'take']	'honour'
*dék̂m̥(t)	'ten'
*dek̂m̥(t)os [*dék̂m̥(t) 'ten']	'tenth'
*dék̂sinos	'right'
*del-	'carve, split, cut'
*del- (WC)	'flow'
*del- (WC) [*del- 'carve']	'aim, compute'
*demelís (C)	'wug'
*dem(h$_a$)-	'build (up)'
*demh$_a$-	'tame, subdue'
*dems-pot- (GA) [*dem(h$_a$)- 'build' + *pótis 'husband']	'master of the house'

*denk̂-	'bite'
*dens- (GA)	'teach, inculcate a skill'
*deph$_x$- (WC)	'strike'
*der-	'sleep'
*der-	'tear off, flay'
*derbh-	'turn, twist'
*dergh- (WC)	'grasp'
*derh$_a$- (WC)	'work'
*derk̂-	'glance at, see'
*derk̂etos (GA) [*derk̂- 'see']	'visible'
*des- (GA)	'enemy'
*deuh$_4$-	'leave, go far away'
*deuk-	'pull'
*deu(s)-	'be lacking'
*(d)h$_2$ék̂ru	'tear'
*d(h$_3$)eu-	'be favourable to'
*dh̥$_3$ĝhmós (GA)	'aslant'
*dibhro- ~ *dībhro- (WC)	'(sacrificial) animal'
*diĝ(h)- (WC)	'tick'
*dih$_1$-	'fly; move swiftly'
*díks	'goat'
*dis- (WC) [*dwéh$_3$(u) 'two']	'apart, asunder'
*dl̥h$_1$ghós	'long'
*dlonghos	'long'
*dm̥pedom (WC)[*dem(h$_a$)- 'build' + *pōds 'foot']	'floor'
*dn̥ĝhuh$_a$-	'tongue'
*do ~ *de	'to, toward'
*dṓm [*dem(h$_a$)- 'build']	'house'
*dṓm (GA) [*dem(h$_a$)- 'build']	'house(hold), nuclear family'
*dóm(h$_a$)os [*dem(h$_a$)- 'build']	'house(hold)'
*dom(h$_a$)unos [*dem(h$_a$)- 'build']	'master'
*domh$_a$yos	'one to be tamed; young bull'
*don- (WC)	'reed'
*dórk^{w}om (WC)	'evening meal'
*dóru	'wood, tree'
*dous-	'(upper) arm, shoulder'
*drap- ~ *drop- [*der- 'tear off']	'clothes, cloak'
*dreh$_a$-	'run'
*drem-	'run'
*drep- [*der- 'tear off']	'scratch, tear, split off'
*dreu-	'run'
*drewentih$_2$- [*dreu- 'run']	(river name)

*dr̥h$_x$weh$_a$-	'± grain'
*dr̥ḱ- (WC) [*derḱ- 'see']	'dragon'
*duh$_a$ros	'long (of time/space)'
*dus-	'bad' (as prefix).
*dusmenēs (GA) [*dus- 'bad' + *men- think']	'hostile', literally 'bad-thought'
*dwéh$_3$(u)	'two'
*dwei- [*dwéh$_3$(u) 'two']	'fear'
*dw(e)i-plos [*dwéh$_3$(u) 'two']	'double, twofold'
*dwi- [*dwéh$_3$(u) 'two']	'bi-'
*dwis [*dwéh$_3$(u) 'two']	'twice'
*dwiyos ~ *dwitos [*dwéh$_3$(u) 'two']	'second'
*dwō deḱm̥(t) [*dwéh$_3$(u) 'two']	'twelve'
*dwoi- [*dwéh$_3$(u) 'two']	'two, group of two'
*dwoyos [*dwéh$_3$(u) 'two']	'double(d), twofold'
*dye(u)- [*dei- 'shine']	'day'
*dyḗus ph$_a$tḗr [*dei- 'shine']	'sky-father'

***dh**

*dhabh-	'put together'
*dhabhros (WC) [*dhabh- 'put together']	'craftsman'
*dhal- (WC)	'sprout'
*dheb-	'thick, packed'
*dhebh-	'harm'
*dhédhh$_1$i- [*dheh$_1$- 'suck(le)']	'± coagulated (sour) milk'
*dhéĝhōm	'earth'
*dheg^{w}h-	'burn'
*dheh$_1$-	'suck(le)'
*dheh$_1$-	'put, place'
*dheh$_1$- (WC)	'uncle'
*dheh$_1$lus- (WC) [*dheh$_1$- 'suck(le)']	'nourishing, suckling'
*dhéh$_1$mi-/men- [*dheh$_1$- 'put']	'what is established, law'
*dhēh$_1$s	'god'
*dhéh$_1$tis [*dheh$_1$- 'put']	'what is established, law'
*dheiĝh-	'work clay; build up'
*dheig^w- (NW)	'stick, set up'
*d(h)ek^{w}s-	'show'
*dhelbh- (NW)	'dig'
*dhelg- (NW)	'sting, pierce'
*dhelg- (NW) [*dhelg- 'sting']	'pin'
*dhen-	'run, flow'
*dhénr̥ (WC)	'palm (of the hand)'
*dher-	'be immobile; support'

**dher-*	'leap, spring'
**dher-* (NW)	'shit'
**dherĝh-*	'bind fast'
**dhers-*	'venture, be bold, brave; undertake'
**dheu-* (GA/PIE?)	'run'
**dheu-* (WC)	'die, breathe one's last'
**dheub-*	'deep'
**dheuĝh-*	'be useful, produce something useful'
**dheu*(h_x)-	'be in (com)motion'
dhĝh*(*e*)*m-en* [dhéĝhōm* 'earth']	'on(to) the ground'
dhĝhm̥ón-* (NW) [dhéĝhōm* 'earth']	'man'
**dhĝhu*h_x- (WC)	'fish'
*(*dh*)*ĝhyes*	'yesterday'
**dhg*^{w}*hei-*	'destroy, perish'
**dhg*^{w}*her-* (GA)	'flow (away)'
dhh*$_1$*ileh*$_a$- [dheh*$_1$- 'suck(le)']	'teat, breast'
dhíĝhs* [dheiĝh-* 'work clay']	'wall, fortification'
**dhl̥gh-* (NW)	'debt'
**dhóh*$_a$*us* (WC)	'± wolf'
**dhoh*$_x$*néh*$_a$-	'(harvested) grain'
**dhólh*$_a$*os*	'valley; vault'
**dh*(*o*)*ngu-*	'dark'
**dhonu-*	'fir'
**dhreg-*	'rain/snow lightly'
**dhreĝ-*	'glide, pull (something) across'
**dhregh-* (NW)	'pull, tear (out)'
**dhregh-* (WC)	'run'
**dhreghes-* (NW)	'berry'
**dhreibh-* (NW)	'drive'
**dhren-* (WC)	'drone' (<'buzz')
**dhreugh-*	'deceive'
**dhrigh-*	'± a (coarse) hair'
**dhrogh-* (WC)	'dregs'
dhroghós* (WC) [dhregh-* 'run']	'wheel'
**dhroughos*	'phantom'
**dhroughós* (NW)	'companion, comrade'
**dhúbhos* (WC)	'wedge, peg'
**dhuĝ*(h_a)*tḗr*	'daughter'
**dhuĝh*$_a$*tḗr diwós*	'sky-daughter'
dhuh*$_2$*mós* [dheu*(h_2)-]	'be in (com)motion'] 'smoke'
**dhūnos* (NW)	'fort'
**dhwen-*	'sound'
dhwenh*$_2$- (GA) [dheu*(h_2)-]	'be in (com)motion'] 'cover over, darken'
**dhwer-*	'pierce'

dhwerh*$_x$- [dhwer*- 'pierce']	'harm'
**dhwerh*$_x$-	'yoke'
**dhwes*-	'breathe'
dhwes*- (NW) [dhwes*- 'breathe']	'spirit'
dhwésmi* [dhwes*- 'breathe']	'breathe, be full of (wild) spirits'
**dhwṓr*	'door, gate'

***e**

**eheu*	'alas'

***g**

**gag*- (WC)	'cackle'
**gal*-	'call out, speak'
**gal*- (NW)	'be physically able'
**ga/ondh*-	'wheat'
**garĝos* (WC)	'frightening, threatening'
**geh*$_1$(*i*)-	'sing'
**geh*$_a$-	'rejoice'
geh*$_a$*dh*- [geh*$_a$- 'rejoice']	'rejoice'
geh*$_a$*u*- [geh*$_a$- 'rejoice']	'rejoice'
**geh*$_x$*ĝh*-	'± enter water, wade'
**geid*- (WC)	'tickle'
**gel*- (NW)	'cold, to freeze'
**gem*- (WC)	'press, squeeze together, squeeze'
**gen*- (WC)	'± compress'
**ger*-	'crane'
**ger*- (WC)	'gather; herd, crowd'
**ger*- (WC)	'± hiss, howl'
**gerg*-	'± crack, resound'
**geu*- ~ **geh*$_x$*u*-	'curve'
**g(e)ulo*-	'fire, glowing coal'
**glaĝh*-	'cry out, lament'
**gleubh*- (WC)	'cut off, cut out'
**gl̥h*$_1$*ís*	'dormouse?'
**glogh*- (WC)	'thorn'
**gloiwos* (WC)	'clay'
**gol*- (WC)	'branch'
**gol(h*$_x$*)wos* (NW/WC?)	'bare, bald'
**gordebhós* (E)	'wild ass'
gów̥r̥* [geu*- 'curve']	'(animal) body hair'
**gras*-	'eat, graze'
**greut*- (NW)	'± compress'
**grōdo*- (WC)	'hail'
**grúĝs* (WC)	'dirt'

gubho/eh*$_a$*-* [geu-* 'curve']	'(store-)room, alcove'
gudóm* [geu-* 'curve']	'intestines'
**gutr̥*	'gullet, throat'
**gwésdos* (WC)	'branch'
***ĝ**	
**ĝar-*	'shout, call'
**ĝelu-*	'leech'
**ĝem-* (WC)	'weep, lament, moan'
**ĝemh*$_x$*-*	'marry'
ĝ(e)m(h*$_x$*)ros* [ĝemh*$_x$*-* 'marry']	'sister's husband'
**ĝenh*$_1$*-*	'beget a child; be born'
ĝénh*$_1$*es-* [ĝenh*$_1$*-* 'beget']	'family'
ĝenh*$_1$*tōr* [ĝenh*$_1$*-* 'beget']	'father; procreator'
ĝenh*$_1$*trih*$_a$*-* [ĝenh*$_1$*-* 'beget']	'mother, procreatrix'
**ĝénu-*	'jaw'
**ĝeP-*	'± eat, masticate'
**ĝerh*$_a$*-*	'grow, age, mature'
**ĝerh*$_a$*ont-*	'old man'
**ĝerh*$_a$*os*	'old man'
**ĝeus-*	'taste, enjoy'
**ĝl̥h*$_3$*wos-*	'husband's sister'
**ĝ(l̥)lákt*	'milk'
ĝm̥h*$_x$*ros* (WC) [ĝemh*$_x$*-* 'marry']	'son-in-law'
**ĝneh*$_3$*-*	'know, be(come) acquainted with'
ĝnéh*$_3$*mn̥* (WC) [ĝneh*$_3$*-* 'know']	'sign'
**ĝómbhos*	'tooth, set/row of teeth'
ĝomh*$_x$*ter-* [ĝemh*$_x$*-* 'marry']	'son-in-law'
**ĝonh*$_a$*dhos* (WC)	'jaw'
**ĝonu*	'knee'
**ĝr̥h*$_a$*nóm*	'grain'
**ĝwelh*$_x$*-*	'burn, glow'
**ĝyeuh*$_x$*-*	'chew'
***gh**	
**ghabh-*	'take, seize'
**ghabhlo/eh*$_a$*-* (NW)	'fork, branch of tree'
**ghaidos* (NW)	'goat'
**ghait(so)-*	'hair, mane'
**ghebhōl*	'head'
**ghedh-*	'join, fit together'
**ghéh*$_a$*(u)mr̥* (NW)	'interior of mouth (gums, palate)'
**gheiĝh-*	'protect, hide'
**ghel-*	'shine'

*ghel- (WC)	'cry out, sing'
*gheldh-	'desire'
*ghelĝheh$_a$- (WC)	'gland'
*ghel(h̥$_2$)d-	'hail'
*ghéluh$_x$s (WC)	'tortoise'
*gheluneh$_a$- (WC)	'lip'
*ghe(n)dh- (WC)	'seize, take in'
*gher-	'± cry (of animals or birds)'
*gherdh-	'gird, surround'
*ghérsos	'asp; pikeperch'?
*gheuĝh-	'protect, hide'
*ghleh$_x$dh(ro)- (NW) [*ghel- 'shine']	'smooth'
*ghleu- (WC)	'revel'
*ghórdhos [*gherdh- 'gird']	'fence, hedge; enclosure, pen, fold'
*ghostis (NW)	'guest; stranger, enemy'
*ghou- (NW)	'perceive, pay heed to'
*ghrebh-	'grasp, take, enclose'
*ghrebh- (NW)	'dig'
*ghredh-	'step, go'
*ghrei- (WC)	'touch lightly'
*ghreib- (NW)	'grip, grasp'
*ghrem-	'rumble'
*ghrendh- (WC)	'grind'
*ghres-	'± threaten, torment'
*g(h)rewom (E)	'reed, rush'
*ghromos (WC) [*ghrem- 'rumble']	'thunder, 'groan'
*g(h)ru(n)(d)- (WC)	'grunt'

***ĝh**

*ĝhaisós [*ĝhi- 'throw']	'throwing spear'
*ĝhalgheh$_a$- (WC)	'pole, stake'
*ĝhalh$_x$ros	'evil, unpleasant, unhealthy'
*ĝhan-s	'goose'
*ĝhasdhos (NW)	'staff'
*ĝhedye/o-	'defecate'
*ĝheh$_1$-	'leave'
*ĝheh$_a$w-	'gape, yawn'
*ĝhei-	'impels'
*ĝheim-	'winter, snow'
*ĝheis-	'frighten'
*ĝhel-	'plough'
*ĝhel- ~ *ghel-	'yellow'
*ĝhengh-	'step, walk'
*ĝher- (NW)	'shine, glow'

*ghḗr (WC) [*ĝhers- 'stiffen (of hair)']	'hedgehog'
*ĝhers-	'stiffen (of hair), bristle'
*ĝhesl(iy)os (GA)	'thousand'
*ĝhésr-	'hand'
*ĝheu-	'pour'
*ĝheud- (NW) [*ĝheu- 'pour']	'pour'
*ĝheu(h_x)-	'call to, invite, invoke'
*ĝheumn- [*ĝheu- 'pour']	'libation'
*ĝh(e)utreh$_a$- (C) [*ĝheu 'pour']	'± pot'
*ĝhéyos [*ĝhei- 'impels']	'horse'
*ĝh(h_1)iyeh$_a$-	'yawn'
*ĝhh̥$_a$wos	'gaping hole'
*ĝhi-	'throw'
*ĝhn̥ghéno/eh$_a$- (GA)	'± buttock'
*ĝhō- (WC)	'behind'
*ĝhóh$_1$ros	'gap, empty space'
*ĝhóln- ~ *ĝhólos [*ĝhel- 'yellow']	'gall'
*ĝhor- (C) [*ĝhers- 'stiffen (of hair)']	'young pig'
*ĝhorh$_x$neh$_a$-	'entrails'
*ĝhor(ye/o)-	'desire'
*ĝhóstos [*ĝhés-r- 'hand']	'hand'
*ĝhrésdh(i)	'barley'
*ĝhwáks (WC)	'torch'
*ĝhwēr	'wild animal'
*ĝhwonos [*ĝheu(h_x)- 'call']	'a sound, voice'
*ĝhy- ~ *ĝyei- (C)	'bird of prey, kite?'

$*g^w$

*g^wabh-	'dip'
*g^wādh-	'dive'
*g^weh$_a$-	'come'
*g^weidh- (WC)	'be foul, purulent'
*g^weih$_3$-	'live'
*g^wel- (WC)	'strike, stab, pierce'
*$g^{(w)}$elbhus	'womb'
*g^welh$_1$-	'throw'
*g^welh$_a$-	'acorn'
g^welōn (WC) [g^wel- 'strike']	'stinger'
*g^wel(s)-	'well up, flow'
*g^wem-	'come'
*g^wén-	'± (swollen) gland'
*g^wénh$_a$	'woman'
*g^werh$_3$-	'swallow'

*g^{w}erh$_{x}$-	'praise'
*g^{w}éru	'spear, spit'
*g^{w}es-	'extinguish'
*g^{w}et-	'say'
*g^{w}étu	'pitch'
*g^{w}étus	'stomach, womb'
*g^{w}ih$_{3}$wo- (WC) [*g^{w}yeh$_{3}$- 'live']	'pitch'
*g^{w}(i)yēh$_{a}$ (GA)	'bowstring; taut thread'
*g^{W}l̥tur-	'vulture'
*g^{w}orh$_{x}$-	'mountain; forest'
*g^{w}ou-k^{w}olos (WC) [*g^{w}ōus 'cow' + *k^{w}el- 'turn']	'cowherd'
*g^{w}ōus	'cow'
*g^{w}reh$_{2}$u-	'heavy'
*g^{w}réh$_{2}$-w-on- [*g^{w}r(e)h$_{a}$(-u)- 'heavy']	'quern'
*g^{w}retsos (NW)	'thick'
*g^{w}rih$_{3}$weh$_{a}$- [*g^{w}erh$_{3}$- 'swallow']	'neck'
*g^{w}uh$_{x}$-	'defecate'
*g^{w}yeh$_{3}$-	'live'
*g^{w}yeh$_{a}$-	'physical power; overcome'
*g^{w}yéh$_{3}$wyom [*g^{w}yeh$_{3}$- 'live']	'animal'

***g^{w}h**

*g^{w}haidrós (WC)	'bright, shining'
*g^{w}hedh-	'ask, pray'
*g^{w}hel- (WC)	'wish, want'
*g^{w}hen-	'strike'
*g^{w}her-	'warm'
*g^{w}hermos [*g^{w}her- 'warm']	'warm'
*g^{w}hih$_{x}$(slo)- (WC)	'± sinew, thread'
*g^{w}honós	'± thick, sufficient'
*g^{w}hren- (WC)	'think'
*g^{w}hrensós [*g^{w}her- 'warm']	'warm'

h

*ha	'surprise'
*ha ha	'laughter'

***h$_{1}$**

*h$_{1}$dónt- [*h$_{1}$édmi 'eat']	'tooth'
*h$_{1}$édmi	'eat'
*h$_{1}$edonom [*h$_{1}$édmi 'eat']	'food'
*h$_{1}$édwōl [*h$_{1}$édmi 'eat']	'pain; evil'
*h$_{1}$eg-	'be in need, lack'

*h$_1$eĝ-	‘say’
*h$_1$eĝ	‘I’
*h$_1$eĝh-	‘cow’
*h$_1$eĝhis	‘hedgehog’
*h$_1$eĝhs (WC)	‘out (of)’
*h$_1$ēg^{w}hmi	‘drink’
*h$_1$eh$_1$tmén-	‘breath’
*h$_1$eh$_1$tr- [*h$_1$eh$_1$tmén- ‘breath’]	‘± lung, internal organ’
*h$_1$éi /*h$_1$ih$_a$- /*h$_1$id	‘this one’
*h$_1$ei-	‘go’
*h$_1$ei-	‘red’
*h$_1$eig-	‘move’
*h$_1$eih$_x$(s)-	‘ice’
*h$_1$eis-	‘set in motion’
*h$_1$éitr̥- [*h$_1$ei- ‘go’]	‘way, road’
*h$_1$eiwos	‘yew’
*h$_1$ekt-	‘net’
*h$_1$éḱweh$_a$- [*h$_1$éḱwos ‘horse’]	‘mare’
*h$_1$éḱwos	‘horse’
*h$_1$el-	‘brown’
*h$_1$el- (WC?)	‘waterbird, swan’
*h$_1$el- (WC)	‘go’
*h$_1$élem (NW)	‘mountain elm (Ulmus mantana)’
*h$_1$elew- (WC)	‘juniper, cedar’
*h$_1$elh$_1$ēn [*h$_1$el- ‘brown’]	‘red deer’
*h$_1$elh$_1$níha- (NW) [*h$_1$el- ‘brown’]	‘hind/cow-elk’
*h$_1$élḱes-	‘± ulcer’
*h$_1$elu-	‘dull red’
*h$_1$em- (NW)	‘take, distribute’
*h$_1$empís (WC)	‘gnat, stinging insect’
*h$_1$en- (WC)	‘year’
*h$_1$en-	‘that’
*h$_1$én-do [*h$_1$en(i) ‘in’]	‘into’
*h$_1$endrós [*h$_1$en(i) ‘in’]	‘egg, scrotum’
*h$_1$eneḱ-	‘attain’
*h$_1$eng^w-	‘swell’
*h$_1$énh$_1$u	‘without’
*h$_1$en(i)	‘in, into’
*h$_1$éni-h$_3$k^w-o/eh$_a$- [*h$_1$en(i) ‘in’ + *h$_3$ek^w- ‘eye’]	‘face’
*h$_1$entér [*h$_1$en(i) ‘in’]	‘into, between’
*h$_1$en-t(e)rom [*h$_1$en(i) ‘in’]	‘innards’
*h$_1$ep-	‘take, seize, grasp’
*h$_1$eperos (NW/WC?)	‘boar’

*$h_1$epi ~ *$h_1$opi	'near, on'
*$h_1$epop	'hoopoe'
*$h_1$er-	'set in motion'
*$h_1$er- (WC)	'earth'
*$h_1$ereg^{w}o- (WC)	'pea'
*$h_1$erh$_1$-	'quiet, at rest'
*$h_1$erh$_1$-	'row'
*$h_1$er(h_1)- (GA)	'separate'
$h_1$erh$_1$trom [$h_1$erh$_1$- 'row']	'oar, paddle'
*$h_1$erh$_a$s-	'be well-disposed to someone'
*$h_1$erh$_x$-	'wash'
*$h_1$eri-	'sheep/goat'
*$h_1$erk^w-	'praise'
*$h_1$ermen-	'sickness'
*$h_1$ers-	'flow'
*$h_1$es-	'be'
*$h_1$es-	'throw, hurl'
h_1ēs- [$h_1$es- 'be']	'sit'
*$h_1$esen-	'autumn'
$h_1$esh$_2$éh$_a$- [$h_1$esh$_2$ós 'master']	'mistress'
*$h_1$esh$_2$ós	'master'
*$h_1$ésh$_2$r̥	'(flowing) blood'
h_1(e)su- [$h_1$es- 'be']	'good'
*$h_1$ét(e)no-	'kernel'
*$h_1$eti	'and, in addition'
($h_1$eti)loik^{w}os [$h_1$eti 'addition' + *leik^w-'leave']	'remains'
*$h_1$eu-	'cover; put on clothes'
*$h_1$eug^{w}h-	'speak solemnly'
*$h_1$eu(h_a)-	'empty, wanting'
*$h_1$euh$_x$dh-	'swell with fluid'
*$h_1$euk-	'become accustomed'
*$h_1$eus-	'burn, singe'
*$h_1$ger-	'awake'
*$h_1$idh$_a$	'here'
$h_1$ísus (GA) [$h_1$eis- 'set in motion']	'arrow'
*$h_1$iteros	'(an)other'
*$h_1$ith$_a$	'thus'
*$h_1$leig-	'jump'
*$h_1$lengh-	'blame, reproach'
*$h_1$le(n)g^{w}h-	'light (of weight)'
$h_1$leudh- [$h_1$el- 'go']	'go (out)'
*$h_1$leudh-	'grow'
$h_1$leudheros (WC) [$h_1$leudh- 'grow']	'people, freeman'

$h_1$leudhos [$h_1$leudh-'grow']	'people, freeman'
*$h_1$neĝh-	'stab'
$h_1$neĝhes- (WC) [$h_1$neĝh- 'stab']	'± spear'
$h_1$newh$_1$m̥ ($h_1$néwh$_1$n̥?)	'nine'
$h_1$newh$_1$m̥m/n̥-mos [$h_1$newh$_1$m̥ 'nine']	'ninth'
*$h_1$nómn̥	'name'
*$h_1$óg^{w}his	'snake
*$h_1$oinos	'one'
$h_1$óistro/eh$_a$- (WC) [$h_1$eis- 'set in motion']	'anger, any strong feeling'
$h_1$óitos [$h_1$ei- 'go']	'a going; oath'
$h_1$óiwo/eh$_a$- (WC) [$h_1$ei- 'red']	'± berry, fruit'
*h_1ōk̂-us	'fast'
*$h_1$ónh$_x$es-	'burden'
$h_1$ónteros (NW) [$h_1$en- 'that']	'other'
$h_1$op (WC?) [$h_1$ep- 'take']	'desire'
*$h_1$orh$_x$deh$_a$- (WC)	'± waterbird'
*$h_1$órs(o)-	'rear-end'
$h_1$óuh$_x$dhr̥ [$h_1$euh$_x$dh- 'swell']	'breast, udder'
$h_1$owes- [$h_1$eu- 'cover']	'(inner) skin'
*$h_1$rebh-	'cover with a roof'
*$h_1$reg^w-es-	'(place of) darkness'
*$h_1$rei-	'move'
$h_1$reih$_x$- [$h_1$rei- 'move']	'move'
*$h_1$reik-	'tear (off)'
*$h_1$reip- (WC)	'tear'
*$h_1$rep- (WC)	'snatch, pluck'
*$h_1$res- ~ *$h_1$ers-	'liquid, moisture'
*$h_1$reudh-	'(bright) red'
*$h_1$reug-	'belch'
$h_1$roudhós [$h_1$reudh- 'red']	'the red metal, i.e. copper'
$h_1$sónt- [$h_1$es- 'be']	'real, true'
$h_1$su-dhh$_1$énos (GA) [$h_1$es- 'be' + *dheh$_1$- 'put']	'rich, well-off'
$h_1$su-menesye/o- (GA) [$h_1$es- 'be' + *men- 'think']	'to be well disposed to'
*$h_1$wers-	'rain'
*$h_1$wes- (NW)	'moist, especially of the ground or plants'
*$h_1$yenh$_a$-ter-	'husband's brother's wife'
(h_1)yēro/eh$_a$- [$h_1$ei- 'go']	'year, new season'

***$h_{1/4}$**

*$h_{1/4}$eis-	'refresh'
*$h_{1/4}$ek-	'rake'

*h$_{1/4}$er-	'ask the gods, consult an oracle'
*h$_{1/4}$óh$_1$(e)s-	'mouth'
*h$_{1/4}$okéteh$_a$- [*h$_{1/4}$ek- 'rake']	'harrow, rake'
*h$_{1/4}$ómsos	'shoulder'
*h$_{1/4}$ōr-	'speak a ritual formula'

***h$_2$**

*h$_2$eb(h)-	'river'
*h$_2$ed- (WC/PIE?)	'grain, barley'
*h$_2$ed(h)-	'hawthorn'
*h$_2$eh$_2$er-	'thresh, rake'
*h$_2$eh$_2$(e)r-	'±kidney'
*h$_2$eh$_x$-	'burn, be hot'
*h$_2$eh$_x$mer- (C) [*h$_2$eh$_x$-'burn']	'day'
*h$_2$éh$_x$ōs [*h$_2$eh$_x$- 'burn']	'ash'
*h$_2$eh$_x$seh$_a$- [*h$_2$eh$_x$- 'burn']	'hearth'
*h$_2$éh$_x$tr̥ [*h$_2$eh$_x$- 'burn']	'fire'
*h$_2$eh$_x$treh$_a$- (WC) [*h$_2$eh$_x$- 'burn']	'hearth'
*h$_2$ēh$_x$tró- (NW) [*h$_2$eh$_x$- 'burn']	'quick, fast'
*h$_2$ēkr̥	'maple'
*h$_2$ek̂-	'sharp, pointed'
*h$_2$élbhit	'barley'
*h$_2$elg^{w}ho/eh$_a$-	'payment, prize'
*h$_2$elwos	'elongated cavity, hollow'
*h$_2$em-	'hold on to, contain'
*h$_2$em-	'raw, bitter'
*h$_2$em-	'mow'
*h$_2$emĝh-	'tie, constrain'
*h$_2$em-h$_a$ek̂s-ih$_a$- [*h$_2$em- 'hold on to' + *h$_a$ek̂s- 'shoulder-joint; axle']	'wagon-chassis'
*h$_2$emros [*h$_2$em- 'raw']	'bitter, sour'
*h$_2$en-	'draw (liquids)'
*h$_2$en-	'father's mother'
*h$_2$éndhes-	'±flower'
*h$_2$enk-	'bend'
*h$_2$ensiyo/eh$_a$- [*h$_2$em- 'hold on to']	'reins; handle'
*h$_2$ent- [*h$_2$enti 'in front']	'forehead'
*h$_2$entbhi- [*h$_2$enti 'in front']	'around, on both sides'
*h$_2$entbhi-k^{w}olos [*h$_2$enti 'in front' + *k^{w}el- 'turn']	'servant'
*h$_2$enti	'in front'
*h$_2$ep-	'fasten, join'

*h_2eP-	'living water'
$h_2$épes- [$h_2$ep- 'fasten']	'limb, part of the body'
*$h_2$er- (WC/PIE?)	'nut'
*$h_2$erdus	'high, lofty'
*$h_2$erĝ-	'white'
$h_2$erĝn̥tom [$h_2$erĝ- 'white']	'white (metal), silver'
*$h_2$erh_x-	'destroy'
*$h_2$erk-	'hold back'
*$h_2$erk-	'rend, destroy'
*$h_2$eru-	'±pray, curse'
*$h_2$éryos	'cavity'
*$h_2$es-	'be/become dry'
*$h_2$eug- (C)	'shine, become bright'
$h_2$euh$_2$ih$_a$- (WC) [$h_2$euh$_2$os- 'grandfather']	'grandmother'
*$h_2$euh$_2$os	'grandfather; uncle'
*$h_2$eu(h_x)s-	'draw water'
*$h_2$lei-	'set in motion'
$h_2$meh$_1$- [$h_2$em- 'mow']	'mow'
$h_2$merg- (WC) [$h_2$em- 'mow']	'gather, harvest'
$h_2$met- (NW) [$h_2$em- 'mow']	'mow'
*$h_2$nobh-	'navel; nave'
*$h_2$omós	'raw, uncooked'
$h_2$ónkos [$h_2$enk- 'bend']	'something bent, hook'
*h_2ó/ép(e)n-	'goods, wealth'
$h_2$ósdos [h_2o 'on' + *sed- 'sit']	'branch'
*$h_2$óst	'bone'
$h_2$owikéh$_a$- [$h_2$ówis 'sheep']	'ewe'
*$h_2$ówis	'sheep'
*$h_2$rétk̂es-	'destruction'
*h_2r̥ĝ-rós (GA)	'fast'
h_2r̥ĝ(u)- [$h_2$erĝ- 'white']	'white'
h_2ŕ̥tk̂os [$h_2$rétk̂es- 'destruction']	'bear'
$h_2$stḗr [$h_2$eh$_x$- 'burn']	'star'
*$h_2$weh$_1$-	'blow'
$h_2$weh$_1$nt- [$h_2$weh$_1$- 'blow']	'wind'
$h_2$weh$_1$yús [$h_2$weh$_1$- 'blow']	'wind'
*(h_2)wer- (NW)	'±attach'
*$h_2$wes-	'dwell, pass the night, stay'
$h_2$wóstu [$h_2$wes- 'dwell']	'dwelling'

***h$_{2/3}$**

*$h_{2/3}$eh$_x$-	'trust in, believe'

*$h_{2/3}$éi$h_1$os	'shaft (of a cart or wagon)'
*$h_{2/3}$(e)lĝ(h)-	'grain' (or 'millet'?)
*$h_{2/3}$enk̂-	'bestow'
*$h_{2/3}$eu-	'weave'
*$h_{2/3}$n̥sis	'large (offensive) knife'
*$h_{2/3}$ónk̂os	'what is bestowed'
*$h_{2/3}$orbhos	'orphan, heir'
*$h_{2/3}$osp-	'aspen, poplar'
*$h_{2/3}$r̥gis	'wheel'
*$h_{2/3}$uh_1e/olo-	'owl'
*$h_{2/3}$uk^w-	'cooking vessel'
*$h_{2/3}$webh-	'weave'
*$h_{2/3}$wed-	'be alive'
*$h_{2/3}$wed(h_2)-	'lead in marriage, marry'
$h_{2/3}$wédr̥ [$h_{2/3}$wed- 'be alive']	'creatures, (wild) animals'
*$h_{2/3}$weg(h)-	'pierce'
*$h_{2/3}$wergh- (NW/PIE?)	'±commit a crime'
$h_{2/3}$wobhseh_a- [$h_{2/3}$webh- 'weave']	'wasp'
*$h_{2/3}$wop-	'treat badly'

***h_3**

*$h_3$ed-	'hate'
*$h_3$ed- (WC)	'give off a smell'
h_3ek^w- [h_3ek^w- 'see']	'eye'
*h_3ek^w- (GA)	'see'
*$h_3$elek- (WC)	'elbow, forearm'
*$h_3$elh_1-	'destroy'
*$h_3$elVn-	'elbow, forearm'
*$h_3$eng^w-	'anoint (with salve), (be)smear'
$h_3$éng^wn̥ (WC) [$h_3$eng^w- 'anoint']	'butter'
*$h_3$enh_2-	'contend, quarrel'
*$h_3$énr̥ (C)	'dream'
*$h_3$ens-	'be gracious to, show favour'
*$h_3$ep-	'roast'
*$h_3$er-	'set in motion (vertically)'
*$h_3$érbhis	'circle, orb'
*$h_3$es(k)-	'ash (tree)'
*$h_3$eu-	'perceive'
*$h_3$eug- (WC)	'cold'
*$h_3$eust(y)o- (NW)	'estuary, river mouth'
h_3ēwis [$h_3$eu- 'perceive']	'obvious'
*$h_3$lem- (WC)	'break'
*$h_3$ligos	'ill; bad'
*$h_3$meigh-	'drizzle, mist'
*$h_3$méiĝhe/o-	'urinate'

*$h_3$merĝ- (GA)	'wipe off'
*$h_3$nobh-	'navel, nave'
*$h_3$nogh(w)-	'(finger- or toe-)nail'
*$h_3$or-	'eagle'
*$h_3$reĝ-	'extend, stretch'
h_3rḗĝs [$h_3$reĝ- 'extend']	'ruler, king'
$h_3$reĝtos [$h_3$reĝ- 'extend']	'right'
*$h_3$reuk-	'dig up'

***h_4**

*$h_4$edhés-	'axe, adze'
*$h_4$ék̂mōn	'stone'
*$h_4$el-	'grind down'
*h_4(e)l̥bh-	'elf'
*$h_4$elbhós	'white'
*$h_4$elh_1-	'burn'
$h_4$elh_1n- [$h_4$elh_1- 'burn']	'sweat' (noun)
*$h_4$eli-	'he-goat'
*$h_4$em-	'mother'
*$h_4$en-	'(old) woman, mother'
$h_4$ep- [$h_4$épo 'back']	fourth generation marker
$h_4$epér- [$h_4$épo 'back']	'back, behind'
*$h_4$épo	'back, behind'
*$h_4$erg^w-	'argue, assert'
*$h_4$er$h_2$os	'border, line, limit'
*$h_4$erós	'member of one's own group'
*$h_4$eu-	'eat'
*$h_4$eu	'away (from)'
*$h_4$loĝ-	'branch'
*$h_4$órĝhei	'mounts'
$h_4$órĝhis [$h_4$órĝhei 'mounts']	'testicle'
*$h_4$upó	'up (from underneath)'
$h_4$upo-sth$_2$i/o- [$h_4$upó 'up' + *(s)teh$_2$- 'stand']	'servant'
*$h_4$welk-	'pull'

***h_a**

*$h_a$ebi- (WC)	'fir'
*$h_a$ebVl-	'apple'
*$h_a$ed (WC)	'at, to'
$h_a$ed-bher- [$h_a$ed 'to' + *bher- 'carry']	'sacrifice
*h_aēgos (GA)	'shame'
*$h_a$egwisy(e)h_a- (WC)	'axe'
*h_aeĝ-	'drive; fight'

h_aeĝilos [h_aeĝ- 'drive']	'fast'
h_aeĝínom [h_aeĝós 'goat']	'hide'
h_aeĝmen- [h_aeĝ- 'drive']	'troop'
*h_aeĝós	'he-goat'
h_aeĝós (GA) [h_aeĝ- 'drive']	'leader'
h_aeĝreh$_a$- [h_aeĝ- 'drive']	'hunt'
h_aeĝros [h_aeĝ- 'drive']	'field, pasture'
*$h_a$egh- (WC)	'be afraid, be downcast'
*$h_a$éghleh$_a$-	'affliction'
$h_a$eghlos [$h_a$egh- 'be afraid']	'unpleasant'
$h_a$eghlu ~h_aeĝhlu (WC)	'rain'
*h_aéĝhr̥	'day'
*$h_a$eg^{w}hnos (WC)	'lamb'
*$h_a$eh$_x$peros (?)(WC)	'river bank, shore of sea'
*$h_a$ei-	'assail, afflict'
*$h_a$ei-	'give'
*$h_a$eid- (WC)	'swell'
*$h_a$eidh-	'burn; fire'
*$h_a$eig- (WC)	'oak'
*$h_a$eiĝs	'goat'
*$h_a$eig^{w}hes- (WC)	'shame'
*$h_a$eik̂-	'possess'
*$h_a$eik̂smo/eh$_a$- (WC)	'spear, pointed stick'
*$h_a$eis-	'wish for, seek out'
*$h_a$ekkeh$_a$-	'mother'
$h_a$ek̂e(tro)- (NW) [$h_a$ek̂- 'sharp']	'sturgeon'
*$h_a$ek̂s-	'shoulder(-joint); axle'
$h_a$ek̂sleh$_a$- [$h_a$ek̂s- 'shoulder']	'shoulder'
$h_a$ek̂stí- [$h_a$ek̂- 'sharp']	'±awn, bristle'
$h_a$ek̂ú- (NW) [$h_a$ek̂- 'sharp']	'perch'
*$h_a$ek^{w}eh$_a$- (NW)	'water'
*$h_a$el- (WC)	'grow'
*$h_a$el-	'wander'
*$h_a$el-	'well up, flow'
*$h_a$el-	'burn'
*$h_a$éliso-	'alder'
$h_a$élmos (E) [$h_a$el- 'well up, flow']	'spring'
*$h_a$elnos (NW)	'beyond, yonder'
*$h_a$elut-	'beer'
*$h_a$élyos	'other'
*$h_a$emesl- (NW)	'blackbird'
*$h_a$emh$_3$- (GA)	'lays hold, grasps; swears'
*$h_a$em(h$_x$)īweh$_a$-	'suffering'
*$h_a$en- (WC)	'that'

*$h_a$endhós	'blind'
$h_a$énĝhes- [$h_a$enĝhu- 'narrow']	'±suffering, grief, fear'
*$h_a$enĝhus-	'narrow'
$h_a$enĝh(w)ēn- (WC) [$h_a$enĝhu- 'narrow']	'neck'
*$h_a$éng^{w}his (WC)	'snake'
*$h_a$énh$_1$-	'breathe'
$h_a$énh$_1$mi [$h_a$énh$_1$- 'breathe']	'breathe'
$h_a$énh$_1$mos [$h_a$énh$_1$- 'breathe']	'breath'
*$h_a$en-h_ae	'up (onto), upwards, along'
*$h_a$énh$_x$t(e)h_a	'doorjamb'
*$h_a$enk-	'bend'
$h_a$enkulos [$h_a$enk- 'bend']	'shoot'
*$h_a$énr̥	'(manly) strength, vitality'
*$h_a$enseh$_a$-	'handle'
*$h_a$énsus	'god, spirit'
*$h_a$en-u (E)	'up (onto), upwards, along'
*$h_a$epus	'weak'
*$h_a$er-	'prepare, put together'
*$h_a$er-	'reed'
*$h_a$érdhis	'point'
*$h_a$éreh$_a$-	'±ryegrass'
$h_a$érh$_3$wr̥ [$h_a$érh$_3$ye/o- 'plough']	'field'
*$h_2$érh$_3$ye/o-	'plough'
*$h_a$érkwos (NW)	'bow and/or arrow'
$h_a$értus [$h_a$er- 'prepare']	'fitting, order'
*$h_a$éru(s)	'wound'
*$h_a$et	'away, beyond'
*$h_a$et-	'go'
$h_a$etnos (NW) [$h_a$et- 'go']	'year'
*$h_a$eu-	'favour'
*$h_a$eug-	'grow, increase'
$h_a$euges- [$h_a$eug- 'grow']	'strength'
$h_a$eusom [$h_a$ewes- 'shine']	'gold'
$h_a$éusōs [$h_a$ewes- 'shine']	'dawn'
h_a(e)ussk̂eti [$h_a$ewes- 'shine']	'it lights up, dawns'
$h_a$eust(e)ro- [$h_a$ewes- 'shine']	'east'
*$h_a$ewei-	'bird'
*$h_a$ewes-	'shine'
*$h_a$ewis	'oats'
*$h_a$eyer-	'early'
*$h_a$eyes-	'metal > copper > bronze'
$h_a$idhrós (GA) [$h_a$eidh- 'burn']	'pure'
*$h_a$lei-	'smear'
*$h_a$leit- (WC)	'± do something hateful or abhorrent'
*$h_a$lek-	'defend, protect'

*(h_a)mauros (WC)	'dark'
*$h_a$melĝ-	'to milk'
*(h_a)mer$h_x g^w$- (WC)	'dark'
*h_anḗr	'man, person'
*h_an̥$h_a$ti-	'duck'
*$h_a$ógeh_a-	'± berry, fruit'
*$h_a$óus-	'ear'
*h_aō(w)i-om	'egg'
*$h_a$óyus	'vital force, life, age of vigour'
$h_a$rei(h_x)- (WC) [$h_a$er- 'prepare']	'number, count (out)'
*(h_a)wiselo- (NW/WC?) [*weis- 'stink']	'weasel'
$h_a$wokséye/o- [$h_a$eug- 'grow']	'grow'
$h_a$yeu- [$h_a$óyus 'vital force']	'young'
$h_a$yuh_x-n̥-ḱós [$h_a$óyus 'vital force']	'youth'

***h_x**

h_xēpis (GA) [$h_2$ep- 'fasten']	'confederate'
*h_xih_xiĝh(e/o)-	'desire (strongly)'
*h_xi$h_x$lu (WC)	'mud; swamp'
*$h_x$leh_ad-	'dear'
*$h_x$náss	'nose'
*(h_x)neid-	'insult'
*h_xn̥g^wnis	'fire'
*h_xoḱtṓ(u)	'eight'
h_xoḱtowós [h_xoḱtō(u) 'eight']	'eighth'
*$h_x$oldhu-	'(dugout) canoe, trough'
*$h_x$óleh_a-	'awl'
*$h_x$ólḱis	'elk/American moose'
*$h_x$olu-	'± spell'
*$h_x$óngl̥	'charcoal'
*$h_x$ópes-	'work' (noun)
*$h_x$orghi- (C)	'nit'
*$h_x$orki- (WC)	'tick'
*$h_x$ósghos	'knot (in wood)'
*$h_x$ousteh_a-	'mouth, lip'
*h_xVnghel- (WC)	'eel'

***i**

*isĝhis-	'loins'
*is$h_1$ros (GA)	'sacred power'
*it-	'thus'

***k**

*kagh- (WC)	'catch, grasp'
*kagh- (NW) [*kagh- 'catch']	'hedge, enclosure'

*kaghlos (WC)	'hail'
*káikos (NW/PIE?)	'one-eyed, cross-eyed'
*kai-welos	'alone'
*káiwr̥(t) (GA)	'cave, fissure (in the earth)'
*kak(k)eh$_a$ye/o- (WC)	'defecate'
*kal- (GA)	'beautiful'
*kamareh$_a$ (GA) [*kam-er-]	'vault'
*kam-er-	'bend'
*kam-p- (WC)	'bend (of terrain)'
*kan- (WC/PIE?)	'sing'
*kannabis (WC)	'hemp'
*kant(h)o- (WC)	'corner, a bending'
*kap-	'seize'
*kap- (NW) [*kap- 'seize']	'hawk, falcon'
*kapōlo-	'± head, skull'
*kápr̥	'penis'
*kápros [*kápr̥ 'penis']	'he-goat'
*kaptos (NW) [*kap- 'seize']	'captive'
*káput (NW)	'head'
*kar-	'praise loudly'
*kar-	'hard'
*karkr(o)-	'crab'
*kars-	'scratch; comb (wool)'
*kāru- (GA) [*kar- 'praise']	'poet'
*kat- (NW)	'cat'
*kath$_a$e	'down'
*katu- (NW)	'fight'
*kắu- (NW)	'howl; owl'
*kau(k)-	'cry out; cry out as a bird'
*kaulós (WC) [*kul- 'hollow']	'± cabbage, stalk'
*kaunos (WC)	'humble, lowly'
*ked-	'± pass through'
*keh$_a$-	'love'
*k(e)h$_a$isVr-	'mane'
*keh$_a$ros (NW) [*keh$_a$- 'love']	'friendly'
*keh$_a$u-	'strike, hew'
*keh$_x$i- (NW)	'hot'
*kei-	'set in motion'
*keḱ-	'polecat'
*kel-	'drive'
*kel-	'strike, hew'
*kel-	'prick'
*kel-	'raise'
*kel- (WC)	'deceive'

*kel(h_1)-	'lift, raise up'
*kelh_1-	'call out to'
*kelh_1- (WC) [*kel- 'strike']	'strike'
*kelp- (WC/PIE?)	'jug, pot'
*kem-	'love'
*kem- (WC)	'± press together'
*kem- (NW)	'hum'
*kemeros (WC)	'± hellebore'
*ken-	'fresh'
*ken-	'love'
*ken$h_x$is	'ash'
*kenk-	'± hock, back of knee'
*kenk-	'gird, wrap around'
*kenk-	'burn'
*kenk- (WC)	'hunger'
*kéntr/n- (WC)	'± patch, patched garment'
*ker-	'± caw'
*ker- (NW)	'burn'
*kerd-	'cut into, carve'
*kerd-	'± defile, defecate'
*kerd- (NW)	'belt'
*kérdos (WC)	'craft'
*kerdheh$_a$- (NW)	'herd, series'
*kergh-	'bind'
*kerh_x- (E)	'propel'
*kerk-	'hen'
*kérmen- [*kerd- 'cut']	'skin'
*kerp- [*kerd- 'cut']	'pluck, harvest'
*kert-	'plait, twine'
*kert- (E) [*kerd- 'cut']	'knife'
*kes-	'comb'
*kēs(k̂)eh$_a$- (WC)	'time'
*ket-	'room'
*keudes- (WC) [*keuh_1- 'perceive']	'magic force'
*keuh_1-	'perceive'
*keu(h_x)-	'curve'
*kéuh_xl̥ [*keu(h_x)- 'curve']	'hernia'
*keu-k-	'curve'
*keul- (NW)	'pig'
*keus-	'hollow out'
*k$h_a$ónks	'honey-coloured, golden'
*kik̂-(y)eh$_a$-	'jay'
*kla(n)g- (WC)	'scream (of birds)'
*kleh$_a$- (NW)	'spread out flat'

*kleh$_a$dhreh$_a$- (WC)	'alder'
*kleh$_a$wis (WC)	'bolt, bar; (wooden) hook'
*kléinus (NW/WC?)	'maple'
*kleng-	'bend, turn'
*klep-	'± lay hand to'
*kl̥h$_x$m(s)- (E)	'be fatigued, sleepy'
*kl̥h$_x$-ro-s (WC) [*kel- 'strike']	'plank'
*kl̥h$_x$wos	'bald'
*kl̥nos	'callosity'
kl̥tḗr [(s)kel- 'cut']	'knife'
*klun-	'resound'
*km̥h$_a$ros	'crayfish'
*km̥h$_x$p-h$_a$- (WC)	'drone'
*knab(h)- (WC)	'pick at, tease out'
*knei-g^{w}h- (NW)	'lean'
*kneu- (NW)	'nut'
*kob- (NW)	'fit, suit, accomplish'
*kobom (NW) [*kob- 'fit']	'success'
*koĝhéh$_a$- (WC)	'goat'
*kóh$_a$ilus (WC)	'healthy, whole'
*kóh$_a$-r̥	'wax'
*koiḱ-	'cut hair'
*kok̂es-	'inner part, nook'
*kók̂so/eh$_a$- [*kok̂es- 'inner part']	'hollow of (major) joint'
*kol- (WC)	'glue'
*kolh$_1$ōn (WC) [*kel(h$_1$)- 'lift']	'hill'
*kolnós	'one-eyed'
*kólsos [*kel- 'raise']	'neck'
*ko(m)	'with, side by side'
*kon-	'do, make'
*ko(n)gos	'hook'
*kónh$_a$m- (WC)	'lower leg, shin'
*kopso- (WC)	'blackbird'
*kóris (WC) [*kerd- 'cut']	'± biting insect'
*korm-	'broth, mash?'
*koryonos (WC) [*koryos 'army']	'leader'
*koryos	'army, people under arms'
*Kos-t-	'hunger'
*kós(V)los (NW)	'hazel'
kouh$_1$ēi(s) (GA) [(s)keuh$_1$- 'perceive']	'priest'
kreb- (NW) [(s)kerbh- 'turn']	'basket'
*kreidhrom (NW) [*kerd- 'cut']	'sieve'
*krek- (WC)	'beat the weft with a stick'
*krek- (NW)	'fish eggs, frogspawn'

*kremh$_x$us (WC)	'(wild) garlic'
*kréps	'body'
*kret- (NW)	'shake'
*kr(e)ubh-	'gather, amass'
*kréuh$_a$	'blood, gore'
*kreuk̂-	'cry out, raise the hue and cry'
*kreup-	'± rough, scabby'
*kreu(-s)-	'strike'
*kreut- (NW)	'± shake'
*kr̥h$_1$pís (WC) [*kerd- 'cut']	'shoe'
*kr̥k̂ós	'thin'
*kr̥nom (WC)	'cherry'
*krob-	'hurry'
*kroku- ~ *krókyeh$_a$- (WC)	'post'
*kr̥sneh$_a$ (WC)	'spring, wave'
*kseros-	'dry'
*kseu-	'rub, whet'
*kseubh-	'shave'
*kseubh- [*skeubh- 'push away']	'shake'
*ksih$_x$róm	'± (skim) milk, whey'
*ksun (WC)	'with'
*ksuróm (GA) [*kseu- 'rub, whet']	'razor'
*(k)sweid-	'milk'
*kswek̂s	'six'
*kswek̂s-k̂omt(h$_a$) [*kswek̂s 'six' + *dék̂m̥(t) 'ten']	'sixty'
*kswek̂sos [*kswek̂s 'six']	'sixth'
*kúh$_x$los	'back'
*kuh$_x$p- (WC)	'water vessel'
*kuh$_x$s-	'hire'
*kukū	'cuckoo'
*kuk̂is	'± (female) pubic hair, vulva'
*kul-	'hollow'
*kumbo/eh$_a$-	'bowl, small vessel'
*kus-	'kiss'
*kus-	'dwelling'
*kutsós	'anus, vulva'
*kVlVk̂-	'cup, drinking vessel'
*kVr-C-	'crow; raven'
*kwat-	'ferment'

***k̂**

*k̂ad-	'fall'
*k̂ámos (WC)	'sheatfish'
*k̂ank-	'branch'

*k̂āpos	'piece of land, garden'
*k̂arh$_x$ka- (NW)	'magpie'
*k̂as-	'grey'
*k̂asos [*k̂as- 'grey']	'hare'
*k̂eh$_1$-	'declare solemnly'
*k̂eh$_1$kom	'edible greens' (< *'foliage'?)
*k̂eh$_1$s- (E) [*k̂eh$_1$- 'declare']	'instruct'
*k̂eh$_a$des-	'±concern; hate'
*k̂eh$_a$k- (WC)	'jump'
*k̂eh$_a$u-	'burn'
*k̂eh$_x$(i)-	'sharpen, hone'
*k̂ei-	'lie'
*k̂eigh- (NW/PIE?)	'fast'
*k̂eir- (NW)	'dull or brownish black'
*k̂éiwos [*k̂ei- 'lie']	'belonging to the household'
*k̂ek^w-	'defecate'
*k̂el- (WC)	'conceal, cover'
*k̂elb- (NW)	'help'
*k̂el(h$_x$)-	'±(spear)point'
*k̂ēls [*k̂el- 'conceal']	'(store)room'
*k̂elto-	'cold'
*k̂em-	'cover'
*k̂em-	'hornless'
*k̂emh$_a$-	'grow tired, tire oneself with work, work'
*k̂enós (C)	'empty'
*k̂e(n)s-	'declare solemnly'
*k̂ent-	'sharp'
*k̂er-	'grow'
*k̂er-	'decay'
*k̂er- ~ *k̂r̥-wos	'greyish blue, greyish green'
*k̂er-	'horn'
*k̂érberos (GA)	'spotted'
*k̂ērd	'heart'
*k̂er(es)- (NW)	'±(rough) hair, bristle'
*k̂érh̥$_2$s [*k̂er- 'horn']	'horn'
*k̂érh̥$_2$sr̥ [*k̂er- 'horn']	'horn'
*k̂erh$_x$-	'mix'
*k̂ers-	'run'
*k̂er(s)no- (WC)	'hoarfrost, frozen snow'
*k̂es-	'cut'
*k̂et- (GA)	'be angry'
*k̂eudh-	'hide'
*k̂euh$_1$-	'swell, grow great with child'
*k̂eu(h$_x$)-	'hollow out'

**k̂éuh$_x$-*	'hernia'
**k̂euk-*	'cry out (to)'
**k̂euk-*	'shine, burn'
k̂ihk̂$_x$won-* (C) [k̂eh$_x$(i)-* 'sharpen']	'pillar, post'
**k̂iker-* (WC)	'chickpea
**k̂is*	'this one'
**k̂lei-*	'lean'
**k̂leu-*	'hear'
**k̂leu-* (WC)	'clean'
k̂leus-* [k̂leu-* 'hear']	'hear'
k̂léutrom* [k̂leu-* 'hear']	'a sound'
k̂léwes-* [k̂leu-* 'hear']	'fame'
k̂líts* [k̂lei-* 'lean']	'post, trimmed log'
**k̂lóunis*	'±haunch, hip'
k̂meh$_a$-* (GA) [k̂emh$_a$-* 'grow tired']	'made, prepared'
**k̂m̥tóm*	'hundred'
**k̂óh$_1$kōh$_2$*	'(forked) branch'
k̂oh$_x$nos* [k̂eh$_x$(i)-* 'sharpen']	'whetstone, hone'
**k̂óimos* (WC)	'household, village'
**k̂oino-* (WC)	'grass'
**k̂oiwis*	'±tube'
**k̂ókolos*	'splinter'
k̂ók^{w}r̥* [k̂ek^w-* 'defecate']	'excrement, dung, manure'
**k̂ólh$_x$ōm*	'stalk, stem, straw'
**k̂(o)nid-* (WC)	'nit, louse egg'
**k̂onk-*	'hang'
k̂onkh$_a$os* [k̂onk-* 'hang']	'mussel(-shell), etc.'
**k̂ónkus*	'a kind of fish'
**k̂oph$_2$ós*	'hoof'
**k̂óph$_a$elos*	'carp'
**k̂ormon-* (NW)	'weasel, ermine/stoat'
k̂óru* [k̂er-* 'horn']	'horn'
**k̂óss*	'(Scotch) pine'
k̂ostrom* ~ **k̂osdhrom* [k̂es-* 'cut']	'knife'
k̂ouh$_1$ros* [k̂euh$_1$-* 'swell']	'powerful'
**k̂óuh$_x$r̥*	'hole, opening'
**k̂óunos*	'red'
**k̂red-*	'framework, beams'
k̂red-dheh$_1$-* [k̂ērd* 'heart' + **dheh$_1$-* 'put']	'believe'
k̂r̥h$_2$sro(h$_x$)on-* (NW) [k̂er-* 'horn']	'hornet'
**k̂ripo-*	'±head and facial hair'
k̂r̥nom* [k̂er-* 'horn']	'horn'
**k̂rópos* (NW)	'roof'
**k̂r̥rēh$_2$*	'head'

*ḱr̥sos (NW) [*ḱers- 'run']	'wagon'
*ḱseh$_1$-	'burn, singe'
*ḱsúlom (WC)	'worked, shaped wood; post, stake'
*ḱuh$_x$dós (WC)	'dung'
*ḱúh$_x$los	'spear, spit'
*ḱ(u)wōn	'dog'
*ḱweitos	'white'
*ḱwéndhr/no- (NW)	'angelica'
*ḱwen(to)- [*ḱeuh$_1$- 'swell']	'holy'
*ḱwesh$_x$-	'±breathe; sigh, groan'
*ḱwésh$_x$mi [*ḱwesh$_x$- 'breathe']	'breathe deeply, sigh'
*ḱyeh$_1$-	'deep intense shade, ±green'
*ḱyeino- (GA)	'bird of prey, kite'

***kh**

*kha-	'laugh'

***k^w**

*k^{w}ap- (WC)	'smoke, seethe'
*k^{w}as- (NW)	'(wicker-) basket'
*k^{w}at- (WC)	'shake'
*- k^{w}e	'and'
*k^{w}ed- (NW)	'whet, sharpen'
*k^{w}eh$_1$(i)-	'fear, revere'
*k^{w}eh$_a$k- (NW)	'of what sort'
*k^{w}eh$_a$li (WC)	'of what sort/size'
*k^{w}eh$_a$m (WC)	'how; as'
*k^{w}eh$_a$s-	'cough'
*k^{w}ei-	'pile up, build'
*k^{w}ei-	'perceive'
*k^{w}ei-	'fine, punish'
*k^{w}eih$_1$-	'rest, quiet'
*k^{w}eḱ/ĝ-	'appear'
*k^{w}ek^{w}lóm [*k^{w}el- 'turn']	'wheel'
*k^{w}el-	'turn'
*k^{w}elp- (WC)	'arch'
*k^{w}em-	'swallow'
*k^{w}ent(h)- (WC)	'suffer'
*k^{w}er-	'cut'
*k^{w}er-	'do, make, build'
*k^{w}erp-	'turn'
*k^{w}erus	'large cooking pot, cauldron'
*k^{w}et- (WC)	'chaff, bran

*k^{w}etwóres	'four'
k^{w}etwor-pod- [k^{w}etwóres 'four' + *pōds 'foot']	'animal'
*k^{w}íd	'what, what one'
*k^{w}ís	'who'
*k(^{w})leik̂-	'suffer'
*k^{w}lep- (E)	'desire'
k^{w}leu- [k^{w}el- 'turn']	'turn'
*k^{w}ód	'what'
*k^{w}odéh_a	'when'
*k^{w}oi$h_x$os	'pertaining to whom/what'
k^{w}oineh_a- [k^{w}ei- 'fine']	'compensation'
*k^{w}óm	'when'
*k^{w}ór	'where'
*k^{w}ós	'who'
*k^{w}óteros	'which (of two)'
*k^{w}óti ~ *k^{w}éti	'how much/many'
*k^{w}rei(h_a)-	'pay'
*k^{w}résnos (NW)	'tree; brush(wood)'
*k^{w}r̥mis	'worm, insect'
*k^{w}r̥snós	'black'
*k^{w}rustēn	'(freezing) cold'
k^{w}r̥wis [k^{w}er- 'do']	'±tool'
*k^{w}sep-	'night'
*k^{w}turyós ~ *k^{w}etwortos [*k^{w}etwóres 'four']	'fourth'
*k^{w}u ~ *k^{w}ū́	'where'

***l**

*lab- (WC)	'lick'
*laiwós	'left'
*lak- (WC)	'lick'
*lak- (WC)	'rend, tear'
*lal-	'babble'
*la(m)bh-	'seize'
*lap-	'shine'
*las-	'be greedy, lascivious'
*lau- (NW)	'benefit, prize'
*leb- (NW)	'lip'
*lebh-	'ivory'
*leg- (WC)	'drip, trickle'
*leĝ-	'gather; see [gather with the eyes]'
*legh-	'lie'
*léghes- [*legh- 'lie']	'place for lying, bed, couch'

*leh$_1$d-	'grow slack, become tired'
*leh$_1$d-	'leave'
*leh$_1$w- (WC)	'stone'
*leh$_2$-	'pour, wet, make flow'
*leh$_2$-	'military action'
*leh$_2$wós [*leh$_2$- 'military action']	'people (under arms)'
*leh$_a$-	'bark'
*leh$_a$- (WC)	'complain, cry out'
*leh$_a$d-	'dear'
*leh$_a$peh$_a$-	'foot, paw'
*leh$_a$t- (NW)	'wet, moist'
*lei-	'bent'
*leib- (WC)	'pour, make a libation'
*leiĝh-	'lick'
*leik^w-	'leave (behind)'
*leip-	'adhere, stick; smear'
*leip- (NW)	'light, cause to shine'
*leis-	'leave a trace on the ground'
*l(e/o)iseh$_a$- (NW) [*leis- 'leave a trace']	'furrow'
*leit(h$_x$)-	'go away, go forth'
*lek-	'jump, scuttle along'
*lem- (WC)	'(nocturnal) spirit'
*lemb- ~ *remb-	'hang down'
*lendh- (NW)	'open land, waste'
*leng-	'bend'
*lenk-	'bend; traverse, divide'
*lēnos (NW)	'quiet'
*lenteh$_a$- (WC)	'linden'
*l(e)nto- (NW)	'soft'
*lep- (WC)	'stone'
*lep- (WC)	'strip, peel'
*lerd- (WC)	'±crooked'
*lesi-	'liver'
*letrom (NW)	'leather'
*leu- (WC)	'dirt'
*leubh-	'love, desire'
*leud- (NW)	'act hypocritically, badly'
*leug-	'grieve, be pained'
*leug- (WC)	'bend; bend together, entwine'
*leuĝ-	'break, break off'
*leugh- (NW)	'lie, tell a lie'
*leuh$_1$- (WC)	'wash, bathe'
*leuh$_x$-	'hunt, release, cut off'
*léuh$_x$ōn [*leuh$_x$- 'hunt']	'animal'

**leuk-*	'shine'
leukós* [leuk-* 'shine']	'light, bright, clear'
leuk-* [leuk-* 'shine']	'see'
**leup-*	'peel'
**linom* (WC)	'flax'
**li(w)-* (WC)	'lion'
**loh*$_a$*po-* (WC)	'cow'
**loid-* (WC)	'play, jest'
lóik*^{w}*nes-* [leik*^{w}*-* 'leave']	'(inherited) possessions'
**lokús* (WC)	'lake, water, pond'
**lōk̂-*	'weasel'
**lók̂s*	'salmonid, salmon (trout)'
**lóndhu*	'loins'
lónko/eh*$_a$*-* [lenk-* 'bend']	'valley'
lōp-* (WC) [lep-* 'strip']	'±strip of cloth, bast, or hide used for clothing'
lord(sk̂)os* (WC) [lerd-* '±crooked']	'crooked of body'
**lorgeh*$_a$*-* (NW?)	'club'
**los-*	'cloth'
**losiwos*	'weak'
**lóubho/eh*$_a$*-* (WC)	'bast, bark'
louh*$_1$*trom* (WC) [leuh*$_1$*-* 'wash']	'(wash-)basin'
lóuk(es)-* [leuk-* 'shine']	'light'
louksneh*$_a$*-* (NW) [leuk-* 'shine']	'moon'
lu-* (lus-*)	'louse'
**luk̂-* (WC)	'lynx'

***m**

**magh-*	'be able'
maghus* [magh-* 'be able']	'young man'
maghwih*$_a$*-* [magh-* 'be able']	'young woman'
**mai-* (NW)	'soil, defile'
**mak-* (WC)	'poppy'
**mak-*	'thin, long'
makrós* (WC) [meh*$_a$*k-* 'thin']	'thin, long'
**mand-*	'enclosure, stall'
**mandh-* or **mant-* (WC)	'chew'
**manu-*	'Man', ancestor of humankind
**márkos* (NW)	'horse'
**masdos* (NW)	'post'
**mat-*	'± worm, maggot'
**mat-*	'hoe, plough'
**māwort-*	'god of war'
**me/o-*	interrogative/relative

**mē*	'not'
**med-*	'measure, weigh'
med-* [med-* 'measure']	'heal, cure'
**médhu*	'mead'
medhwih$_a$-* [médhu* 'mead']	'intoxicator'
**meĝh$_a$-*	'large, great'
**meh$_1$(i)-*	'grow'
**meh$_1$(i)-*	'± mumble'
**meh$_1$l-* (WC)	'small animal'
méh$_1$-nōt* [meh$_1$(i)-* 'grow']	'moon'
meh$_1$ro-* ~moh$_1$ro-* (WC) [**meh$_1$(i)-* 'grow']	'large'
méh$_1$tis* [meh$_1$(i)-* 'grow']	'measure'
**meh$_2$lom*	'apple'
**meh$_a$-*	'wave/trick (with the hand)'
**m(e)h$_a$d-*	'become wet, moist, fat'
**méh$_a$r*	'hand'
**meh$_a$(t)-* (NW)	'good'
**méh$_a$tēr*	'mother'
méh$_a$trōus* (WC) [méh$_a$tēr* 'mother']	'maternal kinsman; maternal uncle'
meh$_a$truh$_a$-* (WC) [méh$_a$tēr* 'mother']	'mother's sister'
**mei-*	'less'
**mei-*	'exchange'
meigh-* ~meik-*	'close the eyes'
**meiĝ(h)-*	'barley' ('grain'?)
**meih$_x$-* (NW)	'go'
**meiḱ-*	'mix'
**meino-*	'opinion'
meit-* [mei-* 'exchange']	'exchange'
mei-wos* [mei-* 'less']	'belonging to little hand'
**mel-*	'argue, contend'
**mel-*	'good'
**mel-*	'fail, harm'
**meldh-*	'pray, speak words to a deity'
**meldh-*	'soft, weak'
**meldh-* (NW)	'lightning'
méles-* [mel-* 'harm']	'fault, mistake'
**méles-* (WC)	'limb'
**mel(h$_1$)-*	'soft'
**melh$_2$-*	'grind'
melh$_2$-* (WC?) [melh$_2$-* 'grind']	'± grain, millet'
**meli-* (NW)	'badger'
**mélit*	'honey'
melítih$_a$-* (C) [mélit* 'honey']	'honey-bee'

**melk-*	'plait, spin'
**mel-n-*	'dull or brownish black'
melo-* [mel-* 'harm']	'bad'
**mḗ(m)s*	'meat'
**men-*	'think, consider'
**men-*	'remain, stay'
**men-*	'project'
men-* [men-* 'project']	'chin'
**mendo/eh$_a$-*	'± (bodily) defect'
**mendyos* (C)	'horse'
**menegh-* (WC/PIE?)	'abundant'
ménes-* (GA) [men-* 'think']	'thought'
**meng-*	'± charm, deceive'
**menk-*	'press'
menk-* [menus/menwos* 'thin']	'lack'
menkus* (C) [menk-* 'press']	'soft'
ménm̥n̥* [men-* 'think']	'thought'
men(s)-dh(e)h$_1$-* [men-* 'think' + **dheh$_1$-* 'put']	'learn'
**menth$_2$-*	'stir'
méntis* [men-* 'think']	'thought'
**menus/menwos*	'thin (in density)'
**mer-*	'crush, pulverize'
**mer-*	'die'
**mer-*	'shine, shimmer'
**mer-*	'disturb, forget'
**mer-* (WC)	'braid, bind'
**merd-*	'± rub, scrape'
merih$_a$-* [méryos* 'young man']	'young woman'
**merk-* (NW)	'± darken'
mers-* [mer-* 'disturb']	'forget'
**méryos*	'young man'
**mesg-*	'intertwine'
**mesg-*	'dip under water, dive'
**meud-*	'be merry'
**meug-* (NW)	'± cheat, deceive'
**m(e)uh$_x$-*	'wash (in urine?)'
**meu(h$_x$)-*	'move'
**méuh$_x$kō(n)* (WC)	'heap'
**meus-*	'move; remove'
**mēus* (NW)	'moss, mould'
**m-h$_4$em-*	'mother'
**misdhós*	'reward, prize'
**míts*	'stake, post'

*ml̥dho/eh$_a$- [*meldh- 'soft']	'clay'
*mleuh$_x$-	'speak'
*ml̥h$_2$dh-o-	'crown of the head'
*ml̥k̂-	'touch lightly'
*mn̥h$_x$- (WC)	'minnow; small fish'
*mōd- (WC)	'meet'
*modheros	'blue/green'
*moisós	'ram, sheep; fleece, skin'
*mok̂o-	'gnat, stinging insect'
*mok̂s	'soon'
*mono- [*men- 'project']	'neck'
*mono/i- [mono- 'neck']	'neck ornament'
*morĝ-	'border'
*móri	'sea'
*mórom	'blackberry'
*móros [*mer- 'die']	'death'
*mórtos (GA) [*mer- 'die']	'person, mortal, man'
*morwi- ~ *morm- ~ *mouro-	'ant'
*mosghos	'marrow, brain'
*móstr̥ (E)	'brain, marrow'
*moud-	'desire strongly'
*mregh- (WC)	'rain softly, drizzle'
*mréghmen- (WC)	'brain'
*mr̥ĝhus	'short'
*mr̥k- (WC)	'± carrot'
*mr̥tís [*mer- 'die']	'death'
*mr̥tóm [*mer- 'die']	'death'
*mr̥tós [*mer- 'die']	'dead; mortal'
*mū-	'dumb'
*mug-	'± make a (low) noise'
*mú(k)skos (WC)	'ass/donkey'
*murmur-	'murmur'
*mus-	'steal'
*mūs [*meus- 'move']	'mouse'
*mus/h$_x$- (WC)	'fly; gnat, midge, mosquito'
*muskós (GA) [*meus- 'move']	'male or female sex organ'
*mustí- (E)	'fist'
*mūs(tlo)- [*meus- 'move']	'(little) mouse; muscle'

***n**

*nak-	'press, squeeze'
*nák(es)- (WC)	'± pelt, hide'
*nant- (NW)	'combat, fight'
*n̥bh(ro/ri)- [*nébhos - 'mist']	'rain'

*n̥dhés ~ *n̥dhero-	'under, low'
*ne	'not'
*ne	'thus'
*nébhes-	'mist, cloud; sky'
*ned-	'knot'
*ned- (WC)	'nettle'
*nedós	'reed, rush'
*nedskéh_a- (NW) [*ned- 'knot']	'tie, ring'
*ne/og^{w}nós	'bare, naked'
neg^{w}hrós (WC) [$h_1$eng^w- 'swell']	'kidney'
*né$h_1$tr- ~ *n$h_1$tr- (NW) [*(s)neh_1- 'twist']	'snake'
*neh_2-	'be timid'
*né$h_a$us	'boat'
*né$h_a$wis	'corpse'
*nei-	'be excited'
*neig^w-	'wash'
*neih_x-	'lead'
*neik-	'begin'
*neik- (WC)	'winnow'
*nek̂-	'perish, die'
*nek̂s [*nek̂- 'die']	'death'
*nék̂us [*nek̂- 'die']	'death; dead'
*nek^{w}t-	'night'
*nem-	'bend'
*nem-	'take/accept legally'
*némos- (WC)	'(sacred) grove'
*népōts	'grandson; (?) nephew'
*neptih_a- [*népōts 'grandson']	'granddaughter; (?) niece'
*neptiyos [*népōts 'grandson']	'descendant'
*neptonos ~ *$h_2$epōm nepōts [*népōts 'grandson']	'grandson of waters'
*ner	'under'
*nes-	'return home'
*neu-	'± cry out'
*neu- (WC/PIE?)	'nod'
*neud- (E)	'push (away)'
*neud- (NW)	'use, enjoy'
*néwos [*nu- 'now']	'new'
*n-$h_4$en-	'(old) woman, mother'
*ni	'downwards'
*nisdos [*ni 'down' + *sed- 'sit']	'nest'
*n̥k^{w}tus [*nek^{w}t- 'night']	'end of the night'
*n̥-mr̥tós (GA) [*ne 'not' + *mer- 'die']	'undying' (drink)
*nóh_1	'we two'

**n*(*o*)*h*$_x$*t*- (WC)	'± rear-end'
noibhos* [nei*- 'be excited']	'holy'
**nu*-	'now'

***o**

**ō*	'O'
**os*(*o*)*nos*	'ass'

***p**

**pad*-	'duck, teal?'
**pandos* (NW)	'curved'
**pano*-	'millet'
**pant*-	'stomach, paunch'
**pap*-	'± mother's breast, teat'
**papa*	'father, papa'
**parikeh*$_a$-	'± concubine; wanton woman'
**pastos*	'firm'
**pau*- (WC)	'little, few'
**ped*-	'fall'
pedom* [pōds* 'foot']	'footprint, track'
**peh*$_1$(*i*)-	'harm'
péh*$_1$*mn̥* (GA) [peh*$_1$(*i*)- 'harm']	'misfortune'
**peh*$_2$-	'guard, cause to graze'
**p*(*e*)*h*$_2$*no/eh*$_a$-	'cloth'
**péh*$_2$*ur*	'fire'
péh*$_2$*usōn* (GA) [peh*$_2$- 'guard']	'pastoral god'
**peh*$_3$(*i*)-	'swallow' > 'drink'
**peh*$_a$*ĝ*- ~ **peh*$_a$*k̂*-	'fasten securely'
**pei*-	'sing'
**peih*$_x$-	'be fat'
**peik/k̂*-	'be hostile, hate'
**peik̂*-	'paint, mark'
**peis*-	'blow to make a noise'
**peis*-	'thresh, grind'
**pek*-	'pull out [wool]'
**pék̂u*	'livestock'
**pek*^{w}-	'cook, bake'
**pel*-	'± sell'
**pel*-	'fold'
**pel*-	'be grey'
**pel*-	'hide'
**peld*-	'felt'
**pelek̂us*	'axe'
**peles*-	'wound'

*pelh$_1$-	'fill'
*pēl(h$_1$)ewis [*pelh$_1$- 'fill']	'container'
*pélh$_1$us [*pelh$_1$- 'fill']	'much'
*pelh$_a$- (NW)	'set in motion'
*pelh$_a$k-	'spread out flat'
*pelh$_x$-	'fort, fortified place'
*pelh$_x$- (WC)	'bear young'
*pel(i)s-	'cliff, stone, rock'
péln- (WC) [(s)pel- 'tear off']	'animal skin, hide'
*pelo/eh$_a$-	'chaff'
*pelpel- (NW)	'butterfly'
*pél(h$_x$)us [*pel- 'be grey']	'mouse'
*pen-	'feed, fatten'
*pen- (NW)	'water'
*penk-	'damp, mud'
*pénk^{w}e	'five'
*penk^{w}e dek̂m̥(t) [*pénk^{w}e 'five' + *dék̂m̥(t) 'ten']	'fifteen'
*penk^{w}ē-k̂omt(h$_a$) [*pénk^{w}e 'five' + *dék̂m̥(t) 'ten']	'fifty'
*pē(n)s-	'dust'
*pēnt-	'heel'
*pent-	'find one's way'
*pent- + *dheh$_1$-/*k^{w}er- [*pent- 'find one's way' + *dheh$_1$- 'put'/*kwer- 'make']	'priest'
*per-	'blow (on a fire)'
*per-	'exchange, barter'
*per-	'strike'
*per-	'pass through'
*per	'over, through, about'
*per-	'appear, bring forth'
*per- [*per- 'appear']	'offspring (of an animal)'
*per- (WC)	'trial, attempt'
*pḗr	'house'
*perd- (GA)	'panther, lion'
*pérde/o-	'fart'
*perg- (NW)	'pole, post'
*per(h$_x$)-	'first'
*peri-h$_1$es- (GA) [*peri 'over' + *h$_1$es- 'be']	'surpass'
*perk-	'fear'
*perk- (NW)	'glowing ash, charcoal'
*perk̂-	'ask, ask for (in marriage)'

**perk̂-*	'speckled'
**perk̂-*	'dig'
**pérk̂us*	'± breast, rib'
**perk*^{w}*unos*	'thunder god'
**pérk*^{w}*us* (NW)	'oak'
**pers-*	'sprinkle'
**pérsneh*$_a$-	'heel'
pértus* [per-* 'pass through']	'passage, way'
**peru-*	'rock'
perut-* [per-* 'over' + **wet-* 'year']	'last year'
**pesd-* (WC)	'fart'
**péses-*	'penis'
**pet-*	'fly'
**pet-*	'stretch'
pet(e)r-* [pet-* 'fly']	'wing, feather'
**peth*$_a$-	'spread out (the arms)'
peth*$_a$- (GA) [pet-* 'fly']	'fly'
pe/oth*$_a$*mo-* (NW) [pet-* 'stretch']	'thread'
**peug-* (WC)	'prick, poke'
**peu(h*$_x$*)-*	'stink, rot'
**peuh*$_x$-	'clean'
**péuk̂s*	'(Scotch) pine, conifer'
**p(h)eu-*	'blow, swell'
phŏ̄l-* (ph*$_x$*ŏ̄l-?*) (WC)	'fall'
**ph̥*$_a$*tḗr*	'father'
ph̥*$_a$*trōus* [ph̥*$_a$*tḗr* 'father']	'paternal kinsman'
**ph̥*$_a$*tr̥wyos*	'father's brother'
**píh*$_x$*wr̥*	'fat(ness)'
pih*$_x$*(y)-* [peh*$_1$*(i)-* 'harm']	'revile'
**pik-* (WC)	'pitch'
**pik̂-sk̂o-*	'spotted'
pik̂sk̂os* [pik̂-sk̂o-* 'spotted']	'trout, fish'
pildo-* (WC) [pilos* 'a hair']	'felt'
**pilos*	'(a single) hair'
**pin-*	'± shaped wood'
pipih*$_x$*usih*$_a$ [peih*$_x$- 'be fat']	'rich in milk'
**pipp-*	'young bird, nestling'
**pis-*	'crush, pound'
pisd-* (GA) [pis-* 'crush']	'press'
pisdo/eh*$_a$- [h*$_1$*epi* 'on' + **sed-* 'sit']	'vulva'
**pit(u)-*	'(some form of) conifer'
pitus* (NW?) [peih*$_x$- 'be fat']	'grain, meal'
**(p)k̂órmos*	'± grief, shame'
pleh*$_1$*dhwéh*$_1$*s* (WC) [pelh*$_1$- 'fill']	'(the mass of) people'

**pleh*$_a$*k-*	'flat'
pleh*$_a$*k-* [pleh*$_a$*k-* 'flat']	'please'
**pleh*$_a$*k/g-* (WC)	'strike, strike one's breasts'
**plek̂-*	'braid, plait'
**plek̂-* (WC)	'± break, tear off'
**plet-*	'broad'
pl(e)t-* [plet-* 'broad']	'shoulder (blade)'
**pleth*$_2$*-*	'spread out'
**pleu-*	'float, swim; wash'
pléumōn* [pleu-* 'float']	'lung'
**pleus-* (NW)	'(pluck) fleece, feathers'
pl̥h*$_1$*nós* [pelh*$_1$*-* 'fill']	'full'
pl̥h*$_1$*u-poik/k̂os* (GA/PIE?) [pelh*$_1$*-* 'fill' + **peik̂-* 'paint']	'many-coloured, variegated'
**pl̥h*$_x$*-*	'grey, pale'
pl̥th*$_2$*w-ih*$_a$*-* [pleth*$_2$*-* 'spread out']	'country, land'
pl̥th*$_2$*ú-* [pleth*$_2$*-* 'spread out']	'broad, wide'
**plus-*	'flea'
**plut-* (NW)	'plank'
**pneu-* (WC)	'snort, sneeze'
pn̥(k*^{w}*)stí-* (NW) [pénk*^{w}*e* 'five']	'fist'
pn̥k*^{w}*tós* [pénk*^{w}*e* 'five']	'fifth'
**pṓds*	'foot'
**poh*$_2$*(i)-*	'watch over cattle'
poh*$_2$*imén-* (WC) [poh*$_2$*(i)-* 'watch over cattle']	'herdsman'
póh*$_2$*iweh*$_a$*-* (WC) [poh*$_2$*(i)-* 'watch over cattle']	'open meadow'
poh*$_3$*tlom* [peh*$_3$*(i)* 'drink']	'drinking vessel'
**poksós*	'side, flank'
**pólh*$_a$*m* (WC)	'palm of the hand'
**pólik(o)s* (NW)	'finger, thumb'
**polk̂éh*$_a$*-* (NW)	'± fallow land'
**polt-* (WC)	'pap, porridge'
póntōh*$_2$*s* [pent-* 'find one's way']	'(untraced) path'
pórk̂os* [perk̂-* 'dig']	'young pig, piglet'
**pos* (WC)	'immediately adjacent; behind, following'
posk*^{w}*o-* [pos* 'behind' + **sek*^{w}*-* 'follow']	'behind'
posti* [pos* 'behind']	'after'
póth*$_a$*r̥* (WC) [peth*$_a$*-* 'spread out']	'shallow dish'
**pótis*	'husband'
potnih*$_a$*-* [pótis* 'husband']	'mistress, lady, wife'
**pótyetoi*	'rules, is master'

*poums-	'(human) body hair'
*prem-	'press down or back'
*prep- (WC)	'appear'
*prest-	'(period of) time'
*preu-	'jump
*preug- [*preu- 'jump']	'jump'
*preus-	'burn'
*preus-	'freeze'
*pr̥h$_3$ḱtós (C)	'anus'
*pr̥(h$_3$)tis [*per- 'exchange']	'what is distributed'
*pr̥h$_a$éh$_1$ [per 'over']	'in front of; before (of time)'
*pr̥h$_a$éi [per 'over']	'in front of; before (of time)'
*prih$_x$eh$_a$- [*prih$_x$ós 'of one's own']	'love'
*prih$_x$eh$_a$- [*prih$_x$ós 'of one's own']	'wife'
*prih$_x$ós	'of one's own'
*pŕ̥ḱeh$_a$- (NW) [*perḱ- 'dig']	'furrow'
*pr̥ḱ(^{w})eh$_a$- (NW) [*pérk^{w}us 'oak']	'pine'
*pro [per 'over']	'forward, ahead, away'
*pro-	third generation marker
*prō- [*per- 'pass through']	'early, morning'
*próḱsom	'grain'
*proti [per 'over']	'against, up to'
*próti-h$_3$(ō)k^{w}o/eh$_a$- [*proti 'against' +*h$_3$ek^w- 'eye']	'face, front'
*psténos	'woman's breast, nipple'
*pster-	'sneeze'
*pteh$_1$- [*pet- 'fall']	'fall'
*pteleyeh$_a$-	'elm?'
*pū- (*puh$_x$- ?)	'stink'
*púh$_x$es- (WC) [*peu(h$_x$)- 'stink']	'putrefaction, pus'
*puh$_x$rós (WC)	'wheat'
*puk(eh$_a$)-	'tail'
*puḱ-	'press together'
*puḱ- (GA)	'headband'
*pulos	'(a single) hair'
*put-	'cut'
*putlós [*pau- 'little']	'son'
*putós	'± vulva, anus'
*pyek-	'strike'

***r**

*rabh-	'± ferocity'
*red-	'gnaw, scrape'
*reg- (GA)	'dye'

*reĝ- /*rek-nos (WC)	'make wet'
*reh$_1$-	'put in order'
*reh$_1$-	'give'
*réh$_1$is [*reh$_1$- 'give']	'possessions'
*reh$_1$mós	'dirty; dirt, soot'
*reh$_1$t- (NW)	'post, pole'
*rei- (NW)	'striped, spotted'
*rei-	'tremble, be unsteady'
*rei-	'scratch'
*reidh- (NW)	'ride'
*reiĝ- (NW)	'extend, stretch out (a body part)'
*reik- [*rei- 'scratch']	'scratch; line'
*rek-	'speak'
*rendh-	'rend, tear open'
*rēp- (NW)	'crawl'
*rēpéh$_a$- (WC)	'turnip'
*resg-	'plait, wattle'
*reth$_2$-	'run'
*reu-	'roar, howl'
*reudh$_a$-	'mourn, lament'
*reudh-	'± push back'
*réughmen-	'cream'
*reu(h$_x$)-	'be open'
*reu(h$_x$)-	'tear out, pluck'
*réuh$_x$es- [*reu(h$_x$)- 'be open']	'open space'
*reuk/g-	'shrink, wrinkle up'
*reumn-	'rumen'
*réumn- [*reu(h$_x$)- 'pluck']	'horsehair' or 'fleece'
*reup-	'break'
*reus-	'± contend with, be angry at'
*rik-	'nit, tick'
*rṓs	'dew, moisture'
*róth$_2$o/eh$_a$- [*reth$_2$- 'run']	'wheel'
*r̥sḗn	'male'
*rughis (NW)	'rye'
*ruk- (NW)	'over-garment'

***s**

*saiwos (NW)	'hard, sharp, rude'
*sakros	'holy'
*sal(i)k- (NW)	'(tree) willow'
*samh̥$_x$dhos (WC)	'sand'
*sap- ~ *sep- (WC)	'± taste, come to know'
*sap- ~*sab-	'sap'

**sausos*	'dry'
*(*s*)*bhond-neha* (WC) [**bhendh-* 'bind']	'strap, sling'
**sed-*	'go'
**sed-*	'sit (down), set'
sedes-* [sed-* 'sit']	'seat'
sedlom* (WC) [sed-* 'sit']	'seat'
sedros* (WC) [sed-* 'sit']	'seat, chairlike object'
**seg-*	'fasten'
**seĝh-*	'hold fast, conquer'
**seh$_1$-*	'sow'
**seh$_1$(i)-*	'throw, neglect'
**seh$_1$(i)-*	'go forward, advance'
**seh$_1$(i)-* (WC)	'sift'
seh$_1$men-* (NW) [seh$_1$-* 'sow']	'seed'
seh$_1$ros* (NW) [seh$_1$(i)-* 'throw']	'long'
**seh$_2$(i)-*	'satisfy, fill up'
séh$_2$tis* (NW) [seh$_2$(i)-* 'satisfy']	'satisfaction'
**seh$_4$i-*	'± be angry at, afflict'
**seh$_a$-(e)l-*	'salt'
**seh$_a$g-*	'perceive acutely, seek out'
**séh$_a$ul*	'sun'
**seik-*	'reach for'
**seik-*	'pour out; overflow'
**sek-*	'cut'
**sek-*	'dry up'
sekūr-* (NW) [sek-* 'cut']	'axe'
**sek^w-*	'follow'
sek^w-* [sek^w-* 'follow']	'see'
**sek^w-* (WC)	'say, recount publicly'
sek^{w}o-* [sek^w-* 'follow']	'following'
**sel-*	'move quickly'
**sel-* (WC)	'seize, take possession of'
sel-* (WC) [sel-* 'move quickly']	'jump'
**selĝ-*	'release, send out'
**selk-*	'pull'
**séles* (GA)	'marsh'
**sélpes-*	'oil, fat, grease'
**sem-*	'at one time, once'
sem-* [sem-* 'once']	'put in order/together'
**sem-*	'summer'
**sem-* (WC)	'draw water'
semgo(lo)s* [sem-* 'once']	'single one'
sēmis* [?sem-* 'once']	'half'
sems* [sem-* 'once']	'united as one, one together'

*seng^{w}h-	'sing, make an incantation'
*sen(h_a)-	'seek, accomplish'
*sen$h_x$dhr- (NW)	'congealed moisture, slag'
*sen-i/u-	'apart'
*senk- (NW) [*sek- 'dry up']	'make/become dry, singe'
*seno-meh$_a$tḗr (NW)	
[sénos 'old' + *méh$_a$tēr 'mother']	'grandmother'
*sénos	'old'
*sent- (NW)	'perceive, think'
*sent-	'go'
*sentos [*sent- 'go']	'way, passage'
*sep-	'handle (skilfully), hold (reverently)'
*sepit	'wheat'
*septḿ̥	'seven'
*septm̥-mós [*septḿ̥ 'seven']	'seventh'
*ser-	'line up'
*ser-	'protect'
*ser- (WC)	'flow'
*seren(y)uh_xs (GA)	name of goddess
*serk-	'make a circle; complete; construct/repair a wall, make restitution'
*serK-	'pass, surpass'
*serp-	'crawl'
*ses-	'rest, sleep, keep quiet'
*ses(y)ó-	'grain, fruit'
*seu-	'boil (something)'
*seu-	'turn'
*seug- (WC)	'be sick'
*seug/k- (NW)	'suck'
*seuh_3-	'set in motion'
*seu(h_x)-	'bear a child'
*seu(h_x)-	'express a liquid'
*seup-	'pure'
*seuyós [*seu- 'turn']	'left'
*séwe	'-self'
*sewos [*séwe '-self']	'own'
*(s)grebh- (WC)	'scratch, cut'
*(s)greh_ab(h)- (WC)	'hornbeam'
*s$h_2$ómen-	'song'
*s$\underset{\circ}{h}_2$tós (WC) [*seh_2(i)- 'satisfy']	'satisfied'
*(s-)$h_4$upér(i)	'over'
s- $h_4$upó [$h_4$upó 'up']	'underneath'
*silVbVr- (NW)	'silver'
*sinĝhós	'leopard'

*_siskus_ [*_sek_- 'dry up']	'dry'
*_skabh_-	'hold up'
*_skaiwós_ (WC)	'left'
*(_s_)_kamb_- (WC)	'curve'
*_skand_-	'jump'
*(_s_)_kand_-	'shine, glitter; moon'
*_skauros_	'± lame'
*_skebh_- (NW) [*_sek_- 'cut']	'scratch, shave'
*(_s_)_ked_-	'scatter'
*_skeh_$_1$_i_(-_d_)- [*_sek_- 'cut']	'cut'
*_skéits_ (NW)	'shield, board'
*_skek_-	'± jump'
*(_s_)_kel_- (WC)	'crooked'
*(_s_)_kel_- [*_sek_- 'cut']	'cut, split apart'
*(_s_)_keng_-	'crooked, limp'
*_sker_-	'± threaten'
*(_s_)_ker_- [*_sek_- 'cut']	'cut apart, cut off'
*_sker_- (WC)	'± hop about'
*(_s_)_kerbh_-	'turn'
*_sket_(_h_)- (WC)	'injure, harm'
*_skeu_-	'sneeze'
*_skeubh_- (NW)	'push away, push ahead'
*(_s_)_keud_-	'throw, shoot'
*(_s_)_keuh_$_1$-	'perceive'
*(_s_)_keu_(_h_$_x$)-	'cover, wrap'
*(_s_)_keup_- (NW)	'bundle'
*_skidrós_ (WC)	'thin'
*(_s_)_koitrós_	'bright, clear'
*(_s_)_koli_- (WC)	'young dog'
skolmeh$_a$- (WC) [(_s_)_kel_- 'cut']	'sword'
(_s_)_kolmos_ [(_s_)_kel_- 'cut']	'boat'
(_s_)_kōlos_ (WC) [(_s_)_kel_- 'cut']	'stake'
*_skótos_ (WC)	'shadow, shade'
*(_s_)_ku_(_n_)_t_- (NW)	'shake, jolt'
(_s_)_kwéh_$_x$_tis_ [(_s_)_keu_(_h_$_x$)- 'cover']	'skin, hide'
*_skwēis_ (NW)	'± needle and/or thorn'
*(_s_)_k̂egos_	'sheep/goat'
*(_s_)_k̂eh_$_1$_w_(_e_)_r_- (WC)	'north wind'
*_sk̂ōyh̥_$_a$	'shade'
*(_s_)_k̂up_-	'shoulder'
*(_s_)_k_^{w}_álos_	'sheatfish, wels'
*(_s_)_lag_- ~ *(_s_)_leh_$_2$_g_- (WC)	'slack'
*(_s_)_lag_^{w}- (WC)	'take, hold'
*_slak_- (NW)	'strike'

*(*s*)*lei-*	'sticky, slimy, slippery'
*(*s*)*lei-* (WC) [*(*s*)*lei-* 'sticky']	'tench'
*(*s*)*leidh-*	'slide'
**sleimak-* (WC) [*(*s*)*lei-* 'sticky']	'snail, slug'
**slenk-* (NW)	'turn, twist (like a snake)'
**sleubh-* (NW)	'slide'
**sli*h_x*u-* (NW)	'plum-coloured'
**slóugos* (NW)	'servant'
*(*s*)*me*	'middle, among'
**smeg-* (NW)	'taste (good)'
**smei-*	'smile, laugh'
**smeid-* (WC)	'smear'
**smeit-*	'throw'
**smek̂-*	'chin, jaw'
*(*s*)*mel-*	'deceive'
*(*s*)*mel-*	'give off light smoke, smoulder'
*(*s*)*meld-* (WC)	'to melt'
*(*s*)*mer-*	'remember, be concerned about'
**sméru-*	'oil, grease'
*(*s*)*meug-* ~ *(*s*)*meuk-*	'slick, slippery'
*(*s*)*m*(*e*)*ug*(*h*)- (WC)	'smoke'
**sm̥-loghos* (WC) [*sem* 'together' + **legh-* 'lie']	'spouse'
sm̥mós* [sem-* 'once']	'some, any'
smók̂wr̥* [smek̂-* 'chin']	'chin, beard'
sm̥teros* (WC) [sem-* 'once']	'one or the other of two'
*(*s*)*ne*h_1-	'twist, turn'
*(*s*)*ne*h_1(*i*)- [*(*s*)*ne*h_1- 'twist']	'twist fibres into thread'
**sne*h_1*u-* [*(*s*)*ne*h_1- 'twist']	'twist fibres into thread'
**snē*h_1*wr̥* [*(*s*)*ne*h_1- 'twist']	'sinew, tendon'
**sne*h_a-	'swim'
**snei*g^w*h-*	'to snow'
*(*s*)*ner-*	'fasten with thread or cord'
**sner-* (WC)	'± rattle, growl'
**sneubh-* (WC)	'marry'
**sneudh-*	'mist, cloud'
sni*g^w*h-s* [snei*g^w*h-* 'snow']	'snow'
**snusós*	'son's wife, brother's wife'
so*/se*h_a/**tód*	'that one'
**soito*/*e*h_a- (NW)	'sorcery'
**sokto-*	'sickness'
**sók̂r̥*	'(human) excrement'
só*k^w-h_2*ōi* [se*k^w- 'follow']	'follower, companion'
**so*k^w*ós*	'sap, resin'

**sók*^{w}*t*	'(upper) leg'
**solh*$_x$-	'dirt; dirty'
**solo/eh*$_a$- ~ *selo-* (NW)	'dwelling, settlement'
**sólwos*	'whole'
som-* [sem-* 'once']	'(together) with'
somo-ĝn̥h*$_1$*-yo-s* (WC) [sem* 'together' + **ĝenh*$_1$- 'beget']	'same (kinship) line'
somo-ph̥*$_a$*tōr* [sem* 'together' + **ph̥*$_a$*tḗr*'father']	'of the same father'
somos* [sem-* 'once']	'same'
**soru*	'booty'
**speh*$_1$-	'be satisfied, be filled, thrive'
*(*s*)*p*(*e*)*iko/eh*$_a$-	'bird, woodpecker'
*(*s*)*pek̂-*	'observe'
*(*s*)*pel-*	'say aloud, recite'
*(*s*)*pel-*	'tear off, strip'
**spelo/eh*$_a$- [*(*s*)*p*(*h*)*el-* 'strip']	'shield'
*(*s*)*pen-*	'draw, spin'
**spend-*	'make an offering'
**sper-*	'?sparrow'
**sper-*	'strew, sow'
**sper-* (WC)	'wrap around'
**sperĝh-*	'move energetically'
**sperh*$_1$-	'kick, spurn'
**sperh*$_x$*g-* (NW)	'strew, sprinkle'
*(*s*)*peud-*	'push, repulse'
**speud-*	'hurry'
sph*$_1$*rós* [speh*$_1$- 'be satisfied']	'± fat, rich'
**sph*$_a$*en-* (WC)	'flat-shaped piece of wood'
*(*s*)*py*(*e*)*uh*$_x$-	'spew, spit'
*(*s*)*pingo-* (WC/PIE?)	'finch'
**spleiĝh-*	'step, go'
*(*s*)*plend-*	'shine'
**sploiĝh*$_2$*-ḗn*	'spleen'
**spoh*$_x$*ino/eh*$_a$	'foam'
*(*s*)*pondh*(*n*)*os* (WC)	'wooden vessel'
*(*s*)*pornóm*	'wing, feather'
*(*s*)*preg-* (WC)	'speak'
*(*s*)*pre*(*n*)*g-*	'wrap up, constrict'
spr̥h*$_1$*ó-* [sperh*$_1$-'kick']	'heel'
*(*s*)*pr̥h*$_x$*g-*	'crackle, sputter'
**srebh-*	'gulp, ingest noisily'
**sre/oh*$_a$*gs* (WC)	'± berry, fruit'
**srenk-* (WC)	'snore'
**srēno/eh*$_a$-	'± hip, thigh'

*sret-	'boil, be agitated, move noisily'
*sreu-	'flow'
*sreumen- (WC) [*sreu- 'flow']	'flowing, streaming (in river names)'
*srīges- (WC)	'cold, frost'
*sromós	'lame'
*sr̥po/eh$_a$-	'sickle'
*stag- (WC)	'seep, drip'
*(s)teg- (WC/PIE?)	'cover'
(s)teg- (WC) [(s)teg- 'cover']	'pole, post'
(s)téges- (WC) [(s)teg- 'cover']	'roof'
*(s)teh$_2$-	'stand'
(s)teh$_2$ist (WC) [(s)teh$_2$- 'stand']	'dough'
stéh$_2$mōn [(s)teh$_2$- 'stand']	'what stands, stature'
stéh$_2$tis [(s)teh$_2$- 'stand']	'place'
stéh$_2$ur [(s)teh$_2$- 'stand']	'post'
*(s)teh$_4$-	'steal'
*steig-	'prick'
*steigh-	'step (up), go'
*stel-	'put in place, (make) stand'
*(s)tel- (NW)	'be still, quiet'
stembh- [(s)teh$_2$- 'stand']	'make stand, prop up'
*sten-	'moan'
*sten- (WC)	'narrow'
*(s)tenh$_x$- [*sten- 'moan']	'groan; thunder'
*ster-	'barren, infertile'
*ster-	'spread out'
*(s)ter-	'stork'
*ster- (WC)	'steal'
*(s)terĝh-	'± crush'
*(s)terh$_1$-	'stiff'
*ster(h$_3$)-	'strew'
*ster(h$_3$)mn̥ [*ster(h$_3$)- 'strew']	'strewn place, ?bed'
*steu- (GA)	'praise'
*(s)teud-	'push, thrust'
*steup-	'strike'
*steuros	'large (domestic) animal'
sth$_2$bho/eh$_a$- (NW) [(s)teh$_2$- 'stand']	'post, pillar'
sth$_2$ei- [(s)teh$_2$- 'stand']	'become hard, fixed'
st(h$_2$)eug- [(s)teh$_2$- 'stand']	'stiff'
*stíghs [steigh- 'step']	'path'
*stl̥neh$_a$- (WC) [*stel- 'put in place']	'post, support'
*stómn̥	'mouth'
*storos (NW)	'starling'
*strenk- (WC)	'string, to pull (tight)'

**(s)trep-* (NW)	'± cry out, dispute'
**streug-*	'be fatigued, exhausted'
**str̥(h$_x$)yon-* (NW)	'sturgeon/salmon'
stup-* [steup-* 'strike']	'± offcut, piece of wood'
su-* [h$_1$es-* 'be']	'good'
**suh$_x$-*	'rain'
suh$_x$nús* [seu(h$_x$)-* 'bear a child']	'son'
**suh$_x$ros* (NW)	'sour, acid'
suh$_x$sos* [seu(h$_x$)-* 'bear a child']	'grandfather'
suh$_x$yús* [seu(h$_x$)-* 'bear a child']	'son'
súleh$_a$-* [seu(h$_x$)-* 'express a liquid']	'± (fermented) juice'
sūs* [?seu(h$_x$)-* 'bear a child']	'pig (wild or domesticated)'
**sward-* (WC)	'laugh'
s(w)ebh-* [swe* '-self']	'lineage'
**s(w)edh-*	'custom, characteristic'
**swedh-o-*	'lineage'
**sweh$_a$de/o-*	'be tasty, please'
sweh$_a$dus* [sweh$_a$de/o-* 'be tasty']	'pleasing (to the senses), tasty'
**(s)weh$_a$gh-* (WC)	'± cry out; resound'
**swei-*	'blow to hiss or buzz'
**sweid-*	'sweat'
**sweid-*	'shine'
**(s)weig-*	'deceive'
swek̂rúh$_a$s* [swék̂uros* 'father-in-law']	'mother-in-law'
**swék̂uros*	'father-in-law'
swēk̂urós* [swék̂uros* 'father-in-law']	'wife's brother'
**swel-* (NW)	'burn'
**swel-* ~ **sel-* (WC)	'plank, board'
**sweliyon-* (WC)	'wife's sister's husband'
**swelno-*	'rise'
swelp-* [swel-* 'burn']	'burn, smoulder'
**swem-* (NW)	'swim'
**swe(n)g-*	'bend, swing'
**swenh$_x$-*	'(re)sound'
**swep-*	'sleep, dream' (vb).
**swep-*	'throw, sweep'
**swer-*	'post, rod'
**swer-*	'darken'
**(s)wer-*	'say, speak'
**swerbh-* (NW)	'turn, move in a twirling motion'
**swergh-*	'be ill'
**swerh$_x$K-*	'watch over, be concerned about'
**swero-*	'(suppurating) wound'
**swésōr*	'sister'

*swesrih$_x$nos (NW) [*swésōr 'sister']	'sister's son'
*swesr(iy)ós [*swésōr 'sister']	'sisterly, sister's son'
*swīg/k- (WC)	'be silent, hush'
*swoiniyeh$_a$- (WC)	'wife's sister', i.e., 'sister-in-law'
*swombhos (WC)	'spongy'
*swópniyom [*swep- 'sleep']	'dream'
*swópnos [*swep- 'sleep']	'sleep, dream' (noun)
*sw(o)r- ~ *sworaks (WC)	'shrew'
*syō(u)ros	'wife's brother'
*syuh$_1$-	'sew'

***t**

*tag- (WC)	'touch'
*tā̆g-	'set in place, arrange'
*tagós [*tā̆g- 'arrange']	'leader'
*tak- (NW)	'be silent'
*taksos	'yew'
*t-at-	'father'
*tauros	'aurochs; bull'
*tegus	'thick, fat'
*t(e)h$_2$us- (NW/PIE?)	'quiet, silent'
*teh$_a$-	'to melt'
*teh$_a$li (WC)	'of that sort or size'
*téh$_a$mot(s) (WC)	'then, at that place'
*téh$_a$wot(s)	'so many, so long'
*teig^w- (WC)	'± side'
*tek-	'bear or beget a child'
*tek-	'run, flow swiftly'
*teknom [*tek- 'bear a child']	'child, offspring'
*tek̂s-	'fabricate'
*tek̂so/eh$_a$- [*tek̂s- 'fabricate']	'axe, adze'
*tek̂steh$_a$- [*tek̂s- 'fabricate']	'plate, bowl'
*tek̂s-(t)or/n- [*tek̂s- 'fabricate']	'one who fabricates'
*telh$_2$-	'lift, raise'
*telh$_x$-	'± pray'
*telh$_x$-om	'floor (of planks)?'
*telk- (NW)	'push, thrust'
*telp-	'have room'
*tem-	'reach, attain'
*temh$_x$-	'be struck, be exhausted'
*temp- [*ten- 'pull']	'stretch'
*ten-	'pull, stretch'
*teng-	'think, feel'
*teng- (WC)	'to moisten, soak'

**tengh-*	'be heavy, difficult'
**teng(h)-*	'pull'
tengh-s-* (NW) [ten-* 'pull']	'pole'
**tenh̥$_a$g-* (WC)	'shallow water?'
**tenk-*	'become firm, thicken; shrink'
tenkl̥* [tenk-* 'become firm']	'buttermilk'
ten-s-* [ten-* 'pull']	'pull'
ténus* [ten-* 'pull']	'thin, long'
**tep-*	'hot'
**ter-*	'±speak out'
**ter-*	'crossover'
**terg^w-*	'scare'
**terh$_1$-*	'pierce, pierce by rubbing'
térh$_1$trom* ~ **térh$_1$dhrom* (WC) [terh$_1$-* 'pierce']	'auger'
**terh$_2$-*	'bring across; overcome, through, above'
ter(i)-* (WC) [terh$_1$-* 'pierce']	'rub, turn'
**TerK-*	'release, allow'
**terk(w)-*	'twist' (< 'spin')
termn-* [ter-* 'cross over']	'end, border; thread-end'
**terp-*	'take (to oneself), satisfy oneself'
térptis* [terp-* 'satisfy oneself']	'satisfaction'
**ters-*	'dry'
**teter-*	'gamebird'
**teu-*	'look on with favour'
**teubh-*	'steal'
**teuh$_a$-*	'swell (with power), grow fat'
**teus-*	'be happy'
**teus-*	'to empty'
teutéh$_a$-* (WC/PIE?) [teuh$_a$-* 'swell']	'the people (?under arms)'
**tih$_x$n-*	'(be) dirty'
**tkeh$_1$-* (GA)	'rule'
**tk̂ei-* (GA)	'settle, dwell'
**tk̂en-* (GA)	'strike'
tk̂ítis* (GA) [tk̂ei-* 'settle']	'settlement'
**tk^{w}reh$_1$yot-*	'clay'
**todéh$_a$*	'then'
**tóksom* (GA)	'bow'
**tolko/eh$_a$-*	'sacrifice, sacrificial meal'
**tolk^w-* (NW)	'speak'
**tómh$_x$es-*	'dark'
**tór*	'there'
**tóti* (WC)	'so much, many'
**trēbs* (WC)	'dwelling'

**treg-*	'gnaw'
**tregh-* (NW)	'run'
**trem-*	'shake, tremble (in fear)'
**trep-*	'turn'
**tres-*	'tremble, shake with fear'
**treud-* (WC)	'thrust, press'
treu*(h_x)- (WC) [terh*$_1$- 'pierce']	'rub away, wear away'
**tréyes*	'three'
**trih*$_a$*tōn* (WC)	'watery (one?)'
trī-k̂omt*(h_a) [tréyes* 'three' + **dék̂m̥*(*t*) 'ten']	'thirty'
tris* [tréyes* 'three']	'thrice'
**tris-* (WC)	'±vine'
triyós* [tréyes* 'three']	'third'
**tŕ̥nu-*	'thorn'
**trosdos* (NW/WC?)	'thrush'
**trus-* (WC)	'reed, rush'
*(*t*)*sel-*	'sneak up on, crawl up on'
tuh*$_a$*s-k̂m̥tyós* (NW) [teuh*$_a$- 'swell' + **k̂m̥tóm* 'hundred']	'thousand'
**túh*$_x$	thou
tussk̂yos* [teus-* 'be empty']	'empty'
**tweis-* (GA)	'shake'
**twéks*	'skin'
**twer-*	'stir, agitate'
**twer-* (WC)	'take, hold'
**twerk-*	'cut off'
**twóh*$_x$*r̥*	'curds, curdled milk'
**twork̂ós*	'boar'
**tyeg*^{w}- (GA)	'give way, pull oneself back (in awe)'

***u**

**ŭ̄d-*	'upward, out (from under)'
udero-* [ud-* 'out']	'abdomen, stomach'
udrós* [wódr̥* 'water']	'otter'
ud*^{s}*tero-* [ud-* 'out']	'abdomen, stomach'
**uk*$^{(w)}$*sēn-*	'ox'
**ul-*	'±howl, hoot'
ulu-* [ul-* 'hoot']	'owl'
**usr-*	'aurochs'

***w**

**wadh-* (NW)	'wade'
**waĝ-*	'split'

wáĝros* (GA) [waĝ-* 'split']	'cudgel'
**wai*	'alas'
wailos* (WC) [wai* 'alas']	'wolf'
**wak-*	'be empty'
**wal-*	'be strong, rule'
**wálsos* (WC/PIE?)	'stake'
**wápōs*	'vapour, steam'
**-wē*	'or'
**wēben*	'cutting weapon, knife'
**webhel-* ~ **wobhel-* (NW)	'weevil, beetle'
**wed-*	'raise one's voice'
**wedmo/eh$_a$-* (WC)	'bride-price'
**wedh-*	'push, strike'
wédhris* [wedh-* 'push']	'castrated'
**weg-*	'plait, weave'
**weĝ-*	'strong'
wegh-* (weĝh-?*)	'shake, set in motion'
**weĝh-*	'bear, carry also ride'
weĝhnos* [weĝh-* 'bear']	'wagon'
weĝhyeh$_a$-* (WC) [weĝh-* 'bear']	'track, road'
**weg^w-* (WC)	'wet'
**weg^{w}h-*	'speak solemnly'
**weh$_1$r-*	'confidence, faithfulness'
weh$_1$ros* (NW) [weh$_1$r-* 'confidence']	'true'
**weh$_a$b-* (NW)	'cry, scream'
**w(e)h$_a$stos* (NW)	'empty'
**weh$_a$t-* (WC)	'(suppurating) wound'
**weh$_x$p-*	'body of water'
**we/oh$_x$r*	'water'
**wéi*	'we'
**weid-*	'see, know (as a fact)'
**weig/k-*	'±turn, yield'
**wei(h$_1$)-*	'plait, wattle'
**wei(h$_x$)-*	'go after'
**weih$_x$-*	'be strong'
wéih$_x$(e)s-* [weih$_x$-* 'be strong']	'strength, vitality, vital force'
**weik-*	'appear'
**weik-*	'consecrate'
**weik-* (NW)	'fight'
**weip-* ~ **weib-*	'turn'
**weip-* (E)	'set in motion, agitate'
**weis-*	'twist, wind around'
**weis-*	'ooze out'
**weis-*	'stink'

**weit-*	'willow'
**weḱ-*	'wish, want'
**wek^w-*	'speak'
**wel-*	'die'
**wel-*	'grass'
**wel-*	'see'
**wel-*	'turn, wind, roll'
**wel-*	'wish, want'
**wel-* (WC)	'warm, heat'
**weld-*	'crush, grind, wear out'
**wel(h_2)-*	'strike, tear at'
**weliko/eh$_a$-* (WC)	'willow'
**welk-* ~ **welg-* (NW)	'wet'
**wels-*	'bulge'
wélsu-* [wel-* 'grass']	'meadow, pasture'
welutrom* [wel-* 'turn']	'case'
**wémh$_x$mi*	'spew, vomit'
**wen-*	'strike, wound'
**wendh-*	'wind, twist'
wendh-* [wendh-* 'wind']	'(a single) hair'
we/ondhso-* [wendh-* 'wind']	'facial hair'
**weng-*	'bend'
**wenh$_x$-*	'desire, strive to obtain'
**wenVst(r)-*	'(ab)omasum'
**wer-* (WC)	'find, take'
**wer-*	'boil, cook'
**wer-*	'crow'
**wer-*	'perceive, give attention to'
**wer-*	'surround, cover, contain'
**wer-*	'burn'
werb(h)-* [wer-* 'perceive']	'oversee, protect'
**werĝ-*	'shave, shear'
**werĝ-*	'work'
**wérh$_x$us*	'broad, wide'
**werno/eh$_a$-*	'alder'
**wers-*	'±thresh'
**wers-*	'peak'
**wersēn*	'male'
**wert-*	'turn'
**werwer-*	'squirrel'
**wes-*	'crush, grind, pound, wear out; wither'
**wes-*	'graze'
**wes-*	'buy'
**wes-*	'be dressed, dress'

*wesno- [*wes- 'buy']	'purchase'
*wésperos ~ *wékeros (WC)	'evening'
*wésr̥	'spring'
*wéstor- [*wes- 'graze']	'herdsman'
*wesu-	'excellent, noble'
*wet-	'year'
*wet-	'see (truly)'
*wételos [*wet- 'year']	'yearling'
*wi-	'apart, in two, asunder'
*widh- [perhaps *wi- 'apart' + *dheh_1- 'put']	'separate, put asunder'
*widheweh_a- [*widh- 'to be separated']	'widow'
*widhu (NW) [*widh- 'to be separated']	'tree, forest'
*wih_1ḗn [*wei(h_1)- 'plait, wattle']	'grapevine'
*wi$h_x$rós [*weih_x- 'be strong']	'man, husband'
*wikso- (WC)	'mistletoe'
*wīk̂m̥tih_1 [*dwi- 'bi' + *dék̂m̥(t) 'ten']	'twenty'
*wik̂pots [*wik̂s- 'extended family' + *pótis 'husband']	'master of the clan'
*wik̂s	'(social unit of) settlement', extended family, clan'
*wi(n)ĝ-	'elm'
*wis-/*ĝ(h)ombhros (NW)	'bison'
*wíss [*weis- 'ooze out']	'poison'
*witeros [*wi- 'apart']	'far'
*wl̥$h_2$neh_a-	'wool'
*wl̥kānos	'smith god'
*wl̥k^wíh_a- [*wl̥k^wós 'dangerous']	'she-wolf'
*wl̥k^wos	'dangerous'
*wl̥k^wos [*wl̥k^wós 'dangerous']	'wolf'
*wl(o)p-	'(red) fox'
*wn̥d^{s}tí-	'bladder'
*w(n̥)nákts	'leader, lord'
*wódr̥	'water'
*wog^{w}hnis (WC)	'ploughshare'
*wóh_1	'you two'
*wóinom (PIE?) [*wei(h_x)- 'plait']	'wine'
*wok̂éh_a-	'cow'
*wōk^ws [*wek^w- 'speak']	'voice'
*wolno/eh_a-	'(bloody) wound'
*wólos	'tail hair (of a horse)'
*wólswom (GA) [*wels- 'bulge']	'gums'
*wórghs	'chain, row, series'
*worh_xd-i/o- (WC) [*wor$h_x$do- 'wart']	'frog'

*worh$_x$do-	'wart'
*worh$_x$dhus	'upright, high'
*wór(h$_x$)ĝs	'nourishment, strength'
*worPo-	'enclosure'
*wortok^w- (GA)	'quail'
*worwos (WC)	'furrow'
*wos(h$_x$)-ko- (NW)	'wax'
*wospo/eh$_a$- [*wes- 'be dressed']	'garment'
*wósu	'goods'
*wōt- (NW) [*wet- see truly']	'poet, seer'
*wōtis [*wet- 'see truly']	'god-inspired'
*wr̥b- (WC)	'branch, sprig, twig'
*wredh-	'grow, stand, take shape'
*wreg-	'track, hunt, follow'
*wreg- (NW)	'press, oppress'
*wreh$_1$ĝ- (WC)	'break, tear to pieces'
*wreh$_a$gh- (WC)	'thorn'
*(w)rep-	'turn, incline'
*wrētos	'flock, herd'
*wr̥h$_1$ēn	'lamb'
*wr(h$_a$)d- (WC)	'root; branch'
*wr̥h$_x$os	'pimple'
*wriyo/eh$_a$-	'fort'
*wr̥mis (WC)	'worm, insect'
*wr̥to/eh$_a$- [*wer- 'surround']	'enclosure'

***y**

*yaĝ- (GA)	'honour, worship'
*yak(k)- (WC)	'± cure, make well'
*yam ~ yau (NW)	'now, already'
*(y)ebh-	'elephant'
*yébhe/o-	'enter, penetrate, copulate'
*yeg-	'ice, icicle'
*yeh$_1$-	'do, make; act vigorously'
*yeh$_1$- (WC)	'throw'
*yeh$_1$g^{w}eh$_a$- (WC)	'power, youthful vigour'
*yéh$_3$s-	'gird'
*yeh$_a$-	'go, travel'
*yeh$_a$- (E)	'ask for, beg'
*yéh$_a$wot(s) (GA)	'as many, as long'
*yek-	'± express, avow'
*yek^{w}r̥(t)	'liver'
*yem- (E)	'hold'
*yemos	'twin'
*yes-	'boil'

**yet-*	'put in the right place'
**yeu-*	'bind, join together'
**yeudh-*	'moved, stirred up; fight'
yeudhmós* [yeudh-* 'fight']	'fighter'
yeug-* [yeu-* 'bind']	'joins, harnesses'
**yeuĝ-*	'stir up, incite; be unquiet'
**yeuh*$_x$-	'mix something moist'
**yéw(e)s-*	'order, law'
**yéw(e)s-*	'grain'
*-*yo*	'and'
**yoinis* (NW)	'reed, rush'
**yóḱu*	'(animal) body hair'
**yórk*s (WC)	'roedeer'
yós*/yéh*$_a$/**yód*	'who, what, that'
**yoteros* (GA)	'which of the two'
**yóti* (GA)	'as much, as many'
**yu-* (WC)	'± shout (for joy)'
yugóm* [yeu-* 'bind']	'yoke'
**yuh*$_x$*-r-* (WC)	'water'
**yuh*$_x$*s* ~ **uswé* ~ **swé*	'ye'
yúh*$_x$*s-* [yeuh*$_x$- 'mix']	'broth'

Appendix 3
An English to Proto-Indo-European Wordlist

ABDOMEN	*udero-, *ud^{s}tero-
ABLE (BE PHYSICALLY)	*magh-, NW *gal-
(AB)OMASUM	*wenVst(r)-
ABOUT	*per
ABOVE	*terh_2-
ABUNDANT	*bhénĝhus, NW/PIE? *menegh-
ACCEPT	*dek̂-, *nem-
ACCOMPLISH	*sen(h_a)-, NW *kob-
ACCUSTOMED	*$h_1$euk-
ACID	NW *suh_x-ros
ACORN	*g^{w}elh_a-
ACQUAINTED WITH	*ĝneh_3-
ACROSS	*terh_2-
ACT HYPOCRITICALLY	NW *leud-
ACT VIGOROUSLY	*yeh_1-
ADDITION (IN)	*$h_1$eti
ADHERE	*leip-
ADJACENT	WC *pos
ADVANCE	*seh_1(i)-
ADZE	*$h_4$edhés-, *tek̂so/eh_a-
AFFLICT	*$h_a$ei-, *seh_4i-
AFFLICTION	*$h_a$éghleh_a-
AFRAID	*bhibhóih_xe, WC *$h_a$egh-
AFTER	*posti
AGAINST	*proti
AGE	*ĝerh_a-
AGE OF VIGOUR	*$h_a$óyus
AGITATE	*twer-, E *weip-
AGITATED	*sret-
AHEAD	*pro
AIM	WC *del-
ALAS	*eheu, wai
ALCOVE	*gubho/eh_a-
ALDER	*$h_a$éliso-, *werno/eh_a-, WC *kle$h_a$dhreh_a-

ALIVE	*$h_{2/3}$wed-
ALLOW	*TerK-
ALONE	*kaiwelos, *$h_1$oinos
ALONG	*$h_a$enh_ae, E *$h_a$en-u
ALREADY	NW *yam/yau
AMASS	*kr(e)u-bh-
AMONG	*(s)me
AND	*ar, *$h_1$eti, *-k^we, *-yo,
ANGELICA	NW *k̂wéndhr/no-
ANGER	WC *$h_1$óistro/eh_a-
ANGRY	*reus-, *seh_4i-, WC *bhorg^{w}o-, GA *k̂et-
ANIMAL	*g^wyé$h_3$wyom, *k^wetwor-pod, *léuh_xōn
ANIMAL (LARGE DOMESTIC)	*steuros
ANIMAL (SMALL)	WC *meh_1l-
ANIMAL (WILD)	*ĝhwēr, *$h_2$wédr̥
ANOINT (WITH SALVE), (BE)SMEAR	*$h_3$eng^w-
(AN)OTHER	*$h_1$iteros, WC *sm̥teros
ANT	*morwi- ~ *morm- ~ *mouro-
ANUS	*kutsós, *putós, C *pr̥h_3k̂tós
ANY	*sm̥mós
APART	*seni/u-, *wi-, WC *dis-
APPEAR	*k^wek̂/ĝ-, *weik-, WC *prep-
APPLE	*$h_a$ebVl-, *me$h_2$lom
APPORTION	*dap-
APPORTION (ER)	*bhagos
ARCH	WC *k^welp-
ARGUE	*$h_4$erg^w-, *mel-
ARM	*dous-, *$h_a$ér$h_x$mos
ARMY	*koryos
AROUND	*$h_2$entbhi-
ARRANGE	*tăg-
ARROW	NW *$h_a$érkwos, GA *$h_1$ísus
AS	WC *k^weh_am
ASH	*h_2éh_xōs, *ken$h_x$is, NW *perk-
ASH (TREE)	*$h_3$es(k)-
ASK FOR	*g^whedh-, *$h_{1/4}$er-, *perk̂-, E *yeh_a-
ASLANT	GA *dl̥h_3ĝhmós
ASP (FISH)	*ghérsos
ASPEN	*$h_{2/3}$osp-
ASS	*os(o)nos, WC *mú(k)skos
ASSAIL	*$h_a$ei-
ASSERT	*$h_4$erg^w-
AT	WC *$h_a$ed
AT ONE TIME	*sem-

ATTACH	*h$_a$ér(h$_x$)-, NW *(h$_2$)wer-
ATTAIN	*h$_1$enek̂-, *tem-
ATTEMPT	WC *per-
ATTENTION (PAY)	*bheudh-, *wer-
AUGER	WC *térh$_1$trom ~ *térh$_1$dhrom
AUROCHS	*tauros, *usr-
AUTUMN	*h$_1$esen-
AVOW	*yek-
AWAKE	*h$_1$ger-
AWAY	*h$_4$eu, *h$_a$et, *pro, NW *dē
AWL	*h$_x$óleh$_a$-
AWN	*h$_a$ek̂stí-
AXE	*h$_4$edhés-, *pelek̂us, *tek̂so/eh$_a$-, NW *sekūr-, WC *h$_a$egwisy(e)h$_a$-
AXLE	*h$_a$ek̂s-
BABBLE	*baba-, lal-
BACK	*h$_4$epér-, *h$_4$épo
BACK (SIDE)	*kúh$_x$los
BAD	*dus-, *h$_3$ligos, *melo-
BADGER	NW *meli-
BAG	*bhólĝhis-
BAKE	*pek^w-, WC *bhōg-
BALD	*kl̥h$_x$wos, NW/WC? *gol(h$_x$)wos
BAR	WC *kleh$_a$wis
BARE	*ne/og^{w}nós, NW/WC? *gol(h$_x$)wos, WC *bhosós
BARK (DOG)	*leh$_a$-, NW *bhereg-, WC *baub-
BARK (TREE)	WC *lóubho/eh$_a$-
BARLEY	*ĝhrésdh(i), *h$_2$élbhit, *meiĝ(h)-, NW *bhares-, WC /PIE? *h$_2$ed-, WC *bhárs
BARREN	*ster-
BARTER	*per-
BASIN	WC *louh$_1$trom
BASKET	NW *kreb-, NW *k^{w}as-
BAST	WC *lōp-, WC *lóubho/eh$_a$-
BATHE	WC *leuh$_1$-
BE	*bheu(h$_x$)-, *h$_1$es-
BEAM	*k̂red-, WC *bhélh$_a$ĝs
BEAN	WC *bhabheh$_a$-, WC *bhak̂ó/eh$_a$-
BEAR (A CHILD)	*bhére/o-, *seu(h$_x$)-,*tek-, WC *pelh$_x$-
BEAR (ANIMAL)	*h$_2$ŕ̥tk̂os
BEAR (VERB)	*bhére/o-, *weĝh-
BEARD	*smók̂wr̥, NW *bhardheh$_a$-
BEAT	NW *bheud-

BEAT THE WEFT WITH A STICK	WC *krek-
BEAUTIFUL	GA *kal-
BEAVER	*bhébhrus
BED	*léghes-, *ster(h_3)mn̥
BEE	NW *bhik^{w}ó-, C *melítih$_a$-
BEECH	WC *bheh$_a$ĝós
BEER	*h$_a$elut-
BEETLE	NW *webhel- ~ *wobhel-
BEFORE	*pr̥h$_a$éh$_1$, *pr̥h$_a$éi
BEG	E *yeh$_a$-
BEGET A CHILD	*ĝenh$_1$-, *tek-
BEGIN	*neik-
BEHIND	*h$_4$epér-, *h$_4$épo, *po-sk^{w}o-, WC *ĝhō-, WC*pos
BEING (COME INTO)	*bheu(h$_x$)-
BELCH	*h$_1$reug-
BELIEVE	*h$_{2/3}$eh$_x$-, *k̂red-dheh$_1$-
BELT	NW *kerd-
BEND	*bheidh-, *bheug-, *bhedh-, *h$_2$enk-, *kamer-, *kleng-, *leng-, *lenk-, *nem-, *weng-, *swe(n)g-, WC *leug-
BEND (OF TERRAIN)	WC *kam-p-
BENEFIT	NW *lau-
BENT	*h$_2$ónkos, *lei-
BERRY	*h$_a$ógeh$_a$-, NW *dhreghes-, WC *h$_1$óiwo/eh$_a$-, WC *sre/oh$_a$gs
BESTOW	*h$_{2/3}$enk̂-
BESTOWED	*h$_{2/3}$ónk̂os
BETWEEN	*h$_1$entér
BEYOND	*h$_a$et, NW *h$_a$elnos
BI-	*dwi-
BIND	*bhendh-, *deh$_1$-, *dherĝh-, *kergh-, *yeu-, WC *mer-
BIRCH	*bherh$_x$ĝos
BIRD	*h$_a$ewei-, *pipp-
BIRD (TYPE OF)	*(s)p(e)iko/eh$_a$-, *teter-
BIRD OF PREY	GA *k̂yeino-, C *ĝhy- ~ *ĝyei-
BISON	NW *wis-/*ĝ(h)ombhros
BITE	*denk̂-
BITTER	*h$_2$em-, *h$_2$em-ro-s
BLACK	*k^{w}r̥snós, *mel-n-, NW *k̂eir-
BLACKBERRY	*mórom
BLACKBIRD	NW *h$_a$emesl-, WC *kopso-

BLADDER	*wn̥d^{s}tí-
BLAME	*$h_1$lengh-
BLEAT	NW *bhleh$_1$-
BLIND	*$h_a$endhós
BLOOD	*$h_1$ésh$_2$r̥, *kréuh$_a$
BLOOM	*bhel-
BLOSSOM	*bhel-
BLOW	*bhel-, *bhes-, *$h_2$weh$_1$-, *peis-, *per-, *p(h)eu-, *swei-, *wet-
BLUE	*k̂er- ~ *k̂r̥-wos, modheros
BOAR	*twork̂ós, NW/WC ?*$h_1$eperos
BOARD	NW *skéits, WC *swel- ~ *sel-
BOAT	*néh$_a$us, *(s)kolmos
BODY	*kréps
BOIL	*seu-, *sret-, *yes-, WC *bhreu-
BOLD	*dhers-
BOLSTER	*bhólĝhis-
BOLT	WC *kleh$_a$wis
BONE	*$h_2$óst
BOOTY	*soru
BORDER	*$h_4$erh$_2$os, *morĝ-, *térmn̥
BORN	*ĝenh$_1$-
BOTH	*bhōu
BOTTOM	*bhudhnó-
BOW	NW *$h_a$érkwos, GA *tóksom
BOWL	*kumbo/eh$_a$-
BOWSTRING	GA *g^w(i)yēh$_a$
BRAID	*plek̂-, WC *mer-
BRAIN	*mosghos, WC *mréghmen-, E *móstr̥
BRAN	WC *k^{w}et-
BRANCH	*$h_2$ósdos, *$h_4$loĝ-, *k̂ank-, *k̂óh$_1$kōh$_2$, NW *ghabhlo/eh$_a$-, WC *gol-, WC *gwésdos, WC *wr̥b-, WC *wr(h_a)d-
BRAVE	*dhers-
BREAK	*bheg-, *bhreu-, *leuĝ-, *reup-, NW *bhreĝ-, WC *bhreus-, WC *$h_3$lem-, WC *plek̂-, WC *wreh$_1$ĝ
BREAST	*dhh$_1$ileh$_a$-, *$h_1$óuh$_x$dhr̥-, *pap-, *pérk̂us, *psténos-
BREATH	*$h_1$eh$_1$tmén-, *$h_a$énh$_1$mos
BREATHE	*dhwes-, *$h_a$énh$_1$-, *$h_a$énh$_1$mi, *k̂wesh$_x$-
BREATHE ONE'S LAST	WC *dheu-
BREW	WC *bhreu -
BRIDE-PRICE	WC *wedmo/eh$_a$-

BRIGHT	*dei-, *ĝhers-, *leukós, *(s)koitrós, WC *g^whaidrós, C *$h_2$eug-
BRING ACROSS	*terh_2-
BRING FORTH	*per-
BRISTLE	*ĝhers -, *h_aeḱstí-, NW *ḱer(es)-
BROAD	*plet-, *pl̥th_2ú-, *wér$h_x$us
BROTH	*korm-, *yúh$_x$s -
BROTHER	*bhré$h_a$ter-
BROTHERHOOD	*bhre$h_a$tríyom
BROTHER´S WIFE	*snusós
BROWN	*bher-, *$h_1$el-, NW *badyos
BRUSH(WOOD)	NW *k^wrésnos
BUBBLE	*bher-
BUCK	*bhuĝos
BUILD	*dem(h_a)-, *dheiĝh-, *k^wei-, *k^wer-
BULGE	*wels-
BULL	*dom$h_a$yos, *tauros
BUNDLE	NW *(s)keup-
BURDEN	*$h_1$ón$h_x$es-
BURN	*bhleg-, *deh_au-, *dheg^{w}h-, *ĝwelh_x-, *$h_1$eus-, *h_2eh_x-, *$h_4$elh_1-, *$h_a$eidh-, *$h_a$el-, *kenk-, *ḱeh_au-, *ḱeuk-, *ḱseh_1-, *preus-, *swelp-, *wer-, NW *ker-, NW *swel-
BURROW	*bhedh-
BUTTER	WC *$h_3$éng^{w}n̥
BUTTERFLY	NW *pelpel -
BUTTERMILK	*tenkl̥
BUTTOCK	GA *ĝhn̥ghéno/eh_a-
BUY	*wes-
CABBAGE	*kaulós
CACKLE	WC *gag-
CALL	*gal-, *ĝar-, *ĝheu(h_x)-, *kelh_1-
CALLOSITY	*kl̥nos
CANOE	*$h_x$oldhu-
CAPTIVE	NW *kaptos
CARP	*ḱóp$h_a$elos
CARROT	WC *mr̥k-
CARRY	*bher-, *weĝh-
CARVE	*del-, *kerd-
CASE	*welutrom
CASTRATED	*wédhris
CAT	NW *kat-

CATCH	WC *kagh-
CAULDRON	*k^werus
CAVE	GA *káiwr̥(t)
CAVITY	*$h_2$elwos, *$h_2$éryos
CAW	*ker-
CEDAR	WC *$h_1$elew-
CHAFF	*pelo/eh_a-, WC *k^wet-
CHAIN	*wórghs
CHARACTERISTIC	*s(w)edh-
CHARCOAL	*$h_x$óngl̥, NW *perk-
CHARM	*meng-
CHEAT	NW *meug-
CHERRY	WC *kr̥nom
CHEW	*ĝyeuh_x-, WC *mandh - or *mant-
CHICKPEA	WC *k̂ik̂er-
CHILD	*teknom
CHIN	*men, *smek̂-, *smók̂wr̥
CIRCLE	*ānos, *$h_3$érbhis, *serk-
CLAN	*wik̂-
CLAY	*ml̥dho/eh_a-, *tk^wre$h_1$yot-, WC *gloiwos
CLEAN	*peuh_x-, WC *k̂leu-
CLEAR	*leukós, *(s)koitrós
CLIFF	*pel(i)s-
CLOAK	*drap- ~ *drop-, NW *ruk-, WC *baitéh_a-
CLOSE THE EYES	*meigh- ~ *meik-
CLOTH	*los-, *p(e)$h_2$no/eh_a-, WC *bhr̥w-, WC *lōp-
CLOTHES	*drap- ~ *drop-, *wospo/eh_a-, WC *kéntr/n-
CLOUD(Y)	*nébhes–, *sneudh-, NW *bhlendh-
CLUB	NW *lorgeh_a-, WC *bak-, GA *wáĝros
COAL	*g(e)ulo-
COLD	*k̂elto-, *k^wrustēn, NW *gel-, WC *$h_3$eug-, WC *srīges-
COLOUR (DEEP INTENSE SHADE)	*k̂yeh_1-
COMB	*kars-, *kes-
COMBAT	NW *nant-
COME	*g^weh_a-, *g^wem-
COMMIT A CRIME	NW/PIE? *$h_{2/3}$wergh-
COMMOTION (BE IN)	*dheu(h_x)-
COMPANION	*sók^w-h_2-ōi, NW *dhroughós, GA *h_2ēpis
COMPEL	WC *bheidh-

COMPENSATION	*$k^{w}oineh_{a}$-
COMPLAIN	WC *leh_{a}-
COMPLETE	*serk-
COMPRESS	NW *greut-, WC *gen-
COMPUTE	WC *del-
CONCEAL	WC *k̂el-
CONCERN	*k̂eh_{a}des-, *(s)mer-, *$swerh_{x}$K-
CONCUBINE	*$parikeh_{a}$-
CONFIDE	WC *bheidh-
CONFIDENCE	*weh_{1}r-
CONGEALED MOISTURE	NW *$senh_{x}$dhr-
CONIFER	*péuk̂s , *pit(u)-
CONQUER	*seĝh-
CONSECRATE	*weik-
CONSIDER	*men-
CONSTRAIN	*h_{2}emĝh-
CONTAIN	*h_{2}em-, *wer-
CONTAINER	*pēl(h_{1})ewis
CONTEND	*$h_{3}enh_{2}$-, *mel-, *reus -
COOK	*pek^{w}-, *wer-
COOT	WC *bhel-
COPPER	*h_{1}roudhós, *h_{a}ey-es-
COPULATE (< EARLY PIE 'ENTER')	*yébhe/o-
CORNER	WC *kan-t(h)o-
CORPSE	*néh_{a}wis
COUCH	*léghes-
COUGH	*$k^{w}eh_{a}s$-
COUNT (OUT)	WC *h_{a}rei(h_{x})-
COUNTRY	*pl̥th_{2}wih_{a}-
COVER	*h_{1}eu-, *h_{1}rebh-, *k̂em-, *(s)keu(h_{x})-, *wer-, WC/PIE? *(s)teg-, WC *k̂el-, GA *dhwenh_{2}-
COW	*g^{w}ōus, *h_{1}eĝh-, *wok̂éh_{a}-, WC *loh_{a}po-
COWHERD	WC *g^{w}ou-k^{w}olos
CRAB	*karkr(o)-
CRACK	*gerg-
CRACKLE	*(s)pr̥ h_{x}g-
CRAFT	WC *kérdos
CRAFTSMAN	WC *dhabhros
CRANE	*ger-
CRAWL	*serp-, *(t)sel-, NW *rēp-
CRAYFISH	*km̥h_{a}ros
CREAM	*réughmen-
CREATURES	*$h_{2/3}$wédr̥

CROOKED	*(s)keng-, WC *lerd-, WC *lord(sḱ)os, WC *(s)kel-
CROSS-EYED	NW/PIE? *káikos
CROSSOVER	*ter-
CROW	*kVr-C -, *wer-
CROWD	WC *ger-
CROWN OF THE HEAD	*ml̥$h_2$dho-
CRUSH	*mer-, *pis-, *(s)terĝh-, *weld-, *wes-
CRY	*glaĝh-, *ĝar-, *gher-, *kau(k)-, *ḱeuk-, *kreuḱ-, *neu-, *wed-, NW *(s)trep-, NW *weh$_a$b-, WC *ghel-, WC *leh$_a$-, WC *(s)weh$_a$gh-
CUCKOO	*kukū
CUP	*kVlVḱ-, *poh$_2$tlom
CURDS	*twóh$_x$r̥
CURE	*med-, WC *bher-, WC *yak(k)
CURSE	*h$_2$eru-
CURVE	*geu- ~*geh$_x$u-, *keu(h$_x$)-, *keu-k-, WC *(s)kamb-
CURVED	NW *pandos
CUSTOM	*s(w)edh-
CUT	*bher-, *bhreh$_x$i-, *bhreu-, *deh$_a$(i)-, *del-, *kerd-, *ḱes-, *k^{w}er-, *put-, *sek-, *skeh$_1$i(-d)-, *(s)kel-, *(s)ker-, *twerk-, WC *gleubh -, WC *(s)grebh-
CUT HAIR	*koiḱ-
CUTTING WEAPON	*wēben
DAMP	*penk-
DANGEROUS	*wl̥k^{w}ós
DARK	*dh(o)ngu-, *tómh$_x$es-, WC *(h$_a$)mauros, WC *(h$_a$)merh$_x$g^w-
DARKEN	*swer-, NW *merk-, GA *dhwenh$_2$-
DARKNESS	*h$_1$reg^w-es-
DAUGHTER	*dhuĝ(h$_a$)tḗr
DAWN	*h$_a$éusōs
DAWNS	*h$_a$(e)us-sḱeti
DAY	*deino-, *dye(u)-, *h$_a$éĝhr̥, C *h$_2$eh$_x$-mer-
DEAD	*mr̥tós, *néḱus
DEAF	*bhodh$_x$rós
DEAR	*h$_x$leh$_a$d-, *leh$_a$d-
DEATH	*móros, *mr̥tís, *mr̥tóm, *neks, *néḱus
DEBT	NW *dhl̥gh-
DECAY	*ḱer-

DECEIVE	*dhreugh-, *meng-, *(s)mel-, *(s)weig-, NW *meug-, WC *kel-
DECLARE SOLEMNLY	*k̂eh$_1$-, *k̂e(n)s-
DEEP	*dheub-
DEER	*h$_1$elh$_1$ēn, WC *yórks
DEFECATE	*ĝhedye/o-, *g^{w}uh$_x$-, *kerd-, *k̂ek^w-, WC *kak(k)eh$_a$ye/o-
DEFECT	*mendo/eh$_a$-
DEFEND	*h$_a$lek-
DEFILE	*kerd-, NW *mai-
DESCENDANT	*neptiyos
DESIRE	*gheldh-, *ĝhor(ye/o)-, *h$_x$ih$_x$iĝh-(e/o)-, *leubh-, *moud -, *wenh$_x$-, WC *h$_1$op, E *k^{w}lep-
DESTROY	*bhreh$_x$i-, *dhg^{w}hei-, *h$_2$erh$_x$-, *h$_2$erk-, *h$_3$elh$_1$-
DESTRUCTION	*h$_2$rétk̂es-
DEW	*rṓs
DIE	*mer-, *nek̂-, *wel-, WC *dheu-
DIFFICULT	*tengh-
DIG UP	*bhedh-, *h$_3$reuk-, *perk̂-, NW *dhelbh-, NW *ghrebh-
DIP	*g^{w}abh-, *mesg-
DIRT(Y)	*reh$_1$mós, *solh$_x$-, *tih$_x$n-, NW *mai -, WC *grúĝs, WC *leu-
DISH	WC *póthḁr
DISPUTE	NW *(s)trep-
DISTRIBUTE	*bhag-, *pr̥(h$_3$)tis, NW *h$_1$em-
DISTURB	*mer-
DIVE	*g^{w}ādh-, *mesg-
DIVIDE	*bhag-, *deh$_a$(i)-, *lenk-
DO	*kon-, *k^{w}er-, *yeh$_1$-
DOG	*k̂(u)wōn, WC *(s)koli-
DONKEY	WC *mú(k)skos
DOOR	*dhwṓr
DOORJAMB	*h$_a$énh$_x$t(e)h$_a$
DORMOUSE	*gl̥h$_1$ís
DO SOMETHING HATEFUL	WC *h$_a$leit-
DOUBLE	*dw(e)i-plos, *dwoyos
DOUGH	WC *(s)teh$_2$ist
DOWN	*kath$_a$e
DOWNCAST	WC *h$_a$egh-
DOWNWARDS	*ni
DRAGON	WC *dr̥k̂-

DRAW (LIQUIDS)	*$h_2$en-, *$h_2$eu(h_x)s-, WC *sem-
DRAW (SPIN)	*(s)pen-
DRAW TOGETHER, BE THICK	*bhénĝh-
DREAM	*swep-, *swópniyom, *swópnos, C *$h_3$énr̥
DREGS	WC *dhrogh-
DRESS(ED)	*wes-
DRINK	*h_1ēg^{w}hmi
DRIP	WC *leg-, WC *stag-
DRIVE	*h_aeĝ-, *kel-, NW *dhreibh-
DRIZZLE	*$h_3$meigh-, WC *mregh-
DRONE (< BUZZ)	WC *dhren-
DRONE (BEE)	WC *km̥h_xp-h_a-
DRY	*$h_2$es-, *kseros, *sausos, *sek-, *sisku-, *ters-, NW *senk-, GA *k̂sēros
DUCK	*h_an̥$h_a$ti-, *pad-
DUMB	*mū-
DUNG	*k̂ók^{w}r̥, *sók̂r̥, NW *dher-, WC *k̂u$h_x$dós
DUST	*pē(n)s-
DWELL	*$h_2$wes-, GA *tk̂ei-
DWELLING	*$h_2$wóstu, *kus-, NW *solo/eh_a- ~ *selo-, WC *trēbs
DYE	GA *reg-
EAGLE	*$h_3$or-
EAR	*$h_a$óus-
EARLY	*$h_a$eyer-, *prō-
EAR OF GRAIN	*$h_a$ek̂es-
EARTH	*dhéĝhōm, WC *$h_1$er-
EAST	*$h_a$eust(e)ro-
EAT	*gras-, *ĝeP-, *$h_1$édmi, *$h_4$eu-
EEL	WC *h_xVnghel-
EGG	*$h_1$endrós, *h_aō(w)i-om
EIGHT	*$h_x$ok̂tṓ(u)
EIGHTH	*$h_x$ok̂to-wós
ELBOW	*$h_3$elVn-, WC *$h_3$elek-
ELEPHANT	?*(y)ebh-
ELF	*h_4(e)l̥bh-
ELK/AMERICAN MOOSE	*$h_x$ólk̂is, NW *$h_1$elh$_1$níha-
ELM	*pteleyeh_a-, *wi(n)ĝ-, NW *$h_1$élem
EMPTY	*$h_1$eu(h_a)-, *teus-, *tussk̂yos, *wak-, NW *w(e)$h_a$stos, C *k̂enós
ENCLOSE	*ghrebh-
ENCLOSURE	*ghórdhos, *mand-, *worPo-, *wr̥to/eh_a-, NW *kagh-

END	*termn-
ENEMY	NW *ghostis, GA *des-
ENJOY	*ĝeus-, NW *neud-
ENTER	*yébhe/o-
ENTRAILS	*ĝhorh$_x$neh$_a$-
ENTWINE	WC *leug-
ERMINE	NW *k̂ormon-
ESTABLISHED	*dhéh$_1$mi-, *dhéh$_1$men-, *dhéh$_1$tis
ESTUARY	NW *h$_3$eust(y)o-
EVENING	WC *wésperos ~ *wékeros
EVENING MEAL	WC *dórk^{w}om
EVIL	*ĝhalh$_x$ros, *h$_1$édwōl
EWE	*h$_2$owikéh$_a$-
EXCELLENT	*wesu-
EXCHANGE	*mei-, *meit-, *per-
EXCITED	*nei-
EXCREMENT	*k̂ók^{w}r̥, *sók̂r̥, NW *dher-
EXHAUSTED	*streug-, *temh$_x$-
EXPRESS	*yek-
EXPRESS A LIQUID	*seu(h$_x$)-
EXTEND	*h$_3$reĝ-, NW *reiĝ-
EXTINGUISH	*g^{w}es-
EYE	*h$_3$ek^w-
EYEBROW	*bhrúh$_x$s
FABRICATE	*tek̂s-
FABRICATOR	*tek̂s-(t)or/n-
FACE	*h$_1$éni-h$_3$k^w-o/eh$_a$-, *próti-h$_3$(ō)k^w-o/eh$_a$-
FACIAL HAIR	*we/ondhso-
FAIL	*mel-
FAITHFULNESS	*weh$_1$r-
FALCON	NW *kap-
FALL	*k̂ad-, *ped-, *pteh$_1$-, WC *phō̂l- (*ph$_x$ō̂l-?)
FALLOW LAND	NW *polk̂éh$_a$-
FAME	*k̂léwes-
FAMILY	*ĝénh$_1$es-, *wik̂-, *wik̂s, GA *dṓm
FAR	*witeros
FART	*pérde/o-, WC *pesd-
FAST	*h$_a$eĝilos, *h$_1$ōk̂-us, NW /PIE? *k̂eigh-, NW *bhris- ~ *bhers-, NW *h$_2$ēh$_x$tro-, GA *h$_2$r̥ĝ-rós
FASTEN	*h$_2$ep-, *peh$_a$ĝ- ~ *peh$_a$k̂-, *seg-, *(s)ner-

FAT(NESS)	*m(e)h_ad-, *peih_x-, *pen-, *pí$h_x$wr̥, *sélpes-, *sp$h_1$rós, *tegus, *teuh_a-
FATHER	*at-, *ĝenh_1tōr, *papa, *ph̥$_a$tḗr, *t-at-
FATHER (OF THE SAME)	*somo-ph̥$_a$tōr
FATHER-IN-LAW	*swék̂uros
FATHER'S BROTHER	*ph̥$_a$tr̥wyos
FATHER'S MOTHER	*$h_2$en-
FATIGUED	*streug-, E *kl̥h_xm(-s)-
FAULT	*méles-
FAVOUR	*d(h_3)eu-, *$h_3$ens-, *$h_a$eu-, *teu-
FEAR	*bhibhóih_xe, *dwei-, *$h_a$énĝhes-, *k^weh_1(i)-, *perk-, *tres-
FEATHER	*pet(e)r-, *(s)pornóm
FEED	*pen-
FELT	*peld-, WC *pildo-
FENCE	*ghórdhos
FERMENT	*kwat-
FEROCITY	*rabh-
FEW	WC *pau-
FIELD	*h_aeĝros, *$h_a$ér$h_3$wr̥
FIFTEEN	*penk^{w}e dek̂m̥(t)
FIFTH	*pn̥k^{w}tós
FIFTY	*penk^{w}ē-k̂omt(h_a)
FIGHT	*h_aeĝ-, *yeudh-, NW *katu-, NW *nant-, NW *weik-
FIGHTER	*yeudhmós
FILL	*pelh_1-, *seh_2(i)-, *speh_1-
FINCH	WC/PIE? *(s)pingo-
FIND	WC *wer-
FIND ONE'S WAY	*pent-
FINE (PUNISHMENT)	*k^wei-
FINGER	NW *pólik(o)s
FIR	*dhonu-, WC *$h_a$ebi-
FIRE	*g(e)ulo-, *h_2é$h_x$tr̥, *$h_a$eidh-, *h_xn̥g^wnis, *pé$h_2$ur
FIRM	*pastos, *tenk-
FIRST	*per(h_x)-
FISH	*pik̂sk̂os, WC *dhĝhuh_x-
FISH (KIND OF)	*k̂ónkus
FISH (SMALL)	WC *mn̥h_x-
FISH EGGS	NW *krek-
FISSURE	GA *káiwr̥(t)
FIST	NW *pn̥(k^w)stí-, E *mustí-
FIT	*ghedh-, *$h_a$ér(h_x)-

FIT (SUIT)	NW *kob-
FITTING	*$h_a$értus
FIVE	*pénk^{w}e
FIXED	*st$h_2$ei-
FLANK	*poksós
FLAT	*pleh_ak-
FLAX	WC *linom
FLAY	*der-
FLEA	*plus-
FLEE	WC *bheug-
FLEECE	*moisós, *réumn-
FLOAT	*pleu-
FLOCK	*wrētos
FLOOR	*tel$h_x$om, WC *dm̥pedom
FLOW	*dhen-, *g^{w}el(s)-, *$h_1$ers-, *$h_a$el-, *leh_2-, *sreu-, *tek-, WC *del-, WC *ser-, GA *dhg^{w}her-
FLOWER	*$h_2$éndhes-, NW *bhlo$h_x$dho-
FLOWING (IN RIVER NAMES)	WC *sreumen-
FLY (INSECT)	WC *mus/h_x-
FLY (VERB)	*dih_1-, *pet-, GA *peth_a-
FOAM	*spo$h_x$ino/eh_a
FOLD	*pel-
FOLLOW	*sek^w-, *wreg-
FOLLOWER	*sók^w-h_2-ōi
FOLLOWING	*sek^{w}o-, WC *pos
FOOD	*$h_1$edonom
FOOT	*pṓds, *le$h_a$peh_a-
FOOTPRINT	*pedom
FOREARM	*bhāĝhus, *$h_3$elVn-, WC *$h_3$elek-
FOREHEAD	*bhólom-, *$h_2$ent-
FORELEG	*bhāĝhus
FOREST	*g^{w}orh_x-, NW *widhu
FORGET	*mer-, *mers-
FORK	NW *ghabhlo/eh_a-
FORT	*dhíĝhs, *pelh_x-, *wriyo/eh_a, NW *dhūnos, WC *bherĝh-
FORWARD	*pro
FOUL	WC *g^{w}eidh-
FOUR	*k^{w}etwóres
FOURTH	*k^{w}turyós ~ *k^{w}etwor-tos
FOX	*wl(o)p-
FRAMEWORK	*k̂red-
FREEZE	*preus-, NW *gel-

FRESH	*ken-
FRIENDLY	NW *keh$_a$ros
FRIGHTEN	*ĝheis-
FRIGHTENING	WC *garĝos
FROG	WC *worh$_x$di/o-
FROGSPAWN	NW *krek-
FRONT	*h$_2$enti, *pr̥h$_a$éh$_1$, *pr̥h$_a$éi, *próti-h$_3$(ō)k^w-o/eh$_a$-
FROST	WC *srīges-
FRUIT	*h$_a$ógeh$_a$-, *ses(y)ó-, WC *h$_1$óiwo/eh$_a$-, WC *sre/oh$_a$gs
FULL	*pl̥h$_1$nós
FURROW	NW *l(o)iseh$_a$-, NW *pŕ̥k̂eh$_a$-, WC *worwos
GALL	*ĝhóln- ~ *ĝhólos
GAMEBIRD	*teter-
GAP	*ĝhóh$_1$ros
GAPE	*ĝheh$_a$w-
GARDEN	*k̂āpos
GARLIC	WC *kremh$_x$us
GATE	*dhwṓr
GATHER	*kr(e)u-bh-, *leĝ-, WC *ger-, WC *h$_2$merg-
GENERATION MARKER (FOURTH)	*h$_4$ep-
GENERATION MARKER (THIRD)	*pro-
GIFT	*déh$_3$r/n-
GIRD	*gherdh-, *kenk-, *yéh$_3$s-
GIVE	*deh$_3$-, *h$_a$ei-, *reh$_1$-
GIVE WAY	GA *tyeg^w-
GLANCE AT	*derk̂-
GLAND	*g^{w}én-, WC *ghelĝheh$_a$-
GLEAM	*bherh$_x$ĝ-
GLIDE	*dhreĝ-
GLITTER	*(s)kand-
GLOW	*ĝwelh$_x$-, NW *ĝher-
GLUE	WC *kol-
GNAT	*mok̂o-, WC *h$_1$empís, WC *mus/h$_x$-
GNAW	*red-, *treg-
GO	*deuh$_4$-, *ghredh-, *h$_1$ei-, *h$_a$et-, *h$_1$leudh-, *leit(h$_x$)-, *seh$_1$(i)-, *sed-, *sent-, *spleiĝh-, *steigh-, *wei(h$_x$)-, *yeh$_a$-, NW *meih$_x$-, WC *h$_1$el-

GOAT	*bhuĝos, *díks, *$h_1$eri, *$h_4$eli-, *h_aeĝós, *$h_a$eiĝs, *kápros, *(s)k̂egos, NW *ghaidos, WC *koĝhéh_a-
GOD	*deiwós, *dhēh_1s, *$h_a$énsus
GODDESS (NAME OF)	GA *seren(y)uh_xs
GOD-INSPIRED	*wōtis
GOD OF WAR	?*māwort-
GOLD	*$h_a$eusom
GOOD	*h_1(e)su-, *mel-, *su-, NW *meh_a(t)-
GOODS	*h_2ó/ép(e)n-, *wósu
GOOSE	*ĝhan-s
GORE	*kréuh_a
GRAIN	*dr̥$h_x$weh_a-, *dho$h_x$néh_a-, *ĝr̥$h_a$nóm, *$h_{2/3}$(e)lĝ(h)-, *meiĝ(h)-, *prók̂som, *ses(y)ó-, *yéw(e)s, NW *pitus, WC/PIE? *$h_2$ed-, WC *melh_2-
GRANDDAUGHTER	*neptih_a-
GRANDFATHER	*$h_2$eu$h_2$os, *su$h_x$sos, NW *$h_2$éuh_2-
GRANDMOTHER	*$h_2$en-, NW *seno-meh_atḗr, WC *$h_2$euh_2ih_a-
GRANDSON	*népōts
GRANDSON OF WATERS	*neptonos ~ *$h_2$epōm nepōts
GRAPEVINE	*wih_1ḗn
GRASP	*ghrebh-, *$h_1$ep-, NW *ghreib-, WC *dergh-, WC *kagh-, GA *$h_a$emh_3-
GRASS	*wel-, WC *k̂oino-
GRAZE	*gras-, *peh_2-, *wes-
GREASE	*sélpes-, *sméru-
GREAT	*meĝh_a-
GREEDY	*las-
GREEN	*k̂er- ~ *k̂r̥-wos, *k̂yeh_1-, *modheros
GREENS (EDIBLE)	*k̂e$h_1$kom
GREY	*k̂as-, *pel-, *pl̥h_x-
GRIEF	*$h_a$énĝhes-, *(p)k̂órmos
GRIEVE	*leug-
GRIND	*$h_4$el-, *melh_2-, *peis-, *weld-, *wes-, WC *ghrendh-
GRIP	NW *ghreib-
GROAN	*k̂wesh_x-, *(s)tenh_x-, WC *ghromos
GROUND (ON[TO] THE)	*dhĝh(e)m-en
GROVE	WC *némos-
GROW	*bheu(h_x)-, *ĝerh_a-, *$h_1$leudh-, *$h_a$eug-, *$h_a$wokséye/o-, *k̂er-, *meh_1(i)-, *wredh-, WC *$h_a$el-
GROWL	NW *bhereg-, WC *sner-

GRUNT	WC *g(h)ru(n)(d)-
GUARD	*peh$_2$-
GUEST	NW *ghostis
GULLET	*gutr̥, WC *bherug-
GULP	*srebh-
GUMS	NW *ghéh$_a$(u)-mr̥, GA *wólswom

HAIL	*ghel(h̥$_2$)d-, WC *grōdo-, WC *kaghlos
HAIR	*dek̂-, *dhrigh-, *gówr̥, *ghait(so)-, *k̂ripo-, *pou-m-s-, *pilos, *pulos, *wendh-, *we/ondhso-, *yók̂u, NW *k̂er(es)-
HALF	*sēmis
HAND	*ĝhésr-, *ĝhóstos, *méh$_a$r
HAND (BELONGING TO LITTLE)	*mei-wos
HANDLE	*h$_2$enseh$_a$-
HANDLE (SKILFULLY)	*sep-
HANG	*lemb- ~ *remb-, *k̂onk-
HAPPY	*meud-, *teus-
HARD	*kar-, *sth$_2$ei-, NW *saiwos
HARE	*k̂asos
HARM	*dhebh-, *dhwerh$_x$-, *mel-, *peh$_1$(i)-, WC *sket(h)-
HARROW	*h$_{1/4}$okéteh$_a$-
HARVEST	*kerp-, WC *h$_2$merg-
HATE	*h$_3$ed-, *k̂eh$_a$des-, *peik/k̂-
HAUNCH	*k̂lóunis
HAWK	NW *kap-
HAWTHORN	*h$_2$ed(h)-
HAZEL	NW *kós(V)los
HEAD	*ghebhōl, *kapōlo-, *k̂r̥rēh$_2$, NW *káput
HEADBAND	GA *déh$_1$mn̥, GA *puk̂-
HEAL	*med-, WC *bher-, WC *yak(k)-
HEALTHY	WC *kóh$_a$ilus
HEAP	WC *méuh$_x$kō(n)
HEAR	*k̂leu-, *k̂leus-
HEART	*k̂ērd
HEARTH	*h$_2$eh$_x$seh$_a$-, WC *h$_2$eh$_x$treh$_a$-
HEAT	WC *wel-
HEAVY	*g^{w}r(e)h$_a$(-u)-, *tengh-
HEDGE	*ghórdhos, NW *kagh-
HEDGEHOG	*h$_1$eĝhis, WC *ghḗr
HEEL	*pēnt-, *pérsneh$_a$-, *spr̥h$_1$ó-
HE-GOAT	*bhuĝos, *h$_a$eĝós, *h$_4$eli-, *kápros

HEIGHT = FORT	WC *bherĝh-
HEIR	*$h_{2/3}$orbhos
HELLEBORE	WC *kemeros
HELP	NW *k̂elb-
HEMP	WC *kannabis
HEN	*kerk-
HENBANE	NW *bhel-
HERD	*wrētos, NW *kerdheh$_a$-
HERDSMAN	*wéstor-, WC *poh$_2$imén-
HERE	*h$_1$idh$_a$
HERNIA	*k̂éuh$_x$-, *kéuh$_x$l̥
HEW	*keh$_a$u-, *kel-
HIDE (CONCEAL)	*gheiĝh-, *gheuĝh-, *k̂eudh-
HIDE (SKIN)	*h$_a$eĝínom, *pel-, *(s)kwéh$_x$tis, WC *nák(es)-, WC *péln-
HIGH	*bherĝh-, *bhr̥ĝhús ~ *bhr̥ĝhént-, *h$_2$erdus, *worh$_x$dhus
HIGH ONE	*bhr̥ĝhn̥tih$_a$-
HILL	*bherĝh-, WC *kolh$_x$ōn
HIND/COW-ELK	NW *h$_1$elh$_1$níh$_a$-
HIP	*k̂lóunis, *srēnos/eh$_a$-
HIRE	*kuh$_x$s-
HISS	WC *ger-
HOARFROST	WC *k̂er(s)no-
HOCK	*kenk-
HOE	*mat-
HOLD	*h$_2$em-, *h$_2$erk-, *seĝh-, *skabh-, WC *(s)lag^w-, WC *twer-, E *yem-
HOLE	*ĝhh̥$_a$wos, *k̂óuh$_x$r̥
HOLLOW	*h$_2$elwos, *kul-
HOLLOW OF (MAJOR) JOINT	*kók̂s-o/eh$_a$-
HOLLOW OUT	*k̂eu(h$_x$)-, *keus-
HOLY	*k̂wen(to)-, *noibhos, *sakros
HONE	*k̂eh$_x$(i)-, *k̂oh$_x$nos
HONEY	*mélit
HONEY-COLOURED, GOLDEN	*kh$_a$ónks
HONOUR	*dek̂es-, GA *yaĝ-
HOOF	*k̂oph$_2$ós
HOOK	*h$_2$ónkos, *ko(n)gos, WC *kleh$_a$wis
HOOPOE	*h$_1$epop
HOOT	*ul-
HOP ABOUT	WC *sker-
HORN	*k̂er-, *k̂érh̥$_2$s, *k̂érh̥$_2$sr̥, *k̂óru, *k̂r̥nom
HORNBEAM	WC *(s)greh$_a$b(h)-

HORNET	NW *k̂r̥$h_2$sro-(h_x)on-
HORNLESS	*k̂em-
HORSE	*ĝhéyos, *$h_1$ék̂wos, NW *márkos, C *mendyos
HORSEHAIR	*réumn-
HOSTILE	*peik/k̂-, GA *dusmenēs
HOT	*h_2eh_x-, *tep-, NW *keh_xi-
HOUSE(HOLD)	*dṓm, *dóm(h_a)os, *k̂éiwos, *pḗr, WC *k̂óimos,
HOW	WC *k^weh_am
HOWL	*bukk-, *bhels-, *reu-, *ul-, NW *kă̄u-, WC *ger-
HOW MUCH/MANY	*k^wóti ~ *k^wéti
HUE AND CRY	*kreuk̂-
HUM	NW *kem-
HUMBLE	WC *kaunos
HUNDRED	*k̂m̥tóm
HUNGER	*Kos-t-, WC *kenk-
HUNT	*h_aeĝreh_a-, *leuh_x-, *wreg-
HURL	*$h_1$es-
HURRY	*krob-, *speud-
HUSBAND	*pótis, *wi$h_x$rós
HUSBAND'S BROTHER	*daih_awḗr
HUSBAND'S BROTHER'S WIFE	*$h_1$yenh_a-ter-
HUSBAND'S SISTER	*ĝl̥$h_3$wos-
HUSH	WC *swīg/k-
I	*h_1eĝ, *$h_1$me
ICE	*$h_1$eih_x(s)-, *yeg-
ICICLE	*yeg-
ILL	*$h_3$ligos, *swergh-, WC *seug-
IMMEDIATELY	WC *pos
IMMOBILE	*dher-
IMPELS	*ĝhei-, *yeuĝ-
IN	*$h_1$éndo, *$h_1$en(i), *$h_1$entér
INCLINE	*(w)rep-
INCREASE	*$h_a$eug-
INFERTILE	*ster-
INFLATED	WC *bhlei-
IN FRONT OF	*$h_2$enti, *pr̥h_aéh_1, *pr̥$h_a$éi
INJURE	WC *sket(h)-
INNARDS	*$h_1$ent(e)rom
INNER PART	*kok̂es-
INSECT	*k^wr̥mis, *mat-, WC *wr̥mis

INSECT (BITING)	WC *kóris
INSECT (STINGING)	*mok̂o-, NW *bhik^{w}ó-, WC *$h_1$empís
INSTRUCT	E *k̂eh_1s-
INSULT	*(h_x)neid-
INTERNAL ORGAN	*h_1e$h_1$tr-
INTERROGATIVE/RELATIVE	*me/o-
INTERTWINE	*mesg-
INTESTINES	*gudóm, *$h_1$ent(e)rom
INTOXICATOR	*medhwih_a-
INVITE	*ĝheu(h_x)-
INVOKE	*ĝheu(h_x)-
IVORY	?*lebh-
JAW	*ĝénu-, *smek̂-, WC *ĝon$h_a$dhos
JAY	*kik̂(y)eh_a-
JEST	WC *loid-
JOIN, FIT TOGETHER	*ghedh-, *$h_2$ep-, *yeu-, *yeug-
JUICE	*súleh_a-
JUG	WC/PIE? *kelp-
JUMP	*$h_1$leig-, *lek-, *preu-, *preug-, *skand-, *skek-, WC *k̂eh_ak-, WC *sel-
JUNIPER	WC *$h_1$elew-
KEEP	NW *bhergh-
KERNEL	*$h_1$ét(e)no-
KICK	*sperh_1-
KIDNEY	*h_2eh_2(e)r-, WC *neg^{w}hrós
KINDLE	*deh_au-
KING	*h_3rḗĝs
KINSHIP LINE (SAME)	WC *somo-ĝn̥h_1-yo-s
KINSMAN (MATERNAL)	WC *mé$h_a$trōus
KINSMAN (PATERNAL)	*p$h̥_a$trōus
KISS	*kus-
KITE	GA *k̂yeino-, C *ĝhy- ~ *ĝyei-
KNEE	*ĝonu
KNEE (BACK OF)	*kenk-
KNIFE	*$h_{2/3}$n̥sis, *kl̥tḗr, *k̂ostrom ~ *k̂osdhrom, *wē-ben, E *kert-
KNOT	*ned-
KNOT (IN WOOD)	*$h_x$ósghos
KNOW	*ĝneh_3-, *weid-, WC *sap- or *sep-
LACK	*das-, *deu(s)-, *$h_1$eg-, *menk-
LADY	*pot-nih_a-

LAKE	WC *lokús
LAMB	*wr̥h_1ēn, WC *$h_a$eg^{w}hnos
LAME	*skauros, *sromós
LAMENT	*glaĝh-, *reudh$_a$-, WC *ĝem-
LAND	*pl̥th$_2$-ih$_a$-
LAND (FALLOW)	NW *polk̂éh$_a$-
LAND (OPEN)	NW *lendh-, WC *póh$_x$iweh$_a$-
LAND (PIECE OF)	*k̂āpos
LARGE	*meĝh$_a$-, WC *meh$_1$ro- ~ *moh$_1$ro-
LASCIVIOUS	*las-
LAUGH	*ha ha, *kha-, *smei-, WC *sward-
LAW	*dhéh$_1$mi/men-, *dhéh$_1$tis, *yéw(e)s-
LAY HAND TO	*klep-, GA *$h_a$emh$_3$-
LEAD	*neih$_x$-
LEADER	*tagós, *w(n̥)nákts, WC *koryonos, GA *h_ae-ĝós
LEAF	*bhlh$_a$d-, WC *bhóliom-
LEAN	*k̂lei-, NW *knei-g^{w}h-
LEAP	*dher-
LEARN	*men(s)-dh(e)h$_1$-
LEATHER	NW *letrom
LEAVE	*deuh$_4$-, *ĝheh$_1$-, *leh$_1$d-, *leik^w-
LEAVE A TRACE ON THE GROUND	*leis-
LEECH	*ĝelu-
LEFT	*laiwós, *seuyós, WC *skaiwós
LEG (LOWER)	WC *kónh$_a$m-
LEG (UPPER)	*sók^{w}t
LEOPARD	*sinĝhós
LEPROSY	*dedrús
LESS	*mei-
LIBATION	*ĝheumn-, WC *leib-
LICK	*leiĝh-, WC *lab-, WC *lak-
LIE	*k̂ei-, *legh-
LIE (DECEIVE)	NW *leugh-
LIFE	*$h_a$óyus
LIFT	*kel(h_x)-, *telh$_2$-
LIGHT (OF WEIGHT)	*$h_1$le(n)g^{w}h-
LIGHT (SHINE)	*leukós, *lóuk(es)-, NW *leip-, GA *bhéh$_2$(e)s-, GA ? *bhéh$_2$tis
LIGHTNING	NW *meldh-
LIMB	*$h_2$épes-, WC *méles-
LIMIT	*$h_4$erh$_2$os
LIMP	*(s)keng-
LINDEN	WC *lenteh$_a$-

LINE	*$h_4$erho-, *reik-
LINEAGE	*s(w)ebh-, *swedh-o-
LINE UP	*ser-
LION	WC *li(w)-, GA *perd-
LIP	*$h_x$ousteh$_a$-, NW *leb-, WC *gheluneh$_a$-
LIQUID	*$h_1$res- ~ *$h_1$ers-
LITTLE	WC *pau-
LIVE	*g^weih$_3$-, *g^wyeh$_3$-
LIVER	*lesi-, *yek^{w}r̥(t)
LIVESTOCK	*pék̂u
LOG (TRIMMED)	*k̂líts
LOINS	*isĝhis-, *lóndhu
LONG (AS)	*yéh$_a$wot(s)
LONG (OF TIME/SPACE)	*dl̥h$_1$ghós, *dlonghos, *duh$_a$ros, *mak-, *ténus, NW *seh$_1$ros, WC *makrós
LORD	*w(n̥)nákts
LOUSE	*lu- (*lus-)
LOUSE EGG	WC *k̂(o)nid-
LOVE	*keh$_a$-, *kem-, *ken-, *leubh-, *prih$_x$eh$_a$-
LOW (NOISE)	WC *baub-
LOW (POSITION)	*n̥dhés ~ *n̥dhero-
LUNG	*h$_1$eh$_1$tr-, *pléumōn
LYING (PLACE FOR)	*léghes-
LYNX	WC *luk̂-
MADE	GA *k̂meh$_a$-
MAGGOT	*mat-
MAGIC FORCE	WC *keudes-
MAGPIE	NW *k̂arh$_x$ka-
MAKE	*kon-, *k^{w}er-, *yeh$_1$-
MALE	*r̥sḗn, *wersēn
MAN	*h$_a$nḗr, *maghus, *méryos, *mVnus, *wih$_x$rós, NW *dhĝhm̥ón, GA *mórtos
MAN (ANCESTOR OF HUMANKIND)	*manu-
MANE	*ghait(so)-, *k(e)h$_a$isVr-
MANY (AS)	GA *yéh$_a$wot(s)
MANY-COLOURED	GA/PIE?*pl̥h$_1$u-poik/k̂os
MAPLE	*h$_2$ēkr̥, NW/WC? *kléinus
MARE	*h$_1$ék̂weh$_a$-
MARK	*peik̂-
MARROW	*mosghos, E *móstr̥
MARRY	*ĝemh$_x$-, *h$_2$wed(h$_2$)-, WC *sneubh-
MARSH	GA *séles
MARTEN	NW *bhel-

MASH (NOUN)	*korm-
MASTER	*dom(h_a)unos, *$h_1$esh$_2$ós, *pótyetoi, *wiḱpots, GA *dems-pot-
MATERNAL KINSMAN	WC *méh$_a$trōus
MEAD	*médhu
MEADOW	*wélsu, WC *póh$_2$iweh$_a$-
MEAL	*dapnom, *tolko/eh$_a$-, NW *pitu, WC *dórk^{w}om,
MEASURE	*deiḱ-, *med-, *méh$_1$tis
MEAT	*mḗ(m)s
MEET	WC *mōd-
MELT	*teh$_a$-, WC *(s)meld-
MEMBER OF ONE'S OWN GROUP	*h$_4$erós
MERRY	*meud-
METAL	*h$_a$eyes-
MIDDLE	*(s)me
MIDGE	WC *mus/h$_x$-
MILITARY ACTION	*leh$_2$-
MILK	*dhédhh$_1$i-, *ĝ(l̥)lákt, *h$_a$melĝ-, *ksih$_x$róm, *(k)sweid-, *pipih$_x$usih$_a$, *twóh$_x$r̥
MILLET	*h$_{2/3}$(e)lĝ(h)-, *pano-, WC *melh$_2$-
MINNOW	WC *mn̥h$_x$-
MISFORTUNE	GA *péh$_1$mn̥
MIST	*h$_3$meigh-, *nébhes -, *sneudh-
MISTAKE	*méles-
MISTLETOE	WC *wikso-
MISTRESS	*h$_1$esh$_2$éh$_a$-, *potnih$_a$-
MIX	*ḱerh$_x$-, *meiḱ-, *yeuh$_x$-
MOAN	*sten-, WC *ĝem-
MOIST(URE)	*h$_1$res- ~ *h$_1$ers-, *m(e)h$_a$d-, *rṓs, NW *h$_1$wes-, NW *leh$_a$t-, NW *senh$_x$dhr-, WC *teng-
MOON	*méh$_1$nōt, *(s)kand-, NW *louksneh$_a$-
MORNING	*prō-
MORTAL	*mr̥tós, GA *mórtos
MOSQUITO	WC *mus/h$_x$-
MOSS	NW *mēus
MOTHER	*ĝenh$_1$trih$_a$-, *h$_4$em-, *h$_4$en-, *h$_a$ekkeh$_a$-, *méh$_a$tēr, *m-h$_4$em-, *n-h$_4$en-
MOTHER-IN-LAW	*sweḱrúh$_a$s
MOTHER'S SISTER	WC *meh$_a$truh$_a$-
MOTION (BE IN)	*dheu(h$_2$)-
MOULD	NW *mēus
MOUNTAIN	*g^{w}orh$_x$-

MOUNTS (SEXUALLY)	*$h_4$órĝhei*
MOURN	*reudh$_a$-*
MOUSE	*mūs*, *mūs(tlo)-*, *pél(h_x)us*
MOUTH	*$h_{1/4}$óh_1(e)s-*, *$h_x$oust-eh$_a$-*, *stómn̥*
MOVE	*dih$_1$-*, *$h_1$rei-*, *$h_1$eig-*, *$h_1$reih$_x$-*, *meu(h_x)-*, *meus-*, *sel-*, *sperĝh-*, *sret-*
MOVED	*yeudh-*
MOW	*$h_2$em-*, *$h_2$meh$_1$-*, NW *$h_2$met-*
MUCH (AS)	*pélh$_1$us*, GA *yóti*
MUD	*penk-*, WC *$h_x$ih$_x$lu*
MUMBLE	*meh$_1$(i)-*
MURMUR	*murmur-*
MUSCLE	*mūs(tlo)-*
MUSSEL(-SHELL), ETC.	*k̂onkh$_a$os*
NAIL	*$h_3$nogh(w)-*
NAKED	*ne/og^{w}nós*, NW/WC? *gol(h_x)wos*, WC *bhosós*
NAME	*$h_1$nómn̥*
NARROW	*$h_a$enĝhus*, WC *sten-*
NAVE	*$h_3$nobh-*
NAVEL	*$h_3$nobh-*
NEAR	*$h_1$epi* ~ *$h_1$opi*
NECK	*g^{w}eih$_3$weh$_a$-*, *mono-*, NW *kólsos*, WC *$h_a$enĝh(w)ēn-*
NECK ORNAMENT	*mono/i-*
NEED	*$h_1$eg-*
NEEDLE	NW *skwēis*
NEGLECT	*seh$_1$(i)-*
NEPHEW	*népōts*
NEST	*nisdos*
NESTLING	*pipp-*
NET	*$h_1$ekt-*
NETTLE	WC *ned-*
NEW	*néwos*
NIECE	*neptih$_a$-*
NIGHT	*k^{w}sep-*, *nek^{w}t-*, *n̥k^{w}tus*
NINE	*$h_1$newh$_1$m̥* (*$h_1$néwh$_1$n̥?*)
NINTH	*$h_1$newh$_1$m̥m/n̥-mos*
NIPPLE	*psténos*, NW *speno-*
NIT	*rik-*, WC *k̂(o)nid-*, C *$h_x$orghi-*
NOBLE	*wesu-*
NOD	WC /PIE? *neu-*
NOISE	*mug-*, WC *b(h)(o)mb(h)-*

NOISE (OF ANIMALS)	*bhrem-
NOOK	*kok̂es-
NORTH WIND	WC *(s)k̂eh_1w(e)r-
NOSE	*$h_x$náss
NOT	*mē, *ne
NOURISHING	*wór(h_x)ĝs, WC *dhe$h_1$lus-
NOW	*nu-, NW *yam/yau
NUMBER	WC *$h_a$rei(h_x)-
NUT	NW *kneu-, WC /PIE?*$h_2$er-
O	*ō
OAK	NW *pérk^{w}us, WC *$h_a$eig-
OAR	*$h_1$er$h_1$trom
OATH	*$h_1$óitos
OATS	*$h_a$ewis
OBSERVE	*bheudh-, *(s)pek̂-
OBVIOUS	*h_3ēwis
OFFER (MAKE AN OFFERING)	*spend-
OFFSPRING (ANIMAL)	*per-
OFFSPRING (HUMAN)	*teknom
OIL	*sélpes-, *sméru-
OLD	*sénos
OLD MAN	*ĝer$h_a$ont-, *ĝer$h_a$os
OLD WOMAN	*$h_4$en-, *n-$h_4$en-
ON	*$h_1$epi ~ *$h_1$opi
ONCE	*sem-
ONE	*$h_1$oinos
ONE-EYED	*kolnós, NW/PIE? *káikos
ONE OR THE OTHER OF TWO	WC *sm̥teros
OOZE OUT	*weis-
OPEN	*reu(h_x)-
OPEN SPACE	*réu$h_x$es-
OPINION	*meino-
OPPRESS	NW *wreg-
OR	*-wē
ORACLE (CONSULT AN)	*$h_{1/4}$er-
ORDER	*$h_a$értus, *yéw(e)s-
ORPHAN	*$h_{2/3}$orbhos
OTHER	*$h_a$élyos, NW *$h_1$ónteros
OTTER	*udrós
OUT	*ud-, WC *h_1eĝhs
OVER	*per, *(s-)$h_4$upér(i)
OVERCOME	*g^{w}yeh_a-, *terh_2-
OVERFLOW	*bhleu-, *seik-

OVERSEE	*werb(h)-
OWL	*b(e)u-, *$h_{2/3}uh_1e$/olo-, *ulu-, NW *kău-
OWN	*prih$_x$ós, *sewos
OX	*uk$^{(w)}$sēn-
PACKED	*dheb-
PADDLE	*h$_1$erh$_1$trom
PAIN	*h$_1$édwōl
PAINT	*peiḱ-
PALE	*bhrodhnós, *pl̥h$_x$-
PALM (OF THE HAND)	WC *dhénr̥, WC *pólh$_a$m
PANTHER	GA *perd-
PAP	WC *polt-
PASS	*per-, *serK-
PASSAGE	*pértus, *sentos
PASS THE NIGHT	*h$_2$wes-
PASS THROUGH	*ked-
PASTORAL GOD	GA *péh$_2$usōn
PASTURE	*wélsu
PATCH	WC *kéntr/n-
PATERNAL KINSMAN	*ph̥$_a$trōus
PATH	*póntōh$_2$s, *stíghs
PAW	*leh$_a$p-eh$_a$-
PAY	*k^{w}rei(h$_a$)-
PAY ATTENTION	*bheudh-
PAYMENT	*h$_2$elg^{w}ho/eh$_a$-
PEA	WC *h$_1$ereg^{w}o-
PEAK	*wers-
PEEL	*leup-, WC *lep-
PEG	WC *dhúbhos
PELT	WC *nák(es)-
PENIS	*kápr̥, *péses-
PEOPLE	WC *déh$_a$mos, *h$_1$leudhos, *leh$_2$wós, WC/PIE? *teutéh$_a$-, WC *h$_1$leudheros, WC *pleh$_1$dhwéh$_1$s
PERCEIVE	*h$_3$eu-, *keuh$_1$-, *k^{w}ei-, *seh$_a$g-, *(s)keuh$_1$-, *wer-, NW *ghou-, NW *sent-
PERCH (FISH)	NW *h$_a$eḱú-
PERISH	*dhg^{w}hei-, *neḱ-
PERSON	*h$_a$nḗr, GA *mórtos
PERSUADE	WC *bheidh-
PERTAINING TO WHOM/WHAT	*k^{w}oih$_x$os
PHANTOM	*dhroughos

PHYSICAL POWER	*g^{w}yeh$_{a}$-
PICK AT	WC *knab(h)-
PIERCE	*dhwer-, *h$_{2/3}$weg(h)-, *terh$_{1}$-, NW *dhelg-, WC *g^{w}el-,
PIG	*pórḱos, *sūs, NW *keul-, C *ĝhor-
PIKEPERCH	*ghérsos
PILE UP	*k^{w}ei-
PILLAR	NW *sth$_{2}$bho/eh$_{a}$-, C *ḱih$_{x}$won-
PIMPLE	*wr̥h$_{x}$os
PIN	NW *dhelg-
PINE	*ḱóss, *péuḱs, NW *pr̥k(^{w})eh$_{a}$-
PITCH	*g^{w}étu, WC *g^{W}ih$_{3}$wo-, WC *pik-
PLACE	*stéh$_{2}$tis
PLAIT	*kert-, *melk-,*pleḱ-, *resg-, *weg-, *wei(h$_{1}$)-
PLANK	NW *plut-, WC *bhélh$_{a}$ĝs, WC *kl̥h$_{x}$ro-s, WC *swel- ~ *sel-
PLATE	*teḱsteh$_{a}$-
PLAY	WC *loid-
PLEASE	*pleh$_{a}$k-, *sweh$_{a}$de/o-
PLEASING (TO THE SENSES)	*sweh$_{a}$dus
PLOUGH	*ĝhel-, *h$_{2}$érh$_{3}$ye/o-, *mat-
PLOUGHSHARE	WC *wog^{w}hnis
PLUCK	*kerp-, *reu(h$_{x}$)-, NW *pleus-, WC *h$_{1}$rep-
PLUM-COLOURED	NW *slih$_{x}$u-
POET	NW *wōt-, GA *kāru-
POINT	*bhr̥stís, *h$_{a}$érdhis
POINTED OBJECT	NW *bharko-
POINT OUT	*bhoudhéye/o-
POISON	*wíss
POKE	WC *peug-
POLE	NW *perg-, NW *reh$_{1}$t-, NW *tenghs-, WC *ĝhalgheh$_{a}$-, WC *(s)teg-
POLECAT	*keḱ-
POND	WC *lokús
POPLAR	*h$_{2/3}$osp-
POPPY	WC *mak-
PORRIDGE	WC *polt-
POSSESS	*h$_{a}$eiḱ-
POSSESSIONS	*lóik^{w}nes-, *réh$_{1}$is
POST	*ḱlíts, *míts, *swer-, *stéh$_{2}$ur, NW *masdos, NW *perg-, NW *reh$_{1}$t-, NW *sth$_{2}$bho/eh$_{a}$-, WC *kroku- ~ *krókyeh$_{a}$-, WC *ḱsúlom, WC *(s)teg-, WC *stl̥neh$_{a}$-, C *ḱih$_{x}$won-

POT	*h$_{2/3}$uk^{w}-, *k^{w}erus-, *poh$_3$tlom, *tek̂steh$_a$-, NW *bhidh-, WC/PIE? *kelp-, WC *kuh$_x$p-, WC *louh$_1$trom, WC *póth$_a$r, WC *(s)pondh(-n)os, C *ĝh(e)utreh$_a$-
POUND	*pis-, *wes-
POUR	*ĝheu-, g^{w}yeh$_a$-, *leh$_2$-, *seik-, NW *ĝheud-, WC *leib-
POWER	WC *yeh$_1$g^{w}eh$_a$-, GA *ish$_1$ros
POWERFUL	*k̂ouh$_1$ros
PRAISE	*g^{w}erh$_x$-, *h$_1$erk^{w}-, *kar-, GA *steu-
PRAY	*g^{w}hedh-, *h$_{1/4}$er-, *h$_2$eru-, *meldh-, *telh$_x$-
PREGNANT	*k̂euh$_1$-
PREPARE(D)	*h$_a$er-, GA *k̂meh$_a$-
PRESS	*menk-, *nak-, *prem-, *puk̂-, NW *māk-, NW *wreg-, WC *gem-, WC *kem-, WC *treud-, GA *pisd-
PRICK	*kel-, *steig-, WC *peug-
PRIEST	*bhertōr, *bhlaĝhmēn, *pent- + *dheh$_1$-/ *k^{w}er-, GA *kouh$_1$ēi(s)
PRIZE	*h$_2$elg^{w}ho/eh$_a$-, *misdhós, NW *lau-
PROJECT	*men-
PROJECTION	NW *bhar-
PROPEL	E *kerh$_x$-
PROPOSE (MARRIAGE)	*perk̂-
PROP UP	*stembh-
PROSPER	*speh$_1$(i)-
PROTECT	*gheiĝh -, *gheuĝh-, *h$_a$lek-, *ser-, *werb(h)-, NW *bhergh-
PUBIC HAIR	*kuk̂is
PULL	*deuk-, *dhreĝ-, *h$_4$welk-, *selk-, *ten-, *teng(h)-, *ten-s-, NW *dhregh-, WC *strenk-
PULL OUT (WOOL)	*pek-, *reu(h$_x$)-
PUNISH	*k^{w}ei-
PURCHASE	*wesno-
PURE	*seup-, GA *h$_a$idhrós
PUS	WC *púh$_x$es-
PUSH	*reudh-, *(s)peud-, *(s)teud-, *wedh-, NW *skeubh-, NW *telk-, E *neud-
PUT ASUNDER	*wi-dhh$_1$-
PUT IN ORDER	*reh$_1$-, *sem-
PUT IN PLACE	*dheh$_1$-, *stel -, *yet-
PUT ON CLOTHES/SHOES	*h$_1$eu-
PUTREFACTION	WC *púh$_x$es-
PUT TOGETHER	*dhabh-, *h$_a$er-

QUAIL	GA *wortok^w-
QUARREL	*h$_3$enh$_2$-
QUERN	*g^{w}réh$_x$-won-
QUICK	NW *h$_2$ēh$_x$tro-
QUIET	*h$_1$erh$_1$-, *k^{w}eih$_1$-, *ses-, NW/PIE? *t(e)h$_2$u-s-, NW *lēnos, NW *(s)tel-
RAIN	*dhreg-, *h$_1$wers-, *n̥bh(ro/ri)-, *suh$_x$-, WC *h$_a$eghlu (ĝh?), WC *mregh-
RAISE	*kel-, *telh$_2$-
RAKE	*h$_{1/4}$ek-, *h$_{1/4}$okéteh$_a$-, *h$_2$eh$_2$er-
RAM	*moisós
RATTLE	WC *sner-
RAVEN	*kVr-C-
RAW	*h$_2$em-, *h$_2$omós
RAZOR	GA *ksuróm
REACH	*tem-
REACH FOR	*seik-
REAL	*h$_1$sónt-
REAR-END	*h$_1$órs(o)-, WC *n(o)h$_x$t-
RECITE	*(s)pel-
RED	*h$_1$ei-, *h$_1$elu-, *h$_1$reudh-, *k̂ounos
RED DEER	*h$_1$elh$_1$ēn
RED FOX	*wl(o)p-
REED	*h$_a$er-, *nedós, NW *yoinis, WC *don-, WC *trus-, E *g(h)rewom
REFRESH	*h$_{1/4}$eis-
REINS	*h$_2$ensiyo/eh$_a$-
REJOICE	*geh$_a$-, *geh$_a$dh-, *geh$_a$u-
RELATION	*bhendhr̥ros
RELEASE	*leuh$_x$-, *selĝ-, *TerK-
REMAIN	*men-
REMAINS	*(h$_1$eti)loik^{w}os
REMEMBER	*(s)mer-
REMOVE	*meus-
REND	*h$_2$erk-, *rendh-, WC *lak-
REPROACH	*h$_1$lengh-
REPULSE	*(s)peud-
RESIN	*sok^{w}ós
RESOUND	*gerg-, *klun-, *swenh$_x$-, WC *(s)weh$_a$gh-
REST	*k^{w}eih$_1$-, *ses-
RESTITUTION	*serk-
RETURN HOME	*nes-
REVEL	WC *ghleu-

REVERE	*k^{w}eh$_1$(i)-
REVILE	*pih$_x$(y)-
REWARD	*misdhós
RIB	*pérk̂us
RICH	GA *h$_1$su-dhh$_1$énos
RICH IN MILK	*pipih$_x$usih$_a$
RIDE	*weĝh-, NW *reidh-
RIGHT	*dék̂sinos, *h$_3$reĝtos
RING	*ānos, NW *nedskéh$_a$-
RISE	*swelno-
RIVER	*deh$_a$nu-, *h$_2$eb(h)-
RIVER BANK	WC *h$_a$eh$_x$peros(?)
RIVER NAME	*drewentih$_2$-
ROAD	*h$_1$éitr̥-, WC *weĝhyeh$_a$-
ROAR	*reu-
ROAST	*bher-, *bhr̥g-, *h$_3$ep-, WC *bhōg-
ROCK	*peru-
ROD	*swer-
ROEDEER	WC *yórks
ROOF	*h$_1$rebh-, NW *k̂rópos, WC *(s)téges-
ROOM	*ket-
ROOM (HAVE)	*telp-
ROOT	*ālu-, WC *wr(h$_a$)d-
ROT	*peu(h$_x$)-
ROUGH	*kreup-
ROW (BOAT)	*h$_1$erh$_1$-
ROW (SERIES)	*wórghs
RUB	*bhes-, *kseu-, *merd-, WC *ter(i)-, WC *treu(h$_x$)-
RUDE	NW *saiwos
RULE	*deik̂-, *pótyetoi, *wal-, GA *tkeh$_1$-
RULER	*h$_3$rḗĝs
RUMBLE	*ghrem-
RUMEN	*reumn-
RUMP	*bulis
RUN	*bhegw-, *dreh$_a$-, *drem-, *dreu-, *dhen-, *k̂ers-, *reth$_2$-, *tek-, NW *tregh-, WC *dhregh-, GA/PIE? *dheu-
RUSH (REED)	*nedós, NW *yoinis, WC *trus-, E *g(h)re-wom
RYE	*h$_a$éreh$_a$-, NW *rughis
SACRED POWER	GA *ish$_1$ros
SACRIFICE	*h$_a$ed-bher-, *tolko/eh$_a$-

SACRIFICIAL ANIMAL	WC *dibhro- ~ *dībhro-
SACRIFICIAL MEAL	*dapnom, *tolko/eh$_a$-
SALMONID	*lóḱs, NW *str̥(h$_x$)yon-
SALT	*seh$_a$-(e)l-
SAME	*somos
SAND	WC *samh̥$_x$dhos
SAP	*sap- ~ *sab-, *sok^{w}ós
SATISFACTION	*térptis, NW *séh$_2$tis
SATISFIED	*speh$_1$-
SATISFY	*seh$_2$(i)-, *terp-, WC *sh̥$_2$tós
SAY	*g^{w}et-, *h$_1$eĝ-, *(s)pel-, *(s)wer-, WC *sek^w-
SAYING	WC *bheh$_a$meh$_a$-
SCABBY	*kreup-
SCARE	*terg^w-
SCATTER	*(s)ked-
SCRAPE	*merd-, *red-
SCRATCH	*drep-, *kars-, *rei-, *reik-, NW *skebh-, WC *(s)grebh-
SCREAM	NW *weh$_a$b-
SCREAM (OF BIRDS)	WC *kla(n)g-
SCROTUM	*h$_1$endrós
SCUTTLE ALONG	*lek-
SEA	*móri
SEASON	*(h$_1$)yēro/eh$_a$-,
SEAT	*sedes-, WC *sedlom, WC *sedros
SECOND	*dwi-yos ~ *dwi-tos
SEE	*derḱ-, *leĝ-, *leuk-, *sek^w-, *weid-, *wel-, *wet-, GA *h$_3$ek^w-
SEED	NW *seh$_1$men-
SEEK	*h$_a$eis-, *seh$_a$g-, *sen(h$_a$)-
SEEP	WC *stag-
SEER	NW *wōt-
SEETHE	*bher-, *bhreu-, WC *k^{w}ap-
SEIZE	*ghabh, *h$_1$ep-, *kap-, *la(m)bh-, WC *ghe(n)dh-, WC *sel-
SELF	*séwe
SELL	*pel-
SEND OUT	*selĝ-
SEPARATE(D)	*widh-, GA *h$_1$er(h$_1$)-
SERVANT	*h$_2$entbhi-k^{w}olos, *h$_4$upo-sth$_2$i/o-, NW *slóugos
SET	*sed-, NW *dheig^w-

SET IN MOTION	*$h_1$eis-, *$h_1$er-, *$h_2$lei-, *$h_3$er-, *kei-, *seuh_3-, *wegh- (*weĝh-?), *yeudh-, NW *pelh_a-, E *weip-
SET IN PLACE	*tắg-
SETTLE	GA *tk̂ei-
SETTLEMENT	*wik̂s, NW *solo/eh_a-/selo-, GA *tk̂ítis
SEVEN	*septḿ̥
SEVENTH	*septm̥-mós
SEW	*syuh_1-
SEX ORGAN	GA *muskós
SHADE	*sk̂ōyh̥$_a$, WC *skótos
SHADOW	WC *skótos
SHAFT (OF A CART OR WAGON)	*$h_{2/3}$éi$h_1$os
SHAKE	*kseubh-, *trem-, *wegh- (*weĝh-?), NW *kret-, NW *kreut, NW *(s)ku(n)t-, WC *k^wat-, GA *tweis-
SHALLOW WATER?	WC *tenh̥$_a$g-
SHAME	*(p)k̂órmos, WC *$h_a$eig^{w}hes-, GA *h_aēgos
SHARP	*$h_2$ek̂-, *k̂ent-, NW *saiwos
SHARPEN	*k̂eh_x(i)-, NW *k^wed-
SHAVE	*kseubh-, *werĝ-, NW *skebh-
SHEATFISH	*(s)k^wálos, WC *k̂ámos
SHEEP	*$h_1$eri-, *$h_2$ówis, *moisós, *(s)k̂egos
SHE-WOLF	*wl̥k^wíh_a-
SHIELD	*spelo/eh_a-, NW *skéits
SHIMMER	*mer-
SHIN	WC *kónh_am
SHINE	*bheh_2-, *bhel-, *bherh_xĝ-, *bhleg, *dei-, *deiw-, *ghel-, *$h_a$ewes-, *k̂euk-, *lap-, *leuk-, *mer-, *(s)kand-, *(s)plend-, *sweid-, NW *ĝher-, NW *leip-, C *$h_2$eug-
SHINING	WC *g^whaidrós
SHOE	WC *kr̥$h_1$pís
SHOOT (PLANT)	*$h_a$enkulos
SHOOT (THROW)	*(s)keud-
SHORE	WC *h_ae$h_x$peros (?)
SHORT	*mr̥ĝhus
SHOULDER	*dous-, *$h_{1/4}$ómsos, *$h_a$ek̂sleh_a-, *pl(e)t-, *(s)k̂up-,
SHOULDER BLADE	*pl(e)t-
SHOULDER JOINT	*$h_a$ek̂s-
SHOUT	*ĝar-, WC *yu-
SHOW	*deik̂-, *d(h)ek^ws-
SHREW	WC *sw(o)r-/*sworaks

SHRINK	*reuk/g-, *tenk-
SICK	WC *seug-
SICKLE	*sr̥po/eh$_a$-
SICKNESS	*h$_1$ermen-, *sokto-
SIDE	*poksós, WC *teig^w-
SIDE BY SIDE	*ko(m)
SIDES (ON BOTH)	*h$_2$entbhi-
SIEVE	NW *kreidhrom
SIFT	WC *seh$_1$(i)-
SIGH	*k̂wesh$_x$-
SIGN	WC *ĝnéh$_3$mn̥
SILENT	*t(e)h$_2$u-s-, NW *tak, WC *swīg/k-
SILVER	*h$_2$erĝn̥tom, NW *silVbVr-
SINEW	*snēh$_1$wr̥, WC *g^{w}hih$_x$(slo)-
SING	*geh$_1$(i)-, *h$_1$eus-, *k̂seh$_1$-, *pei-, *seng^{w}h-, WC/PIE? *kan-, WC *ghel-
SINGE	NW *senk-
SINGLE ONE	*semgo(lo)s
SISTER	*swésōr
SISTERLY	*swesr(iy)ós
SISTER'S HUSBAND	*ĝ(e)m(h$_x$)ros
SISTER'S SON	*swesr(iy)ós, NW *swesrih$_x$nos
SIT	*h$_1$ēs-, *sed-
SIX	*kswek̂s
SIXTH	*kswek̂sos
SIXTY	*kswek̂s- k̂omt(h$_a$)
SKIN	*h$_1$owes-, *kérmen-, *moisós, *(s)kwéh$_x$tis, *twéks, *wer-, WC *péln-
SKIN ERUPTION	*dedrús
SKULL	*kapōlo-
SKY	*nébhes-
SKY DAUGHTER	*dhuĝh$_a$tḗr diwós
SKY FATHER	*dyḗus ph$_a$tḗr
SLACK	WC *(s)lag- ~ *(s)leh$_2$g-
SLAG	NW *senh$_x$dhr-
SLEEP(Y)	*der-, *ses-, *swep-, *swópnos, E *kl̥h$_x$m(-s)-
SLICK	*(s)meug- ~ *(s)meuk-
SLIDE	*(s)leidh-, NW *sleubh-
SLIMY	*(s)lei-
SLING	WC *(s)bhondneh$_a$
SLIPPERY	*(s)lei-, *(s)meug- ~ *(s)meuk-
SLUG	WC *sleimak-
SMASH	WC *bhreus-
SMEAR	*h$_3$eng^w-, *h$_a$lei-, *leip-, WC *smeid-

SMELL (STINK)	WC *$h_3$ed-
SMILE	*smei-
SMITH GOD	*wl̥kānos ~ *wl̥keh$_a$nos
SMOKE	*dhuh$_2$mós, WC *k^{w}ap-, WC *(s)m(e)ug(h)-
SMOOTH	NW *ghleh$_x$dh-(ro)-
SMOULDER	*(s)mel-, *swelp-
SNAIL	WC *sleimak-
SNAKE	*$h_1$óg^{w}his, NW *néh$_1$tr- ~ *nh$_1$tr-, WC *h$_a$éng^{w}his
SNATCH	WC *$h_1$rep-
SNEAK UP ON	*(t)sel-
SNEEZE	*pster-, *skeu-, WC *pneu-
SNORE	WC *srenk-
SNORT	WC *pneu-
SNOW	*dhreg-, *ĝheim-, *sneig^{w}h-, *snig^{w}h-s, WC *k̂er(s)no-
SOAK	WC *teng-
SOFT	*meldh-, *mel(h_1)-, NW *l(e)nto-, C *menkus
SO MANY	*téh$_a$wot(s), WC *tóti
SOME	*sm̥ós
SO MUCH	WC *tóti
SON	*putlós, *suh$_x$nús, *suh$_x$yús
SONG	*sh$_2$ómen-
SON-IN-LAW	*ĝomh$_x$-ter-, WC *ĝm̥h$_x$-ro-s
SON'S WIFE	*snusós
SOON	*mok̂s
SOOT	*reh$_1$mós
SORCERY	NW *soito/eh$_a$-
SORT (OF WHAT)	NW *k^{w}eh$_a$k-, WC *k^{w}eh$_a$li
SORT OR SIZE (OF THAT)	WC *teh$_a$li
SOUND	*dhwen-, *ĝhwonos, *k̂léutrom
SOUR	*$h_2$emros, NW *suh$_x$ros
SOW (VERB)	*seh$_1$-, *sper-
SPARROW	*sper-
SPEAK	*gal, *$h_1$eug^{w}h-, *$h_{1/4}$ōr-, *mleuh$_x$-, *rek-, *(s)wer-, *ter-, *weg^{w}h-, *wek^w-, NW *tolk^w-, WC *bheh$_a$-, WC *(s)preg-
SPEAR	*ĝhaisós, *g^{w}éru, *k̂úh$_x$los, WC *$h_1$neĝhes-, WC *h$_a$eik̂smo/eh$_a$-
SPEARPOINT	*k̂el(h$_x$)-
SPECKLED	*perk̂-
SPELL	*h$_x$olu-
SPEW	*(s)py(e)uh$_x$-, *wémh$_x$mi
SPIN	*melk-, *(s)pen-
SPIRIT	*h$_a$énsus, NW *dhwes-, WC *lem-

SPIT (SPEAR)	*gʷéru, *k̂úh$_x$los, WC *h$_a$eik̂smo/eh$_a$-
SPIT (SPEW)	*(s)py(e)uh$_x$-
SPLEEN	*sploiĝh$_2$-ḗn
SPLINTER	*k̂ókolos
SPLIT	*bheid-, *bher-, *del-, *drep-, *skel-, *waĝ-
SPONGY	WC *swombhos
SPOTTED	*pik̂sk̂o-, NW *rei-, GA *k̂érberos
SPOUSE	WC *sm̥-loghos
SPREAD OUT	*peth$_a$-, *pelh$_a$k-, *pleth$_2$-, *ster-, NW *kleh$_a$-
SPRING (SEASON)	*wésr̥
SPRING (WATER)	WC *bhreh$_1$wr̥, WC *kr̥sneh$_a$, E *h$_a$élmos
SPRINKLE	*pers-, NW *sperh$_x$g-
SPROUT	WC *dhal-
SPURN	*sperh$_1$-
SPUTTER	*(s)pr̥h$_x$g-
SQUEEZE	*bhrak-, *nak-, WC *gem-
SQUIRREL	*werwer-
STAB	*h$_1$neĝh-, WC *gʷel-
STAFF	NW *ĝhasdhos
STAG	WC *bhrentós
STAKE	*míts, WC/PIE? *wálsos, WC *ĝhalgheh$_a$-, WC *k̂súlom, WC *(s)kōlos
STALK	*k̂ólh$_x$ōm, WC *kaulós
STALL	*mand-
STAMMER	*balba- ~ barbar-
STAND	*(s)teh$_2$-, *stembh-, *wredh-
STAR	*h$_2$stḗr
STARLING	NW *storos
STATURE	*stéh$_2$mōn
STEAL	*mus-, *(s)teh$_4$-, *teubh-, WC *ster-
STEAM	*wápōs
STEM	*k̂ólh$_x$ōm
STEP	*ghredh-, *ĝhengh-, *spleiĝh-, *steigh-
STICK (ADHERE)	*leip-, NW *dheigʷ-
STICKY	*(s)lei-
STIFF	*(s)terh$_1$-, *st(h$_2$)eug-
STIFFEN (OF HAIR)	*ĝhers-
STILL	NW *(s)tel-
STING	NW *dhelg-, WC *gʷel-
STINGER	WC *gʷelōn
STINK	*peu(h$_x$)-, *pū- (*puh$_x$-?), *weis-
STIR	*menth$_2$-, *twer-
STIR UP	*yeudh-, *yeuĝ-
STOAT	NW *k̂ormon-

STOMACH	*g^wétus, *pant-, *udero-, *ud^{s}tero-
STONE	*$h_4$ék̂mōn, *pel(i)s, WC *leh_1-w-, WC *lep-
STOREROOM	*gubho/eh_a-, *k̂ēls
STORK	*(s)ter-
STRANGER	NW *ghostis
STRAP	WC *(s)bhondneh_a
STRAW	*k̂ólh_xōm
STRENGTH	*$h_a$énr̥, *$h_a$euges-, *wéih_x(e)s-, *wór(h_x)ĝs
STRETCH	*$h_3$reĝ-, *pet-, *temp-, *ten-, NW *reiĝ-
STREW	*sper-, *ster(h_3)-, NW *sperh_xg-
STREWN PLACE	*ster(h_3)mn̥
STRIKE	*bhei(h_x)-, *bher-, *g^when-, *keh_au-, *kel-, *kreu(-s)-, *per-, *pyek-, *steup-, *wedh-, *wel(h_2)-, *wen-, NW *bheud-, NW *bhlaĝ-, NW *slak-, WC *bhlih_xĝ-, WC *deph_x-, WC *g^wel-, WC *kelh_1-, WC *pleh_ak/g-, GA *tk̂en-
STRIKE ONE'S BREASTS	WC *pleh_ak/g-
STRING	WC *strenk-
STRIP	*(s)pel-, WC *lep-
STRIPED	NW *rei-
STRIVE	*wenh_x-
STRONG	*bélos, *wal-, *weĝ-, *weih_x-
STRUCK	*temh_x-
STURGEON	NW *$h_a$ek̂e(tro)-, NW *str̥(h_x)yon-
SUBDUE	*demh_x-
SUCCESS	NW *kobom
SUCK(LE)	*dheh_1-, NW *seug/k-
SUCKLING	WC *dhe$h_1$lus-
SUFFER	*$k^{(w)}$eik̂-, WC *k^went(h)-
SUFFERING	*$h_a$em(h_x)īweh_a, *$h_a$énĝhes-, GA *pé$h_1$mn̥
SUFFICIENT	*g^whonós
SUMMER	*sem-
SUN	*sé$h_a$ul
SUPPORT	*dher-, WC *stl̥neh_a-
SURPASS	*serK-, GA *peri-$h_1$es-
SURPRISE (SOUND OF)	*ha
SURROUND	*gherdh-, *wer-
SWALLOW	*g^werh_3-, *k^wem-, *peh_3(i)-
SWAMP	WC *h_xi$h_x$lu
SWAN	WC ?*$h_1$el-
SWEAR	GA *$h_a$emh_3-
SWEAT	*$h_4$elh_1n-, *sweid-
SWEEP	*swep-

SWELL	*bhel-, *bhelĝh-, *bhleu-, *$h_1$eng^w-, *$h_1$euh$_x$dh-, *k̂euh$_1$-, *p(h)eu-, NW *bhreus-, WC *$h_a$eid-
SWELL (WITH POWER)	*teuh$_a$-
SWIM	*pleu-, *sneh$_a$-, NW *swem-
SWING	*swe(n)g-
SWORD	WC *skolmeh$_a$-
TAIL	*puk(eh$_a$)-, *wólos
TAKE	*dek̂-, *ghabh-, *ghrebh-, *$h_1$ep-, *nem-, NW *$h_1$em-, WC *(s)lag^w-, WC *twer-
TAKE (TO ONESELF)	*terp-
TAME(D)	*demh$_a$-, *domh$_a$yos
TASTE	*ĝeus-, NW *smeg-, WC *sap- ~ *sep-
TASTY	*sweh$_a$de/o-, *sweh$_a$dus
TEACH	GA *dens-
TEAL	*pad-
TEAR (OFF)	*der-, *drep-, *$h_1$reik-, *rendh-, *reu(h$_x$)-, *(s)pel-, *wel(h$_2$)-, NW *dhregh-, WC *$h_1$reip-, WC *lak-, WC *plek̂-, WC *wreh$_1$ĝ-
TEAR (OF THE EYE)	*(d)$h_2$ék̂ru
TEASE OUT	WC *knab(h)-
TEAT	*dhh$_1$ileh$_a$-, *pap-
TEN	*dék̂m̥(t)
TENCH	WC *(s)lei-
TENDON	*snēh$_1$wr̥
TENTH	*dek̂m̥(t)-os
TESTICLE	*$h_4$órĝhis
TETTER	*dedrús
THAT	*$h_1$en-, WC *$h_a$en-
THAT ONE	*so/*seh$_a$/*tód
THEN	*todéh$_a$, WC *téh$_a$mot(s)
THERE	*tór
THICK	*bhénĝhus, *dheb-, *g^{w}honós, *tegus, *tenk -, NW *g^{w}retsos
THIGH	*srēno/eh$_a$-
THIN	*kr̥k̂ós, *mak-, *menus/menwos, *ténus, WC *makrós, WC *skidrós
THINK	*men-, *teng-, NW *sent-, WC *g^{w}hren-
THIRD	*triyós
THIRTY	*trī-k̂omt(h$_a$)
THIS ONE	*$h_1$éi/*$h_1$ih$_a$- /*$h_1$id, *k̂is
THORN	*tŕ̥nu -, NW *skwēis, WC *glogh-, WC *wreh$_a$gh-

THOU	*te, *túh$_x$
THOUGHT	*ménmn̥, *méntis, GA *ménes-
THOUSAND	NW *tuh$_a$s-k̂m̥tyós, GA *ĝhesl(iy)os
THREAD	*dek̂-, NW *pe/oth$_a$mo-, WC *g^{w}hih$_x$(slo)-, GA *g^w(i)yēh$_a$
THREAD-END	WC *t(e)rmn-
THREATEN	*ghres-, *sker-
THREE	*tréyes
THRESH	*h$_2$eh$_2$er-, *peis-, *wers-
THRICE	*tris
THRIVE	*speh$_1$-
THROAT	*gutr̥
THROUGH	*per, *terh$_2$-
THROW	*ĝhi-, *g^{w}elh$_1$-, *h$_1$es-, *seh$_1$(i)-, *(s)keud-, *smeit-, *swep-, WC *yeh$_1$-
THRUSH	NW /WC?*trosdos
THRUST	*(s)teud-, NW *telk-, WC *treud-
THUMB	NW *pólik(o)s
THUNDER	*(s)tenh$_x$-, WC *ghromos
THUNDER GOD	*perk^{w}unos
THUS	*ar, *h$_1$ith$_a$, *it-, *ne
TICK	*rik-, WC *diĝ(h)-, WC *h$_x$orki-
TICKLE	WC *geid-
TIE	*h$_2$emĝh-, NW *nedskéh$_a$-
TIME	*prest-, WC *kēs(k̂)eh$_a$-
TIMID	*neh$_2$-
TIRED	*k̂emh$_a$-, *leh$_1$d-
TO	*do ~ *de, WC *h$_a$ed
TONGUE	*dn̥ĝhuh$_a$-
TOOL	*k^{w}r̥wis
TOOTH	*ĝómbhos, *h$_1$dónt-
TORCH	WC *ĝhwáks
TORMENT	*ghres-
TORTOISE	WC *ghéluh$_x$s
TOUCH	*deg-, *ml̥k̂-, WC *ghrei-, WC *tag-
TOWARD	*do ~ *de
TRACK (NOUN)	WC *weĝhyeh$_a$-
TRACK (VERB)	*wreg-
TRAVERSE	*lenk-
TREAT BADLY	*h$_{2/3}$wop-
TREE	*dóru, NW *k^{w}résnos, NW *widhu
TREE (TYPE OF)	NW *sal(i)k-
TREMBLE	*rei-, *trem-, *tres-
TRIAL	WC *per-

TRICK (WITH THE HAND)	*meh$_a$-
TROOP	*h$_a$eĝmen-
TROUGH	*h$_x$oldhu-
TROUT	*pik̂sk̂os
TRUE	*h$_1$sónt-, NW *weh$_1$ros
TRUST IN	*h $_{2/3}$eh$_x$-
TUBE	*k̂oiw-is
TURN	-*derbh-, *kleng-, *k^{w}el-, *k^{w}erp-, *k^{w}leu-, *seu-, *(s)kerbh-, *(s)neh$_1$-, *trep-, *weig/k-, *weip- ~ *weib-, *wel-, *wert-, *(w)rep-, NW *slenk-, NW *swerbh-, WC *ter(i)-
TURNIP	WC *rēpéh$_a$-
TWELVE	*dwō dek̂m̥(t)
TWENTY	*wīk̂m̥tih$_1$
TWICE	*dwis
TWIG	WC *wr̥b-
TWIN	*yemos
TWINE	*bher-, *kert-
TWIST FIBRES INTO THREAD	*derbh-, *(s)neh$_1$(i)-, *sneh$_1$u-, *terk(w)-, *weis-, *wendh-, NW *slenk-
TWO	*dwéh$_3$(u)
TWO (GROUP OF)	*dwoi-
TWOFOLD	*dw(e)i-plos, *dwoyos

UDDER	*h$_1$óuh$_x$dhr̥
ULCER	*h$_1$élk̂es-
UNCLE	*ph̥$_a$tr̥wyos, NW *h$_2$éuh$_2$-, WC *dheh$_1$-, WC *méh$_a$trōus
UNDER	*n̥dhés ~ *n̥dhero-, *ner, *s-h$_4$upó
UNDYING (DRINK)	GA *n̥-mr̥-tós
UNHEALTHY	*ĝhalh$_x$ros
UNITED AS ONE	*sem-s
UNPLEASANT	*ĝhalh$_x$ros, *h$_a$egh-los
UNQUIET	*yeuĝ-
UNSTEADY	*rei-
UP(WARD)	*h$_4$upó, *h$_a$en-h$_a$e, *ŭ̄d, E *h$_a$enu
UPRIGHT	*worh$_x$dhus
UP TO	*proti
URINATE	*h$_3$méiĝhe/o-
USE	*bheug-, NW *neud-
USEFUL	*dheuĝh -

VALLEY	*dhólh$_a$os, *lónko/eh$_a$-
VAPOUR	*wápōs

VARIEGATED	GA/PIE? *pl̥h$_1$u-poik/k̂os*
VAULT	**dhólh$_a$os*, GA **kamareh$_a$*
VENTURE	**dhers-*
VILLAGE	WC **k̂óimos*
VINE	W **tris-*
VIOLENT	WC **bhorg^{w}o-*
VISIBLE	GA **derk̂etos*
VITAL FORCE	**h$_a$énr̥*, **h$_a$óyus*, **weih$_x$s*
VOICE	**ĝhwonos*, **wōk^{w}s*
VOMIT	**wémh$_x$mi*
VULTURE	**g^{W}l̥tur-*
VULVA	**kuk̂is*, **kutsós*, **pisdo/eh$_a$-*, **putós*
WADE	**geh$_x$ĝh-*, NW **wadh-*
WAGON	**weĝhnos*, NW **k̂r̥sos*
WAGON-CHASSIS	**h$_2$em-h$_a$ek̂sih$_a$-*
WAKEN	**bhoudhéye/o-*
WALK	**ĝhengh-*
WALL	**dhíĝhs*
WALL (REPAIR)	**serk-*
WANDER	**h$_a$el-*
WANT	**h$_a$eis-*, **wek̂-*, **wel-*, WC **g^{w}hel-*
WANTING	**h$_1$eu(h$_a$)-*
WARM	**g^{w}her-*, **g^{w}hermos*, **g^{w}hrensós*, WC **wel-*
WART	**worh$_x$do-*
WASH	**h$_1$erh$_x$-*, **m(e)uh$_x$-*, **neig^w-*, **pleu-*, WC **leuh$_1$-*
WASP	**h$_{2/3}$wobhseh$_a$-*
WATCH OVER	**swerh$_x$K-*
WATCH OVER CATTLE	**poh$_2$(i)-*
WATER	**h$_2$eP-*, **we/oh$_x$r*, **weh$_x$p-*, **wódr̥*, NW **h$_a$ek^{w}eh$_a$-*, NW **pen-*, WC **tenh̥$_a$g-*, WC **yuh$_x$-r-*
WATERBIRD	WC **h$_1$el-*, WC **h$_1$orh$_x$deh$_a$-*
WATERY (ONE?)	WC **trih$_a$tōn*
WATTLE	**resg-*, **wei(h$_1$)-*
WAVE (NOUN)	WC **kr̥sneh$_a$*
WAVE (VERB)	**meh$_a$-*
WAX	**kóh$_a$-r̥*, NW **wos(h$_x$)ko-*
WAY	**h$_1$éitr̥-*, **pértus*, **sentos*
WE	**nóh$_1$*, **wéi*
WEAK	**h$_a$epus*, **losiwos*, **meldh-*
WEALTH	**h$_2$ó/ép(e)n-*, **wósu*
WEAR AWAY	WC **treu(h$_x$)-*
WEAR OUT	**weld-*, **wes-*

WEASEL	*lōk̂-, NW/WC? *(h$_a$)wiselo-, NW *k̂ormon-
WEAVE	*bher-, *h$_{2/3}$eu-, *h$_{2/3}$webh-, *weg-
WEDGE	WC *dhúbhos
WEEP	WC *ĝem-
WEEVIL	NW *webhel- ~ *wobhel-
WELL-DISPOSED	*h$_1$erh$_a$s-, GA *h$_1$su-menesye/o-
WELL UP	*g^{w}el(s)-, *h$_a$el-
WELS	*(s)k^{w}álos
WET	*leh$_2$-, *m(e)h$_a$d-, NW *leh$_a$t-, NW *welk-/*welg-, WC *reĝ- /*reknos, WC *weg^w-
WHAT	*k^{w}íd, *k^{w}ód
WHEAT	*ga/ondh-, *sepit, WC *puh$_x$rós
WHEEL	*h$_{2/3}$r̥gis, *k^{w}ek^{w}lóm, *róth$_2$o/eh$_a$-, WC *dhro-ghós
WHEN	*k^{w}odéh$_a$, *k^{w}óm
WHERE	*k^{w}ór, *k^{w}u ~ *k^{w}ū́
WHET	*kseu-, NW *k^{w}ed-
WHETSTONE	*k̂oh$_x$nos
WHEY	*ksih$_x$róm
WHICH (OF TWO)	*k^{w}óteros, GA *yoteros
WHITE	*bhelh$_1$-, *h$_2$erĝ-, *h$_2$r̥ ĝ(u), *h$_4$elbhós, *k̂weitos
WHO	*k^{w}ís, *k^{w}ós, *yós/*yéh$_a$/*yód
WHOLE	*sólwos
WIDE	*plet-, *pl̥th$_2$ú-, *wérh$_x$us
WIDOW	*widheweh$_a$-
WIFE	*potnih$_a$-, *prih$_x$eh$_a$-
WIFE'S BROTHER	*swēk̂urós, *syō(u)ros
WIFE'S SISTER, i.e. SISTER-IN-LAW	WC *swoiniyeh$_a$-
WIFE'S SISTER'S HUSBAND	WC *sweliyon-
WILD ANIMAL	*ĝhwēr
WILD ASS	E *gordebhós
WILDCAT	NW *bhel-
WILLOW	*weit-, NW *sal(i)k-, WC *weliko/eh$_a$-
WIND (NOUN)	*h$_2$weh$_1$nt-, *h$_2$weh$_1$yús
WIND (VERB)	*wel-, *wendh-
WINE	*wóinom
WING	*pet(e)r-, *(s)pornóm
WINNOW	WC *neik-
WINTER	*ĝheim-
WIPE OFF	GA *h$_3$merĝ-
WISH	*h$_a$eis-, *wek̂-, *wel-, WC *g^{w}hel-
WITH	*ko(m), *som-, WC *ksun

WITHER	*wes-
WITHOUT	*b(h)eĝh, *$h_1$énh$_1$u
WOLF	*wl̥k^{w}os, WC *dhóh$_a$us, WC *wailos
WOMAN	*g^{w}énh$_a$, *maghwih$_a$-, *merih$_a$-
WOMAN (WANTON)	?*parikeh$_a$-
WOMB	*g$^{(w)}$elbhus, *g^{w}étus
WOOD	*dóru
WOOD (WORKED)	*pin-, *stup-, WC *k̂súlom, WC *sph$_a$en-
WOODEN VESSEL	WC *(s)pondh(n)os
WOODPECKER	*(s)p(e)iko/eh$_a$-
WOOL	*wl̥h$_2$neh$_a$-
WORK	*h$_x$ópes-, *werĝ-, WC *derh$_a$-
WORK CLAY	*dheiĝh-
WORM	*k^{w}r̥mis, *mat-, *wr̥mis
WORSHIP	GA *yaĝ-
WOUND	*h$_a$éru(s), *peles-, *swero-, *wen-, *wolno/eh$_a$-, WC *weh$_a$t-
WRAP	*kenk-, *(s)keu(h$_x$)-, *(s)pre(n)g-, WC *sper-
WRINKLE UP	*reuk/g-
WUG	*k^{w}r̥mis, WC *wr̥mi, C *demelís
YAWN	*ĝheh$_a$w, *ĝh(h$_1$)iy-eh$_a$-
YEAR	*(h$_1$)yēro/eh$_a$-, *wet-, NW *h$_a$etnos, WC *h$_1$en-
YEAR (LAST)	*perut-
YEARLING	*wételos
YELLOW	*ĝhel- ~ *ghel-
YELP	*bhels-
YESTERDAY	*(dh)ĝhyes
YEW	*h$_1$eiwos, *taksos
YIELD	*weig/k-
YOKE	*dhwerh$_x$-, *yugóm
YONDER	NW *h$_a$elnos
YOU	*uswé ~ *swé, *wóh$_1$, *yuh$_x$s
YOUNG	*h$_a$yeu-
YOUNG BIRD	*pipp-
YOUNG DOG	WC *(s)koli-
YOUNG MAN	*maghus, *méryos
YOUNG PIG	*pórk̂os, C *ĝhor-
YOUNG WOMAN	*maghwih$_a$-, *merih$_a$-
YOUTH	*h$_a$yuh$_x$n̥k̂ós

References

Adams, D. Q. (1984). 'Tokharian A *śiśäk*, B *ṣecake*, and the Proto-Indo-European Word for "Lion"', *Zeitschrift für vergleichende Sprachforschung*, 97: 284–6.

—— (1985*a*). 'Designations of the *Cervidae* in Proto-Indo-European', *Journal of Indo-European Studies*, 13: 269–82.

—— (1985*b*). 'PIE **loḱso-* "(Anadromous) Brown Trout" and **koḱso-* "Groin" and their Descendants in Tocharian: A Coda to the Lachsargument', *Indogermanische Forschungen*, 90: 72–82.

—— (1985*c*). 'The Indo-European Word for "Apple" Again', *Indogermanische Forschungen*, 90: 79–82.

—— (1985*d*). 'Sanskrit *púmān*, Latin *pūbēs*, and Related Words', *Die Sprache*, 31: 1–16.

—— (1988*a*). *Tocharian Historical Phonology and Morphology*. New Haven: American Oriental Society.

—— (1988*b*). 'The Indo-European Words for Hair: Reconstructing a Semantic Field', *Journal of Indo-European Studies*, 16: 69–93.

—— (1999). *A Dictionary of Tocharian B*. Amsterdam: Rodopi.

Adrados, F. (1982). *Die räumliche und zeitliche Differenzierung des Indoeuropäischen im Lichte der Vor- und Frühgeschichte*. Innsbruck: Innsbrucker Beiträge zur Sprachwissenschaft.

—— (1985). 'G ἀλώπηξ, O.I. *lopāśá-*, Av *urupis*, Lat *uolpēs* and the IE Laryngeals', in H. Ölberg and G. Schmidt (eds.), *Sprachwissenschaftliche Forschungen: Festschrift Johann Knobloch*. Innsbruck: Institut für Sprachwissenschaft der Universität Innsbruck, 21–8.

Ahyan, S. (1998). 'The Indo-European Mythical Theme of the Final Battle in the "History of the Armenians" by Movses Khorenatsi', *Journal of Indo-European Studies*, 26: 447–57.

Allen, N. J. (1987). 'The Ideology of the Indo-Europeans: Dumézil's Theory and the Idea of a Fourth Function', *International Journal of Moral and Social Studies*, 2(1): 23–39.

—— (2000*a*). 'Argos and Hanuman: Odysseus' Dog in the Light of the *Mahābhārata*', *Journal of Indo-European Studies*, 28: 3–16.

—— (2000*b*). 'Cúchulainn's Women and Some Indo-European Comparisons', *Emania*, 18: 57–64.

—— (2002). 'The Stockmen and the Disciples', *Journal of Indo-European Studies*, 30: 27–40.

Amaladass, A. (1992). 'Jesuits and Sanskrit Studies', in T. R. De Souza and C. J. Borges (eds.), *Jesuits in India: In Historical Perspective*. Goa: Xavier Centre of Historical Research, 209–31.

ANDERSON, E. R. (2003). *Folk-Taxonomies in Early English.* Madison: Fairleigh Dickinson University Press.

ANTHONY, D. (1991). 'The Archaeology of Indo-European Origins', *Journal of Indo-European Studies*, 19: 193–222.

ANTTILA, R. (1972). *An Introduction to Historical and Comparative Linguistics.* New York: Macmillan.

ARUMAA, P. (1949). 'Semantics and Age of Declension', in *Apophoreta Tartuensia.* Stockholm: Societas Litterarum Estonica in Svecia, 73–8.

BADER, F. (1986). 'De Pollux à Deukalion: la racine **deu-k-* "briller, voir"', in A. Etter (ed.), *o-o-pe-ro-si: Festschrift für E. Risch.* Berlin: de Gruyter, 463–88.

—— (1989). *La Langue des dieux, ou l'hermétisme des poètes indo-européens.* Pisa: Giardini.

—— (1992). 'Boire de l'eau', in R. Pearson (ed.), *Perspectives on Indo-European Language, Culture and Religion.* McLean, Va.: Institute for the Study of Man, 380–404.

—— (ed.) (1994). *Langues indo-européennes.* Paris: CNRS.

—— (1997). *Les Langues indo-européennes.* Pans: CNRS.

BAILEY, H. W. (1959). 'Iranian *arya-* and *daha-*', *Transactions of the Philological Society*, 1959: 71–115.

—— (1960). 'Arya II', *Bulletin of the Society for Oriental and African Studies*, 23: 13–39.

—— (1979). *Dictionary of Khotan Saka*, Cambridge: Cambridge University.

BALDI, P. (1974). 'Indo-European **sek^{w}-*', *Journal of Indo-European Studies*, 2: 77–86.

—— (1983). *An Introduction to the Indo-European Languages.* Carbondale: Southern Illinois University.

—— (1999). *The Foundations of Latin.* Berlin: de Gruyter.

BAMMESBERGER, A. (1979). *Beiträge zur einem etymologischen Wörterbuch des Altenglischen.* Heidelberg: C. Winter.

—— (1984). *Lateinische Sprachwissenschaft.* Regensburg: Universität Eichstatt.

—— (1996). 'On Fresh Fish in Some (Indo-)European Languages', *Journal of Indo-European Studies*, 24: 399–408.

BARBER, E. J. W. (1975). 'The PIE Notion of Cloth and Clothing', *Journal of Indo-European Studies*, 3: 294–320.

—— (1991). *Prehistoric Textiles: The Development of Cloth in the Neolithic and Bronze Ages.* Princeton: Princeton University.

—— (2001). 'The Clues in the Clothes: Some Independent Evidence for the Movements of Families', in R. Drews (ed.), *Greater Anatolia and the Indo-Hittite Language Family.* Washington: Institute for the Study of Man, 1–14.

BARRACH, C. (2002). 'The Glottalic Theory Revisited', *Indogermanische Forschungen*, 107: 76–95.

—— (2003). 'The Glottalic Theory Revisited', *Indogermanische Forschungen*, 108: 1–16.

BARTHOLOMAE, C. (1904). *Altiranisches Wörterbuch.* Strassburg: Trübner.

BARTON, C. (1985). 'PIE **swep-* and **ses-*', *Die Sprache*, 31: 17–39.

—— (1989). 'PIE **mer-*, Arm. *meranim* "Die"', *Indogermanische Forschungen*, 94: 135–57.

Beekes, R. S. P. (1976). 'Uncle and Nephew', *Journal of Indo-European Studies*, 4: 43–63.

—— (1982). 'GAv ma: The PIE Word for "Moon, Month" and the Perfect participle', *Journal of Indo-European Studies*, 10: 53–64.

—— (1984). 'PIE "Sun"', *Münchener Studium zur Sprachwissenschaft*, 43: 5–8.

—— (1987*a*). 'On Indo-European "Wine"', *Münchener Studium zur Sprachwissenschaft*, 48: 21–6.

—— (1987*b*). 'The PIE Words for "Name" and "Me"', *Die Sprache*, 33: 1–6.

—— (1988). *A Grammar of Gatha-Avestan*. Leiden: Brill.

—— (1992). 'Widow', *Historische Sprachforschung*, 105: 171–88.

—— (1995). *Comparative Indo-European Linguistics: An Introduction*. Amsterdam: John Benjamins.

—— (2003). 'Indo-European or Substrate? *Φάτνη* and *κῆρυξ*', in A. Bammesberger and T. Vennemann (eds.), *Language in Prehistoric Europe*. Heidelberg: Winter, 109–15.

Beeler, M. (1949). *The Venetic Language*. Berkeley and Los Angeles: University of California.

Benveniste, E. (1935). *Origines de la formation des noms en indo-européen*. Paris: Adrien Maisonneuve.

—— (1945). 'La Doctrine médicale des Indo-Européens', *Revue de l'histoire des religions*, 130: 5–12.

—— (1948). *Noms d'agent et noms d'action en indo-européen*. Paris: Adrien Maisonneuve.

—— (1949). 'Noms d'animaux en indo-européen', *Bulletin de la Société de Linguistique de Paris*, 45: 74–103.

—— (1954). 'Problèmes semantiques de la reconstruction', *Word*, 10: 2–3.

—— (1956*a*). 'Analyse d'un vocable primaire: i.-e. **bhaghu*', *Bulletin de la Société de Linguistique de Paris*, 52: 60–71.

—— (1956*b*). ' "Hiver" et "neige" en indo-européen', in H. Kronasser (ed.), *Gedenkschrift Paul Kretschmer*. Vienna: Wiener Sprachgesellschaft, i. 31–9.

—— (1973*a*). *Indo-European Language and Society*. Coral Gables, Fla.: University of Miami.= (1969) *Vocabulaire des institutions indo-européennes*. Paris: de Minuit.

—— (1973*b*). 'A Lexical Opposition in Need of Revision: sus and porcus', in E. Benveniste, *Indo-European Language and Society*. Coral Gables, Fla.: University of Miami Press, 23–31.

Bergsland, K., and Vogt, H. (1962). 'On the Validity of Glottochronology', *Current Anthropology*, 3: 115–53.

Berlin, B. (1992). *Ethnobiological Classification*. Princeton: Princeton University Press.

—— and Kay, P. (1969). *Basic Color Terms*. Berkeley and Los Angeles: University of California Press.

Bernabé, A. (1982). 'Nombres para el "cerebro" en las lenguas indoeuropeas', *Revista española de linguistica*, 12: 53–68.

Bird, N. (1993). *The Roots and Non-roots of Indo-European: A Lexicostatistic Survey*. Wiesbaden: Harrassowitz.

Blažek, V. (1992). 'Historická Analyza Indoevropské Zoologické Terminologie'. Unpublished Ph.D, Brno.

—— (1999*a*). *Numerals: Comparative-Etymological Analyses and their Implications*. Brno: Masarykova Univerzita v Brne.

—— (1999*b*). 'Is Indo-European *H_1ek̂wos "Horse" Really of Indo-European Origin?', in P. Stalmaszczyk and K. T. Witczak (eds.), *Studia Indogermanica Lodziensia 2*. Łódź: Wydawnictwo uniwersytetu Łodzkiego, 21–32.

—— (2001). 'Indo-European Kinship Terms in *-eter', in O. Šefčik and B. Vykypěl (eds.), *Grammaticus: Studia Linguistica Adolfo Erharto Quinque et Septuagenario Oblatu*. Brno: Masarykova Universita, 24–33.

—— (2005). 'Hic Erant Leones: Indo-European "Lion" *et alii*', *Journal of Indo-European Studies*, 33: 63–101.

Blok, D. (1971). 'Chronologisches zum alteuropäischen Flussnamensystem', *Namn och Bygd*, 59: 149–61.

Bloomfield, L. (1933). *Language*. New York: Holt, Rinehart and Winston.

Bomhard, A. (1977). 'The I.E.–Semitic Hypothesis Re-examined', *Journal of Indo-European Studies*, 5: 55–99.

—— (1986). 'An Etymological Note: PIE *Hs-tér- "Star"', *Journal of Indo-European Studies*, 14: 191–2.

—— (1996). *Indo-European and the Nostratic Hypothesis*. Charleston, SC: Signum.

—— and Kerns, J. C. (1994). *The Nostratic Macrofamily: A Study in Distant Linguistic Relationship*. New York: de Gruyter.

Bonfante, G. (1974). 'Das Problem des Weines und die linguistische Paläontologie', in M. Mayrhofer, W. Meid, B. Schlerath, and R. Schmitt (eds.), *Antiquitates Indogermanicae*. Innsbruck: Innsbrucker Beiträge zur Sprachwissenschaft, 85–90.

—— (1989). 'Il nome della pioggia in indoeuropeo', *Archivo glottologico italiano*, 74: 101.

—— (1996). 'The Etymology of ἵππος', *Journal of Indo-European Studies*, 24: 111–12.

—— and Sebeok, T. (1944). 'Linguistics and the Age and Area Hypothesis', *American Anthropologist*, 46: 382–6.

Brandenstein, W. (1936). *Die erste Indogermanische Wanderung*. Vienna: Gerold.

Bray, D. (2000). 'The End of Mythology: Hesiod's Theogony and the Indo-European Myth of the Final Battle', *Journal of Indo-European Studies*, 28: 359–71.

Bremmer, J. (1976). 'Avunculate and Fosterage', *Journal of Indo-European Studies*, 4: 65–78.

Brixhe, C. (1994). 'Le Phrygien', in F. Bader (ed.), *Langues indo-européennes*. Paris: CNRS: 165–78.

—— and Panayotou, A. (1994). 'Le Thrace', in F. Bader (ed.), *Langues indo-européennes*. Paris: CNRS, 179–203.

Brown, C. (1984). *Language and Living Things: Uniformities in Folk Classification and Naming*. New Brunswick, NJ: Rutgers University Press.

Brugmann, K. (1897–1916). *Grundriss der vergleichenden Grammatik der indogermanischen Sprachen*. Strassburg: Trübner.

Brunner, L. (1969). *Die gemeinsamen Wurzeln des semitischen und indogermanischen Wortschatzes*. Bern: Francke.

Buck, C. (1928). *A Grammar of Oscan and Umbrian*. Boston: Ginn.

—— (1949). *A Dictionary of Selected Synonyms in the Principal Indo-European Languages*. Chicago: University of Chicago.

Burris, H. (1979). 'Geometric Figure Terms: Their Universality and Growth', *Journal of Anthropology*, 1(2): 18–41.

Burrow, T. (1973). *The Sanskrit Language*. London: Faber and Faber.

Bush, A. C. (1987). 'Nepos Again', *Journal of Indo-European Studies*, 15: 285–96.

Buti, G. (1987). 'The Family and the Tribe: Remarks on Indo-European Social Setting', in W. Meid (ed.), *Studien zur indogermansiche Wortschatz*. Innsbruck: Institut für Sprachwissenschaft der Universität, 9–20.

Campanile, E. (1977). *Richerche di cultura poetica indo-europea*. Pisa: Giardini.

—— (1990). *La ricostruzione della cultura indoeuropea*. Pisa: Giardini.

Campbell, L. (1998). *Historical Linguistics: An Introduction*. Edinburgh: Edinburgh University Press.

Carpelan, C., Parpola, A., and Koskikallio, P. (2001). *Early Contacts between Uralic and Indo-European: Linguistic and Archaeological Considerations*. Helsinki: Suomalais-Ugrilainen Seura.

Carroll, J. B. (1971). *The American Heritage Word Frequency Book*. Boston: Houghton Mifflin.

Carruba, O. (1970). *Das Palaische: Texte, Grammatik, Lexikon*. Wiesbaden: Harrassowitz.

—— (1995). 'Die Verwandtschaftsnamen auf *-ter* des Indogermanischen', in W. Smoczynski (ed.), *Kurlyowicz Memorial Volume*. Cracow: Universitas, 143–58.

Chantraine, P. (1968–80). *Dictionnaire étymologique de la langue grecque*. Paris: Klincksieck.

Charlton, T. R. (1991). *Introduction to the Phonological History of the Slavic Languages*. Ann Arbor: Slavica.

Clackson, J. (1994). *The Linguistic Relationship between Armenian and Greek*. Oxford: Blackwell.

Cohen, Y. (2002). *Taboos and Prohibitions in Hittite Society: A Study of the Hittite Expression* natta āra *('Not Permitted')*. Heidelberg: Carl Winter.

Collinder, B. (1974). 'Indo-Uralisch oder gar Nostratisch? Vierzig Jahre auf rauhen Pfaden', in M. Mayrhofer, W. Meid, B. Schlerath, and R. Schmitt (eds.), *Antiquitates Indogermanicae*. Innsbruck: Innsbrucker Beiträge zur Sprachwissenschaft, 363–75.

Comrie, B. (1993). *The Slavonic Languages*. London: Routledge.

Costa, G. (1990). *I composti indoeuropei con *dus- e *su-*. Pisa: Giardini.

Crepajac, L. (1967). 'Die idg. Wortsippe **gh/ghel-* "hell, glänzend" im Griechischen und Slavischen', *Zeitschrift für vergleichende Sprachforschung*, 81: 181–6.

Crevatin, F. (1979). 'Aspetti militari della società IE. e società militari', in F. Crevatin (ed.), *Richerche di antichità indeuropee*. Trieste: Edizioni LINT, 51–76.

Dahllöf, N. (1974). 'Some Semantic Variants of the I.E. Radical Morpheme ok^{w}-', *Indogermanische Forschungen*, 79: 35–52.

Danka, I. R. (1998). 'Two Hymns in Modern Indo-European', in P. Stalmaszczyk and K. T. Witczak (eds.), *Studia Indogermanica Lodziensia 2*. Łódź: Wydawnictwo uniwersytetu Łodzkiego, 173–4.

Darden, B. (2001). 'On the Question of the Anatolian Origin of Indo-Hittite', in R. Drews (ed.), *Greater Anatolia and the Indo-Hittite Language Family*. Washington: Institute for the Study of Man, 184–228.

Das, R., and Meiser, G. (2002). *Geregeltes Ungestüm: Bruderschaften und Jugendbünde bei den indogermanischen Völkern*. Bremen: Hempen Verlag.

Day, J. (2001). *Indo-European Origins: The Anthropological Evidence*. Washington: Institute for the Study of Man.

Delamarre, X. (1991). *Le Vocabulaire indo-européen: Lexique étymologique thématique*. Paris: J. Maisonneuve.

—— (1992). 'Finnois *karhu*, aryen **hr̥ksas*, indo-européen *$*h_2rtkos$*', *Historische Sprachforschung*, 105: 151–4.

—— (2003). *Dictionnaire de la langue gauloise*. Paris: Éditions Errance.

Delbrück, B. (1882). *Introduction to the Study of Language*. Reprinted 1974. Amsterdam: John Benjamins.

—— (1889). *Die indogermanischen Verwandtschaftnamen*. Leipzig: Abhandlungen der Philologisch-historischen Classes der Königlichen Sächsischen Gesellschaft der Wissenschaft 11, 381–606.

Della Volpe, A. (1986). 'Hillfort Nomenclature in Indo-European: The Case of Latin *urbs*', *Journal of Indo-European Studies*, 16: 195–208.

—— (1990). 'From the Hearth to the Creation of Boundaries', *Journal of Indo-European Studies*, 18: 157–84.

—— (1992). 'On Indo-European Ceremonial and Socio-political Elements Underlying the Origin of Formal Boundaries', *Journal of Indo-European Studies*, 20: 71–122.

—— (1993). 'On Evidence of Ranked Status in Indo-European: PIE **wik̂-pot-i-*', *Word*, 44: 255–71.

Demiraj, B. (1993). *Historische Grammatik der albanischen Sprache*. Vienna: Österreichische Akademie der Wissenschaften.

—— (1997). *Albanische Etymologien: Untersuchung zum albanischen Wortschatz*. Amsterdam: Rodopi.

De Simone, C. (1964). 'Die Messapischen Inschriften und ihre Chronologie', in H. Krahe (ed.), *Die Sprache der Illyrer; Zweiter Teil*. Wiesbaden: Harrassowitz.

Detschew, D. (1957). *Die thrakischen Sprachreste*. Vienna: Rohrer.

Devoto, G. (1962). *Origini Indoeuropee*. Florence: Sansoni.

DeVries, J. (1962). *Altnordisches etymologisches Wörterbuch*. Leiden: Brill.

Dexter, M. R. (1996). 'Dawn-Maid and Sun-Maid: Celestial Goddesses among the Proto-Indo-Europeans', in K. Jones-Bley and M. Huld (eds.), *The Indo-Europeanization of Northern Europe*. Washington: Institute for the Study of Man, 228–46.

Diakonoff, I., and Neroznak, V. P. (1985). *Phrygian*. Delmar, NY: Caravan.

D'iakonov, I. M. (1985). 'On the Original Home of the Speakers of Indo-European', *Journal of Indo-European Studies*, 13: 122–40.

Diebold, A. R. (1976). 'Contributions to the Indo-European Salmon Problem', in W. Christie (ed.), *Current Progress in Historical Linguistics*. Amsterdam: North Holland Publishing Company, 341–88.

—— (1985). *The Evolution of the Indo-European Nomenclature for Salmonid Fish: The Case of 'Huchen'*. Washington: Institute for the Study of Man.

—— (1992). 'The Traditional View of the Indo-European Paleoeconomy: Contradictory Evidence from Anthropology and Linguistics', in E. Polomé and W. Winter (eds.), *Reconstructing Languages and Cultures*. Berlin: de Gruyter, 317–67.

DOLGOPOLSKY, A. (1987). 'The Indo-European Homeland and Lexical Contacts of Proto-Indo-European with Other Languages', *Mediterranean Language Review*, 3: 7–31.

—— (1998). *The Nostratic Macrofamily and Linguistic Palaeontology*. Cambridge: McDonald Institute for Archaeological Research.

DREWS, R. (1988). *The Coming of the Greeks*. Princeton: Princeton University.

—— (ed.) (2001). *Greater Anatolia and the Indo-Hittite Language Family*. Washington: Institute for the Study of Man.

DRIESSEN, C. M. (2001). 'On the Etymology of Lat *urbs*', *Journal of Indo-European Studies*, 29: 41–68.

—— (2003). '*h_2é-$h_2$us-o-*, the Proto-Indo-European Term for "Gold"', *Journal of Indo-European Studies*, 31: 347–62.

—— (2004). 'Towards an Indo-European Term for "Felt"', *Journal of Indo-European Studies*, 32: 25–41.

DUBUISSON, D. (1992). 'Les Enjeux d'une exégèse (le mythe dioscurique indo-européen)', in R. Pearson (ed.), *Perspectives on Indo-European Language, Culture and Religion*, vol. ii. McLean, Va.: Institute for the Study of Man, 360–79.

DUHOUX, Y. (1973). 'Indo-Européen **el-eu-dh -/l-eu-dh*, **l-eu-dh-*; grec *eleutheros*, latin *līber*', *Folia Linguistica*, 6: 146–51.

DUMÉZIL, G. (1941). 'Le Nom des "Arya"', *Revue de l'histoire des religions*, 124: 36–59.

—— (1958). '*ari, Aryaman*, à propos de Paul Thieme *ari* "Fremder"', *Journal asiatique*, 246: 67–84.

—— (1970). *The Destiny of the Warrior*. Chicago: University of Chicago.

—— (1968–73). *Mythe et épopée*. Paris: Gallimard.

EILERS, W., and MAYRHOFER, M. (1962). 'Kurdisch *buz* und die indogermanische "Buchen"-Sippe', *Mitteilungen der anthropologischen Gesellschaft in Wien*, 92: 61–92.

ENDZELINS, J. (1971). *Comparative Phonology and Morphology of the Baltic Languages*. The Hague: Mouton.

ERNOUT, A., and MEILLET, A. (1967). *Dictionnaire étymologique de la langage latine: Histoire des mots*. Paris: Klincksieck.

EULER, W. (1987). 'Gab es eine indogermanische Götterfamilie?', in W. Meid (ed.), *Studien zum indogermanischen Wortschatz*. Innsbruck: Institut für Sprachwissenschaft der Universität, 46–51.

FORSSMAN, B. (1969). 'Nachlese zu *ósse*', *Münchener Studium zur Sprachwissenschaft*, 25: 39–50.

FORTSON, B. (2004). *Indo-European Language and Culture*. Oxford: Blackwell.

FRAENKEL, E. (1950). *Die baltischen Sprachen*. Heidelberg: Carl Winter.

—— (1962–5). *Litauisches etymologisches Wörterbuch*. Heidelberg: Carl Winter.

Frake, C. (1961). 'The Diagnosis of Disease among the Subanun of Mindanao', *American Anthropologist*, 63: 113–32.

Friedrich, J., Kammenhuber, A., and Hoffmann, I. (1975–). *Hethitisches Wörterbuch: Zweite, völlig neubearbeitete Auflage auf der Grundlage der edierten hethitischen Texte*. Heidelberg: Winter.

Friedrich, P. (1966). 'Proto-Indo-European Kinship', *Ethnology*, 5: 1–36.

—— (1970). *Proto-Indo-European Trees*. Chicago: University of Chicago.

—— (1975). *Proto-Indo-European Syntax*. Butte, Mont.: Journal of Indo-European Studies.

—— (1987). 'The Proto-Indo-European Adpreps (Spatio-temporal Auxiliaries)', in G. Cardona and N. Zide (eds.), *Festschrift for Henry Hoenigswald: On the Occasion of his Seventieth Birthday*. Tübingen: Gunter Narr, 131–42.

Frisk, H. (1950). 'Zu einigen Verba des Hörens im Indogermanischen', in *Symbolae Philogicae Gotoburgensis*. Göteborg: Wettergren and Kerbor, 1–22.

—— (1960–72). *Griechisches etymologisches Wörterbuch*. Heidelberg: Winter.

Gamkrelidze, T. (1986). 'Indo-European "Apple"', in N. Arhammar et al. (eds.), *Aspects of Language: Studies in Honour of Mario Alinei*. Amsterdam: Rodopi, i. 91–7.

—— and Ivanov, V. (1995). *Indo-European and the Indo-Europeans*. Berlin: Mouton de Gruyter.

Gates, H. P. (1971). 'The Kinship Terminology of Homeric Greek', Supplement to the *International Journal of American Linguistics*, 37(4).

Georgiev, V. (1966). 'Die europäische Makrohydronymie und die Frage nach der Urheimat der Indoeuropäer', in D. Blok (ed.), *Proceedings of the Eighth International Congress of Onomastic Sciences*. The Hague: Mouton, 188–95.

—— (1977). *Trakite i Tehnijat Ezik*. Sofia: Bulgarian Akademy of Sciences.

Gimbutas, M. (1991). *The Civilization of the Goddess*. San Francisco: Harper.

—— (1997). *The Kurgan Culture and the Indo-Europeanization of Europe*. Washington: Institute for the Study of Man.

Godel, R. (1975). *An Introduction to the Study of Classical Armenian*. Wiesbaden: Dr Ludwig Reichert Verlag.

Gonda, J. (1955*a*). 'Die Grundbedeutung der idg. Wurzel **sneig^{w}h-*', *Zeitschrift für vergleichende Sprachforschung*, 73: 228–30.

—— (1995*b*). 'Semantisches zu idg. **rēĝ-* "king" und zur Wurzel **reĝ-*(sich aus) strecken', *Zeitschrift für vergleichende Sprachforschung*, 73: 151–67.

Greenberg, J. (2000–2). *Indo-European and its Closest Relatives: The Eurasiatic Language Family: Lexicon*. Stanford, Calif.: Stanford University Press.

Grottanelli, C. (1986). 'Yoked Horses, Twins and the Powerful Lady: India, Greece, Ireland and Elsewhere', *Journal of Indo-European Studies*, 14: 125–52.

Gvozdanivic, J., (ed.) (1992). *Indo-European Numerals*. Trends in Linguistics 57. Berlin: Mouton de Gruyter.

Haas, O. (1962). *Messapische Studien*. Heidelberg: Winter.

—— (1966). *Die phrygischen Sprachdenkmäler*. Sofia: Akademie Bulgare des sciences.

Häkkinen, K. (2001). 'Prehistoric Finno-Ugric Culture in the Light of Historical Lexicology', in C. Carpelan, A. Parpola, and P. Koskikallio (eds.), *Early Contacts between Uralic and Indo-European: Linguistic and Archaeological Considerations*. Helsinki: Suomalais-Ugrilainen Seura, 169–86.

HALL, R. (1960). 'On Realism in Reconstruction', *Language*, 36: 203–6.

HAMP, E. P. (1960). 'Irish *srón*, Greek ῥίς. ῥῑνός', *Glotta*, 38: 209–11.

—— (1966). 'The Position of Albanian', in H. Birnbaum and J. Puhvel (eds.), *Ancient Indo-European Dialects*. Berkeley and Los Angeles: University of California, 97–121.

—— (1967). 'On the Notions of "Stone" and "Mountain" in Indo-European', *Journal of Linguistics*, 3: 83–90.

—— (1970). 'On the Paradigm of "Knee"', *Glotta*, 48: 72–5.

—— (1971*a*). 'The "Bee" in Irish, Indo-European, and Uralic', *Ériu*, 22: 185–7.

—— (1971*b*). 'Some Colour Words in *-no-*', *International Journal of Slavic Linguistics and Poetics*, 14: 1–5.

—— (1972*a*). 'The Principal (?) Indo-European Constellations', in L. Heilmann (ed.), *Proceedings of the Eleventh International Congress of Linguistics*, Bologna: Società Editrice il Mulino Bologna, 1047–55.

—— (1972*b*). 'On Indo-European Nouns in *e*-reduplication. 5. The Name of the Beaver', *Indogermanische Forschungen*, 77: 164.

—— (1972*c*). 'On Indo-European Nouns in *e*-reduplication. 6. The Word for the Squirrel', *Indogermanische Forschungen*, 77: 159–70.

—— (1973*a*). 'Fish', *Journal of Indo-European Studies*, 1: 507–11.

—— (1973*b*). 'Formations indo-européennes à second élément *(H_o) k^w-', *Bulletin de la Société de Linguistique de Paris*, 68: 77–92.

—— (1974*a*). 'Varia 6. Lith *nasrai*, Slav *nozd(i)ri*, OIr. *srón*, Gk ῥίς', *Ériu*, 25: 275–8.

—— (1974*b*). 'On the Stem Forms of IE "Bone"', *Richerche linguistiche*, 6: 231–5.

—— (1974*c*). 'Varia 2. *enech*, nipé', *Ériu*, 25: 261–8.

—— (1974*d*). 'On the Fundamental IE Orientation', *Eriu*, 25: 253–61.

—— (1975). 'I.E. *$g^w reh_2 uon$-', *Münchener Studium zur Sprachwissenschaft*, 33: 41–3.

—— (1976). '*$g^w eiHo$- "Live"', in A. Morpurgo-Davies and W. Meid (eds.), *Festschrift Palmer*. Innsbruck: Institut für Sprachwissenschaft der Universität Innsbruck, 87–91.

—— (1978). 'Indo-European "Duck"'. *Zeitschrift für vergleichende Sprachforschung*, 92: 29–31.

—— (1979*a*). 'The North European Word for "Apple"', *Zeitschrift für celtische Philologie*, 37: 158–66.

—— (1979*b*). 'Indo-European **kréuh-*', *Indogermanische Forschungen*, 82: 75–6.

—— (1980*a*). 'IE **( )k'uon-* "Dog"', *Indogermanische Forschungen*, 85: 35–42.

—— (1980*b*). 'IE *$kweh_2s$- "Cough"', in K. Čolakova et al. (eds.), *Studia Linguistica in Honorem Vladimir I. Georgiev*. Sofia: Izd na BAN,130–4.

—— (1981*a*). 'Refining Indo-European Lexical Entries. 1. Indo-European "Thrush"', *Zeitschrift für vergleichende Sprachforschung*, 95: 81.

—— (1981*b*). ' "Eat" in Greek', *Glotta*, 59: 155–7.

—— (1982*a*). 'Western Indo-European Notes, 9. **meslH-* "Amsel"', *Indogermanische Forschungen*, 87: 77–9.

—— (1982*b*). 'Arm, Shoulder', *Journal of Indo-European Studies*, 10: 187–9.

Hamp, E. P. (1982*c*). 'The Indo-European Root **bher-* in the Light of Celtic and Albanian', *Zeitschrift für celtische Philologie*, 39: 205–18.

—— (1983). 'IE **meH*$_e$*not-* and the Perfect Participle', *Journal of Indo-European Studies*, 11: 379–82.

—— (1984*a*). 'Indo-European and Balto-Slavic "Sheep"', *Journal of Indo-European Studies*, 12: 192.

—— (1984*b*). 'Indo-European "Bone" Reconsidered', *Zeitschrift für vergleichende Sprachforschung*, 92: 197–201.

—— (1985). 'Indo-European "Gerste, orge, Barley"', *Zeitschrift für vergleichende Sprachforschung* 98: 11–12.

—— (1987*a*). 'The Pig in Northern Europe', in E. Polomé and S. N. Skomal (eds.), *Proto-Indo-European: The Archaeology of a Linguistic Problem*. Washington: Institute for the Study of Man, 185–90.

—— (1987*b*). 'IE *ʕ^w*eui-kV* [fem]', *Journal of Indo-European Studies*, 15: 392.

—— (1987*c*). 'North European IE "Bed"', *North-Western European Language Evolution*, 9: 89–90.

—— (1987*d*). 'Indo-Hittite **men-* "See"', *Journal of Indo-European Studies*, 15: 391.

—— (1988). 'The Indo-European Terms for "Marriage"', in M. A. Jazayery and W. Winter (eds.), *Studies in Honor of Edgar Polomé*. Berlin: Mouton, 179–82.

—— (1989*a*). 'Semantic Divergence in Terms for "Oak"', *Quaderni semantica*, 10: 3–4.

—— (1989*b*). 'Indo-European **(s)dlnghuH*$_a$', in P. Wexler, A. Borg, and S. Somek (eds.), *Studia Linguistica et Orientalia Memoriae Haim Blanc Dedicata*. Wiesbaden: Harrassowitz, 121–4.

—— (1990*a*). 'Albanian *dhe* "Earth"', *Historische Sprachforschung*, 103: 289–92.

(1990*b*). 'On "Sun" in IE', *Historische Sprachforschung*, 103: 193–4.

—— (1990*c*). 'The Indo-European Horse', in T. Markey and J. Greppin (eds.), *When Worlds Collide: Indo-Europeans and Pre-Indo-Europeans*. Ann Arbor: Karoma, 291–302.

—— (1998). 'Whose were the Tocharians? Linguistic Subgrouping and Diagnostic Idiosyncrasy', in V. Mair (ed.), *The Bronze Age and Early Iron Age Peoples of Eastern Central Asia*, 2 vols. Washington: Institute for the Study of Man, 307–46.

—— (2002). 'IE "Spleen"', *Journal of Indo-European Studies*, 30: 145–50.

Hänsel, B., and Zimmer, S. (eds.) (1993). *Die Indogermanen und das Pferd*. Budapest: Archeolingua.

Hansen, L. J. (1980). 'Death and the Indo-Europeans', *Journal of Indo-European Studies*, 8: 31–40.

Haudry, J. (1981). *Les Indo-Européens*. Paris: Presses Universitaires de France.

—— (1987). *La Religion cosmique des Indo-Européens*. Paris: Archè.

—— (1992). 'Notes sur les racines indo-européennes **me-*, **met-*, **med-* "mesurer"', *Études indo-européennes*, 1992: 43–55.

Häusler, A. (2002). 'Ursprung und Ausbreitung der Indogermanen: Alternative Erklärungsmodelle', *Indogermanische Forschungen*, 107: 47–75.

Hendriksen, H. (1981). 'The Words for "Eyebrow" in Indo-Aryan and Indo-European', *Acta Iranica*, 21: 292–5.

Hetterich, H. (1985). 'Indo-European Kinship Terminology', *Anthropological Linguistics*, 27: 453–80.

Hilmarsson, J. (1982). 'Indo-European "Tongue" ', *Journal of Indo-European Studies*, 10: 355–67.

—— (1985). 'Tokh *kāc*, Lat *cutis*, OIcel. *hūþ* < I.E. **kuhtís* "Skin" ', *Zeitschrift für vergleichende Sprachforschung*, 98: 162–3.

Hock, H. H. (1991). *Principles of Historical Linguistics*. Berlin: Mouton de Gruyter.

Hoenigswald, H. (1960). *Language Change and Linguistic Reconstruction*. Chicago: University of Chicago.

Hoffman, K. (1965). 'Idg. **sneigwh*', *Münchener Studium zur Sprachwissenschaft*, 18: 13–28.

Holthausen, F. (1934). *Altenglisches etymologisches Wörterbuch*. Heidelberg: Winter.

Horowitz, F. (1992). 'On the Proto-Indo-European Etymon for "Hand" ', *Word*, 43: 411–19.

Horrocks, G. (1997). *Greek: A History of the Language and its Speakers*. London: Longman.

Hübschmann, H. (1897). *Armenische Grammatik I: Armenische Etymologie*. Leipzig: Breitkopf and Härtel.

Huld, M. E. (1981). 'Cu Chulainn and his IE Kin', *Zeitschrift für celtische Philologie*, 38: 238–41.

—— (1984). *Basic Albanian Etyniologies*, Columbus, Oh.: Slavica.

—— (1986). 'Proto- and Post-Indo-European Designations for "Sun" ', *Zeitschrift für vergleichende Sprachforschung*, 99: 194–202.

—— (1990). 'The Linguistic Typology of the Old European Substrate in North Central Europe', *Journal of Indo-European Studies*, 18: 389–424.

—— (1993). 'Early Indo-European Weapons Terminology', *Word*, 44: 223–34.

—— (1997). 'The Loins of Antimachus', *Journal of Indo-European Studies*, 25: 409–14.

—— (2004). 'An Albanian Reflex of Proto-Indo-European *$*E_1$ék̂u̯o-s* 'Horse', in K. Jones-Bley, M. Huld, A. Della Volpe, and M. R. Dexter (eds.), *Proceedings of the Fifteenth Annual UCLA Indo-European Conference*. Washington: Institute for the Study of Man, 186–95.

Ipsen, G. (1923). 'Sumerisch-akkadische Lehnwörter im Indogermanischen', *Indogermanische Forschungen*, 41: 174–83.

Itkonen, T. (1987). 'Die Bezeichnung der Kiefer in den Sprachen Europas', *Finnisch-ugrische Forschungen*, 48: 1–25.

Ivanov, V. V. (1960). 'L'Organisation sociale des tribus indo-européennes d'après les données linguistiques', *Cahiers d'histoire mondiale*, 5: 789–800.

Jackson, A. V. W. (1968 [1892]). *An Avesta Grammar in Comparison with Sanskrit*. Darmstadt: Wissenschaftliche Buchgesellschaft.

Jakubowicz, M. (1999). 'In the Circle of Love', in P. Stalmaszczyk and K. T. Witczak (eds.), *Studia Indogermanica Lodziensia 2*. Łódź: Wydawnictwo uniwersytetu Łodzkiego, 33–40.

Jamison, S. W. (1982–3). ' "Sleep" in Vedic and Indo-European', *Zeitschrift für vergleichende Sprachforschung*, 96: 6–16.

JASSANOFF, J. (1988). 'PIE *gne- "Recognize, Know"', in A. Bammesberger (ed.), *Die Laryngaltheorie und die Rekonstruktion des indogermanischen Laut- und Formensystems*. Heidelberg: Winter, 227–40.

—— (2003). *Hittite and the Indo-European Verb*. Oxford: Oxford University Press.

JOKI, A. (1963). 'Der wandernde Apfel', *Studia Orientalia*, 28(12): 7–12.

JONES-BLEY, K. (1997). 'Defining Indo-European Burial', in M. R. Dexter and E. Polomé (eds.), *Papers in Memory of Marija Gimbutas*. Washington: Institute for the Study of Man, 194–221.

JOSEPH, B. D., and JANDA, R. D. (2003). *The Handbook of Historical Linguistics*. Oxford: Blackwell.

JUSTUS, C. (1988). 'Indo-European Numerals and Numeral Systems', in Y. Arbeitman (ed.), *A Linguistic Happening in Memory of Ben Schwartz*. Louvain: Peeters, 521–41.

KATIČIĆ, R. (1976). *Ancient Languages of the Balkans*. The Hague: Mouton.

KATZ, H. (1983). 'Zu idg. *mrtó-', *Die Sprache*, 29: 174–7.

KATZ, J. (2003). *Studies in Indo-European Personal Pronouns*. Göttingen: Vandenhoeck and Ruprecht.

KAY, P. and MCDANIEL, C. (1978). 'The Linguistic Significance of the Meanings of Basic Color Terms', *Language*, 54: 610–46.

KAZANAS, N. D. (2001). 'Indo-European Deities and the *R̥gveda*', *Journal of Indo-European Studies*, 29: 257–93.

KENT, R. G. (1953). *Old Persian: Grammar, Texts, Lexicon*. New Haven: American Oriental Society.

KIM, R. (2000). ' "To Drink" in Anatolian, Tocharian and Proto-Indo-European', *Historische Sprachforschung*, 113: 151–70.

KLIMAS, A. (1974). 'Roots **welk-*, **wolk-*, *wl̥k-, *wl̥k^w-: A Case Study of Naming (Wild) Animals in Indo-European Languages', in L. Heilmann (ed.), *Proceedings of the Eleventh International Congress of Linguistics*, Bologna: Società Editrice il Mulino Bologna, 543–7.

KLIMOV, G. A. (1991). 'Some Thoughts on Indo-European–Kartvelian Relations', *Journal of Indo-European Studies*, 19: 325–41.

KLUGE, F. (1975). *Etymologisches Wörterbuch der deutschen Sprache*. Berlin: Walter de Gruyter.

KNOBLOCH, J. (1980). 'Ergologische Etymologien zum Wortschatz des indogermanischen Hausbaus', *Sprachwissenschaft*, 5: 172–200.

—— (1987*a*). '*Ast*, *Ranke* und *Rabe* in indogermanischen Sprachen', *Indogermanische Forschungen*, 92: 29–32.

—— (1987*b*). 'Die Kleidung der Indogermanen und ihrer Erben: Schuhwerk', in W. Meid (ed.), *Studien zum indogermanischen Wortschatz*. Innsbruck: Institut für Sprachwissenschaft der Universität, 65–6.

—— (1992). 'Eine ossetisch-irische Isoglosse: der idg. "Bergschuh"', *Indogermanische Forschungen*, 97: 68–9.

KOLOLIEC, V. T. (1984). 'Nazvanija dorog v indoevropejskich jazykakh', *Etimologija*, 1984: 97–102.

KOWAL, B. (1984). 'Wein oder Bier, eine indogermanische Frage', *Linguistique balkanique*, 27: 73–5.

KRAHE, H. (1964*a*). *Die Sprache der Illyrer*. Wiesbaden: Harrassowitz.

—— (1964*b*). *Unserer ältesten Flussnamen*. Wiesbaden: Harrassowitz.

KRASUKHIN, K. G. (2000). 'The Indo-European Root **dheugh-*: Its Morphology, Meaning, Etymology (in Comparison with Similar Forms)', *Journal of Indo-European Studies*, 28: 37–64.

KRAUSE, W. (1961). 'Zum Namen des Lachses', *Nachrichten der Akademie der Wissenschaften zu Göttingen*, 4: 83–98.

—— and THOMAS, W. (1960–4). *Tocharische Elementarbuch*. Heidelberg: Winter.

KROGMANN, W. (1955). 'Das Buchenargument', *Zeitschrift für vergleichende Sprachforschung*, 72: 1–29.

—— (1957). 'Das Buchenargument', *Zeitschrift für vergleichende Sprachforschung*, 73: 1–25.

—— (1960). 'Das Lachsargument', *Zeitschrift für vergleichende Sprachforschung*, 76: 161–78.

KRONASSER, H. (1962). *Etymologie der hethitischen Sprache*. Wiesbaden: O. Harrassowitz.

KUHN, H. (1954). 'Ablaut, *a* und Altertumskunde', *Zeitschrift für vergleichende Sprachforschung*, 71: 129–61.

—— (1967). 'Re. Hans Krahe, *Unsere ältesten Flussnamen*', *Anzeiger für deutsche Altertum und deutsche Literatur*, 78: 1–22.

KURŁOWICZ, J. (1964). *The Inflexional Categories of Indo-European*. Heidelberg: Winter.

—— (1968). *Indogermanische Grammatik, Akzent, Ablaut*. Heidelberg: Winter.

—— (1975). *Metrik und Sprachgeschichte*. Wrocłlaw: Zakład im Ossolinskich.

LANE, G. S. (1967). 'The Beech Argument: A Re-evaluation of the Linguistic Evidence', *Zeitschrift für vergleichende Sprachforschung*, 81: 197–212.

LAROCHE, É. (1959). *Dictionnaire de la langue louvite*. Paris: Adrien Maisonneuve.

LAZAR-MEYN, H. (1994). 'Colour Terms in *Táin Bó Cúailnge*', in J. P. Mallory and G. Stockman (eds.), *Ulidia: Proceedings of the First International Conference on the Ulster Cycle of Tales*. Belfast: December, 201–5.

LEHMANN, W. P. (1952). *Proto-Indo-European Phonology*. Austin: University of Texas.

—— (1974). *Proto-Indo-European Syntax*. Austin: University of Texas.

—— (1986). *A Gothic Etymological Dictionary Based on the Third Edition of Vergleichendes Wörterbuch der gothischen Sprache by Sigmund Feist*. Leiden: Brill.

—— (1988). ' "The Divine Twins" or "The Twins... Divine" ', in M. Jazayery and W. Winter (eds.), *Language and Cultures in Honor of Edgar C. Polomé*. New York: Mouton de Gruyter, 373–80.

—— (1992). *Historical Linguistics*. London: Routledge.

—— (1993). *Theoretical Bases of Indo-European Linguistics*. London: Routledge.

—— (2002). *Pre-Indo-European*. Washington: Journal of Indo-European Studies.

—— and ZGUSTA, L. (1979). 'Schleicher's Tale after a Century', in B. Brogyanyi (ed.), *Festschrift for Oswald Szemerényi on the Occasion of his 65th Birthday*. Amsterdam: Benjamins, 455–66.

LEHRMAN, A. (1987). 'Anatolian Cognates of the Proto-Indo-European Word for "Wolf"', *Die Sprache*, 33: 13–18.

LEJEUNE, M. (1974). *Manuel de la langue vénète*. Heidelberg: Winter.

—— (1977). '*Dō* "maison"', *Studi micenei ed egeo-anatolici*, 17: 79–84.

LERNER, L. (1951). 'Colour Words in Anglo-Saxon', *Modern Language Review*, 46: 246–9.

LEVIN, S. (1973). *The Indo-European and Semitic Languages*. Albany: State University of New York Press.

LEVINE, M. A. (2005). 'Domestication and Early History of the Horse', in D. S. Mills and S. M. McDonnell (eds.), *The Domestic Horse*. Cambridge: Cambridge University Press, 5–22.

LEWIS, H., and PEDERSEN, H. (1937). *A Concise Comparative Celtic Grammar*. Göttingen: Vandenhoeck and Ruprecht.

LINCOLN, B. (1980). 'The Ferryman of the Dead', *Journal of Indo-European Studies*, 8: 41–59.

—— (1981). *Priests, Warriors, and Cattle: A Study in the Ecology of Religions*. Berkeley and Los Angeles: University of California.

—— (1986). *Myth, Cosmos and Society: Indo-European Themes of Creation and Destruction*. Cambridge, Mass.: Harvard University.

—— (1991). *Death, War and Sacrifice*. Chicago: University of Chicago.

—— (1995). *Priests, Warriors and Cattle*. Berkeley and Los Angeles: University of California.

LINDEMAN, F. O. (1967). 'Indo-Européen **os* "bouche"', in *To Honor Roman Jakobson*. The Hague: Mouton, ii. 1188–90.

—— (1975). 'Note sur le thème i.e. **swad-*', *Norsk Tidsskrift for Sprogvidenskap*, 29: 161–2.

—— (1987). *Introduction to the Laryngeal Theory*. Oslo: Norwegian University Press.

—— (1990*a*). 'A Note on the Phonology of the Word for "Sheep" in Indo-European', *Historische Sprachforschung*, 103: 20–1.

—— (1990*b*). 'On the Word for "Wool" in Indo-European', *Historische Sprachforschung*, 103: 22–4.

—— (2003). 'Indo-European "to See; Eye": A Speculative "Laryngeal" note', *Indogermanische Forschungen*, 108: 47–57.

LINKE, U. (1985). 'Blood as Metaphor in Proto-Indo-European', *Journal of Indo-European Studies*, 13: 333–76.

LITTLETON, C. S. (1973). *The New Comparative Mythology*. Berkeley and Los Angeles: University of California.

LLOYD, A., LÜHR, R., and SPRINGER, O. (1988–). *Etymologisches Wörterbuch des Althochdeutschen*. Göttingen: Vandenhoeck and Ruprecht.

LOCKWOOD, W. B. (1969). *Indo-European Philology*. London: Hutchinson.

—— (1972). *A Panorama of Indo-European Languages*. London: Hutchinson University Library.

LOSADA-BADIA, L. (1992). 'Le Suffixe **-no-* dans les noms de chefs sacrés et guerriers indo-européens', *Études indo-européennes*, 1992: 59–80.

Lunt, H. (2001). *Old Church Slavonic Grammar*. Berlin: de Gruyter.

Lyle, E. (1990). *Archaic Cosmos. Polarity, Space and Time*. Edinburgh: Polygon.

Macdonell, A. (1910). *A Vedic Grammar*. Strassburg: Trübner.

Macjon, J. (1998). 'Drei neuindoeuropäische Hymnen', in P. Stalmaszczyk and K. Witczak (eds.), *Studia Indogermanica Łodziensia*, ii. Łódź: Wydawnictwo uniwersytetu Łodzkiego, 163–170.

McKone, K. (1985). 'Oir *Olc*, *Luch* and IE **wlk^{w}os*, **lúk^{w}os* "Wolf"', *Ériu*, 36: 171–6.

—— (1987). 'Hund, Wolf und Krieger bei den Indogermanen', in W. Meid (ed.), *Studien zum indogermanischen Wortschatz*. Innsbruck: Institut für Sprachwissenschaft der Universität, 101–54.

—— (1996). *Toward a Relative Chronology of Ancient and Medieval Celtic Sound Change*. Maynooth: St Patrick's College.

Maher, J. P. (1973). '*H$_{a}$ek'mon*: "(Stone)Axe" and "Sky" in I-E/Battle-axe Culture', *Journal of Indo-European Studies*, 1: 441–78.

—— (1981). '*Bed* and *Grave* in German and Celtic', *Journal of Indo-European Studies*, 9: 341–7.

—— (1986). 'The Cult of Weapons in Rock Art and Indo-European Languages', in I. Fleming (ed.), *The Thirteenth LACUS Forum 1986*. Lake Bluff: Linguistic Association of Canada and the United States, 53–90.

Makkay, J. (1986). 'Angaben zur Archäologie der Indogermanenfrage, I. Idg. **pel-* und die Grabenanlagen', *Acta Archaeologica*, 38: 13–29.

Mallory, J. P. (1982). Proto-Indo-European and Kurgan Fauna I: Wild Mammals', *Journal of Indo-European Studies*, 10: 193–222.

—— (1983). 'Proto-Indo-European and Kurgan Fauna II: Fish', *Journal of Indo-European Studies*, 11: 263–79.

—— (1989). *In Search of the Indo-Europeans*. London: Thames and Hudson.

—— (1991). 'Kurgan and Indo-European Fauna III: Birds', *Journal of Indo-European Studies*, 19: 223–34.

—— (1995). 'Human Populations and the Indo-European Problem', *Mankind Quarterly*, 33, 131–54.

—— (1997*a*). 'The Homelands of the Indo-Europeans', in R. Blench and M. Spriggs (eds.), *Archaeology and Language I*. London: Routledge, 93–121.

—— (1997*b*). 'Some Aspects of Indo-European Agriculture', in D. Disterheft, M. Huld, and J. Greppin (eds.), *Studies in Honor of Jaan Puhvel*. Washington: Journal of Indo-European Studies, i. 221–40.

—— (2002). 'Indo-Europeans and the Steppelands: The Model of Language Shift', in K. Jones-Bley, M. Huld, A. Della Volpe, and M. R. Dexter (eds.), *Proceedings of the Thirteenth Annual UCLA Indo-European Conference*. Washington: Institute for the Study of Man, 1–27.

—— and Adams, D. Q. (eds.) (1997). *Encyclopedia of Indo-European Culture*. London: Fitzroy Dearborn.

—— and Huld, M. E. (1984). 'Proto-Indo-European "Silver"', *Zeitschrift für vergleichende Sprachforschung*, 97: 1–12.

Mann, S. (1948). *An Historical Albanian–English Dictionary*. London: Longmans.

MANN, S. (1963). *Armenian and Indo-European*. London: Luzac.

—— (1977). *An Albanian Historical Grammar*. Hamburg: Helmut Buske.

—— (1984–7). *An Indo-European Comparative Dictionary*. Hamburg: Helmut Buske.

MARKEY, T. L. (1981). 'Indo-European Theophoric Personal Names and Social Structure', *Journal of Indo-European Studies*, 9: 227–43.

—— (1982). 'Indo-European Etyma for "Left, Left-Handed" and Markedness Reversal', *Mankind Quarterly*, 23: 183–94.

—— (1984*a*). 'IE "Beard" and Related Matters', *Balkansko ezikoznanie*, 27: 71–3.

—— (1984*b*). 'The Grammaticalization and Institutionalization of Indo-European "Hand"', *Journal of Indo-European Studies*, 12: 261–92.

—— (1988). 'Eurasian "Apple" as Arboreal Unit and Item of Culture', *Journal of Indo-European Studies*, 16: 49–68.

—— (1989). 'The Spread of Agriculture in Western Europe: Indo-European and (Non) Pre-Indo-European Linguistic Evidence', in D. Harris and G. Hillman (eds.), *Foraging and Farming*. London: Unwin Hyman, 585–606.

—— (1990). 'Gift, Payment and Reward Revisited', in T. Markey and J. Greppin (eds.), *When Worlds Collide*. Ann Arbor: Karoma, 345–62.

MASICA, C. P. (1991). *The Indo-Aryan Languages*. Cambridge: Cambridge University.

MAYER, A. (1957–9). *Die Sprache der alten Illyrier*, i, ii. Vienna: Österreichische Akademie der Wissenschaften.

MAYRHOFER, M. (1956–80). *Kurzgefasstes etymologisches Wörterbuch des Altindischen*. Heidelberg: Winter.

—— (1974). 'Ein neuer Beleg zu der indogermanischen Sippe für "Halsschumck"', in M. Mayrhofer (ed.), *Antiquitates Indogermanicae: Gedenkschrift für Hermann Güntert*. Innsbruck: Innsbrucker Beiträge zur Sprachwissenschaft, 289–91.

—— (1986). 'Lautlehre', in M. Mayrhofer (ed.), *Indogermanische Grammatik I*. Heidelberg: Carl Winter, 73–181.

—— (1986–2001). *Etymologisches Wörterbuch des Altindoarisches*. Heidelberg: Winter.

MAZJULIS, V. (1986). 'I.E. **ghei-* "svetit, sverkat"', *Etimologija*, 1984: 124–8.

MEID, W. (1975). 'Probleme der räumlichen und zeitlichen Gliederung des Indogermanischen', in H. Rix (ed.), *Flexion und Wortbildung*. Wiesbaden: Reichert, 204–19.

—— (1978). *Dichter und Dichterkunst in indogermanischer Zeit*. Innsbruck: Innsbrucker Beiträge zur Sprachwissenschaft.

—— (1987). 'Zur Vorstellungswelt der Indogermanen anhand des Wortschatzes', in W. Meid (ed.), *Studien zum indogermanischen Wortschatz*. Innsbruck: Institut für Sprachwissenschaft der Universität, 155–66.

—— (1990). *Formen dichtericher Sprache im Keltischen und Germanischen*. Innsbruck: Institut für Sprachwissenschaft der Universität Innsbruck.

MEIER-BRUGGE, M. (2003). *Indo-European Linguistics*. Berlin: de Gruyter.

MEILLET, A. (1937). *Introduction à l'étude comparative des langues indoeuropéennes*. Paris: Hachette.

—— (1967). *The Indo-European Dialects*. University: University of Alabama.

MEISER, G. (1998). *Historische Laut- und Formenlehre der lateinischen Sprache*. Darmstadt: Wissenschaftliche Buchgesellschaft.

Melchert, H. C. (1989). 'PIE "Dog" in Hittite?', *Münchener Studium zur Sprachwissenschaft*: 97–101.

—— (1994). *Anatolian Historical Phonology*. Amsterdam: Rodopi.

—— (2004). *A Dictionary of the Lycian Language*. Ann Arbor: Beech Stave.

Miller, D. (2000). *The Epic Hero*. Baltimore: Johns Hopkins University.

Milewski, T. (1968). 'Die Differenzierung der indoeuropäischen Sprachen', *Lingua Posnaniensis*, 12–13: 37–54.

Moonwomon, B. (1994). 'Color Categorization in Early Greek', *Journal of Indo-European Studies*, 22: 37–65.

Motz, L. (1998). 'The Sky-God of the Indo-Europeans', *Indogermanische Forschungen, 103: 28–39.*

Nagy G. (1974*a*). 'Perkunas and Perun', in M. Mayrhofer, W. Meid, B. Schlerath, and R. Schmitt (eds.), *Antiquitates Indogermanicae*. Innsbruck: Innsbrucker Beiträge zur Sprachwissenschaft, 113–31.

—— (1974*b*). 'Six Studies of Sacral Vocabulary Relating to the Fireplace', *Harvard Studies in Classical Philology*, 78: 71–106.

—— (1974*c*). *Comparative Studies of Greek and Indic Meter*. Cambridge, Mass.: Harvard University.

—— (1987). 'The Indo-European Heritage of Tribal Organization: Evidence from the Greek *polis*', in E. Polomé and S. Skomal (eds.), *Archaeology of a Linguistic Problem: Studies in Honor of Marija Gimbutas*. Washington: Institute for the Study of Man, 245–66.

Narten, J. (1965). 'Ai. *jámbha-*, gr. *gómphos* und Verwandtes', *Zeitschrift für vergleichende Sprachforschung*, 79: 255–64.

Nehring, A. (1936). 'Studien zur indogermanischen Kultur und Urheimat', in W. Koppers (ed.), *Die Indogermanen- und Germanenfrage: Neue Wege zu ihrer Lösung*. Salzburg: Wiener Beiträge zur Kulturgeschichte und Linguistik, 7–229.

Newmark, L. (1982). *Standard Albanian: A Reference Grammar for Students*. Stanford, Calif.: Stanford University.

Nichols, J. (1997). 'The Epicentre of the Indo-European Linguistic Spread', in R. Blench and M. Spriggs (eds.), *Archaeology and Language I*. London: Routledge, 122–48.

—— (1998). 'The Eurasian Spread Zone and the Indo-European Dispersal', in R. Blench and M. Spriggs (eds.), *Archaeology and Language*. London: Routledge, 220–66.

Nielsen, H. (2000). *The Germanic Languages: Origins and Early Dialectal Interrelationships*. Tuscaloosa: University of Alabama.

Niepokuj, M. (1994). 'Reconstructing Semantics, or, a Bad Case of the Bends', in C. Johnson et al. (eds.), *Proceedings of the Twentieth Annual Meeting of the Berkeley Linguistics Society*. Berkeley, 374–86.

Normier, R. (1981). 'Zu Esche und Espe', *Die Sprache*, 27: 22–9.

Nussbaum, A. (1986). *Head and Horn in Indo-European*. Berlin: de Gruyter.

O'Brien, S. (1976). 'Indo-European Eschatology: A Model', *Journal of Indo-European Studies*, 4: 295–320.

Orel, V. (1997). *The Language of the Phrygians*. Delmar, NY: Caravan.

Orel, V. (1998). *Albanian Etymological Dictionary*. Leiden: Brill.

—— (2000). *A Concise Historical Grammar of the Albanian Language*. Leiden: Brill.

Palmer, L. R. (1954). *The Latin Language*. London: Faber and Faber.

—— (1956). 'The Concept of Social Obligation in Indo-European', *Latomus*, 23: 258–69.

Parvulescu, A. (1977). 'Le Nom indo-européen de l'étoile', *Zeitschrift für vergleichende Sprachforschung*, 91: 41–50.

—— (1985). 'Die solare Orientierung im Indogermanischen', *SAIS* 8: 119–25.

—— (1988*a*). 'The Name of the Great Bear', *Journal of Indo-European Studies*, 16: 95–120.

—— (1988*b*). 'Skt *sudhána* "Rich": Grk *euthénia* "Prosperity" and their Cognates', *Indogermanische Forschungen*, 93: 46–51.

—— (1989). 'Blood and IE Kinship Terminology', *Indogermanische Forschungen*, 94: 67–88.

—— (1993*a*). 'IE **dhugheter* "Daughter" and Grassman's Law', *Indogermanische Forschungen*, 98: 55–91.

—— (1993*b*). 'The I-E Horse: A Linguistic Reconstruction', *Word*, 44: 69–76.

—— (1996). 'IE *bhrater* "Brother"', *Indogermanische Forschungen*, 101: 99–106.

Pedersen, H. (1931). *The Discovery of Language*. Reprinted 1962. Bloomington: Indiana University.

Pedrero, R. (1985). 'Las nociones de mano, brazo y codo en indoeuropeo', *Emérita*, 53: 249–67.

Peeters, C. (1974). 'Gothic *kaurus*, Sanskrit *guruh*, Greek *βαρύς*', *Indogermanische Forschungen*, 79: 33–4.

Petrosyan, A. (2002). *The Indo-European and Ancient New Eastern Sources of the Amerian Epic*, Washington: Institute for the study of Man.

Pinault, G.-J. (1982). 'L'Expression indo-européenne de la nomination', *Études indo-européennes*, 3: 15–36.

—— (1989). *Introduction au tokharien*. Paris: LALIES 7: 1–224.

Poetto, M. (1974). 'Hittite *sarap*- and Connected Questions', *Journal of Indo-European Studies*, 2: 435–8.

Pokorny, J. (1959). *Indogermanisches etymologisches Wörterbuch*. Bern: Francke Verlag.

Polomé, E. C. (1980). 'The Gods of the Indo-Europeans', *Mankind Quarterly*, 21: 151–64.

—— (1982). 'Balkan Languages (Illyrian, Thracian and Daco-Moesian)', in J. Boardman et al. (eds.), *Cambridge Ancient History*. Cambridge: Cambridge University, iii/1. 866–88.

—— (1986). 'Der indogermanische Wortschatz auf den Gebiete der Religion', in W. Meid (ed.), *Studien zum indogermanischen Wortschatz*. Innsbruck: Innsbruck Beiträge zur Sprachwissenschaft, 201–17.

—— (1996). 'Beer, Runes and Magic', *Journal of Indo-European Studies*, 24: 99–105.

Porzig, W. (1954). *Die Gliederung des indogermanischen Sprachgebiets*. Heidelberg: Winter.

Porzio Gernia, M. L. (1989). 'Riconstruzione linguistica e ricostruzione culturale: la funzione delle radici *men- e *wat- nell'antica cultura indoeuropea', *Quaderni dell' Istituto di Glottologia*, 1: 79–91.

Prokosch, E. (1938). *A Comparative Germanic Grammar*. Philadelphia: Linguistic Society of America.

Puhvel, J. (1964). 'The Indo-European and Aryan Plough: A Linguistic Study of Technological Diffusion', *Technology and Culture*, 5: 176–90.

—— (1969). ' "Meadow of the Otherworld" in Indo-European Tradition', *Zeitschrift für vergleichende Sprachforschung*, 83: 64–9.

—— (ed.) (1970). *Myth and Law among the Indo-Europeans*. Berkeley and Los Angeles: University of California.

—— (1971). 'Hittite *hurkis* and *hurkel*', *Die Sprache*, 17: 42–5.

—— (1976*a*). 'Latin *area* and Indo-European Threshing Terminology', *California Studies in Classical Antiquity*, 9: 197–202.

—— (1976*b*). ' "Finger" in Greek, Latin and Hittite', *Indogermanische Forschungen*, 81: 25–8.

—— (1984–). *Hittite Etymological Dictionary*. Berlin: Mouton.

—— (1987*a*). *Comparative Mythology*. Baltimore: Johns Hopkins University.

—— (1987*b*). 'All our "Yesterdays" ', in G. Cardona and N. Zide (eds.), *Festschrift for Henry M. Hoenigswald*. Tübingen: Narr, 315–18.

Ramat, A. G., and Ramat, P. (eds.) (1998). *The Indo-European Languages*. London: Routledge.

Ramat, P. (1983). 'L'ideologia indo-europea del dono-obbligo', in E. Campanile (ed.), *Problemi di lingua e di cultura nel campo indo-europeo*. Pisa: Giardini, 85–95.

Rau, W. (1973). *The Meaning of púr in Vedic Literature*. Munich: Abhandlungen der Marburger Gelehrten Gesellschaft.

Raulwing, P. (2000). *Horses, Chariots and Indo-Europeans*. Budapest: Archaeolingua.

Rédei, K. (1988). 'Die ältesten indogermanischen Lehnwörter der uralischen Sprachen', in D. Sinor (ed.), *The Uralic Languages*. Leiden: Brill, 638–64.

Reichelt, H. (1909). *Awestisches Elementarbuch*. Heidelberg: Winter.

Renfrew, C. (1987). *Archaeology and Language*. London: Jonathan Cape.

—— (1996). 'Language Families and the Spread of Farming', in D. Harris (ed.), *The Origins and Spread of Agriculture and Pastoralism in Eurasia*. London: University College, 70–92.

—— (1999). 'Time Depth, Convergence Theory, and Innovation in Proto-Indo-European: "Old Europe" as a PIE Linguistic Area', *Journal of Indo-European Studies*, 27: 257–93.

—— McMahon, A., and Trask, L. (2000). *Time Depth in Historical Linguistics*. 2 vols. Cambridge: McDonald Institute.

—— and Nettle, D. (1999). *Nostratic: Examining a Linguistic Macrofamily*. Cambridge: McDonald Institute.

Ringe, D., Warnow, T., and Taylor, A. (1995). 'Reconstructing Evolutionary History of Natural Languages', *Institute for Research in Cognitive Science Report* 95–16. Philadelphia Institute for Research in Cognitive Science.

Rix, H. (1976). *Historische Grammatik des Griechischen*. Darmstadt: Wissenschaftliche Buchgesellschaft.

—— et al. (eds.) (2001). *Lexikon der indogermanischen Verben*. Wiesbaden: Reichert.

Robins, R. H. (1997). *A Short History of Linguistics*. New York: Longman.

Robinson, O. W. (1992). *Old English and its Closest Relatives: A Survey of the Earliest Germanic Languages*. Stanford, Calif.: Stanford University.

Roider, U. (1981). 'Griech. *thumós* "Mut" - ai. *dhūmáh* "Rauch"', *Zeitschrift für vergleichende Sprachforschung*, 95: 99–109.

Sadowsky, O. (1973). 'The Reconstruction of IE **pisko* and the Extension of its Semantic Sphere', *Journal of Indo-European Studies*, 1: 81–100.

Salmons, J. (1992). *The Glottalic Theory: Survey and Synthesis*. Washington: Institute for the Study of Man.

Scharfe, H. (1985). 'The Vedic Word for "King"', *Journal of the American Oriental Society*, 105: 543–8.

Scheller, M. (1959). *Vedisch priyá- und die Wortsippe frei, freien, Freund: Eine bedeutungsgeschichtliche Studie*. Göttingen: Vandenhoeck and Ruprecht.

Scherer, A. (1953). *Gestirnnamen bei den indogermanischen Völkern*. Heidelberg: Carl Winter.

Schindler, J. (1966). 'Bemerkungen zum idg. Wort für "Schlaf"', *Die Sprache*, 12: 67–76.

—— (1967). 'Das idg. Wort für "Erde" und die dentalen Spiranten', *Die Sprache*, 13: 191–205.

—— (1969). 'Die idg. Wörter "Vogel" und "Ei"', *Die Sprache*, 15: 144–67.

Schleicher, A. (1861–2). *Compendium der vergleichendea Grammatik der indogermanischen Sprachen*. Weimar: Böhlau.

—— (1868). 'Avis akvasas ka', *Beiträge zur vergleichende Sprachforschung*, 5: 206.

Schlerath, B. (1953). 'Über den Hahn', *Zeitschrift für vergleichende Sprachforschung*, 95: 28–32.

—— (1954). 'Der Hund bei den Indogermanen', *Paideuma*, 6: 25–40.

—— (1987). 'Können wir die urindogermanische Sozialstruktur rekonstruieren?', in W. Meid (ed.), *Studien zur indogermanische Wortschatz*. Innsbruck: Institut für Sprachwissenschaft der Universität, 249–64.

—— (1997). 'Metallgegenstände in vedischer Zeit', in C. Becker, M.-L. Dunkelmann, C. Metzner-Nebelsick, H. Peter-Röcher, M. Roeder, and B. Terzan (eds.), *Khrónos: Festschrift für Bernhard Hänsel*. Espelkamp: Marie Leidorf, 819–27.

Schmalstieg, W. (1974). *An Old Prussian Grammar: The Phonology and Morphology of the Three Catechisms*. University Park: Pennsylvania State University.

—— (1980). *Indo-European Linguistics: A New Synthesis*. University Park: University of Pennsylvania.

—— (1988). *A Lithuanian Historical Syntax*. Columbus, Oh.: Slavica.

—— (1995). *An Introduction to Old Russian*. Washington: Institute for the Study of Man.

—— (2000). *The Historical Morphology of the Baltic Verb*. Washington: Institute for the Study of Man.

Schmid, W. P. (1968). *Alteuropäisch und Indogermanisch*. Wiesbaden: Steiner.

—— (1972). 'Baltische Gewässernamen und das vorgeschichtliche Europa', *Indogermanische Forschungen*, 77: 1–18.

—— (1989). *Wort und Zahl: Sprachwissenschaftliche Betrachtungen der Kardinalzahlwörter*. Stuttgart: Steiner.

Schmidt, G. (1978). *Stammbildung und Flexion der indogermanischen Personalpronomina*. Wiesbaden: Harrassowitz.

—— (1992). 'Indogermanische Ordinalzahlen', *Indogermanische Forschungen*, 97: 197–235.

Schmitt, R. (1967). *Dichtung und Dichtersprache in indogermanischer Zeit*. Wiesbaden: Harrassowitz.

—— (1973). *Indogermanische Dichtersprache und Namengebung*. Innsbruck: Institut für vergleichende Sprachforschung.

—— (1977). *Einführung in die griechischen Dialekte*. Darmstadt: Wissenschaftliche Buchgesellschaft.

—— (1981). *Grammatik des Klassisch-Armenischen mit sprachlichen Erläuterungen*. Innsbruck: Innsbrucker Beiträge zur Sprachwissenschaft.

—— (1989). *Compendium Linguarum Iranicarum*. Wiesbaden: Reichert.

Schrader, O., and Nehring, A. (1917–28). *Reallexikon der indogermanischen Altertumskunde*. Berlin: Walter de Gruyter.

Schrijver, P. (1991). *The Reflexes of the Proto-Indo-European Laryngeals in Latin*. Amsterdam: Rodopi.

—— (1995). *Studies in British Celtic Historical Phonology*. Amsterdam: Rodopi.

—— (1998). 'The British Word for "Fox" and its Indo-European Origins', *Journal of Indo-European Studies*, 26: 421–34.

—— (2004). 'The Etymology of English *Weapon*, German *Waffe* and the Indo-European Root **Hwep-*', in I. Hyvärinen, P. Kallio, and J. Korhonen (eds.), *Etymologie: Entlehungen und Entwicklungen*. Helsinki: Société Néophilologique, 355–66.

Schwartz, M. (1992). 'On Proto-Indo-European **penk-* "Hand"', *Word*, 43: 421–7.

Schwenter, E. (1924). *Die primären Interjektionen in den indogermanischen Sprachen*. Heidelberg: Winter.

Seebold, E. (1973). 'Die Stammbildungen der idg. Wurzel **weid-* und deren Bedeutungen', *Die Sprache*, 19: 158–79.

—— (1985). 'Das Benennungsmotiv der Wörter für "Fisch" in den idg. Sprachen', in H. Ölberg and G. Schmidt (eds.), *Sprachwissenschaftliche Forschungen: Festschrift Johann Knobloch*. Innsbruck: Institut für Sprachwissenschaft der Universität Innsbruck, 443–51.

—— (1991). 'Der Himmel, der Tag und die Götter bei den Indogermanen', *Historische Sprachforschung*, 104: 29–45.

Sen, S. K. (1994). 'Proto-Indo-European: a multiangular view', *Journal of Indo-European Studies*, 22: 67–90.

Sergent, B. (1995). *Les Indo-Européens: histoire, langues, mythes*. Paris: Éditions Payot & Rivages.

SEVILLA RODRIGUEZ, M. (1989). 'Indo-European *$(s)k^{w}alo/i$-s "Sheat-fish"', *Journal of Indo-European Studies*, 17: 177–80.

SHERRATT, A. (1981) 'Plough and Pastoralism: Aspects of the Secondary Products Revolution', in I. Hodder, G. Isaac, and N. Hammond (eds.), *Pattern of the Past: Studies in Honour of David Clarke*. Cambridge: Cambridge University Press, 261–305.

—— (1987). 'Cups that Cheered', in W. Waldren and R. Kennard (eds.), *Bell Beakers of the Western Mediterranean*. Oxford, BAR International Series, 81–106.

—— and SHERRATT, S. (1988). 'The Archaeology of Indo-European: An Alternative View', *Antiquity*, 62: 584–95.

SHIELDS, K. (1979). 'Indo-European Basic Colour Terms', *Canadian Journal of Linguistics*, 24: 142–6.

SIHLER, A. (1977). 'The Etymology of PIE *reg'- "King", etc', *Journal of Indo-European Studies*, 5: 221–46.

—— (1995). *New Comparative Grammar of Greek and Latin*. New York: Oxford University.

SOLTA, G. (1963). *Die armenische Sprache*. Leiden: E. J. Brill.

—— (1974). *Zur Stellung der lateinischen Sprache*. Vienna: Verlag der Österreichischen Akademie der Wissenschaften.

SPECHT, F. (1944). *Der Ursprung der indogermanischen Deklination*. Göttingen: Vandenhoeck & Ruprecht.

STALMASZCZYK, P., and WITCZAK, K. T. (1990). 'Celto-Tocharica 1: Three Celtic-Tocharian Terms for Certain Parts of the Body', *Tocharian and Indo-European Studies*, 4: 35–44.

—— —— (1991–2). 'The Celtic word for "Oats, *Avena sativa*" and its Indo-European equivalents', *Lingua Posnaniensis*, 34: 83–7.

STANG, C. S. (1970). *Vergleichende Grammatik der baltischen Sprachen*. Oslo: Universitetsforlaget.

—— (1972). *Lexikalische Sonderübereinstimmungen zwischen dem Slavischen, Baltischen und Germanischen*. Oslo: Universitetsforlaget.

—— (1974). 'Ieur. *swad- /**swad-', *Norsk Tidsskrift for Sprogvidenskap*, 28: 99–101.

STARKE, F. (1985). 'Uridg. *h_1d-tí- "Speise" in Luwischen', *Die Sprache*, 31: 249–55.

—— (1987). 'Die Vertretung von uridg. *dhugh$_2$ter- "Tochter" in den luwischen Sprachen und ihre Stammbildung', *Zeitschrift für vergleichende Sprachforschung*, 100: 243–69.

STERCKX, C. (1994). *Les Dieux protéens des celtes et des indo-européens*. Brussels: Société Belge d'Études Celtiques.

STRUNK, K. (1987). 'Further Evidence for Diachronic Selection: Ved *rYZri*, Lat *regit etc.*', in G. Cardona and N. Zide (eds.), *Festschrift for Henry Hoenigswald: On the Occasion of his Seventieth Birthday*. Tübingen: Gunter Narr, 385–92.

STURTEYANT, E. (1951). *A Comparative Grammar of the Hittite Language*. New Haven: Yale University.

SWADESH, M. (1960). 'Unas correlaciones de arquelogía y lingüística', in P. Bosch-Gimpera, *El problema indoeuropeo*. Mexico: Universidad Autonoma de México, 342–52.

Szemerényi, O. (1958). 'Greek *gála* and the Indo-European Term for Milk', *Zeitschrift für vergleichende Sprachforschung*, 75: 170–90.

—— (1959). 'Latin *hibernus* and Greek *kheimerinós*: The Formation of Time Adjectives in the Classical Languages', *Glotta*, 38: 107–25.

—— (1960). *Studies in the Indo-European System of Numerals*. Heidelberg: Winter.

—— (1970). 'The Indo-European Name for "Heart"', in V. Rūke-Dravina, *Donum Balticum*. Stockholm: Almqvist and Wiksell, 515–33.

—— (1977). 'Studies in the Kinship Terminology of the Indo-European Languages, with Special Reference to Indian, Iranian, Greek and Latin', *Acta Iranica*, Varia 1977: 1–240.

—— (1996). *Introduction to Indo-European Linguistics*. Oxford: Clarendon Press.

Takács, G. (1997). 'Note on the Origin of PIE **pes-* "Penis"', *Journal of Indo-European Studies*, 25: 371–82.

Thieme, P. (1938). *Der Fremdling in Rgveda: Eine Studie über die Bedeutung der Worte ari, arya, aryaman und Arya*. Leipzig: F. A. Brockhaus.

—— (1954). *Die Heimat der indogermanischen Grundsprache*. Wiesbaden: Akademie der Wissenschaften und der Literatur.

—— (1957). '*ari* "Fremder"', *Zeitschrift der Deutschen Morgenländischen Gesellschaft*, 107: 96–104.

—— (1961). 'Idg. **sal-* "Salz" im Sanskrit?', *Zeitschrift der Deutschen Morgenländischen Gesellschaft*, 111: 94–102.

Thompson, D. W. (1895). *A Glossary of Greek Birds*. Oxford: Clarendon Press.

—— (1947). *A Glossary of Greek Fishes*. London: Oxford University.

Thomson, K. (2001). 'The Meaning and Language of the *Rigveda:* Rigvedic *grávan* as a Test Case', *Journal of Indo-European Studies*, 29: 295–349.

Thurneysen, R. (1936). 'Ir *aire*, gen. *airech*', *Zeitschrift für celtische Philologie*, 20: 353–5.

Tichy, E. (2000). *Indogermanisches Grundwissen für Studierende sprachwissenschaftlicher Disziplinen*. Bremen: Hempen Verlag.

Tischler, J. (1973). *Glottochronologie und Lexikostatistik*. Innsbruck: Institut für vergleichende Sprachwissenschaft der Universität Innsbruck.

—— (1977–). *Hethitisches etymologisches Glossar*. Innsbruck: Institut für Sprachwissenschaft der Universität Innsbruck.

Trager, G. (1967). 'The Tanoan Settlement of the Rio Grande Area: A Possible Chronology', in D. Hymes and W. Bittle (eds.), *Studies in Southwestern Ethnolinguistics*. The Hague: Mouton, 335–50.

Trubachev, O. N. (1974–). *Etimologicheskij slovar' slavjanskikh jazykov*. Moscow: Nauka.

Turcan, I. (1982). ' "Dire" et "faire" dans le vocabulaire des institutions indo-européennes', *Études indo-européennes*, 1: 3–21.

Turner, L. (1966–9). *A Comparative Dictionary of the Indo-Aryan Languages*. Oxford: Oxford University.

Untermann, J. (1989). '*arganto-* "Silber" in Keltiberischen', in K. Heller et al. (eds.), *Indogermanica Europaea: Festschrift für Wolfgang Meid*. Graz: Institut für Sprachwissenschaft der Universität, 431–50.

VAILLANT, A. (1950–77). *Grammaire comparée des langues slaves*. 5 vols. Lyon: IAG Klincksieck.

VAN LEEUWEN-TURNOVCOVÁ, J. (1990). *Rechts und Links in Europa*. Wiesbaden: Harrassowitz.

VAN WINDEKENS, A. J. (1976). *Le Tokharien confronté avec les autres langages indo-européennes*. Louvain: Centre Internationale de Dialectologie Générale.

VASMER, M. (1953–8). *Russisches etymologisches Wörterbuch*. Heidelberg: Winter.

VENDRYÈS, J. (1932). 'Sur les verbes de mouvement en indo-européen', *Indian Linguistics*, 2: 21–5.

—— and LAMBERT, P. (1959–). *Lexique étymologique de l'irlandais ancien*. Paris, CNRS.

VENNEMANN, T. (1994). 'Linguistic Reconstruction in the Context of European Prehistory', *Transactions of the Philological Society*, 92: 213–82.

WARD, D. (1968). *The Divine Twins: An Indo-European Myth in Germanic Tradition*. Folklore Studies no. 19. Berkeley and Los Angeles: University of California Press.

WATKINS, C. (1969). 'A Latin–Hittite Etymology', *Language*, 45: 235–42.

—— (1970*a*). 'Studies in Indo-European Legal Language, Institutions, and Mythology', in G. Cardona, H. Hoenigswalld, and A. Senn (eds.), *Indo-European and Indo-Europeans*. Philadelphia: University of Pennsylvania, 321–54.

—— (1970*b*). 'Language of Gods and Language of Men', in J. Puhvel (ed.), *Myth and Law among the Indo-Europeans*. Berkeley and Los Angeles: University of California, 1–17.

—— (1972*a*). 'An Indo-European Word for "Dream" ', in E. Firchow, K. Grimstad, N. Hasselmo, and W. O'Neil (eds.), *Studies for Einar Haugen*. The Hague: Mouton, 554–61.

—— (1972*b*). 'Une désignation indo-européenne de l'eau', *Bulletin de la Société de Linguistique de Paris*, 67: 39–46.

—— (1973). 'An Indo-European Agricultural Term: Latin *ardor*, Hittite *hat-*', *HSPh* 77: 187–93.

—— (1974). 'I.-E. "Star" ', *Die Sprache*, 20: 10–14.

—— (1975). 'Hittite *saru*, Old Irish *serb*, Welsh *herw*: A Hittite-Celtic Etymology', in C. Watkins (ed.), *Indo-European Studies*. Cambridge, Mass.: Havard University, ii. 322–31.

—— (1977). 'Let us now Praise Famous Grains', in C. Watkins (ed.), *Indo-European Studies III*. Cambridge, Mass.: Harvard University, 468–98.

—— (1985). *The American Heritage Dictionary of Indo-European Roots*. Boston: Houghton Mifflin.

—— (1986*a*). 'The Name of Meleager', in A. Etter (ed.), *o-o-pe-ro-si: Festschrift für E. Risch*. Berlin: de Gruyter, 320–8.

—— (1986*b*). ' "In the Interstices of Procedure": Indo-European Legal Language and Comparative Law', *Historiographia Linguistica*, 13: 27–42.

—— (1993). 'Another Thorny Problem', *Linguistica*, 33: 243–8.

—— (1995). *How to Kill a Dragon: Aspects of Indo-European Poetics*. Oxford: Oxford University.

WEITENBERG, J. (1991). 'To Become a Wolf', in R. Pearson (ed.), *Perspectives on Indo-European Language, Culture and Religion*. Washington: Journal of Indo-European Studies, ii: 189–98.

WENNERBERG, C. (1972). 'Indogermanisch **stomen-* "Mund"', *Die Sprache*, 13: 24–33.

WESCOTT, R. W. (1975). 'Proto-Indo-Hittite Color Terms', *Linguistics and Anthropology*: 691–9.

WEST, M. L. (1973). 'Indo-European Metre', *Glotta*, 51: 151–72.

—— (2004). 'An Indo-European Stylistic Feature in Homer', in A. S. A. Bierl and A. Willi (eds.), *Antike Literatur in neuer Deutung*. Munich: K. G. Saur, 33–49.

WIKANDER, S. (1938). *Der arische Männerbund*. Lund: Ohlsson.

WINTER, W. (1970). 'Some Widespread Indo-European Titles', in G. Cardona, H. Hoenigswald, and A. Senn (eds.), *Indo-European and Indo-Europeans*. Philadelphia: University of Pennsylvania, 51–3.

—— (1980). 'OInd. *máhi*: Gr. *méga* "Great" Reconsidered', in K. Klar, M. Langdon, and S. Silver (eds.), *American Indian and Indo-European Studies*. The Hague: Mouton, 487–95.

—— (1982). 'Indo-European Words for "Tongue" and "Fish": A Reappraisal', *Journal of Indo-European Studies*, 10: 167–86.

—— (1988). 'Cardinal Points and Other Directions in Tocharian A and B', in M. Jazayery and W. Winter (eds.), *Language and Cultures in Honor of Edgar C. Polomé*. New York: Mouton de Gruyter, 775–91.

WITCZAK, K. T. (1994*a*). 'Germanic **raih-* "Roedeer", *Capreolus capreolus*: A Proposal for a New Etymology', *Historische Sprachforschung*, 107: 123–42.

—— (1994*b*). ' "Gold" in Mycenaean Greek and Indo-European', *Orpheus*, 4: 55–8.

—— (2003). *Indoeuropejskie nazwy zbóż*. Łódź: Wydawnictwo Uniwersytetu Łódzkiego.

WOJTILLA, G. (1986). 'Notes on Indo-Aryan Terms for "Ploughing" and the "Plough"', *Journal of Indo-European Studies*, 14: 27–37.

WOLFE, S. (1993). 'Reconstructing PIE Terms for Kinship and Marriage', *Word*, 44: 41–51.

WOODHOUSE, R. (2003). 'PIE. **s(w)er(H)K-* "Heed, Care for, Grieve, Lie Ill, Waste Away"?', *Indogermanische Forschungen*, 108: 58–91.

WORDICK, F. (1970). 'A Generative-Extensionist Analysis of the Proto-Indo-European Kinship System'. Unpublished Ph.D. Madison: Xerox Microfilms.

WÜST, W. (1956). *Idg. *péleku- 'Axt, Beil': Eine paläo-linguistische Studie*. Helsinki: Suomalaisen Tiedeakatemian Toimituksia.

YORK, M. (1993). 'Toward a PIE Vocabulary of the Sacred', *Word*, 44: 235–54.

—— (1995). 'The Divine Twins in the Celtic Pantheon', *Journal of Indo-European Studies*, 23: 83–112.

ZIMMER, S. (1981). 'Idg. **ukson-*', *Zeitschrift für vergleichende Sprachforschung*, 95: 84–92.

ZIMMER, S. (1987). 'Indogermanische Sozialstruktur? Zu zwei Thesen Emile Benvenistes', in W. Meid (ed.), *Studien zum indogermanischen Wortschatz*. Innsbruck: Institut für Sprachwissenschaft der Universität, 315–29.

ZIMMER, S. (1988). 'On Dating Proto-Indo-European: A Call for Honesty', *Journal of Indo-European Studies*, 16: 371–5.

ZVELEBIL, M., and ZVELEBIL, K. (1988). 'Agricultural Transition and Indo-European Dispersals', *Antiquity*, 62: 574–83.

General Index

Index Verborum

Proto-Indo-European

Albanian

Albanian [Alb]

a, b, c, ç, d, e, ë, f, g, gj, h, I, j, k, l, ll, m, n, nj, o, p, q, r, rr, s, sh, t, th, u, v, x, xh, y, z, zh

Anatolian Languages

Hittite [Hit]

Baltic Languages

Latvian [Latv]

Lithuanian [Lith]

a, b, c, č, d, e (*ę, ė*), *f, g, h, i* (*į, y*), *j, k, l, m, n, o, p, r, s, š, t, u, ų, ū, v, z, ž*

Old High German [OHG]

Italic languages

French

Italian

Slavic Languages

Tocharian Languages

Lightning Source UK Ltd.
Milton Keynes UK
UKOW03f0803020315

247114UK00002B/4/P

9 780199 296682